# AFQR 2003

# Airline Fleets
# Quick Reference

**Compiled by Tony Pither**

Copyright © Air-Britain (Historians) Ltd 2003

Published by: Air-Britain (Historians) Ltd

Sales Department: 41 Penshurst Road, Leigh,
Tonbridge, Kent TN11 8HL

Membership Enquiries: 1 Rose Cottages, 179 Penn Road,
Hazlemere, Buckinghamshire HP15 7NE

ISBN: 0 85130 337 4

PHOTO CAPTIONS:
Front: Cosmopolitan line-up at Manchester 27th August 2002 including pairs of Bulgarian Air Charter Tu-154Ms, Air 2000 Boeing 757s and Pakistan International Boeing 747s. (Denis Norman)
Back: Electra Airlines DC-10-15 SX-CVP at Manchester on 13.7.02 (Denis Norman)
Qatar Airways Airbus A3--B4 A7-ABN landing at Heathrow on 27th May 2002. (Denis Norman)
Boeing 747-236B G-BDXJ of European Airways at Manchester 21st July 2002. (Denis Norman )

Printed by Bell & Bain Ltd, Glasgow

# AFQR 2003

## Airline Fleets Quick Reference 2003

Welcome to the third edition of Airline Fleets Quick Reference. The comments received from members have been appreciated and some of the suggestions have been included in this edition. Other possible changes are being considered for next year.

Coverage is again worldwide. For Europe, fleets are included for airlines operating aircraft with more than 19 seats (i.e. Jetstream 31/Beech 1900 size). This means that any airliner above that size likely to be seen at a European airport should be included [unless it is in storage]. Also included this year are the larger civilian helicopters used in Western Europe, this means the Pumas/ Tigers/ S-61Ns used on oil or gas related services or Search and Rescue appear for the first time. Again the fleets of the American majors, their feeder services and other operators using jets or large turboprop aircraft are included with the same cut-off size as European operators. The major national and international carriers from the remainder of the world are included but for these the largest aircraft included are usually ATR 42s. The entries for Russian, Ukrainian and other CIS operators tend to be Tupolev Tu-134 and above except where services are operated on a regular basis to Western Europe with smaller aircraft.

Countries are in alphabetical order of nationality prefix, with the airlines in each country also in alphabetical order. Fleets are in alphabetical order of aircraft manufacturer where five or more of the same type occurs; otherwise they are listed in registration order. Information is provided in four columns for each entry – namely registration; type (abridged); constructors' number (and line number for Boeing and McDonnell-Douglas aircraft) plus a column for notes. This last column contains details of fleet number (where appropriate), details of leases between airlines and aircraft stored or on order – where possible this has been restricted to those due in the next 12 months. The types used in AFQR are the marketing names (e.g. Canadair RJ-200) rather than the name on the type certificate (CL-600-2B19) as used in Airline Fleets 2003. Extra data on the airlines and aircraft listed in this book, plus hundreds of other operators, as well as a full decode of airline two and three letter codes will be found in Airline Fleets 2003.

Thanks go to Terry Smith and Chris Chatfield for reading the first draft and offering suggestions and changes and to Dave Partington for preparing the finished article for printing.

Data for this book is identical in content to that in the main book (i.e. believed correct to early February 2003). The decision was taken to leave Buzz and Go as standalone operators this year even though for the 2004 edition they will be incorporated into Ryanair and easyJet respectively. Obviously individual members will have comments to make on the content and concept of this publication and constructive criticism is welcome at the editorial address below but please remember that in common with all Air-Britain publications this has been produced voluntarily in our spare time. Of course, don't forget that this book, like Airline Fleets 2003, can be kept up-to-date through the Commercial Scene section of our monthly flagship magazine Air-Britain News.

Tony Pither, 65 Dacombe Drive, Upton, Poole, Dorset, BH16 5JJ
Fax:            +44 (0)1202 631996
e-mail:        tonypither@aol.com

Abbreviations:

| | |
|---|---|
| o/o | on order (aircraft believed for delivery within the next twelve months) |
| Jow | Joint operations with |
| Lst/Lsf | Leased to or Leased from |
| Opf/Opb | Operated for or operated by |
| Std | stored |

Decodes of airlines and airports are given in the appendices in Airlines Fleets 2003, which is approximately 800 pages in length and available for £22.50 post free (or £18.00 for members) from Air-Britain Sales Department, 41 Penshurst Road, Leigh, Tonbridge, Kent, TN11 8HL. For further details please see the back of this book.

## AP - PAKISTAN

### AERO ASIA INTERNATIONAL — RSO

| | | | |
|---|---|---|---|
| ☐ RA-42345 | Yak-42D | 4520422708304 | Lsf TUL |
| ☐ RA-42354 | Yak-42D | 4520424711397 | Lsf TUL |
| ☐ RA-42415 | Yak-42D | 4520422219089 | Lsf TUL |
| ☐ RA-42417 | Yak-42D | 4520423219110 | Lsf TUL |
| ☐ RA-42425 | Yak-42D | 4520423303016 | Lsf TUL |
| ☐ RA-42433 | Yak-42D | 4520421301017 | Lsf TUL |
| | | | |
| ☐ AP-BFC | BAC One-Eleven 561RC | 401 | std OTP |
| ☐ AP-BFD | BAC One-Eleven 561RC | 404 | std KHI |
| ☐ AP-BFE | BAC One-Eleven 561RC | 406 | std KHI |
| ☐ AP-BFF | BAC One-Eleven 561RC | 407 | std KHI |
| | | | |
| ☐ EX-450 | Boeing 737-281 | 262/20450 | Lsf PHG |
| ☐ EX-451 | Boeing 737-281 | 266/20451 | Lsf PHG |
| ☐ EX-632 | Boeing 737-2T5 | 847/22632 | Lsf PHG |
| ☐ EX-960 | Boeing 737-2T5 | 642/21960 | Lsf PHG |

### PAKISTAN INTERNATIONAL AIRLINES — PIA

| | | |
|---|---|---|
| ☐ AP-BAX | Airbus A300B4-203 | 096 |
| ☐ AP-BAY | Airbus A300B4-203 | 098 |
| ☐ AP-BAZ | Airbus A300B4-203 | 099 |
| ☐ AP-BBA | Airbus A300B4-203 | 114 |
| ☐ AP-BBM | Airbus A300B4-203 | 064 |
| ☐ AP-BBV | Airbus A300B4-203 | 144 |
| ☐ AP-BEL | Airbus A300B4-203 | 269 |
| ☐ AP-BEY | Airbus A300B4-203 | 146 |
| | | |
| ☐ AP-BDZ | Airbus A310-308 | 585 |
| ☐ AP-BEB | Airbus A310-308 | 587 |
| ☐ AP-BEC | Airbus A310-308 | 590 |
| ☐ AP-BEG | Airbus A310-308 | 653 |
| ☐ AP-BEQ | Airbus A310-308 | 656 |
| ☐ AP-BEU | Airbus A310-308 | 691 |
| | | |
| ☐ AP-BCA | Boeing 737-340 | 1114/23294 |
| ☐ AP-BCB | Boeing 737-340 | 1116/23295 |
| ☐ AP-BCC | Boeing 737-340 | 1121/23296 |
| ☐ AP-BCD | Boeing 737-340 | 1122/23297 |
| ☐ AP-BCF | Boeing 737-340 | 1235/23299 |
| ☐ AP-BFT | Boeing 737-340 | 1123/23298 |
| | | |
| ☐ AP-BAK | Boeing 747-240M | 383/21825 |
| ☐ AP-BAT | Boeing 747-240M | 429/22077 |
| ☐ AP-BFU | Boeing 747-367 | 634/23392 |
| ☐ AP-BFV | Boeing 747-367 | 659/23534 |
| ☐ AP-BFW | Boeing 747-367 | 615/23221 |
| ☐ AP-BFX | Boeing 747-367 | 671/23709 |
| ☐ AP-BFY | Boeing 747-367 | 690/23920 |
| ☐ AP-BGG | Boeing 747-367 | 709/24215 |

### PIONEER CARGO AIRLINES

| | | |
|---|---|---|
| ☐ UR-26204 | Antonov An-26 | 57314103 |
| ☐ UR-26676 | Antonov An-26B | 8602 |

### SHAHEEN AIR INTERNATIONAL — SAI

| | | | |
|---|---|---|---|
| ☐ EW-85509 | Tupolev Tu-154B-2 | 81A-509 | Lsf BRU |
| ☐ EW-85538 | Tupolev Tu-154B-2 | 82A-538 | Lsf BRU |
| ☐ EW-85545 | Tupolev Tu-154B-2 | 82A-545 | Lsf BRU |
| ☐ RA-85773 | Tupolev Tu-154M | 93A-955 | Lsf BTC |
| ☐ RA-85816 | Tupolev Tu-154M | 95A-1006 | Lsf BTC |

### STAR AIR AVIATION

| | | |
|---|---|---|
| ☐ AP-BGF | Dornier 228-201 | 8016 |

## A2 - BOTSWANA

### AIR BOTSWANA — BOT

| | | |
|---|---|---|
| ☐ A2-ABD | BAe 146 Srs.100 | E1101 |
| ☐ A2-ABN | ATR 42-500 | 507 |
| ☐ A2-ABO | ATR 42-500 | 511 |
| ☐ A2-ABP | ATR 42-500 | 512 |

## A3 - TONGA

### ROYAN TONGAN AIRLINES — HRH

| | | | |
|---|---|---|---|
| ☐ V8-RBB | Boeing 757-2M6 | 100/23453 | Lsf RBA |

## A40 - OMAN

### GULF AIR — GFA

| | | | |
|---|---|---|---|
| ☐ A4O-EB | Airbus A320-212 | 0325 | 802 |
| ☐ A4O-ED | Airbus A320-212 | 0375 | 804 |
| ☐ A4O-EE | Airbus A320-212 | 0419 | 805 |
| ☐ A4O-EF | Airbus A320-212 | 0421 | 806 |
| ☐ A4O-EG | Airbus A320-212 | 0438 | 807 |
| ☐ A4O-EH | Airbus A320-212 | 0445 | 808 |
| ☐ A4O-EI | Airbus A320-212 | 0459 | 809 |
| ☐ A4O-EJ | Airbus A320-212 | 0466 | 810 |
| ☐ A4O-EL | Airbus A320-212 | 0497 | 812 |
| ☐ A4O-EN | Airbus A320-212 | 0537 | 814 |
| | | | |
| ☐ A4O-KA | Airbus A330-243 | 276 | 501 |
| ☐ A4O-KB | Airbus A330-243 | 281 | 502 |
| ☐ A4O-KC | Airbus A330-243 | 286 | 503 |
| ☐ A4O-KD | Airbus A330-243 | 287 | 504 |
| ☐ A4O-KE | Airbus A330-243 | 334 | 505 |
| ☐ A4O-KF | Airbus A330-243 | 340 | 506 |
| | | | |
| ☐ A4O-LB | Airbus A340-312 | 039 | 402 |
| ☐ A4O-LC | Airbus A340-312 | 040 | 403 |
| ☐ A4O-LD | Airbus A340-312 | 097 | 404 |
| ☐ A4O-LE | Airbus A340-312 | 103 | 405 |
| ☐ A4O-LF | Airbus A340-312 | 133 | 406 |
| | | | |
| ☐ A4O-GI | Boeing 767-3P6ER | 264/24485 | 604 |
| ☐ A4O-GJ | Boeing 767-3P6ER | 267/24495 | 605 |
| ☐ A4O-GK | Boeing 767-3P6ER | 270/24496 | 606 |
| ☐ A4O-GS | Boeing 767-3P6ER | 436/26236 | 613 |
| ☐ A4O-GT | Boeing 767-3P6ER | 440/26238 | 614 |
| ☐ A4O-GU | Boeing 767-3P6ER | 501/36233 | 615 |
| ☐ A4O-GV | Boeing 767-3P6ER | 502/26235 | 616 |
| ☐ A4O-GY | Boeing 767-3P6ER | 538/26234 | 619 |
| ☐ A4O-GZ | Boeing 767-3P6ER | 544/26237 | 620 |

### OMANAIR — OMA

| | | | |
|---|---|---|---|
| ☐ A4O-BN | Boeing 737-8Q8 | 1018/30652 | |
| ☐ A4O-BO | Boeing 737-71M | 1154/33103 | |
| ☐ A4O-BS | Boeing 737-7Q8 | 1048/30649 | |
| ☐ A4O-BT | Boeing 737-7Q8 | 1142/28250 | |
| ☐ OK-TVC | Boeing 737-86Q | 963/30278 | Lsf TVS |
| ☐ A4O-AL | ATR 42-500 | 497 | Lsf CIM |
| ☐ A4O-AM | ATR 42-500 | 501 | Lsf CIM |
| ☐ A4O-AS | ATR 42-500 | 574 | |
| ☐ A4O-AT | ATR 42-500 | 576 | |

## A5 - BHUTAN

### DRUK AIR — DRK

| | | | |
|---|---|---|---|
| ☐ A5-RGD | BAe 146 Srs.100 | E1095 | |
| ☐ A5-RGE | BAe 146 Srs.100 | E1199 | |
| ☐ YL-BAK | Avro RJ70 | E1223 | Lsf BTI |

## A6 - UNITED ARAB EMIRATES

### DOLPHIN AIR

| | | | |
|---|---|---|---|
| ☐ A6-ZYA | Boeing 737-2S2C | 597/21926 | std SHJ |
| ☐ A6-ZYB | Boeing 737-2S2C | 603/21928 | std SHJ |
| ☐ A6-ZYC | Boeing 737-2X2 | 807/22679 | std SHJ |

### EMIRATES                                              UAE

| | | | |
|---|---|---|---|
| ☐ A6-EAA | Airbus A330-243 | 348 | |
| ☐ A6-EAB | Airbus A330-243 | 365 | |
| ☐ A6-EAC | Airbus A330-243 | 372 | |
| ☐ A6-EAD | Airbus A330-243 | 382 | |
| ☐ A6-EAE | Airbus A330-243 | 384 | |
| ☐ A6-EAF | Airbus A330-243 | 392 | |
| ☐ A6-EAG | Airbus A330-243 | 396 | |
| ☐ A6-EAH | Airbus A330-243 | 409 | |
| ■ A6-EAI | Airbus A330-243 | 437 | |
| ☐ A6-EAJ | Airbus A330-243 | 451 | |
| ☐ A6-EAK | Airbus A330-243 | 452 | |
| ☐ A6-EAL | Airbus A330-243 | 462 | |
| ☐ A6-EAM | Airbus A330-243 | 491 | |
| ☐ A6-EAN | Airbus A330-243 | 494 | |
| ☐ A6-EAP | Airbus A330-243 | 509 | |
| ☐ A6- | Airbus A330-243 | 518 | o/o |
| ☐ A6- | Airbus A330-243 | 520 | o/o |
| ☐ A6- | Airbus A330-243 | 525 | o/o |
| ☐ A6- | Airbus A330-243 | 455 | o/o |
| ☐ A6- | Airbus A330-243 | 536 | o/o |
| ☐ A6-EKQ | Airbus A330-243 | 248 | |
| ☐ A6-EKR | Airbus A330-243 | 251 | |
| ☐ A6-EKS | Airbus A330-243 | 283 | |
| ☐ A6-EKT | Airbus A330-243 | 293 | |
| ☐ A6-EKU | Airbus A330-243 | 295 | |
| ☐ A6-EKV | Airbus A330-243 | 314 | |
| ☐ A6-EKW | Airbus A330-243 | 316 | |
| ☐ A6-EKX | Airbus A330-243 | 326 | |
| ☐ A6-EKY | Airbus A330-243 | 328 | |
| ☐ A6-EKZ | Airbus A330-243 | 345 | |
| ☐ A6-ERA | Airbus A340-541 | 457 | |
| ☐ A6-ERB | Airbus A340-541 | 471 | |
| ☐ A6- | Airbus A340-541 | 394 | o/o |
| ☐ A6- | Airbus A340-541 | 485 | o/o |
| ☐ A6- | Airbus A340-541 | 520 | o/o |
| ☐ A6- | Airbus A340-541 | 572 | o/o |
| ☐ A6-EMD | Boeing 777-21H | 30/27247 | |
| ☐ A6-EME | Boeing 777-21H | 33/27248 | |
| ☐ A6-EMF | Boeing 777-21H | 42/27249 | |
| ☐ A6-EMG | Boeing 777-21HER | 63/27252 | |
| ☐ A6-EMH | Boeing 777-21HER | 54/27251 | |
| ☐ A6-EMI | Boeing 777-21HER | 47/27250 | |
| ☐ A6-EMJ | Boeing 777-21HER | 91/27253 | |
| ☐ A6-EMK | Boeing 777-21HER | 171/29324 | |
| ☐ A6-EML | Boeing 777-21HER | 176/29325 | |
| ☐ A6-EMM | Boeing 777-31H | 256/29062 | |
| ☐ A6-EMN | Boeing 777-31H | 262/29063 | |
| ☐ A6-EMO | Boeing 777-31H | 300/28680 | |
| ☐ A6-EMP | Boeing 777-31H | 326/29395 | |
| ☐ A6-EMQ | Boeing 777-31H | 396/32697 | |
| ☐ A6-EMR | Boeing 777-31H | 402/29396 | |
| ☐ A6-EMS | Boeing 777-31H | 408/29067 | |
| ☐ A6-EMT | Boeing 777-31H | 414/32699 | |
| ☐ A6-EMU | Boeing 777-31H | 418/29064 | |
| ☐ A6-EMV | Boeing 777-31H | 432/28687 | |
| ☐ A6- | Boeing 777-31H | 29064 | |
| ☐ A6- | Boeing 777-31H | 32700 | |
| ☐ A6- | Boeing 777-31H | 32702 | |
| ☐ A6-EKL | Airbus A310-308 | 667 | For TSC |

### NOVA GULF

| | | |
|---|---|---|
| ☐ A6-SAA | Boeing 727-294 | 1559/22043 |

## A7 - QATAR

### QATAR AIRWAYS                                         QTR

| | | | |
|---|---|---|---|
| ☐ A7-ABN | Airbus A300B4-622R | 664 | |
| ☐ A7-ABO | Airbus A300B4-622R | 668 | |
| ☐ A7-ABV | Airbus A300B4-622R | 690 | |
| ☐ A7-ABW | Airbus A300B4-622R | 688 | |
| ☐ A7-ABX | Airbus A300B4-622R | 554 | |
| ☐ A7-ABY | Airbus A300B4-622R | 560 | |
| ☐ A7-AFA | Airbus A300B4-622R | 630 | |
| ☐ A7-AFB | Airbus A300B4-622R | 614 | Freighter |
| ☐ A7-AFC | Airbus A300B4-622R | 611 | |
| ☐ A7-AAG | Airbus A320-232 | 0927 | Govt |
| ☐ A7-ABR | Airbus A320-232 | 0928 | |
| ☐ A7-ABS | Airbus A320-232 | 0932 | |
| ☐ A7-ABT | Airbus A320-232 | 0943 | |
| ☐ A7-ABU | Airbus A320-232 | 0977 | |
| ☐ A7-ADA | Airbus A320-232 | 1566 | |
| ☐ A7-ADB | Airbus A320-232 | 1648 | |
| ☐ A7-ADC | Airbus A320-232 | 1773 | |
| ☐ A7-ADD | Airbus A320-232 | 1895 | |
| ☐ A7-ADE | Airbus A320-232 | 1957 | o/o |
| ☐ A7-ADF | Airbus A320-232 | 2112 | o/o |
| ☐ A7-ACA | Airbus A330-203 | 473 | |
| ☐ A7-ACB | Airbus A330-203 | 489 | |
| ☐ A7-ACC | Airbus A330-203 | 511 | o/o |
| ☐ A7-ACD | Airbus A330-203 | 521 | o/o |
| ☐ A7-ACE | Airbus A330-203 | 441 | o/o |
| ☐ A7-ACF | Airbus A330-203 | 571 | o/o |
| ☐ A7-HJJ | Airbus A330-203 | 487 | std TLS |
| ☐ A7-AAF | Airbus A310-324 | 473 | |
| ☐ A7-HHJ | Airbus A319-133X | 1335 | Govt |
| ☐ A7-HHK | Airbus A340-211 | 026 | Govt |
| ☐ A7- | Airbus A340-541 | 495 | o/o |

## A9C - BAHRAIN

### DHL AVIATION                                          DHX

| | | | |
|---|---|---|---|
| ☐ A9C-DHL | Boeing 757-23APF | 258/24635 | Lsf BCS |

## B - CHINA - People's Republic

### AIR CHINA                                             CCA

| | | | |
|---|---|---|---|
| ☐ B- | Airbus A319-132 | 2000 | o/o |
| ☐ B- | Airbus A319-132 | 2007 | o/o |
| ☐ B- | Airbus A319-132 | 2015 | o/o |
| ☐ B- | Airbus A319-132 | | o/o |
| ☐ B- | Airbus A319-132 | | o/o |
| ☐ B-2531 | Boeing 737-3J6 | 1224/23302 | |
| ☐ B-2532 | Boeing 737-3J6 | 1237/23303 | |
| ☐ B-2535 | Boeing 737-3J6 | 2002/25078 | |
| ☐ B-2536 | Boeing 737-3J6 | 2016/25079 | |
| ☐ B-2580 | Boeing 737-3J6 | 2254/25080 | |
| ☐ B-2581 | Boeing 737-3J6 | 2263/25081 | |
| ☐ B-2584 | Boeing 737-3J6 | 2385/25891 | |
| ☐ B-2585 | Boeing 737-3J6 | 2384/27045 | |
| ☐ B-2587 | Boeing 737-3J6 | 2396/25892 | |
| ☐ B-2588 | Boeing 737-3J6 | 2489/25893 | |
| ☐ B-2598 | Boeing 737-3J6 | 2493/27128 | |
| ☐ B-2905 | Boeing 737-33A | 2360/25506 | |
| ☐ B-2906 | Boeing 737-33A | 2373/25507 | |
| ☐ B-2907 | Boeing 737-33A | 2414/25508 | |

| ☐ | B-2947 | Boeing 737-33A | 2599/25511 | |
| ☐ | B-2948 | Boeing 737-3J6 | 2631/27361 | |
| ☐ | B-2949 | Boeing 737-3J6 | 2650/27372 | |
| ☐ | B-2953 | Boeing 737-3J6 | 2710/27523 | |
| ☐ | B-2954 | Boeing 737-3J6 | 2768/27518 | |
| ☐ | B-5035 | Boeing 737-36N | 2976/28672 | |
| ☐ | B- | Boeing 737-36N | 2995/28673 | |
| ☐ | B-2641 | Boeing 737-89L | 337/29876 | |
| ☐ | B-2642 | Boeing 737-89L | 359/29877 | |
| ☐ | B-2643 | Boeing 737-89L | 379/29878 | |
| ☐ | B-2645 | Boeing 737-89L | 427/29879 | |
| ☐ | B-2648 | Boeing 737-89L | 511/29880 | |
| ☐ | B-2649 | Boeing 737-89L | 572/30159 | |
| ☐ | B-2650 | Boeing 737-89L | 594/30160 | |
| ☐ | B-2657 | Boeing 737-89L | 1224/30517 | |
| ☐ | B-2670 | Boeing 737-89L | 1055/30514 | |
| ☐ | B-2671 | Boeing 737-89L | 1165/30515 | |
| ☐ | B-2672 | Boeing 737-89L | 1168/30516 | |
| ☐ | B- | Boeing 737-79L | | o/o |
| ☐ | B- | Boeing 737-79L | | o/o |
| ☐ | B- | Boeing 737-79L | | o/o |
| ☐ | B- | Boeing 737-79L | | o/o |
| ☐ | B-2443 | Boeing 747-4J6 | 957/25881 | |
| ☐ | B-2445 | Boeing 747-4J6 | 1021/25882 | |
| ☐ | B-2446 | Boeing 747-2J6B (SF) | 591/23071 | |
| ☐ | B-2447 | Boeing 747-4J6 | 1054/25883 | |
| ☐ | B-2448 | Boeing 747-2J6B (SF) | 628/23461 | |
| ☐ | B-2450 | Boeing 747-2J6B (SF) | 670/23746 | |
| ☐ | B-2456 | Boeing 747-4J6M | 743/24346 | |
| ☐ | B-2458 | Boeing 747-4J6M | 775/24347 | |
| ☐ | B-2460 | Boeing 747-4J6M | 792/24348 | |
| ☐ | B-2462 | Boeing 747-2J6F | 814/24960 | |
| ☐ | B-2467 | Boeing 747-4J6M | 1119/28754 | |
| ☐ | B-2468 | Boeing 747-4J6M | 1128/28755 | |
| ☐ | B-2469 | Boeing 747-4J6M | 1175/28756 | |
| ☐ | B-2470 | Boeing 747-4J6M | 1181/29070 | |
| ☐ | B-2471 | Boeing 747-4J6M | 1229/29071 | |
| ☐ | B-2472 | Boeing 747-4J6 | 1243/30158 | |
| ☐ | B-2499 | Boeing 767-332ER | 797/30597 | Govt |
| ☐ | B-2551 | Boeing 767-2J6ER | 126/23307 | |
| ☐ | B-2553 | Boeing 767-2J6ER | 155/23744 | |
| ☐ | B-2554 | Boeing 767-2J6ER | 156/23745 | |
| ☐ | B-2555 | Boeing 767-2J6ER | 204/24007 | |
| ☐ | B-2556 | Boeing 767-2J6ER | 253/24157 | |
| ☐ | B-2557 | Boeing 767-3J6 | 429/25875 | |
| ☐ | B-2558 | Boeing 767-3J6 | 478/25876 | |
| ☐ | B-2559 | Boeing 767-3J6 | 530/25877 | |
| ☐ | B-2560 | Boeing 767-3J6 | 569/25878 | |
| ☐ | | Boeing 767-3Q8ER | 692/28132 | o/o |
| ☐ | | Boeing 767-3Q8ER | 762/30301 | o/o |
| ☐ | B-2059 | Boeing 777-2J6 | 168/29153 | |
| ☐ | B-2060 | Boeing 777-2J6 | 173/29154 | |
| ☐ | B-2061 | Boeing 777-2J6 | 179/29155 | |
| ☐ | B-2063 | Boeing 777-2J6 | 214/29156 | |
| ☐ | B-2064 | Boeing 777-2J6 | 240/29157 | |
| ☐ | B-2065 | Boeing 777-2J6 | 280/29744 | |
| ☐ | B-2066 | Boeing 777-2J6 | 290/29745 | |
| ☐ | B-2067 | Boeing 777-2J6 | 338/29746 | |
| ☐ | B-2068 | Boeing 777-2J6 | 344/29747 | |
| ☐ | B-2069 | Boeing 777-2J6 | 349/29748 | |
| ☐ | B-2707 | BAe 146 Srs.100 | E1076 | |
| ☐ | B-2708 | BAe 146 Srs.100 | E1081 | |
| ☐ | B-2709 | BAe 146 Srs.100 | E1083 | |
| ☐ | B-2710 | BAe 146 Srs.100 | E1085 | |
| ☐ | B-2385 | Airbus A340-313X | 192 | Lst CXN |
| ☐ | B-2386 | Airbus A340-313X | 199 | Lst CXN |

## CHINA CARGO AIRLINES    CKK

| ☐ | B-2170 | McDD MD-11F | 475/48461 | Lsf CES |

| ☐ | B-2171 | McDD MD-11 | 461/48495 | o/o |
| ☐ | B-2172 | McDD MD-11 | 496/48496 | o/o |
| ☐ | B-2173 | McDD MD-11F | 512/48497 | Lsf CES |
| ☐ | B-2174 | McDD MD-11F | 522/48498 | Lsf CES |
| ☐ | B-2175 | McDD MD-11 | 541/48520 | o/o |

## CHINA EASTERN AIRLINES    CES

| ☐ | B-2306 | Airbus A300B4-605R | 521 | |
| ☐ | B-2307 | Airbus A300B4-605R | 525 | |
| ☐ | B-2308 | Airbus A300B4-605R | 532 | |
| ☐ | B-2318 | Airbus A300B4-605R | 707 | |
| ☐ | B-2319 | Airbus A300B4-605R | 732 | |
| ☐ | B-2320 | Airbus A300B4-605R | 709 | |
| ☐ | B-2321 | Airbus A300B4-605R | 713 | |
| ☐ | B-2322 | Airbus A300B4-605R | 715 | |
| ☐ | B-2325 | Airbus A300B4-605R | 746 | |
| ☐ | B-2326 | Airbus A300B4-605R | 754 | |
| ☐ | B-2215 | Airbus A319-112 | 1541 | |
| ☐ | B-2216 | Airbus A319-112 | 1551 | |
| ☐ | B-2217 | Airbus A319-112 | 1601 | |
| ☐ | B-2222 | Airbus A319-112 | 1603 | |
| ☐ | B-2226 | Airbus A319-112 | 1786 | |
| ☐ | B-2227 | Airbus A319-112 | 1778 | |
| ☐ | B-2331 | Airbus A319-112 | 1285 | |
| ☐ | B-2332 | Airbus A319-112 | 1303 | |
| ☐ | B-2333 | Airbus A319-112 | 1377 | |
| ☐ | B-2334 | Airbus A319-112 | 1386 | |
| ☐ | B-2201 | Airbus A320-214 | 0914 | |
| ☐ | B-2202 | Airbus A320-214 | 0925 | |
| ☐ | B-2203 | Airbus A320-214 | 1005 | |
| ☐ | B-2207 | Airbus A320-214 | 1028 | |
| ☐ | B-2208 | Airbus A320-214 | 1070 | |
| ☐ | B-2209 | Airbus A320-214 | 1030 | |
| ☐ | B-2219 | Airbus A320-214 | 1532 | |
| ☐ | B-2220 | Airbus A320-214 | 1542 | |
| ☐ | B-2221 | Airbus A320-214 | 1639 | |
| ☐ | B-2228 | Airbus A320-214 | 1906 | |
| ☐ | B-2229 | Airbus A320-214 | 1911 | |
| ☐ | B-2335 | Airbus A320-214 | 1312 | |
| ☐ | B-2336 | Airbus A320-214 | 1330 | |
| ☐ | B-2337 | Airbus A320-214 | 1357 | |
| ☐ | B-2338 | Airbus A320-214 | 1361 | |
| ☐ | B-2360 | Airbus A320-214 | 0772 | |
| ☐ | B-2361 | Airbus A320-214 | 0799 | |
| ☐ | B-2362 | Airbus A320-214 | 0828 | |
| ☐ | B-2363 | Airbus A320-214 | 0883 | |
| ☐ | B-2398 | Airbus A320-214 | 1108 | |
| ☐ | B-2399 | Airbus A320-214 | 1093 | |
| ☐ | B-2400 | Airbus A320-214 | 1072 | |
| ☐ | B- | Airbus A320-214 | | o/o |
| ☐ | B- | Airbus A320-214 | | o/o |
| ☐ | B- | Airbus A320-214 | | o/o |
| ☐ | B- | Airbus A320-214 | | o/o |
| ☐ | B- | Airbus A320-214 | | o/o |
| ☐ | B- | Airbus A320-214 | | o/o |
| ☐ | B-2380 | Airbus A340-313X | 129 | |
| ☐ | B-2381 | Airbus A340-313X | 131 | |
| ☐ | B-2382 | Airbus A340-313X | 141 | |
| ☐ | B-2383 | Airbus A340-313X | 161 | |
| ☐ | B-2384 | Airbus A340-313X | 182 | |
| ☐ | B- | Airbus A340-642 | 488 | o/o |
| ☐ | B- | Airbus A340-642 | 514 | o/o |
| ☐ | B-6050 | Airbus A340-642 | 468 | o/o |
| ☐ | B-6051 | Airbus A340-642 | 488 | o/o |
| ☐ | B-2506 | Boeing 737-2T4 | 1093/23272 | |
| ☐ | B-2507 | Boeing 737-2T4 | 1097/23273 | |
| ☐ | B-2508 | Boeing 737-2T4 | 1099/23274 | |
| ☐ | B-2571 | Boeing 737-39P | 3053/29410 | |
| ☐ | B-2572 | Boeing 737-39P | 3071/29411 | |
| ☐ | B-2573 | Boeing 737-39P | 3080/29412 | |

| | | | |
|---|---|---|---|
| ☐ B-2969 | Boeing 737-36R | 3108/30102 | |
| ☐ B-2977 | Boeing 737-36N | 2888/28560 | |
| ☐ B-2978 | Boeing 737-36N | 2896/28561 | |
| ☐ B-2979 | Boeing 737-36N | 2908/28562 | |
| ☐ B-2988 | Boeing 737-36R | 2970/29087 | |
| ☐ B-2660 | Boeing 737-86R | 786/30494 | |
| ☐ B-2680 | Boeing 737-76Q | 1143/30282 | |
| ☐ B-2681 | Boeing 737-79P | 1198/33037 | |
| ☐ B-2682 | Boeing 737-79P | 1219/33038 | |
| ☐ B-2683 | Boeing 737-79P | 1247/28253 | |
| ☐ B-2684 | Boeing 737-79P | 1227/33039 | |
| ☐ B-2685 | Boeing 737-79P | 1244/33040 | |
| ☐ B-2686 | Boeing 737-8Q8 | 1200/28251 | |
| ☐ B-5030 | Boeing 737-79P | 1267/30651 | |
| ☐ B-5031 | Boeing 737-79P | 28255 | o/o |
| ☐ B-5032 | Boeing 737-79P | 30035 | o/o |
| ☐ B-5033 | Boeing 737-79P | 30657 | o/o |
| | | | |
| ☐ B-2170 | McDD MD-11F | 475/48461 | Lst CKK |
| ☐ B-2171 | McDD MD-11 | 461/48495 | |
| ☐ B-2172 | McDD MD-11 | 496/48496 | |
| ☐ B-2173 | McDD MD-11F | 512/48497 | Lst CKK |
| ☐ B-2174 | McDD MD-11F | 522/48498 | Lst CKK |
| ☐ B-2175 | McDD MD-11 | 541/48520 | |
| | | | |
| ☐ B-2256 | McDD MD-90-30 | 2198/53582 | |
| ☐ B-2257 | McDD MD-90-30 | 2200/53583 | |
| ☐ B-2258 | McDD MD-90-30 | 2203/53584 | |
| ☐ B-2262 | McDD MD-90-30 | 2224/53585 | |
| ☐ B-2263 | McDD MD-90-30 | 2233/53586 | |
| ☐ B-2265 | McDD MD-90-30 | 2240/53587 | |
| ☐ B-2268 | McDD MD-90-30 | 2248/53588 | |
| ☐ B-2269 | McDD MD-90-30 | 2259/53589 | |
| ☐ B-2270 | McDD MD-90-30 | 2261/53590 | |
| ☐ B-2127 | McDD MD-82 | 1537/49511 | |
| ☐ B-2129 | McDD MD-82 | 1568/49513 | |
| ☐ B-2131 | McDD MD-82 | 1609/49515 | |

## CHINA NORTHERN AIRLINES     CSN

| | | | |
|---|---|---|---|
| ☐ B-2315 | Airbus A300B4-622R | 733 | |
| ☐ B-2316 | Airbus A300B4-622R | 734 | Lst NGE |
| ☐ B-2323 | Airbus A300B4-622R | 739 | |
| ☐ B-2327 | Airbus A300B4-622R | 750 | |
| ☐ B-2328 | Airbus A300B4-622R | 756 | |
| ☐ B-2329 | Airbus A300B4-622R | 762 | |
| | | | |
| ☐ B-2280 | Airbus A321-231 | 1596 | |
| ☐ B-2281 | Airbus A321-231 | 1614 | |
| ☐ B-2282 | Airbus A321-231 | 1776 | |
| ☐ B-2283 | Airbus A321-231 | 1788 | |
| ☐ B- | Airbus A321-231 | 1974 | o/o |
| ☐ B- | Airbus A321-231 | 1995 | o/o |
| ☐ B- | Airbus A321-231 | | o/o |
| | | | |
| ☐ B-2104 | McDD MD-82 | 1240/49425 | |
| ☐ B-2105 | McDD MD-82 | 1241/49428 | |
| ☐ B-2108 | McDD MD-82 | 1300/49502 | |
| ☐ B-2121 | McDD MD-82 | 1381/49505 | |
| ☐ B-2122 | McDD MD-82 | 1400/49506 | |
| ☐ B-2126 | McDD MD-82 | 1514/49510 | |
| ☐ B-2128 | McDD MD-82 | 1548/49512 | |
| ☐ B-2130 | McDD MD-82 | 1589/49514 | |
| ☐ B-2132 | McDD MD-82 | 1622/49516 | |
| ☐ B-2134 | McDD MD-82 | 1647/49518 | |
| ☐ B-2136 | McDD MD-82 | 1671/49520 | |
| ☐ B-2139 | McDD MD-82 | 1724/49523 | |
| ☐ B-2140 | McDD MD-82 | 1746/49524 | |
| ☐ B-2142 | McDD MD-82 | 1798/49850 | |
| ☐ B-2143 | McDD MD-82 | 1807/49851 | |
| ☐ B-2145 | McDD MD-82 | 1981/49853 | |
| ☐ B-2146 | McDD MD-82 | 2010/53162 | |
| ☐ B-2147 | McDD MD-82 | 2025/53163 | |
| ☐ B-2148 | McDD MD-82 | 2063/53169 | |
| ☐ B-2149 | McDD MD-82 | 2065/53170 | |

| | | | |
|---|---|---|---|
| ☐ B-2150 | McDD MD-82 | 2067/53171 | |
| ☐ B-2151 | McDD MD-82 | 1959/49852 | |
| ☐ B-2152 | McDD MD-82 | 2041/53164 | |
| | | | |
| ☐ B-2100 | McDD MD-90-30 | 4001/60001 | |
| ☐ B-2103 | McDD MD-90-30 | 4002/60002 | |
| ☐ B-2250 | McDD MD-90-30 | 2143/53523 | |
| ☐ B-2251 | McDD MD-90-30 | 2146/53524 | |
| ☐ B-2252 | McDD MD-90-30 | 2150/53525 | |
| ☐ B-2253 | McDD MD-90-30 | 2170/53526 | |
| ☐ B-2254 | McDD MD-90-30 | 2175/53527 | |
| ☐ B-2255 | McDD MD-90-30 | 2177/53528 | |
| ☐ B-2259 | McDD MD-90-30 | 2220/53529 | |
| ☐ B-2260 | McDD MD-90-30 | 2222/53530 | |
| ☐ B-2261 | McDD MD-90-30 | 2228/53531 | |
| ☐ B-2266 | McDD MD-90-30 | 2253/53532 | |
| ☐ B-2267 | McDD MD-90-30 | 2258/53533 | |
| | | | |
| ☐ B-3446 | Yunshuji Y7-100C | 09703 | |
| ☐ B-3466 | Yunshuji Y7-100 | 04707 | |
| ☐ B-3467 | Yunshuji Y7-100 | 05701 | |
| ☐ B-3468 | Yunshuji Y7-100 | 05703 | |
| ☐ B-3477 | Yunshuji Y7-100C | 06705 | |
| ☐ B-3478 | Yunshuji Y7-100 | 06707 | |
| ☐ B-3484 | Yunshuji Y7-100C | 07703 | |
| ☐ B-3486 | Yunshuji Y7-100C | 07705 | |
| ☐ B-3488 | Yunshuji Y7-100 | 07707 | |
| ☐ B-3495 | Yunshuji Y7-100C | 08706 | |

## CHINA NORTHWEST AIRLINES     CNW

| | | | |
|---|---|---|---|
| ☐ B-2301 | Airbus A310-222 | 311 | |
| ☐ B-2302 | Airbus A310-222 | 320 | |
| ☐ B-2303 | Airbus A310-222 | 419 | |
| ☐ B-2317 | Airbus A300B4-605R | 741 | |
| ☐ B-2324 | Airbus A300B4-622R | 725 | |
| ☐ B-2330 | Airbus A300B4-605R | 763 | |
| | | | |
| ☐ B-2205 | Airbus A320-214 | 0984 | |
| ☐ B-2206 | Airbus A320-214 | 0986 | |
| ☐ B-2211 | Airbus A320-214 | 1041 | |
| ☐ B-2212 | Airbus A320-214 | 1316 | |
| ☐ B-2213 | Airbus A320-214 | 1345 | |
| ☐ B-2214 | Airbus A320-214 | 0548 | |
| ☐ B-2224 | Airbus A320-214 | 0533 | |
| ☐ B-2356 | Airbus A320-214 | 0665 | |
| ☐ B-2357 | Airbus A320-214 | 0754 | |
| ☐ B-2358 | Airbus A320-214 | 0838 | |
| ☐ B-2359 | Airbus A320-214 | 0854 | |
| ☐ B-2372 | Airbus A320-214 | 0897 | |
| ☐ B-2375 | Airbus A320-214 | 0909 | |
| ☐ B-2378 | Airbus A320-214 | 0939 | |
| ☐ B-2379 | Airbus A320-214 | 0967 | |
| ☐ B- | Airbus A320-214 | | o/o |
| | | | |
| ☐ B-2701 | BAe 146 Srs.100 | E1019 | |
| ☐ B-2702 | BAe 146 Srs.100 | E1026 | |
| ☐ B-2703 | BAe 146 Srs.100 | E1032 | |
| ☐ B-2711 | BAe 146 Srs.300 | E3207 | |
| ☐ B-2712 | BAe 146 Srs.300 | E3212 | |
| ☐ B-2715 | BAe 146 Srs.300 | E3214 | |
| ☐ B-2717 | BAe 146 Srs.300 | E3216 | |
| ☐ B-2718 | BAe 146 Srs.300 | E3222 | |
| ☐ B-2719 | BAe 146 Srs.300 | E3218 | |
| ☐ B-2720 | BAe 146 Srs.300 | E3219 | |
| | | | |
| ☐ B- | Tu-204-120C | | o/o |
| ☐ B- | Tu-204-120C | | o/o |

## CHINA SOUTHERN AIRLINES     CSN

| | | | |
|---|---|---|---|
| ☐ B- | Airbus A319-132 | 1971 | o/o |
| ☐ B- | Airbus A319-132 | 1986 | o/o |
| ☐ B- | Airbus A319-132 | 2004 | o/o |
| ☐ B- | Airbus A319-132 | 2008 | o/o |

| | | | |
|---|---|---|---|
| ☐ B-2343 | Airbus A320-232 | 0696 | |
| ☐ B-2345 | Airbus A320-232 | 0698 | |
| ☐ B-2346 | Airbus A320-232 | 0704 | |
| ☐ B-2347 | Airbus A320-232 | 0705 | |
| ☐ B-2350 | Airbus A320-232 | 0712 | |
| ☐ B-2351 | Airbus A320-232 | 0718 | |
| ☐ B-2352 | Airbus A320-232 | 0720 | |
| ☐ B-2353 | Airbus A320-232 | 0722 | |
| ☐ B-2365 | Airbus A320-232 | 0849 | |
| ☐ B-2366 | Airbus A320-232 | 0859 | |
| ☐ B-2367 | Airbus A320-232 | 0881 | |
| ☐ B-2368 | Airbus A320-232 | 0895 | |
| ☐ B-2369 | Airbus A320-232 | 0900 | |
| ☐ B-2391 | Airbus A320-232 | 0950 | |
| ☐ B-2392 | Airbus A320-232 | 0966 | |
| ☐ B-2393 | Airbus A320-232 | 1035 | |
| ☐ B-2395 | Airbus A320-232 | 1039 | |
| ☐ B-2396 | Airbus A320-232 | 1057 | |
| ☐ B-2401 | Airbus A320-232 | 0710 | |
| ☐ B-2448 | Airbus A320-232 | 0709 | |
| | | | |
| ☐ B-2526 | Boeing 737-3Y0 | 2089/25172 | |
| ☐ B-2527 | Boeing 737-3Y0 | 2097/25173 | |
| ☐ B-2528 | Boeing 737-3Y0 | 2168/25174 | |
| ☐ B-2539 | Boeing 737-5Y0 | 2306/26068 | |
| ☐ B-2541 | Boeing 737-5Y0 | 1960/24696 | |
| ☐ B-2542 | Boeing 737-5Y0 | 2003/24897 | |
| ☐ B-2543 | Boeing 737-5Y0 | 2079/24898 | |
| ☐ B-2544 | Boeing 737-5Y0 | 2093/24800 | |
| ☐ B-2516 | Boeing 737-5Y0 | 2095/24900 | |
| ☐ B-2546 | Boeing 737-5Y0 | 2150/25175 | |
| ☐ B-2547 | Boeing 737-5Y0 | 2155/25176 | |
| ☐ B-2548 | Boeing 737-5Y0 | 2211/25182 | |
| ☐ B-2549 | Boeing 737-5Y0 | 2218/25183 | |
| ☐ B-2550 | Boeing 737-5Y0 | 2238/25188 | |
| ☐ B-2574 | Boeing 737-37K | 3100/29407 | |
| ☐ B-2575 | Boeing 737-37K | 3104/29408 | |
| ☐ B-2582 | Boeing 737-31B | 2499/25895 | |
| ☐ B-2583 | Boeing 737-31B | 2554/25897 | |
| ☐ B-2596 | Boeing 737-31B | 2437/27151 | |
| ☐ B-2909 | Boeing 737-3Y0 | 2456/26082 | |
| ☐ B-2910 | Boeing 737-3Y0 | 2459/26083 | |
| ☐ B-2911 | Boeing 737-3Y0 | 2460/26084 | |
| ☐ B-2912 | Boeing 737-5Y0 | 2538/26100 | |
| ☐ B-2915 | Boeing 737-5Y0 | 2544/26101 | |
| ☐ B-2920 | Boeing 737-3Q8 | 2523/27271 | |
| ☐ B-2921 | Boeing 737-3Q8 | 2528/27286 | |
| ☐ B-2922 | Boeing 737-31B | 2555/27272 | |
| ☐ B-2923 | Boeing 737-31B | 2565/27275 | |
| ☐ B-2924 | Boeing 737-31B | 2575/27287 | |
| ☐ B-2926 | Boeing 737-31B | 2593/27289 | |
| ☐ B-2927 | Boeing 737-31B | 2595/27290 | |
| ☐ B-2929 | Boeing 737-31B | 2619/27343 | |
| ☐ B-2935 | Boeing 737-37K | 2547/27283 | |
| ☐ B-2936 | Boeing 737-37K | 2609/27335 | |
| ☐ B-2946 | Boeing 737-37K | 2655/27375 | |
| ☐ B-2941 | Boeing 737-31B | 2622/27344 | |
| ☐ B-2952 | Boeing 737-31B | 2678/27519 | |
| ☐ B-2959 | Boeing 737-31B | 2775/27520 | |
| ☐ N999CZ | Boeing 737-3Y9 | 2405/25604 | |
| | | | |
| ☐ B-2693 | Boeing 737-81B | 1187/32921 | |
| ☐ B-2694 | Boeing 737-81B | 1199/32922 | |
| ☐ B-2695 | Boeing 737-81B | 1213/32923 | |
| ☐ B-2696 | Boeing 737-81B | 1230/32924 | |
| ☐ B-2697 | Boeing 737-81B | 1250/32925 | |
| ☐ B-5020 | Boeing 737-81B | 1268/32926 | |
| ☐ B-5021 | Boeing 737-81B | 32927 | o/o |
| ☐ B- | Boeing 737-81B | | o/o |
| ☐ B- | Boeing 737-81B | | o/o |
| ☐ B- | Boeing 737-81B | | o/o |
| | | | |
| ☐ B-2801 | Boeing 757-21B | 144/24014 | |
| ☐ B-2802 | Boeing 757-21B | 148/24015 | |
| ☐ B-2803 | Boeing 757-21B | 150/24016 | |

| | | | |
|---|---|---|---|
| ☐ B-2804 | Boeing 757-21B | 200/24330 | |
| ☐ B-2805 | Boeing 757-21B | 203/24331 | |
| ☐ B-2806 | Boeing 757-21B | 232/24401 | |
| ☐ B-2807 | Boeing 757-21B | 233/24402 | |
| ☐ B-2811 | Boeing 757-21B | 262/24714 | |
| ☐ B-2815 | Boeing 757-21B | 288/24774 | |
| ☐ B-2816 | Boeing 757-21B | 359/25083 | |
| ☐ B-2817 | Boeing 757-21B | 389/25258 | |
| ☐ B-2818 | Boeing 757-21B | 392/25259 | |
| ☐ B-2822 | Boeing 757-21B | 461/25884 | |
| ☐ B-2823 | Boeing 757-21B | 575/25888 | |
| ☐ B-2824 | Boeing 757-21B | 583/25889 | |
| ☐ B-2825 | Boeing 757-21B | 585/25890 | |
| ☐ B-2835 | Boeing 757-236 | 445/25598 | |
| ☐ B-2838 | Boeing 757-2Z0 | 613/27260 | |
| | | | |
| ☐ B-2051 | Boeing 777-21B | 20/27357 | |
| ☐ B-2052 | Boeing 777-21B | 24/27358 | |
| ☐ B-2053 | Boeing 777-21B | 46/27359 | |
| ☐ B-2054 | Boeing 777-21B | 48/27360 | |
| ☐ B-2055 | Boeing 777-21B | 55/27524 | |
| ☐ B-2056 | Boeing 777-21B | 66/27525 | |
| ☐ B-2057 | Boeing 777-21B | 106/27604 | |
| ☐ B-2058 | Boeing 777-21B | 110/27605 | |
| ☐ N688CZ | Boeing 777-21B | 121/27606 | |
| ☐ | Boeing 777-21B | | o/o |
| | | | |
| ☐ B-2473 | Boeing 747-41BF | 1306/32803 | |
| ☐ B-2461 | Boeing 747-41BF | 1312/32804 | |
| ☐ N412MC | Boeing 747-47UF | 1244/30559 | opb GTI |

### CHINA SOUTHWEST AIRLINES            CXN

| | | | |
|---|---|---|---|
| ☐ B-2519 | Boeing 737-3Z0 | 1168/23448 | |
| ☐ B-2520 | Boeing 737-3Z0 | 1184/23449 | |
| ☐ B-2521 | Boeing 737-3Z0 | 1196/23450 | |
| ☐ B-2522 | Boeing 737-3Z0 | 1240/23451 | |
| ☐ B-2530 | Boeing 737-3Z0 | 2252/27046 | |
| ☐ B-2533 | Boeing 737-3Z0 | 2436/27138 | |
| ☐ B-2537 | Boeing 737-3Z0 | 2027/25089 | |
| ☐ B-2586 | Boeing 737-3Z0 | 2357/27047 | |
| ☐ B-2590 | Boeing 737-3Z0 | 2370/27126 | |
| ☐ B-2597 | Boeing 737-3Z0 | 2495/27176 | |
| ☐ B-2599 | Boeing 737-3Z0 | 2558/25896 | |
| ☐ B-2950 | Boeing 737-3Z0 | 2647/27374 | |
| ☐ B-2951 | Boeing 737-3Z0 | 2658/27373 | |
| ☐ B-2957 | Boeing 737-3Z0 | 2738/27521 | |
| | | | |
| ☐ B-2155 | Boeing 737-66N | 887/28649 | |
| ☐ B-2156 | Boeing 737-66N | 932/28650 | |
| ☐ B-2160 | Boeing 737-66N | 938/28652 | |
| ☐ B-2161 | Boeing 737-86N | 965/28655 | |
| ☐ B-2509 | Boeing 737-8Z0 | 466/30072 | |
| ☐ B-2510 | Boeing 737-8Z0 | 381/30071 | |
| ☐ B-2511 | Boeing 737-8Z0 | 487/30073 | |
| ☐ B-2673 | Boeing 737-86N | 1133/29888 | |
| ☐ B-2690 | Boeing 737-86N | 1153/29889 | |
| ☐ B-5023 | Boeing 737-66N | 1276/29890 | |
| ☐ B-5027 | Boeing 737-66N | 29891 | o/o |
| ☐ B- | Boeing 737-8Z0 | | o/o |
| ☐ B- | Boeing 737-600 | | o/o |
| | | | |
| ☐ B-2820 | Boeing 757-2Z0 | 476/25885 | |
| ☐ B-2821 | Boeing 757-2Z0 | 480/25886 | |
| ☐ B-2826 | Boeing 757-2Y0 | 495/26155 | |
| ☐ B-2832 | Boeing 757-2Z0 | 554/25887 | |
| ☐ B-2836 | Boeing 757-2Z0 | 595/27258 | |
| ☐ B-2837 | Boeing 757-2Z0 | 609/27259 | |
| ☐ B-2839 | Boeing 757-2Z0 | 615/27269 | |
| ☐ B-2840 | Boeing 757-2Z0 | 622/27270 | |
| ☐ B-2841 | Boeing 757-2Z0 | 624/27367 | |
| ☐ B-2844 | Boeing 757-2Z0 | 669/27511 | |
| ☐ B-2845 | Boeing 757-2Z0 | 674/27512 | |
| ☐ B-2855 | Boeing 757-2Z0 | 822/29792 | |
| ☐ B-2856 | Boeing 757-2Z0 | 833/29793 | Lst RNA |

| | | | |
|---|---|---|---|
| ☐ B-2388 | Airbus A340-313X | 242 | |
| ☐ B-2389 | Airbus A340-313X | 243 | |
| ☐ B-2390 | Airbus A340-313X | 264 | |
| ☐ B- | Tupolev Tu-204-120C | | o/o |
| ☐ B- | Tupolev Tu-204-120C | | o/o |
| ☐ B- | Tupolev Tu-204-120C | | o/o |

## CHINA UNITED AIRLINES `CUA`

| | | | |
|---|---|---|---|
| ☐ B-4008 | Boeing 737-3T0 | 1507/23839 | Govt |
| ☐ B-4009 | Boeing 737-3T0 | 1516/23840 | Govt |
| ☐ B-4018 | Boeing 737-33A | 2310/25502 | |
| ☐ B-4019 | Boeing 737-33A | 2313/25503 | |
| ☐ B-4020 | Boeing 737-34N | 2746/28081 | |
| ☐ B-4021 | Boeing 737-34N | 2747/28082 | |
| ☐ B-4052 | Boeing 737-3Q8 | 1957/24701 | |
| ☐ B-4053 | Boeing 737-3Q8 | 1994/24702 | |
| | | | |
| ☐ B-4005 | Canadair RJ-200 | 7138 | Govt |
| ☐ B-4006 | Canadair RJ-200 | 7149 | Govt |
| ☐ B-4007 | Canadair RJ-200 | 7180 | Govt |
| ☐ B-4010 | Canadair RJ-200 | 7189 | Govt |
| ☐ B-4011 | Canadair RJ-200 | 7193 | Govt |
| | | | |
| ☐ B-4030 | Ilyushin Il-76MD | 1013407233 | |
| ☐ B-4031 | Ilyushin Il-76MD | 1013408254 | |
| ☐ B-4032 | Ilyushin Il-76MD | 1013409289 | |
| ☐ B-4033 | Ilyushin Il-76MD | 1033416512 | |
| ☐ B-4034 | Ilyushin Il-76MD | 1033416524 | |
| ☐ B-4035 | Ilyushin Il-76MD | 1033416529 | |
| ☐ B-4036 | Ilyushin Il-76MD | 1033417550 | |
| ☐ B-4037 | Ilyushin Il-76MD | 1033417557 | |
| ☐ B-4038 | Ilyushin Il-76MD | 1033417567 | |
| ☐ B-4039 | Ilyushin Il-76MD | 1043418576 | |
| ☐ B-4040 | Ilyushin Il-76MD | 1053419656 | |
| ☐ B-4041 | Ilyushin Il-76MD | 1053420663 | |
| ☐ B-4042 | Ilyushin Il-76MD | 1063418587 | |
| ☐ B-4043 | Ilyushin Il-76MD | 1063420671 | |
| | | | |
| ☐ B-4001 | Tupolev Tu-154M | 85A-711 | |
| ☐ B-4003 | Tupolev Tu-154M | 85A-713 | std |
| ☐ B-4004 | Tupolev Tu-154M | 85A-714 | |
| ☐ B-4014 | Tupolev Tu-154M | 90A-847 | no titles |
| ☐ B-4015 | Tupolev Tu-154M | 90A-856 | |
| ☐ B-4016 | Tupolev Tu-154M | 91A-872 | |
| ☐ B-4022 | Tupolev Tu-154M | 87A-765 | |
| ☐ B-4023 | Tupolev Tu-154M | 88A-770 | |
| ☐ B-4024 | Tupolev Tu-154M | 88A-789 | |
| ☐ B-4027 | Tupolev Tu-154M | 92A-943 | no titles |
| ☐ B-4028 | Tupolev Tu-154M | 93A-967 | |
| ☐ B-4029 | Tupolev Tu-154M | 93A-950 | |
| ☐ B-4050 | Tupolev Tu-154M | 86A-730 | |
| ☐ B-4051 | Tupolev Tu-154M | 86A-741 | |
| ☐ B-4138 | Tupolev Tu-154M | 85A-712 | |

## CHINA XINHUA AIRLINES `CXH`

| | | | |
|---|---|---|---|
| ☐ B-2908 | Boeing 737-341 | 2303/26854 | |
| ☐ B-2934 | Boeing 737-39K | 2559/27274 | |
| ☐ B-2942 | Boeing 737-332 | 2506/25997 | |
| ☐ B-2943 | Boeing 737-332 | 2510/25998 | |
| ☐ B-2945 | Boeing 737-39K | 2639/27362 | |
| ☐ B-2982 | Boeing 737-36Q | 2859/28657 | |
| ☐ B-2987 | Boeing 737-46Q | 2922/28663 | |
| ☐ B-2989 | Boeing 737-46Q | 2939/28758 | |
| ☐ B-2993 | Boeing 737-46Q | 2981/28759 | |

## CHINA XINJIANG AIRLINES `CSN`

| | | | |
|---|---|---|---|
| ☐ B-3022 | ATR 72-212A | 521 | |
| ☐ B-3023 | ATR 72-212A | 531 | |
| ☐ B-3025 | ATR 72-212A | 547 | |
| ☐ B-3026 | ATR 72-212A | 552 | |
| ☐ B-3027 | ATR 72-212A | 555 | |

| | | | |
|---|---|---|---|
| ☐ B-2162 | Boeing 737-7K9 | 909/30041 | |
| ☐ B-2163 | Boeing 737-7K9 | 931/30042 | |
| ☐ B-2930 | Boeing 737-31L | 2556/27273 | |
| ☐ B-2931 | Boeing 737-31L | 2567/27276 | |
| ☐ B-2698 | Boeing 737-76N | 994/32583 | |
| ☐ B-2699 | Boeing 737-76N | 1028/32596 | |
| | | | |
| ☐ B-2812 | Boeing 757-28S | 961/32341 | |
| ☐ B-2813 | Boeing 757-28S | 966/32342 | |
| ☐ B-2827 | Boeing 757-2Y0 | 503/26156 | |
| ☐ B-2830 | Boeing 757-28S | 1015/32343 | |
| ☐ B-2831 | Boeing 757-2Y0 | 482/26153 | |
| ☐ B-2851 | Boeing 757-28S | 797/29215 | |
| ☐ B-2852 | Boeing 757-2Q8 | 782/28833 | |
| ☐ B-2853 | Boeing 757-28S | 811/29216 | |
| ☐ B-2859 | Boeing 757-28S | 868/29217 | |
| | | | |
| ☐ B-2016 | Ilyushin Il-86 | 51483210097 | std URC |
| ☐ B-2018 | Ilyushin Il-86 | 51483210099 | std URC |
| ☐ B-2019 | Ilyushin Il-86 | 51483210100 | std URC |

## CHINA YUNNAN AIRLINES `CYH`

| | | | |
|---|---|---|---|
| ☐ B-2517 | Boeing 737-3W0 | 1166/23396 | |
| ☐ B-2518 | Boeing 737-3W0 | 1193/23397 | |
| ☐ B-2538 | Boeing 737-3W0 | 2040/25090 | |
| ☐ B-2589 | Boeing 737-3W0 | 2377/27127 | |
| ☐ B-2594 | Boeing 737-341 | 2275/26853 | |
| ☐ B-2955 | Boeing 737-33A | 2687/27453 | |
| ☐ B-2956 | Boeing 737-33A | 2690/27907 | |
| ☐ B-2958 | Boeing 737-3W0 | 2727/27522 | |
| ☐ B-2966 | Boeing 737-33A | 2765/27462 | |
| ☐ B-2981 | Boeing 737-3W0 | 2919/28972 | |
| ☐ B-2983 | Boeing 737-3W0 | 2941/28973 | |
| ☐ B-2985 | Boeing 737-3W0 | 2945/29068 | |
| ☐ B-2986 | Boeing 737-3W0 | 2951/29069 | |
| | | | |
| ☐ B-3013 | Canadair RJ-200 | 7571 | |
| ☐ B-3019 | Canadair RJ-200 | 7581 | |
| ☐ B-3021 | Canadair RJ-200 | 7596 | |
| ☐ B-3070 | Canadair RJ-200 | 7647 | |
| ☐ B-3071 | Canadair RJ-200 | 7684 | |
| ☐ B-3072 | Canadair RJ-200 | 7697 | |
| ☐ B-3078 | Canadair RJ-200 | 7704 | o/o |
| ☐ B- | Canadair RJ-200 | | o/o |
| | | | |
| ☐ B-2502 | Boeing 737-7W0 | 292/30075 | |
| ☐ B-2503 | Boeing 737-7W0 | 311/30074 | |
| ☐ B-2568 | Boeing 767-3W0ER | 620/28148 | |
| ☐ B-2569 | Boeing 767-3W0ER | 627/28149 | |
| ☐ B-2639 | Boeing 737-7W0 | 140/29912 | |
| ☐ B-2640 | Boeing 737-7W0 | 148/29913 | |
| ☐ B-5001 | Boeing 767-3W0ER | 644/28264 | |

## CNAC - ZHEJIANG AIRLINES `CJG`

| | | | |
|---|---|---|---|
| ☐ B-2210 | Airbus A320-214 | 1296 | |
| ☐ B-2354 | Airbus A320-214 | 0707 | |
| ☐ B-2355 | Airbus A320-214 | 0724 | |
| ☐ B-2376 | Airbus A320-214 | 0876 | |
| ☐ B-2377 | Airbus A320-214 | 0921 | |
| | | | |
| ☐ B-2225 | Airbus A319-112 | 1654 | |
| ☐ B-2226 | Airbus A319-112 | 1679 | |
| ☐ B-2339 | Airbus A319-112 | 1753 | |

## HAINAN AIRLINES `CHH`

| | | | |
|---|---|---|---|
| ☐ B-2501 | Boeing 737-44P | 3067/29914 | |
| ☐ B-2576 | Boeing 737-44P | 3106/29915 | |
| ☐ B-2578 | Boeing 737-33A | 2333/25603 | |
| ☐ B-2579 | Boeing 737-33A | 2342/25505 | |
| ☐ B-2937 | Boeing 737-3Q8 | 2557/26295 | |
| ☐ B-2938 | Boeing 737-3Q8 | 2581/26296 | |
| ☐ B-2960 | Boeing 737-4Q8 | 1866/24332 | |

| | | |
|---|---|---|
| B-2963 | Boeing 737-3Q8 | 2769/26325 |
| B-2965 | Boeing 737-4Q8 | 2782/26334 |
| B-2967 | Boeing 737-4Q8 | 2793/26335 |
| B-2970 | Boeing 737-4Q8 | 2811/26337 |
| B-2990 | Boeing 737-48E | 2543/25766 |
| B-2157 | Boeing 737-84P | 1015/32600 |
| B-2158 | Boeing 737-84P | 1033/32601 |
| B-2159 | Boeing 737-84P | 972/32599 |
| B-2636 | Boeing 737-86N | 67/28574 |
| B-2637 | Boeing 737-86N | 103/28576 |
| B-2638 | Boeing 737-8Q8 | 212/28220 |
| B-2646 | Boeing 737-8Q8 | 273/28056 |
| B-2647 | Boeing 737-84P | 345/29947 |
| B-2651 | Boeing 737-84P | 607/30474 |
| B-2652 | Boeing 737-84P | 731/30475 |
| B-2675 | Boeing 737-86Q | 1147/32885 |
| B-2676 | Boeing 737-84P | 1170/32602 |
| B-2677 | Boeing 737-84P | 1191/32604 |
| B-3960 | Dornier 328-300 | 3123 |
| B-3961 | Dornier 328-300 | 3128 |
| B-3962 | Dornier 328-300 | 3143 |
| B-3963 | Dornier 328-300 | 3138 |
| B-3965 | Dornier 328-300 | 3140 |
| B-3966 | Dornier 328-300 | 3135 |
| B-3967 | Dornier 328-300 | 3144 |
| B-3968 | Dornier 328-300 | 3148 |
| B-3969 | Dornier 328-300 | 3153 |
| B-3970 | Dornier 328-300 | 3154 |
| B-3971 | Dornier 328-300 | 3172 |
| B-3972 | Dornier 328-300 | 3175 |
| B-3973 | Dornier 328-300 | 3158 |
| B-3975 | Dornier 328-300 | 3159 |
| B-3976 | Dornier 328-300 | 3177 |
| B-3977 | Dornier 328-300 | 3182 |
| B-3978 | Dornier 328-300 | 3187 |
| B-3979 | Dornier 328-300 | 3191 |
| B-3982 | Dornier 328-300 | 3195 |
| B- | Dornier 328-300 | o/o |
| B- | Dornier 328-300 | o/o |
| B- | Dornier 328-300 | o/o |
| B- | Dornier 328-300 | 3198 o/o |
| B- | Dornier 328-300 | o/o |
| B- | Dornier 328-300 | o/o |
| B- | Dornier 328-300 | o/o |
| B- | Dornier 328-300 | o/o |
| B-2490 | Boeing 767-34PER | 889/33047 |
| B-2491 | Boeing 767-34PER | 891/33048 |
| B-2492 | Boeing 767-34PER | 893/33049 |

## SHANDONG AIRLINES — CDG

| | | |
|---|---|---|
| B-2165 | Boeing 737-3Y0 (QC) | 1242/23499 |
| B-2166 | Boeing 737-3Y0 (QC) | 1243/23500 |
| B-2631 | Boeing 737-3Y0 | 2349/26070 |
| B-2961 | Boeing 737-35N | 2774/28156 |
| B-2962 | Boeing 737-35N | 2778/28157 |
| B-2968 | Boeing 737-35N | 2818/28158 |
| B-2995 | Boeing 737-35N | 3054/29315 |
| B-2996 | Boeing 737-35N | 3065/29316 |
| B-3005 | Canadair RJ-200 | 7435 |
| B-3006 | Canadair RJ-200 | 7443 |
| B-3007 | Canadair RJ-200 | 7498 |
| B-3008 | Canadair RJ-200 | 7512 |
| B-3009 | Canadair RJ-200 | 7522 |
| B-3010 | Canadair RJ-200 | 7557 |
| B-3011 | Canadair RJ-200 | 7556 |
| B-3012 | Canadair RJ-200 | 7565 |
| B-3016 | Canadair RJ-200 | 7614 |
| B-3076 | Canadair RJ-200 | 7690 |
| B-3078 | Canadair RJ-200 | 7704 |
| B- | Canadair RJ-200 | o/o |

| | | |
|---|---|---|
| B-3651 | SAAB SF.340B | 289 |
| B-3652 | SAAB SF.340B | 292 |
| B-3653 | SAAB SF.340B | 296 |
| B-3654 | SAAB SF.340B | 302 |
| B- | Canadair RJ-700 | o/o |
| B- | Canadair RJ-700 | o/o |
| B- | Canadair RJ-700 | o/o |

## SHANGHAI AIRLINES

| | | | |
|---|---|---|---|
| B-2153 | Boeing 737-8Q8 | 942/28242 | |
| B-2167 | Boeing 737-8Q8 | 1047/30631 | |
| B-2168 | Boeing 737-8Q8 | 1086/30632 | |
| B-2577 | Boeing 737-76D | 600/30168 | |
| B-2631 | Boeing 737-7Q8 | 35/28212 | |
| B-2632 | Boeing 737-7Q8 | 122/28216 | |
| B-2663 | Boeing 737-7AD | 72/28437 | |
| B-2686 | Boeing 737-8Q8 | 28251 | o/o |
| B-2913 | Boeing 737-76D | 550/30167 | |
| B-2997 | Boeing 737-7Q8 | 272/28223 | |
| B- | Boeing 737-7Q8 | | o/o |
| B- | Boeing 737-76D | | o/o |
| B- | Boeing 737-76D | | o/o |
| B- | Boeing 737-7Q8 | | o/o |
| B-2688 | Boeing 737-86D | 1192/33471 | |
| B- | Boeing 737-8Q8 | | o/o |
| B-2808 | Boeing 757-26D | 231/24471 | |
| B-2809 | Boeing 757-26D | 235/24472 | |
| B-2810 | Boeing 757-26D | 301/24473 | |
| B-2833 | Boeing 757-26D | 560/27152 | |
| B-2834 | Boeing 757-26D | 576/27183 | |
| B-2842 | Boeing 757-26D | 626/27342 | |
| B-2843 | Boeing 757-26D | 684/27681 | |
| B- | Boeing 757-26D | | o/o |
| B-2498 | Boeing 767-36D | 849/27684 | |
| B-2563 | Boeing 767-36D | 546/27309 | |
| B-2567 | Boeing 767-36D | 686/27685 | |
| B-2570 | Boeing 767-36D | 770/27941 | |
| B- | Boeing 767-3Q8ER | 695/28207 | o/o |
| B-3018 | Canadair RJ-200 | 7453 | |
| B-3020 | Canadair RJ-200 | 7459 | |
| B- | Canadair RJ-200 | | o/o |

## SHENZHEN AIRLINES — CSZ

| | | |
|---|---|---|
| B-2932 | Boeing 737-3K9 | 2302/25787 |
| B-2933 | Boeing 737-3K9 | 2331/25788 |
| B-2939 | Boeing 737-31L | 2625/27345 |
| B-2940 | Boeing 737-31L | 2636/27346 |
| B-2971 | Boeing 737-3Q8 | 2290/25373 |
| B-2972 | Boeing 737-33A | 2831/27463 |
| B-2633 | Boeing 737-79K | 110/29190 |
| B-2635 | Boeing 737-79K | 127/20191 |
| B-2666 | Boeing 737-78S | 631/30169 |
| B-2667 | Boeing 737-78S | 654/30170 |
| B-2668 | Boeing 737-78S | 681/30171 |
| B-2669 | Boeing 737-77L | 1023/32722 |
| B-2678 | Boeing 737-76N | 895/32244 |
| B-2679 | Boeing 737-76N | 710/29893 |
| B-2691 | Boeing 737-8Q8 | 841/28241 |
| B-2692 | Boeing 737-8Q8 | 808/30628 |
| B-5025 | Boeing 737-7BX | 823/30741 |
| B-5026 | Boeing 737-7BX | 864/30742 |

## SICHUAN AIRLINES — CSC

| | | |
|---|---|---|
| B-2340 | Airbus A320-232 | 0540 |
| B-2341 | Airbus A320-232 | 0551 |
| B-2342 | Airbus A320-232 | 0556 |
| B-2370 | Airbus A321-231 | 0878 |
| B-2371 | Airbus A321-231 | 0915 |
| B-2373 | Airbus A320-232 | 0919 |
| B-2397 | Airbus A320-232 | 1013 |

| | | | |
|---|---|---|---|
| ☐ B-3040 | Embraer ERJ-145 | 145317 | |
| ☐ B-3041 | Embraer ERJ-145 | 145349 | |
| ☐ B-3042 | Embraer ERJ-145 | 145352 | |
| ☐ B-3043 | Embraer ERJ-145 | 145377 | |
| ☐ B-3045 | Embraer ERJ-145 | 145470 | |
| ☐ B-3498 | Yunshuji Y7-100C | 06706 | |

## WUHAN AIRLINES — CWU

| | | | |
|---|---|---|---|
| ☐ B-3442 | Yunshuji Y7-100C | 08701 | |
| ☐ B-3443 | Yunshuji Y7-100C | 08702 | |
| ☐ B-3471 | Yunshuji Y7-100C | 05706 | |
| ☐ B-3472 | Yunshuji Y7-100C | 05707 | |
| ☐ B-3490 | Yunshuji Y7-100C | 07709 | |
| ☐ B-3491 | Yunshuji Y7-100C | 07710 | |
| ☐ B-2665 | Boeing 737-86R | 876/30495 | |
| ☐ B-2918 | Boeing 737-3Q8 | 2192/24986 | |
| ☐ B-2919 | Boeing 737-3Q8 | 2268/24987 | |
| ☐ B-2928 | Boeing 737-3Q8 | 2550/26294 | |
| ☐ B-2976 | Boeing 737-3S3 | 3059/29244 | |
| ☐ B- | Boeing 737-86R | | o/o |
| ☐ B- | Boeing 737-86R | | o/o |
| ☐ B- | Embraer ERJ-145 | 145447 | o/o |
| ☐ B- | Embraer ERJ-145 | 145509 | o/o |

## XIAMEN AIRLINES — CXA

| | | | |
|---|---|---|---|
| ☐ B-2516 | Boeing 737-2T4 | 1167/23447 | |
| ☐ B-2524 | Boeing 737-25C | 1585/24236 | |
| ☐ B-2529 | Boeing 737-505 | 2578/26297 | Lsf BRA |
| ☐ B-2591 | Boeing 737-505 | 2353/25792 | Lsf BRA |
| ☐ B-2592 | Boeing 737-505 | 2516/27153 | Lsf BRA |
| ☐ B-2593 | Boeing 737-505 | 2449/27155 | Lsf BRA |
| ☐ B-2655 | Boeing 737-3Q8 | 2480/26288 | |
| ☐ B-2656 | Boeing 737-3Q8 | 2519/26292 | |
| ☐ B-2661 | Boeing 737-3Q8 | 2418/26284 | |
| ☐ B-2662 | Boeing 737-3Q8 | 2466/24988 | |
| ☐ B-2973 | Boeing 737-505 | 2805/26336 | |
| ☐ B-2658 | Boeing 737-75C | 637/30512 | |
| ☐ B-2659 | Boeing 737-75C | 676/30513 | |
| ☐ B-2991 | Boeing 737-75C | 90/29085 | |
| ☐ B-2992 | Boeing 737-75C | 108/29086 | |
| ☐ B-2998 | Boeing 737-75C | 73/29042 | |
| ☐ B-2999 | Boeing 737-75C | 86/29084 | |
| ☐ B-5028 | Boeing 737-75C | 1275/30034 | |
| ☐ B-5029 | Boeing 737-75C | 1229/30634 | |
| ☐ B- | Boeing 737-75C | | o/o |
| ☐ B- | Boeing 737-75C | | o/o |
| ☐ B-2819 | Boeing 757-25C | 475/25898 | |
| ☐ B-2828 | Boeing 757-25C | 565/25899 | |
| ☐ B-2829 | Boeing 757-25C | 574/25900 | |
| ☐ B-2848 | Boeing 757-25C | 685/27513 | |
| ☐ B-2849 | Boeing 757-25C | 698/27517 | |
| ☐ B-2868 | Boeing 757-25C | 993/32941 | |
| ☐ B-2869 | Boeing 757-25C | 1009/32942 | |

## YANGTZE RIVER EXPRESS

| | | | |
|---|---|---|---|
| ☐ B-5035 | Boeing 737-330 | 1465/23835 | |
| ☐ B-5036 | Boeing 737-330 | 1508/23836 | |
| ☐ B-5037 | Boeing 737-330 | 1514/23837 | |
| ☐ B-5055 | Boeing 737-330 | 1677/24283 | |

# B-H, B-K - CHINA - HONG KONG

## AIR HONG KONG — AHK

| | | | |
|---|---|---|---|
| ☐ B-HMD | Boeing 747-2L5SF | 435/22105 | Lsf CPA |
| ☐ N371PC | Airbus A300B4-203F | 157 | Lsf XNA |

## CATHAY PACIFIC AIRWAYS — CPA

| | | | |
|---|---|---|---|
| ☐ B-HLA | Airbus A330-342 | 071 | |
| ☐ B-HLB | Airbus A330-342 | 083 | |
| ☐ B-HLC | Airbus A330-342 | 099 | |
| ☐ B-HLD | Airbus A330-342 | 102 | |
| ☐ B-HLE | Airbus A330-342 | 109 | |
| ☐ B-HLF | Airbus A330-342 | 113 | |
| ☐ B-HLG | Airbus A330-342 | 118 | |
| ☐ B-HLH | Airbus A330-342 | 121 | |
| ☐ B-HLI | Airbus A330-342 | 155 | |
| ☐ B-HLJ | Airbus A330-342 | 012 | |
| ☐ B-HLK | Airbus A330-342 | 017 | |
| ☐ B-HLL | Airbus A330-342 | 244 | |
| ☐ B-HLM | Airbus A330-343X | 386 | |
| ☐ B-HLN | Airbus A330-343X | 389 | |
| ☐ B-HLO | Airbus A330-343X | 393 | |
| ☐ B-HLP | Airbus A330-343X | 418 | |
| ☐ B-HLQ | Airbus A330-343X | 420 | |
| ☐ B-HLR | Airbus A330-343X | 421 | |
| ☐ B-HLS | Airbus A330-343X | 423 | |
| ☐ B-HLT | Airbus A330-343X | 439 | |
| ☐ B- | Airbus A330-343X | 539 | o/o |
| ☐ B- | Airbus A330-343X | 548 | o/o |
| ☐ B-HXA | Airbus A340-313X | 136 | |
| ☐ B-HXB | Airbus A340-313X | 137 | |
| ☐ B-HXC | Airbus A340-313X | 142 | |
| ☐ B-HXD | Airbus A340-313X | 147 | |
| ☐ B-HXE | Airbus A340-313X | 157 | |
| ☐ B-HXF | Airbus A340-313X | 160 | |
| ☐ B-HXG | Airbus A340-313X | 208 | |
| ☐ B-HXH | Airbus A340-313X | 218 | |
| ☐ B-HXI | Airbus A340-313X | 220 | |
| ☐ B-HXJ | Airbus A340-313X | 227 | |
| ☐ B-HXK | Airbus A340-313X | 228 | |
| ☐ B-HXL | Airbus A340-313X | 381 | |
| ☐ B-HXM | Airbus A340-313X | 123 | |
| ☐ B-HXN | Airbus A340-313X | 126 | |
| ☐ B-HXO | Airbus A340-313X | 128 | |
| ☐ B-HQA | Airbus A340-642 | 436 | |
| ☐ B-HQB | Airbus A340-642 | 453 | |
| ☐ B-HQC | Airbus A340-642 | 475 | o/o |
| ☐ B- | Airbus A340-642 | | o/o |
| ☐ B-HIA | Boeing 747-267B | 446/21966 | Lst ABD |
| ☐ B-HIB | Boeing 747-267B | 466/22149 | Lst ABD |
| ☐ B-HIC | Boeing 747-267B | 493/22429 | Lst ABD |
| ☐ B-HID | Boeing 747-267B | 531/22530 | Lst ABD |
| ☐ B-HIE | Boeing 747-267B | 566/22872 | Lst VIR |
| ☐ B-HIF | Boeing 747-267B | 582/23048 | Lst VIR |
| ☐ B-HIH | Boeing 747-267B (SF) | 596/23120 | std |
| ☐ B-HMD | Boeing 747-2L5B (SF) | 435/22105 | Lst AHK |
| ☐ B-HME | Boeing 747-2L5B (SF) | 443/22106 | |
| ☐ B-HMF | Boeing 747-2L5B (SF) | 469/22107 | |
| ☐ B-HOO | Boeing 747-467 | 705/23814 | |
| ☐ B-HOP | Boeing 747-467 | 728/23815 | |
| ☐ B-HOR | Boeing 747-467 | 771/24631 | |
| ☐ B-HOS | Boeing 747-467 | 788/24850 | |
| ☐ B-HOT | Boeing 747-467 | 813/24851 | |
| ☐ B-HOU | Boeing 747-467 | 834/24925 | |
| ☐ B-HOV | Boeing 747-467 | 849/25082 | |
| ☐ B-HOW | Boeing 747-467 | 873/25211 | |
| ☐ B-HOX | Boeing 747-467 | 877/24955 | |
| ☐ B-HOY | Boeing 747-467 | 887/25351 | |
| ☐ B-HOZ | Boeing 747-467 | 925/25871 | |
| ☐ B-HUA | Boeing 747-467 | 930/25872 | |
| ☐ B-HUB | Boeing 747-467 | 937/25873 | |
| ☐ B-HUD | Boeing 747-467 | 949/25874 | |
| ☐ B-HUE | Boeing 747-467 | 970/27117 | |
| ☐ B-HUF | Boeing 747-467 | 993/25869 | |
| ☐ B-HUG | Boeing 747-467 | 1007/25870 | |
| ☐ B-HUH | Boeing 747-467F | 1020/27175 | |
| ☐ B-HUI | Boeing 747-467F | 1033/27230 | |
| ☐ B-HUJ | Boeing 747-467 | 1061/27595 | |
| ☐ B-HUK | Boeing 747-467F | 1065/27503 | |
| ☐ B-HUL | Boeing 747-467F | 1255/30804 | |
| ☐ B-HUO | Boeing 747-467F | 1271/32571 | |

| | | | |
|---|---|---|---|
| ☐ B-HUP | Boeing 747-467F | 1282/30805 | |
| ☐ B-HVX | Boeing 747-267F | 776/24568 | |
| ☐ B-HVY | Boeing 747-236F | 480/22306 | |
| ☐ B-HVZ | Boeing 747-267F | 687/23864 | |
| | | | |
| ☐ B-HNA | Boeing 777-267 | 14/27265 | |
| ☐ B-HNB | Boeing 777-267 | 18/27266 | |
| ☐ B-HNC | Boeing 777-267 | 28/27263 | |
| ☐ B-HND | Boeing 777-267 | 31/27264 | |
| ☐ B-HNE | Boeing 777-267 | 94/27507 | |
| ☐ B-HNF | Boeing 777-367 | 102/27506 | |
| ☐ B-HNG | Boeing 777-367 | 118/27505 | |
| ☐ B-HNH | Boeing 777-367 | 136/27504 | |
| ☐ B-HNI | Boeing 777-367 | 204/27508 | |
| ☐ B-HNJ | Boeing 777-367 | 224/27509 | |
| ☐ B-HNK | Boeing 777-367 | 248/27510 | |
| ☐ B-HNL | Boeing 777-267 | 1/27116 | |
| ☐ B-HNM | Boeing 777-367 | 33702 | o/o |
| ☐ B-HNN | Boeing 777-367 | 33703 | o/o |
| ☐ B- | Boeing 777-367 | | o/o |

## DRAGONAIR — HDA

| | | | |
|---|---|---|---|
| ☐ B-HSD | Airbus A320-232 | 0756 | |
| ☐ B-HSE | Airbus A320-232 | 0784 | |
| ☐ B-HSF | Airbus A320-232 | 0816 | |
| ☐ B-HSG | Airbus A320-232 | 0812 | |
| ☐ B-HSH | Airbus A320-232 | 0877 | |
| ☐ B-HSI | Airbus A320-232 | 0930 | |
| ☐ B-HSJ | Airbus A320-232 | 1253 | |
| ☐ B-HSK | Airbus A320-232 | 1721 | |
| ☐ B-HTD | Airbus A321-231 | 0993 | |
| ☐ B-HTE | Airbus A321-231 | 1024 | |
| ☐ B-HTF | Airbus A321-231 | 0633 | |
| ☐ B-HTG | Airbus A321-231 | 1695 | |
| ☐ B- | Airbus A321-231 | 1984 | o/o |
| ☐ B- | Airbus A321-231 | 2021 | o/o |
| | | | |
| ☐ B-HYA | Airbus A330-342 | 098 | |
| ☐ B-HYB | Airbus A330-342 | 106 | |
| ☐ B-HYD | Airbus A330-342 | 132 | |
| ☐ B-HYE | Airbus A330-342 | 177 | |
| ☐ B-HYF | Airbus A330-342 | 234 | |
| ☐ B-HYG | Airbus A330-343X | 405 | |
| ☐ B-HYH | Airbus A330-343X | 407 | |
| ☐ B-HYI | Airbus A330-343X | 479 | |
| ☐ B-HYJ | Airbus A330-343X | 512 | |
| | | | |
| ☐ B-KAA | Boeing 747-312M | 666/23769 | o/o |
| ☐ B-KAB | Boeing 747-312M | 637/23409 | |
| ☐ B-KAC | Boeing 747-3H6M | 650/23600 | |

## B-M - CHINA - MACAU

### AIR MACAU — AMU

| | | | |
|---|---|---|---|
| ☐ B-MAK | Airbus A319-132 | 1758 | |
| ☐ B-MAL | Airbus A319-132 | 1790 | |
| ☐ B-MAM | Airbus A319-112 | 1893 | |
| ☐ B-MAN | Airbus A319-132 | 1912 | o/o |
| ☐ B-MAO | Airbus A319-132 | 1962 | o/o |
| ☐ B-MAA | Airbus A321-131 | 0550 | |
| ☐ B-MAB | Airbus A321-131 | 0557 | |
| ☐ B-MAD | Airbus A320-232 | 0573 | |
| ☐ B-MAE | Airbus A320-232 | 0582 | |
| ☐ B-MAF | Airbus A321-131 | 0620 | |
| ☐ B-MAG | Airbus A321-131 | 0631 | |
| ☐ B-MAH | Airbus A320-232 | 0805 | |
| ☐ B-MAJ | Airbus A321-131 | 0908 | |
| ☐ B-MAP | Airbus A321-131 | 1850 | |
| ☐ B-MAQ | Airbus A321-131 | 1926 | o/o |
| | | | |
| ☐ B-27013 | Boeing 757-27A | 835/29608 | |
| ☐ 9M-TGA | Boeing 727-2F2F | 1808/22993 | Lsf TSE |
| ☐ 9M-TGB | Boeing 727-2F2F | 1810/22998 | Lsf TSE |

## B - CHINA - TAIWAN

### CHINA AIRLINES — CAL

| | | | |
|---|---|---|---|
| ☐ B-18501 | Airbus A300B4-622R | 767 | |
| ☐ B-18502 | Airbus A300B4-622R | 775 | |
| ☐ B-18503 | Airbus A300B4-622R | 788 | |
| ☐ B-18551 | Airbus A300B4-622R | 666 | |
| ☐ B-18571 | Airbus A300B4-622R | 529 | |
| ☐ B-18572 | Airbus A300B4-622R | 533 | |
| ☐ B-18573 | Airbus A300B4-622R | 536 | |
| ☐ B-18575 | Airbus A300B4-622R | 559 | |
| ☐ B-18756 | Airbus A300B4-622R | 743 | |
| ☐ B-18577 | Airbus A300B4-622R | 677 | |
| ☐ B-18758 | Airbus A300B4-622R | 625 | |
| ☐ B-18579 | Airbus A300B4-622R | 555 | |
| | | | |
| ☐ B-18801 | Airbus A340-313X | 402 | |
| ☐ B-18802 | Airbus A340-313X | 406 | |
| ☐ B-18803 | Airbus A340-313X | 411 | |
| ☐ B-18805 | Airbus A340-313X | 415 | |
| ☐ B-18806 | Airbus A340-313X | 433 | |
| ☐ B- | Airbus A340-313X | 541 | o/o |
| ☐ B- | Airbus A340-313X | 163 | o/o |
| | | | |
| ☐ B-18601 | Boeing 737-809 | 113/28402 | |
| ☐ B-18605 | Boeing 737-809 | 130/28404 | |
| ☐ B-18606 | Boeing 737-809 | 132/28405 | |
| ☐ B-18607 | Boeing 737-809 | 139/29104 | |
| ☐ B-18608 | Boeing 737-809 | 141/28406 | |
| ☐ B-18609 | Boeing 737-809 | 161/28407 | |
| ☐ B-18610 | Boeing 737-809 | 295/29105 | |
| ☐ B-18611 | Boeing 737-809 | 302/29106 | |
| ☐ B-18612 | Boeing 737-809 | 695/30173 | |
| ☐ B-18615 | Boeing 737-809 | 1175/30174 | |
| ☐ B-18616 | Boeing 737-809 | 1182/30175 | |
| | | | |
| ☐ B-18201 | Boeing 747-409 | 1114/28709 | |
| ☐ B-18202 | Boeing 747-409 | 1132/28710 | |
| ☐ B-18203 | Boeing 747-409 | 1136/28711 | |
| ☐ B-18205 | Boeing 747-409 | 1137/28712 | |
| ☐ B-18206 | Boeing 747-409 | 1145/29030 | |
| ☐ B-18207 | Boeing 747-409 | 1176/29219 | |
| ☐ B-18208 | Boeing 747-409 | 1186/29031 | |
| ☐ B-18209 | Boeing 747-409 | 1219/29906 | |
| ☐ B-18251 | Boeing 747-409 | 1063/27965 | |
| ☐ B-18271 | Boeing 747-409 | 766/24309 | |
| ☐ B-18272 | Boeing 747-409 | 778/24310 | |
| ☐ B-18273 | Boeing 747-409 | 869/24311 | |
| ☐ B-18275 | Boeing 747-409 | 954/24312 | |
| ☐ B-18701 | Boeing 747-409F | 1249/30759 | |
| ☐ B-18702 | Boeing 747-409F | 1252/30760 | |
| ☐ B-18703 | Boeing 747-409F | 1254/30761 | |
| ☐ B-18705 | Boeing 747-409F | 1263/30762 | |
| ☐ B-18706 | Boeing 747-409F | 1267/30763 | |
| ☐ B-18707 | Boeing 747-409F | 1269/30764 | |
| ☐ B-18708 | Boeing 747-409F | 1288/30765 | |
| ☐ B-18709 | Boeing 747-409F | 1294/30766 | |
| ☐ B-18710 | Boeing 747-409F | 1300/30767 | |
| ☐ B-18711 | Boeing 747-409F | 1314/30768 | |
| ☐ B-18712 | Boeing 747-409F | 33729 | o/o |
| ☐ B- | Boeing 747-409 | | o/o |
| ☐ B- | Boeing 747-409 | | o/o |
| ☐ B-18752 | Boeing 747-209F | 462/22299 | |
| ☐ B-18771 | Boeing 747-209F | 752/24308 | |
| | | | |
| ☐ B-18172 | McDD MD-11 | 519/48469 | std |

### EVA AIRWAYS — EVA

| | | | |
|---|---|---|---|
| ☐ B-16401 | Boeing 747-45E | 942/27062 | |
| ☐ B-16402 | Boeing 747-45E | 947/27063 | |
| ☐ B-16403 | Boeing 747-45EM | 976/27141 | |
| ☐ B-16405 | Boeing 747-45EM | 982/27142 | |
| ☐ B-16406 | Boeing 747-45EM | 1051/27898 | |
| ☐ B-16407 | Boeing 747-45EM | 1053/27899 | |
| ☐ B-16408 | Boeing 747-45EM | 1076/28092 | |
| ☐ B-16409 | Boeing 747-45EM | 1077/28093 | |

| | | | | |
|---|---|---|---|---|
| ☐ B-16410 | Boeing 747-45E | 1140/29061 | | |
| ☐ B-16411 | Boeing 747-45E | 1151/29111 | | |
| ☐ B-16412 | Boeing 747-45E | 1159/29112 | | |
| ☐ B-16461 | Boeing 747-45EM | 994/27154 | | |
| ☐ B-16462 | Boeing 747-45EM | 998/27173 | | |
| ☐ B-16463 | Boeing 747-45EM | 1004/27174 | | |
| ☐ B-16465 | Boeing 747-45EM | 1016/26062 | | |
| ☐ B-16481 | Boeing 747-45EF | 1251/30607 | | |
| ☐ B-16482 | Boeing 747-45EF | 1279/30608 | | |
| ☐ B-16483 | Boeing 747-45EF | 1309/30609 | | |
| ☐ B- | Boeing 747-45EF | | o/o | |
| | | | | |
| ☐ B-16603 | Boeing 767-35EER | 434/26063 | | |
| ☐ B-16605 | Boeing 767-35EER | 438/26064 | | |
| ☐ B-16621 | Boeing 767-25E | 524/27192 | | |
| ☐ B-16622 | Boeing 767-25E | 527/27193 | | |
| ☐ B-16623 | Boeing 767-25E | 532/27194 | | |
| ☐ B-16625 | Boeing 767-25E | 535/27195 | | |
| ☐ N601EV | Boeing 767-3T7ER | 366/25076 | | |
| ☐ N602EV | Boeing 767-3T7ER | 370/25117 | | |
| | | | | |
| ☐ B-16101 | McDD MD-11 | 570/48542 | | |
| ☐ B-16102 | McDD MD-11 | 572/48543 | | |
| ☐ B-16103 | McDD MD-11 | 576/48415 | | |
| ☐ B-16106 | McDD MD-11F | 587/48545 | | |
| ☐ B-16107 | McDD MD-11F | 589/48546 | | |
| ☐ B-16108 | McDD MD-11F | 619/48778 | | |
| ☐ B-16109 | McDD MD-11F | 620/48779 | | |
| ☐ B-16110 | McDD MD-11F | 630/48786 | | |
| ☐ B-16111 | McDD MD-11F | 631/48787 | | |
| ☐ B-16112 | McDD MD-11F | 633/48789 | | |
| ☐ B-16113 | McDD MD-11F | 634/48790 | | |
| ☐ N105EV | McDD MD-11F | 580/48544 | | |
| | | | | |
| ☐ B- | Airbus A330-203 | 530 | o/o | |
| ☐ B- | Airbus A330-203 | 535 | o/o | |
| ☐ B- | Airbus A330-203 | 542 | o/o | |
| ☐ B- | Airbus A330-203 | 555 | o/o | |
| | | | | |
| ☐ B-27017 | Boeing 757-27A | 904/29610 | Lsf FEA | |
| ☐ B-27021 | Boeing 757-27A | 910/29611 | Lsf FEA | |

### FAR EASTERN AIR TRANSPORT — FEA

| | | | |
|---|---|---|---|
| ☐ B-27001 | Boeing 757-2Q8 | 369/25044 | |
| ☐ B-27007 | Boeing 757-29J | 591/27204 | |
| ☐ B-27011 | Boeing 757-27A | 832/29607 | |
| ☐ B-27013 | Boeing 757-27A | 835/29608 | Lst MAU |
| ☐ B-27015 | Boeing 757-27A | 876/29609 | |
| ☐ B-27017 | Boeing 757-27A | 904/29610 | Lst EVA |
| ☐ B-27021 | Boeing 757-27A | 910/29611 | Lst EVA |
| | | | |
| ☐ B-28007 | McDD MD-83 | 1829/49807 | |
| ☐ B-28011 | McDD MD-82 | 1954/53118 | |
| ☐ B-28017 | McDD MD-82 | 2052/53166 | |
| ☐ B-28021 | McDD MD-82 | 2056/53167 | |
| ☐ B-28023 | McDD MD-83 | 1934/49952 | |
| ☐ B-28025 | McDD MD-83 | 2214/53602 | |
| ☐ B-28027 | McDD MD-83 | 2218/53603 | |
| ☐ B-28031 | McDD MD-83 | 1913/49950 | |
| ☐ B-28033 | McDD MD-82 | 2189/53577 | |
| ☐ B-17918 | McDD MD-90-30 | 2193/53571 | Lsf UIA |
| ☐ B-17923 | McDD MD-90-30 | 2153/53534 | Lsf UIA |

### MANDARIN AIRLINES — MDA

| | | | |
|---|---|---|---|
| ☐ B-12270 | Fokker 50 | 20316 | |
| ☐ B-12271 | Fokker 50 | 20284 | |
| ☐ B-12272 | Fokker 50 | 20286 | |
| ☐ B-12273 | Fokker 50 | 20303 | |
| ☐ B-12275 | Fokker 50 | 20306 | |
| ☐ B-12276 | Fokker 50 | 20312 | |
| ☐ B-12279 | Fokker 50 | 20317 | |
| ☐ B-12291 | Fokker 100 | 11500 | |
| ☐ B-12292 | Fokker 100 | 11496 | |
| | | | |
| ☐ B-16802 | Boeing 737-8Q8 | 739/28236 | Lst PSD |
| ☐ B-16803 | Boeing 737-8Q8 | 743/30664 | |
| ☐ B-16805 | Boeing 737-8Q8 | 768/30636 | |

### TRANSASIA AIRWAYS — TNA

| | | | |
|---|---|---|---|
| ☐ B-22712 | ATR 72-202 | 364 | for sale |
| ☐ B-22715 | ATR 72-201 | 381 | for sale |
| ☐ B-22801 | ATR 72-212 | 517 | |
| ☐ B-22802 | ATR 72-212 | 525 | |
| ☐ B-22803 | ATR 72-212 | 527 | |
| ☐ B-22805 | ATR 72-212A | 558 | |
| ☐ B-22806 | ATR 72-212A | 560 | |
| ☐ B-22807 | ATR 72-212A | 567 | |
| ☐ B-22810 | ATR 72-212A | 642 | |
| | | | |
| ☐ B-22306 | Airbus A320-231 | 0441 | |
| ☐ B-22310 | Airbus A320-232 | 0791 | |
| ☐ B-22311 | Airbus A320-232 | 0822 | |
| ☐ B-22601 | Airbus A321-131 | 0538 | |
| ☐ B-22602 | Airbus A321-131 | 0555 | |
| ☐ B-22603 | Airbus A321-131 | 0602 | |
| ☐ B-22605 | Airbus A321-131 | 0606 | |
| ☐ B-22606 | Airbus A321-131 | 0731 | |
| ☐ B-22607 | Airbus A321-131 | 0746 | |

### UNI AIR — UIA

| | | | |
|---|---|---|---|
| ☐ B-15217 | DHC-8-311A | 379 | |
| ☐ B-15219 | DHC-8-311A | 381 | |
| ☐ B-15221 | DHC-8-311A | 325 | |
| ☐ B-15223 | DHC-8-311B | 404 | |
| ☐ B-15225 | DHC-8-311B | 405 | |
| ☐ B-15227 | DHC-8-311B | 406 | |
| ☐ B-15229 | DHC-8-311B | 407 | |
| ☐ B-15231 | DHC-8-311B | 414 | |
| ☐ B-15233 | DHC-8-311B | 402 | |
| ☐ B-15235 | DHC-8Q-311B | 443 | |
| ☐ B-15237 | DHC-8Q-311B | 467 | |
| ☐ B-15239 | DHC-8Q-311B | 571 | |
| ☐ B-17201 | DHC-8Q-202 | 522 | |
| ☐ B-17503 | DHC-8-402Q | 4007 | |
| ☐ B-17505 | DHC-8-402Q | 4016 | |
| | | | |
| ☐ B-17911 | McDD MD-90-30 | 2158/53535 | |
| ☐ B-17913 | McDD MD-90-30 | 2162/53537 | |
| ☐ B-17915 | McDD MD-90-30 | 2168/53538 | |
| ☐ B-17916 | McDD MD-90-30 | 2172/53539 | |
| ☐ B-17917 | McDD MD-90-30 | 2217/53572 | |
| ☐ B-17918 | McDD MD-90-30 | 2193/53571 | Lst FEA |
| ☐ B-17919 | McDD MD-90-30 | 2173/53569 | |
| ☐ B-17920 | McDD MD-90-30 | 2186/53574 | |
| ☐ B-17921 | McDD MD-90-30 | 2166/53554 | |
| ☐ B-17922 | McDD MD-90-30 | 2243/53601 | |
| ☐ B-17923 | McDD MD-90-30 | 2153/53534 | Lst FEA |
| ☐ B-17925 | McDD MD-90-30 | 2171/53568 | |
| ☐ B-17926 | McDD MD-90-30 | 2169/53567 | |

## C - CANADA

### AIR ALLIANCE — GGN

| | | | |
|---|---|---|---|
| ☐ C-FCMN | Beech 1900D | UE-276 | 962 |
| ☐ C-FCMP | Beech 1900D | UE-271 | 961 |
| ☐ C-GAAR | Beech 1900D | UE-207 | 901 |
| ☐ C-GAAT | Beech 1900D | UE-217 | 903 |
| ☐ C-GCML | Beech 1900D | UE-243 | 960 |
| ☐ C-GGGA | Beech 1900D | UE-291 | 951 |
| ☐ C-GHGA | Beech 1900D | UE-293 | 953 |
| ☐ C-GMGA | Beech 1900D | UE-315 | 956 |
| ☐ C-GORA | Beech 1900D | UE-326 | 957 |
| ☐ C-GORC | Beech 1900D | UE-320 | 959 |
| ☐ C-GORF | Beech 1900D | UE-330 | 958 |
| ☐ C-GVGA | Beech 1900D | UE-292 | 952 |
| ☐ C-GWGA | Beech 1900D | UE-309 | 955 |
| ☐ C-GZGA | Beech 1900D | UE-306 | 954 |
| ☐ C-GKGA | Beech 1900C-1 | UC-117 | 963 |
| ☐ C-GTGA | Beech 1900C-1 | UC-62 | |

| AIR CANADA | | | ACA |
|---|---|---|---|
| ☐ C-FYIY | Airbus A319-114 | 0634 | 252 |
| ☐ C-FYJB | Airbus A319-114 | 0639 | 253 |
| ☐ C-FYJD | Airbus A319-114 | 0649 | 254 |
| ☐ C-FYJE | Airbus A319-114 | 0656 | 255 |
| ☐ C-FYJG | Airbus A319-114 | 0670 | 256 |
| ☐ C-FYJH | Airbus A319-114 | 0672 | 257 |
| ☐ C-FYJI | Airbus A319-114 | 0682 | 258 |
| ☐ C-FYJP | Airbus A319-114 | 0688 | 259 |
| ☐ C-FYKC | Airbus A319-114 | 0691 | 260 |
| ☐ C-FYKR | Airbus A319-114 | 0693 | 261 |
| ☐ C-FYKW | Airbus A319-114 | 0695 | 262 |
| ☐ C-FYNS | Airbus A319-114 | 0572 | 251 |
| ☐ C-FZUG | Airbus A319-114 | 0697 | 263 |
| ☐ C-FZUH | Airbus A319-114 | 0711 | 264 |
| ☐ C-FZUJ | Airbus A319-114 | 0719 | 265 |
| ☐ C-FZUL | Airbus A319-114 | 0721 | 266 |
| ☐ C-GAPY | Airbus A319-114 | 0728 | 267 |
| ☐ C-GAQL | Airbus A319-114 | 0732 | 268 |
| ☐ C-GAQX | Airbus A319-114 | 0736 | 269 |
| ☐ C-GAQZ | Airbus A319-114 | 0740 | 270 |
| ☐ C-GARG | Airbus A319-114 | 0742 | 271 |
| ☐ C-GARJ | Airbus A319-114 | 0752 | 272 |
| ☐ C-GARO | Airbus A319-114 | 0757 | 273 |
| ☐ C-GBHM | Airbus A319-114 | 0769 | 274 |
| ☐ C-GBHN | Airbus A319-114 | 0773 | 275 |
| ☐ C-GBHO | Airbus A319-114 | 0779 | 276 |
| ☐ C-GBHR | Airbus A319-114 | 0785 | 277 |
| ☐ C-GBHY | Airbus A319-114 | 0800 | 278 |
| ☐ C-GBHZ | Airbus A319-114 | 0813 | 279 |
| ☐ C-GBIA | Airbus A319-114 | 0817 | 280 |
| ☐ C-GBIJ | Airbus A319-114 | 0829 | 281 |
| ☐ C-GBIK | Airbus A319-114 | 0831 | 282 |
| ☐ C-GBIM | Airbus A319-114 | 0840 | 283 |
| ☐ C-GBIN | Airbus A319-114 | 0845 | 284 |
| ☐ C-GBIP | Airbus A319-114 | 0546 | 285 |
| ☐ C-GITP | Airbus A319-112 | 1562 | 286 |
| ☐ C-GITR | Airbus A319-112 | 1577 | 287 |
| ☐ C-GITT | Airbus A319-112 | 1630 | 288 |
| ☐ C-GJTA | Airbus A319-112 | 1673 | 290 |
| ☐ C-GJTC | Airbus A319-112 | 1668 | 289 |
| ☐ C-GJVS | Airbus A319-112 | 1718 | 291 |
| ☐ C-GJVY | Airbus A319-112 | 1742 | 292 |
| ☐ C-GJWE | Airbus A319-112 | 1756 | 293 |
| ☐ C-GJWF | Airbus A319-112 | 1765 | 294 |
| ☐ C-GKNW | Airbus A319-112 | 1805 | 295 |
| ☐ C-GKOB | Airbus A319-112 | 1853 | Tango |
| ☐ C-GKOC | Airbus A319-112 | 1886 | 297 o/o |
| ☐ C- | Airbus A319-112 | 1963 | |
| ☐ C- | Airbus A319-112 | 2103 | 298 o/o |
| ☐ C-FDCA | Airbus A320-211 | 0232 | Tango |
| ☐ C-FDQQ | Airbus A320-211 | 0059 | 201 |
| ☐ C-FDQV | Airbus A320-211 | 0068 | 202 |
| ☐ C-FDRH | Airbus A320-211 | 0073 | 203 |
| ☐ C-FDRK | Airbus A320-211 | 0084 | 204 |
| ☐ C-FDRP | Airbus A320-211 | 0122 | 205 |
| ☐ C-FDSN | Airbus A320-211 | 0126 | 206 |
| ☐ C-FDST | Airbus A320-211 | 0127 | 207 |
| ☐ C-FDSU | Airbus A320-211 | 0141 | 208 |
| ☐ C-FFWI | Airbus A320-211 | 0149 | 209 |
| ☐ C-FFWJ | Airbus A320-211 | 0150 | 210 |
| ☐ C-FFWM | Airbus A320-211 | 0154 | 211 |
| ☐ C-FFWN | Airbus A320-211 | 0159 | 212 |
| ☐ C-FGYL | Airbus A320-211 | 0254 | 218 |
| ☐ C-FGYS | Airbus A320-211 | 0255 | 219 |
| ☐ C-FKAJ | Airbus A320-211 | 0333 | 227 |
| ☐ C-FKCK | Airbus A320-211 | 0265 | 220 |
| ☐ C-FKCO | Airbus A320-211 | 0277 | 221 |
| ☐ C-FKCR | Airbus A320-211 | 0290 | 222 |
| ☐ C-FKOJ | Airbus A320-211 | 0330 | 226 |
| ☐ C-FKPO | Airbus A320-211 | 0311 | 224 |
| ☐ C-FKPS | Airbus A320-211 | 0310 | 223 |
| ☐ C-FKPT | Airbus A320-211 | 0324 | 225 |
| ☐ C-FLSF | Airbus A320-211 | 0279 | Tango |
| ☐ C-FLSI | Airbus A320-211 | 0283 | 407 |
| ☐ C-FLSS | Airbus A320-211 | 0284 | 408 |

| | | | |
|---|---|---|---|
| ☐ C-FLSU | Airbus A320-211 | 0309 | Tango |
| ☐ C-FMEQ | Airbus A320-211 | 0302 | Tango |
| ☐ C-FMES | Airbus A320-211 | 0305 | Tango |
| ☐ C-FMJK | Airbus A320-211 | 0342 | 229 |
| ☐ C-FMST | Airbus A320-211 | 0350 | 230 |
| ☐ C-FMSV | Airbus A320-211 | 0359 | 231 |
| ☐ C-FMSX | Airbus A320-211 | 0378 | 232 |
| ☐ C-FMSY | Airbus A320-211 | 0384 | 233 |
| ☐ C-FNNA | Airbus A320-211 | 0426 | 234 |
| ☐ C-FNVU | Airbus A320-211 | 0403 | Tango |
| ☐ C-FNVV | Airbus A320-211 | 0404 | Tango |
| ☐ C-FPDN | Airbus A320-211 | 0341 | 228 |
| ☐ C-FPWD | Airbus A320-211 | 0231 | Tango |
| ☐ C-FPWE | Airbus A320-211 | 0175 | Tango |
| ☐ C-FTJO | Airbus A320-211 | 0183 | 213 |
| ☐ C-FTJP | Airbus A320-211 | 0233 | 214 |
| ☐ C-FTJQ | Airbus A320-211 | 0242 | 215 |
| ☐ C-FTJR | Airbus A320-211 | 0248 | 216 |
| ☐ C-FTJS | Airbus A320-211 | 0253 | 217 |
| ☐ C-FXCD | Airbus A320-211 | | 239 o/o |
| ☐ C-FZUB | Airbus A320-211 | 1940 | 238 o/o |
| ☐ C-GJVT | Airbus A320-211 | 1719 | 235 |
| ☐ C-GKOD | Airbus A320-211 | 1864 | 236 |
| ☐ C-GKOE | Airbus A320-211 | 1874 | 237 |
| ☐ C-GPWG | Airbus A320-211 | 0174 | Tango |
| ☐ C-GQCA | Airbus A320-211 | 0210 | Tango |
| ☐ C- | Airbus A320-211 | 1933 | o/o |
| ☐ C-FZUY | Airbus A321-211 | 1912 | 462 o/o |
| ☐ C-FZVF | Airbus A321-211 | 1794 | 461 |
| ☐ C-GITU | Airbus A321-211 | 1602 | 451 |
| ☐ C-GITY | Airbus A321-211 | 1611 | 452 |
| ☐ C-GIUB | Airbus A321-211 | 1623 | 453 |
| ☐ C-GIUE | Airbus A321-211 | 1632 | 454 |
| ☐ C-GIUF | Airbus A321-211 | 1638 | 455 |
| ☐ C-GJVX | Airbus A321-211 | 1726 | 456 |
| ☐ C-GJWD | Airbus A321-211 | 1748 | 457 |
| ☐ C-GJWI | Airbus A321-211 | 1772 | 458 |
| ☐ C-GJWN | Airbus A321-211 | 1783 | 459 |
| ☐ C-GJWO | Airbus A321-211 | 1811 | 460 |
| ☐ C-GKOH | Airbus A321-211 | 0674 | 465 |
| ☐ C-GKOI | Airbus A321-211 | 0675 | 466 |
| ☐ C-GKOJ | Airbus A321-211 | 0684 | 467 |
| ☐ C-GFAF | Airbus A330-343X | 277 | 931 |
| ☐ C-GFAH | Airbus A330-343X | 279 | 932 |
| ☐ C-GFAJ | Airbus A330-343X | 284 | 933 |
| ☐ C-GFUR | Airbus A330-343X | 344 | 934 |
| ☐ C-GHKR | Airbus A330-343X | 400 | 935 |
| ☐ C-GHKW | Airbus A330-343X | 408 | 936 |
| ☐ C-GHKX | Airbus A330-343X | 412 | 937 |
| ☐ C-GHLM | Airbus A330-343X | 419 | 938 |
| ☐ C-FTNQ | Airbus A340-313 | 088 | |
| ☐ C-FYKX | Airbus A340-313X | 150 | 901 |
| ☐ C-FYKZ | Airbus A340-313X | 154 | 902 |
| ☐ C-FYLC | Airbus A340-313X | 167 | 903 |
| ☐ C-FYLD | Airbus A340-313X | 170 | 904 |
| ☐ C-FYLG | Airbus A340-313X | 175 | 905 |
| ☐ C-FYLU | Airbus A340-313X | 179 | 906 |
| ☐ C-GDVW | Airbus A340-313X | 273 | 909 |
| ☐ C-GDVZ | Airbus A340-313X | 278 | 910 |
| ☐ C-GKOL | Airbus A340-541 | 445 | 951 o/o |
| ☐ C-GKOM | Airbus A340-541 | 464 | 952 o/o |
| ☐ C-GKOO | Airbus A340-642 | | 961 o/o |
| ☐ C-GKOU | Airbus A340-642 | | 962 o/o |
| ☐ C-GKOV | Airbus A340-642 | | 963 o/o |
| ☐ C-FACP | Boeing 737-2L9 | 623/22072 | std YYC |
| ☐ C-FCPM | Boeing 737-2T7 | 850/22761 | AC Jetz |
| ☐ C-FCPN | Boeing 737-2T7 | 856/22762 | |
| ☐ C-FHCP | Boeing 737-2T5 | 641/22024 | Zip |
| ☐ C-GCPM | Boeing 737-217 | 560/21716 | |
| ☐ C-GCPN | Boeing 737-217 | 581/21717 | Zip |
| ☐ C-GCPO | Boeing 737-217 | 584/21718 | Zip |
| ☐ C-GCPP | Boeing 737-217 | 666/22255 | Zip |
| ☐ C-GCPQ | Boeing 737-217 | 672/22256 | |
| ☐ C-GCPS | Boeing 737-217 | 756/22257 | Tango |

| Reg | Type | Serial | Notes |
|---|---|---|---|
| ☐ C-GCPT | Boeing 737-217 | 770/22258 | |
| ☐ C-GCPU | Boeing 737-217 | 771/22259 | Zip |
| ☐ C-GCPV | Boeing 737-217 | 784/22260 | AC Jetz |
| ☐ C-GCPX | Boeing 737-217 | 786/22341 | AC Jetz |
| ☐ C-GCPY | Boeing 737-217 | 810/22342 | |
| ☐ C-GCPZ | Boeing 737-217 | 861/22658 | AC Jetz |
| ☐ C-GEPW | Boeing 737-275 | 425/21115 | std YVR |
| ☐ C-GFCP | Boeing 737-217 | 874/22659 | std YVR |
| ☐ C-GIPW | Boeing 737-275 | 556/21712 | Tango |
| ☐ C-GJCP | Boeing 737-217 | 911/22728 | ZIP |
| ☐ C-GJPW | Boeing 737-275 | 598/21713 | std YVR |
| ☐ C-GKCP | Boeing 737-217 | 915/22729 | |
| ☐ C-GKPW | Boeing 737-275 | 627/21819 | |
| ☐ C-GMCP | Boeing 737-217 | 945/22864 | Zip |
| ☐ C-GNPW | Boeing 737-275 | 684/22159 | std |
| ☐ C-GPPW | Boeing 737-275 | 753/22264 | std |
| ☐ C-GQBB | Boeing 737-296 | 665/22276 | std |
| ☐ C-GQBH | Boeing 737-296 | 759/22516 | std YVR |
| ☐ C-GQCP | Boeing 737-217 | 960/22865 | |
| ☐ C-GRPW | Boeing 737-275 | 765/22266 | std YVR |
| ☐ C-GTPW | Boeing 737-275 | 824/22807 | std |
| ☐ C-GUPW | Boeing 737-275 | 898/22873 | |
| ☐ C-GVPW | Boeing 737-275 | 904/22874 | std |
| ☐ C-GWPW | Boeing 737-275 | 1109/23283 | |
| | | | |
| ☐ C-FBCA | Boeing 747-475 | 912/25422 | 384 |
| ☐ C-FCRA | Boeing 747-475 | 837/24895 | 382 |
| ☐ C-FGHZ | Boeing 747-4F6 | 1038/27827 | 385 |
| ☐ C-GAGL | Boeing 747-433M | 840/24998 | 341 |
| ☐ C-GAGM | Boeing 747-433M | 862/25074 | 342 |
| ☐ C-GAGN | Boeing 747-433M | 868/25075 | 343 |
| ☐ C-GMWW | Boeing 747-475 | 823/24883 | 381; std |
| | | | |
| ☐ C-FBEF | Boeing 767-233ER | 250/24323 | 617 |
| ☐ C-FBEG | Boeing 767-233ER | 252/24324 | 618 |
| ☐ C-FBEM | Boeing 767-233ER | 254/24325 | 619 |
| ☐ C-FCAB | Boeing 767-375ER | 213/24082 | 681 |
| ☐ C-FCAE | Boeing 767-375ER | 215/24083 | 682 |
| ☐ C-FCAF | Boeing 767-375ER | 219/24084 | 683 |
| ☐ C-FCAG | Boeing 767-375ER | 220/24085 | 684 |
| ☐ C-FMWP | Boeing 767-333ER | 508/25583 | 631 |
| ☐ C-FMWQ | Boeing 767-333ER | 596/25584 | 632 |
| ☐ C-FMWU | Boeing 767-333ER | 597/25585 | 633 |
| ☐ C-FMWV | Boeing 767-333ER | 599/25586 | 634 |
| ☐ C-FMWY | Boeing 767-333ER | 604/25587 | 635 |
| ☐ C-FMXC | Boeing 767-333ER | 606/25588 | 636 |
| ☐ C-FOCA | Boeing 767-375ER | 311/24575 | 640 |
| ☐ C-FPCA | Boeing 767-375ER | 258/24306 | 637 |
| ☐ C-FTCA | Boeing 767-375ER | 259/24307 | 638 |
| ☐ C-FUCL | Boeing 767-209ER | 60/22682 | 622 |
| ☐ C-FVNM | Boeing 767-209ER | 18/22681 | 621; std |
| ☐ C-FXCA | Boeing 767-375ER | 302/24574 | 639 |
| ☐ C-GAUB | Boeing 767-233 | 16/22517 | 601 |
| ☐ C-GAUE | Boeing 767-233 | 22/22518 | 602 |
| ☐ C-GAUH | Boeing 767-233 | 40/22519 | 603 |
| ☐ C-GAUN | Boeing 767-233 | 47/22520 | 604 |
| ☐ C-GAUP | Boeing 767-233 | 66/22521 | 605; std |
| ☐ C-GAUS | Boeing 767-233 | 75/22522 | 606 |
| ☐ C-GAUU | Boeing 767-233 | 87/22523 | 607; std |
| ☐ C-GAUW | Boeing 767-233 | 88/22524 | 608; std |
| ☐ C-GAUY | Boeing 767-233ER | 91/22525 | 609; std |
| ☐ C-GAVA | Boeing 767-233ER | 92/22526 | 610 |
| ☐ C-GAVC | Boeing 767-233ER | 102/22527 | 611; std |
| ☐ C-GAVF | Boeing 767-233ER | 105/22528 | 612 |
| ☐ C-GBZR | Boeing 767-38EER | 411/25404 | 645 |
| ☐ C-GDSP | Boeing 767-233ER | 229/24142 | 613; std |
| ☐ C-GDSS | Boeing 767-233ER | 233/24143 | 614 |
| ☐ C-GDSU | Boeing 767-233ER | 234/24144 | 615 |
| ☐ C-GDSY | Boeing 767-233ER | 236/24145 | 616 |
| ☐ C-GDUZ | Boeing 767-38EER | 399/25347 | 646 |
| ☐ C-GEOQ | Boeing 767-375ER | 765/30112 | 647 |
| ☐ C-GEOU | Boeing 767-375ER | 771/30108 | 648 |
| ☐ C-GGBI | Boeing 767-3S1ER | 559/26608 | 650 |
| ☐ C-GGBJ | Boeing 767-35HER | 459/26389 | 651 |
| ☐ C-GGBK | Boeing 767-3S1ER | 384/25120 | 649 |
| ☐ C-GGMX | Boeing 767-3Y0ER | 351/24947 | 652 |
| ☐ C-GGFJ | Boeing 767-3Y0ER | 357/24952 | 653 |
| ☐ C-GGOH | Boeing 767-3Y0ER | 450/26200 | 654; std |
| ☐ C-GHLA | Boeing 767-35HER | 445/26387 | 656 |
| ☐ C-GHLK | Boeing 767-35HER | 456/26388 | 657 |
| ☐ C-GHLQ | Boeing 767-36NER | 832/30846 | 658 |
| ☐ C-GHLT | Boeing 767-36NER | 835/30850 | 659 |
| ☐ C-GHLU | Boeing 767-36NER | 836/30851 | 660 |
| ☐ C-GHLV | Boeing 767-36NER | 843/30852 | 661 |
| ☐ C-GHML | Boeing 767-3Y0ER | 380/24948 | 655 |
| ☐ C-GHPA | Boeing 767-3Y0ER | 386/25000 | 686 |
| ☐ C-GHPD | Boeing 767-3Y0ER | 354/24999 | 687 |
| ☐ C-GLCA | Boeing 767-375ER | 361/25120 | 641 |
| ☐ C-GPWA | Boeing 767-275 | 36/22683 | 671; std |
| ☐ C-GPWB | Boeing 767-275 | 52/22684 | 672 |
| ☐ C-GSCA | Boeing 767-375ER | 372/25121 | 642 |
| | | | |
| ☐ C-FRIA | Canadair RJ-200 | 7045 | 101 |
| ☐ C-FRIB | Canadair RJ-200 | 7047 | 102 |
| ☐ C-FRID | Canadair RJ-200 | 7049 | 103 |
| ☐ C-FRIL | Canadair RJ-200 | 7051 | 104 |
| ☐ C-FSJF | Canadair RJ-200 | 7054 | 105 |
| ☐ C-FSJJ | Canadair RJ-200 | 7058 | 106 |
| ☐ C-FSJU | Canadair RJ-200 | 7060 | 107 |
| ☐ C-FSKE | Canadair RJ-200 | 7065 | 108 |
| ☐ C-FSKM | Canadair RJ-200 | 7071 | 110 |
| ☐ C-FVKM | Canadair RJ-200 | 7074 | 111 |
| ☐ C-FVKN | Canadair RJ-200 | 7078 | 112 |
| ☐ C-FVKR | Canadair RJ-200 | 7083 | 114 |
| ☐ C-FVMD | Canadair RJ-200 | 7082 | 113 |
| ☐ C-FWJB | Canadair RJ-200 | 7087 | 115 |
| ☐ C-FWJF | Canadair RJ-200 | 7095 | 116 |
| ☐ C-FWJI | Canadair RJ-200 | 7096 | 117 |
| ☐ C-FWJS | Canadair RJ-200 | 7097 | 118 |
| ☐ C-FWJT | Canadair RJ-200 | 7098 | 119 |
| ☐ C-FWRR | Canadair RJ-200 | 7107 | 120 |
| ☐ C-FWRS | Canadair RJ-200 | 7112 | 121 |
| ☐ C-FWRT | Canadair RJ-200 | 7118 | 122 |
| ☐ C-FWSC | Canadair RJ-200 | 7120 | 123 |
| ☐ C-FXMY | Canadair RJ-200 | 7124 | 124 |
| ☐ C-FZAQ | Canadair RJ-200 | 7155 | 151 |
| ☐ C-FZSI | Canadair RJ-200 | 7160 | 152 |

## AIR INUIT — AIE

| Reg | Type | Serial | Notes |
|---|---|---|---|
| ☐ C-FCJD | DHC-8-102 | 158 | |
| ☐ C-FDAO | DHC-8-102 | 123 | |
| ☐ C-FDOX | HS.748 Srs.2A /310LFD | 1749 | |
| ☐ C-FGET | HS.748 Srs.2A/244 | 1724 | |
| ☐ C-GCUK | HS.748 Srs.2A /343LFD | 1762 | |
| ☐ C-GEGJ | HS.748 Srs.2A/244 | 1711 | |
| ☐ C-GHQZ | DHC-8-314 | 370 | opf APZ |
| ☐ C-GJNL | DHC-8-311 | 422 | opf APZ |

## AIR NORTH — ANT

| Reg | Type | Serial | Notes |
|---|---|---|---|
| ☐ C-FAGI | HS.748 Srs.2A/276 | 1699 | |
| ☐ C-FJLB | Boeing 737-201 | 680/22273 | |
| ☐ C-FYDU | HS.748 Srs.2A/273 | 1694 | |
| ☐ C-FYDY | HS.748 Srs.2A/233 | 1661 | |
| ☐ C-GNAU | Boeing 737-201 | 602/21817 | |

## AIR TRANSAT — TSC

| Reg | Type | Serial | Notes |
|---|---|---|---|
| ☐ C-FDAT | Airbus A310-308 | 658 | |
| ☐ C-GFAT | Airbus A310-308 | 545 | |
| ☐ C-GLAT | Airbus A310-308 | 588 | |
| ☐ C-GPAT | Airbus A310-308 | 597 | |
| ☐ C-GSAT | Airbus A310-308 | 600 | |
| ☐ C- | Airbus A310-308 | 667 | o/o |
| | | | |
| ☐ C-FTNA | L-1011-150 Tristar | 1019 | |
| ☐ C-FTNG | L-1011-150 Tristar | 1048 | 507 |
| ☐ C-FTNL | L-1011-100 Tristar | 1073 | 512 |
| ☐ C-FTSW | L-1011-100 Tristar | 1246 | 246 |
| ☐ C-GATH | L-1011-500 Tristar | 1235 | 235 |
| ☐ C-GATM | L-1011-500 Tristar | 1236 | 236 |
| ☐ C-GTSP | L-1011-500 Tristar | 1242 | 242 |
| ☐ C-GTSQ | L-1011-500 Tristar | 1243 | 243 |
| ☐ C-GTSR | L-1011-500 Tristar | 1239 | Lst SEU |
| ☐ C-GTSZ | L-1011-100 Tristar | 1103 | 548 |

| | | | |
|---|---|---|---|
| ☐ C-GGTS | Airbus A330-243 | 250 | |
| ☐ C-GITS | Airbus A330-243 | 271 | |
| ☐ C-GKTS | Airbus A330-342 | 111 | |
| ☐ C-GPTS | Airbus A330-243 | 480 | |
| ☐ C-GTSJ | Boeing 757-236ER | 271/24772 | |
| ☐ C-GTSN | Boeing 757-28A | 268/24543 | |
| ☐ C-GTSV | Boeing 757-28A | 530/25622 | Lst HLN |

## ALLCANADA EXPRESS                              CNX

| | | | |
|---|---|---|---|
| ☐ C-FACA | Boeing 727-243F | 1568/22052 | |
| ☐ C-FACJ | Boeing 727-260F | 1534/21979 | Lsf UPS |
| ☐ C-FACK | Boeing 727-217F | 1122/21056 | |
| ☐ C-FACM | Boeing 727-260F | 1789/22759 | Lsf UPS |
| ☐ C-FACN | Boeing 727-221F | 1796/22540 | Lsf LHN |
| ☐ C-FACR | Boeing 727-217F | 1117/21055 | |
| ☐ C-FACW | Boeing 727-227 | 1274/21366 | std |
| ☐ C-FACX | Boeing 727-27F | 448/19500 | Lsf KFA |
| ☐ C-FCJF | Boeing 727-223F | 1653/22011 | |
| ☐ C-GACC | Boeing 727-277F | 1030/20550 | |

## ALTA FLIGHTS                                      ALZ

| | | | |
|---|---|---|---|
| ☐ C-FAFI | SA.227DC Metro 23 | DC-868B | |
| ☐ C-FAFM | SA.227AC Metro III | AC-674B | |
| ☐ C-FAFR | SA.227AC Metro III | AC-684 | |
| ☐ C-FAFW | SA.227AC Metro III | AC-756 | |
| ☐ C-FAFZ | SA.227AC Metro III | AC-676 | |
| ☐ C-FDMR | SA.227DC Metro 23 | DC-889B | |
| ☐ C-GAAF | SA.227DC Metro 23 | DC-891B | |
| ☐ C-GAFQ | SA.227DC Metro 23 | DC-890B | |
| ☐ C-GKAF | SA.227DC Metro 23 | DC-864B | |
| ☐ C-GSAF | SA.227DC Metro 23 | DC-866B | |
| ☐ C- | SA.227AC Metro III | AC-757B | Lst CPH |
| ☐ C- | SA.227AC Metro III | AC-758B | Lst CPH |
| ☐ C-FCCP | BAe Jetstream 3101 | 698 | |
| ☐ C-FZVY | BAe Jetstream 32 | 833 | |
| ☐ C-GCCN | BAe Jetstream 3101 | 704 | std |
| ☐ C-GCCZ | BAe Jetstream 3101 | 712 | std |

## CALM AIR INTERNATIONAL                         CAV

| | | | |
|---|---|---|---|
| ☐ C-FAMO | HS.748 Srs.2A/258LFD | 1669 | |
| ☐ C-FMAK | HS.748 Srs.2A/257 | 1668 | |
| ☐ C-GDOP | HS.748 Srs.2A/283 | 1745 | |
| ☐ C-GEPB | HS.748 Srs.2A/254 | 1686 | 304 |
| ☐ C-GHSC | HS.748 Srs.2B/FAA | 1790 | |
| ☐ C-GSBF | HS.748 Srs.2A/210 | 1662 | |
| ☐ C-FTJV | SAAB SF.340B | 366 | |
| ☐ C-FTJW | SAAB SF.340B | 377 | |
| ☐ C-GTJX | SAAB SF.340B | 165 | |
| ☐ C-GTJY | SAAB SF.340B | 166 | |

## CANADIAN NORTH                                   ANX

| | | | |
|---|---|---|---|
| ☐ C-GDPA | Boeing 737-2T2C | 655/22056 | |
| ☐ C-GFPW | Boeing 737-275C | 481/21294 | |
| ☐ C-GNDU | Boeing 737-242C | 880/22877 | 562 |
| ☐ C-GOPW | Boeing 737-275C | 688/22160 | 582 |
| ☐ C-GSPW | Boeing 737-275C | 813/22618 | |
| ☐ C-FTAR | F.28 Fellowship 1000 | 11047 | |
| ☐ C-FTAY | F.28 Fellowship 1000 | 11084 | |

## CANJET                                             CJA

| | | |
|---|---|---|
| ☐ C-FECJ | Boeing 737-2Q9 | 612/21975 |
| ☐ C-FGCJ | Boeing 737-201 | 728/22352 |
| ☐ C-FJCJ | Boeing 737-201 | 548/21667 |
| ☐ C-FMCJ | Boeing 737-296 | 733/22398 |
| ☐ C-FVCJ | Boeing 737-201 | 731/22353 |

## CARGOJET CANADA                                  WNT

| | | |
|---|---|---|
| ☐ C-FCJP | Boeing 727-223F | 1655/22012 |
| ☐ C-GCJB | Boeing 727-225F | 1535/21855 |
| ☐ C-GCJD | Boeing 727-231F | 1568/21988 |
| ☐ C-GCJQ | Boeing 727-225F | 1682/22437 |

## CENTRAL MOUNTAIN AIR                             GLR

| | | | |
|---|---|---|---|
| ☐ C-FCMB | Beech 1900D | UE-278 | 916 |
| ☐ C-FCME | Beech 1900D | UE-277 | 915 |
| ☐ C-FCMO | Beech 1900D | UE-281 | 917 |
| ☐ C-FCMR | Beech 1900D | UE-283 | 918 |
| ☐ C-FCMU | Beech 1900D | UE-285 | 919 |
| ☐ C-FCMV | Beech 1900D | UE-272 | 913 |
| ☐ C-GCMA | Beech 1900D | UE-289 | 921 |
| ☐ C-GCMY | Beech 1900D | UE-287 | 920 |
| ☐ C-GGBY | Beech 1900D | UE-351 | 923 |
| ☐ C-GGCA | Beech 1900D | UE-359 | 924 |
| ☐ C-GCMJ | Beech 1900C-1 | UC-49 | Lst NTA |
| ☐ C-GCMT | Beech 1900C-1 | UC-120 | Lst NTA |
| ☐ C-GCMZ | Beech 1900C-1 | UC-61 | Lst NTA |

## FIRST AIR                                         FAB

| | | | |
|---|---|---|---|
| ☐ C-FIFA | Boeing 727-225F | 823/20381 | Lst ABR |
| ☐ C-FUFA | Boeing 727-233F | 1128/20941 | |
| ☐ C-GFRB | Boeing 727-27C | 396/19120 | |
| ☐ C-GVFA | Boeing 727-44C | 854/20475 | |
| ☐ C-GXFA | Boeing 727-233F | 1105/20938 | |
| ☐ C-GYFA | Boeing 727-2H3F | 1209/21234 | |
| ☐ C-GBFA | HS.748 Srs.2B/FAA | 1781 | 402 |
| ☐ C-GDUL | HS.748 Srs.2A/215 | 1578 | 403 |
| ☐ C-GFNW | HS.748 Srs.2A /335LFD | 1758 | 405 |
| ☐ C-GGNZ | HS.748 Srs.2A/272 | 1690 | |
| ☐ C-GJVN | HS.748 Srs.2A/209 | 1640 | 406 |
| ☐ C-GTLD | HS.748 Srs.2A/216 | 1722 | 407 |
| ☐ C-GYMX | HS.748 Srs.2A/233 | 1665 | 408 |
| ☐ C-FIQR | ATR 42-300 | 133 | |
| ☐ C-FIQU | ATR 42-300 | 138 | |
| ☐ C-FNVT | Boeing 737-248C | 411/21011 | |
| ☐ C-FTCP | ATR 42-300 | 143 | |
| ☐ C-GCFR | DHC-7-150 | 102 | |
| ☐ C-GHCP | ATR 42-300 | 123 | |
| ☐ C-GHPW | L-100-30 Hercules | 4799 | |
| ☐ C-GNDC | Boeing 737-242C | 580/21728 | |
| ☐ C-GNWM | Boeing 737-210C | 414/21067 | |

## HMY AIRWAYS                                       HMY

| | | |
|---|---|---|
| ☐ C-GMYC | Boeing 757-258 | 152/23917 |
| ☐ C-GMYD | Boeing 757-258 | 185/24254 |

## JAZZ AIR                                          ARN

| | | | |
|---|---|---|---|
| ☐ C-FBAB | BAe 146 Srs.200 | E2090 | 401 |
| ☐ C-FBAE | BAe 146 Srs.200 | E2092 | 402 |
| ☐ C-FBAF | BAe 146 Srs.200 | E2096 | 403 |
| ☐ C-FBAO | BAe 146 Srs.200 | E2111 | 404 |
| ☐ C-FBAV | BAe 146 Srs.200 | E2121 | 405 |
| ☐ C-GRNT | BAe 146 Srs.200 | E2140 | 206 |
| ☐ C-GRNU | BAe 146 Srs.200 | E2139 | 205 |
| ☐ C-GRNV | BAe 146 Srs.200 | E2133 | 204 |
| ☐ C-GRNX | BAe 146 Srs.200 | E2130 | 203 |
| ☐ C-GRNZ | BAe 146 Srs.200 | E2106 | 201 |
| ☐ C-GAAR | Beech 1900D | UE-207 | 901 |
| ☐ C-GAAS | Beech 1900D | UE-209 | 902 |
| ☐ C-GAAT | Beech 1900D | UE-217 | 903 |
| ☐ C-GAAU | Beech 1900D | UE-232 | 904 |
| ☐ C-GAAV | Beech 1900D | UE-235 | 905 |
| ☐ C-GKEJ | Canadair RJ-200 | 7269 | |
| ☐ C-GKEK | Canadair RJ-200 | 7270 | |

| | | | |
|---|---|---|---|
| ☐ C-GKEM | Canadair RJ-200 | 7277 | |
| ☐ C-GKEP | Canadair RJ-200 | 7303 | |
| ☐ C-GKER | Canadair RJ-200 | 7368 | |
| ☐ C-GKEU | Canadair RJ-200 | 7376 | 185 |
| ☐ C-GKEW | Canadair RJ-200 | 7385 | 186 |
| ☐ C-GKEZ | Canadair RJ-200 | 7327 | 187 |
| ☐ C-GKFR | Canadair RJ-200 | 7330 | |
| ☐ C-GKGC | Canadair RJ-200 | 7334 | |
| | | | |
| ☐ C-FABA | DHC-8-102 | 092 | 805 |
| ☐ C-FABG | DHC-8-102 | 147 | 899 |
| ☐ C-FABN | DHC-8-102 | 044 | 803 |
| ☐ C-FABT | DHC-8-102 | 049 | 848 |
| ☐ C-FABW | DHC-8-102 | 097 | 806 |
| ☐ C-FACD | DHC-8-102 | 150 | 808 |
| ☐ C-FACF | DHC-8-311A | 259 | 308 |
| ☐ C-FACT | DHC-8-311A | 262 | 309 |
| ☐ C-FACV | DHC-8-311A | 278 | 311 |
| ☐ C-FADF | DHC-8-311A | 272 | 310 |
| ☐ C-FADJ | DHC-8-102A | 322 | 811 |
| ☐ C-FADK | DHC-8-102A | 324 | 812 |
| ☐ C-FCIZ | DHC-8-102 | 138 | 859; std |
| ☐ C-FCON | DHC-8-102 | 179 | 817 |
| ☐ C-FCTA | DHC-8-102 | 039 | 823 |
| ☐ C-FDND | DHC-8-102 | 129 | 850 |
| ☐ C-FGQI | DHC-8-102 | 185 | 849 |
| ☐ C-FGQK | DHC-8-102 | 193 | 819 |
| ☐ C-FGRC | DHC-8-102 | 195 | 821 |
| ☐ C-FGRM | DHC-8-102 | 199 | 820 |
| ☐ C-FGRP | DHC-8-102 | 207 | 822 |
| ☐ C-FGRY | DHC-8-102 | 212 | 812 |
| ☐ C-FHRA | DHC-8-102 | 206 | 818 |
| ☐ C-FHRC | DHC-8-102 | 209 | 842 |
| ☐ C-FJFM | DHC-8-311A | 240 | 324 |
| ☐ C-FJMG | DHC-8-102A | 255 | 824 |
| ☐ C-FJVV | DHC-8-311A | 271 | 306 |
| ☐ C-FJXZ | DHC-8-311A | 264 | 326 |
| ☐ C-FMDW | DHC-8-311A | 269 | 305 |
| ☐ C-FPON | DHC-8-102 | 171 | 836 |
| ☐ C-FTAK | DHC-8-311A | 246 | 323 |
| ☐ C-FTON | DHC-8-102 | 178 | 838 |
| ☐ C-FVON | DHC-8-102 | 181 | 837 |
| ☐ C-FXON | DHC-8-102 | 183 | 845 |
| ☐ C-GAAC | DHC-8-102 | 047 | 166; std |
| ☐ C-GAAN | DHC-8-102 | 051 | 893; std |
| ☐ C-GABF | DHC-8-102 | 025 | 816 |
| ☐ C-GABH | DHC-8-102 | 211 | 810 |
| ☐ C-GABI | DHC-8-102 | 205 | 809 |
| ☐ C-GABO | DHC-8-311A | 248 | 312 |
| ☐ C-GABP | DHC-8-311A | 257 | 307 |
| ☐ C-GANF | DHC-8-102 | 042 | 802 |
| ☐ C-GANI | DHC-8-102 | 064 | 830 |
| ☐ C-GANK | DHC-8-102 | 087 | 831 |
| ☐ C-GANQ | DHC-8-102 | 096 | 833 |
| ☐ C-GANS | DHC-8-102 | 057 | 828 |
| ☐ C-GCTC | DHC-8-102 | 065 | 846 |
| ☐ C-GESH | DHC-8-102 | 091 | 892 |
| ☐ C-GETA | DHC-8-301 | 186 | 321 |
| ☐ C-GEWQ | DHC-8-311A | 202 | 325 |
| ☐ C-GGOM | DHC-8-102 | 003 | 801; std |
| ☐ C-GHTA | DHC-8-301 | 198 | 316 |
| ☐ C-GION | DHC-8-102 | 127 | 832 |
| ☐ C-GJIG | DHC-8-102 | 068 | 826 |
| ☐ C-GJMI | DHC-8-102 | 077 | 825 |
| ☐ C-GJMK | DHC-8-102 | 081 | 804 |
| ☐ C-GJMO | DHC-8-102 | 079 | 834 |
| ☐ C-GJSV | DHC-8-102 | 085 | 814 |
| ☐ C-GJSX | DHC-8-102 | 088 | 835 |
| ☐ C-GKON | DHC-8-102 | 130 | 815 |
| ☐ C-GKTA | DHC-8-301 | 124 | 317 |
| ☐ C-GLON | DHC-8-102 | 133 | 847 |
| ☐ C-GLTA | DHC-8-301 | 154 | 318 |
| ☐ C-GMON | DHC-8-301 | 131 | 301 |
| ☐ C-GMTA | DHC-8-301 | 174 | 319 |
| ☐ C-GNON | DHC-8-301 | 137 | 302 |
| ☐ C-GOND | DHC-8-102 | 090 | 840 |
| ☐ C-GONH | DHC-8-102 | 093 | 813 |
| ☐ C-GONJ | DHC-8-102 | 095 | 839 |

| | | | |
|---|---|---|---|
| ☐ C-GONN | DHC-8-102 | 101 | 898 |
| ☐ C-GONO | DHC-8-102 | 102 | 807 |
| ☐ C-GONR | DHC-8-102 | 109 | 841 |
| ☐ C-GONW | DHC-8-102 | 112 | 843 |
| ☐ C-GONX | DHC-8-102 | 118 | 829 |
| ☐ C-GONY | DHC-8-102 | 115 | 827 |
| ☐ C-GSTA | DHC-8-301 | 182 | 320 |
| ☐ C-GTAE | DHC-8-102 | 073 | 172 |
| ☐ C-GTAF | DHC-8-103 | 083 | 174 |
| ☐ C-GTAG | DHC-8-301 | 200 | 315 |
| ☐ C-GTAI | DHC-8-102 | 078 | 173 |
| ☐ C-GTAQ | DHC-8-301 | 180 | 313 |
| ☐ C-GTAT | DHC-8-301 | 188 | 314 |
| ☐ C-GTBP | DHC-8-102 | 066 | 175 |
| ☐ C-GTCO | DHC-8-102 | 119 | 856; std |
| ☐ C-GUON | DHC-8-301 | 143 | 303 |
| ☐ C-GVON | DHC-8-301 | 149 | 304 |
| ☐ C-GVTA | DHC-8-301 | 190 | 322 |
| ☐ C-GWRR | DHC-8-102 | 070 | 171 |

## JETSGO   JGO

| | | |
|---|---|---|
| ☐ C-GKLC | McDD MD-83 | 2114/53468 |
| ☐ C-GKLJ | McDD MD-83 | 2102/53467 |
| ☐ C-GKLK | McDD MD-83 | 1991/53124 |
| ☐ C-GKLN | McDD MD-83 | 2130/53486 |
| ☐ C-GKLQ | McDD MD-83 | 2132/53487 |
| ☐ C-GKLR | McDD MD-83 | 2116/53469 |

## KELOWNA FLIGHTCRAFT AIR CHARTER   KFA

| | | | |
|---|---|---|---|
| ☐ C-FMKF | Boeing 727-223 | 1467/21523 | |
| ☐ C-FPKF | Boeing 727-223 | 1473/21524 | |
| ☐ C-GACU | Boeing 727-225F | 775/20152 | 710 |
| ☐ C-GIKF | Boeing 727-227F | 982/20772 | 721 |
| ☐ C-GJKF | Boeing 727-227F | 1106/21042 | 722 |
| ☐ C-GKFA | Boeing 727-22C | 547/19806 | 704 |
| ☐ C-GKFC | Boeing 727-22C | 211/18897 | 701 |
| ☐ C-GKFH | Boeing 727-225F | 779/20153 | 711 |
| ☐ C-GKFN | Boeing 727-25C | 368/19359 | 707 |
| ☐ C-GKFZ | Boeing 727-22C | 436/19204 | 706 |
| ☐ C-GKKF | Boeing 727-227F | 1113/21043 | 723 |
| ☐ C-GLKF | Boeing 727-227F | 1167/21118 | 724 |
| ☐ C-GMKF | Boeing 727-227F | 1175/21119 | 725 |
| ☐ C-GNKF | Boeing 727-227F | 1031/20839 | 726 |
| ☐ C-GOKF | Boeing 727-214 | 715/20162 | |
| ☐ C-GQKF | Boeing 727-243 | 1226/21265 | |
| ☐ C-GTKF | Boeing 727-225F | 1435/21580 | |
| ☐ C-GWKF | Boeing 727-243 | 1231/21270 | |
| | | | |
| ☐ C-FCIB | Convair 580 | 327A | Lst CVA |
| ☐ C-FEKF | Convair 580 | 80 | 45 |
| ☐ C-FFKF | Convair 580 | 179 | 44 |
| ☐ C-FHKF | Convair 580 | 374 | 55 |
| ☐ C-FIWN | Convair 580 | 126 | |
| ☐ C-FKFA | Convair 580 | 100 | 507 |
| ☐ C-FKFL | Convair 580 | 465 | |
| ☐ C-FKFM | Convair 580 | 70 | 54 |
| ☐ C-FKFS | Convair 5800 | 276/004 | |
| ☐ C-FKFY | Convair 580 | 129 | 509 |
| ☐ C-FKFZ | Convair 580 | 151 | 510 |
| ☐ C-GKFF | Convair 580 | 160 | 511 |
| ☐ C-GKFG | Convair 580 | 22 | 516; std |
| ☐ C-GKFJ | Convair 580 | 114 | 508 |
| ☐ C-GKFO | Convair 580 | 78 | 53 |
| ☐ C-GKFP | Convair 580 | 446 | 514 |
| ☐ C-GKFQ | Convair 580 | 86 | 505 |
| ☐ C-GKFU | Convair 580 | 82 | 516 |
| ☐ C-GKFY | Convair 580 | 91 | std |

## MORNINGSTAR AIR EXPRESS   MEI

| | | | |
|---|---|---|---|
| ☐ C-FBWG | Boeing 727-25C | 478/19719 | Opf FDX |
| ☐ C-FBWY | Boeing 727-22F | 349/19085 | Opf FDX |
| ☐ C-GBWH | Boeing 727-116C | 600/19814 | Opf FDX |
| ☐ C-GBWS | Boeing 727-22F | 247/18867 | Opf FDX |

## NT AIR · NTA

| | | | |
|---|---|---|---|
| ☐ C-GCMJ | Beech 1900C-1 | UC-49 | Lsf GLR |
| ☐ C-GCMT | Beech 1900C-1 | UC-120 | Lsf GLR |
| ☐ C-GCMZ | Beech 1900C-1 | UC-61 | Lsf GLR |

## PACIFIC COASTAL AIRLINES · PCO

| | | | |
|---|---|---|---|
| ☐ C-GPCE | Short SD.3-60 | SH3611 | 704 |
| ☐ C-GPCF | Short SD.3-60 | SH3620 | 706 |
| ☐ C-GPCG | Short SD.3-60 | SH3619 | 701 |
| ☐ C-GPCJ | Short SD.3-60 | SH3633 | 705 |
| ☐ C-GPCN | Short SD.3-60 | SH3621 | 702 |
| ☐ C-GPCW | Short SD.3-60 | SH3622 | 703 |
| ☐ C-FPCO | Embraer EMB.110P1 | 110405 | 503 |
| ☐ C-GPCQ | Embraer EMB.110P1 | 110342 | 502 |
| ☐ C-GPCY | Beech 1900C | UB-45 | |

## SKYLINK EXPRESS

| | | |
|---|---|---|
| ☐ C-GSKA | Beech 1900C | UB-32 |
| ☐ C-GSKC | Beech 1900C | UB-27 |
| ☐ C-GSKG | Beech 1900C-1 | UC-22 |
| ☐ C-GSKM | Beech 1900C | UB-21 |
| ☐ C-GSKN | Beech 1900C-1 | UC-54 |
| ☐ C-GSKU | Beech 1900C | UB-35 |
| ☐ C-GSKW | Beech 1900C | UB-33 |

## SKYSERVICE AIRLINES · SSV

| | | | |
|---|---|---|---|
| ☐ C-FRAA | Airbus A320-232 | 1411 | |
| ☐ C-FRAR | Airbus A320-231 | 0447 | |
| ☐ C-FTDA | Airbus A320-212 | 0795 | Lst MYT |
| ☐ C-FTDD | Airbus A320-211 | 0371 | |
| ☐ C-FTDF | Airbus A320-231 | 0437 | |
| ☐ C-FTDQ | Airbus A320-214 | 1686 | |
| ☐ C-GJUK | Airbus A319-112 | 1598 | |
| ☐ C-GJUM | Airbus A320-212 | 0579 | |
| ☐ C-GJUP | Airbus A320-212 | 0645 | |
| ☐ C-GJUQ | Airbus A320-212 | 0671 | |
| ☐ C-GJUU | Airbus A320-212 | 0424 | |
| ☐ C-GTDB | Airbus A320-212 | 0525 | Lst MYT |
| ☐ C-GTDC | Airbus A320-232 | 0496 | |
| ☐ C-GTDG | Airbus A320-214 | 1571 | Lsf AMM |
| ☐ C-GTDH | Airbus A320-214 | 1605 | Lsf AMM |
| ☐ C-GTDK | Airbus A320-231 | 0338 | Lst AIH |
| ☐ C-GTDL | Airbus A320-231 | 0476 | Lst MYT |
| ☐ C-GTDT | Airbus A319-112 | 1884 | |
| ☐ C-GTDX | Airbus A319-112 | 1846 | |
| ☐ C- | Airbus A319-112 | 1901 | o/o |
| ☐ C-FBUS | Airbus A330-322 | 095 | |
| ☐ C-FRAE | Airbus A330-322 | 143 | Lst KZW |
| ☐ C-FRAP | Airbus A330-322 | 087 | |
| ☐ C-FRAV | Airbus A330-322 | 171 | Lst KZW |
| ☐ C-GEOC | BAe Jetstream 31 | 793 | |
| ☐ C-GJPX | BAe Jetstream 31 | 756 | |
| ☐ G-OOOZ | Boeing 757-236 | 466/25593 | Lsf AMM |

## SKYWARD AVIATION

| | | |
|---|---|---|
| ☐ C-FSKJ | Embraer EMB.110P1 | 110272 |
| ☐ C-FSKL | Embraer EMB.110P1 | 110353 |
| ☐ C-FSKO | Beech 1900D | UE-9 |
| ☐ C-FSKR | Embraer EMB.110P1 | 110331 |
| ☐ C-FSKT | Beech 1900D | UE-11 |
| ☐ C-GSKD | Embraer EMB.110P1 | 110329 |

## TRANS CAPITAL AIR

| | | | |
|---|---|---|---|
| ☐ C-FWYU | DHC-7-103 | 12 | Opf UN |
| ☐ C-GGXS | DHC-7-102 | 64 | Opf UN |
| ☐ C-GLPP | DHC-7-102 | 67 | |

## TRANSWEST AIR · ASK

| | | | |
|---|---|---|---|
| ☐ C-FBID | BAe Jetstream 31 | 802 | 301 |
| ☐ C-FBIP | BAe Jetstream 31 | 820 | 305 |
| ☐ C-FSEW | BAe Jetstream 31 | 764 | |
| ☐ C-FVJU | Beech 1900D | UE-156 | |
| ☐ C-FVKC | Beech 1900D | UE-160 | |
| ☐ C-GKCY | SAAB 340A | 133 | |
| ☐ C-GPDC | BAe Jetstream 31 | 766 | |

## VOYAGEUR AIRWAYS · VAL

| | | |
|---|---|---|
| ☐ C-FWZV | DHC-7-103 | 81 |
| ☐ C-FZKM | DHC-7-102 | 61 |
| ☐ C-GCEV | DHC-7-103 | 63 |
| ☐ C-GFFL | DHC-7-102 | 74 |
| ☐ C-GFOF | DHC-7-102 | 37 |
| ☐ C-GGUL | DHC-7-102 | 70 |
| ☐ C-GGUN | DHC-7-110 | 66 |
| ☐ C-GJPI | DHC-7-102 | 36 |
| ☐ C-GLOL | DHC-7-102 | 39 |

## WASAYA AIRWAYS · WSG

| | | | |
|---|---|---|---|
| ☐ C-FFFS | HS.748 Srs.2A/209LFD | 1663 | 806 |
| ☐ C-FTTW | HS.748 Srs.2A/264 | 1681 | 805 |
| ☐ C-GDTD | HS.748 Srs.2B/398 | 1779 | 803 |
| ☐ C-GLTC | HS.748 Srs.2A/244 | 1656 | 801 |
| ☐ C-GMAA | HS.748 Srs.2A/214LFD | 1576 | 807 |
| ☐ C-FWAX | Beech 1900D | UE-297 | |
| ☐ C-GZVJ | Beech 1900D | UE-223 | |

## WEST WIND AVIATION · WEW

| | | |
|---|---|---|
| ☐ C-FCPD | BAe Jetstream 31 | 822 |
| ☐ C-FCSE | HS.748 Srs.2A/269 | 1679 |
| ☐ C-FQVE | HS.748 Srs.2B/378 | 1792 |
| ☐ C-GHGK | BAe Jetstream 31 | 786 |

## WESTEX AIRLINES · WES

| | | | |
|---|---|---|---|
| ☐ C-FVQE | Fairchild F-27F | 89 | Opf DHL |
| ☐ C-GWXC | F.27 Friendship 400 | 10268 | |
| ☐ C-GWXD | F.27 Friendship 300M | 10156 | |
| ☐ C-GWXX | SA.227AC Metro III | AC-738 | |
| ☐ C-GWXZ | SA.227AC Metro III | AC-701 | |

## WESTJET · WJA

| | | | |
|---|---|---|---|
| ☐ C-FAWJ | Boeing 737-281 | 588/21770 | 752 |
| ☐ C-FCWJ | Boeing 737-2E3 | 811/22703 | 748 |
| ☐ C-FIWJ | Boeing 737-2M8 | 659/21955 | 749 |
| ☐ C-FKWJ | Boeing 737-2H4 | 609/21811 | 753 |
| ☐ C-FLWJ | Boeing 737-2Q8 | 1059/23148 | 750 |
| ☐ C-FTWJ | Boeing 737-281 | 585/21767 | 751 |
| ☐ C-GCWJ | Boeing 737-297 | 561/21739 | 723 |
| ☐ C-GEWJ | Boeing 737-2T4 | 633/22055 | 745 |
| ☐ C-GGWJ | Boeing 737-2B4 | 491/21500 | 738 |
| ☐ C-GMWJ | Boeing 737-281 | 594/21771 | 739 |
| ☐ C-GQWJ | Boeing 737-281 | 587/21769 | 740 |
| ☐ C-GSWJ | Boeing 737-2H4 | 544/21593 | 755 |
| ☐ C-GUWJ | Boeing 737-204 | 341/20807 | 743 |
| ☐ C-GVWJ | Boeing 737-281 | 586/21768 | 746 |
| ☐ C-GWJE | Boeing 737-275 | 300/20588 | 735 |
| ☐ C-GWJG | Boeing 737-275 | 315/20670 | 736 |
| ☐ C-GWJK | Boeing 737-269 | 448/21206 | 756 |
| ☐ C-GWJO | Boeing 737-2A3 | 158/20299 | 730 |
| ☐ C-GWJT | Boeing 737-2H4 | 470/21262 | 731 |
| ☐ C-GWJU | Boeing 737-2H4 | 423/21117 | 733 |
| ☐ C-GWWJ | Boeing 737-204 | 542/21694 | 741 |
| ☐ C-GXWJ | Boeing 737-281 | 583/21766 | 742 |
| ☐ C-FIWS | Boeing 737-76N | 851/32404 | |
| ☐ C-FJWS | Boeing 737-76N | 872/28651 | |
| ☐ C-FKWS | Boeing 737-76N | 905/30134 | |

| | | | |
|---|---|---|---|
| ☐ C-FWAD | Boeing 737-7CT | 1222/32753 | |
| ☐ C-FWAF | Boeing 737-7CT | 1239/32747 | |
| ☐ C-FWAI | Boeing 737-7CT | 1246/33656 | |
| ☐ C-FWAO | Boeing 737-7CT | 1254/33657 | |
| ☐ C-FWAQ | Boeing 737-7CT | 1266/32748 | 206 |
| ☐ C-FWBG | Boeing 737-7CT | 32749 | o/o |
| ☐ C-FWBL | Boeing 737-7CT | 32750 | o/o |
| ☐ C-FWBX | Boeing 737-7CT | 32751 | o/o |
| ☐ C-FWBW | Boeing 737-7CT | 33697 | o/o |
| ☐ C-FWCC | Boeing 737-7CT | 32752 | o/o |
| ☐ C-FWCN | Boeing 737-7CT | 33698 | o/o |
| ☐ C-FZWS | Boeing 737-76N | 1044/32371 | |
| ☐ C-GLWS | Boeing 737-76N | 1009/32581 | |
| ☐ C-GRWS | Boeing 737-76N | 1155/32881 | |
| ☐ C-GTWS | Boeing 737-76N | 1179/32883 | |
| ☐ C-GUWS | Boeing 737-76N | 1206/33378 | |
| ☐ C-GWSE | Boeing 737-76N | 1216/33379 | |
| ☐ C-GWSH | Boeing 737-76N | 1258/29886 | |
| ☐ C- | Boeing 737-76N | | o/o |
| ☐ C- | Boeing 737-76N | | o/o |
| ☐ C- | Boeing 737-76N | | o/o |
| ☐ C- | Boeing 737-76N | | o/o |
| ☐ C- | Boeing 737-76N | | o/o |
| ☐ C- | Boeing 737-76N | | o/o |
| ☐ C- | Boeing 737-76N | | o/o |
| ☐ C- | Boeing 737-76N | | o/o |
| ☐ C- | Boeing 737-76N | | o/o |
| ☐ C- | Boeing 737-76N | | o/o |

## CC - CHILE

### LANCHILELAN

| | | | |
|---|---|---|---|
| ☐ CC-COC | Airbus A320-233 | 1304 | |
| ☐ CC-COD | Airbus A320-233 | 1332 | |
| ☐ CC-COE | Airbus A320-233 | 1351 | |
| ☐ CC-COF | Airbus A320-233 | 1355 | |
| ☐ CC-COG | Airbus A320-233 | 1491 | |
| ☐ CC-COH | Airbus A320-233 | 1512 | |
| ☐ CC-COI | Airbus A320-233 | 1526 | |
| ☐ CC-COK | Airbus A320-233 | 1548 | Lst LXP |
| ☐ CC-COM | Airbus A320-233 | 1626 | Lst LXP |
| ☐ CC-COP | Airbus A320-233 | 1858 | |
| ☐ CC-COQ | Airbus A320-233 | 1877 | |
| ☐ CC-COT | Airbus A320-233 | 1903 | |
| ☐ CC- | Airbus A320-233 | | o/o |
| ☐ CC- | Airbus A320-233 | | o/o |
| ☐ CC- | Airbus A320-233 | | o/o |
| ☐ VP-BCK | Airbus A320-233 | 1568 | Lst LPE |
| ☐ VP-BCS | Airbus A320-233 | 1854 | Lst LPE |
| ☐ CC-CQA | Airbus A340-313X | 359 | |
| ☐ CC-CQC | Airbus A340-313X | 363 | |
| ☐ CC-CQE | Airbus A340-313X | 429 | |
| ☐ CC-CQF | Airbus A340-313X | 442 | |
| ☐ CC- | Airbus A340-313X | | o/o |
| ☐ CC- | Airbus A340-313X | | o/o |
| ☐ CC- | Airbus A340-313X | | o/o |
| ☐ CC-CRP | Boeing 737-230 | 777/22134 | |
| ☐ CC-CRQ | Boeing 737-230 | 781/22135 | |
| ☐ CC-CRR | Boeing 737-230 | 657/22114 | |
| ☐ CC-CRS | Boeing 737-230 | 791/22139 | |
| ☐ CC-CSH | Boeing 737-204 | 316/20632 | |
| ☐ CC-CSI | Boeing 737-204 | 318/20633 | |
| ☐ CC-CSP | Boeing 737-204 | 342/20808 | Lst LXP |
| ☐ CC-CVC | Boeing 737-229 | 529/21596 | Lst LXP |
| ☐ CC-CVD | Boeing 737-229 | 617/21840 | |
| ☐ CC-CVG | Boeing 737-291 | 965/23024 | |
| ☐ CC-CVH | Boeing 737-291 | 909/22743 | |
| ☐ CC-CVI | Boeing 737-2Q3 | 706/22367 | |
| ☐ CC-CVJ | Boeing 737-2Q3 | 896/22736 | |
| ☐ CC-CYC | Boeing 737-219 | 428/21131 | |
| ☐ CC-CYK | Boeing 737-205 | 506/21445 | |
| ☐ CC-CZK | Boeing 737-236 | 686/21804 | |
| ☐ CC-CZO | Boeing 737-236 | 693/22030 | |

| | | | |
|---|---|---|---|
| ☐ CC-CBJ | Boeing 767-316ER | 652/27613 | |
| ☐ CC-CDP | Boeing 767-316ER | 602/27597 | |
| ☐ CC-CEB | Boeing 767-316ER | 621/26327 | |
| ☐ CC-CEK | Boeing 767-316ER | 641/26329 | |
| ☐ CC-CRG | Boeing 767-375ER | 430/25865 | |
| ☐ CC-CRH | Boeing 767-375ER | 426/25864 | |
| ☐ CC-CRT | Boeing 767-316ER | 681/27615 | |
| ☐ CC-CZT | Boeing 767-316ER | 699/29228 | |
| ☐ CC-CZU | Boeing 767-316ER | 729/29229 | |
| ☐ CC-CZW | Boeing 767-316ER | 698/29227 | |

### LANCHILE CARGO     LCO

| | | | |
|---|---|---|---|
| ☐ CC-CZX | Boeing 767-316ERF | 778/29881 | Lst TUS |
| ☐ CC-CZY | Boeing 767-316ERF | 806/30780 | |
| ☐ CC-CZZ | Boeing 767-316ERF | 712/25756 | |
| ☐ N312LA | Boeing 767-316ERF | 846/32572 | |
| ☐ N314LA | Boeing 767-316ERF | 848/32573 | Lst MAA |
| ☐ N316LA | Boeing 767-316ERF | 860/30842 | Opb FWL |
| ☐ CC-CEI | Boeing 737-248C | 208/20219 | |
| ☐ N871MY | Douglas DC-8-71F | 343/45970 | Lst MAA |
| ☐ N872SJ | Douglas DC-8-71F | 449/46040 | Lst FWL |

### LANEXPRESS     LXP

| | | |
|---|---|---|
| ☐ CC-CSP | Boeing 737-204 | 342/20808 |
| ☐ CC-CVC | Boeing 737-229 | 529/21596 |
| ☐ CC-COK | Airbus A320-233 | 1548 |
| ☐ CC-COM | Airbus A320-233 | 1626 |

### SKY AIRLINE     SKU

| | | |
|---|---|---|
| ☐ CC-CAP | Boeing 737-236 | 654/22027 |
| ☐ CC-CTB | Boeing 737-2Q3 | 1241/23481 |
| ☐ CC-CTD | Boeing 737-2H6 | 307/20586 |
| ☐ CC-CTH | Boeing 737-230 | 808/22636 |
| ☐ CC-CTK | Boeing 737-230 | 744/22402 |
| ☐ CC-CTM | Boeing 737-2H6 | 302/20582 |
| ☐ CC-CTO | Boeing 737-2H4 | 303/20583 |
| ☐ CC-CTW | Boeing 727-225F | 1554/21861 |

## CN - MOROCCO

### AIR ATLAS EXPRESS     AXP

| | | |
|---|---|---|
| ☐ CN-REB | Boeing 737-4Y0 | 1759/24511 |

### MONDAIR     MMA

| | | |
|---|---|---|
| ☐ CN-RDA | Boeing 737-329 | 1711/24356 |
| ☐ CN-RDB | Boeing 737-329 | 1430/23771 |

### MOROCCO AIRWAYS

| | | | |
|---|---|---|---|
| ☐ CN- | Airbus A320-211 | 0027 | o/o |
| ☐ CN- | Airbus A320-211 | 0029 | o/o |

### REGIONAL AIR LINES     RGL

| | | | |
|---|---|---|---|
| ☐ CN-RLA | Beech 1900D | UE-259 | |
| ☐ CN-RLD | Beech 1900D | UE-267 | |
| ☐ CN-RLF | Embraer ERJ-135ER | 145376 | o/o |
| ☐ CN-RLG | Embraer ERJ-135ER | 145431 | o/o |
| ☐ CN- | Embraer ERJ-135ER | | o/o |
| ☐ CN- | Embraer ERJ-135ER | | o/o |
| ☐ CN- | Embraer ERJ-135ER | | o/o |

### ROYAL AIR MAROC     RAM

| | | |
|---|---|---|
| ☐ CN-RMF | Boeing 737-4B6 | 1880/24807 |
| ☐ CN-RMG | Boeing 737-4B6 | 1888/24808 |
| ☐ CN-RMI | Boeing 737-2B6 | 449/21214 |
| ☐ CN-RMJ | Boeing 737-2B6 | 452/21215 |
| ☐ CN-RML | Boeing 737-2B6 | 851/22767 |
| ☐ CN-RMM | Boeing 737-2B6C | 951/23049 |

| | CN-RMN | Boeing 737-2B6C | 975/23050 | |
|---|---|---|---|---|
| ☐ | CN-RMN | Boeing 737-2B6C | 975/23050 | |
| ☐ | CN-RMV | Boeing 737-5B6 | 2157/25317 | |
| ☐ | CN-RMW | Boeing 737-5B6 | 2166/25364 | |
| ☐ | CN-RMX | Boeing 737-4B6 | 2219/26526 | |
| ☐ | CN-RMY | Boeing 737-5B6 | 2209/26525 | |
| ☐ | CN-RNA | Boeing 737-4B6 | 2453/26531 | |
| ☐ | CN-RNB | Boeing 737-5B6 | 2472/26527 | |
| ☐ | CN-RNC | Boeing 737-4B6 | 2584/26529 | |
| ☐ | CN-RND | Boeing 737-4B6 | 2588/26530 | |
| ☐ | CN-RNF | Boeing 737-4B6 | 2733/27678 | |
| ☐ | CN-RNG | Boeing 737-5B6 | 2734/27679 | |
| ☐ | CN-RNH | Boeing 737-5B6 | 2855/27680 | |
| ☐ | CN-RNJ | Boeing 737-8B6 | 55/28980 | |
| ☐ | CN-RNK | Boeing 737-8B6 | 60/28981 | |
| ☐ | CN-RNL | Boeing 737-7B6 | 236/28982 | |
| ☐ | CN-RNM | Boeing 737-7B6 | 294/28984 | |
| ☐ | CN-RNO | Boeing 737-86N | 285/28595 | |
| ☐ | CN-RNP | Boeing 737-8B6 | 492/28983 | |
| ☐ | CN-RNQ | Boeing 737-7B6 | 501/28985 | |
| ☐ | CN-RNR | Boeing 737-7B6 | 519/28986 | |
| ☐ | CN-RNU | Boeing 737-8B6 | 1095/28987 | |
| ☐ | CN-RNV | Boeing 737-7B6 | 1261/28988 | |
| ☐ | CN- | Boeing 737-86N | | o/o |
| ☐ | CN-CDU | ATR 42-300 | 134 | |
| ☐ | CN-CDV | ATR 42-300 | 137 | |
| ☐ | CN-RGA | Boeing 747-428 | 956/25629 | |
| ☐ | CN-RME | Boeing 747-2B6M | 338/21615 | std |
| ☐ | CN-RMT | Boeing 757-2B6 | 103/23686 | |
| ☐ | CN-RMZ | Boeing 757-2B6 | 106/23687 | |
| ☐ | CN-RNS | Boeing 767-36NER | 863/30115 | |
| ☐ | CN-RNT | Boeing 767-36NER | 867/30843 | |
| ☐ | CN- | Airbus A321-200 | | o/o |

## CP - BOLIVIA

### AEROSUR

| | | | | |
|---|---|---|---|---|
| ☐ | CP-2377 | Boeing 727-23 | 592/20044 | std |
| ☐ | CP- | Boeing 727-264 | 1696/22411 | |
| ☐ | OB-1653 | Yak-40 | 9041860 | Lsf TEA |
| ☐ | XA-HON | Boeing 727-264 | 1416/21617 | Lsf MXA |
| ☐ | XA-HOX | Boeing 727-264 | 1457/21638 | Lsf MXA |

### LAB AIRLINES — LLB

| | | | | |
|---|---|---|---|---|
| ☐ | CP-861 | Boeing 727-1A0 | 748/20279 | |
| ☐ | CP-1223 | Boeing 727-78 | 104/18795 | |
| ☐ | CP-1276 | Boeing 727-2K3 | 1124/21082 | |
| ☐ | CP-1366 | Boeing 727-2K3 | 1373/21494 | |
| ☐ | CP-1367 | Boeing 727-2K3 | 1403/21495 | |
| ☐ | CP-2324 | Boeing 727-2M7 | 1591/21823 | |
| ☐ | CP- | Boeing 727-259 | 1690/22475 | |
| ☐ | CP- | Boeing 767-300ER | | o/o |
| ☐ | CP- | Boeing 767-300ER | | o/o |
| ☐ | CP-2013 | F.27 Friendship 200 | 10138 | |
| ☐ | CP-2232 | Airbus A310-304 | 562 | |
| ☐ | CP-2313 | Boeing 737-3A1 | 2836/28389 | Lsf VSP |
| ☐ | CP-2391 | Boeing 737-382 | 1699/24366 | |

## CS - PORTUGAL

### ACEF CARGO — CFM

| | | | | |
|---|---|---|---|---|
| ☐ | CS-TML | Convair 440 | 484 | Lst AAG |
| ☐ | CS-TMM | Convair 580 | 375 | |

### AEROCONDOR — EAD

| | | | |
|---|---|---|---|
| ☐ | CS-TMH | Short SD.3-60 | SH3694 | |
| ☐ | CS-TMN | Short SD.3-60 | SH3638 | |
| ☐ | CS-TMY | Short SD.3-60 | SH3632 | |
| ☐ | G-EXPS | Short SD.3-60 | SH3661 | |
| ☐ | OY-MUD | Short SD.3-60 | SH3692 | Lsf VIS |

### AIR LUXOR — LXR

| | | | | |
|---|---|---|---|---|
| ☐ | CS-TMW | Airbus A320-214 | 1667 | std |
| ☐ | CS-TNB | Airbus A320-211 | 0191 | |
| ☐ | CS-TNE | Airbus A320-212 | 0395 | Lst NVR |
| ☐ | CS-TQA | Airbus A320-214 | 1439 | |
| ☐ | CS-TQB | Airbus A320-214 | 1450 | |
| ☐ | CS-TQC | Airbus A319-112 | 1494 | |
| ☐ | CS-TMP | L-1011-500 Tristar | 1248 | |
| ☐ | CS-TMR | L-1011-500 Tristar | 1241 | Lst YSS |
| ☐ | CS-TMT | Airbus A330-322 | 096 | |
| ☐ | C9-BAF | Boeing 767-2B1ER | 511/26471 | Jow LAM |

### AIR PORTUGAL — TAP

| | | | |
|---|---|---|---|
| ☐ | CS-TEH | Airbus A310-304 | 483 |
| ☐ | CS-TEI | Airbus A310-304 | 495 |
| ☐ | CS-TEJ | Airbus A310-304 | 494 |
| ☐ | CS-TEW | Airbus A310-304 | 541 |
| ☐ | CS-TEX | Airbus A310-304 | 565 |
| ☐ | CS-TTA | Airbus A319-111 | 0750 |
| ☐ | CS-TTB | Airbus A319-111 | 0755 |
| ☐ | CS-TTC | Airbus A319-111 | 0763 |
| ☐ | CS-TTD | Airbus A319-111 | 0790 |
| ☐ | CS-TTE | Airbus A319-111 | 0821 |
| ☐ | CS-TTF | Airbus A319-111 | 0837 |
| ☐ | CS-TTG | Airbus A319-111 | 0906 |
| ☐ | CS-TTH | Airbus A319-111 | 0917 |
| ☐ | CS-TTI | Airbus A319-111 | 0933 |
| ☐ | CS-TTJ | Airbus A319-111 | 0979 |
| ☐ | CS-TTK | Airbus A319-111 | 1034 |
| ☐ | CS-TTL | Airbus A319-111 | 1100 |
| ☐ | CS-TTM | Airbus A319-111 | 1106 |
| ☐ | CS-TTN | Airbus A319-111 | 1120 |
| ☐ | CS-TTO | Airbus A319-111 | 1127 |
| ☐ | CS-TTP | Airbus A319-111 | 1165 |
| ☐ | CS-TNA | Airbus A320-211 | 0185 |
| ☐ | CS-TNC | Airbus A320-211 | 0234 |
| ☐ | CS-TNG | Airbus A320-214 | 0945 |
| ☐ | CS-TNH | Airbus A320-214 | 0960 |
| ☐ | CS-TNI | Airbus A320-214 | 0982 |
| ☐ | CS-TNJ | Airbus A320-214 | 1181 |
| ☐ | CS-TNK | Airbus A320-214 | 1206 |
| ☐ | CS-TNL | Airbus A320-214 | 1231 |
| ☐ | CS-TNM | Airbus A320-214 | 1799 |
| ☐ | CS-TNN | Airbus A320-214 | 1816 |
| ☐ | CS-TJE | Airbus A321-211 | 1307 |
| ☐ | CS-TJF | Airbus A321-211 | 1399 |
| ☐ | CS-TJG | Airbus A321-211 | 1713 |
| ☐ | CS-TOA | Airbus A340-312 | 041 |
| ☐ | CS-TOB | Airbus A340-312 | 044 |
| ☐ | CS-TOC | Airbus A340-312 | 079 |
| ☐ | CS-TOD | Airbus A340-312 | 091 |

### EUROATLANTIC AIRWAYS — MMZ

| | | | |
|---|---|---|---|
| ☐ | CS-TEB | L-1011-500 Tristar | 1240 |
| ☐ | CS-TMZ | Boeing 737-33A | 1444/23827 |
| ☐ | PR-BRE | Boeing 737-3K9 | 1794/24213 |

### PGA EXPRESS

| | | | | |
|---|---|---|---|---|
| ☐ | CS-TMU | Beech 1900D | UE-335 | Opb OAV |
| ☐ | CS-TMV | Beech 1900D | UE-341 | Opb OAV |

### PORTUGALIA — PGA

| | | | |
|---|---|---|---|
| ☐ | CS-TPG | Embraer ERJ-145 | 145014 |
| ☐ | CS-TPH | Embraer ERJ-145 | 145017 |
| ☐ | CS-TPI | Embraer ERJ-145 | 145031 |
| ☐ | CS-TPJ | Embraer ERJ-145 | 145036 |
| ☐ | CS-TPK | Embraer ERJ-145 | 145041 |
| ☐ | CS-TPL | Embraer ERJ-145 | 145051 |

| | | | |
|---|---|---|---|
| ☐ CS-TPM | Embraer ERJ-145 | 145095 | |
| ☐ CS-TPN | Embraer ERJ-145 | 145099 | |

| | | | |
|---|---|---|---|
| ☐ CS-TPA | Fokker 100 | 11257 | |
| ☐ CS-TPB | Fokker 100 | 11262 | |
| ☐ CS-TPC | Fokker 100 | 11287 | |
| ☐ CS-TPD | Fokker 100 | 11317 | |
| ☐ CS-TPE | Fokker 100 | 11342 | |
| ☐ CS-TPF | Fokker 100 | 11258 | |

### SATA AIR ACORES · SAT

| | | | |
|---|---|---|---|
| ☐ CS-TGL | British Aerospace ATP | 2019 | |
| ☐ CS-TGN | British Aerospace ATP | 2031 | |
| ☐ CS-TGX | British Aerospace ATP | 2025 | |
| ☐ CS-TGY | British Aerospace ATP | 2049 | |

### SATA INTERNACIONAL · RZO

| | | | |
|---|---|---|---|
| ☐ CS-TGP | Boeing 737-3Q8 | 1541/24131 | |
| ☐ CS-TGU | Airbus A310-304 | 571 | |
| ☐ CS-TGV | Airbus A310-304 | 651 | |
| ☐ CS-TGW | Boeing 737-4Y0 | 1678/23981 | |
| ☐ CS-TGZ | Boeing 737-43Q | 2832/28491 | |

### YES · YSS

| | | | |
|---|---|---|---|
| ☐ CS-TMR | L-1011-500 Tristar | 1241 | Lsf LXR |
| ☐ CS-TMX | L-1011-500 Tristar | 1206 | |

## CU - CUBA

### AERO CARIBBEAN · CRN

| | | | |
|---|---|---|---|
| ☐ CU-T1269 | Ilyushin Il-18V | 185007801 | |
| ☐ CU-T1296 | ATR 42-300 | 009 | |
| ☐ CU-T1297 | ATR 42-300 | 014 | |
| ☐ CU-T1512 | ATR 42-300 | 136 | |
| ☐ CU-T1517 | Ilyushin Il-18D | 188010704 | |
| ☐ CU-T1532 | Ilyushin Il-18D | 188010904 | |

### AEROGAVIOTA · GTV

| | | | |
|---|---|---|---|
| ☐ CU-T1240 | ATR 42-500 | 617 | o/o |
| ☐ CU-T1454 | ATR 42-500 | 616 | |
| ☐ CU-T1455 | ATR 42-500 | 618 | |
| ☐ CU-T1456 | ATR 42-500 | 619 | |

### CUBANA DE AVIACION · CUB

| | | | |
|---|---|---|---|
| ☐ CU-T1272 | Yak-42D | 4520424811442 | Lsf WLG |
| ☐ CU-T1273 | Yak-42D | 4520424914340 | |
| ☐ CU-T1274 | Yak-42 | 4520422606204 | Lsf KAZ |
| ☐ CU-T1279 | Yak-42D | 4520424914057 | |
| ☐ CU-T1280 | Ilyushin Il-62M | 3749648 | |
| ☐ CU-T1282 | Ilyushin Il-62M | 2052456 | |
| ☐ CU-T1283 | Ilyushin Il-62M | 4053823 | |
| ☐ CU-T1284 | Ilyushin Il-62M | 4053732 | |
| ☐ EI-CXO | Boeing 767-3G5ER | 612/2811 | Lsf BPA |
| ☐ EI-TAA | Airbus A320-233 | 0912 | Lsf TAI |
| ☐ F-GHOI | Douglas DC-10-30 | 217/46870 | Lsf CUB |
| ☐ N464TA | Airbus A320-233 | 1353 | Lsf TAI |
| ☐ N465TA | Airbus A320-233 | 1374 | Lsf TAI |

## CX - URUGUAY

### PLUNA LINEAS AÉREAS URUGUAYAS · PUA

| | | | |
|---|---|---|---|
| ☐ CX-BON | Boeing 737-2A3 | 830/22737 | |
| ☐ CX-BOO | Boeing 737-2A3 | 834/22738 | |
| ☐ CX-BOP | Boeing 737-2A3 | 844/22739 | |
| ☐ CX-PUA | Boeing 737-3Q8 | 1924/24700 | |
| ☐ CX-PUB | Boeing 767-33AER | 643/28495 | |
| ☐ CX- | Boeing 767-3P6ER | 158/23764 | o/o |

## C2 - NAURU

### AIR NAURU · RON

| | | | |
|---|---|---|---|
| ☐ VH-RON | Boeing 737-4L7 | 2483/26960 | |

## C5 - GAMBIA

### GAMBIA NEW MILLENNIUM AIR · NML

| | | | |
|---|---|---|---|
| ☐ C5-GNM | Ilyushin Il-62M | 3036142 | |

### MAHFOOZ AVIATION · MZS

| | | | |
|---|---|---|---|
| ☐ C5-ABM | Boeing 727-256 | 1501/21781 | std |
| ☐ C5-AMM | Boeing 707-323B | 817/20176 | Lst LAA |
| ☐ C5-DMB | Boeing 727-228 | 847/20411 | Lst TSG |
| ☐ C5-MBM | Boeing 707-347C | 743/19966 | |
| ☐ C5-SBM | Boeing 727-256 | 21610 | |
| ☐ C5-SMM | Boeing 727-251 | 665/19973 | Lst SUD |

## C6 - BAHAMAS

### BAHAMASAIR · BHS

| | | | |
|---|---|---|---|
| ☐ C6-BFG | DHC-8-311A | 288 | |
| ☐ C6-BFH | DHC-8-311A | 291 | |
| ☐ C6-BFI | DHC-8-311A | 295 | |
| ☐ C6-BFN | DHC-8-301 | 159 | |
| ☐ C6-BFO | DHC-8-301 | 164 | |
| ☐ C6-BGK | Boeing 737-275 | 667/22086 | |
| ☐ C6-BGL | Boeing 737-275 | 673/22087 | |

### LAKER AIRWAYS · LBH

| | | | |
|---|---|---|---|
| ☐ N706AA | Boeing 727-223 | 1755/22463 | |
| ☐ N707AA | Boeing 727-223 | 1758/22464 | |

## C9 - MOZAMBIQUE

### LAM – L/A DE MOCAMBIQUE · LAM

| | | | |
|---|---|---|---|
| ☐ C9-BAC | Boeing 737-2B1C | 289/20536 | |
| ☐ C9-BAG | Boeing 737-2N0 | 1313/23677 | Lsf AZW |
| ☐ C9-BAH | Boeing 737-236 | 712/21808 | |
| ☐ C9-BAI | Boeing 737-2K9 | 1178/23405 | |
| ☐ 3D-ZZM | Boeing 737-2H7C | 304/20590 | Lsf ILN |
| ☐ C9-BAF | Boeing 767-2B1ER | 511/26471 | Jow LXR |
| ☐ 3D-ALM | Fokker 100 | 11335 | Lsf ILN |

## D - GERMANY

### AERO LLOYD · AEF

| | | | |
|---|---|---|---|
| ☐ D-ABLB | Airbus A320-214 | 1370 | |
| ☐ D-ALAA | Airbus A320-232 | 0565 | |
| ☐ D-ALAB | Airbus A320-232 | 0575 | Lst RYN |
| ☐ D-ALAC | Airbus A320-232 | 0580 | |
| ☐ D-ALAD | Airbus A320-232 | 0661 | |
| ☐ D-ALAE | Airbus A320-232 | 0659 | Lst RYN |
| ☐ D-ALAF | Airbus A320-232 | 0667 | |
| ☐ D-ALAJ | Airbus A320-232 | 0990 | |
| ☐ D-ALAR | Airbus A320-232 | 1459 | Lst RYN |
| ☐ D-ALAG | Airbus A321-231 | 0787 | |
| ☐ D-ALAH | Airbus A321-231 | 0792 | |
| ☐ D-ALAI | Airbus A321-231 | 0954 | |
| ☐ D-ALAK | Airbus A321-231 | 1004 | |
| ☐ D-ALAL | Airbus A321-231 | 1195 | |
| ☐ D-ALAM | Airbus A321-231 | 1199 | |
| ☐ D-ALAN | Airbus A321-231 | 1218 | |
| ☐ D-ALAO | Airbus A321-231 | 1408 | Lst RYN |
| ☐ D-ALAP | Airbus A321-231 | 1421 | |
| ☐ D-ALAQ | Airbus A321-231 | 1438 | Lst RYN |
| ☐ D-ALAS | Airbus A321-231 | 1487 | Lst RYN |

## AIR BERLIN — BER

| | | | |
|---|---|---|---|
| ☐ D-ABAH | Boeing 737-46J | 2694/27826 | |
| ☐ D-ABAI | Boeing 737-46J | 2794/28038 | |
| ☐ D-ABAK | Boeing 737-46J | 2801/28271 | |
| ☐ D-ABAL | Boeing 737-46J | 2802/28334 | |
| ☐ D-ABAM | Boeing 737-46J | 2879/28867 | |
| ☐ D-ABAC | Boeing 737-86J | 619/30501 | |
| ☐ D-ABAD | Boeing 737-86J | 759/30876 | |
| ☐ D-ABAE | Boeing 737-86J | 782/30877 | |
| ☐ D-ABAF | Boeing 737-86J | 844/30878 | |
| ☐ D-ABAG | Boeing 737-86J | 871/30879 | |
| ☐ D-ABAN | Boeing 737-86J | 36/28068 | |
| ☐ D-ABAO | Boeing 737-86J | 42/28069 | |
| ☐ D-ABAP | Boeing 737-86J | 106/28070 | |
| ☐ D-ABAQ | Boeing 737-86J | 133/28071 | |
| ☐ D-ABAR | Boeing 737-86J | 147/28072 | |
| ☐ D-ABAS | Boeing 737-86J | 200/28073 | |
| ☐ D-ABAT | Boeing 737-86J | 202/29120 | |
| ☐ D-ABAU | Boeing 737-86J | 239/29121 | |
| ☐ D-ABAV | Boeing 737-86J | 450/30498 | |
| ☐ D-ABAW | Boeing 737-86J | 485/30062 | |
| ☐ D-ABAX | Boeing 737-86J | 517/30063 | |
| ☐ D-ABAY | Boeing 737-86J | 567/30499 | |
| ☐ D-ADAZ | Boeing 737-86J | 593/30500 | |
| ☐ D-ABBA | Boeing 737-86J | 879/30570 | |
| ☐ D-ABBB | Boeing 737-86J | 961/32624 | |
| ☐ D-ABBC | Boeing 737-86J | 995/32625 | |
| ☐ D-ABBD | Boeing 737-86J | 1043/30880 | |
| ☐ D-ABBE | Boeing 737-86J | 1067/30881 | |
| ☐ D-ABBF | Boeing 737-86J | 1210/32917 | |
| ☐ D-ABBG | Boeing 737-86J | 1255/32918 | |
| ☐ D-ABBH | Boeing 737-86J | 32919 | o/o |
| ☐ D-ABBI | Boeing 737-86J | 32920 | o/o |
| ☐ D-ABBJ | Boeing 737-86Q | 30286 | o/o |
| ☐ D-AHIE | Boeing 737-73S | 215/29081 | opb HHI |
| ☐ D-A | Boeing 737-73S | 194/29079 | o/o |
| | | | opb HHI |
| ☐ G-XLAE | Boeing 737-8Q8 | 800/30637 | Lsf XLA |
| ☐ PH-HZG | Boeing 737-8K2 | 498/28379 | Lsf TRA |

## AIR OMEGA

| | | | |
|---|---|---|---|
| ☐ D-CAOA | Embraer EMB.120ER | 120013 | |
| ☐ D-CAOB | Embraer EMB.120ER | 120012 | |

## ANTARES AIRTRANSPORT — ANM

| | | | |
|---|---|---|---|
| ☐ D-CLEA | LET L-410UVP-E20 | 902517 | |
| ☐ D-CLED | LET L-410UVP-E20 | 912533 | |
| ☐ D-CLET | LET L-410UVP-E20 | 912603 | |

## ARCUS AIR — AZE

| | | | |
|---|---|---|---|
| ☐ D-CAAM | Dornier 228-212 | 8205 | |
| ☐ D-CUTT | Dornier 228-212 | 8200 | |

## AUGSBURG AIRWAYS — AUB

| | | | |
|---|---|---|---|
| ☐ D-BDTM | DHC-8Q-314 | 545 | |
| ☐ D-BEBA | DHC-8Q-314 | 543 | |
| ☐ D-BHAM | DHC-8-311 | 313 | |
| ☐ D-BHAT | DHC-8Q-311 | 505 | Lst AWS |
| ☐ D-BHOQ | DHC-8Q-311 | 544 | |
| ☐ D-BIER | DHC-8-103 | 310 | Lst RUS |
| ☐ D-BKIM | DHC-8-311 | 356 | |
| ☐ D-BLEJ | DHC-8Q-314 | 521 | |
| ☐ D-BMUC | DHC-8-314A | 350 | |
| ☐ D-BPAD | DHC-8Q-314 | 523 | |
| ☐ D-ADHA | DHC-8-402Q | 4028 | |
| ☐ D-ADHB | DHC-8-402Q | 4029 | |
| ☐ D-ADHC | DHC-8-402Q | 4045 | |
| ☐ D-ADHD | DHC-8-402Q | 4056 | |
| ☐ D-ADHE | DHC-8-402Q | 4066 | |

## AVANTI AIR — EEX

| | | | |
|---|---|---|---|
| ☐ D-BCRP | ATR 42-300QC | 158 | |
| ☐ D-CARA | Beech 1900C | UB-59 | |
| ☐ D-CBIG | Beech 1900D | UE-288 | Lst AWW |
| ☐ D-CBSF | Beech 1900D | UE-8 | Lst AWW |

## BERLINJET

| | | | |
|---|---|---|---|
| ☐ TF-MDB | McDD MD-83 | 1354/49449 | Lsf MDI |

## BLUE WINGS

| | | |
|---|---|---|
| ☐ D-ANNE | Airbus A320-232 | 0530 |

## CIRRUS AIRLINES — RUS

| | | | |
|---|---|---|---|
| ☐ D-ACIR | Embraer ERJ-145 | 145230 | |
| ☐ D-BIER | DHC-8-103 | 310 | Lsf AUB |
| ☐ D-BOBL | DHC-8-102A | 225 | |
| ☐ D-BOBO | DHC-8-102 | 153 | |
| ☐ D-BOBU | DHC-8-311A | 252 | |
| ☐ D-BOBY | DHC-8-102 | 177 | |
| ☐ D-CCIR | Dornier 328-130 | 3100 | |
| ☐ D-COSA | Dornier 328-110 | 3085 | |

## CITY-AIR GERMANY — CIP

| | | | |
|---|---|---|---|
| ☐ D-BKKK | ATR 42-500 | 532 | |
| ☐ D-CEBR | SA.227DC Metro 23 | DC-899B | Lsf EBR |
| ☐ D-CJKO | SA.227DC Metro 23 | DC-900B | |
| ☐ D-COLC | SA.227AC Metro III | AC-689 | Lsf OLT |
| ☐ D- | SAAB SF.340B | | o/o |

## CONDOR BERLIN — CIB

| | | | |
|---|---|---|---|
| ☐ D-AICA | Airbus A320-212 | 0774 | |
| ☐ D-AICB | Airbus A320-212 | 0793 | |
| ☐ D-AICC | Airbus A320-212 | 0809 | |
| ☐ D-AICD | Airbus A320-212 | 0884 | |
| ☐ D-AICE | Airbus A320-212 | 0894 | |
| ☐ D-AICF | Airbus A320-212 | 0905 | Lst TCW |
| ☐ D-AICG | Airbus A320-212 | 0957 | |
| ☐ D-AICH | Airbus A320-212 | 0971 | |
| ☐ D-AICI | Airbus A320-212 | 1381 | |
| ☐ D-AICJ | Airbus A320-212 | 1402 | |
| ☐ D-AICK | Airbus A320-212 | 1416 | |
| ☐ D-AICL | Airbus A320-212 | 1437 | |

## CONDOR FLUG — CFG

| | | | |
|---|---|---|---|
| ☐ D-ABNB | Boeing 757-230 | 274/24738 | Lst DBR |
| ☐ D-ABNC | Boeing 757-230 | 275/24747 | Lst DBR |
| ☐ D-ABND | Boeing 757-230 | 285/24748 | Lst DBR |
| ☐ D-ABNE | Boeing 757-230 | 295/24749 | std |
| ☐ D-ABNF | Boeing 757-230 | 382/25140 | |
| ☐ D-ABNH | Boeing 757-230 | 419/25436 | |
| ☐ D-ABNI | Boeing 757-230 | 422/25437 | |
| ☐ D-ABNK | Boeing 757-230 | 428/25438 | |
| ☐ D-ABNL | Boeing 757-230 | 437/25439 | |
| ☐ D-ABNM | Boeing 757-230 | 443/25440 | |
| ☐ D-ABNN | Boeing 757-230 | 446/25441 | |
| ☐ D-ABNO | Boeing 757-230 | 464/25901 | Lst RYN |
| ☐ D-ABNP | Boeing 757-230 | 521/26433 | std |
| ☐ D-ABNR | Boeing 757-230 | 532/26434 | |
| ☐ D-ABNS | Boeing 757-230 | 537/26435 | Lst RYN |
| ☐ D-ABNT | Boeing 757-230 | 587/26436 | std |
| ☐ D-ABOA | Boeing 757-330 | 804/29016 | std |
| ☐ D-ABOB | Boeing 757-330 | 810/29017 | |
| ☐ D-ABOC | Boeing 757-330 | 818/29015 | |
| ☐ D-ABOE | Boeing 757-330 | 839/29012 | |
| ☐ D-ABOF | Boeing 757-330 | 846/29013 | |
| ☐ D-ABOG | Boeing 757-330 | 849/29014 | |
| ☐ D-ABOH | Boeing 757-330 | 855/30030 | |
| ☐ D-ABOI | Boeing 757-330 | 909/29018 | |
| ☐ D-ABOJ | Boeing 757-330 | 915/29019 | |
| ☐ D-ABOK | Boeing 757-330 | 918/29020 | |

| □ D-ABOL | Boeing 757-330 | 923/29021 |
| □ D-ABOM | Boeing 757-330 | 926/29022 |
| □ D-ABON | Boeing 757-330 | 929/29023 |

| □ D-ABUA | Boeing 767-330ER | 455/26991 |
| □ D-ABUB | Boeing 767-330ER | 466/26987 |
| □ D-ABUC | Boeing 767-330ER | 470/26992 |
| □ D-ABUD | Boeing 767-330ER | 471/26983 |
| □ D-ABUE | Boeing 767-330ER | 518/26984 |
| □ D-ABUF | Boeing 767-330ER | 537/26985 |
| □ D-ABUH | Boeing 767-330ER | 553/26986 |
| □ D-ABUI | Boeing 767-330ER | 562/26988 |
| □ D-ABUZ | Boeing 767-330ER | 382/25209 |

## CONTACT AIR — KIS

| □ D-AFFX | Fokker 50 | 20142 |
| □ D-AFFY | Fokker 50 | 20141 |
| □ D-AFFZ | Fokker 50 | 20133 |
| □ D-AFKK | Fokker 50 | 20205 |
| □ D-AFKL | Fokker 50 | 20213 |
| □ D-AFKM | Fokker 50 | 20214 |
| □ D-AFKN | Fokker 50 | 20223 |
| □ D-AFKO | Fokker 50 | 20234 |
| □ D-AFKP | Fokker 50 | 20235 |
| □ D-AFKU | Fokker 50 | 20236 |

## DEUTSCHE BA — BAG

| □ D-ADBM | Boeing 737-31S | 2942/29057 |
| □ D-ADBN | Boeing 737-31S | 2946/29058 |
| □ D-ADBO | Boeing 737-31S | 2967/29059 |
| □ D-ADBP | Boeing 737-31S | 2979/29060 |
| □ D-ADBQ | Boeing 737-31S | 2982/29099 |
| □ D-ADBR | Boeing 737-31S | 2984/29100 |
| □ D-ADBS | Boeing 737-31S | 3005/29116 |
| □ D-ADBT | Boeing 737-31S | 3070/29264 |
| □ D-ADBU | Boeing 737-31S | 3073/29265 |
| □ D-ADBV | Boeing 737-31S | 3092/29266 |
| □ D-ADBW | Boeing 737-31S | 3093/29267 |
| □ D-ADIA | Boeing 737-33Q | 3117/30333 |
| □ D-ADIB | Boeing 737-36Q | 3120/30334 |
| □ D-ADIC | Boeing 737-36Q | 3129/30335 |
| □ D-ADID | Boeing 737-329 | 1441/23773 |
| □ D-ADIE | Boeing 737-329 | 1443/23774 |

## EUROPEAN AIR EXPRESS — EAL

| □ D-BBBB | ATR 42-300 | 096 |
| □ D-BCRQ | ATR 42-300 | 233 |
| □ D-BCRR | ATR 42-300 | 255 |
| □ D-BCRS | ATR 42-300 | 287 |
| □ D-BCRT | ATR 42-300QC | 289 |
| □ D-BJJJ | ATR 42-300 | 278 |

## EUROWINGS — EWG

| □ D-AEWG | ATR 72-211 | 347 |
| □ D-AEWH | ATR 72-211 | 359 |
| □ D-AEWI | ATR 72-211 | 404 |
| □ D-AEWK | ATR 72-211 | 446 |
| □ D-ANFA | ATR 72-202 | 224 |
| □ D-ANFB | ATR 72-202 | 229 |
| □ D-ANFC | ATR 72-202 | 237 |
| □ D-ANFD | ATR 72-202 | 256 |
| □ D-ANFE | ATR 72-202 | 294 |
| □ D-ANFF | ATR 72-202 | 292 |
| □ D-ANFG | ATR 72-212A | 658 |
| □ D-ANFH | ATR 72-212A | 660 |
| □ D-ANFI | ATR 72-212A | 662 |
| □ D-ANFJ | ATR 72-212A | 664 |
| □ D-ANFK | ATR 72-212A | 666 |
| □ D-ANFL | ATR 72-212A | 668 |

| □ D-BCRO | ATR 42-300QC | 122 |
| □ D-BLLL | ATR 42-500 | 549 |
| □ D-BMMM | ATR 42-500 | 546 |

| □ D-BNNN | ATR 42-500 | 551 |
| □ D-BOOO | ATR 42-500 | 559 |
| □ D-BPPP | ATR 42-500 | 581 |
| □ D-BQQQ | ATR 42-500 | 584 |
| □ D-BRRR | ATR 42-500 | 601 |
| □ D-BSSS | ATR 42-500 | 602 |
| □ D-BTTT | ATR 42-500 | 603 |

| □ D-ACFA | BAe 146 Srs.200 | E2200 |
| □ D-AEWA | BAe 146 Srs.300 | E3163 |
| □ D-AEWB | BAe 146 Srs.300 | E3183 |
| □ D-AEWD | BAe 146 Srs.200 | E2069 |
| □ D-AEWE | BAe 146 Srs.200 | E2077 |
| □ D-AHOI | BAe 146 Srs.300 | E3187 |
| □ D-AJET | BAe 146 Srs.200 | E2201 |
| □ D-ALOA | BAe 146 Srs.200 | E2066 |
| □ D-AQUA | BAe 146 Srs.300 | E3118 |
| □ D-AZUR | BAe 146 Srs.200 | E2060 |

| □ D-ACRA | Canadair RJ-200 | 7567 | |
| □ D-ACRB | Canadair RJ-200 | 7570 | |
| □ D-ACRC | Canadair RJ-200 | 7573 | |
| □ D-ACRD | Canadair RJ-200 | 7583 | |
| □ D-ACRE | Canadair RJ-200 | 7607 | |
| □ D-ACRF | Canadair RJ-200 | 7619 | |
| □ D-ACRG | Canadair RJ-200 | 7630 | |
| □ D-ACRH | Canadair RJ-200 | 7738 | o/o |
| □ D-ACRI | Canadair RJ-200 | | o/o |
| □ D-ACRJ | Canadair RJ-200 | | o/o |
| □ D-ACRK | Canadair RJ-200 | | o/o |
| □ D-ACRL | Canadair RJ-200 | | o/o |
| □ D-ACRM | Canadair RJ-200 | | o/o |
| □ D-ACRN | Canadair RJ-200 | | o/o |
| □ D-AKEN | Canadair RJ-200 | 7489 | |
| □ D-ALIT | Canadair RJ-200 | 7309 | |
| □ D-ALIV | Canadair RJ-200 | 7316 | |

## EXPRESS AIRWAYS

| □ D-CFXD | Short SD.3-60 | SH3749 |
| □ D-CRAS | Short SD.3-60 | SH3744 |

## FARNAIR GERMANY — EPA

| □ D-AFGA | F.27 Friendship 500F | 10341 | o/o |
| □ D-AFGB | F.27 Friendship 500F | 10397 | o/o |
| □ D-AFGC | F.27 Friendship 500F | 10398 | o/o |
| □ D-AFGD | F.27 Friendship 500F | 10449 | o/o |
| □ D-AFGE | F.27 Friendship 500F | 10632 | o/o |
| □ D-AFGF | F.27 Friendship 500F | 10634 | o/o |

## GERMANIA FLUG — GMI

| □ D-AGEG | Boeing 737-35B | 1624/24237 | |
| □ D-AGEJ | Boeing 737-3L9 | 1604/24221 | |
| □ D-AGEK | Boeing 737-3M8 | 1991/25015 | Lst MCS |
| □ D-AGEL | Boeing 737-75B | 5/28110 | |
| □ D-AGEN | Boeing 737-75B | 16/28100 | Lst HLX |
| □ D-AGEP | Boeing 737-75B | 18/28102 | Lst HLX |
| □ D-AGEQ | Boeing 737-75B | 23/28103 | Lst HLX |
| □ D-AGER | Boeing 737-75B | 27/28107 | |
| □ D-AGES | Boeing 737-75B | 28/28108 | |
| □ D-AGET | Boeing 737-75B | 31/28109 | Lst HLX |
| □ D-AGEU | Boeing 737-75B | 39/28104 | |
| □ D-AGEY | Boeing 737-73S | 98/29076 | Lst AZI |
| □ D-AGEZ | Boeing 737-73S | 104/29077 | Lst AZI |

## GERMANWINGS — GWI

| □ D-AIPH | Airbus A320-211 | 0086 | Lsf DLH |
| □ D-AIQR | Airbus A320-211 | 0382 | Lsf DLH |
| □ D-AKNF | Airbus A319-112 | 0646 | |
| □ D-AKNG | Airbus A319-112 | 0654 | |
| □ D-AKNH+ | Airbus A319-112 | 0794 | |
| □ D-AKNI | Airbus A319-112 | 1016 | |
| □ D-AKNJ | Airbus A319-112 | 1172 | |

## HAHN AIR LINES — HHN

| ☐ D-CNAY | SA.227AT Metro III | AT-493 | Lsf NAG |
|---|---|---|---|
| ☐ D-CSAL | SA.227AC Metro III | AC-601 | |
| ☐ D-CSWF | SA.227DC Metro 23 | DC-896B | |

## HAMBURG INTERNATIONAL AIRLINES — HHI

| ☐ D-AHIA | Boeing 737-73S | 229/29082 | |
|---|---|---|---|
| ☐ D-AHIB | Boeing 737-73S | 392/29083 | |
| ☐ D-AHIC | Boeing 737-7BK | 812/30617 | |
| ☐ D-AHID | Boeing 737-73S | 211/29080 | |
| ☐ D-AHIE | Boeing 737-73S | 215/29081 | opf BER |
| ☐ D- | Boeing 737-73S | 194/29079 | opf BER |

## HAPAG-LLOYD — HLF

| ☐ D-AHLC | Airbus A310-308 | 620 | Lst QSC |
|---|---|---|---|
| ☐ D-AHLV | Airbus A310-204 | 430 | |
| ☐ D-AHLW | Airbus A310-204 | 427 | |
| ☐ D-AHLX | Airbus A310-204 | 487 | |
| ☐ D-AHLZ | Airbus A310-204 | 468 | |
| ☐ D-AIDC | Airbus A310-304 | 485 | Lsf DLH |
| ☐ D-AHLF | Boeing 737-5K5 | 1968/24927 | Lst TGZ |
| ☐ D-AHLI | Boeing 737-5K5 | 2022/25037 | Lst TGZ |
| ☐ D-AHLK | Boeing 737-4K5 | 1697/24126 | Lst MNG |
| ☐ D-AHLU | Boeing 737-4K5 | 2677/27831 | Lst ADF |
| ☐ D-AHFA | Boeing 737-8K5 | 7/27981 | |
| ☐ D-AHFB | Boeing 737-8K5 | 8/27982 | |
| ☐ D-AHFC | Boeing 737-8K5 | 9/27977 | |
| ☐ D-AHFD | Boeing 737-8K5 | 40/27978 | |
| ☐ D-AHFE | Boeing 737-8K5 | 44/27979 | |
| ☐ D-AHFF | Boeing 737-8K5 | 45/27980 | |
| ☐ D-AHFG | Boeing 737-8K5 | 59/27989 | |
| ☐ D-AHFH | Boeing 737-8K5 | 218/27983 | |
| ☐ D-AHFI | Boeing 737-8K5 | 220/27984 | |
| ☐ D-AHFJ | Boeing 737-8K5 | 246/27990 | |
| ☐ D-AHFK | Boeing 737-8K5 | 248/27991 | |
| ☐ D-AHFL | Boeing 737-8K5 | 470/27985 | |
| ☐ D-AHFM | Boeing 737-8K5 | 474/27986 | |
| ☐ D-AHFN | Boeing 737-8K5 | 484/28228 | |
| ☐ D-AHFO | Boeing 737-8K5 | 499/27987 | |
| ☐ D-AHFP | Boeing 737-8K5 | 508/27988 | |
| ☐ D-AHFQ | Boeing 737-8K5 | 523/27992 | |
| ☐ D-AHFR | Boeing 737-8K5 | 528/30593 | Lst BLX |
| ☐ D-AHFS | Boeing 737-86N | 556/28623 | |
| ☐ D-AHFT | Boeing 737-8K5 | 636/30413 | |
| ☐ D-AHFU | Boeing 737-8K5 | 703/30414 | |
| ☐ D-AHFV | Boeing 737-8K5 | 719/30415 | |
| ☐ D-AHFW | Boeing 737-8K5 | 760/30882 | |
| ☐ D-AHFX | Boeing 737-8K5 | 778/30416 | |
| ☐ D-AHFY | Boeing 737-8K5 | 781/30417 | |
| ☐ D-AHFZ | Boeing 737-8K5 | 783/30883 | |
| ☐ D-AHLH | Boeing 737-8K5 | 804/30783 | |
| ☐ D-AHLP | Boeing 737-8K5 | 1046/32905 | |
| ☐ D-AHLQ | Boeing 737-8K5 | 1087/32906 | |
| ☐ D-AHLR | Boeing 737-8K5 | 1117/32907 | |
| ☐ D-ATUI | Boeing 737-86Q | 30287 | o/o |

## HAPAG-LLOYD EXPRESS — HLX

| ☐ D-AGEN | Boeing 737-75B | 16/28100 | Lsf GMI |
|---|---|---|---|
| ☐ D-AGEP | Boeing 737-75B | 18/28102 | Lsf GMI |
| ☐ D-AGEQ | Boeing 737-75B | 23/28103 | Lsf GMI |
| ☐ D-AGET | Boeing 737-75B | 31/28109 | Lsf GMI |
| ☐ D- | Boeing 737-7 | | o/o Lsf GMI |
| ☐ D- | Boeing 737-7 | | o/o Lsf GMI |
| ☐ D- | Boeing 737-7 | | o/o Lsf GMI |

## LGW — LGW

| ☐ D-IKBA | Dornier 228-200 | 8066 | |
|---|---|---|---|
| ☐ D-ILKA | Dornier 228-100 | 7005 | |
| ☐ D-ILWB | Dornier 228-200 | 8035 | |
| ☐ D-ILWD | Dornier 228-200 | 8069 | |
| ☐ D-ILWS | Dornier 228-200 | 8002 | |
| ☐ D-IMIK | Dornier 228-200 | 8058 | |

## LTU INTERNATIONAL AIRWAYS — LTU

| ☐ D-ALSA | Airbus A321-211 | 1629 | |
|---|---|---|---|
| ☐ D-ALSB | Airbus A321-211 | 1994 | o/o |
| ☐ D-ALSC | Airbus A321-211 | 2005 | o/o |
| ☐ D-ALTB | Airbus A320-214 | 1385 | |
| ☐ D-ALTC | Airbus A320-214 | 1441 | |
| ☐ D-ALTD+ | Airbus A320-214 | 1493 | |
| ☐ D-ALTE | Airbus A320-214 | 1504 | |
| ☐ D-ALTF | Airbus A320-214 | 1553 | |
| ☐ D-ALTG | Airbus A320-214 | 1762 | |
| ☐ D-ALTH | Airbus A320-214 | 1797 | |
| ☐ D-ALTI | Airbus A320-214 | 1806 | |
| ☐ D-ALTk | Airbus A320-214 | 1931 | |
| ☐ D-ALTL | Airbus A320-214 | | o/o |
| ☐ D-A | Airbus A320-214 | | o/o |
| ☐ D-AERF | Airbus A330-322 | 082 | |
| ☐ D-AERK | Airbus A330-322 | 120 | |
| ☐ D-AERQ | Airbus A330-322 | 127 | |
| ☐ D-ALPA | Airbus A330-223 | 403 | |
| ☐ D-ALPB | Airbus A330-223 | 432 | |
| ☐ D-ALPC | Airbus A330-223 | 444 | |
| ☐ D-ALPD | Airbus A330-223 | 454 | |
| ☐ D-ALPE | Airbus A330-223 | 469 | |
| ☐ D-ALPF | Airbus A330-223 | 476 | |
| ☐ D-ALPG | Airbus A330-223 | 493 | |
| ☐ D-AMUG | Boeing 757-2G5 | 830/29488 | |
| ☐ D-AMUH | Boeing 757-2G5 | 834/29489 | |
| ☐ D-AMUI | Boeing 757-2G5 | 708/28112 | |
| ☐ D-AMUW | Boeing 757-2G5 | 153/23929 | |

## LUFTHANSA CARGO — GEC

| ☐ D-ABYO | Boeing 747-230F | 347/21592 | |
|---|---|---|---|
| ☐ D-ABYU | Boeing 747-230F | 538/22668 | |
| ☐ D-ABYZ | Boeing 747-230B (SF) | 614/23286 | |
| ☐ D-ABZA | Boeing 747-230B (SF) | 617/23287 | |
| ☐ D-ABZB | Boeing 747-230F | 625/23348 | |
| ☐ D-ABZC | Boeing 747-230B (SF) | 633/23393 | |
| ☐ D-ABZF | Boeing 747-230B (SF) | 660/23621 | std |
| ☐ D-ABZI | Boeing 747-230F | 706/24138 | |
| ☐ D-ALCA | McDD MD-11F | 625/48781 | |
| ☐ D-ALCB | McDD MD-11F | 626/48782 | |
| ☐ D-ALCC | McDD MD-11F | 627/48783 | |
| ☐ D-ALCD | McDD MD-11F | 628/48784 | |
| ☐ D-ALCE | McDD MD-11F | 629/48785 | |
| ☐ D-ALCF | McDD MD-11F | 637/48798 | |
| ☐ D-ALCG | McDD MD-11F | 639/48799 | |
| ☐ D-ALCH | McDD MD-11F | 640/48801 | |
| ☐ D-ALCI | McDD MD-11F | 641/48800 | |
| ☐ D-ALCJ | McDD MD-11F | 642/48802 | |
| ☐ D-ALCK | McDD MD-11F | 643/48803 | |
| ☐ D-ALCL | McDD MD-11F | 644/48804 | |
| ☐ D-ALCM | McDD MD-11F | 645/48805 | |
| ☐ D-ALCN | McDD MD-11F | 646/48806 | |

## LUFTHANSA CITYLINE — CLH

| ☐ D-AVRA | Avro RJ85 | E2256 |
|---|---|---|
| ☐ D-AVRB | Avro RJ85 | E2253 |
| ☐ D-AVRC | Avro RJ85 | E2251 |
| ☐ D-AVRD | Avro RJ85 | E2257 |
| ☐ D-AVRE | Avro RJ85 | E2261 |
| ☐ D-AVRF | Avro RJ85 | E2269 |
| ☐ D-AVRG | Avro RJ85 | E2266 |
| ☐ D-AVRH | Avro RJ85 | E2268 |
| ☐ D-AVRI | Avro RJ85 | E2270 |
| ☐ D-AVRJ | Avro RJ85 | E2277 |
| ☐ D-AVRK | Avro RJ85 | E2278 |
| ☐ D-AVRL | Avro RJ85 | E2285 |
| ☐ D-AVRM | Avro RJ85 | E2288 |
| ☐ D-AVRN | Avro RJ85 | E2293 |
| ☐ D-AVRO | Avro RJ85 | E2246 |
| ☐ D-AVRP | Avro RJ85 | E2303 |
| ☐ D-AVRQ | Avro RJ85 | E2304 |
| ☐ D-AVRR | Avro RJ85 | E2317 |

| | | | |
|---|---|---|---|
| ☐ D-ACHA | Canadair RJ-200 | 7378 | |
| ☐ D-ACHB | Canadair RJ-200 | 7391 | |
| ☐ D-ACHC | Canadair RJ-200 | 7394 | |
| ☐ D-ACHD | Canadair RJ-200 | 7403 | |
| ☐ D-ACHE | Canadair RJ-200 | 7407 | |
| ☐ D-ACHF | Canadair RJ-200 | 7431 | |
| ☐ D-ACHG | Canadair RJ-200 | 7439 | |
| ☐ D-ACHH | Canadair RJ-200 | 7449 | |
| ☐ D-ACHI | Canadair RJ-200 | 7464 | |
| ☐ D-ACHK | Canadair RJ-200 | 7499 | |
| ☐ D-ACJA | Canadair RJ-200 | 7122 | |
| ☐ D-ACJB | Canadair RJ-200 | 7128 | |
| ☐ D-ACJC | Canadair RJ-200 | 7130 | |
| ☐ D-ACJD | Canadair RJ-200 | 7135 | |
| ☐ D-ACJE | Canadair RJ-200 | 7165 | |
| ☐ D-ACJF | Canadair RJ-200 | 7200 | |
| ☐ D-ACJG | Canadair RJ-200 | 7220 | |
| ☐ D-ACJH | Canadair RJ-200 | 7266 | |
| ☐ D-ACJI | Canadair RJ-200 | 7282 | |
| ☐ D-ACJJ | Canadair RJ-200 | 7298 | |
| ☐ D-ACJZ | Canadair RJ-200 | 7036 | |
| ☐ D-ACLA | Canadair RJ-200 | 7004 | |
| ☐ D-ACLB | Canadair RJ-200 | 7005 | |
| ☐ D-ACLC | Canadair RJ-200 | 7006 | |
| ☐ D-ACLD | Canadair RJ-200 | 7009 | |
| ☐ D-ACLE | Canadair RJ-200 | 7010 | |
| ☐ D-ACLF | Canadair RJ-200 | 7015 | |
| ☐ D-ACLG | Canadair RJ-200 | 7016 | |
| ☐ D-ACLH | Canadair RJ-200 | 7007 | |
| ☐ D-ACLI | Canadair RJ-200 | 7019 | |
| ☐ D-ACLJ | Canadair RJ-200 | 7021 | |
| ☐ D-ACLK | Canadair RJ-200 | 7023 | |
| ☐ D-ACLL | Canadair RJ-200 | 7024 | |
| ☐ D-ACLM | Canadair RJ-200 | 7025 | |
| ☐ D-ACLP | Canadair RJ-200 | 7064 | |
| ☐ D-ACLQ | Canadair RJ-200 | 7073 | |
| ☐ D-ACLR | Canadair RJ-200 | 7086 | |
| ☐ D-ACLS | Canadair RJ-200 | 7090 | |
| ☐ D-ACLT | Canadair RJ-200 | 7093 | |
| ☐ D-ACLU | Canadair RJ-200 | 7104 | |
| ☐ D-ACLV | Canadair RJ-200 | 7113 | |
| ☐ D-ACLW | Canadair RJ-200 | 7114 | |
| ☐ D-ACLY | Canadair RJ-200 | 7119 | |
| ☐ D-ACLZ | Canadair RJ-200 | 7121 | |
| ☐ D-ACPA | Canadair RJ-700 | 10012 | |
| ☐ D-ACPB | Canadair RJ-700 | 10013 | |
| ☐ D-ACPC | Canadair RJ-700 | 10014 | |
| ☐ D-ACPD | Canadair RJ-700 | 10015 | |
| ☐ D-ACPE | Canadair RJ-700 | 10027 | |
| ☐ D-ACPF | Canadair RJ-700 | 10030 | |
| ☐ D-ACPG | Canadair RJ-700 | 10034 | |
| ☐ D-ACPH | Canadair RJ-700 | 10043 | |
| ☐ D-ACPI | Canadair RJ-700 | 10046 | |
| ☐ D-ACPJ | Canadair RJ-700 | 10040 | |
| ☐ D-ACPK | Canadair RJ-700 | 10063 | |
| ☐ D-ACPL | Canadair RJ-700 | 10076 | o/o |
| ☐ D-ACPM | Canadair RJ-700 | 10080 | o/o |
| ☐ D-ACPN | Canadair RJ-700 | 10083 | o/o |
| ☐ D-ACPO | Canadair RJ-700 | 10085 | o/o |
| ☐ D-ACPP | Canadair RJ-700 | 10086 | o/o |
| ☐ D-ACPQ | Canadair RJ-700 | | o/o |
| ☐ D-ACPR | Canadair RJ-700 | | o/o |
| ☐ D-ACPS | Canadair RJ-700 | | o/o |
| ☐ D-ACPT | Canadair RJ-700 | | o/o |

## LUFTHANSA GERMAN AIRLINES    DLH

| | | | |
|---|---|---|---|
| ☐ D-AIAH | Airbus A300B4-603 | 380 | |
| ☐ D-AIAI | Airbus A300B4-603 | 391 | |
| ☐ D-AIAK | Airbus A300B4-603 | 401 | |
| ☐ D-AIAL | Airbus A300B4-603 | 405 | |
| ☐ D-AIAM | Airbus A300B4-603 | 408 | |
| ☐ D-AIAN | Airbus A300B4-603 | 411 | |
| ☐ D-AIAP | Airbus A300B4-603 | 414 | |
| ☐ D-AIAR | Airbus A300B4-603 | 546 | |
| ☐ D-AIAS | Airbus A300B4-603 | 553 | |
| ☐ D-AIAT | Airbus A300B4-603 | 618 | |
| ☐ D-AIAU | Airbus A300B4-603 | 623 | |

| | | | |
|---|---|---|---|
| ☐ D-AIAW | Airbus A300B4-605R | 764 | |
| ☐ D-AIAX | Airbus A300B4-605R | 773 | |
| ☐ D-AIAY | Airbus A300B4-605R | 608 | |
| ☐ D-AIAZ | Airbus A300B4-605R | 701 | |
| ☐ D-AIDC | Airbus A310-304 | 485 | Lst HLF |
| ☐ D-AIDD | Airbus A310-304 | 488 | |
| ☐ D-AIDF | Airbus A310-304 | 524 | |
| ☐ D-AIDH | Airbus A310-304 | 527 | |
| ☐ D-AIDL | Airbus A310-304 | 547 | |
| ☐ D-AIDM | Airbus A310-304 | 595 | |
| ☐ D-AIDN | Airbus A310-304 | 599 | |
| ☐ D-AILA | Airbus A319-114 | 0609 | |
| ☐ D-AILB | Airbus A319-114 | 0610 | |
| ☐ D-AILC | Airbus A319-114 | 0616 | |
| ☐ D-AILD | Airbus A319-114 | 0623 | |
| ☐ D-AILE | Airbus A319-114 | 0627 | |
| ☐ D-AILF | Airbus A319-114 | 0636 | |
| ☐ D-AILH | Airbus A319-114 | 0641 | Lst KZW |
| ☐ D-AILI | Airbus A319-114 | 0651 | Lst KZW |
| ☐ D-AILK | Airbus A319-114 | 0679 | Lst KZW |
| ☐ D-AILL | Airbus A319-114 | 0689 | |
| ☐ D-AILM | Airbus A319-114 | 0694 | std |
| ☐ D-AILN | Airbus A319-114 | 0700 | |
| ☐ D-AILP | Airbus A319-114 | 0717 | |
| ☐ D-AILR | Airbus A319-114 | 0723 | |
| ☐ D-AILS | Airbus A319-114 | 0729 | |
| ☐ D-AILT | Airbus A319-114 | 0738 | |
| ☐ D-AILU | Airbus A319-114 | 0744 | |
| ☐ D-AILW | Airbus A319-114 | 0853 | |
| ☐ D-AILX | Airbus A319-114 | 0860 | |
| ☐ D-AILY | Airbus A319-114 | 0875 | |
| ☐ D-AIPA | Airbus A320-211 | 0069 | |
| ☐ D-AIPB | Airbus A320-211 | 0070 | |
| ☐ D-AIPC | Airbus A320-211 | 0071 | |
| ☐ D-AIPD | Airbus A320-211 | 0072 | |
| ☐ D-AIPE | Airbus A320-211 | 0078 | |
| ☐ D-AIPF | Airbus A320-211 | 0083 | |
| ☐ D-AIPH | Airbus A320-211 | 0086 | Lst GWI |
| ☐ D-AIPK | Airbus A320-211 | 0093 | std |
| ☐ D-AIPL | Airbus A320-211 | 0094 | Lst KZW |
| ☐ D-AIPM | Airbus A320-211 | 0104 | |
| ☐ D-AIPP | Airbus A320-211 | 0110 | |
| ☐ D-AIPR | Airbus A320-211 | 0111 | |
| ☐ D-AIPS | Airbus A320-211 | 0116 | |
| ☐ D-AIPT | Airbus A320-211 | 0117 | |
| ☐ D-AIPU | Airbus A320-211 | 0135 | |
| ☐ D-AIPW | Airbus A320-211 | 0137 | |
| ☐ D-AIPX | Airbus A320-211 | 0147 | |
| ☐ D-AIPY | Airbus A320-211 | 0161 | |
| ☐ D-AIPZ | Airbus A320-211 | 0162 | |
| ☐ D-AIQA | Airbus A320-211 | 0172 | |
| ☐ D-AIQB | Airbus A320-211 | 0200 | |
| ☐ D-AIQC | Airbus A320-211 | 0201 | |
| ☐ D-AIQD | Airbus A320-211 | 0202 | |
| ☐ D-AIQE | Airbus A320-211 | 0209 | |
| ☐ D-AIQF | Airbus A320-211 | 0216 | |
| ☐ D-AIQH | Airbus A320-211 | 0217 | |
| ☐ D-AIQK | Airbus A320-211 | 0218 | |
| ☐ D-AIQL | Airbus A320-211 | 0267 | |
| ☐ D-AIQM | Airbus A320-211 | 0268 | |
| ☐ D-AIQN | Airbus A320-211 | 0269 | |
| ☐ D-AIQP | Airbus A320-211 | 0346 | |
| ☐ D-AIQR | Airbus A320-211 | 0382 | Lst GWI |
| ☐ D-AIQS | Airbus A320-211 | 0401 | |
| ☐ D-AIQT | Airbus A320-211 | 1337 | |
| ☐ D-AIQU | Airbus A320-211 | 1365 | |
| ☐ D-AIQW | Airbus A320-211 | 1367 | |
| ☐ D-AIRA | Airbus A321-131 | 0458 | |
| ☐ D-AIRB | Airbus A321-131 | 0468 | |
| ☐ D-AIRC | Airbus A321-131 | 0473 | |
| ☐ D-AIRD | Airbus A321-131 | 0474 | |
| ☐ D-AIRE | Airbus A321-131 | 0484 | |
| ☐ D-AIRF | Airbus A321-131 | 0493 | |
| ☐ D-AIRH | Airbus A321-131 | 0412 | |
| ☐ D-AIRK | Airbus A321-131 | 0502 | |

| Reg | Type | c/n | Notes |
|---|---|---|---|
| ☐ D-AIRL | Airbus A321-131 | 0505 | |
| ☐ D-AIRM | Airbus A321-131 | 0518 | |
| ☐ D-AIRN | Airbus A321-131 | 0560 | |
| ☐ D-AIRO | Airbus A321-131 | 0563 | |
| ☐ D-AIRP | Airbus A321-131 | 0564 | |
| ☐ D-AIRR | Airbus A321-131 | 0567 | |
| ☐ D-AIRS | Airbus A321-131 | 0595 | |
| ☐ D-AIRT | Airbus A321-131 | 0652 | |
| ☐ D-AIRU | Airbus A321-131 | 0692 | |
| ☐ D-AIRW | Airbus A321-131 | 0699 | |
| ☐ D-AIRX | Airbus A321-131 | 0887 | |
| ☐ D-AIRY | Airbus A321-131 | 0901 | |
| ☐ D-AISB | Airbus A321-231 | 1080 | |
| ☐ D-AISC | Airbus A321-231 | 1161 | |
| ☐ D-AISD | Airbus A321-231 | 1188 | |
| ☐ D-AISE | Airbus A321-231 | 1214 | |
| ☐ D-AISF | Airbus A321-231 | 1260 | |
| ☐ D-AISG | Airbus A321-231 | 1273 | |
| ☐ D-AIMA | Airbus A330-223 | 305 | |
| ☐ D-AIMB | Airbus A330-223 | 308 | |
| ☐ D-AIMC | Airbus A330-223 | 312 | |
| ☐ D-AIMD | Airbus A330-223 | 322 | |
| ☐ D-AIME | Airbus A330-223 | 324 | |
| ☐ D-AIBA | Airbus A340-211 | 008 | |
| ☐ D-AIBC | Airbus A340-211 | 011 | |
| ☐ D-AIBD | Airbus A340-211 | 018 | |
| ☐ D-AIBE | Airbus A340-211 | 019 | |
| ☐ D-AIBF | Airbus A340-211 | 006 | |
| ☐ D-AIBH | Airbus A340-211 | 021 | |
| ☐ D-AIFA | Airbus A340-313X | 352 | |
| ☐ D-AIFB | Airbus A340-313X | 355 | |
| ☐ D-AIFC | Airbus A340-313X | 379 | |
| ☐ D-AIFD | Airbus A340-313X | 390 | |
| ☐ D-AIFE | Airbus A340-313X | 434 | |
| ☐ D-AIFF | Airbus A340-313X | 447 | |
| ☐ D-AIFG | Airbus A340-313X | o/o | |
| ☐ D-AIFH | Airbus A340-313X | o/o | |
| ☐ D-AIFI | Airbus A340-313X | o/o | |
| ☐ D-AIFJ | Airbus A340-313X | o/o | |
| ☐ D-AIGA | Airbus A340-311 | 020 | |
| ☐ D-AIGB | Airbus A340-311 | 024 | |
| ☐ D-AIGC | Airbus A340-311 | 027 | |
| ☐ D-AIGD | Airbus A340-311 | 028 | |
| ☐ D-AIGF | Airbus A340-311 | 035 | |
| ☐ D-AIGH | Airbus A340-311 | 052 | |
| ☐ D-AIGI | Airbus A340-311 | 053 | |
| ☐ D-AIGK | Airbus A340-311 | 056 | |
| ☐ D-AIGL | Airbus A340-313X | 135 | |
| ☐ D-AIGM | Airbus A340-313X | 158 | |
| ☐ D-AIGN | Airbus A340-313X | 213 | |
| ☐ D-AIGO | Airbus A340-313X | 233 | |
| ☐ D-AIGP | Airbus A340-313X | 252 | |
| ☐ D-AIGR | Airbus A340-313X | 274 | std |
| ☐ D-AIGS | Airbus A340-313X | 297 | |
| ☐ D-AIGT | Airbus A340-313X | 304 | |
| ☐ D-AIGU | Airbus A340-313X | 321 | |
| ☐ D-AIGV | Airbus A340-313X | 325 | |
| ☐ D-AIGW | Airbus A340-313X | 327 | |
| ☐ D-AIGX | Airbus A340-313X | 354 | |
| ☐ D-AIGY | Airbus A340-313X | 335 | |
| ☐ D-AIGZ | Airbus A340-313X | 347 | |
| ☐ D-AIHA | Airbus A340-642 | 482 | o/o |
| ☐ D-AIHB | Airbus A340-642 | 517 | o/o |
| ☐ D-AIHC | Airbus A340-642 | 523 | o/o |
| ☐ D-AIHD | Airbus A340-642 | 537 | o/o |
| ☐ D-AIHE | Airbus A340-642 | 543 | o/o |
| ☐ D-AIHF | Airbus A340-642 | 566 | o/o |
| ☐ D-AIHG | Airbus A340-642 | 569 | o/o |
| ☐ D-AIMF | Airbus A340-311 | 047 | o/o |
| ☐ D-AIMG | Airbus A340-312 | 051 | o/o |
| ☐ D-ABEA | Boeing 737-330 | 1818/24565 | |
| ☐ D-ABEB | Boeing 737-330 | 2077/25148 | |
| ☐ D-ABEC | Boeing 737-330 | 2081/25149 | |
| ☐ D-ABED | Boeing 737-330 | 2082/25215 | |
| ☐ D-ABEE | Boeing 737-330 | 2084/25216 | |
| ☐ D-ABEF | Boeing 737-330 | 2094/25217 | |
| ☐ D-ABEH | Boeing 737-330 | 2102/25242 | |
| ☐ D-ABEI | Boeing 737-330 | 2158/25359 | |
| ☐ D-ABEK | Boeing 737-330 | 2164/25414 | |
| ☐ D-ABEL | Boeing 737-330 | 2175/25415 | |
| ☐ D-ABEM | Boeing 737-330 | 2182/25416 | |
| ☐ D-ABEN | Boeing 737-330 | 2196/26428 | |
| ☐ D-ABEO | Boeing 737-330 | 2207/26429 | std |
| ☐ D-ABEP | Boeing 737-330 | 2216/26430 | |
| ☐ D-ABER | Boeing 737-330 | 2242/26431 | |
| ☐ D-ABES | Boeing 737-330 | 2247/26432 | std |
| ☐ D-ABET | Boeing 737-330 | 2682/27903 | |
| ☐ D-ABEU | Boeing 737-330 | 2691/27904 | |
| ☐ D-ABEW | Boeing 737-330 | 2705/27905 | |
| ☐ D-ABIA | Boeing 737-530 | 1933/24815 | |
| ☐ D-ABIB | Boeing 737-530 | 1958/24816 | |
| ☐ D-ABIC | Boeing 737-530 | 1967/24817 | |
| ☐ D-ABID | Boeing 737-530 | 1974/24818 | |
| ☐ D-ABIE | Boeing 737-530 | 1979/24819 | std |
| ☐ D-ABIF | Boeing 737-530 | 1985/24820 | |
| ☐ D-ABIH | Boeing 737-530 | 1993/24821 | std |
| ☐ D-ABII | Boeing 737-530 | 1997/24822 | |
| ☐ D-ABIK | Boeing 737-530 | 2000/24823 | |
| ☐ D-ABIL | Boeing 737-530 | 2006/24824 | |
| ☐ D-ABIM | Boeing 737-530 | 2011/24937 | |
| ☐ D-ABIN | Boeing 737-530 | 2023/24938 | |
| ☐ D-ABIO | Boeing 737-530 | 2031/24939 | |
| ☐ D-ABIP | Boeing 737-530 | 2034/24940 | |
| ☐ D-ABIR | Boeing 737-530 | 2042/24941 | |
| ☐ D-ABIS | Boeing 737-530 | 2048/24942 | |
| ☐ D-ABIT | Boeing 737-530 | 2049/24943 | |
| ☐ D-ABIU | Boeing 737-530 | 2051/24944 | |
| ☐ D-ABIW | Boeing 737-530 | 2063/24945 | |
| ☐ D-ABIX | Boeing 737-530 | 2070/24946 | |
| ☐ D-ABIY | Boeing 737-530 | 2086/25243 | |
| ☐ D-ABIZ | Boeing 737-530 | 2098/25244 | |
| ☐ D-ABJA | Boeing 737-530 | 2116/25270 | |
| ☐ D-ABJB | Boeing 737-530 | 2117/25271 | |
| ☐ D-ABJC | Boeing 737-530 | 2118/25272 | |
| ☐ D-ABJD | Boeing 737-530 | 2122/25309 | |
| ☐ D-ABJE | Boeing 737-530 | 2126/25310 | |
| ☐ D-ABJF | Boeing 737-530 | 2128/25311 | |
| ☐ D-ABJH | Boeing 737-530 | 2141/25357 | |
| ☐ D-ABJI | Boeing 737-530 | 2151/25358 | std |
| ☐ D-ABWH | Boeing 737-330 (QC) | 1685/24284 | |
| ☐ D-ABXD | Boeing 737-330 (QC) | 1278/23525 | |
| ☐ D-ABXE | Boeing 737-330 | 1282/23526 | |
| ☐ D-ABXF | Boeing 737-330 | 1285/23527 | Lst IAA |
| ☐ D-ABXH | Boeing 737-330 | 1290/23528 | Lst IAA |
| ☐ D-ABXI | Boeing 737-330 | 1293/23529 | Lsd |
| ☐ D-ABXK | Boeing 737-330 | 1297/23530 | Lsd |
| ☐ D-ABXL | Boeing 737-330 | 1307/23531 | |
| ☐ D-ABXM | Boeing 737-330 | 1433/23871 | |
| ☐ D-ABXN | Boeing 737-330 | 1447/23872 | |
| ☐ D-ABXO | Boeing 737-330 | 1489/23873 | |
| ☐ D-ABXP | Boeing 737-330 | 1495/23874 | |
| ☐ D-ABXR | Boeing 737-330 | 1500/23875 | |
| ☐ D-ABXS | Boeing 737-330 | 1656/24280 | |
| ☐ D-ABXT | Boeing 737-330 | 1664/24281 | |
| ☐ D-ABXU | Boeing 737-330 | 1671/24282 | |
| ☐ D-ABXW | Boeing 737-330 | 1785/24561 | |
| ☐ D-ABXX | Boeing 737-330 | 1787/24562 | |
| ☐ D-ABXY | Boeing 737-330 | 1801/24563 | std |
| ☐ D-ABXZ | Boeing 737-330 | 1807/24564 | |
| ☐ D-ABTA | Boeing 747-430M | 747/24285 | |
| ☐ D-ABTB | Boeing 747-430M | 749/24286 | |
| ☐ D-ABTC | Boeing 747-430M | 754/24287 | |
| ☐ D-ABTD | Boeing 747-430M | 785/24715 | |
| ☐ D-ABTE | Boeing 747-430M | 846/24966 | |
| ☐ D-ABTF | Boeing 747-430M | 848/24967 | |
| ☐ D-ABTH | Boeing 747-430M | 856/25047 | |
| ☐ D-ABTK | Boeing 747-430 | 1293/29871 | |
| ☐ D-ABTL | Boeing 747-430 | 1299/29872 | |
| ☐ D-ABTM | Boeing 747-430 | 33430 | o/o |
| ☐ D-ABTN | Boeing 747-430 | 33431 | o/o |
| ☐ D-ABTO | Boeing 747-430 | 33432 | o/o |
| ☐ D-ABTP | Boeing 747-430 | 33433 | o/o |

| | | | |
|---|---|---|---|
| ☐ D-ABVA | Boeing 747-430 | 723/23816 | |
| ☐ D-ABVB | Boeing 747-430 | 700/23817 | |
| ☐ D-ABVC | Boeing 747-430 | 757/24288 | |
| ☐ D-ABVD | Boeing 747-430 | 786/24740 | |
| ☐ D-ABVE | Boeing 747-430 | 787/24741 | |
| ☐ D-ABVF | Boeing 747-430 | 796/24761 | |
| ☐ D-ABVH | Boeing 747-430 | 845/25045 | |
| ☐ D-ABVK | Boeing 747-430 | 847/25046 | |
| ☐ D-ABVL | Boeing 747-430 | 898/26425 | |
| ☐ D-ABVM | Boeing 747-430 | 1143/29101 | |
| ☐ D-ABVN | Boeing 747-430 | 915/26427 | |
| ☐ D-ABVO | Boeing 747-430 | 1080/28086 | |
| ☐ D-ABVP | Boeing 747-430 | 1103/28284 | |
| ☐ D-ABVR | Boeing 747-430 | 1106/28285 | |
| ☐ D-ABVS | Boeing 747-430 | 1109/28286 | |
| ☐ D-ABVT | Boeing 747-430 | 1110/28287 | |
| ☐ D-ABVU | Boeing 747-430 | 1191/29492 | |
| ☐ D-ABVW | Boeing 747-430 | 1205/29493 | |
| ☐ D-ABVX | Boeing 747-430 | 1237/29868 | |
| ☐ D-ABVY | Boeing 747-430 | 1261/29869 | |
| ☐ D-ABVZ | Boeing 747-430 | 1264/29870 | |
| ☐ D-ABYX | Boeing 747-230M | 550/22670 | |
| ☐ D-ABZD | Boeing 747-230B | 639/23407 | std |
| ☐ D-ABZE | Boeing 747-230M | 663/23509 | |
| ☐ D-ABZH | Boeing 747-230B | 665/23622 | std |

### NIGHTEXPRESS — EXT

| | | |
|---|---|---|
| ☐ D-CCAS | Short SD.3-60 | SH3737 |

### NORTHERN AIR CHARTER — NAG

| | | | |
|---|---|---|---|
| ☐ D-CCCC | SA.227AT Merlin IVC | AT-511 | EMS |
| ☐ D-CNAC | SA.227DC Metro 23 | DC-895B | Lst OLT |
| ☐ D-CNAF | SA.227AC Metro III | AC-505B | |
| ☐ D-CNAG | SA.227DC Metro 23 | DC-893B | Lst OLT |
| ☐ D-CNAY | SA.227AT Merlin IVC | AT-493 | Lsd HHN |
| ☐ D-IHBL | SA.227TT Merlin IIIC | TT-512A | |

### OLT — OLT

| | | | |
|---|---|---|---|
| ☐ D-CNAC | SA.227DC Metro 23 | DC-895B | Lsf NAG |
| ☐ D-CNAG | SA.227DC Metro 23 | DC-893B | Lsf NAG |
| ☐ D-COLB | SA.227AC Metro III | AC-754B | |
| ☐ D-COLC | SA.227AC Metro III | AC-689 | Lst CIP |
| ☐ D-COLD | SA.227AC Metro III | AC-421B | |
| ☐ D-COLT | SA.227AC Metro III | AC-690 | |
| ☐ D-AOLT | SAAB 2000 | 037 | |
| ☐ D-CMTM | Dornier 328-110 | 3094 | |
| ☐ D-CMUC | Dornier 328-110 | 3096 | |
| ☐ D-COLE | SAAB SF.340A | 144 | |

### PRIVATE WINGS — PWF

| | | |
|---|---|---|
| ☐ D-COCA | Beech 1900D | UE-224 |

### PTL LUFTFAHRTUNTERNEHMEN — KST

| | | | |
|---|---|---|---|
| ☐ OE-GIF | SAAB SF.340A | 100 | Lsf BCF |

### WDL AVIATION — WDL

| | | | |
|---|---|---|---|
| ☐ D-ADEP | F.27 Friendship 600 | 10318 | |
| ☐ D-ADOP | F.27 Friendship 600 | 10316 | |
| ☐ D-AELC | F.27 Friendship 600 | 10438 | std |
| ☐ D-AELD | F.27 Friendship 600 | 10442 | std |
| ☐ D-AELE | F.27 Friendship 600 | 10477 | |
| ☐ D-AELF | F.27 Friendship 600 | 10323 | std |
| ☐ D-AELG | F.27 Friendship 600 | 10338 | |
| ☐ D-AELH | F.27 Friendship 400 | 10340 | |
| ☐ D-AELJ | F.27 Friendship 600 | 10342 | |
| ☐ D-AELK | F.27 Friendship 600 | 10361 | |
| ☐ D-AELM | F.27 Friendship 600 | 10450 | |
| ☐ D-AISY | F.27 Friendship 600 | 10391 | |
| ☐ D-BAKB | F.27 Friendship 600 | 10261 | |
| ☐ D-BAKC | F.27 Friendship 600 | 10195 | |
| ☐ D-BAKD | F.27 Friendship 600 | 10179 | |

| | | | |
|---|---|---|---|
| ☐ D-AMAJ | BAe 146 Srs.200 | E2028 | |
| ☐ D-AWBA | BAe 146 Srs.300A | E3134 | |
| ☐ D-AWDL | BAe 146 Srs.100 | E1011 | |
| ☐ D-AWUE | BAe 146 Srs.200 | E2050 | |

## DQ - FIJI

### AIR PACIFIC — FJI

| | | | |
|---|---|---|---|
| ☐ DQ-FJC | Boeing 767-3X2ER | 552/26260 | |
| ☐ DQ-FJE | Boeing 747-238B | 464/22614 | Lsf QFA |
| ☐ DQ-FJF | Boeing 737-7X2 | 96/28878 | Lst QFA |
| ☐ DQ-FJG | Boeing 737-8X2 | 275/29968 | |
| ☐ DQ-FJH | Boeing 737-8X2 | 339/29969 | |
| ☐ DQ- | Boeing 747-412 | | o/o Lsf SIA |
| ☐ DQ- | Boeing 747-412 | | o/o Lsf SIA |

## D2 - ANGOLA

### AIR GEMINI — GLL

| | | |
|---|---|---|
| ☐ S9-BAH | Boeing 727-173C | 449/19507 |
| ☐ S9-BAQ | Boeing 727-22C | 293/19093 |
| ☐ S9-BAR | Boeing 727-22C | 318/19098 |
| ☐ S9-BAU | Boeing 727-25C | 367/19358 |
| ☐ S9-BOE | Boeing 727-22C | 388/19192 |

### AIR NACOIA — ANL

| | | | |
|---|---|---|---|
| ☐ D2-FAS | Boeing 727-227 | 983/20773 | std? |
| ☐ D2-FAV | Boeing 707-321C | 366/18717 | |

### AIR TRANSWORLD — PLN

| | | |
|---|---|---|
| ☐ D2-FFA | Boeing 727-22C | 324/19100 |
| ☐ D2-FFB | Boeing 727-51C | 294/19206 |

### ANGOLA AIR CHARTER — AGO

| | | |
|---|---|---|
| ☐ D2-FCI | Boeing 727-23F | 26/18429 |
| ☐ D2-FCK | Boeing 727-44F | 148/18892 |
| ☐ D2-FCM | Ilyushin Il-76TD | |
| ☐ D2-FCN | Ilyushin Il-76TD | |
| ☐ D2-FDX | Ilyushin Il-76T | 063407170 |
| ☐ D2-TBI | Boeing 737-214 | 68/19681 |

### TAAG ANGOLA AIRLINES — DTA

| | | | |
|---|---|---|---|
| ☐ D2-TBC | Boeing 737-2M2C | 447/21173 | |
| ☐ D2-TBD | Boeing 737-2M2 | 567/21723 | Lst GCB |
| ☐ D2-TBO | Boeing 737-2M2 | 891/22776 | |
| ☐ D2-TBP | Boeing 737-2M2 | 1084/23220 | |
| ☐ D2-TBX | Boeing 737-2M2 | 1117/23351 | |
| ☐ D2-TEA | Boeing 747-312M | 653/23410 | |
| ☐ D2-TEB | Boeing 747-357M | 686/23751 | |

## D4 - CAPE VERDE ISLANDS

### TACV – CAPE VERDE AIRLINES — TCV

| | | |
|---|---|---|
| ☐ D4-CBG | Boeing 757-2Q8 | 696/27599 |
| ☐ D4-CBN | Boeing 737-3Q8 | 2786/26333 |

## D6 - COMOROS

### COMOROS AIRLINES — CWK

| | | | |
|---|---|---|---|
| ☐ D6-OZX | Boeing 747SP-27 | 473/22302 | std |

## EC - SPAIN

### AEBAL – AEROLINEAS BALEARES — ABH

| | | |
|---|---|---|
| ☐ EC-HNY | Boeing 717-2CM | 5023/55059 |
| ☐ EC-HNZ | Boeing 717-2CM | 5026/55060 |
| ☐ EC-HOA | Boeing 717-2CM | 5029/55061 |
| ☐ EC-HUZ | Boeing 717-23S | 5054/55066 |

## AERO NOVA — OVA

| | | |
|---|---|---|
| ☐ EC-GVE | SA.227AC Metro III | AC-669 |
| ☐ EC-HCH | SA.227AC Metro III | AC-658B |
| ☐ EC-HZH | SA.227AC Metro III | AC-720 |

## AIR EUROPA LINEAS AEREAS — AEA

| | | | |
|---|---|---|---|
| ☐ EC-FXP" | Boeing 737-4Q8 | 1996/24706 | |
| ☐ EC-FXQ | Boeing 737-4Q8 | 2057/24707 | |
| ☐ EC-GMY | Boeing 737-36Q | 2865/28658 | |
| ☐ EC-GUO | Boeing 737-4Q8 | 2416/26285 | |
| ☐ EC-HNB | Boeing 737-4Q8 | 2239/26280 | |
| ☐ EC-HXT | Boeing 737-4K5 | 1839/24769 | |
| ☐ EC-HBL | Boeing 737-85P | 250/28381 | |
| ☐ EC-HBM | Boeing 737-85P | 256/28382 | |
| ☐ EC-HBN | Boeing 737-85P | 266/28383 | |
| ☐ EC-HGO | Boeing 737-85P | 420/28384 | |
| ☐ EC-HGP | Boeing 737-85P | 421/28385 | |
| ☐ EC-HGQ | Boeing 737-85P | 426/28386 | |
| ☐ EC-HJP | Boeing 737-85P | 480/28535 | |
| ☐ EC-HJQ | Boeing 737-85P | 522/28387 | |
| ☐ EC-HKQ | Boeing 737-85P | 533/28388 | |
| ☐ EC-HKR | Boeing 737-85P | 540/28536 | |
| ☐ EC-HZS | Boeing 737-86Q | 920/30276 | |
| ☐ EC-ICD | Boeing 737-81Q | 1007/30785 | |
| ☐ EC-IDA | Boeing 737-86Q | 1051/32773 | |
| ☐ EC-IDT | Boeing 737-86Q | 1076/30281 | |
| ☐ EC-III | Boeing 737-86Q | 1233/30284 | |
| ☐ EC- | Boeing 737-85P | | o/o |
| G-XLAF | Boeing 737-86N | 1083/29883 | Lsf XLA |
| ☐ EC-FYJ | Boeing 757-256 | 593/26242 | Lst ICE |
| ☐ EC-FYK | Boeing 757-256 | 603/26243 | std |
| ☐ EC-HKS | Boeing 767-3Q8ER | 793/27686 | |
| ☐ EC-HPU | Boeing 767-3Q8ER | 828/30048 | |
| ☐ EC-HSV | Boeing 767-3Q8ER | 840/29387 | |

## AIR NOSTRUM — ANS

| | | | |
|---|---|---|---|
| ☐ EC-HBY | ATR 72-212A | 578 | |
| ☐ EC-HCG | ATR 72-212A | 580 | |
| ☐ EC-HEI | ATR 72-212A | 570 | |
| ☐ EC-HEJ | ATR 72-212A | 565 | |
| ☐ EC-HJI | ATR 72-212A | 562 | |
| ☐ EC-GYI | Canadair RJ-200 | 7249 | |
| ☐ EC-GZA | Canadair RJ-200 | 7252 | |
| ☐ EC-HEK | Canadair RJ-200 | 7320 | |
| ☐ EC-HHI | Canadair RJ-200 | 7343 | |
| ☐ EC-HHV | Canadair RJ-200 | 7350 | |
| ☐ EC-HPR | Canadair RJ-200 | 7430 | |
| ☐ EC-HSH | Canadair RJ-200 | 7466 | |
| ☐ EC-HTZ | Canadair RJ-200 | 7493 | |
| ☐ EC-HXM | Canadair RJ-200 | 7514 | |
| ☐ EC-HYG | Canadair RJ-200 | 7529 | |
| ☐ EC-HZR | Canadair RJ-200 | 7547 | |
| ☐ EC-IAA | Canadair RJ-200 | 7563 | |
| ☐ EC-IBM | Canadair RJ-200 | 7591 | |
| ☐ EC-IDC | Canadair RJ-200 | 7622 | |
| ☐ EC-IGO | Canadair RJ-200 | 7661 | |
| ☐ EC-IJE | Canadair RJ-200 | 7700 | |
| ☐ EC-IJF | Canadair RJ-200 | 7705 | |
| ☐ EC-IJS | Canadair RJ-200 | 7706 | |
| ☐ EC- | Canadair RJ-200 | | o/o |
| ☐ EC- | Canadair RJ-200 | | o/o |
| ☐ EC- | Canadair RJ-200 | | o/o |
| ☐ EC-IBS | DHC-8Q-315 | 560 | |
| ☐ EC-IBT | DHC-8Q-315 | 561 | |
| ☐ EC-ICA | DHC-8Q-315 | 562 | |
| ☐ EC-ICX | DHC-8Q-315 | 563 | |
| ☐ EC-IDK | DHC-8Q-315 | 564 | |
| ☐ EC-IFK | DHC-8Q-315 | 574 | |
| ☐ EC-IGE | DHC-8Q-315 | 576 | |
| ☐ EC-IGS | DHC-8Q-315 | 586 | |
| ☐ EC-IIA | DHC-8Q-315 | 587 | |
| ☐ EC-IIB | DHC-8Q-315 | 588 | |

| | | | |
|---|---|---|---|
| ☐ EC-IJD | DHC-8Q-315 | 589 | |
| ☐ EC-IJP | DHC-8Q-315 | 582 | |
| ☐ PH-DEJ | DHC-8Q-315 | 581 | |
| ☐ EC-IKA | DHC-8Q-315 | 590 | |
| ☐ PH-DMQ | DHC-8Q-315 | 567 | |
| ☐ PH-DMR | DHC-8Q-315 | 569 | |
| ☐ PH-DMU | DHC-8Q-315 | 568 | |
| ☐ PH-DMV | DHC-8Q-315 | 570 | |
| ☐ PH-DMW | DHC-8Q-315 | 573 | |
| ☐ EC-GJY | Fokker 50 | 20265 | |
| ☐ EC-GQT | Fokker 50 | 20136 | |
| ☐ EC-HKA | Fokker 50 | 20203 | |
| ☐ EC-HLC | Fokker 50 | 20137 | |
| ☐ EC-HZA | Fokker 50 | 20202 | Lsf DNM |
| ☐ PH-JXN | Fokker 50 | 20239 | Lsf DNM |

## AIR PLUS COMET — MPD

| | | | |
|---|---|---|---|
| ☐ EC-GMU | Airbus A310-324 | 451 | |
| ☐ EC-GOT | Airbus A310-324 | 455 | |
| ☐ EC-HIF | Airbus A310-325 | 624 | |
| ☐ EC-HLA | Airbus A310-324ET | 489 | |
| ☐ EC-IHV | Airbus A310-325ET | 640 | |
| ☐ EC-I | Airbus A310-325ET | 642 | o/o |
| ☐ | Airbus A310-304 | 520 | o/o |

## ARTAC AVIATION — AVS

| | | |
|---|---|---|
| ☐ EC-GEN | SA.227AC Metro III | AC-688 |
| ☐ EC-GJM | SA.227TC Metro III | BC-772B |

## ATLANTIC AIRWAYS — RCU

| | | |
|---|---|---|
| ☐ EC-GJX | SA.227DC Metro 23 | DC-855B |

## BINTER CANARIAS — IBB

| | | | |
|---|---|---|---|
| ☐ EC-ESS | ATR 72-202 | 154 | |
| ☐ EC-EUJ | ATR 72-202 | 157 | |
| ☐ EC-EYK | ATR 72-202 | 183 | |
| ☐ EC-FIV | ATR 72-201 | 260 | |
| ☐ EC-FJX | ATR 72-201 | 267 | |
| ☐ EC-FKQ | ATR 72-201 | 276 | |
| ☐ EC-GQF | ATR 72-202 | 489 | |
| ☐ EC-GRP | ATR 72-202 | 488 | |
| ☐ EC-GRU | ATR 72-202 | 493 | |
| ☐ EC-HBU | ATR 72-212 | 459 | |
| ☐ EC-HEZ | ATR 72-212A | 582 | |
| ☐ OY-RUB | ATR 72-202 | 301 | Lsd |

## BKS AIR — CKM

| | | |
|---|---|---|
| ☐ EC-HJO | SA.227AC Metro III | AC-615B |
| ☐ EC-HXY | SA.227AC Metro III | AC-461B |

## CYGNUS AIR — RGN

| | | |
|---|---|---|
| ☐ EC-EMD | Douglas DC-8-62F | 407/46023 |
| ☐ EC-EMX | Douglas DC-8-62F | 322/45921 |
| ☐ EC-IGZ | Douglas DC-8-73CF | 46133 |

## EURO CONTINENTAL AIR — ECN

| | | |
|---|---|---|
| ☐ EC-GPS | SA.227AC Metro III | AC-722 |

## FUTURA INTERNATIONAL — FUA

| | | | |
|---|---|---|---|
| ☐ EC-GNZ | Boeing 737-4Y0 | 2199/25178 | |
| ☐ EC-GRX | Boeing 737-46B | 1663/24123 | |
| ☐ EC-GUG | Boeing 737-4S3 | 2061/25116 | |
| ☐ EC-IFN | Boeing 737-46B | 1679/24124 | |
| ☐ EC-IHI | Boeing 737-4S3 | 2083/25134 | std |
| ☐ EC-HHG | Boeing 737-86N | 410/28608 | |
| ☐ EC-HHH | Boeing 737-86N | 449/28610 | |
| ☐ EC-HJJ | Boeing 737-86N | 504/28617 | |

| | | | |
|---|---|---|---|
| ☐ EC-HMJ | Boeing 737-86N | 570/28621 | |
| ☐ EC-HMK | Boeing 737-86N | 585/28624 | |
| ☐ EC-IEN | Boeing 737-86N | 258/28592 | |

## HOLA AIRLINES                    HOA

| | | | |
|---|---|---|---|
| ☐ EC-IEZ | Boeing 737-33A | 1304/23628 | |
| ☐ EC-IFV | Boeing 737-33A | 1284/23626 | |

## IBERIA LINEAS AEREAS DE ESPANA       IBE

| | | | |
|---|---|---|---|
| ☐ EC-HGR | Airbus A319-111 | 1154 | |
| ☐ EC-HGS | Airbus A319-111 | 1180 | |
| ☐ EC-HGT | Airbus A319-111 | 1247 | |
| ☐ EC-HKO | Airbus A319-111 | 1362 | |
| All based Miami, FL | | | |
| ☐ EC-FCB | Airbus A320-211 | 0158 | |
| ☐ EC-FDA | Airbus A320-211 | 0176 | |
| ☐ EC-FDB | Airbus A320-211 | 0173 | |
| ☐ EC-FGH | Airbus A320-211 | 0223 | |
| ☐ EC-FGR | Airbus A320-211 | 0224 | |
| ☐ EC-FGV | Airbus A320-211 | 0207 | |
| ☐ EC-FLP | Airbus A320-211 | 0266 | |
| ☐ EC-FLQ | Airbus A320-211 | 0274 | |
| ☐ EC-FNR | Airbus A320-211 | 0323 | |
| ☐ EC-FQY | Airbus A320-211 | 0356 | |
| ☐ EC-GRE | Airbus A320-211 | 0134 | |
| ☐ EC-GRF | Airbus A320-211 | 0136 | |
| ☐ EC-GRG | Airbus A320-211 | 0143 | |
| ☐ EC-GRH | Airbus A320-211 | 0146 | |
| ☐ EC-GRI | Airbus A320-211 | 0177 | |
| ☐ EC-GRJ+ | Airbus A320-211 | 0246 | |
| ☐ EC-HAB | Airbus A320-214 | 0994 | |
| ☐ EC-HAD | Airbus A320-214 | 0992 | |
| ☐ EC-HAF | Airbus A320-214 | 1047 | |
| ☐ EC-HAG | Airbus A320-214 | 1059 | |
| ☐ EC-HDK | Airbus A320-214 | 1067 | |
| ☐ EC-HDL | Airbus A320-214 | 1063 | |
| ☐ EC-HDN | Airbus A320-214 | 1087 | |
| ☐ EC-HDO | Airbus A320-214 | 1099 | |
| ☐ EC-HDP | Airbus A320-214 | 1101 | |
| ☐ EC-HDT | Airbus A320-214 | 1119 | |
| ☐ EC-HGY | Airbus A320-214 | 1200 | |
| ☐ EC-HGZ | Airbus A320-214 | 1208 | |
| ☐ EC-HHA | Airbus A320-214 | 1221 | |
| ☐ EC-HQG | Airbus A320-214 | 1379 | |
| ☐ EC-HQI | Airbus A320-214 | 1396 | |
| ☐ EC-HQJ | Airbus A320-214 | 1430 | |
| ☐ EC-HQK | Airbus A320-214 | 1454 | |
| ☐ EC-HQL | Airbus A320-214 | 1461 | |
| ☐ EC-HQM | Airbus A320-214 | 1484 | |
| ☐ EC-HSE | Airbus A320-214 | 1229 | |
| ☐ EC-HSF | Airbus A320-214 | 1255 | |
| ☐ EC-HTA | Airbus A320-214 | 1516 | |
| ☐ EC-HTB | Airbus A320-214 | 1530 | |
| ☐ EC-HTC | Airbus A320-214 | 1540 | |
| ☐ EC-HTD | Airbus A320-214 | 1550 | |
| ☐ EC-HUJ | Airbus A320-214 | 1292 | |
| ☐ EC-HUK | Airbus A320-214 | 1318 | |
| ☐ EC-HUL | Airbus A320-214 | 1347 | |
| ☐ EC-HYC | Airbus A320-214 | 1262 | |
| ☐ EC-HYD | Airbus A320-214 | 1288 | |
| ☐ EC-ICQ | Airbus A320-211 | 0199 | |
| ☐ EC-ICR | Airbus A320-211 | 0240 | |
| ☐ EC-ICS | Airbus A320-211 | 0241 | |
| ☐ EC-ICT | Airbus A320-211 | 0264 | |
| ☐ EC-ICU | Airbus A320-211 | 0303 | |
| ☐ EC-ICV | Airbus A320-211 | 0312 | |
| ☐ EC-IEF | Airbus A320-214 | 1655 | |
| ☐ EC-IEG | Airbus A320-214 | 1674 | |
| ☐ EC-IEI | Airbus A320-214 | 1694 | |
| ☐ EC-I | Airbus A320-214 | 1736 | |
| ☐ EC-I | Airbus A320-214 | 1793 | o/o |
| ☐ EC-I | Airbus A320-214 | 1809 | o/o |
| ☐ EC-I | Airbus A320-214 | | o/o |
| ☐ EC-I | Airbus A320-214 | | o/o |

| | | | |
|---|---|---|---|
| ☐ EC-HUH | Airbus A321-211 | 1021 | |
| ☐ EC-HUI | Airbus A321-211 | 1027 | |
| ☐ EC-IGK | Airbus A321-211 | 1572 | |
| ☐ EC-IIG | Airbus A321-211 | 1554 | |
| ☐ EC-IJN | Airbus A321-211 | 1836 | |
| ☐ EC-I | Airbus A321-211 | 1681 | o/o |
| ☐ EC-I | Airbus A321-211 | 1716 | o/o |
| ☐ EC-I | Airbus A321-211 | | o/o |
| ☐ EC-GGS | Airbus A340-313 | 125 | |
| ☐ EC-GHX | Airbus A340-313 | 134 | |
| ☐ EC-GJT | Airbus A340-313 | 145 | |
| ☐ EC-GLE | Airbus A340-313 | 146 | |
| ☐ EC-GPB | Airbus A340-313X | 193 | |
| ☐ EC-GQK | Airbus A340-313X | 197 | |
| ☐ EC-GUP | Airbus A340-313X | 217 | |
| ☐ EC-GUQ | Airbus A340-313X | 221 | |
| ☐ EC-HDQ | Airbus A340-313X | 302 | |
| ☐ EC-HGU | Airbus A340-313X | 318 | |
| ☐ EC-HGV | Airbus A340-313X | 329 | |
| ☐ EC-HGX | Airbus A340-313X | 332 | |
| ☐ EC-HQF | Airbus A340-313X | 378 | |
| ☐ EC-HQH | Airbus A340-313X | 387 | |
| ☐ EC-HQN | Airbus A340-313X | 414 | |
| ☐ EC-ICF | Airbus A340-313X | 459 | |
| ☐ EC-IDF | Airbus A340-313X | 474 | |
| ☐ EC-IIH | Airbus A340-313X | 483 | |
| ☐ EC- | Airbus A340-313 | | o/o |
| ☐ EC- | Airbus A340-642 | 431 | o/o |
| ☐ EC- | Airbus A340-642 | 440 | o/o |
| ☐ EC- | Airbus A340-642 | 460 | o/o |
| ☐ EC-DIA | Boeing 747-256B | 450/22238 | |
| ☐ EC-DIB | Boeing 747-256B | 451/22239 | |
| ☐ EC-DNP | Boeing 747-256B | 554/22764 | |
| ☐ EC-GAG | Boeing 747-256B | 173/20137 | |
| ☐ EC-HVD | Boeing 747-256M | 509/22454 | |
| ☐ EC-IAF | Boeing 747-256M | 515/22455 | |
| ☐ TF-ATI | Boeing 747-341 | 702/24107 | Lsf ABD |
| ☐ TF-ATJ | Boeing 747-341 | 703/24108 | Lsf ABD |
| ☐ EC-FTR | Boeing 757-256 | 553/26239 | |
| ☐ EC-FXV | Boeing 757-256 | 572/26241 | |
| ☐ EC-GZY | Boeing 757-256 | 860/26247 | |
| ☐ EC-GZZ | Boeing 757-256 | 863/26248 | |
| ☐ EC-HAA | Boeing 757-256 | 881/26249 | |
| ☐ EC-HDM | Boeing 757-256 | 889/26250 | |
| ☐ EC-HDR | Boeing 757-256 | 897/26251 | |
| ☐ EC-HDS | Boeing 757-256 | 900/26252 | |
| ☐ EC-HDU | Boeing 757-256 | 902/26253 | |
| ☐ EC-HDV | Boeing 757-256 | 905/26254 | |
| ☐ EC-HIP | Boeing 757-256 | 920/29306 | |
| ☐ EC-HIQ | Boeing 757-256 | 924/29307 | |
| ☐ EC-HIR | Boeing 757-256 | 935/29308 | |
| ☐ EC-HIS | Boeing 757-256 | 936/29309 | |
| ☐ EC-HIT | Boeing 757-256 | 938/29310 | |
| ☐ EC-HIU | Boeing 757-256 | 940/29311 | |
| ☐ EC-HIV | Boeing 757-256 | 943/29312 | |
| ☐ EC-HIX | Boeing 757-256 | 948/30052 | |
| ☐ EC-EXF | McDD MD-87 | 1703/49832 | |
| ☐ EC-EXG | McDD MD-87 | 1706/49833 | |
| ☐ EC-EXM | McDD MD-87 | 1717/49835 | |
| ☐ EC-EXN | McDD MD-87 | 1721/49836 | |
| ☐ EC-EXR | McDD MD-87 | 1714/49834 | |
| ☐ EC-EXT | McDD MD-87 | 1730/49837 | |
| ☐ EC-EYB | McDD MD-87 | 1733/49838 | |
| ☐ EC-EYX | McDD MD-87 | 1739/49839 | |
| ☐ EC-EYY | McDD MD-87 | 1745/49840 | |
| ☐ EC-EYZ | McDD MD-87 | 1751/49841 | |
| ☐ EC-EZA | McDD MD-87 | 1763/49842 | |
| ☐ EC-EZS | McDD MD-87 | 1771/49843 | |
| ☐ EC-FEY | McDD MD-87 | 1865/53208 | |
| ☐ EC-FEZ | McDD MD-87 | 1862/53207 | |
| ☐ EC-FFA | McDD MD-87 | 1867/53209 | |
| ☐ EC-FFH | McDD MD-87 | 1874/53211 | |
| ☐ EC-FFI | McDD MD-87 | 1871/53210 | |
| ☐ EC-FGM | McDD MD-88 | 1890/53193 | |

| | | | |
|---|---|---|---|
| ☐ EC-FHD | McDD MD-87 | 1877/53212 | |
| ☐ EC-FHG | McDD MD-88 | 1911/53194 | |
| ☐ EC-FHK | McDD MD-87 | 1879/53213 | |
| ☐ EC-FIG | McDD MD-88 | 1929/53195 | |
| ☐ EC-FIH | McDD MD-88 | 1930/53196 | |
| ☐ EC-FJE | McDD MD-88 | 1940/53197 | |
| ☐ EC-FLK | McDD MD-88 | 1975/53304 | |
| ☐ EC-FLN | McDD MD-88 | 1974/53303 | |
| ☐ EC-FND | McDD MD-88 | 2001/53305 | |
| ☐ EC-FOF | McDD MD-88 | 2015/53307 | |
| ☐ EC-FOG | McDD MD-88 | 2014/53306 | |
| ☐ EC-FOZ | McDD MD-88 | 2022/53308 | |
| ☐ EC-FPD | McDD MD-88 | 2023/53309 | |
| ☐ EC-FPJ | McDD MD-88 | 2024/53310 | |
| ☐ EC-GRK | McDD MD-87 | 1654/49827 | |
| ☐ EC-GRL | McDD MD-87 | 1667/49828 | |
| ☐ EC-GRM | McDD MD-87 | 1678/49829 | |
| ☐ EC-GRN | McDD MD-87 | 1684/49830 | |
| ☐ EC-GRO | McDD MD-87 | 1688/49831 | |
| | | | |
| ☐ EC-BIS | Douglas DC-9-32 | 262/47312 | Lst AUT |
| ☐ EC-BQU | Douglas DC-9-32 | 563/47447 | Lst AUT |
| ☐ EC-BQX | Douglas DC-9-32 | 567/47454 | Lst AUT |

## IBERTRANS AEREA     *IBT*

| | | | |
|---|---|---|---|
| ☐ EC-GQA | Embraer EMB-120ER | 120027 | |
| ☐ EC-HHN | Embraer EMB-120ER | 120103 | |
| ☐ EC-HFZ | Embraer EMB.120RT | 120261 | Lsf RGI |
| ☐ EC-HSO | Embraer EMB.120ER | 120214 | |
| ☐ EC-HUP | Embraer EMB.120RT | 120209 | |

## IBERWORLD     *IWD*

| | | |
|---|---|---|
| ☐ EC-GZD | Airbus A320-214 | 0879 |
| ☐ EC-GZE | Airbus A320-214 | 0888 |
| ☐ EC-HZU | Airbus A320-214 | 1578 |
| ☐ EC-IAG | Airbus A320-214 | 1597 |
| ☐ EC-ICK | Airbus A320-214 | 1657 |
| ☐ EC-IEQ | Airbus A320-214 | 1767 |
| ☐ EC-HAL | Airbus A310-324 | 594 |
| ☐ EC-IDB | Airbus A330-243 | 461 |
| ☐ EC-IJH | Airbus A330-322 | 072 |

## INTERMEDIACION AEREA     *IEA*

| | | |
|---|---|---|
| ☐ EC-IDG | ATR 42-300 | 003 |

## ISLAS AIRWAYS

| | | | |
|---|---|---|---|
| ☐ EC-IKK | ATR 72-201 | 198 | |
| ☐ EC- | ATR 72-202 | 477 | o/o |

## LTE INTERNATIONAL AIRWAYS     *LTE*

| | | |
|---|---|---|
| ☐ EC-HQV | Boeing 757-2G5 | 36/23118 |
| ☐ EC-HQX | Boeing 757-2G5 | 116/23651 |
| ☐ EC-HRB | Boeing 757-2G5 | 51/23119 |
| ☐ EC-ICN | Airbus A320-214 | 1717 |
| ☐ EC-IEP | Airbus A320-214 | 1775 |
| ☐ EC-ILG | Airbus A321-211 | 1233 |

## NAYSA AEROTAXIS     *NAY*

| | | |
|---|---|---|
| ☐ EC-GTM | Beech 1900C | UB-30 |
| ☐ EC-GUD | Beech 1900C-1 | UC-156 |
| ☐ EC-GZG | Beech 1900C-1 | UC-161 |
| ☐ EC-HCM | Beech 1900C-1 | UC-124 |
| ☐ EC-IAH | Beech 1900C-1 | UC-166 |
| ☐ EC-IJO | Beech 1900D | UE-300 |

## PANAIR LINEAS AEREAS     *PNR*

| | | |
|---|---|---|
| ☐ EC-FZE | BAe 146 Srs.200QT | E2105 |
| ☐ EC-GQO | BAe 146 Srs.200QT | E2086 |

| | | |
|---|---|---|
| ☐ EC-HDH | BAe 146 Srs.200QT | E2056 |
| ☐ EC-HJH | BAe 146 Srs.200QT | E2112 |
| ☐ EC-HQT | Airbus A300B4-203F | 124 |
| ☐ EC-HVZ | Airbus A300B4-203F | 227 |

## SPANAIR     *JKK*

| | | | |
|---|---|---|---|
| ☐ EC-HPM | Airbus A321-231 | 1276 | |
| ☐ EC-HQZ | Airbus A321-231 | 1333 | |
| ☐ EC-HRG | Airbus A321-231 | 1366 | |
| ☐ EC-HRP | Airbus A320-232 | 1349 | |
| ☐ EC-HXA | Airbus A320-232 | 1497 | |
| ☐ EC-IAZ | Airbus A320-232 | 1631 | |
| ☐ EC-ICL | Airbus A320-232 | 1682 | |
| ☐ EC-IEJ | Airbus A320-232 | 1749 | |
| ☐ EC-IIZ | Airbus A320-232 | 1862 | |
| ☐ EC-IJU | Airbus A321-231 | 1843 | |
| ☐ EC- | Airbus A320-232 | 1914 | o/o |
| ☐ EC- | Airbus A320-232 | 1933 | o/o |
| ☐ EC- | Airbus A321-231 | 1946 | o/o |
| ☐ EC- | Airbus A320-232 | | o/o |
| ☐ EC- | Airbus A320-232 | | o/o |
| ☐ EC- | Airbus A320-232 | | o/o |
| | | | |
| ☐ EC-FTS | McDD MD-83 | 1495/49621 | |
| ☐ EC-FXA | McDD MD-83 | 1785/49938 | |
| ☐ EC-FXI | McDD MD-83 | 1591/49630 | |
| ☐ EC-FXY | McDD MD-83 | 1580/49627 | |
| ☐ EC-FZC | McDD MD-83 | 1643/49790 | |
| ☐ EC-GAT | McDD MD-83 | 1542/49709 | |
| ☐ EC-GBA | McDD MD-83 | 1538/49626 | |
| ☐ EC-GCV | McDD MD-82 | 2042/53165 | |
| ☐ EC-GGV | McDD MD-83 | 1644/49791 | |
| ☐ EC-GHE | McDD MD-83 | 1332/49398 | |
| ☐ EC-GHH | McDD MD-83 | 1455/49578 | |
| ☐ EC-GKF | McDD MD-87 | 1333/49389 | |
| ☐ EC-GKG | McDD MD-87 | 1614/49706 | |
| ☐ EC-GNY | McDD MD-83 | 1305/49396 | |
| ☐ EC-GOM | McDD MD-83 | 1465/49579 | |
| ☐ EC-GOU | McDD MD-83 | 1847/53198 | |
| ☐ EC-GQG | McDD MD-83 | 1454/49577 | |
| ☐ EC-GQZ | McDD MD-82 | 1458/49571 | |
| ☐ EC-GTO | McDD MD-82 | 1440/49570 | |
| ☐ EC-GVI | McDD MD-83 | 1778/49936 | |
| ☐ EC-GVO | McDD MD-83 | 1421/49642 | |
| ☐ EC-GXU | McDD MD-83 | 1498/49622 | |
| ☐ EC-HBP | McDD MD-83 | 1583/49629 | |
| ☐ EC-HFP | McDD MD-82 | 2072/53148 | |
| ☐ EC-HFS | McDD MD-82 | 1633/49517 | |
| ☐ EC-HFT | McDD MD-82 | 1690/49521 | |
| ☐ EC-HGA | McDD MD-83 | 1731/53052 | |
| ☐ EC-HGJ | McDD MD-82 | 1658/49519 | |
| ☐ EC-HHF | McDD MD-82 | 1482/49509 | |
| ☐ EC-HHP | McDD MD-82 | 1292/49501 | |
| ☐ EC-HJB | McDD MD-82 | 1425/49507 | |
| ☐ EC-HKP | McDD MD-83 | 1502/49624 | |
| ☐ EC-HMI | McDD MD-87 | 1404/49403 | |
| ☐ EC-HNC | McDD MD-83 | 1484/49620 | |
| ☐ EC-HOV | McDD MD-82 | 1271/49416 | |
| ☐ EC-HVC | McDD MD-83 | 1405/49569 | |
| ☐ EC-HVX | McDD MD-83 | 1468/49572 | |

## SWIFTAIR     *SWT*

| | | | |
|---|---|---|---|
| ☐ EC-HAH | Boeing 727-223F | 1199/21084 | Lsf BCS |
| ☐ EC-HHU | Boeing 727-277F | 1768/22644 | Lsf BCS |
| ☐ EC-HJV | Boeing 727-264F | 1049/20895 | Lsf BCS |
| ☐ EC-HLP | Boeing 727-264F | 1051/20896 | Lsf BCS |
| ☐ EC-IDQ | Boeing 727-223F | 593/19489 | std |
| ☐ EC-IFC | Boeing 727-277F | 1762/22643 | Lsf BCS |
| | | | |
| ☐ EC-GBF | Convair 580 | 458 | Lsf BCS |
| ☐ EC-GDY | Convair 580 | 25 | Lsf BCS |
| ☐ EC-GHN | Convair 580 | 186 | Lsf BCS |
| ☐ EC-GKH | Convair 580 | 135 | Lsf BCS |
| ☐ EC-GSJ | Convair 580 | 130 | Lsf BCS |
| ☐ EC-HJU | Convair 580 | 147 | Lsf BCS |

| | | | |
|---|---|---|---|
| ☐ EC-HLD | Convair 580 | 52 | Lsf BCS |
| ☐ EC-HMR | Convair 580 | 68 | Lsf BCS |
| ☐ EC-HMS | Convair 580 | 459 | Lsf BCS |
| | | | |
| ☐ EC-HAK | Embraer EMB-120RT | 120008 | |
| ☐ EC-HCF | Embraer EMB.120ER | 120007 | |
| ☐ EC-HFK | Embraer EMB.120ER | 120063 | |
| ☐ EC-HMY | Embraer EMB.120ER | 120009 | |
| ☐ EC-HTS | Embraer EMB.120RT | 120168 | |
| | | | |
| ☐ EC-FZB | SA.226TC Metro II | TC-221 | Lsf BCS |
| ☐ EC-GBI | SA.226AT Merlin IVA | AT-041 | Lsf BCS |
| ☐ EC-GXE | SA.227AC Metro III | AC-694 | |
| ☐ EC-GYB | SA.227AC Metro III | AC-699 | |
| ☐ EC- | SA.227AC Metro III | AC-461B | |

## EI - IRELAND

### AER ARANN EXPRESS                                  REA

| | | | |
|---|---|---|---|
| ☐ EI-BYO | ATR 42-310 | 161 | |
| ☐ EI-CBK | ATR 42-310 | 199 | |
| ☐ EI-CPT | ATR 42-300 | 191 | |
| ☐ EI-CVR | ATR 42-300 | 022 | |
| ☐ EI-CVS | ATR 42-300 | 033 | |
| ☐ EI-REA | ATR 72-201 | 441 | |
| ☐ EI-REB | ATR 72-201 | 470 | |
| ☐ PH-PRJ | Fokker 50 | 20212 | Lsf DNM |

### AER LINGUS                                              EIN

| | | | |
|---|---|---|---|
| ☐ EI-CPC | Airbus A321-211 | 0815 | |
| ☐ EI-CPD | Airbus A321-211 | 0841 | |
| ☐ EI-CPE | Airbus A321-211 | 0926 | |
| ☐ EI-CPF | Airbus A321-211 | 0991 | |
| ☐ EI-CPG | Airbus A321-211 | 1023 | |
| ☐ EI-CPH | Airbus A321-211 | 1094 | |
| | | | |
| ☐ EI-CVA | Airbus A320-214 | 1242 | |
| ☐ EI-CVB | Airbus A320-214 | 1394 | |
| ☐ EI-CVC | Airbus A320-214 | 1443 | |
| ☐ EI-CVD | Airbus A320-214 | 1467 | |
| | | | |
| ☐ EI-CRK | Airbus A330-301 | 070 | |
| ☐ EI-DAA | Airbus A330-202 | 397 | |
| ☐ EI-DUB | Airbus A330-301 | 055 | |
| ☐ EI-EWR | Airbus A330-202 | 330 | |
| ☐ EI-JFK | Airbus A330-301 | 086 | |
| ☐ EI-LAX | Airbus A330-202 | 269 | |
| ☐ EI-ORD | Airbus A330-301 | 059 | |
| | | | |
| ☐ EI-BXD | Boeing 737-448 | 1867/24866 | |
| ☐ EI-BXI | Boeing 737-448 | 2036/25052 | Lst RYN |
| ☐ EI-BXK | Boeing 737-448 | 2269/25736 | |
| ☐ EI-CDA | Boeing 737-548 | 1939/24878 | |
| ☐ EI-CDB | Boeing 737-548 | 1970/24919 | |
| ☐ EI-CDC | Boeing 737-548 | 1975/24968 | |
| ☐ EI-CDD | Boeing 737-548 | 1989/24989 | |
| ☐ EI-CDE | Boeing 737-548 | 2050/25115 | |
| ☐ EI-CDF | Boeing 737-548 | 2232/25737 | |
| ☐ EI-CDG | Boeing 737-548 | 2261/25738 | |
| ☐ EI-CDH | Boeing 737-548 | 2271/25739 | |
| | | | |
| ☐ EI-CLG | BAe 146 Srs.300 | E3131 | |
| ☐ EI-CLH | BAe 146 Srs.300 | E3146 | |
| ☐ EI-CLI | BAe 146 Srs.300 | E3159 | |
| ☐ EI-CTM | BAe 146 Srs.300 | E3129 | |
| ☐ EI-CTN | BAe 146 Srs.300 | E3169 | |
| ■ EI-CTO | BAe 146 Srs.300 | E3193 | |

### AIR CONTRACTORS (IRELAND)                 ABR

| | | | |
|---|---|---|---|
| ☐ EI-DHL | Airbus A300B4-203F | 274 | Opf DHL |
| ☐ EI-EAA | Airbus A300B4-203F | 150 | Opf DHL |
| ☐ EI-EAB | Airbus A300B4-203F | 199 | Opf DHL |
| ☐ EI-EAC | Airbus A300B4-203F | 250 | Opf DHL |
| ☐ EI-EAD | Airbus A300B4-203F | 289 | Opf DHL |
| ☐ EI-EAE | Airbus A300B4-203F | 095 | Opf DHL |
| ☐ EI-EAT | Airbus A300B4-203F | 116 | Opf DHL |
| ☐ EI-OZA | Airbus A300B4-103F | 148 | Opf DHL |
| ☐ EI-OZB | Airbus A300B4-103F | 184 | Opf DHL |
| ☐ EI-OZC | Airbus A300B4-103F | 189 | Opf DHL |
| ☐ EI-SAF | Airbus A300B4-203F | 220 | Opf DHL |
| | | | |
| ☐ EI-HCA | Boeing 727-225F | 825/20382 | Opf DHL |
| ☐ EI-HCI | Boeing 727-223F | 705/20183 | Opf DHL |
| ☐ EI-JIV | L-382G Hercules | 4673 | Lsf SFR |
| ☐ EI-JVL | L-382G Hercules | 4676 | Lsf SFR |
| ☐ EI-LCH | Boeing 727-281F | 865/20466 | |
| ☐ EI-SLF | ATR 72-202 | 210 | |

### CHC IRELAND

| | | | |
|---|---|---|---|
| ☐ EI-CNL | Sikorsky S-61N | 61746 | IMES |
| ☐ EI-CXS | Sikorsky S-61N | 61816 | IMES |
| ☐ EI-MES | Sikorsky S-61N | 61776 | IMES |
| ☐ EI-RCG | Sikorsky S-61N | 61807 | IMES |
| ☐ EI-SAR | Sikorsky S-61N | 61143 | IMES |

### CITYJET                                                      BCY

| | | | |
|---|---|---|---|
| ☐ EI-CMS | BAe 146 Srs.200 | E2044 | |
| ☐ EI-CMY | BAe 146 Srs.200 | E2039 | |
| ☐ EI-CNB | BAe 146 Srs.200 | E2046 | |
| ☐ EI-CNQ | BAe 146 Srs.200 | E2031 | |
| ☐ EI-CSK | BAe 146 Srs.200 | E2062 | |
| ☐ EI-CSL | BAe 146 Srs.200 | E2074 | |
| ☐ EI-CWA | BAe 146 Srs.200 | E2058 | |
| ☐ EI-CWB | BAe 146 Srs.200 | E2051 | |
| ☐ EI-CWC | BAe 146 Srs.200 | E2053 | |
| ☐ EI-CWD | BAe 146 Srs.200 | E2108 | |
| ☐ EI-PAT | BAe 146 Srs.200 | E2030 | Lsf AWC |

### IRISH CARGO AIRLINES                             ATT

| | | | |
|---|---|---|---|
| ☐ EI-BNA | Douglas DC-8-63CF | 371/45989 | std |
| ☐ EI-CGO | Douglas DC-8-63F | 392/45924 | |

### RYANAIR                                                    RYR

| | | | |
|---|---|---|---|
| ☐ EI-CJC | Boeing 737-204 | 867/22640 | |
| ☐ EI-CJD | Boeing 737-204 | 946/22966 | |
| ☐ EI-CJE | Boeing 737-204 | 863/22639 | |
| ☐ EI-CJF | Boeing 737-204 | 953/22967 | |
| ☐ EI-CJG | Boeing 737-204 | 629/22058 | |
| ☐ EI-CJH | Boeing 737-204 | 621/22057 | |
| ☐ EI-CJI | Boeing 737-2E7 | 917/22875 | |
| ☐ EI-CKP | Boeing 737-2K2 | 668/22296 | |
| ☐ EI-CKQ | Boeing 737-2K2 | 888/22906 | |
| ☐ EI-CKR | Boeing 737-2K2 | 647/22025 | |
| ☐ EI-CKS | Boeing 737-2T5 | 636/22023 | |
| ☐ EI-CNT | Boeing 737-230 | 694/22115 | |
| ☐ EI-CNV | Boeing 737-230 | 752/22128 | |
| ☐ EI-CNW | Boeing 737-230 | 772/22133 | |
| ☐ EI-CNX | Boeing 737-230 | 745/22127 | |
| ☐ EI-CNY | Boeing 737-230 | 649/22113 | |
| ☐ EI-CNZ | Boeing 737-230 | 735/22126 | |
| ☐ EI-COA | Boeing 737-230 | 848/22637 | |
| ☐ EI-COB | Boeing 737-230 | 727/22124 | |
| ☐ EI-CON | Boeing 737-2T5 | 730/22396 | |
| ☐ EI-COX | Boeing 737-230 | 726/22123 | |
| | | | |
| ☐ EI-CSA | Boeing 737-8AS | 210/29916 | |
| ☐ EI-CSB | Boeing 737-8AS | 298/29917 | |
| ☐ EI-CSC | Boeing 737-8AS | 307/29918 | |
| ☐ EI-CSD | Boeing 737-8AS | 341/29919 | |
| ☐ EI-CSE | Boeing 737-8AS | 362/29920 | |
| ☐ EI-CSF | Boeing 737-8AS | 560/29921 | |
| ☐ EI-CSG | Boeing 737-8AS | 571/29922 | |
| ☐ EI-CSH | Boeing 737-8AS | 576/29923 | |
| ☐ EI-CSI | Boeing 737-8AS | 578/29924 | |
| ☐ EI-CSJ | Boeing 737-8AS | 588/29925 | |

| | | |
|---|---|---|
| ☐ EI-CSM | Boeing 737-8AS | 722/29926 |
| ☐ EI-CSN | Boeing 737-8AS | 727/29927 |
| ☐ EI-CSO | Boeing 737-8AS | 735/29928 |
| ☐ EI-CSP | Boeing 737-8AS | 753/29929 |
| ☐ EI-CSQ | Boeing 737-8AS | 757/29930 |
| ☐ EI-CSR | Boeing 737-8AS | 1020/29931 |
| ☐ EI-CSS | Boeing 737-8AS | 1030/29932 |
| ☐ EI-CST | Boeing 737-8AS | 1038/29933 |
| ☐ EI-CSV | Boeing 737-8AS | 1050/29934 |
| ☐ EI-CSW | Boeing 737-8AS | 1061/29935 |
| ☐ EI-CSX | Boeing 737-8AS | 1140/32778 |
| ☐ EI-CSY | Boeing 737-8AS | 1167/32779 |
| ☐ EI-CSZ | Boeing 737-8AS | 1178/32780 |
| ☐ EI-CTA | Boeing 737-8AS | 1236/29936 |
| ☐ EI-CTB | Boeing 737-8AS | 1238/29937 |
| ☐ EI-DAC | Boeing 737-8AS | 1240/29938 |
| ☐ EI-DAD | Boeing 737-8AS | 1249/33544 |
| ☐ EI-DAE | Boeing 737-8AS | 1252/33545 |
| ☐ EI-DAF | Boeing 737-8AS | 1262/29939 |
| ☐ EI-DAG | Boeing 737-8AS | 1265/29940 |
| ☐ EI-DAH | Boeing 737-8AS | 1269/33546 |
| ☐ EI-DAI | Boeing 737-8AS | 1271/33547 |
| ☐ EI-DAJ | Boeing 737-8AS | 1274/33548 |
| ☐ EI- | Boeing 737-8AS | o/o |
| ☐ EI- | Boeing 737-8AS | o/o |
| ☐ EI- | Boeing 737-8AS | o/o |
| ☐ EI- | Boeing 737-8AS | o/o |
| ☐ EI- | Boeing 737-8AS | o/o |
| ☐ EI- | Boeing 737-8AS | o/o |
| ☐ EI- | Boeing 737-8AS | o/o |
| ☐ EI- | Boeing 737-8AS | o/o |
| ☐ EI- | Boeing 737-8AS | o/o |
| ☐ EI- | Boeing 737-8AS | o/o |

## SKYNET AIRLINES · SIH

| | | |
|---|---|---|
| ☐ EI-CXK | Boeing 737-4S3 | 2255/25596 |
| ☐ EI-CZB | Boeing 737-4Y0 | 1781/24519 |

# EK - ARMENIA

## ARMAVIA · RNV

| | | | |
|---|---|---|---|
| ☐ P4-VNF | Airbus A320-211 | 0726 | Lsf SIB |
| ☐ EK-65575 | Tupolev Tu-134A | 62350 | Lsf CMK |

## ARMENIAN AIRLINES · RME

| | | | |
|---|---|---|---|
| ☐ EK-65044 | Tupolev Tu-134A-3 | 49450 | |
| ☐ EK-65072 | Tupolev Tu-134A-3 | 49972 | Govt |
| ☐ EK-65822 | Tupolev Tu-134A-3 | 09071 | |
| ☐ EK-65831 | Tupolev Tu-134A-3 | 17102 | |
| ☐ EK-65848 | Tupolev Tu-134A-3 | 23136 | |
| ☐ EK-85166 | Tupolev Tu-154B-1 | 76A-166 | std |
| ☐ EK-85279 | Tupolev Tu-154B-1 | 78A-279 | std |
| ☐ EK-85403 | Tupolev Tu-154B-2 | 80A-403 | |
| ☐ EK-85442 | Tupolev Tu-154B-2 | 80A-442 | |
| ☐ EK-85536 | Tupolev Tu-154B-2 | 82A-536 | |
| ☐ EK-85566 | Tupolev Tu-154B-2 | 82A-566 | |
| ☐ RA-85136 | Tupolev Tu-154M | 88A-791 | Lsf BKS |
| ☐ EK-32001 | Airbus A320-212 | 0397 | |
| ☐ EK-86117 | Ilyushin Il-86 | 51483209085 | |
| ☐ EK-86118 | Ilyushin Il-86 | 51483209086 | |

# EL - LIBERIA

Register has been suspended due to illegal registrations and new national registration marks A8 allocated.
No further information at time of going to press.

## DUCOR WORLD AIRWAYS · DWA

| | | | |
|---|---|---|---|
| ☐ 3C-QRL | L-1011-1 Tristar | 1093 | std |
| ☐ 3C-QRQ | L-1011- Tristar | 1101 | |

## SANTA CRUZ IMPERIAL AIRLINES · SNZ

| | | | |
|---|---|---|---|
| ☐ A6-ZYD | Boeing 707-3J6C | 872/20718 | |
| ☐ EL-ALJ | Antonov An-12BP | 8346202 | |

# EP - IRAN

## ARAM AIRLINE · IRW

| | | |
|---|---|---|
| ☐ EP-RAB | Ilyushin Il-76TD | 0053465941 |

## ARIA AIR · IRX

| | | | |
|---|---|---|---|
| ☐ EP-EAA | Tupolev Tu-154M | 90A-897 | Lsf TZK |
| ☐ EP-EAB | Tupolev Tu-154M | 90A-864 | Lsf TZK |
| ☐ EP-EAC | Tupolev Tu-154M | 86A-725 | |
| ☐ EP-EAD | Tupolev Tu-154M | | |

## ATLAS AIR · IRH

| | | |
|---|---|---|
| ☐ EP-ALF | Ilyushin Il-76TD | 0033448407 |
| ☐ EP-ALJ | Ilyushin Il-76TD | 0013434018 |

## CASPIAN AIRLINES · CPN

| | | | |
|---|---|---|---|
| ☐ EP-CPG | Tupolev Tu-154M | 87A-748 | Lsf UDN |
| ☐ EP-CPN | Tupolev Tu-154M | 91A-898 | |
| ☐ EP-CPO | Tupolev Tu-154M | 91A-899 | |

## CHABAHAR AIRLINE · IRU

| | | | |
|---|---|---|---|
| ☐ EP-CFB | Ilyushin Il-76TD | 0093495854 | |
| ☐ EP-CFC | Ilyushin Il-76TD | 0063466981 | Lsf AUV |

## IRAN AIR · IRA

| | | | |
|---|---|---|---|
| ☐ EP-IBA | Airbus A300B4-605R | 723 | |
| ☐ EP-IBB | Airbus A300B4-605R | 727 | |
| ☐ EP-IBS | Airbus A300B2-203 | 080 | |
| ☐ EP-IBT | Airbus A300B2-203 | 185 | |
| ☐ EP-IBV | Airbus A300B2-203 | 187 | |
| ☐ EP-IBZ | Airbus A300B2-203 | 226 | |
| ☐ EP-IBL | Airbus A310-304 | 436 | |
| ☐ EP-IBM | Airbus A310-203 | 338 | |
| ☐ EP-IBN | Airbus A310-203 | 375 | |
| ☐ EP-IBO | Airbus A310-203 | 379 | |
| ☐ EP-IBP | Airbus A310-203 | 370 | |
| ☐ EP-IBQ | Airbus A310-203 | 389 | |
| ☐ EP-IBX | Airbus A310-203 | 390 | |
| ☐ EP-IRB | Boeing 727-86 | 323/19172 | std |
| ☐ EP-IRC | Boeing 727-86 | 505/19816 | |
| ☐ EP-IRP | Boeing 727-286 | 1048/20945 | |
| ☐ EP-IRR | Boeing 727-286 | 1052/20946 | |
| ☐ EP-IRS | Boeing 727-286 | 1070/20947 | |
| ☐ EP-IRT | Boeing 727-286 | 1114/21078 | |
| ☐ EP-IDA | Fokker 100 | 11292 | |
| ☐ EP-IDB | Fokker 100 | 11299 | |
| ☐ EP-IDD | Fokker 100 | 11294 | |
| ☐ EP-IDF | Fokker 100 | 11298 | |
| ☐ EP-IDG | Fokker 100 | 11302 | |
| ☐ EP-IAA | Boeing 747SP-86 | 275/20998 | |
| ☐ EP-IAB | Boeing 747SP-86 | 278/20999 | |
| ☐ EP-IAC | Boeing 747SP-86 | 307/21093 | |
| ☐ EP-IAD | Boeing 747SP-86 | 371/21758 | |
| ☐ EP-IAG | Boeing 747-286M | 291/21217 | |
| ☐ EP-IAH | Boeing 747-286M | 300/21218 | |
| ☐ EP-IAM | Boeing 747-186B | 381/21759 | |
| ☐ EP-ICC | Boeing 747-2J9F | 343/21514 | |
| ☐ EP-IRF | Boeing 737-286C | 283/20498 | |
| ☐ EP-IRH | Boeing 737-286C | 286/20500 | |
| ☐ EP-IRI | Boeing 737-286C | 321/20740 | |

| □ EP-IRK | Boeing 707-321C | 541/19267 |
| □ EP-IRL | Boeing 707-386C | 832/20287 |
| □ EP-IRM | Boeing 707-386C | 839/20288 |
| □ EP-IRN | Boeing 707-386C | 866/20741 |

## IRANAIR TOURS · IRB

| □ EP-MAT | Tupolev Tu-154M | 92A-928 | Lsf OMS |
| □ EP-MBG | Tupolev Tu-154M | 90A-858 | Lsf OMS |
| □ EP-MBJ | Tupolev Tu-154M | 93A-960 | Lsf OMS |
| □ EP-MBK | Tupoelv Tu-154M | 89A-802 | Lsf BKL |
| □ EP-MBL | Tupolev Tu-154M | 89A-799 | |
| □ EP-MBM | Tupolev Tu-154M | 92A-931 | Lsf NKZ |
| □ EP-MBN | Tupolev Tu-154M | 92A-940 | Lsf NKZ |
| □ EP-MBO | Tupolev Tu-154M | 93A-982 | Lsf KAZ |
| □ EP-MBP | Tupolev Tu-154M | 89A-800 | |
| □ EP-MBT | Tupolev Tu-154M | 93A-975 | |
| □ EP-MBU | Tupolev Tu-154M | | |

## IRAN ASEMAN AIRLINES · IRC

| □ EP-ATA | ATR 72-212 | 334 | |
| □ EP-ATH | ATR 72-212 | 339 | |
| □ EP-ATS | ATR 72-212 | 391 | |
| □ EP-ATZ | ATR 72-212 | 398 | |
| □ F-GKOA | ATR 72-202 | 201 | Lsf ARF |
| □ F-GKOC | ATR 72-202 | 307 | Lsf ARF |
| □ F-OIRA | ATR 72-212A | 697 | |
| □ F-OIRB | ATR 72-212A | 573 | |
| | | | |
| □ EP-ASE | F.28 Fellowship 4000 | 11144 | |
| □ EP-ASM | Fokker 100 | | |
| □ EP-PAT | F.28 Fellowship 4000 | 11164 | |
| □ EP-PAU | F.28 Fellowship 4000 | 11166 | |
| □ EP-PAX | F.28 Fellowship 1000C | 11102 | |
| □ EP-PAZ | F.28 Fellowship 1000 | 11104 | Govt |
| □ EP-PBJ | F.28 Fellowship 4000 | 11135 | |
| | | | |
| □ EP-ASA | Boeing 727-228 | 1594/22081 | |
| □ EP-ASB | Boeing 727-228 | 1603/22082 | std |
| □ EP-ASC | Boeing 727-228 | 1638/22084 | |
| □ EP-ASD | Boeing 727-228 | 1665/22085 | |

## KISH AIR · IRK

| □ EP-LBN | Tupolev Tu-154M | 85A-717 |
| □ EP-LBR | Tupolev Tu-154M | 90A-938 |
| □ EP-LBS | Tupolev Tu-154M | 91A-901 |
| □ EP-LBV | Fokker 50 | 20158 |
| □ EP-LCA | Fokker 50 | 20273 |
| □ EP-LCB | Fokker 50 | 20274 |
| □ EP-LCC | Fokker 50 | 20275 |
| □ EP-LCD | Tupolev Tu-154M | |

## MAHAN AIR · IRM

| □ EP-MHE | Airbus A300B4-103 | 035 | |
| □ EP-MHF | Airbus A300B4-103 | 055 | |
| □ EP-MHG | Airbus A300B4-203 | 204 | |
| □ EP-MHH | Airbus A310-304ER | 586 | |
| □ EP-MHI | Airbus A310-304ER | 537 | |
| □ EP- | Airbus A300B4-103F | 042 | o/o |
| | | | |
| □ EP-MHS | Tupolev Tu-154M | | |
| □ EP-MHT | Tupolev Tu-154M | | |
| □ EP-MHV | Tupolev Tu-154M | 92A-932 | Lsf OMS |
| □ EP-MHZ | Tupolev Tu-154M | 91A-890 | Lsf OMS |

## PAYAM INTERNATIONAL AIR · IRP

| □ EP-TPU | Ilyushin Il-76TD | 0093497936 | Lsf BRZ |
| □ EP-TPV | Ilyushin Il-76TD | 0043451523 | Lsf BRZ |

## QESHM AIR · IRQ

| □ EP-TQI | Ilyushin Il-76TD | 1013409321 |
| □ EP-TQJ | Ilyushin Il-76TD | 1013409297 |

## SAHA AIRLINE · IRZ

| □ EP-SHE | Boeing 707-3J9C | 915/21127 |
| □ EP-SHG | Boeing 707-3J9C | 876/20830 |
| □ EP-SHJ | Boeing 707-3J9C | 915/21127 |
| □ EP-SHK | Boeing 707-3J9C | 917/21128 |
| □ EP-SHP | Boeing 707-3J9C | 908/21123 |
| | | |
| □ EP-SHA | Boeing 747-2J9F | 340/21507 |
| □ EP-SHB | Boeing 747-2J9F | 315/21486 |
| □ EP-SHD | Boeing 747-131F | 85/20081 |
| □ EP-SHH | Boeing 747-2J9F | 319/21487 |

# ER - MOLDOVA

## AEROCOM · MCC

| □ ER-ACI | Antonov An-12BP | 6343707 |
| □ ER-ACP | Antonov An-12 | |
| □ ER-ACT | Antonov An-12 | |
| □ ER-ADE | Antonov An-12 | 2340503 |
| □ ER-AXA | Antonov An-12 | 01347907 |
| □ ER-TAI | Tupolev Tu-154M | 82A-546 |

## AIR MOLDOVA · MLD

| □ ER-65036 | Tupolev Tu-134A-3 | 48700 | |
| □ ER-65050 | Tupolev Tu-134A-3 | 49756 | |
| □ ER-65051 | Tupolev Tu-134A-3 | 49758 | |
| □ ER-65094 | Tupolev Tu-134A-3 | 60255 | Govt |
| □ ER-65140 | Tupolev Tu-134A-3 | 60932 | Govt |
| □ ER-65707 | Tupolev Tu-134A-3 | 63435 | |
| □ ER-65791 | Tupolev Tu-134A-3 | 63110 | |
| □ ER-EMA | Embraer EMB.120RT | 120223 | |

## JETLINE INTERNATIONAL · MUL

| □ ER-IBV | Ilyushin Il-76T | 0003423699 | |
| □ P4-ABH | BAC One-Eleven 401AK | 088 | VIP |
| □ VP-BBA | BAC One-Eleven 422EQ | 126 | |

## MOLDAVIAN AIRLINES · MDV

| □ ER-SGB | SAAB SF.340B | 182 | Lsf CRX |
| □ ER-SGC | SAAB SF.340B | 160 | Lsf CRX |
| □ ER-TCF | Tupolev Tu-134A-3 | 62390 | |

## RENAN AIR · RAN

| □ ER-AEJ | Antonov An-72 | 36572094889 | |
| □ ER-AEN | Antonov An-74 | 36547095898 | |
| □ ER-AES | Antonov An-32 | 2509 | Lst SDK |
| □ ER-AEU | Antonov An-32B | 2109 | |
| □ ER-AFI | Antonov An-32B | 3205 | |
| □ ER-AFM | Antonov An-32B | 3305 | |
| □ ER-AFY | Antonov An-24RV | 47309809 | |
| □ ER-ICG | Ilyushin Il-18V | 184007301 | |
| □ ER-ICJ | Ilyushin Il-18E | 186009102 | |
| □ ER-ICM | Ilyushin Il-18D | 182004804 | |

## TIRAMAVIA · TVI

| □ ER-ACA | Antonov An-12BP | 00347102 |
| □ ER-ADN | Antonov An-12BP | 3341606 |
| □ ER-AES | Antonov An-26B | 12001 |

## VICHI AIRLINES · VIH

| □ ER-AFZ | Antonov An-72 | 365722070698 |
| □ ER-AWF | Antonov An-72 | 36572070696 |
| □ ER-75929 | Ilyushin Il-18D | 187010505 |

# ES - ESTONIA

## AERO AIRLINES · EAY

| □ OH-KRE | ATR 72-201 | 174 | Lsf FIN |
| □ OH-KRK | ATR 72-201 | 251 | Lsf FIN |

## AIREST — AIT

| | | | |
|---|---|---|---|
| ☐ ES-LLB | LET L-410UVP-E20C | 912608 | |
| ☐ ES-LLC | LET L-410UVP-E20C | 912609 | |
| ☐ ES-LTA | Tupolev Tu-134A-3 | 60195 | std |
| ☐ ES-LTP | Tupolev Tu-154M | 92A-909 | |
| ☐ ES-PJG | BAe Jetstream 31 | 701 | |

## ENIMEX — ENI

| | | |
|---|---|---|
| ☐ ES-NOB | An-72-100 | 36572080695 |
| ☐ ES-NOC | An-72-100 | 36572010952 |
| ☐ ES-NOG | An-72-100 | 36572080786 |
| ☐ ES-NOH | An-72 | 36572098943 |
| ☐ ES-NOK | An-72-100 | 36572080780 |
| ☐ ES-NOL | An-72-100 | 36572080789 |

## ESTONIAN AIR — ELL

| | | | |
|---|---|---|---|
| ☐ ES-ABC | Boeing 737-5Q8 | 2772/26324 | |
| ☐ ES-ABD | Boeing 737-5Q8 | 2735/26323 | |
| ☐ ES-ABF | Boeing 737-5L9 | 1816/24778 | |
| ☐ ES-AFM | Fokker 50 | 20153 | |
| ☐ ES-AFN | Fokker 50 | 20154 | std |

# ET - ETHIOPIA

## ETHIOPIAN AIRLINES — ETH

| | | |
|---|---|---|
| ☐ ET-AJS | Boeing 757-260PF | 300/24845 |
| ☐ ET-AJX | Boeing 757-260 | 348/25014 |
| ☐ ET-AKC | Boeing 757-260 | 408/25353 |
| ☐ ET-AKE | Boeing 757-260ER | 444/26057 |
| ☐ ET-AKF | Boeing 757-260ER | 496/26058 |
| ☐ ET-AIE | Boeing 767-260ER | 90/23106 |
| ☐ ET-AIF | Boeing 767-260ER | 93/23107 |
| ☐ ET-AKW | Boeing 767-33AER | 403/25346 |
| ☐ ET-ALC | Boeing 767-33AER | 734/28043 |
| ☐ ET-ALH | Boeing 767-3BGER | 802/30565 |
| ☐ ET-AJB | Boeing 737-260 | 1583/23915 |
| ☐ ET-ALE | Boeing 737-2T4 | 1165/23446 |

# EW - BELARUS

## BELAVIA BELARUSSIAN AIRLINES — BRU

| | | | |
|---|---|---|---|
| ☐ EW-65082 | Tupolev Tu-134A-3 | 60081 | |
| ☐ EW-65085 | Tupolev Tu-134A | 60123 | |
| ☐ EW-65106 | Tupolev Tu-134A | 60315 | |
| ☐ EW-65133 | Tupolev Tu-134A-3 | 60645 | |
| ☐ EW-65145 | Tupolev Tu-134A | 60985 | |
| ☐ EW-65754 | Tupolev Tu-134A | 62154 | |
| ☐ EW-65772 | Tupolev Tu-134A-3 | 62472 | |
| ☐ EW-85419 | Tupolev Tu-154B-2 | 80A-419 | std |
| ☐ EW-85509 | Tupolev Tu-154B-2 | 81A-509 | Lst SAI |
| ☐ EW-85538 | Tupolev Tu-154B-2 | 82A-538 | Lst SAI |
| ☐ EW-85545 | Tupolev Tu-154B-2 | 82A-545 | Lst SAI |
| ☐ EW-85703 | Tupolev Tu-154M | 91A-878 | |
| ☐ EW-85706 | Tupolev Tu-154M | 91A-881 | |
| ☐ EW-85741 | Tupolev Tu-154M | 91A-896 | |
| ☐ EW-85748 | Tupolev Tu-154M | 92A-924 | |
| ☐ EW-85815 | Tupolev Tu-154M | 95A-1010 | Govt |

## GOMELAVIA — GOM

| | | |
|---|---|---|
| ☐ EW-85591 | Tupolev Tu-154B-2 | 81A-581 |

## TRANS AVIA EXPORT CARGO AIRLINES — TXC

| | | | |
|---|---|---|---|
| ☐ EW-76709 | Ilyushin Il-76MD | 0063473173 | |
| ☐ EW-76710 | Ilyushin Il-76TD | 0063473182 | |
| ☐ EW-76711 | Ilyushin Il-76TD | 0063473187 | Lst AYZ |
| ☐ EW-76712 | Ilyushin Il-76TD | 0063473190 | Lst ILV |
| ☐ EW-76734 | Ilyushin Il-76TD | 0073476312 | Jow AYZ |
| ☐ EW-76735 | Ilyushin Il-76TD | 0073476314 | |
| ☐ EW-78765 | Ilyushin Il-76MD | 0083486590 | |
| ☐ EW-78769 | Ilyushin Il-76MD | 0083487607 | |
| ☐ EW-78779 | Ilyushin Il-76TD | 0083489662 | Lst AYZ |
| ☐ EW-78787 | Ilyushin Il-76MD | 0083490698 | |
| ☐ EW-78792 | Ilyushin Il-76TD | 0093490718 | |
| ☐ EW-78799 | Ilyushin Il-76TD | 0093491754 | Lst ESL |
| ☐ EW-78801 | Ilyushin Il-76TD | 0093492763 | |
| ☐ EW-78808 | Ilyushin Il-76TD | 0093493794 | Lst ESL |
| ☐ EW-78819 | Ilyushin Il-76TD | 0093495883 | Lst AYZ |
| ☐ EW-78826 | Ilyushin Il-76TD | 1003499991 | Lst ILV |
| ☐ EW-78827 | Ilyushin Il-76TD | 1003499997 | Lst AUV |
| ☐ EW-78828 | Ilyushin Il-76TD | 1003401004 | Lst AUV |
| ☐ EW-78836 | Ilyushin Il-76TD | 0093499986 | |
| ☐ EW-78839 | Ilyushin Il-76TD | 1003402047 | |
| ☐ EW-78843 | Ilyushin Il-76TD | 1003403082 | |
| ☐ EW-78848 | Ilyushin Il-76TD | 1003405159 | Lst ILV |
| ☐ EW-78849 | Ilyushin Il-76TD | 1013405192 | |

# EX - KYRGHYZSTAN

## KYRGHYZSTAN AIRLINES — KGA

| | | | |
|---|---|---|---|
| ☐ EX-65111 | Tupolev Tu-134A-3 | 60346 | std |
| ☐ EX-65119 | Tupolev Tu-134A-3 | 60475 | Lst IKA |
| ☐ EX-65125 | Tupolev Tu-134A-3 | 60575 | std |
| ☐ EX-65778 | Tupolev Tu-134A-3 | 62590 | |
| ☐ EX-65779 | Tupolev Tu-134A-3 | 62602 | |
| ☐ EX-65789 | Tupolev Tu-134A-3 | 62850 | |
| ☐ EX-85252 | Tupolev Tu-154B-2 | 77A-252 | std |
| ☐ EX-85259 | Tupolev Tu-154B-1 | 77A-259 | |
| ☐ EX-85294 | Tupolev Tu-154B-1 | 78A-294 | |
| ☐ EX-85313 | Tupolev Tu-154B-2 | 78A-313 | std |
| ☐ EX-85369 | Tupolev Tu-154B-2 | 79A-369 | Lst IKA |
| ☐ EX-85444 | Tupolev Tu-154B-2 | 80A-444 | |
| ☐ EX-85491 | Tupolev Tu-154B-2 | 81A-491 | std |
| ☐ EX-85497 | Tupolev Tu-154B-2 | 81A-497 | |
| ☐ EX-85519 | Tupolev Tu-154B-2 | 81A-519 | |
| ☐ EX-85590 | Tupolev Tu-154B-2 | 83A-590 | |
| ☐ EX-85762 | Tupolev Tu-154M | 93A-945 | |
| ☐ EX-26036 | Antonov An-26B | 10606 | |
| ☐ EX-76815 | Ilyushin Il-76TD | 1013409310 | |
| ☐ | Airbus A319- | | o/o |
| ☐ | Airbus A319- | | o/o |

## PHOENIX AVIATION — PHG

| | | | |
|---|---|---|---|
| ☐ EX-105 | Ilyushin Il-18D | 188011105 | |
| ☐ EX-201 | Ilyushin Il-18D | 188011201 | |
| ☐ EX-405 | Ilyushin Il-18D | 184007405 | Jow BIO |
| ☐ EX-601 | Ilyushin Il-18E | 185008601 | Lst DJB |
| ☐ EX-75427 | Ilyushin Il-18V | 183005905 | Lsf BFB |
| ☐ EX-75442 | Ilysuhin Il-18D | 187009702 | |
| ☐ EX-75449 | Ilysuhin Il-18D | 187010004 | |
| ☐ EX-75466 | Ilysuhin Il-18D | 187010403 | |
| ☐ EX-75905 | Ilyushin Il-18D | 186008905 | |
| ☐ EX-001 | Antonov An-12 | | |
| ☐ EX-450 | Boeing 737-281 | 262/20450 | Lst RSO |
| ☐ EX-451 | Boeing 737-281 | 266/20451 | Lst RSO |
| ☐ EX-632 | Boeing 737-2T5 | 847/22632 | Lst RSO |
| ☐ EX-960 | Boeing 737-2T5 | 642/21960 | Lst RSO |
| ☐ ST-AQA | Ilyushin Il-76TD | 0023442218 | Jow ETC |
| ☐ ST-AQB | Ilysuhin Il-76TD | 0053460795 | Jow AZZ |
| ☐ ST-CAC | Ilyushin Il-76TD | 0023437076 | Jow BIO |

# EY - TAJIKISTAN

## TAJIKISTAN AIRLINES / TAJIK AIR — TZK

| | | | |
|---|---|---|---|
| ☐ EY-65003 | Tupolev Tu-134A-3 | 44040 | Lst AYZ |
| ☐ EY-65022 | Tupolev Tu-134A-3 | 48395 | |
| ☐ EY-65763 | Tupolev Tu-134A-3 | 62299 | |
| ☐ EY-65788 | Tupolev Tu-134A-3 | 62835 | |
| ☐ EY-65835 | Tupolev Tu-134A-3 | 17112 | |
| ☐ EY-65876 | Tupolev Tu-134A-3 | 31220 | |

| | | | |
|---|---|---|---|
| ☐ EY-85385 | Tupolev Tu-154B-2 | 79A-385 | Lst JAK |
| ☐ EY-85466 | Tupolev Tu-154B-2 | 81A-466 | |
| ☐ EY-85469 | Tupolev Tu-154B-2 | 81A-469 | |
| ☐ EY-85475 | Tupolev Tu-154B-2 | 81A-475 | |
| ☐ EY-85487 | Tupolev Tu-154B-2 | 81A-487 | Lst DAO |
| ☐ EY-85511 | Tupolev Tu-154B-2 | 81A-511 | |
| ☐ EY-85651 | Tupolev Tu-154M | 88A-793 | |
| ☐ EY-85691 | Tupolev Tu-154M | 90A-864 | Lst IRX |
| ☐ EY-85692 | Tupolev Tu-154M | 90A-865 | |
| ☐ EY-85717 | Tupolev Tu-154M | 91A-897 | Lst IRX |

## EZ - TURKMENISTAN

### TURKMENISTAN AIRLINES — TUA

| | | | |
|---|---|---|---|
| ☐ EZ-A001 | Boeing 737-341 | 2305/26855 | |
| ☐ EZ-A002 | Boeing 737-332 | 2439/25994 | |
| ☐ EZ-A003 | Boeing 737-332 | 2455/25995 | |
| ☐ EZ-A010 | Boeing 757-23A | 412/25345 | Govt |
| ☐ EZ-A011 | Boeing 757-22K | 725/28336 | |
| ☐ EZ-A012 | Boeing 757-22K | 726/28337 | |
| ☐ EZ-A014 | Boeing 757-22K | 952/30863 | |
| ☐ EZ-A101 | Boeing 717-22K | 5072/55153 | |
| ☐ EZ-A102 | Boeing 717-22K | 5078/55154 | |
| ☐ EZ-A103 | Boeing 717-22K | 5086/55155 | |
| ☐ EZ-F423 | Ilyushin Il-76TD | 1033418608 | |
| ☐ EZ-F426 | Ilyushin Il-76TD | 1033418609 | |
| ☐ EZ-F427 | Ilyushin Il-76TD | 1033418620 | |
| ☐ EZ-F428 | Ilyushin Il-76TD | 1043418624 | |
| ☐ EZ-J672 | Yak-42D | 4520421316562 | std |
| ☐ EZ-J674 | Yak-42D | 4520421319020 | std |
| ☐ EZ-85549 | Tupolev Tu-154B-2 | 82A-549 | |

## F - FRANCE

### AERIS — AIS

| | | | |
|---|---|---|---|
| ☐ F-GNFC | Boeing 737-36E | 2706/26315 | |
| ☐ F-GNFD | Boeing 737-36E | 2719/26317 | |
| ☐ F-GNFH | Boeing 737-382 | 2241/25162 | |
| ■ F-GNFT | Boeing 737-3Y0 | 1513/23921 | |
| ☐ F-GNFU | Boeing 737-3Y0 | 1629/24256 | |
| ☐ F-GLOV | Boeing 767-304ER | 610/28039 | |
| ☐ F-GOFS | Boeing 767-39HER | 488/26257 | |
| ☐ F- | Boeing 767-300 | | o/o |

### AIGLE AZUR TRANSPORTS AERIENS — AAF

| | | | |
|---|---|---|---|
| ☐ F-GIXH | Boeing 737-3S3 QC) | 1393/23788 | |
| ☐ F-GLXI | Boeing 737-4Y0 | 2301/26066 | |

### AIR ATLANTIQUE — APB

| | | | |
|---|---|---|---|
| ☐ F-GKND | ATR 42-300 | 231 | |
| ☐ F-GPIA | ATR 42-310 | 018 | |
| ☐ F-GPYK | ATR 42-500 | 537 | Lsf LIT |
| ☐ F-GPYM | ATR 42-500 | 520 | Lsf LIT |
| ☐ F-GPYN | ATR 42-500 | 539 | |

### AIR BRETAGNE CENTRAL — BRE

| | | | |
|---|---|---|---|
| ☐ F-GYAB | Beech 1900D | UE-58 | std |

### AIRBUS TRANSPORT INTERNATIONAL — BGA

| | | | |
|---|---|---|---|
| ☐ F-GSTA | A300B4-608ST Beluga | 655/001 | |
| ☐ F-GSTB | A300B4-608ST Beluga | 751/002 | |
| ☐ F-GSTC | A300B4-608ST Beluga | 765/003 | |
| ☐ F-GSTD | A300B4-608ST Beluga | 776/004 | |
| ☐ F-GSTF | A300B4-608ST Beluga | 796/005 | |

### AIR FRANCE — AFR

| | | | |
|---|---|---|---|
| ☐ F-GUGA | Airbus A318-111 | | o/o |
| ☐ F-GUGB | Airbus A318-111 | | o/o |
| ☐ F-GUGC | Airbus A318-111 | | o/o |
| ☐ F-GUGD | Airbus A318-111 | | o/o |
| ☐ F-GUGE | Airbus A318-111 | | o/o |
| ☐ F-GUGF | Airbus A318-111 | | o/o |
| ☐ F-GUGG | Airbus A318-111 | | o/o |
| ☐ F-GUGH | Airbus A318-111 | | o/o |
| ☐ F-GUGI | Airbus A318-111 | | o/o |
| ☐ F-GPMA | Airbus A319-113 | 0598 | |
| ☐ F-GPMB | Airbus A319-113 | 0600 | |
| ☐ F-GPMC | Airbus A319-113 | 0608 | |
| ☐ F-GPMD | Airbus A319-113 | 0618 | |
| ☐ F-GPME | Airbus A319-113 | 0625 | |
| ☐ F-GPMF | Airbus A319-113 | 0637 | |
| ☐ F-GPMG | Airbus A319-113 | 0644 | |
| ☐ F-GPMH | Airbus A319-113 | 0647 | |
| ☐ F-GPMI | Airbus A319-113 | 0660 | |
| ☐ F-GRHA | Airbus A319-111 | 0938 | |
| ☐ F-GRHB | Airbus A319-111 | 0985 | |
| ☐ F-GRHC | Airbus A319-111 | 0998 | |
| ☐ F-GRHD | Airbus A319-111 | 1000 | |
| ☐ F-GRHE | Airbus A319-111 | 1020 | |
| ☐ F-GRHF | Airbus A319-111 | 1025 | |
| ☐ F-GRHG | Airbus A319-111 | 1036 | |
| ☐ F-GRHH | Airbus A319-111 | 1151 | |
| ☐ F-GRHI | Airbus A319-111 | 1169 | |
| ☐ F-GRHJ | Airbus A319-111 | 1176 | |
| ☐ F-GRHK | Airbus A319-111 | 1190 | |
| ☐ F-GRHL | Airbus A319-111 | 1201 | |
| ☐ F-GRHM | Airbus A319-111 | 1216 | |
| ☐ F-GRHN | Airbus A319-111 | 1267 | |
| ☐ F-GRHO | Airbus A319-111 | 1271 | |
| ☐ F-GRHP | Airbus A319-111 | 1344 | |
| ☐ F-GRHQ | Airbus A319-111 | 1404 | |
| ☐ F-GRHR | Airbus A319-111 | 1415 | |
| ☐ F-GRHS | Airbus A319-111 | 1444 | |
| ☐ F-GRHT | Airbus A319-111 | 1449 | |
| ☐ F-GRHU | Airbus A319-111 | 1471 | |
| ☐ F-GRHV | Airbus A319-111 | 1505 | |
| ☐ F-GRHX | Airbus A319-111 | 1524 | |
| ☐ F-GRHY | Airbus A319-111 | 1616 | |
| ☐ F-GRHZ | Airbus A319-111 | 1622 | |
| ☐ F-GRXA | Airbus A319-111 | 1640 | |
| ☐ F-GRXB | Airbus A319-111 | 1645 | |
| ☐ F-GRXC | Airbus A319-111 | 1677 | |
| ☐ F-GRXD | Airbus A319-111 | 1699 | |
| ☐ F-GRXE | Airbus A319-111 | 1733 | |
| ☐ F-GRXF | Airbus A319-111 | 1938 | o/o |
| ☐ F-GRXG | Airbus A319-111 | | o/o |
| ☐ F-GFKA | Airbus A320-111 | 0005 | |
| ☐ F-GFKB | Airbus A320-111 | 0007 | |
| ☐ F-GFKD | Airbus A320-111 | 0014 | |
| ☐ F-GFKE | Airbus A320-111 | 0019 | |
| ☐ F-GFKF | Airbus A320-111 | 0020 | |
| ☐ F-GFKG | Airbus A320-111 | 0021 | |
| ☐ F-GFKH | Airbus A320-211 | 0061 | |
| ☐ F-GFKI | Airbus A320-211 | 0062 | |
| ☐ F-GFKJ | Airbus A320-211 | 0063 | |
| ☐ F-GFKK | Airbus A320-211 | 0100 | |
| ☐ F-GFKL | Airbus A320-211 | 0101 | |
| ☐ F-GFKM | Airbus A320-211 | 0102 | |
| ☐ F-GFKN | Airbus A320-211 | 0128 | |
| ☐ F-GFKO | Airbus A320-211 | 0129 | |
| ☐ F-GFKP | Airbus A320-211 | 0133 | |
| ☐ F-GFKQ | Airbus A320-111 | 0002 | |
| ☐ F-GFKR | Airbus A320-211 | 0186 | |
| ☐ F-GFKS | Airbus A320-211 | 0187 | |
| ☐ F-GFKT | Airbus A320-211 | 0188 | |
| ☐ F-GFKU | Airbus A320-211 | 0226 | |
| ☐ F-GFKV | Airbus A320-211 | 0227 | |
| ☐ F-GFKX | Airbus A320-211 | 0228 | |
| ☐ F-GFKY | Airbus A320-211 | 0285 | |
| ☐ F-GFKZ | Airbus A320-211 | 0286 | |
| ☐ F-GGEA | Airbus A320-111 | 0010 | |
| ☐ F-GGEB | Airbus A320-111 | 0012 | |
| ☐ F-GGEC | Airbus A320-111 | 0013 | |
| ☐ F-GGEE | Airbus A320-111 | 0016 | |

| | | | |
|---|---|---|---|
| ☐ F-GGEF | Airbus A320-111 | 0004 | |
| ☐ F-GGEG | Airbus A320-111 | 0003 | |
| ☐ F-GHQA | Airbus A320-211 | 0033 | |
| ☐ F-GHQB | Airbus A320-211 | 0036 | |
| ☐ F-GHQC | Airbus A320-211 | 0044 | |
| ☐ F-GHQD | Airbus A320-211 | 0108 | |
| ☐ F-GHQE | Airbus A320-211 | 0115 | |
| ☐ F-GHQF | Airbus A320-211 | 0130 | |
| ☐ F-GHQG | Airbus A320-211 | 0155 | |
| ☐ F-GHQH | Airbus A320-211 | 0156 | |
| ☐ F-GHQI | Airbus A320-211 | 0184 | |
| ☐ F-GHQJ | Airbus A320-211 | 0214 | |
| ☐ F-GHQK | Airbus A320-211 | 0236 | |
| ☐ F-GHQL | Airbus A320-211 | 0239 | |
| ☐ F-GHQM | Airbus A320-211 | 0237 | |
| ☐ F-GHQO | Airbus A320-211 | 0278 | |
| ☐ F-GHQP | Airbus A320-211 | 0337 | |
| ☐ F-GHQQ | Airbus A320-211 | 0352 | |
| ☐ F-GHQR | Airbus A320-211 | 0377 | |
| ☐ F-GJVA | Airbus A320-211 | 0144 | |
| ☐ F-GJVB | Airbus A320-211 | 0145 | |
| ☐ F-GJVC | Airbus A320-211 | 0204 | |
| ☐ F-GJVD | Airbus A320-211 | 0211 | |
| ☐ F-GJVE | Airbus A320-211 | 0215 | |
| ☐ F-GJVF | Airbus A320-211 | 0244 | |
| ☐ F-GJVG | Airbus A320-211 | 0270 | |
| ☐ F-GJVW | Airbus A320-211 | 0491 | |
| ☐ F-GKXA | Airbus A320-211 | 0287 | |
| ☐ F-GKXB | Airbus A320-212 | 0235 | |
| ☐ F-GKXC | Airbus A320-214 | 1502 | |
| ☐ F-GKXD | Airbus A320-214 | 1873 | |
| ☐ F-GKXE | Airbus A320-214 | 1879 | |
| ☐ F-GKXF | Airbus A320-214 | 1885 | |
| ☐ F-GKXG | Airbus A320-214 | 1894 | |
| ☐ F-GKXH | Airbus A320-214 | 1924 | |
| ☐ F-GKXI | Airbus A320-214 | 1949 | o/o |
| ☐ F-GKXJ | Airbus A320-214 | 1900 | o/o |
| ☐ F-GLGG | Airbus A320-212 | 0203 | |
| ☐ F-GLGH | Airbus A320-212 | 0220 | |
| ☐ F-GLGM | Airbus A320-212 | 0131 | |
| | | | |
| ☐ F-GMZA | Airbus A321-111 | 0498 | |
| ☐ F-GMZB | Airbus A321-111 | 0509 | |
| ☐ F-GMZC | Airbus A321-211 | 0521 | |
| ☐ F-GMZD | Airbus A321-111 | 0529 | |
| ☐ F-GMZE | Airbus A321-111 | 0544 | |
| ☐ F-GTAD | Airbus A321-211 | 0777 | |
| ☐ F-GTAE | Airbus A321-211 | 0796 | |
| ☐ F-GTAF | Airbus A321-211 | 0761 | |
| ☐ F-GTAG | Airbus A321-211 | 0956 | |
| ☐ F-GTAH | Airbus A321-211 | 1133 | |
| ☐ F-GTAI | Airbus A321-211 | 1299 | |
| ☐ F-GTAJ | Airbus A321-211 | 1476 | |
| ☐ F-GTAK | Airbus A321-211 | 1658 | |
| ☐ F-GTAL | Airbus A321-211 | 1691 | |
| ☐ F-GTAM | Airbus A321-211 | 1859 | |
| ☐ F-GTAN | Airbus A321-211 | 1928 | o/o |
| ☐ F-GTAO | Airbus A321-211 | | o/o |
| | | | |
| ☐ F-GZCA | Airbus A330-203 | 422 | |
| ☐ F-GZCB | Airbus A330-203 | 443 | |
| ☐ F-GZCC | Airbus A330-203 | 448 | |
| ☐ F-GZCD | Airbus A330-203 | 458 | |
| ☐ F-GZCE | Airbus A330-203 | 465 | |
| ☐ F-GZCF | Airbus A330-203 | 481 | |
| ☐ F-GZCG | Airbus A330-203 | 498 | |
| ☐ F-GZCH | Airbus A330-203 | 500 | |
| ☐ F-GZCI | Airbus A330-203 | 502 | |
| ☐ F-GZCJ | Airbus A330-203 | 503 | |
| ☐ F-GZCK | Airbus A330-203 | 516 | o/o |
| ☐ F-GZCL | Airbus A330-203 | 519 | o/o |
| | | | |
| ☐ F-GLZA | Airbus A340-211 | 005 | |
| ☐ F-GLZB | Airbus A340-211 | 007 | |
| ☐ F-GLZC | Airbus A340-211 | 029 | |
| ☐ F-GLZG | Airbus A340-211 | 049 | |
| ☐ F-GLZH | Airbus A340-211 | 078 | |
| ☐ F-GLZI | Airbus A340-211 | 084 | |

| | | | |
|---|---|---|---|
| ☐ F-GLZJ | Airbus A340-313X | 186 | |
| ☐ F-GLZK | Airbus A340-313X | 207 | |
| ☐ F-GLZL | Airbus A340-313X | 210 | |
| ☐ F-GLZM | Airbus A340-313X | 237 | |
| ☐ F-GLZN | Airbus A340-313X | 245 | |
| ☐ F-GLZO | Airbus A340-313X | 246 | |
| ☐ F-GLZP | Airbus A340-313X | 260 | |
| ☐ F-GLZQ | Airbus A340-313X | 289 | |
| ☐ F-GLZR | Airbus A340-313X | 307 | |
| ☐ F-GLZS | Airbus A340-313X | 310 | |
| ☐ F-GLZT | Airbus A340-313X | 319 | |
| ☐ F-GLZU | Airbus A340-313X | 377 | |
| ☐ F-GNIF | Airbus A340-313X | 168 | |
| ☐ F-GNIG | Airbus A340-313X | 174 | |
| ☐ F-GNIH | Airbus A340-313X | 373 | |
| ☐ F-GNII | Airbus A340-313X | 399 | |
| | | | |
| ☐ F-BTSD | Concorde 101 | 213 | |
| ☐ F-BVFA | Concorde 101 | 205 | std |
| ☐ F-BVFB | Concorde 101 | 207 | |
| ☐ F-BVFC | Concorde 101 | 209 | |
| ☐ F-BVFF | Concorde 101 | 215 | |
| | | | |
| ☐ F-GFUA | Boeing 737-33A | 1436/23635 | |
| ☐ F-GFUD | Boeing 737-33A | 1597/24027 | |
| ☐ F-GFUJ | Boeing 737-33A | 2065/25118 | |
| ☐ F-GHVM | Boeing 737-33A | 1595/24026 | |
| ☐ F-GHVO | Boeing 737-33A | 1556/24025 | |
| ☐ F-GHXM | Boeing 737-53A | 1921/24788 | |
| ☐ F-GIXJ | Boeing 737-3Y0 (QC) | 1357/23685 | |
| ☐ F-GJNA | Boeing 737-528 | 2099/25206 | |
| ☐ F-GJNB | Boeing 737-528 | 2108/25227 | |
| ☐ F-GJNC | Boeing 737-528 | 2170/25228 | |
| ☐ F-GJND | Boeing 737-528 | 2180/25229 | |
| ☐ F-GJNE | Boeing 737-528 | 2191/25230 | |
| ☐ F-GJNF | Boeing 737-528 | 2208/25231 | |
| ☐ F-GJNG | Boeing 737-528 | 2231/25232 | |
| ☐ F-GJNH | Boeing 737-528 | 2251/25233 | |
| ☐ F-GJNI | Boeing 737-528 | 2411/25234 | |
| ☐ F-GJNJ | Boeing 737-528 | 2428/25235 | |
| ☐ F-GJNK | Boeing 737-528 | 2443/25236 | |
| ☐ F-GJNL | Boeing 737-5H6 | 2484/26448 | |
| ☐ F-GJNM | Boeing 737-528 | 2464/25237 | |
| ☐ F-GJNN | Boeing 737-528 | 2572/27304 | |
| ☐ F-GJNO | Boeing 737-528 | 2574/27305 | |
| ☐ F-GJNP | Boeing 737-5H6 | 2654/27356 | |
| ☐ F-GJNQ | Boeing 737-5H6 | 2327/26445 | |
| ☐ F-GJNR | Boeing 737-5H6 | 2358/26446 | |
| ☐ F-GJNS | Boeing 737-53S | 3083/29073 | |
| ☐ F-GJNT | Boeing 737-53S | 3086/29074 | |
| ☐ F-GJNU | Boeing 737-53S | 3101/29075 | |
| ☐ F-GJNV | Boeing 737-548 | 2427/26287 | |
| ☐ F-GJNX | Boeing 737-5H6 | 2511/26454 | |
| ☐ F-GJNY | Boeing 737-5H6 | 2527/26456 | |
| ☐ F-GJNZ | Boeing 737-5H6 | 2503/26450 | |
| ☐ F-GJUA | Boeing 737-548 | 2463/25165 | |
| ☐ F-GRFC | Boeing 737-36N | 2996/28569 | |
| | | | |
| ☐ F-BPVR | Boeing 747-228F | 295/21255 | |
| ☐ F-BPVT | Boeing 747-228M | 313/21429 | |
| ☐ F-BPVU | Boeing 747-228B | 333/21537 | |
| ☐ F-BPVX | Boeing 747-228B | 364/21731 | |
| ☐ F-BPVY | Boeing 747-228B | 370/21745 | |
| ☐ F-BPVZ | Boeing 747-228F | 398/21787 | |
| ☐ F-BTDG | Boeing 747-2B3M (EUD) | 518/22514 | |
| ☐ F-BTDH | Boeing 747-2B3M (EUD) | 521/22515 | |
| ☐ F-GBOX | Boeing 747-2B3F | 388/21835 | |
| ☐ F-GCBA | Boeing 747-228B | 428/21982 | |
| ☐ F-GCBB | Boeing 747-228M | 463/22272 | |
| ☐ F-GCBD | Boeing 747-228B (SF) | 503/22428 | |
| ☐ F-GCBE | Boeing 747-228F | 535/22678 | |
| ☐ F-GCBF | Boeing 747-228M | 558/22794 | |
| ☐ F-GCBG | Boeing 747-228F | 569/22939 | |
| ☐ F-GCBH | Boeing 747-228B (SF) | 656/23611 | |
| ☐ F-GCBI | Boeing 747-228M | 661/23676 | |
| ☐ F-GCBJ | Boeing 747-228M | 698/24067 | |
| ☐ F-GCBK | Boeing 747-228F | 714/24158 | |
| ☐ F-GCBL | Boeing 747-228F | 772/24735 | |

| | | | |
|---|---|---|---|
| ☐ F-GCBM | Boeing 747-228F | 822/24879 | |
| ☐ F-GETA | Boeing 747-3B3M | 632/23413 | |
| ☐ F-GETB | Boeing 747-3B3M | 641/23480 | |
| ☐ F-GEXA | Boeing 747-4B3 | 741/24154 | |
| ☐ F-GEXB | Boeing 747-4B3M | 864/24155 | |
| ☐ F-GISA | Boeing 747-428M | 872/25238 | |
| ☐ F-GISB | Boeing 747-428M | 884/25302 | |
| ☐ F-GISC | Boeing 747-428M | 899/25599 | |
| ☐ F-GISD | Boeing 747-428M | 934/25628 | |
| ☐ F-GISE | Boeing 747-428M | 960/25630 | |
| ☐ F-GITA | Boeing 747-428 | 836/24969 | |
| ☐ F-GITB | Boeing 747-428 | 843/24990 | |
| ☐ F-GITC | Boeing 747-428 | 889/25344 | |
| ☐ F-GITD | Boeing 747-428 | 901/25600 | |
| ☐ F-GITE | Boeing 747-428 | 906/25601 | |
| ☐ F-GITF | Boeing 747-428 | 909/25602 | |
| ☐ F-GIUA | Boeing 747-428ERF | 1315/32866 | |
| ☐ F-GIUB | Boeing 747-428ERF | 1317/33096 | |
| ☐ F-GIUC | Boeing 747-428ERF | 1318/32867 | |
| ☐ F- | Boeing 747-428ER | 32868 | o/o |
| ☐ F- | Boeing 747-428ER | 32869 | o/o |
| | | | |
| ☐ F-GSPA | Boeing 777-228ER | 129/29002 | |
| ☐ F-GSPB | Boeing 777-228ER | 133/29003 | |
| ☐ F-GSPC | Boeing 777-228ER | 138/29004 | |
| ☐ F-GSPD | Boeing 777-228ER | 187/29005 | |
| ☐ F-GSPE | Boeing 777-228ER | 189/29006 | |
| ☐ F-GSPF | Boeing 777-228ER | 201/29007 | |
| ☐ F-GSPG | Boeing 777-228ER | 195/27609 | |
| ☐ F-GSPH | Boeing 777-228ER | 210/28675 | |
| ☐ F-GSPI | Boeing 777-228ER | 258/29008 | |
| ☐ F-GSPJ | Boeing 777-228ER | 263/29009 | |
| ☐ F-GSPK | Boeing 777-228ER | 267/29010 | |
| ☐ F-GSPL | Boeing 777-228ER | 284/30457 | |
| ☐ F-GSPM | Boeing 777-228ER | 307/30456 | |
| ☐ F-GSPN | Boeing 777-228ER | 314/29011 | |
| ☐ F-GSPO | Boeing 777-228ER | 320/30614 | |
| ☐ F-GSPP | Boeing 777-228ER | 327/30615 | |
| ☐ F-GSPQ | Boeing 777-228ER | 331/28682 | |
| ☐ F-GSPR | Boeing 777-228ER | 367/28683 | |
| ☐ F-GSPS | Boeing 777-228ER | 370/32306 | |
| ☐ F-GSPT | Boeing 777-228ER | 382/32308 | |
| ☐ F-GSPU | Boeing 777-228ER | 383/32309 | |
| ☐ F-GSPV | Boeing 777-228ER | 385/28684 | |
| ☐ F-GSPX | Boeing 777-228ER | 392/32698 | |
| ☐ F-GSPY | Boeing 777-228ER | 395/32305 | |
| ☐ F-GSPZ | Boeing 777-228ER | 401/32310 | |
| | | | |
| ☐ F-GEMF | Airbus A310-203 | 172 | |
| ☐ F-GHGF | Boeing 767-3Q8ER | 355/24745 | |
| ☐ F-GHGG | Boeing 767-3Q8ER | 378/24746 | |
| ☐ F-GHGH | Boeing 767-37EER | 385/25077 | |
| ☐ F-GHGI | Boeing 767-328ER | 493/27135 | |
| ☐ TF-ELW | Airbus A300C4-605RF | 755 | Lsf ICB |

## AIR FRANCE 'COMMUTER SERVICES'

| | | | |
|---|---|---|---|
| ☐ F-GGLR | ATR 42-300 | 043 | Lst PTN |
| ☐ F-GHJE | ATR 42-300 | 070 | Lst PTN |
| ☐ F-GHPK | ATR 42-300 | 218 | |
| ☐ F-GHPS | ATR 42-300 | 006 | |
| ☐ F-GHPV | ATR 72-201 | 234 | |
| ☐ F-GHPY | ATR 42-300 | 321 | |
| ☐ F-GKPC | ATR 72-201 | 171 | |
| ☐ F-GKPD | ATR 72-201 | 177 | |
| | | | |
| ☐ F-GMAD | Beech 1900D | UE-290 | |
| ☐ F-GPBM | Beech 1900D | UE-305 | |
| ☐ F-GREA | Beech 1900D | UE-307 | |
| ☐ F-GRMD | Beech 1900D | UE-296 | |
| ☐ F-GSFD | Beech 1900D | UE-252 | |
| ☐ F-GTKJ | Beech 1900D | UE-348 | |
| ☐ F-GTVC | Beech 1900D | UE-349 | |
| ☐ F-GUCB | Beech 1900D | UE-308 | |
| | | | |
| ☐ EI-CMS | BAe 146 Srs.200 | E2044 | |
| ☐ EI-CMY | BAe 146 Srs.200 | E2039 | |
| ☐ EI-CNB | BAe 146 Srs.200 | E2046 | |
| ☐ EI-CNQ | BAe 146 Srs.200 | E2031 | |

| | | | |
|---|---|---|---|
| ☐ EI-CSK | BAe 146 Srs.200 | E2062 | |
| ☐ EI-CSL | BAe 146 Srs.200 | E2074 | |
| ☐ EI-CWA | BAe 146 Srs.200 | E2058 | |
| ☐ EI-CWB | BAe 146 Srs.200 | E2051 | |
| ☐ EI-CWC | BAe 146 Srs.200 | E2053 | |
| ☐ EI-CWD | BAe 146 Srs.200 | E2108 | |
| ☐ EI-PAT | BAe 146 Srs.200 | E2030 | |
| ☐ G-JEAK | BAe 146 Srs.200 | E2103 | |
| ☐ G-JEAM | BAe 146 Srs.300 | E3128 | |
| ☐ G-JEAS | BAe 146 Srs.200 | E2020 | |
| ☐ G-JEAT | BAe 146 Srs.100 | E1071 | |
| ☐ G-JEBA | BAe 146 Srs.300 | E3181 | |
| ☐ G-JEBB | BAe 146 Srs.300 | E3185 | |
| | | | |
| ☐ F-GPYP | Canadair RJ-200 | 7126 | |
| ☐ F-GRJA | Canadair RJ-200 | 7070 | |
| ☐ F-GRJB | Canadair RJ-200 | 7076 | |
| ☐ F-GRJC | Canadair RJ-200 | 7085 | |
| ☐ F-GRJD | Canadair RJ-200 | 7088 | |
| ☐ F-GRJE | Canadair RJ-200 | 7106 | |
| ☐ F-GRJF | Canadair RJ-200 | 7108 | |
| ☐ F-GRJG | Canadair RJ-200 | 7143 | |
| ☐ F-GRJH | Canadair RJ-200 | 7162 | |
| ☐ F-GRJI | Canadair RJ-200 | 7147 | |
| ☐ F-GRJJ | Canadair RJ-200 | 7190 | |
| ☐ F-GRJK | Canadair RJ-200 | 7219 | |
| ☐ F-GRJL | Canadair RJ-200 | 722 | |
| ☐ F-GRJM | Canadair RJ-200 | 7222 | |
| ☐ F-GRJN | Canadair RJ-200 | 7262 | |
| ☐ F-GRJO | Canadair RJ-200 | 7296 | |
| ☐ F-GRJP | Canadair RJ-200 | 7301 | |
| ☐ F-GRJQ | Canadair RJ-200 | 7321 | |
| ☐ F-GRJR | Canadair RJ-200 | 7375 | |
| ☐ F-GRJS | Canadair RJ-200 | 7377 | |
| ☐ F-GRJT | Canadair RJ-200 | 7389 | |
| ☐ G-JECA | Canadair RJ-200 | 7345 | |
| ☐ G-JECB | Canadair RJ-200 | 7393 | |
| ☐ G-JECC | Canadair RJ-200 | 7434 | std BHX |
| ☐ G-JECD | Canadair RJ-200 | 7469 | |
| | | | |
| ☐ F-GRZA | Canadair RJ-700 | 10006 | |
| ☐ F-GRZB | Canadair RJ-700 | 10007 | |
| ☐ F-GRZC | Canadair RJ-700 | 10008 | |
| ☐ F-GRZD | Canadair RJ-700 | 10016 | |
| ☐ F-GRZE | Canadair RJ-700 | 10032 | |
| ☐ F-GRZF | Canadair RJ-700 | 10036 | |
| ☐ F-GRZG | Canadair RJ-700 | 10037 | |
| ☐ F-GRZH | Canadair RJ-700 | | o/o |
| ☐ F-GRZI | Canadair RJ-700 | | o/o |
| ☐ F-GRZJ | Canadair RJ-700 | | o/o |
| ☐ F-GRZK | Canadair RJ-700 | | o/o |
| ☐ F-GRZL | Canadair RJ-700 | | o/o |
| | | | |
| ☐ F-GFEO | Embraer EMB.120ER | 120062 | |
| ☐ F-GHIA | Embraer EMB.120ER | 120154 | |
| ☐ F-GHIB | Embraer EMB.120ER | 120162 | |
| ☐ F-GIVK | Embraer EMB.120ER | 120112 | |
| ☐ F-GIYH | Embraer EMB.120ER | 120239 | |
| ☐ F-GIYI | Embraer EMB.120ER | 120244 | |
| ☐ F-GJAK | Embraer EMB.120ER | 120215 | |
| ☐ F-GLRG | Embraer EMB.120ER | 120149 | |
| ☐ F-GMMU | Embraer EMB.120ER | 120253 | |
| ☐ F-GTSG | Embraer EMB.120ER | 120087 | |
| ☐ F-GTSH | Embraer EMB.120ER | 120104 | |
| ☐ F-GTSI | Embraer EMB.120ER | 120123 | |
| ☐ F-GTSJ | Embraer EMB.120ER | 120176 | |
| ☐ F-GTSK | Embraer EMB.120ER | 120213 | |
| ☐ F-GTSN | Embraer EMB.120ER | 120099 | |
| ☐ F-GTSO | Embraer EMB.120ER | 120097 | |
| ☐ F-GTSP | Embraer EMB.120ER | 120235 | |
| | | | |
| ☐ F-GOHA | Embraer ERJ-135 | 145189 | |
| ☐ F-GOHB | Embraer ERJ-135 | 145198 | |
| ☐ F-GOHC | Embraer ERJ-135 | 145243 | |
| ☐ F-GOHD | Embraer ERJ-135 | 145252 | |
| ☐ F-GOHE | Embraer ERJ-135 | 145335 | |
| ☐ F-GOHF | Embraer ERJ-135 | 145347 | |
| ☐ F-GRGP | Embraer ERJ-135 | 145188 | |
| ☐ F-GRGQ | Embraer ERJ-135 | 145233 | |

| | | | |
|---|---|---|---|
| ☐ F-GRGR | Embraer ERJ-135 | 145236 | |
| ☐ F-GRGS | Embraer ERJ-135 | | o/o |
| ☐ F-GRGT | Embraer ERJ-135 | | o/o |
| ☐ F- | Embraer ERJ-135 | | o/o |
| ☐ F- | Embraer ERJ-135 | | o/o |
| ☐ F- | Embraer ERJ-135 | | o/o |
| ☐ F- | Embraer ERJ-135 | | o/o |
| ☐ F- | Embraer ERJ-135 | | o/o |
| ☐ F- | Embraer ERJ-135 | | o/o |
| | | | |
| ☐ F-GRGA | Embraer ERJ-145 | 145008 | |
| ☐ F-GRGB | Embraer ERJ-145 | 145010 | |
| ☐ F-GRGC | Embraer ERJ-145 | 145012 | |
| ☐ F-GRGD | Embraer ERJ-145 | 145043 | |
| ☐ F-GRGE | Embraer ERJ-145 | 145047 | |
| ☐ F-GRGF | Embraer ERJ-145 | 145050 | |
| ☐ F-GRGG | Embraer ERJ-145 | 145118 | |
| ☐ F-GRGH | Embraer ERJ-145 | 145120 | |
| ☐ F-GRGI | Embraer ERJ-145 | 145152 | |
| ☐ F-GRGJ | Embraer ERJ-145 | 145297 | |
| ☐ F-GRGK | Embraer ERJ-145 | 145324 | |
| ☐ F-GRGL | Embraer ERJ-145 | 145375 | |
| ☐ F-GRGM | Embraer ERJ-145 | 145418 | |
| ☐ F-GUAM | Embraer ERJ-145 | 145266 | |
| ☐ F-GUBA | Embraer ERJ-145 | 145398 | |
| ☐ F-GUBB | Embraer ERJ-145 | 145419 | |
| ☐ F-GUBC | Embraer ERJ-145 | 145556 | |
| ☐ F-GUBD | Embraer ERJ-145 | 145333 | |
| ☐ F-GUBE | Embraer ERJ-145 | 145668 | |
| ☐ F-GUBF | Embraer ERJ-145 | 145669 | |
| ☐ F-GUEA | Embraer ERJ-145 | 145342 | |
| ☐ F-GUFD | Embraer ERJ-145 | 145197 | |
| ☐ F-GUJA | Embraer ERJ-145 | 145407 | |
| ☐ F-GUMA | Embraer ERJ-145 | 145405 | |
| ☐ F-GUPT | Embraer ERJ-145 | 145294 | |
| ☐ F-GVGS | Embraer ERJ-145 | 145385 | |
| ☐ F-GVHD | Embraer ERJ-145 | 145178 | |
| | | | |
| ☐ F-GNLJ | Fokker 100 | 11344 | |
| ☐ F-GPNK | Fokker 100 | 11324 | |
| ☐ F-GPNL | Fokker 100 | 11325 | |
| ☐ F-GPXA | Fokker 100 | 11487 | |
| ☐ F-GPXB | Fokker 100 | 11492 | |
| ☐ F-GPXC | Fokker 100 | 11493 | |
| ☐ F-GPXD | Fokker 100 | 11494 | |
| ☐ F-GPXE | Fokker 100 | 11495 | |
| ☐ F-GPXF | Fokker 100 | 11330 | |
| ☐ F-GPXG | Fokker 100 | 11387 | |
| ☐ F-GPXH | Fokker 100 | 11476 | |
| | | | |
| ☐ F-GMVB | SAAB 2000 | 019 | |
| ☐ F-GMVC | SAAB 2000 | 021 | |
| ☐ F-GMVD | SAAB 2000 | 034 | |
| ☐ F-GMVE | SAAB 2000 | 040 | |
| ☐ F-GMVG | SAAB 2000 | 049 | |
| ☐ F-GMVU | SAAB 2000 | 045 | |
| ☐ F-GNEH | SAAB 2000 | 016 | |
| ☐ F-GNEI | SAAB 2000 | 028 | |
| ☐ F-GLIU | Fokker 70 | 11543 | |

## AIR JET — AIJ

| | | | |
|---|---|---|---|
| ☐ F-GLNI | BAe 146 Srs.200QC | E2188 | |
| ☐ F-GOAJ | SAAB 2000 | 017 | |
| ☐ F-GOMA | BAe 146 Srs.200QC | E2211 | |
| ☐ F- | BAe 146 Srs.300 | E3202 | |
| ☐ F-GTSB | SAAB 2000 | 014 | |
| ☐ F-GTSL | SAAB 2000 | 013 | |
| ☐ F- | ATR 42-500 | | o/o |
| ☐ F- | ATR 42-500 | | o/o |
| ☐ F- | ATR 42-500 | | o/o |

## AIRLINAIR — ARF

| | | | |
|---|---|---|---|
| ☐ F-GHPI | ATR 42-310 | 214 | Lsf BZH |
| ☐ F-GKNB | ATR 42-300 | 226 | |
| ☐ F-GKNC | ATR 42-300 | 230 | |
| ☐ F-GKOA | ATR 72-202 | 201 | Lst IRC |
| ☐ F-GKOB | ATR 72-202 | 232 | |
| ☐ F-GKOC | ATR 72-202 | 307 | Lst IRC |
| ☐ F-GKYN | ATR 42-300 | 095 | |
| ☐ F-GPOA | ATR 72-202F | 204 | Opf FPO |
| ☐ F-GPOB | ATR 72-202F | 207 | Opf FPO |
| ☐ F-GPOC | ATR 72-202F | 311 | Opf FPO |
| ☐ F-GPOD | ATR 72-202F | 361 | Opf FPO |
| ☐ F-GVZA | ATR 42-300 | 503 | Opf TDH |
| ☐ F-GVZF | ATR 72-212 | 461 | Opf AFR |
| ☐ F-GVZX | ATR 42-300 | 011 | |
| ☐ F-GVZY | ATR 42-300 | 080 | |
| ☐ F-GVZZ | ATR 42-300 | 055 | |

## AIR LITTORAL — LIT

| | | | |
|---|---|---|---|
| ☐ F-GPYA | ATR 42-500 | 457 | |
| ☐ F-GPYB | ATR 42-500 | 480 | |
| ☐ F-GPYC | ATR 42-500 | 484 | |
| ☐ F-GPYD | ATR 42-500 | 490 | |
| ☐ F-GPYF | ATR 42-500 | 495 | |
| ☐ F-GPYK | ATR 42-500 | 537 | Lst APB |
| ☐ F-GPYL | ATR 42-500 | 542 | |
| ☐ F-GPYM | ATR 42-500 | 520 | Lst APB |
| ☐ F-GPYN | ATR 42-500 | 539 | Lst APB |
| ☐ F-GPYO | ATR 42-500 | 544 | |
| ☐ F-GLIJ | Canadair RJ-200 | 7081 | |
| ☐ F-GLIK | Canadair RJ-200 | 7084 | |
| ☐ F-GLIY | Canadair RJ-200 | 7053 | |
| ☐ F-GLIZ | Canadair RJ-200 | 7057 | |
| ☐ F-GNMN | Canadair RJ-200 | 7003 | |
| ☐ F-GPTB | Canadair RJ-200 | 7177 | |
| ☐ F-GPTC | Canadair RJ-200 | 7182 | |
| ☐ F-GPTD | Canadair RJ-200 | 7184 | |
| ☐ F-GPTE | Canadair RJ-200 | 7183 | |
| ☐ F-GPTF | Canadair RJ-200 | 7197 | |
| ☐ F-GPTG | Canadair RJ-200 | 7223 | |
| ☐ F-GPTJ | Canadair RJ-200 | 7323 | |
| ☐ F-GPTK | Canadair RJ-200 | 7332 | |
| ☐ F-GPTM | Canadair RJ-200 | 7020 | |
| ☐ F-GPYP | Canadair RJ-200 | 7126 | Lst BZH |
| ☐ F-GPYQ | Canadair RJ-200 | 7144 | |
| ☐ F-GPYR | Canadair RJ-200 | 7164 | |
| ☐ F-GLIR | Fokker 100 | 11509 | |
| ☐ F-GLIS | Fokker 70 | 11540 | |
| ☐ F-GLIT | Fokker 70 | 11541 | |
| ☐ F-GLIU | Fokker 70 | 11543 | |
| ☐ F-GLIV | Fokker 70 | 11556 | |
| ☐ F-GLIX | Fokker 70 | 11558 | |

## AIR MEDITERRANEE — BIE

| | | | |
|---|---|---|---|
| ☐ F-GCJL | Boeing 737-222 | 71/19067 | |
| ☐ F-GCSL | Boeing 737-222 | 69/19066 | |
| ☐ F-GGVP | Boeing 737-2K2C | 405/20943 | Opf FPO |
| ☐ F-GGVQ | Boeing 737-2K2C | 408/20944 | Opf FPO |
| ☐ F-GIXA | Boeing 737-2K2C | 354/20836 | Opf FPO |
| ☐ F-GOAF | Boeing 737-242C | 84/19847 | |
| ☐ F-GYAM | Boeing 737-505 | 1917/24652 | |
| ☐ F-GYAN | Airbus A321-111 | 0535 | |
| ☐ F-GYAO | Airbus A321-111 | 0642 | Lst AOM |

## AIR PROVENCE — APR

| | | | |
|---|---|---|---|
| ☐ F-GPDC | HS.748 Srs.2A/232 | 1612 | |

## ALSAIR — LSR

| | | | |
|---|---|---|---|
| ☐ F-HALS | Beech 1900D | UE-379 | |

## ATLANTIQUE AIR ASSISTANCE — TLB

| | | | |
|---|---|---|---|
| ☐ F-GNBR | Beech 1900D | UE-327 | |
| ☐ F-GPYY | Beech 1900C-1 | UC-115 | |

## AXIS AIRWAYS — AXY

| | | |
|---|---|---|
| ☐ F-GIXG | Boeing 737-382 (QC) | 1657/24364 |
| ☐ F-GFUI | Boeing 737-3M8 | 1675/24023 |

## BLUE LINE

| | | |
|---|---|---|
| ☐ F-GNLH | Fokker 100 | 11311 |

## CCM AIRLINES — CCM

| | | |
|---|---|---|
| ☐ F-GKPC | ATR 72-201 | 171 |
| ☐ F-GKPD | ATR 72-201 | 177 |
| ☐ F-GKPE | ATR 72-201 | 192 |
| ☐ F-GKPF | ATR 72-201 | 222 |
| ☐ F-GKPH | ATR 72-202 | 352 |
| ☐ F-GMGK | ATR 72-202 | 365 |
| | | |
| ☐ F-GIOA | Fokker 100 | 11261 |
| ☐ F-GKHD | Fokker 100 | 11381 |
| ☐ F-GKHE | Fokker 100 | 11388 |
| ☐ F-GMPG | Fokker 100 | 11362 |
| ☐ F-GNLJ | Fokker 100 | 11344 |
| | | |
| ☐ F-GYFM | Airbus A319-112 | 1068 |
| ☐ F- | Airbus A319-112 | 1145 o/o |

## CHAMPAGNE AIRLINES — CPH

| | | | |
|---|---|---|---|
| ☐ F-GJPN | SA.227AC Metro III | AC-757B | Lsf ALZ |
| ☐ F-GPSN | SA.227AC Metro III | AC-758B | Lsf ALZ |
| ☐ F-GTRB | SA.227AC Metro III | AC-519 | Lsf FEU |

## CORSAIR — CRL

| | | | |
|---|---|---|---|
| ☐ F-GFUF | Boeing 737-3B3F | 1725/24388 | |
| ☐ F-GFUG | Boeing 737-4B3 | 1916/24750 | |
| ☐ F-GFUH | Boeing 737-4B3 | 2107/24751 | |
| ☐ F-GIXB | Boeing 737-33A (QC) | 1953/24789 | |
| ☐ F-GIXC | Boeing 737-38B (QC) | 2047/25124 | Lsf FPO |
| ☐ F-GIXD | Boeing 737-33A (QC) | 2198/25744 | |
| | | | |
| ☐ F-GSEA | Boeing 747-312 | 603/23032 | |
| ☐ F-GSEX | Boeing 747-312 | 584/23028 | |
| ☐ F-GSKY | Boeing 747-312 | 621/23244 | |
| ☐ F-GSUN | Boeing 747-312 | 593/23030 | |
| ☐ F-HJAC | Boeing 747-312 | 612/23243 | |
| | | | |
| ☐ F-HBIL | Airbus A330-243 | 320 | |
| ☐ F-HCAT | Airbus A330-243 | 285 | |
| ☐ F- | Airbus A330-243 | | o/o |
| ☐ F- | Airbus A330-243 | | o/o |

## CROSSAIR EUROPE — ECC

| | | | |
|---|---|---|---|
| ☐ F-GPKD | SAAB SF.340B | 173 | Lsf CRX |
| ☐ F-GPKG | SAAB SF.340B | 185 | Lsf CRX |
| ☐ F-GPKM | SAAB SF.340B | 221 | Lsf CRX |

## EAGLE AVIATION — EGN

| | | | |
|---|---|---|---|
| ☐ F-GEMO | Airbus A310-304 | 504 | Lst X5 |
| ☐ F-GVVV | Airbus A300B4-103 | 069 | Lst TGA |

## EURALAIR HORIZONS — EUH

| | | |
|---|---|---|
| ☐ F-GRNA | Boeing 737-85F | 174/28823 |
| ☐ F-GRNB | Boeing 737-85F | 180/28824 |
| ☐ F-GRNC | Boeing 737-85F | 151/28821 |
| ☐ F-GRND | Boeing 737-85F | 467/28827 |
| ☐ F-GRNE | Boeing 737-85F | 793/30568 |
| ☐ F-GRNS | Airbus A310-304 | 432 |

## EUROPE AIRPOST — FPO

| | | | |
|---|---|---|---|
| ☐ F-GFUE | Boeing 737-3B3 QC | 1693/24387 | |
| ☐ F-GGVP | Boeing 737-2K2C | 405/20943 | Opb BIE |
| ☐ F-GGVQ | Boeing 737-2K2C | 408/20944 | Opb BIE |
| ☐ F-GIXA | Boeing 737-2K2C | 354/20836 | Opb BIE |
| ☐ F-GIXB | Boeing 737-33A (QC) | 1953/24789 | Opb CRL |
| ☐ F-GIXC | Boeing 737-38B (QC) | 2047/25124 | Opb CRL |
| ☐ F-GIXD | Boeing 737-33A (QC) | 2198/25744 | Opb CRL |
| ☐ F-GIXE | Boeing 737-3B3 (QC) | 2235/26850 | |
| ☐ F-GIXF | Boeing 737-3B3 (QC) | 2267/26851 | |
| ☐ F-GIXI | Boeing 737-348 (QC) | 1458/23809 | |
| ☐ F-GIXJ | Boeing 737-3Y0 (QC) | 1357/23685 | |
| ☐ F-GIXK | Boeing 737-33A (QC) | 1599/24028 | |
| ☐ F-GIXL | Boeing 737-348 (QC) | 1474/23810 | |
| ☐ F-GIXO | Boeing 737-3Q8 (QC) | 1555/24132 | |
| ☐ F-GIXP | Boeing 737-3M8 (QC) | 1630/24021 | |
| ☐ F-GIXR | Boeing 737-3H6F | 2415/27125 | |
| ☐ F-GIXS | Boeing 737-3H6F | 2615/27347 | |
| | | | |
| ☐ F-GPOA | ATR 72-202F | 204 | Opb ARF |
| ☐ F-GPOB | ATR 72-202F | 207 | Opb ARF |
| ☐ F-GPOC | ATR 72-202F | 311 | Opb ARF |
| ☐ F-GPOD | ATR 72-202F | 361 | Opb ARF |

## HEX'AIR — HER

| | | | |
|---|---|---|---|
| ☐ F-GOPE | Beech 1900D | UE-103 | |
| ☐ F-HAPE | Beech 1900D | UE-367 | Lsf PEA |

## OCCITANIA — OJF

| | | | |
|---|---|---|---|
| ☐ F-GRCD | Beech 1900D | UE-311 | std |
| ☐ F-GSAN | Beech 1900D | UE-54 | std |
| ☐ F-HBCA | Beech 1900D | UE-188 | |

## OCTAVIA AIRLINES — OCN

| | | | |
|---|---|---|---|
| ☐ F-GVBR | Embraer EMB.120ER | 120014 | |
| ☐ F-GLPJ | Beech 1900C-1 | UC-40 | |
| ☐ F-HCHA | Beech 1900D | UE-37 | std |

## PAN EUROPÉENNE AIR SERVICE — PEA

| | | | |
|---|---|---|---|
| ☐ F-GOPE | Beech 1900D | UE-103 | |
| ☐ F-GYPE | Embraer ERJ-135LR | 145492 | |
| ☐ F-HAPE | Beech 1900D | UE-367 | Lst HER |

## PREST'AFFAIR — PTF

| | | |
|---|---|---|
| ☐ F-GLNF | Beech 1900D | UE-69 |
| ☐ F-GSAH | Beech 1900D | UE-50 std |

## R-LINES — RLI

| | | |
|---|---|---|
| ☐ F-GLND | Beech 1900D | UE-196 |
| ☐ F-GLNE | Beech 1900D | UE-197 |
| ☐ F-GLNK | Beech 1900D | UE-269 |

## STAR EUROPE — SEU

| | | | |
|---|---|---|---|
| ☐ F-GRSD | Airbus A320-214 | 0653 | |
| ☐ F-GRSE | Airbus A320-214 | 0657 | |
| ☐ F-GRSG | Airbus A320-214 | 0737 | |
| ☐ F-GRSH | Airbus A320-214 | 0749 | |
| ☐ F-GRSI | Airbus A320-214 | 0973 | |
| ☐ F-GRSN | Airbus A320-214 | 1692 | |
| ☐ F-GRSQ | Airbus A330-243 | 501 | |
| ☐ F- | Airbus A330-243 | | o/o |

## TWIN JET — TJT

| | | |
|---|---|---|
| ☐ F-GLNH | Beech 1900D | UE-73 |
| ☐ F-GLPL | Beech 1900C-1 | UC-92 |

## WESTAIR

| | | |
|---|---|---|
| ☐ F-GVAC | Boeing 737-229 | 351/20907 |

## F-O - FRENCH OVERSEAS

### AIR AUSTRAL — REU

| | | | |
|---|---|---|---|
| ☐ F-ODZJ | Boeing 737-53A | 1943/24877 | |
| ☐ F-ODZY | Boeing 737-33A | 2679/27452 | |
| ☐ F-ODZZ | Boeing 737-39M (QC) | 2906/28898 | |
| ☐ EI-CRS | Boeing 777-2Q8ER | 229/29908 | o/o |
| ☐ EI-CRT | Boeing 777-2Q8ER | 246/28676 | o/o |

### AIR CALÉDONIE — TPC

| | | | |
|---|---|---|---|
| ☐ F-ODGN | ATR 42-320 | 097 | |
| ☐ F-ODYD | ATR 42-320 | 221 | |
| ☐ F-ODYE | ATR 42-320 | 335 | |
| ☐ F-OIAM | ATR 42-320 | 403 | |

### AIR CARAIBES — FWI

| | | | |
|---|---|---|---|
| ☐ F-OGUO | ATR 72-212 | 475 | |
| ☐ F-OHQL | ATR 42-500 | 524 | |
| ☐ F-OHQV | ATR 42-500 | 571 | |
| ☐ F-OIJG | ATR 72-212A | 654 | |
| ☐ F-OIJH | ATR 72-212A | 682 | o/o |

### AIR GUYANE — GUY

| | | | |
|---|---|---|---|
| ☐ F-OIJB | ATR 42-500 | 579 | |
| ☐ F-GHPZ | ATR 42-300 | 005 | |
| ☐ TF-ELK | ATR 42-310QC | 059 | Lsf ICB |

### AIR TAHITI — VTA

| | | | |
|---|---|---|---|
| ☐ F-OHJB | ATR 42-500 | 513 | |
| ☐ F-OHJC | ATR 42-500 | 528 | |
| ☐ F-OHJD | ATR 42-500 | 556 | |
| ☐ F-OHJJ | ATR 42-500 | 614 | |
| ☐ F-OHJN | ATR 72-212A | 535 | |
| ☐ F-OHJS | ATR 72-212A | 696 | |
| ☐ F-OHJT | ATR 72-212A | 590 | |
| ☐ F-OHJU | ATR 72-212A | 563 | |

### AIR TAHITI NUI — THT

| | | | |
|---|---|---|---|
| ☐ F-OITN | Airbus A340-211 | 031 | |
| ☐ F-OJGF | Airbus A340-313X | 385 | |
| ☐ F-OJTN | Airbus A340-313X | 395 | |
| ☐ F-OSEA | Airbus A340-313X | 438 | o/o |
| ☐ F-OSUN | Airbus A340-313X | 446 | o/o |

### AIRCALIN – AIR CALÉDONIE INTL — ACI

| | | | |
|---|---|---|---|
| ☐ F-ODGX | Boeing 737-33A | 1729/24094 | |
| ☐ F-OHPX | Airbus A310-325 | 672 | |
| ☐ F-OHSD | Airbus A330-202 | 507 | |
| ☐ F-OHSE | Airbus A330-202 | 510 | o/o |

## G - UNITED KINGDOM

### AIR 2000 — AMM

| | | | |
|---|---|---|---|
| ☐ G-OOAE | Airbus A321-211 | 0852 | |
| ☐ G-OOAF | Airbus A321-211 | 0677 | |
| ☐ G-OOAH | Airbus A321-211 | 0781 | |
| ☐ G-OOAI | Airbus A321-211 | 1006 | |
| ☐ G-OOAJ | Airbus A321-211 | 1017 | |
| ◼ G-OOAP | Airbus A320-214 | 1306 | |
| ☐ G-OOAR | Airbus A320-214 | 1320 | |
| ☐ G-OOAS | Airbus A320-214 | 1571 | Lst SSV |
| ☐ G-OOAT | Airbus A320-214 | 1605 | Lst SSV |
| ☐ G-OOAU | Airbus A320-214 | 1637 | |
| ☐ G-OOAV | Airbus A321-211 | 1720 | |
| ☐ G-OOAW | Airbus A320-214 | 1777 | |
| ☐ G-OOAX | Airbus A320-214 | | o/o |

| | | | |
|---|---|---|---|
| ☐ G-CPEP | Boeing 757-2Y0 | 400/25268 | |
| ☐ G-CPEU | Boeing 757-236 | 864/29941 | |
| ☐ G-CPEV | Boeing 757-236 | 871/29943 | |
| ☐ G-OOBA | Boeing 757-28A | 950/32446 | |
| ☐ G-OOBB | Boeing 757-28A | 951/32447 | Lst RYN |
| ☐ G-OOBC | Boeing 757-28A | 33098 | o/o |
| ☐ G-OOBD | Boeing 757-28A | 33099 | o/o |
| ☐ G-OOBE | Boeing 757-28A | 33100 | o/o |
| ☐ G-OOOB | Boeing 757-28A | 130/23822 | |
| ☐ G-OOOC | Boeing 757-28AER | 162/24017 | |
| ☐ G-OOOD | Boeing 757-28A | 180/24235 | |
| ☐ G-OOOG | Boeing 757-23AER | 219/24292 | |
| ☐ G-OOOI | Boeing 757-23AER | 209/24289 | |
| ☐ G-OOOJ | Boeing 757-23AER | 212/24290 | |
| ☐ G-OOOK | Boeing 757-236 | 362/25054 | |
| ☐ G-OOOM | Boeing 757-225 | 114/22612 | |
| ☐ G-OOOS | Boeing 757-236ER | 221/24397 | |
| ☐ G-OOOU | Boeing 757-2Y0ER | 388/25240 | |
| ☐ G-OOOX | Boeing 757-2Y0ER | 526/26158 | |
| ☐ G-OOOY | Boeing 757-28AER | 802/28203 | |
| ☐ G-OOOZ | Boeing 757-236 | 466/25593 | Lst SSV |
| ☐ G- | Boeing 757-200 | | o/o |
| ☐ G-OOAL | Boeing 767-38AER | 741/29617 | |
| ☐ G-OOAM | Boeing 767-38AER | 792/29618 | |
| ☐ G-OOAN | Boeing 767-39HER | 484/26256 | |

### AIRFREIGHT EXPRESS — AFX

| | | | |
|---|---|---|---|
| ☐ G-INTL | Boeing 747-245F | 242/20826 | std |
| ☐ VP-BRS | Boeing 747-2B5B (SF) | 513/22485 | std |

### AIR SCANDIC — SCY

| | | | |
|---|---|---|---|
| ☐ G-SWJW | Airbus A300B4-203 | 302 | |
| ☐ G-TTMC | Airbus A300B4-203 | 299 | |

### AIR SCOTLAND

| | | | |
|---|---|---|---|
| ☐ SX-BVM | Boeing 757-2G5 | 227/24451 | Lsf ELD |
| ☐ SX-BVN | Boeing 757-2G5 | 228/24497 | Lsf ELD |

### AIR WALES — AWW

| | | | |
|---|---|---|---|
| ☐ D-CBIG | Beech 1900D | UE-288 | Lsf EEX |
| ☐ D-CBSF | Beech 1900D | UE-8 | Lsf EEX |
| ☐ G-BUXT | Dornier 228-202K | 8065 | std |

### ASTRAEUS — AEU

| | | | |
|---|---|---|---|
| ☐ G-STRA | Boeing 737-3S3 | 1517/24059 | |
| ☐ G-STRB | Boeing 737-3Y0 | 1625/24255 | |
| ☐ G-STRC | Boeing 737-7BX | 658/30736 | |
| ☐ G-STRD | Boeing 737-7BX | 687/30737 | |

### ATLANTIC AIR LINES — AAG / ALH

| | | | |
|---|---|---|---|
| ☐ G-FIJR | L-188PF Electra | 1138 | |
| ☐ G-FIJV | L-188CF Electra | 1129 | |
| ☐ G-FIZU | L-188CF Electra | 2014 | |
| ◼ G-LOFB | L-188CF Electra | 1131 | |
| ☐ G-LOFC | L-188CF Electra | 1100 | |
| ☐ G-LOFD | L-188AC Electra | 1143 | |
| ☐ G-LOFE | L-188CF Electra | 1144 | |
| ☐ G-LOFF | L-188CF Electra | 1128 | |
| ☐ G-LOFG | L-188CF Electra | 1116 | std |
| ☐ G-LOFH | L-188CF Electra | 1140 | |
| ☐ G-LOFI | L-188PF Electra | 2010 | o/o |
| ☐ G-AMRA | Douglas DC-3 | 26735 | |
| ☐ G-ANAF | Douglas DC-3 | 16688/33436 | |
| ☐ G-APSA | Douglas DC-6A | 995/45997 | |
| ☐ G-BUKA | SA.227AC Metro III | AC-706B | |
| ☐ G-CONV | Convair 440 | 484 | Lsf GRR |
| ☐ G-SIXC | Douglas DC-6A/B | 1032/45550 | |
| ☐ | Antonov An-26 | | Lsf RAF-Avia |
| ☐ | Antonov An-26 | | Lsf RAF-Avia |
| ☐ | Antonov An-74 | | Lsf CBI |

## AURIGNY AIR SERVICES — AUR

| | | |
|---|---|---|
| ☐ G-BDTN | BN-2A Mk.III Trislander | 1026 |
| ☐ G-BDTO | BN-2A Mk.III Trislander | 1027 |
| ☐ G-BEVT | BN-2A Mk.III Trislander | 1057 |
| ☐ G-FTSE | BN-2A Mk.III Trislander | 1053 |
| ☐ G-JOEY | BN-2A Mk.III Trislander | 1016 |
| ☐ G-PCAM | BN-2A Mk.III Trislander | 1052 |
| ☐ G-RBCI | BN-2A Mk.III Trislander | 1035 |
| ☐ G-RLON | BN-2A Mk.III Trislander | 1008 |
| ☐ G-XTOR | BN-2A Mk.III Trislander | 1065 |
| | | |
| ☐ G-BMLC | Short SD.3-60 | SH3688 |
| ☐ G-GNTB | SAAB SF.340A | 082 |
| ☐ G-GNTC | SAAB SF.340A | 020 |
| ☐ G-RUNG | SAAB SF.340A | 086 Lsf DTR |

## BAC EXPRESS AIRLINES — RPX

| | | |
|---|---|---|
| ☐ G-BKMX | Short SD.3-60 | SH3608 |
| ☐ G-BNMU | Short SD.3-60 | SH3724 std |
| ☐ G-BOEG | Short SD.3-60 | SH3733 |
| ☐ G-BOEI | Short SD.3-60 | SH3735 |
| ☐ G-BPKZ | Short SD.3-60 | SH3756 |
| ■ G-CEAL | Short SD.3-60 | SH3761 |
| ☐ G-CLAS | Short SD.3-60 | SH3635 |
| ☐ G-OBLK | Short SD.3-60 | SH3712 |
| ☐ G-OCEA | Short SD.3-60 | SH3762 |
| ☐ G-OLAH | Short SD.3-60 | SH3604 Lst REA |
| ☐ G-VBAC | Short SD.3-60 | SH3736 |
| ■ G-XPSS | Short SD.3-60 | SH3713 |
| | | |
| ☐ G-BMXD | F.27 Friendship 500 | 10417 |
| ☐ G-BVOB | F.27 Friendship 500 | 10366 |
| ☐ G-JEAD | F.27 Friendship 500 | 10627 |
| ☐ G-JEAE | F.27 Friendship 500F | 10633 Lst EXS |

## BMIBABY

| | | |
|---|---|---|
| ☐ G-BVZH | Boeing 737-5Q8 | 2129/25166 Lsf BMA |
| ☐ G-ECAS | Boeing 737-36N | 2835/28554 Lsf BMA |
| ☐ G-ODSK | Boeing 737-37Q | 2904/28537 Lsf BMA |
| ☐ G-OJTW | Boeing 737-36N | 2876/28558 Lsf BMA |
| ☐ G-OBMP | Boeing 737-3Q8 | 2193/24963 Lsf BMA |

## BMI BRITISH MIDLANDS INTERNATIONAL — BMA

| | | |
|---|---|---|
| ☐ G-MIDA | Airbus A321-231 | 0806 |
| ☐ G-MIDC | Airbus A321-231 | 0835 |
| ☐ G-MIDE | Airbus A321-231 | 0864 |
| ☐ G-MIDF | Airbus A321-231 | 0810 |
| ☐ G-MIDH | Airbus A321-231 | 0968 |
| ☐ G-MIDI | Airbus A321-231 | 0974 |
| ☐ G-MIDJ | Airbus A321-231 | 1045 |
| ☐ G-MIDK | Airbus A321-231 | 1153 |
| ☐ G-MIDL | Airbus A321-231 | 1174 |
| ☐ G-MIDM | Airbus A321-231 | 1207 |
| ☐ G-MIDP | Airbus A320-232 | 1732 |
| ☐ G-MIDR | Airbus A320-232 | 1697 |
| ☐ G-MIDS | Airbus A320-232 | 1424 |
| ☐ G-MIDT | Airbus A320-232 | 1418 |
| ☐ G-MIDU | Airbus A320-232 | 1407 |
| ☐ G-MIDV | Airbus A320-232 | 1383 |
| ☐ G-MIDW | Airbus A320-232 | 1183 |
| ☐ G-MIDX | Airbus A320-232 | 1177 |
| ☐ G-MIDY | Airbus A320-232 | 1014 |
| ☐ G-MIDZ | Airbus A320-232 | 0934 |
| ☐ G- | Airbus A321-231 | o/o |
| ☐ G- | Airbus A320-232 | o/o |
| ☐ G- | Airbus A320-232 | o/o |
| ☐ G- | Airbus A320-232 | o/o |
| ☐ G- | Airbus A320-232 | o/o |
| ☐ G- | Airbus A320-232 | o/o |
| | | |
| ☐ G-BVKA | Boeing 737-59D | 1834/24694 |
| ☐ G-BVKB | Boeing 737-59D | 2592/27268 |
| ☐ G-BVKC | Boeing 737-59D | 1872/24695 |
| ☐ G-BVKD | Boeing 737-59D | 2279/26421 |

| | | |
|---|---|---|
| ☐ G-BVZE | Boeing 737-59D | 2412/26422 |
| ☐ G-BVZG | Boeing 737-5Q8 | 2114/25160 |
| ☐ G-BVZH | Boeing 737-5Q8 | 2129/25166 |
| ☐ G-BVZI | Boeing 737-5Q8 | 2173/25167 |
| ☐ G-BYZJ | Boeing 737-3Q8 | 2139/24962 |
| ☐ G-ECAS | Boeing 737-36N | 2835/28554 |
| ☐ G-OBMM | Boeing 737-4Y0 | 2176/25177 |
| ☐ G-OBMP | Boeing 737-3Q8 | 2193/24963 |
| ☐ G-ODSK | Boeing 737-37Q | 2904/28537 |
| ☐ G-OJTW | Boeing 737-36N | 2876/28558 |
| | | |
| ☐ G-BVJA | Fokker 100 | 11489 |
| ☐ G-BVJB | Fokker 100 | 11488 |
| ☐ G-BVJC | Fokker 100 | 11497 |
| ☐ G-BVJD | Fokker 100 | 11503 |
| ☐ G-BXWE | Fokker 100 | 11327 |
| ☐ G-BXWF | Fokker 100 | 11328 |
| | | |
| ☐ G-WWBB | Airbus A330-243 | 404 Lst SAA |
| ☐ G-WWBC | Airbus A330-243 | 455 o/o |
| ☐ G-WWBD | Airbus A330-243 | 401 Lst SAA |
| ☐ G-WWBM | Airbus A330-243 | 398 |

## BMI REGIONAL — GNT

| | | |
|---|---|---|
| ☐ G-RJXA | Embraer ERJ-145 | 145136 |
| ☐ G-RJXB | Embraer ERJ-145 | 145142 |
| ☐ G-RJXC | Embraer ERJ-145 | 145153 |
| ☐ G-RJXD | Embraer ERJ-145 | 145207 |
| ☐ G-RJXE | Embraer ERJ-145 | 145245 |
| ☐ G-RJXF | Embraer ERJ-145 | 145280 |
| ☐ G-RJXG | Embraer ERJ-145 | 145390 |
| ☐ G-RJXH | Embraer ERJ-145 | 145442 |
| ☐ G-RJXI | Embraer ERJ-145 | 145454 |
| ☐ G-RJXJ | Embraer ERJ-135 | 145473 |
| ☐ G-RJXK | Embraer ERJ-135 | 145494 |
| ☐ G-RJXL | Embraer ERJ-135 | |
| ☐ G-RJXM | Embraer ERJ-145 | o/o |
| ☐ G- | Embraer ERJ-145 | o/o |
| ☐ G- | Embraer ERJ-135 | o/o |

## BRISTOW HELICOPTERS — BMH

| | | |
|---|---|---|
| ☐ G-BLRY | AS.332L Super Puma | 2111 |
| ☐ G-BLXR | AS.332L Super Puma | 2154 |
| ☐ G-BMCW | AS.332L Super Puma | 2161 |
| ☐ G-BMCX | AS.332L Super Puma | 2164 |
| ☐ G-BRXU | AS.332L Super Puma | 2092 |
| ☐ G-BWMG | AS.332L Super Puma | 2046 |
| ☐ G-BWWI | AS.332L Super Puma | 2040 |
| ☐ G-BWZX | AS.332L Super Puma | 2120 |
| ☐ G-JSAR | AS.332L-2 Super Puma | 2576 |
| ☐ G-PUMH | AS.332L Super Puma | 2101 |
| ☐ G-TIGB | AS.332L Super Puma | 2023 |
| ☐ G-TIGC | AS.332L Super Puma | 2024 |
| ☐ G-TIGE | AS.332L Super Puma | 2028 |
| ☐ G-TIGF | AS.332L Super Puma | 2030 |
| ☐ G-TIGG | AS.332L Super Puma | 2032 |
| ☐ G-TIGI | AS.332L Super Puma | 2036 |
| ☐ G-TIGJ | AS.332L Super Puma | 2042 |
| ☐ G-TIGL | AS.332L Super Puma | 2050 |
| ☐ G-TIGM | AS.332L Super Puma | 2045 |
| ☐ G-TIGO | AS.332L Super Puma | 2061 |
| ☐ G-TIGP | AS.332L Super Puma | 2064 |
| ☐ G-TIGR | AS.332L Super Puma | 2071 |
| ☐ G-TIGS | AS.332L Super Puma | 2086 |
| ☐ G-TIGT | AS.332L Super Puma | 2078 |
| ☐ G-TIGV | AS.332L Super Puma | 2099 |
| | | |
| ☐ G-BBHL | Sikorsky S-61N II | 61712 |
| ☐ G-BBVA | Sikorsky S-61N II | 61718 |
| ☐ G-BCLC | Sikorsky S-61N II | 61737 |
| ☐ G-BCLD | Sikorsky S-61L | 61739 std |
| ☐ G-BDIJ | Sikorsky S-61N II | 61751 |
| ☐ G-BDOC | Sikorsky S-61N II | 61765 |
| ☐ G-BFRI | Sikorsky S-61N II | 61809 |
| ☐ G-BGWJ | Sikorsky S-61N II | 61819 |
| ☐ G-BGWK | Sikorsky S-61N II | 61820 |
| ☐ G-BHOG | Sikorsky S-61N II | 61825 |

| ☐ G-BHOH | Sikorsky S-61N II | 61827 |
| ☐ G-BIMU | Sikorsky S-61N II | 61752 |
| ☐ G-BPWB | Sikorsky S-61N II | 61822 |

## BRITANNIA AIRWAYS                                    BAL

| ☐ G-BYAD | Boeing 757-204ER | 450/26963 |
| ☐ G-BYAE | Boeing 757-204ER | 452/26964 |
| ☐ G-BYAF | Boeing 757-204ER | 514/26266 |
| ☐ G-BYAH | Boeing 757-204 | 520/26966 |
| ☐ G-BYAI | Boeing 757-204 | 522/26967 |
| ☐ G-BYAJ | Boeing 757-28AER | 528/25623 |
| ☐ G-BYAK | Boeing 757-204 | 538/26267 |
| ☐ G-BYAL | Boeing 757-204 | 549/25626 |
| ☐ G-BYAN | Boeing 757-204 | 596/27219 |
| ☐ G-BYAO | Boeing 757-204 | 598/27235 |
| ☐ G-BYAP | Boeing 757-204 | 600/27236 |
| ☐ G-BYAS | Boeing 757-204 | 604/27238 |
| ☐ G-BYAT | Boeing 757-204 | 606/27208 |
| ☐ G-BYAU | Boeing 757-204 | 618/27220 |
| ☐ G-BYAW | Boeing 757-204 | 663/27234 |
| ☐ G-BYAX | Boeing 757-204 | 850/28834 |
| ☐ G-BYAY | Boeing 757-204 | 861/28836 |
| ☐ G-CDUO | Boeing 757-236 | 279/24792 |
| ☐ G-CDUP | Boeing 757-236 | 292/24793 |
| | | |
| ☐ G-BRIF | Boeing 767-204ER | 296/24736 |
| ☐ G-BRIG | Boeing 767-204ER | 299/24757 |
| ☐ G-BYAA | Boeing 767-204ER | 362/25058 |
| ☐ G-BYAB | Boeing 767-204ER | 373/25139 |
| ☐ G-OBYB | Boeing 767-304ER | 613/28040 |
| ☐ G-OBYC | Boeing 767-304ER | 614/28041 |
| ☐ G-OBYD | Boeing 767-304ER | 649/28042 |
| ☐ G-OBYE | Boeing 767-304ER | 691/28979 |
| ☐ G-OBYF | Boeing 767-304ER | 705/28208 |
| ☐ G-OBYG | Boeing 767-304ER | 733/29137 |
| ☐ G-OBYH | Boeing 767-304ER | 737/28883 |
| ☐ G-OBYI | Boeing 767-304ER | 783/29138 |
| ■ G-OBYJ | Boeing 767-304ER | 784/29384 |

## BRITISH AIRWAYS                                BAW / SHT

| ☐ G-EUOA | Airbus A319-131 | 1513 | |
| ☐ G-EUOB | Airbus A319-131 | 1529 | |
| ☐ G-EUOC | Airbus A319-131 | 1537 | |
| ☐ G-EUOD | Airbus A319-131 | 1558 | |
| ☐ G-EUOE | Airbus A319-131 | 1574 | |
| ☐ G-EUOF | Airbus A319-131 | 1590 | |
| ☐ G-EUOG | Airbus A319-131 | 1594 | |
| ☐ G-EUOH | Airbus A319-131 | 1604 | |
| ☐ G-EUOI | Airbus A319-131 | 1606 | |
| ☐ G-EUPA | Airbus A319-131 | 1082 | |
| ☐ G-EUPB | Airbus A319-131 | 1115 | |
| ☐ G-EUPC | Airbus A319-131 | 1118 | |
| ☐ G-EUPD | Airbus A319-131 | 1142 | |
| ☐ G-EUPE | Airbus A319-131 | 1193 | |
| ☐ G-EUPF | Airbus A319-131 | 1197 | |
| ☐ G-EUPG | Airbus A319-131 | 1222 | |
| ☐ G-EUPH | Airbus A319-131 | 1225 | |
| ☐ G-EUPJ | Airbus A319-131 | 1232 | |
| ☐ G-EUPK | Airbus A319-131 | 1236 | |
| ☐ G-EUPL | Airbus A319-131 | 1239 | |
| ☐ G-EUPM | Airbus A319-131 | 1258 | |
| ☐ G-EUPN | Airbus A319-131 | 1261 | |
| ☐ G-EUPO | Airbus A319-131 | 1279 | |
| ☐ G-EUPP | Airbus A319-131 | 1295 | |
| ☐ G-EUPR | Airbus A319-131 | 1329 | |
| ☐ G-EUPS | Airbus A319-131 | 1338 | |
| ☐ G-EUPT | Airbus A319-131 | 1380 | |
| ☐ G-EUPU | Airbus A319-131 | 1384 | |
| ☐ G-EUPV | Airbus A319-131 | 1423 | |
| ☐ G-EUPW | Airbus A319-131 | 1440 | |
| ☐ G-EUPX | Airbus A319-131 | 1445 | |
| ☐ G-EUPY | Airbus A319-131 | 1466 | |
| ☐ G-EUPZ | Airbus A319-131 | 1510 | |
| ☐ G- | Airbus A319-131 | | o/o |
| ☐ G- | Airbus A319-131 | | o/o |
| ☐ G- | Airbus A319-131 | | o/o |

| ☐ G-BUSB | Airbus A320-111 | 0006 | |
| ☐ G-BUSC | Airbus A320-111 | 0008 | |
| ☐ G-BUSD | Airbus A320-111 | 0011 | |
| ☐ G-BUSE | Airbus A320-111 | 0017 | |
| ☐ G-BUSF | Airbus A320-111 | 0018 | |
| ☐ G-BUSG | Airbus A320-211 | 0039 | |
| ☐ G-BUSH | Airbus A320-211 | 0042 | |
| ☐ G-BUSI | Airbus A320-211 | 0103 | |
| ☐ G-BUSJ | Airbus A320-211 | 0109 | |
| ☐ G-BUSK | Airbus A320-211 | 0120 | |
| ☐ G-EUUA | Airbus A320-232 | 1661 | |
| ☐ G-EUUB | Airbus A320-232 | 1689 | |
| ☐ G-EUUC | Airbus A320-232 | 1696 | |
| ☐ G-EUUD | Airbus A320-232 | 1760 | |
| ☐ G-EUUE | Airbus A320-232 | 1782 | |
| ☐ G-EUUF | Airbus A320-232 | 1814 | |
| ☐ G-EUUG | Airbus A320-232 | 1829 | |
| ☐ G-EUUH | Airbus A320-232 | 1665 | |
| ☐ G-EUUI | Airbus A320-232 | 1871 | |
| ☐ G-EUUJ | Airbus A320-232 | 1883 | |
| ☐ G-EUUK | Airbus A320-232 | 1899 | |
| ☐ G-EUUL | Airbus A320-232 | 1708 | |
| ☐ G-EUUM | Airbus A320-232 | 1907 | |
| ☐ G-EUUN | Airbus A320-232 | 1910 | |
| ☐ G-EUUO | Airbus A330-232 | 1918 | |
| ☐ G-EUUP | Airbus A330-232 | 2038 | o/o |
| ☐ G-EUUR | Airbus A320-232 | 2040 | o/o |
| | | | |
| ☐ G-BOAA | Concorde 102 | 006 | |
| ☐ G-BOAB | Concorde 102 | 008 | std |
| ☐ G-BOAC | Concorde 102 | 004 | |
| ☐ G-BOAD | Concorde 102 | 010 | |
| ☐ G-BOAE | Concorde 102 | 012 | |
| ☐ G-BOAF | Concorde 102 | 016 | |
| ☐ G-BOAG | Concorde 102 | 014 | |
| | | | |
| ☐ G-BVNM | Boeing 737-4S3 | 1700/24163 | |
| ☐ G-BVNN | Boeing 737-4S3 | 1702/24164 | |
| ☐ G-BVNO | Boeing 737-4S3 | 1736/24167 | |
| ☐ G-DOCA | Boeing 737-436 | 2131/25267 | |
| ☐ G-DOCB | Boeing 737-436 | 2144/25304 | |
| ☐ G-DOCD | Boeing 737-436 | 2156/25349 | |
| ☐ G-DOCE | Boeing 737-436 | 2167/25350 | |
| ☐ G-DOCF | Boeing 737-436 | 2178/25407 | |
| ☐ G-DOCG | Boeing 737-436 | 2183/25408 | |
| ☐ G-DOCH | Boeing 737-436 | 2185/25428 | |
| ■ G-DOCI | Boeing 737-436 | 2188/25839 | |
| ☐ G-DOCL | Boeing 737-436 | 2228/25842 | |
| ☐ G-DOCM | Boeing 737-436 | 2244/25843 | |
| ☐ G-DOCN | Boeing 737-436 | 2379/25848 | |
| ☐ G-DOCO | Boeing 737-436 | 2381/25849 | |
| ☐ G-DOCP | Boeing 737-436 | 2386/25850 | |
| ☐ G-DOCR | Boeing 737-436 | 2387/25851 | |
| ☐ G-DOCS | Boeing 737-436 | 2390/25852 | |
| ☐ G-DOCT | Boeing 737-436 | 2409/25853 | |
| ☐ G-DOCU | Boeing 737-436 | 2417/25854 | |
| ☐ G-DOCV | Boeing 737-436 | 2420/25855 | |
| ☐ G-DOCW | Boeing 737-436 | 2422/25856 | |
| ☐ G-DOCX | Boeing 737-436 | 2451/25857 | |
| ☐ G-DOCY | Boeing 737-436 | 2514/25844 | |
| ☐ G-DOCZ | Boeing 737-436 | 2522/25858 | |
| ☐ G-GBTA | Boeing 737-436 | 2532/25859 | |
| ☐ G-GBTB | Boeing 737-436 | 2545/25860 | |
| ☐ G-GFFA | Boeing 737-59D | 1969/25038 | |
| ☐ G-GFFB | Boeing 737-505 | 2229/25789 | |
| ☐ G-GFFC | Boeing 737-505 | 1923/24272 | |
| ☐ G-GFFD | Boeing 737-59D | 2186/26419 | |
| ☐ G-GFFE | Boeing 737-528 | 2720/27424 | |
| ☐ G-GFFF | Boeing 737-53A | 1868/24754 | |
| ☐ G-GFFG | Boeing 737-505 | 1792/24650 | |
| ☐ G-GFFH | Boeing 737-5H6 | 2637/27354 | |
| ☐ G-GFFI | Boeing 737-528 | 2730/27425 | |
| ☐ G-GFFJ | Boeing 737-5H6 | 2646/27355 | |
| ☐ G-LGTE | Boeing 737-3Y0 | 2015/24908 | |
| ☐ G-LGTF | Boeing 737-382 | 1873/24450 | |
| ☐ G-LGTG | Boeing 737-3Q8 | 1765/24470 | |
| ☐ G-LGTH | Boeing 737-3Y0 | 1542/23924 | |
| ☐ G-LGTI | Boeing 737-3Y0 | 1544/23925 | |

| | | |
|---|---|---|
| ☐ G-BNLA | Boeing 747-436 | 727/23908 |
| ☐ G-BNLB | Boeing 747-436 | 730/23909 |
| ☐ G-BNLC | Boeing 747-436 | 734/23910 |
| ☐ G-BNLD | Boeing 747-436 | 744/23911 |
| ☐ G-BNLE | Boeing 747-436 | 753/24047 |
| ☐ G-BNLF | Boeing 747-436 | 773/24048 |
| ☐ G-BNLG | Boeing 747-436 | 774/24049 |
| ☐ G-BNLH | Boeing 747-436 | 779/24050 |
| ☐ G-BNLI | Boeing 747-436 | 784/24051 |
| ☐ G-BNLJ | Boeing 747-436 | 789/24052 |
| ☐ G-BNLK | Boeing 747-436 | 790/24053 |
| ☐ G-BNLL | Boeing 747-436 | 794/24054 |
| ☐ G-BNLM | Boeing 747-436 | 795/24055 |
| ☐ G-BNLN | Boeing 747-436 | 802/24056 |
| ☐ G-BNLO | Boeing 747-436 | 817/24057 |
| ☐ G-BNLP | Boeing 747-436 | 828/24058 |
| ☐ G-BNLR | Boeing 747-436 | 829/24447 |
| ☐ G-BNLS | Boeing 747-436 | 841/24629 |
| ☐ G-BNLT | Boeing 747-436 | 842/24630 |
| ☐ G-BNLU | Boeing 747-436 | 895/25406 |
| ☐ G-BNLV | Boeing 747-436 | 900/25427 |
| ☐ G-BNLW | Boeing 747-436 | 903/25432 |
| ☐ G-BNLX | Boeing 747-436 | 908/25435 |
| ☐ G-BNLY | Boeing 747-436 | 959/27090 |
| ☐ G-BNLZ | Boeing 747-436 | 964/27091 |
| ☐ G-BYGA | Boeing 747-436 | 1190/28855 |
| ☐ G-BYGB | Boeing 747-436 | 1194/28856 |
| ☐ G-BYGC | Boeing 747-436 | 1195/25823 |
| ☐ G-BYGD | Boeing 747-436 | 1196/28857 |
| ☐ G-BYGE | Boeing 747-436 | 1198/28858 |
| ☐ G-BYGF | Boeing 747-436 | 1200/25824 |
| ☐ G-BYGG | Boeing 747-436 | 1212/28859 |
| ☐ G-CIVA | Boeing 747-436 | 967/27092 |
| ☐ G-CIVB | Boeing 747-436 | 1018/25811 |
| ☐ G-CIVC | Boeing 747-436 | 1022/25812 |
| ☐ G-CIVD | Boeing 747-436 | 1048/27349 |
| ☐ G-CIVE | Boeing 747-436 | 1050/27350 |
| ☐ G-CIVF | Boeing 747-436 | 1058/25434 |
| ☐ G-CIVG | Boeing 747-436 | 1059/25813 |
| ☐ G-CIVH | Boeing 747-436 | 1078/25809 |
| ☐ G-CIVI | Boeing 747-436 | 1079/25814 |
| ☐ G-CIVJ | Boeing 747-436 | 1102/25817 |
| ☐ G-CIVK | Boeing 747-436 | 1104/25818 |
| ☐ G-CIVL | Boeing 747-436 | 1108/27478 |
| ☐ G-CIVM | Boeing 747-436 | 1116/28700 |
| ☐ G-CIVN | Boeing 747-436 | 1129/28848 |
| ☐ G-CIVO | Boeing 747-436 | 1135/28849 |
| ☐ G-CIVP | Boeing 747-436 | 1144/28850 |
| ☐ G-CIVR | Boeing 747-436 | 1146/25820 |
| ☐ G-CIVS | Boeing 747-436 | 1148/28851 |
| ☐ G-CIVT | Boeing 747-436 | 1149/25821 |
| ☐ G-CIVU | Boeing 747-436 | 1154/25810 |
| ☐ G-CIVV | Boeing 747-436 | 1156/25819 |
| ☐ G-CIVW | Boeing 747-436 | 1157/25822 |
| ☐ G-CIVX | Boeing 747-436 | 1172/28852 |
| ☐ G-CIVY | Boeing 747-436 | 1178/28853 |
| ☐ G-CIVZ | Boeing 747-436 | 1183/28854 |
| | | |
| ☐ G-BPEC | Boeing 757-236ER | 323/24882 |
| ☐ G-BPED | Boeing 757-236 | 363/25059 |
| ☐ G-BPEE | Boeing 757-236ER | 364/25060 |
| ☐ G-BPEF | Boeing 757-236ER | 174/24120 |
| ☐ G-BPEI | Boeing 757-236 | 601/25806 |
| ☐ G-BPEJ | Boeing 757-236 | 610/25807 |
| ☐ G-BPEK | Boeing 757-236 | 665/25808 |
| ☐ G-CPEL | Boeing 757-236 | 224/24398 |
| ☐ G-CPEM | Boeing 757-236 | 747/28665 |
| ☐ G-CPEN | Boeing 757-236 | 751/28666 |
| ☐ G-CPEO | Boeing 757-236 | 752/28667 |
| ☐ G-CPER | Boeing 757-236 | 784/29113 |
| ☐ G-CPES | Boeing 757-236 | 793/29114 |
| ☐ G-CPET | Boeing 757-236 | 798/29115 |
| | | |
| ☐ G-BNWA | Boeing 767-336ER | 265/24333 |
| ☐ G-BNWB | Boeing 767-336ER | 281/24334 |
| ☐ G-BNWC | Boeing 767-336ER | 284/24335 |
| ☐ G-BNWD | Boeing 767-336ER | 286/24336 |
| ☐ G-BNWH | Boeing 767-336ER | 335/24340 |

| | | |
|---|---|---|
| ☐ G-BNWI | Boeing 767-336ER | 342/24341 |
| ☐ G-BNWM | Boeing 767-336ER | 376/25204 |
| ☐ G-BNWN | Boeing 767-336ER | 398/25444 |
| ☐ G-BNWO | Boeing 767-336ER | 418/25442 |
| ☐ G-BNWR | Boeing 767-336ER | 421/25732 |
| ☐ G-BNWS | Boeing 767-336ER | 473/25826 |
| ☐ G-BNWT | Boeing 767-336ER | 476/25828 |
| ☐ G-BNWU | Boeing 767-336ER | 483/25829 |
| ☐ G-BNWV | Boeing 767-336ER | 490/27140 |
| ☐ G-BNWW | Boeing 767-336ER | 526/25831 |
| ☐ G-BNWX | Boeing 767-336ER | 529/25832 |
| ☐ G-BNWY | Boeing 767-336ER | 608/25834 |
| ☐ G-BNWZ | Boeing 767-336ER | 648/25733 |
| ☐ G-BZHA | Boeing 767-336ER | 702/29230 |
| ☐ G-BZHB | Boeing 767-336ER | 704/29231 |
| ☐ G-BZHC | Boeing 767-336ER | 708/29232 |
| | | |
| ☐ G-RAES | Boeing 777-236ER | 76/27491 |
| ☐ G-VIIA | Boeing 777-236ER | 41/27483 |
| ■ G-VIIB | Boeing 777-236ER | 49/27484 |
| ☐ G-VIIC | Boeing 777-236ER | 53/27485 |
| ☐ G-VIID | Boeing 777-236ER | 56/27486 |
| ☐ G-VIIE | Boeing 777-236ER | 58/27487 |
| ■ G-VIIF | Boeing 777-236ER | 61/27488 |
| ☐ G-VIIG | Boeing 777-236ER | 65/27489 |
| ☐ G-VIIH | Boeing 777-236ER | 70/27490 |
| ☐ G-VIIJ | Boeing 777-236ER | 111/27492 |
| ☐ G-VIIK | Boeing 777-236ER | 117/28840 |
| ☐ G-VIIL | Boeing 777-236ER | 127/27493 |
| ☐ G-VIIM | Boeing 777-236ER | 130/28841 |
| ☐ G-VIIN | Boeing 777-236ER | 157/29319 |
| ☐ G-VIIO | Boeing 777-236ER | 182/29320 |
| ☐ G-VIIP | Boeing 777-236ER | 193/29321 |
| ☐ G-VIIR | Boeing 777-236ER | 203/29322 |
| ☐ G-VIIS | Boeing 777-236ER | 206/29323 |
| ☐ G-VIIT | Boeing 777-236ER | 217/29962 |
| ☐ G-VIIU | Boeing 777-236ER | 221/29963 |
| ☐ G-VIIV | Boeing 777-236ER | 228/29964 |
| ☐ G-VIIW | Boeing 777-236ER | 233/29965 |
| ☐ G-VIIX | Boeing 777-236ER | 236/29966 |
| ☐ G-VIIY | Boeing 777-236ER | 251/29967 |
| ☐ G-YMMA | Boeing 777-236ER | 242/30302 |
| ☐ G-YMMB | Boeing 777-236ER | 265/30303 |
| ☐ G-YMMC | Boeing 777-236ER | 268/30304 |
| ☐ G-YMMD | Boeing 777-236ER | 269/30305 |
| ☐ G-YMME | Boeing 777-236ER | 275/30306 |
| ☐ G-YMMF | Boeing 777-236ER | 281/30307 |
| ☐ G-YMMG | Boeing 777-236ER | 301/30308 |
| ☐ G-YMMH | Boeing 777-236ER | 303/30309 |
| ☐ G-YMMI | Boeing 777-236ER | 308/30310 |
| ☐ G-YMMJ | Boeing 777-236ER | 311/30311 |
| ☐ G-YMMK | Boeing 777-236ER | 312/30312 |
| ☐ G-YMML | Boeing 777-236ER | 334/30313 |
| ☐ G-YMMM | Boeing 777-236ER | 342/30314 |
| ☐ G-YMMN | Boeing 777-236ER | 346/30316 |
| ☐ G-YMMO | Boeing 777-236ER | 361/30317 |
| ☐ G-YMMP | Boeing 777-236ER | 369/30315 |
| ☐ G-ZZZA | Boeing 777-236 | 6/27105 |
| ☐ G-ZZZB | Boeing 777-236 | 10/27106 |
| ☐ G-ZZZC | Boeing 777-236 | 15/27107 |

## BRITISH AIRWAYS CITIEXPRESS     BRT

| | | |
|---|---|---|
| ☐ G-BVTJ | ATR 72-202 | 342 |
| ☐ G-BVTK | ATR 72-202 | 357 |
| ☐ G-BXTN | ATR 72-202 | 483 |
| ☐ G-BYTO | ATR 72-212 | 472 |
| ☐ G-BYTP | ATR 72-212 | 473 |
| | | |
| ☐ G-BXAR | Avro RJ100 | E3298 |
| ☐ G-BXAS | Avro RJ100 | E3301 |
| ☐ G-BZAT | Avro RJ100 | E3320 |
| ☐ G-BZAU | Avro RJ100 | E3328 |
| ☐ G-BZAV | Avro RJ100 | E3331 |
| ☐ G-BZAW | Avro RJ100 | E3354 |
| ☐ G-BZAX | Avro RJ100 | E3356 |
| ☐ G-BZAY | Avro RJ100 | E3368 |
| ☐ G-BZAZ | Avro RJ100 | E3369 |

| | | | |
|---|---|---|---|
| ☐ G-CFAA | Avro RJ100 | E3373 | |
| ☐ G-CFAB | Avro RJ100 | E3377 | |
| ☐ G-CFAC | Avro RJ100 | E3379 | |
| ☐ G-CFAD | Avro RJ100 | E3380 | |
| ☐ G-CFAE | Avro RJ100 | E3381 | |
| ☐ G-CFAF | Avro RJ100 | E3382 | |
| ☐ G-CFAH | Avro RJ100 | E3384 | |
| | | | |
| ☐ G-GNTZ | BAe 146 Srs.200 | E2036 | |
| ☐ G-MABR | BAe 146 Srs.100 | E1015 | |
| ☐ G-MANS | BAe 146 Srs.200 | E2088 | |
| ☐ G-MIMA | BAe 146 Srs.200 | E2079 | |
| ☐ G-OINV | BAe 146 Srs.300 | E3171 | |
| | | | |
| ■ G-MANA | British Aerospace ATP | 2056 | |
| ☐ G-MANB | British Aerospace ATP | 2055 | |
| ■ G-MANC | British Aerospace ATP | 2054 | |
| ■ G-MANE | British Aerospace ATP | 2045 | |
| ☐ G-MANF | British Aerospace ATP | 2040 | |
| ☐ G-MANG | British Aerospace ATP | 2018 | |
| ☐ G-MANH | British Aerospace ATP | 2017 | |
| ☐ G-MANJ | British Aerospace ATP | 2004 | |
| ■ G-MANL | British Aerospace ATP | 2003 | |
| ☐ G-MANM | British Aerospace ATP | 2005 | |
| ■ G-MANO | British Aerospace ATP | 2006 | |
| ☐ G-MANP | British Aerospace ATP | 2023 | |
| ☐ G-MAUD | British Aerospace ATP | 2002 | |
| | | | |
| ☐ G-BRYI | DHC-8-311A | 256 | |
| ☐ G-BRYJ | DHC-8-311A | 319 | |
| ☐ G-BRYS | DHC-8-311A | 296 | std |
| ☐ G-BRYT | DHC-8-311A | 334 | std |
| ☐ G-BRYU | DHC-8Q-311A | 458 | |
| ☐ G-BRYV | DHC-8Q-311A | 462 | |
| ☐ G-BRYW | DHC-8Q-311A | 474 | |
| ☐ G-BRYX | DHC-8Q-311A | 508 | |
| ☐ G-BRYY | DHC-8Q-311A | 519 | |
| ☐ G-BRYZ | DHC-8Q-311A | 464 | |
| ☐ G-NVSA | DHC-8Q-311A | 451 | |
| ☐ G-NVSB | DHC-8Q-311A | 517 | |
| | | | |
| ☐ G-EMBC | Embraer ERJ-145 | 145024 | |
| ☐ G-EMBD | Embraer ERJ-145 | 145039 | |
| ☐ G-EMBE | Embraer ERJ-145 | 145042 | |
| ☐ G-EMBF | Embraer ERJ-145 | 145088 | |
| ☐ G-EMBG | Embraer ERJ-145 | 145094 | |
| ☐ G-EMBH | Embraer ERJ-145 | 145107 | |
| ☐ G-EMBI | Embraer ERJ-145 | 145126 | |
| ☐ G-EMBJ | Embraer ERJ-145 | 145134 | |
| ☐ G-EMBK | Embraer ERJ-145 | 145167 | |
| ☐ G-EMBL | Embraer ERJ-145 | 145177 | |
| ☐ G-EMBM | Embraer ERJ-145 | 145196 | |
| ☐ G-EMBN | Embraer ERJ-145 | 145201 | |
| ☐ G-EMBO | Embraer ERJ-145 | 145219 | |
| ☐ G-EMBP | Embraer ERJ-145 | 145300 | |
| ☐ G-EMBS | Embraer ERJ-145 | 145357 | |
| ☐ G-EMBT | Embraer ERJ-145 | 145404 | |
| ☐ G-EMBU | Embraer ERJ-145 | 145458 | |
| ☐ G-EMBV | Embraer ERJ-145 | 145482 | |
| ■ G-EMBW | Embraer ERJ-145 | 145546 | |
| ☐ G-EMBX | Embraer ERJ-145 | 145573 | |
| ☐ G-EMBY | Embraer ERJ-145 | 145617 | |
| ☐ G-ERJA | Embraer ERJ-145 | 145229 | |
| ☐ G-ERJB | Embraer ERJ-145 | 145237 | |
| ■ G-ERJC | Embraer ERJ-145 | 145253 | |
| ☐ G-ERJD | Embraer ERJ-145 | 145290 | |
| ■ G-ERJE | Embraer ERJ-145 | 145315 | |
| ☐ G-ERJF | Embraer ERJ-145 | 145325 | |
| ☐ G-ERJG | Embraer ERJ-145 | 145394 | |
| | | | |
| ☐ G-GNTG | SAAB SF.340A | 126 | Opb LOG |
| ☐ G-LGNA | SAAB SF.340B | 199 | Opb LOG |
| ☐ G-LGNB | SAAB SF.340B | 216 | Opb LOG |
| ☐ G-LGNC | SAAB SF.340B | 318 | Opb LOG |
| ☐ G-LGND | SAAB SF.340B | 169 | Opb LOG |
| ☐ G-LGNE | SAAB SF.340B | 172 | Opb LOG |
| ☐ G-LGNF | SAAB SF.340B | 192 | Opb LOG |
| ☐ G-LGNG | SAAB SF.340B | 327 | Opb LOG |

## BRITISH INTERNATIONAL — BIH

| | | | |
|---|---|---|---|
| ☐ G-ATBJ | Sikorsky S-61N | 61269 | Lst SHZ |
| ☐ G-ATFM | Sikorsky S-61N | 61270 | |
| ☐ G-AYOY | Sikorsky S-61N | 61476 | |
| ☐ G-BCEA | Sikorsky S-61N | 61721 | |
| ☐ G-BCEB | Sikorsky S-61NM | 61454 | |
| ☐ G-BFFJ | Sikorsky S-61N | 61777 | |

## BRITISH MEDITERRANEAN AIRWAYS — LAJ

| | | | |
|---|---|---|---|
| ☐ G-MEDA | Airbus A320-231 | 0480 | |
| ☐ G-MEDE | Airbus A320-232 | 1194 | |
| ☐ G-MEDF | Airbus A321-131 | 1690 | |
| ☐ G-MEDG | Airbus A321-131 | 1711 | |
| ☐ G-MEDH | Airbus A320-232 | 1922 | o/o |
| ☐ G- | Airbus A320-232 | | o/o |

## BUZZ — UKA

| | | | |
|---|---|---|---|
| ☐ G-BSNR | BAe 146 Srs.300 | E3165 | |
| ☐ G-BTTP | BAe 146 Srs.300 | E3203 | |
| ☐ G-UKAC | BAe 146 Srs.300 | E3142 | |
| ☐ G-UKAG | BAe 146 Srs.300 | E3162 | |
| ☐ G-UKHP | BAe 146 Srs.300 | E3123 | |
| ☐ G-UKID | BAe 146 Srs.300 | E3157 | |
| ☐ G-UKRC | BAe 146 Srs.300 | E3158 | |
| ☐ G-UKSC | BAe 146 Srs.300 | E3125 | |
| | | | |
| ☐ G-BZZA | Boeing 737-3L9 | 2250/26441 | |
| ☐ G-BZZB | Boeing 737-3L9 | 2059/25125 | |
| ☐ G-BZZE | Boeing 737-3Q8 | 2680/26310 | |
| ☐ G-BZZF | Boeing 737-3Q8 | 2681/26311 | o/o |
| ☐ G-BZZG | Boeing 737-3Q8 | 2693/26312 | o/o |
| ☐ G-BZZH | Boeing 737-3Q8 | 2704/26313 | o/o |
| ☐ G-BZZI | Boeing 737-3Q8 | 2707/26314 | o/o |
| ☐ G-BZZJ | Boeing 737-3Q8 | 2764/26321 | o/o |

## CHANNEL EXPRESS — EXS

| | | | |
|---|---|---|---|
| ☐ G-CELS | Boeing 737-377 | 1294/23660 | Opf Jet 2 |
| ☐ G-CELU | Boeing 737-377 | 1280/23657 | |
| ☐ G-CELV | Boeing 737-377 | 1314/23661 | |
| ☐ G-CELW | Boeing 737-377 (QC) | 1292/23659 | |
| ☐ TF-ELN | Boeing 737-3Q8 (QC) | 1375/23766 | Lsf ISL |
| ☐ TF-ELP | Boeing 737-330 (QC) | 1246/23522 | Opb ISL |
| ☐ TF-ELR | Boeing 737-330 (QC) | 1271/23523 | Opb ISL |
| | | | |
| ☐ G-BNIZ | F.27 Friendship 600F | 10405 | |
| ☐ G-CEXA | F.27 Friendship 500RF | 10503 | |
| ☐ G-CEXB | F.27 Friendship 500RF | 10550 | |
| ☐ G-CEXD | F.27 Friendship 600 | 10351 | |
| ☐ G-CEXE | F.27 Friendship 500 | 10654 | |
| ☐ G-CEXF | F.27 Friendship 500 | 10660 | |
| ☐ G-CEXG | F.27 Friendship 500 | 10459 | |
| ☐ G-JEAE | F.27 Friendship 500F | 10633 | Lsf RPX |
| | | | |
| ☐ G-CEXH | Airbus A300B4-203F | 117 | |
| ☐ G-CEXI | Airbus A300B4-203F | 121 | |
| ☐ G-CEXJ | Airbus A300B4-203F | 147 | |
| ☐ G-CEXK | Airbus A300B4-103F | 105 | |
| ☐ G-CEXS | L-188CF Electra | 1091 | |

## CHC SCOTIA HELICOPTERS — SHZ

| | | | |
|---|---|---|---|
| ☐ G-BKZE | AS.332L Super Puma | 2102 | |
| ☐ G-BKZG | AS.332L Super Puma | 2106 | |
| ☐ G-BKZH | AS.332L Super Puma | 2107 | |
| ☐ G-BOZK | AS.332L Super Puma | 2179 | Lst HBI |
| ☐ G-BUZD | AS.332L Super Puma | 2069 | |
| ☐ G-BWHN | AS.332L Super Puma | 2017 | Lst HBI |
| ☐ G-CHCA | AS.332L Super Puma | 2007 | Lst HBI |
| ☐ G-CHCB | AS.332L Super Puma | 2015 | Lst HBI |
| ☐ G-CHCF | AS.332L2 Super Puma | 2567 | |
| ☐ G-PUMA | AS.332L Super Puma | 2038 | |
| ☐ G-PUMB | AS.332L Super Puma | 2075 | |

| | | | |
|---|---|---|---|
| ☐ G-PUMD | AS.332L Super Puma | 2077 | |
| ☐ G-PUME | AS.332L Super Puma | 2091 | |
| ☐ G-PUMG | AS.332L Super Puma | 2018 | |
| ☐ G-PUMK | AS.332L Super Puma | 2067 | Lsf HKS |
| ☐ G-PUML | AS.332L Super Puma | 2073 | Lsf HKS |
| ☐ G-PUMM | AS.332L2 Super Puma | 2477 | |
| ☐ G-PUMN | AS.332L2 Super Puma | 2474 | Lsf HKS |
| ☐ G-PUMO | AS.332L2 Super Puma | 2467 | |
| ☐ G-PUMS | AS.332L2 Super Puma | 2504 | |
| ☐ G-TIGZ | AS.332L Super Puma | 2115 | |
| | | | |
| ☐ G-ATBJ | Sikorsky S-61N | 61269 | Lsf BIH |
| ☐ G-BEJL | Sikorsky S-61N | 61224 | std |
| ☐ G-BZSN | Sikorsky S-61N | 61807 | Lsf HKS |
| ☐ G-CBKZ | Sikorsky S-61N II | 61816 | |
| ☐ G-CBWC | Sikorsky S-61N | 61740 | Lsf HKS |
| ☐ ZS-RLK | Sikorsky S-61N | 61772 | |
| ☐ ZS-RLL | Sikorsky S-61N | 61778 | |

### DHL AIR — DHK

| | | | |
|---|---|---|---|
| ☐ G-BIKC | Boeing 757-236SF | 11/22174 | Lsf BCS |
| ☐ G-BIKF | Boeing 757-236SF | 16/22177 | |
| ☐ G-BIKG | Boeing 757-236SF | 23/22178 | |
| ☐ G-BIKJ | Boeing 757-236SF | 29/22181 | |
| ☐ G-BIKK | Boeing 757-236SF | 30/22182 | |
| ☐ G-BIKM | Boeing 757-236SF | 33/22184 | |
| ☐ G-BIKN | Boeing 757-236SF | 50/22186 | |
| ☐ G-BIKO | Boeing 757-236SF | 52/22187 | |
| ☐ G-BIKP | Boeing 757-236SF | 54/22188 | |
| ☐ G-BIKR | Boeing 757-236SF | 58/22189 | |
| ☐ G-BIKS | Boeing 757-236SF | 63/22190 | |
| ☐ G-BIKU | Boeing 757-236SF | 78/23399 | |
| ☐ G-BIKV | Boeing 757-236SF | 81/23400 | |
| ☐ G-BIKZ | Boeing 757-236SF | 98/23532 | |
| ☐ G-BMRA | Boeing 757-236SF | 123/23710 | |
| ☐ G-BMRB | Boeing 757-236SF | 145/23975 | |
| ☐ G-BMRC | Boeing 757-236SF | 160/24072 | |
| ☐ G-BMRD | Boeing 757-236SF | 166/24073 | o/o |
| ☐ G-BMRE | Boeing 757-236SF | 168/24074 | o/o |
| ☐ G-BMRF | Boeing 757-236SF | 175/24101 | |
| ☐ G-BMRH | Boeing 757-236SF | 210/24266 | |
| ☐ G-BMRJ | Boeing 757-236SF | 214/24268 | |

### EASTERN AIRWAYS — EZE

| | | | |
|---|---|---|---|
| ☐ G-BUVC | BAe Jetstream 32 | 970 | |
| ☐ G-BUVD | BAe Jetstream 32 | 977 | |
| ☐ G-BYMA | BAe Jetstream 32 | 840 | |
| ☐ G-BYRA | BAe Jetstream 32 | 845 | |
| ☐ G-BYRM | BAe Jetstream 32 | 847 | |
| ☐ G-BZYP | BAe Jetstream 32 | 978 | |
| ☐ G-CBCS | BAe Jetstream 32 | 842 | |
| ☐ G-CBDA | BAe Jetstream 32 | 986 | |
| ☐ G-EEST | BAe Jetstream 31 | 781 | |
| ☐ G-IJYS | BAe Jetstream 31 | 715 | |
| ☐ G-OAKJ | BAe Jetstream 32 | 795 | |
| ☐ G-OEST | BAe Jetstream 32 | 836 | |
| | | | |
| ☐ G-MAJA | BAe Jetstream 41 | 41032 | o/o |
| ☐ G-MAJB | BAe Jetstream 41 | 41018 | o/o |
| ☐ G-MAJC | BAe Jetstream 41 | 41005 | o/o |
| ☐ G-MAJD | BAe Jetstream 41 | 41006 | o/o |
| ☐ G-MAJE | BAe Jetstream 41 | 41007 | |
| ☐ G-MAJF | BAe Jetstream 41 | 41008 | o/o |
| ☐ G-MAJG | BAe Jetstream 41 | 41009 | o/o |
| ☐ G-MAJH | BAe Jetstream 41 | 41010 | o/o |
| ☐ G-MAJI | BAe Jetstream 41 | 41011 | o/o |
| ☐ G-MAJJ | BAe Jetstream 41 | 41024 | o/o |
| ☐ G-MAJL | BAe Jetstream 41 | 41087 | |
| ☐ G-MAJM | BAe Jetstream 41 | 41096 | o/o |
| | | | |
| ☐ G-EMBA | Embraer ERJ-145 | 145016 | o/o |
| ☐ G-EMBB | Embraer ERJ-145 | 145021 | o/o |
| ☐ SE-RAB | Embraer ERJ-135LR | 145453 | |

### EASYJET AIRLINES — EZY

| | | | |
|---|---|---|---|
| ☐ G-EZYB | Boeing 737-3M8 | 1614/24020 | |
| ☐ G-EZYC | Boeing 737-3Y0 | 1691/24462 | |
| ☐ G-EZYD | Boeing 737-3M8 | 1662/24022 | |
| ☐ G-EZYF | Boeing 737-375 | 1395/23708 | |
| ☐ G-EZYG | Boeing 737-33V | 3062/29331 | |
| ☐ G-EZYH | Boeing 737-33V | 3072/29332 | |
| ☐ G-EZYI | Boeing 737-33V | 3084/29333 | |
| ☐ G-EZYJ | Boeing 737-33V | 3089/29334 | |
| ☐ G-EZYK | Boeing 737-33V | 3094/29335 | |
| ☐ G-EZYL | Boeing 737-33V | 3102/29336 | |
| ☐ G-EZYN | Boeing 737-33V | 3114/29338 | Lst EZS |
| ☐ G-EZYO | Boeing 737-33V | 3119/29339 | Lst EZS |
| ☐ G-EZYP | Boeing 737-33V | 3121/29340 | |
| ☐ G-EZYR | Boeing 737-33V | 3125/29341 | |
| ☐ G-EZYS | Boeing 737-33V | 3127/29342 | Lst EZS |
| ☐ G-EZYT | Boeing 737-3Q8 | 2664/26307 | Lsf EZS |
| ☐ HB-IIB | Boeing 737-3M8 | 1689/24024 | Lsf EZS |
| ☐ G-EZJA | Boeing 737-73V | 672/30235 | |
| ☐ G-EZJB | Boeing 737-73V | 715/30236 | |
| ☐ G-EZJC | Boeing 737-73V | 730/30237 | |
| ☐ G-EZJD | Boeing 737-73V | 890/30242 | |
| ☐ G-EZJE | Boeing 737-73V | 913/30238 | |
| ☐ G-EZJF | Boeing 737-73V | 919/30243 | |
| ☐ G-EZJG | Boeing 737-73V | 944/30239 | |
| ☐ G-EZJH | Boeing 737-73V | 974/30240 | |
| ☐ G-EZJI | Boeing 737-73V | 1034/30241 | |
| ☐ G-EZJJ | Boeing 737-73V | 1058/30245 | |
| ☐ G-EZJK | Boeing 737-73V | 1064/30246 | |
| ☐ G-EZJL | Boeing 737-73V | 1066/30247 | |
| ☐ G-EZJM | Boeing 737-73V | 1118/30248 | |
| ☐ G-EZJN | Boeing 737-73V | 1128/30249 | |
| ■ G-EZJO | Boeing 737-73V | 1148/30244 | |
| ☐ G-EZJP | Boeing 737-73V | 1151/32412 | |
| ☐ G-EZJR | Boeing 737-73V | 1202/32413 | |
| ■ G-EZJS | Boeing 737-73V | 1214/32414 | |
| ☐ G-EZJT | Boeing 737-73V | 1260/32415 | |
| ☐ G-EZJU | Boeing 737-73V | 1270/32416 | |
| ☐ G-EZJV | Boeing 737-73V | 32417 | |
| ☐ G-EZJW | Boeing 737-73V | 32418 | |
| ☐ G-EZJX | Boeing 737-73V | 32419 | |
| ■ G-EZJY | Boeing 737-73V | | |
| ☐ G-EZJZ | Boeing 737-73V | | |
| ☐ G- | Boeing 737-73V | | |
| ☐ G-OSLH | Boeing 737-76Q | 1156/30283 | |

### EMERALD AIRWAYS — JEM

| | | | |
|---|---|---|---|
| ☐ G-ATMJ | HS.748 Srs.2A/225 | 1593 | dam |
| ☐ G-AYIM | HS.748 Srs.2A/270 | 1687 | |
| ☐ G-BEJD | HS.748 Srs.1/105 | 1543 | |
| ☐ G-BGMN | HS.748 Srs.2A/347 | 1766 | |
| ☐ G-BGMO | HS.748 Srs.2A/347 | 1767 | |
| ☐ G-BIUV | HS.748 Srs.2A/275LFD | 1701 | |
| ☐ G-BVOU | HS.748 Srs.2A/270 | 1721 | |
| ☐ G-BVOV | HS.748 Srs.2A/372 | 1777 | |
| ☐ G-CLEW | HS.748 Srs.2B/242 | 1647 | |
| ☐ G-OPFW | HS.748 Srs.2A/266 | 1714 | |
| ☐ G-ORAL | HS.748 Srs.2A/334 | 1756 | |
| ☐ G-OSOE | HS.748 Srs.2A/242 | 1697 | |
| ☐ G-OTBA | HS.748 Srs.2A/242 | 1712 | |
| ☐ G-SOEI | HS.748 Srs.2A/242 | 1689 | |
| | | | |
| ☐ G-OBHD | Short SD.3-60 | SH3714 | |
| ☐ G-ROND | Short SD.3-60 | SH3604 | |
| ☐ G-SSWB | Short SD.3-60 | SH3690 | |
| ☐ G-SSWC | Short SD.3-60 | SH3686 | |
| ☐ G-SSWE | Short SD.3-60 | SH3705 | |
| ■ G-SSWM | Short SD.3-60 | SH3648 | |
| ☐ G-SSWO | Short SD.3-60 | SH3609 | |
| ☐ G-SSWR | Short SD.3-60 | SH3670 | |
| ☐ G-SSWX | Short SD.3-60 | SH3715 | |
| ☐ G-SSWA | Short SD.3-30 | SH3042 | |
| ■ G-SSWP | Short SD.3-30 | SH3030 | |

## EUROMANX

| | | |
|---|---|---|
| ☐ PH-RAH | Beech 1900D | UE-31 Opb TRQ |
| ☐ PH-RAR | Beech 1900D | UE-372 Opb TRQ |
| ☐ PH-RAT | Beech 1900D | UE-350 Opb TRQ |

## EUROPEAN AIRWAYS      EAF

| | | |
|---|---|---|
| ☐ G-BYYF | Boeing 737-229C | 576/21738 |
| ☐ G-BZKP | Boeing 737-229C | 401/20915 |
| ☐ G-CEAC | Boeing 737-229 | 360/20911 |
| ☐ G-CEAD | Boeing 737-229 | 421/21137 |
| ☐ G-CEAE | Boeing 737-229 | 365/20912 |
| ☐ G-CEAF | Boeing 737-229 | 358/20910 |
| ☐ G-CEAG | Boeing 737-229 | 420/21136 |
| ☐ G-CEAH | Boeing 737-229 | 418/21135 |
| ☐ G-CEAI | Boeing 737-229 | 431/21176 |
| ☐ G-CEAJ | Boeing 737-229 | 433/21177 |
| | | |
| ☐ G-BDXE | Boeing 747-236B | 321/21350 |
| ☐ G-BDXF | Boeing 747-236B | 323/21351 |
| ☐ G-BDXG | Boeing 747-236B | 328/21536 |
| ☐ G-BDXH | Boeing 747-236B | 365/21635 |
| ☐ G-BDXJ | Boeing 747-236B | 440/21831 |

## EXCEL AIRWAYS      XLA

| | | | |
|---|---|---|---|
| ☐ G-XLAA | Boeing 737-8Q8 | 77/28226 | |
| ☐ G-XLAB | Boeing 737-8Q8 | 160/28218 | |
| ☐ G-XLAC | Boeing 737-81Q | 479/29051 | Lst BSK |
| ☐ G-XLAD | Boeing 737-81Q | 557/29052 | |
| ☐ G-XLAE | Boeing 737-8Q8 | 800/30637 | Lst BER |
| ☐ G-XLAF | Boeing 737-86N | 1083/29883 | Lst AEA |
| ☐ G-XLAG | Boeing 737-86N | 1121/33003 | |
| ☐ G-OXLA | Boeing 737-81Q | 856/30619 | Lsf BSK |
| | | | |
| ☐ TF-ARD | Boeing 757-225 | 74/22211 | Lsf ABD |
| ☐ TF-ARE | Boeing 757-225 | 75/22611 | Lsf ABD |
| ☐ TF-ATD | Boeing 747-267B | 446/21966 | Lsf ABD |
| ☐ TF-ATP | Boeing 767-204ER | 243/24239 | Lsf ABD |
| ☐ TF-ATR | Boeing 767-204ER | 256/24457 | Lsf ABD |

## FLIGHTLINE      FLT

| | | | |
|---|---|---|---|
| ☐ G-BPNT | BAe 146 Srs.300 | E3126 | |
| ☐ G-DEBE | BAe 146 Srs.200 | E2022 | |
| ☐ G-DEFM | BAe 146 Srs.200 | E2016 | |
| ☐ G-FLTA | BAe 146 Srs.200 | E2048 | |
| ☐ G-FLTB | BAe 146 Srs.200 | E2024 | |
| ☐ G-OZRH | BAe 146 Srs.200 | E2047 | Lst CTN |
| ☐ G-TBIC | BAe 146 Srs.200 | E2025 | |
| ☐ G-OFLT | Embraer EMB.110P1 | 110211 | |

## FLYBE. BRITISH EUROPEAN      BEE

| | | | |
|---|---|---|---|
| ☐ G-JEAJ | BAe 146 Srs.200 | E2099 | |
| ☐ G-JEAK | BAe 146 Srs.200 | E2103 | Opb AFR |
| ☐ G-JEAM | BAe 146 Srs.300 | E3128 | Opb AFR |
| ☐ G-JEAS | BAe 146 Srs.200 | E2020 | |
| ☐ G-JEAT | BAe 146 Srs.100 | E1071 | Opb AFR |
| ☐ G-JEAU | BAe 146 Srs.100 | E1035 | |
| ☐ G-JEAV | BAe 146 Srs.200 | E2064 | |
| ☐ G-JEAW | BAe 146 Srs.200 | E2059 | |
| ☐ G-JEAX | BAe 146 Srs.200 | E2136 | |
| ☐ G-JEAY | BAe 146 Srs.200 | E2138 | |
| ☐ G-JEBA | BAe 146 Srs.300 | E3181 | Opb AFR |
| ☐ G-JEBB | BAe 146 Srs.300 | E3185 | Opb AFR |
| ☐ G-JEBC | BAe 146 Srs.300 | E3189 | |
| ☐ G-JEBD | BAe 146 Srs.300 | E3191 | |
| ☐ G-JEBE | BAe 146 Srs.300 | E3206 | |
| ☐ G- | BAe 146 Srs.200 | E2062 | o/o |
| ☐ G- | BAe 146 Srs.200 | E2074 | o/o |
| | | | |
| ☐ G-JEDC | DHC-8Q-311A | 532 | |
| ☐ G-JEDD | DHC-8Q-311A | 533 | |
| ☐ G-JEDE | DHC-8Q-311A | 534 | |
| ☐ G-JEDF | DHC-8Q-311B | 548 | |

| | | | |
|---|---|---|---|
| ☐ G-JEDI | DHC-8-402Q | 4052 | |
| ☐ G-JEDJ | DHC-8-402Q | 4058 | |
| ☒ G-JEDK | DHC-8-402Q | 4065 | |
| ☐ G-JEDL | DHC-8-402Q | 4067 | |
| ☐ G-JEDX | DHC-8Q-201B | 541 | |
| ☐ G-JEDY | DHC-8Q-201B | 542 | |
| ☐ G-JEDZ | DHC-8Q-201B | 547 | |
| | | | |
| ☐ G-JECA | Canadair RJ-200 | 7345 | Opf AFR |
| ☐ G-JECB | Canadair RJ-200 | 7393 | |
| ☐ G-JECC | Canadair RJ-200 | 7434 | |
| ☐ G-JECD | Canadair RJ-200 | 7469 | Opf AFR |

## GB AIRWAYS      GBL

| | | | |
|---|---|---|---|
| ☐ G-TTIA | Airbus A321-231 | 1428 | |
| ☐ G-TTIB | Airbus A321-231 | 1433 | |
| ☐ G-TTIC | Airbus A321-231 | 1869 | |
| | | | |
| ■ G-TTOA | Airbus A320-231 | 1215 | |
| ☐ G-TTOB | Airbus A320-232 | 1687 | |
| ☐ G-TTOC | Airbus A320-232 | 1715 | |
| ☐ G-TTOD | Airbus A320-232 | 1723 | |
| ☐ G-TTOE | Airbus A320-232 | 1754 | o/o |
| ☐ G-TTOF | Airbus A320-232 | 1918 | |
| ☐ G-TTOG | Airbus A320-232 | 1969 | o/o |
| ☐ G-TTOH | Airbus A320-232 | 1993 | o/o |
| ☐ G-TTOI | Airbus A320-232 | | o/o |
| | | | |
| ☐ G-OGBB | Boeing 737-34S | 2983/29108 | For GIA |
| ☐ G-OGBC | Boeing 737-34S | 3001/29109 | For GIA |
| ☐ G-OGBD | Boeing 737-3L9 | 2688/27833 | |
| ☐ G-OGBE | Boeing 737-3L9 | 2692/27834 | |

## GLOBAL SUPPLY SYSTEM      GSS

| | | | |
|---|---|---|---|
| ☐ G-GSSA | Boeing 747-47UF | 1213/29256 | Opb GTI |
| ☐ G-GSSB | Boeing 747-47UF | 1165/29252 | Opb GTI |

## GO FLY      EZY

| | | |
|---|---|---|
| ☐ G-IGOA | Boeing 737-3Y0 | 1853/24678 |
| ☐ G-IGOB | Boeing 737-36Q | 2883/28660 |
| ☐ G-IGOC | Boeing 737-3Y0 | 1811/24546 |
| ☐ G-IGOE | Boeing 737-3Y0 | 1813/24547 |
| ☐ G-IGOF | Boeing 737-3Q8 | 1846/24698 |
| ☐ G-IGOG | Boeing 737-3Y0 | 1580/23927 |
| ☐ G-IGOH | Boeing 737-3Y0 | 1562/23926 |
| ☐ G-IGOI | Boeing 737-33A | 1669/24092 |
| ☐ G-IGOJ | Boeing 737-36N | 3082/28872 |
| ☐ G-IGOK | Boeing 737-36N | 3107/28594 |
| ☐ G-IGOL | Boeing 737-36N | 3112/28596 |
| ☐ G-IGOM | Boeing 737-36N | 3115/28599 |
| ☐ G-IGOO | Boeing 737-36N | 2862/28557 |
| ☐ G-IGOP | Boeing 737-36N | 3118/28602 |
| ☐ G-IGOR | Boeing 737-36N | 3124/28606 |
| ☐ G-IGOS | Boeing 737-3L9 | 2587/27336 |
| ☐ G-IGOT | Boeing 737-3L9 | 1815/24571 |
| ☐ G-IGOU | Boeing 737-3L9 | 2594/27337 |
| ☐ G-IGOV | Boeing 737-3M8 | 2005/25017 |
| ☐ G-IGOW | Boeing 737-3Y0 | 1540/23923 |
| ☐ G-IGOX | Boeing 737-3L9 | 1600/24219 |
| ☐ G-IGOY | Boeing 737-36N | 3010/28570 |
| ☐ G-IGOZ | Boeing 737-3Q8 | 1886/24699 |
| ☐ G-ODUS | Boeing 737-36Q | 2880/28659 |
| ☐ G-OFRA | Boeing 737-36Q | 3023/29327 |
| ☐ G-OHAJ | Boeing 737-36Q | 3035/29141 |
| ☐ G-OMUC | Boeing 737-36Q | 3047/29405 |

## HIGHLAND AIRWAYS      HWY

| | | | |
|---|---|---|---|
| ☐ G-BTXG | BAe Jetstream 31 | 719 | |
| ☐ G-IONA | ATR 42-300 | 017 | |
| ☐ G-JURA | BAe Jetstream 31 | 772 | |
| ☐ G-UIST | BAe Jetstream 31 | 750 | |
| ☐ SE-KCS | SAAB SF.340A | 066 | Lsf SWR |

## JET 2

| | | | |
|---|---|---|---|
| ☐ G-CELS | Boeing 737-377 | 1294/23660 | Opb EXS |
| ☐ G- | Boeing 737-377 | | Opb EXS |

## JMC AIRLINES JMC

| | | | |
|---|---|---|---|
| ☐ G-BVYA | Airbus A320-231 | 0354 | Lst TCW |
| ☐ G-BVYB | Airbus A320-231 | 0357 | Lst TCW |
| ☐ G-BVYC | Airbus A320-231 | 0411 | Lst TCW |
| ☐ G-BXKA | Airbus A320-214 | 0714 | Lst RYN |
| ☐ G-BXKB | Airbus A320-214 | 0716 | |
| ☐ G-BXKC | Airbus A320-214 | 0730 | Lst RYN |
| ☐ G-BXKD | Airbus A320-214 | 0735 | |
| ☐ G-CVYD | Airbus A320-231 | 0393 | |
| ☐ G-CVYE | Airbus A320-231 | 0394 | |
| ☐ G-CVYG | Airbus A320-231 | 0443 | |
| | | | |
| ☐ G-FCLA | Boeing 757-28A | 738/27621 | |
| ☐ G-FCLB | Boeing 757-28A | 749/28164 | |
| ☐ G-FCLC | Boeing 757-28A | 756/28166 | |
| ☐ G-FCLD | Boeing 757-25F | 752/28718 | |
| ☐ G-FCLE | Boeing 757-28A | 805/28171 | |
| ☐ G-FCLF | Boeing 757-28A | 858/28835 | |
| ☐ G-FCLG | Boeing 757-28A | 208/24367 | |
| ■ G-FCLH | Boeing 757-28A | 676/26274 | |
| ☐ G-FCLI | Boeing 757-28A | 672/26275 | |
| ☐ G-FCLJ | Boeing 757-2Y0 | 555/26160 | |
| ☐ G-FCLK | Boeing 757-2Y0 | 557/26161 | |
| ☐ G-JMAA | Boeing 757-3CQ | 960/32241 | |
| ☐ G-JMAB | Boeing 757-3CQ | 963/32242 | |
| ☐ G-JMCD | Boeing 757-25F | 928/30757 | |
| ☐ G-JMCE | Boeing 757-25F | 932/30758 | |
| ☐ G-JMCF | Boeing 757-28A | 226/24369 | |
| ☐ G-JMCG | Boeing 757-2G5 | 671/26278 | |
| | | | |
| ☐ G-OJMB | Airbus A330-243 | 427 | |
| ☐ G-OJMC | Airbus A330-243 | 456 | |

To be renamed **Thomas Cook Airlines** in 2003

## KEENAIR CHARTER JFK

| | | |
|---|---|---|
| ☐ G-BGYT | Embraer EMB.110P1 | 110234 |
| ☐ G-FLTY | Embraer EMB.110P1 | 110215 |
| ☐ G-TABS | Embraer EMB.110P1 | 110212 |

## KLM CITYHOPPER UK

| | | |
|---|---|---|
| ☐ G-UKTB | Fokker 50 | 20247 |
| ☐ G-UKTC | Fokker 50 | 20249 |
| ☐ G-UKTD | Fokker 50 | 20256 |
| ☐ G-UKTE | Fokker 50 | 20270 |
| ☐ G-UKTF | Fokker 50 | 20271 |
| ☐ G-UKTG | Fokker 50 | 20276 |
| ☐ G-UKTH | Fokker 50 | 20277 |
| ☐ G-UKTI | Fokker 50 | 20279 |
| | | |
| ☐ G-UKFA | Fokker 100 | 11246 |
| ☐ G-UKFB | Fokker 100 | 11247 |
| ☐ G-UKFC | Fokker 100 | 11263 |
| ☐ G-UKFD | Fokker 100 | 11259 |
| ☐ G-UKFE | Fokker 100 | 11260 |
| ☐ G-UKFF | Fokker 100 | 11274 |
| ☐ G-UKFG | Fokker 100 | 11275 |
| ☐ G-UKFH | Fokker 100 | 11277 |
| ☐ G-UKFI | Fokker 100 | 11279 |
| ☐ G-UKFJ | Fokker 100 | 11248 |
| ☐ G-UKFK | Fokker 100 | 11249 |
| ☐ G-UKFM | Fokker 100 | 11269 |
| ☐ G-UKFN | Fokker 100 | 11270 |
| ☐ G-UKFO | Fokker 100 | 11271 |
| ☐ G-UKFR | Fokker 100 | 11273 |
| | | |
| ☐ G-UKTK | ATR 72-202 | 519 |
| ☐ G-UKTL | ATR 72-202 | 523 |
| ☐ G-UKTM | ATR 72-202 | 508 |
| ☐ G-UKTN | ATR 72-202 | 496 |

## MAERSK AIR MSK

| | | | |
|---|---|---|---|
| ☐ G-MSKK | Canadair RJ-200 | 7226 | |
| ☐ G-MSKL | Canadair RJ-200 | 7247 | Lst DAN |
| ☐ G-MSKM | Canadair RJ-200 | 7248 | Lst DAN |
| ☐ G-MSKN | Canadair RJ-200 | 7283 | Lst DAN |
| ☐ G-MSKR | Canadair RJ-200 | 7373 | |
| ☐ G-MSKS | Canadair RJ-200 | 7386 | |
| ☐ G-MSKT | Canadair RJ-200 | 7436 | |
| ☐ G-MSKU | Canadair RJ-200 | 7442 | |
| ☐ G-MRSG | Canadair RJ-700 | 10052 | |
| ☐ G-MRSH | Canadair RJ-700 | 10048 | |
| ☐ G-MRSI | Canadair RJ-700 | 10039 | |
| ☐ G-MRSJ | Canadair RJ-700 | 10029 | |
| ☐ G-MRSK | Canadair RJ-700 | 10028 | |

## MONARCH AIRLINES MON

| | | | |
|---|---|---|---|
| ☐ G-MARA | Airbus A321-231 | 0983 | |
| ☐ G-MONX | Airbus A320-212 | 0392 | |
| ☐ G-MPCD | Airbus A320-212 | 0379 | |
| ☐ G-OJEG | Airbus A321-231 | 1015 | |
| ☐ G-OZBB | Airbus A320-212 | 0389 | |
| ☐ G-OZBD | Airbus A321-231 | 1202 | |
| ☐ G-OZBE | Airbus A321-231 | 1707 | |
| ☐ G-OZBF | Airbus A321-231 | 1763 | |
| ☐ G- | Airbus A321-231 | 1941 | o/o |
| ☐ G- | Airbus A321-231 | | o/o |
| | | | |
| ☐ EI-MON | Boeing 757-2Y0 | 472/26151 | std |
| ☐ G-DAJB | Boeing 757-2T7ER | 125/23770 | |
| ☐ G-MONB | Boeing 757-2T7ER | 15/22780 | |
| ☐ G-MONC | Boeing 757-2T7ER | 18/22781 | |
| ☐ G-MOND | Boeing 757-2T7 | 19/22960 | |
| ☐ G-MONE | Boeing 757-2T7ER | 56/23293 | |
| ☐ G-MONJ | Boeing 757-2T7ER | 170/24104 | |
| ■ G-MONK | Boeing 757-2T7ER | 172/24105 | |
| | | | |
| ■ G-EOMA | Airbus A330-242 | 265 | |
| ☐ G-MAJS | Airbus A300B4-605R | 604 | |
| ☐ G-MONR | Airbus A300B4-605R | 540 | |
| ☐ G-MONS | Airbus A300B4-605R | 556 | |
| ☐ G-OJMR | Airbus A300B4-605R | 605 | |
| ☐ G-SMAN | Airbus A330-242 | 261 | |

## MYTRAVEL AIRWAYS MYT

| | | | |
|---|---|---|---|
| ☐ C-FTDA | Airbus A320-212 | 0795 | Lsf SSV |
| ☐ C-GTDB | Airbus A320-212 | 0525 | Lsf SSV |
| ☐ C-GTDK | Airbus A320-231 | 0338 | Lsf SSV |
| ☐ C-GTDL | Airbus A320-231 | 0476 | Lsf SSV |
| ☐ G-BYTH | Airbus A320-231 | 0429 | |
| ☐ G-CRPH | Airbus A320-231 | 0424 | |
| ☐ G-DACR | Airbus A320-212 | 0349 | Lst VKG |
| ☐ G-DHJH | Airbus A321-211 | 1238 | |
| ☐ G-DJAR | Airbus A320-231 | 0164 | |
| ☐ G-DRVE | Airbus A320-212 | 0221 | Lst VKG |
| ☐ G-HBAP | Airbus A320-212 | 0294 | Lst VKG |
| ☐ G-JANM | Airbus A320-212 | 0301 | Lst VKG |
| ☐ G-JDFW | Airbus A320-212 | 0299 | |
| ☐ G-JOEM | Airbus A320-231 | 0449 | |
| ☐ G-JSJX | Airbus A321-211 | 0808 | |
| ☐ G-NIKO | Airbus A321-211 | 1250 | |
| ☐ G-RDVE | Airbus A320-231 | 0163 | |
| ☐ G-RRJE | Airbus A320-212 | 0222 | Lst VKG |
| ☐ G-SSAS | Airbus A320-231 | 0230 | |
| ☐ G-SUEE | Airbus A320-231 | 0363 | |
| ☐ G-TICL | Airbus A320-231 | 0169 | |
| ☐ G-TMDP | Airbus A320-231 | 0168 | |
| ☐ G-TPTT | Airbus A320-212 | 0348 | Lst VKG |
| ☐ G-VCED | Airbus A320-231 | 0193 | |
| ☐ G-VOLH | Airbus A321-211 | 0823 | |
| ☐ G-YJBM | Airbus A320-231 | 0362 | |
| ☐ G- | Airbus A320-214 | 1942 | o/o |
| ☐ G- | Airbus A320-214 | | o/o |
| ☐ G- | Airbus A320-214 | | o/o |
| ☐ G- | Airbus A320-214 | | o/o |

| Reg | Type | c/n | Notes |
|---|---|---|---|
| G- | Airbus A320-214 | | o/o |
| G- | Airbus A320-214 | | o/o |
| G- | Airbus A321-211 | 1887 | o/o |
| G- | Airbus A321-211 | 1960 | o/o |
| G- | Airbus A321-211 | | o/o |
| G- | Airbus A321-211 | | o/o |
| G- | Airbus A320-214 | | o/o |
| G- | Airbus A320-214 | | o/o |
| G- | Airbus A320-214 | | o/o |
| G- | Airbus A320-214 | | o/o |
| G- | Airbus A320-214 | | o/o |
| G- | Airbus A320-214 | | o/o |
| G-MDBD | Airbus A330-243 | 266 | |
| G-MLJL | Airbus A330-243 | 254 | |
| G-MOJO | Airbus A330-243 | 301 | |
| OY-VKF | Airbus A330-243 | 309 | Lsf VKG |
| OY-VKG | Airbus A330-343X | 349 | Lst VKG |
| OY-VKH | Airbus A330-343X | 356 | Lst VKG |
| OY-VKI | Airbus A330-343X | 357 | LstVKG |
| G-CCMY | Boeing 757-23A | 250/24528 | |
| G-JALC | Boeing 757-225 | 5/22194 | |
| G-LCRC | Boeing 757-23AER | 259/24636 | std |
| G-MCEA | Boeing 757-225 | 20/22200 | |
| G-PIDS | Boeing 757-225 | 6/22195 | |
| G-RJGR | Boeing 757-225 | 8/22197 | |
| G-WJAN | Boeing 757-21KER | 746/28674 | |
| G-BYDA | Douglas DC-10-30 | 260/46990 | |
| G-DAJC | Boeing 767-31KER | 533/27206 | |
| G-DIMB | Boeing 767-31KER | 637/28865 | |
| G-DPSP | Douglas DC-10-10 | 285/46646 | |
| G-SJMC | Boeing 767-31KER | 528/27205 | |
| G-TAOS | Douglas DC-10-10 | 318/47832 | |
| G-TDTW | Douglas DC-10-10 | 252/46983 | |

## MYTRAVEL LITE — MYL

| Reg | Type | c/n | Notes |
|---|---|---|---|
| G-JOEM | Airbus A320-231 | 0449 | |
| G-SSAS | Airbus A320-231 | 0230 | |

## PALMAIR

| Reg | Type | c/n | Notes |
|---|---|---|---|
| G-CEAC | Boeing 737-229 | 360/20911 | Lsf EAF |

## REED AVIATION — RAV

| Reg | Type | c/n | Notes |
|---|---|---|---|
| G-BEJD | HS.748 Srs.1/105 | 1543 | Opb JEM |
| G-ORAL | HS.748 Srs.2A/334 | 1756 | Opb JEM |

## SCOTAIRWAYS — SAY

| Reg | Type | c/n | Notes |
|---|---|---|---|
| G-BWIR | Dornier 328-100 | 3023 | |
| G-BWWT | Dornier 328-110 | 3022 | |
| G-BYHG | Dornier 328-110 | 3098 | |
| G-BYMK | Dornier 328-110 | 3062 | |
| G-BYML | Dornier 328-110 | 3069 | |
| G-BYTY | Dornier 328-120 | 3104 | |
| G-BZIF | Dornier 328-110 | 3053 | |

## SKYDRIFT AIRCHARTER — DFT

| Reg | Type | c/n | Notes |
|---|---|---|---|
| G-TABS | Embraer EMB.110P1 | 110212 | Lst JFK |
| PH-DYM | SA.227AC Metro III | AC-523 | |

## THOMAS COOK AIRLINES

See **JMC Airlines**

## TITAN AIRWAYS — AWC

| Reg | Type | c/n | Notes |
|---|---|---|---|
| G-BUPS | ATR 42-300 | 109 | |
| G-ZAPJ | ATR 42-310 | 113 | |
| G-ZAPK | BAe 146 Srs.200QC | E2148 | |
| G-ZAPL | BAe 146 Srs.200 | E2030 | Lst BCY |
| G-ZAPM | Boeing 737-33A | 2608/27285 | |
| G-ZAPN | BAe 146 Srs.200QT | E2119 | |
| G-ZAPO | BAe 146 Srs.200QC | E2176 | |

## VIRGIN ATLANTIC AIRWAYS — VIR

| Reg | Type | c/n | Notes |
|---|---|---|---|
| G-VAEL | Airbus A340-311 | 015 | |
| G-VBUS | Airbus A340-311 | 013 | |
| G-VELD | Airbus A340-313X | 214 | |
| G-VFAR | Airbus A340-313X | 225 | |
| G-VFLY | Airbus A340-311 | 058 | |
| G-VHOL | Airbus A340-311 | 002 | |
| G-VSEA | Airbus A340-311 | 003 | |
| G-VSKY | Airbus A340-311 | 016 | |
| G-VSUN | Airbus A340-311 | 114 | |
| G-VATL | Airbus A340-642 | 376 | |
| G-VEIL | Airbus A340-642 | | o/o |
| G-VFOX | Airbus A340-642 | 449 | |
| G-VGOA | Airbus A340-642 | 371 | |
| G-VMEG | Airbus A340-642 | 391 | |
| G-VOGE | Airbus A340-642 | 416 | |
| G-VSHY | Airbus A340-642 | 383 | |
| G-VSSH | Airbus A340-642 | | o/o |
| G- | Airbus A340-642 | 431 | o/o |
| G- | Airbus A340-642 | | o/o |
| G-VAST | Boeing 747-41R | 1117/28757 | |
| G-VBEE | Boeing 747-219B | 527/22723 | |
| G-VBIG | Boeing 747-4Q8 | 1081/26255 | |
| G-VCAT | Boeing 747-267B | 566/22872 | Lsf CPA |
| G-VFAB | Boeing 747-4Q8 | 1028/24958 | |
| G-VGAL | Boeing 747-443 | 1272/32337 | |
| G-VHOT | Boeing 747-4Q8 | 1043/26326 | |
| G-VIBE | Boeing 747-219B | 568/22791 | |
| G-VLIP | Boeing 747-443 | 1274/32338 | |
| G-VPUF | Boeing 747-219B | 563/22725 | |
| G-VROM | Boeing 747-443 | 1275/32339 | |
| G-VROS | Boeing 747-443 | 1268/30885 | |
| G-VROY | Boeing 747-443 | 1277/32340 | |
| G-VRUM | Boeing 747-267B | 582/23048 | Lsf CPA |
| G-VTOP | Boeing 747-4Q8 | 1100/28194 | |
| G-VWOW | Boeing 747-41R | 1287/32745 | |
| G-VXLG | Boeing 747-41R | 1177/29406 | |
| G-VZZZ | Boeing 747-219B | 523/22722 | |
| G- | Boeing 747-41R | | o/o |
| TF-ATW | Boeing 747-219B | 528/22724 | Opb ABD |

# HA - HUNGARY

## FARNAIR HUNGARY — FAH

| Reg | Type | c/n | Notes |
|---|---|---|---|
| HA-LAC | LET L-410UVP-E3 | 871828 | |
| HA-LAD | LET L-410UVP-E8A | 902516 | |
| HA-LAE | LET L-410UVP-E8A | 902517 | Lst BST |
| HA-LAQ | LET L-410UVP-E4 | 841332 | |
| HA-LAR | LET L-410UVP-E4 | 871923 | Lst LPS |
| HA-YFC | LET L-410FG | 851528 | |
| HA-FAB | F.27 Friendship 500 | 10370 | Lsf FAT |

## HUNAIR HUNGARIAN AIRLINES — HUV

| Reg | Type | c/n | Notes |
|---|---|---|---|
| HA-TCB | Ilyushin Il-76TD | 1013408257 | |

## HUNGARIAN UKRAINIAN HEAVYLIFT — HUK

| Reg | Type | c/n | Notes |
|---|---|---|---|
| HA-TCI | Ilyushin Il-76T | 083410300 | |
| HA-TCJ | Ilyushin Il-76TD | 0083484527 | |

## MALEV – HUNGARIAN AIRLINES — MAH

| Reg | Type | c/n | Notes |
|---|---|---|---|
| HA-LED | Boeing 737-3Y0 | 2021/24909 | |
| HA-LEF | Boeing 737-3Y0 | 2054/24914 | |
| HA-LEG | Boeing 737-3Y0 | 2066/24916 | |
| HA-LEJ | Boeing 737-3Q8 | 2635/26303 | |
| HA-LEN | Boeing 737-4Y0 | 2352/26069 | |
| HA-LEO | Boeing 737-4Y0 | 2361/26071 | |
| HA-LEP | Boeing 737-5K5 | 1848/24776 | |
| HA-LER | Boeing 737-5K5 | 1966/24926 | |
| HA-LES | Boeing 737-3Y0 | 1829/24676 | |
| HA-LET | Boeing 737-3Y0 | 2030/24910 | |

| | | | |
|---|---|---|---|
| ☐ HA-LEU | Boeing 737-4Y0 | 2256/25190 | |
| ☐ HA-LEV | Boeing 737-4Y0 | 1988/24904 | |
| ☐ HA-LEX | Boeing 737-3Y0 | 1973/24902 | |
| ☐ HA-LEY | Boeing 737-4Y0 | 1824/24682 | |
| ☐ HA-LEZ | Boeing 737-4Q8 | 2482/26290 | |
| ☐ HA-LOA | Boeing 737-7Q8 | 28254 | |
| ☐ HA-LOB | Boeing 737-7Q8 | 1264/29346 | |
| ☐ HA-LOC | Boeing 737-7Q8 | 32797 | o/o |
| ☐ HA- | Boeing 737-6Q8 | | o/o |
| ☐ HA- | Boeing 737-8Q8 | | o/o |
| ☐ HA- | Boeing 737-8Q8 | | o/o |
| | | | |
| ☐ HA-LMA | Fokker 70 | 11564 | |
| ☐ HA-LMB | Fokker 70 | 11565 | |
| ☐ HA-LMC | Fokker 70 | 11569 | |
| ☐ HA-LMD | Fokker 70 | 11563 | |
| ☐ HA-LME | Fokker 70 | 11575 | |
| ☐ HA-LMF | Fokker 70 | 11571 | |
| | | | |
| ☐ HA-LHA | Boeing 767-27GER | 475/27048 | |
| ☐ HA-LHB | Boeing 767-27GER | 482/27049 | |
| | | | |
| ☐ HA-LNA | Canadair RJ-200 | 7676 | |
| ☐ HA-LNB | Canadair RJ-200 | 7686 | |
| ☐ HA-LNX | Canadair RJ-200 | 7032 | |

### TRAVEL SERVICE HUNGARY — TVL

| | | | |
|---|---|---|---|
| ☐ HA-LKA | Boeing 737-4Y0 | 2033/24911 | Lsf TVS |
| ☐ HA-LKB | Boeing 737-4Y0 | 1647/23870 | Lsf TVS |

## HB - SWITZERLAND & LICHTENSTEIN

### ASTRA AIRLINES — AWG

| | | | |
|---|---|---|---|
| ☐ HB- | Douglas DC-10-30ER | 352/48285 | o/o |
| ☐ 9G-PHN | Douglas DC-10-30 | 84/46554 | std |
| ☐ V2-SKY | Douglas DC-10-15 | 358/48275 | Lst MLI |

### BELAIR — BHP

| | | | |
|---|---|---|---|
| ☐ HB-IHR | Boeing 757-2Q8ER | 919/29379 | |
| ☐ HB-IHS | Boeing 757-2Q8ER | 922/30394 | |
| ☐ HB-ISE | Boeing 767-3Q8ER | 655/27600 | |

### EASYJET SWITZERLAND — EZS

| | | | |
|---|---|---|---|
| ☐ HB-IIB | Boeing 737-3M8 | 1689/24024 | |
| ☐ HB-IIE | Boeing 737-3Q8 | 2664/26307 | Lst EZY |
| ☐ HB-III | Boeing 737-33V | 3114/29338 | Lsf EZY |
| ☐ HB-IIJ | Boeing 737-33V | 3127/29342 | Lsf EZY |
| ☐ HB-IIK | Boeing 737-33V | 3113/29337 | |
| ☐ HB-IIT | Boeing 737-33V | 3119/29339 | Lsf EZY |

### EDELWEISS AIR — EDW

| | | | |
|---|---|---|---|
| ☐ HB-IHX | Airbus A320-214 | 0942 | |
| ☐ HB-IHY | Airbus A320-214 | 0947 | |
| ☐ HB-IHZ | Airbus A320-214 | 1026 | |
| ☐ HB-IQZ | Airbus A330-243 | 369 | |

### FARNAIR SWITZERLAND — FAT

| | | | |
|---|---|---|---|
| ☐ HB-ILJ | F.27 Friendship 500 | 10596 | |
| ☐ HB-ILQ | F.27 Friendship 500 | 10528 | |
| ☐ HB-ISQ | F.27 Friendship 500 | 10506 | |
| ☐ HB-ISY | F.27 Friendship 500 | 10370 | Lst FAH |
| ☐ HB-ITQ | F.27 Friendship 400 | 10295 | Lst MNL |
| ☐ HB-ITY | F.27 Friendship 500 | 10448 | |
| ☐ HB-IVQ | F.27 Friendship 500 | 10425 | |
| ☐ PH-JLN | F.27 Friendship 500 | 10449 | Lst EPA |
| | | | |
| ☐ HB-AFC | ATR 42-320 | 087 | |
| ☐ HB-AFD | ATR 42-320 | 121 | |
| ☐ HB-AFF | ATR-42-320 | 264 | |
| ☐ HB-AFG | ATR 42-320F | 108 | |

### INTERSKY — ISK

| | | | |
|---|---|---|---|
| ☐ OE-LSB | DHC-8Q-314 | 525 | Lsf RTL |

### ODETTE AIRWAYS — OAW

| | | | |
|---|---|---|---|
| ☐ HB-INV | McDD MD-83 | 1349/49359 | |

### PRIVATAIR — PTI

| | | | |
|---|---|---|---|
| ☐ D- | Airbus A319-131 | 1947 | o/o |
| ☐ D- | Airbus A319-131 | 1955 | o/o |
| | | | |
| ☐ HB-IEE | Boeing 757-23A | 249/24527 | |
| ☐ HB-IIO | Boeing 737-7AK | 241/29865 | [BBJ] |
| ☐ HB-IIP | Boeing 737-7AK | 408/29866 | [BBJ] |
| ☐ HB-IIQ | Boeing 737-7CN | 451/30752 | [BBJ] |

### SWISS INTERNATIONAL AIR LINES

| | | | |
|---|---|---|---|
| ☐ HB-IPR | Airbus A319-112 | 1018 | |
| ☐ HB-IPS | Airbus A319-112 | 0734 | |
| ☐ HB-IPT | Airbus A319-112 | 0727 | |
| ☐ HB-IPU | Airbus A319-112 | 0713 | |
| ☐ HB-IPV | Airbus A319-112 | 0578 | |
| ☐ HB-IPX | Airbus A319-112 | 0612 | |
| ☐ HB-IPY | Airbus A319-112 | 0621 | |
| | | | |
| ☐ HB-IJI | Airbus A320-214 | 0577 | |
| ☐ HB-IJJ | Airbus A320-214 | 0585 | |
| ☐ HB-IJK | Airbus A320-214 | 0596 | |
| ☐ HB-IJL | Airbus A320-214 | 0603 | |
| ☐ HB-IJM | Airbus A320-214 | 0635 | |
| ☐ HB-IJN | Airbus A320-214 | 0643 | |
| ☐ HB-IJO | Airbus A320-214 | 0673 | |
| ☐ HB-IJP | Airbus A320-214 | 0681 | |
| ☐ HB-IJQ | Airbus A320-214 | 0701 | |
| ☐ HB-IJR | Airbus A320-214 | 0703 | |
| ☐ HB-IJS | Airbus A320-214 | 0782 | |
| ☐ HB-IJT | Airbus A320-214 | 0870 | |
| | | | |
| ☐ HB-IOA | Airbus A321-111 | 0517 | |
| ☐ HB-IOB | Airbus A321-111 | 0519 | |
| ☐ HB-IOC | Airbus A321-111 | 0520 | |
| ☐ HB-IOH | Airbus A321-111 | 0664 | |
| ☐ HB-IOI | Airbus A321-111 | 0827 | |
| ☐ HB-IOJ | Airbus A321-111 | 0891 | |
| ☐ HB-IOK | Airbus A321-111 | 0987 | |
| ☐ HB-IOL | Airbus A321-111 | 1144 | |
| | | | |
| ☐ HB-IQB | Airbus A330-223 | 240 | |
| ☐ HB-IQC | Airbus A330-223 | 249 | |
| ☐ HB-IQD | Airbus A330-223 | 253 | |
| ☐ HB-IQE | Airbus A330-223 | 255 | |
| ☐ HB-IQF | Airbus A330-223 | 262 | |
| ☐ HB-IQG | Airbus A330-223 | 275 | |
| ☐ HB-IQH | Airbus A330-223 | 288 | |
| ☐ HB-IQI | Airbus A330-223 | 291 | |
| ☐ HB-IQJ | Airbus A330-223 | 294 | |
| ☐ HB-IQK | Airbus A330-223 | 299 | |
| ☐ HB-IQO | Airbus A330-223 | 343 | |
| ☐ HB-IQP | Airbus A330-223 | 366 | |
| | | | |
| ☐ HB-JMA | Airbus A340-313X | 538 | o/o |
| ☐ HB-JMB | Airbus A340-313X | 545 | o/o |
| ☐ HB-JMC | Airbus A340-313X | 546 | o/o |
| ☐ HB- | Airbus A340-313X | 556 | o/o |
| ☐ HB- | Airbus A340-313X | 559 | o/o |
| ☐ HB- | Airbus A340-313X | 561 | o/o |
| ☐ HB- | Airbus A340-313X | 562 | o/o |
| | | | |
| ☐ HB-IXG | Avro RJ85 | E2231 | |
| ☐ HB-IXH | Avro RJ85 | E2233 | |
| ☐ HB-IXK | Avro RJ85 | E2235 | |
| ☐ HB-IXN | Avro RJ100 | E3286 | |
| ☐ HB-IXO | Avro RJ100 | E3284 | |

| | | | |
|---|---|---|---|
| ☐ HB-IXP | Avro RJ100 | E3283 | |
| ☐ HB-IXQ | Avro RJ100 | E3282 | |
| ☐ HB-IXR | Avro RJ100 | E3281 | |
| ☐ HB-IXS | Avro RJ100 | E3280 | |
| ☐ HB-IXT | Avro RJ100 | E3259 | |
| ☐ HB-IXU | Avro RJ100 | E3276 | |
| ☐ HB-IXV | Avro RJ100 | E3274 | |
| ☐ HB-IXW | Avro RJ100 | E3272 | |
| ☐ HB-IXX | Avro RJ100 | E3262 | |
| ☐ HB-IXY | Avro RJ100 | E3359 | |
| ☐ HB-IYX | Avro RJ100 | E3357 | |
| ☐ HB-IYY | Avro RJ100 | E3339 | |
| ☐ HB-IYZ | Avro RJ100 | E3338 | |
| | | | |
| ☐ HB-JAA | Embraer ERJ-145 | 145232 | |
| ☐ HB-JAB | Embraer ERJ-145 | 145240 | |
| ☐ HB-JAC | Embraer ERJ-145 | 145255 | |
| ☐ HB-JAD | Embraer ERJ-145 | 145269 | |
| ☐ HB-JAE | Embraer ERJ-145 | 145281 | |
| ☐ HB-JAF | Embraer ERJ-145 | 145313 | |
| ☐ HB-JAG | Embraer ERJ-145 | 145321 | |
| ☐ HB-JAH | Embraer ERJ-145 | 145341 | |
| ☐ HB-JAI | Embraer ERJ-145 | 145351 | |
| ☐ HB-JAJ | Embraer ERJ-145 | 145382 | |
| ☐ HB-JAK | Embraer ERJ-145 | 145387 | |
| ☐ HB-JAL | Embraer ERJ-145 | 145400 | |
| ☐ HB-JAM | Embraer ERJ-145 | 145420 | |
| ☐ HB-JAN | Embraer ERJ-145 | 145434 | |
| ☐ HB-JAO | Embraer ERJ-145 | 145456 | |
| ☐ HB-JAP | Embraer ERJ-145 | 145475 | |
| ☐ HB-JAQ | Embraer ERJ-145 | 145498 | |
| ☐ HB-JAR | Embraer ERJ-145 | 145510 | |
| ☐ HB-JAS | Embraer ERJ-145 | 145559 | |
| ☐ HB-JAT | Embraer ERJ-145 | 145564 | |
| ☐ HB-JAU | Embraer ERJ-145 | 145570 | |
| ☐ HB-JAV | Embraer ERJ-145 | 145574 | |
| ☐ HB-JAW | Embraer ERJ-145 | 145580 | |
| ☐ HB-JAX | Embraer ERJ-145 | 145588 | |
| ☐ HB-JAY | Embraer ERJ-145 | 145601 | |
| | | | |
| ☐ HB-JCA | Embraer 170 | | o/o |
| ☐ HB-JCB | Embraer 170 | | o/o |
| ☐ HB-JCC | Embraer 170 | | o/o |
| ☐ HB-JCD | Embraer 170 | | o/o |
| ☐ HB-JCE | Embraer 170 | | o/o |
| | | | |
| ☐ HB-IWA | McDD MD-11 | 458/48443 | |
| ☐ HB-IWB | McDD MD-11 | 459/48444 | |
| ☐ HB-IWC | McDD MD-11 | 460/48445 | |
| ☐ HB-IWD | McDD MD-11 | 463/48446 | |
| ☐ HB-IWE | McDD MD-11 | 464/48447 | |
| ☐ HB-IWI | McDD MD-11 | 477/48454 | |
| ☐ HB-IWK | McDD MD-11 | 487/48455 | |
| ☐ HB-IWL | McDD MD-11 | 494/48456 | |
| ☐ HB-IWM | McDD MD-11 | 498/48457 | |
| ☐ HB-IWN | McDD MD-11 | 571/48539 | |
| ☐ HB-IWO | McDD MD-11 | 611/48540 | |
| ☐ HB-IWP | McDD MD-11 | 614/48634 | |
| ☐ HB-IWQ | McDD MD-11 | 621/48541 | |
| | | | |
| ☐ HB-INR | McDD MD-82 | 1181/49277 | Lst NDC |
| ☐ HB-ISX | McDD MD-83 | 1579/49844 | |
| ☐ HB-ISZ | McDD MD-83 | 1720/49930 | |
| ☐ HB-IUG | McDD MD-83 | 1817/53149 | |
| ☐ HB-IUH | McDD MD-83 | 1831/53150 | |
| ☐ HB-IUM | McDD MD-83 | 1585/49847 | |
| ☐ HB-IUN | McDD MD-83 | 1559/49769 | |
| ☐ HB-IUO | McDD MD-83 | 1687/49857 | |
| ☐ HB-IUP | McDD MD-83 | 1675/49856 | |
| | | | |
| ☐ HB-AKA | SAAB SF.340B | 160 | Lst MDV |
| ☐ HB-AKB | SAAB SF.340B | 161 | Lst SLI |
| ☐ HB-AKC | SAAB SF.340B | 164 | Lst SLI |
| ☐ HB-AKD | SAAB SF.340B | 173 | Lst QE |
| ☐ HB-AKE | SAAB SF.340B | 176 | Lst SLI |
| ☐ HB-AKF | SAAB SF.340B | 182 | Lst MDV |
| ☐ HB-AKG | SAAB SF.340B | 185 | Lst QE |
| ☐ HB-AKH | SAAB SF.340B | 200 | Lst KRP |

| | | | |
|---|---|---|---|
| ☐ HB-AKI | SAAB SF.340B | 208 | Lst KRP |
| ☐ HB-AKL | SAAB SF.340B | 215 | Lst KRP |
| ☐ HB-AKM | SAAB SF.340B | 221 | Lst QE |
| ☐ HB-AKN | SAAB SF.340B | 225 | |
| ☐ HB-AKO | SAAB SF.340B | 228 | Lst KRP |
| ☐ HB-AKP | SAAB SF.340B | 168 | Lst NDC |
| | | | |
| ☐ HB-IYA | SAAB 2000 | 056 | |
| ☐ HB-IYB | SAAB 2000 | 057 | |
| ☐ HB-IYC | SAAB 2000 | 058 | |
| ☐ HB-IYD | SAAB 2000 | 059 | |
| ☐ HB-IYE | SAAB 2000 | 060 | |
| ☐ HB-IYF | SAAB 2000 | 061 | |
| ☐ HB-IYG | SAAB 2000 | 062 | |
| ☐ HB-IYH | SAAB 2000 | 063 | |
| ☐ HB-IZA | SAAB 2000 | 004 | |
| ☐ HB-IZB | SAAB 2000 | 005 | |
| ☐ HB-IZC | SAAB 2000 | 006 | |
| ☐ HB-IZD | SAAB 2000 | 007 | |
| ☐ HB-IZE | SAAB 2000 | 008 | |
| ☐ HB-IZF | SAAB 2000 | 009 | |
| ☐ HB-IZG | SAAB 2000 | 010 | |
| ☐ HB-IZH | SAAB 2000 | 011 | |
| ☐ HB-IZI | SAAB 2000 | 012 | |
| ☐ HB-IZJ | SAAB 2000 | 015 | |
| ☐ HB-IZK | SAAB 2000 | 018 | |
| ☐ HB-IZL | SAAB 2000 | 022 | |
| ☐ HB-IZM | SAAB 2000 | 024 | |
| ☐ HB-IZN | SAAB 2000 | 020 | |
| ☐ HB-IZO | SAAB 2000 | 029 | |
| ☐ HB-IZR | SAAB 2000 | 033 | |
| ☐ HB-IZS | SAAB 2000 | 035 | |
| ☐ HB-IZV | SAAB 2000 | 038 | |
| ☐ HB-IZW | SAAB 2000 | 039 | |
| ☐ HB-IZX | SAAB 2000 | 041 | |
| ☐ HB-IZY | SAAB 2000 | 047 | |
| ☐ HB-IZZ | SAAB 2000 | 048 | |

**SWISS SUN**

| | | | |
|---|---|---|---|
| ☐ HB- | Airbus A320-214 | | o/o |
| ☐ HB- | Airbus A320-214 | | o/o |
| ☐ HB- | Airbus A320-214 | | o/o |
| ☐ HB- | Airbus A320-214 | | o/o |

# HC - ECUADOR

## ICARO EXPRESS

| | | | |
|---|---|---|---|
| ☐ HC-CDA | F.28 Fellowship 4000 | 11230 | |
| ☐ HC-CDG | F.28 Fellowship 4000 | 11240 | |
| ☐ HC- | F.28 Fellowship 4000 | 11222 | o/o |
| ☐ HC- | F.28 Fellowship 4000 | 11224 | o/o |

**TAME** **TAE**

| | | |
|---|---|---|
| ☐ HC-BHM | Boeing 727-2T3 | 1644/22078 |
| ☐ HC-BLE | Boeing 727-134 | 487/19691 |
| ☐ HC-BLV | Boeing 727-17 | 806/20328 |
| ☐ HC-BRI | Boeing 727-230 | 887/20560 |
| ☐ HC-BSC | Boeing 727-230 | 1011/20788 |
| ☐ HC-BZR | Boeing 727-230 | 1404/21618 |
| ☐ HC-BZS | Boeing 727-230 | 1419/21620 |

# HH - HAITI

## HAITI CARIBBEAN AIRLINES

| | | | |
|---|---|---|---|
| ☐ N751PA | Boeing 757-2G5 | 146/23928 | Lsf PCE |

# HI - DOMINICAN REPUBLIC

## AERO CONTINENTE DOMINICANA CND

| | | | |
|---|---|---|---|
| ☐ HI-764CA | Boeing 737-222 | 210/19955 | Lsf ACQ |

## AEROMAR AIRLINES ROM

| | | | |
|---|---|---|---|
| ☐ TF-ATO | Boeing 767-204ER | 210/24013 | Lsf ABD |
| ☐ TF-ATT | Boeing 767-383ER | 263/24358 | Lsf ABD |
| ☐ TF-FIR | Boeing 757-256 | 593/26242 | Lsf ICE |

# HK - COLOMBIA

## ACES COLOMBIA AES

| | | |
|---|---|---|
| ☐ HK-3678X | ATR 42-320 | 261 |
| ☐ HK-3684X | ATR 42-320 | 284 |
| ☐ HK-3943X | ATR 42-320 | 142 |
| ☐ N612VX | ATR 42-500 | 612 |
| ☐ N613VX | ATR 42-500 | 613 |
| ☐ VP-BOD | ATR 42-500 | 506 |
| ☐ VP-BOE | ATR 42-500 | 504 |
| ☐ VP-BOF | ATR 42-500 | 505 |
| ☐ VP-BOH | ATR 42-320 | 406 |
| ☐ VP-BVE | ATR 42-500 | 510 |

| | | | |
|---|---|---|---|
| ☐ VP-BVA | Airbus A320-233 | 0739 | |
| ☐ VP-BVB | Airbus A320-233 | 0743 | |
| ☐ VP-BVC | Airbus A320-233 | 0839 | |
| ☐ VP-BVD | Airbus A320-233 | 0892 | |
| ☐ N635VX | Airbus A320-233 | 1635 | |
| ☐ N834VX | Airbus A320-233 | 1834 | o/o |
| ☐ N892VX | Airbus A320-233 | 1892 | |
| ☐ N902VX | Airbus A320-233 | 1902 | |
| ☐ | Airbus A320-233 | | o/o |
| ☐ | Airbus A320-233 | | o/o |
| ☐ | Airbus A320-233 | | o/o |
| ☐ HK-3738X | Boeing 727-227 | 1573/21997 | |
| ☐ HK-3977X | Boeing 727-277 | 907/20548 | |

## AEROREPUBLICA COLOMBIA RPB

| | | |
|---|---|---|
| ☐ HK-3906X | Douglas DC-9-31 | 444/47401 |
| ☐ HK-3926X | Douglas DC-9-32 | 396/47231 |
| ☐ HK-3928X | Douglas DC-9-32 | 398/47311 |
| ☐ HK-3963X | Douglas DC-9-32 | 544/47437 |
| ☐ HK-3964X | Douglas DC-9-32 | 537/47434 |
| ☐ HK-4084X | Douglas DC-9-31 | 407/47330 |
| ☐ HK-4155X | Douglas DC-9-32 | 632/47524 |
| ☐ HK-4230X | Douglas DC-9-31 | 603/47526 |

| | | |
|---|---|---|
| ☐ HK-4237X | McDD MD-81 | 48008 |
| ☐ HK-4238X | McDD MD-81 | 48009 |
| ☐ HK-4255 | McDD MD-81 | 950/48004 |
| ☐ HK-4259 | McDD MD-81 | 957/48005 |
| ☐ HK-4265 | McDD MD-81 | 938/48002 |

## AEROSUCRE KRE

| | | | |
|---|---|---|---|
| ☐ HK-727 | Boeing 727-59F | 243/19127 | |
| ☐ HK-1717 | Boeing 727-21F | 215/18993 | std |
| ☐ HK-3667X | Boeing 727-23F | 366/19430 | |
| ☐ HK-3985X | Boeing 727-224F | 814/20465 | |
| ☐ HK-4216X | Boeing 737-230C | 223/20253 | |
| ☐ HK-4253 | Boeing 737-2H6C | 436/21109 | |

## AVIANCA – AEROVIAS NACIONALES DE COLOMBIA AVA

| | | |
|---|---|---|
| ☐ N421AV | Boeing 767-2B1ER | 407/25421 |
| ☐ N535AW | Boeing 767-33AER | 491/25535 |
| ☐ N984AN | Boeing 767-383ER | 262/24357 |
| ☐ N985AN | Boeing 767-259ER | 292/24618 |
| ☐ N986AN | Boeing 767-259ER | 321/24835 |
| ☐ N988AN | Boeing 767-284ER | 303/24742 |

| | | |
|---|---|---|
| ☐ PH-AVG | Fokker 50 | 20278 |
| ☐ PH-AVH | Fokker 50 | 20281 |
| ☐ PH-AVJ | Fokker 50 | 20285 |
| ☐ PH-AVN | Fokker 50 | 20296 |
| ☐ PH-AVO | Fokker 50 | 20297 |
| ☐ PH-LXW | Fokker 50 | 20266 |
| ☐ PH-MXJ | Fokker 50 | 20288 |
| ☐ PH-MXS | Fokker 50 | 20299 |

| | | | |
|---|---|---|---|
| ☐ EI-CBR | McDD MD-83 | 1787/49939 | |
| ☐ EI-CBS | McDD MD-83 | 1799/49942 | |
| ☐ EI-CBY | McDD MD-83 | 1888/49944 | |
| ☐ EI-CBZ | McDD MD-83 | 1889/49945 | |
| ☐ EI-CCC | McDD MD-83 | 1898/49946 | |
| ☐ EI-CCE | McDD MD-83 | 1900/49947 | |
| ☐ EI-CDY | McDD MD-83 | 1905/49948 | |
| ☐ EI-CEP | McDD MD-83 | 1984/53122 | |
| ☐ EI-CEQ | McDD MD-83 | 1987/53123 | |
| ☐ EI-CER | McDD MD-83 | 1993/53125 | |
| ☐ EI-CFZ | McDD MD-83 | 1964/53120 | |
| ☐ N190AN | McDD MD-83 | 2148/53190 | |
| ☐ N583AN | McDD MD-83 | 2071/53183 | |
| ☐ N593AN | McDD MD-83 | 2066/53093 | |
| ☐ N632CT | McDD MD-83 | 1603/49632 | |

| | | | |
|---|---|---|---|
| ☐ HK-3480X | Boeing 727-2H3 | 952/20739 | std |
| ☐ EI-CEY | Boeing 757-2Y0ER | 478/26152 | |
| ☐ EI-CEZ | Boeing 757-2Y0ER | 486/26154 | |
| ☐ N227AN | Boeing 757-236 | 57/23227 | |
| ☐ N262CT | Boeing 757-256 | 620/26246 | |
| ☐ N321LF | Boeing 757-2Q8ER | 612/26269 | |
| ☐ N951PG | Boeing 757-236 | 34/22185 | |

## INTERCONTINENTAL DE AVIACION ICT

| | | |
|---|---|---|
| ☐ HK-2865X | Douglas DC-9-15 | 55/45722 |
| ☐ HK-3752X | Douglas DC-9-15 | 101/45781 |
| ☐ HK-3827X | Douglas DC-9-15 | 35/47048 |
| ☐ HK-3859X | Douglas DC-9-14 | 28/45843 |
| ☐ HK-3891X | Douglas DC-9-14 | 72/45776 |
| ☐ HK-3958X | Douglas DC-9-15 | 54/45738 |
| ☐ HK- | Douglas DC-9-14 | 23/45842 |
| ☐ HK- | Douglas DC-9-15 | 46/45841 |

## LINEAS AÉREAS SURAMERICANAS LAU

| | | | |
|---|---|---|---|
| ☐ HK-1271 | Boeing 727-24C | 428/19524 | |
| ☐ HK-1273 | Boeing 727-24C | 442/19526 | |
| ☐ HK-3745 | Boeing 727-1C3F | 819/20420 | std |
| ☐ HK-3814X | Boeing 727-25F | 79/18270 | |
| ☐ HK-4154X | Boeing 727-51F | 162/18804 | |
| ☐ HK-4261X | Boeing 727-251F | 1170/21156 | |
| ☐ HK-4262X | Boeing 727-2F9F | 1291/21427 | |

| | | |
|---|---|---|
| ☐ HK-4245X | Douglas DC-9-15RC | 115/47012 |
| ☐ HK-4246X | Douglas DC-9-15RC | 223/47062 |

## TAMPA AIRLINES TPA

| | | |
|---|---|---|
| ☐ HK-3785X | Douglas DC-8-71F | 462/46066 |
| ☐ HK-3786X | Douglas DC-8-71F | 289/45849 |
| ☐ HK-4176X | Douglas DC-8-71F | 337/45945 |

# HL - SOUTH KOREA

## ASIANA AIRLINES AAR

| | | | |
|---|---|---|---|
| ☐ HL7549 | Airbus A321-231 | 1293 | |
| ☐ HL7588 | Airbus A321-231 | 0771 | |
| ☐ HL7589 | Airbus A321-231 | 0855 | |
| ☐ HL7590 | Airbus A321-231 | 1060 | |
| ☐ HL7594 | Airbus A321-231 | 1356 | |
| ☐ HL7703 | Airbus A321-231 | 1511 | |
| ☐ HL7711 | Airbus A321-231 | 1636 | |
| ☐ HL7712 | Airbus A321-231 | 1670 | |
| ☐ HL7713 | Airbus A321-231 | 1734 | |
| ☐ HL | Airbus A321-231 | | o/o |
| ☐ HL | Airbus A321-231 | | o/o |
| ☐ HL | Airbus A321-231 | | o/o |
| ☐ HL | Airbus A321-231 | | o/o |

| | | |
|---|---|---|
| ☐ HL7227 | Boeing 737-48E | 2314/25764 |
| ☐ HL7228 | Boeing 737-48E | 2335/25765 |
| ☐ HL7232 | Boeing 737-58E | 2614/25767 |
| ☐ HL7233 | Boeing 737-58E | 2724/25768 |

| | | | |
|---|---|---|---|
| ☐ HL7235 | Boeing 737-4Q8 | 2665/26308 | |
| ☐ HL7250 | Boeing 737-58E | 2737/25769 | |
| ☐ HL7251 | Boeing 737-4Y0 | 1639/23869 | |
| ☐ HL7253 | Boeing 737-4Y0 | 1655/23977 | |
| ☐ HL7254 | Boeing 737-4Y0 | 1659/23978 | |
| ☐ HL7257 | Boeing 737-4Y0 | 1749/24469 | |
| ☐ HL7258 | Boeing 737-4Y0 | 1751/24493 | |
| ☐ HL7259 | Boeing 737-4Y0 | 1757/24494 | |
| ☐ HL7260 | Boeing 737-4Y0 | 1803/24520 | |
| ☐ HL7508 | Boeing 737-48E | 2791/25772 | |
| ☐ HL7509 | Boeing 737-48E | 2806/28198 | |
| ☐ HL7510 | Boeing 737-48E | 2816/25771 | |
| ☐ HL7511 | Boeing 737-48E | 2848/27630 | |
| ☐ HL7512 | Boeing 737-48E | 2857/27632 | |
| ☐ HL7513 | Boeing 737-48E | 2860/25776 | |
| ☐ HL7517 | Boeing 737-48E | 2909/25774 | |
| ☐ HL7518 | Boeing 737-48E | 2954/28053 | |
| ☐ HL7527 | Boeing 737-4Q8 | 2602/26299 | |
| ☐ HL7591 | Boeing 737-4Q8 | 2513/26291 | |
| ☐ HL7592 | Boeing 737-4Q8 | 2562/26320 | |
| ☐ HL7593 | Boeing 737-43Q | 2837/28492 | |
| | | | |
| ☐ HL7413 | Boeing 747-48EM | 880/25405 | |
| ☐ HL7414 | Boeing 747-48EM | 892/25452 | |
| ☐ HL7415 | Boeing 747-48EM | 946/25777 | |
| ☐ HL7417 | Boeing 747-48EM | 1006/25779 | |
| ☐ HL7418 | Boeing 747-48E | 1035/25780 | |
| ☐ HL7419 | Boeing 747-48EF | 1044/25781 | |
| ☐ HL7420 | Boeing 747-48EF | 1064/25783 | |
| ☐ HL7421 | Boeing 747-48EM | 1086/25784 | |
| ☐ HL7422 | Boeing 747-48EF | 1096/28367 | |
| ☐ HL7423 | Boeing 747-48EM | 1115/25782 | |
| ☐ HL7426 | Boeing 747-48EF | 1210/27603 | |
| ☐ HL7428 | Boeing 747-48E | 1160/28552 | |
| ☐ HL7436 | Boeing 747-48EF | 1305/29170 | |
| | | | |
| ☐ HL7200 | Boeing 767-328ER | 531/27212 | |
| ☐ HL7247 | Boeing 767-38E | 523/25757 | |
| ☐ HL7248 | Boeing 767-38E | 582/25758 | |
| ☐ HL7263 | Boeing 767-38EER | 328/24797 | |
| ☐ HL7264 | Boeing 767-38EER | 331/24798 | |
| ☐ HL7268 | Boeing 767-38EER | 417/25132 | |
| ☐ HL7506 | Boeing 767-38EFER | 639/25760 | |
| ☐ HL7507 | Boeing 767-38EFER | 616/25761 | |
| ☐ HL7514 | Boeing 767-38E | 656/25763 | |
| ☐ HL7515 | Boeing 767-38E | 658/25762 | |
| ☐ HL7516 | Boeing 767-38E | 668/25759 | |
| ☐ HL7528 | Boeing 767-38E | 693/29129 | |
| ☐ HL7595 | Boeing 767-36NER | 829/30840 | |
| | | | |
| ☐ HL7596 | Boeing 777-28EER | 322/28681 | |
| ☐ HL7597 | Boeing 777-28EER | 359/28686 | |
| ☐ HL7500 | Boeing 777-28EER | 400/28685 | |
| ☐ HL7700 | Boeing 777-28EER | 403/30859 | |
| ☐ HL | Boeing 777-28EER | | o/o |
| ☐ HL | Boeing 777-28EER | | o/o |

## KOREAN AIR  KAL

| | | | |
|---|---|---|---|
| ☐ HL7239 | Airbus A300B4-622R | 627 | |
| ☐ HL7240 | Airbus A300B4-622R | 631 | |
| ☐ HL7241 | Airbus A300B4-622R | 662 | |
| ☐ HL7242 | Airbus A300B4-622R | 685 | |
| ☐ HL7243 | Airbus A300B4-622R | 692 | |
| ☐ HL7244 | Airbus A300B4-622R | 722 | |
| ☐ HL7245 | Airbus A300B4-622R | 731 | |
| ☐ HL7278 | Airbus A300B4-203F | 277 | |
| ☐ HL7279 | Airbus A300B4-203F | 292 | |
| ☐ HL7290 | Airbus A300B4-622 | 388 | For FDX |
| ☐ HL7291 | Airbus A300B4-622 | 417 | For FDX |
| ☐ HL7295 | Airbus A300B4-622R | 582 | |
| ☐ HL7297 | Airbus A300B4-622R | 609 | |
| ☐ HL7299 | Airbus A300B4-622R | 717 | |
| ☐ HL7524 | Airbus A330-322 | 206 | |
| ☐ HL7525 | Airbus A330-322 | 219 | |
| ☐ HL7538 | Airbus A330-223 | 222 | |
| ☐ HL7539 | Airbus A330-223 | 226 | |
| ☐ HL7540 | Airbus A330-322 | 241 | |
| | | | |
| ☐ HL7550 | Airbus A330-322 | 162 | |
| ☐ HL7551 | Airbus A330-322 | 172 | |
| ☐ HL7552 | Airbus A330-223 | 258 | |
| ☐ HL7553 | Airbus A330-322X | 267 | |
| ☐ HL7554 | Airbus A330-322X | 256 | |
| ☐ HL7584 | Airbus A330-322X | 338 | |
| ☐ HL7585 | Airbus A330-322X | 350 | |
| ☐ HL7586 | Airbus A330-322X | 351 | |
| ☐ HL7587 | Airbus A330-322X | 368 | |
| ☐ HL7701 | Airbus A330-323X | 425 | |
| ☐ HL7702 | Airbus A330-323X | 428 | |
| ☐ HL7709 | Airbus A330-323X | 484 | |
| ☐ HL7710 | Airbus A330-323X | 490 | |
| ☐ HL | Airbus A330-323X | 550 | |
| ☐ HL | Airbus A330-323X | | o/o |
| ☐ HL | Airbus A330-323X | | o/o |
| | | | |
| ☐ HL7555 | Boeing 737-86N | 460/30230 | |
| ☐ HL7557 | Boeing 737-86N | 562/28622 | |
| ☐ HL7558 | Boeing 737-86N | 590/28625 | |
| ☐ HL7559 | Boeing 737-86N | 611/28626 | |
| ☐ HL7560 | Boeing 737-8B5 | 622/29981 | |
| ☐ HL7561 | Boeing 737-8B5 | 663/29982 | |
| ☐ HL7562 | Boeing 737-8B5 | 678/29983 | |
| ☐ HL7563 | Boeing 737-86N | 756/28636 | |
| ☐ HL7564 | Boeing 737-86N | 765/28638 | |
| ☐ HL7565 | Boeing 737-8B5 | 848/29984 | |
| ☐ HL7566 | Boeing 737-8B5 | 852/29985 | |
| ☐ HL7567 | Boeing 737-86N | 878/28647 | |
| ☐ HL7568 | Boeing 737-8B5 | 891/29986 | |
| ☐ HL7569 | Boeing 737-8B5 | 999/29987 | |
| ☐ HL7599 | Boeing 737-9B5 | 1026/29988 | |
| ☐ HL7704 | Boeing 737-9B5 | 1082/29989 | |
| ☐ HL7705 | Boeing 737-9B5 | 1162/29990 | |
| ☐ HL7706 | Boeing 737-9B5 | 1188/29991 | |
| ☐ HL7707 | Boeing 737-9B5 | 1190/29992 | |
| ☐ HL7708 | Boeing 737-9B5 | 1208/29993 | |
| ☐ HL7716 | Boeing 737-9B5 | 29994 | o/o |
| ☐ HL7717 | Boeing 737-9B5 | 29995 | o/o |
| ☐ HL7718 | Boeing 737-9B5 | 29996 | o/o |
| ☐ HL | Boeing 737-9B5 | | |
| | | | |
| ☐ HL7400 | Boeing 747-4B5F | 1295/26414 | |
| ☐ HL7402 | Boeing 747-4B5 | 1155/26407 | |
| ☐ HL7403 | Boeing 747-4B5F | 1163/26408 | |
| ☐ HL7404 | Boeing 747-4B5 | 1170/26409 | |
| ☐ HL7405 | Boeing 747-2B5F | 718/24195 | |
| ☐ HL7407 | Boeing 747-4B5 | 729/24198 | |
| ☐ HL7408 | Boeing 747-2B5F | 720/24196 | |
| ☐ HL7409 | Boeing 747-4B5 | 739/24199 | |
| ☐ HL7412 | Boeing 747-4B5 | 748/24200 | |
| ☐ HL7434 | Boeing 747-4B5F | 1316/32809 | |
| ☐ HL7437 | Boeing 747-4B5ERF | 32808 | |
| ☐ HL7438 | Boeing 747-4B5 | 33515 | |
| ☐ HL7443 | Boeing 747-2B5B | 363/21772 | |
| ☐ HL7448 | Boeing 747-4B5F | 1246/26416 | |
| ☐ HL7449 | Boeing 747-4B5F | 1248/26411 | |
| ☐ HL7452 | Boeing 747-2B5F | 454/22481 | |
| ☐ HL7459 | Boeing 747-2B5F | 520/22486 | |
| ☐ HL7460 | Boeing 747-4B5 | 1107/26404 | |
| ☐ HL7461 | Boeing 747-4B5 | 1118/26405 | |
| ☐ HL7462 | Boeing 747-4B5F | 1123/26406 | |
| ☐ HL7465 | Boeing 747-4B5 | 1284/26412 | |
| ☐ HL7466 | Boeing 747-4B5F | 1286/26413 | |
| ☐ HL7467 | Boeing 747-4B5F | 1291/27073 | |
| ☐ HL7469 | Boeing 747-3B5 | 611/22489 | |
| ☐ HL7470 | Boeing 747-3B5SF | 713/24194 | |
| ☐ HL7472 | Boeing 747-4B5 | 1095/26403 | |
| ☐ HL7473 | Boeing 747-4B5 | 1098/28335 | |
| ☐ HL7480 | Boeing 747-4B5M | 793/24619 | |
| ☐ HL7481 | Boeing 747-4B5 | 830/24621 | |
| ☐ HL7482 | Boeing 747-4B5 | 853/25205 | |
| ☐ HL7483 | Boeing 747-4B5 | 874/25275 | |
| ☐ HL7484 | Boeing 747-4B5 | 893/26392 | |
| ☐ HL7485 | Boeing 747-4B5 | 922/26395 | |
| ☐ HL7486 | Boeing 747-4B5 | 951/26396 | |
| ☐ HL7487 | Boeing 747-4B5 | 958/26393 | |
| ☐ HL7488 | Boeing 747-4B5 | 986/26394 | |

| | | | |
|---|---|---|---|
| ☐ HL7489 | Boeing 747-4B5 | 1013/27072 | |
| ☐ HL7490 | Boeing 747-4B5 | 1019/27177 | |
| ☐ HL7491 | Boeing 747-4B5 | 1037/27341 | |
| ☐ HL7492 | Boeing 747-4B5 | 1055/26397 | |
| ☐ HL7493 | Boeing 747-4B5 | 1057/26398 | |
| ☐ HL7494 | Boeing 747-4B5 | 1067/27662 | |
| ☐ HL7495 | Boeing 747-4B5 | 1073/28096 | |
| ☐ HL7497 | Boeing 747-4B5F | 1087/26401 | |
| ☐ HL7498 | Boeing 747-4B5 | 1092/26402 | |
| ☐ HL | Boeing 747-4B5ERF | | o/o |
| ☐ HL | Boeing 747-4B5ERF | | o/o |
| ☐ HL | Boeing 747-4B5ERF | | o/o |
| | | | |
| ☐ HL7526 | Boeing 777-2B5ER | 148/27947 | |
| ☐ HL7530 | Boeing 777-2B5ER | 59/27945 | |
| ☐ HL7531 | Boeing 777-2B5ER | 62/27946 | |
| ☐ HL7532 | Boeing 777-3B5 | 162/28371 | |
| ☐ HL7533 | Boeing 777-3B5 | 178/27948 | |
| ☐ HL7534 | Boeing 777-3B5 | 120/27950 | |
| ☐ HL7573 | Boeing 777-3B5 | 288/27952 | |
| ☐ HL7574 | Boeing 777-2B5ER | 305/28444 | |
| ☐ HL7575 | Boeing 777-2B5ER | 309/28445 | |
| ☐ HL7598 | Boeing 777-2B5ER | 356/27949 | |
| ☐ HL7714 | Boeing 777-2B5ER | 411/27951 | |
| ☐ HL7715 | Boeing 777-2B5ER | 416/28372 | |
| ☐ HL | Boeing 777-2B5ER | | o/o |
| ☐ HL | Boeing 777-3B5 | | o/o |
| ☐ HL | Boeing 777-3B5 | | o/o |
| | | | |
| ☐ HL7206 | Fokker 100 | 11378 | |
| ☐ HL7208 | Fokker 100 | 11388 | |
| ☐ HL7209 | Fokker 100 | 11432 | |
| ☐ HL7210 | Fokker 100 | 11438 | |
| ☐ HL7211 | Fokker 100 | 11439 | |
| ☐ HL7213 | Fokker 100 | 11504 | |
| ☐ HL7214 | Fokker 100 | 11513 | |
| ☐ HL7215 | Fokker 100 | 11519 | |
| ☐ HL7216 | Fokker 100 | 11522 | |
| ☐ HL7217 | Fokker 100 | 11523 | |
| | | | |
| ☐ HL7371 | McDD MD-11F | 456/48407 | |
| ☐ HL7372 | McDD MD-11F | 457/48408 | |
| ☐ HL7374 | McDD MD-11F | 495/48410 | |
| ☐ HL7375 | McDD MD-11F | 521/48523 | |

## HP - PANAMA

### COPA AIRLINES — CMP

| | | | |
|---|---|---|---|
| ☐ | HP-1163CMP | Boeing 737-204 | 541/21693 | |
| ☐ | HP-1195CMP | Boeing 737-204 | 338/20806 | |
| ☐ | HP-1234CMP | Boeing 737-2S3 | 849/22660 | |
| ☐ | HP-1255CMP | Boeing 737-2P6 | 500/21359 | |
| ☐ | HP-1297CMP | Boeing 737-219 | 535/21645 | |
| ☐ | HP-1322CMP | Boeing 737-2P5 | 794/22667 | |
| ☐ | HP-1324CMP | Boeing 737-2P5 | 1010/23113 | |
| ☐ | HP-1339CMP | Boeing 737-2P6 | 538/21677 | |
| ☐ | HP-1340CMP | Boeing 737-2P6 | 528/21612 | |
| ☐ | HP-1369CMP | Boeing 737-71Q | 235/29047 | |
| ☐ | HP-1370CMP | Boeing 737-71Q | 288/29048 | |
| ☐ | HP-1371CMP | Boeing 737-7V3 | 388/30049 | |
| ☐ | HP-1372CMP | Boeing 737-7V3 | 399/28607 | |
| ☐ | HP-1373CMP | Boeing 737-7V3 | 459/30458 | |
| ☐ | HP-1374CMP | Boeing 737-7V3 | 494/30459 | |
| ☐ | HP-1375CMP | Boeing 737-7V3 | 558/30460 | |
| ☐ | HP-1376CMP | Boeing 737-7V3 | 574/30497 | |
| ☐ | HP-1377CMP | Boeing 737-7V3 | 1161/30462 | |
| ☐ | HP-1378CMP | Boeing 737-7V3 | 1173/30461 | |
| ☐ | HP-1379CMP | Boeing 737-7V3 | 1221/30463 | |
| ☐ | HP-1380CMP | Boeing 737-7V3 | 1241/30464 | |
| ☐ | HP-1520CMP | Boeing 737-8V3 | 33709 | o/o |
| ☐ | HP-1521CMP | Boeing 737-8V3 | 33710 | o/o |

### DHL AERO EXPRESSO — DAE

| | | | | |
|---|---|---|---|---|
| ☐ | HP-1310DAE | Boeing 727-264F | 1047/20894 | |
| ☐ | HP-1510DAE | Boeing 727-264F | 950/20709 | Lsf DHL |
| ☐ | HP-1610DAE | Boeing 727-264F | 986/20780 | Lsf DHL |

## HR - HONDURAS

### SOL AIR

| | | | | |
|---|---|---|---|---|
| ☐ | N371FA | Boeing 737-33A | 1337/23631 | Lsf FAO |
| ☐ | N550FA | Boeing 737-3K2 | 1195/23411 | Lsf |
| ☐ | N296SC | Boeing 727-224 | 1756/22449 | Lsf FAO |
| ☐ | N54348 | Boeing 727-231 | 1563/21967 | Lsf FAO |

## HS - THAILAND

### BANGKOK AIRWAYS — BKP

| | | | | |
|---|---|---|---|---|
| ☐ | HS-PGA | ATR 72-202 | 373 | Jow SRH |
| ☐ | HS-PGB | ATR 72-202 | 367 | |
| ☐ | HS-PGC | ATR 72-202 | 452 | Jow SRH |
| ☐ | HS-PGD | ATR 72-202 | 455 | Jow SRH |
| ☐ | HS-PGE | ATR 72-202 | 450 | Jow SRH |
| ☐ | HS-PGF | ATR 72-212A | 700 | Jow SRH |
| ☐ | HS-PGG | ATR 72-212A | 692 | Jow SRH |
| ☐ | HS-PGH | ATR 72-202 | 469 | Jow SRH |
| ☐ | HS-PGK | ATR 72-212A | 680 | Jow SRH |
| ☐ | HS-PGL | ATR 72-212A | 670 | |
| ☐ | HS- | ATR 72-212A | 704 | o/o |
| ☐ | HS- | ATR 72-212A | | o/o |
| | | | | |
| ☐ | HS-PGO | Boeing 717-23S | 5059/55067 | |
| ☐ | HS-PGP | Boeing 717-23S | 5037/55064 | |
| ☐ | HS-PGQ | Boeing 717-231 | 5045/55081 | |
| ☐ | HS-PGR | Boeing 717-231 | 5030/55074 | |

### ORIENT THAI AIRLINES — OEA

| | | | |
|---|---|---|---|
| ☐ | HS-UTA | L-1011-1 Tristar | 1225 |
| ☐ | HS-UTB | Boeing 747-246B | 192/20529 |
| ☐ | HS-UTC | Boeing 747-238B | 341/21658 |
| ☐ | HS-UTH | Boeing 747-146 | 199/20532 |
| ☐ | HS-UTP | Boeing 747-246B | 196/20530 |

### PB AIR — PBA

| | | | |
|---|---|---|---|
| ☐ | HS-PBE | Embraer ERJ-145 | 145597 |
| ☐ | HS-PBF | Embraer ERJ-145 | 145607 |

### PHUKET AIRLINES — VAP

| | | | |
|---|---|---|---|
| ☐ | HS-AKO | Boeing 737-281 | 282/20507 |
| ☐ | HS-AKU | Boeing 737-2B7 | 998/23115 |
| ☐ | HS-VKK | Boeing 737-2B7 | 1039/23131 |
| ☐ | HS-VKU | Boeing 737-281 | 280/20506 |

### THAI AIRWAYS INTERNATIONAL — THA

| | | | | |
|---|---|---|---|---|
| ☐ | HS-TAA | Airbus A300B4-601 | 368 | std |
| ☐ | HS-TAB | Airbus A300B4-601 | 371 | |
| ☐ | HS-TAC | Airbus A300B4-601 | 377 | |
| ☐ | HS-TAD | Airbus A300B4-601 | 384 | |
| ☐ | HS-TAE | Airbus A300B4-601 | 395 | |
| ☐ | HS-TAF | Airbus A300B4-601 | 398 | |
| ☐ | HS-TAG | Airbus A300B4-605R | 464 | |
| ☐ | HS-TAH | Airbus A300B4-605R | 518 | |
| ☐ | HS-TAK | Airbus A300B4-622R | 566 | |
| ☐ | HS-TAL | Airbus A300B4-622R | 569 | |
| ☐ | HS-TAM | Airbus A300B4-622R | 577 | |
| ☐ | HS-TAN | Airbus A300B4-622R | 628 | |
| ☐ | HS-TAO | Airbus A300B4-622R | 629 | |
| ☐ | HS-TAP | Airbus A300B4-622R | 635 | std |
| ☐ | HS-TAR | Airbus A300B4-622R | 681 | |
| ☐ | HS-TAS | Airbus A300B4-622R | 705 | |
| ☐ | HS-TAT | Airbus A300B4-622R | 782 | |
| ☐ | HS-TAW | Airbus A300B4-622R | 784 | |
| ☐ | HS-TAX | Airbus A300B4-622R | 785 | |
| ☐ | HS-TAY | Airbus A300B4-622R | 786 | |
| ☐ | HS-TAZ | Airbus A300B4-622R | 787 | |

| | | |
|---|---|---|
| ☐ HS-TEA | Airbus A330-321 | 050 |
| ☐ HS-TEB | Airbus A330-321 | 060 |
| ☐ HS-TEC | Airbus A330-321 | 062 |
| ☐ HS-TED | Airbus A330-321 | 064 |
| ☐ HS-TEE | Airbus A330-321 | 065 |
| ☐ HS-TEF | Airbus A330-321 | 066 |
| ☐ HS-TEG | Airbus A330-321 | 112 |
| ☐ HS-TEH | Airbus A330-321 | 122 |
| ☐ HS-TEJ | Airbus A330-322 | 209 |
| ☐ HS-TEK | Airbus A330-322 | 224 |
| ☐ HS-TEL | Airbus A330-322 | 231 |
| ☐ HS-TEM | Airbus A330-323X | 346 |
| ☐ HS- | Airbus A330-323X | |
| ☐ HS-TDA | Boeing 737-4D7 | 1899/24830 |
| ☐ HS-TDB | Boeing 737-4D7 | 1922/24831 |
| ☐ HS-TDD | Boeing 737-4D7 | 2318/26611 |
| ☐ HS-TDE | Boeing 737-4D7 | 2330/26612 |
| ☐ HS-TDF | Boeing 737-4D7 | 2338/26613 |
| ☐ HS-TDG | Boeing 737-4D7 | 2481/26614 |
| ☐ HS-TDH | Boeing 737-4D7 | 2962/28703 |
| ☐ HS-TDJ | Boeing 737-4D7 | 2968/28704 |
| ☐ HS-TDK | Boeing 737-4D7 | 2977/28701 |
| ☐ HS-TDL | Boeing 737-4D7 | 2978/28702 |
| ☐ HS-TGA | Boeing 747-4D7 | 1273/32369 |
| ☐ HS-TGB | Boeing 747-4D7 | 1278/32370 |
| ☐ HS-TGD | Boeing 747-3D7 | 681/23721 |
| ☐ HS-TGE | Boeing 747-3D7 | 688/23722 |
| ☐ HS-TGH | Boeing 747-4D7 | 769/24458 |
| ☐ HS-TGJ | Boeing 747-4D7 | 777/24459 |
| ☐ HS-TGK | Boeing 747-4D7 | 833/24993 |
| ☐ HS-TGL | Boeing 747-4D7 | 890/25366 |
| ☐ HS-TGM | Boeing 747-4D7 | 945/27093 |
| ☐ HS-TGN | Boeing 747-4D7 | 950/26615 |
| ☐ HS-TGO | Boeing 747-4D7 | 1001/26609 |
| ☐ HS-TGP | Boeing 747-4D7 | 1047/26610 |
| ☐ HS-TGR | Boeing 747-4D7 | 1071/27723 |
| ☐ HS-TGT | Boeing 747-4D7 | 1097/26616 |
| ☐ HS-TGW | Boeing 747-4D7 | 1111/27724 |
| ☐ HS-TGX | Boeing 747-4D7 | 1134/27725 |
| ☐ HS-TGY | Boeing 747-4D7 | 1164/28705 |
| ☐ HS-TGZ | Boeing 747-4D7 | 1214/28706 |
| ☐ HS-TJA | Boeing 777-2D7 | 25/27726 |
| ☐ HS-TJB | Boeing 777-2D7 | 32/27727 |
| ☐ HS-TJC | Boeing 777-2D7 | 44/27728 |
| ☐ HS-TJD | Boeing 777-2D7 | 51/27729 |
| ☐ HS-TJE | Boeing 777-2D7 | 89/27730 |
| ☐ HS-TJF | Boeing 777-2D7 | 95/27731 |
| ☐ HS-TJG | Boeing 777-2D7 | 100/27732 |
| ☐ HS-TJH | Boeing 777-2D7 | 113/27733 |
| ☐ HS-TKA | Boeing 777-3D7 | 156/29150 |
| ☐ HS-TKB | Boeing 777-3D7 | 170/29151 |
| ☐ HS-TKC | Boeing 777-3D7 | 250/29211 |
| ☐ HS-TKD | Boeing 777-3D7 | 260/29212 |
| ☐ HS-TKE | Boeing 777-3D7 | 304/29213 |
| ☐ HS-TKF | Boeing 777-3D7 | 310/29214 |
| ☐ HS-TMD | McDD MD-11 | 466/48416 |
| ☐ HS-TME | McDD MD-11 | 467/48417 |
| ☐ HS-TMF | McDD MD-11 | 501/48418 |
| ☐ HS-TMG | McDD MD-11 | 505/48451 |
| ☐ HS-TRA | ATR 72-201 | 164 |
| ☐ HS-TRB | ATR 72-201 | 167 |

## HZ - SAUDI ARABIA

### SAUDI ARABIAN AIRLINES SVA

| | | |
|---|---|---|
| ☐ HZ-AJA | Airbus A300B4-620 | 284 |
| ☐ HZ-AJB | Airbus A300B4-620 | 294 |
| ☐ HZ-AJC | Airbus A300B4-620 | 301 |
| ☐ HZ-AJD | Airbus A300B4-620 | 307 |
| ☐ HZ-AJE | Airbus A300B4-620 | 312 |
| ☐ HZ-AJF | Airbus A300B4-620 | 317 |
| ☐ HZ-AJG | Airbus A300B4-620 | 321 |
| ☐ HZ-AJH | Airbus A300B4-620 | 336 |
| ☐ HZ-AJI | Airbus A300B4-620 | 341 |
| ☐ HZ-AJJ | Airbus A300B4-620 | 348 |
| ☐ HZ-AJK | Airbus A300B4-620 | 351 |
| ☐ HZ-AIA | Boeing 747-168B | 512/22498 |
| ☐ HZ-AIB | Boeing 747-168B | 517/22499 |
| ☐ HZ-AIC | Boeing 747-168B | 522/22500 |
| ☐ HZ-AID | Boeing 747-168B | 525/22501 |
| ☐ HZ-AIE | Boeing 747-168B | 530/22502 |
| ☐ HZ-AIF | Boeing 747SP-68 | 529/22503 |
| ☐ HZ-AIG | Boeing 747-168B | 551/22747 |
| ☐ HZ-AII | Boeing 747-168B | 557/22749 |
| ☐ HZ-AIK | Boeing 747-368 | 616/23262 |
| ☐ HZ-AIL | Boeing 747-368 | 619/23263 |
| ☐ HZ-AIM | Boeing 747-368 | 620/23264 |
| ☐ HZ-AIN | Boeing 747-368 | 622/23265 |
| ☐ HZ-AIP | Boeing 747-368 | 630/23267 |
| ☐ HZ-AIQ | Boeing 747-368 | 631/23268 |
| ☐ HZ-AIR | Boeing 747-368 | 643/23269 |
| ☐ HZ-AIS | Boeing 747-368 | 645/23270 |
| ☐ HZ-AIT | Boeing 747-368 | 652/23271 |
| ☐ HZ-AIU | Boeing 747-268F | 724/24359 |
| ☐ HZ-AIV | Boeing 747-468 | 1122/28339 |
| ☐ HZ-AIW | Boeing 747-468 | 1138/28340 |
| ☐ HZ-AIX | Boeing 747-468 | 1182/28341 |
| ☐ HZ-AIY | Boeing 747-468 | 1216/28342 |
| ☐ HZ-AIZ | Boeing 747-468 | 1265/28343 |
| ☐ HZ-AKA | Boeing 777-268ER | 98/28344 |
| ☐ HZ-AKB | Boeing 777-268ER | 99/28345 |
| ☐ HZ-AKC | Boeing 777-268ER | 101/28346 |
| ☐ HZ-AKD | Boeing 777-268ER | 103/28347 |
| ☐ HZ-AKE | Boeing 777-268ER | 109/28348 |
| ☐ HZ-AKF | Boeing 777-268ER | 114/28349 |
| ☐ HZ-AKG | Boeing 777-268ER | 119/28350 |
| ☐ HZ-AKH | Boeing 777-268ER | 124/28351 |
| ☐ HZ-AKI | Boeing 777-268ER | 143/28352 |
| ☐ HZ-AKJ | Boeing 777-268ER | 147/28353 |
| ☐ HZ-AKK | Boeing 777-268ER | 154/28354 |
| ☐ HZ-AKL | Boeing 777-268ER | 166/28355 |
| ☐ HZ-AKM | Boeing 777-268ER | 175/28356 |
| ☐ HZ-AKN | Boeing 777-268ER | 181/28357 |
| ☐ HZ-AKO | Boeing 777-268ER | 186/28358 |
| ☐ HZ-AKP | Boeing 777-268ER | 194/28359 |
| ☐ HZ-AKQ | Boeing 777-268ER | 219/28360 |
| ☐ HZ-AKR | Boeing 777-268ER | 236/28361 |
| ☐ HZ-AKS | Boeing 777-268ER | 255/28362 |
| ☐ HZ-AKT | Boeing 777-268ER | 298/28363 |
| ☐ HZ-AKU | Boeing 777-268ER | 306/29364 |
| ☐ HZ-AKV | Boeing 777-268ER | 323/28365 |
| ☐ HZ-AKW | Boeing 777-268ER | 351/28366 |
| ☐ HZ-APA | McDD MD-90-30 | 2191/53491 |
| ☐ HZ-APB | McDD MD-90-30 | 2205/53492 |
| ☐ HZ-APC | McDD MD-90-30 | 2209/53493 |
| ☐ HZ-APD | McDD MD-90-30 | 2213/53494 |
| ☐ HZ-APE | McDD MD-90-30 | 2215/53495 |
| ☐ HZ-APF | McDD MD-90-30 | 2216/53496 |
| ☐ HZ-APG | McDD MD-90-30 | 2219/53497 |
| ☐ HZ-APH | McDD MD-90-30 | 2221/53498 |
| ☐ HZ-API | McDD MD-90-30 | 2223/53499 |
| ☐ HZ-APJ | McDD MD-90-30 | 2225/53500 |
| ☐ HZ-APK | McDD MD-90-30 | 2226/53501 |
| ☐ HZ-APL | McDD MD-90-30 | 2227/53502 |
| ☐ HZ-APM | McDD MD-90-30 | 2229/53503 |
| ☐ HZ-APN | McDD MD-90-30 | 2230/53504 |
| ☐ HZ-APO | McDD MD-90-30 | 2231/53505 |
| ☐ HZ-APP | McDD MD-90-30 | 2232/53506 |
| ☐ HZ-APQ | McDD MD-90-30 | 2235/53507 |
| ☐ HZ-APR | McDD MD-90-30 | 2237/53508 |
| ☐ HZ-APS | McDD MD-90-30 | 2250/53509 |
| ☐ HZ-APT | McDD MD-90-30 | 2251/53510 |
| ☐ HZ-APU | McDD MD-90-30 | 2255/53511 |
| ☐ HZ-APV | McDD MD-90-30 | 2256/53512 |
| ☐ HZ-APW | McDD MD-90-30 | 2257/53513 |
| ☐ HZ-APX | McDD MD-90-30 | 2260/53514 |
| ☐ HZ-APY | McDD MD-90-30 | 2262/53515 |

| | | | |
|---|---|---|---|
| ☐ HZ-APZ | McDD MD-90-30 | 2263/53516 | |
| ☐ HZ-AP3 | McDD MD-90-30 | 2289/53518 | |
| ☐ HZ-AP4 | McDD MD-90-30 | 2290/53519 | |
| ☐ HZ-AP7 | McDD MD-90-30 | 2288/53517 | |
| ☐ HZ-ANA | McDD MD-11F | 609/48773 | |
| ☐ HZ-ANB | McDD MD-11F | 616/48775 | |
| ☐ HZ-ANC | McDD MD-11F | 617/48776 | |
| ☐ HZ-AND | McDD MD-11F | 618/48777 | |

# I - ITALY

## AIR DOLOMITI — DLA

| | | | |
|---|---|---|---|
| ☐ I-ADLF | ATR 42-500 | 462 | |
| ☐ I-ADLG | ATR 42-500 | 476 | |
| ☐ I-ADLH | ATR 42-500 | 445 | |
| ☐ I-ADLI | ATR 42-500 | 515 | |
| ☐ I-ADLJ | ATR 72-212A | 686 | |
| ☐ I-ADLL | ATR 42-500 | 518 | |
| ☐ I-ADLM | ATR 72-212A | 543 | |
| ☐ I-ADLN | ATR 72-212A | 557 | |
| ☐ I-ADLO | ATR 72-212A | 585 | |
| ☐ I-ADLP | ATR 42-500 | 604 | |
| ☐ I-ADLQ | ATR 42-500 | 606 | |
| ☐ I-ADLS | ATR 72-212A | 634 | |
| ☐ I-ADLT | ATR 72-212A | 638 | |
| ☐ I-ADLU | ATR 42-500 | 609 | |
| ☐ I-ADLV | ATR 42-500 | 610 | |
| ☐ I-ADLZ | ATR 42-500 | 611 | |
| ☐ | ATR 72-212A | | o/o |
| ☐ | ATR 72-212A | | o/o |
| ☐ I-ADJA | Canadair RJ-200 | 7478 | |
| ☐ I-ADJB | Canadair RJ-200 | 7486 | |
| ☐ I-ADJC | Canadair RJ-200 | 7494 | |
| ☐ I-ADJD | Canadair RJ-200 | 7625 | |
| ☐ I-ADJE | Canadair RJ-200 | 7629 | |
| ☐ I-ADJ | Canadair RJ-200 | | o/o |

## AIR EUROPE ITALY — AEL

| | | | |
|---|---|---|---|
| ☐ EI-CRS | Boeing 777-2Q8ER | 229/29908 | For REU |
| ☐ EI-CRT | Boeing 777-2Q8ER | 246/28676 | For REU |

## AIR INDUSTRIA

| | | |
|---|---|---|
| ☐ I-ATRF | ATR 42-300 | 034 |
| ☐ I-ATRG | ATR 42-300 | 042 |
| ☐ I-ATRJ | ATR 42-300 | 057 |
| ☐ I-ATRL | ATR 42-300 | 068 |

## AIR ONE — ADH

| | | | |
|---|---|---|---|
| ☐ D-AGMR | Boeing 737-430 | 2367/27007 | |
| ☐ EI-CLW | Boeing 737-3Y0 | 2248/25187 | |
| ☐ EI-CLZ | Boeing 737-3Y0 | 2205/25179 | |
| ☐ EI-COH | Boeing 737-430 | 2316/27001 | |
| ☐ EI-COI | Boeing 737-430 | 2323/27002 | |
| ☐ EI-COJ | Boeing 737-430 | 2359/27005 | |
| ☐ EI-COK | Boeing 737-430 | 2328/27003 | |
| ☐ EI-CRZ | Boeing 737-36E | 2770/26322 | |
| ☐ EI-CSU | Boeing 737-36E | 2792/27626 | |
| ☐ EI-CWE | Boeing 737-42C | 2060/24232 | |
| ☐ EI-CWF | Boeing 737-42C | 2270/24814 | |
| ☐ EI-CWW | Boeing 737-4Y0 | 2064/24912 | |
| ☐ EI-CWX | Boeing 737-4Y0 | 2009/24906 | |
| ☐ EI-CXH | Boeing 737-4Q8 | 1665/24070 | |
| ☐ EI-CXI | Boeing 737-46Q | 2910/28661 | |
| ☐ EI-CXJ | Boeing 737-4Q8 | 2447/25164 | |
| ☐ EI-CXL | Boeing 737-46N | 2886/28723 | |
| ☐ EI-CXM | Boeing 737-4Q8 | 2620/26302 | |
| ☐ EI-CZG | Boeing 737-4Q8 | 2461/25740 | |
| ☐ F-GKTA | Boeing 737-3M8 | 1884/24413 | |
| ☐ F-GKTB | Boeing 737-3M8 | 1895/24414 | |
| ☐ I-JETA | Boeing 737-229 | 593/21839 | |
| ☐ I-JETC | Boeing 737-230 | 1075/23153 | |
| ☐ I-JETD | Boeing 737-230 | 1089/23158 | |
| ☐ | Boeing 737-43Q | 2838/28493 | o/o |
| ☐ EI-CXP | Boeing 737-883 | 634/30467 | Lsf SAS |
| ☐ EI-CXT | Boeing 737-883 | 668/30468 | |
| ☐ EI-CXU | Boeing 737-883 | 625/28323 | |
| ☐ EI-CXW | Boeing 737-883 | 666/30194 | |
| ☐ TC-APK | Boeing 737-86N | 828/28643 | Lsf PGT |

## AIR SICILIA — SIC

| | | |
|---|---|---|
| ☐ N480AC | McDD MD-81 | 981/48008 |

## AIR VALLEE — RVL

| | | |
|---|---|---|
| ☐ I-AIRH | Dornier 328-300 | 3199 |
| ☐ I-AIRJ | Dornier 328-300 | 3186 |
| ☐ I-AIRX | Dornier 328-300 | 3142 |

## ALISEA — BBG

| | | | |
|---|---|---|---|
| ☐ TF-SUN | Boeing 737-3Q8 | 1301/23535 | Opb ICB |
| ☐ TF-MDD | McDD MD-83 | 1435/49602 | Lsf MDI |

## ALITALIA — AZA

| | | | |
|---|---|---|---|
| ☐ I-BIMA | Airbus A319-112 | 1722 | |
| ☐ I-BIMB | Airbus A319-112 | | o/o |
| ☐ I-BIMC | Airbus A319-112 | | o/o |
| ☐ I-BIMD | Airbus A319-112 | | o/o |
| ☐ I-BIME | Airbus A319-112 | 1740 | |
| ☐ I-BIMF | Airbus A319-112 | | o/o |
| ☐ I-BIMG | Airbus A319-112 | | o/o |
| ☐ I-BIMI | Airbus A319-112 | 1745 | |
| ☐ I-BIMJ | Airbus A319-112 | 1779 | |
| ☐ I-BIMO | Airbus A319-112 | 1770 | |
| ☐ I-BIKA | Airbus A320-214 | 0951 | |
| ☐ I-BIKB | Airbus A320-214 | 1226 | |
| ☐ I-BIKC | Airbus A320-214 | 1448 | |
| ☐ I-BIKD | Airbus A320-214 | 1457 | |
| ☐ I-BIKE | Airbus A320-214 | 0999 | |
| ☐ I-BIKF | Airbus A320-214 | 1473 | |
| ☐ I-BIKG | Airbus A320-214 | 1480 | |
| ☐ I-BIKI | Airbus A320-214 | 1138 | |
| ☐ I-BIKL | Airbus A320-214 | 1489 | |
| ☐ I-BIKO | Airbus A320-214 | 1168 | |
| ☐ I-BIKU | Airbus A320-214 | 1217 | |
| ☐ I-BIXA | Airbus A321-112 | 0477 | |
| ☐ I-BIXB | Airbus A321-112 | 0524 | |
| ☐ I-BIXC | Airbus A321-112 | 0526 | |
| ☐ I-BIXD | Airbus A321-112 | 0532 | |
| ☐ I-BIXE | Airbus A321-112 | 0488 | |
| ☐ I-BIXF | Airbus A321-112 | 0515 | |
| ☐ I-BIXG | Airbus A321-112 | 0516 | |
| ☐ I-BIXH | Airbus A321-112 | 0940 | |
| ☐ I-BIXI | Airbus A321-112 | 0494 | |
| ☐ I-BIXJ | Airbus A321-112 | 0959 | |
| ☐ I-BIXK | Airbus A321-112 | 1220 | |
| ☐ I-BIXL | Airbus A321-112 | 0513 | |
| ☐ I-BIXM | Airbus A321-112 | 0514 | |
| ☐ I-BIXN | Airbus A321-112 | 0576 | |
| ☐ I-BIXO | Airbus A321-112 | 0495 | |
| ☐ I-BIXP | Airbus A321-112 | 0583 | |
| ☐ I-BIXQ | Airbus A321-112 | 0586 | |
| ☐ I-BIXR | Airbus A321-112 | 0593 | |
| ☐ I-BIXS | Airbus A321-112 | 0599 | |
| ☐ I-BIXT | Airbus A321-112 | 0765 | |
| ☐ I-BIXU | Airbus A321-112 | 0434 | |
| ☐ I-BIXV | Airbus A321-112 | 0819 | |
| ☐ I-BIXZ | Airbus A321-112 | 0848 | |
| ☐ I-DEMC | Boeing 747-243M | 492/22506 | |
| ☐ I-DEML | Boeing 747-243B | 536/22511 | std |
| ☐ I-DEMP | Boeing 747-243B | 546/22513 | std |
| ☐ I-DEMR | Boeing 747-243F | 545/22545 | |
| ☐ I-DEMY | Boeing 747-230B | 345/21589 | std |

| | | | |
|---|---|---|---|
| ☐ EI-CRD | Boeing 767-31BER | 534/26259 | |
| ☐ EI-CRF | Boeing 767-31BER | 542/25170 | |
| ☐ EI-CRL | Boeing 767-343ER | 743/30008 | |
| ☐ EI-CRM | Boeing 767-343ER | 746/30009 | |
| ☐ EI-CRO | Boeing 767-3Q8ER | 747/29383 | |
| ☐ EI-CTW | Boeing 767-341ER | 774/30342 | |
| ☐ I-DEIB | Boeing 767-33AER | 560/27376 | |
| ☐ I-DEIC | Boeing 767-33AER | 561/27377 | |
| ☐ I-DEID | Boeing 767-33AER | 584/27468 | |
| ☐ I-DEIF | Boeing 767-33AER | 578/27908 | std |
| ☐ I-DEIG | Boeing 767-33AER | 603/27918 | |
| ☐ I-DEIL | Boeing 767-33AER | 611/28147 | |
| | | | |
| ☐ I-DUPA | McDD MD-11C | 468/48426 | |
| ☐ I-DUPB | McDD MD-11C | 534/48431 | |
| ☐ I-DUPC | McDD MD-11 | 565/48581 | |
| ☐ I-DUPD | McDD MD-11 | 567/48630 | |
| ☐ I-DUPE | McDD MD-11C | 471/48427 | |
| ☐ I-DUPI | McDD MD-11C | 474/48428 | |
| ☐ I-DUPO | McDD MD-11C | 500/48429 | |
| ☐ I-DUPU | McDD MD-11C | 508/48430 | |
| | | | |
| ☐ I-DACM | McDD MD-82 | 1755/49971 | |
| ☐ I-DACN | McDD MD-82 | 1757/49972 | |
| ☐ I-DACP | McDD MD-82 | 1762/49973 | |
| ☐ I-DACQ | McDD MD-82 | 1774/49974 | |
| ☐ I-DACR | McDD MD-82 | 1775/49975 | |
| ☐ I-DACS | McDD MD-82 | 1806/53053 | |
| ☐ I-DACT | McDD MD-82 | 1856/53054 | |
| ☐ I-DACU | McDD MD-82 | 1857/53055 | |
| ☐ I-DACV | McDD MD-82 | 1880/53056 | |
| ☐ I-DACW | McDD MD-82 | 1894/53057 | |
| ☐ I-DACX | McDD MD-82 | 1944/53060 | |
| ☐ I-DACY | McDD MD-82 | 1942/53059 | |
| ☐ I-DACZ | McDD MD-82 | 1927/53058 | |
| ☐ I-DAND | McDD MD-82 | 1957/53061 | |
| ☐ I-DANF | McDD MD-82 | 1960/53062 | |
| ☐ I-DANG | McDD MD-82 | 1972/53176 | |
| ☐ I-DANH | McDD MD-82 | 1973/53177 | |
| ☐ I-DANL | McDD MD-82 | 1994/53178 | |
| ☐ I-DANM | McDD MD-82 | 1997/53179 | |
| ☐ I-DANP | McDD MD-82 | 2002/53180 | |
| ☐ I-DANQ | McDD MD-82 | 2005/53181 | |
| ☐ I-DANR | McDD MD-82 | 2007/53203 | |
| ☐ I-DANU | McDD MD-82 | 2009/53204 | |
| ☐ I-DANV | McDD MD-82 | 2028/53205 | |
| ☐ I-DANW | McDD MD-82 | 2034/53206 | |
| ☐ I-DATA | McDD MD-82 | 2048/53216 | |
| ☐ I-DATB | McDD MD-82 | 2079/53221 | |
| ☐ I-DATC | McDD MD-82 | 2080/53222 | |
| ☐ I-DATD | McDD MD-82 | 2081/53223 | |
| ☐ I-DATE | McDD MD-82 | 2053/53217 | |
| ☐ I-DATF | McDD MD-82 | 2084/53224 | |
| ☐ I-DATG | McDD MD-82 | 2086/53225 | |
| ☐ I-DATH | McDD MD-82 | 2087/53226 | |
| ☐ I-DATI | McDD MD-82 | 2060/53218 | |
| ☐ I-DATJ | McDD MD-82 | 2103/53227 | |
| ☐ I-DATK | McDD MD-82 | 2104/53228 | |
| ☐ I-DATL | McDD MD-82 | 2105/53229 | |
| ☐ I-DATM | McDD MD-82 | 2106/53230 | |
| ☐ I-DATN | McDD MD-82 | 2107/53231 | |
| ☐ I-DATO | McDD MD-82 | 2062/53219 | |
| ☐ I-DATP | McDD MD-82 | 2108/53232 | |
| ☐ I-DATQ | McDD MD-82 | 2110/53233 | |
| ☐ I-DATR | McDD MD-82 | 2111/53234 | |
| ☐ I-DATS | McDD MD-82 | 2113/53235 | |
| ☐ I-DATU | McDD MD-82 | 2073/53220 | |
| ☐ I-DAVA | McDD MD-82 | 1253/49215 | |
| ☐ I-DAVB | McDD MD-82 | 1262/49216 | |
| ☐ I-DAVC | McDD MD-82 | 1268/49217 | |
| ☐ I-DAVD | McDD MD-82 | 1274/49218 | |
| ☐ I-DAVF | McDD MD-82 | 1310/49219 | |
| ☐ I-DAVG | McDD MD-82 | 1319/49220 | |
| ☐ I-DAVH | McDD MD-82 | 1330/49221 | |
| ☐ I-DAVI | McDD MD-82 | 1334/49430 | |
| ☐ I-DAVJ | McDD MD-82 | 1377/49431 | |
| ☐ I-DAVK | McDD MD-82 | 1378/49432 | |
| ☐ I-DAVL | McDD MD-82 | 1428/49433 | |
| ☐ I-DAVM | McDD MD-82 | 1446/49434 | |
| ☐ I-DAVP | McDD MD-82 | 1544/49549 | |

| | | | |
|---|---|---|---|
| ☐ I-DAVR | McDD MD-82 | 1584/49550 | |
| ☐ I-DAVS | McDD MD-82 | 1586/49551 | |
| ☐ I-DAVT | McDD MD-82 | 1597/49552 | |
| ☐ I-DAVU | McDD MD-82 | 1600/49794 | |
| ☐ I-DAVV | McDD MD-82 | 1639/49795 | |
| ☐ I-DAVW | McDD MD-82 | 1713/49796 | |
| ☐ I-DAVX | McDD MD-82 | 1719/49969 | |
| ☐ I-DAVZ | McDD MD-82 | 1737/49970 | |
| ☐ I-DAWA | McDD MD-82 | 1126/49192 | |
| ☐ I-DAWB | McDD MD-82 | 1138/49197 | |
| ☐ I-DAWC | McDD MD-82 | 1142/49198 | |
| ☐ I-DAWD | McDD MD-82 | 1143/49199 | |
| ☐ I-DAWE | McDD MD-82 | 1127/49193 | |
| ☐ I-DAWF | McDD MD-82 | 1147/49200 | |
| ☐ I-DAWG | McDD MD-82 | 1148/49201 | |
| ☐ I-DAWH | McDD MD-82 | 1170/49202 | |
| ☐ I-DAWI | McDD MD-82 | 1130/49194 | |
| ☐ I-DAWJ | McDD MD-82 | 1174/49203 | |
| ☐ I-DAWL | McDD MD-82 | 1179/49204 | |
| ☐ I-DAWM | McDD MD-82 | 1184/49205 | |
| ☐ I-DAWO | McDD MD-82 | 1136/49195 | |
| ☐ I-DAWP | McDD MD-82 | 1188/49206 | |
| ☐ I-DAWQ | McDD MD-82 | 1189/49207 | |
| ☐ I-DAWR | McDD MD-82 | 1190/49208 | |
| ☐ I-DAWS | McDD MD-82 | 1191/49209 | |
| ☐ I-DAWT | McDD MD-82 | 1192/49210 | |
| ☐ I-DAWU | McDD MD-82 | 1137/49196 | |
| ☐ I-DAWV | McDD MD-82 | 1202/49211 | |
| ☐ I-DAWW | McDD MD-82 | 1233/49212 | |
| ☐ I-DAWY | McDD MD-82 | 1243/49213 | |
| ☐ I-DAWZ | McDD MD-82 | 1245/49214 | |
| | | | |
| ☐ I-DISA | Boeing 777-243ER | 413/32855 | |
| ☐ I-DISB | Boeing 777-243ER | 426/32859 | |
| ☐ I-DISD | Boeing 777-243ER | 32860 | o/o |
| ☐ I-DISE | Boeing 777-243ER | 421/32856 | |
| ☐ I-DISO | Boeing 777-243ER | 424/32857 | |
| ☐ I-DISU | Boeing 777-243ER | 425/32858 | |
| ☐ I- | Boeing 777-243ER | | o/o |
| ☐ I- | Boeing 777-243ER | | o/o |
| ☐ I- | Boeing 777-243ER | | o/o |

### ALITALIA EXPRESS                SMX

| | | | |
|---|---|---|---|
| ☐ EI-CLB | ATR 72-212 | 423 | |
| ☐ EI-CLC | ATR 72-212 | 428 | |
| ☐ EI-CLD | ATR 72-212 | 432 | |
| ☐ EI-CMJ | ATR 72-212 | 467 | |
| ☐ I-ATLR | ATR 72-212A | 701 | |
| ☐ I-ATMC | ATR 72-212A | 588 | |
| ☐ I-ATPA | ATR 72-212A | 626 | |
| ☐ I-ATRM | ATR 42-300 | 114 | |
| ☐ I-ATSL | ATR 72-212A | 592 | |
| ☐ I-ATSM | ATR 72-212A | 702 | |
| ☐ I-NOWA | ATR 42-300 | 051 | |
| ☐ I-NOWT | ATR 42-300 | 054 | |
| ☐ I- | ATR 72-212A | | |
| | | | |
| ☐ I-EXMA | Embraer ERJ-145 | 145250 | |
| ☐ I-EXMB | Embraer ERJ-145 | 145330 | |
| ☐ I-EXMC | Embraer ERJ-145 | 145436 | |
| ☐ I-EXMD | Embraer ERJ-145 | 145445 | |
| ☐ I-EXME | Embraer ERJ-145 | 145282 | |
| ☐ I-EXMF | Embraer ERJ-145 | 145641 | |
| ☐ I-EXMG | Embraer ERJ-145 | 145652 | |
| ☐ I-EXMH | Embraer ERJ-145 | 145665 | |
| ☐ I-EXMI | Embraer ERJ-145 | 145286 | |
| ☐ I-EXMO | Embraer ERJ-145 | 145299 | |
| ☐ I-EXMU | Embraer ERJ-145 | 145316 | |
| ☐ I- | Embraer ERJ-145 | | o/o |
| ☐ I- | Embraer ERJ-145 | | o/o |
| ☐ I- | Embraer ERJ-145 | | o/o |
| ☐ I- | Embraer 170 | | o/o |
| ☐ I- | Embraer 170 | | o/o |
| ☐ I- | Embraer 170 | | o/o |
| ☐ I- | Embraer 170 | | o/o |
| ☐ I- | Embraer 170 | | o/o |

## ALPI EAGLES

| | | | |
|---|---|---|---|
| ☐ I-ALPK | Fokker 100 | 11244 | |
| ☐ I-ALPL | Fokker 100 | 11250 | |
| ☐ I-ALPQ | Fokker 100 | 11256 | |
| ☐ I-ALPS | Fokker 100 | 11254 | |
| ☐ I-ALPW | Fokker 100 | 11255 | |
| ☐ I-ALPX | Fokker 100 | 11251 | |
| ☐ I-ALPZ | Fokker 100 | 11252 | |
| ☐ I-ELGF | Fokker 100 | 11253 | |
| | | | |
| ☐ OY-MRI | Boeing 737-7L9 | 766/28014 | Lsf DAN |
| ☐ OY-MRK | Boeing 737-7L9 | 1092/28012 | Lsf DAN |

## AZZURRA AIR       AZI

| | | | |
|---|---|---|---|
| ☐ EI-CNI | Avro RJ-85 | E2299 | |
| ☐ EI-CNJ | Avro RJ-85 | E2300 | |
| ☐ EI-CNK | Avro RJ-85 | E2306 | |
| ☐ EI-COQ | Avro RJ-70 | E1254 | |
| ☐ EI-CPJ | Avro RJ-70 | E1258 | |
| ☐ EI-CPK | Avro RJ-70 | E1260 | |
| ☐ EI-CPL | Avro RJ-70 | E1267 | |
| | | | |
| ☐ D-AGEY | Boeing 737-73S | 98/29076 | Lsf GMI |
| ☐ D-AGEZ | Boeing 737-73S | 104/29077 | Lsf GMI |
| ☐ EI-CXD | Boeing 737-76N | 1120/29885 | |
| ☐ EI-CXE | Boeing 737-76N | 1130/32737 | |
| ☐ OY-MRP | Boeing 737-7L9 | 1092/28012 | Lsf DAN |

## BLUE PANORAMA AIRLINES     BPA

| | | | |
|---|---|---|---|
| ☐ D-AHLU | Boeing 737-4K5 | 2677/27831 | Lst AAW |
| ☐ EI-CUA | Boeing 737-4K5 | 1854/24901 | |
| ☐ EI-CUD | Boeing 737-4Q8 | 2564/26298 | |
| ☐ EI-CUN | Boeing 737-4K5 | 2281/27074 | |
| ☐ I-BPAC | Boeing 737-4Z9 | 2043/25147 | Lst AAW |
| | | | |
| ☐ EI-CXO | Boeing 767-3G5ER | 612/2811 | Lst CUB |
| ☐ EI-CZH | Boeing 767-3G5ER | 720/29435 | |

## CLUBAIR SIXGO     ISG

| | | | |
|---|---|---|---|
| ☐ G-DEFK | BAe 146 Srs.200 | E2012 | |
| ☐ G-DEFL | BAe 146 Srs.200 | E2014 | |
| ☐ I-SIXA | F.27 Friendship 500F | 10637 | |

## EUROFLY     EEZ

| | | | |
|---|---|---|---|
| ☐ I-BIKC | Airbus A320-214 | 1448 | Lsf AZA |
| ☐ I-BIKD | Airbus A320-214 | 1457 | Lsf AZA |
| ☐ I-BIKF | Airbus A320-214 | 1473 | Lsf AZA |
| ☐ I-BIKL | Airbus A320-214 | 1489 | Lsf AZA |
| ☐ I-EEZC | Airbus A320-214 | 1852 | |
| ☐ I- | Airbus A320-214 | 1920 | o/o |
| ☐ I- | Airbus A320-214 | 1937 | o/o |
| ☐ I-EEZA | Airbus A330-223 | 358 | |
| ☐ I-EEZB | Airbus A330-223 | 364 | |

## FREEAIR ITALY

| | | | |
|---|---|---|---|
| ☐ VP-B | McDD MD-83 | 1784/49937 | |
| ☐ EI-CPB | McDD MD-83 | 1788/49940 | |

## GANDALF AIRLINES     GNF

| | | | |
|---|---|---|---|
| ☐ D-BGAB | Dornier 328-300 | 3134 | |
| ☐ D-BGAD | Dornier 328-300 | 3136 | |
| ☐ D-BGAE | Dornier 328-300 | 3146 | |
| ☐ D-BGAF | Dornier 328-300 | 3137 | std |
| ☐ D-BGAG | Dornier 328-300 | 3133 | |
| ☐ D-BGAL | Dornier 328-300 | 3131 | Lst HGS |
| ☐ D-BGAQ | Dornier 328-300 | 3130 | |
| ☐ D-BGAR | Dornier 328-300 | 3152 | |
| ☐ D-BGAS | Dornier 328-300 | 3139 | |

| | | | |
|---|---|---|---|
| ☐ D-CGAC | Dornier 328-110 | 3117 | std |
| ☐ D-CGAN | Dornier 328-110 | 3112 | |
| ☐ D-CGAO | Dornier 328-110 | 3113 | |
| ☐ D-CGAP | Dornier 328-110 | 3107 | |
| ☐ D-CGEP | Dornier 328-110 | 3089 | |

## ICARO     ICA

| | | | |
|---|---|---|---|
| ☐ I-VICY | SA.227DC Metro 23 | DC-849B | |

## ITALY FIRST     IFS

| | | | |
|---|---|---|---|
| ☐ I-RIML | ATR 42-300 | 206 | |
| ☐ I-RIMS | ATR 42-300 | 190 | |

## LAUDA AIR ITALY     LDI

| | | | |
|---|---|---|---|
| ☐ OE-LAT | Boeing 767-31AER | 393/25273 | Lsf LDA |
| ☐ OE-LAW | Boeing 767-3Z9ER | 448/26417 | Lsf LDA |
| ☐ OE-LAX | Boeing 767-3Z9ER | 467/27095 | Lsf LDA |
| | | | |
| ☐ | Airbus A321-231 | 1950 | o/o |
| ☐ | Airbus A321-231 | 1970 | o/o |
| ☐ | Airbus A330-243 | | o/o |

## MERIDIANA     ISS

| | | | |
|---|---|---|---|
| ☐ EI-CIW | McDD MD-83 | 1628/49785 | |
| ☐ EI-CKM | McDD MD-83 | 1655/49792 | |
| ☐ EI-CRE | McDD MD-83 | 1601/49854 | |
| ☐ EI-CRH | McDD MD-83 | 1773/49935 | |
| ☐ EI-CRJ | McDD MD-83 | 1738/53013 | |
| ☐ EI-CRW | McDD MD-83 | 1915/49951 | |
| ☐ I-SMEB | McDD MD-82 | 1908/53064 | |
| ☐ I-SMEC | McDD MD-83 | 1836/49808 | |
| ☐ I-SMED | McDD MD-83 | 2068/53182 | |
| ☐ I-SMEL | McDD MD-82 | 1151/49247 | |
| ☐ I-SMEM | McDD MD-82 | 1152/49248 | |
| ☐ I-SMEP | McDD MD-82 | 1618/49740 | |
| ☐ I-SMER | McDD MD-82 | 1766/49901 | |
| ☐ I-SMES | McDD MD-82 | 1948/49902 | |
| ☐ I-SMET | McDD MD-82 | 1362/49531 | |
| ☐ I-SMEV | McDD MD-82 | 1493/49669 | |
| ☐ I-SMEZ | McDD MD-82 | 1949/49903 | |
| | | | |
| ☐ I-FLRE | BAe 146 Srs.200 | E2210 | |
| ☐ I-FLRI | BAe 146 Srs.200 | E2220 | |
| ☐ I-FLRO | BAe 146 Srs.200 | E2227 | |
| ☐ I-FLRU | BAe 146 Srs.200 | E2204 | |

## MINERVA AIRLINES     MTC

| | | | |
|---|---|---|---|
| ☐ D-CPRP | Dornier 328-110 | 3066 | |
| ☐ D-CPRS | Dornier 328-110 | 3046 | |
| ☐ D-CPRT | Dornier 328-110 | 3042 | |
| ☐ D-CPRU | Dornier 328-110 | 3091 | |
| ☐ D-CPRV | Dornier 328-110 | 3093 | |
| ☐ D-CPRW | Dornier 328-110 | 3097 | |
| ☐ D-CPRX | Dornier 328-110 | 3101 | |
| ☐ D-CPRY | Dornier 328-110 | 3106 | |

## MINILINER     MNL

| | | | |
|---|---|---|---|
| ☐ I-MLQT | F.27 Friendship 400 | 10295 | Lsf FAT |
| ☐ I-MLRT | F.27 Friendship 500 | 10377 | |
| ☐ I-MLTT | F.27 Friendship 500 | 10378 | |
| ☐ I-MLUT | F.27 Friendship 500 | 10369 | |
| ☐ I-MLVT | F.27 Friendship 500 | 10373 | |
| ☐ I- | F.27 Friendship 500 | 10379 | std |
| ☐ I- | F.27 Friendship 500 | 10382 | std |
| ☐ I- | F.27 Friendship 500 | 10390 | |

## MISTRAL AIR     MSA

| | | | |
|---|---|---|---|
| ☐ I-MSAA | BAe 146 Srs.200QT | E2109 | Opf TNT |
| ☐ I-TNTC | BAe 146 Srs.200QT | E2078 | Opf TNT |

## NEOS · NOS

| | | |
|---|---|---|
| ☐ I-NEOS | Boeing 737-86N | 1078/32733 |
| ☐ I-NEOT | Boeing 737-86N | 1144/33004 |
| ☐ I-NEOU | Boeing 737-86N | 1263/29887 |

## PANAIR · PIT

| | | |
|---|---|---|
| ☐ EI-PAM | Boeing 737-4Q8 | 1635/24069 |
| ☐ EI-PAR | Boeing 737-3Q8 | 1666/24300 |

## VOLARE AIRLINES · VLE

| | | | |
|---|---|---|---|
| ☐ EI-CTD | Airbus A320-211 | 0085 | |
| ☐ EI-CUQ | Airbus A320-214 | 1259 | |
| ☐ F-GJVU | Airbus A320-211 | 0436 | |
| ☐ F-GJVX | Airbus A320-211 | 0420 | |
| ☐ F-GLGN | Airbus A320-212 | 0132 | |
| ☐ F-OHFR | Airbus A320-212 | 0189 | |
| ☐ F-OHFT | Airbus A320-212 | 0343 | |
| ☐ F-OHFU | Airbus A320-212 | 0190 | |
| ☐ I-PEKE | Airbus A320-214 | 1308 | |
| ☐ I-PEKF | Airbus A320-214 | 1322 | |
| ☐ I-PEKG | Airbus A320-214 | 1132 | |
| ☐ I-PEKH | Airbus A320-214 | 1162 | |
| ☐ I-PEKI | Airbus A320-214 | 1179 | |
| ☐ I-PEKL | Airbus A320-214 | 1244 | |
| ☐ I-PEKM | Airbus A321-211 | 1451 | |
| ☐ I-PEKN | Airbus A321-211 | 1607 | |
| ☐ I-PEKO | Airbus A320-214 | 1152 | |
| ☐ I-PEKP | Airbus A320-214 | 1198 | |
| ☐ I-PEKQ | Airbus A320-214 | 1757 | |
| ☐ I-VLEA | Airbus A320-214 | 1125 | |
| ☐ I-VLEC | Airbus A330-202 | 205 | |
| ☐ I-VLED | Airbus A330-202 | 211 | |
| ☐ I-VLEE | Airbus A330-202 | 272 | |
| ☐ I-VLEF | Airbus A330-202 | 339 | |
| ☐ I-VLEG | Airbus A330-203 | 463 | |
| ☐ I-VLEH | Airbus A330-203 | 504 | |
| | | | |
| ☐ I-VIMQ | Boeing 767-3Q8ER | 619/27993 | |
| ☐ I- | Airbus A319- | | o/o |
| ☐ I- | Airbus A319- | | o/o |
| ☐ I- | Airbus A319- | | o/o |

# JA - JAPAN

## AIR DO · ADO

| | | |
|---|---|---|
| ☐ JA01HD | Boeing 767-33AER | 689/28159 |
| ☐ JA98AD | Boeing 767-33AER | 687/27476 |

## AIR JAPAN · AJX

| | | | |
|---|---|---|---|
| ☐ JA8323 | Boeing 767-381ER | 463/25654 | Lsf ANA |
| ☐ JA8356 | Boeing 767-381ER | 379/25136 | Lsf ANA |
| ☐ JA8362 | Boeing 767-381ER | 285/24632 | Lsf ANA |
| ☐ JA8664 | Boeing 767-381ER | 556/27339 | Lsf ANA |
| ☐ JA8970 | Boeing 767-381ER | 645/25619 | Lsf ANA |
| ☐ JA603A | Boeing 767-381 | 877/32972 | Lsf ANA |
| ☐ JA604A | Boeing 767-381 | 881/32973 | Lsf ANA |
| ☐ JA605A | Boeing 767-381 | 882/32974 | Lsf ANA |
| ☐ JA606A | Boeing 767-381 | 883/32975 | Lsf ANA |
| ☐ JA607A | Boeing 767-381 | 884/32976 | Lsf ANA |
| ☐ JA608A | Boeing 767-381 | 886/32977 | Lsf ANA |

## AIR NIPPON · ANK

| | | | |
|---|---|---|---|
| ☐ JA8389 | Airbus A320-211 | 0219 | Lsf ANA |
| ☐ JA8390 | Airbus A320-211 | 0245 | Lsf ANA |
| ☐ JA8391 | Airbus A320-211 | 0300 | Lsf ANA |
| ☐ JA8393 | Airbus A320-211 | 0365 | Lsf ANA |
| | | | |
| ☐ JA300K | Boeing 737-54K | 2872/27434 | |
| ☐ JA301K | Boeing 737-54K | 2875/27435 | |
| ☐ JA302K | Boeing 737-54K | 3002/28990 | |

| | | | |
|---|---|---|---|
| ☐ JA303K | Boeing 737-54K | 3017/28991 | |
| ☐ JA304K | Boeing 737-54K | 3030/28992 | |
| ☐ JA305K | Boeing 737-54K | 3075/28993 | |
| ☐ JA306K | Boeing 737-54K | 3109/29794 | |
| ☐ JA307K | Boeing 737-54K | 3116/29795 | |
| ☐ JA351K | Boeing 737-5Y0 | 2240/25189 | |
| ☐ JA352K | Boeing 737-5Y0 | 2534/26097 | |
| ☐ JA353K | Boeing 737-5Y0 | 2552/26104 | |
| ☐ JA354K | Boeing 737-5Y0 | 2553/26105 | |
| ☐ JA355K | Boeing 737-5L9 | 2823/28129 | |
| ☐ JA356K | Boeing 737-5L9 | 2784/28083 | |
| ☐ JA357K | Boeing 737-5L9 | 2828/28131 | |
| ☐ JA358K | Boeing 737-5L9 | 2825/28130 | |
| ☐ JA359K | Boeing 737-5L9 | 2817/28128 | |
| ☐ JA391K | Boeing 737-4Y0 | 1805/24545 | |
| ☐ JA392K | Boeing 737-46M | 2847/28550 | |
| ☐ JA8195 | Boeing 737-54K | 2815/27433 | |
| ☐ JA8196 | Boeing 737-54K | 2824/27966 | |
| ☐ JA8404 | Boeing 737-54K | 2708/27381 | |
| ☐ JA8419 | Boeing 737-54K | 2723/27430 | |
| ☐ JA8500 | Boeing 737-54K | 2751/27431 | |
| ☐ JA8504 | Boeing 737-54K | 2783/27432 | |
| ☐ JA8595 | Boeing 737-54K | 2850/28461 | |
| ☐ JA8596 | Boeing 737-54K | 2853/28462 | |
| | | | |
| ☐ JA8735 | NAMC YS-11A-213 | 2108 | std |
| ☐ JA8744 | NAMC YS-11A-213 | 2116 | |
| ☐ JA8761 | NAMC YS-11A-513 | 2133 | |
| ☐ JA8772 | NAMC YS-11A-523 | 2146 | |
| All for sale in Thailand | | | |

## ALL NIPPON AIRWAYS · ANA

| | | | |
|---|---|---|---|
| ☐ JA201A | Airbus A320-211 | 1973 | o/o |
| ☐ JA202A | Airbus A320-211 | 2054 | o/o |
| ☐ JA203A | Airbus A320-211 | 2061 | o/o |
| ☐ JA8300 | Airbus A320-211 | 0549 | |
| ☐ JA8304 | Airbus A320-211 | 0531 | |
| ☐ JA8313 | Airbus A320-211 | 0534 | |
| ☐ JA8381 | Airbus A320-211 | 0138 | |
| ☐ JA8382 | Airbus A320-211 | 0139 | |
| ☐ JA8383 | Airbus A320-211 | 0148 | |
| ☐ JA8384 | Airbus A320-211 | 0151 | |
| ☐ JA8385 | Airbus A320-211 | 0167 | |
| ☐ JA8386 | Airbus A320-211 | 0170 | |
| ☐ JA8387 | Airbus A320-211 | 0196 | Lst ANK |
| ☐ JA8388 | Airbus A320-211 | 0212 | |
| ☐ JA8389 | Airbus A320-211 | 0219 | Lst ANK |
| ☐ JA8390 | Airbus A320-211 | 0245 | Lst ANK |
| ☐ JA8391 | Airbus A320-211 | 0300 | Lst ANK |
| ☐ JA8392 | Airbus A320-211 | 0328 | |
| ☐ JA8393 | Airbus A320-211 | 0365 | Lst ANK |
| ☐ JA8394 | Airbus A320-211 | 0383 | |
| ☐ JA8395 | Airbus A320-211 | 0413 | |
| ☐ JA8396 | Airbus A320-211 | 0482 | |
| ☐ JA8400 | Airbus A320-211 | 0554 | |
| ☐ JA8609 | Airbus A320-211 | 0501 | |
| ☐ JA8654 | Airbus A320-211 | 0507 | |
| ☐ JA8946 | Airbus A320-211 | 0669 | |
| ☐ JA8947 | Airbus A320-211 | 0685 | |
| ☐ JA8948 | Airbus A320-211 | | o/o |
| ☐ JA8949 | Airbus A320-211 | | o/o |
| ☐ JA8950 | Airbus A320-211 | | o/o |
| ☐ JA8997 | Airbus A320-211 | 0658 | |
| | | | |
| ☐ JA101A | Airbus A321-131 | 0802 | |
| ☐ JA102A | Airbus A321-131 | 0811 | |
| ☐ JA103A | Airbus A321-131 | 0963 | |
| ☐ JA104A | Airbus A321-131 | 1008 | |
| ☐ JA105A | Airbus A321-131 | 1042 | |
| ☐ JA106A | Airbus A321-131 | 1204 | |
| ☐ JA107A | Airbus A321-131 | 1227 | |
| | | | |
| ☐ JA401A | Boeing 747-481 | 1133/28282 | |
| ☐ JA402A | Boeing 747-481 | 1142/28283 | |
| ☐ JA403A | Boeing 747-481 | 1199/29262 | |
| ☐ JA404A | Boeing 747-481 | 1204/29263 | |

| | | | |
|---|---|---|---|
| ☐ JA405A | Boeing 747-481 | 1250/30322 | |
| ☐ JA8094 | Boeing 747-481 | 805/24801 | |
| ☐ JA8095 | Boeing 747-481 | 812/24833 | |
| ☐ JA8096 | Boeing 747-481 | 832/24920 | |
| ☐ JA8097 | Boeing 747-481 | 863/25135 | |
| ☐ JA8098 | Boeing 747-481 | 870/25207 | |
| ☐ JA8099 | Boeing 747-481D | 891/25292 | |
| ☐ JA8146 | Boeing 747SR-81 | 456/22292 | |
| ☐ JA8147 | Boeing 747SR-81 | 477/22293 | |
| ☐ JA8148 | Boeing 747SR-81 | 481/22294 | |
| ☐ JA8152 | Boeing 747SR-81 | 511/22594 | |
| ☐ JA8153 | Boeing 747SR-81 | 516/22595 | |
| ☐ JA8156 | Boeing 747SR-81 | 541/22709 | |
| ☐ JA8157 | Boeing 747SR-81 | 544/22710 | |
| ☐ JA8159 | Boeing 747SR-81 | 572/22712 | |
| ☐ JA8174 | Boeing 747-281B | 648/23501 | |
| ☐ JA8175 | Boeing 747-281B | 649/23502 | |
| ☐ JA8192 | Boeing 747-2D3B (SF) | 514/22579 | Lst NCA |
| ☐ JA8955 | Boeing 747-481D | 914/25639 | |
| ☐ JA8956 | Boeing 747-481D | 920/25640 | |
| ☐ JA8957 | Boeing 747-481D | 927/25642 | |
| ☐ JA8958 | Boeing 747-481 | 928/25641 | |
| ☐ JA8959 | Boeing 747-481D | 952/25646 | |
| ☐ JA8960 | Boeing 747-481D | 972/25643 | |
| ☐ JA8961 | Boeing 747-481D | 975/25644 | |
| ☐ JA8962 | Boeing 747-481 | 979/25645 | |
| ☐ JA8963 | Boeing 747-481D | 991/25647 | |
| ☐ JA8964 | Boeing 747-481D | 996/27163 | |
| ☐ JA8965 | Boeing 747-481D | 1060/27436 | |
| ☐ JA8966 | Boeing 747-481D | 1066/27442 | |
| | | | |
| ☐ JA601A | Boeing 767-381 | 669/27943 | |
| ☐ JA601F | Boeing 767-381ERF | 885/33404 | |
| ☐ JA602A | Boeing 767-381 | 684/27944 | |
| ☐ JA603A | Boeing 767-381 | 877/32972 | |
| ☐ JA604A | Boeing 767-381 | 881/32973 | |
| ☐ JA605A | Boeing 767-381 | 882/32974 | |
| ☐ JA606A | Boeing 767-381 | 883/32975 | |
| ☐ JA607A | Boeing 767-381 | 884/32976 | |
| ☐ JA608A | Boeing 767-381 | 886/32977 | |
| ☐ JA609A | Boeing 767-381 | 888/32978 | o/o |
| ☐ JA610A | Boeing 767-381 | 895/32979 | o/o |
| ☐ JA611A | Boeing 767-381 | 32980 | o/o |
| ☐ JA8240 | Boeing 767-281 | 110/23142 | |
| ☐ JA8244 | Boeing 767-281 | 121/23146 | |
| ☐ JA8245 | Boeing 767-281 | 123/23147 | |
| ☐ JA8251 | Boeing 767-281 | 143/23431 | |
| ☐ JA8252 | Boeing 767-281 | 145/23432 | |
| ☐ JA8255 | Boeing 767-281 | 171/23434 | |
| ☐ JA8256 | Boeing 767-381 | 176/23756 | |
| ☐ JA8257 | Boeing 767-381 | 177/23757 | |
| ☐ JA8258 | Boeing 767-381 | 179/23758 | |
| ☐ JA8259 | Boeing 767-381 | 185/23759 | |
| ☐ JA8271 | Boeing 767-381 | 199/24002 | |
| ☐ JA8272 | Boeing 767-381 | 212/24003 | |
| ☐ JA8273 | Boeing 767-381 | 218/24004 | |
| ☐ JA8274 | Boeing 767-381 | 222/24005 | |
| ☐ JA8275 | Boeing 767-381 | 223/24006 | |
| ☐ JA8285 | Boeing 767-381 | 245/24350 | |
| ☐ JA8286 | Boeing 767-381ER | 269/24400 | |
| ☐ JA8287 | Boeing 767-381 | 271/24351 | |
| ☐ JA8288 | Boeing 767-381 | 276/24415 | |
| ☐ JA8289 | Boeing 767-381 | 280/24416 | |
| ☐ JA8290 | Boeing 767-381 | 290/24417 | |
| ☐ JA8291 | Boeing 767-381 | 295/24755 | |
| ☐ JA8322 | Boeing 767-381 | 458/25618 | |
| ☐ JA8323 | Boeing 767-381ER | 463/25654 | |
| ☐ JA8324 | Boeing 767-381 | 465/25655 | |
| ☐ JA8342 | Boeing 767-381 | 573/27445 | |
| ☐ JA8356 | Boeing 767-381ER | 379/25136 | |
| ☐ JA8357 | Boeing 767-381 | 401/25293 | |
| ☐ JA8358 | Boeing 767-381ER | 432/25616 | |
| ☐ JA8359 | Boeing 767-381 | 439/25617 | |
| ☐ JA8360 | Boeing 767-381 | 352/25055 | |
| ☐ JA8362 | Boeing 767-381ER | 285/24632 | |
| ☐ JA8363 | Boeing 767-381 | 300/24756 | |
| ☐ JA8368 | Boeing 767-381 | 336/24880 | |
| ☐ JA8567 | Boeing 767-381 | 510/25656 | |

| | | | |
|---|---|---|---|
| ☐ JA8568 | Boeing 767-381 | 515/25657 | |
| ☐ JA8569 | Boeing 767-381 | 516/27050 | |
| ☐ JA8578 | Boeing 767-381 | 519/25658 | |
| ☐ JA8579 | Boeing 767-381 | 520/25659 | |
| ☐ JA8664 | Boeing 767-381ER | 556/27339 | |
| ☐ JA8669 | Boeing 767-381 | 567/27444 | |
| ☐ JA8670 | Boeing 767-381 | 539/25660 | |
| ☐ JA8674 | Boeing 767-381 | 543/25661 | |
| ☐ JA8677 | Boeing 767-381 | 551/25662 | |
| ☐ JA8970 | Boeing 767-381ER | 645/25619 | |
| ☐ JA8971 | Boeing 767-381ER | 651/27942 | |
| | | | |
| ☐ JA701A | Boeing 777-281 | 77/27938 | |
| ☐ JA702A | Boeing 777-281 | 75/27033 | |
| ☐ JA703A | Boeing 777-281 | 81/27034 | |
| ☐ JA704A | Boeing 777-281 | 131/27035 | |
| ☐ JA705A | Boeing 777-281 | 137/29029 | |
| ☐ JA706A | Boeing 777-281 | 141/27036 | |
| ☐ JA707A | Boeing 777-281ER | 247/27037 | |
| ☐ JA708A | Boeing 777-281ER | 278/28277 | |
| ☐ JA709A | Boeing 777-281ER | 286/28278 | |
| ☐ JA710A | Boeing 777-281ER | 302/28279 | |
| ☐ JA751A | Boeing 777-381 | 142/28272 | |
| ☐ JA752A | Boeing 777-381 | 160/28274 | |
| ☐ JA753A | Boeing 777-381 | 132/28273 | |
| ☐ JA754A | Boeing 777-381 | 172/27939 | |
| ☐ JA755A | Boeing 777-381 | 104/28275 | |
| ☐ JA756A | Boeing 777-381 | 27039 | o/o |
| ☐ JA757A | Boeing 777-381 | 27040 | o/o |
| ☐ JA8197 | Boeing 777-281 | 16/27027 | |
| ☐ JA8198 | Boeing 777-281 | 21/27028 | |
| ☐ JA8199 | Boeing 777-281 | 29/27029 | |
| ☐ JA8967 | Boeing 777-281 | 37/27030 | |
| ☐ JA8968 | Boeing 777-281 | 38/27031 | |
| ☐ JA8969 | Boeing 777-281 | 50/27032 | |

| FAIR LINK | | | FRI |
|---|---|---|---|
| ☐ JA01RJ | Canadair RJ-200 | 7052 | |
| ☐ JA02RJ | Canadair RJ-200 | 7033 | |
| ☐ JA03RJ | Canadair RJ-200 | 7624 | |
| ☐ JA04RJ | Canadair RJ-200 | 7817 | o/o |

| J-AIR | | | |
|---|---|---|---|
| ☐ JA201J | Canadair RJ-200 | 7452 | |
| ☐ JA202J | Canadair RJ-200 | 7484 | |
| ☐ JA203J | Canadair RJ-200 | 7626 | |
| ☐ JA204J | Canadair RJ-200 | 7643 | |
| ☐ JA205J | Canadair RJ-200 | | o/o |
| ☐ JA206J | Canadair RJ-200 | | o/o |

| JAL EXPRESS | | | JEX |
|---|---|---|---|
| ☐ JA8991 | Boeing 737-446 | 2718/27916 | |
| ☐ JA8992 | Boeing 737-446 | 2729/27917 | |
| ☐ JA8993 | Boeing 737-446 | 2812/28087 | |
| ☐ JA8994 | Boeing 737-446 | 2907/28097 | |
| ☐ JA8995 | Boeing 737-446 | 2911/28831 | |
| ☐ JA8996 | Boeing 737-446 | 2953/28832 | |
| ☐ JA8998 | Boeing 737-446 | 3044/28994 | |
| ☐ JA8999 | Boeing 737-446 | 3111/29864 | |

| JAL WAYS | | | JAZ |
|---|---|---|---|
| ☐ JA8127 | Boeing 747-246B | 255/21031 | |
| ☐ JA8140 | Boeing 747-246B | 407/22064 | |
| ☐ JA8149 | Boeing 747-246B | 489/22478 | |
| ☐ JA8150 | Boeing 747-246B | 496/22479 | Lst JAL |
| ☐ JA8187 | Boeing 747-346 | 695/24019 | |
| ☐ JA8539 | Douglas DC-10-40 | 304/47822 | |
| ☐ JA8541 | Douglas DC-10-40 | 308/47824 | Lst JAL |
| ☐ JA8544 | Douglas DC-10-40 | 340/47852 | |
| ☐ JA8547 | Douglas DC-10-40 | 366/47856 | |

## JAPAN AIR COMMUTER       JAC

| | | | |
|---|---|---|---|
| ☐ JA841C | DHC-8Q-402 | 4072 | |
| ☐ JA842C | DHC-8Q-402 | 4073 | |
| ☐ JA843C | DHC-8Q-402 | 4076 | o/o |
| ☐ JA844C | DHC-8Q-402 | | o/o |
| ☐ JA845C | DHC-8Q-402 | | o/o |
| ☐ JA846C | DHC-8Q-402 | | o/o |
| | | | |
| ☐ JA8717 | NAMC YS-11A-217 | 2092 | Lsf JAS |
| ☐ JA8759 | NAMC YS-11A-227 | 2152 | Lsf JAS |
| ☐ JA8763 | NAMC YS-11A-227 | 2135 | Lsf JAS |
| ☐ JA8766 | NAMC YS-11A-227 | 2142 | Lsf JAS |
| ☐ JA8768 | NAMC YS-11A-222 | 2147 | Lsf JAS |
| ☐ JA8771 | NAMC YS-11A-227 | 2149 | Lsf JAS |
| ☐ JA8777 | NAMC YS-11A-227 | 2163 | Lsf JAS |
| ☐ JA8781 | NAMC YS-11A-217 | 2166 | Lsf JAS |
| ☐ JA8788 | NAMC YS-11A-217 | 2176 | Lsf JAS |
| ☐ JA8809 | NAMC YS-11A-202 | 2054 | Lsf JAS |
| | | | |
| ☐ JA001C | SAAB SF.340B | 419 | |
| ☐ JA002C | SAAB SF.340B | 459 | |
| ☐ JA8594 | SAAB SF.340B | 399 | |
| ☐ JA8642 | SAAB SF.340B | 365 | |
| ☐ JA8649 | SAAB SF.340B | 368 | |
| ☐ JA8703 | SAAB SF.340B | 355 | |
| ☐ JA8704 | SAAB SF.340B | 361 | |
| ☐ JA8886 | SAAB SF.340B | 281 | |
| ☐ JA8887 | SAAB SF.340B | 308 | |
| ☐ JA8888 | SAAB SF.340B | 331 | |
| ☐ JA8900 | SAAB SF.340B | 378 | |

## JAPAN AIR LINES       JAL

| | | | |
|---|---|---|---|
| ☐ JA8993 | Boeing 737-446 | 2812/28087 | |
| ☐ JA8994 | Boeing 737-446 | 2907/28097 | |
| ☐ JA8995 | Boeing 737-446 | 2911/28831 | |
| ☐ JA8996 | Boeing 737-446 | 2953/28832 | |
| ☐ JA8998 | Boeing 737-446 | 3044/28994 | |
| ☐ JA8999 | Boeing 737-446 | 3111/29864 | |
| | | | |
| ☐ JA811J | Boeing 747-246F | 571/22989 | |
| ☐ JA812J | Boeing 747-346 | 588/23067 | |
| ☐ JA813J | Boeing 747-346 | 589/23068 | |
| ☐ JA8071 | Boeing 747-446 | 758/24423 | |
| ☐ JA8072 | Boeing 747-446 | 760/24424 | |
| ☐ JA8073 | Boeing 747-446 | 767/24425 | |
| ☐ JA8074 | Boeing 747-446 | 768/24426 | |
| ☐ JA8075 | Boeing 747-446 | 780/24427 | |
| ☐ JA8076 | Boeing 747-446 | 797/24777 | |
| ☐ JA8077 | Boeing 747-446 | 798/24784 | |
| ☐ JA8078 | Boeing 747-446 | 821/24870 | |
| ☐ JA8079 | Boeing 747-446 | 824/24885 | |
| ☐ JA8080 | Boeing 747-446 | 825/24886 | |
| ☐ JA8081 | Boeing 747-446 | 851/25064 | |
| ☐ JA8082 | Boeing 747-446 | 871/25212 | |
| ☐ JA8083 | Boeing 747-446D | 844/25213 | |
| ☐ JA8084 | Boeing 747-446D | 879/25214 | |
| ☐ JA8085 | Boeing 747-446 | 876/25260 | |
| ☐ JA8086 | Boeing 747-446 | 885/25308 | |
| ☐ JA8087 | Boeing 747-446 | 897/26346 | |
| ☐ JA8088 | Boeing 747-446 | 902/26341 | |
| ☐ JA8089 | Boeing 747-446 | 905/26342 | |
| ☐ JA8090 | Boeing 747-446D | 907/26347 | |
| ☐ JA8128 | Boeing 747-146A | 259/21029 | |
| ☐ JA8130 | Boeing 747-246B | 376/21679 | |
| ☐ JA8131 | Boeing 747-246B | 380/21680 | |
| ☐ JA8132 | Boeing 747-246F | 382/21681 | |
| ☐ JA8141 | Boeing 747-246B | 411/22065 | |
| ☐ JA8150 | Boeing 747-246B | 496/22479 | |
| ☐ JA8160 | Boeing 747-221F | 392/21744 | |
| ☐ JA8161 | Boeing 747-246B (SF) | 579/22990 | |
| ☐ JA8162 | Boeing 747-246B | 581/22991 | |
| ☐ JA8163 | Boeing 747-346 | 599/23149 | |
| ☐ JA8164 | Boeing 747-146B | 601/23150 | |
| ☐ JA8165 | Boeing 747-221F | 384/21743 | |
| ☐ JA8166 | Boeing 747-346 | 607/23151 | |
| | | | |
| ☐ JA8169 | Boeing 747-246B (SF) | 635/23389 | |
| ☐ JA8170 | Boeing 747-346SR | 636/23390 | |
| ☐ JA8171 | Boeing 747-246F | 654/23391 | |
| ☐ JA8173 | Boeing 747-346 | 640/23482 | |
| ☐ JA8176 | Boeing 747-346SR | 655/23637 | |
| ☐ JA8177 | Boeing 747-346 | 658/23638 | |
| ☐ JA8178 | Boeing 747-346 | 664/23639 | |
| ☐ JA8179 | Boeing 747-346 | 668/23640 | |
| ☐ JA8180 | Boeing 747-246F | 684/23641 | |
| ☐ JA8183 | Boeing 747-346 | 692/23967 | |
| ☐ JA8184 | Boeing 747-346 | 693/23968 | |
| ☐ JA8185 | Boeing 747-346 | 691/23969 | |
| ☐ JA8186 | Boeing 747-346 | 694/24018 | |
| ☐ JA8193 | Boeing 747-212B (SF) | 457/21940 | |
| ☐ JA8901 | Boeing 747-446 | 918/26343 | |
| ☐ JA8902 | Boeing 747-446 | 929/26344 | |
| ☐ JA8903 | Boeing 747-446D | 935/26345 | |
| ☐ JA8904 | Boeing 747-446D | 941/26348 | |
| ☐ JA8905 | Boeing 747-446D | 948/26349 | |
| ☐ JA8906 | Boeing 747-446 | 961/26350 | |
| ☐ JA8907 | Boeing 747-446D | 963/26351 | |
| ☐ JA8908 | Boeing 747-446D | 978/26352 | |
| ☐ JA8909 | Boeing 747-446 | 980/26353 | |
| ☐ JA8910 | Boeing 747-446 | 1024/26355 | |
| ☐ JA8911 | Boeing 747-446 | 1026/26356 | |
| ☐ JA8912 | Boeing 747-446 | 1031/27099 | |
| ☐ JA8913 | Boeing 747-446 | 1153/26359 | |
| ☐ JA8914 | Boeing 747-446 | 1166/26360 | |
| ☐ JA8915 | Boeing 747-446 | 1188/26361 | |
| ☐ JA8916 | Boeing 747-446 | 1202/26362 | |
| ☐ JA8917 | Boeing 747-446 | 1208/29899 | |
| ☐ JA8918 | Boeing 747-446 | 1234/27650 | |
| ☐ JA8919 | Boeing 747-446 | 1236/27100 | |
| ☐ JA8920 | Boeing 747-446 | 1253/27648 | |
| ☐ JA8921 | Boeing 747-446 | 1262/27645 | |
| ☐ JA8922 | Boeing 747-446 | 1280/27646 | |
| ☐ JA8923 | Boeing 747-446 | | o/o |
| ☐ JA8924 | Boeing 747-446 | | o/o |
| ☐ JA8925 | Boeing 747-446 | | o/o |
| ☐ JA8937 | Boeing 747-246F | 494/22477 | |
| | | | |
| ☐ JA601J | Boeing 767-346ER | 875/32886 | |
| ☐ JA602J | Boeing 767-346ER | 879/32887 | |
| ☐ JA603J | Boeing 767-346ER | 880/32888 | |
| ☐ JA604J | Boeing 767-346ER | 33493 | o/o |
| ☐ JA605J | Boeing 767-346ER | 33494 | o/o |
| ☐ JA606J | Boeing 767-346ER | 33495 | o/o |
| ☐ JA607J | Boeing 767-346ER | 33496 | o/o |
| ☐ JA8233 | Boeing 767-246 | 122/23214 | |
| ☐ JA8234 | Boeing 767-346 | 148/23216 | |
| ☐ JA8235 | Boeing 767-346 | 150/23217 | |
| ☐ JA8236 | Boeing 767-346 | 132/23215 | |
| ☐ JA8253 | Boeing 767-346 | 174/23645 | |
| ☐ JA8264 | Boeing 767-346 | 186/23965 | |
| ☐ JA8265 | Boeing 767-346 | 192/23961 | |
| ☐ JA8267 | Boeing 767-346 | 193/23962 | |
| ☐ JA8268 | Boeing 767-346 | 224/23963 | |
| ☐ JA8269 | Boeing 767-346 | 225/23964 | |
| ☐ JA8299 | Boeing 767-346 | 277/24498 | |
| ☐ JA8364 | Boeing 767-346 | 327/24782 | |
| ☐ JA8365 | Boeing 767-346 | 329/24783 | |
| ☐ JA8397 | Boeing 767-346 | 547/27311 | |
| ☐ JA8398 | Boeing 767-346 | 548/27312 | |
| ☐ JA8399 | Boeing 767-346 | 554/27313 | |
| ☐ JA8975 | Boeing 767-346 | 581/27658 | |
| ☐ JA8980 | Boeing 767-346 | 673/28837 | |
| ☐ JA8986 | Boeing 767-346 | 680/28838 | |
| ☐ JA8988 | Boeing 767-346 | 772/29863 | |
| | | | |
| ☐ JA701J | Boeing 777-246ER | 410/32889 | |
| ☐ JA702J | Boeing 777-246ER | 417/32890 | |
| ☐ JA703J | Boeing 777-246ER | 427/32891 | |
| ☐ JA704J | Boeing 777-246ER | 32892 | o/o |
| ☐ JA705J | Boeing 777-246ER | 32893 | o/o |
| ☐ JA731J | Boeing 777-346ER | 423/32430 | o/o |
| ☐ JA732J | Boeing 777-346ER | 429/32431 | o/o |
| ☐ JA733J | Boeing 777-346ER | 32432 | o/o |
| ☐ JA771J | Boeing 777-246ER | 27656 | o/o |

| | | | |
|---|---|---|---|
| ☐ JA8941 | Boeing 777-346 | 152/28393 | |
| ☐ JA8942 | Boeing 777-346 | 158/28394 | |
| ☐ JA8943 | Boeing 777-346 | 196/28395 | |
| ☐ JA8944 | Boeing 777-346 | 212/28396 | |
| ☐ JA8945 | Boeing 777-346 | 238/28397 | |
| ☐ JA8981 | Boeing 777-246 | 23/27364 | |
| ☐ JA8982 | Boeing 777-246 | 26/27365 | |
| ☐ JA8983 | Boeing 777-246 | 39/27366 | |
| ☐ JA8984 | Boeing 777-246 | 68/27651 | |
| ☐ JA8985 | Boeing 777-246 | 72/27652 | |
| | | | |
| ☐ JA8531 | Douglas DC-10-40 | 216/46923 | |
| ☐ JA8532 | Douglas DC-10-40 | 220/46660 | |
| ☐ JA8534 | Douglas DC-10-40 | 206/46913 | |
| ☐ JA8535 | Douglas DC-10-40 | 230/46662 | |
| ☐ JA8537 | Douglas DC-10-40 | 265/46967 | |
| ☐ JA8538 | Douglas DC-10-40 | 274/46974 | |
| ☐ JA8541 | Douglas DC-10-40 | 308/47824 | |
| ☐ JA8542 | Douglas DC-10-40 | 310/47825 | |
| ☐ JA8543 | Douglas DC-10-40 | 313/47826 | |
| ☐ JA8545 | Douglas DC-10-40 | 343/47853 | |
| ☐ JA8548 | Douglas DC-10-40 | 367/47857 | |
| ☐ JA8549 | Douglas DC-10-40 | 381/48301 | |
| | | | |
| ☐ JA8582 | McDD MD-11 | 559/48573 | |
| ☐ JA8584+ | McDD MD-11 | 568/48575 | |
| ☐ JA8586+ | McDD MD-11 | 583/48577 | |
| ☐ JA8587+ | McDD MD-11 | 588/48578 | |
| ☐ JA8588 | McDD MD-11 | 599/48579 | |
| ☐ JA8589 | McDD MD-11 | 610/48774 | |

## JAPAN AIR SYSTEM — JAS

| | | | |
|---|---|---|---|
| ☐ JA011D | Airbus A300B4-622R | 783 | |
| ☐ JA012D | Airbus A300B4-622R | 797 | |
| ☐ JA014D | Airbus A300B4-622R | 836 | |
| ☐ JA015D | Airbus A300B4-622R | 837 | |
| ☐ JA016D | Airbus A300B4-622R | 838 | |
| ☐ JA8237 | Airbus A300C4-2C | 256 | |
| ☐ JA8263 | Airbus A300B4-2C | 151 | |
| ☐ JA8292 | Airbus A300B4-2C | 110 | |
| ☐ JA8293 | Airbus A300B4-2C | 194 | |
| ☐ JA8369 | Airbus A300B4-203 | 239 | |
| ☐ JA8375 | Airbus A300B4-622R | 602 | |
| ☐ JA8376 | Airbus A300B4-622R | 617 | |
| ☐ JA8377 | Airbus A300B4-622R | 621 | |
| ☐ JA8464 | Airbus A300B2K-3C | 082 | |
| ☐ JA8466 | Airbus A300B2K-3C | 090 | |
| ☐ JA8471 | Airbus A300B2K-3C | 160 | |
| ☐ JA8472 | Airbus A300B2K-3C | 163 | |
| ☐ JA8473 | Airbus A300B2K-3C | 176 | |
| ☐ JA8476 | Airbus A300B2K-3C | 209 | |
| ☐ JA8477 | Airbus A300B2K-3C | 244 | |
| ☐ JA8478 | Airbus A300B2K-3C | 253 | |
| ☐ JA8527 | Airbus A300B4-622R | 724 | |
| ☐ JA8529 | Airbus A300B4-622R | 729 | |
| ☐ JA8558 | Airbus A300B4-622R | 637 | |
| ☐ JA8559 | Airbus A300B4-622R | 641 | |
| ☐ JA8560 | Airbus A300B4-2C | 178 | |
| ☐ JA8561 | Airbus A300B4-622R | 670 | |
| ☐ JA8562 | Airbus A300B4-622R | 679 | |
| ☐ JA8563 | Airbus A300B4-622R | 683 | |
| ☐ JA8564 | Airbus A300B4-622R | 703 | |
| ☐ JA8565 | Airbus A300B4-622R | 711 | |
| ☐ JA8566 | Airbus A300B4-622R | 730 | |
| ☐ JA8573 | Airbus A300B4-622R | 737 | |
| ☐ JA8574 | Airbus A300B4-622R | 740 | |
| ☐ JA8657 | Airbus A300B4-622R | 753 | |
| ☐ JA8659 | Airbus A300B4-622R | 770 | |
| | | | |
| ☐ JA007D | Boeing 777-289 | 134/27639 | |
| ☐ JA008D | Boeing 777-289 | 146/27640 | |
| ☐ JA009D | Boeing 777-289 | 159/27641 | |
| ☐ JA010D | Boeing 777-289 | 213/27642 | |
| ☐ JA8977 | Boeing 777-289 | 45/27636 | |
| ☐ JA8978 | Boeing 777-289 | 79/27637 | |
| ☐ JA8979 | Boeing 777-289 | 107/27638 | |

| | | | |
|---|---|---|---|
| ☐ JA8260 | McDD MD-81 | 1359/49461 | |
| ☐ JA8261 | McDD MD-81 | 1477/49462 | |
| ☐ JA8262 | McDD MD-81 | 1488/49463 | |
| ☐ JA8278 | McDD MD-87 | 1476/49464 | |
| ☐ JA8279 | McDD MD-87 | 1604/49465 | |
| ☐ JA8280 | McDD MD-87 | 1727/49466 | |
| ☐ JA8281 | McDD MD-87 | 1742/49467 | |
| ☐ JA8294 | McDD MD-81 | 1598/49820 | |
| ☐ JA8295 | McDD MD-81 | 1615/49821 | |
| ☐ JA8296 | McDD MD-81 | 1734/49907 | |
| ☐ JA8297 | McDD MD-81 | 1749/49908 | |
| ☐ JA8370 | McDD MD-87 | 1881/53039 | |
| ☐ JA8371 | McDD MD-87 | 1897/53040 | |
| ☐ JA8372 | McDD MD-87 | 1945/53041 | |
| ☐ JA8373 | McDD MD-87 | 1969/53042 | |
| ☐ JA8374 | McDD MD-81 | 1982/53043 | |
| ☐ JA8496 | McDD MD-81 | 1194/49280 | |
| ☐ JA8497 | McDD MD-81 | 1200/49281 | |
| ☐ JA8498 | McDD MD-81 | 1282/49282 | |
| ☐ JA8499 | McDD MD-81 | 1299/49283 | |
| ☐ JA8552 | McDD MD-81 | 2040/53297 | |
| ☐ JA8553 | McDD MD-81 | 2045/53298 | |
| ☐ JA8554 | McDD MD-81 | 2075/53299 | |
| ☐ JA8555 | McDD MD-81 | 2076/53300 | |
| ☐ JA8556 | McDD MD-81 | 2082/53301 | |
| ☐ JA8557 | McDD MD-81 | 2085/53302 | |
| | | | |
| ☐ JA001D | McDD MD-90-30 | 2210/53555 | |
| ☐ JA002D | McDD MD-90-30 | 2207/53556 | |
| ☐ JA003D | McDD MD-90-30 | 2211/53557 | |
| ☐ JA004D | McDD MD-90-30 | 2212/53558 | |
| ☐ JA005D | McDD MD-90-30 | 2236/53559 | |
| ☐ JA006D | McDD MD-90-30 | 2245/53560 | |
| ☐ JA8004 | McDD MD-90-30 | 2184/53359 | |
| ☐ JA8020 | McDD MD-90-30 | 2190/53360 | |
| ☐ JA8029 | McDD MD-90-30 | 2202/53361 | |
| ☐ JA8062 | McDD MD-90-30 | 2098/53352 | |
| ☐ JA8063 | McDD MD-90-30 | 2120/53353 | |
| ☐ JA8064 | McDD MD-90-30 | 2125/53354 | |
| ☐ JA8065 | McDD MD-90-30 | 2131/53355 | |
| ☐ JA8066 | McDD MD-90-30 | 2157/53356 | |
| ☐ JA8069 | McDD MD-90-30 | 2164/53357 | |
| ☐ JA8070 | McDD MD-90-30 | 2179/53358 | |
| | | | |
| ☐ JA8717 | NAMC YS-11A-217 | 2092 | Lst JAC |
| ☐ JA8759 | NAMC YS-11A-227 | 2152 | Lst JAC |
| ☐ JA8763 | NAMC YS-11A-227 | 2135 | Lst JAC |
| ☐ JA8766 | NAMC YS-11A-227 | 2142 | Lst JAC |
| ☐ JA8768 | NAMC YS-11A-222 | 2147 | Lst JAC |
| ☐ JA8771 | NAMC YS-11A-227 | 2149 | Lst JAC |
| ☐ JA8777 | NAMC YS-11A-227 | 2163 | Lst JAC |
| ☐ JA8781 | NAMC YS-11A-217 | 2166 | Lst JAC |
| ☐ JA8788 | NAMC YS-11A-217 | 2176 | Lst JAC |
| ☐ JA8809 | NAMC YS-11A-202 | 2054 | Lst JAC |

## JAPAN ASIA AIRWAYS — JAA

| | | | |
|---|---|---|---|
| ☐ JA8128 | Boeing 747-146A | 259/21029 | Lst JAL |
| ☐ JA8129 | Boeing 747-246B | 361/21678 | |
| ☐ JA8154 | Boeing 747-246B | 547/22745 | |
| ☐ JA8155 | Boeing 747-246B | 548/22746 | |
| ☐ JA8189 | Boeing 747-346 | 716/24156 | |
| ☐ JA8266 | Boeing 767-346 | 191/23966 | |
| ☐ JA8531 | Douglas DC-10-40 | 216/46923 | Lst JAL |
| ☐ JA8532 | Douglas DC-10-40 | 220/46660 | Lst JAL |
| ☐ JA8534 | Douglas DC-10-40 | 206/46913 | Lst JAL |
| ☐ JA8537 | Douglas DC-10-40 | 255/46967 | Lst JAL |
| ☐ JA8976 | Boeing 767-346 | 667/27659 | |
| ☐ JA8987 | Boeing 767-346 | 668/28553 | |

## JAPAN TRANSOCEAN AIR — JTA

| | | | |
|---|---|---|---|
| ☐ JA8523 | Boeing 737-4Q3 | 2618/26603 | |
| ☐ JA8524 | Boeing 737-4Q3 | 2684/26604 | |
| ☐ JA8525 | Boeing 737-4Q3 | 2752/26605 | |
| ☐ JA8526 | Boeing 737-4Q3 | 2898/26606 | |
| ☐ JA8597 | Boeing 737-4Q3 | 3043/27660 | |

| | | | |
|---|---|---|---|
| ☐ JA8930 | Boeing 737-4K5 | 2394/27102 | |
| ☐ JA8931 | Boeing 737-429 | 2106/25247 | |
| ☐ JA8932 | Boeing 737-429 | 2120/25248 | |
| ☐ JA8933 | Boeing 737-429 | 2104/25226 | |
| ☐ JA8934 | Boeing 737-4K5 | 2670/27830 | |
| ☐ JA8938 | Boeing 737-4Q3 | 3085/29485 | |
| ☐ JA8939 | Boeing 737-4Q3 | 3088/29486 | |
| ☐ JA8940 | Boeing 737-4Q3 | 3122/29487 | |
| ☐ JA8953 | Boeing 737-4K5 | 1783/24129 | |
| ☐ JA8954 | Boeing 737-4K5 | 1827/24130 | |

### LEQUOIS AIRLINES

| | | | |
|---|---|---|---|
| ☐ JA01LQ | Boeing 767-36NER | 30847 | o/o |

### NAKANIHON AIRLINE SERVICE

| | | |
|---|---|---|
| ☐ JA01NV | Fokker 50 | 20257 |
| ☐ JA8200 | Fokker 50 | 20307 |
| ☐ JA8875 | Fokker 50 | 20196 |
| ☐ JA8889 | Fokker 50 | 20259 |

### NIPPON CARGO AIRLINES     NCA

| | | | |
|---|---|---|---|
| ☐ JA8158 | Boeing 747SR-81 (SF) | 559/22711 | |
| ☐ JA8167 | Boeing 747-281F | 604/23138 | |
| ☐ JA8168 | Boeing 747-281F | 608/23139 | |
| ☐ JA8172 | Boeing 747-281F | 623/23350 | |
| ☐ JA8181 | Boeing 747-281B (SF) | 667/23698 | |
| ☐ JA8182 | Boeing 747-281B (SF) | 683/23813 | |
| ☐ JA8188 | Boeing 747-281F | 689/23919 | |
| ☐ JA8190 | Boeing 747-281B (SF) | 750/24399 | |
| ☐ JA8191 | Boeing 747-281F | 818/24576 | |
| ☐ JA8192 | Boeing 747-2D3B (SF) | 514/22579 | Lsf ANA |
| ☐ JA8194 | Boeing 747-281F | 886/25171 | |
| ☐ JA601F | Boeing 767-381ERF | 33404 | Jow ANA |

### ORIENTAL AIR BRIDGE     NGK

| | | |
|---|---|---|
| ☐ JA801B | DHC-8Q-201 | 566 |
| ☐ JA802B | DHC-8Q-201 | 579 |

### RYUKYU AIR COMMUTER

| | | |
|---|---|---|
| ☐ JA8972 | DHC-8-103 | 472 |
| ☐ JA8973 | DHC-8Q-103 | 501 |
| ☐ JA8974 | DHC-8Q-103B | 540 |
| ☐ JA | DHC-8Q-103B | 593 |

### SKYMARK AIRLINES     SKY

| | | |
|---|---|---|
| ☐ JA767A | Boeing 767-3Q8ER | 714/27616 |
| ☐ JA767B | Boeing 767-3Q8ER | 722/27617 |
| ☐ JA767C | Boeing 767-3Q8ER | 870/29390 |

### SKYNET ASIA AIRLINES     SNJ

| | | |
|---|---|---|
| ☐ JA737A | Boeing 737-46Q | 3033/29000 |
| ☐ JA737B | Boeing 737-46Q | 3040/29001 |

## JU - MONGOLIA

### MIAT – MONGOLIAN AIRLINES     MGL

| | | |
|---|---|---|
| ☐ EI-CXV | Boeing 737-8CX | 1166/32364 |
| ☐ JU-1036 | Boeing 727-281 | 881/20572 |
| ☐ JU-1037 | Boeing 727-281 | 888/20573 |
| ☐ F-OHPT | Airbus A310-304 | 526 |

## JY - JORDAN

### JORDANIAN AVIATION     JAV

| | | | |
|---|---|---|---|
| ☐ JY-JAA | Boeing 707-321B | 774/20022 | |
| ☐ JY-JAB | Boeing 737-33A | 1312/23630 | Lst UKM |

### ROYAL JORDANIAN     RJA

| | | | |
|---|---|---|---|
| ☐ F-ODVF | Airbus A310-304F | 445 | |
| ☐ F-ODVG | Airbus A310-304 | 490 | |
| ☐ F-ODVH | Airbus A310-304 | 491 | |
| ☐ F-ODVI | Airbus A310-304 | 531 | |
| ☐ JY-AGK | Airbus A310-304 | 573 | |
| ☐ JY-AGL | Airbus A310-304 | 661 | |
| ☐ JY-AGP | Airbus A310-304 | 416 | |
| ☐ JY-AGU | Airbus A310-203 | 295 | Lst LAA |
| ☐ JY-AGV | Airbus A310-203 | 306 | Lst LAA |
| ☐ F-OGYC | Airbus A320-212 | 0569 | |
| ☐ F-OHGB | Airbus A320-211 | 0289 | |
| ☐ F-OHGC | Airbus A320-211 | 0407 | |
| ☐ JY-AYA | Airbus A320-211 | 0087 | |
| ☐ JY-AYB | Airbus A320-211 | 0088 | |
| ☐ JY-AIA | Airbus A340-211 | 038 | |
| ☐ JY-AIB | Airbus A340-211 | 043 | |
| ☐ JY-AJN | Boeing 707-3J6C | 874/20720 | |
| ☐ JY-AJO | Boeing 707-3J6C | 879/20723 | |

## J2 - DJIBOUTI

### DAALLO AIRLINES     DAO

| | | | |
|---|---|---|---|
| ☐ EY-85487 | Tupolev Tu-154B-2 | 81A-487 | Lsf TZK |
| ☐ UR-CAN | McDD MD-83 | 1539/49822 | Lsf KHO |

## LN - NORWAY

### AIRLIFT

| | | |
|---|---|---|
| ☐ LN-OMX | AS.332L1 Super Puma | 2351 |

### ARCTIC AIR     AKR

| | | |
|---|---|---|
| ☐ LN-AAO | Dornier 228-201 | 8108 |
| ☐ LN-BER | Dornier 228-212 | 8192 |

### BRAATHENS AIRWAYS     BRA

| | | | |
|---|---|---|---|
| ☐ LN-BRD | Boeing 737-505 | 1842/24651 | |
| ☐ LN-BRE | Boeing 737-405 | 1860/24643 | |
| ☐ LN-BRH | Boeing 737-505 | 1925/24828 | |
| ☐ LN-BRI | Boeing 737-405 | 1938/24644 | |
| ☐ LN-BRJ | Boeing 737-505 | 2018/24273 | |
| ☐ LN-BRK | Boeing 737-505 | 2035/24274 | |
| ☐ LN-BRN | Boeing 737-505 | 2138/24646 | |
| ☐ LN-BRO | Boeing 737-505 | 2143/24647 | |
| ☐ LN-BRP | Boeing 737-405 | 2137/25303 | |
| ☐ LN-BRQ | Boeing 737-405 | 2148/25348 | |
| ☐ LN-BRR | Boeing 737-505 | 2213/24648 | |
| ☐ LN-BRS | Boeing 737-505 | 2225/24649 | |
| ☐ LN-BRV | Boeing 737-505 | 2351/25791 | |
| ☐ LN-BRX | Boeing 737-505 | 2434/25797 | |
| ☐ LN-BUC | Boeing 737-505 | 2649/26304 | |
| ☐ LN-BUD | Boeing 737-505 | 2803/25794 | |
| ☐ LN-BUE | Boeing 737-505 | 2800/27627 | |
| ☐ LN-BUF | Boeing 737-405 | 2867/25795 | |
| ☐ LN-BUG | Boeing 737-505 | 2866/27631 | |
| ☐ LN-TUA | Boeing 737-705 | 33/28211 | |
| ☐ LN-TUD | Boeing 737-705 | 142/28217 | std |
| ☐ LN-TUE | Boeing 737-705 | 230/29091 | |
| ☐ LN-TUF | Boeing 737-705 | 245/28222 | |
| ☐ LN-TUG | Boeing 737-705 | 260/29092 | std |
| ☐ LN-TUH | Boeing 737-705 | 471/29093 | std |
| ☐ LN-TUI | Boeing 737-705 | 507/29094 | std |
| ☐ LN-TUJ | Boeing 737-705 | 773/28095 | |
| ☐ LN-TUK | Boeing 737-705 | 794/28096 | |
| ☐ LN-TUL | Boeing 737-705 | 1072/29097 | |
| ☐ LN-TUM | Boeing 737-705 | 1116/29098 | |

### CHC HELICOPTER SERVICE     HKS

| | | |
|---|---|---|
| ☐ LN-OAW | AS.332L Super Puma | 2053 |
| ☐ LN-OBF | AS.332L Super Puma 2 | 2381 |

| | | | |
|---|---|---|---|
| ☐ LN-OBQ | AS.332L Super Puma 2 | 2312 | |
| ☐ LN-ODA | AS.332L Super Puma | 2073 | Lst SHZ |
| ☐ LN-OHA | AS.332L Super Puma 2 | 2396 | |
| ☐ LN-OHB | AS.332L Super Puma 2 | 2398 | |
| ☐ LN-OHC | AS.332L Super Puma 2 | 2393 | |
| ☐ LN-OHD | AS.322L Super Puma 2 | 2395 | |
| ☐ LN-OHF | AS.332L2 Super Puma | 2474 | Lst SHZ |
| ☐ LN-OHG | AS.332L2 Super Puma | 2493 | |
| ☐ LN-OHH | AS.332L2 Super Puma | 2366 | |
| ☐ LN-OLB | AS.332L Super Puma | 2082 | |
| ☐ LN-OLD | AS.332L Super Puma | 2103 | |
| ☐ LN-OMF | AS.332L Super Puma | 2067 | Lst SHZ |
| ☐ LN-OMH | AS.332L Super Puma | 2113 | |
| ☐ LN-OMT | AS.332L1 Super Puma | 2468 | |
| ☐ LN-OPH | AS.332L1 Super Puma | 2347 | |
| | | | |
| ☐ LN-OQB | Sikorsky S-61N II | 61807 | Lst SHZ |
| ☐ LN-OQM | Sikorsky S-61N II | 61764 | |
| ☐ LN-OQQ | Sikorsky S-61N II | 61814 | |
| ☐ LN-ORC | Sikorsky S-61N II | 61817 | |
| ☐ LN-OSJ | Sikorsky S-61N II | 61715 | |
| ☐ LN-OST | Sikorsky S-61N II | 61738 | |
| ☐ LN-OSU | Sikorsky S-61N II | 61740 | Lst SHZ |

### COAST AIR — CST

| | | |
|---|---|---|
| ☐ LN-FAI | ATR 42-300 | 331 |
| ☐ LN-FAJ | BAe Jetstream 31 | 621 |
| ☐ LN-FAM | BAe Jetstream 31 | 740 |
| ☐ LN-FAO | ATR 42-320 | 148 |
| ☐ LN-FAP | ATR 42-320 | 110 |
| ☐ LN-FAV | BAe Jetstream 31 | 606 |

### KATO AIRLINE — KAT

| | | |
|---|---|---|
| ☐ LN-HTA | Dornier 228-202 | 8127 |

### LUFTTRANSPORT — LTR

| | | | |
|---|---|---|---|
| ☐ LN-LYR | Dornier 228-202K | 8166 | |
| ☐ LN-MOL | Dornier 228-202K | 8156 | Lsf ISL |

### NORSK HELICOPTER — NPR

| | | | |
|---|---|---|---|
| ☐ LN-OBA | AS.332L1 Super Puma | 2384 | |
| ☐ LN-OLC | AS.332L Super Puma | 2083 | |
| ☐ LN-OMI | AS.332L Super Puma | 2123 | |
| ☐ LN-ONB | AS.332L Super Puma | 2122 | Lsf BHL |
| ☐ LN-OND | AS.322L Super Puma | 2157 | Lsf BHL |
| ☐ LN-ONE | AS.332L1 Super Puma | 9002 | |
| ☐ LN-ONH | AS.332L2 Super Puma | 2488 | |
| ☐ LN-ONI | AS.332L2 Super Puma | 2500 | |

### NORWEGIAN AIR SHUTTLE — NAX

| | | |
|---|---|---|
| ☐ LN-BRU | Boeing 737-505 | 2245/25790 |
| ☐ LN-KKF | Boeing 737-3K2 | 1683/24326 |
| ☐ LN-KKG | Boeing 737-3K2 | 1712/24327 |
| ☐ LN-KKH | Boeing 737-3K2 | 1856/24328 |
| ☐ LN-KKI | Boeing 737-3K2 | 1858/24329 |
| ☐ LN-KKJ | Boeing 737-36N | 2936/28564 |
| ☐ LN-KKL | Boeing 737-36N | 2955/28671 |
| | | |
| ☐ LN-BBA | Fokker 50 | 20130 |
| ☐ LN-BBB | Fokker 50 | 20131 |
| ☐ LN-BBC | Fokker 50 | 20134 |
| ☐ LN-KKA | Fokker 50 | 20117 |
| ☐ LN-KKD | Fokker 50 | 20230 |
| ☐ LN-KKE | Fokker 50 | 20226 |

### SCANDINAVIAN AIRLINE SYSTEM — SAS

See fleet details under **Sweden (SE-)**

### TEDDY AIR

| | | | |
|---|---|---|---|
| ☐ SE-LEP | SAAB SF.340A | 127 | Lsf GAO |
| ☐ SE-LES | SAAB SF.340A | 129 | Lsf GAO |

### WIDERØE'S FLYVESELSKAP — WIF

| | | |
|---|---|---|
| ☐ LN-WDA | DHC-8Q-402 | 4069 |
| ☐ LN-WDB | DHC-8Q-402 | 4070 |
| ☐ LN-WDC | DHC-8Q-402 | 4071 |
| ☐ LN-WDS | DHC-8Q-402 | 4016 |
| ☐ LN-WFA | DHC-8-311A | 342 |
| ☐ LN-WFB | DHC-8-311A | 293 |
| ☐ LN-WFC | DHC-8-311A | 236 |
| ☐ LN-WFE | DHC-8Q-311 | 491 |
| ☐ LN-WFH | DHC-8-311A | 238 |
| ☐ LN-WFO | DHC-8Q-311 | 493 |
| ☐ LN-WFP | DHC-8Q-311 | 495 |
| ☐ LN-WFR | DHC-8Q-311 | 385 |
| ☐ LN-WFS | DHC-8Q-311 | 535 |
| ☐ LN-WIA | DHC-8-103B | 359 |
| ☐ LN-WIB | DHC-8-103B | 360 |
| ☐ LN-WIC | DHC-8-103B | 367 |
| ☐ LN-WID | DHC-8-103B | 369 |
| ☐ LN-WIE | DHC-8-103B | 371 |
| ☐ LN-WIF | DHC-8-103B | 372 |
| ☐ LN-WIG | DHC-8-103B | 382 |
| ☐ LN-WIH | DHC-8-103B | 383 |
| ☐ LN-WII | DHC-8-103B | 384 |
| ☐ LN-WIJ | DHC-8-103B | 386 |
| ☐ LN-WIK | DHC-8-103B | 394 |
| ☐ LN-WIL | DHC-8-103B | 398 |
| ☐ LN-WIM | DHC-8-103B | 403 |
| ☐ LN-WIN | DHC-8-103B | 409 |
| ☐ LN-WIO | DHC-8-103B | 417 |
| ☐ LN-WIP | DHC-8-103A | 239 |
| ☐ LN-WIR | DHC-8-103A | 273 |

## LV - ARGENTINA

### AEROLINEAS ARGENTINAS — ARG

| | | | |
|---|---|---|---|
| ☐ LV-JMX | Boeing 737-287 | 243/20404 | std EZE |
| ☐ LV-JMY | Boeing 737-287 | 248/20405 | std EZE |
| ☐ LV-JND | Boeing 737-287C | 263/20407 | |
| ☐ LV-JTD | Boeing 737-287F | 285/20523 | |
| ☐ LV-JTO | Boeing 737-287 | 291/20537 | |
| ☐ LV-LEB | Boeing 737-287 | 331/20768 | |
| ☐ LV-LIV | Boeing 737-287 | 381/20965 | |
| ☐ LV-WSU | Boeing 737-2A8 | 503/21496 | |
| ☐ LV-WSY | Boeing 737-281 | 293/20562 | |
| ☐ LV-WTG | Boeing 737-2A8 | 505/21498 | |
| ☐ LV-WTX | Boeing 737-281 | 292/20561 | |
| ☐ LV-ZEC | Boeing 737-236 | 648/21796 | |
| ☐ LV-ZIE | Boeing 737-236 | 658/21798 | |
| ☐ LV-ZRE | Boeing 737-236 | 1077/23168 | |
| ☐ LV-ZRO | Boeing 737-236 | 1060/23164 | |
| ☐ LV-ZSD | Boeing 737-236 | 1088/23171 | |
| ☐ LV-ZSW | Boeing 737-236 | 1086/23170 | |
| ☐ LV-ZTD | Boeing 737-236 | 1102/23225 | |
| ☐ LV-ZTG | Boeing 737-236 | 1081/23169 | |
| ☐ LV-ZTJ | Boeing 737-236 | 1091/23172 | |
| ☐ LV-ZTT | Boeing 737-236 | 699/21806 | |
| ☐ LV-ZTY | Boeing 737-236 | 1047/23159 | |
| ☐ LV-ZXC | Boeing 737-236 | 1053/23160 | |
| ☐ LV-ZXU | Boeing 737-236 | 1105/23226 | |
| ☐ LV-ZYG | Boeing 737-236 | 645/21795 | |
| ☐ LV-ZYN | Boeing 737-236 | 643/21794 | |
| ☐ LV-ZYY | Boeing 737-236 | 660/21799 | |

Operated as **Aerolineas Executive Jet**

| | | |
|---|---|---|
| ☐ LV-MLO | Boeing 747-287B | 349/21725 |
| ☐ LV-MLP | Boeing 747-287B | 403/21726 |
| ☐ LV-MLR | Boeing 747-287B | 404/21727 |
| ☐ LV-OEP | Boeing 747-287B | 487/22297 |
| ☐ LV-OOZ | Boeing 747-287B | 532/22592 |
| ☐ LV-OPA | Boeing 747-287B | 552/22593 |
| ☐ LV-YPC | Boeing 747-212B | 436/21938 |
| | | |
| ☐ LV-VBX | McDD MD-88 | 2016/53047 |
| ☐ LV-VBZ | McDD MD-88 | 2031/53049 |
| ☐ LV-VCB | McDD MD-88 | 2043/53351 |
| ☐ LV-VGB | McDD MD-88 | 2046/53446 |
| ☐ LV-VGC | McDD MD-88 | 2064/53447 |

| | | |
|---|---|---|
| ☐ LV-ZPJ | Airbus A340-211 | 074 |
| ☐ LV-ZPO | Airbus A340-211 | 063 |
| ☐ LV-ZPX | Airbus A340-211 | 080 |
| ☐ LV-ZRA | Airbus A340-211 | 085 |

### AMERICAN FALCON — AFB

| | | |
|---|---|---|
| ☐ LV-WGX | Boeing 737-2P6 | 498/21358 |
| ☐ LV-WZC | F.28 Fellowship 1000 | 11017 |
| ☐ LV-ZYJ | Boeing 737-291 | 923/22744 |

### CIELOS DEL SUR – AUSTRAL — AUT

| | | |
|---|---|---|
| ☐ LV-ZTE | Boeing 737-228 | 1135/23349 |
| ☐ LV-ZTI | Boeing 737-228 | 937/23002 |
| ☐ LV-ZXB | Boeing 737-228 | 958/23009 |
| ☐ LV-ZXH | Boeing 737-228 | 1256/23503 |
| ☐ LV-ZXP | Boeing 737-228 | 939/23003 |
| ☐ LV-ZXV | Boeing 737-228 | 1426/23793 |
| ☐ LV-ZYI | Boeing 737-228 | 959/23010 |
| ☐ LV- | Boeing 737-228 | 971/23011 |
| | | |
| ☐ LV-VAG | McDD MD-83 | 1951/53117 |
| ☐ LV-WFN | McDD MD-81 | 952/48025 |
| ☐ LV-WGM | McDD MD-83 | 1627/49784 |
| ☐ LV-WGN | McDD MD-83 | 1764/49934 |
| ☐ LV-WPY | McDD MD-81 | 948/48024 |
| | | |
| ☐ LV-WGU | Douglas DC-9-32 | 567/47454Lsf IBE; std |
| ☐ LV-WHL | Douglas DC-9-32 | 505/47368Lsf IBE; std |
| ☐ LV-WIS | Douglas DC-9-32 | 262/47312Lsf IBE; std |

### DINAR LINEAS AEREAS — RDN

| | | | |
|---|---|---|---|
| ☐ LV-YNA | Douglas DC-9-41 | 747/47614 | |
| ☐ LV-YOA | Douglas DC-9-41 | 727/47606 | |
| ☐ LV-YPA | Douglas DC-9-41 | 742/47613 | std |
| ☐ LV-ZXS | Boeing 737-201 | 141/20211 | |

### LAPA – LINEA PRIVADA ARGENTINA — LPR

| | | |
|---|---|---|
| ☐ LV-VGF | Boeing 737-2M6 | 422/21138 |
| ☐ LV-YBS | Boeing 737-266 | 453/21193 |
| ☐ LV-YGB | Boeing 737-2S3 | 746/22633 |
| ☐ LV-YXB | Boeing 737-204 | 487/21335 |
| ☐ LV-YZA | Boeing 737-204 | 489/21336 |
| ☐ LV-ZRM | Boeing 737-7Q8 | 369/28224 |

### SOUTHERN WINDS AIRLINES — SWD

| | | |
|---|---|---|
| ☐ LV-WPF | Canadair RJ-200 | 7115 |
| ☐ LV-WSB | Canadair RJ-200 | 7154 |
| ☐ LV-WXT | Canadair RJ-200 | 7041 |
| | | |
| ☐ LV-ZTX | Boeing 737-228 | 1267/23504 |
| ☐ LV-ZZA | Boeing 737-205 | 460/21219 |
| ☐ LV-ZYX | Boeing 737-2M6 | 399/20913 |
| ☐ LV-ZZC | Boeing 737-2E1 | 424/21112 |
| | | |
| ☐ TF-ARA | Boeing 767-3Q8ER | 694/28206 Opb ABD |
| ☐ TF-ARB | Boeing 767-3Q8ER | 570/26265 Opb ABD |

## LX - LUXEMBOURG

### CARGOLUX AIRLINES INTERNATIONAL — CLX

| | | |
|---|---|---|
| ☐ LX-FCV | Boeing 747-4R7F | 1002/25866 |
| ☐ LX-GCV | Boeing 747-4R7F | 1008/25867 |
| ☐ LX-ICV | Boeing 747-428F | 968/25632 |
| ☐ LX-KCV | Boeing 747-4R7F | 1125/25868 |
| ☐ LX-LCV | Boeing 747-4R7F | 1139/29053 |
| ☐ LX-MCV | Boeing 747-4R7F | 1189/29729 |
| ☐ LX-NCV | Boeing 747-4R7F | 1203/29730 |
| ☐ LX-OCV | Boeing 747-4R7F | 1222/29731 |
| ☐ LX-PCV | Boeing 747-4R7F | 1231/29732 |

| | | |
|---|---|---|
| ☐ LX-RCV | Boeing 747-4R7F | 1235/30400 |
| ☐ LX-SCV | Boeing 747-4R7F | 1281/29733 |
| ☐ LX-TCV | Boeing 747-4R7F | 1311/30401 |

### LUXAIR — LGL

| | | |
|---|---|---|
| ☐ LX-LGF | Boeing 737-4C9 | 2215/25429 |
| ☐ LX-LGG | Boeing 737-4C9 | 2249/26437 |
| ☐ LX-LGN | Boeing 737-59D | 2028/25065 |
| ☐ LX-LGO | Boeing 737-5C9 | 2413/26438 |
| ☐ LX-LGP | Boeing 737-5C9 | 2444/26439 |
| | | |
| ☐ LX-LGI | Embraer ERJ-145 | 145369 |
| ☐ LX-LGJ | Embraer ERJ-145 | 145395 |
| ☐ LX-LGU | Embraer ERJ-145 | 145084 |
| ☐ LX-LGV | Embraer ERJ-145 | 145129 |
| ☐ LX-LGW | Embraer ERJ-145 | 145135 |
| ☐ LX-LGX | Embraer ERJ-145 | 145147 |
| ☐ LX-LGY | Embraer ERJ-145 | 145242 |
| ☐ LX-LGZ | Embraer ERJ-145 | 145258 |
| | | |
| ☒ LX-LGC | Fokker 50 | 20168 |
| ☐ LX-LGD | Fokker 50 | 20171 |
| ☐ LX-LGE | Fokker 50 | 20180 |

### LUX AVIATION

| | | |
|---|---|---|
| ☐ LX-GDE | Embraer EMB.120ER | 120184 |

## LY - LITHUANIA

### AIR LITHUANIA — KLA

| | | |
|---|---|---|
| ☐ LY-ARI | ATR 42-300 | 012A |

### LITHUANIAN AIRLINES — LIL

| | | |
|---|---|---|
| ☐ LY-AGP | Boeing 737-375 | 1434/23808 |
| ☐ LY-BAG | Boeing 737-382 | 1857/24449 |
| ☐ LY-BSD | Boeing 737-2T4 | 886/22701 |
| ☐ LY-BSG | Boeing 737-2T2 | 892/22793 |
| | | |
| ☐ LY-SBC | SAAB 2000 | 025 |
| ☐ LY-SBD | SAAB 2000 | 023 |
| ☐ LY-SBG | SAAB 2000 | 032 |

## LZ - BULGARIA

### AIR SOFIA — SFB

| | | |
|---|---|---|
| ☐ LZ-SFA | Antonov An-12BP | 02348007 |
| ☐ LZ-SFK | Antonov An-12BP | 2341901 Lst ALK |
| ☐ LZ-SFL | Antonov An-12BP | 4342101 |
| ☐ LZ-SFN | Antonov An-12BP | 2340806 |
| ☐ LZ-SFS | Antonov An-12BP | 6344308 |
| ☐ LZ-SFT | Antonov An-12BP | 9346904 |
| ☐ LZ-SFH | Antonov An-26 | 3904Lst Mandala |
| ☐ TC-APJ | Boeing 737-86N | 1104/32735 Lsf PGT |

### BALKAN AIR TOUR

| | | |
|---|---|---|
| ☐ LZ-BOG | Boeing 737-330 | 1293/23529 Lsf DLH |
| ☐ LZ-BOH | Boeing 737-330 | 1297/23530 Lsf DLH |

### BF AIRLINES — BFB

| | | |
|---|---|---|
| ☐ LZ-BFE | Antonov An-12BP | 9346308 |
| ☐ LZ-BFU | Ilyushin Il-18V | 183005905 Lst PHG |

### BH AIR — BGH

| | | |
|---|---|---|
| ☐ LZ-HMI | Tupolev Tu-154M | 85A-706 Lsf HMS |
| ☐ LZ-HMN | Tupolev Tu-154M | 90A-832 Lsf HMS |
| ☐ LZ-HMQ | Tupolev Tu-154M | 87A-743 Lsf HMS |

## BRIGHT AVIATION SERVICES — BRW

| | | |
|---|---|---|
| ☐ LZ-BRA | Antonov An-12BP | 8346006 |
| ☐ LZ-BRC | Antonov An-12BP | 8345510 |
| ☐ LZ-BRW | Antonov An-12BP | |

## BULGARIAN AIR CHARTER — BUC

| | | |
|---|---|---|
| ☐ LZ-LCA | Tupolev Tu-154M | 89A-829 Lsf VARZ |
| ☐ LZ-LCC | Tupolev Tu-154M | 92A-921 Lsf VARZ |
| ☐ LZ-LCI | Tupolev Tu-154M | 88A-788  Lsf BKL |
| ☐ LZ-LCS | Tupolev Tu-154M | 86A-727  Lsf URN |
| ☐ LZ-LCV | Tupolev Tu-154M | 86A-733  Lsf URN |
| ☐ LZ-LCX | Tupolev Tu-154M | 86A-744 Lsf VARZ |
| | | |
| ☐ LZ- | McDD MD-80 | o/o |
| ☐ LZ- | McDD MD-80 | o/o |
| ☐ LZ- | McDD MD-80 | o/o |

## HEMUS AIR — HMS

| | | |
|---|---|---|
| ☐ LZ-TUH | Tupolev Tu-134A | 60142 Opf ADA |
| ☐ LZ-TUJ | Tupolev Tu-134A | 49913 Lst LBC |
| ☐ LZ-TUL | Tupolev Tu-134A-3 | 4352303 |
| ☐ LZ-TUN | Tupolev Tu-134A-3 | 4352307 |
| ☐ LZ-TUT | Tupolev Tu-134B-3 | 63987 |
| ☐ LZ-HMI | Tupolev Tu-154M | 85A-706 Lst BGS |
| ☐ LZ-HMN | Tupolev Tu-154M | 90A-832 Lst BGS |
| ☐ LZ-HMQ | Tupolev Tu-154M | 87A-743 Lst BGS |
| ☐ LZ-HMS | Tupolev Tu-154M | 87A-751 Lst LBC |
| ☐ LZ-HMW | Tupolev Tu-154M | 85A-707 |
| ☐ LZ-HMY | Tupolev Tu-154M | 91A-875 |
| ☐ ZA-MAL | BAe 146 Srs.200 | E2054 Opf ADA |

## INTER TRANS AIR — ITT

| | | |
|---|---|---|
| ☐ LZ-ITA | Antonov An-12BP | 3341004 |
| ☐ LZ-ITS | Antonov An-12BP | 3341505 |

## RILA AIRLINES — RAB

| | | |
|---|---|---|
| ☐ LZ-RAA | Antonov An-12BP | 402410 |

## VEGA AIRLINES — VEA

| | | |
|---|---|---|
| ☐ LZ-VEA | Antonov An-12BP | 01340106 |
| ☐ LZ-VEC | Antonov An-12 | 06344610 |
| ☐ LZ-VED | Antonov An-12B | 02348207 |

## VIA – AIR VIA BULGARIAN AIRWAYS — VIM

| | | |
|---|---|---|
| ☐ LZ-MIG | Tupolev Tu-154M | 90A-840 |
| ☐ LZ-MIK | Tupolev Tu-154M | 90A-844 |
| ☐ LZ-MIL | Tupolev Tu-154M | 90A-845 |
| ☐ LZ-MIR | Tupolev Tu-154M | 90A-852 |
| ☐ LZ-MIS | Tupolev Tu-154M | 90A-863 |

# N - UNITED STATES OF AMERICA

## AIRBORNE EXPRESS — ABX

| | | |
|---|---|---|
| ☐ N702AX | Boeing 767-231ER | 29/22566 |
| ☐ N707AX | Boeing 767-231ER | 63/22570 |
| ☐ N708AX | Boeing 767-231ER | 64/22571 |
| ☐ N709AX | Boeing 767-231ER | 65/22572 |
| ☐ N713AX | Boeing 767-205ER | 101/23058 |
| ☐ N767AX | Boeing 767-281 | 51/22785 |
| ☐ N768AX | Boeing 767-281 | 54/22786 |
| ☐ N769AX | Boeing 767-281 | 58/22787 |
| ☐ N773AX | Boeing 767-281 | 61/22788 |
| ☐ N774AX | Boeing 767-281 | 67/22789 |
| ☐ N775AX | Boeing 767-281 | 69/22790 |
| ☐ N783AX | Boeing 767-281 | 80/23016 |
| ☐ N784AX | Boeing 767-281 | 82/23017 |
| ☐ N785AX | Boeing 767-281 | 84/23018 |
| ☐ N786AX | Boeing 767-281 | 85/23019 |
| ☐ N787AX | Boeing 767-281 | 96/23020 |
| ☐ N788AX | Boeing 767-281 | 103/23021 |
| ☐ N789AX | Boeing 767-281 | 104/23022 |
| ☐ N790AX | Boeing 767-281 | 106/23140 |
| ☐ N791AX | Boeing 767-281 | 108/23141 |
| ☐ N792AX | Boeing 767-281 | 110/23142 o/o |
| ☐ N793AX | Boeing 767-281 | 114/23143 |
| ☐ N794AX | Boeing 767-281 | 115/23144 |
| ☐ N795AX | Boeing 767-281 | 116/23145 |
| ☐ N | Boeing 767-281 | 121/23146 o/o |
| ☐ N | Boeing 767-281 | 123/23147 o/o |
| ☐ N | Boeing 767-281 | 143/23431 o/o |
| ☐ N | Boeing 767-281 | 145/23432 o/o |
| ☐ N | Boeing 767-281 | 167/23433 o/o |
| ☐ N | Boeing 767-281 | 171/23434 o/o |
| ☐ N | Boeing 767-231ER | o/o |
| | | |
| ☐ N801AX | Douglas DC-8-62F | 470/46077 |
| ☐ N811AX | Douglas DC-8-63F | 521/46113 |
| ☐ N812AX | Douglas DC-8-63F | 524/46126 |
| ☐ N813AX | Douglas DC-8-63F | 509/46136 |
| ☐ N814AX | Douglas DC-8-63F | 439/46041 |
| ☐ N815AX | Douglas DC-8-63PF | 503/46097 |
| ☐ N816AX | Douglas DC-8-63PF | 496/46093 |
| ☐ N817AX | Douglas DC-8-63F | 334/45928 std |
| ☐ N818AX | Douglas DC-8-63F | 484/46075 |
| ☐ N819AX | Douglas DC-8-63F | 327/45927 |
| ☐ N820AX | Douglas DC-8-63F | 529/46155 |
| ☐ N821AX | Douglas DC-8-63F | 518/46116 std |
| ☐ N822AX | Douglas DC-8-63F | 476/46079 |
| ☐ N823AX | Douglas DC-8-63F | 506/46122 std |
| ☐ N824AX | Douglas DC-8-63F | 533/46141 std |
| ☐ N825AX | Douglas DC-8-63F | 530/46115 |
| ☐ N826AX | Douglas DC-8-63CF | 480/46061 |
| ☐ N828AX | Douglas DC-8-63F | 377/45999 |
| ☐ N842AX | Douglas DC-8-61F | 405/46015 |
| ☐ N843AX | Douglas DC-8-61F | 418/46017 |
| ☐ N847AX | Douglas DC-8-61F | 435/46031 |
| ☐ N848AX | Douglas DC-8-61F | 436/46032 |
| ☐ N849AX | Douglas DC-8-61F | 305/45891 |
| ☐ N850AX | Douglas DC-8-61F | 297/45894 |
| ☐ N853AX | Douglas DC-8-61F | 419/46037 |
| | | |
| ☐ N900AX | Douglas DC-9-32 | 514/47380 |
| ☐ N901AX | Douglas DC-9-32 | 519/47381 |
| ☐ N902AX | Douglas DC-9-32 | 572/47426 |
| ☐ N903AX | Douglas DC-9-32 | 573/47427 |
| ☐ N904AX | Douglas DC-9-32CF | 172/47040 |
| ☐ N905AX | Douglas DC-9-32CF | 208/47147 |
| ☐ N906AX | Douglas DC-9-31 | 270/47072 |
| ☐ N907AX | Douglas DC-9-31 | 401/47203 |
| ☐ N908AX | Douglas DC-9-31F | 98/47008 |
| ☐ N909AX | Douglas DC-9-32CF | 246/47148 |
| ☐ N923AX | Douglas DC-9-31 | 260/47165 |
| ☐ N924AX | Douglas DC-9-31 | 507/47403 |
| ☐ N925AX | Douglas DC-9-15 | 14/45728 |
| ☐ N927AX | Douglas DC-9-15 | 20/45717 |
| ☐ N928AX | Douglas DC-9-33RC | 447/47392 |
| ☐ N929AX | Douglas DC-9-31 | 351/45874 |
| ☐ N930AX | Douglas DC-9-33RC | 445/47363 |
| ☐ N931AX | Douglas DC-9-33F | 543/47384 |
| ☐ N932AX | Douglas DC-9-33RC | 584/47465 |
| ☐ N933AX | Douglas DC-9-33RC | 343/47291 |
| ☐ N934AX | Douglas DC-9-33RC | 564/47462 |
| ☐ N935AX | Douglas DC-9-33F | 521/47413 |
| ☐ N936AX | Douglas DC-9-31 | 371/47269 |
| ☐ N937AX | Douglas DC-9-31 | 376/47074 |
| ☐ N938AX | Douglas DC-9-31 | 152/47009 |
| ☐ N939AX | Douglas DC-9-32 | 459/47201 |
| ☐ N941AX | Douglas DC-9-31 | 602/47419 |
| ☐ N943AX | Douglas DC-9-31 | 617/47528 |
| ☐ N944AX | Douglas DC-9-31 | 623/47550 |
| ☐ N945AX | Douglas DC-9-31 | 634/47551 |
| ☐ N946AX | Douglas DC-9-31 | 86/47003 |
| ☐ N947AX | Douglas DC-9-31 | 81/47004 |
| ☐ N948AX | Douglas DC-9-31 | 269/47065 |
| ☐ N949AX | Douglas DC-9-31 | 515/47325 |

| | | | |
|---|---|---|---|
| ☐ N952AX | Douglas DC-9-41 | 751/47615 | |
| ☐ N953AX | Douglas DC-9-41 | 732/47608 | |
| ☐ N954AX | Douglas DC-9-41 | 736/47612 | |
| ☐ N955AX | Douglas DC-9-41 | 768/47619 | |
| ☐ N956AX | Douglas DC-9-41 | 777/47620 | |
| ☐ N957AX | Douglas DC-9-41 | 871/47759 | |
| ☐ N958AX | Douglas DC-9-41 | 874/47760 | |
| ☐ N959AX | Douglas DC-9-41 | 875/47761 | |
| ☐ N960AX | Douglas DC-9-41 | 876/47762 | |
| ☐ N962AX | Douglas DC-9-41 | 887/47768 | |
| ☐ N963AX | Douglas DC-9-41 | 894/47780 | |
| ☐ N964AX | Douglas DC-9-41 | 895/47781 | |
| ☐ N965AX | Douglas DC-9-41 | 566/47498 | |
| ☐ N966AX | Douglas DC-9-41 | 645/47510 | |
| ☐ N967AX | Douglas DC-9-41 | 643/47509 | |
| ☐ N968AX | Douglas DC-9-41 | 568/47499 | |
| ☐ N969AX | Douglas DC-9-41 | 575/47464 | |
| ☐ N970AX | Douglas DC-9-41 | 601/47494 | |
| ☐ N971AX | Douglas DC-9-41 | 604/47497 | |
| ☐ N972AX | Douglas DC-9-41 | 743/47631 | |
| ☐ N973AX | Douglas DC-9-41 | 677/47511 | |
| ☐ N974AX | Douglas DC-9-41 | 728/47623 | |
| ☐ N975AX | Douglas DC-9-41 | 678/47512 | |
| ☐ N976AX | Douglas DC-9-41 | 714/47596 | |
| ☐ N977AX | Douglas DC-9-41 | 679/47513 | |
| ☐ N978AX | Douglas DC-9-41 | 740/47628 | |
| ☐ N979AX | Douglas DC-9-41 | 559/47492 | |
| ☐ N980AX | Douglas DC-9-32 | 314/47176 | |
| ☐ N981AX | Douglas DC-9-32 | 347/47273 | |
| ☐ N982AX | Douglas DC-9-32 | 385/47317 | |
| ☐ N983AX | Douglas DC-9-32 | 386/47257 | |
| ☐ N984AX | Douglas DC-9-32 | 387/47258 | |
| ☐ N985AX | Douglas DC-9-32 | 606/47522 | |
| ☐ N986AX | Douglas DC-9-32 | 654/47543 | |
| ☐ N987AX | Douglas DC-9-32 | 484/47364 | |
| ☐ N988AX | Douglas DC-9-32 | 179/47084 | |
| ☐ N989AX | Douglas DC-9-32 | 279/47314 | |
| ☐ N990AX | Douglas DC-9-41 | 562/47493 | |

## AIR MIDWEST     AMW

| | | | |
|---|---|---|---|
| ☐ N5YV | Beech 1900D | UE-5 | Lsf ASH |
| ☐ N6YV | Beech 1900D | UE-6 | Lsf ASH |
| ☐ N13ZV | Beech 1900D | UE-13 | Lsf ASH |
| ☐ N15YV | Beech 1900D | UE-15 | Lsf ASH |
| ☐ N23YV | Beech 1900D | UE-23 | Lsf ASH |
| ☐ N26YV | Beech 1900D | UE-26 | Lsf ASH |
| ☐ N107YV | Beech 1900D | UE-107 | Lsf ASH |
| ☐ N131YV | Beech 1900D | UE-131 | Lsf ASH |
| ☐ N133YV | Beech 1900D | UE-133 | Lsf ASH |
| ☐ N135YV | Beech 1900D | UE-135 | Lsf ASH |
| ☐ N138YV | Beech 1900D | UE-138 | Lsf ASH |
| ☐ N139ZV | Beech 1900D | UE-139 | Lsf ASH |
| ☐ N140ZV | Beech 1900D | UE-140 | Lsf ASH |
| ☐ N143YV | Beech 1900D | UE-143 | Lsf ASH |
| ☐ N144ZV | Beech 1900D | UE-144 | Lsf ASH |
| ☐ N146ZV | Beech 1900D | UE-146 | Lsf ASH |
| ☐ N155ZV | Beech 1900D | UE-155 | Lsf ASH |
| ☐ N161YV | Beech 1900D | UE-161 | Lsf ASH |
| ☐ N162ZV | Beech 1900D | UE-162 | Lsf ASH |
| ☐ N163YV | Beech 1900D | UE-163 | Lsf ASH |
| ☐ N165YV | Beech 1900D | UE-165 | Lsf ASH |
| ☐ N166YV | Beech 1900D | UE-166 | Lsf ASH |
| ☐ N167YV | Beech 1900D | UE-167 | Lsf ASH |
| ☐ N171ZV | Beech 1900D | UE-171 | Lsf ASH |
| ☐ N173YV | Beech 1900D | UE-173 | Lsf ASH |
| ☐ N174YV | Beech 1900D | UE-174 | Lsf ASH |
| ☐ N176YV | Beech 1900D | UE-176 | Lsf ASH |
| ☐ N182YV | Beech 1900D | UE-182 | Lsf ASH |
| ☐ N190YV | Beech 1900D | UE-190 | Lsf ASH |
| ☐ N218YV | Beech 1900D | UE-218 | Lsf ASH |
| ☐ N231YV | Beech 1900D | UE-231 | Lsf ASH |
| ☐ N237YV | Beech 1900D | UE-237 | Lsf ASH |
| ☐ N244YV | Beech 1900D | UE-244 | Lsf ASH |
| ☐ N3199Q | Beech 1900D | UE-213 | Lsf ASH |
| ☐ N10675 | Beech 1900D | UE-229 | Lsf ASH |

## AIR TRANSPORT INTERNATIONAL     ATN

| | | | |
|---|---|---|---|
| ☐ N21CX | Douglas DC-8-62F | 365/45955 | |
| ☐ N31CX | Douglas DC-8-62F | 318/45911 | |
| ☐ N41CX | Douglas DC-8-62CF | 523/46129 | Opf BAX |
| ☐ N603AL | Douglas DC-8-73F | 401/46003 | |
| ☐ N605AL | Douglas DC-8-73F | 490/46106 | |
| ☐ N606AL | Douglas DC-8-73F | 432/46044 | Opf BAX |
| ☐ N728PL | Douglas DC-8-62F | 353/45918 | |
| ☐ N786AL | Douglas DC-8-63CF | 500/46121 | |
| ☐ N799AL | Douglas DC-8-62F | 335/45922 | Opf BAX |
| ☐ N820BX+ | Douglas DC-8-71F | 460/46065 | Opf BAX |
| ☐ N821BX | Douglas DC-8-71F | 262/45811 | Opf BAX |
| ☐ N822BX | Douglas DC-8-71F | 284/45813 | Opf BAX |
| ☐ N823BX | Douglas DC-8-71F | 459/46064 | Opf BAX |
| ☐ N824BX | Douglas DC-8-71F | 339/45946 | Opf BAX |
| ☐ N825BX | Douglas DC-8-71F | 381/45978 | Opf BAX |
| ☐ N826BX | Douglas DC-8-71F | 399/45998 | std |
| ☐ N827BX | Douglas DC-8-71F | 356/45971 | Opf BAX |
| ☐ N828BX | Douglas DC-8-71F | 382/45993 | Opf BAX |
| ☐ N829BX | Douglas DC-8-71F | 387/45994 | Opf BAX |
| ☐ N830BX | Douglas DC-8-71F | 358/45973 | Opf BAX |
| ☐ N867BX | Douglas DC-8-63CF | 479/46049 | Opf BAX |
| ☐ N870BX | Douglas DC-8-63F | 445/46036 | Opf BAX |

## AIRTRAN AIRWAYS     TRS

| | | | |
|---|---|---|---|
| ☐ N940AT | Boeing 717-2BD | 5005/55004 | 702 |
| ☐ N942AT | Boeing 717-2BD | 5006/55005 | 703 |
| ☐ N943AT | Boeing 717-2BD | 5007/55006 | 704 |
| ☐ N944AT | Boeing 717-2BD | 5008/55007 | 705 |
| ☐ N945AT | Boeing 717-2BD | 5009/55008 | 706 |
| ☐ N946AT | Boeing 717-2BD | 5010/55009 | 707 |
| ☐ N947AT | Boeing 717-2BD | 5011/55010 | 708 |
| ☐ N948AT | Boeing 717-2BD | 5012/55011 | 709 |
| ☐ N949AT | Boeing 717-2BD | 5004/55003 | 701 |
| ☐ N950AT | Boeing 717-2BD | 5018/55012 | 710 |
| ☐ N951AT | Boeing 717-2BD | 5021/55013 | 711 |
| ☐ N952AT | Boeing 717-2BD | 5027/55014 | 712 |
| ☐ N953AT | Boeing 717-2BD | 5033/55015 | 713 |
| ☐ N954AT | Boeing 717-2BD | 5036/55016 | 714 |
| ☐ N955AT | Boeing 717-2BD | 5040/55017 | 715 |
| ☐ N956AT | Boeing 717-2BD | 5044/55018 | 716 |
| ☐ N957AT | Boeing 717-2BD | 5047/55019 | 717 |
| ☐ N958AT | Boeing 717-2BD | 5051/55020 | 718 |
| ☐ N959AT | Boeing 717-2BD | 5057/55021 | 719 |
| ☐ N960AT | Boeing 717-2BD | 5058/55022 | 720 |
| ☐ N961AT | Boeing 717-2BD | 5062/55023 | 721 |
| ☐ N963AT | Boeing 717-2BD | 5066/55024 | |
| ☐ N964AT | Boeing 717-2BD | 5071/55025 | |
| ☐ N965AT | Boeing 717-2BD | 5076/55026 | |
| ☐ N966AT | Boeing 717-2BD | 5081/55027 | |
| ☐ N967AT | Boeing 717-2BD | 5082/55028 | |
| ☐ N968AT | Boeing 717-2BD | 5091/55029 | |
| ☐ N969AT | Boeing 717-2BD | 5094/55030 | |
| ☐ N970AT | Boeing 717-2BD | 5096/55031 | |
| ☐ N971AT | Boeing 717-2BD | 5097/55032 | |
| ☐ N972AT | Boeing 717-2BD | 5099/55033 | |
| ☐ N974AT | Boeing 717-2BD | 5101/55034 | |
| ☐ N975AT | Boeing 717-2BD | 5102/55035 | |
| ☐ N977AT | Boeing 717-2BD | 5106/55036 | |
| ☐ N978AT | Boeing 717-2BD | 5108/55037 | |
| ☐ N979AT | Boeing 717-2BD | 5109/55038 | |
| ☐ N980AT | Boeing 717-2BD | 5111/55039 | |
| ☐ N981AT | Boeing 717-2BD | 5113/55040 | |
| ☐ N982AT | Boeing 717-2BD | 5114/55051 | |
| ☐ N983AT | Boeing 717-2BD | 5115/55042 | |
| ☐ N986AT | Boeing 717-231 | 5067/55089 | |
| ☐ N988AT | Boeing 717-23S | 5065/55068 | |
| ☐ N989AT | Boeing 717-23S | 5085/55152 | |
| ☐ N990AT | Boeing 717-23S | 5088/55134 | |
| ☐ N991AT | Boeing 717-23S | 5090/55135 | |
| ☐ N992AT | Boeing 717-2BD | 5100/55136 | |
| ☐ N993AT | Boeing 717-2BD | 5103/55137 | |
| ☐ N994AT | Boeing 717-2BD | 5104/55138 | |
| ☐ N995AT | Boeing 717-2BD | 5105/55139 | |
| ☐ N996AT | Boeing 717-2BD | 5107/55140 | |

| | | | |
|---|---|---|---|
| ☐ N997AT | Boeing 717-23S | 5110/55141 | |
| ☐ N998AT | Boeing 717-2BD | 5112/55142 | |
| ☐ N | Boeing 717-231 | 5017/55058 | o/o |
| ☐ N | Boeing 717-231 | 5019/55069 | o/o |
| ☐ N | Boeing 717-231 | 5022/55070 | o/o |
| ☐ N | Boeing 717-231 | 5025/55072 | o/o |
| ☐ N | Boeing 717-231 | 5028/55073 | o/o |
| ☐ N | Boeing 717-231 | 5032/55075 | o/o |
| ☐ N | Boeing 717-231 | 5035/55076 | o/o |
| ☐ N | Boeing 717-231 | 5039/55078 | o/o |
| ☐ N | Boeing 717-231 | 5042/55079 | o/o |
| ☐ N | Boeing 717-231 | 5043/55080 | o/o |
| ☐ N | Boeing 717-231 | 5046/55082 | o/o |
| ☐ N | Boeing 717-231 | 5049/55083 | o/o |
| ☐ N | Boeing 717-231 | 5055/55085 | o/o |
| ☐ N | Boeing 717-231 | 5060/55087 | o/o |
| ☐ N | Boeing 717-231 | 5068/55090 | o/o |
| ☐ N | Boeing 717-231 | 5075/55091 | o/o |
| ☐ N | Boeing 717-231 | 5024/55071 | o/o |
| ☐ N | Boeing 717-231 | 5038/55077 | o/o |
| ☐ N | Boeing 717-231 | 5052/55084 | o/o |
| ☐ N | Boeing 717-231 | 5056/55086 | o/o |
| ☐ N | Boeing 717-231 | 5063/55088 | o/o |
| | | | |
| ☐ N821AT | Douglas DC-9-32 | 413/47284 | |
| ☐ N823AT | Douglas DC-9-32 | 625/47529 | |
| ☐ N828AT | Douglas DC-9-32 | 348/47274 | |
| ☐ N830AT | Douglas DC-9-32 | 838/47723 | |
| ☐ N831AT | Douglas DC-9-32 | 793/47674 | |
| ☐ N832AT | Douglas DC-9-32 | 547/47451 | |
| ☐ N833AT | Douglas DC-9-32 | 528/47489 | |
| ☐ N834AT | Douglas DC-9-32 | 527/47488 | |
| ☐ N835AT | Douglas DC-9-32 | 644/47534 | |
| ☐ N836AT | Douglas DC-9-32 | 636/47397 | |
| ☐ N837AT | Douglas DC-9-32 | 336/45774 | |
| ☐ N839AT | Douglas DC-9-32 | 189/47089 | |
| ☐ N840AT | Douglas DC-9-32 | 593/47523 | |
| ☐ N845AT | Douglas DC-9-32 | 465/47238 | |
| ☐ N846AT | Douglas DC-9-32 | 333/47226 | |
| ☐ N847AT | Douglas DC-9-32 | 667/47555 | |
| ☐ N848AT | Douglas DC-9-32 | 672/47559 | |
| ☐ N849AT | Douglas DC-9-32 | 648/47484 | |
| ☐ N866AT | Douglas DC-9-32 | 423/47168 | |
| ☐ N867AT | Douglas DC-9-32 | 425/47170 | |

## AIRTRAN CONNECT

| | | |
|---|---|---|
| ☐ N433AW | Canadair RJ-200 | 7289 |

## ALASKA AIRLINES     ASA

| | | |
|---|---|---|
| ☐ N703AS | Boeing 737-490 | 3039/28893 |
| ☐ N705AS | Boeing 737-490 | 3043/29318 |
| ☐ N706AS | Boeing 737-490 | 3050/28894 |
| ☐ N708AS | Boeing 737-490 | 3058/28895 |
| ☐ N709AS | Boeing 737-490 | 3099/28896 |
| ☐ N713AS | Boeing 737-490 | 3110/30161 |
| ☐ N730AS | Boeing 737-290C | 760/22577 |
| ☐ N740AS | Boeing 737-290C | 767/22578 |
| ☐ N741AS | Boeing 737-2Q8C | 610/21959 |
| ☐ N742AS | Boeing 737-290C | 1032/23136 |
| ☐ N743AS | Boeing 737-210C | 590/21821 |
| ☐ N744AS | Boeing 737-210C | 605/21822 |
| ☐ N745AS | Boeing 737-298C | 346/20794 |
| ☐ N746AS | Boeing 737-2X6C | 1042/23123 |
| ☐ N747AS | Boeing 737-2X6C | 1046/23124 |
| ☐ N754AS | Boeing 737-4Q8 | 2266/25095 |
| ☐ N755AS | Boeing 737-4Q8 | 2278/25096 |
| ☐ N756AS | Boeing 737-4Q8 | 2299/25097 |
| ☐ N760AS | Boeing 737-4Q8 | 2320/25098 |
| ☐ N762AS | Boeing 737-4Q8 | 2334/25099 |
| ☐ N763AS | Boeing 737-4Q8 | 2346/25100 |
| ☐ N764AS | Boeing 737-4Q8 | 2348/25101 |
| ☐ N765AS | Boeing 737-4Q8 | 2350/25102 |
| ☐ N767AS | Boeing 737-490 | 2354/27081 |
| ☐ N768AS | Boeing 737-490 | 2350/27082 |
| ☐ N769AS | Boeing 737-4Q8 | 2452/25103 |

| | | | |
|---|---|---|---|
| ☐ N771AS | Boeing 737-4Q8 | 2476/25104 | |
| ☐ N772AS | Boeing 737-4Q8 | 2505/25105 | |
| ☐ N773AS | Boeing 737-4Q8 | 2518/25106 | |
| ☐ N774AS | Boeing 737-4Q8 | 2526/25107 | |
| ☐ N775AS | Boeing 737-4Q8 | 2551/25108 | |
| ☐ N776AS | Boeing 737-4Q8 | 2561/25109 | |
| ☐ N778AS | Boeing 737-4Q8 | 2586/25110 | |
| ☐ N779AS | Boeing 737-4Q8 | 2605/25111 | |
| ☐ N780AS | Boeing 737-4Q8 | 2638/25112 | |
| ☐ N782AS | Boeing 737-4Q8 | 2656/25113 | |
| ☐ N783AS | Boeing 737-4Q8 | 2666/25114 | |
| ☐ N784AS | Boeing 737-4Q8 | 2826/28199 | |
| ☐ N785AS | Boeing 737-4Q8 | 2858/27628 | |
| ☐ N786AS | Boeing 737-4S3 | 1870/24795 | |
| ☐ N788AS | Boeing 737-490 | 2891/28885 | |
| ☐ N791AS | Boeing 737-490 | 2902/28886 | |
| ☐ N792AS | Boeing 737-490 | 2903/28887 | |
| ☐ N793AS | Boeing 737-490 | 2990/28888 | |
| ☐ N794AS | Boeing 737-490 | 3000/28889 | |
| ☐ N795AS | Boeing 737-490 | 3006/28890 | |
| ☐ N796AS | Boeing 737-490 | 3027/28891 | |
| ☐ N797AS | Boeing 737-490 | 3036/28892 | |
| ☐ N799AS | Boeing 737-490 | 3038/29270 | |
| | | | |
| ☐ N607AS | Boeing 737-790 | 313/29751 | |
| ☐ N609AS | Boeing 737-790 | 350/29752 | |
| ☐ N611AS | Boeing 737-790 | 385/29753 | |
| ☐ N612AS | Boeing 737-790 | 406/30162 | |
| ☐ N613AS | Boeing 737-790 | 430/30163 | |
| ☐ N614AS | Boeing 737-790 | 439/30343 | |
| ☐ N615AS | Boeing 737-790 | 472/30344 | |
| ☐ N617AS | Boeing 737-790 | 532/30542 | |
| ☐ N618AS | Boeing 737-790 | 536/30543 | |
| ☐ N619AS | Boeing 737-790 | 597/30164 | |
| ☐ N622AS | Boeing 737-790 | 661/30165 | |
| ☐ N623AS | Boeing 737-790 | 700/30166 | |
| ☐ N624AS | Boeing 737-790 | 724/30778 | |
| ☐ N625AS | Boeing 737-790 | 754/30792 | |
| ☐ N626AS | Boeing 737-790 | 763/30793 | |
| ☐ N627AS | Boeing 737-790 | 796/30794 | |
| ☐ N629AS | Boeing 737-7BK | 1273/30626 | |
| ☐ N644AS | Boeing 737-790 | 30795 | o/o |
| ☐ N645AS | Boeing 737-7BK | 33011 | o/o |
| ☐ N647AS | Boeing 737-7BK | 33012 | o/o |
| ☐ N | Boeing 737-7Q8 | 30662 | o/o |
| ☐ N | Boeing 737-7Q8 | 30663 | o/o |
| | | | |
| ☐ N302AS | Boeing 737-990 | 596/30017 | |
| ☐ N303AS | Boeing 737-990 | 683/30016 | |
| ☐ N305AS | Boeing 737-990 | 774/30013 | |
| ☐ N306AS | Boeing 737-990 | 802/30014 | |
| ☐ N307AS | Boeing 737-990 | 838/30015 | |
| ☐ N309AS | Boeing 737-990 | 902/30857 | |
| ☐ N315AS | Boeing 737-990 | 1218/30019 | |
| ☐ N317AS | Boeing 737-990 | 30856 | o/o |
| ☐ N318AS | Boeing 737-990 | 30018 | o/o |
| ☐ N319AS | Boeing 737-990 | 33679 | o/o |
| ☐ N320AS | Boeing 737-990 | 33680 | o/o |
| ☐ N | Boeing 737-990 | | o/o |
| | | | |
| ☐ N931AS | McDD MD-82 | 1178/49232 | |
| ☐ N933AS | McDD MD-83 | 1204/49234 | |
| ☐ N934AS | McDD MD-83 | 1234/49235 | |
| ☐ N935AS | McDD MD-83 | 1235/49236 | |
| ☐ N937AS | McDD MD-82 | 1276/49364 | |
| ☐ N943AS | McDD MD-83 | 1779/53018 | |
| ☐ N944AS | McDD MD-83 | 1783/53019 | |
| ☐ N947AS | McDD MD-83 | 1789/53020 | |
| ☐ N948AS | McDD MD-83 | 1801/53021 | |
| ☐ N949AS | McDD MD-83 | 1809/53022 | |
| ☐ N950AS | McDD MD-83 | 1821/53023 | |
| ☐ N951AS | McDD MD-82 | 1064/49111 | |
| ☐ N953AS | McDD MD-82 | 1287/49386 | |
| ☐ N954AS | McDD MD-82 | 1288/49387 | |
| ☐ N958AS | McDD MD-83 | 1825/53024 | |
| ☐ N960AS | McDD MD-83 | 1976/53074 | |
| ☐ N961AS | McDD MD-83 | 1977/53075 | |
| ☐ N962AS | McDD MD-83 | 1988/53076 | |

| | | | | |
|---|---|---|---|---|
| ☐ N964AS | McDD MD-83 | 1996/53078 | | |
| ☐ N965AS | McDD MD-83 | 2004/53079 | | |
| ☐ N967AS | McDD MD-82 | 1083/49103 | | |
| ☐ N968AS | McDD MD-83 | 1850/53016 | | |
| ☐ N969AS | McDD MD-83 | 1851/53063 | | |
| ☐ N972AS | McDD MD-83 | 2074/53448 | | |
| ☐ N973AS | McDD MD-83 | 2077/53449 | | |
| ☐ N974AS | McDD MD-83 | 2078/53450 | | |
| ☐ N975AS | McDD MD-83 | 2083/53451 | | |
| ☐ N976AS | McDD MD-83 | 2109/53452 | | |
| ☐ N977AS | McDD MD-83 | 2112/53453 | | |
| ☐ N979AS | McDD MD-83 | 2139/53471 | | |
| ☐ N981AS | McDD MD-83 | 2178/53472 | | |
| ☐ N982AS | McDD MD-83 | 2183/53473 | | |

## ALLEGIANT AIR                                      AAY

| | | | |
|---|---|---|---|
| ☐ N127NK | Douglas DC-9-21 | 488/47361 | |
| ☐ N860GA | McDD MD-83 | 1631/49786 | |
| ☐ N945MA | McDD MD-87 | 1552/49725 | |
| ☐ N948MA | McDD MD-87 | 1646/49778 | |
| ☐ N | McDD MD-83 | 1415/49556 | o/o |
| ☐ N | McDD MD-83 | 1436/49557 | o/o |

## ALOHA AIRLINES                                     AAH

| | | | |
|---|---|---|---|
| ☐ N802AL | Boeing 737-2S5C | 663/22148 | std |
| ☐ N805AL | Boeing 737-2M6C | 637/21809 | |
| ☐ N806AL | Boeing 737-2S2C | 600/21927 | |
| ☐ N807AL | Boeing 737-2T4 | 1151/23443 | |
| ☐ N808AL | Boeing 737-2T4 | 1155/23445 | |
| ☐ N809AL | Boeing 737-2Q9 | 552/21720 | |
| ☐ N810AL | Boeing 737-2Y5 | 1523/24031 | |
| ☐ N816AL | Boeing 737-2X6C | 1036/23122 | |
| ☐ N817AL | Boeing 737-2X6C | 1113/23292 | |
| ☐ N818AL | Boeing 737-230 | 703/22117 | |
| ☐ N819AL | Boeing 737-25A | 1486/23791 | |
| ☐ N820AL | Boeing 737-230 | 790/22138 | |
| ☐ N821AL | Boeing 737-230 | 1079/23155 | |
| ☐ N823AL | Boeing 737-230 | 1078/23154 | |
| ☐ N824AL | Boeing 737-282 | 978/23045 | |
| ☐ N826AL | Boeing 737-282C | 1002/23051 | |
| ☐ N827AL | Boeing 737-209 | 1579/23913 | |
| ☐ N738AL | Boeing 737-73A | 390/28499 | |
| ☐ N739AL | Boeing 737-73A | 414/28500 | |
| ☐ N740AL | Boeing 737-76N | 799/28640 | |
| ☐ N741AL | Boeing 737-76N | 809/28641 | |
| ☐ N742AL | Boeing 737-76N | 855/30830 | |
| ☐ N743AL | Boeing 737-76N | 986/28654 | |
| ☐ N744AL | Boeing 737-76N | 1013/32582 | |
| ☐ N745AL | Boeing 737-76N | 347/29904 | |
| ☐ N746AL | Boeing 737-76N | 372/29905 | |
| ☐ N748AL | Boeing 737-76N | 429/30050 | |

## ALPINE AIR EXPRESS                                 AIP

| | | |
|---|---|---|
| ☐ N17ZV | Beech 1900C-1 | UC-17 |
| ☐ N125BA | Beech 1900C | UB-6 |
| ☐ N127BA | Beech 1900C | UB-7 |
| ☐ N153GA | Beech 1900C | UB-34 |
| ☐ N154GA | Beech 1900C | UB-25 |
| ☐ N172GA | Beech 1900C | UB-11 |
| ☐ N190GA | Beech 1900C | UB-1 |
| ☐ N192GA | Beech 1900C | UB-17 |
| ☐ N194GA | Beech 1900C | UB-8 |
| ☐ N195GA | Beech 1900C | UB-65 |
| ☐ N197GA | Beech 1900C | UB-16 |
| ☐ N198GA | Beech 1900C | UB-5 |
| ☐ N410UB | Beech 1900C-1 | UC-70 |
| ☐ N565M | Beech 1900C | UB-43 |
| ☐ N31764 | Beech 1900C | UC-53 |
| ☐ N2YV | Beech 1900D | UE-2 |

## AMERICAN AIRLINES                                  AAL

| | | | |
|---|---|---|---|
| ☐ N3075A | Airbus A300B4-605R | 606 | 075 |
| ☐ N7055A | Airbus A300B4-605R | 462 | 055 |

| | | | |
|---|---|---|---|
| ☐ N7062A | Airbus A300B4-605R | 474 | 062 |
| ☐ N7076A | Airbus A300B4-605R | 610 | 076 |
| ☐ N7082A | Airbus A300B4-605R | 643 | 082 |
| ☐ N7083A | Airbus A300B4-605R | 645 | 083 |
| ☐ N8067A | Airbus A300B4-605R | 510 | 067; std |
| ☐ N11060 | Airbus A300B4-605R | 470 | 060 |
| ☐ N14056 | Airbus A300B4-605R | 463 | 056 |
| ☐ N14061 | Airbus A300B4-605R | 471 | 061 |
| ☐ N14065 | Airbus A300B4-605R | 508 | 065; std |
| ☐ N14068 | Airbus A300B4-605R | 511 | 068 |
| ☐ N14077 | Airbus A300B4-605R | 612 | 077 |
| ☐ N18066 | Airbus A300B4-605R | 509 | 066 |
| ☐ N19059 | Airbus A300B4-605R | 469 | 059 |
| ☐ N25071 | Airbus A300B4-605R | 514 | 071 |
| ☐ N33069 | Airbus A300B4-605R | 512 | 069 |
| ☐ N34078 | Airbus A300B4-605R | 615 | 078 |
| ☐ N40064 | Airbus A300B4-605R | 507 | 064 |
| ☐ N41063 | Airbus A300B4-605R | 506 | 063 |
| ☐ N50051 | Airbus A300B4-605R | 459 | 051 |
| ☐ N59081 | Airbus A300B4-605R | 639 | 081 |
| ☐ N70054 | Airbus A300B4-605R | 461 | 054 |
| ☐ N70072 | Airbus A300B4-605R | 515 | 072 |
| ☐ N70073 | Airbus A300B4-605R | 516 | 073 |
| ☐ N70074 | Airbus A300B4-605R | 517 | 074 |
| ☐ N70079 | Airbus A300B4-605R | 619 | 079 |
| ☐ N77080 | Airbus A300B4-605R | 626 | 080 |
| ☐ N80052 | Airbus A300B4-605R | 460 | 052 |
| ☐ N80057 | Airbus A300B4-605R | 465 | 057 |
| ☐ N80058 | Airbus A300B4-605R | 466 | 058 |
| ☐ N80084 | Airbus A300B4-605R | 675 | 084 |
| ☐ N90070 | Airbus A300B4-605R | 513 | 070 |
| ☐ N91050 | Airbus A300B4-605R | 423 | 050 |

| | | | |
|---|---|---|---|
| ☐ N901AN | Boeing 737-823 | 184/29503 | 3AA |
| ☐ N902AN | Boeing 737-823 | 190/29504 | 3AB |
| ☐ N903AN | Boeing 737-823 | 196/29505 | 3AC |
| ☐ N904AN | Boeing 737-823 | 207/29506 | 3AD |
| ☐ N905AN | Boeing 737-823 | 231/29507 | 3AE |
| ☐ N906AN | Boeing 737-823 | 240/29508 | 3AF |
| ☐ N907AN | Boeing 737-823 | 254/29509 | 3AG |
| ☐ N908AN | Boeing 737-823 | 263/29510 | 3AH |
| ☐ N909AN | Boeing 737-823 | 267/29511 | 3AJ |
| ☐ N910AN | Boeing 737-823 | 271/29512 | 3AK |
| ☐ N912AN | Boeing 737-823 | 289/29513 | 3AL |
| ☐ N913AN | Boeing 737-823 | 293/29514 | 3AM |
| ☐ N914AN | Boeing 737-823 | 316/29515 | 3AN |
| ☐ N915AN | Boeing 737-823 | 322/29516 | 3AP |
| ☐ N916AN | Boeing 737-823 | 332/29517 | 3AR |
| ☐ N917AN | Boeing 737-823 | 344/29518 | 3AS |
| ☐ N918AN | Boeing 737-823 | 353/29519 | 3AT |
| ☐ N919AN | Boeing 737-823 | 363/29520 | 3AU |
| ☐ N920AN | Boeing 737-823 | 378/29521 | 3AV |
| ☐ N921AN | Boeing 737-823 | 383/29522 | 3AW |
| ☐ N922AN | Boeing 737-823 | 398/29523 | 3AX |
| ☐ N923AN | Boeing 737-823 | 405/29524 | 3AY |
| ☐ N924AN | Boeing 737-823 | 434/29525 | 3BA |
| ☐ N925AN | Boeing 737-823 | 440/29526 | 3BB |
| ☐ N926AN | Boeing 737-823 | 453/29527 | 3BC |
| ☐ N927AN | Boeing 737-823 | 462/30077 | 3BD |
| ☐ N928AN | Boeing 737-823 | 473/29528 | 3BE |
| ☐ N929AN | Boeing 737-823 | 488/30078 | 3BF |
| ☐ N930AN | Boeing 737-823 | 503/29529 | 3BG |
| ☐ N931AN | Boeing 737-823 | 509/30079 | 3BH |
| ☐ N932AN | Boeing 737-823 | 527/29530 | 3BJ |
| ☐ N933AN | Boeing 737-823 | 531/30080 | 3BK |
| ☐ N934AN | Boeing 737-823 | 553/29531 | 3BL |
| ☐ N935AN | Boeing 737-823 | 559/30081 | 3BM |
| ☐ N936AN | Boeing 737-823 | 575/29532 | 3BN |
| ☐ N937AN | Boeing 737-823 | 579/30082 | 3BP |
| ☐ N938AN | Boeing 737-823 | 608/29533 | 3BR |
| ☐ N939AN | Boeing 737-823 | 612/30083 | 3BS |
| ☐ N940AN | Boeing 737-823 | 616/30598 | 3BT |
| ☐ N941AN | Boeing 737-823 | 624/29534 | 3BU |
| ☐ N942AN | Boeing 737-823 | 629/30084 | 3BV |
| ☐ N943AN | Boeing 737-823 | 635/30599 | 3BW |
| ☐ N944AN | Boeing 737-823 | 645/29535 | 3BX |
| ☐ N945AN | Boeing 737-823 | 649/30085 | 3BY |
| ☐ N946AN | Boeing 737-823 | 655/30600 | 3CA |

| | Registration | Type | Line/Serial | Code |
|---|---|---|---|---|
| ☐ | N947AN | Boeing 737-823 | 671/29536 | 3CB |
| ☐ | N948AN | Boeing 737-823 | 679/30086 | 3CC |
| ☐ | N949AN | Boeing 737-823 | 699/29537 | 3CD |
| ☐ | N950AN | Boeing 737-823 | 704/30087 | 3CE |
| ☐ | N951AA | Boeing 737-823 | 720/29538 | 3CF |
| ☐ | N952AA | Boeing 737-823 | 726/30088 | 3CG |
| ☐ | N953AN | Boeing 737-823 | 741/29539 | 3CH |
| ☐ | N954AN | Boeing 737-823 | 745/30089 | 3CJ |
| ☐ | N955AN | Boeing 737-823 | 762/29540 | 3CK |
| ☐ | N956AN | Boeing 737-823 | 764/30090 | 3CL |
| ☐ | N957AN | Boeing 737-823 | 788/29541 | 3CM |
| ☐ | N958AN | Boeing 737-823 | 797/30091 | 3CN |
| ☐ | N959AN | Boeing 737-823 | 801/30828 | 3CP |
| ☐ | N960AN | Boeing 737-823 | 818/29542 | 3CR |
| ☐ | N961AN | Boeing 737-823 | 822/30092 | 3CS |
| ☐ | N962AN | Boeing 737-823 | 825/30858 | 3CT |
| ☐ | N963AN | Boeing 737-823 | 834/29543 | 3CU |
| ☐ | N964AN | Boeing 737-823 | 837/30093 | 3CV |
| ☐ | N965AN | Boeing 737-823 | 860/29544 | 3CW |
| ☐ | N966AN | Boeing 737-823 | 863/30094 | 3CX |
| ☐ | N967AN | Boeing 737-823 | 883/29545 | 3CY |
| ☐ | N968AN | Boeing 737-823 | 886/30095 | 3DA |
| ☐ | N969AN | Boeing 737-823 | 910/29546 | 3DB |
| ☐ | N970AN | Boeing 737-823 | 915/30096 | 3DC |
| ☐ | N971AN | Boeing 737-823 | 937/29547 | 3DD |
| ☐ | N972AN | Boeing 737-823 | 941/30097 | 3DE |
| ☐ | N973AN | Boeing 737-823 | 971/29548 | 3DF |
| ☐ | N974AN | Boeing 737-823 | 977/30098 | 3DG |
| ☐ | N975AN | Boeing 737-823 | 992/29549 | 3DH |
| ☐ | N976AN | Boeing 737-823 | 1001/30099 | 3DJ |
| ☐ | N977AN | Boeing 737-823 | 1019/29550 | 3DK |
| ☐ | N978AN | Boeing 737-823 | 1022/30100 | 3DL |
| ☐ | N172AJ | Boeing 757-223 | 1012/32400 | 5FT |
| ☐ | N173AN | Boeing 757-223 | 1005/32399 | 5FS |
| ☐ | N174AA | Boeing 757-223 | 968/31308 | 5FR |
| ☐ | N175AN | Boeing 757-223 | 992/32394 | 5FK |
| ☐ | N176AA | Boeing 757-223 | 994/32395 | 5FL |
| ☐ | N177AN | Boeing 757-223 | 996/32396 | 5FM |
| ☐ | N178AA | Boeing 757-223 | 1002/32397 | 5FN |
| ☐ | N179AA | Boeing 757-223 | 1000/32398 | 5FP |
| ☐ | N181AN | Boeing 757-223 | 852/29591 | 5EN |
| ☐ | N182AN | Boeing 757-223 | 853/29592 | 5EP |
| ☐ | N183AN | Boeing 757-223ER | 862/29593 | 5ER |
| ☐ | N184AN | Boeing 757-223ER | 866/29594 | 5ES |
| ☐ | N185AN | Boeing 757-223 | 962/32379 | 5ET |
| ☐ | N186AN | Boeing 757-223 | 964/32380 | 5EU |
| ☐ | N187AN | Boeing 757-223 | 965/32381 | 5EV |
| ☐ | N188AN | Boeing 757-223 | 969/32382 | 5EW |
| ☐ | N189AN | Boeing 757-223 | 970/32383 | 5EX |
| ☐ | N190AA | Boeing 757-223 | 973/32384 | 5EY |
| ☐ | N191AN | Boeing 757-223 | 977/32385 | 5FA |
| ☐ | N192AN | Boeing 757-223 | 979/32386 | 5FB |
| ☐ | N193AN | Boeing 757-223 | 981/32387 | 5FC |
| ☐ | N194AA | Boeing 757-223 | 983/32388 | 5FD |
| ☐ | N195AN | Boeing 757-223 | 984/32389 | 5FE |
| ☐ | N196AA | Boeing 757-223 | 986/32390 | 5FF |
| ☐ | N197AN | Boeing 757-223 | 988/32391 | 5FG |
| ☐ | N198AA | Boeing 757-223 | 989/32392 | 5FH |
| ☐ | N199AN | Boeing 757-223 | 991/32393 | 5FJ |
| ☐ | N601AN | Boeing 757-223 | 661/27052 | 5DU |
| ☐ | N602AN | Boeing 757-223 | 664/27053 | 5DV |
| ☐ | N603AA | Boeing 757-223 | 670/27054 | 5DW |
| ☐ | N604AA | Boeing 757-223 | 677/27055 | 5DX |
| ☐ | N605AA | Boeing 757-223 | 680/27056 | 5DY |
| ☐ | N606AA | Boeing 757-223 | 707/27057 | 5EA |
| ☐ | N607AM | Boeing 757-223 | 712/27058 | 5EB |
| ☐ | N608AA | Boeing 757-223ER | 720/27446 | 5EC |
| ☐ | N609AA | Boeing 757-223ER | 722/27447 | 5ED |
| ☐ | N610AA | Boeing 757-223 | 234/24486 | 610 |
| ☐ | N611AM | Boeing 757-223 | 236/24487 | 611 |
| ☐ | N612AA | Boeing 757-223 | 240/24488 | 612 |
| ☐ | N613AA | Boeing 757-223 | 242/24489 | 613 |
| ☐ | N614AA | Boeing 757-223 | 243/24490 | 614 |
| ☐ | N615AM | Boeing 757-223 | 245/24491 | 615 |
| ☐ | N616AA | Boeing 757-223 | 248/24524 | 616 |
| ☐ | N617AM | Boeing 757-223 | 253/24525 | 617 |
| ☐ | N618AA | Boeing 757-223 | 260/24526 | 618 |
| ☐ | N619AA | Boeing 757-223 | 269/24577 | 619 |
| ☐ | N620AA | Boeing 757-223 | 276/24578 | 620 |
| ☐ | N621AM | Boeing 757-223 | 283/24579 | 621 |
| ☐ | N622AA | Boeing 757-223 | 289/24580 | 622 |
| ☐ | N623AA | Boeing 757-223 | 296/24581 | 623 |
| ☐ | N624AA | Boeing 757-223 | 297/24582 | 624 |
| ☐ | N625AA | Boeing 757-223 | 303/24583 | 625 |
| ☐ | N626AA | Boeing 757-223 | 304/24584 | 626 |
| ☐ | N627AA | Boeing 757-223 | 308/24585 | 627 |
| ☐ | N628AA | Boeing 757-223 | 309/24586 | 628 |
| ☐ | N629AA | Boeing 757-223 | 315/24587 | 629 |
| ☐ | N630AA | Boeing 757-223 | 316/24588 | 630 |
| ☐ | N631AA | Boeing 757-223 | 317/24589 | 631 |
| ☐ | N632AA | Boeing 757-223 | 321/24590 | 632 |
| ☐ | N633AA | Boeing 757-223 | 324/24591 | 633 |
| ☐ | N634AA | Boeing 757-223 | 327/24592 | 634 |
| ☐ | N635AA | Boeing 757-223 | 328/24593 | 635 |
| ☐ | N636AM | Boeing 757-223 | 336/24594 | 636 |
| ☐ | N637AM | Boeing 757-223 | 337/24595 | 637 |
| ☐ | N638AA | Boeing 757-223 | 344/24596 | 638 |
| ☐ | N639AA | Boeing 757-223 | 345/24597 | 639 |
| ☐ | N640A | Boeing 757-223 | 350/24598 | 640 |
| ☐ | N641AA | Boeing 757-223 | 351/24599 | 641 |
| ☐ | N642AA | Boeing 757-223 | 357/24600 | 642 |
| ☐ | N643AA | Boeing 757-223 | 360/24601 | 643 |
| ☐ | N645AA | Boeing 757-223 | 370/24603 | 5BR |
| ☐ | N646AA | Boeing 757-223 | 375/24604 | 5BS |
| ☐ | N647AM | Boeing 757-223 | 378/24605 | 5BT |
| ☐ | N648AA | Boeing 757-223 | 379/24606 | 5BU |
| ☐ | N649AA | Boeing 757-223 | 383/24607 | 5BV |
| ☐ | N650AA | Boeing 757-223 | 384/24608 | 5BW |
| ☐ | N652AA | Boeing 757-223 | 391/24610 | 5BY |
| ☐ | N653A | Boeing 757-223 | 397/24611 | 5CA |
| ☐ | N654A | Boeing 757-223 | 398/24612 | 5CB |
| ☐ | N655AA | Boeing 757-223 | 402/24613 | 5CC |
| ☐ | N656AA | Boeing 757-223 | 404/24614 | 5CD |
| ☐ | N657AM | Boeing 757-223 | 409/24615 | 5CE |
| ☐ | N658AA | Boeing 757-223 | 410/24616 | 5CF |
| ☐ | N659AA | Boeing 757-223 | 417/24617 | 5CG |
| ☐ | N660AM | Boeing 757-223 | 418/25294 | 5CH |
| ☐ | N661AA | Boeing 757-223 | 423/25295 | 5CJ |
| ☐ | N662AA | Boeing 757-223 | 425/25296 | 5CK |
| ☐ | N663AM | Boeing 757-223 | 432/25297 | 5CL |
| ☐ | N664AA | Boeing 757-223 | 433/25298 | 5CM |
| ☐ | N665AA | Boeing 757-223 | 436/25299 | 5CN |
| ☐ | N666A | Boeing 757-223 | 451/25300 | 5CP |
| ☐ | N668AA | Boeing 757-223 | 460/25333 | 5CS |
| ☐ | N669AA | Boeing 757-223 | 463/25334 | 5CT |
| ☐ | N670AA | Boeing 757-223 | 468/25335 | 5CU |
| ☐ | N671AA | Boeing 757-223 | 473/25336 | 5CV |
| ☐ | N672AA | Boeing 757-223 | 474/25337 | 5CW |
| ☐ | N673AN | Boeing 757-223 | 812/29423 | 5EE |
| ☐ | N674AN | Boeing 757-223 | 816/29424 | 5EF |
| ☐ | N675AN | Boeing 757-223 | 817/29425 | 5EG |
| ☐ | N676AN | Boeing 757-223 | 827/29426 | 5EH |
| ☐ | N677AN | Boeing 757-223 | 828/29427 | 5EJ |
| ☐ | N678AN | Boeing 757-223 | 837/29428 | 5EK |
| ☐ | N679AN | Boeing 757-223 | 842/29589 | 5EL |
| ☐ | N680AN | Boeing 757-223 | 847/29590 | 5EM |
| ☐ | N681AA | Boeing 757-223 | 483/25338 | 5CX |
| ☐ | N682AA | Boeing 757-223 | 484/25339 | 5CY |
| ☐ | N683A | Boeing 757-223 | 491/25340 | 5DA |
| ☐ | N684AA | Boeing 757-223 | 504/25341 | 5DB |
| ☐ | N685AA | Boeing 757-223 | 507/25342 | 5DC |
| ☐ | N686AA | Boeing 757-223 | 509/25343 | 5DD |
| ☐ | N687AA | Boeing 757-223ER | 536/25695 | 5DE |
| ☐ | N688AA | Boeing 757-223ER | 548/25730 | 5DF |
| ☐ | N689AA | Boeing 757-223ER | 562/25731 | 5DG |
| ☐ | N690AA | Boeing 757-223ER | 566/25696 | 5DH |
| ☐ | N691AA | Boeing 757-223ER | 568/25697 | 5DJ |
| ☐ | N692AA | Boeing 757-223 | 578/26972 | 5DK |
| ☐ | N693AA | Boeing 757-223 | 580/26973 | 5DL |
| ☐ | N694AN | Boeing 757-223 | 582/26974 | 5DM |
| ☐ | N695AN | Boeing 757-223 | 621/26975 | 5DN |
| ☐ | N696AN | Boeing 757-223 | 627/26976 | 5DP |
| ☐ | N697AN | Boeing 757-223 | 633/26977 | 5DR |
| ☐ | N698AN | Boeing 757-223 | 635/26980 | 5DS |
| ☐ | N699AN | Boeing 757-223 | 660/27051 | 5DT |

| | Registration | Type | Ser/Line | Code |
|---|---|---|---|---|
| ☐ | N701TW | Boeing 757-2Q8 | 721/28160 | 5TA |
| ☐ | N702TW | Boeing 757-2Q8 | 732/28162 | 5TB |
| ☐ | N703TW | Boeing 757-2Q8ER | 736/27620 | 5TC |
| ☐ | N704X | Boeing 757-2Q8 | 741/28163 | 5TD |
| ☐ | N705TW | Boeing 757-231 | 742/28479 | 5TE |
| ☐ | N706TW | Boeing 757-2Q8 | 743/28165 | 5TF |
| ☐ | N707TW | Boeing 757-2Q8ER | 744/27625 | 5TG |
| ☐ | N708TW | Boeing 757-231 | 750/28480 | 5TH |
| ☐ | N709TW | Boeing 757-2Q8 | 754/28168 | 5TJ |
| ☐ | N710TW | Boeing 757-2Q8 | 757/28169 | 5TK |
| ☐ | N711ZX | Boeing 757-231 | 758/28481 | 5TL |
| ☐ | N712TW | Boeing 757-2Q8ER | 760/27624 | 5TM |
| ☐ | N713TW | Boeing 757-2Q8 | 764/28173 | 5TN |
| ☐ | N714P | Boeing 757-231 | 770/28482 | 5TP |
| ☐ | N715TW | Boeing 757-231 | 777/28483 | 5TR |
| ☐ | N716TW | Boeing 757-231 | 825/28484 | 5TS |
| ☐ | N717TW | Boeing 757-231 | 854/28485 | 5TT |
| ☐ | N718TW | Boeing 757-231 | 869/28486 | 5TU |
| ☐ | N719TW | Boeing 757-231 | 878/28487 | 5TV |
| ☐ | N720TW | Boeing 757-231 | 883/30319 | 5TW |
| ☐ | N721TW | Boeing 757-231 | 874/29954 | 5TX |
| ☐ | N722TW | Boeing 757-231 | 893/29385 | 5TY |
| ☐ | N723TW | Boeing 757-231 | 907/29378 | 5WA |
| ☐ | N724TW | Boeing 757-231 | 884/28488 | 5WB |
| ☐ | N725TW | Boeing 757-231 | 891/30338 | 5WC |
| ☐ | N726TW | Boeing 757-231 | 896/30339 | 5WD |
| ☐ | N727TW | Boeing 757-231 | 901/30340 | 5WE |
| ☐ | N7667A | Boeing 757-223 | 459/25301 | 5CR |
| | | | | |
| ☐ | N301AA | Boeing 767-223 | 8/22307 | 301 |
| ☐ | N302AA | Boeing 767-223 | 19/22308 | 302 |
| ☐ | N303AA | Boeing 767-223 | 23/22309 | 303 |
| ☐ | N304AA | Boeing 767-223 | 25/22310 | 304 |
| ☐ | N305AA | Boeing 767-223 | 34/22311 | 305 |
| ☐ | N306AA | Boeing 767-223 | 44/22312 | 306 |
| ☐ | N307AA | Boeing 767-223 | 72/22313 | 307 |
| ☐ | N308AA | Boeing 767-223 | 73/22314 | 308 |
| ☐ | N312AA | Boeing 767-223ER | 94/22315 | 312 |
| ☐ | N313AA | Boeing 767-223ER | 95/22316 | 313 |
| ☐ | N315AA | Boeing 767-223ER | 109/22317 | 315 |
| ☐ | N316AA | Boeing 767-223ER | 111/22318 | 316 |
| ☐ | N317AA | Boeing 767-223ER | 112/22319 | 317 |
| ☐ | N319AA | Boeing 767-223ER | 128/22320 | 319 |
| ☐ | N320AA | Boeing 767-223ER | 130/22321 | 320 |
| ☐ | N321AA | Boeing 767-223ER | 139/22322 | 321 |
| ☐ | N322AA | Boeing 767-223ER | 140/22323 | 322 |
| ☐ | N323AA | Boeing 767-223ER | 146/22324 | 323 |
| ☐ | N324AA | Boeing 767-223ER | 147/22325 | 324 |
| ☐ | N325AA | Boeing 767-223ER | 157/22326 | 325 |
| ☐ | N327AA | Boeing 767-223ER | 159/22327 | 327 |
| ☐ | N328AA | Boeing 767-223ER | 160/22328 | 328 |
| ☐ | N329AA | Boeing 767-223ER | 164/22329 | 329 |
| ☐ | N330AA | Boeing 767-223ER | 166/22330 | 330 |
| ☐ | N332AA | Boeing 767-223ER | 168/22331 | 332 |
| ☐ | N335AA | Boeing 767-223ER | 194/22333 | 335 |
| ☐ | N336AA | Boeing 767-223ER | 195/22334 | 336 |
| ☐ | N338AA | Boeing 767-223ER | 196/22335 | 338 |
| ☐ | N339AA | Boeing 767-223ER | 198/22336 | 339 |
| ☐ | N342AN | Boeing 767-323 | 896/33081 | 342 |
| ☐ | N343AN | Boeing 767-323 | 33082 | 343 o/o |
| ☐ | N344AN | Boeing 767-323 | 33083 | 344 o/O |
| ☐ | N345AN | Boeing 767-323 | 33084 | 345 o/o |
| ☐ | N346AN | Boeing 767-323 | 33085 | 346 o/o |
| ☐ | N347AN | Boeing 767-323 | 33086 | 347 o/o |
| ☐ | N348AN | Boeing 767-323 | 33087 | 348 o/o |
| ☐ | N349AN | Boeing 767-323 | 33088 | 349 o/o |
| ☐ | N350AN | Boeing 767-323 | 33089 | 350 o/o |
| ☐ | N351AA | Boeing 767-323ER | 202/24032 | 351 |
| ☐ | N352AA | Boeing 767-323ER | 205/24033 | 352 |
| ☐ | N353AA | Boeing 767-323ER | 206/24034 | 353 |
| ☐ | N354AA | Boeing 767-323ER | 211/24035 | 354 |
| ☐ | N355AA | Boeing 767-323ER | 221/24036 | 355 |
| ☐ | N357AA | Boeing 767-323ER | 227/24038 | 357 |
| ☐ | N358AA | Boeing 767-323ER | 228/24039 | 358 |
| ☐ | N359AA | Boeing 767-323ER | 230/24040 | 359 |
| ☐ | N360AA | Boeing 767-323ER | 232/24041 | 360 |
| ☐ | N361AA | Boeing 767-323ER | 235/24042 | 361 |
| ☐ | N362AA | Boeing 767-323ER | 237/24043 | 362 |
| ☐ | N363AA | Boeing 767-323ER | 238/24044 | 363 |
| ☐ | N366AA | Boeing 767-323ER | 388/25193 | 366 |
| ☐ | N368AA | Boeing 767-323ER | 404/25195 | 368 |
| ☐ | N369AA | Boeing 767-323ER | 422/25196 | 369 |
| ☐ | N370AA | Boeing 767-323ER | 425/25197 | 370 |
| ☐ | N371AA | Boeing 767-323ER | 431/25198 | 371 |
| ☐ | N372AA | Boeing 767-323ER | 433/25199 | 372 |
| ☐ | N373AA | Boeing 767-323ER | 435/25200 | 373 |
| ☐ | N374AA | Boeing 767-323ER | 437/25201 | 374 |
| ☐ | N376AN | Boeing 767-323ER | 447/25445 | 376 |
| ☐ | N377AN | Boeing 767-323ER | 453/25446 | 377 |
| ☐ | N378AN | Boeing 767-323ER | 469/25447 | 378 |
| ☐ | N379AA | Boeing 767-323ER | 481/25448 | 379 |
| ☐ | N380AN | Boeing 767-323ER | 489/25449 | 380 |
| ☐ | N381AN | Boeing 767-323ER | 495/25450 | 381 |
| ☐ | N382AN | Boeing 767-323ER | 498/25451 | 382 |
| ☐ | N383AN | Boeing 767-323ER | 500/26995 | 383 |
| ☐ | N384AA | Boeing 767-323ER | 512/26996 | 384 |
| ☐ | N385AM | Boeing 767-323ER | 536/27059 | 385 |
| ☐ | N386AA | Boeing 767-323ER | 540/27060 | 386 |
| ☐ | N387AN | Boeing 767-323ER | 541/27184 | 387 |
| ☐ | N388AA | Boeing 767-323ER | 563/27448 | 388 |
| ☐ | N389AA | Boeing 767-323ER | 564/27449 | 389 |
| ☐ | N390AA | Boeing 767-323ER | 565/27450 | 390 |
| ☐ | N391AA | Boeing 767-323ER | 566/27451 | 391 |
| ☐ | N392AN | Boeing 767-323ER | 700/29429 | 392 |
| ☐ | N393AN | Boeing 767-323ER | 701/29430 | 393 |
| ☐ | N394AN | Boeing 767-323ER | 703/29431 | 394 |
| ☐ | N395AN | Boeing 767-323ER | 709/29432 | 395 |
| ☐ | N396AN | Boeing 767-323ER | 739/29603 | 396 |
| ☐ | N397AN | Boeing 767-323ER | 744/29604 | 397 |
| ☐ | N398AN | Boeing 767-323ER | 748/29605 | 398 |
| ☐ | N399AN | Boeing 767-323ER | 752/29606 | 399 |
| ☐ | N7375A | Boeing 767-323ER | 441/25202 | 375 |
| ☐ | N39356 | Boeing 767-323ER | 226/24034 | 356 |
| ☐ | N39364 | Boeing 767-323ER | 240/24045 | 364 |
| ☐ | N39365 | Boeing 767-323ER | 241/24046 | 365 |
| ☐ | N39367 | Boeing 767-323ER | 394/25194 | 367 |
| | | | | |
| ☐ | N750AN | Boeing 777-223ER | 332/30259 | 7BJ |
| ☐ | N751AN | Boeing 777-223ER | 333/30798 | 7BK |
| ☐ | N752AN | Boeing 777-223ER | 339/30260 | 7BL |
| ☐ | N753AN | Boeing 777-223ER | 341/30261 | 7BM |
| ☐ | N754AN | Boeing 777-223ER | 345/30262 | 7BN |
| ☐ | N755AN | Boeing 777-223ER | 354/30263 | 7BP |
| ☐ | N756AM | Boeing 777-223ER | 358/30264 | 7BR |
| ☐ | N757AN | Boeing 777-223ER | 363/32636 | 7BS |
| ☐ | N758AN | Boeing 777-223ER | 371/32637 | 7BT |
| ☐ | N759AN | Boeing 777-223ER | 376/32638 | 7BU |
| ☐ | N760AN | Boeing 777-223ER | 379/31477 | 7BV |
| ☐ | N761AJ | Boeing 777-223ER | 393/31478 | 7BW |
| ☐ | N762AN | Boeing 777-223ER | 399/31479 | 7BX |
| ☐ | N763AN | Boeing 777-223ER | 31480 | 7BY o/o |
| ☐ | N764AN | Boeing 777-223ER | 32439 | 7CA o/o |
| ☐ | N770AN | Boeing 777-223ER | 185/29578 | 7AA |
| ☐ | N771AN | Boeing 777-223ER | 190/29579 | 7AB |
| ☐ | N772AN | Boeing 777-223ER | 198/29580 | 7AC |
| ☐ | N773AN | Boeing 777-223ER | 199/29583 | 7AD |
| ☐ | N774AN | Boeing 777-223ER | 208/29581 | 7AE |
| ■ | N775AN | Boeing 777-223ER | 209/29584 | 7AF |
| ☐ | N776AN | Boeing 777-223ER | 215/29582 | 7AG |
| ☐ | N777AN | Boeing 777-223ER | 218/29585 | 7AH |
| ☐ | N778AN | Boeing 777-223ER | 223/29587 | 7AJ |
| ☐ | N779AN | Boeing 777-223ER | 225/29955 | 7AK |
| ☐ | N780AN | Boeing 777-223ER | 241/29956 | 7AL |
| ☐ | N781AN | Boeing 777-223ER | 266/29586 | 7AM |
| ☐ | N782AN | Boeing 777-223ER | 270/30003 | 7AN |
| ☐ | N783AN | Boeing 777-223ER | 271/30004 | 7AP |
| ☐ | N784AN | Boeing 777-223ER | 272/29588 | 7AR |
| ☐ | N785AN | Boeing 777-223ER | 274/30005 | 7AS |
| ☐ | N786AN | Boeing 777-223ER | 276/30250 | 7AT |
| ☐ | N787AL | Boeing 777-223ER | 277/30010 | 7AU |
| ☐ | N788AN | Boeing 777-223ER | 283/30011 | 7AV |
| ☐ | N789AN | Boeing 777-223ER | 285/30252 | 7AW |
| ☐ | N790AN | Boeing 777-223ER | 287/30251 | 7AX |
| ☐ | N791AN | Boeing 777-223ER | 289/30254 | 7AY |
| ☐ | N792AN | Boeing 777-223ER | 292/30253 | 7BA |
| ☐ | N793AN | Boeing 777-223ER | 299/30255 | 7BB |

| | | | | | | | | | |
|---|---|---|---|---|---|---|---|---|---|
| ☐ N794AN | Boeing 777-223ER | 313/30256 | 7BC | | ☐ N1472B | Fokker 100 | | 11514 | 2DG |
| ☐ N795AN | Boeing 777-223ER | 315/30257 | 7BD | | ☐ N1473K | Fokker 100 | | 11515 | 2DH |
| ☐ N796AN | Boeing 777-223ER | 316/30796 | 7BE | | ☐ N1474D | Fokker 100 | | 11520 | 2DJ; std |
| ☐ N797AN | Boeing 777-223ER | 321/30012 | 7BF | | | | | | |
| ☐ N798AN | Boeing 777-223ER | 324/30797 | 7BG | | ☐ N110HM | McDD MD-83 | | 1636/49787 | 4WT |
| ☐ N799AN | Boeing 777-223ER | 328/30258 | 7BH | | ☐ N203AA | McDD MD-82 | | 1097/49145 | 203 |
| | | | | | ☐ N205AA | McDD MD-82 | | 1103/49155 | 205 |
| ☐ N1400H | Fokker 100 | 11340 | 2AA | | ☐ N207AA | McDD MD-82 | | 1106/49158 | 207 |
| ☐ N1401G | Fokker 100 | 11352 | 2AB | | ☐ N208AA | McDD MD-82 | | 1107/49159 | 208 |
| ☐ N1402K | Fokker 100 | 11353 | 2AC | | ☐ N210AA | McDD MD-82 | | 1109/49161 | 210 |
| ☐ N1403M | Fokker 100 | 11354 | 2AD | | ☐ N214AA | McDD MD-82 | | 1110/49162 | 214 |
| ☐ N1404D | Fokker 100 | 11355 | 2AE | | ☐ N216AA | McDD MD-82 | | 1099/49167 | 216 |
| ☐ N1405J | Fokker 100 | 11356 | 2AF | | ☐ N218AA | McDD MD-82 | | 1100/49168 | 218 |
| ☐ N1406A | Fokker 100 | 11359 | 2AG | | ☐ N219AA | McDD MD-82 | | 1112/49171 | 219 |
| ☐ N1407D | Fokker 100 | 11360 | 2AH | | ☐ N221AA | McDD MD-82 | | 1113/49172 | 221 |
| ☐ N1408B | Fokker 100 | 11361 | 2AJ | | ☐ N223AA | McDD MD-82 | | 1114/49173 | 223 |
| ☐ N1409B | Fokker 100 | 11367 | 2AK | | ☐ N224AA | McDD MD-82 | | 1115/49174 | 224 |
| ☐ N1410E | Fokker 100 | 11368 | 2AL | | ☐ N225AA | McDD MD-82 | | 1116/49175 | 225 |
| ☐ N1411G | Fokker 100 | 11369 | 2AM | | ☐ N226AA | McDD MD-82 | | 1120/49176 | 226 |
| ☐ N1412A | Fokker 100 | 11370 | 2AN | | ☐ N227AA | McDD MD-82 | | 1121/49177 | 227 |
| ☐ N1413A | Fokker 100 | 11376 | 2AP | | ☐ N228AA | McDD MD-82 | | 1122/49178 | 228 |
| ☐ N1414D | Fokker 100 | 11377 | 2AR | | ☐ N232AA | McDD MD-82 | | 1123/49179 | 232 |
| ☐ N1415K | Fokker 100 | 11385 | 2AS | | ☐ N233AA | McDD MD-82 | | 1124/49180 | 233 |
| ☐ N1416A | Fokker 100 | 11395 | 2AT | | ☐ N234AA | McDD MD-82 | | 1125/49181 | 234 |
| ☐ N1417D | Fokker 100 | 11396 | 2AU | | ☐ N236AA | McDD MD-82 | | 1154/49251 | 236 |
| ☐ N1418A | Fokker 100 | 11397 | 2AV | | ☐ N237AA | McDD MD-82 | | 1155/49253 | 237 |
| ☐ N1420D | Fokker 100 | 11403 | 2AX | | ☐ N241AA | McDD MD-82 | | 1156/49254 | 241 |
| ☐ N1421K | Fokker 100 | 11404 | 2AY | | ☐ N242AA | McDD MD-82 | | 1157/49255 | 242 |
| ☐ N1422J | Fokker 100 | 11405 | 2BA | | ☐ N244AA | McDD MD-82 | | 1158/49256 | 244 |
| ☐ N1423A | Fokker 100 | 11406 | 2BB | | ☐ N245AA | McDD MD-82 | | 1160/49257 | 245 |
| ☐ N1424M | Fokker 100 | 11407 | 2BC | | ☐ N246AA | McDD MD-82 | | 1161/49258 | 246 |
| ☐ N1425A | Fokker 100 | 11408 | 2BD | | ☐ N248AA | McDD MD-82 | | 1162/49259 | 248 |
| ☐ N1426A | Fokker 100 | 11411 | 2BE | | ☐ N249AA | McDD MD-82 | | 1164/49269 | 249 |
| ☐ N1427A | Fokker 100 | 11412 | 2BF | | ☐ N251AA | McDD MD-82 | | 1165/49270 | 251 |
| ☐ N1428D | Fokker 100 | 11413 | 2BG | | ☐ N253AA | McDD MD-82 | | 1175/49286 | 253 |
| ☐ N1429G | Fokker 100 | 11414 | 2BH | | ☐ N255AA | McDD MD-82 | | 1176/49287 | 255 |
| ☐ N1430D | Fokker 100 | 11415 | 2BJ | | ☐ N258AA | McDD MD-82 | | 1187/49288 | 258 |
| ☐ N1431B | Fokker 100 | 11416 | 2BK | | ☐ N259AA | McDD MD-82 | | 1193/49289 | 269 |
| ☐ N1432A | Fokker 100 | 11417 | 2BL | | ☐ N262AA | McDD MD-82 | | 1195/49290 | 262 |
| ☐ N1433B | Fokker 100 | 11418 | 2BM | | ☐ N266AA | McDD MD-82 | | 1210/49291 | 266 |
| ☐ N1434A | Fokker 100 | 11419 | 2BN | | ☐ N269AA | McDD MD-82 | | 1211/49292 | 269 |
| ☐ N1435D | Fokker 100 | 11425 | 2BP | | ☐ N271AA | McDD MD-82 | | 1212/49293 | 271 |
| ☐ N1436A | Fokker 100 | 11426 | 2BR | | ☐ N274AA | McDD MD-82 | | 1166/49271 | 274 |
| ☐ N1437B | Fokker 100 | 11427 | 2BS | | ☐ N275AA | McDD MD-82 | | 1167/49272 | 275 |
| ☐ N1438H | Fokker 100 | 11428 | 2BT | | ☐ N276AA | McDD MD-82 | | 1168/49273 | 276 |
| ☐ N1439A | Fokker 100 | 11434 | 2BU; std | | ☐ N278AA | McDD MD-82 | | 1213/49294 | 278 |
| ☐ N1440A | Fokker 100 | 11435 | 2BV | | ☐ N279AA | McDD MD-82 | | 1214/49295 | 279 |
| ☐ N1441A | Fokker 100 | 11436 | 2BW | | ☐ N283AA | McDD MD-82 | | 1215/49296 | 283 |
| ☐ N1442E | Fokker 100 | 11437 | 2BX | | ☐ N285AA | McDD MD-82 | | 1216/49297 | 285 |
| ☐ N1443A | Fokker 100 | 11446 | 2BY | | ☐ N286AA | McDD MD-82 | | 1217/49298 | 286 |
| ☐ N1444N | Fokker 100 | 11447 | 2CA | | ☐ N287AA | McDD MD-82 | | 1218/49299 | 287 |
| ☐ N1445B | Fokker 100 | 11448 | 2CB; std | | ☐ N288AA | McDD MD-82 | | 1219/49300 | 288 |
| ☐ N1446A | Fokker 100 | 11449 | 2CC | | ☐ N289AA | McDD MD-82 | | 1220/49301 | 289 |
| ☐ N1447L | Fokker 100 | 11456 | 2CD | | ☐ N290AA | McDD MD-82 | | 1221/49302 | 290 |
| ☐ N1448A | Fokker 100 | 11457 | 2CE | | ☐ N291AA | McDD MD-82 | | 1222/49303 | 291 |
| ☐ N1449D | Fokker 100 | 11458 | 2CF | | ☐ N292AA | McDD MD-82 | | 1223/49304 | 292 |
| ☐ N1450A | Fokker 100 | 11459 | 2CG | | ☐ N293AA | McDD MD-82 | | 1226/49305 | 293 |
| ☐ N1451N | Fokker 100 | 11460 | 2CH | | ☐ N294AA | McDD MD-82 | | 1227/49306 | 294 |
| ☐ N1452B | Fokker 100 | 11464 | 2CJ | | ☐ N295AA | McDD MD-82 | | 1228/49307 | 295 |
| ☐ N1453D | Fokker 100 | 11465 | 2CK | | ☐ N296AA | McDD MD-82 | | 1229/49308 | 296 |
| ☐ N1454D | Fokker 100 | 11466 | 2CL | | ☐ N297AA | McDD MD-82 | | 1246/49309 | 297 |
| ☐ N1455K | Fokker 100 | 11467 | 2CM | | ☐ N298AA | McDD MD-82 | | 1247/49310 | 298 |
| ☐ N1456D | Fokker 100 | 11468 | 2CN | | ☐ N400AA | McDD MD-82 | | 1248/49311 | 400 |
| ☐ N1457B | Fokker 100 | 11469 | 2CP | | ☐ N402A | McDD MD-82 | | 1255/49313 | 402 |
| ☐ N1458H | Fokker 100 | 11478 | 2CR | | ☐ N403A | McDD MD-82 | | 1256/49314 | 403 |
| ☐ N1459A | Fokker 100 | 11479 | 2CS | | ☐ N405A | McDD MD-82 | | 1258/49316 | 405 |
| ☐ N1460A | Fokker 100 | 11480 | 2CT | | ☐ N406A | McDD MD-82 | | 1259/49317 | 406 |
| ☐ N1461C | Fokker 100 | 11481 | 2CU | | ☐ N407AA | McDD MD-82 | | 1265/49318 | 407 |
| ☐ N1462C | Fokker 100 | 11482 | 2CV | | ☐ N408AA | McDD MD-82 | | 1266/49319 | 408 |
| ☐ N1463A | Fokker 100 | 11483 | 2CW | | ☐ N409AA | McDD MD-82 | | 1267/49320 | 409 |
| ☐ N1464A | Fokker 100 | 11490 | 2CX | | ☐ N410AA | McDD MD-82 | | 1273/49321 | 410 |
| ☐ N1465K | Fokker 100 | 11491 | 2CY | | ☐ N411AA | McDD MD-82 | | 1280/49322 | 411 |
| ☐ N1466A | Fokker 100 | 11498 | 2DA | | ☐ N412AA | McDD MD-82 | | 1281/49323 | 412 |
| ☐ N1467A | Fokker 100 | 11499 | 2DB | | ☐ N413AA | McDD MD-82 | | 1289/49324 | 413 |
| ☐ N1468A | Fokker 100 | 11501 | 2DC | | ☐ N415AA | McDD MD-82 | | 1295/49326 | 415 |
| ☐ N1469D | Fokker 100 | 11502 | 2DD | | ☐ N416AA | McDD MD-82 | | 1296/49327 | 416 |
| ☐ N1470K | Fokker 100 | 11506 | 2DE | | ☐ N417AA | McDD MD-82 | | 1301/49328 | 417 |
| ☐ N1471G | Fokker 100 | 11507 | 2DF; std | | ☐ N418AA | McDD MD-82 | | 1302/49329 | 418 |

| | Reg | Type | Line/Serial | Fleet |
|---|---|---|---|---|
| ☐ | N419AA | McDD MD-82 | 1306/49331 | 419 |
| ☐ | N420AA | McDD MD-82 | 1307/49332 | 420 |
| ☐ | N422AA | McDD MD-82 | 1312/49334 | 422 |
| ☐ | N423AA | McDD MD-82 | 1320/49335 | 423 |
| ☐ | N424AA | McDD MD-82 | 1321/49336 | 424 |
| ☐ | N426AA | McDD MD-82 | 1327/49338 | 426 |
| ☐ | N427AA | McDD MD-82 | 1328/49339 | 427 |
| ☐ | N428AA | McDD MD-82 | 1329/49340 | 428 |
| ☐ | N429AA | McDD MD-82 | 1336/49341 | 429 |
| ☐ | N430AA | McDD MD-82 | 1337/49342 | 430 |
| ☐ | N431AA | McDD MD-82 | 1339/49343 | 431 |
| ☐ | N432AA | McDD MD-82 | 1376/49350 | 432 |
| ☐ | N433AA | McDD MD-83 | 1388/49451 | 433 |
| ☐ | N434AA | McDD MD-83 | 1389/49452 | 434 |
| ☐ | N435AA | McDD MD-83 | 1390/49453 | 435 |
| ☐ | N436AA | McDD MD-83 | 1391/49454 | 436 |
| ☐ | N437AA | McDD MD-83 | 1392/49455 | 437 |
| ☐ | N438AA | McDD MD-83 | 1393/49456 | 438 |
| ☐ | N439AA | McDD MD-83 | 1398/49457 | 439 |
| ☐ | N440AA | McDD MD-82 | 1407/49459 | 440 |
| ☐ | N441AA | McDD MD-82 | 1408/49460 | 441 |
| ☐ | N442AA | McDD MD-82 | 1409/49468 | 442 |
| ☐ | N443AA | McDD MD-82 | 1410/49469 | 443 |
| ☐ | N445AA | McDD MD-82 | 1418/49471 | 445 |
| ☐ | N446AA | McDD MD-82 | 1426/49472 | 446 |
| ☐ | N447AA | McDD MD-82 | 1427/49473 | 447 |
| ☐ | N448AA | McDD MD-82 | 1431/49474 | 448 |
| ☐ | N449AA | McDD MD-82 | 1432/49475 | 449 |
| ☐ | N450AA | McDD MD-82 | 1439/49476 | 450 |
| ☐ | N451AA | McDD MD-82 | 1441/49477 | 451 |
| ☐ | N452AA | McDD MD-82 | 1450/49553 | 452 |
| ☐ | N453AA | McDD MD-82 | 1451/49558 | 453 |
| ☐ | N454AA | McDD MD-82 | 1460/49559 | 454 |
| ☐ | N455AA | McDD MD-82 | 1462/49560 | 455 |
| ☐ | N456AA | McDD MD-82 | 1474/49561 | 456 |
| ☐ | N457AA | McDD MD-82 | 1475/49562 | 457 |
| ☐ | N458AA | McDD MD-82 | 1485/49563 | 458 |
| ☐ | N459AA | McDD MD-82 | 1486/49564 | 459 |
| ☐ | N460AA | McDD MD-82 | 1496/49565 | 460 |
| ☐ | N461AA | McDD MD-82 | 1497/49566 | 461 |
| ☐ | N462AA | McDD MD-82 | 1505/49592 | 462 |
| ☐ | N463AA | McDD MD-82 | 1506/49593 | 463 |
| ☐ | N464AA | McDD MD-82 | 1507/49594 | 464 |
| ☐ | N465A | McDD MD-82 | 1509/49595 | 465 |
| ☐ | N466AA | McDD MD-82 | 1510/49596 | 466 |
| ☐ | N467AA | McDD MD-82 | 1511/49597 | 467 |
| ☐ | N468AA | McDD MD-82 | 1513/49598 | 468 |
| ☐ | N469AA | McDD MD-82 | 1515/49599 | 469 |
| ☐ | N470AA | McDD MD-82 | 1516/49600 | 470 |
| ☐ | N471AA | McDD MD-82 | 1518/49601 | 471 |
| ☐ | N472AA | McDD MD-82 | 1520/49647 | 472 |
| ☐ | N473AA | McDD MD-82 | 1521/49648 | 473 |
| ☐ | N474 | McDD MD-82 | 1526/49649 | 474 |
| ☐ | N475AA | McDD MD-82 | 1527/49650 | 475 |
| ☐ | N476AA | McDD MD-82 | 1528/49651 | 476 |
| ☐ | N477AA | McDD MD-82 | 1529/49652 | 477 |
| ☐ | N478AA | McDD MD-82 | 1534/49653 | 478 |
| ☐ | N479AA | McDD MD-82 | 1535/49654 | 479 |
| ☐ | N480AA | McDD MD-82 | 1536/49655 | 480 |
| ☐ | N481AA | McDD MD-82 | 1545/49656 | 481 |
| ☐ | N482AA | McDD MD-82 | 1546/49675 | 482 |
| ☐ | N483A | McDD MD-82 | 1550/49676 | 483 |
| ☐ | N484AA | McDD MD-82 | 1551/49677 | 484 |
| ☐ | N485AA | McDD MD-82 | 1555/49678 | 485 |
| ☐ | N486AA | McDD MD-82 | 1557/49679 | 486 |
| ☐ | N487AA | McDD MD-82 | 1558/49680 | 487 |
| ☐ | N488AA | McDD MD-82 | 1560/49681 | 488 |
| ☐ | N489AA | McDD MD-82 | 1562/49682 | 489 |
| ☐ | N490AA | McDD MD-82 | 1563/49683 | 490 |
| ☐ | N491AA | McDD MD-82 | 1564/49684 | 491 |
| ☐ | N492AA | McDD MD-82 | 1565/49730 | 492 |
| ☐ | N493AA | McDD MD-82 | 1566/49731 | 493 |
| ☐ | N494AA | McDD MD-82 | 1567/49732 | 494 |
| ☐ | N495AA | McDD MD-82 | 1607/49733 | 495 |
| ☐ | N496AA | McDD MD-82 | 1619/49734 | 496 |
| ☐ | N497AA | McDD MD-82 | 1635/49735 | 497 |
| ☐ | N498AA | McDD MD-82 | 1640/49736 | 498 |
| ☐ | N499AA | McDD MD-82 | 1641/49737 | 499 |
| ☐ | N501AA | McDD MD-82 | 1648/49738 | 501 |
| ☐ | N505AA | McDD MD-82 | 1652/49799 | 505 |
| ☐ | N510AM | McDD MD-82 | 1669/49804 | 510 |
| ☐ | N513AA | McDD MD-82 | 1686/49890 | 513 |
| ☐ | N516AM | McDD MD-82 | 1696/49893 | 516 |
| ☐ | N552AA | McDD MD-82 | 1826/53034 | 552 |
| ☐ | N553AA | McDD MD-82 | 1828/53083 | 553 |
| ☐ | N554AA | McDD MD-82 | 1830/53084 | 554 |
| ☐ | N555AN | McDD MD-82 | 1839/53085 | 555 |
| ☐ | N556AA | McDD MD-82 | 1840/53086 | 556 |
| ☐ | N557AN | McDD MD-82 | 1841/53087 | 557 |
| ☐ | N558AA | McDD MD-82 | 1852/53088 | 558 |
| ☐ | N559AA | McDD MD-82 | 1853/53089 | 559 |
| ☐ | N560AA | McDD MD-82 | 1858/53090 | 560 |
| ☐ | N561AA | McDD MD-82 | 1863/53091 | 561 |
| ☐ | N562AA | McDD MD-83 | 1370/49344 | 562 |
| ☐ | N563AA | McDD MD-83 | 1371/49345 | 563 |
| ☐ | N564AA | McDD MD-83 | 1372/49346 | 564 |
| ☐ | N565AA | McDD MD-83 | 1373/49347 | 565 |
| ☐ | N566AA | McDD MD-83 | 1374/49348 | 566 |
| ☐ | N567AM | McDD MD-83 | 2021/53293 | 567 |
| ☐ | N568AA | McDD MD-83 | 1375/49349 | 568 |
| ☐ | N569AA | McDD MD-83 | 1385/49351 | 569 |
| ☐ | N570AA | McDD MD-83 | 1386/49352 | 570 |
| ☐ | N571AA | McDD MD-83 | 1387/49353 | 571 |
| ☐ | N572AA | McDD MD-83 | 1406/49458 | 572 |
| ☐ | N573AA | McDD MD-82 | 1864/53092 | 573 |
| ☐ | N574AA | McDD MD-82 | 1866/53151 | 574 |
| ☐ | N575AM | McDD MD-82 | 1875/53152 | 575 |
| ☐ | N576AA | McDD MD-82 | 1876/53153 | 576 |
| ☐ | N577AA | McDD MD-82 | 1878/53154 | 577 |
| ☐ | N578AA | McDD MD-82 | 1883/53155 | 578 |
| ☐ | N579AA | McDD MD-82 | 1884/53156 | 579 |
| ☐ | N580AA | McDD MD-82 | 1885/53157 | 580 |
| ☐ | N581AA | McDD MD-82 | 1891/53158 | 581 |
| ☐ | N582AA | McDD MD-82 | 1892/53159 | 582 |
| ☐ | N583AA | McDD MD-82 | 1893/53160 | 583 |
| ☐ | N584AA | McDD MD-82 | 1902/53247 | 584 |
| ☐ | N585AA | McDD MD-82 | 1903/53248 | 585 |
| ☐ | N586AA | McDD MD-82 | 1904/53249 | 586 |
| ☐ | N587AA | McDD MD-82 | 1907/53250 | 587 |
| ☐ | N588AA | McDD MD-83 | 1909/53251 | 588 |
| ☐ | N589AA | McDD MD-83 | 1910/53252 | 589 |
| ☐ | N590AA | McDD MD-83 | 1919/53253 | 590 |
| ☐ | N591AA | McDD MD-83 | 1920/53254 | 591 |
| ☐ | N592AA | McDD MD-83 | 1932/53255 | 592 |
| ☐ | N593AA | McDD MD-83 | 1933/53256 | 593 |
| ☐ | N594AA | McDD MD-83 | 1966/53284 | 594 |
| ☐ | N595AA | McDD MD-83 | 1989/53285 | 595 |
| ☐ | N596AA | McDD MD-83 | 2000/53286 | 596 |
| ☐ | N597AA | McDD MD-83 | 2006/53287 | 597 |
| ☐ | N598AA | McDD MD-83 | 2011/53288 | 598 |
| ☐ | N599AA | McDD MD-83 | 2012/53289 | 599 |
| ☐ | N752RA | McDD MD-87 | 1674/49780 | R5 |
| ☐ | N901TW | McDD MD-82 | 1098/49166 | 4TA |
| ☐ | N902TW | McDD MD-82 | 1101/49153 | 4TB |
| ☐ | N903TW | McDD MD-82 | 1102/49154 | 4TC |
| ☐ | N904TW | McDD MD-82 | 1104/49156 | 4TD |
| ☐ | N905TW | McDD MD-82 | 1105/49157 | 4TE |
| ☐ | N906TW | McDD MD-82 | 1108/49160 | 4TF |
| ☐ | N907TW | McDD MD-82 | 1117/49165 | 4TG |
| ☐ | N908TW | McDD MD-82 | 1118/49169 | 4TH |
| ☐ | N909TW | McDD MD-82 | 1119/49170 | 4TJ |
| ☐ | N911TW | McDD MD-82 | 1128/49182 | 4TK |
| ☐ | N912TW | McDD MD-82 | 1129/49183 | 4TL |
| ☐ | N913TW | McDD MD-82 | 1131/49184 | 4TM; std |
| ☐ | N914TW | McDD MD-82 | 1132/49185 | 4TN |
| ☐ | N915TW | McDD MD-82 | 1133/49186 | 4TP |
| ☐ | N916TW | McDD MD-82 | 1134/49187 | 4TR |
| ☐ | N917TW | McDD MD-82 | 1196/49366 | 4TS |
| ☐ | N918TW | McDD MD-82 | 1197/49367 | 4TT |
| ☐ | N919TW | McDD MD-82 | 1198/49368 | 4TU |
| ☐ | N920TW | McDD MD-82 | 1199/49369 | 4TV |
| ☐ | N921TW | McDD MD-82 | 1051/49101 | 4UL |
| ☐ | N922TW | McDD MD-82 | 1000/48013 | 4UM |
| ☐ | N923TW | McDD MD-82 | 1205/49379 | 4UN |
| ☐ | N924TW | McDD MD-82 | 1025/49100 | 4UP |
| ☐ | N925TW | McDD MD-82 | 1251/49357 | 4UR; std |

| | Registration | Type | Fleet/MSN | Code |
|---|---|---|---|---|
| ☐ | N926TW | McDD MD-82 | 1250/49356 | 4US |
| ☐ | N927TW | McDD MD-82 | 1294/49358 | 4UT |
| ☐ | N928TW | McDD MD-82 | 997/48012 | 4UU |
| ☐ | N929TW | McDD MD-82 | 1013/48014 | 4UV |
| ☐ | N939AS | McDD MD-83 | 1459/49657 | 4WH |
| ☐ | N940AS | McDD MD-83 | 1577/49825 | 4UJ |
| ☐ | N941AS | McDD MD-83 | 1616/49925 | 4UK |
| ☐ | N948TW | McDD MD-83 | 1414/49575 | 4WS |
| ☐ | N950U | McDD MD-82 | 1141/49230 | 4TW |
| ☐ | N951TW | McDD MD-83 | 2135/53470 | 4XA |
| ☐ | N951U | McDD MD-82 | 1145/49245 | 4TX |
| ☐ | N952U | McDD MD-82 | 1238/49266 | 4TY |
| ☐ | N953U | McDD MD-82 | 1239/49267 | 4UA |
| ☐ | N954U | McDD MD-82 | 1399/49426 | 4UB |
| ☐ | N955U | McDD MD-82 | 1401/49427 | 4UC |
| ☐ | N956U | McDD MD-82 | 1478/49701 | 4UD |
| ☐ | N957U | McDD MD-82 | 1479/49702 | 4UE |
| ☐ | N958U | McDD MD-82 | 1489/49703 | 4UF |
| ☐ | N959U | McDD MD-82 | 1490/49704 | 4UG |
| ☐ | N960TW | McDD MD-82 | 1177/49231 | 4UH |
| ☐ | N961TW | McDD MD-83 | 2264/53611 | 4XT |
| ☐ | N962TW | McDD MD-83 | 2265/53612 | 4XU |
| ☐ | N963TW | McDD MD-83 | 2266/53613 | 4XV |
| ☐ | N964TW | McDD MD-83 | 2267/53614 | 4XW |
| ☐ | N965TW | McDD MD-83 | 2268/53615 | 4XX |
| ☐ | N966TW | McDD MD-83 | 2269/53616 | 4XY |
| ☐ | N967TW | McDD MD-83 | 2270/53617 | 4YA |
| ☐ | N968TW | McDD MD-83 | 2271/53618 | 4YB |
| ☐ | N969TW | McDD MD-83 | 2272/53619 | 4YC; std |
| ☐ | N970TW | McDD MD-83 | 2273/53620 | 4YD; std |
| ☐ | N971TW | McDD MD-83 | 2274/53621 | 4YE; std |
| ☐ | N972TW | McDD MD-83 | 2275/53622 | 4YF |
| ☐ | N973TW | McDD MD-83 | 2276/53623 | 4YG |
| ☐ | N974TW | McDD MD-83 | 2277/53624 | 4YH |
| ☐ | N975TW | McDD MD-83 | 2278/53625 | 4YJ |
| ☐ | N976TW | McDD MD-83 | 2279/53626 | 4YK |
| ☐ | N978TW | McDD MD-83 | 2281/53628 | 4YM |
| ☐ | N979TW | McDD MD-83 | 2282/53629 | 4YN |
| ☐ | N980TW | McDD MD-83 | 2283/53630 | 4YP |
| ☐ | N982TW | McDD MD-83 | 2285/53632 | 4YR |
| ☐ | N983TW | McDD MD-83 | 2286/53633 | 4YS |
| ☐ | N984TW | McDD MD-83 | 2287/53634 | 4YT |
| ☐ | N9302B | McDD MD-83 | 1383/49528 | 4WB |
| ☐ | N3507A | McDD MD-82 | 1661/49801 | 507 |
| ☐ | N3515 | McDD MD-82 | 1695/49892 | 515 |
| ☐ | N7506 | McDD MD-82 | 1660/49800 | 506 |
| ☐ | N7508 | McDD MD-82 | 1662/49802 | 508 |
| ☐ | N7509 | McDD MD-82 | 1663/49803 | 509 |
| ☐ | N7512A | McDD MD-82 | 1673/49806 | 512 |
| ☐ | N7514A | McDD MD-82 | 1694/49891 | 514 |
| ☐ | N7517A | McDD MD-82 | 1697/49894 | 517 |
| ☐ | N7518A | McDD MD-82 | 1698/49895 | 518 |
| ☐ | N7519A | McDD MD-82 | 1707/49896 | 519 |
| ☐ | N7520A | McDD MD-82 | 1708/49897 | 520 |
| ☐ | N7521A | McDD MD-82 | 1709/49898 | 521 |
| ☐ | N7522A | McDD MD-82 | 1722/49899 | 522 |
| ☐ | N7525A | McDD MD-82 | 1735/49917 | 525 |
| ☐ | N7526A | McDD MD-82 | 1743/49918 | 526 |
| ☐ | N7527A | McDD MD-82 | 1744/49919 | 527 |
| ☐ | N7528A | McDD MD-82 | 1750/49920 | 528 |
| ☐ | N7530 | McDD MD-82 | 1753/49922 | 530 |
| ☐ | N7531A | McDD MD-82 | 1758/49923 | 531 |
| ☐ | N7532A | McDD MD-82 | 1759/49924 | 532 |
| ☐ | N7533A | McDD MD-82 | 1760/49987 | 533 |
| ☐ | N7534A | McDD MD-82 | 1768/49988 | 534 |
| ☐ | N7535A | McDD MD-82 | 1769/49989 | 535 |
| ☐ | N7536A | McDD MD-82 | 1770/49990 | 536 |
| ☐ | N7537A | McDD MD-82 | 1780/49991 | 537 |
| ☐ | N7538A | McDD MD-82 | 1781/49992 | 538 |
| ☐ | N7539A | McDD MD-82 | 1782/49993 | 539 |
| ☐ | N7540A | McDD MD-82 | 1790/49994 | 540 |
| ☐ | N7541A | McDD MD-82 | 1791/49995 | 541 |
| ☐ | N7542A | McDD MD-82 | 1792/49996 | 542 |
| ☐ | N7543A | McDD MD-82 | 1802/53025 | 543 |
| ☐ | N7544A | McDD MD-82 | 1804/53026 | 544 |
| ☐ | N7546A | McDD MD-82 | 1813/53028 | 546 |
| ☐ | N7547A | McDD MD-82 | 1814/53029 | 547 |
| ☐ | N7548A | McDD MD-82 | 1816/53030 | 548 |
| ☐ | N7549A | McDD MD-82 | 1819/53031 | 549 |
| ☐ | N7550 | McDD MD-82 | 1820/53032 | 550 |
| ☐ | N9304C | McDD MD-83 | 1397/49530 | 4WD |
| ☐ | N9305N | McDD MD-83 | 1286/49355 | 4WE |
| ☐ | N9306T | McDD MD-83 | 1367/49567 | 4WF |
| ☐ | N9307R | McDD MD-83 | 1437/49663 | 4WG |
| ☐ | N9401W | McDD MD-83 | 1872/53137 | 4WJ |
| ☐ | N9402W | McDD MD-83 | 1886/53138 | 4WK |
| ☐ | N9403W | McDD MD-83 | 1899/53139 | 4WL |
| ☐ | N9404V | McDD MD-83 | 1923/53140 | 4WM |
| ☐ | N9405T | McDD MD-83 | 1935/53141 | 4WN |
| ☐ | N9406W | McDD MD-83 | 2026/53126 | 4WP |
| ☐ | N9407R | McDD MD-83 | 1356/49400 | 4WR |
| ☐ | N9409F | McDD MD-83 | 1971/53121 | 4WS |
| ☐ | N9412W | McDD MD-83 | 2118/53187 | 4WU |
| ☐ | N9413T | McDD MD-83 | 2119/53188 | 4WV |
| ☐ | N9414W | McDD MD-83 | 2121/53189 | 4WX |
| ☐ | N9420D | McDD MD-83 | 1554/49824 | 4WY |
| ☐ | N9615W | McDD MD-83 | 2192/53562 | 4XB |
| ☐ | N9616G | McDD MD-83 | 219/653563 | 4XC |
| ☐ | N9617R | McDD MD-83 | 2199/53564 | 4XD |
| ☐ | N9618A | McDD MD-83 | 2201/53565 | 4XE |
| ☐ | N9619V | McDD MD-83 | 2206/53566 | 4XF |
| ☐ | N9620D | McDD MD-83 | 2208/53591 | 4XG |
| ☐ | N9621A | McDD MD-83 | 2234/53592 | 4XH; std |
| ☐ | N9622A | McDD MD-83 | 2239/53593 | 4XJ; std |
| ☐ | N9624T | McDD MD-83 | 2241/53594 | 4XK |
| ☐ | N9625W | McDD MD-83 | 2244/53595 | 4XL |
| ☐ | N9626F | McDD MD-83 | 2247/53596 | 4XM |
| ☐ | N9627R | McDD MD-83 | 2249/53597 | 4XN |
| ☐ | N9628W | McDD MD-83 | 2252/53598 | 4XP |
| ☐ | N9629H | McDD MD-83 | 2254/53599 | 4XR |
| ☐ | N9630A | McDD MD-83 | 2174/53561 | 4XS |
| ☐ | N9677W | McDD MD-83 | 2280/53627 | 4YL |
| ☐ | N9681B | McDD MD-83 | 2284/53631 | 4XT |
| ☐ | N14551 | McDD MD-82 | 1822/53033 | 551 |
| ☐ | N16545 | McDD MD-82 | 1805/53027 | 545 |
| ☐ | N33414 | McDD MD-82 | 1290/49325 | 414 |
| ☐ | N33502 | McDD MD-82 | 1649/49739 | 502 |
| ☐ | N44503 | McDD MD-82 | 1650/49797 | 503 |
| ☐ | N59523 | McDD MD-82 | 1723/49915 | 523 |
| ☐ | N70401 | McDD MD-82 | 1249/49312 | 401 |
| ☐ | N70404 | McDD MD-82 | 1257/49315 | 404 |
| ☐ | N70425 | McDD MD-82 | 1325/49337 | 425 |
| ☐ | N70504 | McDD MD-82 | 1651/49798 | 504 |
| ☐ | N70524 | McDD MD-82 | 1729/49916 | 524 |
| ☐ | N70529 | McDD MD-82 | 1752/49921 | 529 |
| ☐ | N73444 | McDD MD-82 | 1417/49470 | 444 |
| ☐ | N76200 | McDD MD-83 | 2013/53290 | 200 |
| ☐ | N76201 | McDD MD-83 | 2019/53291 | 201 |
| ☐ | N76202 | McDD MD-83 | 2020/53292 | 202 |
| ☐ | N77421 | McDD MD-82 | 1311/49333 | 421 |
| ☐ | N90511 | McDD MD-82 | 1672/49805 | 511 |

| | AMERICAN CONNECTION | | | RBD |
|---|---|---|---|---|
| ☐ | N4AE | ATR 72-212 | 244 | |
| ☐ | N47AE | ATR 42-300 | 047 | std |
| ☐ | N135MQ | ATR 42-310 | 135 | |
| ☐ | N141AE | ATR 42-300 | 141 | |
| ☐ | N213AT | ATR 42-300 | 211 | std |
| ☐ | N216AT | ATR 42-300 | 216 | |
| ☐ | N233RM | ATR 42-310 | 235 | std |
| ☐ | N242AT | ATR 42-300 | 242 | |
| ☐ | N246AE | ATR 42-320 | 243 | |
| ☐ | N248AT | ATR 72-212 | 248 | |
| ☐ | N249AT | ATR 42-320 | 249 | std |
| ☐ | N251AE | ATR 42-320 | 250 | |
| ☐ | N252AM | ATR 72-212 | 253 | |
| ☐ | N255AE | ATR 42-300 | 254 | |
| ☐ | N260AE | ATR 72-201 | 263 | |
| ☐ | N262AT | ATR 42-300 | 262 | |
| ☐ | N265AE | ATR 42-320 | 266 | |
| ☐ | N269AT | ATR 42-320 | 269 | |
| ☐ | N270AT | ATR 72-212 | 270 | |
| ☐ | N271AT | ATR 42-320 | 273 | |
| ☐ | N274AT | ATR 72-212 | 274 | std |
| ☐ | N275BC | ATR 42-300 | 275 | |

| | | | |
|---|---|---|---|
| ☐ N277AT | ATR 42-300 | 277 | |
| ☐ N282AT | ATR 42-320 | 282 | std |
| ☐ N288AM | ATR 72-212 | 288 | |
| ☐ N293AT | ATR 42-300 | 293 | std |
| ☐ N308AE | ATR 72-212 | 309 | |
| ☐ N310DK | ATR 42-300 | 310 | |
| ☐ N314AM | ATR 42-300 | 314 | |
| ☐ N319AM | ATR 42-300 | 319 | |
| ☐ N322AC | ATR 72-212 | 320 | std |
| ☐ N325AT | ATR 42-320 | 325 | |
| ☐ N327AT | ATR 42-320 | 327 | |
| ☐ N342AT | ATR 72-212 | 345 | |
| ☐ N348AE | ATR 72-212 | 349 | |
| ☐ N351AT | ATR 42-320 | 354 | |
| ☐ N355AT | ATR 72-212 | 355 | |
| ☐ N369AT | ATR 72-212 | 369 | |
| ☐ N377AT | ATR 72-212 | 377 | |
| ☐ N399AT | ATR 72-212 | 399 | |
| ☐ N407AT | ATR 72-212 | 407 | |
| ☐ N408AT | ATR 72-212 | 408 | |
| ☐ N410AT | ATR 72-212 | 410 | |
| ☐ N414WF | ATR 72-212 | 414 | |
| ☐ N417AT | ATR 72-212 | 417 | |
| ☐ N420AT | ATR 72-212 | 420 | |
| ☐ N421TE | ATR 42-300 | 102 | |
| ☐ N422TE | ATR 42-300 | 106 | |
| ☐ N423TE | ATR 42-300 | 119 | |
| ☐ N424TE | ATR 42-300 | 124 | |
| ☐ N425MJ | ATR 72-212 | 425 | |
| ☐ N426AT | ATR 72-212 | 426 | |
| ☐ N426TE | ATR 42-300 | 228 | |
| ☐ N429AT | ATR 72-212 | 429 | |
| ☐ N431AT | ATR 72-212 | 431 | |
| ☐ N434AT | ATR 72-212 | 434 | |
| ☐ N438AT | ATR 72-212 | 438 | |
| ☐ N440AM | ATR 72-212 | 440 | |
| ☐ N447AM | ATR 72-212 | 447 | |
| ☐ N448AM | ATR 72-212 | 448 | |
| ☐ N451AT | ATR 72-212 | 451 | |
| ☐ N494AE | ATR 72-212A | 494 | |
| ☐ N498AT | ATR 72-212A | 498 | |
| ☐ N499AT | ATR 72-212A | 499 | |
| ☐ N529AM | ATR 72-212A | 529 | |
| ☐ N533AT | ATR 72-212A | 533 | |
| ☐ N536AT | ATR 72-212A | 536 | |
| ☐ N538AT | ATR 72-212A | 538 | |
| ☐ N540AM | ATR 72-212A | 540 | |
| ☐ N541AT | ATR 72-212A | 541 | |
| ☐ N545AT | ATR 72-212A | 545 | |
| ☐ N548AT | ATR 72-212A | 548 | |
| ☐ N550LL | ATR 72-212A | 550 | |
| ☐ N721TE | ATR 72-202 | 217 | |
| ☐ N722TE | ATR 72-202 | 220 | |
| ☐ N723TE | ATR 72-202 | 283 | |
| ☐ N557HK | BAe Jetstream 41 | 41074 | |
| ☐ N558HK | BAe Jetstream 41 | 41071 | |
| ☐ N560HK | BAe Jetstream 41 | 41076 | |
| ☐ N561HK | BAe Jetstream 41 | 41077 | |
| ☐ N562HK | BAe Jetstream 41 | 41078 | |
| ☐ N563HK | BAe Jetstream 41 | 41079 | |
| ☐ N564HK | BAe Jetstream 41 | 41081 | |
| ☐ N565HK | BAe Jetstream 41 | 41082 | |
| ☐ N566HK | BAe Jetstream 41 | 41084 | |
| ☐ N567HK | BAe Jetstream 41 | 41085 | |
| ☐ N568HK | BAe Jetstream 41 | 41086 | |
| ☐ N569HK | BAe Jetstream 41 | 41088 | |
| ☐ N570HK | BAe Jetstream 41 | 41089 | |
| ☐ N571HK | BAe Jetstream 41 | 41090 | |
| ☐ N572HK | BAe Jetstream 41 | 41091 | |
| ☐ N573HK | BAe Jetstream 41 | 41092 | |
| ☐ N574HK | BAe Jetstream 41 | 41093 | |
| ☐ N551HK | BAe Jetstream 41 | 41040 | |
| ☐ N552HK | BAe Jetstream 41 | 41057 | |
| ☐ M553HK | BAe Jetstream 41 | 41066 | |
| ☐ N555HK | BAe Jetstream 41 | 41072 | |
| ☐ N556HK | BAe Jetstream 41 | 41073 | |
| ☐ N559HK | BAe Jetstream 41 | 41075 | |

| | | |
|---|---|---|
| ☐ N560HK | BAe Jetstream 41 | 41076 |
| ☐ N561HK | BAe Jetstream 41 | 41077 |
| ☐ N565HK | BAe Jetstream 41 | 41082 |
| ☐ N566HK | BAe Jetstream 41 | 41084 |
| ☐ N567HK | BAe Jetstream 41 | 41085 |
| ☐ N568HK | BAe Jetstream 41 | 41086 |
| ☐ N569HK | BAe Jetstream 41 | 41088 |
| ☐ N570HK | BAe Jetstream 41 | 41089 |
| ☐ N571HK | BAe Jetstream 41 | 41090 |
| ☐ N573HK | BAe Jetstream 41 | 41092 |
| ☐ N574HK | BAe Jetstream 41 | 41093 |
| ☐ N295SK | Embraer ERJ-140 | 145513 |
| ☐ N297SK | Embraer ERJ-140 | 145522 |
| ☐ N299SK | Embraer ERJ-140 | 145532 |
| ☐ N371SK | Embraer ERJ-140 | 145535 |
| ☐ N372SK | Embraer ERJ-140 | 145538 |
| ☐ N373SK | Embraer ERJ-140 | 145543 |
| ☐ N374SK | Embraer ERJ-140 | 145544 |
| ☐ N375SK | Embraer ERJ-140 | 145569 |
| ☐ N376SK | Embraer ERJ-140 | 145578 |
| ☐ N377SK | Embraer ERJ-140 | 145579 |
| ☐ N378SK | Embraer ERJ-140 | 145593 |
| ☐ N379SK | Embraer ERJ-140 | 145606 |
| ☐ N380SK | Embraer ERJ-140 | 145613 |
| ☐ N381SK | Embraer ERJ-140 | 145619 |
| ☐ N382SK | Embraer ERJ-140 | 145624 |
| ☐ N270SK | Embraer ERJ-145 | 145304 |
| ☐ N271SK | Embraer ERJ-145 | 145305 |
| ☐ N272SK | Embraer ERJ-145 | 145306 |
| ☐ N274SK | Embraer ERJ-145 | 145344 |
| ☐ N276SK | Embraer ERJ-145 | 145348 |
| ☐ N277SK | Embraer ERJ-145 | 145355 |
| ☐ N278SK | Embraer ERJ-145 | 145370 |
| ☐ N279SK | Embraer ERJ-145 | 145379 |
| ☐ N296SK | Embraer ERJ-145 | 145497 |
| ☐ N801HK | Embraer ERJ-145 | 145053 |
| ☐ N802HK | Embraer ERJ-145 | 145066 |
| ☐ N803HK | Embraer ERJ-145 | 145077 |
| ☐ N804HK | Embraer ERJ-145 | 145082 |
| ☐ N805HK | Embraer ERJ-145 | 145096 |
| ☐ N806HK | Embraer ERJ-145 | 145112 |
| ☐ N807HK | Embraer ERJ-145 | 145119 |
| ☐ N808HK | Embraer ERJ-145 | 145157 |
| ☐ N809HK | Embraer ERJ-145 | 145187 |
| ☐ N810HK | Embraer ERJ-145 | 145231 |
| ☐ N811HK | Embraer ERJ-145 | 145256 |
| ☐ N812HK | Embraer ERJ-145 | 145373 |
| ☐ N813HK | Embraer ERJ-145 | 145044 Lsf EGF |
| ☐ N814HK | Embraer ERJ-145 | 145046 Lsf EGF |
| ☐ N815HK | Embraer ERJ-145 | 145048 Lsf EGF |
| ☐ N816HK | Embraer ERJ-145 | 145055 Lsf EGF |
| ☐ N817HK | Embraer ERJ-145 | 145058 Lsf EGF |
| ☐ N818HK | Embraer ERJ-145 | 145059 Lsf EGF |

| AMERICAN EAGLE | | | EGF |
|---|---|---|---|
| ☐ N500AE | Canadair RJ-700 | 10025 | |
| ☐ N501BG | Canadair RJ-700 | 10017 | |
| ☐ N502AE | Canadair RJ-700 | 10018 | |
| ☐ N503AE | Canadair RJ-700 | 10021 | |
| ☐ N504AE | Canadair RJ-700 | 10044 | |
| ☐ N505AE | Canadair RJ-700 | 10053 | |
| ☐ N506AE | Canadair RJ-700 | 10056 | |
| ☐ N507AE | Canadair RJ-700 | 10059 | |
| ☐ N508AE | Canadair RJ-700 | | o/o |
| ☐ N509AE | Canadair RJ-700 | | o/o |
| ☐ N510AE | Canadair RJ-700 | | o/o |
| ☐ N511AE | Canadair RJ-700 | | o/o |
| ☐ N512AE | Canadair RJ-700 | | o/o |
| ☐ N513AE | Canadair RJ-700 | | o/o |
| ☐ N514AE | Canadair RJ-700 | | o/o |
| ☐ N515AE | Canadair RJ-700 | | o/o |
| ☐ N516AE | Canadair RJ-700 | | o/o |
| ☐ N517AE | Canadair RJ-700 | | o/o |
| ☐ N518AE | Canadair RJ-700 | | o/o |

| Reg | Type | c/n | |
|---|---|---|---|
| ☐ N519AE | Canadair RJ-700 | | o/o |
| ☐ N520AE | Canadair RJ-700 | | o/o |
| ☐ N521AE | Canadair RJ-700 | | o/o |
| ☐ N700LE | Embraer ERJ-135 | 145156 | |
| ☐ N701MH | Embraer ERJ-135 | 145162 | |
| ☐ N702AE | Embraer ERJ-135 | 145164 | |
| ☐ N703MR | Embraer ERJ-135 | 145173 | |
| ☐ N704PG | Embraer ERJ-135 | 145174 | |
| ☐ N705AE | Embraer ERJ-135 | 145184 | |
| ☐ N706RG | Embraer ERJ-135 | 145194 | |
| ☐ N707EB | Embraer ERJ-135 | 145195 | |
| ☐ N708AE | Embraer ERJ-135 | 145205 | |
| ☐ N709GB | Embraer ERJ-135 | 145211 | |
| ☐ N710TB | Embraer ERJ-135 | 145224 | |
| ☐ N711PH | Embraer ERJ-135 | 145235 | |
| ☐ N712AE | Embraer ERJ-135 | 145247 | |
| ☐ N713AE | Embraer ERJ-135 | 145249 | |
| ☐ N714BZ | Embraer ERJ-135 | 145260 | |
| ☐ N715AE | Embraer ERJ-135 | 145262 | |
| ☐ N716AE | Embraer ERJ-135 | 145264 | |
| ☐ N717AE | Embraer ERJ-135 | 145272 | |
| ☐ N718AE | Embraer ERJ-135 | 145275 | |
| ☐ N719AE | Embraer ERJ-135 | 145276 | |
| ☐ N720AE | Embraer ERJ-135 | 145279 | |
| ☐ N721HS | Embraer ERJ-135 | 145283 | |
| ☐ N722AE | Embraer ERJ-135 | 145287 | |
| ☐ N723AE | Embraer ERJ-135 | 145288 | |
| ☐ N724AE | Embraer ERJ-135 | 145301 | |
| ☐ N725AE | Embraer ERJ-135 | 145312 | |
| ☐ N726AE | Embraer ERJ-135 | 145314 | |
| ☐ N727AE | Embraer ERJ-135 | 145326 | |
| ☐ N728AE | Embraer ERJ-135 | 145328 | |
| ☐ N729AE | Embraer ERJ-135 | 145343 | |
| ☐ N730KW | Embraer ERJ-135 | 145346 | |
| ☐ N731BE | Embraer ERJ-135 | 145 | o/o |
| ☐ N732DH | Embraer ERJ-135 | 145 | o/o |
| ☐ N733KR | Embraer ERJ-135 | 145368 | |
| ☐ N734EK | Embraer ERJ-135 | 145371 | |
| ☐ N735TS | Embraer ERJ-135 | 145386 | |
| ☐ N736DT | Embraer ERJ-135 | 145388 | |
| ☐ N737MW | Embraer ERJ-135 | 145396 | |
| ☐ N738NR | Embraer ERJ-135 | 145401 | |
| ☐ N739AE | Embraer ERJ-135 | 145402 | |
| ☐ N800AE | Embraer ERJ-140 | 145425 | |
| ☐ N801AE | Embraer ERJ-140 | 145469 | |
| ☐ N802AE | Embraer ERJ-140 | 145471 | |
| ☐ N803AE | Embraer ERJ-140 | 145483 | |
| ☐ N804AE | Embraer ERJ-140 | 145487 | |
| ☐ N805AE | Embraer ERJ-140 | 145489 | |
| ☐ N806AE | Embraer ERJ-140 | 145503 | |
| ☐ N807AE | Embraer ERJ-140 | 145506 | |
| ☐ N808AE | Embraer ERJ-140 | 145519 | |
| ☐ N809AE | Embraer ERJ-140 | 145521 | |
| ☐ N810AE | Embraer ERJ-140 | 145525 | |
| ☐ N811AE | Embraer ERJ-140 | 145529 | |
| ☐ N812AE | Embraer ERJ-140 | 145531 | |
| ☐ N813AE | Embraer ERJ-140 | 145539 | |
| ☐ N814AE | Embraer ERJ-140 | 145541 | |
| ☐ N815AE | Embraer ERJ-140 | 145545 | |
| ☐ N816AE | Embraer ERJ-140 | 145552 | |
| ☐ N817AE | Embraer ERJ-140 | 145554 | |
| ☐ N818AE | Embraer ERJ-140 | 145561 | |
| ☐ N819AE | Embraer ERJ-140 | 145569 | |
| ☐ N820AE | Embraer ERJ-140 | 145576 | |
| ☐ N821AE | Embraer ERJ-140 | 145577 | |
| ☐ N822AE | Embraer ERJ-140 | 145581 | |
| ☐ N823AE | Embraer ERJ-140 | 145582 | |
| ☐ N824AE | Embraer ERJ-140 | 145584 | |
| ☐ N825AE | Embraer ERJ-140 | 145589 | |
| ☐ N826AE | Embraer ERJ-140 | 145592 | |
| ☐ N827AE | Embraer ERJ-140 | 145602 | |
| ☐ N828AE | Embraer ERJ-140 | 145604 | |
| ☐ N829AE | Embraer ERJ-140 | 145609 | |
| ☐ N830AE | Embraer ERJ-140 | 145615 | |
| ☐ N831AE | Embraer ERJ-140 | 145616 | |
| ☐ N832AE | Embraer ERJ-140 | 145627 | |
| ☐ N833AE | Embraer ERJ-140 | 145629 | |
| ☐ N834AE | Embraer ERJ-140 | 145631 | |
| ☐ N835AE | Embraer ERJ-140 | 145634 | |
| ☐ N836AE | Embraer ERJ-140 | 145635 | |
| ☐ N837AE | Embraer ERJ-140 | 145647 | |
| ☐ N838AE | Embraer ERJ-140 | 145651 | |
| ☐ N839AE | Embraer ERJ-140 | 145653 | |
| ☐ N840AE | Embraer ERJ-140 | 145656 | |
| ☐ N841AE | Embraer ERJ-140 | 145667 | |
| ☐ N842AE | Embraer ERJ-140 | 145673 | |
| ☐ N843AE | Embraer ERJ-140 | 145680 | |
| ☐ N844AE | Embraer ERJ-140 | 145682 | |
| ☐ N845AE | Embraer ERJ-140 | | o/o |
| ☐ N846AE | Embraer ERJ-140 | | o/o |
| ☐ N847AE | Embraer ERJ-140 | | o/o |
| ☐ N848AE | Embraer ERJ-140 | | o/o |
| ☐ N849AE | Embraer ERJ-140 | | o/o |
| ☐ N850AE | Embraer ERJ-140 | | o/o |
| ☐ N851AE | Embraer ERJ-140 | | o/o |
| ☐ N852AE | Embraer ERJ-140 | | o/o |
| ☐ N853AE | Embraer ERJ-140 | | o/o |
| ☐ N854AE | Embraer ERJ-140 | | o/o |
| ☐ N855AE | Embraer ERJ-140 | | o/o |
| ☐ N856AE | Embraer ERJ-140 | | o/o |
| ☐ N857AE | Embraer ERJ-140 | | o/o |
| ☐ N858AE | Embraer ERJ-140 | | o/o |
| ☐ N859AE | Embraer ERJ-140 | | o/o |
| ☐ N960AE | Embraer ERJ-140 | | o/o |
| ☐ N861AE | Embraer ERJ-140 | | o/o |
| ☐ N862AE | Embraer ERJ-140 | | o/o |
| ☐ N863AE | Embraer ERJ-140 | | o/o |
| ☐ N864AE | Embraer ERJ-140 | | o/o |
| ☐ N865AE | Embraer ERJ-140 | | o/o |
| ☐ N600BK | Embraer ERJ-145 | 145044 | |
| ☐ N601GH | Embraer ERJ-145 | 145046 | |
| ☐ N602AE | Embraer ERJ-145 | 145048 | |
| ☐ N603AE | Embraer ERJ-145 | 145055 | |
| ☐ N604DG | Embraer ERJ-145 | 145058 | |
| ☐ N605RR | Embraer ERJ-145 | 145059 | |
| ☐ N606AE | Embraer ERJ-145 | 145062 | |
| ☐ N607AE | Embraer ERJ-145 | 145064 | |
| ☐ N608AE | Embraer ERJ-145 | 145068 | |
| ☐ N609AE | Embraer ERJ-145 | 145069 | |
| ☐ N610AE | Embraer ERJ-145 | 145073 | |
| ☐ N611AE | Embraer ERJ-145 | 145074 | |
| ☐ N612AE | Embraer ERJ-145 | 145079 | |
| ☐ N613AE | Embraer ERJ-145 | 145081 | |
| ☐ N614AE | Embraer ERJ-145 | 145086 | |
| ☐ N615AE | Embraer ERJ-145 | 145087 | |
| ☐ N616AE | Embraer ERJ-145 | 145092 | |
| ☐ N617AE | Embraer ERJ-145 | 145093 | |
| ☐ N618AE | Embraer ERJ-145 | 145097 | |
| ☐ N619AE | Embraer ERJ-145 | 145101 | |
| ☐ N620AE | Embraer ERJ-145 | 145102 | |
| ☐ N621AE | Embraer ERJ-145 | 145105 | |
| ☐ N622AE | Embraer ERJ-145 | 145108 | |
| ☐ N623AE | Embraer ERJ-145 | 145109 | |
| ☐ N624AE | Embraer ERJ-145 | 145111 | |
| ☐ N625AE | Embraer ERJ-145 | 145115 | |
| ☐ N626AE | Embraer ERJ-145 | 145117 | |
| ☐ N627AE | Embraer ERJ-145 | 145121 | |
| ☐ N628AE | Embraer ERJ-145 | 145124 | |
| ☐ N629AE | Embraer ERJ-145 | 145130 | |
| ☐ N630AE | Embraer ERJ-145 | 145132 | |
| ☐ N631AE | Embraer ERJ-145 | 145139 | |
| ☐ N632AE | Embraer ERJ-145 | 145143 | |
| ☐ N633AE | Embraer ERJ-145 | 145148 | |
| ☐ N634AE | Embraer ERJ-145 | 145150 | |
| ☐ N635AE | Embraer ERJ-145 | 145158 | |
| ☐ N636AE | Embraer ERJ-145 | 145160 | |
| ☐ N637AE | Embraer ERJ-145 | 145170 | |
| ☐ N638AE | Embraer ERJ-145 | 145172 | |
| ☐ N639AE | Embraer ERJ-145 | 145182 | |
| ☐ N640AE | Embraer ERJ-145 | 145183 | |
| ☐ N641AE | Embraer ERJ-145 | 145191 | |
| ☐ N642AE | Embraer ERJ-145 | 145193 | |
| ☐ N643AE | Embraer ERJ-145 | 145200 | |

| | | | |
|---|---|---|---|
| ☐ N644AE | Embraer ERJ-145 | 145204 | |
| ☐ N645AE | Embraer ERJ-145 | 145212 | |
| ☐ N646AE | Embraer ERJ-145 | 145213 | |
| ☐ N647AE | Embraer ERJ-145 | 145222 | |
| ☐ N648AE | Embraer ERJ-145 | 145225 | |
| ☐ N649PP | Embraer ERJ-145 | 145234 | |
| ☐ N650AE | Embraer ERJ-145 | 145417 | |
| ☐ N651AE | Embraer ERJ-145 | 145422 | |
| ☐ N652RS | Embraer ERJ-145 | 145432 | |
| ☐ N653AE | Embraer ERJ-145 | 145433 | |
| ☐ N654AE | Embraer ERJ-145 | 145437 | |
| ☐ N655AE | Embraer ERJ-145 | 145452 | |
| | | | |
| ☐ N211NE | SAAB SF.340B | 211 | |
| ☐ N218AE | SAAB SF.340B | 218 | std |
| ☐ N219AE | SAAB SF.340B | 219 | std |
| ☐ N222NE | SAAB SF.340B | 222 | |
| ☐ N227AE | SAAB SF.340B | 227 | |
| ☐ N231LN | SAAB SF.340B | 231 | std |
| ☐ N232AE | SAAB SF.340B | 232 | std |
| ☐ N234AE | SAAB SF.340B | 234 | |
| ☐ N235AE | SAAB SF.340B | 235 | |
| ☐ N236AE | SAAB SF.340B | 236 | std |
| ☐ N238AE | SAAB SF.340B | 238 | std |
| ☐ N240DS | SAAB SF.340B | 240 | std |
| ☐ N241AE | SAAB SF.340B | 241 | |
| ☐ N243AE | SAAB SF.340B | 243 | |
| ☐ N244AE | SAAB SF.340B | 244 | |
| ☐ N245AE | SAAB SF.340B | 245 | std |
| ☐ N247AE | SAAB SF.340B | 247 | |
| ☐ N250AE | SAAB SF.340B | 250 | std |
| ☐ N253AE | SAAB SF.340B | 253 | std |
| ☐ N254AE | SAAB SF.340B | 254 | |
| ☐ N256AE | SAAB SF.340B | 256 | |
| ☐ N259AE | SAAB SF.340B | 259 | std |
| ☐ N261AE | SAAB SF.340B | 261 | std |
| ☐ N263AE | SAAB SF.340B | 263 | |
| ☐ N264AE | SAAB SF.340B | 264 | |
| ☐ N266AE | SAAB SF.340B | 266 | |
| ☐ N268AE | SAAB SF.340B | 268 | |
| ☐ N272AE | SAAB SF.340B | 272 | |
| ☐ N273AE | SAAB SF.340B | 273 | |
| ☐ N278AE | SAAB SF.340B | 278 | |
| ☐ N280AE | SAAB SF.340B | 280 | |
| ☐ N283AE | SAAB SF.340B | 283 | std |
| ☐ N284AE | SAAB SF.340B | 284 | |
| ☐ N286AE | SAAB SF.340B | 286 | std |
| ☐ N297AE | SAAB SF.340B | 297 | std |
| ☐ N298AE | SAAB SF.340B | 298 | std |
| ☐ N301AE | SAAB SF.340B | 301 | std |
| ☐ N304AE | SAAB SF.340B | 304 | std |
| ☐ N305AE | SAAB SF.340B | 305 | |
| ☐ N306AE | SAAB SF.340B | 306 | std |
| ☐ N307AE | SAAB SF.340B | 307 | |
| ☐ N309AE | SAAB SF.340B | 309 | |
| ☐ N312AE | SAAB SF.340B | 312 | |
| ☐ N313AE | SAAB SF.340B | 313 | |
| ☐ N317AE | SAAB SF.340B | 317 | std |
| ☐ N320AE | SAAB SF.340B | 320 | |
| ☐ N323AE | SAAB SF.340B | 323 | std |
| ☐ N324AE | SAAB SF.340B | 324 | |
| ☐ N326AE | SAAB SF.340B | 326 | |
| ☐ N329AE | SAAB SF.340B | 329 | |
| ☐ N330AE | SAAB SF.340B | 330 | |
| ☐ N332AE | SAAB SF.340B | 332 | |
| ☐ N338SB | SAAB SF.340B | 338 | |
| ☐ N339SB | SAAB SF.340B | 339 | |
| ☐ N340RC | SAAB SF.340B | 340 | |
| ☐ N341SB | SAAB SF.340B | 341 | |
| ☐ N344SB | SAAB SF.340B | 344 | |
| ☐ N345SB | SAAB SF.340B | 345 | |
| ☐ N346SB | SAAB SF.340B | 346 | std |
| ☐ N347SB | SAAB SF.340B | 347 | |
| ☐ N349BE | SAAB SF.340B | 196 | |
| ☐ N349SB | SAAB SF.340B | 349 | std |
| ☐ N350CF | SAAB SF.340B | 350 | |
| ☐ N352SB | SAAB SF.340B | 352 | std |
| ☐ N354SB | SAAB SF.340B | 354 | |

| | | | |
|---|---|---|---|
| ☐ N356SB | SAAB SF.340B | 356 | |
| ☐ N358BE | SAAB SF.340B | 279 | std |
| ☐ N359BE | SAAB SF.340B | 285 | std |
| ☐ N359SB | SAAB SF.340B | 359 | |
| ☐ N361BE | SAAB SF.340B | 290 | |
| ☐ N362BE | SAAB SF.340B | 291 | |
| ☐ N363BE | SAAB SF.340B | 293 | std |
| ☐ N371AE | SAAB SF.340B | 371 | std |
| ☐ N373AE | SAAB SF.340B | 373 | |
| ☐ N375AE | SAAB SF.340B | 375 | std |
| ☐ N376AE | SAAB SF.340B | 376 | std |
| ☐ N380AE | SAAB SF.340B | 380 | std |
| ☐ N381AE | SAAB SF.340B | 381 | |
| ☐ N382AE | SAAB SF.340B | 382 | |
| ☐ N383AE | SAAB SF.340B | 383 | |
| ☐ N384AE | SAAB SF.340B | 384 | |
| ☐ N386AE | SAAB SF.340B | 386 | |
| ☐ N387AE | SAAB SF.340B | 387 | |
| ☐ N388AE | SAAB SF.340B | 388 | |
| ☐ N389AE | SAAB SF.340B | 389 | |
| ☐ N390AE | SAAB SF.340B | 390 | |
| ☐ N391AE | SAAB SF.340B | 391 | |
| ☐ N392AE | SAAB SF.340B | 392 | |
| ☐ N393AE | SAAB SF.340B | 393 | |
| ☐ N394AE | SAAB SF.340B | 394 | |
| ☐ N396AE | SAAB SF.340B | 396 | |
| ☐ N397AE | SAAB SF.340B | 397 | |
| ☐ N398AM | SAAB SF.340B | 398 | |
| ☐ N400BR | SAAB SF.340B | 400 | |
| ☐ N901AE | SAAB SF.340B | 401 | |
| ☐ N902AE | SAAB SF.340B | 269 | |
| ☐ N903AE | SAAB SF.340B | 282 | |
| ☐ N904AE | SAAB SF.340B | 314 | |
| ☐ N905AE | SAAB SF.340B | 319 | |

## AMERICAN TRANS AIR – ATA      AMT

| | | | |
|---|---|---|---|
| ☐ N301TZ | Boeing 737-83N | 847/28239 | |
| ☐ N302TZ | Boeing 737-83N | 875/32576 | |
| ☐ N303TZ | Boeing 737-83N | 888/28648 | |
| ☐ N304TZ | Boeing 737-83N | 898/30675 | |
| ☐ N305TZ | Boeing 737-83N | 929/30706 | |
| ☐ N306TZ | Boeing 737-83N | 933/32348 | |
| ☐ N307TZ | Boeing 737-83N | 948/28653 | |
| ☐ N308TZ | Boeing 737-83N | 958/28244 | |
| ☐ N309TZ | Boeing 737-83N | 973/32577 | |
| ☐ N310TZ | Boeing 737-83N | 984/28243 | |
| ☐ N311TZ | Boeing 737-83N | 998/32578 | |
| ☐ N312TZ | Boeing 737-83N | 1002/32579 | |
| ☐ N313TZ | Boeing 737-83N | 1024/32580 | |
| ☐ N314TZ | Boeing 737-83N | 1035/30640 | |
| ☐ N315TZ | Boeing 737-83N | 1054/28245 | |
| ☐ N316TZ | Boeing 737-83N | 1059/32609 | |
| ☐ N317TZ | Boeing 737-83N | 1081/28246 | |
| ☐ N318TZ | Boeing 737-83N | 1091/28247 | |
| ☐ N319TZ | Boeing 737-83N | 1106/30643 | |
| ☐ N320TZ | Boeing 737-83N | 1110/32610 | |
| ☐ N321TZ | Boeing 737-83N | 1123/28249 | |
| ☐ N322TZ | Boeing 737-83N | 1135/32611 | |
| ☐ N323TZ | Boeing 737-83N | 1149/30033 | |
| ☐ N324TZ | Boeing 737-83N | 1163/32882 | |
| ☐ N325TZ | Boeing 737-83N | 1181/32884 | |
| ☐ N326TZ | Boeing 737-83N | 1184/32612 | |
| ☐ N327TZ | Boeing 737-83N | 1197/32613 | |
| ☐ N328TZ | Boeing 737-83N | 1201/32614 | |
| ☐ N329TZ | Boeing 737-83N | 1207/32615 | |
| ☐ N330TZ | Boeing 737-83N | 1212/32616 | |
| ☐ N331TZ | Boeing 737-83N | 30660 | o/o |
| ☐ N332TZ | Boeing 737-83N | 32618 | o/o |
| ☐ N333TZ | Boeing 737-83N | 32619 | o/o |
| ☐ N334TZ | Boeing 737-83N | 32620 | o/o |
| ☐ N335TZ | Boeing 737-83N | 32621 | o/o |
| ☐ N337TZ | Boeing 737-83N | 32622 | o/o |
| ☐ N338TZ | Boeing 737-83N | 32623 | o/o |
| | | | |
| ☐ N513AT | Boeing 757-28A | 974/32449 | |
| ☐ N514AT | Boeing 757-23N | 690/27971 | |
| ☐ N515AT | Boeing 757-23N | 692/27598 | |

| | | | |
|---|---|---|---|
| ☐ N516AT | Boeing 757-23N | 694/27972 | |
| ☐ N517AT | Boeing 757-23N | 735/27973 | |
| ☐ N518AT | Boeing 757-23N | 737/27974 | |
| ☐ N519AT | Boeing 757-23N | 779/27975 | |
| ☐ N520AT | Boeing 757-23N | 814/27976 | |
| ☐ N521AT | Boeing 757-28AER | 213/24368 | |
| ☐ N522AT | Boeing 757-23N | 843/29330 | |
| ☐ N523AT | Boeing 757-23N | 888/30232 | |
| ☐ N524AT | Boeing 757-23N | 895/30233 | |
| ☐ N525AT | Boeing 757-23N | 930/30548 | |
| ☐ N526AT | Boeing 757-23N | 931/30735 | |
| ☐ N527AT | Boeing 757-23N | 945/30886 | |
| ☐ N528AT | Boeing 757-23N | 946/30887 | |
| ☐ N550TZ | Boeing 757-33N | 972/32584 | |
| ☐ N551TZ | Boeing 757-33N | 976/32585 | |
| ☐ N552TZ | Boeing 757-33N | 978/32586 | |
| ☐ N553TZ | Boeing 757-33N | 980/32587 | |
| ☐ N554TZ | Boeing 757-33N | 985/32588 | |
| ☐ N555TZ | Boeing 757-33N | 1003/32589 | |
| ☐ N556TZ | Boeing 757-33N | 1017/32590 | |
| ☐ N557TZ | Boeing 757-33N | 1007/32591 | |
| ☐ N558TZ | Boeing 757-33N | 1008/32592 | |
| ☐ N559TZ | Boeing 757-33N | 1018/32593 | |
| ☐ N560TZ | Boeing 757-33N | 33525 | o/o |
| ☐ N561TZ | Boeing 757-33N | 33526 | o/o |
| | | | |
| ☐ N160AT | L-1011-500 Tristar | 1217 | std |
| ☐ N161AT | L-1011-500 Tristar | 1219 | |
| ☐ N162AT | L-1011-500 Tristar | 1220 | |
| ☐ N163AT | L-1011-500 Tristar | 1229 | |
| ☐ N164AT | L-1011-500 Tristar | 1238 | |
| ☐ N186AT | L-1011-50 Tristar | 1074 | |
| ☐ N188AT | L-1011-50 Tristar | 1078 | |
| ☐ N189AT | L-1011-50 Tristar | 1081 | std |
| ☐ N191AT | L-1011-50 Tristar | 1084 | |
| ☐ N194AT | L-1011-100 Tristar | 1230 | |
| ☐ N195AT | L-1011-150 Tristar | 1041 | std |
| ☐ N196AT | L-1011-50 Tristar | 1076 | std |
| ☐ N197AT | L-1011-50 Tristar | 1082 | |
| ☐ N198AT | L-1011-500 Tristar | 1111 | |

## AMERICA WEST AIRLINES　　　　AWE

| | | | |
|---|---|---|---|
| ☐ N801AW | Airbus A319-132 | 0889 | |
| ☐ N802AW | Airbus A319-132 | 0924 | |
| ☐ N803AW | Airbus A319-132 | 0931 | |
| ☐ N804AW | Airbus A319-132 | 1043 | |
| ☐ N805AW | Airbus A319-132 | 1049 | |
| ☐ N806AW | Airbus A319-132 | 1056 | |
| ☐ N807AW | Airbus A319-132 | 1064 | |
| ☐ N808AW | Airbus A319-132 | 1088 | |
| ☐ N809AW | Airbus A319-132 | 1111 | |
| ☐ N810AW | Airbus A319-132 | 1116 | |
| ☐ N812AW | Airbus A319-132 | 1178 | |
| ☐ N813AW | Airbus A319-132 | 1223 | |
| ☐ N814AW | Airbus A319-132 | 1281 | |
| ☐ N815AW | Airbus A319-132 | 1323 | |
| ☐ N816AW | Airbus A319-132 | 1350 | |
| ☐ N817AW | Airbus A319-132 | 1373 | |
| ☐ N818AW | Airbus A319-132 | 1375 | |
| ☐ N819AW | Airbus A319-132 | 1395 | |
| ☐ N820AW | Airbus A319-132 | 1397 | |
| ☐ N821AW | Airbus A319-132 | 1406 | |
| ☐ N822AW | Airbus A319-132 | 1410 | |
| ☐ N823AW | Airbus A319-132 | 1463 | |
| ☐ N824AW | Airbus A319-132 | 1490 | |
| ☐ N825AW | Airbus A319-132 | 1527 | |
| ☐ N826AW | Airbus A319-132 | 1534 | |
| ☐ N827AW | Airbus A319-132 | 1547 | |
| ☐ N828AW | Airbus A319-132 | 1552 | |
| ☐ N829AW | Airbus A319-132 | 1563 | |
| ☐ N830AW | Airbus A319-132 | 1565 | |
| ☐ N831AW | Airbus A319-132 | 1576 | |
| ☐ N832AW | Airbus A319-132 | 1643 | |
| ☐ N833AW | Airbus A319-132 | 1844 | |
| ☐ N834AW | Airbus A319-132 | | o/o |
| ☐ N | Airbus A319-132 | | o/o |

| | | | |
|---|---|---|---|
| ☐ N604AW | Airbus A320-232 | 1196 | |
| ☐ N605AW | Airbus A320-232 | 0543 | |
| ☐ N619AW | Airbus A320-232 | 0527 | |
| ☐ N620AW | Airbus A320-231 | 0052 | |
| ☐ N621AW | Airbus A320-231 | 0053 | |
| ☐ N622AW | Airbus A320-231 | 0054 | |
| ☐ N624AW | Airbus A320-231 | 0055 | |
| ☐ N625AW | Airbus A320-231 | 0064 | |
| ☐ N626AW | Airbus A320-231 | 0065 | |
| ☐ N627AW | Airbus A320-231 | 0066 | |
| ☐ N628AW | Airbus A320-231 | 0067 | |
| ☐ N629AW | Airbus A320-231 | 0076 | |
| ☐ N631AW | Airbus A320-231 | 0077 | |
| ☐ N632AW | Airbus A320-231 | 0081 | |
| ☐ N633AW | Airbus A320-231 | 0082 | |
| ☐ N634AW | Airbus A320-231 | 0091 | |
| ☐ N635AW | Airbus A320-231 | 0092 | dbr? |
| ☐ N636AW | Airbus A320-231 | 0098 | |
| ☐ N637AW | Airbus A320-231 | 0099 | |
| ☐ N638AW | Airbus A320-232 | 0455 | |
| ☐ N639AW | Airbus A320-232 | 0471 | |
| ☐ N640AW | Airbus A320-232 | 0448 | |
| ☐ N642AW | Airbus A320-232 | 0584 | |
| ☐ N643AW | Airbus A320-231 | 0315 | |
| ☐ N644AW | Airbus A320-231 | 0317 | |
| ☐ N645AW | Airbus A320-231 | 0238 | |
| ☐ N646AW | Airbus A320-231 | 0271 | std |
| ☐ N647AW | Airbus A320-232 | 0762 | |
| ☐ N648AW | Airbus A320-232 | 0770 | |
| ☐ N649AW | Airbus A320-232 | 0803 | |
| ☐ N650AW | Airbus A320-232 | 0856 | |
| ☐ N651AW | Airbus A320-232 | 0866 | |
| ☐ N652AW | Airbus A320-232 | 0953 | |
| ☐ N653AW | Airbus A320-232 | 1003 | |
| ☐ N654AW | Airbus A320-232 | 1050 | |
| ☐ N655AW | Airbus A320-232 | 1075 | |
| ☐ N656AW | Airbus A320-232 | 1079 | |
| ☐ N657AW | Airbus A320-232 | 1083 | |
| ☐ N658AW | Airbus A320-232 | 1110 | |
| ☐ N659AW | Airbus A320-232 | 1166 | |
| ☐ N660AW | Airbus A320-232 | 1234 | |
| ☐ N661AW | Airbus A320-232 | 1284 | |
| ☐ N662AW | Airbus A320-232 | 1274 | |
| ☐ N663AW | Airbus A320-232 | 1419 | |
| ☐ N664AW | Airbus A320-232 | 1621 | |
| ☐ N665AW | Airbus A320-232 | 1644 | |
| ☐ N667AW | Airbus A320-232 | 1710 | |
| ☐ N668AW | Airbus A320-232 | 1764 | |
| ☐ N669AW | Airbus A320-232 | 1792 | |
| ☐ N669AW | Airbus A320-232 | | o/o |
| ☐ N670AW | Airbus A320-232 | | o/o |
| ☐ N672AW | Airbus A320-232 | | o/o |
| ☐ N673AW | Airbus A320-232 | | o/o |
| ☐ N674AW | Airbus A320-232 | | o/o |
| ☐ N675AW | Airbus A320-232 | | o/o |
| | | | |
| ☐ N138AW | Boeing 737-2E3 | 887/22792 | std |
| ☐ N149AW | Boeing 737-2U9 | 749/22575 | std |
| ☐ N150AW | Boeing 737-3G7 | 1076/23218 | |
| ☐ N151AW | Boeing 737-3G7 | 1090/23219 | |
| ☐ N154AW | Boeing 737-3G7 | 1417/23776 | |
| ☐ N155AW | Boeing 737-3G7 | 1419/23777 | |
| ☐ N156AW | Boeing 737-3G7 | 1455/23778 | |
| ☐ N157AW | Boeing 737-3G7 | 1457/23779 | |
| ☐ N158AW | Boeing 737-3G7 | 1459/23780 | |
| ☐ N160AW | Boeing 737-3G7 | 1496/23782 | |
| ☐ N164AW | Boeing 737-33A | 1283/23625 | |
| ☐ N166AW | Boeing 737-33A | 1302/23627 | |
| ☐ N168AW | Boeing 737-33A | 1311/23629 | |
| ☐ N173AW | Boeing 737-33A | 1344/23632 | |
| ☐ N174AW | Boeing 737-33A | 1421/23633 | |
| ☐ N175AW | Boeing 737-33A | 1423/23634 | |
| ☐ N178AW | Boeing 737-277 | 768/22645 | |
| ☐ N179AW | Boeing 737-277 | 778/22646 | |
| ☐ N180AW | Boeing 737-277 | 785/22647 | |
| ☐ N182AW | Boeing 737-277 | 801/22649 | |
| ☐ N183AW | Boeing 737-277 | 806/22650 | |
| ☐ N184AW | Boeing 737-277 | 819/22651 | |

| | | | |
|---|---|---|---|
| ☐ N185AW | Boeing 737-277 | 831/22652 | |
| ☐ N186AW | Boeing 737-277 | 832/22653 | |
| ☐ N187AW | Boeing 737-277 | 862/22654 | |
| ☐ N188AW | Boeing 737-277 | 872/22655 | |
| ☐ N189AW | Boeing 737-277 | 876/22656 | |
| ☐ N302AW | Boeing 737-3G7 | 1578/24009 | |
| ☐ N303AW | Boeing 737-3G7 | 1606/24010 | |
| ☐ N305AW | Boeing 737-3G7 | 1612/24012 | |
| ☐ N306AW | Boeing 737-3G7 | 1809/24633 | |
| ☐ N307AW | Boeing 737-3G7 | 1823/24634 | |
| ☐ N308AW | Boeing 737-3G7 | 1825/24710 | |
| ☐ N309AW | Boeing 737-3G7 | 1843/24711 | |
| ☐ N311AW | Boeing 737-3G7 | 1869/24712 | |
| ☐ N312AW | Boeing 737-3S3 | 1519/24060 | |
| ☐ N313AW | Boeing 737-3S3 | 1336/23712 | |
| ☐ N314AW | Boeing 737-3S3 | 1345/23733 | |
| ☐ N315AW | Boeing 737-3S3 | 1359/23734 | |
| ☐ N316AW | Boeing 737-3S3 | 1341/23713 | |
| ☐ N322AW | Boeing 737-3G7 | 2112/25400 | |
| ☐ N323AW | Boeing 737-3Y0 | 1353/23684 | |
| ☐ N324AW | Boeing 737-301 | 1157/23261 | |
| ☐ N325AW | Boeing 737-301 | 1146/23260 | |
| ☐ N326AW | Boeing 737-301 | 1126/23258 | |
| ☐ N327AW | Boeing 737-3Q8 | 1252/23507 | |
| ☐ N328AW | Boeing 737-3B7 | 1320/23377 | |
| ☐ N331AW | Boeing 737-3Y0 | 1363/23747 | |
| ☐ N332AW | Boeing 737-3B7 | 1427/23384 | |
| ☐ N334AW | Boeing 737-3Y0 | 1381/23748 | |
| ☐ N335AW | Boeing 737-3U3 | 3003/28740 | |
| ☐ N336AW | Boeing 737-375 | 1388/23707 | |
| | | | |
| ☐ N901AW | Boeing 757-2S7 | 76/23321 | |
| ☐ N902AW | Boeing 757-2S7 | 79/23322 | |
| ☐ N903AW | Boeing 757-2S7 | 80/23323 | |
| ☐ N904AW | Boeing 757-2S7 | 96/23566 | |
| ☐ N905AW | Boeing 757-2S7 | 97/23567 | |
| ☐ N906AW | Boeing 757-2S7 | 99/23568 | |
| ☐ N907AW | Boeing 757-225 | 155/22691 | |
| ☐ N908AW | Boeing 757-2G7 | 244/24233 | |
| ☐ N909AW | Boeing 757-2G7 | 252/24522 | |
| ☐ N910AW | Boeing 757-2G7 | 256/24523 | |
| ☐ N913AW | Boeing 757-225 | 35/22207 | |
| ☐ N914AW | Boeing 757-225 | 38/22208 | |
| ☐ N915AW | Boeing 757-225 | 40/22209 | |

### AMERICA WEST EXPRESS

| | | | |
|---|---|---|---|
| ☐ N7264V | Canadair RJ-200 | 7264 | |
| ☐ N7291Z | Canadair RJ-200 | 7291 | |
| ☐ N7305V | Canadair RJ-200 | 7305 | |
| ☐ N17156 | Canadair RJ-200 | 7156 | |
| ☐ N17217 | Canadair RJ-200 | 7217 | |
| ☐ N17231 | Canadair RJ-200 | 7231 | |
| ☐ N17275 | Canadair RJ-200 | 7275 | |
| ☐ N17337 | Canadair RJ-200 | 7337 | |
| ☐ N17358 | Canadair RJ-200 | 7358 | |
| ☐ N27172 | Canadair RJ-200 | 7172 | |
| ☐ N27173 | Canadair RJ-200 | 7173 | |
| ☐ N27185 | Canadair RJ-200 | 7185 | |
| ☐ N27191 | Canadair RJ-200 | 7191 | |
| ☐ N27314 | Canadair RJ-200 | 7314 | |
| ☐ N27318 | Canadair RJ-200 | 7318 | |
| ☐ N37178 | Canadair RJ-200 | 7178 | |
| ☐ N37208 | Canadair RJ-200 | 7208 | |
| ☐ N37218 | Canadair RJ-200 | 7218 | |
| ☐ N37228 | Canadair RJ-200 | 7228 | |
| ☐ N47202 | Canadair RJ-200 | 7202 | |
| ☐ N47239 | Canadair RJ-200 | 7239 | |
| ☐ N77181 | Canadair RJ-200 | 7181 | |
| ☐ N77195 | Canadair RJ-200 | 7195 | |
| ☐ N77260 | Canadair RJ-200 | 7260 | |
| ☐ N77278 | Canadair RJ-200 | 7278 | |
| ☐ N77286 | Canadair RJ-200 | 7286 | |
| ☐ N77302 | Canadair RJ-200 | 7302 | |
| ☐ N77331 | Canadair RJ-200 | 7331 | |
| ☐ N87353 | Canadair RJ-200 | 7353 | |
| ☐ N97325 | Canadair RJ-200 | 7325 | |
| ☐ N | Canadair RJ-200 | | o/o |

| | | | |
|---|---|---|---|
| ☐ N501MJ | Canadair RJ-700 | 10047 | |
| ☐ N502MJ | Canadair RJ-700 | 10050 | |
| ☐ N503MJ | Canadair RJ-700 | 10058 | |
| ☐ N504MJ | Canadair RJ-700 | 10066 | |
| ☐ N505MJ | Canadair RJ-700 | 10070 | |
| ☐ N506MJ | Canadair RJ-700 | 10073 | |
| ☐ N | Canadair RJ-900 | 15002 | o/o |
| ☐ N | Canadair RJ-900 | | o/o |
| ☐ N | Canadair RJ-900 | | o/o |
| ☐ N | Canadair RJ-900 | | o/o |
| ☐ N | Canadair RJ-900 | | o/o |
| | | | |
| ☐ N436YV | DHC-8-202 | 436 | |
| ☐ N437YV | DHC-8-202 | 437 | |
| ☐ N445YV | DHC-8Q-202 | 445 | |
| ☐ N446YV | DHC-8Q-202 | 446 | |
| ☐ N449YV | DHC-8Q-202 | 449 | |
| ☐ N454YV | DHC-8Q-202 | 454 | |
| ☐ N455YV | DHC-8Q-202 | 455 | |
| ☐ N456YV | DHC-8Q-202 | 456 | |
| | | | |
| ☐ N107YV | Beech 1900D | UE-107 | |
| ☐ N123YV | Beech 1900D | UE-123 | |
| ☐ N135YV | Beech 1900D | UE-135 | |
| | | | |
| ☐ N273SK | Embraer ERJ-145 | 145331 | |
| ☐ N292SK | Embraer ERJ-145 | 145488 | |
| ☐ N294SK | Embraer ERJ-145 | 145497 | |
| ☐ N296SK | Embraer ERJ-145 | 145514 | |

### AMERIFLIGHT — AMF

| | | | |
|---|---|---|---|
| ☐ N330AF | Beech 1900C | UB-38 | |
| ☐ N331AF | Beech 1900C | UB-44 | |
| ☐ N3052K | Beech 1900C | UB-70 | |
| ☐ N3071A | Beech 1900C | UB-46 | |
| ☐ N3229A | Beech 1900C | UB-51 | |
| ☐ N7203C | Beech 1900C | UB-28 | |
| ☐ N31701 | Beech 1900C | UB-2 | |
| ☐ N31702 | Beech 1900C | UB-3 | |
| ☐ N31703 | Beech 1900C | UB-10 | |
| ☐ N31704 | Beech 1900C | UB-12 | |
| ☐ N31705 | Beech 1900C | UB-60 | |

### AMERIJET INTERNATIONAL — AJT

| | | | |
|---|---|---|---|
| ☐ N196AJ | Boeing 727-227F | 1017/20838 | |
| ☐ N199AJ | Boeing 727-2F9F | 1285/21426 | |
| ☐ N395AJ | Boeing 727-233F | 1148/21100 | |
| ☐ N495AJ | Boeing 727-233F | 1103/20937 | std |
| ☐ N598AJ | Boeing 727-212F | 1506/21947 | |
| ☐ N794AJ | Boeing 727-227F | 1197/21243 | |
| ☐ N994AJ | Boeing 727-233F | 1130/20942 | |

### AMERISTAR JET CHARTER — AJI

| | | | |
|---|---|---|---|
| ☐ N568PC | Douglas DC-9-15RC | 219/47086 | |
| ☐ N737TW | Boeing 737-230C | 274/20257 | |
| ☐ N767TW | Boeing 737-230C | 276/20258 | |
| ☐ N783TW | Douglas DC-9-15F | 97/47010 | |
| ☐ N784TW | Douglas DC-9-15F | 141/47014 | |
| ☐ N785TW | Douglas DC-9-15F | 156/47015 | |

### ASIA PACIFIC AIRLINES — MGE

| | | | |
|---|---|---|---|
| ☐ N319NE | Boeing 727-212F | 1289/21349 | |
| ☐ N86425 | Boeing 727-212F | 1329/21459 | |

### ATLAS AIR — GTI

| | | | |
|---|---|---|---|
| ☐ N354MC | Boeing 747-341SF | 627/23394 | Lst PAC |
| ☐ N355MC | Boeing 747-341SF | 629/23395 | Lst PAC |
| ☐ N408MC | Boeing 747-47UF | 1192/29261 | |
| ☐ N409MC | Boeing 747-47UF | 1242/30558 | Lst PAC |
| ☐ N412MC | Boeing 747-47UF | 1244/30559 | |
| ☐ N415MC | Boeing 747-47UF | 1304/32837 | |
| ☐ N416MC | Boeing 747-47UF | 1307/32838 | |
| ☐ N418MC | Boeing 747-47UF | 1319/32840 | |

| | | | |
|---|---|---|---|
| ☐ N491MC | Boeing 747-47UF | 1165/29252 | Lst GSS |
| ☐ N492MC | Boeing 747-47UF | 1169/29253 | |
| ☐ N493MC | Boeing 747-47UF | 1179/29254 | |
| ☐ N494MC | Boeing 747-47UF | 1184/29255 | Lst TAY |
| ☐ N495MC | Boeing 747-47UF | 1213/29256 | Lst GSS |
| ☐ N496MC | Boeing 747-47UF | 1217/29257 | Lst PAC |
| ☐ N497MC | Boeing 747-47UF | 1220/29258 | |
| ☐ N498MC | Boeing 747-47UF | 1227/29259 | |
| ☐ N499MC | Boeing 747-47UF | 1240/29260 | |
| ☐ N | Boeing 747-47UF | | |
| ☐ N505MC | Boeing 747-2D3M | 296/21251 | Lst PAC |
| ☐ N506MC | Boeing 747-2D3M | 297/21252 | |
| ☐ N507MC | Boeing 747-230M | 320/21380 | |
| ☐ N508MC | Boeing 747-230M | 356/21644 | |
| ☐ N509MC | Boeing 747-230M | 299/21221 | |
| ☐ N512MC | Boeing 747-230M | 294/21220 | |
| ☐ N516MC | Boeing 747-243M | 497/22507 | |
| ☐ N517MC | Boeing 747-243B (SF) | 613/23300 | |
| ☐ N518MC | Boeing 747-243M | 647/23476 | |
| ☐ N522MC | Boeing 747-2D7B (SF) | 417/21783 | |
| ☐ N523MC | Boeing 747-2D7B (SF) | 402/21782 | |
| ☐ N524MC | Boeing 747-2D7B (SF) | 424/21784 | |
| ☐ N526MC | Boeing 747-2D7B (SF) | 479/22337 | |
| ☐ N527MC | Boeing 747-2D7B (SF) | 504/22471 | |
| ☐ N528MC | Boeing 747-2D7B (SF) | 597/22472 | |
| ☐ N534MC | Boeing 747-2F6B (SF) | 421/21832 | |
| ☐ N535MC | Boeing 747-2F6B (SF) | 423/21833 | |
| ☐ N536MC | Boeing 747-228F | 334/21576 | |
| ☐ N537MC | Boeing 747-271C | 524/22403 | Lst CLX |
| ☐ N538MC | Boeing 747-271C | 416/21964 | Lst ICL |
| ☐ N539MC | Boeing 747-271C | 438/21965 | Lst ICL |
| ☐ N540MC | Boeing 747-243M | 499/22508 | |
| ☐ N808MC | Boeing 747-212B (SF) | 253/21048 | |
| ☐ N809MC | Boeing 747-228F | 245/20887 | |
| ☐ N24837 | Boeing 747-329M | 810/24837 | Lst PAC |

### BAX GLOBAL

| | | | |
|---|---|---|---|
| ☐ N41CX | Douglas DC-8-62CF | 523/46129 | |
| ☐ N606AL | Douglas DC-8-73F | 432/46044 | Opb ATN |
| ☐ N799AL | Douglas DC-8-62F | 335/45922 | Opb ATN |
| ☐ N820BX | Douglas DC-8-71F | 460/46065 | Opb ATN |
| ☐ N821BX | Douglas DC-8-71F | 262/45811 | Opb ATN |
| ☐ N822BX | Douglas DC-8-71F | 284/45813 | Opb ATN |
| ☐ N823BX | Douglas DC-8-71F | 459/46064 | Opb ATN |
| ☐ N824BX | Douglas DC-8-71F | 339/45946 | Opb ATN |
| ☐ N825BX | Douglas DC-8-71F | 381/45978 | Opb ATN |
| ☐ N826BX | Douglas DC-8-71F | 399/45998 | Opb ATN |
| ☐ N827BX | Douglas DC-8-71F | 356/45971 | Opb ATN |
| ☐ N828BX | Douglas DC-8-71F | 382/45993 | Opb ATN |
| ☐ N829BX | Douglas DC-8-71F | 387/45994 | Opb ATN |
| ☐ N830BX | Douglas DC-8-71F | 358/45973 | Opb ATN |
| ☐ N867BX | Douglas DC-8-63CF | 479/46049 | Lst ATN |
| ☐ N868BX | Douglas DC-8-63F | 434/46034 | std |
| ☐ N869BX | Douglas DC-8-63F | 438/46035 | std |
| ☐ N870BX | Douglas DC-8-63F | 445/46036 | Lst ATN |
| | | | |
| ☐ N858AA | Boeing 727-223F | 1200/21085 | Opb KHA |
| ☐ N6806 | Boeing 727-223F | 548/19481 | Opb KHA |
| ☐ N6816 | Boeing 727-223F | 611/19491 | Opb KHA |
| ☐ N6831 | Boeing 727-223F | 707/20184 | Opb KHA |

### BIG SKY AIRLINES  BSY

| | | |
|---|---|---|
| ☐ N60NE | SA.227AC Metro III | AC-760B |
| ☐ N158MC | SA.227AC Metro III | AC-726B |
| ☐ N159MC | SA.227AC Metro III | AC-728B |
| ☐ N160MC | SA.227AC Metro III | AC-733B |
| ☐ N430MA | SA.227AC Metro III | AC-710 |
| ☐ N453LA | SA.227DC Metro 23 | DC-852B |
| ☐ N459AM | SA.227AC Metro III | AC-700 |
| ☐ N702M | SA.227AC Metro III | AC-702 |
| ☐ N704C | SA.227AC Metro III | AC-704 |
| ☐ N850LS | SA.227DC Metro 23 | DC-850B |
| ☐ N853LS | SA.227DC Metro 23 | DC-853B |
| ☐ N854LS | SA.227DC Metro 23 | DC-854B |
| ☐ N27465 | SA.227AC Metro III | AC-755B |

| | | |
|---|---|---|
| ☐ N16731 | Embraer EMB.120ER | 120190 |
| ☐ N15732 | Embraer EMB.120ER | 120195 |
| ☐ N58733 | Embraer EMB.120ER | 120197 |
| ☐ N57734 | Embraer EMB.120ER | 120199 |

### BOSTON-MAINE AIRWAYS  CXS / NLE

| | | |
|---|---|---|
| ☐ N161PC | BAe Jetstream 31 | 675 |
| ☐ N162PC | BAe Jetstream 31 | 677 |
| ☐ N163PC | BAe Jetstream 31 | 678 |
| ☐ N164PC | BAe Jetstream 31 | 682 |
| ☐ N300PX | BAe Jetstream 31 | 652 |
| ☐ N301PX | BAe Jetstream 31 | 654 |
| ☐ N304PX | BAe Jetstream 31 | 663 |
| ☐ N305PX | BAe Jetstream 31 | 666 |
| ☐ N306PX | BAe Jetstream 31 | 670 |
| ☐ N307PX | BAe Jetstream 31 | 673 |
| ☐ N308PX | BAe Jetstream 31 | 674 |
| ☐ N332PX | BAe Jetstream 31 | 702 |
| ☐ N529PA | BAe Jetstream 31 | 771 |
| ☐ N530PA | BAe Jetstream 31 | 732 |
| ☐ N531PA | BAe Jetstream 31 | 748 |
| ☐ N532PA | BAe Jetstream 31 | 750 |
| ☐ N534PA | BAe Jetstream 31 | 731 |
| ☐ N535PA | BAe Jetstream 31 | 687 |
| ☐ N536PA | BAe Jetstream 31 | 681 |
| ☐ N537PA | BAe Jetstream 31 | 684 |
| ☐ N538PA | BAe Jetstream 31 | 751 |
| ☐ N539PA | BAe Jetstream 31 | 741 |
| ☐ N658BA | BAe Jetstream 31 | 658 |

### CAPITAL CARGO INTL AIRLINES  CCI

| | | |
|---|---|---|
| ☐ N227JL | Boeing 727-214F | 1020/30875 |
| ☐ N286SC | Boeing 727-2A1F | 1694/21601 |
| ☐ N287SC | Boeing 727-2A1F | 1673/21345 |
| ☐ N308AS | Boeing 727-227F | 1627/22002 |
| ☐ N357KP | Boeing 727-230F | 924/20675 |
| ☐ N708AA | Boeing 727-223F | 1761/22465 |
| ☐ N713AA | Boeing 727-223F | 1769/22469 |
| ☐ N715AA | Boeing 727-223F | 1771/22470 |
| ☐ N808EA | Boeing 727-225F | 1689/22439 |
| ☐ N879AA | Boeing 727-223F | 1367/21391 |
| ☐ N898AA | Boeing 727-223F | 1663/22014 |
| ☐ N899AA | Boeing 727-223F | 1666/22015 |
| ☐ N89427 | Boeing 727-227F | 1273/21365 |

### CASINO EXPRESS  CXP

| | | |
|---|---|---|
| ☐ N233TM | Boeing 737-282 | 972/23043 |
| ☐ N344TM | Boeing 737-282 | 973/23044 |
| ☐ N789TM | Boeing 737-282 | 981/23046 |

### CENTURION AIR CARGO  CWC

| | | |
|---|---|---|
| ☐ N140WE | Douglas DC-10-40F | 212/46920 |
| ☐ N141WE | Douglas DC-10-40F | 224/46661 |
| ☐ N142WE | Douglas DC-10-40F | 262/46966 |

### CHAMPION AIR  CCP

| | | | |
|---|---|---|---|
| ☐ N292AS | Boeing 727-212 | 1327/21458 | |
| ☐ N293AS | Boeing 727-212 | 1287/21348 | |
| ☐ N294AS | Boeing 727-290 | 1621/22146 | |
| ☐ N295AS | Boeing 727-290 | 1623/22147 | |
| ☐ N681CA | Boeing 727-2S7 | 1592/22020 | |
| ☐ N682CA | Boeing 727-2S7 | 1584/22019 | |
| ☐ N683CA | Boeing 727-2S7 | 1721/22490 | Lsf NWA |
| ☐ N684CA | Boeing 727-2S7 | 1726/22491 | Lsf NWA |
| ☐ N685CA | Boeing 727-2S7 | 1729/22492 | Lsf NWA |
| ☐ N686CA | Boeing 727-2S7 | 1617/22021 | Lsf NWA |
| ☐ N688CA | Boeing 727-2S7 | 1654/22344 | Lsf NWA |
| ☐ N696CA | Boeing 727-2J4 | 1733/22574 | |
| ☐ N697CA | Boeing 727-270 | 1817/23052 | |
| ☐ N705CA | Boeing 727-223 | 544/19479 | |

## CHICAGO EXPRESS AIRLINES

| | | |
|---|---|---|
| ☐ N300CE | SAAB SF.340B | 184 |
| ☐ N301CE | SAAB SF.340B | 191 |
| ☐ N302CE | SAAB SF.340B | 193 |
| ☐ N303CE | SAAB SF.340B | 194 |
| ☐ N304CE | SAAB SF.340B | 198 |
| ☐ N305CE | SAAB SF.340B | 202 |
| ☐ N306CE | SAAB SF.340B | 203 |
| ☐ N307CE | SAAB SF.340B | 204 |
| ☐ N308CE | SAAB SF.340B | 210 |
| ☐ N309CE | SAAB SF.340B | 201 |
| ☐ N311CE | SAAB SF.340B | 214 |
| ☐ N312CE | SAAB SF.340B | 334 |
| ☐ N314CE | SAAB SF.340B | 335 |
| ☐ N315CE | SAAB SF.340B | 343 |
| ☐ N316CE | SAAB SF.340B | 348 |
| ☐ N317CE | SAAB SF.340B | 352 |
| ☐ N318CE | SAAB SF.340B | 358 |

## COLGAN AIR

| | | | |
|---|---|---|---|
| ☐ N60MJ | Beech 1900D | UE-60 | |
| ☐ N116YV | Beech 1900D | UE-116 | |
| ☐ N119CJ | Beech 1900C-1 | UC-19 | LVC |
| ☐ N129CJ | Beech 1900C-1 | UC-129 | LVE |
| ☐ N136MJ | Beech 1900D | UE-36 | |
| ☐ N149CJ | Beech 1900D | UE-49 | |
| ☐ N152MJ | Beech 1900D | UE-52 | |
| ☐ N155CJ | Beech 1900D | UE-55 | |
| ☐ N171CJ | Beech 1900D | UE-71 | |
| ☐ N172MJ | Beech 1900D | UE-72 | |
| ☐ N191CJ | Beech 1900D | UE-19 | |
| ☐ N207CJ | Beech 1900C-1 | UC-107 | |
| ☐ N210CJ | Beech 1900C-1 | UC-110 | LVD |
| ☐ N221CJ | Beech 1900D | UE-221 | |
| ☐ N243CJ | Beech 1900D | UE-43 | |
| ☐ N550CJ | Beech 1900C-1 | UC-50 | LVA |
| ☐ N15031 | Beech 1900C-1 | UC-103 | |
| ☐ N32017 | Beech 1900C-1 | UC-37 | |

## COMMUTAIR — UCA

| | | | |
|---|---|---|---|
| ☐ N830CA | Beech 1900D | UE-393 | |
| ☐ N831CA | Beech 1900D | UE-395 | std |
| ☐ N832CA | Beech 1900D | UE-406 | std |
| ☐ N833CA | Beech 1900D | UE-377 | std |
| ☐ N834CA | Beech 1900D | UE-378 | std |
| ☐ N835CA | Beech 1900D | UE-400 | std |
| ☐ N836CA | Beech 1900D | UE-407 | std |
| ☐ N837CA | Beech 1900D | UE-397 | |
| ☐ N838CA | Beech 1900D | UE-396 | |
| ☐ N839CA | Beech 1900D | UE-385 | std |
| ☐ N840CA | Beech 1900D | UE-401 | |
| ☐ N841CA | Beech 1900D | UE-391 | std |
| ☐ N842CA | Beech 1900D | UE-402 | std |
| ☐ N843CA | Beech 1900D | UE-382 | std |
| ☐ N844CA | Beech 1900D | UE-410 | |
| ☐ N845CA | Beech 1900D | UE-388 | std |
| ☐ N846CA | Beech 1900D | UE-363 | std |
| ☐ N847CA | Beech 1900D | UE-386 | std |
| ☐ N848CA | Beech 1900D | UE-387 | std |
| ☐ N850CA | Beech 1900D | UE-215 | |
| ☐ N852CA | Beech 1900D | UE-389 | |
| ☐ N853CA | Beech 1900D | UE-390 | std |
| ☐ N854CA | Beech 1900D | UE-399 | |
| ☐ N855CA | Beech 1900D | UE-392 | |
| ☐ N856CA | Beech 1900D | UE-405 | |
| ☐ N857CA | Beech 1900D | UE-403 | |
| ☐ N858CA | Beech 1900D | UE-408 | |
| ☐ N859CA | Beech 1900D | UE-128 | std |
| ☐ N860CA | Beech 1900D | UE-134 | std |
| ☐ N861CA | Beech 1900D | UE-164 | 791; std |
| ☐ N862CA | Beech 1900D | UE-180 | 789; std |

## CONTINENTAL AIRLINES — COA

| | | | |
|---|---|---|---|
| ☐ N16301 | Boeing 737-3T0 | 1119/23352 | 301 |
| ☐ N59302 | Boeing 737-3T0 | 1129/23353 | 302 |
| ☐ N77303 | Boeing 737-3T0 | 1130/23354 | 303 |
| ☐ N61304 | Boeing 737-3T0 | 1131/23355 | 304 |
| ☐ N63305 | Boeing 737-3T0 | 1133/23356 | 305 |
| ☐ N17306 | Boeing 737-3T0 | 1141/23357 | 306 |
| ☐ N14307 | Boeing 737-3T0 | 1142/23358 | 307 |
| ☐ N14308 | Boeing 737-3T0 | 1144/23359 | 308 |
| ☐ N17309 | Boeing 737-3T0 | 1147/23360 | 309 |
| ☐ N16310 | Boeing 737-3T0 | 1150/23361 | 310 |
| ☐ N69311 | Boeing 737-3T0 | 1152/23362 | 311 |
| ☐ N60312 | Boeing 737-3T0 | 1153/23363 | 312 |
| ☐ N12313 | Boeing 737-3T0 | 1158/23364 | 313 |
| ☐ N71314 | Boeing 737-3T0 | 1159/23365 | 314 |
| ☐ N34315 | Boeing 737-3T0 | 1174/23366 | 315 |
| ☐ N17316 | Boeing 737-3T0 | 1180/23367 | 316 |
| ☐ N17317 | Boeing 737-3T0 | 1181/23368 | 317 |
| ☐ N12318 | Boeing 737-3T0 | 1188/23369 | 318 |
| ☐ N12319 | Boeing 737-3T0 | 1190/23370 | 319 |
| ☐ N14320 | Boeing 737-3T0 | 1191/23371 | 320 |
| ☐ N17321 | Boeing 737-3T0 | 1192/23372 | 321 |
| ☐ N12322 | Boeing 737-3T0 | 1202/23373 | 322 |
| ☐ N10323 | Boeing 737-3T0 | 1204/23374 | 323 |
| ☐ N14324 | Boeing 737-3T0 | 1207/23375 | 324 |
| ☐ N14325 | Boeing 737-3T0 | 1228/23455 | 325 |
| ☐ N17326 | Boeing 737-3T0 | 1230/23456 | 326 |
| ☐ N12327 | Boeing 737-3T0 | 1238/23457 | 327 |
| ☐ N17328 | Boeing 737-3T0 | 1244/23458 | 328 |
| ☐ N17329 | Boeing 737-3T0 | 1247/23459 | 329 |
| ☐ N70330 | Boeing 737-3T0 | 1253/23460 | 330 |
| ☐ N13331 | Boeing 737-3T0 | 1258/23569 | 331; std |
| ☐ N47332 | Boeing 737-3T0 | 1263/23570 | 332 |
| ☐ N69333 | Boeing 737-3T0 | 1276/23571 | 333 |
| ☐ N14334 | Boeing 737-3T0 | 1296/23572 | 334 |
| ☐ N14335 | Boeing 737-3T0 | 1298/23573 | 335 |
| ☐ N14336 | Boeing 737-3T0 | 1328/23574 | 336 |
| ☐ N14337 | Boeing 737-3T0 | 1333/23575 | 337 |
| ☐ N59338 | Boeing 737-3T0 | 1338/23576 | 338 |
| ☐ N16339 | Boeing 737-3T0 | 1340/23577 | 339 |
| ☐ N39340 | Boeing 737-3T0 | 1358/23578 | 340; std |
| ☐ N14341 | Boeing 737-3T0 | 1368/23579 | 341 |
| ☐ N14342 | Boeing 737-3T0 | 1373/23580 | 342 |
| ☐ N39343 | Boeing 737-3T0 | 1376/23581 | 343 |
| ☐ N17344 | Boeing 737-3T0 | 1383/23582 | 344 |
| ☐ N17345 | Boeing 737-3T0 | 1385/23583 | 345 |
| ☐ N14346 | Boeing 737-3T0 | 1396/23584 | 346 |
| ☐ N14347 | Boeing 737-3T0 | 1404/23585 | 347 |
| ☐ N69348 | Boeing 737-3T0 | 1411/23586 | 348 |
| ☐ N12349 | Boeing 737-3T0 | 1413/23587 | 349 |
| ☐ N18350 | Boeing 737-3T0 | 1448/23588 | 350 |
| ☐ N69351 | Boeing 737-3T0 | 1466/23589 | 351 |
| ☐ N70352 | Boeing 737-3T0 | 1468/23590 | 352 |
| ☐ N70353 | Boeing 737-3T0 | 1472/23591 | 353 |
| ☐ N76354 | Boeing 737-3T0 | 1476/23592 | 354 |
| ☐ N76355 | Boeing 737-3T0 | 1478/23593 | 355 |
| ☐ N17356 | Boeing 737-3T0 | 1522/23942 | 356 |
| ☐ N19357 | Boeing 737-3T0 | 1518/23841 | 357 |
| ☐ N14358 | Boeing 737-3T0 | 1558/23943 | 358 |
| ☐ N73380 | Boeing 737-3Q8 | 2674/26309 | 380; std |
| ☐ N14601 | Boeing 737-524 | 2566/27314 | 601 |
| ☐ N69602 | Boeing 737-524 | 2571/27315 | 602 |
| ☐ N69603 | Boeing 737-524 | 2573/27316 | 603 |
| ☐ N14604 | Boeing 737-524 | 2576/27317 | 604 |
| ☐ N14605 | Boeing 737-524 | 2582/27318 | 605 |
| ☐ N58606 | Boeing 737-524 | 2590/27319 | 606 |
| ☐ N16607 | Boeing 737-524 | 2596/27320 | 607 |
| ☐ N33608 | Boeing 737-524 | 2597/27321 | 608 |
| ☐ N14609 | Boeing 737-524 | 2607/27322 | 609 |
| ☐ N27610 | Boeing 737-524 | 2616/27323 | 610 |
| ☐ N18611 | Boeing 737-524 | 2621/27324 | 611 |
| ☐ N11612 | Boeing 737-524 | 2630/27325 | 612 |
| ☐ N14613 | Boeing 737-524 | 2633/27326 | 613 |
| ☐ N17614 | Boeing 737-524 | 2634/27327 | 614 |
| ☐ N37615 | Boeing 737-524 | 2640/27328 | 615 |
| ☐ N52616 | Boeing 737-524 | 2641/27329 | 616 |
| ☐ N16617 | Boeing 737-524 | 2648/27330 | 617 |
| ☐ N16618 | Boeing 737-524 | 2652/27331 | 618 |
| ☐ N17619 | Boeing 737-524 | 2659/27332 | 619 |
| ☐ N17620 | Boeing 737-524 | 2660/27333 | 620 |
| ☐ N19621 | Boeing 737-524 | 2661/27334 | 621 |

| | Reg | Type | Serial | Fleet |
|---|---|---|---|---|
| ☐ | N18622 | Boeing 737-524 | 2669/27526 | 622 |
| ☐ | N19623 | Boeing 737-524 | 2672/27527 | 623 |
| ☐ | N13624 | Boeing 737-524 | 2675/27528 | 624 |
| ☐ | N46625 | Boeing 737-524 | 2683/27529 | 625 |
| ☐ | N32626 | Boeing 737-524 | 2686/27530 | 626 |
| ☐ | N17627 | Boeing 737-524 | 2700/27531 | 627 |
| ☐ | N14628 | Boeing 737-524 | 2712/27532 | 628 |
| ☐ | N14629 | Boeing 737-524 | 2725/27533 | 629 |
| ☐ | N59630 | Boeing 737-524 | 2726/27534 | 630 |
| ☐ | N62631 | Boeing 737-524 | 2728/27535 | 631 |
| ☐ | N16632 | Boeing 737-524 | 2736/27900 | 632 |
| ☐ | N24633 | Boeing 737-524 | 2743/27901 | 633 |
| ☐ | N33635 | Boeing 737-524 | 2771/26339 | 635 |
| ☐ | N19636 | Boeing 737-524 | 2777/26340 | 636 |
| ☐ | N33637 | Boeing 737-524 | 2776/27540 | 637 |
| ☐ | N19638 | Boeing 737-524 | 2912/28899 | 638 |
| ☐ | N14639 | Boeing 737-524 | 2913/28900 | 639 |
| ☐ | N17640 | Boeing 737-524 | 2924/28901 | 640 |
| ☐ | N11641 | Boeing 737-524 | 2926/28902 | 641 |
| ☐ | N16642 | Boeing 737-524 | 2927/28903 | 642 |
| ☐ | N17644 | Boeing 737-524 | 2934/28905 | 644 |
| ☐ | N14645 | Boeing 737-524 | 2935/28906 | 645 |
| ☐ | N16646 | Boeing 737-524 | 2956/28907 | 646 |
| ☐ | N16647 | Boeing 737-524 | 2958/28908 | 647 |
| ☐ | N16648 | Boeing 737-524 | 2960/28909 | 648 |
| ☐ | N16649 | Boeing 737-524 | 2972/28910 | 649 |
| ☐ | N16650 | Boeing 737-524 | 2973/28911 | 650 |
| ☐ | N11651 | Boeing 737-524 | 2980/28912 | 651 |
| ☐ | N14652 | Boeing 737-524 | 2985/28913 | 652 |
| ☐ | N14653 | Boeing 737-524 | 2986/28914 | 653 |
| ☐ | N14654 | Boeing 737-524 | 2993/28915 | 654 |
| ☐ | N14655 | Boeing 737-524 | 2994/28916 | 655 |
| ☐ | N11656 | Boeing 737-524 | 3019/28917 | 656 |
| ☐ | N23657 | Boeing 737-524 | 3026/28918 | 657 |
| ☐ | N18658 | Boeing 737-524 | 3045/28919 | 658 |
| ☐ | N15659 | Boeing 737-524 | 3048/28920 | 659 |
| ☐ | N14660 | Boeing 737-524 | 3052/28921 | 660 |
| ☐ | N23661 | Boeing 737-524 | 3055/28922 | 661 |
| ☐ | N14662 | Boeing 737-524 | 3060/28923 | 662 |
| ☐ | N17663 | Boeing 737-524 | 3063/28924 | 663 |
| ☐ | N14664 | Boeing 737-524 | 3066/28925 | 664 |
| ☐ | N13665 | Boeing 737-524 | 3069/28926 | 665 |
| ☐ | N14667 | Boeing 737-524 | 3074/28927 | 667 |
| ☐ | N14668 | Boeing 737-524 | 3077/28928 | 668 |
| ☐ | N16701 | Boeing 737-724 | 29/28762 | 701 |
| ☐ | N24702 | Boeing 737-724 | 32/28763 | 702 |
| ☐ | N16703 | Boeing 737-724 | 37/28764 | 703 |
| ☐ | N14704 | Boeing 737-724 | 43/28765 | 704 |
| ☐ | N25705 | Boeing 737-724 | 46/28766 | 705 |
| ☐ | N24706 | Boeing 737-724 | 47/28767 | 706 |
| ☐ | N23707 | Boeing 737-724 | 48/28768 | 707 |
| ☐ | N23708 | Boeing 737-724 | 52/28769 | 708 |
| ☐ | N16709 | Boeing 737-724 | 93/28779 | 709 |
| ☐ | N15710 | Boeing 737-724 | 94/28780 | 710 |
| ☐ | N54711 | Boeing 737-724 | 97/28782 | 711 |
| ☐ | N15712 | Boeing 737-724 | 105/28783 | 712 |
| ☐ | N16713 | Boeing 737-724 | 107/28784 | 713 |
| ☐ | N33714 | Boeing 737-724 | 119/28785 | 714 |
| ☐ | N24715 | Boeing 737-724 | 125/28786 | 715 |
| ☐ | N13716 | Boeing 737-724 | 156/28787 | 716 |
| ☐ | N29717 | Boeing 737-724 | 182/28936 | 717 |
| ☐ | N13718 | Boeing 737-724 | 185/28937 | 718 |
| ☐ | N17719 | Boeing 737-724 | 195/28938 | 719 |
| ☐ | N13720 | Boeing 737-724 | 214/28939 | 720 |
| ☐ | N23721 | Boeing 737-724 | 219/28940 | 721 |
| ☐ | N27722 | Boeing 737-724 | 247/28789 | 722 |
| ☐ | N21723 | Boeing 737-724 | 253/28790 | 723 |
| ☐ | N27724 | Boeing 737-724 | 283/28791 | 724 |
| ☐ | N39726 | Boeing 737-724 | 315/28796 | 726 |
| ☐ | N38727 | Boeing 737-724 | 317/28797 | 727 |
| ☐ | N39728 | Boeing 737-724 | 321/28944 | 728 |
| ☐ | N24729 | Boeing 737-724 | 325/28945 | 729 |
| ☐ | N17730 | Boeing 737-724 | 338/28798 | 730 |
| ☐ | N14731 | Boeing 737-724 | 346/28799 | 731 |
| ☐ | N16732 | Boeing 737-724 | 352/28948 | 732 |
| ☐ | N27733 | Boeing 737-724 | 364/28800 | 733 |
| ☐ | N27734 | Boeing 737-724 | 371/28949 | 734 |
| ☐ | N14735 | Boeing 737-724 | 376/28950 | 735 |
| ☐ | N24736 | Boeing 737-724 | 380/28803 | 736 |
| ☐ | N13750 | Boeing 737-724 | 286/28941 | 750 |
| ☐ | N15751 | Boeing 737-724 | | 751 o/o |
| ☐ | N17752 | Boeing 737-724 | | 752 o/o |
| ☐ | N17753 | Boeing 737-724 | | 753 o/o |
| ☐ | N12754 | Boeing 737-724 | | 754 o/o |
| ☐ | N13755 | Boeing 737-724 | | 755 o/o |
| ☐ | N16756 | Boeing 737-724 | | 756 o/o |
| ☐ | N18757 | Boeing 737-724 | | 757 o/o |
| ☐ | N15758 | Boeing 737-724 | | 758 o/o |
| ☐ | N25201 | Boeing 737-824 | 443/28958 | 201 |
| ☐ | N24202 | Boeing 737-824 | 581/30429 | 202 |
| ☐ | N33203 | Boeing 737-824 | 591/30613 | 203 |
| ☐ | N35204 | Boeing 737-824 | 606/30576 | 204 |
| ☐ | N27205 | Boeing 737-824 | 615/30577 | 205 |
| ☐ | N11206 | Boeing 737-824 | 618/30578 | 206 |
| ☐ | N36207 | Boeing 737-824 | 627/30579 | 207 |
| ☐ | N26208 | Boeing 737-824 | 644/30580 | 208 |
| ☐ | N33209 | Boeing 737-824 | 647/30581 | 209 |
| ☐ | N26210 | Boeing 737-824 | 56/28770 | 210 |
| ☐ | N24211 | Boeing 737-824 | 58/28771 | 211 |
| ☐ | N24212 | Boeing 737-824 | 63/28772 | 212 |
| ☐ | N27213 | Boeing 737-824 | 65/28773 | 213 |
| ☐ | N14214 | Boeing 737-824 | 74/28774 | 214 |
| ☐ | N26215 | Boeing 737-824 | 76/28775 | 215 |
| ☐ | N12216 | Boeing 737-824 | 79/28776 | 216 |
| ☐ | N16217 | Boeing 737-824 | 81/28777 | 217 |
| ☐ | N12218 | Boeing 737-824 | 84/28778 | 218 |
| ☐ | N14219 | Boeing 737-824 | 88/28781 | 219 |
| ☐ | N18220 | Boeing 737-824 | 134/28929 | 220 |
| ☐ | N12221 | Boeing 737-824 | 153/28930 | 221 |
| ☐ | N34222 | Boeing 737-824 | 159/28931 | 222 |
| ☐ | N18223 | Boeing 737-824 | 162/28932 | 223 |
| ☐ | N24224 | Boeing 737-824 | 165/28933 | 224 |
| ☐ | N12225 | Boeing 737-824 | 168/28934 | 225 |
| ☐ | N26226 | Boeing 737-824 | 171/28935 | 226 |
| ☐ | N13227 | Boeing 737-824 | 262/28788 | 227 |
| ☐ | N14228 | Boeing 737-824 | 281/28792 | 228 |
| ☐ | N17229 | Boeing 737-824 | 287/28793 | 229 |
| ☐ | N14230 | Boeing 737-824 | 296/28794 | 230 |
| ☐ | N14231 | Boeing 737-824 | 300/28795 | 231 |
| ☐ | N26232 | Boeing 737-824 | 304/28942 | 232 |
| ☐ | N17233 | Boeing 737-824 | 328/28943 | 233 |
| ☐ | N16234 | Boeing 737-824 | 334/28946 | 234 |
| ☐ | N14235 | Boeing 737-824 | 342/28947 | 235 |
| ☐ | N35236 | Boeing 737-824 | 367/28801 | 236 |
| ☐ | N14237 | Boeing 737-824 | 374/28802 | 237 |
| ☐ | N12238 | Boeing 737-824 | 386/28804 | 238 |
| ☐ | N27239 | Boeing 737-824 | 391/28951 | 239 |
| ☐ | N14240 | Boeing 737-824 | 394/28952 | 240 |
| ☐ | N54241 | Boeing 737-824 | 395/28953 | 241 |
| ☐ | N14242 | Boeing 737-824 | 402/28805 | 242 |
| ☐ | N18243 | Boeing 737-824 | 403/28806 | 243 |
| ☐ | N17244 | Boeing 737-824 | 409/28954 | 244 |
| ☐ | N17245 | Boeing 737-824 | 411/28955 | 245 |
| ☐ | N27246 | Boeing 737-824 | 413/28956 | 246 |
| ☐ | N36247 | Boeing 737-824 | 431/28807 | 247 |
| ☐ | N13248 | Boeing 737-824 | 435/28808 | 248 |
| ☐ | N14249 | Boeing 737-824 | 438/28809 | 249 |
| ☐ | N14250 | Boeing 737-824 | 441/28957 | 250 |
| ☐ | N73251 | Boeing 737-824 | 650/30582 | 251 |
| ☐ | N37252 | Boeing 737-824 | 656/30583 | 252 |
| ☐ | N37253 | Boeing 737-824 | 660/30584 | 253 |
| ☐ | N76254 | Boeing 737-824 | 667/30779 | 254 |
| ☐ | N37255 | Boeing 737-824 | 686/30610 | 255 |
| ☐ | N73256 | Boeing 737-824 | 692/30611 | 256 |
| ☐ | N38257 | Boeing 737-824 | 706/30612 | 257 |
| ☐ | N77258 | Boeing 737-824 | 708/30802 | 258 |
| ☐ | N73259 | Boeing 737-824 | 854/30803 | 259 |
| ☐ | N35260 | Boeing 737-824 | 862/30855 | 260 |
| ☐ | N77261 | Boeing 737-824 | 897/31582 | 261 |
| ☐ | N33262 | Boeing 737-824 | 901/32402 | 262 |
| ☐ | N37263 | Boeing 737-824 | 906/31583 | 263 |
| ☐ | N33264 | Boeing 737-824 | 916/31584 | 264 |
| ☐ | N76265 | Boeing 737-824 | 928/31585 | 265 |
| ☐ | N33266 | Boeing 737-824 | 930/32403 | 266 |

| Reg | Type | Line/MSN | Fleet |
|---|---|---|---|
| N37267 | Boeing 737-824 | 939/31586 | 267 |
| N38268 | Boeing 737-824 | 957/31587 | 268 |
| N76269 | Boeing 737-824 | 966/31588 | 269 |
| N73270 | Boeing 737-824 | 970/31632 | 270 |
| N35271 | Boeing 737-824 | 982/31589 | 271 |
| N36272 | Boeing 737-824 | 987/31590 | 272 |
| N37273 | Boeing 737-824 | 1012/31591 | 273 |
| N37274 | Boeing 737-824 | 1062/31592 | 274 |
| N73275 | Boeing 737-824 | 1077/31593 | 275 |
| N73276 | Boeing 737-824 | 1079/31594 | 276 |
| N37277 | Boeing 737-824 | 1099/31595 | 277 |
| N73278 | Boeing 737-824 | | 278 o/o |
| N79279 | Boeing 737-824 | | 279 o/o |
| N36280 | Boeing 737-824 | | 280 o/o |
| N37281 | Boeing 737-824 | | 281 o/o |
| N34282 | Boeing 737-824 | | 282 o/o |
| N73283 | Boeing 737-824 | | 283 o/o |
| N33284 | Boeing 737-824 | | 284 o/o |
| N78285 | Boeing 737-824 | | 285 o/o |
| N33286 | Boeing 737-824 | | 286 o/o |
| N37287 | Boeing 737-824 | | 287 o/o |
| N76288 | Boeing 737-824 | | 288 o/o |
| N33289 | Boeing 737-824 | | 289 o/o |
| N37290 | Boeing 737-824 | | 290 o/o |
| N73291 | Boeing 737-824 | | 291 o/o |
| N33292 | Boeing 737-824 | | 292 o/o |
| N30401 | Boeing 737-924 | 820/30118 | 401 |
| N79402 | Boeing 737-924 | 857/30119 | 402 |
| N38403 | Boeing 737-924 | 884/30120 | 403 |
| N32404 | Boeing 737-924 | 893/30121 | 404 |
| N72405 | Boeing 737-924 | 911/30122 | 405 |
| N73406 | Boeing 737-924 | 943/30123 | 406 |
| N35407 | Boeing 737-924 | 951/30124 | 407 |
| N37408 | Boeing 737-924 | 962/30125 | 408 |
| N37409 | Boeing 737-924 | 1004/30126 | 409 |
| N75410 | Boeing 737-924 | 1021/30127 | 410 |
| N71411 | Boeing 737-924 | 1052/30128 | 411 |
| N31412 | Boeing 737-924 | 1112/30129 | 412 |
| N37413 | Boeing 737-924 | | 413 o/o |
| N30414 | Boeing 737-924 | | 414 o/o |
| N73415 | Boeing 737-924 | | 415 o/o |
| N58101 | Boeing 757-224 | 614/27291 | 101 |
| N14102 | Boeing 757-224 | 619/27292 | 102 |
| N33103 | Boeing 757-224 | 623/27293 | 103 |
| N17104 | Boeing 757-224 | 629/27294 | 104 |
| N17105 | Boeing 757-224 | 632/27295 | 105 |
| N14106 | Boeing 757-224 | 637/27296 | 106 |
| N14107 | Boeing 757-224 | 641/27297 | 107 |
| N21108 | Boeing 757-224 | 645/27298 | 108 |
| N12109 | Boeing 757-224 | 648/27299 | 109 |
| N13110 | Boeing 757-224 | 650/27300 | 110 |
| N57111 | Boeing 757-224 | 652/27301 | 111 |
| N18112 | Boeing 757-224 | 653/27302 | 112 |
| N13113 | Boeing 757-224 | 668/27555 | 113 |
| N12114 | Boeing 757-224 | 682/27556 | 114 |
| N14115 | Boeing 757-224 | 686/27557 | 115 |
| N12116 | Boeing 757-224 | 702/27558 | 116 |
| N19117 | Boeing 757-224 | 706/27559 | 117 |
| N14118 | Boeing 757-224 | 748/27560 | 118 |
| N18119 | Boeing 757-224 | 753/27561 | 119 |
| N14120 | Boeing 757-224 | 761/27562 | 120 |
| N14121 | Boeing 757-224 | 766/27563 | 121 |
| N17122 | Boeing 757-224 | 768/27564 | 122 |
| N26123 | Boeing 757-224 | 781/28966 | 123 |
| N29124 | Boeing 757-224 | 786/27565 | 124 |
| N12125 | Boeing 757-224 | 788/28967 | 125 |
| N17126 | Boeing 757-224ER | 790/27566 | 126 |
| N48127 | Boeing 757-224ER | 791/28968 | 127 |
| N17128 | Boeing 757-224ER | 795/27567 | 128 |
| N29129 | Boeing 757-224ER | 796/28969 | 129 |
| N19130 | Boeing 757-224ER | 799/28970 | 130 |
| N34131 | Boeing 757-224 | 806/28971 | 131 |
| N33132 | Boeing 757-224 | 809/29281 | 132 |
| N17133 | Boeing 757-224 | 840/29282 | 133 |
| N67134 | Boeing 757-224 | 848/29283 | 134 |
| N41135 | Boeing 757-224 | 851/29284 | 135 |
| N19136 | Boeing 757-224 | 856/29285 | 136 |
| N34137 | Boeing 757-224 | 899/30229 | 137 |
| N13138 | Boeing 757-224 | 903/30351 | 138 |
| N17139 | Boeing 757-224 | 911/30352 | 139 |
| N41140 | Boeing 757-224 | 913/30353 | 140 |
| N19141 | Boeing 757-224 | 933/30354 | 141 |
| N75851 | Boeing 757-324 | 990/32810 | 851 |
| N57852 | Boeing 757-324 | 995/32811 | 852 |
| N75853 | Boeing 757-324 | 997/32812 | 853 |
| N75854 | Boeing 757-324 | 999/32813 | 854 |
| N57855 | Boeing 757-324 | 32814 | 855 o/o |
| N74856 | Boeing 757-324 | 32815 | 856 o/o |
| N57857 | Boeing 757-324 | | 857 o/o |
| N75858 | Boeing 757-324 | | 858 o/o |
| N56859 | Boeing 757-324 | | 859 o/o |
| N73860 | Boeing 757-324 | | 860 o/o |
| N75861 | Boeing 757-324 | | 861 o/o |
| N57862 | Boeing 757-324 | | 862 o/o |
| N57863 | Boeing 757-324 | | 863 o/o |
| N57864 | Boeing 757-324 | | 864 o/o |
| N77865 | Boeing 757-324 | | 865 o/o |
| N76151 | Boeing 767-224ER | 811/30430 | 151 |
| N73152 | Boeing 767-224ER | 815/30431 | 152 |
| N76153 | Boeing 767-224ER | 819/30432 | 153 |
| N69154 | Boeing 767-224ER | 823/30433 | 154 |
| N68155 | Boeing 767-224ER | 825/30434 | 155 |
| N76156 | Boeing 767-224ER | 827/30435 | 156 |
| N67157 | Boeing 767-224ER | 833/30436 | 157 |
| N67158 | Boeing 767-224ER | 839/30437 | 158 |
| N68159 | Boeing 767-224ER | 845/30438 | 159 |
| N68160 | Boeing 767-224ER | 851/30439 | 160 |
| N66051 | Boeing 767-424ER | 799/29446 | 051 |
| N67052 | Boeing 767-424ER | 805/29447 | 052 |
| N59053 | Boeing 767-424ER | 809/29448 | 053 |
| N76054 | Boeing 767-424ER | 816/29449 | 054 |
| N76055 | Boeing 767-424ER | 826/29450 | 055 |
| N66056 | Boeing 767-424ER | 842/29451 | 056 |
| N66057 | Boeing 767-424ER | 859/29452 | 057 |
| N67058 | Boeing 767-424ER | 862/29453 | 058 |
| N69059 | Boeing 767-424ER | 864/29454 | 059 |
| N78060 | Boeing 767-424ER | 866/29455 | 060 |
| N68061 | Boeing 767-424ER | 868/29456 | 061 |
| N76062 | Boeing 767-424ER | 869/29457 | 062 |
| N69063 | Boeing 767-424ER | 872/29458 | 063 |
| N76064 | Boeing 767-424ER | 873/29459 | 064 |
| N76065 | Boeing 767-424ER | 876/29460 | 065 |
| N77066 | Boeing 767-424ER | 878/29461 | 066 |
| N78001 | Boeing 777-224ER | 161/27577 | 001 |
| N78002 | Boeing 777-224ER | 165/27578 | 002 |
| N78003 | Boeing 777-224ER | 167/27579 | 003 |
| N78004 | Boeing 777-224ER | 169/27580 | 004 |
| N78005 | Boeing 777-224ER | 177/27581 | 005 |
| N77006 | Boeing 777-224ER | 183/29476 | 006 |
| N74007 | Boeing 777-224ER | 197/29477 | 007 |
| N78008 | Boeing 777-224ER | 200/29478 | 008 |
| N78009 | Boeing 777-224ER | 211/29479 | 009 |
| N76010 | Boeing 777-224ER | 220/29480 | 010 |
| N79011 | Boeing 777-224ER | 227/29859 | 011 |
| N77012 | Boeing 777-224ER | 234/29860 | 012 |
| N78013 | Boeing 777-224ER | 243/29861 | 013 |
| N77014 | Boeing 777-224ER | 253/29862 | 014 |
| N27015 | Boeing 777-224ER | 273/28678 | 015 |
| N57016 | Boeing 777-224ER | 279/28679 | 016 |
| N87017 | Boeing 777-224ER | 391/31679 | 017 |
| N37018 | Boeing 777-224ER | 397/31680 | 018 |
| N477AC | McDD MD-82 | 1015/48062 | 885; std |
| N478AC | McDD MD-82 | 1020/48063 | 886; std |
| N819NY | McDD MD-82 | 1297/49479 | 819 |
| N936AS | McDD MD-83 | 1275/49363 | 842; std |
| N937MC | McDD MD-82 | 1324/49450 | 877; std |
| N938AS | McDD MD-83 | 1277/49365 | 843; std |
| N938MC | McDD MD-83 | 1340/49525 | 878; std |
| N10801 | McDD MD-82 | 1082/49127 | 801; std |
| N33805 | McDD MD-82 | 1149/49249 | 805; std |

| | | | |
|---|---|---|---|
| ☐ N16806 | McDD MD-82 | 1150/49260 | 806 |
| ☐ N16807 | McDD MD-82 | 1153/49261 | 807; std |
| ☐ N14810 | McDD MD-82 | 1171/49264 | 810 |
| ☐ N12811 | McDD MD-82 | 1185/49265 | 811 |
| ☐ N17812 | McDD MD-82 | 1186/49250 | 812; std |
| ☐ N14816 | McDD MD-82 | 1206/49370 | 816 |
| ☐ N33817 | McDD MD-82 | 1207/49371 | 817 |
| ☐ N14818 | McDD MD-82 | 1293/49478 | 818; std |
| ☐ N15820 | McDD MD-82 | 1298/49480 | 820 |
| ☐ N72821 | McDD MD-82 | 1308/49481 | 821 |
| ☐ N72822 | McDD MD-82 | 1309/49482 | 822 |
| ☐ N76823 | McDD MD-82 | 1314/49483 | 823 |
| ☐ N72824 | McDD MD-82 | 1315/49484 | 824; std |
| ☐ N72825 | McDD MD-82 | 1316/49485 | 825 |
| ☐ N69826 | McDD MD-82 | 1317/49486 | 826 |
| ☐ N77827 | McDD MD-82 | 1335/49487 | 827 |
| ☐ N71828 | McDD MD-82 | 1350/49488 | 828 |
| ☐ N72829 | McDD MD-82 | 1351/49489 | 829; std |
| ☐ N72830 | McDD MD-82 | 1352/49490 | 830 |
| ☐ N14831 | McDD MD-82 | 1360/49491 | 831 |
| ☐ N35832 | McDD MD-82 | 1361/49492 | 832 |
| ☐ N18833 | McDD MD-82 | 1364/49493 | 833 |
| ☐ N10834 | McDD MD-82 | 1368/49494 | 834; std |
| ☐ N18835 | McDD MD-82 | 1318/49439 | 835 |
| ☐ N35836 | McDD MD-82 | 1322/49441 | 836; std |
| ☐ N57837 | McDD MD-82 | 1411/49582 | 837; std |
| ☐ N34838 | McDD MD-82 | 1419/49634 | 838 |
| ☐ N14839 | McDD MD-82 | 1420/49635 | 839 |
| ☐ N14840 | McDD MD-82 | 1369/49580 | 840 |
| ☐ N15841 | McDD MD-82 | 1384/49581 | 841 |
| ☐ N83870 | McDD MD-82 | 1012/48056 | 870; std |
| ☐ N14871 | McDD MD-82 | 1079/48022 | 871 |
| ☐ N92874 | McDD MD-82 | 1073/49122 | 874 |
| ☐ N98876 | McDD MD-82 | 1323/49444 | 876; std |
| ☐ N14879 | McDD MD-83 | 1342/49526 | 879; std |
| ☐ N14880 | McDD MD-81 | 967/48044 | 880; std |
| ☐ N13881 | McDD MD-81 | 970/48045 | 881; std |
| ☐ N37882 | McDD MD-81 | 973/48027 | 882; std |
| ☐ N16883 | McDD MD-81 | 1018/48073 | 883 |
| ☐ N16887 | McDD MD-82 | 1061/49116 | 887; std |
| ☐ N35888 | McDD MD-82 | 1063/49117 | 888; std |
| ☐ N14889 | McDD MD-82 | 1065/49118 | 889; std |
| ☐ N14890 | McDD MD-82 | 1066/49114 | 890; std |
| ☐ N13891 | McDD MD-82 | 1076/49102 | 891; std |
| ☐ N16893 | McDD MD-82 | 1272/49392 | 893; std |

### CONTINENTAL EXPRESS — BTA

| | | | |
|---|---|---|---|
| ☐ N25811 | ATR 42-300 | 094 | 477; std |
| ☐ N19812 | ATR 42-300 | 099 | 465; std |
| ☐ N14813 | ATR 42-300 | 100 | std |
| ☐ N18814 | ATR 42-300 | 103 | 463; std |
| ☐ N14815 | ATR 42-300 | 104 | 462; std |
| ☐ N15816 | ATR 42-300 | 105 | 466; std |
| ☐ N34817 | ATR 42-300 | 152 | 489; std |
| ☐ N15818 | ATR 42-300 | 153 | std |
| ☐ N14819 | ATR 42-300 | 156 | for FDX |
| ☐ N34820 | ATR 42-300 | 159 | 490; std |
| ☐ N14821 | ATR 42-300 | 160 | 491; std |
| ☐ N14822 | ATR 42-300 | 163 | std |
| ☐ N15823 | ATR 42-300 | 165 | std |
| ☐ N16824 | ATR 42-300 | 166 | for FDX |
| ☐ N14825 | ATR 42-300 | 170 | for FDX |
| ☐ N26826 | ATR 42-300 | 172 | 486?; std |
| ☐ N15827 | ATR 42-300 | 175 | 457; std |
| ☐ N14828 | ATR 42-300 | 179 | for FDX |
| ☐ N14830 | ATR 42-300 | 184 | for FDX |
| ☐ N17831 | ATR 42-300 | 185 | 485; std |
| ☐ N14832 | ATR 42-300 | 187 | 487; std |
| ☐ N14833 | ATR 42-300 | 188 | 479; std |
| ☐ N14834 | ATR 42-300 | 193 | 460; std |
| ☐ N11835 | ATR 42-300 | 194 | std |
| ☐ N42836 | ATR 42-300 | 200 | 487; std |
| ☐ N21837 | ATR 42-300 | 202 | 488; std |
| ☐ N99838 | ATR 42-320 | 259 | for FDX |
| ☐ N93840 | ATR 42-300 | 271 | for FDX |
| ☐ N97841 | ATR 42-300 | 280 | |
| ☐ N86842 | ATR 42-300 | 286 | 486?; std |

| | | | |
|---|---|---|---|
| ☐ N34712 | Embraer EMB.120ER | 120111 | 286; std |
| ☐ N15713 | Embraer EMB.120ER | 120114 | 287; std |
| ☐ N12715 | Embraer EMB.120ER | 120125 | std |
| ☐ N27716 | Embraer EMB.120ER | 120128 | std |
| ☐ N40717 | Embraer EMB.120ER | 120133 | 291; std |
| ☐ N16718 | Embraer EMB.120ER | 120136 | std |
| ☐ N17720 | Embraer EMB.120ER | 120142 | std |
| ☐ N16723 | Embraer EMB.120ER | 120169 | std |
| ☐ N15725 | Embraer EMB.120ER | 120173 | std |
| ☐ N51726 | Embraer EMB.120ER | 120174 | std |
| ☐ N22727 | Embraer EMB.120ER | 120177 | 271; std |
| ☐ N17728 | Embraer EMB.120ER | 120182 | std |
| ☐ N16729 | Embraer EMB.120ER | 120185 | std |
| ☐ N15730 | Embraer EMB.120ER | 120187 | std |
| ☐ N16731 | Embraer EMB.120ER | 120190 | std |
| ☐ N15732 | Embraer EMB.120ER | 120195 | std |
| ☐ N58733 | Embraer EMB.120ER | 120197 | std |
| ☐ N57734 | Embraer EMB.120ER | 120199 | std |

| | | | |
|---|---|---|---|
| ☐ N16501 | Embraer ERJ-135 | 145145 | 501 |
| ☐ N16502 | Embraer ERJ-135 | 145166 | 502 |
| ☐ N19503 | Embraer ERJ-135 | 145176 | 503 |
| ☐ N22504 | Embraer ERJ-135 | 145186 | 504 |
| ☐ N14505 | Embraer ERJ-135 | 145192 | 505 |
| ☐ N27506 | Embraer ERJ-135 | 145206 | 506 |
| ☐ N17507 | Embraer ERJ-135 | 145215 | 507 |
| ☐ N14508 | Embraer ERJ-135 | 145220 | 508 |
| ☐ N15509 | Embraer ERJ-135 | 145238 | 509 |
| ☐ N16510 | Embraer ERJ-135 | 145251 | 510 |
| ☐ N16511 | Embraer ERJ-135 | 145267 | 511 |
| ☐ N27512 | Embraer ERJ-135 | 145274 | 512 |
| ☐ N17513 | Embraer ERJ-135 | 145292 | 513 |
| ☐ N14514 | Embraer ERJ-135 | 145303 | 514 |
| ☐ N29515 | Embraer ERJ-135 | 145309 | 515 |
| ☐ N14516 | Embraer ERJ-135 | 145323 | 516 |
| ☐ N24517 | Embraer ERJ-135 | 145332 | 517 |
| ☐ N28518 | Embraer ERJ-135 | 145334 | 518 |
| ☐ N12519 | Embraer ERJ-135 | 145366 | 519 |
| ☐ N16520 | Embraer ERJ-135 | 145372 | 520 |
| ☐ N17521 | Embraer ERJ-135 | 145378 | 521 |
| ☐ N14522 | Embraer ERJ-135 | 145383 | 522 |
| ☐ N27523 | Embraer ERJ-135 | 145389 | 523 |
| ☐ N17524 | Embraer ERJ-135 | 145399 | 524 |
| ☐ N16525 | Embraer ERJ-135 | 145403 | 525 |
| ☐ N11526 | Embraer ERJ-135 | 145410 | 526 |
| ☐ N15527 | Embraer ERJ-135 | 145413 | 527 |
| ☐ N12528 | Embraer ERJ-135 | 145504 | 528 |
| ☐ N28529 | Embraer ERJ-135 | 145512 | 529 |
| ☐ N12530 | Embraer ERJ-135 | 145533 | 530 |
| ☐ N13531 | Embraer ERJ-135 | | 531 o/o |
| ☐ N16532 | Embraer ERJ-135 | | 532 o/o |
| ☐ N16533 | Embraer ERJ-135 | | 533 o/o |
| ☐ N21534 | Embraer ERJ-135 | | 534 o/o |
| ☐ N | Embraer ERJ-135 | | o/o |
| ☐ N | Embraer ERJ-135 | | o/o |
| ☐ N | Embraer ERJ-135 | | o/o |
| ☐ N | Embraer ERJ-135 | | o/o |
| ☐ N | Embraer ERJ-135 | | o/o |
| ☐ N | Embraer ERJ-135 | | o/o |
| ☐ N | Embraer ERJ-135 | | o/o |
| ☐ N | Embraer ERJ-135 | | o/o |
| ☐ N | Embraer ERJ-135 | | o/o |
| ☐ N | Embraer ERJ-135 | | o/o |
| ☐ N | Embraer ERJ-135 | | o/o |
| ☐ N | Embraer ERJ-135 | | o/o |
| ☐ N | Embraer ERJ-135 | | o/o |
| ☐ N | Embraer ERJ-135 | | o/o |
| ☐ N | Embraer ERJ-135 | | o/o |
| ☐ N | Embraer ERJ-135 | | o/o |

| | | | |
|---|---|---|---|
| ☐ N11535 | Embraer ERJ-145 | 145518 | 535 |
| ☐ N11536 | Embraer ERJ-145 | 145520 | 536 |
| ☐ N21537 | Embraer ERJ-145 | 145523 | 537 |
| ☐ N12538 | Embraer ERJ-145 | 145527 | 538 |
| ☐ N11539 | Embraer ERJ-145 | 145536 | 539 |
| ☐ N12540 | Embraer ERJ-145 | 145537 | 540 |
| ☐ N16541 | Embraer ERJ-145 | 145542 | 541 |
| ☐ N14542 | Embraer ERJ-145 | 145547 | 542 |

| | Reg | Type | c/n | Fleet |
|---|---|---|---|---|
| ☐ | N14543 | Embraer ERJ-145 | 145553 | 543 |
| ☐ | N11544 | Embraer ERJ-145 | 145557 | 544 |
| ☐ | N26545 | Embraer ERJ-145 | 144558 | 545 |
| ☐ | N16546 | Embraer ERJ-145 | 145562 | 546 |
| ☐ | N11547 | Embraer ERJ-145 | 145563 | 547 |
| ☐ | N11548 | Embraer ERJ-145 | 145565 | 548 |
| ☐ | N26549 | Embraer ERJ-145 | 145571 | 549 |
| ☐ | N13550 | Embraer ERJ-145 | 145575 | 550 |
| ☐ | N11551 | Embraer ERJ-145 | 145411 | 551 |
| ☐ | N12552 | Embraer ERJ-145 | 145583 | 552 |
| ☐ | N13553 | Embraer ERJ-145 | 145585 | 553 |
| ☐ | N19554 | Embraer ERJ-145 | 145587 | 554 |
| ☐ | N15555 | Embraer ERJ-145 | 145594 | 555 |
| ☐ | N18556 | Embraer ERJ-145 | 145595 | 556 |
| ☐ | N18557 | Embraer ERJ-145 | 145596 | 557 |
| ☐ | N14558 | Embraer ERJ-145 | 145598 | 558 |
| ☐ | N16559 | Embraer ERJ-145 | 145603 | 559 |
| ☐ | N17560 | Embraer ERJ-145 | 145605 | 560 |
| ☐ | N16561 | Embraer ERJ-145 | 145610 | 561 |
| ☐ | N14562 | Embraer ERJ-145 | 145611 | 562 |
| ☐ | N12563 | Embraer ERJ-145 | 145612 | 563 |
| ☐ | N12564 | Embraer ERJ-145 | 145618 | 564 |
| ☐ | N11565 | Embraer ERJ-145 | 145621 | 565 |
| ☐ | N13566 | Embraer ERJ-145 | 145622 | 566 |
| ☐ | N12567 | Embraer ERJ-145 | 145623 | 567 |
| ☐ | N14558 | Embraer ERJ-145 | 145628 | 568 |
| ☐ | N12569 | Embraer ERJ-145 | 145630 | 569 |
| ☐ | N14570 | Embraer ERJ-145 | 145632 | 570 |
| ☐ | N16571 | Embraer ERJ-145 | 145633 | 571 |
| ☐ | N15572 | Embraer ERJ-145 | 145636 | 572 |
| ☐ | N14573 | Embraer ERJ-145 | 145638 | 573 |
| ☐ | N15574 | Embraer ERJ-145 | 145639 | 574 |
| ☐ | N10575 | Embraer ERJ-145 | 145640 | 575 |
| ☐ | N12576 | Embraer ERJ-145 | | 576 o/o |
| ☐ | N15577 | Embraer ERJ-145 | | 577 o/o |
| ☐ | N14578 | Embraer ERJ-145 | | 578 o/o |
| ☐ | N14579 | Embraer ERJ-145 | | 579 o/o |
| ☐ | N17580 | Embraer ERJ-145 | | 580 o/o |
| ☐ | N12581 | Embraer ERJ-145 | | 581 o/o |
| ☐ | N11582 | Embraer ERJ-145 | | 582 o/o |
| ☐ | N12900 | Embraer ERJ-145 | 145511 | 900 |
| ☐ | N48901 | Embraer ERJ-145 | 145501 | 901 |
| ☐ | N14902 | Embraer ERJ-145 | 145496 | 902 |
| ☐ | N13903 | Embraer ERJ-145 | 145479 | 903 |
| ☐ | N12904 | Embraer ERJ-145 | 145477 | 904 |
| ☐ | N14905 | Embraer ERJ-145 | 145476 | 905 |
| ☐ | N29906 | Embraer ERJ-145 | 145472 | 906 |
| ☐ | N10907 | Embraer ERJ-145 | 145468 | 907 |
| ☐ | N13908 | Embraer ERJ-145 | 145465 | 908 |
| ☐ | N22909 | Embraer ERJ-145 | 145459 | 909 |
| ☐ | N15910 | Embraer ERJ-145 | 145455 | 910 |
| ☐ | N16911 | Embraer ERJ-145 | 145446 | 911 |
| ☐ | N14912 | Embraer ERJ-145 | 145439 | 912 |
| ☐ | N13913 | Embraer ERJ-145 | 145438 | 913 |
| ☐ | N13914 | Embraer ERJ-145 | 145430 | 914 |
| ☐ | N36915 | Embraer ERJ-145 | 145421 | 915 |
| ☐ | N14916 | Embraer ERJ-145 | 145415 | 916 |
| ☐ | N29917 | Embraer ERJ-145 | 145414 | 917 |
| ☐ | N16918 | Embraer ERJ-145 | 145397 | 918 |
| ☐ | N16919 | Embraer ERJ-145 | 145393 | 919 |
| ☐ | N14920 | Embraer ERJ-145 | 145380 | 920 |
| ☐ | N12921 | Embraer ERJ-145 | 145354 | 921 |
| ☐ | N12922 | Embraer ERJ-145 | 145338 | 922 |
| ☐ | N14923 | Embraer ERJ-145 | 145318 | 923 |
| ☐ | N12924 | Embraer ERJ-145 | 145311 | 924 |
| ☐ | N14925 | Embraer ERJ-145 | 145004 | 925 |
| ☐ | N15926 | Embraer ERJ-145 | 145005 | 926 |
| ☐ | N16927 | Embraer ERJ-145 | 145006 | 927 |
| ☐ | N17928 | Embraer ERJ-145 | 145007 | 928 |
| ☐ | N13929 | Embraer ERJ-145 | 145009 | 929 |
| ☐ | N14930 | Embraer ERJ-145 | 145011 | 930 |
| ☐ | N15932 | Embraer ERJ-145 | 145015 | 932 |
| ☐ | N14933 | Embraer ERJ-145 | 145018 | 933 |
| ☐ | N12934 | Embraer ERJ-145 | 145019 | 934 |
| ☐ | N13935 | Embraer ERJ-145 | 145022 | 935 |
| ☐ | N13936 | Embraer ERJ-145 | 145025 | 936 |
| ☐ | N14937 | Embraer ERJ-145 | 145026 | 937 |
| ☐ | N14938 | Embraer ERJ-145 | 145029 | 938 |
| ☐ | N14939 | Embraer ERJ-145 | 145030 | 939 |
| ☐ | N14940 | Embraer ERJ-145 | 145033 | 940 |
| ☐ | N15941 | Embraer ERJ-145 | 145035 | 941 |
| ☐ | N14942 | Embraer ERJ-145 | 145037 | 942 |
| ☐ | N14943 | Embraer ERJ-145 | 145040 | 943 |
| ☐ | N16944 | Embraer ERJ-145 | 145045 | 944 |
| ☐ | N14945 | Embraer ERJ-145 | 145049 | 945 |
| ☐ | N14947 | Embraer ERJ-145 | 145054 | 947 |
| ☐ | N12946 | Embraer ERJ-145 | 145052 | 946 |
| ☐ | N15948 | Embraer ERJ-145 | 145056 | 948 |
| ☐ | N13949 | Embraer ERJ-145 | 145057 | 949 |
| ☐ | N14950 | Embraer ERJ-145 | 145061 | 950 |
| ☐ | N16951 | Embraer ERJ-145 | 145063 | 951 |
| ☐ | N14952 | Embraer ERJ-145 | 145067 | 952 |
| ☐ | N14953 | Embraer ERJ-145 | 145071 | 953 |
| ☐ | N16954 | Embraer ERJ-145 | 145072 | 954 |
| ☐ | N13955 | Embraer ERJ-145 | 145075 | 955 |
| ☐ | N13956 | Embraer ERJ-145 | 145078 | 956 |
| ☐ | N12957 | Embraer ERJ-145 | 145080 | 957 |
| ☐ | N13958 | Embraer ERJ-145 | 145085 | 958 |
| ☐ | N14959 | Embraer ERJ-145 | 145091 | 959 |
| ☐ | N14960 | Embraer ERJ-145 | 145100 | 960 |
| ☐ | N16961 | Embraer ERJ-145 | 145103 | 961 |
| ☐ | N27962 | Embraer ERJ-145 | 145110 | 962 |
| ☐ | N16963 | Embraer ERJ-145 | 145116 | 963 |
| ☐ | N13964 | Embraer ERJ-145 | 145123 | 964 |
| ☐ | N13965 | Embraer ERJ-145 | 145125 | 965 |
| ☐ | N19966 | Embraer ERJ-145 | 145131 | 966 |
| ☐ | N12967 | Embraer ERJ-145 | 145133 | 967 |
| ☐ | N13968 | Embraer ERJ-145 | 145138 | 968 |
| ☐ | N13969 | Embraer ERJ-145 | 145141 | 969 |
| ☐ | N13970 | Embraer ERJ-145 | 145146 | 970 |
| ☐ | N22971 | Embraer ERJ-145 | 145149 | 971 |
| ☐ | N14972 | Embraer ERJ-145 | 145151 | 972 |
| ☐ | N15973 | Embraer ERJ-145 | 145159 | 973 |
| ☐ | N14974 | Embraer ERJ-145 | 145161 | 974 |
| ☐ | N13975 | Embraer ERJ-145 | 145163 | 975 |
| ☐ | N16976 | Embraer ERJ-145 | 145171 | 976 |
| ☐ | N14977 | Embraer ERJ-145 | 145175 | 977 |
| ☐ | N13978 | Embraer ERJ-145 | 145180 | 978 |
| ☐ | N13979 | Embraer ERJ-145 | 145181 | 979 |
| ☐ | N15980 | Embraer ERJ-145 | 145202 | 980 |
| ☐ | N16981 | Embraer ERJ-145 | 145208 | 981 |
| ☐ | N18982 | Embraer ERJ-145 | 145223 | 982 |
| ☐ | N15983 | Embraer ERJ-145 | 145239 | 983 |
| ☐ | N17984 | Embraer ERJ-145 | 145246 | 984 |
| ☐ | N15985 | Embraer ERJ-145 | 145248 | 985 |
| ☐ | N15986 | Embraer ERJ-145 | 145254 | 986 |
| ☐ | N16987 | Embraer ERJ-145 | 145261 | 987 |
| ☐ | N13988 | Embraer ERJ-145 | 145265 | 988 |
| ☐ | N13989 | Embraer ERJ-145 | 145271 | 989 |
| ☐ | N13990 | Embraer ERJ-145 | 145277 | 990 |
| ☐ | N14991 | Embraer ERJ-145 | 145278 | 991 |
| ☐ | N13992 | Embraer ERJ-145 | 145284 | 992 |
| ☐ | N13993 | Embraer ERJ-145 | 145289 | 993 |
| ☐ | N13994 | Embraer ERJ-145 | 145291 | 994 |
| ☐ | N13995 | Embraer ERJ-145 | 145295 | 995 |
| ☐ | N12996 | Embraer ERJ-145 | 145296 | 996 |
| ☐ | N13997 | Embraer ERJ-145 | 145298 | 997 |
| ☐ | N14998 | Embraer ERJ-145 | 145302 | 998 |
| ☐ | N16999 | Embraer ERJ-145 | 145307 | 999 |
| ☐ | N18101 | Embraer ERJ-145XR | 145590 | |
| ☐ | N18102 | Embraer ERJ-145XR | 145643 | |
| ☐ | N24103 | Embraer ERJ-145XR | 145645 | |
| ☐ | N41104 | Embraer ERJ-145XR | 145646 | |
| ☐ | N14105 | Embraer ERJ-145XR | 145649 | |
| ☐ | N11106 | Embraer ERJ-145XR | 145650 | |
| ☐ | N11107 | Embraer ERJ-145XR | 145654 | |
| ☐ | N17108 | Embraer ERJ-145XR | 145655 | |
| ☐ | N11109 | Embraer ERJ-145XR | 145657 | |
| ☐ | N34110 | Embraer ERJ-145XR | 145658 | |
| ☐ | N34111 | Embraer ERJ-145XR | 145659 | |
| ☐ | N16112 | Embraer ERJ-145XR | 145660 | |
| ☐ | N11113 | Embraer ERJ-145XR | 145662 | |
| ☐ | N18114 | Embraer ERJ-145XR | 145664 | |
| ☐ | N17115 | Embraer ERJ-145XR | 145666 | |
| ☐ | N14116 | Embraer ERJ-145XR | 145672 | |
| ☐ | N14117 | Embraer ERJ-145XR | 145674 | |
| ☐ | N13118 | Embraer ERJ-145XR | 145675 | |
| ☐ | N11121 | Embraer ERJ-145XR | 145683 | |

| | | | |
|---|---|---|---|
| ☐ N | Embraer ERJ-145XR | | o/o |
| ☐ N | Embraer ERJ-145XR | | o/o |
| ☐ N | Embraer ERJ-145XR | | o/o |
| ☐ N | Embraer ERJ-145XR | | o/o |
| ☐ N | Embraer ERJ-145XR | | o/o |
| ☐ N | Embraer ERJ-145XR | | o/o |
| ☐ N | Embraer ERJ-145XR | | o/o |
| ☐ N | Embraer ERJ-145XR | | o/o |
| ☐ N | Embraer ERJ-145XR | | o/o |
| ☐ N | Embraer ERJ-145XR | | o/o |
| ☐ N | Embraer ERJ-145XR | | o/o |
| ☐ N | Embraer ERJ-145XR | | o/o |
| ☐ N | Embraer ERJ-145XR | | o/o |
| ☐ N | Embraer ERJ-145XR | | o/o |
| ☐ N | Embraer ERJ-145XR | | o/o |
| ☐ N | Embraer ERJ-145XR | | o/o |
| ☐ N | Embraer ERJ-145XR | | o/o |
| ☐ N | Embraer ERJ-145XR | | o/o |
| ☐ N | Embraer ERJ-145XR | | o/o |
| ☐ N | Embraer ERJ-145XR | | o/o |
| ☐ N | Embraer ERJ-145XR | | o/o |
| ☐ N | Embraer ERJ-145XR | | o/o |
| ☐ N | Embraer ERJ-145XR | | o/o |
| ☐ N | Embraer ERJ-145XR | | o/o |

## CONTINENTAL MICRONESIA — CMI

A subsidiary of **Continental Airlines** and operates
Boeing 737-824's leased from the parent as required

## CONRACT AIR CARGO — TSU

| | | |
|---|---|---|
| ☐ N211FL | Boeing 727-172C | 575/19807 |
| ☐ N221FL | Boeing 727-22C | 543/19805 |
| ☐ N231FL | Boeing 727-22C | 438/19205 |

## CSA AIR — IRO

Operates Cessna 208s for **FedEx** (q.v.)

## CUSTOM AIR TRANSPORT — CTT

| | | | |
|---|---|---|---|
| ☐ N220NE | Boeing 727-31F | 160/18905 | |
| ☐ N511PE | Boeing 727-232F | 917/20634 | |
| ☐ N721RW | Boeing 727-2M7F | 1206/21200 | std |
| ☐ N902PG | Boeing 727-281F | 958/20725 | |
| ☐ N920PG | Boeing 727-287F | 1415/21688 | |
| ☐ N8887Z | Boeing 727-281F | 1537/21856 | |
| ☐ N24343 | Boeing 727-231F | 1458/21630 | |
| ☐ N54354 | Boeing 727-231F | 1580/21986 | |

Some operated for **Charter America** as and when reqd

## DELTA AIR LINES — DAL

| | | | |
|---|---|---|---|
| ☐ N282WA | Boeing 727-247 | 1362/21484 | 579; std |
| ☐ N283WA | Boeing 727-247 | 1364/21485 | 580 |
| ☐ N291WA | Boeing 727-247 | 1589/22109 | 583 |
| ☐ N292WA | Boeing 727-247 | 1613/22110 | 584; std |
| ☐ N294WA | Boeing 727-247 | 1618/22112 | 586; std |
| ☐ N295WA | Boeing 727-247 | 1730/22532 | 587; std |
| ☐ N296WA | Boeing 727-247 | 1736/22533 | 588 |
| ☐ N297WA | Boeing 727-247 | 1738/22534 | 589 |
| ☐ N504DA | Boeing 727-232 | 1270/21306 | 504 |
| ☐ N509DA | Boeing 727-232 | 1300/21311 | 509; std |
| ☐ N516DA | Boeing 727-232 | 1381/21432 | 516 |
| ☐ N518DA | Boeing 727-232 | 1398/21469 | 518 |
| ☐ N521DA | Boeing 727-232 | 1413/21472 | 521 |
| ☐ N522DA | Boeing 727-232 | 1422/21582 | 522 |
| ☐ N523DA | Boeing 727-232 | 1423/21583 | 523 |
| ☐ N532DA | Boeing 727-232 | 1602/22045 | 532 |
| ☐ N533DA | Boeing 727-232 | 1604/22046 | 533 |
| ☐ N544DA | Boeing 727-232 | 1741/22493 | 544 |
| ☐ N545DA | Boeing 727-232 | 1749/22494 | 545; std |
| ☐ N546DA | Boeing 727-232 | 1785/22677 | 546; std |
| ☐ N805EA | Boeing 727-225 | 1677/22436 | 590 |
| ☐ N830WA | Boeing 727-247 | 1341/21482 | 577 |

| | | | |
|---|---|---|---|
| ☐ N8873Z | Boeing 727-225 | 1239/21291 | 445 |
| ☐ N8875Z | Boeing 727-225 | 1241/21293 | 441 |
| ☐ N8882Z | Boeing 727-225 | 1412/21579 | 591 |
| ☐ N8891Z | Boeing 727-225 | 1546/21860 | 439 |
| | | | |
| ☐ N235WA | Boeing 737-2J8 | 890/22859 | 359; std |
| ☐ N236WA | Boeing 737-247 | 1061/23184 | 360; std |
| ☐ N237WA | Boeing 737-247 | 1065/23185 | 361; std |
| ☐ N238WA | Boeing 737-247 | 1066/23186 | 362; std |
| ☐ N239WA | Boeing 737-247 | 1070/23187 | 363; std |
| ☐ N242WA | Boeing 737-247 | 1257/23516 | 364; std |
| ☐ N243WA | Boeing 737-247 | 1261/23517 | 365; std |
| ☐ N244WA | Boeing 737-247 | 1265/23518 | 366; std |
| ☐ N245WA | Boeing 737-247 | 1299/23519 | 372 |
| ☐ N301DL | Boeing 737-232 | 991/23073 | 301; std |
| ☐ N302DL | Boeing 737-232 | 993/23074 | 302; std |
| ☐ N303DL | Boeing 737-232 | 994/23075 | 303 |
| ☐ N304DL | Boeing 737-232 | 995/23076 | 304 |
| ☐ N305DL | Boeing 737-232 | 996/23077 | 305 |
| ☐ N306DL | Boeing 737-232 | 1000/23078 | 306 |
| ☐ N307DL | Boeing 737-232 | 1003/23079 | 307 |
| ☐ N308DL | Boeing 737-232 | 1004/23080 | 308 |
| ☐ N309DL | Boeing 737-232 | 1005/23081 | 309; std |
| ☐ N310DA | Boeing 737-232 | 1006/23082 | 310 |
| ☐ N311DL | Boeing 737-232 | 1008/23083 | 311 |
| ☐ N312DL | Boeing 737-232 | 1009/23084 | 312 |
| ☐ N313DL | Boeing 737-232 | 1011/23085 | 313 |
| ☐ N314DA | Boeing 737-232 | 1012/23086 | 314 |
| ☐ N315DL | Boeing 737-232 | 1013/23087 | 315 |
| ☐ N316DL | Boeing 737-232 | 1018/23088 | 316; std |
| ☐ N317DL | Boeing 737-232 | 1019/23089 | 317 |
| ☐ N318DL | Boeing 737-232 | 1020/23090 | 318 |
| ☐ N319DL | Boeing 737-232 | 1021/23091 | 319; std |
| ☐ N320DL | Boeing 737-232 | 1023/23092 | 320 |
| ☐ N321DL | Boeing 737-232 | 1024/23093 | 321 |
| ☐ N322DL | Boeing 737-232 | 1026/23094 | 322; std |
| ☐ N323DL | Boeing 737-232 | 1027/23095 | 323 |
| ☐ N324DL | Boeing 737-232 | 1028/23096 | 324; std |
| ☐ N325DL | Boeing 737-232 | 1029/23097 | 325 |
| ☐ N326DL | Boeing 737-232 | 1031/23098 | 326; std |
| ☐ N327DL | Boeing 737-232 | 1035/23099 | 327 |
| ☐ N328DL | Boeing 737-232 | 1038/23100 | 328; std |
| ☐ N329DL | Boeing 737-232 | 1041/23101 | 329; std |
| ☐ N330DL | Boeing 737-232 | 1045/23102 | 330; std |
| ☐ N331DL | Boeing 737-232 | 1051/23103 | 331; std |
| ☐ N332DL | Boeing 737-232 | 1062/23104 | 332; std |
| ☐ N334DL | Boeing 737-232 | 1068/23105 | 334; std |
| ☐ N367DL | Boeing 737-2S3 | 563/21774 | 367; std |
| ☐ N369DL | Boeing 737-2S3 | 577/21776 | 369; std |
| ☐ N373DL | Boeing 737-247 | 1329/23520 | 373 |
| ☐ N374DL | Boeing 737-247 | 1342/23521 | 374; std |
| ☐ N375DL | Boeing 737-247 | 1347/23602 | 375 |
| ☐ N376DL | Boeing 737-247 | 1361/23603 | 376 |
| ☐ N377DL | Boeing 737-247 | 1369/23604 | 377 |
| ☐ N378DL | Boeing 737-247 | 1371/23605 | 378 |
| ☐ N379DL | Boeing 737-247 | 1379/23606 | 379 |
| ☐ N380DL | Boeing 737-247 | 1387/23607 | 380 |
| ☐ N381DL | Boeing 737-247 | 1399/23608 | 381; std |
| ☐ N382DL | Boeing 737-247 | 1403/23609 | 382 |
| ☐ N221DL | Boeing 737-35B | 1467/23970 | 221; std |
| ☐ N222DZ | Boeing 737-35B | 1482/23971 | 222; std |
| ☐ N223DZ | Boeing 737-35B | 1537/23972 | 223; std |
| ☐ N224DA | Boeing 737-35B | 1628/24269 | 224; std |
| ☐ N225DL | Boeing 737-35B | 2053/25069 | 225; std |
| ☐ N231DN | Boeing 737-35B | 1365/23717 | 231; std |
| ☐ N232DZ | Boeing 737-35B | 1602/24220 | 232; std |
| ☐ N241DL | Boeing 737-330 | 1439/23833 | 241; std |
| ☐ N242DL | Boeing 737-330 | 1454/23834 | 242; std |
| ☐ N302WA | Boeing 737-347 | 1106/23182 | 202 |
| ☐ N303WA | Boeing 737-347 | 1108/23183 | 203 |
| ☐ N304WA | Boeing 737-347 | 1170/23345 | 204 |
| ☐ N305WA | Boeing 737-347 | 1172/23346 | 205 |
| ☐ N306WA | Boeing 737-347 | 1173/23347 | 206 |
| ☐ N307WA | Boeing 737-347 | 1218/23440 | 207 |
| ☐ N308WA | Boeing 737-347 | 1220/23441 | 208 |
| ☐ N309WA | Boeing 737-347 | 1239/23442 | 209 |
| ☐ N311WA | Boeing 737-347 | 1287/23597 | 211 |
| ☐ N312WA | Boeing 737-347 | 1289/23598 | 212 |

| | | | |
|---|---|---|---|
| ☐ N313WA | Boeing 737-347 | 1324/23599 | 213 |
| ☐ N947WP | Boeing 737-3B7 | 1308/23376 | 253 |
| ☐ N948WP | Boeing 737-301 | 1132/23259 | 252 |
| ☐ N951WP | Boeing 737-3B7 | 1007/22951 | 251 |
| ☐ N952WP | Boeing 737-3B7 | 1339/23378 | 254 |
| ☐ N2310 | Boeing 737-347 | 1269/23596 | 210 |
| ☐ N3301 | Boeing 737-347 | 1087/23181 | 201 |
| | | | |
| ☐ N371DA | Boeing 737-832 | 115/29619 | 3701; std |
| ☐ N372DA | Boeing 737-832 | 118/29620 | 3702 |
| ☐ N373DA | Boeing 737-832 | 123/29621 | 3703; std |
| ☐ N374DA | Boeing 737-832 | 128/29622 | 3704; std |
| ☐ N375DA | Boeing 737-832 | 145/29623 | 3705; std |
| ☐ N376DA | Boeing 737-832 | 176/29624 | 3706; std |
| ☐ N377DA | Boeing 737-832 | 264/29625 | 3707; std |
| ☐ N378DA | Boeing 737-832 | 340/30265 | 3708; std |
| ☐ N379DA | Boeing 737-832 | 351/30349 | 3709 |
| ☐ N380DA | Boeing 737-832 | 361/30266 | 3710 |
| ☐ N381DN | Boeing 737-832 | 365/30350 | 3711 |
| ☐ N382DA | Boeing 737-832 | 389/30345 | 3712 |
| ☐ N383DN | Boeing 737-832 | 393/30346 | 3713 |
| ☐ N384DA | Boeing 737-832 | 412/30347 | 3714 |
| ☐ N385DA | Boeing 737-832 | 418/30348 | 3715 |
| ☐ N386DA | Boeing 737-832 | 446/30373 | 3716 |
| ☐ N387DA | Boeing 737-832 | 457/30374 | 3717 |
| ☐ N388DA | Boeing 737-832 | 469/30375 | 3718 |
| ☐ N389DA | Boeing 737-832 | 513/30376 | 3719 |
| ☐ N390DA | Boeing 737-832 | 518/30536 | 3720 |
| ☐ N391DA | Boeing 737-832 | 535/30560 | 3721 |
| ☐ N392DA | Boeing 737-832 | 564/30561 | 3722 |
| ☐ N393DA | Boeing 737-832 | 584/30377 | 3723 |
| ☐ N394DA | Boeing 737-832 | 589/30562 | 3724 |
| ☐ N395DN | Boeing 737-832 | 604/30773 | 3725 |
| ☐ N396DA | Boeing 737-832 | 632/30378 | 3726 |
| ☐ N397DA | Boeing 737-832 | 638/30537 | 3727 |
| ☐ N398DA | Boeing 737-832 | 641/30774 | 3728 |
| ☐ N399DA | Boeing 737-832 | 657/30379 | 3729 |
| ☐ N3730B | Boeing 737-832 | 662/30538 | 3730 |
| ☐ N3731T | Boeing 737-832 | 665/30775 | 3731 |
| ☐ N3732J | Boeing 737-832 | 674/30380 | 3732 |
| ☐ N3733Z | Boeing 737-832 | 685/30539 | 3733 |
| ☐ N3734B | Boeing 737-832 | 689/30776 | 3734 |
| ☐ N3735D | Boeing 737-832 | 694/30381 | 3735 |
| ☐ N3736C | Boeing 737-832 | 709/30540 | 3736 |
| ☐ N3737C | Boeing 737-832 | 712/30799 | 3737 |
| ☐ N3738B | Boeing 737-832 | 723/30382 | 3738 |
| ☐ N3739P | Boeing 737-832 | 729/30541 | 3739 |
| ☐ N3740C | Boeing 737-832 | 732/30800 | 3740 |
| ☐ N3741S | Boeing 737-832 | 750/30487 | 3741 |
| ☐ N3742C | Boeing 737-832 | 755/30835 | 3742 |
| ☐ N3743H | Boeing 737-832 | 770/30836 | 3743 |
| ☐ N3744F | Boeing 737-832 | 805/30837 | 3744 |
| ☐ N3745B | Boeing 737-832 | 831/32373 | 3745 |
| ☐ N3746H | Boeing 737-832 | 842/30488 | 3746 |
| ☐ N3747D | Boeing 737-832 | 846/32374 | 3747 |
| ☐ N3748Y | Boeing 737-832 | 865/30489 | 3748 |
| ☐ N3749D | Boeing 737-832 | 867/30490 | 3749 |
| ☐ N3750D | Boeing 737-832 | 870/32375 | 3750 |
| ☐ N3751B | Boeing 737-832 | 892/30491 | 3751 |
| ☐ N3752 | Boeing 737-832 | 894/30492 | 3752 |
| ☐ N3753 | Boeing 737-832 | 899/32626 | 3753 |
| ☐ N3754A | Boeing 737-832 | 907/29626 | 3754 |
| ☐ N3755D | Boeing 737-832 | 914/29627 | 3755 |
| ☐ N3756 | Boeing 737-832 | 917/30493 | 3756 |
| ☐ N3757D | Boeing 737-832 | 921/30813 | 3757 |
| ☐ N3758Y | Boeing 737-832 | 923/30814 | 3758 |
| ☐ N3759 | Boeing 737-832 | 949/30815 | 3759 |
| ☐ N3760C | Boeing 737-832 | 952/30816 | 3760 |
| ☐ N3761R | Boeing 737-832 | 964/29628 | 3761 |
| ☐ N3762Y | Boeing 737-832 | 968/30817 | 3762 |
| ☐ N3763D | Boeing 737-832 | 1003/29629 | 3763 |
| ☐ N3764D | Boeing 737-832 | 1006/30818 | 3764 |
| ☐ N3765 | Boeing 737-832 | 1008/30819 | 3765 |
| ☐ N3766 | Boeing 737-832 | 1029/30820 | 3766 |
| ☐ N3767 | Boeing 737-832 | 1031/30821 | 3767 |
| ☐ N3768 | Boeing 737-832 | 1053/29630 | 3768 |
| ☐ N3769L | Boeing 737-832 | 1057/30822 | 3769 |
| ☐ N3771K | Boeing 737-832 | 1103/29632 | 3771 |
| ☐ N3772H | Boeing 737-832 | 29633 | 3772 o/o |
| ☐ N3773C | Boeing 737-832 | 29634 | 3773 o/o |
| ☐ N3774C | Boeing 737-832 | 30824 | 3774 o/o |
| ☐ N3775 | Boeing 737-832 | 30826 | 3775 o/o |
| ☐ N3776D | Boeing 737-832 | 29635 | 3776 o/o |
| ☐ N37700 | Boeing 737-832 | 1074/29631 | 3770 |
| | | | |
| ☐ N601DL | Boeing 757-232 | 37/22808 | 601 |
| ☐ N602DL | Boeing 757-232 | 39/22809 | 602 |
| ☐ N603DL | Boeing 757-232 | 41/22810 | 603 |
| ☐ N604DL | Boeing 757-232 | 43/22811 | 604 |
| ☐ N605DL | Boeing 757-232 | 46/22812 | 605 |
| ☐ N606DL | Boeing 757-232 | 49/22813 | 606 |
| ☐ N607DL | Boeing 757-232 | 61/22814 | 607 |
| ☐ N608DA | Boeing 757-232 | 64/22815 | 608 |
| ☐ N609DL | Boeing 757-232 | 65/22816 | 609 |
| ☐ N610DL | Boeing 757-232 | 66/22817 | 610 |
| ☐ N611DL | Boeing 757-232 | 71/22818 | 611 |
| ☐ N612DL | Boeing 757-232 | 73/22819 | 612 |
| ☐ N613DL | Boeing 757-232 | 84/22820 | 613 |
| ☐ N614DL | Boeing 757-232 | 85/22821 | 614 |
| ☐ N615DL | Boeing 757-232 | 87/22822 | 615 |
| ☐ N616DL | Boeing 757-232 | 91/22823 | 616 |
| ☐ N617DL | Boeing 757-232 | 92/22907 | 617 |
| ☐ N618DL | Boeing 757-232 | 95/22908 | 618 |
| ☐ N619DL | Boeing 757-232 | 101/22909 | 619 |
| ☐ N620DL | Boeing 757-232 | 111/22910 | 620 |
| ☐ N621DL | Boeing 757-232 | 112/22911 | 621 |
| ☐ N622DL | Boeing 757-232 | 113/22912 | 622 |
| ☐ N623DL | Boeing 757-232 | 118/22913 | 623 |
| ☐ N624DL | Boeing 757-232 | 120/22914 | 624 |
| ☐ N625DL | Boeing 757-232 | 126/22915 | 625 |
| ☐ N626DL | Boeing 757-232 | 128/22916 | 626 |
| ☐ N627DL | Boeing 757-232 | 129/22917 | 627 |
| ☐ N628DL | Boeing 757-232 | 133/22918 | 628 |
| ☐ N629DL | Boeing 757-232 | 134/22919 | 629 |
| ☐ N630DL | Boeing 757-232 | 135/22920 | 630 |
| ☐ N631DL | Boeing 757-232 | 138/23612 | 631 |
| ☐ N632DL | Boeing 757-232 | 154/23613 | 632 |
| ☐ N633DL | Boeing 757-232 | 157/23614 | 633 |
| ☐ N634DL | Boeing 757-232 | 158/23615 | 634 |
| ☐ N635DL | Boeing 757-232 | 159/23762 | 635 |
| ☐ N636DL | Boeing 757-232 | 164/23763 | 636 |
| ☐ N637DL | Boeing 757-232 | 171/23760 | 637 |
| ☐ N638DL | Boeing 757-232 | 177/23761 | 638 |
| ☐ N639DL | Boeing 757-232 | 198/23993 | 638 |
| ☐ N640DL | Boeing 757-232 | 201/23994 | 640 |
| ☐ N641DL | Boeing 757-232 | 202/23995 | 641 |
| ☐ N642DL | Boeing 757-232 | 205/23996 | 642 |
| ☐ N643DL | Boeing 757-232 | 206/23997 | 643 |
| ☐ N644DL | Boeing 757-232 | 207/23998 | 644 |
| ☐ N645DL | Boeing 757-232 | 216/24216 | 645 |
| ☐ N646DL | Boeing 757-232 | 217/24217 | 646 |
| ☐ N647DL | Boeing 757-232 | 222/24218 | 647 |
| ☐ N648DL | Boeing 757-232 | 223/24372 | 648 |
| ☐ N649DL | Boeing 757-232 | 229/24389 | 649 |
| ☐ N650DL | Boeing 757-232 | 230/24390 | 650 |
| ☐ N651DL | Boeing 757-232 | 238/24391 | 651 |
| ☐ N652DL | Boeing 757-232 | 239/24392 | 652 |
| ☐ N653DL | Boeing 757-232 | 261/24393 | 653 |
| ☐ N654DL | Boeing 757-232 | 264/24394 | 654 |
| ☐ N655DL | Boeing 757-232 | 265/24395 | 655 |
| ☐ N656DL | Boeing 757-232 | 266/24396 | 656 |
| ☐ N657DL | Boeing 757-232 | 286/24419 | 657 |
| ☐ N658DL | Boeing 757-232 | 287/24420 | 658 |
| ☐ N659DL | Boeing 757-232 | 293/24421 | 659 |
| ☐ N660DL | Boeing 757-232 | 294/24422 | 660 |
| ☐ N661DN | Boeing 757-232 | 335/24972 | 661 |
| ☐ N662DN | Boeing 757-232 | 342/24991 | 662 |
| ☐ N663DN | Boeing 757-232 | 343/24992 | 663 |
| ☐ N664DN | Boeing 757-232 | 347/25012 | 664 |
| ☐ N665DN | Boeing 757-232 | 349/25013 | 665 |
| ☐ N666DN | Boeing 757-232 | 354/25034 | 666 |
| ☐ N667DN | Boeing 757-232 | 355/25035 | 667 |
| ☐ N668DN | Boeing 757-232 | 376/25141 | 668 |
| ☐ N669DN | Boeing 757-232 | 377/25142 | 669 |
| ☐ N670DN | Boeing 757-232 | 415/25331 | 670 |
| ☐ N671DN | Boeing 757-232 | 416/25332 | 671 |

| | Registration | Type | c/n | Fleet No. |
|---|---|---|---|---|
| ☐ | N672DL | Boeing 757-232 | 429/25977 | 672 |
| ☐ | N673DL | Boeing 757-232 | 430/25978 | 673 |
| ☐ | N674DL | Boeing 757-232 | 439/25979 | 674 |
| ☐ | N675DL | Boeing 757-232 | 448/25980 | 675 |
| ☐ | N676DL | Boeing 757-232 | 455/25981 | 676 |
| ☐ | N677DL | Boeing 757-232 | 456/25982 | 677 |
| ☐ | N678DL | Boeing 757-232 | 465/25983 | 678 |
| ☐ | N679DA | Boeing 757-232 | 500/26955 | 679 |
| ☐ | N680DA | Boeing 757-232 | 502/26956 | 680 |
| ☐ | N681DA | Boeing 757-232 | 516/26957 | 681 |
| ☐ | N682DA | Boeing 757-232 | 518/26958 | 682 |
| ☐ | N683DA | Boeing 757-232 | 533/27103 | 683 |
| ☐ | N684DA | Boeing 757-232 | 535/27104 | 684 |
| ☐ | N685DA | Boeing 757-232 | 667/27588 | 685 |
| ☐ | N686DA | Boeing 757-232 | 689/27589 | 686 |
| ☐ | N687DL | Boeing 757-232 | 800/27586 | 687 |
| ☐ | N688DL | Boeing 757-232 | 803/27587 | 688 |
| ☐ | N689DL | Boeing 757-232 | 807/27172 | 689 |
| ☐ | N690DL | Boeing 757-232 | 808/27585 | 690 |
| ☐ | N692DL | Boeing 757-232 | 820/29724 | 692 |
| ☐ | N693DL | Boeing 757-232 | 826/29725 | 693 |
| ☐ | N694DL | Boeing 757-232 | 831/29726 | 694 |
| ☐ | N695DL | Boeing 757-232 | 838/29727 | 695 |
| ☐ | N696DL | Boeing 757-232 | 845/29728 | 696 |
| ☐ | N697DL | Boeing 757-232 | 880/30318 | 697 |
| ☐ | N698DL | Boeing 757-232 | 885/29911 | 698 |
| ☐ | N699DL | Boeing 757-232 | 887/29970 | 699 |
| ☐ | N750AT | Boeing 757-212ER | 45/23126 | 6902 |
| ☐ | N751AT | Boeing 757-212ER | 44/23125 | 6901 |
| ☐ | N752AT | Boeing 757-212ER | 48/23128 | 6904 |
| ☐ | N757AT | Boeing 757-212ER | 47/23127 | 6903 |
| ☐ | N900PC | Boeing 757-26D | 740/28446 | 691 |
| ☐ | N6700 | Boeing 757-232 | 890/30337 | 6700 |
| ☐ | N6701 | Boeing 757-232 | 892/30187 | 6701 |
| ☐ | N6702 | Boeing 757-232 | 898/30188 | 6702 |
| ☐ | N6703D | Boeing 757-232 | 908/30234 | 6703 |
| ☐ | N6704Z | Boeing 757-232 | 914/30396 | 6704 |
| ☐ | N6705Y | Boeing 757-232 | 917/30397 | 6705 |
| ☐ | N6706Q | Boeing 757-232 | 921/30422 | 6706 |
| ☐ | N6707A | Boeing 757-232 | 927/30395 | 6707 |
| ☐ | N6708D | Boeing 757-232 | 934/30480 | 6708 |
| ☐ | N6709 | Boeing 757-232 | 937/30481 | 6709 |
| ☐ | N6710E | Boeing 757-232 | 939/30482 | 6710 |
| ☐ | N6711M | Boeing 757-232 | 941/30483 | 6711 |
| ☐ | N6712B | Boeing 757-232 | 942/30484 | 6712 |
| ☐ | N6713Y | Boeing 757-232 | 944/30777 | 6713 |
| ☐ | N6714Q | Boeing 757-232 | 949/30485 | 6714 |
| ☐ | N6715C | Boeing 757-232 | 953/30486 | 6715 |
| ☐ | N6716C | Boeing 757-232 | 955/30838 | 6716 |
| ☐ | N67171 | Boeing 757-232 | 959/30839 | 6717 |
| ☐ | N101DA | Boeing 767-232 | 6/22213 | 101 |
| ☐ | N102DA | Boeing 767-232 | 12/22214 | 102 |
| ☐ | N103DA | Boeing 767-232 | 17/22215 | 103 |
| ☐ | N104DA | Boeing 767-232 | 26/22216 | 104 |
| ☐ | N105DA | Boeing 767-232 | 27/22217 | 105 |
| ☐ | N106DA | Boeing 767-232 | 31/22218 | 106 |
| ☐ | N107DL | Boeing 767-232 | 37/22219 | 107 |
| ☐ | N108DL | Boeing 767-232 | 38/22220 | 108 |
| ☐ | N109DL | Boeing 767-232 | 53/22221 | 109 |
| ☐ | N110DL | Boeing 767-232 | 56/22222 | 110 |
| ☐ | N111DN | Boeing 767-232 | 74/22223 | 111 |
| ☐ | N112DL | Boeing 767-232 | 76/22224 | 112; std |
| ☐ | N113DA | Boeing 767-232 | 77/22225 | 113 |
| ☐ | N114DL | Boeing 767-232 | 78/22226 | 114; std |
| ☐ | N115DA | Boeing 767-232 | 83/22227 | 115; std |
| ☐ | N116DL | Boeing 767-332 | 136/23275 | 116 |
| ☐ | N117DL | Boeing 767-332 | 151/23276 | 117 |
| ☐ | N118DL | Boeing 767-332 | 152/23277 | 118 |
| ☐ | N119DL | Boeing 767-332 | 153/23278 | 119 |
| ☐ | N120DL | Boeing 767-332 | 154/23279 | 120 |
| ☐ | N121DE | Boeing 767-332 | 162/23435 | 121 |
| ☐ | N122DL | Boeing 767-332 | 163/23436 | 122 |
| ☐ | N123DN | Boeing 767-332 | 188/23437 | 123 |
| ☐ | N124DE | Boeing 767-332 | 189/23438 | 124 |
| ☐ | N125DL | Boeing 767-332 | 200/24075 | 125 |
| ☐ | N126DL | Boeing 767-332 | 201/24076 | 126 |
| ☐ | N127DL | Boeing 767-332 | 203/24077 | 127 |
| ☐ | N128DL | Boeing 767-332 | 207/24078 | 128 |
| ☐ | N129DL | Boeing 767-332 | 209/24079 | 129 |
| ☐ | N130DL | Boeing 767-332 | 216/24080 | 130 |
| ☐ | N131DN | Boeing 767-332 | 320/24852 | 131 |
| ☐ | N132DN | Boeing 767-332 | 345/24981 | 132 |
| ☐ | N133DN | Boeing 767-332 | 348/24982 | 133 |
| ☐ | N134DL | Boeing 767-332 | 353/25123 | 134 |
| ☐ | N135DL | Boeing 767-332 | 356/25145 | 135 |
| ☐ | N136DL | Boeing 767-332 | 374/25146 | 136 |
| ☐ | N137DL | Boeing 767-332 | 392/25306 | 137 |
| ☐ | N138DL | Boeing 767-332 | 410/25409 | 138 |
| ☐ | N139DL | Boeing 767-332 | 427/25984 | 139 |
| ☐ | N140LL | Boeing 767-332 | 499/25988 | 1401 |
| ☐ | N143DA | Boeing 767-332 | 721/25991 | 1403 |
| ☐ | N144DA | Boeing 767-332 | 751/27584 | 1404 |
| ☐ | N152DL | Boeing 767-3P6ER | 339/24984 | 1502 |
| ☐ | N153DL | Boeing 767-3P6ER | 340/24985 | 1503 |
| ☐ | N154DL | Boeing 767-3P6ER | 389/25241 | 1504 |
| ☐ | N155DL | Boeing 767-3P6ER | 390/25269 | 1505 |
| ☐ | N156DL | Boeing 767-3P6ER | 406/25354 | 1506 |
| ☐ | N169DL | Boeing 767-332ER | 706/29689 | 1601 |
| ☐ | N171DN | Boeing 767-332ER | 304/24759 | 171 |
| ☐ | N171DZ | Boeing 767-332ER | 717/29690 | 1701 |
| ☐ | N172DN | Boeing 767-332ER | 312/24775 | 172 |
| ☐ | N172DZ | Boeing 767-332ER | 719/29691 | 1702 |
| ☐ | N173DN | Boeing 767-332ER | 313/24800 | 173 |
| ☐ | N173DZ | Boeing 767-332ER | 723/29692 | 1703 |
| ☐ | N174DN | Boeing 767-332ER | 317/24802 | 174 |
| ☐ | N174DZ | Boeing 767-332ER | 725/29693 | 1704 |
| ☐ | N175DN | Boeing 767-332ER | 318/24803 | 175 |
| ☐ | N175DZ | Boeing 767-332ER | 740/29696 | 1705 |
| ☐ | N176DN | Boeing 767-332ER | 341/25061 | 176 |
| ☐ | N176DZ | Boeing 767-332ER | 745/29697 | 1706 |
| ☐ | N177DN | Boeing 767-332ER | 346/25122 | 177 |
| ☐ | N177DZ | Boeing 767-332ER | 750/29698 | 1707 |
| ☐ | N178DN | Boeing 767-332ER | 349/25143 | 178 |
| ☐ | N178DZ | Boeing 767-332ER | 795/30596 | 1708 |
| ☐ | N179DN | Boeing 767-332ER | 350/25144 | 179 |
| ☐ | N180DN | Boeing 767-332ER | 428/25985 | 180 |
| ☑ | N181DN | Boeing 767-332ER | 446/25986 | 181 |
| ☐ | N182DN | Boeing 767-332ER | 461/25987 | 182 |
| ☐ | N183DN | Boeing 767-332ER | 492/27110 | 183 |
| ☐ | N184DN | Boeing 767-332ER | 496/27111 | 184 |
| ☐ | N185DN | Boeing 767-332ER | 576/27961 | 185 |
| ☐ | N186DN | Boeing 767-332ER | 585/27962 | 186 |
| ☐ | N187DN | Boeing 767-332ER | 617/27582 | 187 |
| ☐ | N188DN | Boeing 767-332ER | 631/27583 | 188 |
| ☐ | N189DN | Boeing 767-332ER | 646/25990 | 189 |
| ☐ | N190DN | Boeing 767-332ER | 653/28447 | 190 |
| ☐ | N191DN | Boeing 767-332ER | 654/28448 | 191 |
| ☐ | N192DN | Boeing 767-332ER | 664/28449 | 192 |
| ☐ | N193DN | Boeing 767-332ER | 671/28450 | 193 |
| ☐ | N194DN | Boeing 767-332ER | 675/28451 | 194 |
| ☐ | N195DN | Boeing 767-332ER | 676/28452 | 195 |
| ☐ | N196DN | Boeing 767-332ER | 679/28453 | 196 |
| ☐ | N197DN | Boeing 767-332ER | 683/28454 | 197 |
| ☐ | N198DN | Boeing 767-332ER | 685/28455 | 198 |
| ☐ | N199DN | Boeing 767-332ER | 690/28456 | 199 |
| ☐ | N394DL | Boeing 767-324ER | 572/27394 | 1521 |
| ☑ | N1200K | Boeing 767-332ER | 696/28457 | 200 |
| ☐ | N1201P | Boeing 767-332ER | 697/28458 | 201 |
| ☐ | N1402A | Boeing 767-332 | 506/25989 | 1402 |
| ☐ | N1501P | Boeing 767-3P6ER | 334/24983 | 1501 |
| ☐ | N1602 | Boeing 767-332ER | 735/29694 | 1602 |
| ☐ | N1603 | Boeing 767-332ER | 739/29695 | 1603 |
| ☐ | N1604R | Boeing 767-332ER | 749/30180 | 1604 |
| ☐ | N1605 | Boeing 767-332ER | 753/30198 | 1605 |
| ☐ | N1607B | Boeing 767-332ER | 787/30388 | 1607 |
| ☐ | N1608 | Boeing 767-332ER | 788/30573 | 1608 |
| ☐ | N1609 | Boeing 767-332ER | 789/30574 | 1609 |
| ☐ | N1610D | Boeing 767-332ER | 790/30594 | 1610 |
| ☐ | N1611B | Boeing 767-332ER | 794/30595 | 1611 |
| ☐ | N1612T | Boeing 767-332ER | 838/30575 | 1612 |
| ☐ | N1613B | Boeing 767-332ER | 847/32776 | 1613 |
| ☐ | N16065 | Boeing 767-332ER | 755/30199 | 1606 |
| ☐ | N825MH | Boeing 767-432ER | 758/29703 | 1801 |
| ☐ | N826MH | Boeing 767-432ER | 769/29713 | 1802 |

| Reg | Type | Line/MSN | Fleet |
|---|---|---|---|
| ☐ N827MH | Boeing 767-432ER | 773/29705 | 1803 |
| ☐ N828MH | Boeing 767-432ER | 791/29699 | 1804 |
| ☐ N829MH | Boeing 767-432ER | 801/29700 | 1805 |
| ☐ N830MH | Boeing 767-432ER | 803/29701 | 1806 |
| ☐ N831MH | Boeing 767-432ER | 804/29702 | 1807 |
| ☐ N832MH | Boeing 767-432ER | 807/29704 | 1808 |
| ☐ N833MH | Boeing 767-432ER | 810/29706 | 1809 |
| ☐ N834MH | Boeing 767-432ER | 813/29707 | 1810 |
| ☐ N835MH | Boeing 767-432ER | 814/29708 | 1811 |
| ☐ N836MH | Boeing 767-432ER | 818/29709 | 1812 |
| ☐ N837MH | Boeing 767-432ER | 820/29710 | 1813 |
| ☐ N838MH | Boeing 767-432ER | 821/29711 | 1814 |
| ☐ N839MH | Boeing 767-432ER | 824/29712 | 1815 |
| ☐ N840MH | Boeing 767-432ER | 830/29718 | 1816 |
| ☐ N841MH | Boeing 767-432ER | 855/29714 | 1817 |
| ☐ N842MH | Boeing 767-432ER | 856/29715 | 1818 |
| ☐ N843MH | Boeing 767-432ER | 865/29716 | 1819 |
| ☐ N844MH | Boeing 767-432ER | 871/29717 | 1820 |
| ☐ N845MH | Boeing 767-432ER | 874/29719 | 1821 |
| ☐ N860DA | Boeing 777-232ER | 202/29951 | 7001 |
| ☐ N861DA | Boeing 777-232ER | 207/29952 | 7002 |
| ☐ N862DA | Boeing 777-232ER | 235/29734 | 7003 |
| ☐ N863DA | Boeing 777-232ER | 245/29735 | 7004 |
| ☐ N864DA | Boeing 777-232ER | 249/29736 | 7005 |
| ☐ N865DA | Boeing 777-232ER | 257/29737 | 7006 |
| ☐ N866DA | Boeing 777-232ER | 261/29738 | 7007 |
| ☐ N867DA | Boeing 777-232ER | 387/29743 | 7008 |
| ☐ N801DE | McDD MD-11 | 480/48472 | 801 |
| ☐ N802DE | McDD MD-11 | 481/48473 | 802 |
| ☐ N803DE | McDD MD-11 | 485/48474 | 803 |
| ☐ N804DE | McDD MD-11 | 489/48475 | 804 |
| ☐ N805DE | McDD MD-11 | 510/48476 | 805; std |
| ☐ N806DE | McDD MD-11 | 511/48477 | 806 |
| ☐ N807DE | McDD MD-11 | 514/48478 | 807 |
| ☐ N808DE | McDD MD-11 | 536/48479 | 808 |
| ☐ N809DE | McDD MD-11 | 538/48480 | 809 |
| ☐ N810DE | McDD MD-11 | 542/48565 | 810 |
| ☐ N811DE | McDD MD-11 | 543/48566 | 811 |
| ☐ N812DE | McDD MD-11 | 560/48600 | 812 |
| ☐ N813DE | McDD MD-11 | 562/48601 | 813 |
| ☐ N814DE | McDD MD-11 | 605/48623 | 814 |
| ☐ N815DE | McDD MD-11 | 622/48624 | 815 |
| ☐ N900DE | McDD MD-88 | 1970/53372 | 9000 |
| ☐ N901DE | McDD MD-88 | 1980/53378 | 9001 |
| ☐ N901DL | McDD MD-88 | 1338/49532 | 901 |
| ☐ N902DE | McDD MD-88 | 1983/53379 | 9002 |
| ☐ N902DL | McDD MD-88 | 1341/49533 | 902 |
| ☐ N903DE | McDD MD-88 | 1986/53380 | 9003 |
| ☐ N903DL | McDD MD-88 | 1344/49534 | 903 |
| ☐ N904DE | McDD MD-88 | 1990/53409 | 9004 |
| ☐ N904DL | McDD MD-88 | 1347/49535 | 904 |
| ☐ N905DE | McDD MD-88 | 1992/53410 | 9005 |
| ☐ N905DL | McDD MD-88 | 1348/49536 | 905 |
| ☐ N906DE | McDD MD-88 | 2027/53415 | 9006 |
| ☐ N906DL | McDD MD-88 | 1355/49537 | 906 |
| ☐ N907DE | McDD MD-88 | 2029/53416 | 9007 |
| ☐ N907DL | McDD MD-88 | 1365/49538 | 907 |
| ☐ N908DE | McDD MD-88 | 2032/53417 | 9008 |
| ☐ N908DL | McDD MD-88 | 1366/49539 | 908 |
| ☐ N909DE | McDD MD-88 | 2033/53418 | 9009 |
| ☐ N909DL | McDD MD-88 | 1395/49540 | 909 |
| ☐ N910DE | McDD MD-88 | 2036/53419 | 9010 |
| ☐ N910DL | McDD MD-88 | 1416/49541 | 910 |
| ☐ N911DE | McDD MD-88 | 2037/49967 | 9011 |
| ☐ N911DL | McDD MD-88 | 1433/49542 | 911 |
| ☐ N912DE | McDD MD-88 | 2038/49997 | 9012 |
| ☐ N912DL | McDD MD-88 | 1434/49543 | 912 |
| ☐ N913DE | McDD MD-88 | 2039/49956 | 9013 |
| ☐ N913DL | McDD MD-88 | 1443/49544 | 913 |
| ☐ N914DE | McDD MD-88 | 2049/49957 | 9014 |
| ☐ N914DL | McDD MD-88 | 1444/49545 | 914 |
| ☐ N915DE | McDD MD-88 | 2050/53420 | 9015 |
| ☐ N915DL | McDD MD-88 | 1447/49546 | 915 |
| ☐ N916DE | McDD MD-88 | 2051/53421 | 9016 |
| ☐ N916DL | McDD MD-88 | 1448/49591 | 916 |
| ☐ N917DE | McDD MD-88 | 2054/49958 | 9017 |
| ☐ N917DL | McDD MD-88 | 1469/49573 | 917 |
| ☐ N918DE | McDD MD-88 | 2055/49959 | 9018 |
| ☐ N918DL | McDD MD-88 | 1470/49583 | 918 |
| ☐ N919DE | McDD MD-88 | 2058/53422 | 9019 |
| ☐ N919DL | McDD MD-88 | 1471/49584 | 919 |
| ☐ N920DE | McDD MD-88 | 2059/53423 | 9020 |
| ☐ N920DL | McDD MD-88 | 1473/49644 | 920 |
| ☐ N921DL | McDD MD-88 | 1480/49645 | 921 |
| ☐ N922DL | McDD MD-88 | 1481/49646 | 922 |
| ☐ N923DL | McDD MD-88 | 1491/49705 | 923 |
| ☐ N924DL | McDD MD-88 | 1492/49711 | 924 |
| ☐ N925DL | McDD MD-88 | 1500/49712 | 925 |
| ☐ N926DL | McDD MD-88 | 1523/49713 | 926 |
| ☐ N927DA | McDD MD-88 | 1524/49714 | 927 |
| ☐ N928DL | McDD MD-88 | 1530/49715 | 928 |
| ☐ N929DL | McDD MD-88 | 1531/49716 | 929 |
| ☐ N930DL | McDD MD-88 | 1532/49717 | 930 |
| ☐ N931DL | McDD MD-88 | 1533/49718 | 931 |
| ☐ N932DL | McDD MD-88 | 1570/49719 | 932 |
| ☐ N933DL | McDD MD-88 | 1571/49720 | 933 |
| ☐ N934DL | McDD MD-88 | 1574/49721 | 934 |
| ☐ N935DL | McDD MD-88 | 1575/49722 | 935 |
| ☐ N936DL | McDD MD-88 | 1576/49723 | 936 |
| ☐ N937DL | McDD MD-88 | 1588/49810 | 937 |
| ☐ N938DL | McDD MD-88 | 1590/49811 | 938 |
| ☐ N939DL | McDD MD-88 | 1593/49812 | 939 |
| ☐ N940DL | McDD MD-88 | 1599/49813 | 940 |
| ☐ N941DL | McDD MD-88 | 1602/49814 | 941 |
| ☐ N942DL | McDD MD-88 | 1605/49815 | 942 |
| ☐ N943DL | McDD MD-88 | 1608/49816 | 943 |
| ☐ N944DL | McDD MD-88 | 1612/49817 | 944 |
| ☐ N945DL | McDD MD-88 | 1613/49818 | 945 |
| ☐ N946DL | McDD MD-88 | 1629/49819 | 946 |
| ☐ N947DL | McDD MD-88 | 1664/49878 | 947 |
| ☐ N948DL | McDD MD-88 | 1666/49879 | 948 |
| ☐ N949DL | McDD MD-88 | 1676/49880 | 949 |
| ☐ N950DL | McDD MD-88 | 1677/49881 | 950 |
| ☐ N951DL | McDD MD-88 | 1679/49882 | 951 |
| ☐ N952DL | McDD MD-88 | 1683/49883 | 952 |
| ☐ N953DL | McDD MD-88 | 1685/49884 | 953 |
| ☐ N954DL | McDD MD-88 | 1689/49885 | 954 |
| ☐ N955DL | McDD MD-88 | 1691/49886 | 955 |
| ☐ N956DL | McDD MD-88 | 1699/49887 | 956 |
| ☐ N957DL | McDD MD-88 | 1700/49976 | 957 |
| ☐ N958DL | McDD MD-88 | 1701/49977 | 958 |
| ☐ N959DL | McDD MD-88 | 1710/49978 | 959 |
| ☐ N960DL | McDD MD-88 | 1711/49979 | 960 |
| ☐ N961DL | McDD MD-88 | 1712/49980 | 961 |
| ☐ N962DL | McDD MD-88 | 1725/49981 | 962 |
| ☐ N963DL | McDD MD-88 | 1726/49982 | 963 |
| ☐ N964DL | McDD MD-88 | 1747/49983 | 964 |
| ☐ N965DL | McDD MD-88 | 1748/49984 | 965 |
| ☐ N966DL | McDD MD-88 | 1795/53115 | 966 |
| ☐ N967DL | McDD MD-88 | 1796/53116 | 967 |
| ☐ N968DL | McDD MD-88 | 1808/53161 | 968 |
| ☐ N969DL | McDD MD-88 | 1810/53172 | 969 |
| ☐ N970DL | McDD MD-88 | 1811/53173 | 970 |
| ☐ N971DL | McDD MD-88 | 1823/53214 | 971 |
| ☐ N972DL | McDD MD-88 | 1824/53215 | 972 |
| ☐ N973DL | McDD MD-88 | 1832/53241 | 973 |
| ☐ N974DL | McDD MD-88 | 1833/53242 | 974 |
| ☐ N975DL | McDD MD-88 | 1834/53243 | 975 |
| ☐ N976DL | McDD MD-88 | 1845/53257 | 976 |
| ☐ N977DL | McDD MD-88 | 1848/53258 | 977 |
| ☐ N978DL | McDD MD-88 | 1849/53259 | 978 |
| ☐ N979DL | McDD MD-88 | 1859/53266 | 979 |
| ☐ N980DL | McDD MD-88 | 1860/53267 | 980 |
| ☐ N981DL | McDD MD-88 | 1861/53268 | 981 |
| ☐ N982DL | McDD MD-88 | 1870/53273 | 982 |
| ☐ N983DL | McDD MD-88 | 1873/53274 | 983 |
| ☐ N984DL | McDD MD-88 | 1912/53311 | 984 |
| ☐ N985DL | McDD MD-88 | 1914/53312 | 985 |
| ☐ N986DL | McDD MD-88 | 1924/53313 | 986 |
| ☐ N987DL | McDD MD-88 | 1926/53338 | 987 |
| ☐ N988DL | McDD MD-88 | 1928/53339 | 988; std |
| ☐ N989DL | McDD MD-88 | 1936/53341 | 989 |
| ☐ N990DL | McDD MD-88 | 1939/53342 | 990 |

| | | | |
|---|---|---|---|
| ☐ N991DL | McDD MD-88 | 1941/53343 | 991 |
| ☐ N992DL | McDD MD-88 | 1943/53344 | 992 |
| ☐ N993DL | McDD MD-88 | 1950/53345 | 993 |
| ☐ N994DL | McDD MD-88 | 1952/53346 | 994 |
| ☐ N995DL | McDD MD-88 | 1955/53362 | 995 |
| ☐ N996DL | McDD MD-88 | 1958/53363 | 996 |
| ☐ N997DL | McDD MD-88 | 1961/53364 | 997 |
| ☐ N998DL | McDD MD-88 | 1963/53370 | 998 |
| ☐ N999DN | McDD MD-88 | 1965/53371 | 999 |
| | | | |
| ☐ N901DA | McDD MD-90-30 | 2100/53381 | 9201 |
| ☐ N902DA | McDD MD-90-30 | 2094/53382 | 9202 |
| ☐ N903DA | McDD MD-90-30 | 2095/53383 | 9203 |
| ☐ N904DA | McDD MD-90-30 | 2096/53384 | 9204 |
| ☐ N905DA | McDD MD-90-30 | 2097/53385 | 9205 |
| ☐ N906DA | McDD MD-90-30 | 2098/53386 | 9206 |
| ☐ N907DA | McDD MD-90-30 | 2115/53387 | 9207 |
| ☐ N908DA | McDD MD-90-30 | 2117/53388 | 9208 |
| ☐ N909DA | McDD MD-90-30 | 2122/53389 | 9209 |
| ☐ N910DN | McDD MD-90-30 | 2123/53390 | 9210 |
| ☐ N911DA | McDD MD-90-30 | 2126/53391 | 9211 |
| ☐ N912DN | McDD MD-90-30 | 2136/53392 | 9212 |
| ☐ N913DN | McDD MD-90-30 | 2154/53393 | 9213 |
| ☐ N914DN | McDD MD-90-30 | 2156/53394 | 9214 |
| ☐ N915DN | McDD MD-90-30 | 2159/53395 | 9215 |
| ☐ N916DN | McDD MD-90-30 | 2161/53396 | 9216 |

### DELTA CONNECTION — DAL

| | | | |
|---|---|---|---|
| ☐ N530AS | ATR 72-212 | 453 | |
| ☐ N531AS | ATR 72-212 | 454 | |
| ☐ N532AS | ATR 72-212 | 458 | |
| ☐ N533AS | ATR 72-212 | 460 | |
| ☐ N534AS | ATR 72-212 | 463 | |
| ☐ N535AS | ATR 72-212 | 464 | |
| ☐ N536AS | ATR 72-212 | 465 | |
| ☐ N630AS | ATR 72-212 | 336 | |
| ☐ N631AS | ATR 72-212 | 362 | |
| ☐ N632AS | ATR 72-212 | 338 | |
| ☐ N633AS | ATR 72-212 | 344 | |
| ☐ N634AS | ATR 72-212 | 370 | |
| ☐ N635AS | ATR 72-212 | 372 | |
| ☐ N636AS | ATR 72-212 | 375 | |
| ☐ N637AS | ATR 72-212 | 383 | |
| ☐ N640AS | ATR 72-212 | 405 | |
| ☐ N641AS | ATR 72-212 | 387 | |
| ☐ N642AS | ATR 72-212 | 395 | |
| ☐ N643AS | ATR 72-212 | 413 | |
| | | | |
| ☐ N403CA | Canadair RJ-200 | 7428 | |
| ☐ N408CA | Canadair RJ-200 | 7440 | |
| ☐ N409CA | Canadair RJ-200 | 7441 | |
| ☐ N420CA | Canadair RJ-200 | 7451 | |
| ☐ N427CA | Canadair RJ-200 | 7460 | |
| ☐ N430CA | Canadair RJ-200 | 7461 | |
| ☐ N431CA | Canadair RJ-200 | 7472 | |
| ☐ N435CA | Canadair RJ-200 | 7473 | |
| ☐ N436CA | Canadair RJ-200 | 7482 | |
| ☐ N442CA | Canadair RJ-200 | 7483 | Lst SKW |
| ☐ N443CA | Canadair RJ-200 | 7539 | |
| ☐ N446CA | Canadair RJ-200 | 7546 | |
| ☐ N447CA | Canadair RJ-200 | 7552 | |
| ☐ N451CA | Canadair RJ-200 | 7562 | |
| ☐ N455CA | Canadair RJ-200 | 7592 | |
| ☐ N457CA | Canadair RJ-200 | 7612 | |
| ☐ N458CA | Canadair RJ-200 | | o/o |
| ☐ N466CA | Canadair RJ-200 | 7627 | |
| ☐ N467CA | Canadair RJ-200 | 7637 | |
| ☐ N468CA | Canadair RJ-200 | 7649 | |
| ☐ N470CA | Canadair RJ-200 | 7650 | |
| ☐ N471CA | Canadair RJ-200 | 7655 | |
| ☐ N472CA | Canadair RJ-200 | 7667 | |
| ☐ N473CA | Canadair RJ-200 | 7668 | |
| ☐ N477CA | Canadair RJ-200 | 7670 | |
| ☐ N478CA | Canadair RJ-200 | 7671 | |
| ☐ N479CA | Canadair RJ-200 | 7675 | |
| ☐ N483CA | Canadair RJ-200 | 7689 | |
| ☐ N484CA | Canadair RJ-200 | 7702 | |

| | | | |
|---|---|---|---|
| ☐ N486CA | Canadair RJ-200 | 7707 | |
| ☐ N487CA | Canadair RJ-200 | | o/o |
| ☐ N488CA | Canadair RJ-200 | | o/o |
| ☐ N489CA | Canadair RJ-200 | | o/o |
| ☐ N491CA | Canadair RJ-200 | | o/o |
| ☐ N492CA | Canadair RJ-200 | | o/o |
| ☐ N708CA | Canadair RJ-200 | 7235 | |
| ☐ N709CA | Canadair RJ-200 | 7238 | |
| ☐ N710CA | Canadair RJ-200 | 7241 | |
| ☐ N712CA | Canadair RJ-200 | 7244 | |
| ☐ N713CA | Canadair RJ-200 | 7245 | |
| ☐ N716CA | Canadair RJ-200 | 7250 | |
| ☐ N719CA | Canadair RJ-200 | 7253 | |
| ☐ N721CA | Canadair RJ-200 | 7259 | |
| ☐ N729CA | Canadair RJ-200 | 7265 | |
| ☐ N735CA | Canadair RJ-200 | 7267 | |
| ☐ N739CA | Canadair RJ-200 | 7273 | |
| ☐ N759CA | Canadair RJ-200 | 7279 | Lst SKW |
| ☐ N767CA | Canadair RJ-200 | 7285 | Lst SKW |
| ☐ N769CA | Canadair RJ-200 | 7292 | Lst SKW |
| ☐ N776CA | Canadair RJ-200 | 7293 | Lst SKW |
| ☐ N778CA | Canadair RJ-200 | 7297 | Lst SKW |
| ☐ N779CA | Canadair RJ-200 | 7306 | |
| ☐ N781CA | Canadair RJ-200 | 7312 | |
| ☐ N783CA | Canadair RJ-200 | 7315 | |
| ☐ N784CA | Canadair RJ-200 | 7319 | |
| ☐ N785CA | Canadair RJ-200 | 7326 | |
| ☐ N786CA | Canadair RJ-200 | 7333 | |
| ☐ N796CA | Canadair RJ-200 | 7338 | |
| ☐ N797CA | Canadair RJ-200 | 7344 | |
| ☐ N798CA | Canadair RJ-200 | 7348 | |
| ☐ N804CA | Canadair RJ-200 | 7352 | |
| ☐ N805CA | Canadair RJ-200 | 7354 | |
| ☐ N806CA | Canadair RJ-200 | 7359 | |
| ☐ N807CA | Canadair RJ-200 | 7364 | |
| ☐ N809CA | Canadair RJ-200 | 7366 | |
| ☐ N810CA | Canadair RJ-200 | 7370 | |
| ☐ N811CA | Canadair RJ-200 | 7380 | |
| ☐ N812CA | Canadair RJ-200 | 7381 | |
| ☐ N814CA | Canadair RJ-200 | 7387 | |
| ☐ N815CA | Canadair RJ-200 | 7397 | |
| ☐ N818CA | Canadair RJ-200 | 7408 | |
| ☐ N819CA | Canadair RJ-200 | 7415 | |
| ☐ N820AS | Canadair RJ-200 | 7188 | |
| ☐ N821AS | Canadair RJ-200 | 7194 | |
| ☐ N821CA | Canadair RJ-200 | 7420 | |
| ☐ N823AS | Canadair RJ-200 | 7196 | |
| ☐ N824AS | Canadair RJ-200 | 7203 | |
| ☐ N825AS | Canadair RJ-200 | 7207 | |
| ☐ N826AS | Canadair RJ-200 | 7210 | |
| ☐ N827AS | Canadair RJ-200 | 7212 | |
| ☐ N828AS | Canadair RJ-200 | 7213 | |
| ☐ N829AS | Canadair RJ-200 | 7232 | |
| ☐ N830AS | Canadair RJ-200 | 7236 | |
| ☐ N832AS | Canadair RJ-200 | 7243 | |
| ☐ N833AS | Canadair RJ-200 | 7246 | |
| ☐ N834AS | Canadair RJ-200 | 7254 | |
| ☐ N835AS | Canadair RJ-200 | 7258 | |
| ☐ N836AS | Canadair RJ-200 | 7263 | |
| ☐ N837AS | Canadair RJ-200 | 7271 | |
| ☐ N838AS | Canadair RJ-200 | 7276 | |
| ☐ N839AS | Canadair RJ-200 | 7284 | |
| ☐ N840AS | Canadair RJ-200 | 7290 | |
| ☐ N841AS | Canadair RJ-200 | 7300 | |
| ☐ N842AS | Canadair RJ-200 | 7304 | |
| ☐ N843AS | Canadair RJ-200 | 7310 | |
| ☐ N844AS | Canadair RJ-200 | 7317 | |
| ☐ N845AS | Canadair RJ-200 | 7324 | |
| ☐ N846AS | Canadair RJ-200 | 7328 | |
| ☐ N847AS | Canadair RJ-200 | 7335 | |
| ☐ N848AS | Canadair RJ-200 | 7339 | |
| ☐ N849AS | Canadair RJ-200 | 7347 | |
| ☐ N850AS | Canadair RJ-200 | 7355 | |
| ☐ N851AS | Canadair RJ-200 | 7360 | |
| ☐ N852AS | Canadair RJ-200 | 7369 | |
| ☐ N853AS | Canadair RJ-200 | 7374 | |
| ☐ N854AS | Canadair RJ-200 | 7382 | |
| ☐ N855AS | Canadair RJ-200 | 7395 | |

| Reg | Type | c/n | Notes |
|---|---|---|---|
| N856AS | Canadair RJ-200 | 7404 | |
| N857AS | Canadair RJ-200 | 7411 | |
| N858AS | Canadair RJ-200 | 7417 | |
| N859AS | Canadair RJ-200 | 7421 | |
| N860AS | Canadair RJ-200 | 7433 | |
| N861AS | Canadair RJ-200 | 7445 | |
| N862AS | Canadair RJ-200 | 7476 | |
| N863AS | Canadair RJ-200 | 7487 | |
| N864AS | Canadair RJ-200 | 7502 | |
| N865AS | Canadair RJ-200 | 7507 | |
| N866AS | Canadair RJ-200 | 7517 | |
| N867AS | Canadair RJ-200 | 7463 | |
| N868CA | Canadair RJ-200 | 7427 | |
| N868AS | Canadair RJ-200 | 7474 | |
| N869AS | Canadair RJ-200 | 7479 | |
| N870AS | Canadair RJ-200 | 7530 | |
| N871AS | Canadair RJ-200 | 7537 | |
| N872AS | Canadair RJ-200 | 7542 | |
| N873AS | Canadair RJ-200 | 7549 | |
| N874AS | Canadair RJ-200 | 7551 | |
| N875AS | Canadair RJ-200 | 7559 | |
| N876AS | Canadair RJ-200 | 7576 | |
| N877AS | Canadair RJ-200 | 7579 | |
| N878AS | Canadair RJ-200 | 7590 | |
| N879AS | Canadair RJ-200 | 7600 | |
| N880AS | Canadair RJ-200 | 7606 | |
| N881AS | Canadair RJ-200 | 7496 | |
| N882AS | Canadair RJ-200 | 7503 | |
| N883AS | Canadair RJ-200 | 7504 | |
| N884AS | Canadair RJ-200 | 7513 | |
| N885AS | Canadair RJ-200 | 7521 | |
| N886AS | Canadair RJ-200 | 7531 | |
| N889AS | Canadair RJ-200 | 7538 | |
| N901EV | Canadair RJ-200 | 7616 | |
| N902EV | Canadair RJ-200 | 7620 | |
| N903EV | Canadair RJ-200 | 7621 | |
| N904EV | Canadair RJ-200 | 7628 | |
| N905EV | Canadair RJ-200 | 7632 | |
| N906EV | Canadair RJ-200 | 7642 | |
| N907EV | Canadair RJ-200 | 7648 | |
| N908EV | Canadair RJ-200 | 7654 | |
| N909EV | Canadair RJ-200 | 7658 | |
| N910EV | Canadair RJ-200 | 7727 | |
| N912EV | Canadair RJ-200 | 7728 | |
| N913EV | Canadair RJ-200 | 7731 | |
| N912CA | Canadair RJ-200 | 7011 | |
| N914CA | Canadair RJ-200 | 7012 | |
| N915CA | Canadair RJ-200 | 7013 | |
| N916CA | Canadair RJ-200 | 7014 | |
| N917CA | Canadair RJ-200 | 7017 | |
| N918CA | Canadair RJ-200 | 7018 | |
| N920CA | Canadair RJ-200 | 7022 | |
| N924CA | Canadair RJ-200 | 7026 | |
| N926CA | Canadair RJ-200 | 7027 | |
| N927CA | Canadair RJ-200 | 7031 | |
| N929CA | Canadair RJ-200 | 7035 | |
| N931CA | Canadair RJ-200 | 7037 | |
| N932CA | Canadair RJ-200 | 7038 | |
| N933CA | Canadair RJ-200 | 7040 | |
| N934CA | Canadair RJ-200 | 7042 | |
| N936CA | Canadair RJ-200 | 7043 | |
| N937CA | Canadair RJ-200 | 7044 | |
| N938CA | Canadair RJ-200 | 7046 | |
| N940CA | Canadair RJ-200 | 7048 | |
| N941CA | Canadair RJ-200 | 7050 | |
| N943CA | Canadair RJ-200 | 7062 | Lst SKW |
| N945CA | Canadair RJ-200 | 7069 | Lst SKW |
| N946CA | Canadair RJ-200 | 7072 | Lst SKW |
| N947CA | Canadair RJ-200 | 7077 | Lst SKW |
| N948CA | Canadair RJ-200 | 7079 | Lst SKW |
| N949CA | Canadair RJ-200 | 7080 | |
| N951CA | Canadair RJ-200 | 7091 | |
| N952CA | Canadair RJ-200 | 7092 | |
| N954CA | Canadair RJ-200 | 7100 | |
| N956CA | Canadair RJ-200 | 7105 | |
| N957CA | Canadair RJ-200 | 7109 | |
| N958CA | Canadair RJ-200 | 7111 | |
| N959CA | Canadair RJ-200 | 7116 | |
| N960CA | Canadair RJ-200 | 7117 | |
| N962CA | Canadair RJ-200 | 7123 | |
| N963CA | Canadair RJ-200 | 7127 | |
| N964CA | Canadair RJ-200 | 7129 | |
| N965CA | Canadair RJ-200 | 7131 | |
| N966CA | Canadair RJ-200 | 7132 | |
| N967CA | Canadair RJ-200 | 7134 | |
| N969CA | Canadair RJ-200 | 7141 | |
| N971CA | Canadair RJ-200 | 7145 | |
| N973CA | Canadair RJ-200 | 7146 | |
| N975CA | Canadair RJ-200 | 7150 | |
| N976CA | Canadair RJ-200 | 7151 | |
| N977CA | Canadair RJ-200 | 7157 | |
| N978CA | Canadair RJ-200 | 7158 | |
| N979CA | Canadair RJ-200 | 7159 | |
| N981CA | Canadair RJ-200 | 7163 | |
| N982CA | Canadair RJ-200 | 7168 | |
| N983CA | Canadair RJ-200 | 7169 | |
| N984CA | Canadair RJ-200 | 7171 | |
| N986CA | Canadair RJ-200 | 7174 | |
| N987CA | Canadair RJ-200 | 7199 | |
| N988CA | Canadair RJ-200 | 7204 | |
| N989CA | Canadair RJ-200 | 7215 | |
| N991CA | Canadair RJ-200 | 7216 | |
| N995CA | Canadair RJ-200 | 7229 | |
| N999CA | Canadair RJ-200 | 7230 | |
| N | Canadair RJ-200 | | o/o |
| N | Canadair RJ-200 | | o/o |
| N | Canadair RJ-200 | | o/o |
| N | Canadair RJ-200 | | o/o |
| N | Canadair RJ-200 | | o/o |
| N | Canadair RJ-200 | | o/o |
| N | Canadair RJ-200 | | o/o |
| N | Canadair RJ-200 | | o/o |
| N | Canadair RJ-200 | | o/o |
| N | Canadair RJ-200 | | o/o |
| N | Canadair RJ-200 | | o/o |
| N | Canadair RJ-200 | | o/o |
| N | Canadair RJ-200 | | o/o |
| N | Canadair RJ-200 | | o/o |
| N | Canadair RJ-200 | | o/o |
| N | Canadair RJ-200 | | o/o |
| N | Canadair RJ-200 | | o/o |
| N | Canadair RJ-200 | | o/o |
| N | Canadair RJ-200 | | o/o |
| N | Canadair RJ-200 | | o/o |
| N | Canadair RJ-200 | | o/o |
| N | Canadair RJ-200 | | o/o |
| N | Canadair RJ-200 | | o/o |
| N | Canadair RJ-200 | | o/o |
| N | Canadair RJ-200 | | o/o |
| N | Canadair RJ-200 | | o/o |
| N317CA | Canadair RJ-700 | 10055 | |
| N331CA | Canadair RJ-700 | 10061 | |
| N340CA | Canadair RJ-700 | 10062 | |
| N354CA | Canadair RJ-700 | 10064 | |
| N355CA | Canadair RJ-700 | 10067 | |
| N367CA | Canadair RJ-700 | 10069 | |
| N701EV | Canadair RJ-700 | 10020 | |
| N702EV | Canadair RJ-700 | 10035 | |
| N703EV | Canadair RJ-700 | 10038 | |
| N705EV | Canadair RJ-700 | 10051 | |
| N706EV | Canadair RJ-700 | 10054 | |
| N707EV | Canadair RJ-700 | 10057 | |
| N708EV | Canadair RJ-700 | 10060 | |
| N709EV | Canadair RJ-700 | 10068 | |
| N710EV | Canadair RJ-700 | 10071 | |
| N712EV | Canadair RJ-700 | | o/o |
| N713EV | Canadair RJ-700 | | o/o |
| N716EV | Canadair RJ-700 | | o/o |
| N717EV | Canadair RJ-700 | | o/o |
| N718EV | Canadair RJ-700 | | o/o |
| N719EV | Canadair RJ-700 | | o/o |
| N720EV | Canadair RJ-700 | | o/o |
| N722EV | Canadair RJ-700 | | o/o |
| N723EV | Canadair RJ-700 | | o/o |
| N724EV | Canadair RJ-700 | | o/o |
| N727EV | Canadair RJ-700 | | o/o |

| Reg | Type | c/n | Notes |
|---|---|---|---|
| ☐ N730EV | Canadair RJ-700 | | o/o |
| ☐ N738EV | Canadair RJ-700 | | o/o |
| ☐ N740EV | Canadair RJ-700 | | o/o |
| ☐ N741EV | Canadair RJ-700 | | o/o |
| ☐ N744EV | Canadair RJ-700 | | o/o |
| ☐ N748EV | Canadair RJ-700 | | o/o |
| ☐ N | Canadair RJ-700 | | o/o |
| ☐ N | Canadair RJ-700 | | o/o |
| ☐ N | Canadair RJ-700 | | o/o |
| ☐ N | Canadair RJ-700 | | o/o |
| ☐ N | Canadair RJ-700 | | o/o |
| ☐ N | Canadair RJ-700 | | o/o |
| ☐ N | Canadair RJ-700 | | o/o |
| ☐ N | Canadair RJ-700 | | o/o |
| ☐ N | Canadair RJ-700 | | o/o |
| ☐ N | Canadair RJ-700 | | o/o |
| ☐ N | Canadair RJ-700 | | o/o |
| ☐ N | Canadair RJ-700 | | o/o |
| ☐ N | Canadair RJ-700 | | o/o |
| ☐ N | Canadair RJ-700 | | o/o |

| Reg | Type | c/n |
|---|---|---|
| ☐ N401FJ | Dornier 328-310 | 3145 |
| ☐ N402FJ | Dornier 328-310 | 3147 |
| ☐ N403FJ | Dornier 328-310 | 3149 |
| ☐ N404FJ | Dornier 328-310 | 3150 |
| ☐ N405FJ | Dornier 328-310 | 3155 |
| ☐ N406FJ | Dornier 328-310 | 3156 |
| ☐ N407FJ | Dornier 328-310 | 3157 |
| ☐ N408FJ | Dornier 328-310 | 3160 |
| ☐ N409FJ | Dornier 328-310 | 3161 |
| ☐ N410FJ | Dornier 328-310 | 3165 |
| ☐ N411FJ | Dornier 328-310 | 3166 |
| ☐ N412FJ | Dornier 328-310 | 3167 |
| ☐ N413FJ | Dornier 328-310 | 3168 |
| ☐ N414FJ | Dornier 328-300 | 3169 |
| ☐ N415FJ | Dornier 328-310 | 3170 |
| ☐ N416FJ | Dornier 328-310 | 3171 |
| ☐ N417FJ | Dornier 328-310 | 3174 |
| ☐ N418FJ | Dornier 328-310 | 3176 |
| ☐ N419FJ | Dornier 328-310 | 3173 |
| ☐ N420FJ | Dornier 328-310 | 3178 |
| ☐ N421FJ | Dornier 328-310 | 3189 |
| ☐ N422FJ | Dornier 328-310 | 3180 |
| ☐ N423FJ | Dornier 328-310 | 3181 |
| ☐ N424FJ | Dornier 328-310 | 3185 |
| ☐ N425FJ | Dornier 328-310 | 3189 |
| ☐ N426FJ | Dornier 328-310 | 3190 |
| ☐ N427FJ | Dornier 328-310 | 3192 |
| ☐ N428FJ | Dornier 328-310 | 3193 |
| ☐ N429FJ | Dornier 328-310 | 3194 |
| ☐ N430FJ | Dornier 328-310 | 3209 |

| Reg | Type | c/n |
|---|---|---|
| ☐ N229AS | Embraer EMB.120RT | 120042 |
| ☐ N230AS | Embraer EMB.120RT | 120032 |
| ☐ N232AS | Embraer EMB.120RT | 120036 |
| ☐ N235AS | Embraer EMB.120RT | 120047 |
| ☐ N237AS | Embraer EMB.120RT | 120051 |
| ☐ N238AS | Embraer EMB.120RT | 120053 |
| ☐ N239AS | Embraer EMB.120RT | 120057 |
| ☐ N240AS | Embraer EMB.120RT | 120060 |
| ☐ N244AS | Embraer EMB.120RT | 120073 |
| ☐ N245AS | Embraer EMB.120RT | 120075 |
| ☐ N246AS | Embraer EMB.120RT | 120100 |
| ☐ N257AS | Embraer EMB.120RT | 120126 |
| ☐ N258AS | Embraer EMB.120RT | 120131 |
| ☐ N260AS | Embraer EMB.120RT | 120132 |
| ☐ N261AS | Embraer EMB.120RT | 120141 |
| ☐ N262AS | Embraer EMB.120RT | 120146 |
| ☐ N263AS | Embraer EMB.120RT | 120157 |
| ☐ N264AS | Embraer EMB.120RT | 120165 |
| ☐ N265AS | Embraer EMB.120RT | 120170 |
| ☐ N266AS | Embraer EMB.120RT | 120188 |
| ☐ N267AS | Embraer EMB.120RT | 120198 |
| ☐ N268AS | Embraer EMB.120RT | 120202 |
| ☐ N268CA | Embraer EMB.120RT | 120262 |
| ☐ N269AS | Embraer EMB.120RT | 120210 |
| ☐ N273AS | Embraer EMB.120RT | 120222 |

| Reg | Type | c/n |
|---|---|---|
| ☐ N274AS | Embraer EMB.120RT | 120229 |
| ☐ N275AS | Embraer EMB.120ER | 120234 |
| ☐ N280AS | Embraer EMB.120RT | 120231 |
| ☐ N281AS | Embraer EMB.120RT | 120224 |
| ☐ N282AS | Embraer EMB.120RT | 120226 |
| ☐ N283AS | Embraer EMB.120RT | 120236 |
| ☐ N284AS | Embraer EMB.120RT | 120249 |
| ☐ N285AS | Embraer EMB.120RT | 120265 |
| ☐ N286AS | Embraer EMB.120RT | 120268 |
| ☐ N463CA | Embraer EMB.120RT | 120267 |
| ☐ N500AS | Embraer EMB.120RT | 120272 |
| ☐ N501AS | Embraer EMB.120RT | 120273 |
| ☐ N502AS | Embraer EMB.120RT | 120274 |
| ☐ N503AS | Embraer EMB.120RT | 120275 |
| ☐ N504AS | Embraer EMB.120RT | 120278 |
| ☐ N505AS | Embraer EMB.120RT | 120279 |
| ☐ N638AS | Embraer EMB.120RT | 120282 |
| ☐ N639AS | Embraer EMB.120RT | 120283 |

| Reg | Type | c/n | Notes |
|---|---|---|---|
| ☐ N831RP | Embraer ERJ-140 | 145663 | |
| ☐ N832RP | Embraer ERJ-140 | 145676 | |
| ☐ N | Embraer ERJ-140 | | o/o |
| ☐ N | Embraer ERJ-140 | | o/o |
| ☐ N | Embraer ERJ-140 | | o/o |
| ☐ N | Embraer ERJ-140 | | o/o |
| ☐ N | Embraer ERJ-140 | | o/o |
| ☐ N | Embraer ERJ-140 | | o/o |
| ☐ N | Embraer ERJ-140 | | o/o |
| ☐ N | Embraer ERJ-140 | | o/o |
| ☐ N | Embraer ERJ-140 | | o/o |
| ☐ N | Embraer ERJ-140 | | o/o |
| ☐ N | Embraer ERJ-140 | | o/o |
| ☐ N | Embraer ERJ-140 | | o/o |
| ☐ N561RP | Embraer ERJ-145 | 145447 | |
| ☐ N562RP | Embraer ERJ-145 | 145451 | |
| ☐ N563RP | Embraer ERJ-145 | 145509 | |
| ☐ N564RP | Embraer ERJ-145 | 145524 | |
| ☐ N | Embraer ERJ-145 | | o/o |
| ☐ N | Embraer ERJ-145 | | o/o |
| ☐ N | Embraer ERJ-145 | | o/o |

## DHL AIRWAYS — DHL

| Reg | Type | c/n | Notes |
|---|---|---|---|
| ☐ N362DH | Airbus A300B4-103F | 084 | |
| ☐ N363DH | Airbus A300B4-103F | 085 | |
| ☐ N364DH | Airbus A300B4-203F | 141 | |
| ☐ N365DH | Airbus A300B4-203F | 149 | |
| ☐ N366DH | Airbus A300B4-203F | 249 | |
| ☐ N367DH | Airbus A300B4-203F | 265 | |
| ☐ N622DH | Boeing 727-264F | 1051/20896 | Opb SWT |
| ☐ N623DH | Boeing 727-264F | 1049/20895 | Opb SWT |
| ☐ N624DH | Boeing 727-264F | 950/20709 | Opb DAE |
| ☐ N625DH | Boeing 727-264F | 986/20780 | Opb DAE |
| ☐ N626DH | Boeing 727-277F | 1768/22644 | Opb SWT |
| ☐ N627DH | Boeing 727-277F | 1753/22641 | Opb SWT |
| ☐ N701DH | Boeing 727-30C | 387/19011 | std |
| ☐ N702DH | Boeing 727-30C | 519/19793 | std |
| ☐ N703DH | Boeing 727-30C | 382/19010 | std |
| ☐ N705DH | Boeing 727-22C | 386/19191 | std |
| ☐ N708DH | Boeing 727-25F | 101/18275 | |
| ☐ N709DH | Boeing 727-82C | 660/19968 | |
| ☐ N712DH | Boeing 727-29F | 419/19401 | std |
| ☐ N715DH | Boeing 727-155C | 461/19618 | std |
| ☐ N717DH | Boeing 727-23F | 343/19389 | std |
| ☐ N720DH | Boeing 727-228F | 562/19544 | |
| ☐ N721DH | Boeing 727-228F | 564/19545 | |
| ☐ N724DH | Boeing 727-228F | 685/19862 | std |
| ☐ N726DH | Boeing 727-228F | 845/20409 | |
| ☐ N727DH | Boeing 727-228F | 778/20204 | |
| ☐ N740DH | Boeing 727-2Q9F | 1508/21930 | |
| ☐ N741DH | Boeing 727-2Q9F | 1531/21931 | |
| ☐ N742DH | Boeing 727-225F | 1238/21290 | |
| ☐ N743DH | Boeing 727-225F | 1685/22438 | |
| ☐ N745DH | Boeing 727-224F | 1149/20665 | |
| ☐ N746DH | Boeing 727-224F | 1697/22252 | |

| ☐ N747DH | Boeing 727-224F | 1702/22253 |
| ☐ N748DH | Boeing 727-225F | 1692/22440 |
| ☐ N749DH | Boeing 727-223F | 1659/22013 |
| ☐ N750DH | Boeing 727-2M7 | 1680/21951 |
| ☐ N751DH | Boeing 727-264 | 1802/22982 |
| ☐ N752DH | Boeing 727-223F | 1763/22466 |
| ☐ N753DH | Boeing 727-223F | 1766/22468 |
| ☐ N754DH | Boeing 727-223F | 1646/22008 |
| ☐ N755DH | Boeing 727-225F | 1539/21857 |
| ☐ N780DH | Boeing 727-223F | 1636/22006 |
| | | |
| ☐ N801DH | Douglas DC-8-73AF | 431/46033 |
| ☐ N802DH | Douglas DC-8-73AF | 451/46076 |
| ☐ N803DH | Douglas DC-8-73AF | 508/46123 |
| ☐ N804DH | Douglas DC-8-73AF | 511/46124 |
| ☐ N805DH | Douglas DC-8-73AF | 515/46125 |
| ☐ N806DH | Douglas DC-8-73CF | 394/46002 |
| ☐ N807DH | Douglas DC-8-73CF | 375/45990 |
| ☐ N873SJ | Douglas DC-8-73F | 519/46091 |

### DISCOVER AIR       DCV

| ☐ N205CA | Embraer EMB.120RT | 120205 |
| ☐ N241CA | Embraer EMB.120RT | 120211 |
| ☐ N427UE | BAe Jetstream 31 | 811 |
| ☐ N431AM | BAe Jetstream 32EP | 881 |
| ☐ N873JX | BAe Jetstream 32EP | 873 |
| ☐ N3108 | BAe Jetstream 32 | 824 |

### EVERGREEN INTERNATIONAL AIRLINES   EIA

| ☐ N470EV | Boeing 747-273C | 237/20653 | |
| ☐ N471EV | Boeing 747-273C | 209/20651 | |
| ☐ N477EV | Boeing 747SR-46 | 231/20784 | |
| ☐ N478EV | Boeing 747SR-46 | 254/21033 | |
| ☐ N479EV | Boeing 747-132 | 94/19898 | |
| ☐ N480EV | Boeing 747-121 | 106/20348 | |
| ☐ N481EV | Boeing 747-132 | 72/19896 | |
| ☐ N482EV | Boeing 747-212B | 219/20713 | |
| ☐ N485EV | Boeing 747-212B | 218/20712 | |
| ☐ N486EV | Boeing 747-212B | 240/20888 | |
| ☐ N3203Y | Boeing 747-128 | 39/19751 | std |
| All SCD conversions | | | |
| | | | |
| ☐ N915F | Douglas DC-9-15RC | 207/47061 | |
| ☐ N916F | Douglas DC-9-15RC | 165/47044 | |
| ☐ N933F | Douglas DC-9-33RC | 280/47191 | |
| ☐ N941F | Douglas DC-9-33F | 311/47193 | |
| ☐ N942F | Douglas DC-9-33F | 467/47408 | |
| ☐ N944F | Douglas DC-9-33RC | 324/47194 | std |
| ☐ N945F | Douglas DC-9-33RC | 337/47279 | |

### EXECUTIVE AIRLINES       ORA

| ☐ N16EN | BAe Jetstream 31 | 743 |
| ☐ N16EX | BAe Jetstream 31 | 826 |
| ☐ N404GJ | BAe Jetstream 31 | 754 |

### EXPRESS.NET AIRLINES       XNA

| ☐ N224KW | Airbus A300B4-203F | 073 | |
| ☐ N307FV | Airbus A300B4-203F | 235 | |
| ☐ N370PC | Airbus A300B4-203F | 134 | |
| ☐ N371PC | Airbus A300B4-203F | 157 | Lst AHK |
| ☐ N372PC | Airbus A300B4-203F | 196 | |
| ☐ N373PC | Airbus A300B4-203F | 218 | |
| ☐ N472AS | Airbus A300B4-203F | 125 | |
| ☐ N473AS | Airbus A300B4-203F | 203 | |
| ☐ N474AS | Airbus A300B4-203F | 219 | |
| ☐ N13974 | Airbus A300B4-203F | 126 | |
| | | | |
| ☐ N704A | Boeing 727-173C | 427/19504 | |
| ☐ N792A | Boeing 727-22C | 406/19195 | |
| ☐ N793A | Boeing 727-227 | 997/20774 | |
| ☐ N76753 | Boeing 727-227F | 1219/21249 | |

### EXPRESS ONE INTERNATIONAL    LHN

| ☐ N263US | Boeing 727-251F | 737/19982 | |
| ☐ N275WC | Boeing 727-277F | 989/20549 | |
| ☐ N290NE | Boeing 727-25F | 242/18972 | |
| ☐ N310NE | Boeing 727-2A7F | 726/20241 | |
| ☐ N311NE | Boeing 727-223F | 684/19703 | std |
| ☐ N312NE | Boeing 727-223F | 755/20193 | std |
| ☐ N313NE | Boeing 727-223F | 680/19702 | std |
| ☐ N314NE | Boeing 727-223F | 664/19495 | std |
| ☐ N315NE | Boeing 727-223F | 738/20190 | std |
| ☐ N316NE | Boeing 727-223F | 511/19475 | std |
| ☐ N352PA | Boeing 727-225F | 899/20616 | |
| ☐ N353PA | Boeing 727-225F | 933/20622 | |
| ☐ N354PA | Boeing 727-225F | 940/20624 | |
| ☐ N356PA | Boeing 727-225F | 946/20626 | |
| ☐ N361KP | Boeing 727-225F | 947/20627 | |
| ☐ N368PA | Boeing 727-221F | 1796/22540 | Lst CNX |
| ☐ N695CA | Boeing 727-224 | 1064/20661 | Lst SWT |
| ☐ N702NE | Boeing 727-223 | 1746/22460 | |
| ☐ N707CA | Boeing 727-224 | 1072/20662 | Lst SWT |
| ☐ N742RW | Boeing 727-2MF | 1693/21952 | |
| ☐ N6813 | Boeing 727-223F | 588/19488 | |
| ☐ N6815 | Boeing 727-223F | 602/19490 | |
| ☐ N6826 | Boeing 727-223F | 689/19704 | |
| ☐ N6839 | Boeing 727-223F | 752/20192 | |
| ☐ N12305 | Boeing 727-231F | 576/19562 | |
| ☐ N17410 | Boeing 727-243F | 1438/21663 | |
| ☐ N74318 | Boeing 727-231F | 708/20051 | |

### FALCON AIR EXPRESS       FAO

| ☐ N203AV | Boeing 727-259 | 1688/22474 | std |
| ☐ N266US | Boeing 727-251 | 745/19985 | std |
| ☐ N296SC | Boeing 727-224 | 1756/22449 | |
| ☐ N705AA | Boeing 727-223 | 1751/22462 | std |
| ☐ N908PG | Boeing 727-276F | 1101/20951 | |
| ☐ N54348 | Boeing 727-231 | 1563/21967 | |
| ☐ N64346 | Boeing 727-231 | 1464/21633 | |
| ☐ N79749 | Boeing 727-224 | 1767/22451 | |
| ☐ N79750 | Boeing 727-224 | 1772/22452 | |
| ☐ N371FA | Boeing 737-33A | 1337/23631 | Lst Sol Air |

### FEDEX EXPRESS       FDX

| ☐ N14819 | ATR 42-300 | 156 | |
| ☐ N16824 | ATR 42-300 | 166 | |
| ☐ N14825 | ATR 42-300 | 170 | |
| ☐ N14828 | ATR 42-300 | 179 | |
| ☐ N14830 | ATR 42-300 | 184 | |
| ☐ N99838 | ATR 42-320 | 259 | |
| ☐ N93840 | ATR 42-300 | 271 | |
| ☐ N | ATR 42-300 | | o/o |
| | | | |
| ☐ N650FE | Airbus A300F4-605R | 726 | |
| ☐ N651FE | Airbus A300F4-605R | 728 | |
| ☐ N652FE | Airbus A300F4-605R | 735 | |
| ☐ N653FE | Airbus A300F4-605R | 736 | |
| ☐ N654FE | Airbus A300F4-605R | 738 | |
| ☐ N655FE | Airbus A300F4-605R | 742 | |
| ☐ N656FE | Airbus A300F4-605R | 745 | |
| ☐ N657FE | Airbus A300F4-605R | 748 | |
| ☐ N658FE | Airbus A300F4-605R | 752 | |
| ☐ N659FE | Airbus A300F4-605R | 757 | |
| ☐ N660FE | Airbus A300F4-605R | 759 | |
| ☐ N661FE | Airbus A300F4-605R | 760 | |
| ☐ N662FE | Airbus A300F4-605R | 761 | |
| ☐ N663FE | Airbus A300F4-605R | 766 | |
| ☐ N664FE | Airbus A300F4-605R | 768 | |
| ☐ N665FE | Airbus A300F4-605R | 769 | |
| ☐ N667FE | Airbus A300F4-605R | 771 | |
| ☐ N668FE | Airbus A300F4-605R | 772 | |
| ☐ N669FE | Airbus A300F4-605R | 774 | |
| ☐ N792FE | Airbus A300F4-605R | 777 | |
| ☐ N670FE | Airbus A300F4-605R | 778 | |
| ☐ N671FE | Airbus A300F4-605R | 778 | |
| ☐ N672FE | Airbus A300F4-605R | 779 | |
| ☐ N673FE | Airbus A300F4-605R | 780 | |

| Reg | Type | c/n | Note |
|---|---|---|---|
| ☐ N674FE | Airbus A300F4-605R | 781 | |
| ☐ N675FE | Airbus A300F4-605R | 789 | |
| ☐ N676FE | Airbus A300F4-605R | 790 | |
| ☐ N677FE | Airbus A300F4-605R | 791 | |
| ☐ N678FE | Airbus A300F4-605R | 792 | |
| ☐ N679FE | Airbus A300F4-605R | 793 | |
| ☐ N680FE | Airbus A300F4-605R | 794 | |
| ☐ N681FE | Airbus A300F4-605R | 799 | |
| ☐ N682FE | Airbus A300F4-605R | 800 | |
| ☐ N683FE | Airbus A300F4-605R | 801 | |
| ☐ N684FE | Airbus A300F4-605R | 802 | |
| ☐ N685FE | Airbus A300F4-605R | 803 | |
| ☐ N686FE | Airbus A300F4-605R | 804 | |
| ☐ N716FD | Airbus A300B4-622 | 358 | |
| ☐ N717FD | Airbus A300B4-622 | 361 | |
| ☐ N718FD | Airbus A300B4-622 | 365 | |
| ☐ N719FD | Airbus A300B4-622 | 388 | |
| ☐ N720FD | Airbus A300B4-622 | 417 | |
| ☐ N721FD | Airbus A300B4-622RF | 477 | |
| ☐ N722FD | Airbus A300B4-622RF | 479 | |
| ☐ N723FD | Airbus A300B4-622RF | 543 | |
| ☐ N401FE | Airbus A310-203F | 191 | |
| ☐ N402FE | Airbus A310-203F | 201 | |
| ☐ N403FE | Airbus A310-203F | 230 | |
| ☐ N404FE | Airbus A310-203F | 233 | |
| ☐ N405FE | Airbus A310-203F | 237 | |
| ☐ N407FE | Airbus A310-203F | 254 | |
| ☐ N408FE | Airbus A310-203F | 257 | |
| ☐ N409FE | Airbus A310-203F | 273 | |
| ☐ N410FE | Airbus A310-203F | 356 | |
| ☐ N411FE | Airbus A310-203F | 359 | |
| ☐ N412FE | Airbus A310-203F | 360 | |
| ☐ N413FE | Airbus A310-203F | 397 | |
| ☐ N414FE | Airbus A310-203F | 400 | |
| ☐ N415FE | Airbus A310-203F | 349 | |
| ☐ N416FE | Airbus A310-222F | 288 | |
| ☐ N417FE | Airbus A310-222F | 333 | |
| ☐ N418FE | Airbus A310-222F | 343 | |
| ☐ N419FE | Airbus A310-222F | 345 | |
| ☐ N420FE | Airbus A310-222F | 339 | |
| ☐ N421FE | Airbus A310-222F | 342 | |
| ☐ N422FE | Airbus A310-222F | 346 | |
| ☐ N423FE | Airbus A310-203F | 281 | |
| ☐ N424FE | Airbus A310-203F | 241 | |
| ☐ N425FE | Airbus A310-203F | 264 | |
| ☐ N426FE | Airbus A310-203F | 245 | |
| ☐ N427FE | Airbus A310-203F | 362 | |
| ☐ N428FE | Airbus A310-203F | 248 | |
| ☐ N429FE | Airbus A310-203F | 364 | |
| ☐ N430FE | Airbus A310-203F | 394 | |
| ☐ N431FE | Airbus A310-203 | 316 | |
| ☐ N432FE | Airbus A310-203 | 326 | |
| ☐ N433FE | Airbus A310-203 | 335 | |
| ☐ N434FE | Airbus A310-203 | 355 | |
| ☐ N435FE | Airbus A310-203 | 369 | |
| ☐ N436FE | Airbus A310-203 | 454 | |
| ☐ N442FE | Airbus A310-203F | 353 | |
| ☐ N443FE | Airbus A310-203F | 283 | |
| ☐ N445FE | Airbus A310-203F | 297 | |
| ☐ N446FE | Airbus A310-222F | 224 | |
| ☐ N447FE | Airbus A310-222F | 251 | |
| ☐ N448FE | Airbus A310-222F | 260 | |
| ☐ N449FE | Airbus A310-222F | 217 | |
| ☐ N450FE | Airbus A310-222F | 162 | |
| ☐ N451FE | Airbus A310-222F | 303 | |
| ☐ N452FE | Airbus A310-222F | 313 | |
| ☐ N453FE | Airbus A310-222F | 267 | |
| ☐ N454FE | Airbus A310-222F | 278 | |
| ☐ N455FE | Airbus A310-222F | 331 | |
| ☐ N456FE | Airbus A310-222F | 318 | |
| ☐ N801FD | Airbus A310-324F | 539 | |
| ☐ N802FD | Airbus A310-324F | 542 | |
| ☐ N102FE | Boeing 727-22C | 392/19193 | |
| ☐ N103FE | Boeing 727-22C | 414/19199 | |
| ☐ N105FE | Boeing 727-22C | 394/19194 | |
| ☐ N107FE | Boeing 727-22C | 424/19202 | |
| ☐ N112FE | Boeing 727-22C | 630/19890 | |
| ☐ N113FE | Boeing 727-22C | 647/19894 | |
| ☐ N114FE | Boeing 727-24C | 460/19527 | |
| ☐ N115FE | Boeing 727-116C | 600/19814 | Lst MAL |
| ☐ N116FE | Boeing 727-25C | 335/19298 | |
| ☐ N119FE | Boeing 727-25C | 352/19301 | |
| ☐ N120FE | Boeing 727-25C | 356/19356 | |
| ☐ N124FE | Boeing 727-25C | 371/19360 | |
| ☐ N127FE | Boeing 727-25C | 478/19719 | Lst MAL |
| ☐ N133FE | Boeing 727-25C | 510/19851 | |
| ☐ N135FE | Boeing 727-25C | 522/19853 | |
| ☐ N136FE | Boeing 727-25C | 632/19855 | |
| ☐ N143FE | Boeing 727-21C | 314/19136 | |
| ☐ N144FE | Boeing 727-21C | 316/19137 | |
| ☐ N147FE | Boeing 727-22F | 270/19080 | |
| ☐ N148FE | Boeing 727-22F | 353/19086 | |
| ☐ N149FE | Boeing 727-22F | 359/19087 | |
| ☐ N150FE | Boeing 727-22F | 370/19141 | |
| ☐ N151FE | Boeing 727-22F | 472/19147 | |
| ☐ N152FE | Boeing 727-25F | 172/18285 | |
| ☐ N166FE | Boeing 727-22F | 227/18863 | |
| ☐ N168FE | Boeing 727-22F | 232/18865 | |
| ☐ N169FE | Boeing 727-22F | 241/18866 | |
| ☐ N180FE | Boeing 727-22F | 247/18867 | Lst MAL |
| ☐ N185FE | Boeing 727-22F | 259/18871 | |
| ☐ N186FE | Boeing 727-22F | 261/18872 | |
| ☐ N187FE | Boeing 727-22F | 268/19079 | |
| ☐ N188FE | Boeing 727-22F | 275/19081 | |
| ☐ N189FE | Boeing 727-22F | 279/19082 | |
| ☐ N190FE | Boeing 727-22F | 281/19083 | |
| ☐ N191FE | Boeing 727-22F | 337/19084 | |
| ☐ N192FE | Boeing 727-22F | 349/19085 | Lst MAL |
| ☐ N193FE | Boeing 727-22F | 440/19142 | |
| ☐ N194FE | Boeing 727-22F | 446/19143 | |
| ☐ N198FE | Boeing 727-22F | 512/19154 | |
| ☐ N199FE | Boeing 727-173C | 459/19509 | |
| ☐ N201FE | Boeing 727-2S2FRE | 1818/22924 | |
| ☐ N203FE | Boeing 727-2S2F | 1819/22925 | |
| ☐ N204FE | Boeing 727-2S2F | 1820/22926 | |
| ☐ N205FE | Boeing 727-2S2FRE | 1821/22927 | |
| ☐ N206FE | Boeing 727-2S2FRE | 1822/22928 | |
| ☐ N207FE | Boeing 727-2S2FRE | 1823/22929 | |
| ☐ N208FE | Boeing 727-2S2FRE | 1824/22930 | |
| ☐ N209FE | Boeing 727-2S2FRE | 1825/22931 | |
| ☐ N210FE | Boeing 727-2S2FRE | 1826/22932 | |
| ☐ N211FE | Boeing 727-2S2F | 1827/22933 | |
| ☐ N212FE | Boeing 727-2S2FRE | 1828/22934 | |
| ☐ N213FE | Boeing 727-2S2F | 1829/22935 | |
| ☐ N215FE | Boeing 727-2S2FRE | 1830/22936 | |
| ☐ N216FE | Boeing 727-2S2FRE | 1831/22937 | |
| ☐ N217FE | Boeing 727-2S2FRE | 1832/22938 | |
| ☐ N218FE | Boeing 727-233F | 1150/21101 | |
| ☐ N219FE | Boeing 727-233F | 1152/21102 | |
| ☐ N220FE | Boeing 727-233F | 1074/20934 | |
| ☐ N221FE | Boeing 727-233F | 1069/20932 | |
| ☐ N222FE | Boeing 727-233F | 1071/20933 | |
| ☐ N223FE | Boeing 727-233F | 1076/20935 | |
| ☐ N233FE | Boeing 727-247F | 1249/21327 | |
| ☐ N234FE | Boeing 727-247F | 1251/21328 | |
| ☐ N235FE | Boeing 727-247F | 1254/21329 | |
| ☐ N236FE | Boeing 727-247F | 1260/21330 | |
| ☐ N237FE | Boeing 727-247F | 1266/21331 | |
| ☐ N240FE | Boeing 727-277F | 1083/20978 | |
| ☐ N241FE | Boeing 727-277F | 1098/20979 | |
| ☐ N242FE | Boeing 727-277F | 1237/21178 | |
| ☐ N243FE | Boeing 727-277F | 1352/21480 | |
| ☐ N244FE | Boeing 727-277F | 1436/21647 | |
| ☐ N245FE | Boeing 727-277F | 1566/22016 | |
| ☐ N246FE | Boeing 727-277F | 1660/22068 | |
| ☐ N254FE | Boeing 727-233F | 1078/20936 | |
| ☐ N257FE | Boeing 727-233F | 1112/20939 | |
| ☐ N258FE | Boeing 727-233F | 1120/20940 | |
| ☐ N262FE | Boeing 727-233F | 1468/21624 | |
| ☐ N263FE | Boeing 727-233F | 1470/21625 | |
| ☐ N264FE | Boeing 727-233F | 1472/21626 | |
| ☐ N265FE | Boeing 727-233F | 1523/21671 | |
| ☐ N266FE | Boeing 727-233F | 1538/21672 | |
| ☐ N267FE | Boeing 727-233F | 1541/21673 | |
| ☐ N268FE | Boeing 727-233F | 1543/21674 | |
| ☐ N269FE | Boeing 727-233F | 1555/21675 | |

| | Registration | Type | Serial | Operator |
|---|---|---|---|---|
| ☐ | N270FE | Boeing 727-233F | 1578/22035 | |
| ☐ | N271FE | Boeing 727-233F | 1596/22036 | |
| ☐ | N272FE | Boeing 727-233F | 1600/22037 | |
| ☐ | N273FE | Boeing 727-233F | 1612/22038 | |
| ☐ | N274FE | Boeing 727-233F | 1614/22039 | |
| ☐ | N275FE | Boeing 727-233F | 1626/22040 | |
| ☐ | N276FE | Boeing 727-233F | 1628/22041 | |
| ☐ | N277FE | Boeing 727-233F | 1630/22042 | |
| ☐ | N278FE | Boeing 727-233F | 1699/22345 | |
| ☐ | N279FE | Boeing 727-233F | 1704/22346 | |
| ☐ | N280FE | Boeing 727-223F | 1708/22347 | |
| ☐ | N281FE | Boeing 727-233F | 1714/22348 | |
| ☐ | N282FE | Boeing 727-233F | 1722/22349 | |
| ☐ | N283FE | Boeing 727-233F | 1745/22350 | |
| ☐ | N284FE | Boeing 727-233F | 1791/22621 | |
| ☐ | N285FE | Boeing 727-233F | 1792/22622 | |
| ☐ | N286FE | Boeing 727-233F | 1803/22623 | |
| ☐ | N287FE | Boeing 727-2D4F | 1527/21849 | |
| ☐ | N288FE | Boeing 727-2D4F | 1536/21850 | |
| ☐ | N461FE | Boeing 727-225F | 1734/22548 | |
| ☐ | N462FE | Boeing 727-225F | 1739/22550 | |
| ☐ | N463FE | Boeing 727-225F | 1744/22551 | |
| ☐ | N464FE | Boeing 727-225F | 1234/21288 | |
| ☐ | N465FE | Boeing 727-225F | 1235/21289 | |
| ☐ | N466FE | Boeing 727-225F | 1240/21292 | |
| ☐ | N467FE | Boeing 727-225F | 1306/21449 | |
| ☐ | N468FE | Boeing 727-225F | 1312/21452 | |
| ☐ | N469FE | Boeing 727-225F | 1437/21581 | |
| ☐ | N477FE | Boeing 727-227F | 1281/21394 | |
| ☐ | N478FE | Boeing 727-227F | 1283/21395 | |
| ☐ | N479FE | Boeing 727-227F | 1337/21461 | |
| ☐ | N480FE | Boeing 727-227F | 1342/21462 | |
| ☐ | N481FE | Boeing 727-227F | 1353/21463 | |
| ☐ | N482FE | Boeing 727-227F | 1355/21464 | |
| ☐ | N483FE | Boeing 727-227F | 1363/21465 | |
| ☐ | N484FE | Boeing 727-227F | 1372/21466 | |
| ☐ | N485FE | Boeing 727-227F | 1388/21488 | |
| ☐ | N486FE | Boeing 727-227F | 1390/21489 | |
| ☐ | N487FE | Boeing 727-227F | 1396/21490 | |
| ☐ | N488FE | Boeing 727-227F | 1402/21491 | |
| ☐ | N489FE | Boeing 727-227F | 1440/21492 | |
| ☐ | N490FE | Boeing 727-227F | 1442/21493 | |
| ☐ | N491FE | Boeing 727-227F | 1444/21529 | |
| ☐ | N492FE | Boeing 727-227F | 1446/21530 | |
| ☐ | N493FE | Boeing 727-227F | 1450/21531 | |
| ☐ | N494FE | Boeing 727-227F | 1453/21532 | |
| ☐ | N495FE | Boeing 727-227F | 1484/21669 | |
| ☐ | N496FE | Boeing 727-227F | 1486/21670 | |
| ☐ | N498FE | Boeing 727-232F | 1068/20867 | |
| ☐ | N499FE | Boeing 727-232F | 1095/21018 | |
| ☐ | N700FX | Cessna 208B | 208B0419 | Opb CFS |
| ☐ | N701FX | Cessna 208B | 208B0420 | Opb WIG |
| ☐ | N702FX | Cessna 208B | 208B0422 | Opb BVN |
| ☐ | N703FX | Cessna 208B | 208B0423 | Opb IRO |
| ☐ | N705FX | Cessna 208B | 208B0425 | Opb CFS |
| ☐ | N706FX | Cessna 208B | 208B0426 | Opb IRO |
| ☐ | N707FX | Cessna 208B | 208B0427 | Opb PCM |
| ☐ | N708FX | Cessna 208B | 208B0429 | Opb MTN |
| ☐ | N709FX | Cessna 208B | 208B0430 | Opb CFS |
| ☐ | N710FX | Cessna 208B | 208B0431 | Opb CPT |
| ☐ | N711FX | Cessna 208B | 208B0433 | Opb CFS |
| ☐ | N712FX | Cessna 208B | 208B0435 | Opb IRO |
| ☐ | N713FX | Cessna 208B | 208B0438 | Opb PCM |
| ☐ | N715FX | Cessna 208B | 208B0440 | Opb MTN |
| ☐ | N716FX | Cessna 208B | 208B0442 | Opb CPT |
| ☐ | N717FX | Cessna 208B | 208B0445 | Opb IRO |
| ☐ | N718FX | Cessna 208B | 208B0448 | Opb BVN |
| ☐ | N719FX | Cessna 208B | 208B0450 | Opb BVN |
| ☐ | N720FX | Cessna 208B | 208B0452 | Opb CFS |
| ☐ | N721FX | Cessna 208B | 208B0453 | Opb MTN |
| ☐ | N722FX | Cessna 208B | 208B0454 | Opb PCM |
| ☐ | N723FX | Cessna 208B | 208B0456 | Opb BVN |
| ☐ | N724FX | Cessna 208B | 208B0458 | Opb CPT |
| ☐ | N725FX | Cessna 208B | 208B0460 | Opb WIG |
| ☐ | N726FX | Cessna 208B | 208B0465 | Opb PCM |
| ☐ | N727FX | Cessna 208B | 208B0468 | Opb IRO |
| ☐ | N728FX | Cessna 208B | 208B0471 | Opb CFS |
| ☐ | N729FX | Cessna 208B | 208B0474 | Opb MTN |
| ☐ | N730FX | Cessna 208B | 208B0477 | Opb CPT |
| ☐ | N731FX | Cessna 208B | 208B0480 | Opb WIG |
| ☐ | N738FX | Cessna 208B | 208B0482 | Opb BVN |
| ☐ | N740FX | Cessna 208B | 208B0484 | Opb MTN |
| ☐ | N741FX | Cessna 208B | 208B0486 | Opb BVN |
| ☐ | N742FX | Cessna 208B | 208B0489 | Opb MTN |
| ☐ | N744FX | Cessna 208B | 208B0492 | Opb PCM |
| ☐ | N745FX | Cessna 208B | 208B0495 | Opb BVN |
| ☐ | N746FX | Cessna 208B | 208B0498 | Opb CFS |
| ☐ | N747FE | Cessna 208B | 208B0238 | Opb MTN |
| ☐ | N747FX | Cessna 208B | 208B0501 | Opb MTN |
| ☐ | N748FE | Cessna 208B | 208B0241 | Opb WIG |
| ☐ | N748FX | Cessna 208B | 208B0503 | Opb PCM |
| ☐ | N749FE | Cessna 208B | 208B0242 | Opb BVN |
| ☐ | N749FX | Cessna 208B | 208B0508 | Opb MAL |
| ☐ | N750FX | Cessna 208B | 208B0511 | Opb PCM |
| ☐ | N751FE | Cessna 208B | 208B0245 | Opb CPT |
| ☐ | N751FX | Cessna 208B | 208B0514 | Opb BVN |
| ☐ | N752FE | Cessna 208B | 208B0247 | Opb IRO |
| ☐ | N752FX | Cessna 208B | 208B0517 | Opb CFS |
| ☐ | N753FE | Cessna 208B | 208B0248 | Opb CFS |
| ☐ | N753FX | Cessna 208B | 208B0520 | Opb BVN |
| ☐ | N754FX | Cessna 208B | 208B0526 | Opb PCM |
| ☐ | N755FE | Cessna 208B | 208B0250 | Opb MTN |
| ☐ | N755FX | Cessna 208B | 208B0529 | Opb WIG |
| ☐ | N756FE | Cessna 208B | 208B0251 | Opb BVN |
| ☐ | N756FX | Cessna 208B | 208B0532 | Opb CFS |
| ☐ | N757FX | Cessna 208B | 208B0535 | Opb WIG |
| ☐ | N758FX | Cessna 208B | 208B0539 | Opb MAL |
| ☐ | N759FX | Cessna 208B | 208B0542 | Opb MAL |
| ☐ | N760FE | Cessna 208B | 208B0252 | Opb Corp Air |
| ☐ | N761FE | Cessna 208B | 208B0254 | Opb IRO |
| ☐ | N762FE | Cessna 208B | 208B0255 | Opb PCM |
| ☐ | N763FE | Cessna 208B | 208B0256 | Opb PCM |
| ☐ | N764FE | Cessna 208B | 208B0258 | Opb MTN |
| ☐ | N765FE | Cessna 208B | 208B0259 | Opb BVN |
| ☐ | N766FE | Cessna 208B | 208B0260 | Opb Corp Air |
| ☐ | N767FE | Cessna 208B | 208B0262 | Opb IRO |
| ☐ | N768FE | Cessna 208B | 208B0263 | Opb PCM |
| ☐ | N769FE | Cessna 208B | 208B0264 | Opb MTN |
| ☐ | N770FE | Cessna 208B | 208B0265 | Opb BVN |
| ☐ | N771FE | Cessna 208B | 208B0267 | Opb PCM |
| ☐ | N772FE | Cessna 208B | 208B0268 | Opb PCM |
| ☐ | N773FE | Cessna 208B | 208B0269 | Opb BVN |
| ☐ | N774FE | Cessna 208B | 208B0271 | Opb BVN |
| ☐ | N775FE | Cessna 208B | 208B0272 | Opb CFS |
| ☐ | N776FE | Cessna 208B | 208B0273 | Opb MTN |
| ☐ | N778FE | Cessna 208B | 208B0275 | Opb CFS |
| ☐ | N779FE | Cessna 208B | 208B0276 | Opb CFS |
| ☐ | N780FE | Cessna 208B | 208B0277 | Opb WIG |
| ☐ | N781FE | Cessna 208B | 208B0278 | Opb PCM |
| ☐ | N782FE | Cessna 208B | 208B0280 | Opb PCM |
| ☐ | N783FE | Cessna 208B | 208B0281 | Opb WIG |
| ☐ | N784FE | Cessna 208B | 208B0282 | Opb IRO |
| ☐ | N785FE | Cessna 208B | 208B0283 | Opb PCM |
| ☐ | N786FE | Cessna 208B | 208B0284 | Opb BVN |
| ☐ | N787FE | Cessna 208B | 208B0285 | Opb MTN |
| ☐ | N788FE | Cessna 208B | 208B0286 | Opb CFS |
| ☐ | N789FE | Cessna 208B | 208B0287 | Opb WIG |
| ☐ | N790FE | Cessna 208B | 208B0288 | Opb PCM |
| ☐ | N791FE | Cessna 208B | 208B0289 | Opb CPT |
| ☐ | N792FE | Cessna 208B | 208B0290 | Opb MTN |
| ☐ | N793FE | Cessna 208B | 208B0291 | Opb BVN |
| ☐ | N794FE | Cessna 208B | 208B0292 | Opb CPT |
| ☐ | N795FE | Cessna 208B | 208B0293 | Opb IRO |
| ☐ | N796FE | Cessna 208B | 208B0212 | Opb CPT |
| ☐ | N797FE | Cessna 208B | 208B0042 | Opb CPT |
| ☐ | N798FE | Cessna 208B | 208B0174 | Opb CPT |
| ☐ | N799FE | Cessna 208A | 20800065 | Opb CPT |
| ☐ | N800FE | Cessna 208 | 20800007 | Opb CPT |
| ☐ | N801FE | Cessna 208A | 20800009 | Opb MTN |
| ☐ | N804FE | Cessna 208B | 208B0039 | Opb WIG |
| ☐ | N807FE | Cessna 208B | 208B0041 | Opb WIG |
| ☐ | N812FE | Cessna 208A | 20800040 | Opb CPT |
| ☐ | N819FE | Cessna 208A | 20800056 | Opb MTN |
| ☐ | N820FE | Cessna 208B | 208B0111 | Opb MTN |
| ☐ | N827FE | Cessna 208A | 20800072 | Opb CPT |
| ☐ | N828FE | Cessna 208B | 208B0122 | Opb IRO |
| ☐ | N830FE | Cessna 208A | 20800075 | Opb IRO |

| Reg | Type | Serial | Operator |
|---|---|---|---|
| ☐ N831FE | Cessna 208B | 208B0225 | Opb MTN |
| ☐ N832FE | Cessna 208 | 20800081 | Opb BVN |
| ☐ N833FE | Cessna 208A | 20800084 | Opb CFS |
| ☐ N835FE | Cessna 208A | 20800016 | Opb WIG |
| ☐ N841FE | Cessna 208B | 208B0144 | Opb BVN |
| ☐ N842FE | Cessna 208B | 208B0146 | Opb MTN |
| ☐ N843FE | Cessna 208B | 208B0147 | Opb IRO |
| ☐ N844FE | Cessna 208B | 208B0149 | Opb PCM |
| ☐ N845FE | Cessna 208B | 208B0152 | Opb BVN |
| ☐ N846FE | Cessna 208B | 208B0154 | Opb CPT |
| ☐ N847FE | Cessna 208B | 208B0156 | Opb MTN |
| ☐ N848FE | Cessna 208B | 208B0158 | Opb MTN |
| ☐ N849FE | Cessna 208B | 208B0162 | Opb MTN |
| ☐ N850FE | Cessna 208B | 208B0164 | Opb CFS |
| ☐ N851FE | Cessna 208B | 208B0166 | Opb CPT |
| ☐ N852FE | Cessna 208B | 208B0168 | Opb MTN |
| ☐ N853FE | Cessna 208B | 208B0170 | Opb MTN |
| ☐ N855FE | Cessna 208B | 208B0203 | Opb MTN |
| ☐ N856FE | Cessna 208B | 208B0176 | Opb CFS |
| ☐ N857FE | Cessna 208B | 208B0177 | Opb PCM |
| ☐ N858FE | Cessna 208B | 208B0178 | Opb IRO |
| ☐ N859FE | Cessna 208B | 208B0181 | Opb CFS |
| ☐ N860FE | Cessna 208B | 208B0182 | Opb Corp Air |
| ☐ N861FE | Cessna 208B | 208B0183 | Opb BVN |
| ☐ N862FE | Cessna 208B | 208B0184 | Opb MTN |
| ☐ N863FE | Cessna 208B | 208B0186 | Opb CPT |
| ☐ N864FE | Cessna 208B | 208B0187 | Opb CPT |
| ☐ N865FE | Cessna 208B | 208B0188 | Opb WIG |
| ☐ N866FE | Cessna 208B | 208B0189 | Opb BVN |
| ☐ N867FE | Cessna 208B | 208B0191 | Opb CPT |
| ☐ N869FE | Cessna 208B | 208B0195 | Opb MTN |
| ☐ N870FE | Cessna 208B | 208B0196 | Opb WIG |
| ☐ N871FE | Cessna 208B | 208B0198 | Opb IRO |
| ☐ N872FE | Cessna 208B | 208B0200 | Opb PCM |
| ☐ N873FE | Cessna 208B | 208B0202 | Opb CFS |
| ☐ N874FE | Cessna 208B | 208B0205 | Opb MTN |
| ☐ N875FE | Cessna 208B | 208B0206 | Opb CFS |
| ☐ N876FE | Cessna 208B | 208B0207 | Opb CFS |
| ☐ N877FE | Cessna 208B | 208B0232 | Opb CPT |
| ☐ N878FE | Cessna 208B | 208B0211 | Opb MTN |
| ☐ N879FE | Cessna 208B | 208B0213 | Opb PCM |
| ☐ N880FE | Cessna 208B | 208B0215 | Opb CFS |
| ☐ N881FE | Cessna 208B | 208B0204 | Opb MTN |
| ☐ N882FE | Cessna 208B | 208B0208 | Opb CFS |
| ☐ N883FE | Cessna 208B | 208B0210 | Opb IRO |
| ☐ N884FE | Cessna 208B | 208B0233 | Opb IRO |
| ☐ N885FE | Cessna 208B | 208B0185 | Opb CPT |
| ☐ N886FE | Cessna 208B | 208B0190 | Opb PCM |
| ☐ N887FE | Cessna 208B | 208B0216 | Opb MTN |
| ☐ N888FE | Cessna 208B | 208B0217 | Opb WIG |
| ☐ N889FE | Cessna 208B | 208B0218 | Opb BVN |
| ☐ N890FE | Cessna 208B | 208B0219 | Opb CPT |
| ☐ N891FE | Cessna 208B | 208B0221 | Opb PCM |
| ☐ N892FE | Cessna 208B | 208B0222 | Opb PCM |
| ☐ N893FE | Cessna 208B | 208B0223 | Opb IRO |
| ☐ N894FE | Cessna 208B | 208B0224 | Opb BVN |
| ☐ N895FE | Cessna 208B | 208B0015 | Opb CFS |
| ☐ N896FE | Cessna 208B | 208B0226 | Opb MAL |
| ☐ N897FE | Cessna 208B | 208B0227 | Opb CFS |
| ☐ N898FE | Cessna 208B | 208B0228 | Opb WIG |
| ☐ N899FE | Cessna 208B | 208B0235 | Opb CFS |
| ☐ N900FE | Cessna 208B | 208B0054 | Opb BVN |
| ☐ N901FE | Cessna 208B | 208B0001 | Opb WIG |
| ☐ N902FE | Cessna 208B | 208B0002 | Opb BVN |
| ☐ N903FE | Cessna 208B | 208B0003 | Opb CPT |
| ☐ N904FE | Cessna 208B | 208B0004 | Opb CPT |
| ☐ N905FE | Cessna 208B | 208B0005 | Opb MTN |
| ☐ N906FE | Cessna 208B | 208B0006 | Opb IRO |
| ☐ N907FE | Cessna 208B | 208B0007 | Opb IRO |
| ☐ N908FE | Cessna 208B | 208B0008 | Opb PCM |
| ☐ N909FE | Cessna 208B | 208B0009 | Opb WIG |
| ☐ N910FE | Cessna 208B | 208B0010 | Opb CPT |
| ☐ N911FE | Cessna 208B | 208B0011 | Opb WIG |
| ☐ N912FE | Cessna 208B | 208B0012 | Opb BVN |
| ☐ N914FE | Cessna 208B | 208B0014 | Opb IRO |
| ☐ N916FE | Cessna 208B | 208B0016 | Opb CPT |
| ☐ N917FE | Cessna 208B | 208B0017 | Opb MTN |
| ☐ N918FE | Cessna 208B | 208B0018 | Opb CFS |
| ☐ N919FE | Cessna 208B | 208B0019 | Opb WIG |
| ☐ N920FE | Cessna 208B | 208B0020 | Opb PCM |
| ☐ N921FE | Cessna 208B | 208B0021 | Opb MTN |
| ☐ N922FE | Cessna 208B | 208B0022 | Opb BVN |
| ☐ N923FE | Cessna 208B | 208B0023 | Opb IRO |
| ☐ N924FE | Cessna 208B | 208B0024 | Opb CPT |
| ☐ N925FE | Cessna 208B | 208B0025 | Opb IRO |
| ☐ N926FE | Cessna 208B | 208B0026 | Opb CPT |
| ☐ N927FE | Cessna 208B | 208B0027 | Opb IRO |
| ☐ N928FE | Cessna 208B | 208B0028 | Opb BVN |
| ☐ N929FE | Cessna 208B | 208B0029 | Opb BVN |
| ☐ N930FE | Cessna 208B | 208B0030 | Opb PCM |
| ☐ N931FE | Cessna 208B | 208B0031 | Opb WIG |
| ☐ N933FE | Cessna 208B | 208B0033 | Opb CPT |
| ☐ N934FE | Cessna 208B | 208B0034 | Opb BVN |
| ☐ N935FE | Cessna 208B | 208B0035 | Opb WIG |
| ☐ N936FE | Cessna 208B | 208B0036 | Opb CPT |
| ☐ N937FE | Cessna 208B | 208B0037 | Opb WIG |
| ☐ N938FE | Cessna 208B | 208B0038 | Opb MTN |
| ☐ N939FE | Cessna 208B | 208B0180 | Opb BVN |
| ☐ N940FE | Cessna 208B | 208B0040 | Opb CFS |
| ☐ N943FE | Cessna 208B | 208B0043 | Opb MTN |
| ☐ N944FE | Cessna 208B | 208B0044 | Opb BVN |
| ☐ N946FE | Cessna 208B | 208B0048 | Opb IRO |
| ☐ N947FE | Cessna 208B | 208B0050 | Opb WIG |
| ☐ N950FE | Cessna 208B | 208B0056 | Opb BVN |
| ☐ N952FE | Cessna 208B | 208B0060 | Opb CPT |
| ☐ N953FE | Cessna 208B | 208B0062 | Opb CFS |
| ☐ N954FE | Cessna 208B | 208B0064 | Opb IRO |
| ☐ N955FE | Cessna 208B | 208B0066 | Opb MTN |
| ☐ N956FE | Cessna 208B | 208B0068 | Opb CFS |
| ☐ N957FE | Cessna 208B | 208B0070 | Opb BVN |
| ☐ N958FE | Cessna 208B | 208B0071 | Opb WIG |
| ☐ N959FE | Cessna 208B | 208B0073 | Opb WIG |
| ☐ N960FE | Cessna 208B | 208B0075 | Opb CFS |
| ☐ N961FE | Cessna 208B | 208B0077 | Opb BVN |
| ☐ N962FE | Cessna 208B | 208B0078 | Opb MTN |
| ☐ N963FE | Cessna 208B | 208B0080 | Opb WIG |
| ☐ N964FE | Cessna 208B | 208B0083 | Opb CPT |
| ☐ N965FE | Cessna 208B | 208B0084 | Opb CFS |
| ☐ N966FE | Cessna 208B | 208B0086 | Opb WIG |
| ☐ N967FE | Cessna 208B | 208B0088 | Opb MTN |
| ☐ N968FE | Cessna 208B | 208B0090 | Opb PCM |
| ☐ N969FE | Cessna 208B | 208B0092 | Opb PCM |
| ☐ N970FE | Cessna 208B | 208B0093 | Opb BVN |
| ☐ N971FE | Cessna 208B | 208B0094 | Opb CPT |
| ☐ N972FE | Cessna 208B | 208B0096 | Opb CPT |
| ☐ N973FE | Cessna 208B | 208B0098 | Opb MTN |
| ☐ N975FE | Cessna 208B | 208B0101 | Opb MTN |
| ☐ N976FE | Cessna 208B | 208B0103 | Opb CFS |
| ☐ N977FE | Cessna 208B | 208B0104 | Opb CPT |
| ☐ N978FE | Cessna 208B | 208B0105 | Opb BVN |
| ☐ N979FE | Cessna 208B | 208B0106 | Opb MTN |
| ☐ N980FE | Cessna 208B | 208B0108 | Opb CPT |
| ☐ N981FE | Cessna 208B | 208B0110 | Opb WIG |
| ☐ N983FE | Cessna 208B | 208B0113 | Opb CFS |
| ☐ N984FE | Cessna 208B | 208B0115 | Opb PCM |
| ☐ N985FE | Cessna 208B | 208B0117 | Opb PCM |
| ☐ N986FE | Cessna 208B | 208B0194 | Opb IRO |
| ☐ N987FE | Cessna 208B | 208B0201 | Opb PCM |
| ☐ N989FE | Cessna 208B | 208B0124 | Opb WIG |
| ☐ N990FE | Cessna 208B | 208B0125 | Opb CPT |
| ☐ N991FE | Cessna 208B | 208B0127 | Opb CPT |
| ☐ N992FE | Cessna 208B | 208B0128 | Opb CFS |
| ☐ N993FE | Cessna 208B | 208B0130 | Opb IRO |
| ☐ N994FE | Cessna 208B | 208B0132 | Opb BVN |
| ☐ N995FE | Cessna 208B | 208B0133 | Opb PCM |
| ☐ N996FE | Cessna 208B | 208B0135 | Opb WIG |
| ☐ N997FE | Cessna 208B | 208B0197 | Opb CPT |
| ☐ N998FE | Cessna 208B | 208B0139 | Opb WIG |
| ☐ N999FE | Cessna 208B | 208B0231 | Opb MTN |
| ☐ N701FE | F.27 Friendship 600 | 10419 | Opb CFS |
| ☐ N702FE | F.27 Friendship 600 | 10350 | Opb CFS |
| ☐ N703FE | F.27 Friendship 600 | 10420 | Opb CFS |
| ☐ N705FE | F.27 Friendship 500 | 10367 | Opb MTN |
| ☐ N706FE | F.27 Friendship 500 | 10384 | Opb MTN |
| ☐ N707FE | F.27 Friendship 500 | 10371 | Opb CFS |
| ☐ N708FE | F.27 Friendship 500 | 10372 | Opb CFS |
| ☐ N709FE | F.27 Friendship 500 | 10375 | Opb MTN |

| | | | |
|---|---|---|---|
| ☐ N710FE | F.27 Friendship 500 | 10380 | Opb MTN |
| ☐ N711FE | F.27 Friendship 500 | 10383 | Opb CFS |
| ☐ N712FE | F.27 Friendship 500F | 10613 | Opb MTN |
| ☐ N713FE | F.27 Friendship 500F | 10615 | Opb MTN |
| ☐ N714FE | F.27 Friendship 500 | 10461 | Opb MTN |
| ☐ N715FE | F.27 Friendship 500 | 10468 | Opb MTN |
| ☐ N716FE | F.27 Friendship 500 | 10471 | Opb MTN |
| ☐ N717FE | F.27 Friendship 500 | 10455 | Opb MTN |
| ☐ N718FE | F.27 Friendship 500 | 10470 | Opb MTN |
| ☐ N719FE | F.27 Friendship 500 | 10467 | Opb MTN |
| ☐ N720FE | F.27 Friendship 500 | 10464 | Opb CFS |
| ☐ N721FE | F.27 Friendship 500 | 10460 | Opb MTN |
| ☐ N722FE | F.27 Friendship 500 | 10472 | Opb MTN |
| ☐ N723FE | F.27 Friendship 500 | 10682 | Opb MTN |
| ☐ N724FE | F.27 Friendship 500 | 10677 | Opb MTN |
| ☐ N725FE | F.27 Friendship 500 | 10658 | Opb MTN |
| ☐ N726FE | F.27 Friendship 500 | 10683 | Opb MTN |
| ☐ N727FE | F.27 Friendship 500 | 10661 | Opb MTN |
| ☐ N728FE | F.27 Friendship 500 | 10657 | Opb MTN |
| ☐ N729FE | F.27 Friendship 600 | 10385 | Opb CFS |
| ☐ N730FE | F.27 Friendship 600 | 10386 | Opb CFS |
| ☐ N740FE | F.27 Friendship 600 | 10329 | Opb CFS |
| ☐ N741FE | F.27 Friendship 600 | 10387 | Opb CFS |
| ☐ N742FE | F.27 Friendship 600 | 10349 | Opb CFS |
| | | | |
| ☐ N131AA | Douglas DC-10-10 | 273/46994 | std |
| ☐ N132AA | Douglas DC-10-10 | 294/47827 | std |
| ☐ N134AA | Douglas DC-10-10F | 321/47829 | |
| ☐ N135AA | Douglas DC-10-10 | 323/47830 | std |
| ☐ N167AA | Douglas DC-10-10 | 112/40930 | std |
| ☐ N168AA | Douglas DC-10-10 | 153/46938 | std |
| ☐ N301FE | McDD MD-10-30CF | 96/46800 | |
| ☐ N302FE | Douglas DC-10-30CF | 103/46801 | |
| ☐ N303FE | McDD MD-10-30CF | 110/46802 | |
| ☐ N304FE | Douglas DC-10-30CF | 257/46992 | |
| ☐ N305FE | Douglas DC-10-30F | 339/47870 | |
| ☐ N306FE | Douglas DC-10-30F | 409/48287 | |
| ☐ N307FE | Douglas DC-10-30F | 412/48291 | |
| ☐ N308FE | Douglas DC-10-30F | 416/48297 | |
| ☐ N309FE | Douglas DC-10-30F | 419/48298 | |
| ☐ N310FE | Douglas DC-10-30F | 422/48299 | |
| ☐ N311FE | McDD MD-10-30CF | 219/46871 | |
| ☐ N312FE | McDD MD-10-30CF | 433/48300 | |
| ☐ N313FE | Douglas DC-10-30F | 440/48311 | |
| ☐ N314FE | Douglas DC-10-30F | 442/48312 | |
| ☐ N315FE | Douglas DC-10-30F | 443/48313 | |
| ☐ N316FE | McDD MD-10-30F | 444/48314 | |
| ☐ N317FE | Douglas DC-10-30CF | 277/46835 | |
| ☐ N318FE | Douglas DC-10-30CF | 282/46837 | |
| ☐ N319FE | Douglas DC-10-30CF | 317/47820 | |
| ☐ N320FE | Douglas DC-10-30F | 326/47835 | |
| ☐ N321FE | Douglas DC-10-30F | 330/47836 | |
| ☐ N322FE | Douglas DC-10-30CF | 215/47908 | |
| ☐ N323FE | Douglas DC-10-30F | 302/47811 | |
| ☐ N326FE | Douglas DC-10-30F | 312/47813 | |
| ☐ N358FE | McDD MD-10-10F | 297/46633 | |
| ☐ N359FE | Douglas DC-10-10 | 307/46635 | |
| ☐ N360FE | McDD MD-10-10F | 309/46636 | |
| ☐ N361FE | McDD MD-10-10F | 344/48260 | |
| ☐ N362FE | McDD MD-10-10F | 347/48261 | |
| ☐ N363FE | McDD MD-10-10F | 353/48263 | |
| ☐ N364FE | McDD MD-10-10F | 4/46600 | |
| ☐ N365FE | Douglas DC-10-10F | 6/46601 | |
| ☐ N366FE | Douglas DC-10-10F | 8/46602 | |
| ☐ N367FE | Douglas DC-10-10F | 15/46605 | |
| ☐ N368FE | Douglas DC-10-10F | 17/46606 | |
| ☐ N369FE | Douglas DC-10-10 | 25/46607 | |
| ☐ N370FE | Douglas DC-10-10F | 26/46608 | |
| ☐ N371FE | Douglas DC-10-10F | 27/46609 | |
| ☐ N372FE | McDD MD-10-10F | 32/46610 | |
| ☐ N373FE | Douglas DC-10-10F | 35/46611 | |
| ☐ N374FE | Douglas DC-10-10 | 39/46612 | |
| ☐ N375FE | Douglas DC-10-10 | 42/46613 | |
| ☐ N377FE | McDD MD-10-10F | 59/47965 | |
| ☐ N381FE | Douglas DC-10-10 | 76/46615 | |
| ☐ N383FE | Douglas DC-10-10F | 86/46616 | |
| ☐ N384FE | Douglas DC-10-10F | 89/46617 | |
| ☐ N385FE | Douglas DC-10-10F | 119/46619 | |
| ☐ N386FE | McDD MD-10-10F | 138/46620 | |

| | | | |
|---|---|---|---|
| ☐ N387FE | Douglas DC-10-10F | 140/46621 | |
| ☐ N388FE | Douglas DC-10-10F | 144/46622 | |
| ☐ N389FE | Douglas DC-10-10F | 154/46623 | |
| ☐ N390FE | Douglas DC-10-10F | 155/46624 | |
| ☐ N391FE | McDD MD-10-10F | 169/46625 | |
| ☐ N392FE | Douglas DC-10-10F | 198/46626 | |
| ☐ N393FE | McDD MD-10-10F | 205/46627 | |
| ☐ N395FE | Douglas DC-10-10F | 208/46630 | |
| ☐ N396FE | McDD MD-10-10F | 209/46631 | |
| ☐ N397FE | Douglas DC-10-10F | 210/46632 | |
| ☐ N398FE | McDD MD-10-10F | 298/46634 | |
| ☐ N399FE | McDD MD-10-10F | 351/48262 | |
| ☐ N550FE | McDD MD-10-10F | 55/46521 | |
| ☐ N566FE | McDD MD-10-10F | 271/46989 | |
| | | | |
| ☐ N1829U | Douglas DC-10-10 | 207/46629 | std |
| ☐ N1849U | Douglas DC-10-10 | 203/46939 | std |
| ☐ N1853U | Douglas DC-10-30F | 303/47812 | std |
| ☐ N10060 | Douglas DC-10-10F | 269/46970 | |
| ☐ N40061 | Douglas DC-10-10F | 272/46973 | |
| ☐ N68049 | Douglas DC-10-10CF | 139/47803 | |
| ☐ N68050 | Douglas DC-10-10CF | 142/47804 | |
| ☐ N68051 | Douglas DC-10-10CF | 145/47805 | |
| ☐ N68052 | Douglas DC-10-10CF | 148/47806 | |
| ☐ N68053 | Douglas DC-10-10CF | 173/47807 | |
| ☐ N68054 | Douglas DC-10-10CF | 177/47808 | |
| ☐ N68056 | Douglas DC-10-10CF | 194/47810 | |
| ☐ N68057 | Douglas DC-10-10CF | 379/48264 | |
| ☐ N68058 | Douglas DC-10-10F | 33/40705 | |
| ☐ N68059 | Douglas DC-10-10F | 78/46907 | |
| ☐ N | Douglas DC-10-10 | 70/46710 | std |
| ☐ N | Douglas DC-10-10 | 207/46628 | std |
| ☐ N | Douglas DC-10-30 | 61/46707 | std |
| ☐ N | Douglas DC-10-10 | 62/46708 | std |
| | | | |
| ☐ N578FE | McDD MD-11F | 449/48458 | |
| ☐ N579FE | McDD MD-11 | 546/48470 | |
| ☐ N580FE | McDD MD-11F | 558/48471 | |
| ☐ N582FE | McDD MD-11F | 451/48420 | |
| ☐ N583FE | McDD MD-11F | 452/48421 | |
| ☐ N584FE | McDD MD-11F | 483/48436 | |
| ☐ N585FE | McDD MD-11F | 482/48481 | |
| ☐ N586FE | McDD MD-11F | 469/48487 | |
| ☐ N587FE | McDD MD-11F | 492/48489 | |
| ☐ N588FE | McDD MD-11F | 499/48490 | |
| ☐ N589FE | McDD MD-11F | 503/48491 | |
| ☐ N590FE | McDD MD-11F | 462/48505 | |
| ☐ N591FE | McDD MD-11F | 504/48527 | |
| ☐ N592FE | McDD MD-11F | 526/48550 | |
| ☐ N593FE | McDD MD-11F | 527/48551 | |
| ☐ N594FE | McDD MD-11F | 530/48552 | |
| ☐ N595FE | McDD MD-11F | 531/48553 | |
| ☐ N596FE | McDD MD-11F | 535/48554 | |
| ☐ N597FE | McDD MD-11F | 537/48596 | |
| ☐ N598FE | McDD MD-11F | 540/48597 | |
| ☐ N599FE | McDD MD-11F | 550/48598 | |
| ☐ N601FE | McDD MD-11F | 447/48401 | |
| ☐ N602FE | McDD MD-11F | 448/48402 | |
| ☐ N603FE | McDD MD-11F | 470/48459 | |
| ☐ N604FE | McDD MD-11F | 497/48460 | |
| ☐ N605FE | McDD MD-11F | 515/48514 | |
| ☐ N606FE | McDD MD-11F | 549/48602 | |
| ☐ N607FE | McDD MD-11F | 517/48547 | |
| ☐ N608FE | McDD MD-11F | 521/48548 | |
| ☐ N609FE | McDD MD-11F | 545/48549 | |
| ☐ N610FE | McDD MD-11F | 551/48603 | |
| ☐ N612FE | McDD MD-11F | 555/48605 | |
| ☐ N613FE | McDD MD-11F | 598/48749 | |
| ☐ N614FE | McDD MD-11F | 507/48528 | |
| ☐ N615FE | McDD MD-11F | 602/48767 | |
| ☐ N616FE | McDD MD-11F | 594/48747 | |
| ☐ N617FE | McDD MD-11F | 595/48748 | |
| ☐ N618FE | McDD MD-11F | 604/48754 | |
| ☐ N619FE | McDD MD-11F | 607/48770 | |
| ☐ N620FE | McDD MD-11F | 635/48791 | |
| ☐ N621FE | McDD MD-11F | 636/48792 | |
| ☐ N623FE | McDD MD-11F | 638/48794 | |

## FINE AIR SERVICES APW

| | | | |
|---|---|---|---|
| ☐ N29UA | Douglas DC-8-61F | 544/46159 | |
| ☐ N30UA | Douglas DC-8-61F | 290/45888 | |
| ☐ N44UA | Douglas DC-8F-54 | 234/45800 | std |
| ☐ N54FA | Douglas DC-8F-54 | 157/45637 | std |
| ☐ N55FB | Douglas DC-8F-55 | 218/45678 | std |
| ☐ N345JW | Douglas DC-8-63F | 421/46042 | |
| ☐ N426FB | Douglas DC-8F-54 | 185/45667 | |
| ☐ N427FB | Douglas DC-8F-54 | 195/45684 | std |
| ☐ N441J | Douglas DC-8-63CF | 416/45988 | |
| ☐ N505FB | Douglas DC-8-51F | 21/45410 | std |
| ☐ N508DC | Douglas DC-8-51F) | 330/45935 | std |
| ☐ N661AV | Douglas DC-8-63CF | 396/45969 | |
| ☐ N784AL | Douglas DC-8-63F | 531/46135 | |
| ☐ N791AL | Douglas DC-8-62F | 539/46150 | |
| ☐ N802BN | Douglas DC-8-62F | 307/45909 | |
| ☐ N810BN | Douglas DC-8-62F | 298/45905 | |
| ☐ N906R | Douglas DC-8-63F | 454/46087 | |
| ☐ N1804 | Douglas DC-8-62F | 303/45896 | |
| ☐ N1808E | Douglas DC-8-62F | 494/46105 | |
| ☐ N7046H | Douglas DC-8F-54 | 408/46011 | std |
| ☐ N8968U | Douglas DC-8-62F | 465/46069 | |
| ☐ N8969U | Douglas DC-8-62F | 467/46070 | |
| ☐ N8974U | Douglas DC-8-62F | 487/46110 | |
| | | | |
| ☐ N260FA | L-1011-200F Tristar | 1158 | std |
| ☐ N306GB | L-1011-200F Tristar | 1138 | std |
| ☐ N307GB | L-1011-200F Tristar | 1131 | |
| ☐ N308GB | L-1011-200F Tristar | 1133 | |

## FLORIDA WEST INTL AIRLINES FWL

| | | | |
|---|---|---|---|
| ☐ N316LA | Boeing 767-316ERF | 860/30842 | Lsf LCO |
| ☐ N872SJ | Douglas DC-8-71F | 449/46040 | Lsf LCO |

## FRONTIER AIRLINES FFT

| | | | |
|---|---|---|---|
| ☐ N801FR | Airbus A318-111 | 1939 | o/o |
| ☐ N802FR | Airbus A318-111 | 1991 | o/o |
| ☐ N803FR | Airbus A318-111 | | o/o |
| ☐ N804FR | Airbus A318-111 | | o/o |
| ☐ N805FR | Airbus A318-111 | | o/o |
| ☐ N901FR | Airbus A319-111 | 1488 | |
| ☐ N902FR | Airbus A319-111 | 1515 | |
| ☐ N903FR | Airbus A319-111 | 1560 | |
| ☐ N904FR | Airbus A319-111 | 1579 | |
| ☐ N905FR | Airbus A319-111 | 1583 | |
| ☐ N906FR | Airbus A319-111 | 1684 | |
| ☐ N907FR | Airbus A319-111 | 1743 | |
| ☐ N908FR | Airbus A319-111 | 1759 | |
| ☐ N909FR | Airbus A319-111 | 1761 | |
| ☐ N910FR | Airbus A319-111 | 1781 | |
| ☐ N912FR | Airbus A319-111 | 1803 | |
| ☐ N913FR | Airbus A319-111 | 1863 | |
| ☐ N914FR | Airbus A319-111 | 1841 | |
| ☐ N915FR | Airbus A319-111 | 1851 | |
| ☐ N916FR | Airbus A319-111 | 1876 | |
| ☐ N917FR | Airbus A319-111 | 1890 | |
| ☐ N918FR | Airbus A319-111 | 1943 | o/o |
| ☐ N919FR | Airbus A319-111 | 1980 | o/o |
| ☐ N920FR | Airbus A319-111 | 1991 | o/o |
| ☐ N921FR | Airbus A319-111 | 1997 | o/o |
| ☐ N922FR | Airbus A319-111 | 2010 | o/o |
| ☐ N923FR | Airbus A319-111 | 2012 | o/o |
| ☐ N924FR | Airbus A319-111 | | o/o |
| ☐ N925FR | Airbus A319-111 | | o/o |
| ☐ N926FR | Airbus A319-111 | | o/o |
| ☐ N927FR | Airbus A319-111 | | o/o |
| | | | |
| ☐ N1PC | Boeing 737-2P6 | 530/21613 | |
| ☐ N118RW | Boeing 737-2Y5 | 955/23040 | 276 |
| ☐ N237TR | Boeing 737-228 | 948/23007 | |
| ☐ N270FL | Boeing 737-2L9 | 812/22733 | 270; std |
| ☐ N271FL | Boeing 737-2L9 | 818/22734 | 271; std |
| ☐ N578US | Boeing 737-301 | 1124/23257 | 301 |
| ☐ N302FL | Boeing 737-317 | 1216/23177 | 302 |

| | | | |
|---|---|---|---|
| ☐ N303FL | Boeing 737-3M8 | 2007/25039 | 303 |
| ☐ N304FL | Boeing 737-3Q8 | 2878/27633 | 304 |
| ☐ N305FA | Boeing 737-36Q | 2914/28662 | 305 |
| ☐ N306FL | Boeing 737-36N | 2921/28563 | 306 |
| ☐ N307FL | Boeing 737-36Q | 2989/28760 | 307 |
| ☐ N310FL | Boeing 737-3L9 | 2234/26440 | 310 |
| ☐ N311FL | Boeing 737-3S1 | 1911/24856 | 311 |
| ☐ N312FL | Boeing 737-3L9 | 1775/24569 | 312 |
| ☐ N313FL | Boeing 737-3L9 | 2277/26442 | 313 |
| ☐ N314FL | Boeing 737-36E | 2123/25256 | 314 |
| ☐ N315FL | Boeing 737-36E | 2068/25159 | 315 |
| ☐ N316FL | Boeing 737-36E | 2194/25264 | 316 |
| ☐ N317FL | Boeing 737-36E | 2187/25263 | 317 |
| ☐ N318FL | Boeing 737-3Q8 | 2541/26293 | 318 |
| ☐ N319FL | Boeing 737-3Q8 | 2623/26301 | 319 |
| ☐ N921WA | Boeing 737-2Y5 | 954/23039 | |

## FRONTIER JETEXPRESS FFT

| | | | |
|---|---|---|---|
| ☐ N17156 | Canadair RJ-200 | 7156 | Opb ASH |
| ☐ N17175 | Canadair RJ-200 | 7175 | Opb ASH |
| ☐ N37342 | Canadair RJ-200 | 7342 | Opb ASH |

## GEMINI AIR CARGO GCO

| | | | |
|---|---|---|---|
| ☐ N600GC | Douglas DC-10-30F | 245/46965 | |
| ☐ N601GC | Douglas DC-10-30F | 117/47921 | |
| ☐ N602GC | Douglas DC-10-30F | 123/47923 | |
| ☐ N603GC | Douglas DC-10-30F | 122/47922 | |
| ☐ N604GC | Douglas DC-10-30F | 129/47924 | |
| ☐ N605GC | Douglas DC-10-30F | 166/47925 | |
| ☐ N606GC | Douglas DC-10-30F | 196/47929 | |
| ☐ N607GC | Douglas DC-10-30F | 256/46978 | |
| ☐ N608GC | Douglas DC-10-30F | 214/46921 | |
| ☐ N609GC | Douglas DC-10-30F | 158/46932 | |
| ☐ N612GC | Douglas DC-10-30F | 337/47840 | |
| ☐ N614GC | Douglas DC-10-30F | 137/46931 | |
| | | | |
| ☐ N701GC | McDD MD-11F | 476/48434 | |
| ☐ N702GC | McDD MD-11F | 478/48435 | |
| ☐ N703GC | McDD MD-11F | 453/48411 | |
| ☐ N705GC | McDD MD-11F | 454/48412 | |

## GREAT LAKES AIRLINES GLA

| | | | |
|---|---|---|---|
| ☐ N94GL | Beech 1900D | UE-94 | |
| ☐ N96UX | Beech 1900D | UE-96 | |
| ☐ N97UX | Beech 1900D | UE-97 | |
| ☐ N100UX | Beech 1900D | UE-100 | |
| ☐ N101UX | Beech 1900D | UE-101 | |
| ☐ N118GL | Beech 1900D | UE-118 | |
| ☐ N122UX | Beech 1900D | UE-122 | |
| ☐ N150GL | Beech 1900D | UE-150 | |
| ☐ N153GL | Beech 1900D | UE-153 | |
| ☐ N154GL | Beech 1900D | UE-154 | |
| ☐ N169GL | Beech 1900D | UE-169 | |
| ☐ N170GL | Beech 1900D | UE-170 | |
| ☐ N179GL | Beech 1900D | UE-179 | |
| ☐ N184UX | Beech 1900D | UE-184 | |
| ☐ N192GL | Beech 1900D | UE-192 | |
| ☐ N195GL | Beech 1900D | UE-195 | |
| ☐ N201GL | Beech 1900D | UE-201 | |
| ☐ N202UX | Beech 1900D | UE-202 | |
| ☐ N204GL | Beech 1900D | UE-204 | |
| ☐ N208GL | Beech 1900D | UE-208 | |
| ☐ N210GL | Beech 1900D | UE-210 | |
| ☐ N211GL | Beech 1900D | UE-211 | |
| ☐ N219GL | Beech 1900D | UE-219 | |
| ☐ N220UX | Beech 1900D | UE-220 | |
| ☐ N226GL | Beech 1900D | UE-226 | |
| ☐ N228GL | Beech 1900D | UE-228 | |
| ☐ N240GL | Beech 1900D | UE-240 | |
| ☐ N245GL | Beech 1900D | UE-245 | |
| ☐ N247GL | Beech 1900D | UE-247 | |
| ☐ N249GL | Beech 1900D | UE-249 | |
| ☐ N251GL | Beech 1900D | UE-251 | |
| ☐ N253GL | Beech 1900D | UE-253 | |

| | | | |
|---|---|---|---|
| ☐ N254GL | Beech 1900D | UE-254 | |
| ☐ N255GL | Beech 1900D | UE-255 | |
| ☐ N257GL | Beech 1900D | UE-257 | |
| ☐ N260GL | Beech 1900D | UE-260 | |
| ☐ N261GL | Beech 1900D | UE-261 | |
| | | | |
| ☐ N71GL | Embraer EMB.120ER | 120071 | |
| ☐ N85GL | Embraer EMB.120ER | 120085 | |
| ☐ N96ZK | Embraer EMB.120ER | 120096 | |
| ☐ N108UX | Embraer EMB.120ER | 120108 | |
| ☐ N293UX | Embraer EMB.120ER | 120293 | |
| ☐ N297UX | Embraer EMB.120ER | 120297 | |
| ☐ N299UX | Embraer EMB.120RT | 120299 | |
| ☐ N101UE | Beech 1900C-1 | UC-101 | |
| ☐ N167GL | Beech 1900C-1 | UC-167 | std |

## GREAT PLAINS AIRLINES                    OZR

| | | | |
|---|---|---|---|
| ☐ N410Z | Dornier 328-300 | 3125 | |
| ☐ N430Z | Dornier 328-300 | 3127 | |
| ☐ N | Dornier 328-300 | | o/o |
| ☐ N | Dornier 328-300 | | o/o |
| ☐ N | Dornier 328-300 | | o/o |
| ☐ N | Dornier 328-300 | | o/o |

## GULFSTREAM INTERNATIONAL              GFT

| | | | |
|---|---|---|---|
| ☐ N16540 | Beech 1900D | UE-172 | |
| ☐ N17534 | Beech 1900D | UE-141 | |
| ☐ N17541 | Beech 1900D | UE-203 | |
| ☐ N38537 | Beech 1900D | UE-158 | |
| ☐ N47542 | Beech 1900D | UE-198 | |
| ☐ N48544 | Beech 1900D | UE-183 | |
| ☐ N49543 | Beech 1900D | UE-181 | |
| ☐ N53545 | Beech 1900D | UE-185 | |
| ☐ N69547 | Beech 1900D | UE-189 | |
| ☐ N69548 | Beech 1900D | UE-193 | std |
| ☐ N69549 | Beech 1900D | UE-194 | |
| ☐ N81533 | Beech 1900D | UE-137 | |
| ☐ N81535 | Beech 1900D | UE-147 | |
| ☐ N81536 | Beech 1900D | UE-152 | |
| ☐ N81538 | Beech 1900D | UE-199 | |
| ☐ N81546 | Beech 1900D | UE-187 | |
| ☐ N81553 | Beech 1900D | UE-222 | |
| ☐ N81556 | Beech 1900D | UE-239 | |
| ☐ N82539 | Beech 1900D | UE-168 | |
| ☐ N87550 | Beech 1900D | UE-205 | |
| ☐ N87551 | Beech 1900D | UE-206 | |
| ☐ N87552 | Beech 1900D | UE-216 | |
| ☐ N87554 | Beech 1900D | UE-227 | |
| ☐ N87555 | Beech 1900D | UE-234 | |
| ☐ N87557 | Beech 1900D | UE-246 | |

## HAWAIIAN AIRLINES                         HAL

| | | |
|---|---|---|
| ☐ N475HA | Boeing 717-22A | 5050/55121 |
| ☐ N476HA | Boeing 717-22A | 5053/55118 |
| ☐ N477HA | Boeing 717-22A | 5061/55122 |
| ☐ N478HA | Boeing 717-22A | 5064/55123 |
| ☐ N479HA | Boeing 717-22A | 5069/55124 |
| ☐ N480HA | Boeing 717-22A | 5070/55125 |
| ☐ N481HA | Boeing 717-22A | 5073/55126 |
| ☐ N482HA | Boeing 717-22A | 5074/55127 |
| ☐ N483HA | Boeing 717-22A | 5079/55128 |
| ☐ N484HA | Boeing 717-22A | 5080/55129 |
| ☐ N485HA | Boeing 717-22A | 5089/55130 |
| ☐ N486HA | Boeing 717-22A | 5092/55131 |
| ☐ N487HA | Boeing 717-22A | 5098/55132 |
| | | |
| ☐ N580HA | Boeing 767-33AER | 850/28140 |
| ☐ N581HA | Boeing 767-33AER | 853/28141 |
| ☐ N581LF | Boeing 767-3G5ER | 612/28111 |
| ☐ N582HA | Boeing 767-33AER | 857/28139 |
| ☐ N583HA | Boeing 767-33AER | 423/25531 |
| ☐ N584HA | Boeing 767-3G5ER | 255/24258 |
| ☐ N585HA | Boeing 767-3G5ER | 251/24257 |
| ☐ N586HA | Boeing 767-3G5ER | 268/24259 |

| | | | |
|---|---|---|---|
| ☐ N587HA | Boeing 767-33AER | 887/33421 | |
| ☐ N588HA | Boeing 767-3CBER | 890/33466 | |
| ☐ N589HA | Boeing 767-33AER | 892/33422 | |
| ☐ N590HA | Boeing 767-3CBER | 894/33467 | |
| ☐ N591HA | Boeing 767-33AER | 897/33423 | |
| ☐ N592HA | Boeing 767-3CBER | 898/33468 | |
| ☐ N593HA | Boeing 767-33AER | 33424 | |
| ☐ N594HA | Boeing 767-3CBER | 33469 | |
| ☐ N595HA | Boeing 767-33AER | 33425 | |
| | | | |
| ☐ N126AA | Douglas DC-10-10 | 247/46947 | Lsf AAL |
| ☐ N127AA | Douglas DC-10-10 | 249/46948 | Lsf AAL |
| ☐ N129AA | Douglas DC-10-10 | 270/46996 | Lsf AAL |
| ☐ N140AA | Douglas DC-10-30 | 106/46712 | |
| ☐ N141AA | Douglas DC-10-30 | 165/46713 | |

## HORIZON AIRLINES                          QXE

| | | | |
|---|---|---|---|
| ☐ N600QX | Canadair RJ-700 | 10005 | 600 |
| ☐ N601QX | Canadair RJ-700 | 10009 | 601 |
| ☐ N602QX | Canadair RJ-700 | 10010 | 602 |
| ☐ N603QX | Canadair RJ-700 | 10011 | 603 |
| ☐ N604QX | Canadair RJ-700 | 10019 | 604 |
| ☐ N605QX | Canadair RJ-700 | 10022 | 605 |
| ☐ N606QX | Canadair RJ-700 | 10023 | 606 |
| ☐ N607QX | Canadair RJ-700 | 10024 | 607 |
| ☐ N608QX | Canadair RJ-700 | 10026 | 608 |
| ☐ N609QX | Canadair RJ-700 | 10031 | 609 |
| ☐ N610QX | Canadair RJ-700 | 10033 | 610 |
| ☐ N611QX | Canadair RJ-700 | 10041 | 611 |
| ☐ N612QX | Canadair RJ-700 | 10042 | 612 |
| ☐ N613QX | Canadair RJ-700 | 10045 | 613 |
| ☐ N614QX | Canadair RJ-700 | 10049 | 614 |
| ☐ N615QX | Canadair RJ-700 | 10065 | 615 |
| ☐ N616QX | Canadair RJ-700 | | o/o |
| ☐ N617QX | Canadair RJ-700 | | o/o |
| ☐ N618QX | Canadair RJ-700 | | o/o |
| | | | |
| ☐ N345PH | DHC-8Q-202 | 476 | |
| ☐ N346PH | DHC-8Q-202 | 477 | |
| ☐ N347PH | DHC-8Q-202 | 480 | |
| ☐ N348PH | DHC-8Q-202 | 484 | |
| ☐ N349PH | DHC-8Q-202 | 486 | |
| ☐ N350PH | DHC-8Q-202 | 488 | |
| ☐ N351PH | DHC-8Q-202 | 490 | |
| ☐ N352PH | DHC-8Q-202 | 494 | |
| ☐ N353PH | DHC-8Q-202 | 496 | |
| ☐ N354PH | DHC-8Q-202 | 498 | |
| ☐ N355PH | DHC-8Q-202 | 500 | |
| ☐ N356PH | DHC-8Q-202 | 502 | |
| ☐ N357PH | DHC-8Q-202 | 504 | |
| ☐ N358PH | DHC-8Q-202 | 506 | |
| ☐ N359PH | DHC-8Q-202 | 514 | |
| ☐ N360PH | DHC-8Q-202 | 515 | |
| ☐ N361PH | DHC-8Q-202 | 516 | |
| ☐ N362PH | DHC-8Q-202 | 518 | |
| ☐ N363PH | DHC-8Q-202 | 520 | |
| ☐ N364PH | DHC-8Q-202 | 524 | |
| ☐ N365PH | DHC-8Q-202 | 526 | |
| ☐ N366PH | DHC-8Q-202 | 510 | |
| ☐ N367PH | DHC-8Q-202 | 511 | |
| ☐ N368PH | DHC-8Q-202 | 512 | |
| ☐ N369PH | DHC-8Q-202 | 513 | |
| ☐ N374PH | DHC-8Q-202 | 528 | |
| ☐ N375PH | DHC-8Q-202 | 529 | |
| ☐ N379PH | DHC-8Q-202 | 530 | |
| ☐ N824PH | DHC-8-102 | 157 | |
| ☐ N825PH | DHC-8-102 | 213 | |
| ☐ N826PH | DHC-8-102 | 214 | |
| ☐ N827PH | DHC-8-102A | 275 | |
| ☐ N828PH | DHC-8-102A | 287 | |
| ☐ N829PH | DHC-8-102A | 304 | |
| ☐ N830PH | DHC-8-102A | 314 | |
| ☐ N831PH | DHC-8-102A | 328 | |
| ☐ N400QX | DHC-8-401Q | 4030 | |
| ☐ N401QX | DHC-8-401Q | 4031 | |
| ☐ N402QX | DHC-8-401Q | 4032 | |
| N403QX | DHC-8-401Q | 4037 | |

| | | | |
|---|---|---|---|
| ☐ N404QX | DHC-8-401Q | 4046 | |
| ☐ N405QX | DHC-8-401Q | 4047 | |
| ☐ N406QX | DHC-8-401Q | 4048 | |
| ☐ N407QX | DHC-8-401Q | 4049 | |
| ☐ N408QX | DHC-8-401Q | 4050 | |
| ☐ N409QX | DHC-8-401Q | 4051 | |
| ☐ N410QX | DHC-8-401Q | 4053 | |
| ☐ N411QX | DHC-8-401Q | 4055 | |
| ☐ N412QX | DHC-8-401Q | 4059 | |
| ☐ N413QX | DHC-8-401Q | 4060 | |
| ☐ N414QX | DHC-8-401Q | 4061 | |
| | | | |
| ☐ N477AU | F.28 Fellowship 4000 | 11226 | std |
| ☐ N479AU | F.28 Fellowship 4000 | 11228 | |
| ☐ N482US | F.28 Fellowship 4000 | 11231 | |
| ☐ N484US | F.28 Fellowship 4000 | 11234 | |
| ☐ N490US | F.28 Fellowship 4000 | 11152 | |
| ☐ N491US | F.28 Fellowship 4000 | 11156 | |
| ☐ N492US | F.28 Fellowship 4000 | 11159 | |
| ☐ N493US | F.28 Fellowship 4000 | 11161 | |
| ☐ N494US | F.28 Fellowship 4000 | 11167 | std |
| ☐ N496US | F.28 Fellowship 4000 | 11169 | |
| ☐ N497US | F.28 Fellowship 4000 | 11173 | |
| ☐ N498US | F.28 Fellowship 4000 | 11181 | |
| ☐ N499US | F.28 Fellowship 4000 | 11182 | |

## ISLAND AIR HONOLULU — PRI

| | | | |
|---|---|---|---|
| ☐ N805WP | DHC-8-102A | 353 | |
| ☐ N806WP | DHC-8-102A | 357 | |
| ☐ N807WP | DHC-8-102 | 023 | |
| ☐ N808WP | DHC-8-103 | 026 | |

## JETBLUE AIRWAYS — JBU

| | | | |
|---|---|---|---|
| ☐ N503JB | Airbus A320-232 | 1123 | |
| ☐ N504JB | Airbus A320-232 | 1156 | |
| ☐ N505JB | Airbus A320-232 | 1173 | |
| ☐ N506JB | Airbus A320-232 | 1235 | |
| ☐ N507JB | Airbus A320-232 | 1240 | |
| ☐ N508JB | Airbus A320-232 | 1257 | |
| ☐ N509JB | Airbus A320-232 | 1270 | |
| ☐ N510JB | Airbus A320-232 | 1280 | |
| ☐ N516JB | Airbus A320-232 | 1302 | |
| ☐ N517JB | Airbus A320-232 | 1327 | |
| ☐ N519JB | Airbus A320-232 | 1398 | |
| ☐ N520JB | Airbus A320-232 | 1446 | |
| ☐ N521JB | Airbus A320-232 | 1452 | |
| ☐ N522JB | Airbus A320-232 | 1464 | |
| ☐ N523JB | Airbus A320-232 | 1506 | |
| ☐ N524JB | Airbus A320-232 | 1528 | |
| ☐ N526JB | Airbus A320-232 | 1546 | |
| ☐ N527JB | Airbus A320-232 | 1557 | |
| ☐ N528JB | Airbus A320-232 | 1591 | |
| ☐ N529JB | Airbus A320-232 | 1610 | |
| ☐ N531JB | Airbus A320-232 | 1650 | |
| ☐ N533JB | Airbus A320-232 | 1652 | |
| ☐ N534JB | Airbus A320-232 | 1705 | |
| ☐ N535JB | Airbus A320-232 | 1739 | |
| ☐ N536JB | Airbus A320-232 | 1784 | |
| ☐ N537JB | Airbus A320-232 | 1785 | |
| ☐ N542JB | Airbus A320-232 | 1802 | |
| ☐ N543JB | Airbus A320-232 | 1823 | |
| ☐ N544JB | Airbus A320-232 | 1835 | |
| ☐ N546JB | Airbus A320-232 | 1827 | |
| ☐ N547JB | Airbus A320-232 | 1849 | |
| ☐ N548JB | Airbus A320-232 | 1868 | |
| ☐ N550JB | Airbus A320-232 | 1891 | |
| ☐ N552JB | Airbus A320-232 | 1861 | |
| ☐ N553JB | Airbus A320-232 | 1896 | |
| ☐ N554JB | Airbus A320-232 | 1898 | |
| ☐ N556JB | Airbus A320-232 | 1904 | |
| ☐ N558JB | Airbus A320-232 | 1915 | |
| ☐ N559JB | Airbus A320-232 | 1917 | |
| ☐ N561JB | Airbus A320-232 | 1927 | |
| ☐ N562JB | Airbus A320-232 | 1948 | |
| ☐ N | Airbus A320-232 | | o/o |
| ☐ N | Airbus A320-232 | | o/o |
| ☐ N | Airbus A320-232 | | o/o |
| ☐ N | Airbus A320-232 | | o/o |
| ☐ N | Airbus A320-232 | | o/o |
| ☐ N | Airbus A320-232 | | o/o |

## KALITTA AIR — CKS

| | | | |
|---|---|---|---|
| ☐ N702CK | Boeing 747-146 | 161/20332 | |
| ☐ N705CK | Boeing 747-246 | 243/21034 | |
| ☐ N707CK | Boeing 747-269B | 332/21541 | |
| ☐ N709CK | Boeing 747-132 | 159/20247 | |
| ☐ N712CK | Boeing 747-122 | 60/19754 | |
| ☐ N713CK | Boeing 747-2B4B | 264/21099 | |
| ☐ N714CK | Boeing 747-209B | 519/22446 | |
| ☐ N715CK | Boeing 747-209B | 556/22447 | |
| ☐ N716CK | Boeing 747-122 | 52/19753 | |
| ☐ N | Boeing 747-246B | 116/19823 | |
| All SCD or SF conversions | | | |
| | | | |
| ☐ N718AA | Boeing 727-227 | 894/20611 | |
| ☐ N866AA | Boeing 727-223 | 1277/21371 | |

## KITTY HAWK AIR CARGO — KHA

| | | | |
|---|---|---|---|
| ☐ N90AX | Boeing 727-222F | 729/20040 | |
| ☐ N180AX | Boeing 727-222F | 732/20041 | |
| ☐ N252US | Boeing 727-251F | 655/19971 | |
| ☐ N255US | Boeing 727-251F | 667/19974 | |
| ☐ N264US | Boeing 727-251F | 741/19983 | |
| ☐ N278US | Boeing 727-251F | 1173/21157 | |
| ☐ N279US | Boeing 727-251F | 1177/21158 | |
| ☐ N281KH | Boeing 727-2J0F | 1158/21105 | |
| ☐ N284KH | Boeing 727-2J0F | 1174/21108 | |
| ☐ N579PE | Boeing 727-243F | 1421/21662 | |
| ☐ N750US | Boeing 727-214F | 1343/21512 | std |
| ☐ N751US | Boeing 727-214F | 1365/21513 | std |
| ☐ N854AA | Boeing 727-223 | 1192/20995 | |
| ☐ N855AA | Boeing 727-223F | 1193/20996 | |
| ☐ N856AA | Boeing 727-223F | 1195/20997 | |
| ☐ N858AA | Boeing 727-223F | 1200/21085 | |
| ☐ N901RF | Boeing 727-259F | 1747/22476 | std |
| ☐ N902RF | Boeing 727-225F | 1737/22549 | std |
| ☐ N916PG | Boeing 727-287F | 1469/21690 | |
| ☐ N936PG | Boeing 727-225F | 1695/22441 | |
| ☐ N1269Y | Boeing 727-2A1F | 1230/21269 | |
| ☐ N6806 | Boeing 727-223F | 548/19481 | |
| ☐ N6807 | Boeing 727-223F | 557/19482 | |
| ☐ N6808 | Boeing 727-223F | 558/19483 | |
| ☐ N6809 | Boeing 727-223F | 560/19484 | |
| ☐ N6810 | Boeing 727-223F | 571/19485 | |
| ☐ N6811 | Boeing 727-223F | 578/19486 | std |
| ☐ N6812 | Boeing 727-223F | 579/19487 | |
| ☐ N6816 | Boeing 727-223F | 611/19491 | |
| ☐ N6821 | Boeing 727-223F | 669/19496 | |
| ☐ N6827 | Boeing 727-223F | 698/20180 | |
| ☐ N6831 | Boeing 727-223F | 707/20184 | |
| ☐ N6833 | Boeing 727-223F | 721/20186 | |
| ☐ N6834 | Boeing 727-223F | 722/20187 | std |
| ☐ N6838 | Boeing 727-223F | 739/20191 | |
| ☐ N69735 | Boeing 727-224F | 1079/20664 | |
| ☐ N69739 | Boeing 727-224F | 1153/20667 | |
| ☐ N69740 | Boeing 727-224F | 1154/20668 | |
| ☐ N77780 | Boeing 727-232F | 918/20635 | |
| ☐ N79748 | Boeing 727-224F | 1760/22450 | |
| | | | |
| ☐ N563PC | Douglas DC-9-15RC | 194/47055 | std |
| ☐ N564PC | Douglas DC-9-15RC | 223/47062 | std |

## LYNDEN AIR CARGO — LYC

| | | | |
|---|---|---|---|
| ☐ N401LC | L-100-30 Hercules | 4606 | |
| ☐ N402LC | L-100-30 Hercules | 4698 | |
| ☐ N403LC | L-100-30 Hercules | 4590 | |
| ☐ N404LC | L-100-30 Hercules | 4763 | |
| ☐ N405LC | L-100-30 Hercules | 5025 | |

## MESA AIRLINES ASH

| | | | |
|---|---|---|---|
| ☐ N193YV | Embraer EMB.120ER | 120193 | |
| ☐ N203YV | Embraer EMB.120ER | 120203 | |
| ☐ N221YV | Embraer EMB.120RT | 120221 | |
| ☐ N244CA | Embraer EMB.120RT | 120217 | |
| ☐ N251YV | Embraer EMB.120ER | 120251 | |
| ☐ N270YV | Embraer EMB.120ER | 120270 | |
| ☐ N298YV | Embraer EMB.120RT | 120298 | |
| ☐ N301YV | Embraer EMB.120RT | 120301 | |

## MIAMI AIR INTERNATIONAL BSK

| | | | |
|---|---|---|---|
| ☐ G-XLAC | Boeing 737-81Q | 479/29051 | Lsf XLA |
| ☐ N732MA | Boeing 737-81Q | 830/30618 | |
| ☐ N733MA | Boeing 737-81Q | 856/30619 | Lst XLA |
| ☐ N802MA | Boeing 727-225 | 1668/22433 | |
| ☐ N803MA | Boeing 727-225 | 1671/22434 | |
| ☐ N804MA | Boeing 727-225 | 1674/22435 | |
| ☐ N889MA | Boeing 727-225 | 1532/21854 | std |

## MIDATLANTIC AIRWAYS

| | | |
|---|---|---|
| ☐ N592ML | Canadair RJ-200 | 7410 |

## MIDWEST CONNECT

| | | | |
|---|---|---|---|
| ☐ N79SK | Beech 1900D | UE-79 | |
| ☐ N81SK | Beech 1900D | UE-81 | |
| ☐ N85SK | Beech 1900D | UE-85 | |
| ☐ N87SK | Beech 1900D | UE-87 | |
| ☐ N91SK | Beech 1900D | UE-91 | |
| ☐ N92SK | Beech 1900D | UE-92 | |
| ☐ N118SK | Beech 1900D | UE-108 | |
| ☐ N145SK | Beech 1900D | UE-145 | |
| ☐ N148SK | Beech 1900D | UE-148 | |
| ☐ N801SK | Beech 1900D | UE-80 | |
| ☐ N831SK | Beech 1900D | UE-83 | |
| ☐ N841SK | Beech 1900D | UE-84 | |
| ☐ N881SK | Beech 1900D | UE-88 | |
| ☐ N891SK | Beech 1900D | UE-89 | |
| ☐ N901SK | Beech 1900D | UE-90 | |
| ☐ N351SK | Dornier 328-300 | 3108 | |
| ☐ N352SK | Dornier 328-300 | 3111 | |
| ☐ N353SK | Dornier 328-300 | 3122 | |
| ☐ N354SK | Dornier 328-300 | 3126 | |
| ☐ N355SK | Dornier 328-300 | 3124 | |
| ☐ N356SK | Dornier 328-300 | 3163 | |
| ☐ N357SK | Dornier 328-300 | 3164 | |
| ☐ N358SK | Dornier 328-300 | 3188 | |
| ☐ N359SK | Dornier 328-300 | 3202 | |
| ☐ N360SK | Dornier 328-300 | 3136 | |
| ☐ N | Dornier 328-300 | | o/o |
| ☐ N | Dornier 328-300 | | o/o |
| ☐ N530RJ | Embraer ERJ-140 | 145 | o/o |
| ☐ N531RJ | Embraer ERJ-140 | 145 | o/o |
| ☐ N532RJ | Embraer ERJ-140 | 145 | o/o |
| ☐ N533RJ | Embraer ERJ-140 | 145 | o/o |
| ☐ N534RJ | Embraer ERJ-140 | 145 | o/o |
| ☐ N535RJ | Embraer ERJ-140 | 145 | o/o |
| ☐ N536RJ | Embraer ERJ-140 | 145 | o/o |
| ☐ N537RJ | Embraer ERJ-140 | 145 | o/o |

## MIDWEST EXPRESS MEP

| | | | |
|---|---|---|---|
| ☐ N902ME | Boeing 717-2 | 5116/55166 | |
| ☐ N903ME | Boeing 717-2 | 55167 | o/o |
| ☐ N904ME | Boeing 717-2 | 55168 | o/o |
| ☐ N905ME | Boeing 717-2 | 55169 | o/o |
| ☐ N906ME | Boeing 717-2 | 55170 | o/o |
| ☐ N907ME | Boeing 717-2 | 55171 | o/o |
| ☐ N908ME | Boeing 717-2 | 55172 | o/o |
| ☐ N909ME | Boeing 717-2 | 55173 | o/o |
| ☐ N910ME | Boeing 717-2 | 55174 | o/o |
| ☐ N912ME | Boeing 717-2 | 55175 | o/o |
| ☐ N913ME | Boeing 717-2 | 55176 | o/o |
| ☐ N914ME | Boeing 717-2 | 55177 | o/o |
| ☐ N916ME | Boeing 717-2 | 55178 | o/o |
| ☐ N917ME | Boeing 717-2 | 55179 | o/o |
| ☐ N202ME | Douglas DC-9-32 | 778/47672 | |
| ☐ N203ME | Douglas DC-9-32 | 779/47673 | |
| ☐ N204ME | Douglas DC-9-32 | 781/47680 | |
| ☐ N205ME | Douglas DC-9-32 | 715/47601 | |
| ☐ N206ME | Douglas DC-9-32 | 908/47791 | |
| ☐ N207ME | Douglas DC-9-32 | 915/47794 | |
| ☐ N209ME | Douglas DC-9-32 | 828/47730 | |
| ☐ N212ME | Douglas DC-9-32 | 822/47701 | |
| ☐ N215ME | Douglas DC-9-32 | 837/47744 | |
| ☐ N216ME | Douglas DC-9-32 | 835/47740 | |
| ☐ N300ME | Douglas DC-9-15 | 17/45718 | |
| ☐ N301ME | Douglas DC-9-32 | 240/47190 | |
| ☐ N302ME | Douglas DC-9-32 | 198/47102 | |
| ☐ N401ME | Douglas DC-9-32 | 230/47133 | |
| ☐ N500ME | Douglas DC-9-14 | 4/45711 | |
| ☐ N501ME | Douglas DC-9-32 | 229/47132 | |
| ☐ N502ME | Douglas DC-9-32 | 956/48132 | |
| ☐ N600ME | Douglas DC-9-14 | 19/45725 | |
| ☐ N602ME | Douglas DC-9-32 | 959/48133 | |
| ☐ N700ME | Douglas DC-9-14 | 2/45696 | |
| ☐ N601ME | McDD MD-88 | 1624/49762 | |
| ☐ N701ME | McDD MD-88 | 1620/49760 | |
| ☐ N803ME | McDD MD-81 | 953/48029 | |
| ☐ N804ME | McDD MD-81 | 962/48030 | |
| ☐ N805ME | McDD MD-81 | 969/48031 | |
| ☐ N806ME | McDD MD-81 | 978/48032 | |
| ☐ N807ME | McDD MD-81 | 988/48033 | |
| ☐ N808ME | McDD MD-82 | 999/48070 | |
| ☐ N809ME | McDD MD-82 | 1004/48071 | |
| ☐ N810ME | McDD MD-81 | 1011/48072 | |
| ☐ N812ME | McDD MD-81 | 966/48006 | |
| ☐ N813ME | McDD MD-81 | 971/48007 | |
| ☐ N814ME | McDD MD-81 | 992/48010 | |

## NORTH AMERICAN AIRLINES NAO

| | | |
|---|---|---|
| ☐ N750NA | Boeing 757-28A | 658/26277 |
| ☐ N752NA | Boeing 757-28A | 865/28174 |
| ☐ N754NA | Boeing 757-28A | 958/29381 |
| ☐ N756NA | Boeing 757-28A | 967/32448 |
| ☐ N767NA | Boeing 767-324ER | 601/27569 |
| ☐ N768NA | Boeing 767-36NER | 754/29898 |

## NORTHERN AIR CARGO NAC

| | | |
|---|---|---|
| ☐ N190AJ | Boeing 727-46F | 236/18878 |
| ☐ N930FT | Boeing 727-23F | 329/19387 |
| ☐ N992AJ | Boeing 727-23F | 358/19428 |

## NORTHWEST AIRLINES NWA

| | | | |
|---|---|---|---|
| ☐ N301NB | Airbus A319-114 | 1058 | 3101 |
| ☐ N302NB | Airbus A319-114 | 1062 | 3102 |
| ☐ N303NB | Airbus A319-114 | 1071 | 3103 |
| ☐ N304NB | Airbus A319-114 | 1078 | 3104 |
| ☐ N305NB | Airbus A319-114 | 1090 | 3105 |
| ☐ N306NB | Airbus A319-114 | 1091 | 3106 |
| ☐ N307NB | Airbus A319-114 | 1126 | 3107 |
| ☐ N308NB | Airbus A319-114 | 1129 | 3108 |
| ☐ N309NB | Airbus A319-114 | 1131 | 3109 |
| ☐ N310NB | Airbus A319-114 | 1149 | 3110 |
| ☐ N311NB | Airbus A319-114 | 1164 | 3111 |
| ☐ N312NB | Airbus A319-114 | 1167 | 3112 |
| ☐ N313NB | Airbus A319-114 | 1186 | 3113 |
| ☐ N314NB | Airbus A319-114 | 1191 | 3114 |
| ☐ N315NB | Airbus A319-114 | 1230 | 3115 |
| ☐ N316NB | Airbus A319-114 | 1249 | 3116 |
| ☐ N317NB | Airbus A319-114 | 1324 | 3117 |
| ☐ N318NB | Airbus A319-114 | 1325 | 3118 |
| ☐ N319NB | Airbus A319-114 | 1346 | 3119 |

| | Registration | Type | Serial | Fleet No. |
|---|---|---|---|---|
| ☐ | N320NB | Airbus A319-114 | 1392 | 3120 |
| ☐ | N321NB | Airbus A319-114 | 1414 | 3121 |
| ☐ | N322NB | Airbus A319-114 | 1434 | 3122 |
| ☐ | N323NB | Airbus A319-114 | 1453 | 3123 |
| ☐ | N324NB | Airbus A319-114 | 1456 | 3124 |
| ☐ | N325NB | Airbus A319-114 | 1483 | 3125 |
| ☐ | N326NB | Airbus A319-114 | 1498 | 3126 |
| ☐ | N327NB | Airbus A319-114 | 1501 | 3127 |
| ☐ | N328NB | Airbus A319-114 | 1520 | 3128 |
| ☐ | N329NB | Airbus A319-114 | 1543 | 3129 |
| ☐ | N330NB | Airbus A319-114 | 1549 | 3130 |
| ☐ | N331NB | Airbus A319-114 | 1567 | 3131 |
| ☐ | N332NB | Airbus A319-114 | 1570 | 3132 |
| ☐ | N333NB | Airbus A319-114 | 1582 | 3133 |
| ☐ | N334NB | Airbus A319-114 | 1659 | 3134 |
| ☐ | N335NB | Airbus A319-114 | 1662 | 3135 |
| ☐ | N336NB | Airbus A319-114 | 1683 | 3136 |
| ☐ | N337NB | Airbus A319-114 | 1685 | 3137 |
| ☐ | N338NB | Airbus A319-114 | 1693 | 3138 |
| ☐ | N339NB | Airbus A319-114 | 1709 | 3139 |
| ☐ | N340NB | Airbus A319-114 | 1714 | 3140 |
| ☐ | N341NB | Airbus A319-114 | 1738 | 3141 |
| ☐ | N342NB | Airbus A319-114 | 1746 | 3142 |
| ☐ | N343NB | Airbus A319-114 | 1752 | 3143 |
| ☐ | N344NB | Airbus A319-114 | 1766 | 3144 |
| ☐ | N345NB | Airbus A319-114 | 1774 | 3145 |
| ☐ | N346NB | Airbus A319-114 | 1796 | 3146 |
| ☐ | N347NB | Airbus A319-114 | 1800 | 3147 |
| ☐ | N348NB | Airbus A319-114 | 1810 | 3148 |
| ☐ | N350NB | Airbus A319-114 | 1819 | 3150 |
| ☐ | N351NB | Airbus A319-114 | 1820 | 3151 |
| ☐ | N352NB | Airbus A319-114 | 1824 | 3152 |
| ☐ | N353NB | Airbus A319-114 | 1828 | 3153 |
| ☐ | N354NB | Airbus A319-114 | 1833 | 3154 |
| ☐ | N355NB | Airbus A319-114 | 1839 | 3155 |
| ☐ | N356NB | Airbus A319-114 | 1870 | 3156 |
| ☐ | N357NB | Airbus A319-114 | 1875 | 3157 |
| ☐ | N358NB | Airbus A319-114 | 1897 | 3158 |
| ☐ | N359NB | Airbus A319-114 | 1923 | 3159 |
| ☐ | N | Airbus A319-114 | 1959 | o/o |
| ☐ | N | Airbus A319-114 | 1976 | o/o |
| ☐ | N | Airbus A319-114 | 1982 | o/o |
| ☐ | N | Airbus A319-114 | 1990 | o/o |
| ☐ | N | Airbus A319-114 | 2002 | o/o |
| ☐ | N | Airbus A319-114 | 2013 | o/o |
| ☐ | N301US | Airbus A320-211 | 0031 | 3201 |
| ☐ | N302US | Airbus A320-211 | 0032 | 3202 |
| ☐ | N303US | Airbus A320-211 | 0034 | 3203 |
| ☐ | N304US | Airbus A320-211 | 0040 | 3204 |
| ☐ | N305US | Airbus A320-211 | 0041 | 3205 |
| ☐ | N306US | Airbus A320-211 | 0060 | 3206 |
| ☐ | N307US | Airbus A320-211 | 0106 | 3207 |
| ☐ | N308US | Airbus A320-211 | 0107 | 3208 |
| ☐ | N309US | Airbus A320-211 | 0118 | 3209 |
| ☐ | N310NW | Airbus A320-211 | 0121 | 3210 |
| ☐ | N311US | Airbus A320-211 | 0125 | 3211 |
| ☐ | N312US | Airbus A320-211 | 0152 | 3212 |
| ☐ | N313US | Airbus A320-211 | 0153 | 3213 |
| ☐ | N314US | Airbus A320-211 | 0160 | 3214 |
| ☐ | N315US | Airbus A320-211 | 0171 | 3215 |
| ☐ | N316US | Airbus A320-211 | 0192 | 3216 |
| ☐ | N317US | Airbus A320-211 | 0197 | 3217 |
| ☐ | N318US | Airbus A320-211 | 0206 | 3218 |
| ☐ | N319US | Airbus A320-211 | 0208 | 3219 |
| ☐ | N320US | Airbus A320-211 | 0213 | 3220 |
| ☐ | N321US | Airbus A320-211 | 0262 | 3221 |
| ☐ | N322US | Airbus A320-211 | 0263 | 3222 |
| ☐ | N323US | Airbus A320-211 | 0272 | 3223 |
| ☐ | N324US | Airbus A320-211 | 0273 | 3224 |
| ☐ | N325US | Airbus A320-211 | 0281 | 3225 |
| ☐ | N326US | Airbus A320-211 | 0282 | 3226 |
| ☐ | N327NW | Airbus A320-211 | 0297 | 3227 |
| ☐ | N328NW | Airbus A320-211 | 0298 | 3228 |
| ☐ | N329NW | Airbus A320-211 | 0306 | 3229 |
| ☐ | N330NW | Airbus A320-211 | 0307 | 3230 |
| ☐ | N331NW | Airbus A320-211 | 0318 | 3231 |
| ☐ | N332NW | Airbus A320-211 | 0319 | 3232 |
| ☐ | N333NW | Airbus A320-211 | 0329 | 3233 |
| ☐ | N334NW | Airbus A320-212 | 0339 | 3234 |
| ☐ | N335NW | Airbus A320-212 | 0340 | 3235 |
| ☐ | N336NW | Airbus A320-212 | 0355 | 3236 |
| ☐ | N337NW | Airbus A320-212 | 0358 | 3237 |
| ☐ | N338NW | Airbus A320-212 | 0360 | 3238 |
| ☐ | N339NW | Airbus A320-212 | 0367 | 3239 |
| ☐ | N340NW | Airbus A320-212 | 0372 | 3240 |
| ☐ | N341NW | Airbus A320-212 | 0380 | 3241 |
| ☐ | N342NW | Airbus A320-212 | 0381 | 3242 |
| ☐ | N343NW | Airbus A320-212 | 0387 | 3243 |
| ☐ | N344NW | Airbus A320-212 | 0388 | 3244 |
| ☐ | N345NW | Airbus A320-212 | 0399 | 3245 |
| ☐ | N346NW | Airbus A320-212 | 0400 | 3246 |
| ☐ | N347NW | Airbus A320-212 | 0408 | 3247 |
| ☐ | N348NW | Airbus A320-212 | 0410 | 3248 |
| ☐ | N349NW | Airbus A320-212 | 0417 | 3249 |
| ☐ | N350NA | Airbus A320-212 | 0418 | 3250 |
| ☐ | N351NW | Airbus A320-212 | 0766 | 3251 |
| ☐ | N352NW | Airbus A320-212 | 0778 | 3252 |
| ☐ | N353NW | Airbus A320-212 | 0786 | 3253 |
| ☐ | N354NW | Airbus A320-212 | 0801 | 3254 |
| ☐ | N355NW | Airbus A320-212 | 0807 | 3255 |
| ☐ | N356NW | Airbus A320-212 | 0818 | 3256 |
| ☐ | N357NW | Airbus A320-212 | 0830 | 3257 |
| ☐ | N358NW | Airbus A320-212 | 0832 | 3258 |
| ☐ | N359NW | Airbus A320-212 | 0846 | 3259 |
| ☐ | N360NW | Airbus A320-212 | 0903 | 3260 |
| ☐ | N361NW | Airbus A320-212 | 0907 | 3261 |
| ☐ | N362NW | Airbus A320-212 | 0911 | 3262 |
| ☐ | N363NW | Airbus A320-212 | 0923 | 3263 |
| ☐ | N364NW | Airbus A320-212 | 0962 | 3264 |
| ☐ | N365NW | Airbus A320-212 | 0964 | 3265 |
| ☐ | N366NW | Airbus A320-212 | 0981 | 3266 |
| ☐ | N367NW | Airbus A320-212 | 0988 | 3267 |
| ☐ | N368NW | Airbus A320-212 | 0996 | 3268 |
| ☐ | N369NW | Airbus A320-212 | 1011 | 3269 |
| ☐ | N370NW | Airbus A320-212 | 1037 | 3270 |
| ☐ | N371NW | Airbus A320-212 | 1535 | 3271 |
| ☐ | N372NW | Airbus A320-212 | 1633 | 3272 |
| ☐ | N373NW | Airbus A320-212 | 1641 | 3273 |
| ☐ | N374NW | Airbus A320-212 | 1646 | 3274 |
| ☐ | N375NC | Airbus A320-212 | 1789 | 3275 |
| ☐ | N376NW | Airbus A320-212 | 1812 | 3276 |
| ☐ | N377NW | Airbus A320-212 | | 3277 o/o |
| ☐ | N378NW | Airbus A320-212 | | 3278 o/o |
| ☐ | N379NW | Airbus A320-212 | | 3279 o/o |
| ☐ | N380NW | Airbus A320-212 | | 3280 o/o |
| ☐ | N381NW | Airbus A320-212 | | 3281 o/o |
| ☐ | N382NW | Airbus A320-212 | | 3282 o/o |
| ☐ | N801NW | Airbus A330-323X | 524 | o/o |
| ☐ | N | Airbus A330-323X | 533 | o/o |
| ☐ | N | Airbus A330-323X | 542 | o/o |
| ☐ | N | Airbus A330-323X | 549 | o/o |
| ☐ | N | Airbus A330-323X | | o/o |
| ☐ | N | Airbus A330-323X | | o/o |
| ☐ | N201US | Boeing 727-251 | 1645/22154 | 2201 |
| ☐ | N202US | Boeing 727-251 | 1648/22155 | 2202 |
| ☐ | N204US | Boeing 727-251 | 1703/22544 | 2204 |
| ☐ | N275US | Boeing 727-251 | 1168/21154 | 2275 |
| ☐ | N284US | Boeing 727-251 | 1284/21323 | 2284 |
| ☐ | N285US | Boeing 727-251 | 1286/21324 | 2285 |
| ☐ | N286US | Boeing 727-251 | 1288/21325 | 2286 |
| ☐ | N287US | Boeing 727-251 | 1290/21375 | 2287 |
| ☐ | N288US | Boeing 727-251 | 1293/21376 | 2288; std |
| ☐ | N289US | Boeing 727-251 | 1295/21377 | 2289 |
| ☐ | N290US | Boeing 727-251 | 1297/21378 | 2290 |
| ☐ | N291US | Boeing 727-251 | 1299/21379 | 2291 |
| ☐ | N292US | Boeing 727-251 | 1317/21503 | 2292 |
| ☐ | N293US | Boeing 727-251 | 1319/21504 | 2293 |
| ☐ | N295US | Boeing 727-251 | 1392/21506 | 2295 |
| ☐ | N296US | Boeing 727-251 | 1495/21788 | 2296 |
| ☐ | N297US | Boeing 727-251 | 1496/21789 | 2297 |
| ☐ | N298US | Boeing 727-251 | 1599/22152 | 2298 |
| ☐ | N299US | Boeing 727-251 | 1601/22153 | 2299 |

| Reg | Type | Line/Serial | Code |
|---|---|---|---|
| ☐ N716RC | Boeing 727-2S7 | 1617/22021 | 2713 |
| ☐ N718RC | Boeing 727-2S7 | 1654/22344 | 2714 |
| ☐ N719RC | Boeing 727-2S7 | 1721/22490 | 2715 |
| ☐ N720RC | Boeing 727-2S7 | 1726/22491 | 2716 |
| ☐ N721RC | Boeing 727-2S7 | 1729/22492 | 2717 |
| ☐ N722RW | Boeing 727-2M7 | 1220/21201 | 2762 |
| ☐ N727RW | Boeing 727-2M7 | 1455/21656 | 2767; std |
| ☐ N728RW | Boeing 727-2M7 | 1491/21741 | 2768 |
| ☐ N729RW | Boeing 727-2M7 | 1514/21742 | 2769 |
| ☐ N816EA | Boeing 727-225 | 1775/22553 | 2707 |
| ☐ N817EA | Boeing 727-225 | 1781/22554 | 2708 |
| ☐ N818EA | Boeing 727-225 | 1783/22555 | 2709 |
| ☐ N820EA | Boeing 727-225 | 1795/22557 | 2710 |
| ☐ N8877Z | Boeing 727-225 | 1308/21450 | 2702 |
| ☐ N612US | Boeing 747-251B | 135/20357 | 6612; std |
| ☐ N613US | Boeing 747-251B | 141/20358 | 6613 |
| ☐ N615US | Boeing 747-251B | 165/20360 | 6615 |
| ☐ N616US | Boeing 747-251F | 258/21120 | 6716 |
| ☐ N617US | Boeing 747-251F | 261/21121 | 6717 |
| ☐ N618US | Boeing 747-251F | 269/21122 | 6718 |
| ☐ N619US | Boeing 747-251F | 308/21321 | 6719 |
| ☐ N622US | Boeing 747-251B | 357/21704 | 6622 |
| ☐ N623US | Boeing 747-251B | 374/21705 | 6623 |
| ☐ N624US | Boeing 747-251B | 377/21706 | 6624 |
| ☐ N625US | Boeing 747-251B | 378/21707 | 6625 |
| ☐ N626US | Boeing 747-251B | 379/21708 | 6626 |
| ☐ N627US | Boeing 747-251B | 412/21709 | 6627 |
| ☐ N628US | Boeing 747-251B | 442/22389 | 6628 |
| ☐ N629US | Boeing 747-251F | 444/22388 | 6729 |
| ☐ N630US | Boeing 747-2J9F | 400/21668 | 6730 |
| ☐ N631US | Boeing 747-251B | 594/23111 | 6631 |
| ☐ N632US | Boeing 747-251B | 595/23112 | 6632 |
| ☐ N633US | Boeing 747-227B | 437/21991 | 6633 |
| ☐ N634US | Boeing 747-227B | 465/22234 | 6634 |
| ☐ N635US | Boeing 747-227B | 375/21682 | 6635 |
| ☐ N636US | Boeing 747-251B | 642/23547 | 6636 |
| ☐ N637US | Boeing 747-251B | 644/23548 | 6637 |
| ☐ N638US | Boeing 747-251B | 651/23549 | 6638 |
| ☐ N639US | Boeing 747-251F | 680/23887 | 6739 |
| ☐ N640US | Boeing 747-251F | 682/23888 | 6740 |
| ☐ N641NW | Boeing 747-212B | 470/21941 | 6641 |
| ☐ N642NW | Boeing 747-212B | 471/21942 | 6642 |
| ☐ N643NW | Boeing 747-249F | 458/22245 | 6743 |
| ☐ N644NW | Boeing 747-212F | 710/24177 | 6744 |
| ☐ N645NW | Boeing 747-222B (SF) | 673/23736 | 6745 |
| ☐ N646NW | Boeing 747-222B (SF) | 675/23737 | 6746 |
| ☐ N661US | Boeing 747-451 | 696/23719 | 6301 |
| ☐ N662US | Boeing 747-451 | 708/23720 | 6302 |
| ☐ N663US | Boeing 747-451 | 715/23818 | 6303 |
| ☐ N664US | Boeing 747-451 | 721/23819 | 6304 |
| ☐ N665US | Boeing 747-451 | 726/23820 | 6305 |
| ☐ N666US | Boeing 747-451 | 742/23821 | 6306 |
| ☐ N667US | Boeing 747-451 | 799/24222 | 6307 |
| ☐ N668US | Boeing 747-451 | 800/24223 | 6308 |
| ☐ N669US | Boeing 747-451 | 803/24224 | 6309 |
| ☐ N670US | Boeing 747-451 | 804/24225 | 6310 |
| ☐ N671US | Boeing 747-451 | 1206/26477 | 6311 |
| ☐ N672US | Boeing 747-451 | 1223/30267 | 6312 |
| ☐ N673US | Boeing 747-451 | 1226/30268 | 6313 |
| ☐ N674US | Boeing 747-451 | 1232/30269 | 6314 |
| ☐ N675US | Boeing 747-451 | 1297/33001 | 6315 |
| ☐ N676NW | Boeing 747-451 | 1303/33002 | 6316 |
| ☐ N | Boeing 747-357M | 570/22704 | std |
| ☐ N | Boeing 747-357M | 576/22705 | std |
| ☐ N501US | Boeing 757-251 | 53/23190 | 5501 |
| ☐ N502US | Boeing 757-251 | 55/23191 | 5502 |
| ☐ N503US | Boeing 757-251 | 59/23192 | 5503 |
| ☐ N504US | Boeing 757-251 | 60/23193 | 5504 |
| ☐ N505US | Boeing 757-251 | 62/23194 | 5505 |
| ☐ N506US | Boeing 757-251 | 67/23195 | 5506 |
| ☐ N507US | Boeing 757-251 | 68/23196 | 5507 |
| ☐ N508US | Boeing 757-251 | 69/23197 | 5508 |
| ☐ N509US | Boeing 757-251 | 70/23198 | 5509 |
| ☐ N511US | Boeing 757-251 | 72/23199 | 5511 |
| ☐ N512US | Boeing 757-251 | 82/23200 | 5512 |
| ☐ N513US | Boeing 757-251 | 83/23201 | 5513 |
| ☐ N514US | Boeing 757-251 | 86/23202 | 5514 |
| ☐ N515US | Boeing 757-251 | 88/23203 | 5515 |
| ☐ N516US | Boeing 757-251 | 104/23204 | 5516 |
| ☐ N517US | Boeing 757-251 | 105/23205 | 5517 |
| ☐ N518US | Boeing 757-251 | 107/23206 | 5518 |
| ☐ N519US | Boeing 757-251 | 108/23207 | 5519 |
| ☐ N520US | Boeing 757-251 | 109/23208 | 5520 |
| ☐ N521US | Boeing 757-251 | 110/23209 | 5521 |
| ☐ N522US | Boeing 757-251 | 119/23616 | 5522 |
| ☐ N523US | Boeing 757-251 | 121/23617 | 5523 |
| ☐ N524US | Boeing 757-251 | 122/23618 | 5524 |
| ☐ N525US | Boeing 757-251 | 124/23619 | 5525 |
| ☐ N526US | Boeing 757-251 | 131/23620 | 5526 |
| ☐ N527US | Boeing 757-251 | 136/23842 | 5527 |
| ☐ N528US | Boeing 757-251 | 137/23843 | 5528 |
| ☐ N529US | Boeing 757-251 | 140/23844 | 5529 |
| ☐ N530US | Boeing 757-251 | 188/23845 | 5530 |
| ☐ N531US | Boeing 757-251 | 190/23846 | 5531 |
| ☐ N532US | Boeing 757-251 | 192/24263 | 5532 |
| ☐ N533US | Boeing 757-251 | 194/24264 | 5533 |
| ☐ N534US | Boeing 757-251 | 196/24265 | 5534 |
| ☐ N535US | Boeing 757-251 | 693/26482 | 5635 |
| ☐ N536US | Boeing 757-251 | 695/26483 | 5636 |
| ☐ N537US | Boeing 757-251 | 697/26484 | 5637 |
| ☐ N538US | Boeing 757-251 | 699/26485 | 5638 |
| ☐ N539US | Boeing 757-251 | 700/26486 | 5639 |
| ☐ N540US | Boeing 757-251 | 701/26487 | 5640 |
| ☐ N541US | Boeing 757-251 | 703/26488 | 5641 |
| ☐ N542US | Boeing 757-251 | 705/26489 | 5642 |
| ☐ N543US | Boeing 757-251 | 709/26490 | 5643 |
| ☐ N544US | Boeing 757-251 | 710/26491 | 5644 |
| ☐ N545US | Boeing 757-251 | 711/26492 | 5645 |
| ☐ N546US | Boeing 757-251 | 713/26493 | 5646 |
| ☐ N547US | Boeing 757-251 | 714/26494 | 5647 |
| ☐ N548US | Boeing 757-251 | 715/26495 | 5648 |
| ☐ N549US | Boeing 757-251 | 716/26496 | 5649 |
| ☐ N550NW | Boeing 757-251 | 968/26497 | 5550 |
| ☐ N551NW | Boeing 757-251 | 971/26498 | 5551 |
| ☐ N552NW | Boeing 757-251 | 975/26499 | 5552 |
| ☐ N553NW | Boeing 757-251 | 982/26500 | 5553 |
| ☐ N554NW | Boeing 757-251 | 987/26501 | 5554 |
| ☐ N555NW | Boeing 757-251 | 1011/33391 | 5555 |
| ☐ N556NW | Boeing 757-251 | 1013/33392 | 5556 |
| ☐ N557NW | Boeing 757-251 | 1016/33393 | 5557 |
| ☐ N581NW | Boeing 757-351 | 1001/32982 | |
| ☐ N582NW | Boeing 757-351 | 1014/32981 | |
| ☐ N583NW | Boeing 757-351 | 1019/32983 | |
| ☐ N584NW | Boeing 757-351 | 1020/32984 | |
| ☐ N585NW | Boeing 757-351 | 1021/32985 | |
| ☐ N586NW | Boeing 757-351 | 1022/32987 | |
| ☐ N587NW | Boeing 757-351 | 1023/32986 | |
| ☐ N588NW | Boeing 757-351 | 1024/32988 | |
| ☐ N589NW | Boeing 757-351 | 1025/32989 | |
| ☐ N590NW | Boeing 757-351 | 32990 | o/o |
| ☐ N591NW | Boeing 757-351 | 32991 | o/o |
| ☐ N592NW | Boeing 757-351 | 32992 | o/o |
| ☐ N593NW | Boeing 757-351 | 32993 | o/o |
| ☐ N594NW | Boeing 757-351 | 32994 | o/o |
| ☐ N595NW | Boeing 757-351 | 32995 | o/o |
| ☐ N596NW | Boeing 757-351 | 32996 | o/o |
| ☐ N89S | Douglas DC-9-31 | 486/47042 | 9930 |
| ☐ N90S | Douglas DC-9-31 | 498/47244 | 9931 |
| ☐ N401EA | Douglas DC-9-51 | 788/47682 | 9885 |
| ☐ N600TR | Douglas DC-9-51 | 899/47783 | 9886 |
| ☐ N601NW | Douglas DC-9-32 | 136/47038 | 9601 |
| ☐ N602NW | Douglas DC-9-32 | 168/47046 | 9602 |
| ☐ N603NW | Douglas DC-9-32 | 195/47101 | 9603 |
| ☐ N604NW | Douglas DC-9-32 | 299/47222 | 9604 |
| ☐ N605NW | Douglas DC-9-32 | 300/47223 | 9605 |
| ☐ N606NW | Douglas DC-9-32 | 317/47225 | 9606 |
| ☐ N607NW | Douglas DC-9-32 | 428/47232 | 9607 |
| ☐ N608NW | Douglas DC-9-32 | 429/47233 | 9608 |
| ☐ N609NW | Douglas DC-9-32 | 435/47234 | 9609 |
| ☐ N610NW | Douglas DC-9-32 | 525/47432 | 9610 |
| ☐ N611NA | Douglas DC-9-32 | 540/47435 | 9611 |
| ☐ N612NW | Douglas DC-9-32 | 541/47436 | 9612 |
| ☐ N613NW | Douglas DC-9-32 | 545/47438 | 9613 |

| Reg | Type | Line/MSN | Fleet |
|---|---|---|---|
| ☐ N614NW | Douglas DC-9-32 | 210/47128 | 9614 |
| ☐ N615NW | Douglas DC-9-32 | 225/47129 | 9615 |
| ☐ N616NW | Douglas DC-9-32 | 356/47229 | 9616 |
| ☐ N617NW | Douglas DC-9-32 | 436/47235 | 9617 |
| ☐ N618NW | Douglas DC-9-32 | 526/47433 | 9618 |
| ☐ N619NW | Douglas DC-9-32 | 614/47518 | 9619 |
| ☐ N620NW | Douglas DC-9-32 | 641/47533 | 9620 |
| ☐ N621NW | Douglas DC-9-32 | 676/47544 | 9621 |
| ☐ N622NW | Douglas DC-9-32 | 680/47575 | 9622 |
| ☐ N623NW | Douglas DC-9-32 | 706/47591 | 9623 |
| ☐ N670MC | Douglas DC-9-51 | 807/47659 | 9882 |
| ☐ N671MC | Douglas DC-9-51 | 810/47660 | 9883 |
| ☐ N675MC | Douglas DC-9-51 | 780/47651 | 9880 |
| ☐ N676MC | Douglas DC-9-51 | 798/47652 | 9881 |
| ☐ N677MC | Douglas DC-9-51 | 873/47756 | 9884 |
| ☐ N750NW | Douglas DC-9-41 | 218/47114 | 9750 |
| ☐ N751NW | Douglas DC-9-41 | 261/47115 | 9751 |
| ☐ N752NW | Douglas DC-9-41 | 308/47116 | 9752 |
| ☐ N753NW | Douglas DC-9-41 | 319/47117 | 9753 |
| ☐ N754NW | Douglas DC-9-41 | 323/47178 | 9754 |
| ☐ N755NW | Douglas DC-9-41 | 335/47179 | 9755 |
| ☐ N756NW | Douglas DC-9-41 | 354/47180 | 9756 |
| ☐ N758NW | Douglas DC-9-41 | 359/47286 | 9758 |
| ☐ N759NW | Douglas DC-9-41 | 364/47287 | 9759 |
| ☐ N760NC | Douglas DC-9-51 | 813/47708 | 9851 |
| ☐ N760NW | Douglas DC-9-41 | 369/47288 | 9760 |
| ☐ N761NC | Douglas DC-9-51 | 814/47709 | 9852 |
| ☐ N762NC | Douglas DC-9-51 | 818/47710 | 9853 |
| ☐ N762NW | Douglas DC-9-41 | 555/47395 | 9762 |
| ☐ N763NC | Douglas DC-9-51 | 832/47716 | 9854 |
| ☐ N763NW | Douglas DC-9-41 | 557/47396 | 9763 |
| ☐ N764NC | Douglas DC-9-51 | 833/47717 | 9855 |
| ☐ N765NC | Douglas DC-9-51 | 834/47718 | 9856 |
| ☐ N766NC | Douglas DC-9-51 | 852/47739 | 9857 |
| ☐ N767NC | Douglas DC-9-51 | 853/47724 | 9858 |
| ☐ N768NC | Douglas DC-9-51 | 854/47729 | 9859 |
| ☐ N769NC | Douglas DC-9-51 | 877/47757 | 9860 |
| ☐ N770NC | Douglas DC-9-51 | 880/47758 | 9861 |
| ☐ N771NC | Douglas DC-9-51 | 881/47769 | 9862 |
| ☐ N772NC | Douglas DC-9-51 | 884/47774 | 9863 |
| ☐ N773NC | Douglas DC-9-51 | 888/47775 | 9864 |
| ☐ N774NC | Douglas DC-9-51 | 889/47776 | 9865 |
| ☐ N775NC | Douglas DC-9-51 | 904/47785 | 9866 |
| ☐ N776NC | Douglas DC-9-51 | 905/47786 | 9867 |
| ☐ N777NC | Douglas DC-9-51 | 912/47787 | 9868 |
| ☐ N778NC | Douglas DC-9-51 | 927/48100 | 9869 |
| ☐ N779NC | Douglas DC-9-51 | 931/48101 | 9870 |
| ☐ N780NC | Douglas DC-9-51 | 932/48102 | 9871 |
| ☐ N781NC | Douglas DC-9-51 | 935/48121 | 9872 |
| ☐ N782NC | Douglas DC-9-51 | 936/48107 | 9873 |
| ☐ N783NC | Douglas DC-9-51 | 937/48108 | 9874 |
| ☐ N784NC | Douglas DC-9-51 | 939/48109 | 9875 |
| ☐ N785NC | Douglas DC-9-51 | 945/48110 | 9876 |
| ☐ N786NC | Douglas DC-9-51 | 984/48148 | 9877 |
| ☐ N787NC | Douglas DC-9-51 | 990/48149 | 9878 |
| ☐ N908H | Douglas DC-9-31 | 583/47517 | 9937 |
| ☐ N914RW | Douglas DC-9-31 | 492/47362 | 9962 |
| ☐ N915RW | Douglas DC-9-31 | 169/47139 | 9957 |
| ☐ N916RW | Douglas DC-9-31 | 239/47144 | 9952 |
| ☐ N917RW | Douglas DC-9-31 | 247/47145 | 9958 |
| ☐ N918RW | Douglas DC-9-31 | 248/47158 | 9953 |
| ☐ N919RW | Douglas DC-9-31 | 255/47162 | 9959 |
| ☐ N920RW | Douglas DC-9-31 | 256/47163 | 9960 |
| ☐ N921RW | Douglas DC-9-31 | 259/47164 | 9954 |
| ☐ N922RW | Douglas DC-9-31 | 271/47182 | 9955 |
| ☐ N923RW | Douglas DC-9-31 | 272/47183 | 9956 |
| ☐ N924RW | Douglas DC-9-31 | 275/47185 | 9961 |
| ☐ N925US | Douglas DC-9-32 | 596/47472 | 9925 |
| ☐ N926NW | Douglas DC-9-32 | 589/47425 | 9926 |
| ☐ N926RC | Douglas DC-9-32 | 598/47473 | 9924 |
| ☐ N927RC | Douglas DC-9-32 | 590/47469 | 9923 |
| ☐ N940N | Douglas DC-9-32 | 708/47572 | 9918 |
| ☐ N941N | Douglas DC-9-32 | 535/47450 | 9919 |
| ☐ N942N | Douglas DC-9-32 | 549/47459 | 9920 |
| ☐ N943N | Douglas DC-9-32 | 773/47647 | 9921 |
| ☐ N945N | Douglas DC-9-32 | 775/47664 | 9922 |
| ☐ N949N | Douglas DC-9-32 | 691/47566 | 9916 |
| ☐ N952N | Douglas DC-9-31 | 161/47073 | 9902; std |
| ☐ N953N | Douglas DC-9-31 | 177/47083 | 9903 |
| ☐ N955N | Douglas DC-9-31 | 241/47160 | 9905 |
| ☐ N956N | Douglas DC-9-31 | 294/47252 | 9906 |
| ☐ N957N | Douglas DC-9-31 | 295/47253 | 9907 |
| ☐ N958N | Douglas DC-9-31 | 301/47254 | 9908 |
| ☐ N959N | Douglas DC-9-31 | 310/47255 | 9909 |
| ☐ N960N | Douglas DC-9-31 | 326/47256 | 9910 |
| ☐ N961N | Douglas DC-9-31 | 487/47405 | 9911 |
| ☐ N962N | Douglas DC-9-31 | 499/47406 | 9912 |
| ☐ N963N | Douglas DC-9-31 | 511/47415 | 9913 |
| ☐ N964N | Douglas DC-9-31 | 512/47416 | 9914 |
| ☐ N965N | Douglas DC-9-31 | 518/47417 | 9915 |
| ☐ N967N | Douglas DC-9-32 | 694/47573 | 9917 |
| ☐ N982US | Douglas DC-9-32 | 264/45790 | 9982 |
| ☐ N983US | Douglas DC-9-32 | 446/47282 | 9983 |
| ☐ N984US | Douglas DC-9-32 | 538/47383 | 9984 |
| ☐ N985US | Douglas DC-9-32 | 605/47479 | 9985 |
| ☐ N986US | Douglas DC-9-32 | 607/47480 | 9986 |
| ☐ N987US | Douglas DC-9-32 | 646/47458 | 9987 |
| ☐ N994Z | Douglas DC-9-32 | 193/47097 | 9981 |
| ☐ N1308T | Douglas DC-9-31 | 433/47315 | 9943 |
| ☐ N1309T | Douglas DC-9-31 | 439/47316 | 9944 |
| ☐ N1332U | Douglas DC-9-31 | 554/47404 | 9935 |
| ☐ N1334U | Douglas DC-9-31 | 597/47280 | 9933 |
| ☐ N1798U | Douglas DC-9-31 | 529/47369 | 9938 |
| ☐ N1799U | Douglas DC-9-31 | 551/47370 | 9936 |
| ☐ N3322L | Douglas DC-9-32 | 187/47031 | 9940 |
| ☐ N3324L | Douglas DC-9-32 | 205/47103 | 9941 |
| ☐ N3991C | Douglas DC-9-32 | 298/47175 | 9942 |
| ☐ N8908E | Douglas DC-9-14 | 50/45749 | 9150 |
| ☐ N8909E | Douglas DC-9-14 | 57/45770 | 9151 |
| ☐ N8911E | Douglas DC-9-14 | 67/45825 | 9152 |
| ☐ N8912E | Douglas DC-9-14 | 68/45829 | 9153 |
| ☐ N8913E | Douglas DC-9-14 | 75/45830 | 9154 |
| ☐ N8914E | Douglas DC-9-14 | 76/45831 | 9155 |
| ☐ N8915E | Douglas DC-9-14 | 84/45832 | 9156 |
| ☐ N8920E | Douglas DC-9-31 | 95/45835 | 9927 |
| ☐ N8921E | Douglas DC-9-31 | 96/45836 | 9928 |
| ☐ N8923E | Douglas DC-9-31 | 104/45838 | 9929 |
| ☐ N8925E | Douglas DC-9-31 | 117/45840 | 9945 |
| ☐ N8926E | Douglas DC-9-31 | 124/45863 | 9946 |
| ☐ N8928E | Douglas DC-9-31 | 137/45865 | 9949 |
| ☐ N8929E | Douglas DC-9-31 | 138/45866 | 9948 |
| ☐ N8932E | Douglas DC-9-31 | 227/47141 | 9996 |
| ☐ N8933E | Douglas DC-9-31 | 232/47142 | 9997 |
| ☐ N8934E | Douglas DC-9-31 | 238/47143 | 9998 |
| ☐ N8938E | Douglas DC-9-31 | 249/47161 | 9947 |
| ☐ N8944E | Douglas DC-9-31 | 266/47167 | 9988 |
| ☐ N8945E | Douglas DC-9-31 | 267/47181 | 9989 |
| ☐ N8950E | Douglas DC-9-31 | 276/47186 | 9990 |
| ☐ N8957E | Douglas DC-9-31 | 313/47215 | 9991 |
| ☐ N8960E | Douglas DC-9-31 | 331/45869 | 9992 |
| ☐ N8978E | Douglas DC-9-31 | 391/47327 | 9995 |
| ☐ N8979E | Douglas DC-9-31 | 392/47328 | 9994 |
| ☐ N8986E | Douglas DC-9-31 | 482/47402 | 9993 |
| ☐ N9330 | Douglas DC-9-31 | 318/47138 | 9966 |
| ☐ N9331 | Douglas DC-9-31 | 320/47263 | 9967 |
| ☐ N9332 | Douglas DC-9-31 | 329/47264 | 9968 |
| ☐ N9333 | Douglas DC-9-31 | 292/47246 | 9969 |
| ☐ N9334 | Douglas DC-9-31 | 342/47247 | 9970 |
| ☐ N9335 | Douglas DC-9-31 | 415/47337 | 9971 |
| ☐ N9336 | Douglas DC-9-31 | 416/47338 | 9972 |
| ☐ N9337 | Douglas DC-9-31 | 464/47346 | 9973 |
| ☐ N9338 | Douglas DC-9-31 | 478/47347 | 9974 |
| ☐ N9339 | Douglas DC-9-31 | 479/47382 | 9975 |
| ☐ N9340 | Douglas DC-9-31 | 489/47389 | 9976 |
| ☐ N9341 | Douglas DC-9-31 | 490/47390 | 9977 |
| ☐ N9342 | Douglas DC-9-31 | 491/47391 | 9978 |
| ☐ N9343 | Douglas DC-9-31 | 501/47439 | 9979 |
| ☐ N9344 | Douglas DC-9-31 | 502/47440 | 9980 |
| ☐ N9346 | Douglas DC-9-32 | 517/47376 | 9950 |
| ☐ N9347 | Douglas DC-9-32 | 135/45827 | 9951 |
| ☐ N9348 | Douglas DC-9-15 | 127/45787 | 9138 |
| ☐ N211NW | Douglas DC-10-30 | 171/46868 | 1211 |
| ☐ N221NW | Douglas DC-10-30 | 132/46579 | 1221 |
| ☐ N223NW | Douglas DC-10-30 | 183/46580 | 1223 |
| ☐ N224NW | Douglas DC-10-30 | 184/46581 | 1224 |

| | | | |
|---|---|---|---|
| ☐ N225NW | Douglas DC-10-30 | 187/46582 | 1225 |
| ☐ N226NW | Douglas DC-10-30ER | 292/46583 | 1226 |
| ☐ N227NW | Douglas DC-10-30 | 241/46969 | 1227 |
| ☐ N228NW | Douglas DC-10-30 | 131/46578 | 1228 |
| ☐ N229NW | Douglas DC-10-30 | 60/46551 | 1229 |
| ☐ N230NW | Douglas DC-10-30 | 71/46552 | 1230 |
| ☐ N232NW | Douglas DC-10-30 | 236/46961 | 1232 |
| ☐ N233NW | Douglas DC-10-30 | 240/46640 | 1233 |
| ☐ N234NW | Douglas DC-10-30 | 188/46912 | 1234 |
| ☐ N235NW | Douglas DC-10-30 | 199/46915 | 1235 |
| ☐ N236NW | Douglas DC-10-30 | 160/46934 | 1236 |
| ☒ N237NW | Douglas DC-10-30 | 336/47844 | 1237 |
| ☐ N238NW | Douglas DC-10-30ER | 434/48267 | 1238 |
| ☐ N239NW | Douglas DC-10-30ER | 435/48290 | 1239 |
| ☐ N240NW | Douglas DC-10-30ER | 438/48319 | 1240 |
| ☐ N241NW | Douglas DC-10-30 | 355/48282 | 1241 |
| ☐ N242NW | Douglas DC-10-30 | 356/47845 | 1242 |
| ☐ N243NW | Douglas DC-10-30ER | 436/48315 | 1243 |
| ☐ N244NW | Douglas DC-10-30ER | 437/48316 | 1244 |

## NORTHWEST AIRLINK — NWA

| | | | |
|---|---|---|---|
| ☐ N501XJ | Avro RJ85 | E2208 | 501 |
| ☐ N502XJ | Avro RJ85 | E2307 | 502 |
| ☐ N503XJ | Avro RJ85 | E2310 | 503 |
| ☐ N504XJ | Avro RJ85 | E2311 | 504 |
| ☐ N505XJ | Avro RJ85 | E2313 | 505 |
| ☐ N506XJ | Avro RJ85 | E2314 | 506 |
| ☐ N507XJ | Avro RJ85 | E2316 | 507 |
| ☐ N508XJ | Avro RJ85 | E2318 | 508 |
| ☐ N509XJ | Avro RJ85 | E2321 | 509 |
| ☐ N510XJ | Avro RJ85 | E2323 | 510 |
| ☐ N511XJ | Avro RJ85 | E2325 | 511 |
| ☐ N512XJ | Avro RJ85 | E2326 | 512 |
| ☐ N513XJ | Avro RJ85 | E2329 | 513 |
| ☐ N514XJ | Avro RJ85 | E2330 | 514 |
| ☐ N515XJ | Avro RJ85 | E2333 | 515 |
| ☐ N516XJ | Avro RJ85 | E2334 | 516 |
| ☐ N517XJ | Avro RJ85 | E2335 | 517 |
| ☐ N518XJ | Avro RJ85 | E2337 | 518 |
| ☐ N519XJ | Avro RJ85 | E2344 | 519 |
| ☐ N520XJ | Avro RJ85 | E2345 | 520 |
| ☐ N521XJ | Avro RJ85 | E2346 | 521 |
| ☐ N522XJ | Avro RJ85 | E2347 | 522 |
| ☐ N523XJ | Avro RJ85 | E2348 | 523 |
| ☐ N524XJ | Avro RJ85 | E2349 | 524 |
| ☐ N525XJ | Avro RJ85 | E2350 | 525 |
| ☐ N526XJ | Avro RJ85 | E2351 | 526 |
| ☐ N527XJ | Avro RJ85 | E2352 | 527 |
| ☐ N528XJ | Avro RJ85 | E2353 | 528 dam |
| ☐ N529XJ | Avro RJ85 | E2363 | 529 |
| ☐ N530XJ | Avro RJ85 | E2364 | 530 |
| ☐ N531XJ | Avro RJ85 | E2365 | 531 |
| ☐ N532XJ | Avro RJ85 | E2366 | 532 |
| ☐ N533XJ | Avro RJ85 | E2367 | 533 |
| ☐ N534XJ | Avro RJ85 | E2370 | |
| ☐ N535XJ | Avro RJ85 | E2371 | |
| ☐ N536XJ | Avro RJ85 | E2372 | |

| | | | |
|---|---|---|---|
| ☐ N8390A | Canadair RJ-200 | 7390 | 8390 |
| ☐ N8396A | Canadair RJ-200 | 7396 | 8396 |
| ☐ N8409N | Canadair RJ-200 | 7409 | 8409 |
| ☐ N8412F | Canadair RJ-200 | 7412 | 8412 |
| ☐ N8416B | Canadair RJ-200 | 7416 | 8416 |
| ☐ N8423C | Canadair RJ-200 | 7423 | 8423 |
| ☐ N8432A | Canadair RJ-200 | 7432 | 8432 |
| ☐ N8444F | Canadair RJ-200 | 7444 | 8444 |
| ☐ N8458A | Canadair RJ-200 | 7458 | 8458 |
| ☐ N8475B | Canadair RJ-200 | 7475 | 8475 |
| ☐ N8477R | Canadair RJ-200 | 7477 | 8477 |
| ☐ N8488D | Canadair RJ-200 | 7488 | 8488 |
| ☐ N8492C | Canadair RJ-200 | 7492 | 8492 |
| ☐ N8495B | Canadair RJ-200 | 7495 | 8495 |
| ☐ N8501F | Canadair RJ-200 | 7501 | 8501 |
| ☐ N8505Q | Canadair RJ-200 | 7505 | 8505 |
| ☐ N8506C | Canadair RJ-200 | 7506 | 8506 |
| ☐ N8515F | Canadair RJ-200 | 7515 | 8515 |

| | | | |
|---|---|---|---|
| ☐ N8516C | Canadair RJ-200 | 7516 | 8516 |
| ☐ N8524A | Canadair RJ-200 | 7524 | 8524 |
| ☐ N8525B | Canadair RJ-200 | 7525 | 8525 |
| ☐ N8532G | Canadair RJ-200 | 7532 | 8532 |
| ☐ N8533D | Canadair RJ-200 | 7533 | 8533 |
| ☐ N8541D | Canadair RJ-200 | 7541 | 8541 |
| ☐ N8543F | Canadair RJ-200 | 7543 | 8543 |
| ☐ N8554A | Canadair RJ-200 | 7554 | 8554 |
| ☐ N8560F | Canadair RJ-200 | 7560 | 8560 |
| ☐ N8577D | Canadair RJ-200 | 7577 | 8577 |
| ☐ N8580A | Canadair RJ-200 | 7580 | 8580 |
| ☐ N8587E | Canadair RJ-200 | 7587 | 8587 |
| ☐ N8588D | Canadair RJ-200 | 7588 | 8588 |
| ☐ N8598B | Canadair RJ-200 | 7598 | 8598 |
| ☐ N8604C | Canadair RJ-200 | 7604 | 8604 |
| ☐ N8611A | Canadair RJ-200 | 7611 | 8611 |
| ☐ N8623A | Canadair RJ-200 | 7623 | 8623 |
| ☐ N8631E | Canadair RJ-200 | 7631 | 8631 |
| ☐ N8646A | Canadair RJ-200 | 7646 | 8646 |
| ☐ N8659B | Canadair RJ-200 | 7659 | 8659 |
| ☐ N8665A | Canadair RJ-200 | 7665 | 8665 |
| ☐ N8672A | Canadair RJ-200 | 7672 | 8672 |
| ☐ N8673D | Canadair RJ-200 | 7673 | 8673 |
| ☐ N8674A | Canadair RJ-200 | 7674 | 8674 |
| ☐ N8683B | Canadair RJ-200 | 7683 | 8683 |
| ☐ N8688C | Canadair RJ-200 | 7688 | 6888 |
| ☐ N8694A | Canadair RJ-200 | 7694 | 8694 |
| ☐ N8696C | Canadair RJ-200 | 7696 | 8696 |
| ☐ N8698A | Canadair RJ-200 | 7698 | 8698 |
| ☐ N8709A | Canadair RJ-200 | 7709 | 8709 |
| ☐ N8710A | Canadair RJ-200 | 7710 | 8710 |
| ☐ N8718E | Canadair RJ-200 | 7718 | 8718 |
| ☐ N8721B | Canadair RJ-200 | 7721 | 8721 |
| ☐ N | Canadair RJ-200 | 7733 | 8733 o/o |
| ☐ N | Canadair RJ-200 | 7736 | 8736 o/o |

| | | | |
|---|---|---|---|
| ☐ N27XJ | SAAB SF.340A | 027 | |
| ☐ N46XJ | SAAB SF.340A | 046 | |
| ☐ N48XJ | SAAB SF.340A | 048 | |
| ☐ N68XJ | SAAB SF.340A | 068 | |
| ☐ N76XJ | SAAB SF.340A | 076 | |
| ☐ N79XJ | SAAB SF.340A | 079 | |
| ☐ N89XJ | SAAB SF.340A | 089 | |
| ☐ N98XJ | SAAB SF.340A | 098 | |
| ☐ N99XJ | SAAB SF.340A | 099 | |
| ☐ N102XJ | SAAB SF.340A | 102 | |
| ☐ N106XJ | SAAB SF.340A | 106 | |
| ☐ N107PX | SAAB SF.340A | 010 | |
| ☐ N107XJ | SAAB SF.340A | 107 | |
| ☐ N108PX | SAAB SF.340A | 012 | |
| ☐ N109PX | SAAB SF.340A | 021 | |
| ☐ N110PX | SAAB SF.340A | 023 | |
| ☐ N110XJ | SAAB SF.340A | 110 | dam |
| ☐ N111PX | SAAB SF.340A | 024 | |
| ☐ N112PX | SAAB SF.340A | 025 | |
| ☐ N112XJ | SAAB SF.340A | 112 | |
| ☐ N114XJ | SAAB SF.340A | 114 | |
| ☐ N115XJ | SAAB SF.340A | 115 | |
| ☐ N119XJ | SAAB SF.340A | 119 | |
| ☐ N142XJ | SAAB SF.340A | 142 | |
| ☐ N325PX | SAAB SF.340A | 051 | |
| ☐ N326PX | SAAB SF.340A | 054 | |
| ☐ N327PX | SAAB SF.340A | 059 | |
| ☐ N344AM | SAAB SF.340A | 030 | |
| ☐ N347AM | SAAB SF.340A | 039 | |
| ☐ N360PX | SAAB SF.340B | 220 | |
| ☐ N361PX | SAAB SF.340B | 249 | |
| ☐ N362PX | SAAB SF.340B | 258 | |
| ☐ N363PX | SAAB SF.340B | 260 | |
| ☐ N364PX | SAAB SF.340B | 262 | |
| ☐ N365PX | SAAB SF.340B | 265 | |
| ☐ N366PX | SAAB SF.340B | 267 | |
| ☐ N367PX | SAAB SF.340B | 271 | |
| ☐ N368PX | SAAB SF.340B | 274 | |
| ☐ N369PX | SAAB SF.340B | 295 | |
| ☐ N370PX | SAAB SF.340B | 300 | |
| ☐ N402XJ | SAAB SF.340B | 402 | |
| ☐ N403BH | SAAB SF.340A | 060 | |

| | | | |
|---|---|---|---|
| □ N403XJ | SAAB SF.340B | 403 | |
| □ N404BH | SAAB SF.340A | 061 | |
| □ N404XJ | SAAB SF.340B | 404 | |
| □ N406BH | SAAB SF.340A | 074 | |
| □ N406XJ | SAAB SF.340B | 406 | |
| □ N407BH | SAAB SF.340A | 078 | |
| □ N407XJ | SAAB SF.340B | 407 | |
| □ N408XJ | SAAB SF.340B | 408 | |
| □ N410XJ | SAAB SF.340B | 410 | |
| □ N411XJ | SAAB SF.340B | 411 | |
| □ N412XJ | SAAB SF.340B | 412 | |
| □ N413XJ | SAAB SF.340B | 413 | |
| □ N414XJ | SAAB SF.340B | 414 | |
| □ N415XJ | SAAB SF.340B | 415 | |
| □ N416XJ | SAAB SF.340B | 416 | |
| □ N417XJ | SAAB SF.340B | 417 | |
| □ N418XJ | SAAB SF.340B | 418 | |
| □ N420XJ | SAAB SF.340B | 420 | |
| □ N421XJ | SAAB SF.340B | 421 | |
| □ N422XJ | SAAB SF.340B | 422 | |
| □ N423XJ | SAAB SF.340B | 423 | |
| □ N424XJ | SAAB SF.340B | 424 | |
| □ N425XJ | SAAB SF.340B | 425 | |
| □ N426XJ | SAAB SF.340B | 426 | |
| □ N427XJ | SAAB SF.340B | 427 | |
| □ N428XJ | SAAB SF.340B | 428 | |
| □ N429XJ | SAAB SF.340B | 429 | |
| □ N430XJ | SAAB SF.340B | 430 | |
| □ N433XJ | SAAB SF.340B | 433 | |
| □ N434XJ | SAAB SF.340B | 434 | |
| □ N435XJ | SAAB SF.340B | 435 | |
| □ N436XJ | SAAB SF.340B | 436 | |
| □ N437XJ | SAAB SF.340B | 437 | |
| □ N438XJ | SAAB SF.340B | 438 | |
| □ N439XJ | SAAB SF.340B | 439 | |
| □ N441XJ | SAAB SF.340B | 441 | s |
| □ N442XJ | SAAB SF.340B | 442 | |
| □ N443XJ | SAAB SF.340B | 443 | |
| □ N444XJ | SAAB SF.340B | 444 | |
| □ N445XJ | SAAB SF.340B | 445 | |
| □ N446XJ | SAAB SF.340B | 446 | std |
| □ N447XJ | SAAB SF.340B | 447 | |
| □ N448XJ | SAAB SF.340B | 448 | |
| □ N449XJ | SAAB SF.340B | 449 | |
| □ N450XJ | SAAB SF.340B | 450 | |
| □ N451XJ | SAAB SF.340B | 451 | |
| □ N452XJ | SAAB SF.340B | 452 | |
| □ N453XJ | SAAB SF.340B | 453 | |
| □ N454XJ | SAAB SF.340B | 454 | |
| □ N456XJ | SAAB SF.340B | 456 | |
| □ N457XJ | SAAB SF.340B | 457 | |
| □ N922MA | SAAB SF.340A | 077 | |
| □ N935MA | SAAB SF.340A | 073 | |
| □ N991XJ | SAAB SF.340A | 091 | |

## OMNI AIR INTERNATIONAL   OAE

| | | | |
|---|---|---|---|
| □ N189AX | Douglas DC-10-30F | 354/48277 | |
| □ N279AX | Douglas DC-10-30F | 316/47816 | |
| □ N360AX | Douglas DC-10-10 | 38/46706 | std |
| □ N450AX | Douglas DC-10-10 | 162/46942 | std |
| □ N540AX | Douglas DC-10-30 | 299/46595 | |
| □ N630AX | Douglas DC-10-30 | 301/46596 | |
| □ N720AX | Douglas DC-10-30 | 342/48252 | |
| □ N17085 | Douglas DC-10-30 | 201/47957 | |
| □ N59083 | Douglas DC-10-30 | 170/47926 | |
| □ N48277 | Douglas DC-10-30F | 354/48277 | |
| □ N | Boeing 757-2Q8 | 457/25621 | o/o |
| □ N | Boeing 757-2Q8 | 723/28161 | o/o |

## PACE AIRLINES   PCE

| | | | |
|---|---|---|---|
| □ N37NY | Boeing 737-4Y0 | 1651/23976 | |
| □ N159PL | Boeing 737-242 | 438/21186 | |
| □ N219PA | Boeing 737-222 | 211/19956 | |
| □ N249TR | Boeing 737-2K5 | 792/22598 | |

| | | | |
|---|---|---|---|
| □ N250TR | Boeing 737-2K5 | 779/22597 | |
| □ N251TR | Boeing 737-228 | 1397/23792 | |
| □ N | Boeing 737-228 | 936/23001 | |
| □ N370PA | Boeing 737-3L9 | 2760/27294 | |
| □ N371PA | Boeing 737-306 | 1325/23543 | |
| □ N372PA | Boeing 737-306 | 1349/23546 | |
| □ N373PA | Boeing 737-3Y0 | 1389/23749 | |
| □ N374PA | Boeing 737-36M | 2810/28333 | |
| □ N375PA | Boeing 737-3Y0 | 1511/23812 | |
| □ N377PA | Boeing 737-3L9 | 1402/23718 | |
| □ N920WA | Boeing 737-236 | 626/21791 | |
| □ N751PA | Boeing 757-2G5 | 146/23928 | ex |
| □ N801DM | Boeing 757-256 | 561/26240 | |

## PAN AM – PAN AMERICAN AIRWAYS   PAA

| | | | |
|---|---|---|---|
| □ N342PA | Boeing 727-222 | 1503/21893 | |
| □ N343PA | Boeing 727-222 | 1505/21894 | |
| □ N346PA | Boeing 727-222 | 1528/21904 | |
| □ N357PA | Boeing 727-222 | 1511/21896 | |
| □ N361PA | Boeing 727-225 | 939/20623 | |
| □ N362PA | Boeing 727-2J0 | 1160/21106 | |
| □ N363PA | Boeing 727-221 | 1764/22535 | |
| □ N364PA | Boeing 727-2J0 | 1172/21107 | |
| □ N365PA | Boeing 727-225 | 948/20628 | |
| □ N367PA | Boeing 727-221 | 1794/22539 | |
| □ N369PA | Boeing 727-282 | 1579/21950 | |
| □ N7254U | Boeing 727-222 | 1311/21401 | |
| □ N7255U | Boeing 727-222 | 1313/21402 | std |
| □ N7257U | Boeing 727-222 | 1321/21404 | |
| □ N7259U | Boeing 727-222 | 1325/21406 | |
| □ N7261U | Boeing 727-222 | 1334/21408 | |
| □ N7266U | Boeing 727-222 | 1351/21413 | o/o |
| □ N7283U | Boeing 727-222 | 1408/21561 | |
| □ N7441U | Boeing 727-222 | 1507/21895 | |
| □ N7444U | Boeing 727-222 | 1515/21898 | |
| □ N7445U | Boeing 727-222 | 1517/21899 | std |
| □ N7446U | Boeing 727-222 | 1519/21900 | |
| □ N7448U | Boeing 727-222 | 1524/21902 | |
| □ N7449U | Boeing 727-222 | 1526/21903 | o/o |
| □ N7456U | Boeing 727-222 | 1570/21910 | |
| □ N7457U | Boeing 727-222 | 1572/21911 | o/o |
| □ N7458U | Boeing 727-222 | 1575/21912 | |
| □ N7459U | Boeing 727-222 | 1593/21913 | o/o |
| □ N7464U | Boeing 727-222 | 1625/21918 | std |
| □ N7467U | Boeing 727-222 | 1639/21921 | |

## PLANET AIRWAYS   PLZ

| | | | |
|---|---|---|---|
| □ N893AA | Boeing 727-223 | 1649/22009 | |
| □ N894AA | Boeing 727-223 | 1650/22010 | |
| □ N1910 | Boeing 727-23 | 311/19385 | |
| □ N69741 | Boeing 727-224 | 1684/22250 | |
| □ N69742 | Boeing 727-224 | 1687/22251 | |
| □ N79745 | Boeing 727-224 | 1740/22448 | |

## POLAR AIR CARGO   PAC

| | | | |
|---|---|---|---|
| □ N354MC | Boeing 747-341SF | 627/23394 | Lsf GTI |
| □ N355MC | Boeing 747-341SF | 629/23395 | Lsf GTI |
| □ N409MC | Boeing 747-47UF | 1242/30558 | Lsf GTI |
| □ N450PA | Boeing 747-46NF | 1257/30808 | |
| □ N451PA | Boeing 747-46NF | 1259/30809 | |
| □ N452PA | Boeing 747-46NF | 1260/30810 | |
| □ N453PA | Boeing 747-46NF | 1283/30811 | |
| □ N454PA | Boeing 747-46NF | 1310/30812 | |
| □ N496MC | Boeing 747-47UF | 1217/29257 | Lsf GTI |
| □ N505MC | Boeing 747-2D3M | 296/21251 | Lsf GTI |
| □ N524UP | Boeing 747-237B | 318/21446 | Lsf UPS |
| □ N806FT | Boeing 747-249F | 406/21827 | |
| □ N858FT | Boeing 747-123 | 90/20109 | std |
| □ N859FT | Boeing 747-123 | 133/20326 | |
| □ N920FT | Boeing 747-249F | 460/22237 | |
| □ N159PL | Boeing 747-283M | 358/21575 | |
| □ N921FT | Boeing 747-2U3B | 561/22768 | |
| □ N922FT | Boeing 747-2U3B | 562/22769 | |
| □ N923FT | Boeing 747-2U3B | 562/22769 | |

| | | | |
|---|---|---|---|
| ☐ N924FT | Boeing 747-259B | 372/21730 | Lst UPS |
| ☐ N638FE | Boeing 747-245F | 396/21841 | |
| ☐ N926FT | Boeing 747-2R7F | 354/21650 | |
| ☐ N24837 | Boeing 747-329M | 810/24837 | Lsf GTI |

All model −100s and −200s are SCD or SF conversions

## QUEST CARGO INTERNATIONAL

| | | | |
|---|---|---|---|
| ☐ N802MA | Boeing 727-225 | 1668/22433 | |
| ☐ N803MA | Boeing 727-225 | 1671/22434 | std |
| ☐ N804MA | Boeing 727-225 | 1674/22435 | |
| ☐ N889MA | Boeing 727-225 | 1532/21854 | std |

## RYAN INTERNATIONAL AIRLINES          RYN

| | | | |
|---|---|---|---|
| ☐ D-ALAB | Airbus A320-232 | 0575 | Lsf AEF |
| ☐ D-ALAE | Airbus A320-232 | 0659 | Lsf AEF |
| ☐ D-ALAO | Airbus A321-231 | 1408 | Lsf AEF |
| ☐ D-ALAQ | Airbus A321-231 | 1438 | Lsf AEF |
| ☐ D-ALAR | Airbus A320-232 | 1459 | Lsf AEF |
| ☐ D-ALAS | Airbus A321-231 | 1487 | Lsf AEF |
| ☐ G-BXKA | Airbus A320-214 | 0714 | Lsf JMC |
| ☐ G-BXKC | Airbus A320-214 | 0730 | Lsf JMC |
| ☐ N29SW | Boeing 737-2H4 | 499/21340 | |
| ☐ N54SW | Boeing 737-2H4 | 543/21535 | |
| ☐ N251RY | Boeing 737-4Y0 | 2201/25180 | |
| ☐ N255RY | Boeing 737-86N | 534/28619 | Lsf FUA |
| ☐ EC-HVY | Boeing 737-4Y0 | 1885/24690 | Lsf FUA |
| ☐ EI-BXI | Boeing 737-448 | 2036/25052 | Lsf EIN |
| ☐ EI-CDG | Boeing 737-548 | 2261/25738 | Lsf EIN |
| ☐ D-ABNO | Boeing 757-230 | 464/25901 | Lsf CFG |
| ☐ D-ABNS | Boeing 757-230 | 537/26435 | Lsf CFG |
| ☐ G-JMCD | Boeing 757-25F | 928/30757 | Lsf JMC |
| ☐ G-JMCE | Boeing 757-25F | 932/30758 | Lsf JMC |
| ☐ G-OOBB | Boeing 757-28A | 951/32447 | Lsf AMM |
| ☐ N571RY | Douglas DC-10-10 | 283/46645 | |
| ☐ N572RY | Douglas DC-10-10 | 251/46977 | |
| ☐ N951LF | Airbus A320-233 | 0460 | |
| ☐ N253TR | Boeing 737-228 | 943/23005 | |

## SCENIC AIRLINES          SCE

| | | | |
|---|---|---|---|
| ☐ N278MA | F.27 Friendship 200 | 10280 | |
| ☐ N279MA | F.27 Friendship 200 | 10297 | |
| ☐ N280EA | F.27 Friendship 600 | 10394 | |
| ☐ N283EA | F.27 Friendship 500F | 10522 | |
| ☐ N284MA | F.27 Friendship 500F | 10560 | |

## SKYWEST AIRLINES          SKW

| | | | |
|---|---|---|---|
| ☐ N403SW | Canadair RJ-200 | 7028 | |
| ☐ N405SW | Canadair RJ-200 | 7029 | |
| ☐ N406SW | Canadair RJ-200 | 7030 | |
| ☐ N407SW | Canadair RJ-200 | 7034 | |
| ☐ N408SW | Canadair RJ-200 | 7055 | |
| ☐ N409SW | Canadair RJ-200 | 7056 | |
| ☐ N410SW | Canadair RJ-200 | 7066 | |
| ☐ N411SW | Canadair RJ-200 | 7067 | |
| ☐ N412SW | Canadair RJ-200 | 7101 | |
| ☐ N413SW | Canadair RJ-200 | 7102 | |
| ☐ N416SW | Canadair RJ-200 | 7089 | |
| ☐ N417SW | Canadair RJ-200 | 7400 | |
| ☐ N418SW | Canadair RJ-200 | 7446 | |
| ☐ N423SW | Canadair RJ-200 | 7456 | |
| ☐ N426SW | Canadair RJ-200 | 7468 | |
| ☐ N427SW | Canadair RJ-200 | 7497 | |
| ☐ N429SW | Canadair RJ-200 | 7518 | |
| ☐ N430SW | Canadair RJ-200 | 7523 | |
| ☐ N431SW | Canadair RJ-200 | 7536 | |
| ☐ N432SW | Canadair RJ-200 | 7548 | |
| ☐ N433SW | Canadair RJ-200 | 7550 | |
| ☐ N435SW | Canadair RJ-200 | 7555 | |
| ☐ N437SW | Canadair RJ-200 | 7564 | |

| | | | |
|---|---|---|---|
| ☐ N438SW | Canadair RJ-200 | 7574 | |
| ☐ N439SW | Canadair RJ-200 | 7578 | |
| ☐ N440SW | Canadair RJ-200 | 7589 | |
| ☐ N441SW | Canadair RJ-200 | 7602 | |
| ☐ N442SW | Canadair RJ-200 | 7609 | |
| ☐ N442CA< | Canadair RJ-200 | 7483 | Lsf COM |
| ☐ N443SW | Canadair RJ-200 | 7638 | |
| ☐ N445SW | Canadair RJ-200 | 7651 | |
| ☐ N446SW | Canadair RJ-200 | 7666 | |
| ☐ N447SW | Canadair RJ-200 | 7677 | |
| ☐ N448SW | Canadair RJ-200 | 7678 | |
| ☐ N449SW | Canadair RJ-200 | 7699 | |
| ☐ N452SW | Canadair RJ-200 | 7716 | |
| ☐ N493SW | Canadair RJ-200 | 7450 | |
| ☐ N498SW | Canadair RJ-200 | 7483 | Lsf COM |
| ☐ N499SW | Canadair RJ-200 | 7398 | |
| ☐ N587SW | Canadair RJ-200 | 7062 | Lsf COM |
| ☐ N588SW | Canadair RJ-200 | 7069 | Lsf COM |
| ☐ N589SW | Canadair RJ-200 | 7072 | Lsf COM |
| ☐ N590SW | Canadair RJ-200 | 7077 | Lsf COM |
| ☐ N591SW | Canadair RJ-200 | 7079 | Lsf COM |
| ☐ N592SW | Canadair RJ-200 | 7279 | Lsf COM |
| ☐ N594SW | Canadair RJ-200 | 7285 | Lsf COM |
| ☐ N595SW | Canadair RJ-200 | 7292 | Lsf COM |
| ☐ N597SW | Canadair RJ-200 | 7293 | Lsf COM |
| ☐ N720SW | Canadair RJ-200 | 7297 | Lsf COM |
| ☐ N | Canadair RJ-200 | | o/o |
| ☐ N | Canadair RJ-200 | | o/o |
| ☐ N | Canadair RJ-200 | | o/o |
| ☐ N | Canadair RJ-200 | | o/o |
| ☐ N | Canadair RJ-200 | | o/o |
| ☐ N | Canadair RJ-200 | | o/o |
| ☐ N | Canadair RJ-200 | | o/o |
| ☐ N903SW | Canadair RJ-200 | 7425 | |
| ☐ N905SW | Canadair RJ-200 | 7437 | |
| ☐ N906SW | Canadair RJ-200 | 7510 | |
| ☐ N907SW | Canadair RJ-200 | 7511 | |
| ☐ N908SW | Canadair RJ-200 | 7540 | |
| ☐ N909SW | Canadair RJ-200 | 7558 | |
| ☐ N910SW | Canadair RJ-200 | 7566 | |
| ☐ N912SW | Canadair RJ-200 | 7595 | |
| ☐ N913SW | Canadair RJ-200 | 7597 | |
| ☐ N915SW | Canadair RJ-200 | 7615 | |
| ☐ N916SW | Canadair RJ-200 | 7634 | |
| ☐ N917SW | Canadair RJ-200 | 7641 | |
| ☐ N918SW | Canadair RJ-200 | 7645 | |
| ☐ N919SW | Canadair RJ-200 | 7657 | |
| ☐ N920SW | Canadair RJ-200 | 7660 | |
| ☐ N923SW | Canadair RJ-200 | 7664 | |
| ☐ N924SW | Canadair RJ-200 | 7681 | |
| ☐ N925SW | Canadair RJ-200 | 7682 | |
| ☐ N926SW | Canadair RJ-200 | 7687 | |
| ☐ N927SW | Canadair RJ-200 | 7693 | |
| ☐ N928SW | Canadair RJ-200 | 7701 | |
| ☐ N929SW | Canadair RJ-200 | 7703 | |
| ☐ N930SW | Canadair RJ-200 | 7713 | |
| ☐ N932SW | Canadair RJ-200 | 7714 | |
| ☐ N934SW | Canadair RJ-200 | 7722 | |
| ☐ N935SW | Canadair RJ-200 | 7725 | |
| ☐ N936SW | Canadair RJ-200 | 7726 | |
| ☐ N | Canadair RJ-200 | | o/o |
| ☐ N | Canadair RJ-200 | | o/o |
| ☐ N | Canadair RJ-200 | | o/o |
| ☐ N981ML | Canadair RJ-200 | 7388 | |
| ☐ N | Canadair RJ-200 | | o/o |
| ☐ N | Canadair RJ-200 | | o/o |
| ☐ N | Canadair RJ-200 | | o/o |
| ☐ N | Canadair RJ-200 | | o/o |
| ☐ N | Canadair RJ-200 | | o/o |
| ☐ N | Canadair RJ-200 | | o/o |
| ☐ N | Canadair RJ-200 | | o/o |
| ☐ N | Canadair RJ-200 | | o/o |
| ☐ N | Canadair RJ-200 | | o/o |
| ☐ N | Canadair RJ-200 | | o/o |

| | Reg | Type | C/n | |
|---|---|---|---|---|
| ☐ | N | Canadair RJ-200 | | o/o |
| ☐ | N | Canadair RJ-200 | | o/o |
| ☐ | N | Canadair RJ-200 | | o/o |
| ☐ | N | Canadair RJ-200 | | o/o |
| ☐ | N | Canadair RJ-200 | | o/o |
| ☐ | N | Canadair RJ-200 | | o/o |
| ☐ | N | Canadair RJ-200 | | o/o |
| ☐ | N | Canadair RJ-200 | | o/o |
| ☐ | N | Canadair RJ-200 | | o/o |
| ☐ | N130G | Embraer EMB.120ER | 120130 | |
| ☐ | N137H | Embraer EMB.120ER | 120137 | |
| ☐ | N156CA | Embraer EMB.120ER | 120156 | |
| ☐ | N161CA | Embraer EMB.120ER | 120143 | |
| ☐ | N162CA | Embraer EMB.120ER | 120150 | |
| ☐ | N186SW | Embraer EMB.120ER | 120034 | |
| ☐ | N187SW | Embraer EMB.120ER | 120037 | |
| ☐ | N188SW | Embraer EMB.120ER | 120039 | |
| ☐ | N189SW | Embraer EMB.120ER | 120048 | |
| ☐ | N190SW | Embraer EMB.120ER | 120050 | |
| ☐ | N194SW | Embraer EMB.120ER | 120120 | |
| ☐ | N195SW | Embraer EMB.120ER | 120127 | |
| ☐ | N196CA | Embraer EMB.120ER | 120196 | |
| ☐ | N196SW | Embraer EMB.120ER | 120151 | |
| ☐ | N197SW | Embraer EMB.120ER | 120186 | |
| ☐ | N198SW | Embraer EMB.120ER | 120227 | |
| ☐ | N199SW | Embraer EMB.120ER | 120237 | |
| ☐ | N203SW | Embraer EMB.120ER | 120240 | |
| ☐ | N204SW | Embraer EMB.120ER | 120243 | |
| ☐ | N207SW | Embraer EMB.120ER | 120266 | |
| ☐ | N209SW | Embraer EMB.120ER | 120269 | |
| ☐ | N212SW | Embraer EMB.120ER | 120276 | |
| ☐ | N213SW | Embraer EMB.120ER | 120277 | |
| ☐ | N214SW | Embraer EMB.120ER | 120280 | |
| ☐ | N215SW | Embraer EMB.120ER | 120281 | |
| ☐ | N216SW | Embraer EMB.120ER | 120285 | |
| ☐ | N217SW | Embraer EMB.120ER | 120286 | |
| ☐ | N218SW | Embraer EMB.120ER | 120287 | |
| ☐ | N220SW | Embraer EMB.120ER | 120288 | |
| ☐ | N221SW | Embraer EMB.120ER | 120290 | |
| ☐ | N223SW | Embraer EMB.120ER | 120291 | |
| ☐ | N224SW | Embraer EMB.120ER | 120294 | |
| ☐ | N226SW | Embraer EMB.120ER | 120296 | |
| ☐ | N227SW | Embraer EMB.120ER | 120304 | |
| ☐ | N229SW | Embraer EMB.120ER | 120305 | |
| ☐ | N232SW | Embraer EMB.120ER | 120306 | |
| ☐ | N233SW | Embraer EMB.120ER | 120307 | |
| ☐ | N234SW | Embraer EMB.120ER | 120308 | |
| ☐ | N235SW | Embraer EMB.120ER | 120310 | |
| ☐ | N236SW | Embraer EMB.120ER | 120312 | |
| ☐ | N237SW | Embraer EMB.120ER | 120314 | |
| ☐ | N250YV | Embraer EMB.120ER | 120250 | |
| ☐ | N251UE | Embraer EMB.120RT | 120108 | |
| ☐ | N251YV | Embraer EMB.120ER | 120251 | |
| ☐ | N268UE | Embraer EMB.120ER | 120207 | |
| ☐ | N269UE | Embraer EMB.120ER | 120194 | |
| ☐ | N270YV | Embraer EMB.120ER | 120270 | |
| ☐ | N271YV | Embraer EMB.120ER | 120271 | |
| ☐ | N284YV | Embraer EMB.120ER | 120284 | |
| ☐ | N288SW | Embraer EMB.120ER | 120316 | |
| ☐ | N290SW | Embraer EMB.120ER | 120317 | |
| ☐ | N291SW | Embraer EMB.120ER | 120318 | |
| ☐ | N292SW | Embraer EMB.120ER | 120319 | |
| ☐ | N292UX | Embraer EMB.120ER | 120292 | |
| ☐ | N293SW | Embraer EMB.120ER | 120320 | |
| ☐ | N294SW | Embraer EMB.120ER | 120321 | |
| ☐ | N295SW | Embraer EMB.120ER | 120322 | |
| ☐ | N295UX | Embraer EMB.120ER | 120295 | |
| ☐ | N296SW | Embraer EMB.120ER | 120325 | |
| ☐ | N297SW | Embraer EMB.120ER | 120327 | |
| ☐ | N298SW | Embraer EMB.120ER | 120328 | |
| ☐ | N299SW | Embraer EMB.120ER | 120329 | |
| ☐ | N308SW | Embraer EMB.120ER | 120326 | |
| ☐ | N393SW | Embraer EMB.120ER | 120330 | |
| ☐ | N560SW | Embraer EMB.120ER | 120334 | |
| ☐ | N561SW | Embraer EMB.120ER | 120335 | |
| ☐ | N562SW | Embraer EMB.120ER | 120336 | |
| ☐ | N563SW | Embraer EMB.120ER | 120338 | |
| ☐ | N564SW | Embraer EMB.120ER | 120339 | |
| ☐ | N565SW | Embraer EMB.120ER | 120340 | |
| ☐ | N566SW | Embraer EMB.120ER | 120341 | |
| ☐ | N567SW | Embraer EMB.120ER | 120342 | |
| ☐ | N568SW | Embraer EMB.120ER | 120343 | |
| ☐ | N569SW | Embraer EMB.120ER | 120344 | |
| ☐ | N576SW | Embraer EMB.120ER | 120345 | |
| ☐ | N578SW | Embraer EMB.120ER | 120346 | |
| ☐ | N579SW | Embraer EMB.120ER | 120347 | |
| ☐ | N580SW | Embraer EMB.120ER | 120348 | |
| ☐ | N581SW | Embraer EMB.120ER | 120349 | |
| ☐ | N582SW | Embraer EMB.120ER | 120350 | |
| ☐ | N583SW | Embraer EMB.120ER | 120351 | |
| ☐ | N584SW | Embraer EMB.120ER | 120352 | |
| ☐ | N585SW | Embraer EMB.120ER | 120353 | |
| ☐ | N586SW | Embraer EMB.120ER | 120354 | |
| ☐ | N593SW | Embraer EMB.120ER | 120191 | |
| ☐ | N595SW | Embraer EMB.120ER | 120289 | |
| ☐ | N1105G | Embraer EMB.120ER | 120105 | |
| ☐ | N1110J | Embraer EMB.120ER | 120110 | |
| ☐ | N1117H | Embraer EMB.120ER | 120117 | |

## SOUTHEAST AIRLINES     SNK

| ☐ | N920LG | Douglas DC-9-32 | 913/47797 | |
| ☐ | N921LG | Douglas DC-9-32 | 914/47798 | |
| ☐ | N932MJ | Douglas DC-9-31 | 1052/48156 | |
| ☐ | N933JK | Douglas DC-9-31 | 1058/48159 | |
| ☐ | N934LK | Douglas DC-9-31 | 1054/48157 | |
| ☐ | N935DS | Douglas DC-9-31 | 1056/48158 | |
| ☐ | N12532 | Douglas DC-9-32 | 349/45791 | |
| ☐ | N11FQ | McDD MD-88 | 1606/49759 | |
| ☐ | N12FQ | McDD MD-88 | 1657/49766 | |
| ☐ | N374GE | McDD MD-82 | 1208/49374 | |
| ☐ | N418GE | McDD MD-82 | 1394/49418 | |

## SOUTHERN AIR     SOO

| ☐ | N742SA | Boeing 747-230M | 549/22669 | |
| ☐ | N743SA | Boeing 747-230M | 574/22671 | |
| ☐ | N744SA | Boeing 747-230M | 490/22363 | |
| ☐ | N745SA | Boeing 747-2F6B (SF) | 498/22382 | std |

## SOUTHWEST AIRLINES     SWA

| ☐ | N68SW | Boeing 737-2H4 | 725/22357 | std |
| ☐ | N71SW | Boeing 737-2H4 | 732/22358 | |
| ☐ | N73SW | Boeing 737-2H4 | 826/22673 | |
| ☐ | N74SW | Boeing 737-2H4 | 827/22674 | |
| ☐ | N80SW | Boeing 737-2H4 | 839/22675 | |
| ☐ | N81SW | Boeing 737-2H4 | 841/22730 | |
| ☐ | N82SW | Boeing 737-2H4 | 864/22731 | |
| ☐ | N83SW | Boeing 737-2H4 | 877/22732 | |
| ☐ | N85SW | Boeing 737-2H4 | 878/22826 | |
| ☐ | N86SW | Boeing 737-2H4 | 882/22827 | |
| ☐ | N87SW | Boeing 737-2H4 | 905/22903 | |
| ☐ | N89SW | Boeing 737-2H4 | 913/22904 | |
| ☐ | N90SW | Boeing 737-2H4 | 918/22905 | |
| ☐ | N91SW | Boeing 737-2H4 | 929/22963 | |
| ☐ | N92SW | Boeing 737-2H4 | 933/22964 | |
| ☐ | N93SW | Boeing 737-2H4 | 942/22965 | |
| ☐ | N94SW | Boeing 737-2H4 | 968/23053 | |
| ☐ | N95SW | Boeing 737-2H4 | 969/23054 | |
| ☐ | N96SW | Boeing 737-2H4 | 970/23055 | |
| ☐ | N102SW | Boeing 737-2H4 | 1014/23108 | |
| ☐ | N103SW | Boeing 737-2H4 | 1016/23109 | |
| ☐ | N104SW | Boeing 737-2H4 | 1017/23110 | |
| ☐ | N105SW | Boeing 737-2H4 | 1095/23249 | |
| ☐ | N129SW | Boeing 737-2K6 | 678/22340 | |
| ☐ | N130SW | Boeing 737-2T4 | 855/22699 | |
| ☐ | N702ML | Boeing 737-2T4 | 624/22054 | |
| ☐ | N721WN | Boeing 737-2T4 | 817/22697 | |
| ☐ | N722WN | Boeing 737-2T4 | 823/22698 | |
| ☐ | N300SW | Boeing 737-3H4 | 1037/22940 | |
| ☐ | N301SW | Boeing 737-3H4 | 1048/22941 | |

| | | |
|---|---|---|
| ☐ N302SW | Boeing 737-3H4 | 1052/22942 |
| ☐ N303SW | Boeing 737-3H4 | 1101/22943 |
| ☐ N304SW | Boeing 737-3H4 | 1138/22944 |
| ☐ N305SW | Boeing 737-3H4 | 1139/22945 |
| ☐ N306SW | Boeing 737-3H4 | 1148/22946 |
| ☐ N307SW | Boeing 737-3H4 | 1156/22947 |
| ☐ N308SA | Boeing 737-3Y0 | 1233/23498 |
| ☐ N309SW | Boeing 737-3H4 | 1160/22948 |
| ☐ N310SW | Boeing 737-3H4 | 1161/22949 |
| ☐ N311SW | Boeing 737-3H4 | 1183/23333 |
| ☐ N312SW | Boeing 737-3H4 | 1185/23334 |
| ☐ N313SW | Boeing 737-3H4 | 1201/23335 |
| ☐ N314SW | Boeing 737-3H4 | 1229/23336 |
| ☐ N315SW | Boeing 737-3H4 | 1231/23337 |
| ☐ N316SW | Boeing 737-3H4 | 1232/23338 |
| ☐ N317WN | Boeing 737-3Q8 | 1506/24068 |
| ☐ N318SW | Boeing 737-3H4 | 1255/23339 |
| ☐ N319SW | Boeing 737-3H4 | 1348/23340 |
| ☐ N320SW | Boeing 737-3H4 | 1350/23341 |
| ☐ N321SW | Boeing 737-3H4 | 1351/23342 |
| ☐ N322SW | Boeing 737-3H4 | 1377/23343 |
| ☐ N323SW | Boeing 737-3H4 | 1378/23344 |
| ☐ N324SW | Boeing 737-3H4 | 1384/23414 |
| ☐ N325SW | Boeing 737-3H4 | 1398/23689 |
| ☐ N326SW | Boeing 737-3H4 | 1400/23690 |
| ☐ N327SW | Boeing 737-3H4 | 1407/23691 |
| ☐ N328SW | Boeing 737-3H4 | 1521/23692 |
| ☐ N329SW | Boeing 737-3H4 | 1525/23693 |
| ☐ N330SW | Boeing 737-3H4 | 1529/23694 |
| ☐ N331SW | Boeing 737-3H4 | 1536/23695 |
| ☐ N332SW | Boeing 737-3H4 | 1545/23696 |
| ☐ N333SW | Boeing 737-3H4 | 1547/23697 |
| ☐ N334SW | Boeing 737-3H4 | 1549/23938 |
| ☐ N335SW | Boeing 737-3H4 | 1553/23939 |
| ☐ N336SW | Boeing 737-3H4 | 1557/23940 |
| ☐ N337SW | Boeing 737-3H4 | 1567/23959 |
| ☐ N338SW | Boeing 737-3H4 | 1571/23960 |
| ☐ N339SW | Boeing 737-3H4 | 1591/24090 |
| ☐ N340LV | Boeing 737-3K2 | 1360/23738 |
| ☐ N341SW | Boeing 737-3H4 | 1593/24091 |
| ☐ N342SW | Boeing 737-3H4 | 1682/24133 |
| ☐ N343SW | Boeing 737-3H4 | 1686/24151 |
| ☐ N344SW | Boeing 737-3H4 | 1688/24152 |
| ☐ N345SA | Boeing 737-3K2 | 1386/23786 |
| ☐ N346SW | Boeing 737-3H4 | 1690/24153 |
| ☐ N347SW | Boeing 737-3H4 | 1708/24374 |
| ☐ N348SW | Boeing 737-3H4 | 1710/24375 |
| ☐ N349SW | Boeing 737-3H4 | 1734/24408 |
| ☐ N350SW | Boeing 737-3H4 | 1748/24409 |
| ☐ N351SW | Boeing 737-3H4 | 1790/24572 |
| ☐ N352SW | Boeing 737-3H4 | 1942/24888 |
| ☐ N353SW | Boeing 737-3H4 | 1947/24889 |
| ☐ N354SW | Boeing 737-3H4 | 2092/25219 |
| ☐ N355SW | Boeing 737-3H4 | 2103/25250 |
| ☐ N356SW | Boeing 737-3H4 | 2105/25251 |
| ☐ N357SW | Boeing 737-3H4 | 2294/26594 |
| ☐ N358SW | Boeing 737-3H4 | 2295/26595 |
| ☐ N359SW | Boeing 737-3H4 | 2297/26596 |
| ☐ N360SW | Boeing 737-3H4 | 2307/26571 |
| ☐ N361SW | Boeing 737-3H4 | 2309/26572 |
| ☐ N362SW | Boeing 737-3H4 | 2322/26573 |
| ☐ N363SW | Boeing 737-3H4 | 2429/26574 |
| ☐ N364SW | Boeing 737-3H4 | 2430/26575 |
| ☐ N365SW | Boeing 737-3H4 | 2433/26576 |
| ☐ N366SW | Boeing 737-3H4 | 2469/26577 |
| ☐ N367SW | Boeing 737-3H4 | 2470/26578 |
| ☐ N368SW | Boeing 737-3H4 | 2473/26579 |
| ☐ N369SW | Boeing 737-3H4 | 2477/26580 |
| ☐ N370SW | Boeing 737-3H4 | 2497/26597 |
| ☐ N371SW | Boeing 737-3H4 | 2500/26598 |
| ☐ N372SW | Boeing 737-3H4 | 2504/26599 |
| ☐ N373SW | Boeing 737-3H4 | 2509/26581 |
| ☐ N374SW | Boeing 737-3H4 | 2515/26582 |
| ☐ N375SW | Boeing 737-3H4 | 2520/26583 |
| ☐ N376SW | Boeing 737-3H4 | 2570/26584 |
| ☐ N378SW | Boeing 737-3H4 | 2579/26585 |
| ☐ N379SW | Boeing 737-3H4 | 2580/26586 |
| ☐ N380SW | Boeing 737-3H4 | 2610/26587 |
| ☐ N382SW | Boeing 737-3H4 | 2611/26588 |
| ☐ N383SW | Boeing 737-3H4 | 2612/26589 |
| ☐ N384SW | Boeing 737-3H4 | 2613/26590 |
| ☐ N385SW | Boeing 737-3H4 | 2617/26600 |
| ☐ N386SW | Boeing 737-3H4 | 2626/26601 |
| ☐ N387SW | Boeing 737-3H4 | 2627/26602 |
| ☐ N388SW | Boeing 737-3H4 | 2628/26591 |
| ☐ N389SW | Boeing 737-3H4 | 2629/26592 |
| ☐ N390SW | Boeing 737-3H4 | 2642/26593 |
| ☐ N391SW | Boeing 737-3H4 | 2643/27378 |
| ☐ N392SW | Boeing 737-3H4 | 2644/27379 |
| ☐ N394SW | Boeing 737-3H4 | 2645/27380 |
| ☐ N395SW | Boeing 737-3H4 | 2667/27689 |
| ☐ N396SW | Boeing 737-3H4 | 2668/27690 |
| ☐ N397SW | Boeing 737-3H4 | 2695/27691 |
| ☐ N398SW | Boeing 737-3H4 | 2696/27692 |
| ☐ N399WN | Boeing 737-3H4 | 2697/27693 |
| ☐ N600WN | Boeing 737-3H4 | 2699/27694 |
| ☐ N601WN | Boeing 737-3H4 | 2702/27695 |
| ☐ N602SW | Boeing 737-3H4 | 2713/27953 |
| ☐ N603SW | Boeing 737-3H4 | 2714/27954 |
| ☐ N604SW | Boeing 737-3H4 | 2715/27955 |
| ☐ N605SW | Boeing 737-3H4 | 2716/27956 |
| ☐ N606SW | Boeing 737-3H4 | 2740/27926 |
| ☐ N607SW | Boeing 737-3H4 | 2741/27927 |
| ☐ N608SW | Boeing 737-3H4 | 2742/27928 |
| ☐ N609SW | Boeing 737-3H4 | 2744/27929 |
| ☐ N610WN | Boeing 737-3H4 | 2745/27606 |
| ☐ N611SW | Boeing 737-3H4 | 2750/27697 |
| ☐ N612SW | Boeing 737-3H4 | 2753/27930 |
| ☐ N613SW | Boeing 737-3H4 | 2754/27931 |
| ☐ N614SW | Boeing 737-3H4 | 2755/28033 |
| ☐ N615SW | Boeing 737-3H4 | 2757/27698 |
| ☐ N616SW | Boeing 737-3H4 | 2758/27699 |
| ☐ N617SW | Boeing 737-3H4 | 2759/27700 |
| ☐ N618WN | Boeing 737-3H4 | 2761/28034 |
| ☐ N619SW | Boeing 737-3H4 | 2762/28035 |
| ☐ N620SW | Boeing 737-3H4 | 2766/28036 |
| ☐ N621SW | Boeing 737-3H4 | 2767/28037 |
| ☐ N622SW | Boeing 737-3H4 | 2779/27932 |
| ☐ N623SW | Boeing 737-3H4 | 2780/27933 |
| ☐ N624SW | Boeing 737-3H4 | 2781/27934 |
| ☐ N625SW | Boeing 737-3H4 | 2787/27701 |
| ☐ N626SW | Boeing 737-3H4 | 2789/27702 |
| ☐ N627SW | Boeing 737-3H4 | 2790/27935 |
| ☐ N628SW | Boeing 737-3H4 | 2795/27703 |
| ☐ N629SW | Boeing 737-3H4 | 2796/27704 |
| ☐ N630WN | Boeing 737-3H4 | 2797/27705 |
| ☐ N631SW | Boeing 737-3H4 | 2798/27706 |
| ☐ N632SW | Boeing 737-3H4 | 2799/27707 |
| ☐ N633SW | Boeing 737-3H4 | 2807/27936 |
| ☐ N634SW | Boeing 737-3H4 | 2808/27937 |
| ☐ N635SW | Boeing 737-3H4 | 2813/27708 |
| ☐ N636WN | Boeing 737-3H4 | 2814/27709 |
| ☐ N637SW | Boeing 737-3H4 | 2819/27710 |
| ☐ N638SW | Boeing 737-3H4 | 2820/27711 |
| ☐ N639SW | Boeing 737-3H4 | 2821/27712 |
| ☐ N640SW | Boeing 737-3H4 | 2840/27713 |
| ☐ N641SW | Boeing 737-3H4 | 2841/27714 |
| ☐ N642WN | Boeing 737-3H4 | 2842/27715 |
| ☐ N643SW | Boeing 737-3H4 | 2843/27716 |
| ☐ N644SW | Boeing 737-3H4 | 2869/28329 |
| ☐ N645SW | Boeing 737-3H4 | 2870/28330 |
| ☐ N646SW | Boeing 737-3H4 | 2871/28331 |
| ☐ N647SW | Boeing 737-3H4 | 2892/27717 |
| ☐ N648SW | Boeing 737-3H4 | 2893/27718 |
| ☐ N649SW | Boeing 737-3H4 | 2894/27719 |
| ☐ N650SW | Boeing 737-3H4 | 2901/27720 |
| ☐ N651SW | Boeing 737-3H4 | 2915/27721 |
| ☐ N652SW | Boeing 737-3H4 | 2916/27722 |
| ☐ N653SW | Boeing 737-3H4 | 2917/28398 |
| ☐ N654SW | Boeing 737-3H4 | 2918/28399 |
| ☐ N655SW | Boeing 737-3H4 | 2931/28400 |
| ☐ N656SW | Boeing 737-3H4 | 2932/28401 |
| ☐ N657SW | Boeing 737-3L9 | 1111/23331 |
| ☐ N658SW | Boeing 737-3L9 | 1118/23332 |
| ☐ N659SW | Boeing 737-301 | 1112/23229 |
| ☐ N660SW | Boeing 737-301 | 1115/23230 |

| | | | |
|---|---|---|---|
| ☐ N661SW | Boeing 737-317 | 1098/23173 | |
| ☐ N662SW | Boeing 737-3Q8 | 1125/23255 | |
| ☐ N663SW | Boeing 737-3Q8 | 1128/23256 | |
| ☐ N664WN | Boeing 737-3Y0 | 1206/23495 | |
| ☐ N665WN | Boeing 737-3Y0 | 1227/23497 | |
| ☐ N667SW | Boeing 737-3T5 | 1092/23063 | |
| ☐ N669SW | Boeing 737-3A4 | 1484/23752 | |
| ☐ N670SW | Boeing 737-3G7 | 1533/23784 | |
| ☐ N671SW | Boeing 737-3G7 | 1535/23785 | |
| ☐ N672SW | Boeing 737-3Q8 | 1215/23406 | |
| ☐ N673AA | Boeing 737-3A4 | 1063/23251 | |
| ☐ N674AA | Boeing 737-3A4 | 1094/23252 | |
| ☐ N675AA | Boeing 737-3A4 | 1096/23253 | |
| ☐ N676SW | Boeing 737-3A4 | 1100/23288 | |
| ☐ N677AA | Boeing 737-3A4 | 1182/23289 | |
| ☐ N678AA | Boeing 737-3A4 | 1205/23290 | |
| ☐ N679AA | Boeing 737-3A4 | 1211/23291 | |
| ☐ N680AA | Boeing 737-3A4 | 1318/23505 | |
| ☐ N682SW | Boeing 737-3Y0 | 1217/23496 | |
| ☐ N683SW | Boeing 737-3G7 | 1576/24008 | |
| ☐ N684WN | Boeing 737-3T0 | 1520/23941 | |
| ☐ N685SW | Boeing 737-3Q8 | 1209/23401 | |
| ☐ N686SW | Boeing 737-317 | 1110/23175 | |
| ☐ N687SW | Boeing 737-3Q8 | 1187/23388 | |
| ☐ N688SW | Boeing 737-3Q8 | 1107/23254 | |
| ☐ N689SW | Boeing 737-3Q8 | 1163/23387 | |
| ☐ N690SW | Boeing 737-3G7 | 1531/23783 | |
| ☐ N691WN | Boeing 737-3G7 | 1494/23781 | |
| ☐ N692SW | Boeing 737-3T5 | 1083/23062 | |
| ☐ N693SW | Boeing 737-317 | 1104/23174 | |
| ☐ N694SW | Boeing 737-3T5 | 1080/23061 | |
| ☐ N695SW | Boeing 737-3Q8 | 1249/23506 | |
| ☐ N696SW | Boeing 737-3T5 | 1527/23064 | |
| ☐ N697SW | Boeing 737-3T0 | 1505/23838 | |
| ☐ N698SW | Boeing 737-317 | 1213/23176 | |
| ☐ N699SW | Boeing 737-3Y0 | 1372/23826 | |
| | | | |
| ☐ N501SW | Boeing 737-5H4 | 1718/24178 | |
| ☐ N502SW | Boeing 737-5H4 | 1744/24179 | |
| ☐ N503SW | Boeing 737-5H4 | 1766/24180 | |
| ☐ N504SW | Boeing 737-5H4 | 1804/24181 | |
| ☐ N505SW | Boeing 737-5H4 | 1826/24182 | |
| ☐ N506SW | Boeing 737-5H4 | 1852/24183 | |
| ☐ N507SW | Boeing 737-5H4 | 1864/24184 | |
| ☐ N508SW | Boeing 737-5H4 | 1932/24185 | |
| ☐ N509SW | Boeing 737-5H4 | 1934/24186 | |
| ☐ N510SW | Boeing 737-5H4 | 1940/24187 | |
| ☐ N511SW | Boeing 737-5H4 | 2029/24188 | |
| ☐ N512SW | Boeing 737-5H4 | 2056/24189 | |
| ☐ N513SW | Boeing 737-5H4 | 2058/24190 | |
| ☐ N514SW | Boeing 737-5H4 | 2078/25153 | |
| ☐ N515SW | Boeing 737-5H4 | 2080/25154 | |
| ☐ N519SW | Boeing 737-5H4 | 2121/25318 | |
| ☐ N520SW | Boeing 737-5H4 | 2134/25319 | |
| ☐ N521SW | Boeing 737-5H4 | 2136/25320 | |
| ☐ N522SW | Boeing 737-5H4 | 2202/26564 | |
| ☐ N523SW | Boeing 737-5H4 | 2204/26565 | |
| ☐ N524SW | Boeing 737-5H4 | 2224/26566 | |
| ☐ N525SW | Boeing 737-5H4 | 2283/26567 | |
| ☐ N526SW | Boeing 737-5H4 | 2285/26568 | |
| ☐ N527SW | Boeing 737-5H4 | 2287/26569 | |
| ☐ N528SW | Boeing 737-5H4 | 2292/26570 | |
| | | | |
| ☐ N400WN | Boeing 737-7H4 | 806/27891 | |
| ☐ N401WN | Boeing 737-7H4 | 810/29813 | |
| ☐ N402WN | Boeing 737-7H4 | 811/29814 | |
| ☐ N403WN | Boeing 737-7H4 | 821/29815 | |
| ☐ N404WN | Boeing 737-7H4 | 880/27892 | |
| ☐ N405WN | Boeing 737-7H4 | 881/27893 | |
| ☐ N406WN | Boeing 737-7H4 | 885/27894 | |
| ☐ N407WN | Boeing 737-7H4 | 903/29817 | |
| ☐ N408WN | Boeing 737-7H4 | 934/27895 | |
| ☐ N409WN | Boeing 737-7H4 | 945/27896 | |
| ☐ N410WN | Boeing 737-7H4 | 946/27897 | |
| ☐ N411WN | Boeing 737-7H4 | 950/29821 | |
| ☐ N412WN | Boeing 737-7H4 | 956/29818 | |
| ☐ N413WN | Boeing 737-7H4 | 960/29819 | |
| ☐ N414WN | Boeing 737-7H4 | 967/29820 | |
| ☐ N415WN | Boeing 737-7H4 | 980/29836 | |
| ☐ N416WN | Boeing 737-7H4 | 990/33453 | |
| ☐ N417WN | Boeing 737-7H4 | 993/29822 | |
| ☐ N418WN | Boeing 737-7H4 | 1000/29823 | |
| ☐ N419WN | Boeing 737-7H4 | 1017/29824 | |
| ☐ N420WN | Boeing 737-7H4 | 1039/29825 | |
| ☐ N421LV | Boeing 737-7H4 | 1040/33452 | |
| ☐ N422WN | Boeing 737-7H4 | 1093/29826 | |
| ☐ N423WN | Boeing 737-7H4 | 1101/29827 | |
| ☐ N424WN | Boeing 737-7H4 | 1105/29828 | |
| ☐ N425LV | Boeing 737-7H4 | 1109/29829 | |
| ☐ N426WN | Boeing 737-7H4 | 1114/29830 | |
| ☐ N427WN | Boeing 737-7H4 | 1119/29831 | |
| ☐ N428WN | Boeing 737-7H4 | 1243/29844 | |
| ☐ N429WN | Boeing 737-7H4 | 1256/33658 | |
| ☐ N430WN | Boeing 737-7H4 | 1257/33659 | |
| ☐ N431WN | Boeing 737-7H4 | 1259/29845 | |
| ☐ N432WN | Boeing 737-7H4 | 33715 | o/o |
| ☐ N433LV | Boeing 737-7H4 | 33716 | o/o |
| ☐ N434WN | Boeing 737-7H4 | 32454 | o/o |
| ☐ N435WN | Boeing 737-7H4 | 32455 | o/o |
| ☐ N436WN | Boeing 737-7H4 | 32456 | o/o |
| ☐ N437WN | Boeing 737-7H4 | | o/o |
| ☐ N438WN | Boeing 737-7H4 | | o/o |
| ☐ N439WN | Boeing 737-7H4 | | o/o |
| ☐ N4440LV | Boeing 737-7H4 | | o/o |
| ☐ N441WN | Boeing 737-7H4 | | o/o |
| ☐ N442WN | Boeing 737-7H4 | | o/o |
| ☐ N443WN | Boeing 737-7H4 | | o/o |
| ☐ N444WN | Boeing 737-7H4 | | o/o |
| ☐ N445WN | Boeing 737-7H4 | | o/o |
| ☐ N446WN | Boeing 737-7H4 | | o/o |
| ☐ N447WN | Boeing 737-7H4 | | o/o |
| ☐ N448WN | Boeing 737-7H4 | | o/o |
| ☐ N449WN | Boeing 737-7H4 | | o/o |
| ☐ N450WN | Boeing 737-7H4 | | o/o |
| ☐ N451WN | Boeing 737-7H4 | | o/o |
| ☐ N452WN | Boeing 737-7H4 | | o/o |
| ☐ N453WN | Boeing 737-7H4 | | o/o |
| ☐ N454WN | Boeing 737-7H4 | | o/o |
| ☐ N455WN | Boeing 737-7H4 | | o/o |
| ☐ N456WN | Boeing 737-7H4 | | o/o |
| ☐ N457WN | Boeing 737-7H4 | | o/o |
| ☐ N458WN | Boeing 737-7H4 | | o/o |
| ☐ N459WN | Boeing 737-7H4 | | o/o |
| ☐ N460WN | Boeing 737-7H4 | | o/o |
| ☐ N700GS | Boeing 737-7H4 | 4/27835 | |
| ☐ N701GS | Boeing 737-7H4 | 6/27836 | |
| ☐ N703SW | Boeing 737-7H4 | 12/27837 | |
| ☐ N704SW | Boeing 737-7H4 | 15/27838 | |
| ☐ N705SW | Boeing 737-7H4 | 20/27839 | |
| ☐ N706SW | Boeing 737-7H4 | 24/27840 | |
| ☐ N707SA | Boeing 737-7H4 | 1/27841 | |
| ☐ N708SW | Boeing 737-7H4 | 2/27842 | |
| ☐ N709SW | Boeing 737-7H4 | 3/27843 | |
| ☐ N710SW | Boeing 737-7H4 | 34/27844 | |
| ☐ N711HK | Boeing 737-7H4 | 38/27845 | |
| ☐ N712SW | Boeing 737-7H4 | 53/27846 | |
| ☐ N713SW | Boeing 737-7H4 | 54/27847 | |
| ☐ N714CB | Boeing 737-7H4 | 61/27848 | |
| ☐ N715SW | Boeing 737-7H4 | 62/27849 | |
| ☐ N716SW | Boeing 737-7H4 | 64/27850 | |
| ☐ N717SA | Boeing 737-7H4 | 70/27851 | |
| ☐ N718SW | Boeing 737-7H4 | 71/27852 | |
| ☐ N719SW | Boeing 737-7H4 | 82/27853 | |
| ☐ N720WN | Boeing 737-7H4 | 121/27854 | |
| ☐ N723SW | Boeing 737-7H4 | 199/27855 | |
| ☐ N724SW | Boeing 737-7H4 | 201/27856 | |
| ☐ N725SW | Boeing 737-7H4 | 208/27857 | |
| ☐ N726SW | Boeing 737-7H4 | 213/27858 | |
| ☐ N727SW | Boeing 737-7H4 | 274/27859 | |
| ☐ N728SW | Boeing 737-7H4 | 276/27860 | |
| ☐ N729SW | Boeing 737-7H4 | 278/27861 | |
| ☐ N730SW | Boeing 737-7H4 | 284/27862 | |
| ☐ N731SA | Boeing 737-7H4 | 318/27863 | |
| ☐ N732SW | Boeing 737-7H4 | 319/27864 | |
| ☐ N733SA | Boeing 737-7H4 | 320/27865 | |
| ☐ N734SA | Boeing 737-7H4 | 324/27866 | |

| | | | |
|---|---|---|---|
| ☐ N735SA | Boeing 737-7H4 | 354/27867 | |
| ☐ N736SA | Boeing 737-7H4 | 357/27868 | |
| ☐ N737JW | Boeing 737-7H4 | 358/27869 | |
| ☐ N738CB | Boeing 737-7H4 | 360/27870 | |
| ☐ N739GB | Boeing 737-7H4 | 144/29275 | |
| ☐ N740SW | Boeing 737-7H4 | 155/29276 | |
| ☐ N741SA | Boeing 737-7H4 | 157/29277 | |
| ☐ N742SW | Boeing 737-7H4 | 172/29278 | |
| ☐ N743SW | Boeing 737-7H4 | 175/29279 | |
| ☐ N744SW | Boeing 737-7H4 | 232/29490 | |
| ☐ N745SW | Boeing 737-7H4 | 237/29491 | |
| ☐ N746SW | Boeing 737-7H4 | 299/29798 | |
| ☐ N747SA | Boeing 737-7H4 | 306/29799 | |
| ☐ N748SW | Boeing 737-7H4 | 331/29800 | |
| ☐ N749SW | Boeing 737-7H4 | 343/29801 | |
| ☐ N750SA | Boeing 737-7H4 | 366/29802 | |
| ☐ N751SW | Boeing 737-7H4 | 373/29803 | |
| ☐ N752SW | Boeing 737-7H4 | 387/29804 | |
| ☐ N753SW | Boeing 737-7H4 | 400/29848 | |
| ☐ N754SW | Boeing 737-7H4 | 416/29849 | |
| ☐ N755SA | Boeing 737-7H4 | 419/27871 | |
| ☐ N756SA | Boeing 737-7H4 | 422/27872 | |
| ☐ N757LV | Boeing 737-7H4 | 425/29850 | |
| ☐ N758SW | Boeing 737-7H4 | 437/27873 | |
| ☐ N759GS | Boeing 737-7H4 | 448/30544 | |
| ☐ N760SW | Boeing 737-7H4 | 468/27874 | |
| ☐ N761RR | Boeing 737-7H4 | 495/27875 | |
| ☐ N762SW | Boeing 737-7H4 | 512/27876 | |
| ☐ N763SW | Boeing 737-7H4 | 520/27877 | |
| ☐ N764SW | Boeing 737-7H4 | 521/27878 | |
| ☐ N765SW | Boeing 737-7H4 | 525/29805 | |
| ☐ N766SW | Boeing 737-7H4 | 537/29806 | |
| ☐ N767SW | Boeing 737-7H4 | 541/29807 | |
| ☐ N768SW | Boeing 737-7H4 | 580/30587 | |
| ☐ N769SW | Boeing 737-7H4 | 592/30588 | |
| ☐ N770SA | Boeing 737-7H4 | 595/30589 | |
| ☐ N771SA | Boeing 737-7H4 | 599/27879 | |
| ☐ N772SW | Boeing 737-7H4 | 601/27880 | |
| ☐ N773SA | Boeing 737-7H4 | 603/27881 | |
| ☐ N774SW | Boeing 737-7H4 | 609/27882 | |
| ☐ N775SW | Boeing 737-7H4 | 617/30590 | |
| ☐ N776WN | Boeing 737-7H4 | 620/30591 | |
| ☐ N777QC | Boeing 737-7H4 | 621/30592 | |
| ☐ N778SW | Boeing 737-7H4 | 626/27883 | |
| ☐ N779SW | Boeing 737-7H4 | 628/27884 | |
| ☐ N780SW | Boeing 737-7H4 | 643/27885 | |
| ☐ N781WN | Boeing 737-7H4 | 646/30601 | |
| ☐ N782SA | Boeing 737-7H4 | 670/29808 | |
| ☐ N783SW | Boeing 737-7H4 | 675/29809 | |
| ☐ N784SW | Boeing 737-7H4 | 677/29810 | |
| ☐ N785SW | Boeing 737-7H4 | 693/30602 | |
| ☐ N786SW | Boeing 737-7H4 | 698/29811 | |
| ☐ N787SA | Boeing 737-7H4 | 705/29812 | |
| ☐ N788SA | Boeing 737-7H4 | 707/30603 | |
| ☐ N789SW | Boeing 737-7H4 | 718/29816 | |
| ☐ N790SW | Boeing 737-7H4 | 721/30604 | |
| ☐ N791SW | Boeing 737-7H4 | 736/27886 | |
| ☐ N792SW | Boeing 737-7H4 | 737/27887 | |
| ☐ N793SA | Boeing 737-7H4 | 744/27888 | |
| ☐ N794SW | Boeing 737-7H4 | 748/30605 | |
| ☐ N795SW | Boeing 737-7H4 | 780/30606 | |
| ☐ N796SW | Boeing 737-7H4 | 784/27889 | |
| ☐ N797MX | Boeing 737-7H4 | 803/27890 | |
| ☐ N798SW | Boeing 737-7AD | 41/28436 | |
| ☐ N799SW | Boeing 737-7Q8 | 14/28209 | |

### SPIRIT AIRLINES — NKS

| | | | |
|---|---|---|---|
| ☐ N130NK | Douglas DC-9-41 | 722/47604 | std |
| ☐ N131NK | Douglas DC-9-41 | 724/47605 | |
| ☐ N133NK | Douglas DC-9-32 | 923/48111 | |
| ☐ N969ML | Douglas DC-9-31 | 370/47268 | |
| ☐ N12536 | Douglas DC-9-32 | 213/47113 | |
| | | | |
| ☐ N800NK | McDD MD-82 | 1096/49144 | |
| ☐ N801NK | McDD MD-82 | 1005/48048 | |
| ☐ N802NK | McDD MD-82 | 2061/53168 | |

| | | | |
|---|---|---|---|
| ☐ N803NK | McDD MD-82 | 1035/48087 | |
| ☐ N804NK | McDD MD-82 | 1085/49104 | |
| ☐ N805NK | McDD MD-81 | 991/48058 | |
| ☐ N806NK | McDD MD-81 | 975/48051 | |
| ☐ N807NK | McDD MD-87 | 1634/49777 | |
| ☐ N808NK | McDD MD-82 | 1363/49504 | |
| ☐ N809NK | McDD MD-82 | 1346/49503 | |
| ☐ N810NK | McDD MD-82 | 924/48015 | |
| ☐ N811NK | McDD MD-82 | 958/48017 | |
| ☐ N812NK | McDD MD-82 | 1078/48021 | |
| ☐ N814NK | McDD MD-82 | 1483/49619 | |
| ☐ N815NK | McDD MD-82 | 1260/49415 | |
| ☐ N816NK | McDD MD-82 | 1092/49140 | |
| ☐ N817NK | McDD MD-82 | 1093/49141 | std |
| ☐ N818NK | McDD MD-81 | 995/48018 | |
| ☐ N819NK | McDD MD-81 | 941/48016 | |
| ☐ N820NK | McDD MD-82 | 1080/49126 | |
| ☐ N821NK | McDD MD-82 | 1449/49508 | |
| ☐ N822NK | McDD MD-83 | 1272/49392 | |
| ☐ N823NK | McDD MD-82 | 1045/48020 | |
| ☐ N824NK | McDD MD-83 | 1818/53015 | |
| ☐ N825NK | McDD MD-83 | 1736/53012 | |
| ☐ N826NK | McDD MD-82 | 1270/49391 | |
| ☐ N827NK | McDD MD-83 | 1658/49793 | |

### SUN COUNTRY AIRLINES — SCX

| | | | |
|---|---|---|---|
| ☐ N801SY | Boeing 737-8Q8 | 777/30332 | |
| ☐ N804SY | Boeing 737-8Q8 | 908/30689 | |
| ☐ N805SY | Boeing 737-8Q8 | 985/30032 | |
| ☐ N806SY | Boeing 737-8Q8 | 76/28215 | |
| ☐ PH-HZE | Boeing 737-8K2 | 277/28377 | Lsf TRA |
| ☐ PH-HZI | Boeing 737-8K2 | 524/28380 | Lsf TRA |
| ☐ PH-HZV | Boeing 737-8K2 | 1158/30650 | Lsf TRA |
| ☐ N281SC | Boeing 727-282 | 1494/21949 | |
| ☐ N284SC | Boeing 727-2J4 | 1301/21438 | |

### TRADEWINDS AIRLINES — TDX

| | | | |
|---|---|---|---|
| ☐ N501TR | Airbus A300B4-203F | 053 | |
| ☐ N502TA | Airbus A300B4-203F | 075 | |
| ☐ N504TA | Airbus A300B4-203F | 216 | |
| ☐ N505TA | Airbus A300B4-203F | 271 | |
| ☐ N506TA | Airbus A300B4-203F | 207 | |
| ☐ N510TA | Airbus A300B4-203F | 100 | |
| ☐ N511TA | Airbus A300B4-203F | 173 | |
| ☐ N512TA | Airbus A300B4-203F | 183 | |
| ☐ N820SC | Airbus A300B4-203F | 154 | |
| ☐ N311EA | L-1011-1 Tristar | 1012 | |

### TRANSMERIDIAN AIRLINES — TRZ

| | | | |
|---|---|---|---|
| ☐ N288SC | Boeing 727-2J4 | 984/20765 | |
| ☐ N906PG | Boeing 727-281 | 969/20728 | |
| ☐ N910PG | Boeing 727-287 | 1812/22606 | |
| ☐ N919PG | Boeing 727-287 | 1777/22604 | |
| ☐ N54344 | Boeing 727-231 | 1460/21631 | |
| | | | |
| ☐ N521NA | Boeing 757-236 | 453/25592 | |
| ☐ N958PG | Boeing 757-236 | 163/24118 | Lst SDO |

### TRANS STATES AIRLINES — LOF

| | | | |
|---|---|---|---|
| ☐ N421TE | ATR 42-300 | 102 | |
| ☐ N422TE | ATR 42-300 | 106 | |
| ☐ N423TE | ATR 42-300 | 119 | |
| ☐ N424TE | ATR 42-300 | 124 | |
| ☐ N426TE | ATR 42-300 | 228 | |
| ☐ N721TE | ATR 72-202 | 217 | |
| ☐ N722TE | ATR 72-202 | 220 | |
| ☐ N723TE | ATR 72-202 | 283 | |
| | | | |
| ☐ N550HK | BAe Jetstream 41 | 41039 | |
| ☐ N551HK | BAe Jetstream 41 | 41040 | |
| ☐ N552HK | BAe Jetstream 41 | 41057 | |
| ☐ N553HK | BAe Jetstream 41 | 41066 | |

| | | | |
|---|---|---|---|
| ☐ N554HK | BAe Jetstream 41 | 41067 | |
| ☐ N555HK | BAe Jetstream 41 | 41072 | |
| ☐ N556HK | BAe Jetstream 41 | 41073 | |
| ☐ N557HK | BAe Jetstream 41 | 41074 | |
| ☐ N558HK | BAe Jetstream 41 | 41071 | |
| ☐ N559HK | BAe Jetstream 41 | 41075 | |
| ☐ N560HK | BAe Jetstream 41 | 41076 | |
| ☐ N561HK | BAe Jetstream 41 | 41077 | |
| ☐ N562HK | BAe Jetstream 41 | 41078 | |
| ☐ N563HK | BAe Jetstream 41 | 41079 | |
| ☐ N564HK | BAe Jetstream 41 | 41081 | |
| ☐ N565HK | BAe Jetstream 41 | 41082 | |
| ☐ N566HK | BAe Jetstream 41 | 41084 | |
| ☐ N567HK | BAe Jetstream 41 | 41085 | |
| ☐ N568HK | BAe Jetstream 41 | 41086 | |
| ☐ N569HK | BAe Jetstream 41 | 41088 | |
| ☐ N570HK | BAe Jetstream 41 | 41089 | |
| ☐ N571HK | BAe Jetstream 41 | 41090 | |
| ☐ N572HK | BAe Jetstream 41 | 41091 | |
| ☐ N573HK | BAe Jetstream 41 | 41092 | |
| ☐ N574HK | BAe Jetstream 41 | 41093 | |
| | | | |
| ☐ N801HK | Embraer ERJ-145 | 145053 | |
| ☐ N802HK | Embraer ERJ-145 | 145066 | |
| ☐ N803HK | Embraer ERJ-145 | 145077 | |
| ☐ N804HK | Embraer ERJ-145 | 145082 | |
| ☐ N805HK | Embraer ERJ-145 | 145096 | |
| ☐ N806HK | Embraer ERJ-145 | 145112 | |
| ☐ N807HK | Embraer ERJ-145 | 145119 | |
| ☐ N808HK | Embraer ERJ-145 | 145157 | |
| ☐ N809HK | Embraer ERJ-145 | 145187 | |
| ☐ N810HK | Embraer ERJ-145 | 145231 | |
| ☐ N811HK | Embraer ERJ-145 | 145256 | |
| ☐ N812HK | Embraer ERJ-145 | 145373 | |
| ☐ N813HK | Embraer ERJ-145 | 145044 | |
| ☐ N814HK | Embraer ERJ-145 | 145046 | |
| ☐ N815HK | Embraer ERJ-145 | 145048 | |
| ☐ N816HK | Embraer ERJ-145 | 145055 | |
| ☐ N817HK | Embraer ERJ-145 | 145058 | |
| ☐ N818HK | Embraer ERJ-145 | 145059 | |
| ☐ N819HK | Embraer ERJ-145 | 145062 | |
| ☐ N820HK | Embraer ERJ-145 | 145064 | |
| ☐ N821HK | Embraer ERJ-145 | 145068 | |

## UNITED AIR LINES — UAL

| | | | |
|---|---|---|---|
| ☐ N801UA | Airbus A319-131 | 0686 | 4001 |
| ☐ N802UA | Airbus A319-131 | 0690 | 4002 |
| ☐ N803UA | Airbus A319-131 | 0748 | 4003 |
| ☐ N804UA | Airbus A319-131 | 0759 | 4004 |
| ☐ N805UA | Airbus A319-131 | 0783 | 4005 |
| ☐ N806UA | Airbus A319-131 | 0788 | 4006 |
| ☐ N807UA | Airbus A319-131 | 0798 | 4007 |
| ☐ N808UA | Airbus A319-131 | 0804 | 4008 |
| ☐ N809UA | Airbus A319-131 | 0825 | 4009 |
| ☐ N810UA | Airbus A319-131 | 0843 | 4010 |
| ☐ N811UA | Airbus A319-131 | 0847 | 4011 |
| ☐ N812UA | Airbus A319-131 | 0850 | 4012 |
| ☐ N813UA | Airbus A319-131 | 0858 | 4013 |
| ☐ N814UA | Airbus A319-131 | 0862 | 4014 |
| ☐ N815UA | Airbus A319-131 | 0867 | 4015 |
| ☐ N816UA | Airbus A319-131 | 0871 | 4016 |
| ☐ N817UA | Airbus A319-131 | 0873 | 4017 |
| ☐ N818UA | Airbus A319-131 | 0882 | 4018 |
| ☐ N819UA | Airbus A319-131 | 0893 | 4019 |
| ☐ N820UA | Airbus A319-131 | 0898 | 4020 |
| ☐ N821UA | Airbus A319-131 | 0944 | 4021 |
| ☐ N822UA | Airbus A319-131 | 0948 | 4022 |
| ☐ N823UA | Airbus A319-131 | 0952 | 4023 |
| ☐ N824UA | Airbus A319-131 | 0965 | 4024 |
| ☐ N825UA | Airbus A319-131 | 0980 | 4025 |
| ☐ N826UA | Airbus A319-131 | 0989 | 4026 |
| ☐ N827UA | Airbus A319-131 | 1022 | 4027 |
| ☐ N828UA | Airbus A319-131 | 1031 | 4028 |
| ☐ N829UA | Airbus A319-131 | 1211 | 4029 |
| ☐ N830UA | Airbus A319-131 | 1243 | 4030 |
| ☐ N831UA | Airbus A319-131 | 1291 | 4031 |
| ☐ N832UA | Airbus A319-131 | 1321 | 4032 |
| ☐ N833UA | Airbus A319-131 | 1401 | 4033 |
| ☐ N834UA | Airbus A319-131 | 1420 | 4034 |
| ☐ N835UA | Airbus A319-131 | 1426 | 4035 |
| ☐ N836UA | Airbus A319-131 | 1460 | 4036 |
| ☐ N837UA | Airbus A319-131 | 1474 | 4037 |
| ☐ N838UA | Airbus A319-131 | 1477 | 4038 |
| ☐ N839UA | Airbus A319-131 | 1507 | 4039 |
| ☐ N840UA | Airbus A319-131 | 1522 | 4040 |
| ☐ N841UA | Airbus A319-131 | 1545 | 4041 |
| ☐ N842UA | Airbus A319-131 | 1569 | 4042 |
| ☐ N843UA | Airbus A319-131 | 1573 | 4043 |
| ☐ N844UA | Airbus A319-131 | 1581 | 4044 |
| ☐ N845UA | Airbus A319-131 | 1585 | 4045 |
| ☐ N846UA | Airbus A319-131 | 1600 | 4046 |
| ☐ N847UA | Airbus A319-131 | 1627 | 4047 |
| ☐ N848UA | Airbus A319-131 | 1647 | 4048 |
| ☐ N849UA | Airbus A319-131 | 1649 | 4049 |
| ☐ N850UA | Airbus A319-131 | 1653 | 4050 |
| ☐ N851UA | Airbus A319-131 | 1664 | 4051 |
| ☐ N852UA | Airbus A319-131 | 1671 | 4052 |
| ☐ N853UA | Airbus A319-131 | 1688 | 4053 |
| ☐ N854UA | Airbus A319-131 | 1731 | 4054 |
| ☐ N855UA | Airbus A319-131 | 1737 | 4055 |
| ☐ N856UA | Airbus A319-131 | 1778 | 4056 |
| ☐ N857UA | Airbus A319-131 | | 4057 |
| | | | |
| ☐ N401UA | Airbus A320-232 | 0435 | 4701 |
| ☐ N402UA | Airbus A320-232 | 0439 | 4702 |
| ☐ N403UA | Airbus A320-232 | 0442 | 4703 |
| ☐ N404UA | Airbus A320-232 | 0450 | 4704 |
| ☐ N405UA | Airbus A320-232 | 0452 | 4705 |
| ☐ N406UA | Airbus A320-232 | 0454 | 4706 |
| ☐ N407UA | Airbus A320-232 | 0456 | 4707 |
| ☐ N408UA | Airbus A320-232 | 0457 | 4708 |
| ☐ N409UA | Airbus A320-232 | 0462 | 4709 |
| ☐ N410UA | Airbus A320-232 | 0463 | 4710 |
| ☐ N411UA | Airbus A320-232 | 0464 | 4711 |
| ☐ N412UA | Airbus A320-232 | 0465 | 4712 |
| ☐ N413UA | Airbus A320-232 | 0470 | 4713 |
| ☐ N414UA | Airbus A320-232 | 0472 | 4614 |
| ☐ N415UA | Airbus A320-232 | 0475 | 4615 |
| ☐ N416UA | Airbus A320-232 | 0479 | 4616 |
| ☐ N417UA | Airbus A320-232 | 0483 | 4617 |
| ☐ N418UA | Airbus A320-232 | 0485 | 4618 |
| ☐ N419UA | Airbus A320-232 | 0487 | 4619 |
| ☐ N420UA | Airbus A320-232 | 0489 | 4620 |
| ☐ N421UA | Airbus A320-232 | 0500 | 4621 |
| ☐ N422UA | Airbus A320-232 | 0503 | 4622 |
| ☐ N423UA | Airbus A320-232 | 0504 | 4623 |
| ☐ N424UA | Airbus A320-232 | 0506 | 4624 |
| ☐ N425UA | Airbus A320-232 | 0508 | 4625 |
| ☐ N426UA | Airbus A320-232 | 0510 | 4626 |
| ☐ N427UA | Airbus A320-232 | 0512 | 4627 |
| ☐ N428UA | Airbus A320-232 | 0523 | 4628 |
| ☐ N429UA | Airbus A320-232 | 0539 | 4629 |
| ☐ N430UA | Airbus A320-232 | 0568 | 4630 |
| ☐ N431UA | Airbus A320-232 | 0571 | 4631 |
| ☐ N432UA | Airbus A320-232 | 0587 | 4632 |
| ☐ N433UA | Airbus A320-232 | 0589 | 4633 |
| ☐ N434UA | Airbus A320-232 | 0592 | 4634 |
| ☐ N435UA | Airbus A320-232 | 0613 | 4635 |
| ☐ N436UA | Airbus A320-232 | 0638 | 4636 |
| ☐ N437UA | Airbus A320-232 | 0655 | 4637 |
| ☐ N438UA | Airbus A320-232 | 0678 | 4638 |
| ☐ N439UA | Airbus A320-232 | 0683 | 4639 |
| ☐ N440UA | Airbus A320-232 | 0702 | 4640 |
| ☐ N441UA | Airbus A320-232 | 0751 | 4641 |
| ☐ N442UA | Airbus A320-232 | 0780 | 4642 |
| ☐ N443UA | Airbus A320-232 | 0820 | 4643 |
| ☐ N444UA | Airbus A320-232 | 0824 | 4644 |
| ☐ N445UA | Airbus A320-232 | 0826 | 4645 |
| ☐ N446UA | Airbus A320-232 | 0834 | 4646 |
| ☐ N447UA | Airbus A320-232 | 0836 | 4647 |
| ☐ N448UA | Airbus A320-232 | 0842 | 4648 |
| ☐ N449UA | Airbus A320-232 | 0851 | 4649 |
| ☐ N450UA | Airbus A320-232 | 0857 | 4650 |
| ☐ N451UA | Airbus A320-232 | 0865 | 4651 |
| ☐ N452UA | Airbus A320-232 | 0955 | 4652 |

| | Reg | Type | c/n | Fleet |
|---|---|---|---|---|
| ☐ | N453UA | Airbus A320-232 | 1001 | 4653 |
| ☐ | N454UA | Airbus A320-232 | 1104 | 4654 |
| ☐ | N455UA | Airbus A320-232 | 1105 | 4655 |
| ☐ | N456UA | Airbus A320-232 | 1128 | 4656 |
| ☐ | N457UA | Airbus A320-232 | 1146 | 4657 |
| ☐ | N458UA | Airbus A320-232 | 1163 | 4658 |
| ☐ | N459UA | Airbus A320-232 | 1192 | 4659 |
| ☐ | N460UA | Airbus A320-232 | 1248 | 4660 |
| ☐ | N461UA | Airbus A320-232 | 1266 | 4661 |
| ☐ | N462UA | Airbus A320-232 | 1272 | 4662 |
| ☐ | N463UA | Airbus A320-232 | 1282 | 4663 |
| ☐ | N464UA | Airbus A320-232 | 1290 | 4664 |
| ☐ | N465UA | Airbus A320-232 | 1341 | 4665 |
| ☐ | N466UA | Airbus A320-232 | 1343 | 4666; std |
| ☐ | N467UA | Airbus A320-232 | 1359 | 4667 |
| ☐ | N468UA | Airbus A320-232 | 1363 | 4668 |
| ☐ | N469UA | Airbus A320-232 | 1409 | 4669 |
| ☐ | N470UA | Airbus A320-232 | 1427 | 4670 |
| ☐ | N471UA | Airbus A320-232 | 1432 | 4671 |
| ☐ | N472UA | Airbus A320-232 | 1435 | 4672 |
| ☐ | N473UA | Airbus A320-232 | 1469 | 4673 |
| ☐ | N474UA | Airbus A320-232 | 1475 | 4674 |
| ☐ | N475UA | Airbus A320-232 | 1495 | 4675 |
| ☐ | N476UA | Airbus A320-232 | 1508 | 4676 |
| ☐ | N477UA | Airbus A320-232 | 1514 | 4677 |
| ☐ | N478UA | Airbus A320-232 | 1533 | 4678 |
| ☐ | N479UA | Airbus A320-232 | 1538 | 4679 |
| ☐ | N480UA | Airbus A320-232 | 1555 | 4680 |
| ☐ | N481UA | Airbus A320-232 | 1559 | 4681 |
| ☐ | N482UA | Airbus A320-232 | 1584 | 4682 |
| ☐ | N483UA | Airbus A320-232 | 1586 | 4683 |
| ☐ | N484UA | Airbus A320-232 | 1609 | 4684 |
| ☐ | N485UA | Airbus A320-232 | 1617 | 4685 |
| ☐ | N486UA | Airbus A320-232 | 1620 | 4686 |
| ☐ | N487UA | Airbus A320-232 | 1669 | 4687 |
| ☐ | N488UA | Airbus A320-232 | 1680 | 4688 |
| ☐ | N489UA | Airbus A320-232 | 1702 | 4689 |
| ☐ | N490UA | Airbus A320-232 | 1728 | 4690 |
| ☐ | N491UA | Airbus A320-232 | 1741 | 4691 |
| ☐ | N492UA | Airbus A320-232 | 1755 | 4692 |
| ☐ | N493UA | Airbus A320-232 | 1821 | 4693 |
| ☐ | N494UA | Airbus A320-232 | 1840 | 4694 |
| ☐ | N495UA | Airbus A320-232 | 1842 | 4695 |
| ☐ | N496UA | Airbus A320-232 | 1845 | 4696 |
| ☐ | N497UA | Airbus A320-232 | 1847 | 4697 |
| ☐ | N498UA | Airbus A320-232 | 1865 | 4968 |
| ☐ | N | Airbus A320-232 | | o/o |
| ☐ | N | Airbus A320-232 | | o/o |
| ☐ | N | Airbus A320-232 | | o/o |
| ☐ | N202UA | Boeing 737-322 | 1930/24717 | 1002 |
| ☐ | N203UA | Boeing 737-322 | 1937/24718 | 1003 |
| ☐ | N301UA | Boeing 737-322 | 1300/23642 | 9901 |
| ☐ | N302UA | Boeing 737-322 | 1315/23643 | 9902 |
| ☐ | N303UA | Boeing 737-322 | 1322/23644 | 9903 |
| ☐ | N304UA | Boeing 737-322 | 1330/23665 | 9904 |
| ☐ | N305UA | Boeing 737-322 | 1332/23666 | 9905 |
| ☐ | N306UA | Boeing 737-322 | 1334/23667 | 9906 |
| ☐ | N307UA | Boeing 737-322 | 1346/23668 | 9907 |
| ☐ | N308UA | Boeing 737-322 | 1354/23669 | 9908 |
| ☐ | N309UA | Boeing 737-322 | 1364/23670 | 9909 |
| ☐ | N310UA | Boeing 737-322 | 1370/23671 | 9910 |
| ☐ | N311UA | Boeing 737-322 | 1470/23672 | 9911 |
| ☐ | N312UA | Boeing 737-322 | 1479/23673 | 9912 |
| ☐ | N313UA | Boeing 737-322 | 1481/23674 | 9913 |
| ☐ | N314UA | Boeing 737-322 | 1483/23675 | 9914 |
| ☐ | N315UA | Boeing 737-322 | 1485/23947 | 9915 |
| ☐ | N316UA | Boeing 737-322 | 1491/23948 | 9916 |
| ☐ | N317UA | Boeing 737-322 | 1493/23949 | 9917 |
| ☐ | N318UA | Boeing 737-322 | 1504/23950 | 9918 |
| ☐ | N319UA | Boeing 737-322 | 1532/23951 | 9919 |
| ☐ | N320UA | Boeing 737-322 | 1534/23952 | 9920 |
| ☐ | N321UA | Boeing 737-322 | 1546/23953 | 9921 |
| ☐ | N322UA | Boeing 737-322 | 1548/23954 | 9922 |
| ☐ | N323UA | Boeing 737-322 | 1550/23955 | 9923 |
| ☐ | N324UA | Boeing 737-322 | 1564/23956 | 9924 |
| ☐ | N325UA | Boeing 737-322 | 1566/23957 | 9925 |
| ☐ | N326UA | Boeing 737-322 | 1568/23958 | 9926 |
| ☐ | N327UA | Boeing 737-322 | 1570/24147 | 9927 |
| ☐ | N328UA | Boeing 737-322 | 1572/24148 | 9928 |
| ☐ | N329UA | Boeing 737-322 | 1574/24149 | 9929 |
| ☐ | N330UA | Boeing 737-322 | 1588/24191 | 9930 |
| ☐ | N331UA | Boeing 737-322 | 1590/24192 | 9931 |
| ☐ | N332UA | Boeing 737-322 | 1592/24193 | 9932 |
| ☐ | N333UA | Boeing 737-322 | 1594/24228 | 9933 |
| ☐ | N334UA | Boeing 737-322 | 1605/24229 | 9934 |
| ☐ | N335UA | Boeing 737-322 | 1607/24230 | 9935 |
| ☐ | N336UA | Boeing 737-322 | 1609/24240 | 9936 |
| ☐ | N337UA | Boeing 737-322 | 1611/24241 | 9937 |
| ☐ | N338UA | Boeing 737-322 | 1613/24242 | 9938 |
| ☐ | N339UA | Boeing 737-322 | 1615/24243 | 9939 |
| ☐ | N340UA | Boeing 737-322 | 1617/24244 | 9940 |
| ☐ | N341UA | Boeing 737-322 | 1619/24245 | 9941 |
| ☐ | N342UA | Boeing 737-322 | 1632/24246 | 9942 |
| ☐ | N343UA | Boeing 737-322 | 1634/24247 | 9943 |
| ☐ | N344UA | Boeing 737-322 | 1636/24248 | 9944 |
| ☐ | N345UA | Boeing 737-322 | 1638/24249 | 9945 |
| ☐ | N346UA | Boeing 737-322 | 1644/24250 | 9946 |
| ☐ | N347UA | Boeing 737-322 | 1646/24251 | 9947 |
| ☐ | N348UA | Boeing 737-322 | 1648/24252 | 9948 |
| ☐ | N349UA | Boeing 737-322 | 1650/24253 | 9949 |
| ☐ | N350UA | Boeing 737-322 | 1652/24301 | 9950 |
| ☐ | N351UA | Boeing 737-322 | 1668/24319 | 9951 |
| ☐ | N352UA | Boeing 737-322 | 1670/24320 | 9952 |
| ☐ | N353UA | Boeing 737-322 | 1672/24321 | 9953 |
| ☐ | N354UA | Boeing 737-322 | 1692/24360 | 9954 |
| ☐ | N355UA | Boeing 737-322 | 1694/24361 | 9955 |
| ☐ | N356UA | Boeing 737-322 | 1696/24362 | 9956 |
| ☐ | N357UA | Boeing 737-322 | 1704/24378 | 9957 |
| ☐ | N358UA | Boeing 737-322 | 1724/24379 | 1358 |
| ☐ | N359UA | Boeing 737-322 | 1728/24452 | 9959 |
| ☐ | N360UA | Boeing 737-322 | 1730/24453 | 9960 |
| ☐ | N361UA | Boeing 737-322 | 1750/24454 | 9961 |
| ☐ | N362UA | Boeing 737-322 | 1752/24455 | 9962 |
| ☐ | N363UA | Boeing 737-322 | 1754/24532 | 9963 |
| ☐ | N364UA | Boeing 737-322 | 1756/24533 | 9964 |
| ☐ | N365UA | Boeing 737-322 | 1758/24534 | 9965 |
| ☐ | N366UA | Boeing 737-322 | 1760/24535 | 1366 |
| ☐ | N367UA | Boeing 737-322 | 1762/24536 | 1367 |
| ☐ | N368UA | Boeing 737-322 | 1774/24537 | 9968 |
| ☐ | N369UA | Boeing 737-322 | 1776/24538 | 1369 |
| ☐ | N370UA | Boeing 737-322 | 1778/24539 | 1370 |
| ☐ | N371UA | Boeing 737-322 | 1780/24540 | 1371 |
| ☐ | N372UA | Boeing 737-322 | 1782/24637 | 1372 |
| ☐ | N373UA | Boeing 737-322 | 1784/24638 | 1373 |
| ☐ | N374UA | Boeing 737-322 | 1786/24639 | 1374 |
| ☐ | N375UA | Boeing 737-322 | 1798/24640 | 1375 |
| ☐ | N376UA | Boeing 737-322 | 1802/24641 | 1376 |
| ☐ | N377UA | Boeing 737-322 | 1806/24642 | 1377 |
| ☐ | N378UA | Boeing 737-322 | 1810/24653 | 1378 |
| ☐ | N379UA | Boeing 737-322 | 1812/24654 | 1379 |
| ☐ | N380UA | Boeing 737-322 | 1814/24655 | 1380 |
| ☐ | N381UA | Boeing 737-322 | 1822/24656 | 1381 |
| ☐ | N382UA | Boeing 737-322 | 1830/24657 | 1382 |
| ☐ | N383UA | Boeing 737-322 | 1832/24658 | 1383 |
| ☐ | N384UA | Boeing 737-322 | 1836/24659 | 1384 |
| ☐ | N385UA | Boeing 737-322 | 1838/24660 | 1385 |
| ☐ | N386UA | Boeing 737-322 | 1840/24661 | 1386 |
| ☐ | N387UA | Boeing 737-322 | 1862/24662 | 1387 |
| ☐ | N388UA | Boeing 737-322 | 1875/24663 | 1388 |
| ☐ | N389UA | Boeing 737-322 | 1877/24664 | 1389 |
| ☐ | N390UA | Boeing 737-322 | 1889/24665 | 1390 |
| ☐ | N391UA | Boeing 737-322 | 1891/24666 | 1391 |
| ☐ | N392UA | Boeing 737-322 | 1893/24667 | 1392 |
| ☐ | N393UA | Boeing 737-322 | 1905/24668 | 1393 |
| ☐ | N394UA | Boeing 737-322 | 1907/24669 | 1394 |
| ☐ | N395UA | Boeing 737-322 | 1909/24670 | 1395 |
| ☐ | N396UA | Boeing 737-322 | 1913/24671 | 1396 |
| ☐ | N397UA | Boeing 737-322 | 1915/24672 | 1397 |
| ☐ | N398UA | Boeing 737-322 | 1920/24673 | 1398 |
| ☐ | N399UA | Boeing 737-322 | 1928/24674 | 1399 |
| ☐ | N901UA | Boeing 737-522 | 1948/25001 | 1601 |
| ☐ | N902UA | Boeing 737-522 | 1950/25002 | 1602 |
| ☐ | N903UA | Boeing 737-522 | 1952/25003 | 1603 |
| ☐ | N904UA | Boeing 737-522 | 1965/25004 | 1604 |

| | | | | | | | | |
|---|---|---|---|---|---|---|---|---|
| ☐ N905UA | Boeing 737-522 | 1976/25005 | 1605 | | ☐ N181UA | Boeing 747-422 | 881/25278 | 8181 |
| ☐ N906UA | Boeing 737-522 | 1981/25006 | 1606 | | ☐ N182UA | Boeing 747-422 | 882/25279 | 8182 |
| ☐ N907UA | Boeing 737-522 | 1983/25007 | 1607 | | ☐ N183UA | Boeing 747-422 | 911/25379 | 8183; std |
| ☐ N908UA | Boeing 737-522 | 1987/25008 | 1608 | | ☐ N184UA | Boeing 747-422 | 913/25380 | 8184; std |
| ☐ N909UA | Boeing 737-522 | 1999/25009 | 1609 | | ☐ N185UA | Boeing 747-422 | 919/25395 | 8185; std |
| ☐ N910UA | Boeing 737-522 | 2073/25254 | 9710 | | ☐ N186UA | Boeing 747-422 | 931/26875 | 8186; std |
| ☐ N911UA | Boeing 737-522 | 2075/25255 | 9711 | | ☐ N187UA | Boeing 747-422 | 939/26876 | 8187; std |
| ☐ N912UA | Boeing 737-522 | 2096/25290 | 9712 | | ☐ N188UA | Boeing 747-422 | 944/26877 | 8188; std |
| ☐ N913UA | Boeing 737-522 | 2101/25291 | 9713 | | ☐ N189UA | Boeing 747-422 | 966/26878 | 8189; std |
| ☐ N914UA | Boeing 737-522 | 2110/25381 | 9714 | | ☐ N190UA | Boeing 747-422 | 973/26879 | 8190; std |
| ☐ N915UA | Boeing 737-522 | 2119/25382 | 9715 | | ☐ N191UA | Boeing 747-422 | 984/26880 | 8191; std |
| ☐ N916UA | Boeing 737-522 | 2146/25383 | 9716 | | ☐ N192UA | Boeing 747-422 | 989/26881 | 8192 |
| ☐ N917UA | Boeing 737-522 | 2149/25384 | 9717 | | ☐ N193UA | Boeing 747-422 | 1085/26890 | 8193 |
| ☐ N918UA | Boeing 737-522 | 2152/25385 | 9718 | | ☐ N194UA | Boeing 747-422 | 1088/26892 | 8194; std |
| ☐ N919UA | Boeing 737-522 | 2154/25386 | 9719 | | ☐ N195UA | Boeing 747-422 | 1113/26899 | 8195; std |
| ☐ N920UA | Boeing 737-522 | 2179/25387 | 9720 | | ☐ N196UA | Boeing 747-422 | 1120/28715 | 8196 |
| ☐ N921UA | Boeing 737-522 | 2181/25388 | 9721 | | ☐ N197UA | Boeing 747-422 | 1121/26901 | 8197; std |
| ☐ N922UA | Boeing 737-522 | 2189/26642 | 9722 | | ☐ N198UA | Boeing 747-422 | 1124/28716 | 8198 |
| ☐ N923UA | Boeing 737-522 | 2190/26643 | 9723 | | ☐ N199UA | Boeing 747-422 | 1126/28717 | 8199 |
| ☐ N924UA | Boeing 737-522 | 2212/26645 | 9724 | | | | | |
| ☐ N925UA | Boeing 737-522 | 2214/26646 | 9725 | | ☐ N501UA | Boeing 757-222 | 241/24622 | 5401 |
| ☐ N926UA | Boeing 737-522 | 2230/26648 | 9726 | | ☐ N502UA | Boeing 757-222 | 246/24623 | 5402 |
| ☐ N927UA | Boeing 737-522 | 2246/26649 | 9727 | | ☐ N503UA | Boeing 757-222 | 247/24624 | 5403 |
| ☐ N928UA | Boeing 737-522 | 2257/26651 | 9728 | | ☐ N504UA | Boeing 757-222 | 251/24625 | 5404 |
| ☐ N929UA | Boeing 737-522 | 2259/26652 | 9729 | | ☐ N505UA | Boeing 757-222 | 254/24626 | 5405 |
| ☐ N930UA | Boeing 737-522 | 2274/26655 | 9730 | | ☐ N506UA | Boeing 757-222 | 263/24627 | 5406 |
| ☐ N931UA | Boeing 737-522 | 2289/26656 | 9731 | | ☐ N507UA | Boeing 757-222 | 270/24743 | 5407 |
| ☐ N932UA | Boeing 737-522 | 2291/26658 | 9732 | | ☐ N508UA | Boeing 757-222 | 277/24744 | 5408 |
| ☐ N933UA | Boeing 737-522 | 2293/26659 | 9733 | | ☐ N509UA | Boeing 757-222 | 284/24763 | 5409 |
| ☐ N934UA | Boeing 737-522 | 2312/26662 | 9734 | | ☐ N510UA | Boeing 757-222 | 290/24780 | 5410 |
| ☐ N935UA | Boeing 737-522 | 2315/26663 | 1635 | | ☐ N511UA | Boeing 757-222 | 291/24799 | 5411 |
| ☐ N936UA | Boeing 737-522 | 2325/26667 | 1636 | | ☐ N512UA | Boeing 757-222 | 298/24809 | 5412 |
| ☐ N937UA | Boeing 737-522 | 2329/26668 | 1637 | | ☐ N513UA | Boeing 757-222 | 299/24810 | 5413 |
| ☐ N938UA | Boeing 737-522 | 2336/26671 | 1638 | | ☐ N514UA | Boeing 757-222 | 305/24839 | 5414 |
| ☐ N939UA | Boeing 737-522 | 2343/26672 | 1639 | | ☐ N515UA | Boeing 757-222 | 306/24840 | 5415 |
| ☐ N940UA | Boeing 737-522 | 2345/26675 | 1640 | | ☐ N516UA | Boeing 757-222 | 307/24860 | 5416 |
| ☐ N941UA | Boeing 737-522 | 2364/26676 | 1641 | | ☐ N517UA | Boeing 757-222 | 310/24861 | 5417 |
| ☐ N942UA | Boeing 737-522 | 2365/26679 | 1642 | | ☐ N518UA | Boeing 757-222 | 311/24871 | 5418 |
| ☐ N943UA | Boeing 737-522 | 2366/26680 | 1643 | | ☐ N519UA | Boeing 757-222 | 312/24872 | 5419; std |
| ☐ N944UA | Boeing 737-522 | 2368/26683 | 1644 | | ☐ N520UA | Boeing 757-222 | 313/24890 | 5420 |
| ☐ N945UA | Boeing 737-522 | 2388/26684 | 1645 | | ☐ N521UA | Boeing 757-222 | 319/24891 | 5421 |
| ☐ N946UA | Boeing 737-522 | 2402/26687 | 1646 | | ☐ N522UA | Boeing 757-222 | 320/24931 | 5422 |
| ☐ N947UA | Boeing 737-522 | 2404/26688 | 1647 | | ☐ N523UA | Boeing 757-222 | 329/24932 | 5423 |
| ☐ N948UA | Boeing 737-522 | 2408/26691 | 1648 | | ☐ N524UA | Boeing 757-222 | 331/24977 | 5424 |
| ☐ N949UA | Boeing 737-522 | 2421/26692 | 1649 | | ☐ N525UA | Boeing 757-222 | 338/24978 | 5425 |
| ☐ N950UA | Boeing 737-522 | 2423/26695 | 1650 | | ☐ N526UA | Boeing 757-222 | 339/24994 | 5426 |
| ☐ N951UA | Boeing 737-522 | 2440/26696 | 1651 | | ☐ N527UA | Boeing 757-222 | 341/24995 | 5427 |
| ☐ N952UA | Boeing 737-522 | 2485/26699 | 1652 | | ☐ N528UA | Boeing 757-222 | 346/25018 | 5428 |
| ☐ N953UA | Boeing 737-522 | 2490/26700 | 1653 | | ☐ N529UA | Boeing 757-222 | 352/25019 | 5429 |
| ☐ N954UA | Boeing 737-522 | 2494/26739 | 1654 | | ☐ N530UA | Boeing 757-222 | 353/25043 | 5430 |
| ☐ N955UA | Boeing 737-522 | 2498/26703 | 1655 | | ☐ N531UA | Boeing 757-222 | 361/25042 | 5431 |
| ☐ N956UA | Boeing 737-522 | 2508/26704 | 1656 | | ☐ N532UA | Boeing 757-222 | 366/25072 | 5432 |
| ☐ N957UA | Boeing 737-522 | 2512/26707 | 1657 | | ☐ N533UA | Boeing 757-222 | 367/25073 | 5433 |
| | | | | | ☐ N534UA | Boeing 757-222 | 372/25129 | 5434 |
| ☐ N104UA | Boeing 747-422 | 1141/26902 | 8104 | | ☐ N535UA | Boeing 757-222 | 373/25130 | 5435 |
| ☐ N105UA | Boeing 747-451 | 985/26473 | 8105 | | ☐ N536UA | Boeing 757-222 | 380/25156 | 5436 |
| ☐ N106UA | Boeing 747-451 | 988/26474 | 8106 | | ☐ N537UA | Boeing 757-222 | 381/25157 | 5437 |
| ☐ N107UA | Boeing 747-422 | 1168/26900 | 8107 | | ☐ N538UA | Boeing 757-222 | 385/25222 | 5438 |
| ☐ N108UA | Boeing 747-422 | 1171/26903 | 8108 | | ☐ N539UA | Boeing 757-222 | 386/25223 | 5439 |
| ☐ N109UA | Boeing 747-422 | 1185/26906 | 8109 | | ☐ N540UA | Boeing 757-222 | 393/25252 | 5440 |
| ☐ N116UA | Boeing 747-422 | 1193/26908 | 8116 | | ☐ N541UA | Boeing 757-222 | 394/25253 | 5441 |
| ☐ N117UA | Boeing 747-422 | 1197/28810 | 8117 | | ☐ N542UA | Boeing 757-222 | 396/25276 | 5442 |
| ☐ N118UA | Boeing 747-422 | 1201/28811 | 8118 | | ☐ N543UA | Boeing 757-222ER | 401/25698 | 5543 |
| ☐ N119UA | Boeing 747-422 | 1207/28812 | 8119 | | ☐ N544UA | Boeing 757-222ER | 405/25322 | 5544 |
| ☐ N120UA | Boeing 747-422 | 1209/29166 | 8120 | | ☐ N545UA | Boeing 757-222ER | 406/25323 | 5545 |
| ☐ N121UA | Boeing 747-422 | 1211/29167 | 8121 | | ☐ N546UA | Boeing 757-222ER | 413/25367 | 5546 |
| ☐ N122UA | Boeing 747-422 | 1218/29168 | 8122 | | ☐ N547UA | Boeing 757-222ER | 414/25368 | 5547 |
| ☐ N127UA | Boeing 747-422 | 1221/28813 | 8127 | | ☐ N548UA | Boeing 757-222ER | 420/25396 | 5548 |
| ☐ N128UA | Boeing 747-422 | 1245/30023 | 8128 | | ☐ N549UA | Boeing 757-222ER | 421/25397 | 5549 |
| ☐ N171UA | Boeing 747-422 | 733/24322 | 8171 | | ☐ N550UA | Boeing 757-222ER | 426/25398 | 5550 |
| ☐ N172UA | Boeing 747-422 | 740/24363 | 8172 | | ☐ N551UA | Boeing 757-222ER | 427/25399 | 5551 |
| ☐ N173UA | Boeing 747-422 | 759/24380 | 8173 | | ☐ N552UA | Boeing 757-222ER | 431/26641 | 5552 |
| ☐ N174UA | Boeing 747-422 | 762/24381 | 8174 | | ☐ N553UA | Boeing 757-222 | 434/25277 | 5453 |
| ☐ N175UA | Boeing 747-422 | 806/24382 | 8175 | | ☐ N554UA | Boeing 757-222 | 435/26644 | 5454 |
| ☐ N176UA | Boeing 747-422 | 811/24383 | 8176 | | ☐ N555UA | Boeing 757-222 | 442/26647 | 5455 |
| ☐ N177UA | Boeing 747-422 | 819/24384 | 8177 | | ☐ N556UA | Boeing 757-222 | 447/26650 | 5456 |
| ☐ N178UA | Boeing 747-422 | 820/24385 | 8178 | | ☐ N557UA | Boeing 757-222 | 454/26653 | 5457 |
| ☐ N179UA | Boeing 747-422 | 866/25158 | 8179; std | | ☐ N558UA | Boeing 757-222 | 462/26654 | 5458 |
| ☐ N180UA | Boeing 747-422 | 867/25224 | 8180 | | ☐ N559UA | Boeing 757-222 | 467/26657 | 5459 |

| | Registration | Type | c/n | Fleet No. |
|---|---|---|---|---|
| ☐ | N560UA | Boeing 757-222 | 469/26660 | 5460 |
| ☐ | N561UA | Boeing 757-222 | 479/26661 | 5461 |
| ☐ | N562UA | Boeing 757-222 | 487/26664 | 5462 |
| ☐ | N563UA | Boeing 757-222 | 488/26665 | 5463 |
| ☐ | N564UA | Boeing 757-222 | 490/26666 | 5464 |
| ☐ | N565UA | Boeing 757-222 | 492/26669 | 5465 |
| ☐ | N566UA | Boeing 757-222 | 494/26670 | 5466 |
| ☐ | N567UA | Boeing 757-222 | 497/26673 | 5467 |
| ☐ | N568UA | Boeing 757-222 | 498/26674 | 5468 |
| ☐ | N569UA | Boeing 757-222 | 499/26677 | 5469 |
| ☐ | N570UA | Boeing 757-222 | 501/26678 | 5470 |
| ☐ | N571UA | Boeing 757-222 | 506/26681 | 5471 |
| ☐ | N572UA | Boeing 757-222 | 508/26682 | 5472 |
| ☐ | N573UA | Boeing 757-222 | 512/26685 | 5473 |
| ☐ | N574UA | Boeing 757-222 | 513/26686 | 5474 |
| ☐ | N575UA | Boeing 757-222 | 515/26689 | 5475 |
| ☐ | N576UA | Boeing 757-222 | 524/26690 | 5676 |
| ☐ | N577UA | Boeing 757-222 | 527/26693 | 5677 |
| ☐ | N578UA | Boeing 757-222 | 531/26694 | 5678 |
| ☐ | N579UA | Boeing 757-222 | 539/26697 | 5679 |
| ☐ | N580UA | Boeing 757-222 | 542/26698 | 5680 |
| ☐ | N581UA | Boeing 757-222 | 543/26701 | 5681 |
| ☐ | N582UA | Boeing 757-222 | 550/26702 | 5682 |
| ☐ | N583UA | Boeing 757-222 | 556/26705 | 5683 |
| ☐ | N584UA | Boeing 757-222 | 559/26706 | 5684 |
| ☐ | N585UA | Boeing 757-222 | 563/26709 | 5685 |
| ☐ | N586UA | Boeing 757-222 | 567/26710 | 5686 |
| ☐ | N587UA | Boeing 757-222 | 570/26713 | 5007 |
| ☐ | N588UA | Boeing 757-222 | 571/26717 | 5688 |
| ☐ | N589UA | Boeing 757-222ER | 773/28707 | 5589 |
| ☐ | N590UA | Boeing 757-222ER | 785/28708 | 5590 |
| ☐ | N592UA | Boeing 757-222 | 719/28143 | 5492 |
| ☐ | N593UA | Boeing 757-222 | 724/28144 | 5493 |
| ☐ | N594UA | Boeing 757-222 | 727/28145 | 5494 |
| ☐ | N595UA | Boeing 757-222ER | 789/28748 | 5595 |
| ☐ | N596UA | Boeing 757-222ER | 794/28749 | 5596 |
| ☐ | N597UA | Boeing 757-222ER | 841/28750 | 5597 |
| ☐ | N598UA | Boeing 757-222ER | 844/28751 | 5598 |
| ☐ | N601UA | Boeing 767-222 | 2/21862 | 6201 |
| ☐ | N602UA | Boeing 767-222ER | 3/21863 | 6002 |
| ☐ | N603UA | Boeing 767-222 | 4/21864 | 6203; std |
| ☐ | N604UA | Boeing 767-222 | 5/21865 | 6204 |
| ☐ | N605UA | Boeing 767-222ER | 7/21866 | 6005; std |
| ☐ | N606UA | Boeing 767-222ER | 9/21867 | 6006 |
| ☐ | N607UA | Boeing 767-222ER | 10/21868 | 6007 |
| ☐ | N608UA | Boeing 767-222ER | 11/21869 | 6008 |
| ☐ | N609UA | Boeing 767-222ER | 13/21870 | 6009 |
| ☐ | N610UA | Boeing 767-222ER | 15/21871 | 6010; std |
| ☐ | N611UA | Boeing 767-222ER | 20/21872 | 6011 |
| ☐ | N613UA | Boeing 767-222 | 42/21874 | 6213 |
| ☐ | N614UA | Boeing 767-222 | 43/21875 | 6214 |
| ☐ | N615UA | Boeing 767-222 | 45/21876 | 6215 |
| ☐ | N617UA | Boeing 767-222 | 46/21877 | 6217 |
| ☐ | N618UA | Boeing 767-222 | 48/21878 | 6218 |
| ☐ | N619UA | Boeing 767-222 | 49/21879 | 6219; std |
| ☐ | N620UA | Boeing 767-222 | 50/21880 | 6220 |
| ☐ | N641UA | Boeing 767-322ER | 360/25091 | 6341 |
| ☐ | N642UA | Boeing 767-322ER | 367/25092 | 6342 |
| ☐ | N643UA | Boeing 767-322ER | 368/25093 | 6343 |
| ☐ | N644UA | Boeing 767-322ER | 369/25094 | 6344 |
| ☐ | N645UA | Boeing 767-322ER | 391/25280 | 6345 |
| ☐ | N646UA | Boeing 767-322ER | 420/25283 | 6346 |
| ☐ | N647UA | Boeing 767-322ER | 424/25284 | 6347 |
| ☐ | N648UA | Boeing 767-322ER | 443/25285 | 6348 |
| ☐ | N649UA | Boeing 767-322ER | 444/25286 | 6349 |
| ☐ | N650UA | Boeing 767-322ER | 449/25287 | 6350 |
| ☐ | N651UA | Boeing 767-322ER | 452/25389 | 6351 |
| ☐ | N652UA | Boeing 767-322ER | 457/25390 | 6352 |
| ☐ | N653UA | Boeing 767-322ER | 460/25391 | 6353 |
| ☐ | N654UA | Boeing 767-322ER | 462/25392 | 6354 |
| ☐ | N655UA | Boeing 767-322ER | 468/25393 | 6355 |
| ☐ | N656UA | Boeing 767-322ER | 472/25394 | 6356 |
| ☐ | N657UA | Boeing 767-322ER | 479/27112 | 6357 |
| ☐ | N658UA | Boeing 767-322ER | 480/27113 | 6358 |
| ☐ | N659UA | Boeing 767-322ER | 485/27114 | 6359 |
| ☐ | N660UA | Boeing 767-322ER | 494/27115 | 6360 |
| ☐ | N661UA | Boeing 767-322ER | 507/27158 | 6361 |
| ☐ | N662UA | Boeing 767-322ER | 513/27159 | 6362 |
| ☐ | N663UA | Boeing 767-322ER | 514/27160 | 6363 |
| ☐ | N664UA | Boeing 767-322ER | 707/29236 | 6764 |
| ☐ | N665UA | Boeing 767-322ER | 711/29237 | 6765 |
| ☐ | N666UA | Boeing 767-322ER | 715/29238 | 6766 |
| ☐ | N667UA | Boeing 767-322ER | 716/29239 | 6767 |
| ☐ | N668UA | Boeing 767-322ER | 742/30024 | 6768 |
| ☐ | N669UA | Boeing 767-322ER | 757/30025 | 6769 |
| ☐ | N670UA | Boeing 767-322ER | 763/29240 | 6770 |
| ☐ | N671UA | Boeing 767-322ER | 766/30026 | 6771 |
| ☐ | N672UA | Boeing 767-322ER | 777/30027 | 6772 |
| ☐ | N673UA | Boeing 767-322ER | 779/29241 | 6773 |
| ☐ | N674UA | Boeing 767-322ER | 782/29242 | 6774; std |
| ☐ | N675UA | Boeing 767-322ER | 800/29243 | 6775 |
| ☐ | N676UA | Boeing 767-322ER | 834/30028 | 6776 |
| ☐ | N677UA | Boeing 767-322ER | 852/30029 | 6777 |
| ☐ | N204UA | Boeing 777-222ER | 191/28713 | 2704 |
| ☐ | N205UA | Boeing 777-222ER | 205/28714 | 2705 |
| ☐ | N206UA | Boeing 777-222ER | 216/30212 | 2706 |
| ☐ | N207UA | Boeing 777-222ER | 232/30213 | 2707 |
| ☐ | N208UA | Boeing 777-222ER | 254/30214 | 2708 |
| ☐ | N209UA | Boeing 777-222ER | 259/30215 | 2809 |
| ☐ | N210UA | Boeing 777-222ER | 264/30216 | 2510 |
| ☐ | N211UA | Boeing 777-222 | 282/30217 | 2511 |
| ☐ | N212UA | Boeing 777-222 | 293/30218 | 2512 |
| ☐ | N213UA | Boeing 777-222 | 295/30219 | 2513 |
| ☐ | N214UA | Boeing 777-222 | 296/30220 | 2514 |
| ☐ | N215UA | Boeing 777-222 | 297/30221 | 2515 |
| ☐ | N216UA | Boeing 777-222ER | 291/30549 | 2816 |
| ☐ | N217UA | Boeing 777-222ER | 294/30550 | 2817 |
| ☐ | N218UA | Boeing 777-222ER | 317/30222 | 2818 |
| ☐ | N219UA | Boeing 777-222ER | 318/30551 | 2819 |
| ☐ | N220UA | Boeing 777-222ER | 340/30223 | 2820 |
| ☐ | N221UA | Boeing 777-222ER | 347/30552 | 2821 |
| ☐ | N222UA | Boeing 777-222ER | 352/30553 | 2822 |
| ☐ | N223UA | Boeing 777-222ER | 357/30224 | 2823 |
| ☐ | N224UA | Boeing 777-222ER | 375/30225 | 2824 |
| ☐ | N225UA | Boeing 777-222ER | 377/30554 | 2825 |
| ☐ | N226UA | Boeing 777-222ER | 380/30226 | 2826 |
| ☐ | N227UA | Boeing 777-222ER | 381/30555 | 2827 |
| ☐ | N228UA | Boeing 777-222ER | 384/30556 | 2828 |
| ☐ | N229UA | Boeing 777-222ER | 388/30557 | 2829 |
| ☐ | N230UA | Boeing 777-222ER | 30227 | 2830 |
| ☐ | N766UA | Boeing 777-222 | 8/26917 | 2366 |
| ☐ | N767UA | Boeing 777-222 | 9/26918 | 2367 |
| ☐ | N768UA | Boeing 777-222 | 11/26919 | 2368 |
| ☐ | N769UA | Boeing 777-222 | 12/26921 | 2369 |
| ☐ | N770UA | Boeing 777-222 | 13/26925 | 2370 |
| ☐ | N771UA | Boeing 777-222 | 3/26932 | 2371 |
| ☐ | N772UA | Boeing 777-222 | 5/26930 | 2372 |
| ☐ | N773UA | Boeing 777-222 | 4/26929 | 2373 |
| ☐ | N774UA | Boeing 777-222 | 2/26936 | 2374 |
| ☐ | N775UA | Boeing 777-222 | 22/26947 | 2375 |
| ☐ | N776UA | Boeing 777-222 | 27/26937 | 2376 |
| ☐ | N777UA | Boeing 777-222 | 7/26916 | 2377 |
| ☐ | N778UA | Boeing 777-222 | 34/26940 | 2378 |
| ☐ | N779UA | Boeing 777-222 | 35/26941 | 2379 |
| ☐ | N780UA | Boeing 777-222 | 36/26944 | 2380 |
| ☐ | N781UA | Boeing 777-222 | 40/26945 | 2381 |
| ☐ | N782UA | Boeing 777-222ER | 57/26948 | 2782 |
| ☐ | N783UA | Boeing 777-222ER | 60/26950 | 2783 |
| ☐ | N784UA | Boeing 777-222ER | 69/26951 | 2784 |
| ☐ | N785UA | Boeing 777-222ER | 73/26954 | 2785 |
| ☐ | N786UA | Boeing 777-222ER | 52/26938 | 2786 |
| ☐ | N787UA | Boeing 777-222ER | 43/26939 | 2787 |
| ☐ | N788UA | Boeing 777-222ER | 82/26942 | 2788 |
| ☐ | N789UA | Boeing 777-222ER | 88/26935 | 2789 |
| ☐ | N790UA | Boeing 777-222ER | 92/26943 | 2790 |
| ☐ | N791UA | Boeing 777-222ER | 93/26933 | 2791 |
| ☐ | N792UA | Boeing 777-222ER | 96/26934 | 2792 |
| ☐ | N793UA | Boeing 777-222ER | 97/26946 | 2793 |
| ☐ | N794UA | Boeing 777-222ER | 105/26953 | 2794 |
| ☐ | N795UA | Boeing 777-222ER | 108/26927 | 2795 |
| ☐ | N796UA | Boeing 777-222ER | 112/26931 | 2796 |
| ☐ | N797UA | Boeing 777-222ER | 116/26924 | 2797 |
| ☐ | N798UA | Boeing 777-222ER | 123/26928 | 2798 |
| ☐ | N799UA | Boeing 777-222ER | 139/26926 | 2799 |

| UNITED EXPRESS | | UAL |
|---|---|---|
| ☐ N301UE | BAe Jetstream 41 | 41012 |
| ☐ N302UE | BAe Jetstream 41 | 41013 |
| ☐ N303UE | BAe Jetstream 41 | 41015 |
| ☐ N305UE | BAe Jetstream 41 | 41019 |
| ☐ N306UE | BAe Jetstream 41 | 41020 |
| ☐ N307UE | BAe Jetstream 41 | 41021 |
| ☐ N308UE | BAe Jetstream 41 | 41023 |
| ☐ N309UE | BAe Jetstream 41 | 41022 |
| ☐ N311UE | BAe Jetstream 41 | 41029 |
| ☐ N312UE | BAe Jetstream 41 | 41025 |
| ☐ N313UE | BAe Jetstream 41 | 41026 |
| ☐ N314UE | BAe Jetstream 41 | 41027 |
| ☐ N315UE | BAe Jetstream 41 | 41033 |
| ☐ N316UE | BAe Jetstream 41 | 41055 |
| ☐ N317UE | BAe Jetstream 41 | 41031 |
| ☐ N318UE | BAe Jetstream 41 | 41041 |
| ☐ N319UE | BAe Jetstream 41 | 41042 |
| ☐ N320UE | BAe Jetstream 41 | 41043 |
| ☐ N321UE | BAe Jetstream 41 | 41045 |
| ☐ N322UE | BAe Jetstream 41 | 41058 |
| ☐ N324UE | BAe Jetstream 41 | 41017 |
| ☐ N325UE | BAe Jetstream 41 | 41063 |
| ☐ N326UE | BAe Jetstream 41 | 41064 |
| ☐ N327UE | BAe Jetstream 41 | 41080 |
| ☐ N328UE | BAe Jetstream 41 | 41083 |
| ☐ N329UE | BAe Jetstream 41 | 41097 |
| ☐ N330UE | BAe Jetstream 41 | 41098 |
| ☐ N331UE | BAe Jetstream 41 | 41099 |
| ☐ N332UE | BAe Jetstream 41 | 41100 |
| ☐ N333UE | BAe Jetstream 41 | 41101 |
| | | |
| ☐ N156TR | BAe 146 Srs.200 | E2156 |
| ☐ N179US | BAe 146 Srs.200 | E2041 |
| ☐ N181US | BAe 146 Srs.200 | E2042 |
| ☐ N183US | BAe 146 Srs.200 | E2043 |
| ☐ N291UE | BAe 146 Srs.200 | E2084 |
| ☐ N292UE | BAe 146 Srs.200 | E2087 |
| ☐ N290UE | BAe 146 Srs.200 | E2080 |
| ☐ N463AP | BAe 146 Srs.100 | E1063 |
| ☐ N606AW | BAe 146 Srs.200 | E2033 |
| ☐ N607AW | BAe 146 Srs.200 | E2052 |
| ☐ N608AW | BAe 146 Srs.200 | E2049 |
| ☐ N609AW | BAe 146 Srs.200 | E2070 |
| ☐ N610AW | BAe 146 Srs.200 | E2082 |
| ☐ N611AW | BAe 146 Srs.300 | E3120 |
| ☐ N612AW | BAe 146 Srs.300 | E3122 |
| ☐ N614AW | BAe 146 Srs.300 | E3132 |
| ☐ N615AW | BAe 146 Srs.300 | E3141 |
| ☐ N616AW | BAe 146 Srs.300 | E3145 |
| | | |
| ☐ N401AW | Canadair RJ-200 | 7280 |
| ☐ N402AW | Canadair RJ-200 | 7281 |
| ☐ N403AW | Canadair RJ-200 | 7288 |
| ☐ N404AW | Canadair RJ-200 | 7294 |
| ☐ N405AW | Canadair RJ-200 | 7362 |
| ☐ N406AW | Canadair RJ-200 | 7402 |
| ☐ N407AW | Canadair RJ-200 | 7424 |
| ☐ N408AW | Canadair RJ-200 | 7568 |
| ☐ N409AW | Canadair RJ-200 | 7447 |
| ☐ N410AW | Canadair RJ-200 | 7490 |
| ☐ N411ZW | Canadair RJ-200 | 7569 |
| ☐ N412AW | Canadair RJ-200 | 7582 |
| ☐ N413AW | Canadair RJ-200 | 7585 |
| ☐ N414ZW | Canadair RJ-200 | 7586 |
| ☐ N415AW | Canadair RJ-200 | 7593 |
| ☐ N416AW | Canadair RJ-200 | 7603 |
| ☐ N417AW | Canadair RJ-200 | 7610 |
| ☐ N418AW | Canadair RJ-200 | 7618 |
| ☐ N419AW | Canadair RJ-200 | 7633 |
| ☐ N420AW | Canadair RJ-200 | 7640 |
| ☐ N421ZW | Canadair RJ-200 | 7346 |
| ☐ N422AW | Canadair RJ-200 | 7341 |
| ☐ N423AW | Canadair RJ-200 | 7636 |
| ☐ N424AW | Canadair RJ-200 | 7656 |
| ☐ N425AW | Canadair RJ-200 | 7663 |
| ☐ N426AW | Canadair RJ-200 | 7669 |
| ☐ N427ZW | Canadair RJ-200 | 7685 |
| ☐ N428AW | Canadair RJ-200 | 7695 |
| ☐ N429AW | Canadair RJ-200 | 7711 |
| ☐ N430AW | Canadair RJ-200 | 7719 |
| ☐ N431AW | Canadair RJ-200 | 7256 |
| ☐ N432AW | Canadair RJ-200 | 7257 |
| ☐ N434AW | Canadair RJ-200 | 7322 |
| ☐ N435AW | Canadair RJ-200 | 7724 |
| ☐ N436AW | Canadair RJ-200 | o/o |
| ☐ N620BR | Canadair RJ-200 | 7179 |
| ☐ N621BR | Canadair RJ-200 | 7186 |
| ☐ N622BR | Canadair RJ-200 | 7187 |
| ☐ N623BR | Canadair RJ-200 | 7192 |
| ☐ N624BR | Canadair RJ-200 | 7211 |
| ☐ N625BR | Canadair RJ-200 | 7214 |
| ☐ N626BR | Canadair RJ-200 | 7225 |
| ☐ N627BR | Canadair RJ-200 | 7233 |
| ☐ N628BR | Canadair RJ-200 | 7240 |
| ☐ N629BR | Canadair RJ-200 | 7251 |
| ☐ N630BR | Canadair RJ-200 | 7255 |
| ☐ N631BR | Canadair RJ-200 | 7261 |
| ☐ N632BR | Canadair RJ-200 | 7268 |
| ☐ N633BR | Canadair RJ-200 | 7274 |
| ☐ N634BR | Canadair RJ-200 | 7287 |
| ☐ N635BR | Canadair RJ-200 | 7295 |
| ☐ N636BR | Canadair RJ-200 | 7307 |
| ☐ N637BR | Canadair RJ-200 | 7308 |
| ☐ N638BR | Canadair RJ-200 | 7311 |
| ☐ N639BR | Canadair RJ-200 | 7313 |
| ☐ N640BR | Canadair RJ-200 | 7340 |
| ☐ N641BR | Canadair RJ-200 | 7349 |
| ☐ N642BR | Canadair RJ-200 | 7356 |
| ☐ N643BR | Canadair RJ-200 | 7363 |
| ☐ N644BR | Canadair RJ-200 | 7379 |
| ☐ N645BR | Canadair RJ-200 | 7383 |
| ☐ N646BR | Canadair RJ-200 | 7392 |
| ☐ N647BR | Canadair RJ-200 | 7399 |
| ☐ N648BR | Canadair RJ-200 | 7406 |
| ☐ N649BR | Canadair RJ-200 | 7414 |
| ☐ N650BR | Canadair RJ-200 | 7418 |
| ☐ N651BR | Canadair RJ-200 | 7426 |
| ☐ N652BR | Canadair RJ-200 | 7429 |
| ☐ N653BR | Canadair RJ-200 | 7438 |
| ☐ N654BR | Canadair RJ-200 | 7454 |
| ☐ N655BR | Canadair RJ-200 | 7457 |
| ☐ N656BR | Canadair RJ-200 | 7485 |
| ☐ N657BR | Canadair RJ-200 | 7491 |
| ☐ N658BR | Canadair RJ-200 | 7500 |
| ☐ N659BR | Canadair RJ-200 | 7509 |
| ☐ N660BR | Canadair RJ-200 | 7519 |
| ☐ N661BR | Canadair RJ-200 | 7520 |
| ☐ N662BR | Canadair RJ-200 | 7526 |
| ☐ N663BR | Canadair RJ-200 | 7527 |
| ☐ N664BR | Canadair RJ-200 | 7528 |
| ☐ N665BR | Canadair RJ-200 | 7534 |
| ☐ N667BR | Canadair RJ-200 | 7535 |
| ☐ N668BR | Canadair RJ-200 | 7544 |
| ☐ N669BR | Canadair RJ-200 | 7545 |
| ☐ N670BR | Canadair RJ-200 | 7561 |
| ☐ N671BR | Canadair RJ-200 | 7572 |
| ☐ N672BR | Canadair RJ-200 | 7594 |
| ☐ N673BR | Canadair RJ-200 | 7599 |
| ☐ N674BR | Canadair RJ-200 | 7601 |
| ☐ N675BR | Canadair RJ-200 | 7635 |
| ☐ N676BR | Canadair RJ-200 | 7644 |
| ☐ N677BR | Canadair RJ-200 | 7652 |
| ☐ N678BR | Canadair RJ-200 | 7653 |
| ☐ N679BR | Canadair RJ-200 | 7662 |
| ☐ N680BR | Canadair RJ-200 | 7679 |
| ☐ N681BR | Canadair RJ-200 | 7680 |
| ☐ N682BR | Canadair RJ-200 | 7691 |
| ☐ N683BR | Canadair RJ-200 | 7692 |
| ☐ N684BR | Canadair RJ-200 | 7708 |
| ☐ N685BR | Canadair RJ-200 | 7712 |
| ☐ N686BR | Canadair RJ-200 | 7715 |
| ☐ N687BR | Canadair RJ-200 | 7720 |
| ☐ N688BR | Canadair RJ-200 | 7723 |
| ☐ N689BR | Canadair RJ-200 | 7737 |

| | | | |
|---|---|---|---|
| ☐ N701BR | Canadair RJ-200 | 7448 | |
| ☐ N702BR | Canadair RJ-200 | 7462 | |
| ☐ N703BR | Canadair RJ-200 | 7467 | |
| ☐ N705BR | Canadair RJ-200 | 7470 | |
| ☐ N706BR | Canadair RJ-200 | 7553 | |
| ☐ N708BR | Canadair RJ-200 | 7575 | |
| ☐ N | Canadair RJ-200 | | o/o |
| ☐ N | Canadair RJ-200 | | o/o |
| ☐ N | Canadair RJ-200 | | o/o |
| ☐ N | Canadair RJ-200 | | o/o |
| ☐ N | Canadair RJ-200 | | o/o |
| ☐ N | Canadair RJ-200 | | o/o |
| ☐ N | Canadair RJ-200 | | o/o |
| ☐ N | Canadair RJ-200 | | o/o |
| ☐ N | Canadair RJ-200 | | o/o |
| ☐ N | Canadair RJ-200 | | o/o |
| ☐ N | Canadair RJ-200 | | o/o |
| ☐ N | Canadair RJ-200 | | o/o |
| ☐ N | Canadair RJ-200 | | o/o |
| ☐ N | Canadair RJ-200 | | o/o |
| ☐ N | Canadair RJ-200 | | o/o |
| ☐ N | Canadair RJ-200 | | o/o |
| ☐ N | Canadair RJ-200 | | o/o |
| ☐ N | Canadair RJ-200 | | o/o |
| ☐ N | Canadair RJ-200 | | o/o |
| ☐ N | Canadair RJ-200 | | o/o |
| ☐ N | Canadair RJ-200 | | o/o |

| | | | |
|---|---|---|---|
| ☐ N328LS | Dornier 328-100 | 3025 | |
| ☐ N328MX | Dornier 238-120 | 3071 | |
| ☐ N329MX | Dornier 328-120 | 3049 | |
| ☐ N330MX | Dornier 328-120 | 3067 | |
| ☐ N331MX | Dornier 328-120 | 3074 | |
| ☐ N334PH | Dornier 328-110 | 3012 | |
| ☐ N335PC | Dornier 328-120 | 3013 | |
| ☐ N335PH | Dornier 328-120 | 3035 | |
| ☐ N336PH | Dornier 328-110 | 3014 | |
| ☐ N337PH | Dornier 328-110 | 3020 | |
| ☐ N338PH | Dornier 328-110 | 3029 | |
| ☐ N339PH | Dornier 328-110 | 3015 | |
| ☐ N340LS | Dornier 328-120 | 3040 | |
| ☐ N341PH | Dornier 328-110 | 3065 | |
| ☐ N350AD | Dornier 328-120 | 3050 | |
| ☐ N453FJ | Dornier 328-310 | 3215 | |
| ☐ N454FJ | Dornier 328-310 | 3216 | |
| ☐ N455FJ | Dornier 328-310 | 3200 | |
| ☐ N456FJ | Dornier 328-310 | 32.. | o/o |
| ☐ N457FJ | Dornier 328-310 | 32.. | o/o |
| ☐ N200CD | Embraer EMB.120RT | 120200 | |

| UPS AIRLINES | | | UPS |
|---|---|---|---|
| ☐ N120UP | Airbus A300F4-622R | 805 | |
| ☐ N121UP | Airbus A300F4-622R | 806 | |
| ☐ N122UP | Airbus A300F4-622R | 807 | |
| ☐ N124UP | Airbus A300F4-622R | 808 | |
| ☐ N125UP | Airbus A300F4-622R | 809 | |
| ☐ N126UP | Airbus A300F4-622R | 810 | |
| ☐ N127UP | Airbus A300F4-622R | 811 | |
| ☐ N128UP | Airbus A300F4-622R | 812 | |
| ☐ N129UP | Airbus A300F4-622R | 813 | |
| ☐ N130UP | Airbus A300F4-622R | 814 | |
| ☐ N131UP | Airbus A300F4-622R | 815 | |
| ☐ N133UP | Airbus A300F4-622R | 816 | |
| ☐ N134UP | Airbus A300F4-622R | 817 | |
| ☐ N135UP | Airbus A300F4-622R | 818 | |
| ☐ N136UP | Airbus A300F4-622R | 819 | |
| ☐ N137UP | Airbus A300F4-622R | 820 | |
| ☐ N138UP | Airbus A300F4-622R | 821 | |
| ☐ N139UP | Airbus A300F4-622R | 822 | |
| ☐ N140UP | Airbus A300F4-622R | 823 | |
| ☐ N141UP | Airbus A300F4-622R | 824 | |
| ☐ N142UP | Airbus A300F4-622R | 825 | |
| ☐ N143UP | Airbus A300F4-622R | 826 | |
| ☐ N144UP | Airbus A300F4-622R | 827 | |
| ☐ N145UP | Airbus A300F4-622R | 828 | |
| ☐ N146UP | Airbus A300F4-622R | 829 | |

| | | | |
|---|---|---|---|
| ☐ N147UP | Airbus A300F4-622R | 830 | |
| ☐ N148UP | Airbus A300F4-622R | 831 | |
| ☐ N149UP | Airbus A300F4-622R | 832 | |
| ☐ N150UP | Airbus A300F4-622R | 833 | |
| ☐ N151UP | Airbus A300F4-622R | 834 | |
| ☐ N152UP | Airbus A300F4-622R | 835 | |
| ☐ N153UP | Airbus A300F4-622R | 839 | |
| ☐ N154UP | Airbus A300F4-622R | 840 | |
| ☐ N155UP | Airbus A300F4-622R | 841 | |
| ☐ N | Airbus A300F4-622R | 845 | |
| ☐ N | Airbus A300F4-622R | 846 | |
| ☐ N | Airbus A300F4-622R | 847 | |

| | | | |
|---|---|---|---|
| ☐ N211UP | Boeing 727-247F | 1489/21700 | |
| ☐ N212UP | Boeing 727-247F | 1305/21392 | |
| ☐ N902UP | Boeing 727-51C | 244/18898 | |
| ☐ N903UP | Boeing 727-51C | 263/18945 | |
| ☐ N904UP | Boeing 727-51C | 274/18946 | |
| ☐ N905UP | Boeing 727-51C | 286/18947 | |
| ☐ N906UP | Boeing 727-30C | 437/19314 | |
| ☐ N907UP | Boeing 727-27C | 379/19118 | |
| ☐ N908UP | Boeing 727-27C | 312/19114 | |
| ☐ N909UP | Boeing 727-27C | 328/19115 | |
| ☐ N910UP | Boeing 727-27C | 376/19117 | |
| ☐ N911UP | Boeing 727-27C | 393/19119 | |
| ☐ N912UP | Boeing 727-62C | 338/19244 | |
| ☐ N913UP | Boeing 727-62C | 342/19245 | |
| ☐ N914UP | Boeing 727-62C | 423/19246 | |
| ☐ N915UP | Boeing 727-27C | 475/19533 | |
| ☐ N916UP | Boeing 727-172C | 615/19808 | |
| ☐ N917UP | Boeing 727-30C | 395/19310 | |
| ☐ N918UP | Boeing 727-30C | 364/19008 | |
| ☐ N919UP | Boeing 727-30C | 391/19012 | |
| ☐ N920UP | Boeing 727-180C | 604/19873 | |
| ☐ N921UP | Boeing 727-180C | 534/19874 | |
| ☐ N922UP | Boeing 727-31C | 404/19231 | |
| ☐ N923UP | Boeing 727-31C | 390/19229 | |
| ☐ N924UP | Boeing 727-31C | 463/19234 | |
| ☐ N925UP | Boeing 727-31C | 402/19230 | |
| ☐ N926UP | Boeing 727-31C | 458/19233 | Lst SRR |
| ☐ N927UP | Boeing 727-31C | 425/19232 | Lst SRR |
| ☐ N928UP | Boeing 727-22C | 280/19091 | |
| ☐ N929UP | Boeing 727-22C | 291/19092 | |
| ☐ N930UP | Boeing 727-22C | 305/19096 | |
| ☐ N931UP | Boeing 727-25C | 645/19858 | |
| ☐ N932UP | Boeing 727-25C | 635/19856 | |
| ☐ N933UP | Boeing 727-25C | 641/19857 | |
| ☐ N934UP | Boeing 727-21C | 301/19135 | |
| ☐ N935UP | Boeing 727-1A7C | 619/20143 | |
| ☐ N936UP | Boeing 727-108C | 420/19503 | |
| ☐ N937UP | Boeing 727-25QC | 354/19302 | |
| ☐ N938UP | Boeing 727-173C | 447/19506 | |
| ☐ N939UP | Boeing 727-27C | 469/19532 | |
| ☐ N940UP | Boeing 727-185C | 546/19826 | |
| ☐ N941UP | Boeing 727-22C | 407/19196 | |
| ☐ N942UP | Boeing 727-22C | 333/19101 | |
| ☐ N943UP | Boeing 727-22C | 336/19102 | Lst SRR |
| ☐ N944UP | Boeing 727-22C | 341/19103 | Lst SRR |
| ☐ N945UP | Boeing 727-22C | 295/19094 | |
| ☐ N946UP | Boeing 727-25C | 490/19721 | |
| ☐ N947UP | Boeing 727-25C | 493/19722 | |
| ☐ N948UP | Boeing 727-25C | 360/19357 | |
| ☐ N949UP | Boeing 727-25C | 468/19717 | |
| ☐ N950UP | Boeing 727-25C | 474/19718 | |
| ☐ N951UP | Boeing 727-25C | 497/19850 | |
| ☐ N954UP | Boeing 727-185C | 527/19827 | |

| | | | |
|---|---|---|---|
| ☐ N520UP | Boeing 747-212SF | 475/21943 | |
| ☐ N521UP | Boeing 747-212SF | 510/21944 | |
| ☐ N522UP | Boeing 747-237SF | 401/21936 | |
| ☐ N523UP | Boeing 747-283SF | 500/22381 | |
| ☐ N524UP | Boeing 747-237SF | 318/21446 | |
| ☐ N525UP | Boeing 747-212SF | 449/21939 | |
| ☐ N526UP | Boeing 747-212SF | /21937 | |
| ☐ N527UP | Boeing 747-259B (SCD) | 372/21730 | |
| ☐ N528UP | Boeing 747-256M | 699/24071 | |
| ☐ N671UP | Boeing 747-123SF | 115/20323 | |
| ☐ N672UP | Boeing 747-123SF | 119/20324 | |

| | | |
|---|---|---|
| ☐ N673UP | Boeing 747-123SF | 125/20325 |
| ☐ N674UP | Boeing 747-123SF | 46/20100 |
| ☐ N675UP | Boeing 747-123SF | 136/20390 |
| ☐ N676UP | Boeing 747-123SF | 57/20101 |
| ☐ N677UP | Boeing 747-123SF | 143/20391 |
| ☐ N680UP | Boeing 747SR-46SF | 234/20923 |
| ☐ N681UP | Boeing 747-121SF | 70/19661 |
| ☐ N682UP | Boeing 747-121SF | 110/20349 |
| ☐ N683UP | Boeing 747-121SF | 131/20353 |
| | | |
| ☐ N401UP | Boeing 757-24APF | 139/23723 |
| ☐ N402UP | Boeing 757-24APF | 141/23724 |
| ☐ N403UP | Boeing 757-24APF | 143/23725 |
| ☐ N404UP | Boeing 757-24APF | 147/23726 |
| ☐ N405UP | Boeing 757-24APF | 149/23727 |
| ☐ N406UP | Boeing 757-24APF | 176/23728 |
| ☐ N407UP | Boeing 757-24APF | 181/23729 |
| ☐ N408UP | Boeing 757-24APF | 184/23730 |
| ☐ N409UP | Boeing 757-24APF | 186/23731 |
| ☐ N410UP | Boeing 757-24APF | 189/23732 |
| ☐ N411UP | Boeing 757-24APF | 191/23851 |
| ☐ N412UP | Boeing 757-24APF | 193/23852 |
| ☐ N413UP | Boeing 757-24APF | 195/23853 |
| ☐ N414UP | Boeing 757-24APF | 197/23854 |
| ☐ N415UP | Boeing 757-24APF | 199/23855 |
| ☐ N416UP | Boeing 757-24APF | 318/23903 |
| ☐ N417UP | Boeing 757-24APF | 322/23904 |
| ☐ N418UP | Boeing 757-24APF | 326/23905 |
| ☐ N419UP | Boeing 757-24APF | 330/23906 |
| ☐ N420UP | Boeing 757-24APF | 334/23907 |
| ☐ N421UP | Boeing 757-24APF | 395/25281 |
| ☐ N422UP | Boeing 757-24APF | 399/25324 |
| ☐ N423UP | Boeing 757-24APF | 403/25325 |
| ☐ N424UP | Boeing 757-24APF | 407/25369 |
| ☐ N425UP | Boeing 757-24APF | 411/25370 |
| ☐ N426UP | Boeing 757-24APF | 477/25457 |
| ☐ N427UP | Boeing 757-24APF | 481/25458 |
| ☐ N428UP | Boeing 757-24APF | 485/25459 |
| ☐ N429UP | Boeing 757-24APF | 489/25460 |
| ☐ N430UP | Boeing 757-24APF | 493/25461 |
| ☐ N431UP | Boeing 757-24APF | 569/25462 Lst SRR |
| ☐ N432UP | Boeing 757-24APF | 573/25463 Lst SRR |
| ☐ N433UP | Boeing 757-24APF | 577/25464 Lst SRR |
| ☐ N434UP | Boeing 757-24APF | 579/25465 Lst SRR |
| ☐ N435UP | Boeing 757-24APF | 581/25466 |
| ☐ N436UP | Boeing 757-24APF | 625/25467 |
| ☐ N437UP | Boeing 757-24APF | 628/25468 |
| ☐ N438UP | Boeing 757-24APF | 631/25469 |
| ☐ N439UP | Boeing 757-24APF | 634/25470 |
| ☐ N440UP | Boeing 757-24APF | 636/25471 |
| ☐ N441UP | Boeing 757-24APF | 638/27386 |
| ☐ N442UP | Boeing 757-24APF | 640/27387 |
| ☐ N443UP | Boeing 757-24APF | 642/27388 |
| ☐ N444UP | Boeing 757-24APF | 644/27389 |
| ☐ N445UP | Boeing 757-24APF | 646/27390 |
| ☐ N446UP | Boeing 757-24APF | 649/27735 |
| ☐ N447UP | Boeing 757-24APF | 651/27736 |
| ☐ N448UP | Boeing 757-24APF | 654/27737 |
| ☐ N449UP | Boeing 757-24APF | 656/27738 |
| ☐ N450UP | Boeing 757-24APF | 659/25472 |
| ☐ N451UP | Boeing 757-24APF | 675/27739 |
| ☐ N452UP | Boeing 757-24APF | 679/25473 |
| ☐ N453UP | Boeing 757-24APF | 683/25474 |
| ☐ N454UP | Boeing 757-24APF | 687/25475 |
| ☐ N455UP | Boeing 757-24APF | 691/25476 |
| ☐ N456UP | Boeing 757-24APF | 728/25477 |
| ☐ N457UP | Boeing 757-24APF | 729/25478 |
| ☐ N458UP | Boeing 757-24APF | 730/25479 |
| ☐ N459UP | Boeing 757-24APF | 733/25480 |
| ☐ N460UP | Boeing 757-24APF | 734/25481 |
| ☐ N461UP | Boeing 757-24APF | 755/28265 |
| ☐ N462UP | Boeing 757-24APF | 759/28266 |
| ☐ N463UP | Boeing 757-24APF | 763/28267 |
| ☐ N464UP | Boeing 757-24APF | 765/28268 |
| ☐ N465UP | Boeing 757-24APF | 767/28269 |
| ☐ N466UP | Boeing 757-24APF | 769/25482 |
| ☐ N467UP | Boeing 757-24APF | 771/25483 |
| ☐ N468UP | Boeing 757-24APF | 774/25484 |
| | | |
| ☐ N469UP | Boeing 757-24APF | 776/25485 |
| ☐ N470UP | Boeing 757-24APF | 778/25486 |
| ☐ N471UP | Boeing 757-24APF | 813/28842 |
| ☐ N472UP | Boeing 757-24APF | 815/28843 |
| ☐ N473UP | Boeing 757-24APF | 823/28846 |
| ☐ N474UP | Boeing 757-24APF | 879/28844 |
| ☐ N475UP | Boeing 757-24APF | 882/28845 |
| | | |
| ☐ N301UP | Boeing 767-34AFER | 580/27239 |
| ☐ N302UP | Boeing 767-34AFER | 590/27240 |
| ☐ N303UP | Boeing 767-34AFER | 594/27241 |
| ☐ N304UP | Boeing 767-34AFER | 598/27242 |
| ☐ N305UP | Boeing 767-34AFER | 600/27243 |
| ☐ N306UP | Boeing 767-34AFER | 622/27759 |
| ☐ N307UP | Boeing 767-34AFER | 624/27760 |
| ☐ N308UP | Boeing 767-34AFER | 626/27761 |
| ☐ N309UP | Boeing 767-34AFER | 628/27740 |
| ☐ N310UP | Boeing 767-34AFER | 630/27762 |
| ☐ N311UP | Boeing 767-34AFER | 632/27741 |
| ☐ N312UP | Boeing 767-34AFER | 634/27763 |
| ☐ N313UP | Boeing 767-34AFER | 636/27764 |
| ☐ N314UP | Boeing 767-34AFER | 638/27742 |
| ☐ N315UP | Boeing 767-34AFER | 640/27743 |
| ☐ N316UP | Boeing 767-34AFER | 660/27744 |
| ☐ N317UP | Boeing 767-34AFER | 666/27745 |
| ☐ N318UP | Boeing 767-34AFER | 670/27746 |
| ☐ N319UP | Boeing 767-34AFER | 672/27758 |
| ☐ N320UP | Boeing 767-34AFER | 674/27747 |
| ☐ N322UP | Boeing 767-34AFER | 678/27748 |
| ☐ N323UP | Boeing 767-34AFER | 682/27749 |
| ☐ N324UP | Boeing 767-34AFER | 724/27750 |
| ☐ N325UP | Boeing 767-34AFER | 726/27751 |
| ☐ N326UP | Boeing 767-34AFER | 728/27752 |
| ☐ N327UP | Boeing 767-34AFER | 730/27753 |
| ☐ N328UP | Boeing 767-34AFER | 732/27754 |
| ☐ N329UP | Boeing 767-34AFER | 756/27755 |
| ☐ N330UP | Boeing 767-34AFER | 760/27756 |
| ☐ N331UP | Boeing 767-34AFER | 764/27757 |
| ☐ N332UP | Boeing 767-34AFER | 854/32843 |
| ☐ N334UP | Boeing 767-34AFER | 858/32844 |
| | | |
| ☐ N700UP | Douglas DC-8-71CF | 316/45900 |
| ☐ N701UP | Douglas DC-8-71CF | 331/45938 |
| ☐ N702UP | Douglas DC-8-71CF | 294/45902 |
| ☐ N703UP | Douglas DC-8-71CF | 351/45939 |
| ☐ N705UP | Douglas DC-8-71CF | 329/45949 |
| ☐ N706UP | Douglas DC-8-71F | 495/46056 |
| ☐ N707UP | Douglas DC-8-71F | 288/45907 |
| ☐ N708UP | Douglas DC-8-71F | 450/46048 |
| ☐ N709UP | Douglas DC-8-71F | 292/45914 |
| ☐ N713UP | Douglas DC-8-71F | 400/46014 |
| ☐ N715UP | Douglas DC-8-71F | 295/45915 |
| ☐ N718UP | Douglas DC-8-71F | 420/46018 |
| ☐ N729UP | Douglas DC-8-71F | 425/46029 |
| ☐ N730UP | Douglas DC-8-71F | 426/46030 |
| ☐ N744UP | Douglas DC-8-71F | 326/45944 |
| ☐ N748UP | Douglas DC-8-71CF | 321/45948 |
| ☐ N750UP | Douglas DC-8-71CF | 354/45950 |
| ☐ N752UP | Douglas DC-8-71CF | 338/45952 |
| ☐ N755UP | Douglas DC-8-71F | 492/46055 |
| ☐ N772UP | Douglas DC-8-71F | 477/46072 |
| ☐ N779UP | Douglas DC-8-71F | 363/45979 |
| ☐ N797UP | Douglas DC-8-71CF | 313/45897 |
| ☐ N798UP | Douglas DC-8-71CF | 320/45898 |
| ☐ N801UP | Douglas DC-8-73CF | 489/46101 |
| ☐ N802UP | Douglas DC-8-73AF | 502/46100 |
| ☐ N803UP | Douglas DC-8-73CF | 485/46073 |
| ☐ N804UP | Douglas DC-8-73AF | 403/46004 |
| ☐ N805UP | Douglas DC-8-73CF | 525/46117 |
| ☐ N806UP | Douglas DC-8-73AF | 413/46006 |
| ☐ N807UP | Douglas DC-8-73AF | 422/46007 |
| ☐ N808UP | Douglas DC-8-73AF | 423/46008 |
| ☐ N809UP | Douglas DC-8-73CF | 493/46109 |
| ☐ N810UP | Douglas DC-8-73CF | 395/46001 |
| ☐ N811UP | Douglas DC-8-73CF | 501/46089 |
| ☐ N812UP | Douglas DC-8-73CF | 520/46112 |
| ☐ N813UP | Douglas DC-8-73CF | 456/46059 |
| ☐ N814UP | Douglas DC-8-73CF | 504/46090 |

| | | | |
|---|---|---|---|
| ☐ N818UP | Douglas DC-8-73CF | 522/46108 | |
| ☐ N819UP | Douglas DC-8-73F | 411/46019 | |
| ☐ N836UP | Douglas DC-8-73CF | 344/45936 | |
| ☐ N840UP | Douglas DC-8-73CF | 528/46140 | |
| ☐ N851UP | Douglas DC-8-73CF | 440/46051 | |
| ☐ N852UP | Douglas DC-8-73CF | 442/46052 | |
| ☐ N866UP | Douglas DC-8-73CF | 393/45966 | |
| ☐ N867UP | Douglas DC-8-73CF | 385/45967 | |
| ☐ N868UP | Douglas DC-8-73CF | 389/45968 | |
| ☐ N874UP | Douglas DC-8-73PF | 468/46074 | |
| ☐ N880UP | Douglas DC-8-73F | 466/46080 | |
| ☐ N894UP | Douglas DC-8-73CF | 482/46094 | |
| | | | |
| ☐ N250UP | McDD MD-11F | 596/48745 | |
| ☐ N251UP | McDD MD-11F | 592/48744 | |
| ☐ N252UP | McDD MD-11 | 601/48768 | |
| ☐ N253UP | McDD MD-11F | 554/48439 | |
| ☐ N254UP | McDD MD-11F | 547/48406 | |
| ☐ N270UP | McDD MD-11F | 574/48576 | |
| ☐ N271UP | McDD MD-11F | 556/48572 | |
| ☐ N272UP | McDD MD-11F | 552/48571 | |
| ☐ N273UP | McDD MD-11F | 566/48574 | |
| ☐ N | McDD MD-11F | 559/48573 | |
| ☐ N | McDD MD-11F | 568/48575 | |
| ☐ N | McDD MD-11F | 583/48577 | |
| ☐ N | McDD MD-11F | 588/48578 | |
| ☐ N | McDD MD-11F | 599/48579 | |
| ☐ N | McDD MD-11F | 610/48774 | |

## US AIRWAYS                                       USA

| | | | |
|---|---|---|---|
| ☐ N700UW | Airbus A319-112 | 0885 | |
| ☐ N701UW | Airbus A319-112 | 0890 | |
| ☐ N702UW | Airbus A319-112 | 0896 | |
| ☐ N703UW | Airbus A319-112 | 0904 | |
| ☐ N704US | Airbus A319-112 | 0922 | |
| ☐ N705UW | Airbus A319-112 | 0929 | |
| ☐ N706US | Airbus A319-112 | 0946 | |
| ☐ N707UW | Airbus A319-112 | 0949 | |
| ☐ N708UW | Airbus A319-112 | 0972 | |
| ☐ N709UW | Airbus A319-112 | 0997 | |
| ☐ N710UW | Airbus A319-112 | 1019 | |
| ☐ N711UW | Airbus A319-112 | 1033 | |
| ☐ N712US | Airbus A319-112 | 1038 | |
| ☐ N713UW | Airbus A319-112 | 1040 | |
| ☐ N714US | Airbus A319-112 | 1046 | |
| ☐ N715UW | Airbus A319-112 | 1051 | |
| ☐ N716UW | Airbus A319-112 | 1055 | |
| ☐ N717UW | Airbus A319-112 | 1069 | |
| ☐ N718UW | Airbus A319-112 | 1077 | |
| ☐ N719US | Airbus A319-112 | 1084 | |
| ☐ N720US | Airbus A319-112 | 1089 | |
| ☐ N721UW | Airbus A319-112 | 1095 | |
| ☐ N722UW | Airbus A319-112 | 1097 | |
| ☐ N723UW | Airbus A319-112 | 1109 | |
| ☐ N724UW | Airbus A319-112 | 1122 | |
| ☐ N725UW | Airbus A319-112 | 1135 | |
| ☐ N726US | Airbus A319-112 | 1136 | std |
| ☐ N727UW | Airbus A319-112 | 1147 | std |
| ☐ N728UW | Airbus A319-112 | 1155 | |
| ☐ N729US | Airbus A319-112 | 1170 | std |
| ☐ N730US | Airbus A319-112 | 1182 | |
| ☐ N732US | Airbus A319-112 | 1203 | std |
| ☐ N733UW | Airbus A319-112 | 1205 | |
| ☐ N736US | Airbus A319-112 | 1209 | |
| ☐ N737US | Airbus A319-112 | 1245 | |
| ☐ N738US | Airbus A319-112 | 1254 | |
| ☐ N739US | Airbus A319-112 | 1263 | |
| ☐ N740UW | Airbus A319-112 | 1265 | |
| ☐ N741UW | Airbus A319-112 | 1269 | |
| ☐ N742US | Airbus A319-112 | 1275 | std |
| ☐ N743UW | Airbus A319-112 | 1277 | |
| ☐ N744US | Airbus A319-112 | 1287 | |
| ☐ N745UW | Airbus A319-112 | 1289 | |
| ☐ N746UW | Airbus A319-112 | 1297 | std |
| ☐ N747UW | Airbus A319-112 | 1301 | |
| ☐ N748UW | Airbus A319-112 | 1311 | |
| ☐ N749US | Airbus A319-112 | 1313 | |

| | | | |
|---|---|---|---|
| ☐ N750UW | Airbus A319-112 | 1315 | |
| ☐ N751UW | Airbus A319-112 | 1317 | |
| ☐ N752US | Airbus A319-112 | 1319 | |
| ☐ N753US | Airbus A319-112 | 1326 | |
| ☐ N754UW | Airbus A319-112 | 1328 | |
| ☐ N755US | Airbus A319-112 | 1331 | |
| ☐ N756US | Airbus A319-112 | 1340 | |
| ☐ N757UW | Airbus A319-112 | 1342 | |
| ☐ N758US | Airbus A319-112 | 1348 | |
| ☐ N760US | Airbus A319-112 | 1354 | |
| ☐ N762US | Airbus A319-112 | 1358 | |
| ☐ N763US | Airbus A319-112 | 1360 | |
| ☐ N764US | Airbus A319-112 | 1369 | std |
| ☐ N765US | Airbus A319-112 | 1371 | |
| ☐ N766US | Airbus A319-112 | 1378 | |
| ☐ N767UW | Airbus A319-112 | 1382 | std |
| ☐ N768US | Airbus A319-112 | 1389 | |
| ☐ N769US | Airbus A319-112 | 1391 | |
| ☐ N770UW | Airbus A319-112 | 1393 | std |
| ☐ N771UW | Airbus A319-112 | 1668 | o/o |
| ☐ N772UW | Airbus A319-112 | | o/o |
| ☐ N773US | Airbus A319-112 | | o/o |
| ☐ N774US | Airbus A319-112 | | o/o |
| ☐ N775UW | Airbus A319-112 | | o/o |
| | | | |
| ☐ N101UW | Airbus A320-214 | 0936 | |
| ☐ N102UW | Airbus A320-214 | 0844 | |
| ☐ N103US | Airbus A320-214 | 0861 | |
| ☐ N104UW | Airbus A320-214 | 0863 | |
| ☐ N105UW | Airbus A320-214 | 0868 | |
| ☐ N106US | Airbus A320-214 | 1044 | |
| ☐ N107US | Airbus A320-214 | 1052 | |
| ☐ N108UW | Airbus A320-214 | 1061 | |
| ☐ N109UW | Airbus A320-214 | 1065 | |
| ☐ N110UW | Airbus A320-214 | 1112 | |
| ☐ N111US | Airbus A320-214 | 1114 | |
| ☐ N112US | Airbus A320-214 | 1134 | |
| ☐ N113UW | Airbus A320-214 | 1141 | |
| ☐ N114UW | Airbus A320-214 | 1148 | |
| ☐ N115US | Airbus A320-214 | 1171 | |
| ☐ N116US | Airbus A320-214 | 1210 | |
| ☐ N117UW | Airbus A320-214 | 1224 | |
| ☐ N118US | Airbus A320-214 | 1264 | |
| ☐ N119US | Airbus A320-214 | 1268 | |
| ☐ N120US | Airbus A320-214 | 1286 | |
| ☐ N121UW | Airbus A320-214 | 1294 | |
| ☐ N122US | Airbus A320-214 | 1298 | |
| ☐ N123UW | Airbus A320-214 | 1310 | |
| ☐ N124US | Airbus A320-214 | 1314 | |
| ☐ N125US | Airbus A320-214 | | o/o |
| ☐ N126US | Airbus A320-214 | 1694 | o/o |
| ☐ N127US | Airbus A320-214 | | o/o |
| ☐ N128US | Airbus A320-214 | | o/o |
| ☐ N129US | Airbus A320-214 | | o/o |
| ☐ N130US | Airbus A320-214 | | o/o |
| ☐ N131US | Airbus A320-214 | | o/o |
| ☐ N132US | Airbus A320-214 | | o/o |
| ☐ N133US | Airbus A320-214 | | o/o |
| | | | |
| ☐ N161UW | Airbus A321-211 | 1403 | |
| ☐ N162UW | Airbus A321-211 | 1412 | |
| ☐ N163US | Airbus A321-211 | 1417 | |
| ☐ N164UW | Airbus A321-211 | 1425 | |
| ☐ N165US | Airbus A321-211 | 1431 | |
| ☐ N166US | Airbus A321-211 | 1436 | std |
| ☐ N167US | Airbus A321-211 | 1442 | |
| ☐ N168US | Airbus A321-211 | 1447 | |
| ☐ N169UW | Airbus A321-211 | 1455 | |
| ☐ N170US | Airbus A321-211 | 1462 | |
| ☐ N171US | Airbus A321-211 | 1465 | |
| ☐ N172US | Airbus A321-211 | 1472 | |
| ☐ N173US | Airbus A321-211 | 1481 | |
| ☐ N174US | Airbus A321-211 | 1492 | |
| ☐ N175US | Airbus A321-211 | 1496 | |
| ☐ N176US | Airbus A321-211 | 1499 | |
| ☐ N177US | Airbus A321-211 | 1517 | |
| ☐ N178US | Airbus A321-211 | 1519 | |
| ☐ N179UW | Airbus A321-211 | 1521 | std |

| Reg | Type | Serial | Note |
|---|---|---|---|
| N180US | Airbus A321-211 | 1525 | |
| N181UW | Airbus A321-211 | 1531 | |
| N182UW | Airbus A321-211 | 1536 | |
| N183UW | Airbus A321-211 | 1539 | |
| N184US | Airbus A321-211 | 1651 | |
| N185UW | Airbus A321-211 | 1666 | |
| N186US | Airbus A321-211 | 1701 | |
| N187US | Airbus A321-211 | 1704 | |
| N188US | Airbus A321-211 | 1724 | |
| N670UW | Airbus A330-323X | 315 | |
| N671UW | Airbus A330-323X | 323 | |
| N672UW | Airbus A330-323X | 333 | |
| N673UW | Airbus A330-323X | 337 | |
| N674UW | Airbus A330-323X | 342 | |
| N675US | Airbus A330-323X | 370 | |
| N676UW | Airbus A330-323X | 375 | |
| N677UW | Airbus A330-323X | 380 | |
| N678US | Airbus A330-323X | 388 | |
| N679US | Airbus A330-323X | | |
| N300AU | Boeing 737-301 | 1103/23228 | |
| N334US | Boeing 737-301 | 1164/23231 | std |
| N335US | Boeing 737-301 | 1169/23232 | |
| N340US | Boeing 737-301 | 1222/23237 | std |
| N341US | Boeing 737-301 | 1248/23510 | |
| N342US | Boeing 737-301 | 1268/23511 | |
| N346US | Boeing 737-301 | 1355/23515 | std |
| N349US | Boeing 737-301 | 1382/23552 | std |
| N350US | Boeing 737-301 | 1406/23553 | |
| N351US | Boeing 737-301 | 1408/23554 | std |
| N352US | Boeing 737-301 | 1428/23555 | std |
| N353US | Boeing 737-301 | 1435/23556 | |
| N354US | Boeing 737-301 | 1437/23557 | |
| N355US | Boeing 737-301 | 1449/23558 | std |
| N356US | Boeing 737-301 | 1451/23559 | std |
| N371US | Boeing 737-3B7 | 1001/22950 | |
| N373US | Boeing 737-3B7 | 1015/22952 | |
| N374US | Boeing 737-3B7 | 1022/22953 | |
| N375US | Boeing 737-3B7 | 1030/22954 | |
| N376US | Boeing 737-3B7 | 1043/22955 | |
| N383US | Boeing 737-3B7 | 1057/22956 | |
| N384US | Boeing 737-3B7 | 1127/22957 | |
| N385US | Boeing 737-3B7 | 1137/22958 | |
| N387US | Boeing 737-3B7 | 1140/22959 | |
| N389US | Boeing 737-3B7 | 1149/23311 | |
| N390US | Boeing 737-3B7 | 1162/23312 | std |
| N391US | Boeing 737-3B7 | 1177/23313 | |
| N392US | Boeing 737-3B7 | 1179/23314 | |
| N393US | Boeing 737-3B7 | 1210/23315 | |
| N394US | Boeing 737-3B7 | 1212/23316 | |
| N395US | Boeing 737-3B7 | 1221/23317 | |
| N396US | Boeing 737-3B7 | 1234/23318 | |
| N397US | Boeing 737-3B7 | 1250/23319 | |
| N504AU | Boeing 737-3B7 | 1362/23379 | |
| N505AU | Boeing 737-3B7 | 1366/23380 | |
| N506AU | Boeing 737-3B7 | 1394/23381 | std |
| N511AU | Boeing 737-3B7 | 1442/23594 | |
| N512AU | Boeing 737-3B7 | 1450/23595 | |
| N514AU | Boeing 737-3B7 | 1461/23700 | |
| N515AU | Boeing 737-3B7 | 1464/23701 | |
| N516AU | Boeing 737-3B7 | 1475/23702 | |
| N517AU | Boeing 737-3B7 | 1480/23703 | |
| N518AU | Boeing 737-3B7 | 1488/23704 | std |
| N519AU | Boeing 737-3B7 | 1497/23705 | |
| N520AU | Boeing 737-3B7 | 1499/23706 | |
| N521AU | Boeing 737-3B7 | 1501/23856 | |
| N522AU | Boeing 737-3B7 | 1503/23857 | |
| N523AU | Boeing 737-3B7 | 1509/23858 | |
| N524AU | Boeing 737-3B7 | 1551/23859 | |
| N525AU | Boeing 737-3B7 | 1560/23860 | |
| N526AU | Boeing 737-3B7 | 1584/23861 | |
| N527AU | Boeing 737-3B7 | 1586/23862 | std |
| N528AU | Boeing 737-3B7 | 1703/24410 | |
| N529AU | Boeing 737-3B7 | 1713/24411 | |
| N530AU | Boeing 737-3B7 | 1735/24412 | |
| N531AU | Boeing 737-3B7 | 1743/24478 | |
| N532AU | Boeing 737-3B7 | 1745/24479 | |
| N533AU | Boeing 737-3B7 | 1767/24515 | |
| N534AU | Boeing 737-3B7 | 1769/24516 | std |
| N558AU | Boeing 737-301 | 1291/23512 | |
| N559AU | Boeing 737-301 | 1327/23513 | std |
| N560AU | Boeing 737-301 | 1331/23514 | |
| N562AU | Boeing 737-301 | 1367/23550 | std |
| N563AU | Boeing 737-301 | 1380/23551 | std |
| N573US | Boeing 737-301 | 1463/23560 | |
| N574US | Boeing 737-301 | 1469/23739 | |
| N575US | Boeing 737-301 | 1477/23740 | std |
| N576US | Boeing 737-301 | 1498/23741 | |
| N577US | Boeing 737-301 | 1502/23742 | |
| N584US | Boeing 737-301 | 1510/23743 | |
| N585US | Boeing 737-301 | 1539/23930 | |
| N586US | Boeing 737-301 | 1552/23931 | |
| N587US | Boeing 737-301 | 1554/23932 | |
| N588US | Boeing 737-301 | 1559/23933 | |
| N589US | Boeing 737-301 | 1563/23934 | |
| N590US | Boeing 737-301 | 1569/23935 | |
| N591US | Boeing 737-301 | 1575/23936 | |
| N592US | Boeing 737-301 | 1587/23937 | |
| N404US | Boeing 737-401 | 1487/23886 | std |
| N405US | Boeing 737-401 | 1512/23885 | std |
| N406US | Boeing 737-401 | 1528/23876 | |
| N407US | Boeing 737-401 | 1543/23877 | std |
| N408US | Boeing 737-401 | 1561/23878 | std |
| N409US | Boeing 737-401 | 1573/23879 | std |
| N411US | Boeing 737-401 | 1596/23880 | std |
| N412US | Boeing 737-401 | 1610/23881 | std |
| N413US | Boeing 737-401 | 1621/23882 | std |
| N415US | Boeing 737-401 | 1631/23883 | std |
| N417US | Boeing 737-401 | 1674/23984 | |
| N418US | Boeing 737-401 | 1676/23985 | |
| N419US | Boeing 737-401 | 1684/23986 | |
| N420US | Boeing 737-401 | 1698/23987 | |
| N421US | Boeing 737-401 | 1714/23988 | |
| N422US | Boeing 737-401 | 1716/23989 | |
| N423US | Boeing 737-401 | 1732/23990 | |
| N424US | Boeing 737-401 | 1746/23991 | |
| N425US | Boeing 737-401 | 1764/23992 | |
| N426US | Boeing 737-4B7 | 1789/24548 | |
| N427US | Boeing 737-4B7 | 1791/24549 | |
| N428US | Boeing 737-4B7 | 1793/24550 | |
| N429US | Boeing 737-4B7 | 1795/24551 | |
| N430US | Boeing 737-4B7 | 1797/24552 | |
| N431US | Boeing 737-4B7 | 1799/24553 | std |
| N432US | Boeing 737-4B7 | 1817/24554 | |
| N433US | Boeing 737-4B7 | 1819/24555 | |
| N434US | Boeing 737-4B7 | 1821/24556 | |
| N435US | Boeing 737-4B7 | 1835/24557 | |
| N436US | Boeing 737-4B7 | 1845/24558 | |
| N437US | Boeing 737-4B7 | 1847/24559 | |
| N441US | Boeing 737-4B7 | 1892/24812 | |
| N442US | Boeing 737-4B7 | 1906/24841 | |
| N443US | Boeing 737-4B7 | 1908/24842 | std |
| N445US | Boeing 737-4B7 | 1914/24863 | |
| N446US | Boeing 737-4B7 | 1931/24873 | std |
| N447US | Boeing 737-4B7 | 1936/24874 | |
| N448US | Boeing 737-4B7 | 1944/24892 | |
| N449US | Boeing 737-4B7 | 1946/24893 | |
| N775AU | Boeing 737-4B7 | 1954/24933 | |
| N776AU | Boeing 737-4B7 | 1956/24934 | |
| N777AU | Boeing 737-4B7 | 1980/24979 | |
| N778AU | Boeing 737-4B7 | 1982/24980 | |
| N779AU | Boeing 737-4B7 | 1986/24996 | |
| N780AU | Boeing 737-4B7 | 1990/24997 | |
| N781AU | Boeing 737-4B7 | 1992/25020 | |
| N782AU | Boeing 737-4B7 | 1995/25021 | |
| N783AU | Boeing 737-4B7 | 2010/25022 | |
| N784AU | Boeing 737-4B7 | 2020/25023 | |
| N785AU | Boeing 737-4B7 | 2026/25024 | |
| N600AU | Boeing 757-225 | 3/22192 | |
| N601AU | Boeing 757-225 | 4/22193 | |
| N602AU | Boeing 757-225 | 7/22196 | |
| N603AU | Boeing 757-225 | 12/22198 | |
| N604AU | Boeing 757-225 | 17/22199 | |

| | | | |
|---|---|---|---|
| ☐ N605AU | Boeing 757-225 | 21/22201 | |
| ☐ N606AU | Boeing 757-225 | 22/22202 | |
| ☐ N607AU | Boeing 757-225 | 26/22203 | |
| ☐ N608AU | Boeing 757-225 | 27/22204 | |
| ☐ N609AU | Boeing 757-225 | 28/22205 | |
| ☐ N610AU | Boeing 757-2B7 | 525/27122 | |
| ☐ N611AU | Boeing 757-2B7 | 534/27123 | |
| ☐ N612AU | Boeing 757-2B7 | 540/27143 | |
| ☐ N613AU | Boeing 757-2B7 | 544/27144 | |
| ☐ N614AU | Boeing 757-2B7 | 546/27145 | |
| ☐ N615AU | Boeing 757-2B7 | 551/27146 | std |
| ☐ N616AU | Boeing 757-2B7 | 552/27147 | std |
| ☐ N617AU | Boeing 757-2B7 | 564/27148 | |
| ☐ N618AU | Boeing 757-225 | 42/22210 | |
| ☐ N619AU | Boeing 757-2B7 | 584/27198 | |
| ☐ N620AU | Boeing 757-2B7 | 586/27199 | |
| ☐ N621AU | Boeing 757-2B7 | 589/27200 | |
| ☐ N622AU | Boeing 757-2B7 | 605/27201 | |
| ☐ N623AU | Boeing 757-2B7 | 607/27244 | |
| ☐ N624AU | Boeing 757-2B7 | 630/27245 | |
| ☐ N625VJ | Boeing 757-2B7 | 643/27246 | |
| ☐ N626AU | Boeing 757-2B7 | 647/27303 | |
| ☐ N627AU | Boeing 757-2B7 | 655/27805 | |
| ☐ N628AU | Boeing 757-2B7 | 657/27806 | |
| ☐ N629AU | Boeing 757-2B7 | 662/27807 | |
| ☐ N630AU | Boeing 757-2B7 | 666/27808 | |
| ☐ N631AU | Boeing 757-2B7 | 673/27809 | |
| ☐ N632AU | Boeing 757-2B7 | 678/27810 | |
| ☐ N633AU | Boeing 757-2B7 | 681/27811 | |
| | | | |
| ☐ N645US | Boeing 767-201ER | 173/23897 | |
| ☐ N646US | Boeing 767-201ER | 175/23898 | |
| ☐ N647US | Boeing 767-201ER | 182/23899 | std |
| ☐ N648US | Boeing 767-201ER | 190/23900 | |
| ☐ N649US | Boeing 767-201ER | 197/23901 | |
| ☐ N650US | Boeing 767-201ER | 217/23902 | |
| ☐ N651US | Boeing 767-2B7ER | 306/24764 | |
| ☐ N652US | Boeing 767-2B7ER | 308/24765 | |
| ☐ N653US | Boeing 767-2B7ER | 338/24894 | |
| ☐ N655US | Boeing 767-2B7ER | 383/25257 | |
| ☐ N656US | Boeing 767-2B7ER | 486/26847 | |

## US AIRWAYS EXPRESS                                      USX

| | | |
|---|---|---|
| ☐ N550HK | BAe Jetstream 41 | 41039 |
| ☐ N553HK | BAe Jetstream 41 | 41066 |
| ☐ N554HK | BAe Jetstream 41 | 41067 |
| ☐ N555HK | BAe Jetstream 41 | 41072 |
| ☐ N556HK | BAe Jetstream 41 | 41073 |
| ☐ N558HK | BAe Jetstream 41 | 41071 |
| ☐ N559HK | BAe Jetstream 41 | 41075 |
| ☐ N562HK | BAe Jetstream 41 | 41078 |
| ☐ N563HK | BAe Jetstream 41 | 41079 |
| ☐ N564HK | BAe Jetstream 41 | 41081 |
| ☐ N572HK | BAe Jetstream 41 | 41091 |
| | | |
| ☐ N5YV | Beech 1900D | UE-5 |
| ☐ N6YV | Beech 1900D | UE-6 |
| ☐ N13ZV | Beech 1900D | UE-13 |
| ☐ N23YV | Beech 1900D | UE-23 |
| ☐ N62ZV | Beech 1900D | UE-62 |
| ☐ N64YV | Beech 1900D | UE-64 |
| ☐ N65YV | Beech 1900D | UE-65 |
| ☐ N67YV | Beech 1900D | UE-67 |
| ☐ N123YV | Beech 1900D | UE-123 |
| ☐ N126YV | Beech 1900D | UE-126 |
| ☐ N127ZV | Beech 1900D | UE-127 |
| ☐ N131YV | Beech 1900D | UE-131 |
| ☐ N133YV | Beech 1900D | UE-133 |
| ☐ N135YV | Beech 1900D | UE-135 |
| ☐ N138YV | Beech 1900D | UE-138 |
| ☐ N140ZV | Beech 1900D | UE-140 |
| ☐ N142ZV | Beech 1900D | UE-142 |
| ☐ N143YV | Beech 1900D | UE-143 |
| ☐ N144ZV | Beech 1900D | UE-144 |
| ☐ N146ZV | Beech 1900D | UE-146 |
| ☐ N155ZV | Beech 1900D | UE-155 |
| ☐ N159YV | Beech 1900D | UE-159 |

| | | | |
|---|---|---|---|
| ☐ N161YV | Beech 1900D | UE-161 | |
| ☐ N162ZV | Beech 1900D | UE-162 | |
| ☐ N165YV | Beech 1900D | UE-165 | |
| ☐ N167YV | Beech 1900D | UE-167 | |
| ☐ N173YV | Beech 1900D | UE-173 | |
| ☐ N190YV | Beech 1900D | UE-190 | |
| ☐ N218YV | Beech 1900D | UE-218 | |
| ☐ N3199Q | Beech 1900D | UE-213 | |
| ☐ N10675 | Beech 1900D | UE-229 | |
| | | | |
| ☐ N17156 | Canadair RJ-200 | 7156 | |
| ☐ N17175 | Canadair RJ-200 | 7175 | |
| ☐ N27172 | Canadair RJ-200 | 7172 | |
| ☐ N27173 | Canadair RJ-200 | 7173 | |
| ☐ N | Canadair RJ-200 | | o/o |
| ☐ N | Canadair RJ-200 | | o/o |
| ☐ N | Canadair RJ-200 | | o/o |
| ☐ N | Canadair RJ-200 | | o/o |
| ☐ N | Canadair RJ-200 | | o/o |
| | | | |
| ☐ EI-CHP | DHC-8-102A | 258 | |
| ☐ N326EN | DHC-8-311 | 234 | |
| ☐ N327EN | DHC-8-311A | 261 | |
| ☐ N328EN | DHC-8-311A | 281 | |
| ☐ N329EN | DHC-8-311 | 290 | |
| ☐ N330EN | DHC-8-311A | 274 | |
| ☐ N331EN | DHC-8-311A | 279 | |
| ☐ N336EN | DHC-8-311A | 336 | |
| ☐ N337EN | DHC-8-311A | 284 | |
| ☐ N342EN | DHC-8-311A | 395 | |
| ☐ N343EN | DHC-8-311A | 340 | |
| ☐ N434YV | DHC-8-202 | 434 | |
| ☐ N444YV | DHC-8Q-202 | 444 | |
| ☐ N447YV | DHC-8Q-202 | 447 | |
| ☐ N448YV | DHC-8Q-202 | 448 | |
| ☐ N803SA | DHC-8-311 | 221 | |
| ☐ N804EX | DHC-8-102A | 227 | |
| ☐ N805EX | DHC-8-102A | 228 | |
| ☐ N806EX | DHC-8-102A | 263 | |
| ☐ N807EX | DHC-8-102A | 292 | |
| ☐ N808EX | DHC-8-102A | 299 | |
| ☐ N809EX | DHC-8-102A | 302 | |
| ☐ N810EX | DHC-8-102A | 308 | |
| ☐ N811AW | DHC-8-102A | 201 | |
| ☐ N812EX | DHC-8-102A | 312 | |
| ☐ N814EX | DHC-8-102A | 318 | |
| ☐ N815EX | DHC-8-102A | 321 | |
| ☐ N816EX | DHC-8-102A | 329 | |
| ☐ N817EX | DHC-8-102A | 191 | |
| ☐ N818EX | DHC-8-102A | 235 | |
| ☐ N819EX | DHC-8-102 | 016 | |
| ☐ N820EX | DHC-8-102 | 019 | |
| ☐ N821EX | DHC-8-102 | 173 | |
| ☐ N822EX | DHC-8-102 | 187 | |
| ☐ N824EX | DHC-8-102 | 387 | |
| ☐ N825EX | DHC-8-102A | 388 | |
| ☐ N826EX | DHC-8-102A | 389 | |
| ☐ N827EX | DHC-8-102A | 390 | |
| ☐ N828EX | DHC-8-102A | 392 | |
| ☐ N829EX | DHC-8-102 | 146 | |
| ☐ N830EX | DHC-8-102 | 155 | |
| ☐ N831EX | DHC-8-102 | 160 | |
| ☐ N832EX | DHC-8-102A | 280 | |
| ☐ N833EX | DHC-8-102A | 282 | |
| ☐ N834EX | DHC-8-102A | 285 | |
| ☐ N835EX | DHC-8-102A | 289 | |
| ☐ N836EX | DHC-8-102A | 297 | |
| ☐ N837EX | DHC-8-102A | 217 | |
| ☐ N838EX | DHC-8-102A | 220 | |
| ☐ N839EX | DHC-8-102A | 226 | |
| ☐ N840EX | DHC-8-102A | 327 | |
| ☐ N841EX | DHC-8-102A | 249 | |
| ☐ N842EX | DHC-8-102 | 341 | |
| ☐ N843EX | DHC-8-102 | 335 | |
| ☐ N844EX | DHC-8-102A | 339 | |
| ☐ N845EX | DHC-8-102 | 344 | |
| ☐ N846EX | DHC-8-102A | 326 | |
| ☐ N847EX | DHC-8-102A | 333 | |
| ☐ N848EX | DHC-8-102A | 331 | |

| Reg | Type | Serial |
|---|---|---|
| ☐ N849EX | DHC-8-102A | 337 |
| ☐ N906HA | DHC-8-102 | 009 |
| ☐ N907HA | DHC-8-102 | 011 |
| ☐ N908HA | DHC-8-102 | 015 |
| ☐ N910HA | DHC-8-102 | 022 |
| ☐ N911HA | DHC-8-102 | 034 |
| ☐ N912HA | DHC-8-102 | 040 |
| ☐ N914HA | DHC-8-102 | 053 |
| ☐ N915HA | DHC-8-102 | 069 |
| ☐ N916HA | DHC-8-102 | 072 |
| ☐ N917HA | DHC-8-102 | 075 |
| ☐ N920HA | DHC-8-102 | 084 |
| ☐ N921HA | DHC-8-102 | 089 |
| ☐ N923HA | DHC-8-102 | 099 |
| ☐ N925HA | DHC-8-102 | 111 |
| ☐ N926HA | DHC-8-102 | 114 |
| ☐ N927HA | DHC-8-102 | 117 |
| ☐ N928HA | DHC-8-102 | 120 |
| ☐ N930HA | DHC-8-102 | 126 |
| ☐ N931HA | DHC-8-102 | 132 |
| ☐ N933HA | DHC-8-102 | 134 |
| ☐ N934HA | DHC-8-102 | 139 |
| ☐ N935HA | DHC-8-102 | 142 |
| ☐ N936HA | DHC-8-102 | 145 |
| ☐ N937HA | DHC-8-102 | 148 |
| ☐ N938HA | DHC-8-102 | 152 |
| ☐ N940HA | DHC-8-102 | 156 |
| ☐ N941HA | DHC-8-102 | 161 |
| ☐ N942HA | DHC-8-102 | 163 |
| ☐ N943HA | DHC-8-102 | 167 |
| ☐ N964HA | DHC-8-102 | 343 |
| ☐ N965HA | DHC-8Q-202 | 450 |
| ☐ N966HA | DHC-8Q-202 | 452 |
| ☐ N968HA | DHC-8Q-202 | 465 |
| ☐ N969HA | DHC-8Q-202 | 468 |
| ☐ N975HA | DHC-8-102 | 176 |
| ☐ N979HA | DHC-8-102A | 373 |
| ☐ N980HA | DHC-8-102A | 376 |
| ☐ N981HA | DHC-8-102A | 378 |
| ☐ N982HA | DHC-8-102A | 380 |
| ☐ N983HA | DHC-8Q-201 | 478 |
| ☐ N984HA | DHC-8-102A | 377 |
| ☐ N985HA | DHC-8Q-201 | 479 |
| ☐ N986HA | DHC-8-201 | 421 |
| ☐ N987HA | DHC-8-201 | 425 |
| ☐ N988HA | DHC-8-201 | 426 |
| ☐ N989HA | DHC-8-201 | 427 |
| ☐ N990HA | DHC-8-201 | 428 |
| ☐ N991HA | DHC-8-201 | 431 |
| ☐ N992HA | DHC-8-201 | 432 |
| ☐ N993HA | DHC-8-201 | 457 |
| ☐ N994HA | DHC-8-201 | 459 |
| ☐ N995HA | DHC-8-201 | 460 |
| ☐ N996HA | DHC-8Q-201 | 497 |
| ☐ N997HA | DHC-8Q-202 | 507 |
| ☐ N998HA | DHC-8Q-202 | 509 |
| ☐ N | DHC-8-314 | 290 |
| | | |
| ☐ N328JS | Dornier 328-100 | 3030 |
| ☐ N422JS | Dornier 328-100 | 3018 |
| ☐ N423JS | Dornier 328-100 | 3032 |
| ☐ N424JS | Dornier 328-100 | 3033 |
| ☐ N425JS | Dornier 328-100 | 3037 |
| ☐ N426JS | Dornier 328-100 | 3038 |
| ☐ N427JS | Dornier 328-100 | 3039 |
| ☐ N429JS | Dornier 328-100 | 3043 |
| ☐ N430JS | Dornier 328-100 | 3044 |
| ☐ N431JS | Dornier 328-100 | 3028 |
| ☐ N432JS | Dornier 328-100 | 3045 |
| ☐ N433JS | Dornier 328-100 | 3047 |
| ☐ N434JS | Dornier 328-100 | 3051 |
| ☐ N436JS | Dornier 328-100 | 3052 |
| ☐ N437JS | Dornier 328-100 | 3055 |
| ☐ N439JS | Dornier 328-100 | 3057 |
| ☐ N440JS | Dornier 328-100 | 3058 |
| ☐ N441JS | Dornier 328-100 | 3059 |
| ☐ N442JS | Dornier 328-100 | 3060 |
| ☐ N457PS | Dornier 328-100 | 3048 |
| ☐ N458PS | Dornier 328-100 | 3068 |
| ☐ N459PS | Dornier 328-100 | 3070 |
| ☐ N460PS | Dornier 328-100 | 3061 |
| ☐ N461PS | Dornier 328-100 | 3075 |
| ☐ N462PS | Dornier 328-110 | 3084 |
| ☐ N463PS | Dornier 328-110 | 3087 |
| ☐ N470PS | Dornier 328-110 | 3006 |
| ☐ N471PS | Dornier 328-110 | 3007 |
| ☐ N472PS | Dornier 328-110 | 3008 |
| ☐ N473PS | Dornier 328-110 | 3010 |
| | | |
| ☐ N260SK | Embraer ERJ-145 | 145128 |
| ☐ N261SK | Embraer ERJ-145 | 145144 |
| ☐ N262SK | Embraer ERJ-145 | 145168 |
| ☐ N263SK | Embraer ERJ-145 | 145199 |
| ☐ N264SK | Embraer ERJ-145 | 145221 |
| ☐ N265SK | Embraer ERJ-145 | 145226 |
| ☐ N266SK | Embraer ERJ-145 | 145241 |
| ☐ N267SK | Embraer ERJ-145 | 145268 |
| ☐ N268SK | Embraer ERJ-145 | 145270 |
| ☐ N269SK | Embraer ERJ-145 | 145293 |
| ☐ N280SK | Embraer ERJ-145 | 145381 |
| ☐ N281SK | Embraer ERJ-145 | 145391 |
| ☐ N282SK | Embraer ERJ-145 | 145409 |
| ☐ N283SK | Embraer ERJ-145 | 145424 |
| ☐ N284SK | Embraer ERJ-145 | 145427 |
| ☐ N285SK | Embraer ERJ-145 | 145435 |
| ☐ N286SK | Embraer ERJ-145 | 145443 |
| ☐ N287SK | Embraer ERJ-145 | 145460 |
| ☐ N288SK | Embraer ERJ-145 | 145461 |
| ☐ N289SK | Embraer ERJ-145 | 145463 |
| ☐ N290SK | Embraer ERJ-145 | 145474 |
| ☐ N291SK | Embraer ERJ-145 | 145486 |
| ☐ N293SK | Embraer ERJ-145 | 145500 |
| ☐ N298SK | Embraer ERJ-145 | 145508 |
| ☐ N370SK | Embraer ERJ-145 | 145515 |
| ☐ N | Embraer ERJ-145 | o/o |
| ☐ N | Embraer ERJ-145 | o/o |
| ☐ N | Embraer ERJ-145 | o/o |
| ☐ N | Embraer ERJ-145 | o/o |
| ☐ N | Embraer ERJ-145 | o/o |
| ☐ N | Embraer ERJ-145 | o/o |
| ☐ N | Embraer ERJ-145 | o/o |
| ☐ N825MJ | Embraer ERJ-145 | 145179 |
| ☐ N826MJ | Embraer ERJ-145 | 145214 |
| ☐ N827MJ | Embraer ERJ-145 | 145217 |
| ☐ N828MJ | Embraer ERJ-145 | 145218 |
| ☐ N829MJ | Embraer ERJ-145 | 145228 |
| ☐ N830MJ | Embraer ERJ-145 | 145259 |
| ☐ N831MJ | Embraer ERJ-145 | 145273 |
| ☐ N832MJ | Embraer ERJ-145 | 145310 |
| ☐ N833MJ | Embraer ERJ-145 | 145327 |
| ☐ N834MJ | Embraer ERJ-145 | 145340 |
| ☐ N835MJ | Embraer ERJ-145 | 145353 |
| ☐ N836MJ | Embraer ERJ-145 | 145359 |
| ☐ N837MJ | Embraer ERJ-145 | 145367 |
| ☐ N838MJ | Embraer ERJ-145 | 145384 |
| ☐ N839MJ | Embraer ERJ-145 | o/o |
| ☐ N840MJ | Embraer ERJ-145 | 145429 |
| ☐ N841MJ | Embraer ERJ-145 | 145448 |
| ☐ N842MJ | Embraer ERJ-145 | 145457 |
| ☐ N843MJ | Embraer ERJ-145 | 145478 |
| ☐ N844MJ | Embraer ERJ-145 | 145481 |
| ☐ N845MJ | Embraer ERJ-145 | 145502 |
| ☐ N846MJ | Embraer ERJ-145 | 145507 |
| ☐ N847MJ | Embraer ERJ-145 | 145517 |
| ☐ N848MJ | Embraer ERJ-145 | 145530 |
| ☐ N849MJ | Embraer ERJ-145 | 145534 |
| ☐ N850MJ | Embraer ERJ-145 | 145568 |
| ☐ N851MJ | Embraer ERJ-145 | 145572 |
| ☐ N852MJ | Embraer ERJ-145 | 145567 |
| ☐ N853MJ | Embraer ERJ-145 | 145464 |
| ☐ N854MJ | Embraer ERJ-145 | 145490 |
| ☐ N855MJ | Embraer ERJ-145 | 145614 |
| ☐ N856MJ | Embraer ERJ-145 | 145626 |
| ☐ N857MJ | Embraer ERJ-145 | o/o |
| ☐ N858MJ | Embraer ERJ-145 | o/o |
| ☐ N859MJ | Embraer ERJ-145 | o/o |
| ☐ N860MJ | Embraer ERJ-145 | o/o |

| ☐ N19XS | SAAB SF.340A | 019 |
| ☐ N35SZ | SAAB SF.340A | 035 |
| ☐ N40SZ | SAAB SF.340A | 040 |
| ☐ N43SZ | SAAB SF.340A | 043 |
| ☐ N95CQ | SAAB SF.340A | 095 |
| ☐ N96CN | SAAB SF.340A | 096 |
| ☐ N101CN | SAAB SF.340A | 101 |
| ☐ N104CQ | SAAB SF.340A | 104 |
| ☐ N108CQ | SAAB SF.340A | 108 |
| ☐ N118SD | SAAB SF.340A | 118 |
| ☐ N121CQ | SAAB SF.340A | 121 |
| ☐ N123XS | SAAB SF.340A | 123 |
| ☐ N125CH | SAAB SF.340A | 125 |
| ☐ N128CH | SAAB SF.340A | 128 |
| ☐ N138SD | SAAB SF.340A | 138 |
| ☐ N140CQ | SAAB SF.340A | 140 |
| ☐ N146SD | SAAB SF.340A | 146 |
| ☐ N148SD | SAAB SF.340A | 148 |
| ☐ N149SZ | SAAB SF.340A | 149 |
| ☐ N150CN | SAAB SF.340A | 150 |
| ☐ N152CQ | SAAB SF.340A | 152 |
| ☐ N157SD | SAAB SF.340A | 157 |
| ☐ N158SD | SAAB SF.340A | 158 |
| ☐ N237MJ | SAAB SF.340B | 237 |
| ☐ N239CJ | SAAB SF.340B | 239 |
| ☐ N242CJ | SAAB SF.340B | 242 |
| ☐ N252CJ | SAAB SF.340B | 252 |
| ☐ N275CJ | SAAB SF.340B | 275 |
| ☐ N277MJ | SAAB SF.340B | 277 |
| ☐ N294CJ | SAAB SF.340B | 294 |
| ☐ N299CJ | SAAB SF.340B | 299 |
| ☐ N340SZ | SAAB SF.340A | 004 |
| ☐ N340SF | SAAB SF.340A | 014 |
| ☐ N360SZ | SAAB SF.340A | 006 |

## USA 3000 AIRLINES — GWY

| ☐ N260AV | Airbus A320-214 | 1564 |
| ☐ N261AV | Airbus A320-214 | 1615 |
| ☐ N262AV | Airbus A320-214 | 1725 |
| ☐ N263AV | Airbus A320-214 | 1860 |
| ☐ N264AV | Airbus A320-214 | 1867 |
| ☐ N265AV | Airbus A320-214 | 0427 |

## WORLD AIRWAYS — WOA

| ☐ N107WA | Douglas DC-10-30CF | 280/46836 | |
| ☐ N117GB | Douglas DC-10-30 | 446/48318 | |
| ☐ N304WL | Douglas DC-10-30F | 192/47928 | |
| ☐ N352WL | Douglas DC-10-30F | 338/47838 | |
| ☐ N526MD | Douglas DC-10-30F | 267/46998 | |
| ☐ N14075 | Douglas DC-10-30F | 221/46922 | |
| ☐ N47888 | Douglas DC-10-30F | 291/47888 | |
| | | | |
| ☐ N271WA | McDD MD-11 | 525/48518 | |
| ☐ N272WA | McDD MD-11 | 506/48437 | |
| ☐ N273WA | McDD MD-11 | 539/48519 | |
| ☐ N274WA | McDD MD-11F | 563/48633 | |
| ☐ N275WA | McDD MD-11CF | 579/48631 | |
| ☐ N276WA | McDD MD-11CF | 582/48632 | Lst STU |
| ☐ N277WA | McDD MD-11ER | 590/48743 | |
| ☐ N278WA | McDD MD-11ER | 597/48746 | |
| ☐ N279WA | McDD MD-11 | 623/48756 | |

## OB - PERU

### AERO CONTINENTE — ACQ

| ☐ OB-1546 | Boeing 727-22 | 485/19150 | |
| ☐ OB-1570 | Boeing 727-22 | 508/19153 | |
| ☐ OB-1601 | Boeing 727-51 | 203/18943 | |
| ☐ OB-1728 | Boeing 727-23 | 44/18433 | Lst VND |
| ☐ OB-1738 | Boeing 727-23 | 381/19432 | |
| ☐ OB-1759 | Boeing 727-22 | 507/19152 | |
| | | | |
| ☐ CC-CJM | Boeing 737-201 | 159/20212 | |
| ☐ OB-1544 | Boeing 737-2A9 | 386/20956 | |
| ☐ OB-1620 | Boeing 737-247 | 125/19615 | std |

| ☐ OB-1723 | Boeing 737-204 | 162/19712 | |
| ☐ OB-1729 | Boeing 737-247 | 145/20128 | |
| ☐ OB-1730 | Boeing 737-201 | 61/19422 | Lst VND |
| ☐ OB-1733 | Boeing 737-222 | 50/19059 | |
| ☐ OB-1742 | Boeing 737-247 | 126/19616 | |
| ☐ OB-1745 | Boeing 737-130 | 3/19014 | |
| ☐ OB-1746 | Boeing 737-281 | 235/20277 | |
| ☐ OB-1747 | Boeing 737-201 | 244/20414 | std |
| ☐ OB-1751 | Boeing 737-205 | 128/19409 | |
| ☐ OB-1752 | Boeing 737-205 | 320/20711 | |
| ☐ OB-1753 | Boeing 737-201 | 172/20214 | |
| ☐ OB-1754 | Boeing 737-201 | 207/20215 | |
| ☐ OB-1755 | Boeing 737-222 | 210/19955 | Lst CND |
| ☐ OB-1763 | Boeing 737-222 | 19059 | |
| ☐ OB-1764 | Boeing 737-201 | 20212 | |
| | | | |
| ☐ OB-1636 | F.28 Fellowship 1000 | 11009 | |
| ☐ OB-1750 | F.28 Fellowship 1000 | 11097 | |
| ☐ OB-1758 | Boeing 767-205 | 81/23057 | |
| ☐ OB-1765 | Boeing 767-2Q8B | 272/24448 | |
| ☐ OB-1766 | Boeing 767-219ER | 239/24150 | |

### AVIADINA — VND

| ☐ OB-1728 | Boeing 727-23 | 44/18433 | Lsf ACQ |
| ☐ OB-1730 | Boeing 737-201 | 61/19422 | Lsf ACQ |
| ☐ OB-1731 | Boeing 727-23 | 43/18432 | |
| ☐ OB-1738 | Boeing 727-23 | 381/19432 | Lsf ACQ |
| ☐ OB-1748 | Boeing 737-247 | 107/19547 | |

### CIELOS DEL PERU — CIU

| ☐ N831LA | Douglas DC-10-30F | 147/46936 |
| ☐ N833LA | Douglas DC-10-30F | 152/46937 |
| ☐ OB-1749 | Douglas DC-10-30CF | 127/46891 |

### LAN PERU — LPE

| ☐ VP-BCK | Airbus A320-233 | 1568 | Lsf LAN |
| ☐ VP-BCS | Airbus A320-233 | 1854 | Lsf LAN |

### TACA PERU — TPU

| ☐ N471TA | Airbus A319-132 | 1066 | Lsf TAI |
| ☐ N472TA | Airbus A319-132 | 1113 | Lsf TAI |
| ☐ N473TA | Airbus A319-132 | 1140 | Lsf TAI |
| ☐ N474TA | Airbus A319-132 | 1159 | Lsf TAI |

### TANS — ELV

| ☐ OB-1713 | Boeing 737-244 | 82/19707 | 350 |
| ☐ OB-1718 | Boeing 737-248 | 147/19424 | |
| ☐ OB-1719 | Boeing 737-248 | 227/20221 | |
| ☐ OB-1724 | Boeing 737-282 | 967/23042 | 352 |

## OD - LEBANON

### MIDDLE EAST AIRLINES — MEA

| ☐ F-OHLO | Airbus A320-232 | 0760 | |
| ☐ F-OHMO | Airbus A320-232 | 0640 | |
| ☐ F-OHMP | Airbus A321-231 | 0663 | |
| ☐ F-OHMQ | Airbus A321-231 | 0668 | |
| ☐ F-OHMR | Airbus A320-232 | 0676 | |
| ☐ F- | Airbus A321-231 | 1878 | o/o |
| ☐ F- | Airbus A321-231 | 1953 | o/o |
| ☐ F- | Airbus A321-231 | 1956 | o/o |
| ☐ F- | Airbus A321-231 | 1967 | o/o |
| ☐ F- | Airbus A321-231 | 1977 | o/o |
| ☐ F- | Airbus A321-231 | | o/o |
| | | | |
| ☐ F-OHLN | Airbus A300B4-605R | 747 | |
| ☐ 3B-STI | Airbus A310-222 | 347 | |
| ☐ 3B-STJ | Airbus A310-222 | 350 | |
| ☐ 3B-STK | Airbus A310-222 | 357 | |
| ☐ | Airbus A330-243 | 527 | o/o |
| ☐ | Airbus A330-2 | | o/o |
| ☐ | Airbus A330-2 | | o/o |

## TMA CARGO — TMA

| | | | |
|---|---|---|---|
| ☐ OD-AGD | Boeing 707-323C | 437/18939 | |
| ☐ OD-AGO | Boeing 707-321C | 570/19269 | Lst LAA |
| ☐ OD-AGP | Boeing 707-321C | 594/19274 | |
| ☐ OD-AGS | Boeing 707-331C | 626/19214 | std |
| ☐ OD-AGX | Boeing 707-327C | 498/19104 | std |
| ☐ OD-AGY | Boeing 707-327C | 499/19105 | std |
| ☐ TF-ELS | Airbus A310-304F | 552 | Opb ICB |

# OE - AUSTRIA

## AERO LLOYD AUSTRIA

| | | |
|---|---|---|
| ☐ OE- | Airbus A320-2 | o/o |
| ☐ OE- | Airbus A320-2 | o/o |
| ☐ OE- | Airbus A320-2 | o/o |

## AIR ALPS AVIATION — LPV

| | | |
|---|---|---|
| ☐ OE-LKA | Dornier 328-110 | 3110 |
| ☐ OE-LKB | Dornier 328-110 | 3036 |
| ☐ OE-LKC | Dornier 328-110 | 3119 |
| ☐ OE-LKD | Dornier 328-110 | 3072 |
| ☐ OE-LKE | Dornier 328-110 | 3063 |
| ☐ OE-LKF | Dornier 328-110 | 3073 |

## AMERER AIR — AMK

| | | |
|---|---|---|
| ☐ OE-ILA | L-188AF Electra | 1145 |
| ☐ OE-ILB | L-188AF Electra | 1039 |
| ☐ OE-ILW | F-27 Friendship 500 | 10681 |

## AUSTRIAN AIRLINES — AUA

| | | |
|---|---|---|
| ☐ OE- | Airbus A319- | o/o |
| ☐ OE- | Airbus A319- | o/o |
| ☐ OE- | Airbus A319- | o/o |
| ☐ OE- | Airbus A319- | o/o |
| ☐ OE- | Airbus A319- | o/o |
| ☐ OE- | Airbus A319- | o/o |
| ☐ OE- | Airbus A319- | o/o |
| | | |
| ☐ OE-LBN | Airbus A320-214 | 0768 |
| ☐ OE-LBO | Airbus A320-214 | 0776 |
| ☐ OE-LBP | Airbus A320-214 | 0797 |
| ☐ OE-LBQ | Airbus A320-214 | 1137 |
| ☐ OE-LBR | Airbus A320-214 | 1150 |
| ☐ OE-LBS | Airbus A320-214 | 1189 |
| ☐ OE-LBT | Airbus A320-214 | 1387 |
| ☐ OE-LBU | Airbus A320-214 | 1478 |
| | | |
| ☐ OE-LBA | Airbus A321-111 | 0552 |
| ☐ OE-LBB | Airbus A321-111 | 0570 |
| ☐ OE-LBC | Airbus A321-111 | 0581 |
| ☐ OE-LBD | Airbus A321-211 | 0920 |
| ☐ OE-LBE | Airbus A321-211 | 0935 |
| ☐ OE-LBF | Airbus A321-211 | 1458 |
| | | |
| ☐ OE-LAG | Airbus A340-212 | 075 |
| ☐ OE-LAH | Airbus A340-212 | 081 |
| ☐ OE-LAK | Airbus A340-313X | 169 |
| ☐ OE-LAL | Airbus A340-313X | 263 |
| | | |
| ☐ OE-LAM | Airbus A330-223 | 223 |
| ☐ OE-LAN | Airbus A330-223 | 195 |
| ☐ OE-LAO | Airbus A330-223 | 181 |
| ☐ OE-LAP | Airbus A330-223 | 317 |
| | | |
| ☐ OE-LFO | Fokker 70 | 11559 |
| ☐ OE-LFP | Fokker 70 | 11560 |
| ☐ OE-LFQ | Fokker 70 | 11568 |
| ☐ OE-LFR | Fokker 70 | 11572 |
| | | |
| ☐ OE-LMA | McDD MD-82 | 1183/49278 |
| ☐ OE-LMB | McDD MD-82 | 1230/49279 |

| | | |
|---|---|---|
| ☐ OE-LMC | McDD MD-82 | 1252/49372 |
| ☐ OE-LMD | McDD MD-83 | 1837/49933 |
| ☐ OE-LME | McDD MD-83 | 2057/53377 |
| ☐ OE-LMK | McDD MD-87 (ER) | 1412/49411 |
| ☐ OE-LML | McDD MD-87 (ER) | 1424/49412 |
| ☐ OE-LMN | McDD MD-87 | 1682/49414 |
| ☐ OE-LMO | McDD MD-87 | 1692/49888 |

## BACHFLUG — BCF

| | | | |
|---|---|---|---|
| ☐ OE-GIF | SAAB SF.340A | 100 | Lst KST |

## EAGLE AIRLINES — EAV

| | | |
|---|---|---|
| ☐ OE-LEO | BAe Jetstream 31 | 604 |

## GROSSMAN AIR SERVICES — HTG

| | | | |
|---|---|---|---|
| ☐ D-BGAL | Dornier 328-300 | 3131 | Lsf GNF |
| ☐ OE-HTG | Dornier 328-300 | 3162 | |

## JETALLIANCE

| | | | |
|---|---|---|---|
| ☐ D-BIER | DHC-8-103 | 310 | Lsf RUS |

## LAUDA AIR — LDA

| | | | |
|---|---|---|---|
| ☐ OE-LNJ | Boeing 737-8Z9 | 69/28177 | |
| ☐ OE-LNK | Boeing 737-8Z9 | 222/28178 | |
| ☐ OE-LNL | Boeing 737-6Z9 | 526/30137 | |
| ☐ OE-LNM | Boeing 737-6Z9 | 546/30138 | |
| ☐ OE-LNO | Boeing 737-7Z9 | 815/30418 | |
| ☐ OE-LNP | Boeing 737-7Z9 | 874/30419 | |
| ☐ OE-LNP | Boeing 737-8Z9 | 1100/30420 | |
| ☐ OE-LNQ | Boeing 737-8Z9 | 30421 | o/o |
| | | | |
| ☐ OE-LAE | Boeing 767-3Z9ER | 812/30383 | |
| ☐ OE-LAT | Boeing 767-31AER | 393/25273 | Lst LDI |
| ☐ OE-LAU | Boeing 767-3Z9ER | 165/23765 | Lst LDI |
| ☐ OE-LAW | Boeing 767-3Z9ER | 448/26417 | Lst LDI |
| ☐ OE-LAX | Boeing 767-3Z9ER | 467/27095 | Lst LDI |
| ☐ OE-LAY | Boeing 767-3Z9ER | 731/29867 | |
| ☐ OE-LAZ | Boeing 767-3Z9ER | 759/30331 | |
| | | | |
| ☐ OE-ILF | Boeing 737-3Z9 | 1254/23601 | |
| ☐ OE-LNH | Boeing 737-4Z9 | 2043/25147 | Lst BPA |
| ☐ OE-LNI | Boeing 737-4Z9 | 2432/27094 | |
| ☐ OE-LPA | Boeing 777-2Z9ER | 87/28698 | |
| ☐ OE-LPB | Boeing 777-2Z9ER | 163/28699 | |
| ☐ OE-LPC | Boeing 777-2Z9ER | 386/29313 | |
| | | | |
| ☐ OE-LRE | Canadair RJ-200 | 7059 | |
| ☐ OE-LRF | Canadair RJ-200 | 7061 | |
| ☐ OE-LRG | Canadair RJ-200 | 7063 | |
| ☐ OE-LRH | Canadair RJ-200 | 7125 | |
| ☐ OE- | Airbus A321-231 | | Lsf SALE |
| ☐ OE- | Airbus A321-231 | | Lsf SALE |

## TYROLEAN AIRWAYS — TYR

| | | |
|---|---|---|
| ☐ OE-LCF | Canadair RJ-200 | 7094 |
| ☐ OE-LCG | Canadair RJ-200 | 7103 |
| ☐ OE-LCH | Canadair RJ-200 | 7110 |
| ☐ OE-LCI | Canadair RJ-200 | 7133 |
| ☐ OE-LCJ | Canadair RJ-200 | 7142 |
| ☐ OE-LCK | Canadair RJ-200 | 7148 |
| ☐ OE-LCL | Canadair RJ-200 | 7167 |
| ☐ OE-LCM | Canadair RJ-200 | 7205 |
| ☐ OE-LCN | Canadair RJ-200 | 7365 |
| ☐ OE-LCO | Canadair RJ-200 | 7371 |
| ☐ OE-LCP | Canadair RJ-200 | 7480 |
| ☐ OE-LCQ | Canadair RJ-200 | 7605 |
| | | |
| ☐ OE-LGA | DHC-8-402Q | 4014 |
| ☐ OE-LGB | DHC-8-402Q | 4015 |
| ☐ OE-LGC | DHC-8-402Q | 4026 |

| | | | |
|---|---|---|---|
| ☐ OE-LGD | DHC-8-402Q | 4027 | |
| ☐ OE-LGE | DHC-8-402Q | 4042 | |
| ☐ OE-LGF | DHC-8-402Q | 4068 | |
| ☐ OE-LGG | DHC-8-402Q | 4074 | |
| ☐ OE-LGH | DHC-8-402Q | 4075 | |
| ☐ OE-LLE | DHC-8-106B | 355 | |
| ☐ OE-LTG | DHC-8Q-314 | 438 | |
| ☐ OE-LTH | DHC-8Q-314 | 442 | |
| ☐ OE-LTI | DHC-8Q-314 | 466 | |
| ☐ OE-LTJ | DHC-8Q-314 | 481 | |
| ☐ OE-LTK | DHC-8Q-314 | 483 | |
| ☐ OE-LTL | DHC-8Q-314 | 485 | |
| ☐ OE-LTM | DHC-8Q-314 | 527 | |
| ☐ OE-LTN | DHC-8Q-314 | 531 | |
| ☐ OE-LTO | DHC-8Q-314 | 553 | |
| ☐ OE-LTP | DHC-8Q-314 | 554 | |
| | | | |
| ☐ OE-LFG | Fokker 70 | 11549 | |
| ☐ OE-LFH | Fokker 70 | 11554 | |
| ☐ OE-LFI | Fokker 70 | 11529 | |
| ☐ OE-LFJ | Fokker 70 | 11532 | for KLC |
| ☐ OE-LFK | Fokker 70 | 11555 | |
| ☐ OE-LFL | Fokker 70 | 11573 | |
| | | | |
| ☐ OE-LSM | Embraer ERJ-145 | 145322 | |
| ☐ OE-LSP | Embraer ERJ-145 | 145337 | |
| ☐ OE-LSR | Embraer ERJ-145 | 145203 | |

### TEAMLINE AIR

| | | | |
|---|---|---|---|
| ☐ OE-GIF | SAAB SF.340A | 100 | Lsf BCF |

### TYROLEAN JET SERVICE — TJS

| | | | |
|---|---|---|---|
| ☐ OE-GBB | Dornier 328-110 | 3078 | Jow WLC |
| ☐ OE-HMS | Dornier 328-300 | 3121 | |
| ☐ OE-HTJ | Dornier 328-300 | 3114 | |

### WELCOME AIR — WLC

| | | | |
|---|---|---|---|
| ☐ OE-GBB | Dornier 328-110 | 3078 | Jow TJS |
| ☐ OE-LIR | Dornier 328-110 | 3115 | |
| ☐ OE-LJR | Dornier 328-310 | 3213 | |

## OH - FINLAND

### AIR BOTNIA — KFB

| | | | |
|---|---|---|---|
| ☐ OH-SAH | Avro RJ-85 | E2383 | |
| ☐ OH-SAI | Avro RJ-85 | E2385 | |
| ☐ OH-SAJ | Avro RJ-85 | E2388 | |
| ☐ OH-SAK | Avro RJ-85 | E2389 | |
| ☐ OH-SAL | Avro RJ-85 | E2392 | |
| | | | |
| ☐ OH-SAS | SAAB 2000 | 044 | |
| ☐ OH-SAT | SAAB 2000 | 042 | |
| ☐ OH-SAU | SAAB 2000 | 043 | |
| ☐ OH-SAW | SAAB 2000 | 046 | |
| ☐ OH-SAX | SAAB 2000 | 055 | |

### AIR FINLAND

| | | | |
|---|---|---|---|
| ☐ OH- | Boeing 757-2 | | |

### FINNAIR — FIN

| | | | |
|---|---|---|---|
| ☐ OH-KRA | ATR 72-201 | 126 | |
| ☐ OH-KRB | ATR 72-201 | 140 | |
| ☐ OH-KRC | ATR 72-201 | 145 | |
| ☐ OH-KRD | ATR 72-201 | 162 | |
| ☐ OH-KRE | ATR 72-201 | 174 | Lst EAY |
| ☐ OH-KRF | ATR 72-201 | 324 | |
| ☐ OH-KRH | ATR 72-201 | 212 | |
| ☐ OH-KRK | ATR 72-201 | 251 | Lst EAY |
| ☐ OH-KRL | ATR 72-201 | 332 | |

| | | | |
|---|---|---|---|
| ☐ OH-LVA | Airbus A319-112 | 1073 | |
| ☐ OH-LVB | Airbus A319-112 | 1107 | |
| ☐ OH-LVC | Airbus A319-112 | 1309 | |
| ☐ OH-LVD | Airbus A319-112 | 1352 | |
| ☐ OH-LVE | Airbus A319-112 | 1791 | |
| ☐ OH-LVF | Airbus A319-112 | 1808 | |
| ☐ OH-LVG | Airbus A319-112 | 1916 | |
| ☐ OH-LVH | Airbus A319-112 | 1184 | |
| ☐ OH-LVI | Airbus A319-112 | 1364 | o/o |
| | | | |
| ☐ OH-LXA | Airbus A320-214 | 1405 | |
| ☐ OH-LXB | Airbus A320-214 | 1470 | |
| ☐ OH-LXC | Airbus A320-214 | 1544 | |
| ☐ OH-LXD | Airbus A320-214 | 1588 | |
| ☐ OH-LXE | Airbus A320-214 | 1678 | |
| ☐ OH-LXF | Airbus A320-214 | 1712 | |
| ☐ OH-LXG | Airbus A320-214 | 1735 | |
| ☐ OH-LXH | Airbus A320-214 | 1913 | |
| ☐ OH-LXI | Airbus A320-214 | | o/o |
| ☐ OH-LXJ | Airbus A320-214 | | o/o |
| ☐ OH-LXK | Airbus A320-214 | | o/o |
| | | | |
| ☐ OH-LZA | Airbus A321-211 | 0941 | |
| ☐ OH-LZB | Airbus A321-211 | 0961 | |
| ☐ OH-LZC | Airbus A321-211 | 1185 | |
| ☐ OH-LZD | Airbus A321-211 | 1241 | |
| ☐ OH-LZE | Airbus A321-211 | 1978 | o/o |
| | | | |
| ☐ OH-LBO | Boeing 757-2Q8 | 772/28172 | |
| ☐ OH-LBR | Boeing 757-2Q8 | 775/28167 | |
| ☐ OH-LBS | Boeing 757-2Q8 | 792/27623 | |
| ☐ OH-LBT | Boeing 757-2Q8 | 801/28170 | |
| ☐ OH-LBU | Boeing 757-2Q8 | 857/29377 | |
| ☐ OH-LBV | Boeing 757-2Q8 | 1006/30046 | |
| ☐ OH-LBX | Boeing 757-2Q8 | 1010/29382 | |
| ☐ OH- | Boeing 757-2K2 | 717/26330 | |
| | | | |
| ☐ OH-LYP | Douglas DC-9-51 | 808/47696 | |
| ☐ OH-LYR | Douglas DC-9-51 | 827/47736 | |
| ☐ OH-LYS | Douglas DC-9-51 | 829/47737 | |
| ☐ OH-LYT | Douglas DC-9-51 | 830/47738 | Lst LAV |
| ☐ OH-LYU | Douglas DC-9-51 | 883/47771 | Lst LAV |
| ☐ OH-LYV | Douglas DC-9-51 | 890/47772 | |
| ☐ OH-LYW | Douglas DC-9-51 | 891/47773 | |
| ☐ OH-LYX | Douglas DC-9-51 | 980/48134 | |
| ☐ OH-LYY | Douglas DC-9-51 | 987/48135 | |
| ☐ OH-LYZ | Douglas DC-9-51 | 993/48136 | |
| | | | |
| ☐ OH-LMG | McDD MD-83 | 1503/49625 | |
| ☐ OH-LMH | McDD MD-82 | 1978/53245 | |
| ☐ OH-LMR | McDD MD-83 | 1209/49284 | |
| ☐ OH-LMS | McDD MD-83 | 1169/49252 | |
| ☐ OH-LMT | McDD MD-82 | 1594/49877 | |
| ☐ OH-LMW | McDD MD-82 | 1767/49905 | |
| ☐ OH-LMX | McDD MD-82 | 1786/49906 | |
| ☐ OH-LMY | McDD MD-82 | 1901/53244 | |
| ☐ OH-LMZ | McDD MD-82 | 1918/53246 | |
| ☐ OH-LPA | McDD MD-82 | 1765/49900 | |
| ☐ OH-LPB | McDD MD-83 | 2047/49966 | |
| ☐ OH-LPC | McDD MD-83 | 2044/49965 | |
| ☐ OH-LPD | McDD MD-83 | 1547/49710 | |
| ☐ OH-LPE | McDD MD-83 | 1357/49401 | |
| ☐ OH-LPF | McDD MD-83 | 1413/49574 | |
| ☐ OH-LPG | McDD MD-83 | 1561/49708 | |
| ☐ OH-LPH | McDD MD-83 | 1499/49623 | |
| ☐ OH-FAE | SAAB SF.340A/QC | 139 | Lst GAO |
| ☐ OH-FAF | SAAB SF.340B | 167 | Lst GAO |
| ☐ OH-LGA | McDD MD-11 | 455/48449 | |
| ☐ OH-LGB | McDD MD-11 | 479/48450 | |
| ☐ OH-LGC | McDD MD-11 | 529/48512 | |
| ☐ OH-LGD | McDD MD-11 | 564/48513 | |
| ☐ OH-LGE | McDD MD-11 | 624/48780 | o/o |

## OK - CZECH REPUBLIC

### ABA-AIR — ABP

| | | | |
|---|---|---|---|
| ☐ OK-ABA | F.27 Friendship 500CRF | 10530 | Opf UPS |
| ☐ OK-ABB | F.27 Friendship 500CRF | 10531 | Opf UPS |

## CSA CZECH AIRLINES — CSA

| | | |
|---|---|---|
| ☐ OK-AFE | ATR 42-420 | 487 |
| ☐ OK-AFF | ATR 42-420 | 491 |
| ☐ OK-BFG | ATR 42-320 | 409 |
| ☐ OK-BFH | ATR 42-320 | 412 |
| ☐ OK-VFI | ATR 42-320 | 173 |
| ☐ OK-XFA | ATR 72-201 | 285 |
| ☐ OK-XFB | ATR 72-202 | 297 |
| ☐ OK-XFC | ATR 72-202 | 299 |
| ☐ OK-XFD | ATR 72-201 | 303 |
| | | |
| ☐ OK-BGQ | Boeing 737-43Q | 2839/28494 |
| ☐ OK-CGH | Boeing 737-55S | 2849/28469 |
| ☐ OK-CGI | Boeing 737-49R | 2845/28882 |
| ☐ OK-CGJ | Boeing 737-55S | 2861/28470 |
| ☐ OK-CGK | Boeing 737-55S | 2885/28471 |
| ☐ OK-CGT | Boeing 737-46M | 2844/28549 |
| ☐ OK-DGL | Boeing 737-55S | 3004/28472 |
| ☐ OK-DGM | Boeing 737-45S | 3014/28473 |
| ☐ OK-DGN | Boeing 737-45S | 3028/28474 |
| ☐ OK-EGO | Boeing 737-55S | 3096/28475 |
| ☐ OK-EGP | Boeing 737-45S | 3103/28476 |
| ☐ OK-FGR | Boeing 737-45S | 3131/28477 |
| ☐ OK-FGS | Boeing 737-45S | 3132/28478 |
| ☐ OK-WGF | Boeing 737-4Y0 | 1978/24903 |
| ☐ OK-WGG | Boeing 737-4Y0 | 1972/24693 |
| ☐ OK-XGA | Boeing 737-55S | 2300/26539 |
| ☐ OK-XGB | Boeing 737-55S | 2317/26540 |
| ☐ OK-XGC | Boeing 737-55S | 2319/26541 |
| ☐ OK-XGD | Boeing 737-55S | 2337/26542 |
| ☐ OK-XGE | Boeing 737-55S | 2339/26543 |
| ☐ OK- | Boeing 737-4Q8 | 2486/26289 |
| | | |
| ☐ OK-WAA | Airbus A310-304 | 564 |
| ☐ OK-WAB | Airbus A310-304 | 567 |

## FISCHER AIR — FFR

| | | |
|---|---|---|
| ☐ OK-FAN | Boeing 737-33A | 2864/27469 |
| ☐ OK-FIT | Boeing 737-36N | 3097/28590 |
| ☐ OK-FUN | Boeing 737-33A | 2873/27910 |

## TRAVEL SERVICE AIRLINES — TVS

| | | | |
|---|---|---|---|
| ☐ OK-TVA | Boeing 737-86N | 869/32243 | |
| ☐ OK-TVB | Boeing 737-8CX | 1125/32362 | |
| ☐ OK-TVC | Boeing 737-86Q | 963/30278 | Lst OMA |
| ☐ OK-TVQ | Boeing 737-86N | 514/28618 | |
| ☐ OK-TVR | Boeing 737-4Y0 | 1647/23870 | |
| ☐ OK-TVS | Boeing 737-4Y0 | 2033/24911 | |

# OM - SLOVAKIA

## AIR SLOVAKIA — SVK

| | | |
|---|---|---|
| ☐ OM-ALK | Boeing 737-230 | 1085/23157 |
| ☐ OM-ERA | Boeing 737-2H4 | 568/21722 |
| ☐ OM-RAN | Boeing 737-230 | 1082/23156 |

## SKY EUROPE AIRLINES — ESK

| | | | |
|---|---|---|---|
| ☐ OM-SKY | Embraer EMB.120ER | 120175 | Lsf MPS |
| ☐ OM-SPY | Embraer EMB.120ER | 120092 | |
| ☐ OM- | Boeing 737-300 | | o/o |

## SLOVAK AIRLINES — SLL

| | | |
|---|---|---|
| ☐ OM-AAA | Tupolev Tu-154M | 98A-1014 |
| ☐ OM-AAB | Tupolev Tu-154M | 98A-1015 |
| ☐ OM-AAC | Tupolev Tu-154M | 98A-1018 |
| ☐ OM-AAD | Boeing 737-33A | 23636 |

## SLOVAK GOVT FLYING SERVICE — SSG

| | | |
|---|---|---|
| ☐ OM-BYE | Yakovlev Yak-40 | 9440338 |
| ☐ OM-BYL | Yakovlev Yak-40 | 9940560 |
| ☐ OM-BYO | Tupolev Tu-154M | 89A-803 |
| ☐ OM-BYR | Tupolev Tu-154M | 98A-1012 |

# OO - BELGIUM

## BIRDY AIRLINES

| | | | |
|---|---|---|---|
| ☐ OO-SFM | Airbus A330-301 | 030 | Opf SAB |
| ☐ OO-SFN | Airbus A330-301 | 037 | Opf SAB |
| ☐ OO-SFO | Airbus A330-301 | 045 | Opf SAB |

## EUROPEAN AIR TRANSPORT — BCS

| | | | |
|---|---|---|---|
| ☐ EI-DHL | Airbus A300B4-203F | 274 | |
| ☐ EI-SAF | Airbus A300B4-203F | 220 | |
| ☐ OO-DLC | Airbus A300B4-203F | 152 | Lsf SFR |
| ☐ OO-DLD | Airbus A300B4-203F | 259 | Lsf SFR |
| ☐ OO-DLE | Airbus A300B4-203F | 236 | Lsf SFR |
| ☐ OO-DLG | Airbus A300B4-203F | 208 | Lsf SFR |
| ☐ OO-DLI | Airbus A300B4-203F | 234 | Lsf SFR |
| ☐ OO-DLL | Airbus A300B4-203F | 093 | |
| ☐ OO-DLR | Airbus A300B4-203F | 095 | Lsf ABR |
| ☐ OO-DLT | Airbus A300B4-203F | 250 | Lsf ABR |
| ☐ OO-DLU | Airbus A300B4-203F | 289 | Lsf ABR |
| ☐ OO-DLV | Airbus A300B4-203F | 150 | Lsf ABR |
| ☐ OO-DLW | Airbus A300B4-203F | 199 | Lsf ABR |
| ☐ OO-DLY | Airbus A300B4-203F | 116 | Lsf ABR |
| | | | |
| ☐ EC-HHU | Boeing 727-277F | 1768/22644 | Lst SWT |
| ☐ EC-HIG | Boeing 727-277F | 1753/22641 | Lst XME |
| ☐ EC-HJV | Boeing 727-264F | 1049/20895 | Lst SWT |
| ☐ EC-HLP | Boeing 727-264F | 1051/20896 | Lst SWT |
| ☐ EC-IDQ | Boeing 727-223F | 593/19489 | Lst SWT |
| ☐ EC-IFC | Boeing 727-277F | 1762/22643 | Lst SWT |
| ☐ OO-DHN | Boeing 727-31F | 711/20113 | |
| ☐ OO-DHO | Boeing 727-31F | 700/20112 | |
| ☐ OO-DHQ | Boeing 727-35F | 325/19167 | Lst VEC |
| ☐ OO-DHR | Boeing 727-35F | 489/19834 | |
| ☐ OO-DHS | Boeing 727-223F | 733/20189 | |
| ☐ OO-DHU | Boeing 727-223F | 1187/20992 | |
| ☐ OO-DHV | Boeing 727-223F | 1199/21084 | Lst SWT |
| ☐ OO-DHW | Boeing 727-223F | 1189/20993 | |
| ☐ OO-DHX | Boeing 727-223F | 1190/20994 | |
| ☐ OO-DHY | Boeing 727-230F | 1091/20905 | |
| ☐ OO-DHZ | Boeing 727-2Q4F | 1683/22424 | Lst SWT |
| ☐ OO-DLB | Boeing 727-277F | 1759/22642 | Lst XME |
| | | | |
| ☐ OO-DLJ | Boeing 757-23APF | 340/24971 | |
| ☐ OO-DLN | Boeing 757-236SF | 9/22172 | |
| ☐ OO-DLP | Boeing 757-236SF | 24/22179 | |
| ☐ OO-DLQ | Boeing 757-236SF | 13/22175 | |
| ☐ OO-DPB | Boeing 757-236SF | 32/22183 | |
| ☐ OO-DPF | Boeing 757-236SF | 10/22173 | |
| ☐ OO-DPI | Boeing 757-236SF | 179/24102 | |
| ☐ OO-DPJ | Boeing 757-236SF | 90/23493 | |
| ☐ OO-DPL | Boeing 757-236SF | 211/24267 | |
| ☐ OO-DPN | Boeing 757-236SF | 93/23533 | |
| ☐ OO-DPO | Boeing 757-236SF | 77/23398 | |
| ☐ OO-DPW | Boeing 757-236SF | 89/23492 | |
| | | | |
| ☐ OO-DHB | Convair 580 | 458 | Lst SWT |
| ☐ OO-DHC | Convair 580 | 68 | Lst SWT |
| ☐ OO-DHD | Convair 580 | 135 | Lst SWT |
| ☐ OO-DHE | Convair 580 | 52 | Lst SWT |
| ☐ OO-DHF | Convair 580 | 147 | Lst SWT |
| ☐ OO-DHG | Convair 580 | 25 | Lst SWT |
| ☐ OO-DHH | Convair 580 | 186 | Lst SWT |
| ☐ OO-DHL | Convair 580 | 459 | Lst SWT |
| ☐ OO-HUB | Convair 580 | 130 | Lst SWT |

## SKY SERVICE — SKS

| | | |
|---|---|---|
| ☐ OO-SKW | Embraer EMB.110P1 | 110381 |

## SN BRUSSELS AIRLINES DAT

| | | | |
|---|---|---|---|
| ☐ OO-DJE | BAe 146 Srs.200 | E2164 | |
| ☐ OO-DJF | BAe 146 Srs.200 | E2167 | |
| ☐ OO-DJG | BAe 146 Srs.200 | E2180 | |
| ☐ OO-DJH | BAe 146 Srs.200 | E2172 | |
| ☐ OO-DJJ | BAe 146 Srs.200 | E2196 | |
| | | | |
| ☐ OO-DJK | Avro RJ-85 | E2271 | |
| ☐ OO-DJL | Avro RJ-85 | E2273 | |
| ☐ OO-DJN | Avro RJ-85 | E2275 | |
| ☐ OO-DJO | Avro RJ-85 | E2279 | |
| ☐ OO-DJP | Avro RJ-85 | E2287 | |
| ☐ OO-DJQ | Avro RJ-85 | E2289 | |
| ☐ O-DJR | Avro RJ-85 | E2290 | |
| ☐ OO-DJS | Avro RJ-85 | E2292 | |
| ☐ OO-DJT | Avro RJ-85 | E2294 | |
| ☐ OO-DJV | Avro RJ-85 | E2295 | |
| ☐ OO-DJW | Avro RJ-85 | E2296 | |
| ☐ OO-DJX | Avro RJ-85 | E2297 | |
| ☐ OO-DJY | Avro RJ-85 | E2302 | |
| ☐ OO-DJZ | Avro RJ-85 | E2305 | |
| | | | |
| ☐ OO-DWA | Avro RJ-100 | E3308 | |
| ☐ OO-DWB | Avro RJ-100 | E3315 | |
| ☐ OO-DWC | Avro RJ-100 | E3322 | |
| ☐ OO-DWD | Avro RJ-100 | E3324 | |
| ☐ OO-DWE | Avro RJ-100 | E3327 | |
| ☐ OO-DWF | Avro RJ-100 | E3332 | |
| ☐ OO-DWG | Avro RJ-100 | E3336 | |
| ☐ OO-DWH | Avro RJ-100 | E3340 | |
| ☐ OO-DWI | Avro RJ-100 | E3342 | |
| ☐ OO-DWJ | Avro RJ-100 | E3355 | |
| ☐ OO-DWK | Avro RJ-100 | E3360 | |
| ☐ OO-DWL | Avro RJ-100 | E3361 | |
| | | | |
| ☐ OO-MJE | BAe 146 Srs.200 | E2192 | |
| ☐ OO-SSK | Airbus A319-132 | 1336 | o/o |
| ☐ OO-SSG | Airbus A319-132 | 1160 | o/o |
| ☐ OO-SSH | Airbus A319-132 | 1184 | o/o |

## SOBELAIR SLR

| | | | |
|---|---|---|---|
| ☐ OO-RMV | Boeing 737-408 | 1705/24352 | |
| ☐ OO-SBJ | Boeing 737-46B | 1844/24573 | |
| ☐ OO-SBM | Boeing 737-429 | 2217/25729 | |
| ☐ OO-SBX | Boeing 737-3M8 | 2017/25040 | |
| ☐ OO-SBZ | Boeing 737-329 | 1412/23775 | |
| ☐ OO-SLW | Boeing 737-448 | 1742/24474 | |
| | | | |
| ☐ OO-IHV | Boeing 767-3BGER | 798/30564 | |
| ☐ OO-SLR | Boeing 767-3BGER | 786/30563 | |
| ☐ OO-SLS | Boeing 767-3BGER | 817/30566 | |
| ☐ OO-VAS | Boeing 737-86Q | 1237/30285 | |

## THOMAS COOK AIRLINES BELGIUM TCW

| | | | |
|---|---|---|---|
| ☐ D-AICF | Airbus A320-212 | 0905 | Lsf CIB |
| ☐ OO-TCB | Airbus A320-231 | 0357 | Lsf JMC |
| ☐ OO-TCC | Airbus A320-231 | 0411 | Lsf JMC |
| ☐ OO-TCF | Airbus A320-231 | 0354 | Lsf JMC |
| ☐ OO-TCH | Airbus A320-214 | 1929 | o/o |

## TNT AIRWAYS TAY

| | | | |
|---|---|---|---|
| ☐ EC-HQT | Airbus A300B4-203F | 124 | Opb PNR |
| ☐ EC-HVZ | Airbus A300B4-203F | 227 | Opb PNR |
| ☐ OO-TZA | Airbus A300B4-203F | 155 | |
| ☐ OO-TZB | Airbus A300B4-203F | 261 | |
| ☐ OO-TZC | Airbus A300B4-203F | 210 | |
| ☐ OO-TZD | Airbus A300B4-203F | 247 | |
| | | | |
| ☐ EC-ELT | BAe 146 Srs.200QT | E2102 | Opb PNR |
| ☐ EC-FVY | BAe 146 Srs.200QT | E2117 | Opb PNR |
| ☐ EC-FZE | BAe 146 Srs.200QT | E2105 | Opb PNR |
| ☐ EC-GQO | BAe 146 Srs.200QT | E2086 | Opb PNR |
| ☐ EC-HDH | BAe 146 Srs.200QT | E2056 | Opb PNR |
| ☐ EC-HJH | BAe 146 Srs.200QT | E2112 | Opb PNR |
| ☐ I-TNTC | BAe 146 Srs.200QT | E2078 | Opb MSA |
| ☐ I-MSAA | BAe 146 Srs.200QT | E2109 | Opb MSA |
| ☐ OO-TAA | BAe 146 Srs.300QT | E3151 | |
| ☐ OO-TAD | BAe 146 Srs.300QT | E3166 | |
| ☐ OO-TAE | BAe 146 Srs.300QT | E3182 | |
| ☐ OO-TAF | BAe 146 Srs.300QT | E3186 | |
| ☐ OO-TAH | BAe 146 Srs.300QT | E3168 | |
| ☐ OO-TAJ | BAe 146 Srs.300QT | E3153 | |
| ☐ OO-TAK | BAe 146 Srs.300QT | E3150 | |
| ☐ OO-TAR | BAe 146 Srs.200QT | E2067 | |
| ☐ OO-TAS | BAe 146 Srs.300QT | E3154 | |
| ☐ OO-TAU | BAe 146 Srs.200QT | E2100 | |
| ☐ OO-TAW | BAe 146 Srs.200QT | E2089 | |
| ☐ OO-TJA | Boeing 747-47UF | 1184/29255 | OpbGTI |
| | | | |
| ☐ RA-64032 | Tu-204-120C | 1450743164032 | |
| ☐ SU-EAG | Tu-204-120C | 1450743764028 | Lsf CCE |
| ☐ SU-EAJ | Tu-204-120S | 1450743164029 | Lsf CCE |
| ☐ SU-EAK | Tu-204-120S | 1450743164033 | Lsf CCE |

## VIRGIN EXPRESS VEX

| | | | |
|---|---|---|---|
| ☐ OO-LTM | Boeing 737-3M8 | 2037/25070 | |
| ☐ OO-LTU | Boeing 737-33A | 2709/27455 | |
| ☐ OO-VBR | Boeing 737-4Y0 | 1680/24314 | |
| ☐ OO-VED | Boeing 737-46M | 2847/28550 | |
| ☐ OO-VEF | Boeing 737-430 | 2311/27000 | |
| ☐ OO-VEG | Boeing 737-36N | 2987/28568 | |
| ☐ OO-VEH | Boeing 737-36N | 3022/28571 | |
| ☐ OO-VEJ | Boeing 737-405 | 1738/24271 | |
| ☐ OO-VEK | Boeing 737-405 | 1726/24270 | |
| ☐ OO-VEN | Boeing 737-36N | 3090/28586 | |
| ☐ OO-VEO | Boeing 737-4Y0 | 1876/24688 | |
| ☐ OO-VEP | Boeing 737-43Q | 2827/28489 | |
| ☐ OO-VES | Boeing 737-43Q | 2838/28493 | o/o |
| ☐ OO-VEX | Boeing 737-36N | 2948/28670 | |
| ☐ OO-VJO | Boeing 737-4Y0 | 1667/23980 | |

## VLM AIRLINES VLM

| | | | |
|---|---|---|---|
| ☐ OO-VLE | Fokker 50 | 20132 | |
| ☐ OO-VLJ | Fokker 50 | 20105 | |
| ☐ OO-VLK | Fokker 50 | 20122 | |
| ☐ OO-VLM | Fokker 50 | 20135 | |
| ☐ OO-VLN | Fokker 50 | 20145 | |
| ☐ OO-VLO | Fokker 50 | 20127 | |
| ☐ OO-VLQ | Fokker 50 | 20159 | |
| ☐ OO-VLR | Fokker 50 | 20121 | |
| ☐ OO-VLS | Fokker 50 | 20109 | |
| ☐ OO-VLV | Fokker 50 | 20160 | |

## OY - DENMARK

## AIR GREENLAND GRL

| | | | |
|---|---|---|---|
| ☐ OY-CBT | DHC-7-103 | 10 | |
| ☐ OY-CBU | DHC-7-103 | 20 | |
| ☐ OY-CTC | DHC-7-102 | 101 | |
| ☐ OY-GRD | DHC-7-103 | 9 | |
| ☐ OY-GRE | DHC-7-103 | 106 | |
| ☐ OY-GRF | DHC-7-102 | 113 | |
| | | | |
| ☐ OY-GRL | Boeing 757-236 | 449/25620 | |
| ☐ OY-GRN | Airbus A330-223 | 230 | |
| ☐ OY-HAF | Sikorsky S-61N | 61267 | |
| ☐ OY-HAG | Sikorsky S-61N | 61268 | |

## ATLANTIC AIRWAYS FLI

| | | | |
|---|---|---|---|
| ☐ OY-CRG | BAe 146 Srs.200A | E2075 | |
| ☐ OY-RCA | BAe 146 Srs.200 | E2045 | |

## AVIATION ASSISTANCE VIS

| | | | |
|---|---|---|---|
| ☐ OY-BVI | Beech 1900C-1 | UC-55 | |
| ☐ OY-GEG | Beech 1900C-1 | UC-132 | std CNL |
| ☐ OY-GEP | Beech 1900D | UE-31 | Lst TRQ |

| | | | |
|---|---|---|---|
| ☐ OY-GMP | Beech 1900D | UE-29 | Lst TRQ |
| ☐ OY- | Beech 1900D | UE-35 | |
| ☐ OY-MUD | Shorts SD.3-60 | SH3692 | Lst EAD |

### BENAIR AIR SERVICE — BDI

| | | |
|---|---|---|
| ☐ OY-BJP | SA.227AC Metro III | AC-499 |
| ☐ OY-PBH | LET L-410UVP-E20 | 972736 |
| ☐ OY-PBI | LET L-410UVP-E20 | 871936 |

### CHC DENMARK — HBI

| | | |
|---|---|---|
| ☐ OY-HDT | AS.332L Super Puma | 2017 |
| ☐ OY-HEO | AS.332L Super Puma | 2007 |
| ☐ OY-HHA | AS.332L Super Puma | 2015 |
| ☐ OY-HHC | AS.332L Super Puma | 2179 |

### CIMBER AIR — CIM

| | | | |
|---|---|---|---|
| ☐ OY-CIB | ATR 42-300 | 007 | |
| ☐ OY-CID | ATR 42-300 | 079 | |
| ☐ OY-CIE | ATR 42-300 | 082 | |
| ☐ OY-CIG | ATR 42-300 | 019 | |
| ☐ OY-CIH | ATR 42-300 | 238 | |
| ☐ OY-CIJ | ATR 42-500 | 497 | Lst OMA |
| ☐ OY-CIK | ATR 42-500 | 501 | Lst OMA |
| ☐ OY-CIL | ATR 42-500 | 514 | |
| ☐ OY-CIM | ATR 72-212A | 468 | |
| ☐ OY-CIN | ATR 72-212A | 568 | |
| ☐ OY-CIO | ATR 72-212A | 595 | |
| ☐ OY-CIP | ATR 72-201 | 147 | |
| ☐ OY-CIT | ATR 42-310 | 196 | |
| ☐ OY-CIV | ATR 72-201 | 150 | |
| | | | |
| ☐ OY-RJA | Canadair RJ-200 | 7413 | |
| ☐ OY-RJB | Canadair RJ-200 | 7419 | |

### DANISH AIR TRANSPORT

| | | | |
|---|---|---|---|
| ☐ OY-CIA | ATR 42-300 | 005 | Lst GUY |
| ☐ OY-CIR | ATR 42-310 | 107 | |
| ☐ OY-CIU | ATR 42-310 | 112 | |
| ☐ OY-JRJ | ATR 42-320 | 036 | |
| ☐ OY-JRY | ATR 42-300 | 063 | |
| ☐ OY-MUK | ATR 42-300 | 176 | |
| ☐ OY-RUB | ATR 72-202 | 301 | Lst IBB |
| ☐ OY- | ATR 72-201 | 227 | |
| ☐ OY-RUM | ATR 42-300 | 010 | |
| | | | |
| ☐ G-RUNG | SAAB SF.340A | 086 | Lst AUR |
| ☐ OY-JRF | Beech 1900C | UB-66 | |
| ☐ OY-JRI | Beech 1900C-1 | UC-44 | |
| ☐ OY-JRK | Short SC.7 Skyliner | SH1901 | |
| ☐ OY-JRV | Beech 1900D | UE-338 | |

### MAERSK AIR — DAN

| | | | |
|---|---|---|---|
| ☐ OY-APB | Boeing 737-5L9 | 2788/28084 | |
| ☐ OY-APH | Boeing 737-5L9 | 2856/28721 | |
| ☐ OY-API | Boeing 737-5L9 | 2868/28722 | |
| ☐ OY-APK | Boeing 737-5L9 | 2947/28995 | |
| ☐ OY-APL | Boeing 737-5L9 | 2998/28996 | Lst LOT |
| ☐ OY-APN | Boeing 737-5L9 | 3008/28997 | |
| ☐ OY-APP | Boeing 737-5L9 | 3068/29234 | |
| ☐ OY-APR | Boeing 737-5L9 | 3076/29235 | |
| ☐ OY-MAC | Boeing 737-5L9 | 1919/24859 | |
| ☐ OY-MAD | Boeing 737-5L9 | 1961/24928 | |
| ☐ OY-MAE | Boeing 737-5L9 | 2038/25066 | |
| ☐ OY-MAO | Boeing 737-3L9 | 2587/27336 | Lst BAG |
| ☐ OY-MAP | Boeing 737-3L9 | 2594/27337 | Lst BAG |
| ☐ OY-MAS | Boeing 737-3L9 | 2692/27834 | Lst GBL |
| ☐ OY-MRC | Boeing 737-7L9 | 26/28006 | |
| ☐ OY-MRD | Boeing 737-7L9 | 136/28007 | |
| ☐ OY-MRE | Boeing 737-7L9 | 203/28008 | |
| ☐ OY-MRF | Boeing 737-7L9 | 221/28009 | |
| ☐ OY-MRG | Boeing 737-7L9 | 396/28010 | |

| | | | |
|---|---|---|---|
| ☐ OY-MRH | Boeing 737-7L9 | 682/28013 | |
| ☐ OY-MRI | Boeing 737-7L9 | 766/28014 | Lst ELG |
| ☐ OY-MRJ | Boeing 737-7L9 | 785/28015 | |
| ☐ OY-MRK | Boeing 737-7L9 | 1092/28012 | Lst ELG |
| ☐ OY-MRL | Boeing 737-7L9 | 1203/28011 | |
| | | | |
| ☐ OY-MBP | Canadair RJ-200 | 7247 | Lsf MSK |
| ☐ OY-MBR | Canadair RJ-200 | 7248 | Lsf MSK |
| ☐ OY-MBS | Canadair RJ-200 | 7283 | Lsf MSK |
| ☐ OY-MBT | Canadair RJ-200 | 7617 | |
| ☐ OY-MMU | Fokker 50 | 20153 | Lst ELL |
| ☐ OY-MMV | Fokker 50 | 20154 | Lst ELL |

### NEWAIR AIRSERVICE — NAW

| | | | |
|---|---|---|---|
| ☐ OY-EBB | Fokker 50 | 20118 | |
| ☐ OY-EBC | F-27 Friendship 200 | 10675 | Lst RAE |
| ☐ OY-EBD | Fokker 50 | 20119 | |
| ☐ OY-EBG | Fokker 50 | 20227 | |
| ☐ OY-MMS | Fokker 50 | 20148 | |

### NORTH FLYING — NFA

| | | | |
|---|---|---|---|
| ☐ OY-NPB | SA.227AC Metro III | AC-420 | |
| ☐ OY-NPD | SA.227DC Metro 23 | DC-865B | Lsf DAX |
| ☐ OY-NPE | SA.227DC Metro 23 | DC-867B | Lsf DAX |

### MYTRAVEL AIRWAYS — VKG

| | | | |
|---|---|---|---|
| ☐ OY-CNB | Airbus A320-212 | 0221 | Lsf AIH |
| ☐ OY-CNC | Airbus A320-212 | 0222 | Lsf AIH |
| ☐ OY-CNM | Airbus A320-212 | 0301 | Lsf AIH |
| ☐ OY-CNN | Airbus A320-212 | 0348 | Lsf AIH |
| ☐ OY-CNP | Airbus A320-212 | 0294 | Lsf AIH |
| ☐ OY-CNR | Airbus A320-212 | 0349 | Lsf AIH |
| ☐ OY-VKA | Airbus A321-211 | 1881 | |
| ☐ OY-VKB | Airbus A321-211 | 1921 | |
| ☐ OY-VKC | Airbus A321-211 | 1932 | |
| ☐ OY-VKL | Airbus A320-231 | 1780 | |
| ☐ OY-VKM | Airbus A320-231 | 1889 | |
| ☐ OY-VKN | Airbus A320-231 | | o/o |
| ☐ OY-VKT | Airbus A320-231 | | o/o |
| ☐ OY-VKF | Airbus A330-243 | 309 | Lst AIH |
| ☐ OY-VKG | Airbus A330-343X | 349 | Lsf AIH |
| ☐ OY-VKH | Airbus A330-343X | 356 | Lsf AIH |
| ☐ OY-VKI | Airbus A330-343X | 357 | Lsf AIH |
| ☐ OY-CNO | Douglas DC-10-30 | 260/46990 | Lst AIH |
| ☐ OY-CNS | Douglas DC-10-10 | 285/46646 | Lst AIH |
| ☐ OY-CNU | Douglas DC-10-10 | 318/47832 | Lst AIH |
| ☐ OY-CNY | Douglas DC-10-10 | 252/46983 | Lst AIH |

### SCANDINAVIAN AIRLINE SYSTEM — SAS

For details see under **Sweden (SE-)**

### SCAN-CON AIRWAYS

| | | |
|---|---|---|
| ☐ OY-ASY | Embraer EMB.110P1 | 110308 |
| ☐ OY-BHT | Embraer EMB.110P2 | 110161 |
| ☐ OY-MUG | Shorts SD.3-60 | SH3716 |
| ☐ OY-SCF | SAAB 340A | 007 |
| ☐ OY-IVA | Nord 262A/Mohawk 298 | 57 |

### STAR AIR — SRR

| | | | |
|---|---|---|---|
| ☐ OY-UPA | Boeing 727-31C | 458/19233 | Lsf UPS |
| ☐ OY-UPD | Boeing 727-22C | 341/19103 | Lsf UPS |
| ☐ OY-UPJ | Boeing 727-22C | 336/19102 | Lsf UPS |
| ☐ OY-UPS | Boeing 727-31C | 425/19232 | Lsf UPS |
| | | | |
| ☐ OY-USA | Boeing 757-24APF | 569/25462 | Lsf UPS |
| ☐ OY-USB | Boeing 757-24APF | 573/25463 | Lsf UPS |
| ☐ OY-USC | Boeing 757-24APF | 577/25464 | Lsf UPS |
| ☐ OY-USD | Boeing 757-24APF | 579/25465 | Lsf UPS |

## STERLING EUROPEAN AIRLINES     *SNB*

| | | |
|---|---|---|
| OY-SEA | Boeing 737-8Q8 | 50/28213 |
| OY-SEB | Boeing 737-8Q8 | 78/28214 |
| OY-SEC | Boeing 737-8Q8 | 226/28221 |
| OY-SED | Boeing 737-8Q8 | 769/28237 |
| OY-SEH | Boeing 737-85H | 178/29444 |
| OY-SEI | Boeing 737-85H | 186/29445 |
| OY-SEJ | Boeing 737-85H | 29446 | o/o |

## SUN-AIR OF SCANDINAVIA     *SUS*

| | | |
|---|---|---|
| OY-MUE | BAe Jetstream 31 | 758 |
| OY-SVF | BAe Jetstream 31 | 686 |
| OY-SVI | BAe ATP | 2061 |
| OY-SVJ | BAe Jetstream 31 | 711 |
| OY-SVK | BAe Jetstream 31 | 772 |
| OY-SVS | BAe Jetstream 41 | 41014 |
| OY-SVT | BAe ATP | 2062 |
| OY-SVU | BAe ATP | 2063 |
| OY-SVW | BAe Jetstream 41 | 41047 |

# P - NORTH KOREA

## AIR KORYO

| | | | |
|---|---|---|---|
| P-551 | Tupolev Tu-154B | 75A-129 | |
| P-552 | Tupolev Tu-154B | 76A-143 | |
| P-553 | Tupolev Tu-154B | 77A-191 | |
| P-561 | Tupolev Tu-154B-2 | 83A-573 | |
| P-618 | Ilyushin Il-62M | 2546624 | Govt |
| P-813 | Tupolev Tu-134B-3 | 66215 | |
| P-814 | Tupolev Tu-134B-3 | 66368 | |
| P-835 | Ilyushin Il-18D | 188011205 | |
| P-836 | Ilyushin Il-18V | 185008204 | |
| P-881 | Ilyushin Il-62M | 3647853 | |
| P-882 | Ilyushin Il-62M | 2850236 | Govt |
| P-885 | Ilyushin Il-62M | 3933913 | |
| P-912 | Ilyushin Il-76MD | 1003403104 | |
| P-913 | Ilyushin Il-76TD | 1003404126 | |
| P-914 | Ilyushin Il-76TD | 1003404146 | |

# PH - NETHERLANDS

## AIR HOLLAND     *HLN*

| | | | |
|---|---|---|---|
| PH-AHE | Boeing 757-27B | 165/2413 | |
| PH-AHR | Boeing 767-328ER | 497/27136 | |
| PH-AHS | Boeing 757-28A | 530/25622 | Lsf TSC |

## DENIM AIR     *DNM*

| | | | |
|---|---|---|---|
| PH-DEI | DHC-8Q-315 | 586 | Lst ANS |
| PH-DEJ | DHC-8Q-315 | 581 | |
| PH-DME | DHC-8Q-315 | 560 | Lst ANS |
| PH-DMI | DHC-8Q-315 | 561 | Lst ANS |
| PH-DML | DHC-8Q-315 | 562 | Lst ANS |
| PH-DMM | DHC-8Q-315 | 563 | Lst ANS |
| PH-DMP | DHC-8Q-315 | 564 | Lst ANS |
| PH-DMQ | DHC-8Q-315 | 567 | Lst ANS |
| PH-DMR | DHC-8Q-315 | 569 | Lst ANS |
| PH-DMU | DHC-8Q-315 | 568 | Lst ANS |
| PH-DMV | DHC-8Q-315 | 570 | Lst ANS |
| PH-DMW | DHC-8Q-315 | 573 | Lst ANS |
| PH-DMX | DHC-8Q-315 | 574 | Lst ANS |
| PH-DMY | DHC-8Q-315 | 576 | Lst ANS |
| PH-DMZ | DHC-8Q-315 | 582 | Lst ANS |
| PH-- | DHC-8Q-315 | 589 | Lst ANS |
| PH- | DHC-8Q-315 | 590 | Lst ANS |
| PH-FZE | Fokker 50 | 20182 | |
| PH-FZG | Fokker 50 | 20202 | Lst ANS |
| PH-FZH | Fokker 50 | 20210 | |
| PH-JXN | Fokker 50 | 20239 | Lst ANS |
| PH-LMT | Fokker 50 | 20192 | |
| PH-PRG | Fokker 50 | 20155 | std |
| PH-PRH | Fokker 50 | 20200 | |

| | | | |
|---|---|---|---|
| PH-PRI | Fokker 50 | 20201 | |
| PH-PRJ | Fokker 50 | 20212 | Lst REA |
| PH-RRF | Fokker 50 | 20220 | |
| PH-WXH | Fokker 50 | 20251 | |

## DUTCHBIRD     *DBR*

| | | | |
|---|---|---|---|
| PH-DBA | Boeing 757-230 | 274/24738 | Lsf CFG |
| PH-DBB | Boeing 757-230 | 275/24747 | Lsf CFG |
| PH-DBH | Boeing 757-230 | 285/24748 | Lsf CFG |
| PH- | Airbus A320-214 | 1081 | o/o |
| PH- | Airbus A320-214 | 1370 | o/o |

## FARNAIR NETHERLANDS     *FRN*

| | | | |
|---|---|---|---|
| D-AAAC | F-27 Friendship 500 | 10378 | Lst EPA |
| PH-FHL | F-27 Friendship 500F | 10634 | |
| PH-FLM | F-27 Friendship 500F | 10341 | |
| PH-FNV | F-27 Friendship 500 | 10397 | Lst MNL |
| PH-FNW | F-27 Friendship 500 | 10398 | |
| PH-FYC | F-27 Friendship 500F | 10632 | |
| PH-JLN | F-27 Friendship 500 | 10449 | |
| PH-CLA | Airbus A300B4-103F | 044 | |
| PH-EAN | Airbus A300B4-103F | 041 | |
| PH-GIR | Airbus A300B4-103F | 042 | |

## KLM CITYHOPPER     *KLC*

| | | |
|---|---|---|
| PH-JXJ | Fokker 50 | 20232 |
| PH-KVA | Fokker 50 | 20189 |
| PH-KVB | Fokker 50 | 20190 |
| PH-KVC | Fokker 50 | 20191 |
| PH-KVD | Fokker 50 | 20197 |
| PH-KVE | Fokker 50 | 20206 |
| PH-KVF | Fokker 50 | 20207 |
| PH-KVG | Fokker 50 | 20211 |
| PH-KVH | Fokker 50 | 20217 |
| PH-KVI | Fokker 50 | 20218 |
| PH-KVK | Fokker 50 | 20219 |
| PH-KXM | Fokker 50 | 20252 |
| PH-JCH | Fokker 70 | 11528 |
| PH-JCT | Fokker 70 | 11537 |
| PH-KZA | Fokker 70 | 11567 |
| PH-KZB | Fokker 70 | 11562 |
| PH-KZC | Fokker 70 | 11566 |
| PH-KZD | Fokker 70 | 11582 |
| PH-KZE | Fokker 70 | 11576 |
| PH-KZF | Fokker 70 | 11577 |
| PH-KZG | Fokker 70 | 11578 |
| PH-KZH | Fokker 70 | 11583 |
| PH-KZI | Fokker 70 | 11579 |
| PH-KZK | Fokker 70 | 11581 |
| PH-KZL | Fokker 70 | 11536 |
| PH-KZM | Fokker 70 | 11561 |
| PH-KZN | Fokker 70 | 11553 |
| PH-KZO | Fokker 70 | 11538 |
| PH-KZ | Fokker 70 | 11539 |
| PH-KZR | Fokker 70 | 11551 |
| PH-WXA | Fokker 70 | 11570 |
| PH-WXC | Fokker 70 | 11574 |
| PH-WXG | Fokker 70 | 11532 |

## KLM EXCEL     *AXL*

| | | | |
|---|---|---|---|
| PH-XLE | ATR 42-320 | 090 | |
| PH-XLH | ATR 72-201 | 195 | |
| PH-XLI | ATR 42-320 | 066 | |
| PH-XLK | ATR 42-320 | 093 | |
| PH-XLL | ATR 42-320 | 374 | |
| PH-XLM | ATR 42-320 | 78 | |
| PH-RXA | Embraer ERJ-145 | 145216 | |
| PH-RXB | Embraer ERJ-145 | 145320 | |
| PH-RXC | Embraer ERJ-145 | 145106 | Lst MLD |
| PH-XLB | Embraer EMB.120RT | 120091 | |

## KLM – ROYAL DUTCH AIRLINES                    KLM

| | | | |
|---|---|---|---|
| ☐ | PH-BDA | Boeing 737-306 | 1275/23537 |
| ☐ | PH-BDB | Boeing 737-306 | 1288/23538 |
| ☐ | PH-BDC | Boeing 737-306 | 1295/23539 |
| ☐ | PH-BDD | Boeing 737-306 | 1303/23540 |
| ☐ | PH-BDE | Boeing 737-306 | 1309/23541 |
| ☐ | PH-BDG | Boeing 737-306 | 1317/23542 |
| ☐ | PH-BDI | Boeing 737-306 | 1335/23544 |
| ☐ | PH-BDK | Boeing 737-306 | 1343/23545 |
| ☐ | PH-BDN | Boeing 737-306 | 1640/24261 |
| ☐ | PH-BDO | Boeing 737-306 | 1642/24262 |
| ☐ | PH-BDP | Boeing 737-306 | 1681/24404 |
| ☐ | PH-BDR | Boeing 737-406 | 1768/24514 |
| ☐ | PH-BDS | Boeing 737-406 | 1770/24529 |
| ☐ | PH-BDT | Boeing 737-406 | 1772/24530 |
| ☐ | PH-BDU | Boeing 737-406 | 1902/24857 |
| ☐ | PH-BDW | Boeing 737-406 | 1903/24858 |
| ☐ | PH-BDY | Boeing 737-406 | 1949/24959 |
| ☐ | PH-BDZ | Boeing 737-406 | 2132/25355 |
| ☐ | PH-BPB | Boeing 737-4Y0 | 1723/24344 |
| ☐ | PH-BPC | Boeing 737-4Y0 | 1747/24468 |
| ☐ | PH-BTA | Boeing 737-406 | 2161/25412 |
| ☐ | PH-BTB | Boeing 737-406 | 2184/25423 |
| ☐ | PH-BTC | Boeing 737-406 | 2200/25424 |
| ☐ | PH-BTD | Boeing 737-306 | 2406/27420 |
| ☐ | PH-BTE | Boeing 737-306 | 2438/27421 |
| ☐ | PH-BTF | Boeing 737-406 | 2591/27232 |
| ☐ | PH-BTG | Boeing 737-406 | 2601/27233 |
| ☐ | PH-BTH | Boeing 737-306 | 2930/28719 |
| ☐ | PH-BTI | Boeing 737-306 | 2957/28720 |
| ☐ | PH-BXA | Boeing 737-8K2 | 198/29131 |
| ☐ | PH-BXB | Boeing 737-8K2 | 261/29132 |
| ☐ | PH-BXC | Boeing 737-8K2 | 305/29133 |
| ☐ | PH-BXD | Boeing 737-8K2 | 355/29134 |
| ☐ | PH-BXE | Boeing 737-8K2 | 552/29595 |
| ☐ | PH-BXF | Boeing 737-8K2 | 583/29596 |
| ☐ | PH-BXG | Boeing 737-8K2 | 605/30357 |
| ☐ | PH-BXH | Boeing 737-8K2 | 630/29597 |
| ☐ | PH-BXI | Boeing 737-8K2 | 633/30358 |
| ☐ | PH-BXK | Boeing 737-8K2 | 639/29598 |
| ☐ | PH-BXL | Boeing 737-8K2 | 659/30359 |
| ☐ | PH-BXM | Boeing 737-8K2 | 714/30355 |
| ☐ | PH-BXN | Boeing 737-8K2 | 728/30356 |
| ☐ | PH-BXO | Boeing 737-9K2 | 866/29599 |
| ☐ | PH-BXP | Boeing 737-9K2 | 924/29600 |
| ☐ | PH-BXR | Boeing 737-9K2 | 959/29601 |
| ☐ | PH-BXS | Boeing 737-9K2 | 982/29602 |
| | | | |
| ☐ | PH-BFA | Boeing 747-406 | 725/23999 |
| ☐ | PH-BFB | Boeing 747-406 | 732/24000 |
| ☐ | PH-BFC | Boeing 747-406M | 735/23982 |
| ☐ | PH-BFD | Boeing 747-406M | 737/24001 |
| ☐ | PH-BFE | Boeing 747-406M | 763/24201 |
| ☐ | PH-BFF | Boeing 747-406M | 770/24202 |
| ☐ | PH-BFG | Boeing 747-406 | 782/24517 |
| ☐ | PH-BFH | Boeing 747-406M | 783/24518 |
| ☐ | PH-BFI | Boeing 747-406M | 850/25086 |
| ☐ | PH-BFK | Boeing 747-406 | 854/25087 |
| ☐ | PH-BFL | Boeing 747-406 | 888/25356 |
| ☐ | PH-BFM | Boeing 747-406M | 896/26373 |
| ☐ | PH-BFN | Boeing 747-406 | 969/26372 |
| ☐ | PH-BFO | Boeing 747-406M | 938/25413 |
| ☐ | PH-BFP | Boeing 747-406M | 992/26374 |
| ☐ | PH-BFR | Boeing 747-406M | 1014/27202 |
| ☐ | PH-BFS | Boeing 747-406 | 1090/28195 |
| ☐ | PH-BFT | Boeing 747-406 | 1112/28459 |
| ☐ | PH-BFU | Boeing 747-406 | 1127/28196 |
| ☐ | PH-BFV | Boeing 747-406 | 1225/28460 |
| ☐ | PH-BFW | Boeing 747-406 | 1258/30454 |
| ☐ | PH-BFY | Boeing 747-406 | 1302/30455 |
| ☐ | PH-BUH | Boeing 747-206M (EUD/SF)271/21110 |  |
| ☐ | PH-BUI | Boeing 747-206M (EUD/SF)276/21111 |  |
| ☐ | PH-BUK | Boeing 747-206M (EUD)336/21549 |  |
| ☐ | PH-BUL | Boeing 747-206M (EUD)344/21550 |  |
| ☐ | PH-BUM | Boeing 747-206M (EUD)369/21659 |  |
| ☐ | PH-BUN | Boeing 747-206M (EUD)389/21660 |  |
| ☐ | PH-BUO | Boeing 747-206B (EUD)397/21848 |  |

| | | | |
|---|---|---|---|
| ☐ | PH-BUR | Boeing 747-206B (EUD)491/22379 |  |
| ☐ | PH-BUT+ | Boeing 747-206M (EUD)539/22380 |  |
| ☐ | PH-BUU+ | Boeing 747-306M | 587/23056 |
| ☐ | PH-BUV | Boeing 747-306M | 600/23137 |
| ☐ | PH-BUW | Boeing 747-306M | 657/23508 |
| ☐ | PH-CKA | Boeing 747-406ERF | 33694 |
| ☐ | PH-CKB | Boeing 747-406ERF | 33695 |
| ☐ | PH-CKC | Boeing 747-406ERF | 33696 |
| | | | |
| ☐ | PH-BZA | Boeing 767-306ER | 587/27957 |
| ☐ | PH-BZB | Boeing 767-306ER | 589/27958 |
| ☐ | PH-BZC | Boeing 767-306ER | 592/26263 |
| ☐ | PH-BZD | Boeing 767-306ER | 605/27610 |
| ☐ | PH-BZE | Boeing 767-306ER | 607/28098 |
| ☐ | PH-BZF | Boeing 767-306ER | 609/27959 |
| ☐ | PH-BZG | Boeing 767-306ER | 625/27960 |
| ☐ | PH-BZH | Boeing 767-306ER | 633/27611 |
| ☐ | PH-BZI | Boeing 767-306ER | 647/27612 |
| ☐ | PH-BZK | Boeing 767-306ER | 661/27614 |
| ☐ | PH-BZM | Boeing 767-306ER | 738/28884 |
| ☐ | PH-BZO | Boeing 767-306ER | 781/30393 |
| ☐ | PH- | Boeing 777-206ER | o/c |
| ☐ | PH- | Boeing 777-206ER | o/c |
| | | | |
| ☐ | PH-KCA | McDD MD-11 | 557/48555 |
| ☐ | PH-KCB | McDD MD-11 | 561/48556 |
| ☐ | PH-KCC | McDD MD-11 | 569/48557 |
| ☐ | PH-KCD | McDD MD-11 | 573/48558 |
| ☐ | PH-KCE | McDD MD-11 | 575/48559 |
| ☐ | PH-KCF | McDD MD-11 | 578/48560 |
| ☐ | PH-KCG | McDD MD-11 | 585/48561 |
| ☐ | PH-KCH | McDD MD-11 | 591/48562 |
| ☐ | PH-KCI | McDD MD-11 | 593/48563 |
| ☐ | PH-KCK | McDD MD-11 | 612/48564 |

## MARTINAIR HOLLAND                    MPH

| | | | |
|---|---|---|---|
| ☐ | PH-MCG | Boeing 767-31AER | 279/24428 |
| ☐ | PH-MCH | Boeing 767-31AER | 294/24429 |
| ☐ | PH-MCI | Boeing 767-31AER | 400/25312 |
| ☐ | PH-MCL | Boeing 767-31AER | 415/26469 |
| ☐ | PH-MCM | Boeing 767-31AER | 416/26470 |
| ☐ | PH-MCV | Boeing 767-31AER | 595/27619 |
| | | | |
| ☐ | PH-MCP | McDD MD-11CF | 577/48616 |
| ☐ | PH-MCR | McDD MD-11CF | 581/48617 |
| ☐ | PH-MCS | McDD MD-11CF | 584/48618 |
| ☐ | PH-MCT | McDD MD-11CF | 586/48629 |
| ☐ | PH-MCU | McDD MD-11F | 606/48757 |
| ☐ | PH-MCW | McDD MD-11CF | 632/48788 |
| | | | |
| ☐ | PH-AHI | Boeing 757-27B | 178/24137 |
| ☐ | PH-BUH | Boeing 747-206M (EUD/SF) 271/21110 o/o |  |
| ☐ | PH-MCE | Boeing 747-21AC | 669/23652 |
| ☐ | PH-MCF | Boeing 747-21AM | 712/24134 |
| ☐ | PH-MCN | Boeing 747-228F | 878/25266 |
| ☐ | PH-MPD | Airbus A320-232 | 1944 o/o |
| ☐ | PH-MPE | Airbus A320-232 | 1945 |

## METROPOLIS REGIONAL AIRLINES                    MPS

| | | | |
|---|---|---|---|
| ☐ | PH-BRL | Embraer EMB.120RT | 120083 |
| ☐ | PH-BRM | Embraer EMB.120RT | 120090 |
| ☐ | PH-BRP | Embraer EMB.120RT | 120175 Lst ESK |

## ROSSAIR EUROPE                    ROS

| | | | |
|---|---|---|---|
| ☐ | PH-ACY | Beech 1900D | UE-44 |
| ☐ | PH-RAG | Beech 1900D | UE-29 |
| ☐ | PH-RAH | Beech 1900D | UE-31 Lst Euromanx |
| ☐ | PH-RAE | Beech 1900D | UE-21 |
| ☐ | PH-RAR | Beech 1900D | UE-372 Lst EuroManx |
| ☐ | PH-RAT | Beech 1900D | UE-350 Lst Euromanx |
| ☐ | PH-RAK | ATR 42-300 | 032 |
| ☐ | PH-RAQ | ATR 42-300 | 139 |

## SCHREINER AIRWAYS — SCH

| | | | |
|---|---|---|---|
| ☐ PH-SDH | DHC-8-102 | 222 | |
| ☐ PH-SDK | DHC-8-311A | 254 | |
| ☐ PH-SDM | DHC-8-311A | 298 | |
| ☐ PH-SDU | DHC-8-311A | 232 | |
| ☐ PH-SDV | DHC-8-311A | 267 | |
| ☐ PH-TTA | DHC-8-102A | 237 | Lst AQB |

## SCHREINER NORTHSEA HELICOPTERS

| | | |
|---|---|---|
| ☐ PH-NZD | Sikorsky S-61N | 61489 |
| ☐ PH-NZG | Sikorsky S-61N | 61753 |
| ☐ PH-NZK | Sikorsky S-61N | 61773 |
| ☐ PH-NZL | Sikorsky S-61N | 61775 |

## TRANSAVIA AIRLINES — TRA

| | | | |
|---|---|---|---|
| ☐ PH-HZA | Boeing 737-8K2 | 51/28373 | |
| ☐ PH-HZB | Boeing 737-8K2 | 57/28374 | |
| ☐ PH-HZC | Boeing 737-8K2 | 85/28375 | |
| ☐ PH-HZD | Boeing 737-8K2 | 252/28376 | |
| ☐ PH-HZE | Boeing 737-8K2 | 277/28377 | Lst SCX |
| ☐ PH-HZF | Boeing 737-8K2 | 291/28378 | |
| ☐ PH-HZG | Boeing 737-8K2 | 498/28379 | Lst BER |
| ☐ PH-HZI | Boeing 737-8K2 | 524/28380 | Lst SCX |
| ☐ PH-HZJ | Boeing 737-8K2 | 549/30389 | |
| ☐ PH-HZK | Boeing 737-8K2 | 555/30390 | |
| ☐ PH-HZL | Boeing 737-8K2 | 814/30391 | |
| ☐ PH-HZM | Boeing 737-8K2 | 833/30392 | |
| ☐ PH-HZN | Boeing 737-8K2 | 32943 | o/o |
| ☐ PH-HZO | Boeing 737-8K2 | 32944 | o/o |
| ☐ PH-HZP | Boeing 737-8K2 | 1122/30646 | |
| ☐ PH-HZV | Boeing 737-8K2 | 1158/30650 | Lst SCX |
| ☐ PH-HZW | Boeing 737-8K2 | 1132/29345 | |
| ☐ PH-HZX | Boeing 737-8K2 | 1126/28248 | |
| ☐ PH-HZY | Boeing 737-8K2 | 1122/30646 | |
| ☐ PH-HZX | Boeing 737-8K2 | 1126/28248 | |
| ☐ PH-XRA | Boeing 737-7K2 | 873/30784 | |
| ☐ PH-XRB | Boeing 737-7K2 | 28256 | o/o |
| ☐ PH-XRC | Boeing 737-7K2 | 29347 | o/o |
| ☐ PH-XRD | Boeing 737-7K2 | 30659 | o/o |
| ☐ PH-XRW | Boeing 737-7K2 | 33465 | o/o |
| ☐ PH-XRX | Boeing 737-7K2 | 33464 | o/o |
| ☐ PH-XRY | Boeing 737-7K2 | 33463 | o/o |
| ☐ PH-XRZ | Boeing 737-7K2 | 33462 | o/o |
| ☐ PH-TKA | Boeing 757-2K2 | 519/26633 | |
| ☐ PH-TKB | Boeing 757-2K2 | 545/26634 | |
| ☐ PH-TKC | Boeing 757-2K2 | 608/26635 | |

## TRANS TRAVEL AIRLINES — TRQ

| | | | |
|---|---|---|---|
| ☐ PH-RAG | Beech 1900D | UE-29 | Lsf ROS |
| ☐ PH-RAR | Beech 1900D | UE-372 | Lsf ROS |
| ☐ PH-RAE | Beech 1900D | UE-21 | Lsf ROS |
| ☐ PH-RAK | ATR 42-300 | 032 | Lsf ROS |
| ☐ PH-RAQ | ATR 42-300 | 139 | Lsf ROS |
| ☐ ZS-ORE | ATR 42-300F | 086 | Lsf ROS |

## TULIP AIR — TLP

| | | |
|---|---|---|
| ☐ PH-KJG | BAe Jetstream 31 | 690 |

# PJ - NETHERLANDS ANTILLES

## DUTCH CARIBBEAN AIRLINES — ALM

| | | |
|---|---|---|
| ☐ PJ-SEF | McDD MD-82 | 1075/49123 |
| ☐ PJ-SEG | McDD MD-82 | 1077/49124 |
| ☐ PJ-SEH | McDD MD-82 | 1452/49661 |
| ☐ PJ-SNK | Douglas DC-9-31 | 1039/48144 |
| ☐ PJ- | Douglas DC-9-31 | 1046/48154 |
| ☐ PJ- | Douglas DC-9-31 | 1024/48139 |

## DUTCH CARIBBEAN EXPRESS — DCE

| | | |
|---|---|---|
| ☐ PJ-DHE | DHC-8-311A | 242 |
| ☐ PJ-DHI | DHC-8-311A | 230 |

## DUTCH EAGLE EXPRESS

| | | |
|---|---|---|
| ☐ PH- | Embraer EMB.120 | o/o |
| ☐ PH- | Embraer EMB.120 | o/o |
| ☐ PH- | ATR 42- | o/o |
| ☐ PH- | ATR 42- | o/o |

# PK - INDONESIA

## AIRFAST INDONESIA — AFE

| | | |
|---|---|---|
| ☐ PK-OCI | Boeing 737-230C | 234/20255 |
| ☐ PK-OCP | Boeing 737-27A | 1424/23794 |
| ☐ PK-OCQ | Boeing 737-2Q8 | 554/21687 |

## AIR MARK INDONESIA AVIATION

| | | |
|---|---|---|
| ☐ PK-AIG | Boeing 737-204 | 696/22364 |

## AIR PARADISE INTERNATIONAL

| | | | |
|---|---|---|---|
| ☐ PK-KDW | Airbus A310-324 | 534 | o/o |

## BATAVIA AIR — BTV

| | | | |
|---|---|---|---|
| ☐ PK-YCM | F-28 Fellowship 4000 | 11158 | |
| ☐ PK-YTA | Boeing 737-266 | 451/21192 | |
| ☐ PK-YTF | Boeing 737-2T5 | 737/22397 | |
| ☐ PK-YTI | Boeing 737-2L9 | 698/22407 | |
| ☐ PK-YTK | Boeing 737-4Y0 | 1865/24687 | o/o |
| ☐ PK-YTP | Boeing 737-4Y0 | 1731/24345 | o/o |

## BAYU INDONESIA AIR — BYU

| | | |
|---|---|---|
| ☐ PK-BYD | Boeing 737-2Q8 | 522/21518 |

## BOURAQ INDONESIA AIRLINES — BOU

| | | | |
|---|---|---|---|
| ☐ PK-IJH | Boeing 737-2K2 | 507/21397 | |
| ☐ PK-IJI | Boeing 737-230 | 734/22125 | |
| ☐ PK-IJJ | Boeing 737-230 | 762/22130 | |
| ☐ PK-IJK | Boeing 737-230 | 838/22143 | |
| ☐ PK-IJM | Boeing 737-230 | 764/22131 | |
| ☐ PK-IJN | Boeing 737-230 | 769/22132 | |
| ☐ PK-KJK | Boeing 737-266 | 457/21195 | Lsf MSR |
| ☐ PK-KJM | Boeing 737-2H6 | 559/21732 | |
| ☐ PK-KJN | Boeing 737-2K5 | 814/22599 | |
| ☐ PK-YGM | Boeing 737-2A9C | 249/20206 | |
| ☐ PK-NAI | F-28 Fellowship 4000 | 11142 | Opb NIN |

## CITYLINK

| | | | |
|---|---|---|---|
| ☐ PK-GFS | F-28 Fellowship 3000R | 11119 | Lsf MNA |
| ☐ PK-GFT | F-28 Fellowship 3000R | 11129 | Lsf MNA |
| ☐ PK-GFW | F-28 Fellowship 3000RC | 11134 | Lsf MNA |
| ☐ PK-GKZ | F-28 Fellowship 4000 | 11216 | Lsf MNA |
| ☐ PK-GQB | F-28 Fellowship 4000 | 11218 | Lsf MNA |

## GARUDA INDONESIA — GIA

| | | |
|---|---|---|
| ☐ PK-GPA | Airbus A330-341 | 138 |
| ☐ PK-GPC | Airbus A330-341 | 140 |
| ☐ PK-GPD | Airbus A330-341 | 144 |
| ☐ PK-GPE | Airbus A330-341 | 148 |
| ☐ PK-GPF | Airbus A330-341 | 153 |
| ☐ PK-GPG | Airbus A330-341 | 165 |
| ☐ PK-GGA | Boeing 737-5U3 | 2920/28726 |
| ☐ PK-GGC | Boeing 737-5U3 | 2937/28727 |
| ☐ PK-GGD | Boeing 737-5U3 | 2938/28728 |
| ☐ PK-GGE | Boeing 737-5U3 | 2950/28729 |

| | | | |
|---|---|---|---|
| ☐ PK-GGF | Boeing 737-5U3 | 2952/28730 | |
| ☐ PK-GGG | Boeing 737-3U3 | 2949/28731 | |
| ☐ PK-GGN | Boeing 737-3U3 | 3029/28735 | |
| ☐ PK-GGO | Boeing 737-3U3 | 3032/28736 | |
| ☐ PK-GGP | Boeing 737-3U3 | 3037/28737 | |
| ☐ PK-GGQ | Boeing 737-3U3 | 3064/28739 | |
| ☐ PK-GGR | Boeing 737-3U3 | 3079/28741 | |
| ☐ PK-GGS | Boeing 737-33A | 2153/25138 | |
| ☐ PK-GGT | Boeing 737-36N | 2964/28566 | |
| ☐ PK- | Boeing 737-341 | 2971/28567 | o/o |
| ☐ PK- | Boeing 737-34S | 2983/29108 | o/o |
| ☐ PK- | Boeing 737-34S | 3001/29109 | o/o |
| ☐ PK-GWK | Boeing 737-4U3 | 2531/25713 | |
| ☐ PK-GWL | Boeing 737-4U3 | 2535/25714 | |
| ☐ PK-GWM | Boeing 737-4U3 | 2537/25715 | |
| ☐ PK-GWN | Boeing 737-4U3 | 2540/25716 | |
| ☐ PK-GWO | Boeing 737-4U3 | 2546/25717 | |
| ☐ PK-GWP | Boeing 737-4U3 | 2548/25718 | |
| ☐ PK-GWQ | Boeing 737-4U3 | 2549/25719 | |
| ☐ PK-GWT | Boeing 737-4K5 | 2711/26316 | |
| ☐ PK-GWU | Boeing 737-4Q8 | 2076/24708 | |
| ☐ PK-GWV | Boeing 737-4Y0 | 1777/24512 | |
| ☐ PK-GWW | Boeing 737-470 | 1901/24683 | |
| ☐ PK-GWX | Boeing 737-4Y0 | 1904/24691 | |
| ☐ PK-GWY | Boeing 737-43Q | 2830/28490 | |
| ☐ PK-GWZ | Boeing 737-49R | 2833/28881 | |
| ☐ PK-GZA | Boeing 737-497 | 2382/25663 | |
| ☐ PK-GZC | Boeing 737-497 | 2393/25664 | |
| | | | |
| ☐ PK-GSA | Boeing 747-2U3B | 452/22246 | |
| ☐ PK-GSB | Boeing 747-2U3B | 459/22247 | |
| ☐ PK-GSC | Boeing 747-2U3B | 461/22248 | |
| ☐ PK-GSD | Boeing 747-2U3B | 468/22249 | |
| ☐ PK-GSG | Boeing 747-4U3 | 1011/25704 | |
| ☐ PK-GSH | Boeing 747-4U3 | 1029/25705 | |
| ☐ PK-GSI | Boeing 747-441 | 917/24956 | |
| | | | |
| ☐ PK-GIA | Douglas DC-10-30 | 223/46918 | |
| ☐ PK-GIB | Douglas DC-10-30 | 226/46919 | |
| ☐ PK-GIC | Douglas DC-10-30 | 239/46964 | |
| ☐ PK-GID | Douglas DC-10-30 | 246/46951 | |
| ☐ PK-GIF | Douglas DC-10-30 | 286/46686 | |

### INDONESIAN AIRLINES    IAA

| | | | |
|---|---|---|---|
| ☐ PK-IAA | Boeing 737-330 | 1290/23528 | Lsf DLH |
| ☐ PK-IAB | Boeing 737-330 | 1285/23527 | Lsf DLH |
| ☐ PK-IAT | Boeing 747-312 | 626/23245 | |

### JATAYU AIR    JTY

| | | | |
|---|---|---|---|
| ☐ PK-JGC | Boeing 727-227 | 974/20736 | |
| ☐ PK-JGS | Boeing 737-222 | 197/19949 | |
| ☐ PK-JGT | Boeing 727-247 | 889/20580 | |
| ☐ PK-JGU | Boeing 727-227 | 929/20613 | |
| ☐ PK-JGV | Boeing 737-266 | 466/21227 | |
| ☐ PK-JGW | Boeing 737-2N7 | 458/21226 | |
| ☐ PK-J | Boeing 727-200 | | |
| ☐ PK-J | Boeing 737-200 | | |

### LION AIRLINES    LNI

| | | | |
|---|---|---|---|
| ☐ PK-LIA | Boeing 737-2P5 | 502/21440 | |
| ☐ PK-LMD | McDD MD-82 | 1069/49113 | |
| ☐ PK-LME | McDD MD-82 | 2145/53481 | |
| ☐ PK-LMF | McDD MD-82 | 2069/53147 | |
| ☐ PK-LMG | McDD MD-82 | 1278/49417 | |
| ☐ PK-LMH | McDD MD-82 | 1403/49419 | |
| ☐ PK- | McDD MD-82 | 1201/49373 | |
| ☐ PK- | McDD MD-82 | 1068/49112 | |
| ☐ PK- | McDD MD-82 | 1159/49262 | |
| ☐ PK- | McDD MD-82 | 1163/49263 | |
| ☐ PK- | McDD MD-82 | 1043/48083 | |
| ☐ PK- | McDD MD-82 | 1032/48089 | |
| ☐ PK- | McDD MD-82 | 1019/48066 | |
| ☐ PK- | McDD MD-82 | 1173/49189 | |
| ☐ PK- | McDD MD-82 | 1159/49262 | |

### MANDALA AIRLINES    MDL

| | | | |
|---|---|---|---|
| ☐ PK-RIA | Boeing 737-2P6 | 497/21357 | |
| ☐ PK-RIC | Boeing 737-2S3 | 646/22278 | |
| ☐ PK-RID | Boeing 737-2T4 | 906/22803 | |
| ☐ PK-RIE | Boeing 737-2T4 | 908/22804 | |
| ☐ PK-RIF | Boeing 737-2L9 | 549/21685 | |
| ☐ PK-RIH | Boeing 737-4Y0 | 1616/23868 | |
| ☐ PK-RII | Boeing 737-2E7 | 922/22876 | |
| ☐ PK-RIJ | Boeing 737-210 | 578/21820 | |
| ☐ PK-RIK | Boeing 737-2V5 | 724/22531 | |
| ☐ PK-RIL | Boeing 737-230 | 788/22137 | |
| ☐ PK-RIM | Boeing 737-230 | 783/22136 | |
| ☐ PK-RIP | Boeing 737-2H4 | 905/22903 | |
| ☐ PK-RIQ | Boeing 737-291 | 957/23023 | |
| ☐ PK-RIR | Boeing 737-2L9 | 825/22735 | |

### MERPATI NUSANTARA AIRLINES    MNA

| | | | |
|---|---|---|---|
| ☐ PK-MBC | Boeing 737-230 | 754/22129 | |
| ☐ PK-MBD | Boeing 737-230 | 795/22141 | |
| ☐ PK-MBE | Boeing 737-230 | 797/22142 | |
| ☐ PK-MBF | Boeing 737-2T4 | 707/22368 | |
| ☐ PK-MBG | Boeing 737-2T4 | 708/22369 | |
| ☐ PK-MBH | Boeing 737-2S3 | 650/22279 | |
| ☐ PK-MBJ | Boeing 737-2U4 | 761/22576 | |
| ☐ PK-MBK | Boeing 737-4Y0 | 1883/24689 | |
| ☐ PK- | Boeing 737-4Y0 | 1733/24467 | |
| ☐ PK- | Boeing 737-4Y0 | 1779/24513 | |
| | | | |
| ☐ PK- | Fokker 50 | 20187 | o/o |
| ☐ PK- | Fokker 50 | 20188 | o/o |
| ☐ PK- | Fokker 50 | 20193 | o/o |
| ☐ PK- | Fokker 50 | 20195 | o/o |
| ☐ PK- | Fokker 50 | 20198 | o/o |
| | | | |
| ☐ PK-MJA | Fokker 100 | 11453 | |
| ☐ PK-MJC | Fokker 100 | 11463 | |
| ☐ PK-MJD | Fokker 100 | 11474 | |

### NURMAN AIR    NIN

| | | | |
|---|---|---|---|
| ☐ PK-NAI | F-28 Fellowship 4000 | 11142 | Op for BOU |
| ☐ PK-NAJ | F-28 Fellowship 4000 | 11133 | |

### PELITA AIR    PAS

| | | |
|---|---|---|
| ☐ PK-PCN | C.212-A4 | 56N/CC4-8-216 |
| ☐ PK-PCO | C.212-A4 | 55N/CC4-7-215 |
| ☐ PK-PCP | C.212-A4 | 48N/AB4-20-208 |
| ☐ PK-PCQ | C.212-A4 | 47N/AB4-19-207 |
| ☐ PK-PCR | C.212-A4 | 46N/AB4-18-206 |
| ☐ PK-PCS | C.212-A4 | 45N/AB4-17-205 |
| ☐ PK-PCT | C.212-A4 | 44N/AB4-16-204 |
| ☐ PK-PCU | C.212-A4 | 43N/AB4-15-203 |
| | | |
| ☐ PK-PSV | DHC-7-103 | 105 |
| ☐ PK-PSW | DHC-7-103 | 100 |
| ☐ PK-PSX | DHC-7-103 | 94 |
| ☐ PK-PSY | DHC-7-103 | 86 |
| ☐ PK-PSZ | DHC-7-103 | 75 |
| | | |
| ☐ PK-PFF | Fokker 100 | 11475 |
| ☐ PK-PFG | Fokker 100 | 11477 |
| ☐ PK-PFH | Fokker 50 | 20237 |
| ☐ PK-PFJ | Fokker 50 | 20260 |
| ☐ PK-PFK | Fokker 50 | 20283 |
| ☐ PK- | Fokker 50 | 20237 |
| ☐ PK-PJJ | Avro RJ85 | E2239 |
| ☐ PK-PJK | F-28 Fellowship 4000 | 11192 |
| ☐ PK-PJL | F-28 Fellowship 4000 | 11111 |
| ☐ PK-PJM | F-28 Fellowship 4000 | 11178 |
| ☐ PK-PJY | F-28 Fellowship 4000 | 11146 |

### REPUBLIC EXPRESS – RPX AIRLINES    RPH

| | | | |
|---|---|---|---|
| ☐ PK-RPX | Boeing 737-230C | 238/20256 | Lsd |

## SEULAWAH AIR

| | | | |
|---|---|---|---|
| ☐ PK-NAD | Boeing 737-209 | 1581/24197 | Lsf TSE |

## STAR AIR    STQ

| | | |
|---|---|---|
| ☐ PK-ALC | Boeing 737-2H6 | 1120/23320 |
| ☐ PK-ALK | Boeing 737-236 | 742/22032 |
| ☐ PK-ALN | Boeing 737-2B7 | 1044/23132 |

## TRANSAIR

| | | |
|---|---|---|
| ☐ PK-BAR | Boeing 727-25 | 229/18970 |

# PP-, PR-, PS-, PT- BRAZIL

## ABSA CARGO    TUS

| | | | |
|---|---|---|---|
| ☐ PR-ABA | Douglas DC-8-61F | 374/45980 | |
| ☐ PR-ABB | Boeing 767-316FER | 778/29881 | Lsf LDC |

## BETA CARGO AIR    BET

| | | |
|---|---|---|
| ☐ PP-BRG | Boeing 707-323C | 670/19586 |
| ☐ PP-BRR | Boeing 707-323C | 727/20088 |
| ☐ PP-BSE | Boeing 707-330C | 557/19317 |

## BRA – BRASIL RODO AEREO    BRB

| | | | |
|---|---|---|---|
| ☐ PR-BRA | Boeing 737-33A | 1462/23830 | |
| ☐ PR-BRB | Boeing 737-3Q4 | 1577/24210 | |
| ☐ PR-BRC | Boeing 737-46B | 2088/25262 | |
| ☐ PR-BRD | Boeing 737-3M8 | 1717/24376 | |
| ☐ PR-BRE | Boeing 737-3K9 | 1794/24213 | Lst MMZ |

## BRASMEX

| | | |
|---|---|---|
| ☐ PR-BME | Douglas DC-10-30F | 314/47819 |

## FLY LINHAS AEREAS    FLB

| | | | |
|---|---|---|---|
| ☐ PP-BLR | Boeing 727-243 | 1394/21661 | |
| ☐ PP-BLS | Boeing 727-224 | 934/20655 | |
| ☐ PP-JUB | Boeing 727-227 | 1196/21242 | std |
| ☐ PP-LBF | Boeing 727-2B6 | 945/20705 | |
| ☐ PP-LBO | Boeing 727-2B6 | 1633/22377 | std |

## GOL TRANSPORTES AEREOS    GLO

| | | |
|---|---|---|
| ☐ PR-GOA | Boeing 737-7L9 | 11/28005 |
| ☐ PR-GOB | Boeing 737-75B | 13/28099 |
| ☐ PR-GOC | Boeing 737-75B | 17/28101 |
| ☐ PR-GOD | Boeing 737-75B | 66/28105 |
| ☐ PR-GOE | Boeing 737-75B | 68/28106 |
| ☐ PR-GOF | Boeing 737-76Q | 843/30273 |
| ☐ PR-GOG | Boeing 737-76Q | 900/30275 |
| ☐ PR-GOH | Boeing 737-76N | 954/32440 |
| ☐ PR-GOI | Boeing 737-76N | 983/32574 |
| ☐ PR-GOJ | Boeing 737-8CX | 1041/32359 |
| ☐ PR-GOK | Boeing 737-8CX | 1084/32360 |
| ☐ PR-GOL | Boeing 737-7L9 | 10/28004 |
| ☐ PR-GOM | Boeing 737-76N | 463/28613 |
| ☐ PR-GON | Boeing 737-76N | 436/30051 |
| ☐ PR-GOO | Boeing 737-76N | 1068/30135 |
| ☐ PR-GOP | Boeing 737-8BK | 1194/30621 |
| ☐ PR-GOQ | Boeing 737-76N | 1215/33417 |
| ☐ PR-GOR | Boeing 737-76N | 1231/33380 |
| ☐ PR-GOT | Boeing 737-8BK | 1248/30625 |
| ☐ PR-GOU | Boeing 737-7Q8 | 183/28219 |
| ☐ PR-GOV | Boeing 737-76N | 135/28580 |
| ☐ PR-GOW | Boeing 737-76N | 170/28584 |

## NORDESTE L/A REGIONAIS    NES

| | | |
|---|---|---|
| ☐ PT-MND | Boeing 737-53A | 1898/24786 |
| ☐ PT-MNE | Boeing 737-53A | 1900/24787 |
| ☐ PT-MNH | Boeing 737-5Y0 | 2304/26067 |
| ☐ PT-MNI | Boeing 737-53A | 2177/25425 |
| ☐ PT-MNK | Boeing 737-33A | 2756/27457 |
| ☐ PT-MNL | Boeing 737-33A | 2959/27458 |
| ☐ PT-MNB | Fokker 50 | 20302 |
| ☐ PT-MNF | Embraer EMB.120ER | 120332 |
| ☐ PT-MNG | Embraer EMB.120ER | 120333 |
| ☐ PT-SLX | Fokker 50 | 20283 |
| ☐ PT-SRA | Fokker 50 | 20261 |

## PANTANAL    PTN

| | | | |
|---|---|---|---|
| ☐ PT-MFI | ATR 42-320 | 302 | |
| ☐ PT-MFJ | ATR 42-320 | 343 | |
| ☐ PT-MFK | ATR 42-300 | 225 | |
| ☐ PT-MFM | ATR 42-300 | 376 | |
| ☐ PT-MFT | ATR 42-320 | 306 | Lsf BZH |
| ☐ PT-MFU | ATR 42-310 | 070 | Lsf BZH |
| ☐ PT-MFV | ATR 42-300 | 043 | |
| ☐ PT-MFX | ATR 42-320 | 329 | |

## RIO-SUL    RSL

| | | |
|---|---|---|
| ☐ PT-MNJ | Boeing 737-33A | 2046/25057 |
| ☐ PT-SLU | Boeing 737-5Y0 | 2236/25186 |
| ☐ PT-SLW | Boeing 737-53A | 1964/24922 |
| ☐ PT-SSB | Boeing 737-5Q8 | 2834/27629 |
| ☐ PT-SSC | Boeing 737-5Q8 | 2889/27634 |
| ☐ PT-SSD | Boeing 737-56N | 2944/28565 |
| ☐ PT-SSE | Boeing 737-5Q8 | 2965/28052 |
| ☐ PT-SSF | Boeing 737-5Q8 | 2999/28201 |
| ☐ PT-SSG | Boeing 737-5Q8 | 3024/28055 |
| ☐ PT-SSH | Boeing 737-58E | 2991/29122 |
| ☐ PT-SSI | Boeing 737-53A | 1882/24785 |
| ☐ PT-SSJ | Boeing 737-33A | 1984/24791 |
| ☐ PT-SSK | Boeing 737-3Y0 | 1538/23922 |
| ☐ PT-SSL | Boeing 737-5Y0 | 2220/25185 |
| ☐ PT-SSM | Boeing 737-5Y0 | 2260/25191 |
| ☐ PT-SSN | Boeing 737-53A | 1945/24881 |
| ☐ PT-SSO | Boeing 737-53A | 1962/24921 |
| ☐ PT-SSP | Boeing 737-33A | 1741/24097 |
| ☐ PT-SSQ | Boeing 737-33A | 2703/27454 |
| ☐ PT-SPA | Embraer ERJ-145 | 145020 |
| ☐ PT-SPB | Embraer ERJ-145 | 145023 |
| ☐ PT-SPC | Embraer ERJ-145 | 145027 |
| ☐ PT-SPD | Embraer ERJ-145 | 145028 |
| ☐ PT-SPF | Embraer ERJ-145 | 145034 |
| ☐ PT-SPG | Embraer ERJ-145 | 145038 |
| ☐ PT-SPH | Embraer ERJ-145 | 145060 |
| ☐ PT-SPI | Embraer ERJ-145 | 145065 |
| ☐ PT-SPJ | Embraer ERJ-145 | 145083 |
| ☐ PT-SPK | Embraer ERJ-145 | 145089 |
| ☐ PT-SPL | Embraer ERJ-145 | 145090 |
| ☐ PT-SPM | Embraer ERJ-145 | 145114 |
| ☐ PT-SPN | Embraer ERJ-145 | 145127 |
| ☐ PT-SPO | Embraer ERJ-145 | 145137 |
| ☐ PT-SPP | Embraer ERJ-145 | 145350 |
| ☐ PR-SAA | Boeing 737-76Q | 947/30277 |
| ☐ PR-SAE | Boeing 737-73S | 187/29078 |
| ☐ PR-SAF | Boeing 737-7Q8 | 713/30635 |
| ☐ PR-SAG | Boeing 737-7Q8 | 369/28224 |
| ☐ PR-SAH | Boeing 737-76Q | 740/30271 |
| ☐ PT-SRD | Embraer EMB.120ER | 120315 |
| ☐ PT-SRE | Embraer EMB.120ER | 120324 |
| ☐ PT-SRG | Embraer EMB.120ER | 120331 |

## SKYMASTER AIRLINES    SKC

| | | |
|---|---|---|
| ☐ PT-MTR | Boeing 707-369C | 758/20084 |
| ☐ PT-WSZ | Boeing 707-338C | 404/18808 |
| ☐ PT-WUS | Boeing 707-324C | 576/19352 |
| ☐ PR-SKC | Douglas DC-8-63F | 547/46143 |
| ☐ PR-SKM | Douglas DC-8-63F | 527/46137 |

## TAM LINHAS AEREAS — TAM

| Reg | Type | c/n | Notes |
|---|---|---|---|
| PR-MAH | Airbus A319-132 | 1608 | |
| PR-MAI | Airbus A319-132 | 1703 | |
| PR-MAL | Airbus A319-132 | 1801 | |
| PR-MAM | Airbus A319-132 | 1826 | |
| PR-MAN | Airbus A319-132 | 1831 | |
| PR-MAO | Airbus A319-132 | 1837 | |
| PR-MAQ | Airbus A319-132 | 1855 | |
| PR-M | Airbus A319-132 | 1919 | o/o |
| PR-M | Airbus A319-132 | 1930 | o/o |
| PR-M | Airbus A319-132 | 1934 | o/o |
| PR-M | Airbus A319-132 | 1952 | o/o |
| PR-M | Airbus A319-132 | 1985 | o/o |
| PT-MZA | Airbus A319-132 | 0976 | |
| PT-MZB | Airbus A319-132 | 1010 | |
| PT-MZC | Airbus A319-132 | 1092 | |
| PT-MZD | Airbus A319-132 | 1096 | |
| PT-MZE | Airbus A319-132 | 1103 | |
| PT-MZF | Airbus A319-132 | 1139 | |
| | | | |
| PR-MAA | Airbus A320-232 | 1595 | |
| PR-MAB | Airbus A320-232 | 1663 | |
| PR-MAC | Airbus A320-232 | 1672 | |
| PR-MAD | Airbus A320-232 | 1771 | |
| PR-MAE | Airbus A320-232 | 1804 | |
| PR-MAF | Airbus A320-231 | 0249 | |
| PR-MAG | Airbus A320-232 | 1832 | |
| PR-MAJ | Airbus A320-232 | 1818 | |
| PR-MAK | Airbus A320-232 | 1825 | |
| PR-MAP | Airbus A320-232 | 1857 | |
| PR-MAR | Airbus A320-232 | 1888 | |
| PR-MA | Airbus A320-232 | | o/o |
| PR-M | Airbus A320-232 | | o/o |
| PR-M | Airbus A320-232 | | o/o |
| PT-MZG | Airbus A320-232 | 1143 | |
| PT-MZH | Airbus A320-232 | 1158 | |
| PT-MZI | Airbus A320-232 | 1246 | |
| PT-MZJ | Airbus A320-232 | 1251 | |
| PT-MZK | Airbus A320-232 | 1368 | |
| PT-MZL | Airbus A320-232 | 1376 | |
| PT-MZM | Airbus A320-232 | 0453 | |
| PT-MZN | Airbus A320-231 | 0440 | |
| PT-MZO | Airbus A320-231 | 0250 | |
| PT-MZP | Airbus A320-231 | 0243 | |
| PT-MZQ | Airbus A320-231 | 0335 | |
| PT-MZR | Airbus A320-231 | 0334 | |
| PT-MZS | Airbus A320-231 | 0251 | |
| PT-MZT | Airbus A320-232 | 1486 | |
| PT-MZU | Airbus A320-232 | 1518 | |
| PT-MZV | Airbus A320-232 | 0758 | |
| PT-MZW | Airbus A320-232 | 1580 | |
| PT-MZX | Airbus A320-232 | 1613 | |
| PT-MZY | Airbus A320-232 | 1628 | |
| PT-MZZ | Airbus A320-232 | 1593 | |
| | | | |
| PT-MVA | Airbus A330-222 | 232 | |
| PT-MVB | Airbus A330-222 | 238 | |
| PT-MVC | Airbus A330-222 | 247 | |
| PT-MVD | Airbus A330-222 | 259 | |
| PT-MVE | Airbus A330-223 | 361 | |
| PT-MVF | Airbus A330-223 | 466 | |
| PT-MVG | Airbus A330-223 | 472 | |
| PT-MVH | Airbus A330-223 | 477 | |
| PT-MVK | Airbus A330-223 | 486 | |
| PT- | Airbus A330-223 | | o/o |
| PT- | Airbus A330-223 | 527 | o/o |
| | | | |
| PT-MQA | Fokker 100 | 11296 | |
| PT-MQB | Fokker 100 | 11350 | |
| PT-MQC | Fokker 100 | 11371 | std |
| PT-MQD | Fokker 100 | 11383 | |
| PT-MQE | Fokker 100 | 11389 | |
| PT-MQF | Fokker 100 | 11401 | |
| PT-MQG | Fokker 100 | 11527 | |
| PT-MQI | Fokker 100 | 11517 | |
| PT-MQJ | Fokker 100 | 11347 | |
| PT-MQK | Fokker 100 | 11336 | |
| PT-MQL | Fokker 100 | 11394 | |
| PT-MQM | Fokker 100 | 11301 | |
| PT-MQN | Fokker 100 | 11409 | |
| PT-MQO | Fokker 100 | 11423 | |
| PT-MQP | Fokker 100 | 11430 | std |
| PT-MQQ | Fokker 100 | 11265 | |
| PT-MQR | Fokker 100 | 11421 | |
| PT-MQS | Fokker 100 | 11431 | |
| PT-MQT | Fokker 100 | 11429 | |
| PT-MQU | Fokker 100 | 11264 | |
| PT-MQV | Fokker 100 | 11326 | |
| PT-MQW | Fokker 100 | 11332 | |
| PT-MRA | Fokker 100 | 11284 | std |
| PT-MRB | Fokker 100 | 11285 | std |
| PT-MRC | Fokker 100 | 11320 | |
| PT-MRD | Fokker 100 | 11322 | std |
| PT-MRE | Fokker 100 | 11348 | std |
| PT-MRF | Fokker 100 | 11351 | std |
| PT-MRG | Fokker 100 | 11304 | std |
| PT-MRH | Fokker 100 | 11305 | |
| PT-MRI | Fokker 100 | 11442 | |
| PT-MRJ | Fokker 100 | 11451 | std |
| PT-MRL | Fokker 100 | 11441 | |
| PT-MRN | Fokker 100 | 11443 | |
| PT-MRO | Fokker 100 | 11470 | |
| PT-MRP | Fokker 100 | 11472 | |
| PT-MRQ | Fokker 100 | 11473 | |
| PT-MRR | Fokker 100 | 11461 | |
| PT-MRS | Fokker 100 | 11462 | |
| PT-MRT | Fokker 100 | 11505 | |
| PT-MRU | Fokker 100 | 11511 | |
| PT-MRV | Fokker 100 | 11516 | |
| PT-MRW | Fokker 100 | 11518 | |
| PT-MRX | Fokker 100 | 11341 | std |
| PT-MRY | Fokker 100 | 11343 | |
| PT-MRZ | Fokker 100 | 11290 | |
| PT-WHK | Fokker 100 | 11452 | std |
| PT-WHL | Fokker 100 | 11471 | |
| PT- | Fokker 100 | 11424 | o/o |
| PT- | Fokker 100 | 11433 | o/o |
| PT- | Fokker 100 | 11454 | o/o |
| PT- | Fokker 100 | 11455 | o/o |

## VARIG BRASIL — VRG

| Reg | Type | c/n | Notes |
|---|---|---|---|
| PP-CJR | Boeing 737-2C3 | 404/21015 | std |
| PP-CJT | Boeing 737-2C3 | 410/21017 | |
| PP-VME | Boeing 737-241 | 378/21000 | |
| PP-VMF | Boeing 737-241 | 384/21001 | std |
| PP-VMG | Boeing 737-241 | 385/21002 | std |
| PP-VMH | Boeing 737-241 | 389/21003 | |
| PP-VMI | Boeing 737-241 | 390/21004 | std |
| PP-VMJ | Boeing 737-241 | 394/21005 | std |
| PP-VML | Boeing 737-241 | 400/21007 | std |
| PP-VMM | Boeing 737-241 | 402/21008 | std |
| PP-VNM | Boeing 737-241 | 417/21009 | |
| PP-VNT | Boeing 737-33A | 1446/23828 | |
| PP-VNX | Boeing 737-33A | 1460/23829 | |
| PP-VNY | Boeing 737-3K9 | 1918/24864 | |
| PP-VNZ | Boeing 737-3K9 | 1926/24869 | |
| PP-VOH | Boeing 737-341 | 1673/24279 | std |
| PP-VON | Boeing 737-341 | 1935/24935 | |
| PP-VOO | Boeing 737-341 | 1951/24936 | |
| PP-VOR | Boeing 737-33A | 1727/24093 | |
| PP-VOS | Boeing 737-341 | 2085/25048 | |
| PP-VOT | Boeing 737-341 | 2091/25049 | |
| PP-VOU | Boeing 737-341 | 2125/25050 | |
| PP-VOV | Boeing 737-341 | 2127/25051 | |
| PP-VOW | Boeing 737-3Q8 | 2133/24961 | |
| PP-VOY | Boeing 737-3K9 | 2090/25210 | |
| PP-VOZ | Boeing 737-3K9 | 2100/25239 | |
| PP-VPA | Boeing 737-341 | 2273/26852 | |
| PP-VPB | Boeing 737-341 | 2321/26856 | |
| PP-VPC | Boeing 737-341 | 2326/26857 | |
| PP-VPF | Boeing 737-3S1 | 1896/24834 | |
| PP-VPQ | Boeing 737-36Q | 2940/28664 | |
| PP-VPR | Boeing 737-36Q | 3011/28761 | |
| PP-VPX | Boeing 737-33R | 2899/28870 | |
| PP-VPY | Boeing 737-33R | 2900/28871 | |
| PP-VPZ | Boeing 737-3S3 | 3061/29245 | |

| | | | |
|---|---|---|---|
| ☐ PP-VQN | Boeing 737-33A | 1763/24098 | |
| ☐ PP-VQO | Boeing 737-3M8 | 1719/24377 | |
| ☐ PP-VQW | Boeing 737-3S3 | 1374/23787 | |
| ☐ PP-VQZ | Boeing 737-33A | 2606/27284 | |
| ☐ PP- | Boeing 737-76N | 28872 | o/o |
| ☐ PP- | Boeing 737-81R | | o/o |
| ☐ PP- | Boeing 737-81R | | o/o |
| ☐ PP- | Boeing 737-741 | | o/o |
| ☐ PP- | Boeing 737-741 | | o/o |
| ☐ PP- | Boeing 737-741 | | o/o |
| ☐ PP- | Boeing 737-741 | | o/o |
| ☐ PP-VSA | Boeing 737-85F | 936/30571 | |
| ☐ PP-VSB | Boeing 737-85F | 976/30477 | |
| ☐ PP-VSC | Boeing 737-841 | | o/o |
| ☐ PP- | Boeing 737-841 | | o/o |
| ☐ PP-VNN | Boeing 767-241ER | 161/23803 | dbf? |
| ☐ PP-VNO | Boeing 767-241ER | 170/23801 | |
| ☐ PP-VNP | Boeing 767-241ER | 172/23802 | |
| ☐ PP-VNQ | Boeing 767-241ER | 178/23804 | |
| ☐ PP-VNR | Boeing 767-241ER | 180/23805 | |
| ☐ PP-VNS | Boeing 767-241ER | 181/23806 | |
| ☐ PP-VOI | Boeing 767-341ER | 289/24752 | |
| ☐ PP-VOJ | Boeing 767-341ER | 291/24753 | |
| ☐ PP-VOK | Boeing 767-341ER | 314/24843 | |
| ☐ PP-VOL | Boeing 767 341FR | 324/24844 | |
| ☐ PP-VPV | Boeing 767-375ER | 248/24080 | |
| ☐ PP-VPW | Boeing 767-375ER | 249/24087 | |
| ☐ PP- | Boeing 767-341ER | | o/o |
| ☐ PP- | Boeing 767-341ER | | o/o |
| ☐ PP- | Boeing 767-341ER | | o/o |
| ☐ PP- | Boeing 767-341ER | | o/o |
| ☐ PP- | Boeing 767-341ER | | o/o |
| ☐ PP- | Boeing 767-341ER | | o/o |
| ☐ PP-VRA | Boeing 777-2Q8ER | 365/28689 | |
| ☐ PP-VRB | Boeing 777-2Q8ER | 373/28692 | |
| ☐ PP- | Boeing 777-2Q8ER | | o/o |
| ☐ PP- | Boeing 777-2Q8ER | | o/o |
| ☐ PP- | Boeing 777-2Q8ER | | o/o |
| ☐ PP- | Boeing 777-2Q8ER | | o/o |
| ☐ PP-VPJ | McDD MD-11 | 523/48404 | |
| ☐ PP-VPK | McDD MD-11 | 524/48405 | |
| ☐ PP-VPN | McDD MD-11 | 486/48499 | |
| ☐ PP-VPO | McDD MD-11 | 493/48500 | |
| ☐ PP-VPP | McDD MD-11 | 513/48501 | |
| ☐ PP-VQF | McDD MD-11 | 520/48502 | |
| ☐ PP-VQG | McDD MD-11 | 528/48503 | |
| ☐ PP-VQH | McDD MD-11 | 548/48504 | |
| ☐ PP-VQI | McDD MD-11ER | 608/48753 | |
| ☐ PP-VQJ | McDD MD-11ER | 613/48755 | |
| ☐ PP-VQK | McDD MD-11ER | 615/48758 | |
| ☐ PP-VQL | McDD MD-11 | 488/48413 | |
| ☐ PP-VQM | McDD MD-11 | 491/48414 | |
| ☐ PP-VQX | McDD MD-11 | 603/48769 | |

### VARIG LOGISTICA — VLO

| | | | |
|---|---|---|---|
| ☐ PP-VLD | Boeing 727-41F | 824/20425 | |
| ☐ PP-VLE | Boeing 727-172C | 480/19666 | |
| ☐ PP-VLG | Boeing 727-41F | 810/20423 | |
| ☐ PP-VLS | Boeing 727-173C | 457/19508 | |
| ☐ PP-VQU | Boeing 727-2J7F | 1037/20880 | |
| ☐ PP-VQV | Boeing 727-243F | 1725/22166 | |
| ☐ PR-LGB | Boeing 727-2A1F | 1253/21341 | |
| ☐ PR-LGC | Boeing 727-2A1F | 1256/21342 | o/o |
| ☐ PP-VMT | Douglas DC-10-30CF | 329/47841 | |
| ☐ PP-VMU | Douglas DC-10-30CF | 332/47842 | std |
| ☐ PP-VQY | Douglas DC-10-30F | 179/46949 | |

### VASP — VSP

| | | | |
|---|---|---|---|
| ☐ CP-2313 | Boeing 737-3A1 | 2836/28389 | Lst LLB |
| ☐ PP-SFI | Boeing 737-2Q3 | 591/21478 | |
| ☐ PP-SFJ | Boeing 737-3K9 | 1633/24212 | |
| ☐ PP-SFN | Boeing 737-3L9 | 2763/27925 | |
| ☐ PP-SMA | Boeing 737-2A1 | 161/20092 | |

| | | | |
|---|---|---|---|
| ☐ PP-SMB | Boeing 737-2A1F | 169/20093 | VASPEX |
| ☐ PP-SMC | Boeing 737-2A1 | 182/20094 | |
| ☐ PP-SMF | Boeing 737-2A1 | 301/20589 | |
| ☐ PP-SMG | Boeing 737-2A1 | 324/20777 | |
| ☐ PP-SMH | Boeing 737-2A1 | 325/20778 | |
| ☐ PP-SMP | Boeing 737-2A1 | 327/20779 | |
| ☐ PP-SMQ | Boeing 737-214 | 180/20155 | |
| ☐ PP-SMR | Boeing 737-214 | 189/20157 | |
| ☐ PP-SMS | Boeing 737-214 | 193/20159 | |
| ☐ PP-SMT | Boeing 737-214 | 195/20160 | |
| ☐ PP-SMU | Boeing 737-2A1 | 364/20967 | |
| ☐ PP-SMW | Boeing 737-2H4C | 258/20346 | VASPEX |
| ☐ PP-SMZ | Boeing 737-2A1 | 382/20971 | |
| ☐ PP-SNA | Boeing 737-2A1 | 412/21094 | |
| ☐ PP-SNB | Boeing 737-2A1F | 432/21095 | VASPEX |
| ☐ PP-SOT | Boeing 737-3L9 | 2074/25150 | |
| ☐ PP-SOU | Boeing 737-3L9 | 2140/25360 | |
| ☐ PP-SPF | Boeing 737-2L7C | 419/21073 | |
| ☐ PP-SPG | Boeing 737-2L7 | 533/21616 | |
| ☐ PP-SPH | Boeing 737-2L9 | 614/22070 | |
| ☐ PP-SPI | Boeing 737-2Q3 | 519/21476 | |
| ☐ PP-SPJ | Boeing 737-2M9 | 461/21236 | |
| ☐ PP-SFC | Boeing 727-264F | 1143/21071 | VASPEX |
| ☐ PP-SFG | Boeing 727-2Q4F | 1698/22425 | VASPEX |
| ☐ PP-SFQ | Boeing 727-2J4F | 1588/22079 | VASPEX |
| ☐ PP-SNL | Airbus A300B2-203 | 202 | |
| ☐ PP-SNM | Airbus A300B2-203 | 205 | |
| ☐ PP-SNN | Airbus A300B2-203 | 225 | |

### PZ - SURINAME

#### SURINAM AIRWAYS — SLM

| | | | |
|---|---|---|---|
| ☐ PZ-TCK | Douglas DC-9-51 | 763/47655 | |

### P2 - PAPUA NEW GUINEA

#### AIR NIUGINI — ANG

| | | | |
|---|---|---|---|
| ☐ P2-AND | F-28 Fellowship 4000 | 11118 | |
| ☐ P2-ANE | F-28 Fellowship 1000 | 11033 | |
| ☐ P2-ANF | F-28 Fellowship 1000 | 11038 | |
| ☐ P2-ANI | F-28 Fellowship 4000 | 11223 | |
| ☐ P2-ANR | F-28 Fellowship 4000 | 11207 | |
| ☐ P2-ANS | F-28 Fellowship 4000 | 11195 | |
| ☐ P2-ANU | F-28 Fellowship 1000 | 11041 | |

### RA - RUSSIA

#### AEROFLOT DON AIRLINES — ROV

| | | | |
|---|---|---|---|
| ☐ RA-85295 | Tupolev Tu-154B-1 | 78A-295 | |
| ☐ RA-85308 | Tupolev Tu-154B-2 | 78A-308 | |
| ☐ RA-85409 | Tupolev Tu-154B-2 | 80A-409 | Lst KIL |
| ☐ RA-85425 | Tupolev Tu-154B-2 | 80A-425 | |
| ☐ RA-85435 | Tupolev Tu-154B-2 | 80A-435 | |
| ☐ RA-85436 | Tupolev Tu-154B-2 | 80A-436 | |
| ☐ RA-85452 | Tupolev Tu-154B-2 | 80A-452 | |
| ☐ RA-85453 | Tupolev Tu-154B-2 | 80A-453 | |
| ☐ RA-85527 | Tupolev Tu-154B-2 | 82A-527 | |
| ☐ RA-85626 | Tupolev Tu-154M | 87A-753 | Lsf AFL |
| ☐ RA-85640 | Tupolev Tu-154M | 88A-772 | Lsf AFL |
| ☐ RA-85726 | Tupolev Tu-154M | 86A-725 | |
| ☐ RA-12974 | Antonov An-12BP | 9346506 | Lsf FRT |
| ☐ RA-12994 | Antonov An-12V | 00347401 | Lsf FRT |
| ☐ RA-65100 | Tupolev Tu-134A-3 | 60258 | |
| ☐ RA-65666 | Tupolev Tu-134A-3 | 1351202 | |
| ☐ RA-65796 | Tupolev Tu-134A-3 | 63150 | |
| ☐ RA-65863 | Tupolev Tu-134A-3 | 28283 | |

#### AEROFLOT RUSSIAN AIRLINES — AFL

| | | | |
|---|---|---|---|
| ☐ F-OGQQ | Airbus A310-308 | 592 | |
| ☐ F-OGQR | Airbus A310-308 | 593 | |
| ☐ F-OGQT | Airbus A310-308 | 622 | |

| | | | |
|---|---|---|---|
| ☐ F-OGQU | Airbus A310-308 | 646 | |
| ☐ F-OGYP | Airbus A310-324 | 442 | |
| ☐ F-OGYQ | Airbus A310-324 | 453 | |
| ☐ F-OGYT | Airbus A310-324 | 660 | |
| ☐ F-OGYU | Airbus A310-324 | 687 | |
| ☐ F-OGYV | Airbus A310-324 | 689 | |
| ☐ VP-BAF | Airbus A310-304 | 472 | |
| ☐ VP-BAG | Airbus A310-304 | 475 | |
| ☐ VP-BAH | Boeing 737-4M0 | 3018/29201 | |
| ☐ VP-BAI | Boeing 737-4M0 | 3025/29202 | |
| ☐ VP-BAJ | Boeing 737-4M0 | 3049/29203 | |
| ☐ VP-BAL | Boeing 737-4M0 | 3051/29204 | |
| ☐ VP-BAM | Boeing 737-4M0 | 3056/29205 | |
| ☐ VP-BAN | Boeing 737-4M0 | 3058/29206 | |
| ☐ VP-BAO | Boeing 737-4M0 | 3078/29207 | |
| ☐ VP-BAP | Boeing 737-4M0 | 3081/29208 | |
| ☐ VP-BAQ | Boeing 737-4M0 | 3087/29209 | |
| ☐ VP-BAR | Boeing 737-4M0 | 3091/29210 | |
| ☐ VP-BAS | Boeing 777-2Q8ER | 135/27607 | |
| ☐ VP-BAU | Boeing 777-2Q8ER | 164/27608 | |
| ☐ VP-BAV | Boeing 767-36NER | 761/30107 | |
| ☐ VP-BAX | Boeing 767-36NER | 767/30109 | |
| ☐ VP-BAY | Boeing 767-36NER | 775/30110 | |
| ☐ VP-BAZ | Boeing 767-36NER | 776/30111 | |
| ☐ VP-BDE | Douglas DC-10-40F | 306/47823 | |
| ☐ VP-BDF | Douglas DC-10-40F | 349/47855 | |
| ☐ VP- | Douglas DC-10-40F | | o/o |
| ☐ VP- | Douglas DC-10-40F | | o/o |
| ☐ RA-86517 | Ilyushin Il-62M | 3139732 | |
| ☐ RA-86518 | Ilyushin Il-62M | 3139956 | |
| ☐ RA-86520 | Ilyushin Il-62M | 1241314 | |
| ☐ RA-86523 | Ilyushin Il-62M | 2241647 | |
| ☐ RA-86524 | Ilyushin Il-62M | 3242321 | |
| ☐ RA-86532 | Ilyushin Il-62M | 4243111 | |
| ☐ RA-86533 | Ilyushin Il-62M | 1343123 | |
| ☐ RA-76467 | Ilyushin Il-76TD | 0023440157 | |
| ☐ RA-76468 | Ilyushin Il-76TD | 0023441195 | |
| ☐ RA-76469 | Ilyushin Il-76TD | 0033444286 | |
| ☐ RA-76470 | Ilyushin Il-76TD | 0033445291 | |
| ☐ RA-76476 | Ilyushin Il-76TD | 0043451528 | Lsf ASE |
| ☐ RA-76478 | Ilyushin Il-76TD | 0053459788 | |
| ☐ RA-76479 | Ilyushin Il-76TD | 0053460790 | |
| ☐ RA-76482 | Ilyushin Il-76TD | 0053460832 | |
| ☐ RA-76488 | Ilyushin Il-76TD | 0073479371 | |
| ☐ RA-76750 | Ilyushin Il-76TD | 0083485561 | Lsf ASE |
| ☐ RA-76785 | Ilyushin Il-76TD | 0093495863 | |
| ☐ RA-76795 | Ilyushin Il-76TD | 0093498962 | |
| ☐ RA-86002 | Ilyushin Il-86 | 0103 | |
| ☐ RA-86015 | Ilyushin Il-86 | 51483202013 | |
| ☐ RA-86054 | Ilyushin Il-86 | 51483203021 | |
| ☐ RA-86058 | Ilyushin Il-86 | 51483203025 | |
| ☐ RA-86066 | Ilyushin Il-86 | 51483204033 | Lst VSO |
| ☐ RA-86067 | Ilyushin Il-86 | 51483204034 | |
| ☐ RA-86075 | Ilyushin Il-86 | 51483205044 | |
| ☐ RA-86079 | Ilyushin Il-86 | 51483206050 | |
| ☐ RA-86087 | Ilyushin Il-86 | 51483206058 | |
| ☐ RA-86088 | Ilyushin Il-86 | 51483206059 | |
| ☐ RA-86095 | Ilyushin Il-86 | 51483207066 | |
| ☐ RA-86096 | Ilyushin Il-86 | 51483207067 | |
| ☐ RA-86103 | Ilyushin Il-86 | 51483208071 | |
| ☐ RA-86110 | Ilyushin Il-86 | 51483208078 | |
| ☐ RA-86113 | Ilyushin Il-86 | 51483209081 | |
| ☐ RA-86124 | Ilyushin Il-86 | 51483210092 | |
| ☐ RA-96005 | Ilyushin Il-96-300 | 74393201002 | |
| ☐ RA-96007 | Ilyushin Il-96-300 | 74393201004 | |
| ☐ RA-96008 | Ilyushin Il-96-300 | 74393201005 | |
| ☐ RA-96010 | Ilyushin Il-96-300 | 74393201007 | |
| ☐ RA-96011 | Ilyushin Il-96-300 | 74393201008 | |
| ☐ RA-96015 | Ilyushin Il-96-300 | 74393201012 | |
| ☐ RA-65148 | Tupolev Tu-134A-3 | 61025 | Lsf KMV |
| ☐ RA-65559 | Tupolev Tu-134A | 49909 | |
| ☐ RA-65566 | Tupolev Tu-134A | 63952 | |
| ☐ RA-65567 | Tupolev Tu-134A | 63967 | |

| | | | |
|---|---|---|---|
| ☐ RA-65568 | Tupolev Tu-134A | 66135 | |
| ☐ RA-65612 | Tupolev Tu-134A-3 | 3352102 | Lsf KMV |
| ☐ RA-65623 | Tupolev Tu-134A | 49985 | |
| ☐ RA-65697 | Tupolev Tu-134A-3 | 63307 | |
| ☐ RA-65717 | Tupolev Tu-134A-3 | 63657 | |
| ☐ RA-65769 | Tupolev Tu-134A-3 | 62415 | |
| ☐ RA-65770 | Tupolev Tu-134A-3 | 62430 | |
| ☐ RA-65777 | Tupolev Tu-134A-3 | 62552 | |
| ☐ RA-65781 | Tupolev Tu-134A-3 | 62645 | |
| ☐ RA-65783 | Tupolev Tu-134A-3 | 62713 | |
| ☐ RA-65784 | Tupolev Tu-134A-3 | 62715 | |
| ☐ RA-65793 | Tupolev Tu-134A-3 | 63128 | |
| ☐ RA-85570 | Tupolev Tu-154B-2 | 83A-570 | |
| ☐ RA-85626 | Tupolev Tu-154M | 87A-753 | Lst DNV |
| ☐ RA-85637 | Tupolev Tu-154M | 87A-767 | |
| ☐ RA-85638 | Tupolev Tu-154M | 88A-768 | |
| ☐ RA-85639 | Tupolev Tu-154M | 88A-771 | |
| ☐ RA-85640 | Tupolev Tu-154M | 88A-772 | Lst DNV |
| ☐ RA-85642 | Tupolev Tu-154M | 88A-778 | |
| ☐ RA-85643 | Tupolev Tu-154M | 88A-779 | |
| ☐ RA-85644 | Tupolev Tu-154M | 88A-780 | |
| ☐ RA-85646 | Tupolev Tu-154M | 88A-784 | |
| ☐ RA-85647 | Tupolev Tu-154M | 88A-785 | |
| ☐ RA-85649 | Tupolev Tu-154M | 88A-787 | |
| ☐ RA-85661 | Tupolev Tu-154M | 89A-811 | |
| ☐ RA-85662 | Tupolev Tu-154M | 89A-816 | |
| ☐ RA-85663 | Tupolev Tu-154M | 89A-817 | |
| ☐ RA-85665 | Tupolev Tu-154M | 89A-819 | |
| ☐ RA-85668 | Tupolev Tu-154M | 89A-826 | |
| ☐ RA-85669 | Tupolev Tu-154M | 89A-827 | |
| ☐ RA-85670 | Tupolev Tu-154M | 89A-828 | |
| ☐ RA-85810 | Tupolev Tu-154M | 89A-824 | |
| ☐ RA-85811 | Tupolev Tu-154M | 89A-831 | |

## AEROFREIGHT AIRLINES — FRT

| | | | |
|---|---|---|---|
| ☐ RA-11115 | Antonov An-12BP | 01348003 | |
| ☐ RA-11116 | Antonov An-12B | 01348006 | |
| ☐ RA-11124 | Antonov An-12B | 02348106 | Jow TIS |
| ☐ RA-11128 | Antonov An-12B | 02348203 | |
| ☐ RA-11408 | Antonov An-12BP | 3341209 | |
| ☐ RA-11529 | Antonov An-12BP | 6344109 | Jow FUE |
| ☐ RA-12974 | Antonov An-12BP | 9346506 | Lst DNV |
| ☐ RA-12992 | Antonov An-12B | 00347306 | |
| ☐ RA-12994 | Antonov An-12V | 00347401 | Lst DNV |
| ☐ RA-48984 | Antonov An-12BP | 402603 | |
| ☐ RA-85312 | Tupolev Tu-154B-1 | 78A-312 | |
| ☐ RA-86531 | Ilyushin Il-62M | 4242654 | |
| ☐ RA-86565 | Ilyushin Il-62M | 2546812 | |
| ☐ RA-86935 | Ilyushin Il-62M | 1545951 | |

## AIRLINES 400 — VAZ

| | | | |
|---|---|---|---|
| ☐ RA-85634 | Tupolev Tu-154M | 87A-763 | Lst IRK |
| ☐ RA-85650 | Tupolev Tu-154M | 88A-788 | Lst BUC |
| ☐ RA-85653 | Tupolev Tu-154M | 88A-795 | |
| ☐ RA-85671 | Tupolev Tu-154M | 90A-829 | Lsf MVL |
| ☐ RA-85847 | Tupolev Tu-154M | 88A-792 | Lsf BTC |
| ☐ RA-64021 | Tu-204-100S | 1450743164021 | |
| ☐ RA-76472 | Ilyushin Il-76TD | 0033446350 | Lsf AYZ |
| ☐ RA-76483 | Ilyushin Il-76TD | 0063468042 | Lst TIS |
| ☐ RA-76787 | Ilyushin Il-76TD | 0093495854 | |

## AIRSTAN — JSC

| | | | |
|---|---|---|---|
| ☐ RA-76842 | Ilyushin Il-76TD | 1033418616 | |
| ☐ UK 76831 | Ilyushin Il-76TD | 1013409287 | Lsf TPR |

## AJT AIR INTERNATIONAL — TRJ

| | | | |
|---|---|---|---|
| ☐ RA-85832 | Tupolev Tu-154M | 92A-908 | |
| ☐ RA-86065 | Ilyushin Il-86 | 51483203032 | |
| ☐ RA-86115 | Ilyushin Il-86 | 51483209083 | |
| ☐ RA-86140 | Ilyushin Il-86 | 51483211102 | |
| ☐ RA-86141 | Ilyushin Il-86 | 51483211103 | |

## ALROSA AVIATION LRO

| | | |
|---|---|---|
| ☐ RA-65146 | Tupolev Tu-134B-3 | 61000 |
| ☐ RA-65693 | Tupolev Tu-134B-3 | 63221 |
| ☐ RA-65715 | Tupolev Tu-134B-3 | 63536 |
| ☐ RA-65738 | Tupolev Tu-134A | 2351507 |
| ☐ RA-65907 | Tupolev Tu-134A | 63996 |
| ☐ RA-85757 | Tupolev Tu-154M | 92A-939 |
| ☐ RA-85654 | Tupolev Tu-154M | 89A-796 |
| ☐ RA-85675 | Tupolev Tu-154M | 90A-835 |
| ☐ RA-85684 | Tupolev Tu-154M | 90A-851 |
| ☐ RA-85728 | Tupolev Tu-154M | 92A-910 |

## ASTRAKHAN AIRLINES ASZ

| | | | |
|---|---|---|---|
| ☐ RA-65055 | Tupolev Tu-134A | 49856 | Lst KGL |
| ☐ RA-65080 | Tupolev Tu-134A-3 | 60065 | |
| ☐ RA-65102 | Tupolev Tu-134A-3 | 60267 | Lst BTC |
| ☐ RA-65825 | Tupolev Tu-134A-3 | 09078 | |
| ☐ RA-65828 | Tupolev Tu-134A | 12086 | |

## ATLANT – SOYUZ AIRLINES AYZ

| | | | |
|---|---|---|---|
| ☐ EW-76711 | Ilyushin Il-76TS | 0063473187 | Lsf TXC |
| ☐ EW-76734 | Ilyushin Il-76TD | 0073476312 | Lsf TXC |
| ☐ EW-78779 | Ilyushin Il-76TD | 0083489662 | Lsf TXC |
| ☐ EW-78819 | Ilyushin Il-76TD | 0093495883 | Lsf TXC |
| ☐ RA-76367 | Ilyushin Il-76TD | 1033414474 | |
| ☐ RA-76370 | Ilyushin Il-76TD | 1033414458 | Jow GZP |
| ☐ RA-76401 | Ilyushin Il-76TD | 1023412399 | Lsf UHS |
| ☐ RA-76402 | Ilyushin Il-76TD | 1023413430 | Jow GZP |
| ☐ RA-76409 | Ilyushin Il-76TD | 1023410355 | Lsf KNM |
| ☐ RA-76425 | Ilyushin Il-76TD | 1003405167 | Lsf KNM |
| ☐ RA-76445 | Ilyushin Il-76TD | 1023410330 | Jow GZP |
| ☐ RA-76446 | Ilyushin Il-76TD | 1023412418 | Jow GZP |
| ☐ RA-76472 | Ilyushin Il-76TD | 0033446350 | Jow VAZ |
| ☐ RA-76494 | Ilyushin Il-76TD | 0053465956 | |
| ☐ RA-76783 | Ilyushin Il-76TD | 0093498974 | Lsf UHS |
| ☐ RA-76798 | Ilyushin Il-76TD | 1003403063 | Lsf BRZ |
| ☐ RA-78731 | Ilyushin Il-76T | 0013428831 | |
| | | | |
| ☐ RA-86062 | Ilyushin Il-86 | 51483203029 | Lsf UHS |
| ☐ RA-86139 | Ilyushin Il-86 | 51483210098 | Jow ESL |
| ☐ RA-96002 | Ilyushin Il-96-300 | 74393201001 | |

## ATRAN – AVIATRANS CARGO AIRLINES VAS

| | | | |
|---|---|---|---|
| ☐ RA-11868 | Antonov An-12B | 9346310 | |
| ☐ RA-12990 | Antonov An-12B | 00347304 | |
| ☐ RA-93912 | Antonov An-12B | 4341709 | |
| ☐ RA-93913 | Antonov An-12B | 4342609- | |
| ☐ RA-93915 | Antonov An-12B | 4342103 | |
| ☐ RA-98117 | Antonov An-12B | 402301 | |
| ☐ RA-98118 | Antonov An-12B | 6344304 | |
| ☐ RA-76809 | Ilyushin Il-76TD | 1013408252 | Lsf DOB |

## ATRUVERA AIR TRANSPORT AUV

| | | | |
|---|---|---|---|
| ☐ EW-76737 | Ilyushin Il-76TD | 0073477323 | Lsf TXC |
| ☐ EW-78827 | Ilyushin Il-76TD | 1003499997 | Lsf TXC |
| ☐ RA-76471 | Ilyushin Il-76TD | 0033446345 | |
| ☐ RA-76659 | Ilyushin Il-76MD | 0053463908 | |
| ☐ RA-76672 | Ilyushin Il-76TD | 0063466981 | Lst IRU |

## AVIACON ZITOTRANS AZS

| | | | |
|---|---|---|---|
| ☐ RA-76352 | Ilyushin Il-76TD | 1023411378 | |
| ☐ RA-76510 | Ilyushin Il-76T | 083414432 | Lsf TYM |
| ☐ RA-76514 | Ilyushin Il-76T | 083415453 | Lsf TYM |
| ☐ RA-76518 | Ilyushin Il-76T | 093420594 | Lsf TYM |
| ☐ RA-76527 | Ilyushin Il-76T | 0003427796 | Lsf TYM |
| ☐ RA-76666 | Ilyushin Il-76MD | 0053464934 | Lst ESL |
| ☐ RA-76807 | Ilyushin Il-76TD | 1013405176 | Lsf TYM |

## AVIAEXPRESSKRUIZ BKS

| | | |
|---|---|---|
| ☐ RA-85101 | Tupolev Tu-154M | 88A-783 |
| ☐ RA-85109 | Tupolev Tu-154M | 88A-790 |

---

| | | | |
|---|---|---|---|
| ☐ RA-85136 | Tupolev Tu-154M | 88A-791 | Lst RME |
| ☐ RA-85149 | Tupolev Tu-154M | 88A-797 | |
| ☐ RA-85609 | Tupolev Tu-154M | 85A-704 | |

## AVIAST VVA

| | | | |
|---|---|---|---|
| ☐ RA-76485 | Ilyushin Il-76TD | 0063470088 | |
| ☐ RA-76486 | Ilyushin Il-76TD | 0073476281 | |
| ☐ RA-76487 | Ilyushin Il-76TD | 0073479367 | |
| ☐ RA-76754 | Ilyushin Il-76T | 093421637 | |
| ☐ RA-76796 | Ilyushin Il-76MD | 0093491735 | |
| ☐ RA-76797 | Ilyushin Il-76TD | 1003403052 | |
| ☐ RA-76814 | Ilyushin Il-76TD | 1013408269 | |
| ☐ RA-76820 | Ilyushin Il-76TD | 1013409295 | |
| ☐ RA-76849 | Ilyushin Il-76TD | 0023440161 | |
| ☐ EW-78820 | Ilyushin Il-76TD | 0093496907 | |
| | | | |
| ☐ RA-11756 | Antonov An-12BP | 4342208 | |
| ☐ RA-11962 | Antonov An-12BP | 5543007 | |
| ☐ RA-69314 | Antonov An-12BP | 5343004 | Jow FUE |

## AVIASTAR FUE

| | | | |
|---|---|---|---|
| ☐ RA-11529 | Antonov An-12B | 6344109 | Jow FRT |
| ☐ RA-64006 | Tu-204 | 1450743164006 | |
| ☐ RA-64017 | Tu-204-100 | 1450742564017 | Lst SBI |
| ☐ RA-69314 | Antonov An-12BP | 5343004 | Jow VVA |
| ☐ RA-76491 | Ilyushin Il-76T | 093421630 | |

## AVL – ARKHANGELSKIE LINII AUL

| | | | |
|---|---|---|---|
| ☐ RA-65066 | Tupolev Tu-134A-3 | 49898 | |
| ☐ RA-65084 | Tupolev Tu-134A-3 | 60115 | std |
| ☐ RA-65096 | Tupolev Tu-134A-3 | 60257 | |
| ☐ RA-65103 | Tupolev Tu-134A-3 | 60297 | |
| ☐ RA-65116 | Tupolev Tu-134A-3 | 60420 | |
| | | | |
| ☐ RA-85302 | Tupolev Tu-154B-2 | 78A-302 | |
| ☐ RA-85365 | Tupolev Tu-154B-2 | 79A-365 | |
| ☐ RA-85386 | Tupolev Tu-154B-2 | 79A-386 | |
| ☐ RA-85468 | Tupolev Tu-154B-2 | 81A-468 | |
| ☐ RA-85551 | Tupolev Tu-154B-2 | 82A-551 | Lst ESL |

## BAIKAL AIRLINES BKL

| | | | |
|---|---|---|---|
| ☐ RA-85462 | Tupolev Tu-154B-2 | 80A-462 | Lst TIS |
| ☐ RA-85503 | Tupolev Tu-154B-2 | 81A-503 | Lst TIS |
| ☐ RA-85512 | Tupolev Tu-154B-2 | 81A-512 | |
| ☐ RA-85613 | Tupolev Tu-154M | 86A-722 | Lst SBI |
| ☐ RA-85652 | Tupolev Tu-154M | 88A-794 | Lst SBI |
| ☐ RA-85657 | Tupolev Tu-154M | 89A-802 | Lst IRB |
| ☐ RA-85690 | Tupolev Tu-154M | 90A-861 | Lst SBI |
| | | | |
| ☐ RA-76484 | Ilyushin Il-76TD | 0063469081 | Lst TIS |
| ☐ RA-76808 | Ilyushin Il-76TD | 1013405177 | Lst TIS |

## BAL – BASHKIRSKIE AVIALINII BTC

| | | | |
|---|---|---|---|
| ☐ RA-85450 | Tupolev Tu-154B-1 | 80A-450 | |
| ☐ RA-85773 | Tupolev Tu-154M | 93A-955 | Lst SAI |
| ☐ RA-85777 | Tupolev Tu-154M | 93A-959 | |
| ☐ RA-85824 | Tupolev Tu-154M | 88A-769 | |
| ☐ RA-85825 | Tupolev Tu-154M | 88A-776 | |
| ☐ RA-85826 | Tupolev Tu-154M | 89A-812 | |
| ☐ RA-85831 | Tupolev Tu-154M | 88A-774 | |
| ☐ RA-85846 | Tupolev Tu-154M | 89A-807 | |
| ☐ RA-85847 | Tupolev Tu-154M | 88A-792 | Lst VAZ |
| ☐ RA-85848 | Tupolev Tu-154M | 89A-804 | |
| | | | |
| ☐ RA-65028 | Tupolev Tu-134A | 48490 | |
| ☐ RA-65040 | Tupolev Tu-134A | 49100 | Govt |
| ☐ RA-65102 | Tupolev Tu-134A-3 | 60267 | Lsf ASZ |
| ☐ RA-74014 | An-74-200 | 36547098968 | |
| ☐ RA-74015 | An-74-200 | 36547098969 | |
| ☐ RA-74046 | Antonov An-74 | 36547097935 | |

### CHERNOMOR AVIA — CMK

| | | | |
|---|---|---|---|
| ☐ RA-65565 | Tupolev Tu-134A | 63998 | |
| ☐ RA-65604 | Tupolev Tu-134A | 62561 | Lsf EFR |
| ☐ RA-65939 | Tupolev Tu-134A-3 | 1351409 | |
| ☐ RA-85291 | Tupolev Tu-154B-1 | 78A-291 | |
| ☐ RA-85332 | Tupolev Tu-154B-2 | 79A-332 | |
| ☐ RA-85384 | Tupolev Tu-154B-2 | 79A-384 | |

### CHITAAVIA — CHF

| | | | |
|---|---|---|---|
| ☐ RA-85235 | Tupolev Tu-154B-1 | 77A-235 | |
| ☐ RA-85280 | Tupolev Tu-154B-2 | 78A-280 | |
| ☐ RA-85506 | Tupolev Tu-154B-2 | 81A-506 | |
| ☐ RA-85766 | Tupolev Tu-154M | 92A-923 | |

### CONTINENTAL AIRWAYS — PVV

| | | | |
|---|---|---|---|
| ☐ RA-85696 | Tupolev Tu-154M | 91A-869 | Lsf MVL |
| ☐ RA-85760 | Tupolev Tu-154M | 92A-942 | |
| ☐ RA-86138 | Ilyushin Il-86 | 51483210096 | |

### DALAVIA — KHB

| | | | |
|---|---|---|---|
| ☐ RA-86128 | Ilyushin Il-62M | 2255719 | |
| ☐ RA-86131 | Ilyushin Il-62M | 4255244 | |
| ☐ RA-86471 | Ilyushin Il-62M | 72504 | |
| ☐ RA-86479 | Ilyushin Il-62M | 4728118 | Lsf KHB |
| ☐ RA-86481 | Ilyushin Il-62M | 1829415 | |
| ☐ RA-86486 | Ilyushin Il-62M | 3830123 | |
| ☐ RA-86493 | Ilyushin Il-62M | 4140748 | |
| ☐ RA-86525 | Ilyushin Il-62M | 4851612 | |
| ☐ RA-86560 | Ilyushin Il-62M | 2153347 | |
| ☐ RA-85178 | Tupolev Tu-154B-1 | 76A-178 | |
| ☐ RA-85190 | Tupolev Tu-154B-1 | 76A-190 | |
| ☐ RA-85205 | Tupolev Tu-154B-1 | 77A-205 | |
| ☐ RA-85206 | Tupolev Tu-154B-1 | 77A-206 | |
| ☐ RA-85207 | Tupolev Tu-154B-1 | 77A-207 | |
| ☐ RA-85216 | Tupolev Tu-154B-1 | 77A-216 | |
| ☐ RA-85220 | Tupolev Tu-154B-2 | 77A-220 | |
| ☐ RA-85266 | Tupolev Tu-154B-2 | 78A-266 | |
| ☐ RA-85336 | Tupolev Tu-154B-2 | 79A-336 | |
| ☐ RA-85341 | Tupolev Tu-154B-2 | 79A-341 | |
| ☐ RA-85443 | Tupolev Tu-154B-2 | 80A-443 | |
| ☐ RA-85477 | Tupolev Tu-154B-2 | 81A-477 | |
| ☐ RA-85607 | Tupolev Tu-154M | 85A-702 | |
| ☐ RA-85734 | Tupolev Tu-154M | 92A-916 | |
| ☐ RA-64502 | Tupolev Tu-214 | 42625002 | |
| ☐ RA-64503 | Tupolev Tu-214 | 42103003 | |

### DOBROLET AIRLINES — DOB

| | | | |
|---|---|---|---|
| ☐ RA-76388 | Ilyushin Il-76TD | 1013406204 | Lst TUP |
| ☐ RA-76389 | Ilyushin Il-76TD | 1013407212 | |
| ☐ RA-76418 | Ilyushin Il-76T | 073409237 | |
| ☐ RA-76809 | Ilyushin Il-76TD | 1013408252 | Lsf VAS |

### DOMODEDOVO AIRLINES — DMO

| | | | |
|---|---|---|---|
| ☐ RA-86127 | Ilyushin Il-62M | 1254851 | |
| ☐ RA-86129 | Ilyushin Il-62M | 2255525 | |
| ☐ RA-86475 | Ilyushin Il-62M | 3727113 | std |
| ☐ RA-86494 | Ilyushin Il-62M | 4140952 | |
| ☐ RA-86499 | Ilyushin Il-62M | 2932637 | |
| ☐ RA-86516 | Ilyushin Il-62M | 2139524 | |
| ☐ RA-86519 | Ilyushin Il-62M | 4140212 | |
| ☐ RA-86521 | Ilyushin Il-62M | 1241425 | |
| ☐ RA-86526 | Ilyushin Il-62M | 2951447 | |
| ☐ RA-86530 | Ilyushin Il-62M | 4242543 | |
| ☐ RA-86535 | Ilyushin Il-62M | 2444455 | |
| ☐ RA-86541 | Ilyushin Il-62M | 3951359 | |
| ☐ RA-86552 | Ilyushin Il-62M | 2052345 | |
| ☐ RA-86673 | Ilyushin Il-62M | 3154416 | |
| ☐ RA-76786 | Ilyushin Il-76TD | 0093496923 | Lst ASE |
| ☐ RA-76799 | Ilyushin Il-76TD | 1003403037 | Lst ASE |

| | | | |
|---|---|---|---|
| ☐ RA-76806 | Ilyushin Il-76TD | 1003403121 | |
| ☐ RA-76812 | Ilyushin Il-76TD | 1013407230 | Lst ASE |
| ☐ RA-96006 | Ilyushin Il-96-300 | 74393201003 | |
| ☐ RA-96009 | Ilyushin Il-96-300 | 74393201006 | |
| ☐ RA-96013 | Ilyushin Il-96-300 | 74393201010 | |

### EAST LINE EXPRESS — ESL

| | | | |
|---|---|---|---|
| ☐ EW-78799 | Ilyushin Il-76MD | 0093491754 | Lsf TXC |
| ☐ EW-78808 | Ilyushin Il-76MD | 0093493794 | Lsf TXC |
| ☐ RA-76369 | Ilyushin Il-76TD | 1033414480 | |
| ☐ RA-76381 | Ilyushin Il-76TD | 1033418596 | |
| ☐ RA-76400 | Ilyushin Il-76TD | 1023413438 | Lsf VLK |
| ☐ RA-76403 | Ilyushin Il-76TD | 1023412414 | Lsf VLK |
| ☐ RA-76462 | Ilyushin Il-76T | 0012432955 | |
| ☐ RA-76492 | Ilyushin Il-76T | 093418548 | Lsf VLK |
| ☐ RA-76666 | Ilyushin Il-76MD | 0053464934 | Lsf ASZ |
| ☐ RA-76817 | Ilyushin Il-76TD | 1023412387 | |
| ☐ UK-76353 | Ilyushin Il-76TD | 1023414454 | Lsf UZB |
| ☐ UK 76448 | Ilyushin Il-76TD | 1023413443 | Lsf UZB |
| ☐ RA-65798 | Tupolev Tu-134A-3 | 63179 | |
| ☐ RA-85551 | Tupolev Tu-154B-2 | 82A-551 | Lsf AUL |
| ☐ RA-85799 | Tupolev Tu-154M | 93A-983 | |
| ☐ RA-85827 | Tupolev Tu-154M | 87A-745 | Lsf ENK |
| ☐ RA-85829 | Tupolev Tu-154M | 89A-755 | Lsf ENK |
| ☐ RA-86567 | Ilyushin Il-62M | 4256314 | |
| ☐ RA-86139 | Ilyushin Il-86 | 51483210098 | Jow AYZ |
| ☐ RA-86144 | Ilyushin Il-86 | 51483204035 | Jow KZK |
| ☐ UR-BWM | Antonov An-12BP | 00347004 | |
| ☐ UR-SVG | Antonov An-12BK | 4342409 | Jow VRE |

### ENKOR — ENK

| | | | |
|---|---|---|---|
| ☐ RA-85514 | Tupolev Tu-154B-2 | 81A-514 | |
| ☐ RA-85724 | Tupolev Tu-154M | 92A-906 | |
| ☐ RA-85725 | Tupolev Tu-154M | 92A-907 | |
| ☐ RA-85754 | Tupolev Tu-154M | 92A-936 | |
| ☐ RA-85827 | Tupolev Tu-154M | 87A-745 | Lst ESL |
| ☐ RA-85829 | Tupolev Tu-154M | 89A-755 | Lst ESL |
| ☐ RA-65131 | Tupolev Tu-134A-3 | 60637 | |
| ☐ RA-65786 | Tupolev Tu-134A-3 | 62775 | |

### GAZPROMAVIA — GZP

| | | | |
|---|---|---|---|
| ☐ RA-74005 | An-74TK-100 | 36547095892 | |
| ☐ RA-74008 | An-74T-100 | 36547095900 | |
| ☐ RA-74012 | An-74D | 36547098959 | |
| ☐ RA-74016 | An-74TK-100 | 365470991034 | |
| ☐ RA-74031 | An-74-200 | 36547098961 | |
| ☐ RA-74032 | An-74TK-100 | 36547098962 | |
| ☐ RA-74035 | An-74TK-100 | 36547098963 | |
| ☐ RA-74036 | An-74-200 | 36547098965 | |
| ☐ RA-74044 | An-74TK-100 | 36547097936 | |
| ☐ RA-74056 | An-74-200 | 36547098951 | |
| ☐ RA-74058 | An-74-200 | 36547098956 | |
| ☐ RA-76370 | Ilyushin Il-76TD | 1033414458 | Jow AYZ |
| ☐ RA-76402 | Ilyushin Il-76TD | 1023413430 | Jow AYZ |
| ☐ RA-76445 | Ilyushin Il-76TD | 1023410330 | Jow AYZ |
| ☐ RA-76446 | Ilyushin Il-76TD | 1023412418 | Jow AYZ |
| ☐ RA-65045 | Tupolev Tu-134A | 49500 | |
| ☐ RA-65983 | Tupolev Tu-134A-3 | 63350 | |
| ☐ RA-85625 | Tupolev Tu-154M | 87A-752 | |
| ☐ RA-85751 | Tupolev Tu-154M | 92A-933 | |
| ☐ RA-85774 | Tupolev Tu-154M | 93A-956 | |
| ☐ RA-85778 | Tupolev Tu-154M | 93A-962 | |

### GROMOV AIR — GAI

| | | | |
|---|---|---|---|
| ☐ RA-65047 | Tupolev Tu-134A | 49600 | |
| ☐ RA-65682 | Tupolev Tu-134A | 62120 | Jow FLV |
| ☐ RA-65721 | Tupolev Tu-134A-3M | 66130 | |
| ☐ RA-65740 | Tupolev Tu-134A | 2351510 | |

| | | | |
|---|---|---|---|
| ☐ RA-65926 | Tupolev Tu-134A-1 | 66101 | |
| ☐ RA-65927 | Tupolev Tu-134A | 66198 | |
| ☐ RA-65932 | Tupolev Tu-134A-3 | 66405 | Lsf SDB |
| ☐ RA-85317 | Tupolev Tu-154M | 78A-317 | |

## IL-AVIA                                                ILV

| | | | |
|---|---|---|---|
| ☐ EW-76712 | Ilyushin Il-76MD | 0063473190 | Lsf TXC |
| ☐ EW-78826 | Ilyushin Il-76TD | 1003499991 | Lsf TXC |
| ☐ EW-78848 | Ilyushin Il-76TD | 1003405159 | Lsf TXC |
| ☐ RA-76474 | Ilyushin Il-76TD | 0033448407 | |
| ☐ RA-76578 | Ilyushin Il-76TD | 0043449468 | |
| ☐ RA-88294 | Yakovlev Yak-40 | 9331329 | |

## IRON DRAGON FLY                              IDF

| | | | |
|---|---|---|---|
| ☐ RA-76495 | Ilyushin Il-76TD | 073410292 | |
| ☐ RA-85358 | Tupolev Tu-154B-2 | 79A-358 | Lst AKT |
| ☐ RA-85842 | Tupolev Tu-154B-2 | 80A-420 | Lst LLM |
| ☐ RA-86538 | Ilyushin Il-62M | 2241758 | Lsf CHD |

## KALININGRAD AVIA                            KLN

| | | | |
|---|---|---|---|
| ☐ RA-65010 | Tupolev Tu-134A | 46130 | |
| ☐ RA-65011 | Tupolev Tu-134A | 46140 | |
| ☐ RA-65019 | Tupolev Tu-134A | 48375 | |
| ☐ RA-65027 | Tupolev Tu-134A | 48485 | |
| ☐ RA-65054 | Tupolev Tu-134A | 49840 | |
| ☐ RA-65087 | Tupolev Tu-134A | 60155 | |
| ☐ RA-65090 | Tupolev Tu-134A-3 | 60185 | |
| ☐ RA-65824 | Tupolev Tu-134A-3 | 09074 | |
| ☐ RA-65870 | Tupolev Tu-134A-3 | 28310 | |
| ☐ RA-85789 | Tupolev Tu-154M | 93A-973 | |

## KMV – KAVMINVODY AVIA               MVD

| | | | |
|---|---|---|---|
| ☐ RA-65074 | Tupolev Tu-134A-3 | 49987 | |
| ☐ RA-65126 | Tupolev Tu-134A-3 | 60588 | |
| ☐ RA-65139 | Tupolev Tu-134A | 60915 | |
| ☐ RA-65844 | Tupolev Tu-134A | 18125 | |
| ☐ RA-65887 | Tupolev Tu-134A | 36170 | |
| ☐ RA-85226 | Tupolev Tu-154B-1 | 77A-226 | Lsf NGL |
| ☐ RA-85287 | Tupolev Tu-154B-1 | 78A-287 | Lsf NGL |
| ☐ RA-85303 | Tupolev Tu-154B-2 | 78A-303 | |
| ☐ RA-85307 | Tupolev Tu-154B-2 | 78A-307 | |
| ☐ RA-85330 | Tupolev Tu-154B-2 | 79A-330 | |
| ☐ RA-85340 | Tupolev Tu-154B-2 | 79A-340 | |
| ☐ RA-85371 | Tupolev Tu-154B-2 | 79A-371 | |
| ☐ RA-85373 | Tupolev Tu-154B-2 | 79A-373 | |
| ☐ RA-85382 | Tupolev Tu-154B-2 | 79A-382 | |
| ☐ RA-85393 | Tupolev Tu-154B-2 | 80A-393 | |
| ☐ RA-85457 | Tupolev Tu-154B-2 | 80A-457 | |
| ☐ RA-85494 | Tupolev Tu-154B-2 | 81A-494 | |
| ☐ RA-85715 | Tupolev Tu-154M | 91A-891 | |
| ☐ RA-85722 | Tupolev Tu-154M | 92A-904 | |
| ☐ RA-85746 | Tupolev Tu-154M | 92A-929 | |
| ☐ RA-64016 | Tu-204-100 | 1450742364016 | |
| ☐ RA-64022 | Tu-204-100 | 1450743164022 | |

## KOMIINTERAVIA                               KMV

| | | | |
|---|---|---|---|
| ☐ RA-65005 | Tupolev Tu-134A | 44065 | Lst CGI |
| ☐ RA-65148 | Tupolev Tu-134A-3 | 61025 | Lst TMN |
| ☐ RA-65606 | Tupolev Tu-134A | 46300 | |
| ☐ RA-65607 | Tupolev Tu-134A | 48560 | |
| ☐ RA-65608 | Tupolev Tu-134A | 38040 | |
| ☐ RA-65609 | Tupolev Tu-134A-3 | 46155 | Lst TMN |
| ☐ RA-65611 | Tupolev Tu-134A | 3351903 | |
| ☐ RA-65612 | Tupolev Tu-134A | 3352102 | Lst AFL |
| ☐ RA-65614 | Tupolev Tu-134A | 4352207 | Lst TMN |
| ☐ RA-65620 | Tupolev Tu-134A | 35180 | |
| ☐ RA-65716 | Tupolev Tu-134B-3 | 63595 | |
| ☐ RA-65755 | Tupolev Tu-134A-3 | 62165 | |
| ☐ RA-65777 | Tupolev Tu-134A-3 | 62552 | Lst KJC |

| | | | |
|---|---|---|---|
| ☐ RA-65780 | Tupolev Tu-134A-3 | 62622 | |
| ☐ RA-65793 | Tupolev Tu-134A-3 | 63128 | Lst AFL |
| ☐ RA-65901 | Tupolev Tu-134A-3 | 63731 | |
| ☐ RA-65902 | Tupolev Tu-134A-3 | | |
| ☐ RA-65977 | Tupolev Tu-134A-3 | 63245 | |

## KRAS AIR                                          KJC

| | | | |
|---|---|---|---|
| ☐ RA-76459 | Ilyushin Il-76T | 0013430890 | |
| ☐ RA-76463 | Ilyushin Il-76T | 0013432960 | |
| ☐ RA-76464 | Ilyushin Il-76TD | 0023437090 | |
| ☐ RA-76465 | Ilyushin Il-76TD | 0023438101 | |
| ☐ RA-76509 | Ilyushin Il-76T | 083413415 | std KJA |
| ☐ RA-76516 | Ilyushin Il-76T | 093418566 | |
| ☐ RA-76517 | Ilyushin Il-76T | 093418560 | std KJA |
| ☐ RA-76524 | Ilyushin Il-76T | 0003425746 | |
| ☐ RA-76792 | Ilyushin Il-76TD | 0093497942 | |
| ☐ RA-86085 | Ilyushin Il-86 | 51483206056 | |
| ☐ RA-86121 | Ilyushin Il-86 | 51483209089 | |
| ☐ RA-86122 | Ilyushin Il-86 | 51483210090 | std KJA |
| ☐ RA-86137 | Ilyushin Il-86 | 51483210095 | |
| ☐ RA-86145 | Ilyushin Il-86 | 51483211101 | |
| ☐ | McDD MD-82 | 1181/49277 | o/o |
| ☐ | McDD MD-83 | 1579/49844 | o/o |
| ☐ | McDD MD-83 | 1720/49930 | o/o |
| ☐ | McDD MD-83 | 1817/53149 | o/o |
| ☐ | McDD MD-83 | 1831/53150 | u/o |
| ☐ | McDD MD-83 | 1585/49847 | o/o |
| ☐ | McDD MD-83 | 1405/49569 | o/o |
| ☐ | McDD MD-83 | 1468/49572 | o/o |
| ☐ RA-65605 | Tupolev Tu-134A | 09070 | |
| ☐ RA-65608 | Tupolev Tu-134A | 38040 | Lsf KMV |
| ☐ RA-65618 | Tupolev Tu-134A-3 | 12095 | Lsf KMV |
| ☐ RA-65777 | Tupolev Tu-134A-3 | 62552 | Lsf KMV |
| ☐ RA-65780 | Tupolev Tu-134A-3 | 62622 | Lsf KMV |
| ☐ RA-65960 | Tupolev Tu-134A | 3351806 | |
| ☐ RA-85201 | Tupolev Tu-154B-1 | 77A-201 | |
| ☐ RA-85417 | Tupolev Tu-154B-2 | 80A-417 | |
| ☐ RA-85418 | Tupolev Tu-154B-2 | 80A-418 | |
| ☐ RA-85505 | Tupolev Tu-154B-2 | 81A-505 | |
| ☐ RA-85529 | Tupolev Tu-154B-2 | 82A-529 | |
| ☐ RA-85672 | Tupolev Tu-154M | 90A-830 | |
| ☐ RA-85676 | Tupolev Tu-154M | 90A-836 | Lsf BKN |
| ☐ RA-85678 | Tupolev Tu-154M | 90A-841 | |
| ☐ RA-85679 | Tupolev Tu-154M | 90A-842 | |
| ☐ RA-85681 | Tupolev Tu-154M | 90A-848 | Lsf BKN |
| ☐ RA-85682 | Tupolev Tu-154M | 90A-849 | |
| ☐ RA-85683 | Tupolev Tu-154M | 90A-850 | |
| ☐ RA-85694 | Tupolev Tu-154M | 91A-867 | |
| ☐ RA-85702 | Tupolev Tu-154M | 91A-877 | |
| ☐ RA-85704 | Tupolev Tu-154M | 91A-879 | |
| ☐ RA-85708 | Tupolev Tu-154M | 91A-883 | Jow BKN |
| ☐ RA-85720 | Tupolev Tu-154M | 91A-902 | |
| ☐ RA-85759 | Tupolev Tu-154M | 92A-941 | |
| ☐ RA-64014 | Tu-204-100 | | |
| ☐ RA-64015 | Tu-204-100 | | |
| ☐ RA-64018 | Tu-204-110 | 1450743164018 | |
| ☐ RA-64019 | Tu-204-110 | 1450743164019 | |
| ☐ RA-64020 | Tu-204-100 | 1450743164029 | |
| ☐ RA-64024 | Tu-204-110 | | |
| ☐ RA-86453 | Ilyushin Il-62 | 1622323 | |
| ☐ RA-86709 | Ilyushin Il-62 | 62204 | |
| ☐ VH-RMK | Boeing 767-204 | 79/22981 | |
| ☐ | Boeing 767-216ER | 144/23624 | o/o |
| ☐ P4-ABA | Boeing 767-277 | 22694 | |

## MAVIAL – MAGADAN AIRLINES        MVL

| | | | |
|---|---|---|---|
| ☐ RA-85540 | Tupolev Tu-154B-2 | 82A-540 | |
| ☐ RA-85562 | Tupolev Tu-154B-2 | 82A-562 | Lsf VLK |
| ☐ RA-85567 | Tupolev Tu-154B-2 | 82A-567 | |

☐ RA-85584 Tupolev Tu-154B-2 83A-584
☐ RA-85667 Tupolev Tu-154M 89A-825
☐ RA-85671 Tupolev Tu-154M 90A-829 Lst BUC
☐ RA-85677 Tupolev Tu-154M 90A-839 Lst LDF
☐ RA-85680 Tupolev Tu-154M 90A-843 Lst BUC
☐ RA-85696 Tupolev Tu-154M 91A-869 Lst PVV

☐ RA-86590 Ilyushin Il-62M 2647737

## OMSKAVIA AIRLINE OMS

☐ RA-85714 Tupolev Tu-154M 91A-890 Lst IRM
☐ RA-85730 Tupolev Tu-154M 92A-912
☐ RA-85745 Tupolev Tu-154M 92A-928 Lst IRB
☐ RA-85750 Tupolev Tu-154M 92A-932 Lst IRB
☐ RA-85752 Tupolev Tu-154M 92A-934
☐ RA-85763 Tupolev Tu-154M 92A-946
☐ RA-85801 Tupolev Tu-154M 93A-960 Lst IRB
☐ RA-85818 Tupolev Tu-154M 85A-719
☐ RA-85830 Tupolev Tu-154M 89A-821
☐ RA-85841 Tupolev Tu-154M 90A-858 Lst IRB

## ORENBURG AVIA ORB

☐ RA-65049 Tupolev Tu-134A 49755
☐ RA-65110 Tupolev Tu-134A-3 60343
☐ RA-65136 Tupolev Tu-134A-3 60885

☐ RA-85595 Tupolev Tu-154B-2 84A-595
☐ RA-85602 Tupolev Tu-154B-2 84A-602 Jow TMN
☐ RA-85604 Tupolev Tu-154B-2 85A-604 Jow TMN
☐ RA-85768 Tupolev Tu-154M 94A-949

## PERM AIRLINES PGP

☐ RA-65046 Tupolev Tu-134A-3 49550
☐ RA-65059 Tupolev Tu-134A 49870
☐ RA-65064 Tupolev Tu-134A-3 49886
☐ RA-65118 Tupolev Tu-134A-3 60462
☐ RA-65751 Tupolev Tu-134A-3 61066
☐ RA-65775 Tupolev Tu-134A-3 62530

☐ RA-85217 Tupolev Tu-154B-1 77A-217
☐ RA-85284 Tupolev Tu-154B-1 78A-284

## POLET AVIAKOMPANIA POT

☐ RA-82010 An-124-100 9773053616017
☐ RA-82013 An-124 977305.73203.
☐ RA-82014 An-124 9773054732039 std
☐ RA-82024 An-124 19530502033
☐ RA-82026 An-124-100 19530502127
☐ RA-82075 An-124-100 9773053459147
☐ RA-82077 An-124-100 9773054459151
☐ RA-82080 An-124-100 o/o

## PULKOVO AIRLINES PLK

☐ RA-86050 Ilyushin Il-86 51483202017
☐ RA-86061 Ilyushin Il-86 51483203028
☐ RA-86063 Ilyushin Il-86 51483203030
☐ RA-86070 Ilyushin Il-86 51483204037
☐ RA-86073 Ilyushin Il-86 51483204040
☐ RA-86092 Ilyushin Il-86 51483207063
☐ RA-86094 Ilyushin Il-86 51483207065
☐ RA-86106 Ilyushin Il-86 51483208074

☐ RA-65004 Tupolev Tu-134A-3 44060
☐ RA-65042 Tupolev Tu-134A-3 49350
☐ RA-65068 Tupolev Tu-134A-3 49907
☐ RA-65088 Tupolev Tu-134A 60172
☐ RA-65093 Tupolev Tu-134A-3 60215
☐ RA-65109 Tupolev Tu-134A-3 60339
☐ RA-65112 Tupolev Tu-134A-3 60350
☐ RA-65113 Tupolev Tu-134A 60380
☐ RA-65128 Tupolev Tu-134A-3 60628

☐ RA-65144 Tupolev Tu-134A-3 60977
☐ RA-65759 Tupolev Tu-134A 62239

☐ RA-85171 Tupolev Tu-154M 92A-893
☐ RA-85185 Tupolev Tu-154M 91A-894
☐ RA-85187 Tupolev Tu-154M 91A-919
☐ RA-85204 Tupolev Tu-154M 91A-896
☐ RA- Tupolev Tu-154M 93A-954 o/o
☐ RA-85334 Tupolev Tu-154B-2 79A-334
☐ RA-85377 Tupolev Tu-154B-2 79A-377
☐ RA-85441 Tupolev Tu-154B-2 80A-441
☐ RA-85442 Tupolev Tu-154B-2
☐ RA-85530 Tupolev Tu-154B-2 82A-530
☐ RA-85542 Tupolev Tu-154B-2 82A-542
☐ RA-85552 Tupolev Tu-154B-2 82A-552
☐ RA-85553 Tupolev Tu-154B-2 82A-553
☐ RA-85579 Tupolev Tu-154B-2 83A-579
☐ RA-85658 Tupolev Tu-154M 89A-808
☐ RA-85695 Tupolev Tu-154M 91A-868
☐ RA-85753 Tupolev Tu-154M 92A-935
☐ RA-85767 Tupolev Tu-154M 93A-948
☐ RA-85769 Tupolev Tu-154M 93A-951
☐ RA-85770 Tupolev Tu-154M 93A-952
☐ RA-85771 Tupolev Tu-154M 93A-953
☐ RA-85779 Tupolev Tu-154M 93A-963
☐ RA-85785 Tupolev Tu-154M 93A-969
☐ RA-85800 Tupolev Tu-154M 94A-984

## ROSSIA STATE TRANSPORT CO SDM

☐ RA-86466 Ilyushin Il-62M 2749316
☐ RA-86467 Ilyushin Il-62M 3749733
☐ RA-86468 Ilyushin Il-62M 4749857
☐ RA-86536 Ilyushin Il-62M 4445948
☐ RA-86537 Ilyushin Il-62M 3546733
☐ RA-86540 Ilyushin Il-62M 3546548
☐ RA-86559 Ilyushin Il-62M 2153258
☐ RA-86561 Ilyushin Il-62M 4154841
☐ RA-86710 Ilyushin Il-62M 2647646
☐ RA-86712 Ilyushin Il-62M 4648339

☐ RA-65553 Tupolev Tu-134A-3 66300
☐ RA-65555 Tupolev Tu-134A-3 66350
☐ RA-65904 Tupolev Tu-134A-3 63953
☐ RA-65905 Tupolev Tu-134A-3 63965
☐ RA-65911 Tupolev Tu-134A-3 63972
☐ RA-65912 Tupolev Tu-134A-3 63985
☐ RA-65921 Tupolev Tu-134A-3 63997
☐ RA-65978 Tupolev Tu-134A-3 63357
☐ RA-65979 Tupolev Tu-134A-3 63158
☐ RA-65994 Tupolev Tu-134A 66207
☐ RA-65995 Tupolev Tu-134A-3 66400

☐ RA-85629 Tupolev Tu-154M 87A-758
☐ RA-85645 Tupolev Tu-154M 88A-782
☐ RA-85659 Tupolev Tu-154M 89A-809
☐ RA-85666 Tupolev Tu-154M 89A-820
☐ RA-85686 Tupolev Tu-154M 90A-854
☐ RA-85843 Tupolev Tu-154M 95A-991
☐ RA-85844 Tupolev Tu-154M 95A-992 o/o

☐ RA-75453 Ilyushin Il-18D 187010103
☐ RA-75454 Ilyushin Il-18D 187010104
☐ RA-75464 Ilyushin Il-18D 187010401
☐ RA-96012 Ilyushin Il-96-300 74393201009
☐ RA-96014 Ilyushin Il-96-300 74393201011
☐ RA-96016 Ilyushin Il-96-300 74393202010 c

## SMARA AIRLINES BRZ

☐ RA-65105 Tupolev Tu-134A-3 60308
☐ RA-65122 Tupolev Tu-134A-3 60518
☐ RA-65753 Tupolev Tu-134A-3 61099
☐ RA-65758 Tupolev Tu-134A-3 62230
☐ RA-65792 Tupolev Tu-134A-3 63121
☐ RA-65797 Tupolev Tu-134A-3 63173
☐ RA-65800 Tupolev Tu-134A 3352009
☐ RA-65935 Tupolev Tu-134A-3 66180 Lst PSS

| | | | |
|---|---|---|---|
| ☐ RA-85264 | Tupolev Tu-154B-2 | 78A-264 | |
| ☐ RA-85267 | Tupolev Tu-154B-1 | 78A-267 | |
| ☐ RA-85472 | Tupolev Tu-154B-2 | 81A-472 | |
| ☐ RA-85500 | Tupolev Tu-154B-2 | 81A-500 | |
| ☐ RA-85585 | Tupolev Tu-154B-2 | 83A-585 | |
| ☐ RA-85716 | Tupolev Tu-154M | 91A-892 | |
| ☐ RA-85723 | Tupolev Tu-154M | 92A-905 | |
| ☐ RA-85731 | Tupolev Tu-154M | 92A-913 | |
| ☐ RA-85739 | Tupolev Tu-154M | 92A-922 | |
| ☐ RA-85792 | Tupolev Tu-154M | 93A-976 | |
| ☐ RA-85817 | Tupolev Tu-154M | 95A-1007 | Lst IRK |
| ☐ RA-85821 | Tupolev Tu-154M | 89A-805 | |
| ☐ RA-85822 | Tupolev Tu-154M | 89A-806 | |
| ☐ RA-85823 | Tupolev Tu-154M | 88A-775 | |
| ☐ RA- | Tupolev Tu-154M | 88A-777 | |

| | | |
|---|---|---|
| ☐ RA-76475 | Ilyushin Il-76TD | 0043451523 |
| ☐ RA-76791 | Ilyushin Il-76TD | 0093497936 |
| ☐ RA-76798 | Ilyushin Il-76TD | 1003403063 | Lst AYZ |

## SAT – SAKHALIN AIRLINES    SHU

| | | | |
|---|---|---|---|
| ☐ RA-67251 | DHC-8-102 | 215 | |
| ☐ RA- | DHC-8-102 | | o/o |
| ☐ RA-86566 | Ilyushin Il-62M | 4255152 | |

## SIBAVIATRANS    SIB

| | | | |
|---|---|---|---|
| ☐ RA-65615 | Tupolev Tu-134A-3 | 4352205 | |
| ☐ RA-65771 | Tupolev Tu-134A-3 | 62445 | |
| ☐ RA-65845 | Tupolev Tu-134A-3 | 23131 | |
| ☐ RA-65881 | Tupolev Tu-134A-3 | 35220 | |
| ☐ RA-74041 | An-74-200 | 36547096924 | |
| ☐ UR-85395 | Tupolev Tu-154B-2 | 80A-395 | Lsf LHS |
| ☐ RA- | Antonov An-140 | | o/o |
| ☐ RA- | Antonov An-140 | | o/o |
| ☐ RA- | Antonov An-140 | | o/o |

## SIBIR AIRLINES    SBI

| | | | |
|---|---|---|---|
| ☐ RA-86006 | Ilyushin Il-86 | 51483200004 | |
| ☐ RA-86081 | Ilyushin Il-86 | 51483206052 | |
| ☐ RA-86089 | Ilyushin Il-86 | 51483207060 | |
| ☐ RA-86091 | Ilyushin Il-86 | 51483207062 | |
| ☐ RA-86102 | Ilyushin Il-86 | 51483207070 | std OVB |
| ☐ RA-86104 | Ilyushin Il-86 | 51483208072 | std OVB |
| ☐ RA-86105 | Ilyushin Il-86 | 51483208073 | |
| ☐ RA-86107 | Ilyushin Il-86 | 51483208075 | |
| ☐ RA-86108 | Ilyushin Il-86 | 51483208076 | |
| ☐ RA-86109 | Ilyushin Il-86 | 51483208077 | |
| ☐ RA-86112 | Ilyushin Il-86 | 51483208080 | std OVB |
| ☐ RA-86120 | Ilyushin Il-86 | 51483209088 | |

| | | | |
|---|---|---|---|
| ☐ RA-85237 | Tupolev Tu-154B-1 | 77A-237 | |
| ☐ RA-85402 | Tupolev Tu-154B-2 | 80A-402 | |
| ☐ RA-85421 | Tupolev Tu-154B-2 | 80A-421 | |
| ☐ RA-85437* | Tupolev Tu-154B-2 | 80A-437 | |
| ☐ RA-85451* | Tupolev Tu-154B-2 | 80A-451 | |
| ☐ RA-85461 | Tupolev Tu-154B-2 | 80A-461 | |
| ☐ RA-85471 | Tupolev Tu-154B-2 | 81A-471 | |
| ☐ RA-85485 | Tupolev Tu-154B-2 | 81A-485 | |
| ☐ RA-85495* | Tupolev Tu-154B-2 | 81A-495 | |
| ☐ RA-85556 | Tupolev Tu-154B-2 | 82A-556 | |
| ☐ RA-85583 | Tupolev Tu-154B-2 | 83A-583 | |
| ☐ RA-85610 | Tupolev Tu-154M | 84A-705 | |
| ☐ RA-85613 | Tupolev Tu-154M | 86A-722 | Lsf BKL |
| ☐ RA-85615 | Tupolev Tu-154M | 86A-731 | |
| ☐ RA-85618 | Tupolev Tu-154M | 86A-737 | |
| ☐ RA-85619 | Tupolev Tu-154M | 86A-738 | |
| ☐ RA-85620 | Tupolev Tu-154M | 86A-739 | |
| ☐ RA-85622 | Tupolev Tu-154M | 87A-746 | |
| ☐ RA-85623 | Tupolev Tu-154M | 87A-749 | |
| ☐ RA-85624 | Tupolev Tu-154M | 87A-750 | |
| ☐ RA-85632 | Tupolev Tu-154M | 87A-761 | |
| ☐ RA-85635 | Tupolev Tu-154M | 87A-764 | |
| ☐ RA-85652 | Tupolev Tu-154M | 88A-794 | Lsf BKL |
| ☐ RA-85673 | Tupolev Tu-154M | 90A-833 | |

| | | | |
|---|---|---|---|
| ☐ RA-85674 | Tupolev Tu-154M | 90A-834 | |
| ☐ RA-85687 | Tupolev Tu-154M | 90A-857 | |
| ☐ RA-85688 | Tupolev Tu-154M | 90A-859 | |
| ☐ RA-85690 | Tupolev Tu-154M | 90A-861 | Lsf BKL |
| ☐ RA-85697 | Tupolev Tu-154M | 91A-870 | |
| ☐ RA-85699 | Tupolev Tu-154M | 91A-874 | |
| ☐ RA-85705 | Tupolev Tu-154M | 91A-880 | |
| ☐ RA-85709 | Tupolev Tu-154M | 91A-884 | |
| ☐ RA-85736 | Tupolev Tu-154M | 92A-918 | |
| ☐ RA-85743 | Tupolev Tu-154M | 92A-926 | |

| | | | |
|---|---|---|---|
| ☐ P4-VNF | Airbus A320-211 | 0726 | Lst RNV |
| ☐ RA-64011 | Tu-204 | 1450741364011 | |
| ☐ RA-64017 | Tu-204-100 | 19450742564017 | |

## TATARSTAN AIR    KAZ

| | | | |
|---|---|---|---|
| ☐ RA-85412 | Tupolev Tu-154B-2 | 80A-412 | Lst AKT |
| ☐ RA-85488 | Tupolev Tu-154B-2 | 81A-488 | std |
| ☐ RA-85504 | Tupolev Tu-154B-2 | 81A-504 | |
| ☐ RA-85798 | Tupolev Tu-154M | 93A-982 | Lst IRB |
| ☐ RA-85804 | Tupolev Tu-154B-2 | 81A-517 | |

| | | | |
|---|---|---|---|
| ☐ RA-65033 | Tupolev Tu-134A-3 | 48540 | Lsf CBK |
| ☐ RA-65691 | Tupolev Tu-134A | 63195 | |
| ☐ RA-65973 | Tupolev Tu-134A | 3352003 | |

## TESIS    TIS

| | | | |
|---|---|---|---|
| ☐ RA-76373 | Ilyushin Il-76TD | 1033415507 | Lsf DRU |
| ☐ RA-76420 | Ilyushin Il-76TD | 1023413446 | Lsf DRU |
| ☐ RA-76483 | Ilyushin Il-76TD | 0063468042 | Lsf VAZ |
| ☐ RA-76484 | Ilyushin Il-76TD | 0063469081 | Lsf BKL |
| ☐ RA-76808 | Ilyushin Il-76TD | 1013405177 | Lsf BKL |
| ☐ UN-76371 | Ilyushin Il-76TD | 1033414485 | Jow KZK |
| ☐ UN-76384 | Ilyushin Il-76TD | 1003401015 | Jow SAH |
| ☐ UN-76385 | Ilyushin Il-76TD | 1033416515 | Jow SAH |
| ☐ UN-76434 | Ilyushin Il-76 | 1023412395 | Jow SAH |
| ☐ UN-76442 | Ilyushin Il-76TD | 1023414450 | Jow SAH |

| | | | |
|---|---|---|---|
| ☐ RA-11124 | Antonov An-12B | 02348106 | Jow FRT |
| ☐ RA-85462 | Tupolev Tu-154B-2 | 80A-462 | Lsf BKL |
| ☐ RA-85503 | Tupolev Tu-154B-2 | 81A-503 | Lsf BKL |

## TRANSAERO AIRLINES    TSO

| | | | |
|---|---|---|---|
| ☐ EI-CXN | Boeing 737-329 | 1432/23772 | |
| ☐ EI-CXR | Boeing 737-329 | 1709/24335 | |
| ☐ N100UN | Boeing 737-7K9 | 19/28088 | |
| ☐ N101UN | Boeing 737-7K9 | 25/28089 | |
| ☐ RA-73000 | Boeing 737-2C9 | 516/21444 | |
| ☐ RA-73001 | Boeing 737-236 | 656/22028 | |
| ☐ RA-73002 | Boeing 737-236 | 751/22034 | |
| ☐ VP-BTA | Boeing 737-2C9 | 501/21443 | |

| | | | |
|---|---|---|---|
| ☐ EI-CXZ | Boeing 767-216ER | 347/24973 | |
| ☐ EI-CZD | Boeing 767-216ER | 142/23623 | |
| ☐ RA-86123 | Ilyushin Il-86 | 51483210091 | Lst VSO |

## TRETYAKOVO AIRLINES    TKO

| | | | |
|---|---|---|---|
| ☐ RA-65057 | Tupolev Tu-134A-3 | 49865 | |
| ☐ RA-65550 | Tupolev Tu-134A-3 | 66200 | |
| ☐ RA-65564 | Tupolev Tu-134A-3 | 63165 | |

| | | | |
|---|---|---|---|
| ☐ RA-74296 | Ilyushin Il-18D | 187010603 | |
| ☐ RA-75834 | Ilyushin Il-18V | 182005104 | |
| ☐ RA-86503 | Ilyushin Il-62M | 4934512 | |
| ☐ RA-86542 | Ilyushin Il-62M | 3952714 | |
| ☐ RA-86568 | Ilyushin Il-62M | 4256223 | |
| ☐ UN-75111 | Ilyushin Il-18V | 184007105 | Lsf GDR |

## TYUMEN AIRLINES    TYM

| | | | |
|---|---|---|---|
| ☐ RA-65009 | Tupolev Tu-134A-3 | 46120 | |
| ☐ RA-65012 | Tupolev Tu-134A | 46175 | |
| ☐ RA-65017 | Tupolev Tu-134A | 48360 | |
| ☐ RA-65038 | Tupolev Tu-134A | 48950 | |

| | | | |
|---|---|---|---|
| ☐ RA-65063 | Tupolev Tu-134A-3 | 49880 | |
| ☐ RA-65127 | Tupolev Tu-134A-3 | 60627 | |
| ☐ RA-65802 | Tupolev Tu-134A | 3352101 | |
| ☐ RA-65899 | Tupolev Tu-134A-3 | 42225 | |
| | | | |
| ☐ RA-85255 | Tupolev Tu-154B-1 | 77A-255 | |
| ☐ RA-85335 | Tupolev Tu-154B-2 | 79A-335 | Lst KGL |
| ☐ RA-85366 | Tupoled Tu-154B-2 | 79A-366 | |
| ☐ RA-85481 | Tupolev Tu-154B-2 | 81A-481 | |
| ☐ RA-85498 | Tupolev Tu-154B-2 | 81A-498 | |
| ☐ RA-85502 | Tupolev Tu-154B-2 | 81A-502 | |
| ☐ RA-85522 | Tupolev Tu-154B-2 | 82A-522 | |
| | | | |
| ☐ RA-12976 | Antonov An-12V | 9346510 | |
| ☐ RA-76510 | Ilyushin Il-76T | 083414432 | Lst AZS |
| ☐ RA-76514 | Ilyushin Il-76T | 083415433 | Lst AZS |
| ☐ RA-76518 | Ilyushin Il-76T | 093420594 | Lst AZS |
| ☐ RA-76527 | Ilyushin Il-76T | 0003427796 | Lst AZS |
| ☐ RA-76807 | Ilyushin Il-76TD | 1013405176 | Lst AZS |

## TYUMENAVIATRANS                                   TMN

| | | | |
|---|---|---|---|
| ☐ RA-65052 | Tupolev Tu-134A | 49825 | |
| ☐ RA-65083 | Tupolev Tu-134A-3 | 60090 | |
| ☐ RA-65101 | Tupolev Tu-134A-3 | 60260 | |
| ☐ RA-65117 | Tupolev Tu-134A-3 | 60450 | |
| ☐ RA-65148 | Tupolev Tu-134A-3 | 61025 | Lsf KMV |
| ☐ RA-65609 | Tupolev Tu-134A-3 | 46155 | Lsf KMV |
| ☐ RA-65614 | Tupolev Tu-134A | 4352207 | Lsf KMV |
| ☐ RA-65616 | Tupolev Tu-134A-3 | 4352206 | |
| ☐ RA-65621 | Tupolev Tu-134A-3 | 48320 | |
| ☐ RA-65847 | Tupolev Tu-134A-3 | 23135 | |
| | | | |
| ☐ RA-85557 | Tupolev Tu-154B-2 | 82A-557 | |
| ☐ RA-85602 | Tupolev Tu-154B-2 | 84A-602 | Jow ORB |
| ☐ RA-85604 | Tupolev Tu-154B-2 | 85A-604 | Jow ORB |
| ☐ RA-85733 | Tupolev Tu-154M | 92A-915 | |
| ☐ RA-85755 | Tupolev Tu-154M | 92A-937 | |
| ☐ RA-85796 | Tupolev Tu-154M | 93A-980 | |
| ☐ RA-85805 | Tupolev Tu-154M | 94A-986 | |
| ☐ RA-85806 | Tupolev Tu-154M | 94A-987 | |
| ☐ RA-85808 | Tupolev Tu-154M | 94A-989 | |
| ☐ RA-85813 | Tupolev Tu-154M | 9.A-990 | |
| ☐ RA-85820 | Tupolev Tu-154M | 9.A-995 | |

## ULYANOVSK HIGHER CIVIL AVIATION SCHOOL                               UHS

| | | | |
|---|---|---|---|
| ☐ RA-85013 | Tupolev Tu-154B | 71A-013 | |
| ☐ RA-85016 | Tupolev Tu-154B | 71A-016 | |
| ☐ RA-85025 | Tupolev Tu-154B | 72A-025 | |
| ☐ RA-85078 | Tupolev Tu-154A | 74A-078 | |
| ☐ RA-85091 | Tupolev Tu-154A | 74A-091 | |
| ☐ RA-85315 | Tupolev Tu-154B-2 | 78A-315 | |
| ☐ RA-85388 | Tupolev Tu-154B-2 | 79A-388 | |
| ☐ RA-85470 | Tupolev Tu-154B-2 | 81A-470 | |
| ☐ RA-85636 | Tupolev Tu-154M | 87A-766 | |
| ☐ RA-65018 | Tupolev Tu-134A | 48365 | |
| | | | |
| ☐ RA-76401 | Ilyushin Il-76TD | 1023412399 | |
| ☐ RA-76783 | Ilyushin Il-76TD | 0093498974 | |
| ☐ RA-86062 | Ilyushin Il-86 | 51483203029 | |
| ☐ RA-86458 | Ilyushin Il-62M | 62303 | |
| ☐ RA-86507 | Ilyushin Il-62M | 2035546 | |

## URAL AIRLINES                                     SVR

| | | | |
|---|---|---|---|
| ☐ RA-85193 | Tupolev Tu-154B-2 | 77A-193 | |
| ☐ RA-85219 | Tupolev Tu-154B-2 | 77A-219 | |
| ☐ RA-85310 | Tupolev Tu-154B-2 | 78A-310 | |
| ☐ RA-85319 | Tupolev Tu-154B-2 | 78A-319 | |
| ☐ RA-85328 | Tupolev Tu-154B-2 | 79A-328 | |
| ☐ RA-85357 | Tupolev Tu-154B-2 | 79A-357 | |
| ☐ RA-85374 | Tupolev Tu-154B-2 | 79A-374 | |
| ☐ RA-85375 | Tupolev Tu-154B-2 | 79A-375 | |
| ☐ RA-85432 | Tupolev Tu-154B-2 | 80A-432 | |

| | | | |
|---|---|---|---|
| ☐ RA-85439 | Tupolev Tu-154B-2 | 80A-439 | |
| ☐ RA-85459 | Tupolev Tu-154B-2 | 80A-459 | |
| ☐ RA-85489 | Tupolev Tu-154B-2 | 81A-489 | |
| ☐ RA-85508 | Tupolev Tu-154B-2 | 81A-508 | |
| ☐ RA-85807 | Tupolev Tu-154M | 94A-988 | |
| ☐ RA-85814 | Tupolev Tu-154M | 9.A-994 | |
| ☐ RA-85833 | Tupolev Tu-154M | 01A-1017 | |
| | | | |
| ☐ RA-86078 | Ilyushin Il-86 | 51483205049 | |
| ☐ RA-86093 | Ilyushin Il-86 | 51483207064 | |
| ☐ RA-86114 | Ilyushin Il-86 | 51483209082 | |

## VASO AIRLINES                                     VSO

| | | | |
|---|---|---|---|
| ☐ RA-86066 | Ilyushin Il-86 | 51483204033 | Lsf AFL |
| ☐ RA-86123 | Ilyushin Il-86 | 51483210091 | Lsf TSO |

## VOLGA-DNEPR AIRLINES                               VDA

| | | | |
|---|---|---|---|
| ☐ RA-82003 | An-124-100 | 19530502792 | |
| ☐ RA-82042 | An-124-100 | 9773054055093 | |
| ☐ RA-82043 | An-124-100 | 9773054155101 | |
| ☐ RA-82044 | An-124-100 | 9773054155109 | |
| ☐ RA-82045 | An-124-100 | 9773052255113 | |
| ☐ RA-82046 | An-124-100 | 9773052255117 | |
| ☐ RA-82047 | An-124-100 | 9773053259121 | |
| ☐ RA-82074 | An-124-100 | 9773051459142 | |
| ☐ RA-82078 | An-124-100 | 97730543559143 | |
| ☐ RA-82079 | An-124-100 | 9773052062157 | |
| ☐ RA-82 | An-124-100 | | o/o |
| ☐ RA-76788 | Ilyushin Il-76TD | 0033446325 | |

## VORONEZH AVIA                                      VRN

| | | | |
|---|---|---|---|
| ☐ RA-65062 | Tupolev Tu-134A | 49875 | |
| ☐ RA-65065 | Tupolev Tu-134A-3 | 49890 | |
| ☐ RA-65067 | Tupolev Tu-134A-3 | 49905 | |
| ☐ RA-65762 | Tupolev Tu-134A-3 | 62279 | |
| ☐ RA-65794 | Tupolev Tu-134A-3 | 63135 | Lst CIG |
| ☐ RA-65880 | Tupolev Tu-134A-3 | 35200 | Lst CIG |
| ☐ RA-65918 | Tupolev Tu-134A-3 | 63995 | |
| ☐ RA-65929 | Tupolev Tu-134A | 66495 | |

## YAMAL AIRLINES                                     LLM

| | | | |
|---|---|---|---|
| ☐ RA-65132 | Tupolev Tu-134A-3 | 60639 | |
| ☐ RA-65143 | Tupolev Tu-134A | 60967 | |
| ☐ RA-65552 | Tupolev Tu-134A-3 | 66270 | |
| ☐ RA-65554 | Tupolev Tu-134A-3 | 66320 | Lst NZP |
| ☐ RA-65906 | Tupolev Tu-134A | 66175 | |
| ☐ RA-65914 | Tupolev Tu-134A-3 | 66109 | |
| ☐ RA-65915 | Tupolev Tu-134A-3 | 66120 | |
| ☐ RA-65916 | Tupolev Tu-134A-3 | 66152 | |
| | | | |
| ☐ RA-74027 | An-74-200 | 36547096920 | Lst NZP |
| ☐ RA-74043 | An-74-200 | 36547096923 | Lst NZP |
| ☐ RA-74052 | An-74-200 | 36547098444 | Lst NZP |
| | | | |
| ☐ RA-85324 | Tupolev Tu-154B-2 | 79A-324 | |
| ☐ RA-85819 | Tupolev Tu-154M | 97A-1008 | |
| ☐ RA-85842 | Tupolev Tu-154B-2 | 80A-420 | Lsf IDF |

## RP - PHILIPPINES

## ABOITIZ AIR TRANSPORT                              BOI

| | | | |
|---|---|---|---|
| ☐ RP-C2253 | NAMC YS-11A | 2020 | Lst RIT |
| ☐ RP-C3202 | NAMC YS-11A | 2128 | std |
| ☐ RP-C3205 | NAMC YS-11 | 2010 | |
| ☐ RP-C3208 | NAMC YS-11A | 2138 | Lst RIT |
| ☐ RP-C3212 | NAMC YS-11A | 2111 | std |
| ☐ RP-C3214 | NAMC YS-11A | 2158 | Lst RIT |
| ☐ RP-C3215 | NAMC YS-11A | 2021 | |
| ☐ RP-C | NAMC YS-11A | 2078 | |

## AIR PHILIPPINES — GAP

| | | |
|---|---|---|
| ☐ EI-BZM | Boeing 737-3Y0 | 1929/24681 |
| ☐ EI-BZN | Boeing 737-3Y0 | 1941/24770 |
| ☐ RP-C2020 | Boeing 737-222 | 179/19943 |
| ☐ RP-C2021 | Boeing 737-222 | 6/19039 |
| ☐ RP-C2022 | Boeing 737-222 | 175/19942 |
| ☐ RP-C2023 | Boeing 737-222 | 187/19947 |
| ☐ RP-C2025 | Boeing 737-222 | 103/19077 |
| ☐ RP-C3011 | Boeing 737-2H4 | 524/21533 |
| ☐ RP-C3012 | Boeing 737-2H4 | 509/21448 |
| ☐ RP-C3015 | Boeing 737-2H4 | 526/21534 |

## ASIAN SPIRIT — RIT

| | | | |
|---|---|---|---|
| ☐ RP-C2015 | NAMC YS-11A | 2067 | |
| ☐ RP-C2253 | NAMC YS-11A | 2020 | Lsf BOI |
| ☐ RP-C3208 | NAMC YS-11A | 2138 | Lsf BOI |
| ☐ RP-C3214 | NAMC YS-11A | 2158 | Lsf BOI |
| ☐ RP-C3217 | NAMC YS-11A | 2083 | |
| ☐ RP-C3587 | NAMC YS-11A | 2069 | |
| ☐ RP-C3588 | NAMC YS-11A | 2168 | std |

## CEBU PACIFIC AIR — CEB

| | | |
|---|---|---|
| ☐ RP-C1503 | Douglas DC-9-32 | 906/47789 |
| ☐ RP-C1504 | Douglas DC-9-32 | 910/47792 |
| ☐ RP-C1505 | Douglas DC-9-32 | 911/47793 |
| ☐ RP-C1506 | Douglas DC-9-32 | 916/47795 |
| ☐ RP-C1508 | Douglas DC-9-32 | 176/47070 |
| ☐ RP-C1509 | Douglas DC-9-32 | 188/47071 |
| ☐ RP-C1535 | Douglas DC-9-32 | 352/47266 |
| ☐ RP-C1536 | Douglas DC-9-32 | 471/47353 |
| ☐ RP-C1537 | Douglas DC-9-32 | 684/47570 |
| ☐ RP-C1538 | Douglas DC-9-32 | 466/47239 |
| ☐ RP-C1539 | Douglas DC-9-32 | 666/47485 |
| ☐ RP-C1540 | Douglas DC-9-32 | 868/47734 |
| ☐ RP-C1541 | Douglas DC-9-31 | 1036/48143 |
| ☐ RP-C1543 | Douglas DC-9-31 | 921/48116 |
| ☐ RP-C1544 | Douglas DC-9-31 | 922/48117 |
| ☐ RP-C | Douglas DC-9-31 | 920/48115 |
| ☐ RP-C2714 | Boeing 757-236 | 218/24370 |
| ☐ RP-C2715 | Boeing 757-236 | 225/24371 |
| ☐ RP-C2716 | Boeing 757-236 | 441/25597 |

## PHILIPPINE AIRLINES — PAL

| | | |
|---|---|---|
| ☐ F-OHZM | Airbus A330-301 | 183 |
| ☐ F-OHZN | Airbus A330-301 | 184 |
| ☐ F-OHZO | Airbus A330-301 | 188 |
| ☐ F-OHZP | Airbus A330-301 | 191 |
| ☐ F-OHZQ | Airbus A330-301 | 189 |
| ☐ F-OHZR | Airbus A330-301 | 198 |
| ☐ F-OHZS | Airbus A330-301 | 200 |
| ☐ F-OHZT | Airbus A330-301 | 203 |
| ☐ F-OHPJ | Airbus A340-313X | 173 |
| ☐ F-OHPK | Airbus A340-313X | 176 |
| ☐ F-OHPL | Airbus A340-313X | 187 |
| ☐ F-OHPM | Airbus A340-313X | 196 |
| ☐ RP-C3221 | Airbus A320-214 | 0706 |
| ☐ RP-C3223 | Airbus A320-214 | 0745 |
| ☐ RP-C3224 | Airbus A320-214 | 0753 |
| ☐ EI-BZE | Boeing 737-3Y0 | 1753/24464 |
| ☐ EI-BZF | Boeing 737-3Y0 | 1755/24465 |
| ☐ EI-BZJ | Boeing 737-3Y0 | 1837/24677 |
| ☐ EI-BZL | Boeing 737-3Y0 | 1927/24680 |
| ☐ EI-CUL | Boeing 737-36N | 2882/28559 |
| ☐ EI-CVN | Boeing 737-4Y0 | 1841/24684 |
| ☐ EI-CVO | Boeing 737-4S3 | 2223/25594 |
| ☐ EI-CVP | Boeing 737-4Y0 | 2442/26081 |
| ☐ RP-C4007 | Boeing 737-332 | 2488/25996 |
| ☐ RP-C4008 | Boeing 737-33A | 2025/25033 |

| | | | |
|---|---|---|---|
| ☐ N751PR | Boeing 747-4F6 | 1005/27261 | |
| ☐ N752PR | Boeing 747-4F6 | 1012/27262 | |
| ☐ N753PR | Boeing 747-4F6 | 1039/27828 | |
| ☐ N754PR | Boeing 747-469M | 1068/27663 | |

# SE - SWEDEN

## BRITANNIA AIRWAYS SWEDEN — BLX

| | | | |
|---|---|---|---|
| ☐ D-AHFR | Boeing 737-8K5 | 528/30593 | Lsf HLF |
| ☐ SE-DZH | Boeing 737-804 | 452/28227 | |
| ☐ SE-DZI | Boeing 737-804 | 478/28229 | Lst WEA |
| ☐ SE-DZK | Boeing 737-804 | 538/28231 | |
| ☐ SE-DZL | Boeing 737-804 | 502/30465 | |
| ☐ SE-DZM | Boeing 737-804 | 505/30466 | |
| ☐ SE-DZN | Boeing 737-804 | 1127/32903 | |
| ☐ SE-DZV | Boeing 737-804 | 32904 | o/o |

## CITY AIRLINE — SDR

| | | | |
|---|---|---|---|
| ☐ F-GTSL | SAAB 2000 | 013 | Lst FIN |
| ☐ SE-RAA | Embraer ERJ-135 | 145210 | |
| ☐ SE-RAB | Embraer ERJ-135 | 145453 | Lst EZE |
| ☐ SE-RAC | Embraer ERJ-135 | 145098 | |

## EUROPEAN EXECUTIVE EXPRESS — EXC

| | | | |
|---|---|---|---|
| ☐ SE-LDI | BAe Jetstream 31 | 785 | |
| ☐ SE-LGB | BAe Jetstream 31 | 639 | |
| ☐ SE-LGC | BAe Jetstream 31 | 645 | |
| ☐ SE-LGH | BAe Jetstream 31 | 773 | |
| ☐ SE-LNT | BAe Jetstream 32EP | 948 | |
| ☐ SE-LNU | BAe Jetstream 32EP | 949 | |
| ☐ SE-LNV | BAe Jetstream 32EP | 951 | |
| ☐ SE-LNY | BAe ATP | 2058 | o/o |
| ☐ SE-LNZ | BAe ATP | 2060 | o/o |

## FALCON AVIATION — FCN

| | | |
|---|---|---|
| ☐ SE-DPA | Boeing 737-33A (QC) | 2067/25401 |
| ☐ SE-DPB | Boeing 737-33A (QC) | 2159/25402 |
| ☐ SE-DPC | Boeing 737-33A (QC) | 2172/25426 |

## GOLDEN AIR — GAO

| | | | |
|---|---|---|---|
| ☐ OH-FAE | SAAB SF.340A/QC | 139 | Lsf FIN |
| ☐ OH-FAF | SAAB SF.340B | 167 | Lsf FIN |
| ☐ SE-ISD | SAAB SF.340A | 145 | |
| ☐ SE-ISE | SAAB SF.340A | 156 | |
| ☐ SE-ISG | SAAB SF.340B | 162 | |
| ☐ SE-KTE | SAAB SF.340B | 230 | |
| ☐ SE-KTK | SAAB SF.340B | 276 | |
| ☐ SE-LEP | SAAB SF.340A | 127 | |
| ☐ SE-LES | SAAB SF.340A | 129 | |
| ☐ SE-LHO | SAAB SF.340B | 364 | |
| ☐ SE-LMR | SAAB SF.340A | 141 | |
| ☐ F-GTSL | SAAB 2000 | 013 | Lst SDR |
| ☐ SE-LOG | SAAB 2000 | 031 | |

## INTERNATIONAL BUSINESS AIR — IBZ

| | | |
|---|---|---|
| ☐ SE-LEF | SA.227AC Metro III | AC-451B |
| ☐ SE-LIL | SA.227AC Metro III | AC-432B |
| ☐ SE-LKC | Embraer EMB.120ER | 120046 |

## MALMÖ AVIATION — SCW

| | | |
|---|---|---|
| ☐ SE-DRD | BAe 146 Srs 200 | E2094 |
| ☐ SE-DSO | Avro RJ100 | E3221 |
| ☐ SE-DSP | Avro RJ100 | E3242 |
| ☐ SE-DSR | Avro RJ100 | E3244 |
| ☐ SE-DSS | Avro RJ100 | E3245 |
| ☐ SE-DST | Avro RJ100 | E3247 |

| | | | |
|---|---|---|---|
| ☐ SE-DSU | Avro RJ100 | E3248 | |
| ☐ SE-DSV | Avro RJ100 | E3250 | |
| ☐ SE-DSX | Avro RJ100 | E3255 | |
| ☐ SE-DSY | Avro RJ100 | E3263 | |

## NORDIC AIRLINK · NDC

| | | | |
|---|---|---|---|
| ☐ HB-AKP | SAAB SF.340B | 168 | Lsf CRX |
| ☐ HB-INR | McDD MD-82 | | |
| ☐ SE-DMT | McDD MD-81 | 944/48003 | |
| ☐ SE-RBE | McDD MD-82 | 1089/49152 | |

## NOVAIR · NVR

| | | | |
|---|---|---|---|
| ☐ CS-TNE | Airbus A320-212 | 0395 | Lsf LXR |
| ☐ SE-DVO | Boeing 737-85F | 166/28822 | |
| ☐ SE-DVR | Boeing 737-85F | 238/28826 | |
| ☐ SE-DVU | Boeing 737-85F | 188/28825 | |
| ☐ SE-RBF | Airbus A330-223 | 353 | |
| ☐ SE-RBG | Airbus A330-223 | 362 | |

## SCANDINAVIAN AIRLINES SYTEM · SAS

| | | | |
|---|---|---|---|
| ☐ LN-RKI | Airbus A321-232 | 1817 | |
| ☐ LN-RKK | Airbus A321-232 | | o/o |
| ☐ LN-RKL | Airbus A321-232 | | o/o |
| ☐ OY-KBB | Airbus A321-232 | 1642 | |
| ☐ OY-KBE | Airbus A321-232 | 1798 | |
| ☐ OY-KBF | Airbus A321-232 | 1807 | |
| ☐ OY-KBH | Airbus A321-232 | 1675 | |
| ☐ OY-KBK | Airbus A321-232 | 1587 | |
| ☐ OY-KBL | Airbus A321-232 | 1619 | |
| ☐ SE-REG | Airbus A321-232 | 1848 | |
| ☐ SE-REH | Airbus A321-232 | | o/o |
| ☐ SE-REL | Airbus A321-232 | | o/o |
| | | | |
| ☐ LN-RKH | Airbus A330-343X | 497 | |
| ☐ OY-KBN | Airbus A330-343X | 496 | |
| ☐ OY-KBS | Airbus A330-343X | | o/o |
| ☐ SE-REE | Airbus A330-343X | 515 | |
| | | | |
| ☐ LN-RKF | Airbus A340-313X | 413 | |
| ☐ LN-RKG | Airbus A340-313X | 424 | |
| ☐ OY-KBA | Airbus A340-313X | 435 | |
| ☐ OY-KBC | Airbus A340-313X | 467 | |
| ☐ OY-KBD | Airbus A340-313X | 470 | |
| ☐ OY-KBI | Airbus A340-313X | 430 | |
| ☐ OY-KBM | Airbus A340-313X | 450 | |
| | | | |
| ☐ LN-RCN | Boeing 737-883 | 529/28318 | |
| ☐ LN-RCO | Boeing 737-883 | 548/28319 | |
| ☐ LN-RCR | Boeing 737-883 | 577/28321 | |
| ☐ LN-RCS | Boeing 737-883 | 587/30193 | |
| ☐ LN-RCT | Boeing 737-683 | 303/30189 | |
| ☐ LN-RCU | Boeing 737-683 | 335/30190 | |
| ☐ LN-RCW | Boeing 737-683 | 333/28308 | |
| ☐ LN-RCX | Boeing 737-883 | 733/28309 | |
| ☐ LN-RCY | Boeing 737-883 | 767/28324 | |
| ☐ LN-RCZ | Boeing 737-883 | 798/30197 | |
| ☐ LN-RPA | Boeing 737-683 | 100/28290 | |
| ☐ LN-RPB | Boeing 737-683 | 137/28294 | |
| ☐ LN-RPD | Boeing 737-883 | 625/28323 | Lst ADH |
| ☐ LN-RPF | Boeing 737-683 | 330/28307 | |
| ☐ LN-RPG | Boeing 737-683 | 255/28310 | |
| ☐ LN-RPH | Boeing 737-683 | 375/28605 | |
| ☐ LN-RPJ | Boeing 737-783 | 486/30192 | |
| ☐ LN-RPK | Boeing 737-783 | 500/28317 | |
| ☐ LN-RPL | Boeing 737-883 | 673/30469 | |
| ☐ LN-RPM | Boeing 737-883 | 696/30195 | |
| ☐ LN-RPN | Boeing 737-883 | 717/30470 | |
| ☐ LN-RPO | Boeing 737-883 | 634/30467 | Lst ADH |
| ☐ LN-RPP | Boeing 737-883 | 666/30194 | Lst ADH |
| ☐ LN-RPS | Boeing 737-683 | 191/28298 | |
| ☐ LN-RPT | Boeing 737-683 | 193/28299 | |
| ☐ LN-RPU | Boeing 737-683 | 407/28312 | |
| ☐ LN-RPW | Boeing 737-683 | 92/28289 | |
| ☐ LN-RPX | Boeing 737-683 | 112/28291 | |

| | | | |
|---|---|---|---|
| ☐ LN-RPY | Boeing 737-683 | 116/28292 | |
| ☐ LN-RPZ | Boeing 737-683 | 120/28293 | |
| ☐ LN-RRN | Boeing 737-783 | 404/30191 | |
| ☐ LN-RRO | Boeing 737-683 | 49/28288 | |
| ☐ LN-RRP | Boeing 737-683 | 382/28311 | |
| ☐ LN-RRR | Boeing 737-683 | 368/28309 | |
| ☐ LN-RRS | Boeing 737-883 | 1014/28325 | |
| ☐ LN-RRT | Boeing 737-883 | 1036/28326 | |
| ☐ LN-RRU | Boeing 737-883 | 1070/28327 | |
| ☐ LN-RRX | Boeing 737-683 | 21/28296 | |
| ☐ LN-RRY | Boeing 737-683 | 30/28297 | |
| ☐ LN-RRZ | Boeing 737-683 | 149/28295 | |
| ☐ OY-KKE | Boeing 737-683 | 290/28305 | |
| ☐ OY-KKG | Boeing 737-683 | 209/28300 | |
| ☐ OY-KKH | Boeing 737-683 | 227/28301 | |
| ☐ OY-KKI | Boeing 737-783 | 464/28315 | |
| ☐ OY-KKR | Boeing 737-783 | 476/28316 | |
| ☐ OY-KKS | Boeing 737-683 | 614/28322 | |
| ☐ OY-KKT | Boeing 737-883 | 668/30468 | Lst ADH |
| ☐ OY-KKU | Boeing 737-883 | 551/28320 | |
| ☐ OY-KKY | Boeing 737-683 | 329/28306 | |
| ☐ SE-DNT | Boeing 737-683 | 243/28302 | |
| ☐ SE-DNU | Boeing 737-683 | 257/28303 | |
| ☐ SE-DNX | Boeing 737-683 | 270/28304 | |
| ☐ SE-DTH | Boeing 737-683 | 447/28313 | |
| ☐ SE-DTI | Boeing 737-783 | 458/28314 | |
| ☐ SE-DTR | Boeing 737-683 | 32277 | o/o |
| ☐ SE-DYC | Boeing 737-883 | 32276 | o/o |
| ☐ SE-DYD | Boeing 737-883 | 30471 | o/o |
| ☐ SE-DYG | Boeing 737-883 | 1169/32278 | |
| ☐ SE-DYT | Boeing 737-883 | 28328 | o/o |
| | | | |
| ☐ LN-RCD | Boeing 767-383ER | 315/24847 | |
| ☐ LN-RCE | Boeing 767-383ER | 309/24846 | |
| ☐ LN-RCF | Boeing 767-383ER | 330/24849 | |
| ☐ LN-RCG | Boeing 767-383ER | 273/24475 | |
| ☐ LN-RCH | Boeing 767-383ER | 257/24318 | |
| ☐ LN-RCL | Boeing 767-383ER | 395/25365 | |
| ☐ LN-RCM | Boeing 767-383ER | 412/26544 | |
| ☐ OY-KDN | Boeing 767-383ER | 325/24848 | |
| | | | |
| ☐ LN-RLE | McDD MD-82 | 1232/49382 | |
| ☐ LN-RLF | McDD MD-82 | 1236/49383 | |
| ☐ LN-RLG | McDD MD-82 | 1283/49423 | |
| ☐ LN-RLR | McDD MD-82 | 1345/49437 | |
| ☐ LN-RMA | McDD MD-82 | 1379/49554 | |
| ☐ LN-RMD | McDD MD-82 | 1402/49555 | |
| ☐ LN-RMG | McDD MD-87 | 1522/49611 | |
| ☐ LN-RMH | McDD MD-87 | 1827/49612 | |
| ☐ LN-RMJ | McDD MD-82 | 1659/49912 | |
| ☐ LN-RMK | McDD MD-87 | 1705/49610 | |
| ☐ LN-RML | McDD MD-82 | 1835/53002 | |
| ☐ LN-RMM | McDD MD-82 | 1855/53005 | |
| ☐ LN-RMN | McDD MD-82 | 1922/53295 | |
| ☐ LN-RMO | McDD MD-81 | 1947/53315 | |
| ☐ LN-RMP | McDD MD-87 | 1962/53337 | |
| ☐ LN-RMR | McDD MD-81 | 1998/53365 | |
| ☐ LN-RMS | McDD MD-81 | 2003/53368 | |
| ☐ LN-RMT | McDD MD-81 | 1815/53001 | |
| ☐ LN-RMU | McDD MD-87 | 1967/53340 | |
| ☐ LN-ROM | McDD MD-81 | 1895/53008 | |
| ☐ LN-RON | McDD MD-81 | 1979/53347 | |
| ☐ LN-ROO | McDD MD-81 | 1999/53366 | |
| ☐ LN-ROP | McDD MD-82 | 1237/49384 | |
| ☐ LN-ROR | McDD MD-82 | 1244/49385 | |
| ☐ LN-ROS | McDD MD-82 | 1263/49421 | |
| ☐ LN-ROT | McDD MD-82 | 1264/49422 | |
| ☐ LN-ROU | McDD MD-82 | 1284/49424 | |
| ☐ LN-ROW | McDD MD-82 | 1353/49438 | |
| ☐ LN-ROX | McDD MD-82 | 1442/49603 | |
| ☐ LN-ROY | McDD MD-82 | 1543/49615 | |
| ☐ LN-ROZ | McDD MD-87 | 1572/49608 | |
| ☐ OY-KGT | McDD MD-82 | 1225/49380 | |
| ☐ OY-KGY | McDD MD-81 | 1254/49420 | |
| ☐ OY-KGZ | McDD MD-81 | 1231/49381 | |
| ☐ OY-KHC | McDD MD-82 | 1303/49436 | |
| ☐ OY-KHE | McDD MD-82 | 1456/49604 | |
| ☐ OY-KHF | McDD MD-87 | 1517/49609 | |

| | | |
|---|---|---|
| ☐ OY-KHG | McDD MD-82 | 1519/49613 |
| ☐ OY-KHI | McDD MD-87 | 1556/49614 |
| ☐ OY-KHK | McDD MD-82 | 1638/49910 |
| ☐ OY-KHL | McDD MD-82 | 1653/49911 |
| ☐ OY-KHM | McDD MD-82 | 1693/49914 |
| ☐ OY-KHN | McDD MD-81 | 1812/53000 |
| ☐ OY-KHP | McDD MD-81 | 1882/53007 |
| ☐ OY-KHR | McDD MD-81 | 1896/53275 |
| ☐ OY-KHT | McDD MD-82 | 1937/53296 |
| ☐ OY-KHU | McDD MD-87 | 1953/53336 |
| ☐ OY-KHW | McDD MD-87 | 1985/53348 |
| ☐ SE-DIB | McDD MD-87 | 1501/49605 |
| ☐ SE-DIC | McDD MD-87 | 1512/49607 |
| ☐ SE-DIF | McDD MD-87 | 1569/49606 |
| ☐ SE-DII | McDD MD-82 | 1625/49909 |
| ☐ SE-DIK | McDD MD-82 | 1553/49728 |
| ☐ SE-DIL | McDD MD-82 | 1665/49913 |
| ☐ SE-DIN | McDD MD-82 | 1803/49999 |
| ☐ SE-DIP | McDD MD-87 | 1921/53010 |
| ☐ SE-DIR | McDD MD-81 | 1846/53004 |
| ☐ SE-DIS | McDD MD-81 | 1869/53006 |
| ☐ SE-DIU | McDD MD-87 | 1931/53011 |
| ☐ SE-DIX | McDD MD-82 | 1800/49998 |
| ☐ SE-DIZ | McDD MD-82 | 1917/53294 |
| ☐ SE-DMB | McDD MD-81 | 1946/53314 |

| | | |
|---|---|---|
| ☐ LN-ROA | McDD MD-90-30 | 2141/53459 |
| ☐ LN-ROB | McDD MD-90-30 | 2149/53462 |
| ☐ OY-KIL | McDD MD-90-30 | 2140/53458 |
| ☐ OY-KIM | McDD MD-90-30 | 2142/53460 |
| ☐ OY-KIN | McDD MD-90-30 | 2197/53544 |
| ☐ SE-DMF | McDD MD-90-30 | 2138/53457 |
| ☐ SE-DMG | McDD MD-90-30 | 2147/53461 |
| ☐ SE-DMH | McDD MD-90-30 | 2194/53543 |

| | | |
|---|---|---|
| ☐ LN-RDA | DHC-8-402Q | 4013 |
| ☐ LN-RDB | DHC-8-402Q | 4018 |
| ☐ LN-RDC | DHC-8-402Q | 4019 |
| ☐ LN-RDD | DHC-8-402Q | 4009 |
| ☐ LN-RDE | DHC-8-402Q | 4020 |
| ☐ LN-RDF | DHC-8-402Q | 4021 |
| ☐ LN-RDG | DHC-8-402Q | 4022 |
| ☐ LN-RDH | DHC-8-402Q | 4023 |
| ☐ LN-RDI | DHC-8-402Q | 4024 |
| ☐ LN-RDJ | DHC-8-402Q | 4010 |
| ☐ LN-RDK | DHC-8-402Q | 4025 |
| ☐ LN-RDL | DHC-8-402Q | 4011 |
| ☐ LN-RDM | DHC-8-402Q | 4033 |
| ☐ LN-RDO | DHC-8-402Q | 4036 |
| ☐ LN-RDP | DHC-8-402Q | 4012 |
| ☐ LN-RDQ | DHC-8-402Q | 4008 |
| ☐ LN-RDR | DHC-8-402Q | 4034 |
| ☐ LN-RDS | DHC-8-402Q | 4035 |
| ☐ LN-RDT | DHC-8-402Q | 4038 |
| ☐ OY-KCD | DHC-8-402Q | 4054 |
| ☐ OY-KCE | DHC-8-402Q | 4057 |
| ☐ OY-KCF | DHC-8-402Q | 4062 |
| ☐ OY-KCG | DHC-8-402Q | 4063 |
| ☐ OY-KCH | DHC-8-402Q | 4064 |

| | | |
|---|---|---|
| ☐ LN-RNC | Fokker 50 | 20176 |
| ☐ LN-RND | Fokker 50 | 20178 |
| ☐ LN-RNE | Fokker 50 | 20179 |
| ☐ LN-RNF | Fokker 50 | 20183 |
| ☐ LN-RNG | Fokker 50 | 20184 |
| ☐ OY-KAE | Fokker 50 | 20162 |
| ☐ OY-KAF | Fokker 50 | 20163 |

## SKYWAYS EXPRESS — SKX

| | | |
|---|---|---|
| ☐ SE-DZA | Embraer ERJ-145 | 145070 |
| ☐ SE-DZB | Embraer ERJ-145 | 145113 |
| ☐ SE-DZC | Embraer ERJ-145 | 145169 |
| ☐ SE-DZD | Embraer ERJ-145 | 145185 |
| ☐ SE-KTC | Fokker 50 | 20124 |
| ☐ SE-KTD | Fokker 50 | 20125 |

| | | |
|---|---|---|
| ☐ SE-LEA | Fokker 50 | 20116 |
| ☐ SE-LEB | Fokker 50 | 20120 |
| ☐ SE-LEC | Fokker 50 | 20112 |
| ☐ SE-LED | Fokker 50 | 20111 |
| ☐ SE-LEH | Fokker 50 | 20108 |
| ☐ SE-LEL | Fokker 50 | 20110 |
| ☐ SE-LEU | Fokker 50 | 20115 |
| ☐ SE-LEZ | Fokker 50 | 20128 |
| ☐ SE-LIN | Fokker 50 | 20138 |
| ☐ SE-LIO | Fokker 50 | 20146 |
| ☐ SE-LIP | Fokker 50 | 20147 |
| ☐ SE-LIR | Fokker 50 | 20151 |
| ☐ SE-LIS | Fokker 50 | 20152 |
| ☐ SE-LIT | Fokker 50 | 20194 |

| | | | |
|---|---|---|---|
| ☐ SE-ISL | SAAB SF.340A | 130 | |
| ☐ SE-ISP | SAAB SF.340A | 015 | |
| ☐ SE-ISR | SAAB SF.340A | 017 | |
| ☐ SE-ISV | SAAB SF.340A | 045 | |
| ☐ SE-ISY | SAAB SF.340A | 080 | |
| ☐ SE-KCR | SAAB SF.340A/QC | 065 | |
| ☐ SE-KCS | SAAB SF.340A/QC | 066 | |
| ☐ SE-KCT | SAAB SF.340A/QC | 070 | Lst SRL |
| ☐ SE-KCU | SAAB SF.340A | 135 | |
| ☐ SE-KPD | SAAB SF.340A | 037 | |
| ☐ SE-KPE | SAAB SF.340A | 055 | |
| ☐ SE-KRN | SAAB SF.340A | 159 | Lst SRL |
| ☐ SE-KSI | SAAB SF.340B | 223 | |
| ☐ SE-KSK | SAAB SF.340B | 229 | |
| ☐ SE-KUT | SAAB SF.340A | 087 | Lst SRL |

## SVENSKA DIREKTFLYG — HSV

| | | |
|---|---|---|
| ☐ SE-LHB | BAe Jetstream 32 | 844 |
| ☐ SE-LHC | BAe Jetstream 32 | 846 |
| ☐ SE-LHE | BAe Jetstream 32 | 854 |
| ☐ SE-LHF | BAe Jetstream 32 | 855 |
| ☐ SE-LHG | BAe Jetstream 32EP | 857 |
| ☐ SE-LHH | BAe Jetstream 32EP | 848 |
| ☐ SE-LHI | BAe Jetstream 32EP | 841 |
| ☐ SE-LHK | BAe Jetstream 32 | 864 |
| ☐ SE-KKX | Dornier 228-100 | 7004 |

## SWEDLINE EXPRESS — SRL

| | | | |
|---|---|---|---|
| ☐ SE-KCT | SAAB SF.340A/QC | 070 | Lsf SKX |
| ☐ SE-KCV | SAAB SF.340B | 310 | |
| ☐ SE-KRN | SAAB SF.340A | 159 | Lsf SKX |
| ☐ SE-KUT | SAAB SF.340A | 087 | Lsf SKX |
| ☐ SE-LGS | SAAB SF.340A | 071 | |
| ☐ SE-LCX | Beech 1900D | UE-275 | |

## WEST AIR SWEDEN — SWN

| | | | |
|---|---|---|---|
| ☐ SE-LEG | HS.748 Srs.2A/244 | 1723 | |
| ☐ SE-LEK | HS.748 Srs.2A/244 | 1725 | |
| ☐ SE-LEX | HS.748 Srs.2A/244 | 1727 | |
| ☐ SE-LIA | HS.748 Srs.2A/264 | 1717 | |
| ☐ SE-LIB | HS.748 Srs.2B/371LFD | 1776 | |
| ☐ SE-LIC | HS.748 Srs.2B/399LFD | 1778 | |
| ☐ SE-LID | HS.748 Srs.2A/333 | 1760 | |
| ☐ SE-LIE | HS.748 Srs.2A/229 | 1595 | |
| ☐ SE-LIF | HS.748 Srs.2A/229 | 1596 | |
| ☐ SE-LGU | BAe ATP | 2022 | |
| ☐ SE-LGV | BAe ATP | 2034 | |
| ☐ SE-LGX | BAe ATP | 2036 | |
| ☐ SE-LGY | BAe ATP | 2035 | |
| ☐ SE-LGZ | BAe ATP (F) | 2021 | |
| ☐ SE-LHX | BAe ATP | 2020 | |
| ☐ SE-LHZ | BAe ATP | 2059 | |
| ☐ SE-LNY | BAe ATP | 2058 | o/o |
| ☐ SE-LNZ | BAe ATP | 2060 | o/o |
| ☐ SE-LPR | BAe ATP | 2057 | |
| ☐ SE-LPS | BAe ATP | 2043 | |

## SP - POLAND

### AIR POLONIA APN

| | | | |
|---|---|---|---|
| □ SP-KPY | LET L-410UVP | 902439 | |
| □ SP-KPZ | LET L-410UVP | 902431 | |
| □ SP- | Boeing 737-4Q8 | 2653/26306 | o/o |
| □ SP- | Boeing 737-4Q8 | 3009/28202 | o/o |

### EUROLOT ELO

| | | |
|---|---|---|
| □ SP-EDA | ATR 42-500 | 516 |
| □ SP-EDB | ATR 42-500 | 522 |
| □ SP-EDC | ATR 42-500 | 526 |
| □ SP-EDD | ATR 42-500 | 530 |
| □ SP-EDE | ATR 42-500 | 443 |
| □ SP-LFA | ATR 72-202 | 246 |
| □ SP-LFB | ATR 72-202 | 265 |
| □ SP-LFC | ATR 72-202 | 272 |
| □ SP-LFD | ATR 72-202 | 279 |
| □ SP-LFE | ATR 72-202 | 328 |
| □ SP-LFF | ATR 72-202 | 402 |
| □ SP-LFG | ATR 72-202 | 411 |
| □ SP-LFH | ATR 72-202 | 478 |

### LOT – POLISH AIRLINES LOT

| | | | |
|---|---|---|---|
| □ SP-LKA | Boeing 737-55D | 2389/27416 | |
| □ SP-LKB | Boeing 737-55D | 2392/27417 | |
| □ SP-LKC | Boeing 737-55D | 2397/27418 | |
| □ SP-LKD | Boeing 737-55D | 2401/27419 | |
| □ SP-LKE | Boeing 737-55D | 2448/27130 | |
| ■ SP-LKF | Boeing 737-55D | 2603/27368 | |
| □ SP-LKG | Boeing 737-53C | 1894/24825 | |
| □ SP-LKH | Boeing 737-53C | 2041/24826 | |
| □ SP-LKI | Boeing 737-53C | 2243/24827 | |
| □ SP-LKK | Boeing 737-5L9 | 2998/28996 | Lsf DAN |
| □ SP-LLA | Boeing 737-45D | 2458/27131 | |
| □ SP-LLB | Boeing 737-45D | 2492/27156 | |
| □ SP-LLC | Boeing 737-45D | 2502/27157 | |
| □ SP-LLD | Boeing 737-45D | 2589/27256 | |
| □ SP-LLE | Boeing 737-45D | 2804/27914 | |
| □ SP-LLF | Boeing 737-45D | 2874/28672 | |
| □ SP-LLG | Boeing 737-45D | 2895/28753 | |
| □ SP-LMC | Boeing 737-36N | 2890/28668 | |
| □ SP-LMD | Boeing 737-36N | 2897/28669 | |
| □ SP- | Boeing 737-85D | | o/o |
| □ SP- | Boeing 737-85D | | o/o |
| □ SP-LOA | Boeing 767-25DER | 261/24733 | |
| □ SP-LOB | Boeing 767-25DER | 266/24734 | |
| □ SP-LPA | Boeing 767-35DER | 322/24865 | |
| □ SP-LPB | Boeing 767-35DER | 577/27902 | Lst UVG |
| □ SP-LPC | Boeing 767-35DER | 659/28656 | |
| □ SP-LGA | Embraer ERJ-145 | 145155 | |
| □ SP-LGB | Embraer ERJ-145 | 145165 | |
| □ SP-LGC | Embraer ERJ-145 | 145227 | |
| □ SP-LGD | Embraer ERJ-145 | 145244 | |
| □ SP-LGE | Embraer ERJ-145 | 145285 | |
| □ SP-LGF | Embraer ERJ-145 | 145308 | |
| □ SP-LGG | Embraer ERJ-145 | 145319 | |
| □ SP-LGH | Embraer ERJ-145 | 145329 | |
| □ SP-LGI | Embraer ERJ-145 | 145336 | |
| □ SP-LGK | Embraer ERJ-145 | 145339 | |
| □ SP-LGL | Embraer ERJ-145 | 145406 | |
| □ SP-LGM | Embraer ERJ-145 | 145408 | |
| □ SP-LGN | Embraer ERJ-145 | 145441 | |
| □ SP-LGO | Embraer ERJ-145 | 145560 | |
| □ SP-LGP | Embraer ERJ-145 | | o/o |
| □ SP- | Embraer ERJ-145 | | o/o |

### SILESIAN AIR

| | | | |
|---|---|---|---|
| □ SP-KTL | LET L-410UVP-E16A | 902414 | |
| □ SP-KTM | Beech 1900D | | o/o |
| □ SP-KTN | Beech 1900D | | o/o |
| □ SP-KTO | Beech 1900D | | o/o |
| □ SP-KTP | Beech 1900D | | o/o |

### WHITE EAGLE GENERAL AVIATION WFA

| | | | |
|---|---|---|---|
| □ SP-FTN | LET L-410UVP-E10 | 902515 | |
| □ SP-FTV | LET L-410UVP-E | 882038 | |
| □ SP-FTX | LET L-410UVP-E10 | 892301 | |
| □ SP-FTY | LET L-410UVP-E10 | 892317 | |
| □ SP-KTB | LET L-410UVP-E | 902504 | Opf DHL |
| □ SP-KTC | LET L-410UVP-E | 902425 | o/o |
| □ SE-DZI | Boeing 737-804 | 478/28229 | Lsf BLX |
| □ SP-KCA | ATR 42-300 | 085 | |
| □ SP- | ATR 42-300 | 092 | o/o |
| □ SP-KDK | Boeing 737-8K5 | 59/27989 | Lsf HLF |
| □ SP-KEI | Boeing 737-4K5 | 1687/24125 | |
| □ SP-KEK | Boeing 737-4K5 | 1707/24127 | |
| □ SP-KEN | Boeing 737-4K5 | 1715/24128 | |

## ST - SUDAN

### AZZA AIR TRANSPORT AZZ

| | | |
|---|---|---|
| □ ER-AXC | Antonov An-12 | 7345209 |
| □ ST-AKW | Boeing 707-330C | 788/20123 |
| □ ST-APS | Ilyushin Il-76TD | 1023409316 |
| □ ST-AQB | Ilyushin Il-76TD | 0053460795 |
| □ ST-AQG | Antonov An-12 | |
| □ ST-JCC | Boeing 707-384C | 495/18948 |

### SPIRIT OF AFRICA SDN

| | | |
|---|---|---|
| □ ST-AQI | Boeing 707-307C | 756/19999 |
| □ ST-AQW | Boeing 707-300 | 854/20517 |
| □ 3C-QRG | Douglas DC-8F-54 | 274/45858 |

### SUDAN AIRWAYS SUD

| | | | |
|---|---|---|---|
| □ C5-SMM | Boeing 727-251 | 665/19973 | Lsf |
| □ F-ODTK | Airbus A300B4-622 | 252 | |
| □ F-OHIA | Airbus A300B4-605R | 530 | std CHR |
| □ ST-AFA | Boeing 707-3J8C | 885/20897 | |
| □ ST-AFB | Boeing 707-3J8C | 887/20898 | |
| □ ST-AFK | Boeing 737-2J8C | 429/21169 | |
| □ ST-AIX | Boeing 707-369C | 764/20086 | std KRT |
| □ TC-FLA | Airbus A300B4-203 | 127 | Lsf FLM |
| □ TS-IOE | Boeing 737-2H3 | 758/22624 | Lsf TAR |
| □ TS-IOF | Boeing 737-2H3 | 776/22625 | Lsf TAR |

### TAAT – TRANS ARABIAN AIR TRANSPORT

| | | |
|---|---|---|
| □ ST-AMF | Boeing 707-321C | 637/19367 |

### TRANS ATTICO ETC

| | | |
|---|---|---|
| □ ST-AQA | Ilyushin Il-76TD | 0023442218 Jow PHG |
| □ ST-CAC | Ilyushin Il-76TD | 0023437076 Jow PHG |

### UNITED ARABIAN COMPANY UAB

| | | |
|---|---|---|
| □ ST-AQE | Antonov An-12BP | 1400196 |

## SU - EGYPT

### AIR CAIRO CCE

| | | | |
|---|---|---|---|
| □ SU-EAF | Tu-204-120 | 1450743764027 | |
| □ SU-EAG | Tu-204-120S | 1450743764028 | Lst TAY |
| □ SU-EAH | Tu-204-120 | 1450743164023 | |
| □ SU-EAI | Tu-204-120 | 1450743164025 | |
| □ SU-EAJ | Tu-204-120S | 1450743164029 | Lst TAY |
| □ SU-EAK | Tu-204-120S | 1450743164033 | Lst TAY |

### AIR MEMPHIS — MHS

| | | | |
|---|---|---|---|
| ☐ SU-AVZ | Boeing 707-366C | 868/20762 | |
| ☐ SU-PBB | Boeing 707-336C | 762/19916 | std |
| ☐ SU-PBO | Douglas DC-9-31 | 940/48131 | |

### AIR SINAI — ASD

| | | | |
|---|---|---|---|
| ☐ SU-GBK | Boeing 737-566 | 2276/26052 | Lsf MSR |

### AMC AVIATION — AMV

| | | | |
|---|---|---|---|
| ☐ SU-AYK | Boeing 737-266 | 455/21194 | |
| ☐ SU-BMM | Airbus A300B4-203 | 175 | Lst MLI |
| ☐ SU-BMQ | McDD MD-90-30 | 2195/53576 | |
| ☐ SU-BOW | Airbus A310-322 | 437 | Lst MLI |

### EGYPTAIR — MSR

| | | | |
|---|---|---|---|
| ☐ SU- | ATR 42-500 | | Lsf LIT |
| ☐ SU- | ATR 42-500 | | Lsf LIT |
| ☐ SU- | ATR 42-500 | | Lsf LIT |
| ☐ SU- | ATR 42-500 | | Lsf ROT |
| ☐ SU- | ATR 42-500 | | Lsf ROT |
| ☐ SU- | ATR 42-500 | | Lsf ROT |
| ☐ SU-BDG | Airbus A300B4-203F | 200 | |
| ☐ SU-GAC | Airbus A300B4-203F | 255 | |
| ☐ SU-GAR | Airbus A300B4-622R | 557 | |
| ☐ SU-GAS | Airbus A300B4-622R | 561 | |
| ☐ SU-GAT | Airbus A300B4-622R | 572 | |
| ☐ SU-GAU | Airbus A300B4-622R | 575 | |
| ☐ SU-GAV | Airbus A300B4-622R | 579 | |
| ☐ SU-GAW | Airbus A300B4-622R | 581 | |
| ☐ SU-GAY | Airbus A300B4-622R | 607 | |
| ☐ SU-GBA | Airbus A320-231 | 0165 | |
| ☐ SU-GBB | Airbus A320-231 | 0166 | |
| ☐ SU-GBC | Airbus A320-231 | 0178 | |
| ☐ SU-GBD | Airbus A320-231 | 0194 | |
| ☐ SU-GBE | Airbus A320-231 | 0198 | |
| ☐ SU-GBF | Airbus A320-231 | 0351 | |
| ☐ SU-GBG | Airbus A320-231 | 0366 | |
| ☐ SU-GBT | Airbus A321-231 | 0680 | |
| ☐ SU-GBU | Airbus A321-231 | 0687 | |
| ☐ SU-GBV | Airbus A321-231 | 0715 | |
| ☐ SU-GBW | Airbus A321-231 | 0725 | |
| ☐ SU-GBM | Airbus A340-212 | 156 | |
| ☐ SU-GBN | Airbus A340-212 | 159 | |
| ☐ SU-GBO | Airbus A340-212 | 178 | |
| ☐ SU- | Airbus A340-642 | | |
| ☐ SU- | Airbus A340-642 | | |
| ☐ SU-AYL | Boeing 737-266 | 457/21195 | Lst BOU |
| ☐ SU-GBH | Boeing 737-566 | 2019/25084 | |
| ☐ SU-GBJ | Boeing 737-566 | 2169/25352 | |
| ☐ SU-GBK | Boeing 737-566 | 2276/26052 | Lst ASD |
| ☐ SU-GBL | Boeing 737-566 | 2282/26051 | |
| ☐ SU-GBP | Boeing 777-266 | 71/28423 | |
| ☐ SU-GBR | Boeing 777-266 | 80/28424 | |
| ☐ SU-GBS | Boeing 777-266 | 85/28425 | |
| ☐ SU-GBX | Boeing 777-266ER | 362/32629 | |
| ☐ SU-GBY | Boeing 777-266ER | 368/32630 | |
| ☐ SU-APD | Boeing 707-366C | 834/20341 | |
| ☐ SU-GAL | Boeing 747-366M | 704/24161 | |
| ☐ SU-GAM | Boeing 747-366M | 707/24162 | |

### FLASH AIRLINES — FSH

| | | | |
|---|---|---|---|
| ☐ SU-ZCD | Boeing 737-3Q8 | 2424/26286 | |
| ☐ SU-ZCF | Boeing 737-3Q8 | 2383/26283 | |

### LOTUS AIR — TAS

| | | | |
|---|---|---|---|
| ☐ SU-LBB | Airbus A320-212 | 0814 | |
| ☐ SU-LBC | Airbus A320-214 | 0937 | |
| ☐ SU-LBD | Airbus A320-214 | 1372 | Lst GHA |
| ☐ SU-LBE | Airbus A320-214 | 1413 | |
| ☐ SU- | Airbus A320-214 | | o/o |
| ☐ SU- | Airbus A320-214 | | o/o |

### LUXOR AIR

| | | | |
|---|---|---|---|
| ☐ SU-BMF | McDD MD-83 | 1968/53199 | |
| ☐ SU- | McDD MD-83 | 2151/53191 | |
| ☐ SU- | McDD MD-83 | 2155/53192 | |

### MIDWEST AIRLINES EGYPT — MWA

| | | | |
|---|---|---|---|
| ☐ SU-MWA | Airbus A310-304 | 652 | |
| ☐ SU-MWB | Airbus A310-304 | 671 | |
| ☐ SU- | Airbus A320-214 | | o/o |
| ☐ SU- | Airbus A320-214 | | o/o |

### PHAROAH AIRLINES — PHR

| | | |
|---|---|---|
| ☐ SU-PMA | Boeing 737-222 | 63/19064 |

### SHOROUK AIR — SHK

| | | |
|---|---|---|
| ☐ SU-RAA | Airbus A320-231 | 0322 |
| ☐ SU-RAB | Airbus A320-231 | 0326 |
| ☐ SU-RAC | Airbus A320-231 | 0478 |
| ☐ SU-RAD | Airbus A320-231 | 0344 |

### TRISTAR AIR — TSY

| | | |
|---|---|---|
| ☐ SU-BMZ | Airbus A300B4-203F | 129 |

## SU-Y - PALESTINE

### PALESTINIAN AIRLINES — PNW

| | | |
|---|---|---|
| ☐ SU-YAH | Fokker 50 | 20123 |
| ☐ SU-YAI | Fokker 50 | 20143 |
| ☐ SU-YAK | Boeing 727-230 | 1425/21621 |

## SX - GREECE

### AEGEAN CRONUS AIRLINES — CUS

| | | |
|---|---|---|
| ☐ SX-DVA | Avro RJ100 | E3341 |
| ☐ SX-DVB | Avro RJ100 | E3343 |
| ☐ SX-DVC | Avro RJ100 | E3358 |
| ☐ SX-DVD | Avro RJ100 | E3362 |
| ☐ SX-DVE | Avro RJ100 | E3374 |
| ☐ SX-DVF | Avro RJ100 | E3375 |
| ☐ SX-BBT | Boeing 737-33A | 2012/25011 |
| ☐ SX-BBU | Boeing 737-33A | 2206/25743 |
| ☐ SX-BGH | Boeing 737-4Y0 | 1589/23866 |
| ☐ SX-BGJ | Boeing 737-4S3 | 2233/25595 |
| ☐ SX-BGK | Boeing 737-3Y0 | 1897/24679 |
| ☐ SX-BGR | Boeing 737-408 | 2032/25063 |
| ☐ SX-BLM | Boeing 737-42C | 2062/24813 |
| ☐ SX-BAO | ATR 72-202 | 326 |
| ☐ SX-BAP | ATR 72-202 | 330 |
| ☐ SX-BFK | ATR 72-202 | 313 |

### AVIATOR AIRWAYS — AVW

| | | |
|---|---|---|
| ☐ SX-BST | Beech 1900D | UE-236 |

### ELECTRA AIRLINES — ELD

| | | | |
|---|---|---|---|
| ☐ SX-CVC | Douglas DC-10-30F | 335/47843 | std |
| ☐ SX-CVH | Douglas DC-10-15 | 346/48258 | |

| | | | |
|---|---|---|---|
| SX-CVP | Douglas DC-10-15 | 372/48294 | |
| SX-BVM | Boeing 757-2G5 | 227/24451 | |
| SX-BVN | Boeing 757-2G5 | 228/24497 | |

## HELLAS JET

| | | | |
|---|---|---|---|
| SX- | Airbus A320-232 | 1992 | o/o |
| SX- | Airbus A320-232 | 2016 | o/o |
| N340LA | Airbus A320-232 | 0425 | o/o |

## HELLAS WINGS — LJR

| | | |
|---|---|---|
| SX-BNJ | BAe Jetstream 31 | 829 |

## HELLENIC STAR AVIATION — HST

| | | |
|---|---|---|
| SX-BNA | DHC-7-102 | 090 |
| SX-BSR | BAe Jetstream 31 | 718 |
| SX-BTD | SAAB SF.340B | 360 |
| SX-BTE | SAAB SF.340B | 357 |

## MACEDONIAN AIRLINES — MCS

| | | | |
|---|---|---|---|
| SX-BLB | Boeing 737-3M8 | 1991/25015 | Lsf GMI |
| SX-BMA | Boeing 737-46J | 2465/27171 | |
| SX-BMB | Boeing 737-46J | 2585/27213 | |
| SX-BMC | Boeing 737-42J | 2457/27143 | |

## OLYMPIC AIRWAYS — OAL

| | | | |
|---|---|---|---|
| SX-BCA | Boeing 737-284 | 463/21224 | std |
| SX-BCB | Boeing 737-284 | 464/21225 | std |
| SX-BCC | Boeing 737-284 | 474/21301 | std |
| SX-BCD | Boeing 737-284 | 475/21302 | std |
| SX-BCE | Boeing 737-284 | 674/22300 | std |
| SX-BCF | Boeing 737-284 | 683/22301 | std |
| SX-BCG | Boeing 737-284 | 691/22338 | std |
| SX-BCH | Boeing 737-284 | 692/22339 | std |
| SX-BCI | Boeing 737-284 | 695/22343 | std |
| SX-BCK | Boeing 737-284 | 766/22400 | std |
| SX-BCL | Boeing 737-284 | 780/22401 | std |
| SX-BKA | Boeing 737-484 | 2109/25313 | |
| SX-BKB | Boeing 737-484 | 2124/25314 | |
| SX-BKC | Boeing 737-484 | 2130/25361 | |
| SX-BKD | Boeing 737-484 | 2142/25362 | |
| SX-BKE | Boeing 737-484 | 2160/25417 | |
| SX-BKF | Boeing 737-484 | 2174/25430 | |
| SX-BKG | Boeing 737-484 | 2471/27149 | |
| SX-BKH | Boeing 737-4Q8 | 1828/24703 | |
| SX-BKI | Boeing 737-4Q8 | 1855/24704 | |
| SX-BKK | Boeing 737-4Q8 | 2195/25371 | |
| SX-BKL | Boeing 737-4Y0 | 2055/24915 | |
| SX-BKM | Boeing 737-4Q8 | 2115/24709 | |
| SX-BKN | Boeing 737-4Q8 | 2380/26281 | |
| SX-BLA | Boeing 737-33R | 2887/28869 | |
| SX-BEK | Airbus A300B4-605R | 632 | |
| SX-BEL | Airbus A300B4-605R | 696 | |
| SX-BEM | Airbus A300B4-605R | 603 | |
| SX-DFA | Airbus A340-313X | 235 | |
| SX-DFB | Airbus A340-313X | 239 | |
| SX-DFC | Airbus A340-313X | 280 | |
| SX-DFD | Airbus A340-313X | 292 | |
| SX-OAC | Boeing 747-212B | 387/21683 | |
| SX-OAE | Boeing 747-212B | 399/21935 | |

## OLYMPIC AVIATION — OLY

| | | |
|---|---|---|
| SX-BIA | ATR 42-320 | 169 |
| SX-BIB | ATR 42-320 | 182 |
| SX-BIC | ATR 42-320 | 197 |
| SX-BID | ATR 42-320 | 219 |
| SX-BIE | ATR 72-202 | 239 |
| SX-BIF | ATR 72-202 | 241 |
| SX-BIG | ATR 72-202 | 290 |

| | | |
|---|---|---|
| SX-BIH | ATR 72-202 | 305 |
| SX-BII | ATR 72-202 | 353 |
| SX-BIK | ATR 72-202 | 350 |
| SX-BIL | ATR 72-202 | 437 |
| SX-BIM | ATR 72-202 | 291 |
| SX-BIN | ATR 72-202 | 337 |
| SX-BHC | Dornier 228-201 | 8030 |
| SX-BHD | Dornier 228-201 | 8034 |
| SX-BHE | Dornier 228-201 | 8050 |
| SX-BHF | Dornier 228-201 | 8057 |
| SX-BHH | Dornier 228-201 | 8079 |
| SX-BHI | Dornier 228-201 | 8080 |
| SX-BOA | Boeing 717-2K9 | 5015/55056 |
| SX-BOB | Boeing 717-2K9 | 5016/55053 |
| SX-BOC | Boeing 717-23S | 5048/55065 |

## TRANSEUROPEAN AIRLINES — TEG

| | | |
|---|---|---|
| SX-BNL | Embraer EMB.110P1 | 110224 |

## VER-AVIA — GRV

| | | |
|---|---|---|
| SX-BBX | SA.227AC Metro III | AC-657 |
| SX-BMM | SA.227AC Metro III | BC-774B |
| SX-BNN | SA.227AC Metro III | BC-771B |

# S2 - BANGLADESH

## BIMAN BANGLADESH AIRLINES — BBC

| | | | |
|---|---|---|---|
| S2-ACO | Douglas DC-10-30 | 263/46993 | |
| S2-ACP | Douglas DC-10-30 | 275/46995 | |
| S2-ACQ | Douglas DC-10-30 | 300/47817 | |
| S2-ACR | Douglas DC-10-30 | 445/48317 | |
| S2-ACS | Douglas DC-10-30ER | 341/46543 | |
| S2-ADN | Douglas DC-10-30ER | 295/46542 | |
| S2-ACH | F-28 Fellowship 4000 | 11172 | |
| S2-ACV | F-28 Fellowship 4000 | 11124 | |
| S2-ACW | F-28 Fellowship 4000 | 11148 | |
| S2-ADE | Airbus A310-325 | 698 | |
| S2-ADF | Airbus A310-325 | 700 | |
| S2-ADG | Airbus A310-324 | 433 | Lsf SIA |
| S2-ADH | Airbus A310-325 | 650 | |

## BISMILLAH AIRLINES — BML

| | | | |
|---|---|---|---|
| S2-ADR | L-1011- Tristar | | o/o |

# S5 - SLOVENIA

## ADRIA AIRWAYS — ADR

| | | |
|---|---|---|
| S5-AAA | Airbus A320-231 | 043 |
| S5-AAB | Airbus A320-231 | 113 |
| S5-AAC | Airbus A320-231 | 114 |
| S5-AAD | Canadair RJ-200 | 7166 |
| S5-AAE | Canadair RJ-200 | 7170 |
| S5-AAF | Canadair RJ-200 | 7272 |
| S5-AAG | Canadair RJ-200 | 7384 |

## ALPE AIR — LPS

| | | | |
|---|---|---|---|
| HA-LAR | LET L-410UVP-E4 | 871923 | Lsf FAH |

## SOLINAIR — SOP

| | | | |
|---|---|---|---|
| S5-BAE | LET L-410UVP-E | 902503 | Opf DHL |
| S5-BAF | LET L-410UVP-E8C | 912540 | |

## S7 - SEYCHELLES

### AIR SEYCHELLES SEY

| | | |
|---|---|---|
| ☐ S7-AHM | Boeing 767-37DER | 637/26328 |
| ☐ S7-ASY | Boeing 767-3Q8ER | 831/29386 |
| ☐ S7-SEZ | Boeing 737-7Q8 | 1005/30727 |

### REGIONAIR RGA

| | | | |
|---|---|---|---|
| ☐ S7-ABA | Boeing 737-377 | 1641/24305 | |
| ☐ S7-ABB | Boeing 737-377 | 1618/24302 | |
| ☐ S7-ABC | Boeing 737-377 | 1622/24304 | |
| ☐ S7-RGJ | Airbus A320-131 | 0604 | Lst PIC |
| ☐ S7-RGK | Airbus A320-131 | 0614 | Lst PIC |
| ☐ S7-RGL | Airbus A320-232 | 0542 | Lst PIC |
| ☐ S7-RGM | Boeing 737-3Q8 | 1598/24299 | Lst UBA |
| ☐ S7-RGO | Airbus A300B4-605R | 584 | Lst PIC |
| ☐ S7-RGP | Airbus A310-324 | 549 | Lst PIC |
| ☐ S7-RGR | Airbus A310-322 | 409 | |
| ☐ S7- | Airbus A310-322 | 410 | |

## S9 - SAO TOME

### BRITISH GULF INTL AIRLINES BGI

| | | | |
|---|---|---|---|
| ☐ EX-160 | Antonov An-12BP | 401901 | |
| ☐ S9-BOS | Antonov An-12B | 01347704 | |
| ☐ S9-BOT | Antonov An-12BP | 543305 | Lst SRW |
| ☐ S9-CAQ | Antonov An-12BP | 3341408 | Lst SVN |

### TRANSAFRIK INTERNATIONAL

| | | |
|---|---|---|
| ☐ S9-BAE | Boeing 727-31F | 147/18903 |
| ☐ S9-BAG | Boeing 727-30C | 411/19313 |
| ☐ S9-BAV | Boeing 727-223 | 1324/21383 |
| ☐ S9-BOC | Boeing 727-23F | 127/18447 |
| ☐ S9-BOD | Boeing 727-25F | 223/18968 |
| ☐ S9-BOG | Boeing 727-90C | 332/19170 |
| ☐ S9-CAA | Boeing 727-95F | 494/19836 |
| ☐ S9-CAB | Boeing 727-23F | 266/19182 |
| ☐ S9-TAO | Boeing 727-23F | 350/19390 |
| ☐ S9-TBA | Boeing 727-51 | 120/18801 |
| ☐ S9-BAS | L-382G Hercules | 4472 |
| ☐ S9-BOF | L-382G Hercules | 4586 |
| ☐ S9-BOQ | L-382E Hercules | 4388 |
| ☐ S9-BOR | L-382E Hercules | 4362 |
| ☐ S9-CAI | L-382E Hercules | 4562 |
| ☐ S9-CAJ | L-382E Hercules | 4565 |
| ☐ S9-CAV | L-382E Hercules | 4301 |
| ☐ S9-CAW | L-382E Hercules | 4300 |
| ☐ S9-CAX | L-382E Hercules | 4248 |
| ☐ S9-CAY | L-382E Hercules | 4208 |
| ☐ S9-NAL | L-382E Hercules | 4385 |
| ☐ S9-TAJ | L-382G Hercules | 4134 |
| ☐ S9- | L-382G Hercules | 4299 |

## TC - TURKEY

### AIR ANATOLIA NTL

| | | |
|---|---|---|
| ☐ TC-ANI | Airbus A300B4-203 | 046 |

### ATLAS INTERNATIONAL OGE

| | | |
|---|---|---|
| ☐ TC-OGA | Boeing 757-225 | 115/22688 |
| ☐ TC-OGB | Boeing 757-225 | 117/22689 |
| ☐ TC-OGC | Boeing 757-2G5 | 161/23983 |
| ☐ TC-OGZ | Boeing 737-46B | 2088/25262 |

### BOSPHORUS EUROPEAN AIRWAYS BHY

| | | | |
|---|---|---|---|
| ☐ TC-COA | Airbus A300B4-120 | 128 | |
| ☐ TC-OIM | Airbus A300B4-120 | 094 | Std |
| ☐ TC-OYC | Airbus A300B4-120 | 079 | |

### FLY AIRLINES FLM

| | | | |
|---|---|---|---|
| ☐ TC-FLA | Airbus A300B4-203 | 127 | Lst SUD |

### FREEBIRD AIRLINES FHY

| | | | |
|---|---|---|---|
| ☐ TC-FBB | McDD MD-83 | 2090/53185 | |
| ☐ TC-FBD | McDD MD-83 | 2092/53186 | |
| ☐ TC-FBG | McDD MD-83 | 2088/53184 | |
| ☐ TC-FBT | McDD MD-83 | 1906/49949 | |
| ☐ TC- | Boeing 737-800 | | o/o |
| ☐ TC- | Boeing 737-800 | | o/o |
| ☐ TC- | Boeing 737-800 | | o/o |

### INTER EXPRESS INX

| | | | |
|---|---|---|---|
| ☐ TC-IEA | Boeing 737-8CX | 1098/32361 | |
| ☐ TC-IEB | Boeing 737-8CX | 1139/32363 | |
| ☐ TC-IEC | Boeing 737-8CX | | o/o |

### KTHY CYPRUS TURKISH AIRLINES KYV

| | | | |
|---|---|---|---|
| ☐ TC-JBF | Boeing 727-2F2 | 1085/20980 | std |
| ☐ TC-JCO | Airbus A310-203 | 386 | |
| ☐ TC-JYK | Airbus A310-203 | 172 | Lsf AFR |
| ☐ TC-MAO | Boeing 737-86N | 840/28645 | |
| ☐ TC-MSO | Boeing 737-8S3 | 475/29246 | |
| ☐ TC-MZZ | Boeing 737-8S3 | 493/29247 | |

### MNG CARGO AIRLINES MNB

| | | | |
|---|---|---|---|
| ☐ TC-MNA | Airbus A300B4-203F | 019 | |
| ☐ TC-MNB | Airbus A300B4-203F | 292 | Lsf KAL |
| ☐ TC-MNC | Airbus A300B4-203F | 277 | Lsf KAL |
| ☐ TC-MND | Airbus A300C4-203F | 212 | |
| ☐ TC-MNE | Airbus A300B4-203 | 222 | |
| ☐ TC-MNG | Airbus A300C4-203 | 083 | |
| ☐ TC- | Airbus A300B4-203F | 123 | |
| ☐ TC-MNF | Boeing 737-4K5 | 1697/24126 | Lsf HLF |
| ☐ TC-MNH | Boeing 737-448 | 1850/24773 | |
| ☐ TC-MNI | Boeing 737-4K5 | 1715/24128 | |
| ☐ TC-MNL | Boeing 737-4Q8 | 2562/25374 | |
| ☐ TC-MNM | Boeing 737-4Q8 | 2598/25375 | |

### ONUR AIR OHY

| | | |
|---|---|---|
| ☐ TC-OAA | Airbus A300B4-605R | 744 |
| ☐ TC-OAB | Airbus A300B4-605R | 749 |
| ☐ TC-ONK | Airbus A300B4-103 | 086 |
| ☐ TC-ONL | Airbus A300B4-103 | 087 |
| ☐ TC-ONT | Airbus A300B4-203 | 138 |
| ☐ TC-ONU | Airbus A300B4-203 | 192 |
| ☐ TC-ONY | Airbus A300B2K-3C | 037 |
| ☐ TC-ONM | McDD MD-88 | 2167/53546 |
| ☐ TC-ONN | McDD MD-88 | 2170/53547 |
| ☐ TC-ONO | McDD MD-88 | 2180/53548 |
| ☐ TC-ONP | McDD MD-88 | 2185/53549 |
| ☐ TC-ONR | McDD MD-88 | 2187/53550 |
| ☐ TC-OAC | Airbus A320-212 | 0313 |
| ☐ TC-OAD | Airbus A320-212 | 0345 |
| ☐ TC-ONJ | Airbus A321-131 | 0385 |
| ☐ TC-ONS | Airbus A321-131 | 0364 |

### PEGASUS AIRLINES PGT

| | | | |
|---|---|---|---|
| ☐ TC-AFJ | Boeing 737-4Y0 | 1661/23979 | Lst KZW |
| ☐ TC-AFM | Boeing 737-4Q8 | 2221/26279 | |
| ☐ TC-APD | Boeing 737-42R | 2997/29107 | Lst KZW |
| ☐ TC-APR | Boeing 737-4Y0 | 1859/24685 | |
| ☐ TC-AAP | Boeing 737-86N | 1113/32736 | |
| ☐ TC-APF | Boeing 737-86N | 813/28642 | |
| ☐ TC-APG | Boeing 737-82R | 224/29329 | |

| | | | |
|---|---|---|---|
| ☐ TC-APH | Boeing 737-8S3 | 792/29250 | |
| ☐ TC-API | Boeing 737-86N | 1056/32732 | |
| ☐ TC-APJ | Boeing 737-86N | 1104/32735 | Lst SFB |
| ☐ TC-APK | Boeing 737-86N | 828/28643 | |
| ☐ TC-APL | Boeing 737-86N | 515/30231 | |
| ☐ TC-APM | Boeing 737-809 | 117/28403 | Lst KZW |
| ☐ TC-APN | Boeing 737-86N | 573/28628 | |
| ☐ TC-APU | Boeing 737-82R | 849/29344 | |
| ☐ TC-APV | Boeing 737-86N | 772/28639 | |
| ☐ TC-APY | Boeing 737-86N | 233/28591 | Lst KZW |
| ☐ TC-APZ | Boeing 737-809 | 129/29103 | |

## SKY AIRLINES — SHY

| | | | |
|---|---|---|---|
| ☐ SKY AIRLINES | | SHY | |
| ☐ TC-SKA | Boeing 737-4Y0 | 1582/23865 | |
| ☐ TC-SKB | Boeing 737-430 | 2344/27004 | |
| ☐ TC-SKC | Boeing 737-85F | 997/30478 | |
| ☐ TC-SKD | Boeing 737-4Q8 | 2280/25372 | |

## SUNEXPRESS AIR — SXS

| | | | |
|---|---|---|---|
| ☐ TC-SUA | Boeing 737-86N | 455/28612 | |
| ☐ TC-SUB | Boeing 737-86N | 477/28614 | |
| ☐ TC-SUC | Boeing 737-86N | 483/28616 | |
| ☐ TC-SUD | Boeing 737-86N | 542/28620 | |
| ☐ TC-SUG | Boeing 737-8CX | 1209/32365 | |
| ☐ TC-SUH | Boeing 737-8CX | 1235/32366 | |
| ☐ TC-SUI | Boeing 737-8CX | 1253/32367 | |
| ☐ TC-SUJ | Boeing 737-8CX | 32368 | o/o |

## TURKISH AIRLINES — THY

| | | |
|---|---|---|
| ☐ TC-JCV | Airbus A310-304 | 476 |
| ☐ TC-JCY | Airbus A310-304 | 478 |
| ☐ TC-JCZ | Airbus A310-304 | 480 |
| ☐ TC-JDA | Airbus A310-304 | 496 |
| ☐ TC-JDB | Airbus A310-304ER | 497 |
| ☐ TC-JDJ | Airbus A340-311 | 023 |
| ☐ TC-JDK | Airbus A340-311 | 025 |
| ☐ TC-JDL | Airbus A340-311 | 057 |
| ☐ TC-JDM | Airbus A340-311 | 115 |
| ☐ TC-JDN | Airbus A340-313X | 180 |
| ☐ TC-JIH | Airbus A340-313X | 270 |
| ☐ TC-JII | Airbus A340-313X | 331 |
| ☐ TC-THA | Avro RJ100 | E3232 |
| ☐ TC-THB | Avro RJ100 | E3234 |
| ☐ TC-THC | Avro RJ100 | E3236 |
| ☐ TC-THD | Avro RJ100 | E3237 |
| ☐ TC-THE | Avro RJ100 | E3238 |
| ☐ TC-THH | Avro RJ100 | E3243 |
| ☐ TC-THI | Avro RJ70 | E1229 |
| ☐ TC-THJ | Avro RJ70 | E1230 |
| ☐ TC-THM | Avro RJ100 | E3264 |
| ☐ TC-THN | Avro RJ70 | E1252 |
| ☐ TC-THO | Avro RJ100 | E3265 |
| ☐ TC-JDF | Boeing 737-4Y0 | 2071/24917 |
| ☐ TC-JDG | Boeing 737-4Y0 | 2203/25181 |
| ☐ TC-JDH | Boeing 737-4Y0 | 2227/25184 |
| ☐ TC-JDT | Boeing 737-4Y0 | 2258/25261 |
| ☐ TC-JDU | Boeing 737-5Y0 | 2286/25288 |
| ☐ TC-JDV | Boeing 737-5Y0 | 2288/25289 |
| ☐ TC-JDY | Boeing 737-4Y0 | 2284/26065 |
| ☐ TC-JEN | Boeing 737-4Q8 | 2689/25376 |
| ☐ TC-JEO | Boeing 737-4Q8 | 2717/25377 |
| ☐ TC-JER | Boeing 737-4Y0 | 2735/26073 |
| ☐ TC-JET | Boeing 737-4Y0 | 2425/26077 |
| ☐ TC-JEU | Boeing 737-4Y0 | 2431/26078 |
| ☐ TC-JEV | Boeing 737-4Y0 | 2468/26085 |
| ☐ TC-JEY | Boeing 737-4Y0 | 2475/26086 |
| ☐ TC-JEZ | Boeing 737-4Y0 | 2487/26088 |
| ☐ TC-JKA | Boeing 737-4Y0 | 2604/26300 |
| ☐ TC-JFC | Boeing 737-8F2 | 80/29765 |
| ☐ TC-JFD | Boeing 737-8F2 | 87/29766 |

| | | |
|---|---|---|
| ☐ TC-JFE | Boeing 737-8F2 | 95/29767 |
| ☐ TC-JFF | Boeing 737-8F2 | 99/29768 |
| ☐ TC-JFG | Boeing 737-8F2 | 102/29769 |
| ☐ TC-JFH | Boeing 737-8F2 | 114/29770 |
| ☐ TC-JFI | Boeing 737-8F2 | 228/29771 |
| ☐ TC-JFJ | Boeing 737-8F2 | 242/29772 |
| ☐ TC-JFK | Boeing 737-8F2 | 259/29773 |
| ☐ TC-JFL | Boeing 737-8F2 | 269/29774 |
| ☐ TC-JFM | Boeing 737-8F2 | 279/29775 |
| ☐ TC-JFN | Boeing 737-8F2 | 308/29776 |
| ☐ TC-JFO | Boeing 737-8F2 | 309/29777 |
| ☐ TC-JFP | Boeing 737-8F2 | 349/29778 |
| ☐ TC-JFR | Boeing 737-8F2 | 370/29779 |
| ☐ TC-JFT | Boeing 737-8F2 | 454/29780 |
| ☐ TC-JFU | Boeing 737-8F2 | 461/29781 |
| ☐ TC-JFV | Boeing 737-8F2 | 490/29782 |
| ☐ TC-JFY | Boeing 737-8F2 | 497/29783 |
| ☐ TC-JFZ | Boeing 737-8F2 | 539/29784 |
| ☐ TC-JGA | Boeing 737-8F2 | 544/29785 |
| ☐ TC-JGB | Boeing 737-8F2 | 566/29786 |
| ☐ TC-JGC | Boeing 737-8F2 | 771/29787 |
| ☐ TC-JGD | Boeing 737-8F2 | 791/29788 |
| ☐ TC-JGE | Boeing 737-8F2 | 1065/29789 |
| ☐ TC-JGF | Boeing 737-8F2 | 1088/29790 |
| ☐ TC-JGG | Boeing 737-8F2 | 29791 |
| ☐ TC-JCA | Boeing 727-2F2F | 1804/22992 |

# TF - ICELAND

## AIR ATLANTA ICELAND — ABD

| | | | |
|---|---|---|---|
| ☐ TF-ABA | Boeing 747-267B | 531/22530 | Lsf CPA |
| ☐ TF-ABP | Boeing 747-267B | 493/22429 | Lsf CPA |
| ☐ TF-ARF | Boeing 747-236B | 506/22305 | |
| ☐ TF-ARG | Boeing 747-236B | 495/22303 | |
| ☐ TF-ARJ | Boeing 747-236M | 674/23735 | |
| ☐ TF-AR | Boeing 747-236B | 21238 | |
| ☐ TF-ATC | Boeing 747-267B | 466/22149 | Lsf CPA |
| ☐ TF-ATD | Boeing 747-267B | 446/21966 | Lst XLA |
| ☐ TF-ATE | Boeing 747-246B | 197/20531 | |
| ☐ TF-ATF | Boeing 747-246B | 137/19825 | |
| ☐ TF-ATH | Boeing 747-341 | 701/24106 | |
| ☐ TF-ATI | Boeing 747-341 | 702/24107 | Lst IBE |
| ☐ TF-ATJ | Boeing 747-341 | 703/24108 | Lst IBE |
| ☐ TF-ATN | Boeing 747-219B | 527/22723 | Lst VIR |
| ☐ TF-ATW | Boeing 747-219B | 528/22724 | Lst VIR |
| ☐ TF-ATX | Boeing 747-236B (SF) | 672/23711 | |
| ☐ TF-ATZ | Boeing 747-236B (SF) | 697/24088 | Lst MAS |
| ☐ TF-ARA | Boeing 767-3Q8ER | 694/28206 | Lst SWD |
| ☐ TF-ARB | Boeing 767-3Q8ER | 570/26265 | Lst SWD |
| ☐ TF-ATO | Boeing 767-204ER | 210/24013 | Lst ROM |
| ☐ TF-ATP | Boeing 767-204ER | 243/24239 | Lst XLA |
| ☐ TF-ATR | Boeing 767-204ER | 256/24457 | Lst XLA |
| ☐ TF-ATT | Boeing 767-383ER | 263/24358 | Lst ROM |
| ☐ TF-ATU | Boeing 767-3Y0ER | 464/26204 | |
| ☐ TF-ATY | Boeing 767-204ER | 107/23072 | |
| ☐ TF-ARD | Boeing 757-225 | 74/22211 | Lst XLA |
| ☐ TF-ARE | Boeing 757-225 | 75/22611 | Lst XLA |

## BLUEBIRD CARGO — BBD

| | | | |
|---|---|---|---|
| ☐ TF-BBC | Boeing 737-3Q4 | 1493/24209 | |
| ☐ TF-BBD | Boeing 737-3Y0F | 1701/24463 | Opf UPS |

## ICEBIRD AIRWAYS — ICB

| | | |
|---|---|---|
| ■ TF-ELL | Boeing 737-210C | 173/20138 |
| ☐ TF-ELN | Boeing 737-3Q8QC | 1375/23766 |

## ICELANDAIR — ICE

| | | |
|---|---|---|
| ☐ TF-FIG | Boeing 757-23APF | 237/24456 |
| ☐ TF-FIH | Boeing 757-208 | 273/24739 |

| | | | |
|---|---|---|---|
| ❏ TF-FII | Boeing 757-208 | 281/24760 | |
| ❏ TF-FIJ | Boeing 757-208 | 368/25085 | |
| ❏ TF-FIK | Boeing 757-28A | 704/26276 | |
| ❏ TF-FIN | Boeing 757-208 | 780/28989 | |
| ❏ TF-FIO | Boeing 757-208 | 859/29436 | |
| ❏ TF-FIP | Boeing 757-208 | 916/30423 | |
| ❏ TF-FIR | Boeing 757-256 | 593/26242 | Lst ROM |
| ❏ TF-FIV | Boeing 757-208 | 956/30424 | |
| ❏ TF-FIW | Boeing 757-27B | 302/24838 | |
| ❏ TF-FIX | Boeing 757-308 | 1004/29434 | |
| | | | |
| ❏ TF-FIA | Boeing 737-408 | 1705/24352 | Lst BXI |
| ❏ TF-FIE | Boeing 737-3S3QC | 1445/23811 | Opf TNT |

## ISLANDSFLUG — ICB

| | | | |
|---|---|---|---|
| ❏ TF-ELP | Boeing 737-330 (QC) | 1246/23522 | Opf EXS |
| ❏ TF-ELR | Boeing 737-330 (QC) | 1271/23523 | Opf EXS |
| ❏ TF-ELS | Airbus A310-304F | 552 | Opf TMA |
| ❏ TF-ELU | Airbus A300B4-622RF | 657 | |
| ❏ TF-ELV | Boeing 737-4S3 | 24796 | |
| ❏ TF-ELW | Airbus A300C4-605R | 755 | Opf AFR |
| ❏ TF-SUN | Boeing 737-3Q8 | 1301/23535 | Opf BBG |

## MD AIRLINES — MDI

| | | | |
|---|---|---|---|
| ❏ TF-MDB | McDD MD-83 | 1354/49449 | |
| ❏ TF-MDC | McDD MD-83 | 1740/53014 | std |
| ❏ TF-MDD | McDD MD-83 | 1435/49602 | Lst BBG |

# TG - GUATEMALA

## AVIATECA GUATEMALA — GUG

| | | | |
|---|---|---|---|
| ❏ N123GU | Boeing 737-2H6 | 308/20587 | |
| ❏ N127GU | Boeing 737-242 | 619/22074 | |

# TI - COSTA RICA

## LACSA COSTA RICA — LRC

| | | | |
|---|---|---|---|
| ❏ N340LA | Airbus A320-232 | 0425 | Lsf TAI |
| ❏ N481TA | Airbus A320-233 | 1500 | Lsf TAI |
| ❏ N482TA | Airbus A320-233 | 1482 | Lsf TAI |
| ❏ N941LF | Airbus A320-233 | 0461 | Lsf TAI |
| ❏ N981LR | Airbus A320-233 | 0558 | Lsf TAI |
| ❏ N991LR | Airbus A320-233 | 0561 | Lsf TAI |
| | | | |
| ❏ N238TA | Boeing 737-242 | 630/22075 | Lsf TAI |
| ❏ N251LF | Boeing 737-2L9 | 705/22408 | Lsf TAI |
| ❏ N261LR | Boeing 737-230 | 744/22402 | Lsf TAI |
| ❏ N281LF | Boeing 737-2L9 | 620/22071 | Lsf TAI |

# TJ - CAMEROON

## CAMEROON AIRLINES — UYC

| | | | |
|---|---|---|---|
| ❏ TJ-AIO | Boeing 737-229 | 437/21139 | Lsf |
| ❏ TJ-CAC | Boeing 767-33AER | 822/28138 | |
| ❏ TJ-CAD | Boeing 767-231ER | 14/22564 | |
| ❏ TJ-CAE | Boeing 747-312 | 23033 | |
| ❏ TJ-CAF | Boeing 757-23APF | 314/24868 | |
| ❏ TJ-CAG | Boeing 757-23A | 220/24293 | |
| ❏ TJ-CAH | Boeing 757-23A | 333/24924 | |
| | | | |
| ❏ TJ-CBI | Canadair RJ-200 | 7584 | o/o |
| ❏ F-GPTB | Canadair RJ-200 | 7177 | Lsf LIT |

# TN - CONGO BRAZZAVILLE

## LINA CONGO — GCB

| | | | |
|---|---|---|---|
| ❏ TN-AGR | Boeing 737-217 | 149/20197 | |

## TRANSAIR CONGO — TSG

| | | | |
|---|---|---|---|
| ❏ C5-DMB | Boeing 727-228 | 847/20411 | Lsf MSZ |
| ❏ TN-AFY | Boeing 727-35 | 486/19833 | std |
| ❏ TN-AFZ | Boeing 727-23 | 542/19839 | |
| ❏ 3C-QQL | Antonov An-12BP | 4341803 | |

# TR - GABON

## AIR GABON — AGN

| | | | |
|---|---|---|---|
| ❏ F-ODJG | Boeing 747-2Q2M | 324/21468 | |
| ❏ TR-LEV | Boeing 727-228 | 1605/22083 | |
| ❏ TR-LFH | Boeing 767-266ER | 97/23178 | |
| ❏ TR-LFU | Boeing 737-408 | 1721/24353 | |
| ❏ TR-LFZ | Boeing 737-3Y0 | 1431/23750 | |
| ❏ TR-LXL | Boeing 737-2Q2C | 515/21467 | |
| ❏ 3D-AAJ | Boeing 737-222 | 97/19075 | |

# TS - TUNISIA

## KARTHAGO AIRLINES — KAJ

| | | | |
|---|---|---|---|
| ❏ TS-IEC | Boeing 737-33A | 2008/25010 | |
| ❏ TS-IED | Boeing 737-33A | 2014/25032 | |

## MEDITERRANEAN AIR SERVICE

| | | | |
|---|---|---|---|
| ❏ TS-IOD | Boeing 737-2H3C | 615/21974 | Lsf TAR |

## NOUVELAIR — LBT

| | | | |
|---|---|---|---|
| ❏ TS-INA | Airbus A320-214 | 1121 | |
| ❏ TS-INB | Airbus A320-214 | 1175 | |
| ❏ TS-INC | Airbus A320-214 | 1744 | |
| ❏ EI-CEK | McDD MD-83 | 1596/49631 | |
| ❏ EI-CNO | McDD MD-83 | 1494/49672 | |
| ❏ F-GHEC | McDD MD-83 | 1429/49662 | |

## TUNINTER — TUI

| | | | |
|---|---|---|---|
| ❏ TS-LBA | ATR 42-300 | 245 | std |
| ❏ TS-LBB | ATR 72-202 | 258 | |
| ❏ TS-LBC | ATR 72-202 | 281 | |

## TUNISAIR — TAR

| | | | |
|---|---|---|---|
| ❏ TS-IMB | Airbus A320-211 | 0119 | |
| ❏ TS-IMC | Airbus A320-211 | 0124 | |
| ❏ TS-IMD | Airbus A320-211 | 0205 | |
| ❏ TS-IME | Airbus A320-211 | 0123 | |
| ❏ TS-IMF | Airbus A320-211 | 0370 | |
| ❏ TS-IMG | Airbus A320-211 | 0390 | |
| ❏ TS-IMH | Airbus A320-211 | 0402 | |
| ❏ TS-IMI | Airbus A320-211 | 0511 | |
| ❏ TS-IMJ | Airbus A319-114 | 0869 | |
| ❏ TS-IMK | Airbus A319-114 | 0880 | |
| ❏ TS-IML | Airbus A320-211 | 0958 | |
| ❏ TS-IMM | Airbus A320-211 | 0975 | |
| ❏ TS-IMN | Airbus A320-211 | 1187 | |
| ❏ TS-IMO | Airbus A319-114 | 1479 | |
| ❏ TS-IMP | Airbus A320-211 | 1700 | |
| | | | |
| ❏ TS-IOC | Boeing 737-2H3 | 607/21973 | Lst DEI |
| ❏ TS-IOD | Boeing 737-2H3C | 615/21974 | Lst DR |
| ❏ TS-IOE | Boeing 737-2H3 | 758/22624 | Lst SUD |
| ❏ TS-IOF | Boeing 737-2H3 | 776/22625 | Lst SUD |
| ❏ TS-IOG | Boeing 737-5H3 | 2253/26639 | |
| ❏ TS-IOH | Boeing 737-5H3 | 2474/26640 | |
| ❏ TS-IOI | Boeing 737-5H3 | 2583/27257 | |
| ❏ TS-IOJ | Boeing 737-5H3 | 2701/27912 | |
| ❏ TS-IOK | Boeing 737-6H3 | 268/29496 | |
| ❏ TS-IOL | Boeing 737-6H3 | 282/29497 | |
| ❏ TS-IOM | Boeing 737-6H3 | 310/29498 | |
| ❏ TS-ION | Boeing 737-6H3 | 510/29499 | |

| | | | |
|---|---|---|---|
| ☐ TS-IOP | Boeing 737-6H3 | 543/29500 | |
| ☐ TS-IOQ | Boeing 737-6H3 | 563/29501 | |
| ☐ TS-IOR | Boeing 737-6H3 | 816/29502 | |
| ☐ TS-IAX | Airbus A300B4-622R | 601 | Lst LAA |
| ☐ TS-IPA | Airbus A300B4-605R | 558 | |
| ☐ TS-IPB | Airbus A300B4-605R | 563 | |
| ☐ TS-IPC | Airbus A300B4-605R | 505 | |
| ☐ TS-JHR | Boeing 727-2H3 | 1171/21179 | |

## TY - BENIN

### AFRIQUE AIRLINES

| | | | |
|---|---|---|---|
| ☐ F-GEMO | Airbus A310-304 | 504 | FLsf EGN |

## TZ - MALI

### AIR MALI — MLI

| | | | |
|---|---|---|---|
| ☐ SU-BMM | Airbus A300B4-203 | 175 | Lsf AMV |
| ☐ SU-BOW | Airbus A310-322 | 437 | Lsf AMV |
| ☐ V2-SKY | Douglas DC-10-15 | 358/48275 | Lsf AWG |

## T9 - BOSNIA-HERZEGOVINA

### AIR BOSNIA — BON

| | | | |
|---|---|---|---|
| ☐ T9-AAC | McDD MD-81 | 1049/48093 | |
| ☐ T9-ABD | Yak-42D | 4520422016201 | Lsf UDC |
| ☐ T9- | McDD MD-82 | 1055/4895 | o/ |

### AIR SERPSKA — SBK

| | | | |
|---|---|---|---|
| ☐ YU-ALP | ATR 72-201 | 189 | Lsf JAT |

### BIOAIR — BIO

| | | | |
|---|---|---|---|
| ☐ EX-405 | Ilyushin Il-18D | 184007405 | Jow PHG |
| ☐ T9-ABE | Antonov An-74 | 36547097932 | |
| ☐ T9-CAD | Antonov An-12BP | 4342202 | Lst KHO |

## UK - UZBEKISTAN

### AVIALEASING — TWN

| | | | |
|---|---|---|---|
| ☐ UK 11109 | Antonov An-12BP | 01348005 | |
| ☐ UK 11418 | Antonov An-12BP | 7344705 | |
| ☐ UK 76410 | Ilyushin Il-76TD | 1023412411 | Lst AHC |
| ☐ UK 76447 | Ilyushin Il-76TD | 1023412389 | Lst AHC |
| ☐ 4K-86810 | Ilyushin Il-76MD | 053404094 | |

### TAPO-AVIA — TPR

| | | | |
|---|---|---|---|
| ☐ UK 11807 | Antonov An-12BP | 00346910 | |
| ☐ UK 58644 | Antonov An-12BP | 2340303 | |
| ☐ UK 76375 | Ilyushin Il-76TD | 1033414496 | |
| ☐ UK 76427 | Ilyushin Il-76TD | 1013406207 | Lst ASE |
| ☐ UK 76821 | Ilyushin Il-76TD | 0023441200 | Lst ASE |
| ☐ UK 76831 | Ilyushin Il-76TD | 1013409287 | Lst AJC |

### UZBEKISTAN AIRWAYS — UZB

| | | | |
|---|---|---|---|
| ☐ UK 86569 | Ilyushin Il-62M | 1356234 | Govt |
| ☐ UK 86573 | Ilyushin Il-62M | 4140536 | |
| ☐ UK 86574 | Ilyushin Il-62M | 3344833 | std |
| ☐ UK 86575 | Ilyushin Il-62M | 1647928 | |
| ☐ UK 86576 | Ilyushin Il-62M | 4546257 | std |
| ☐ UK 86577 | Ilyushin Il-62M | 2748552 | std |
| ☐ UK 86578 | Ilyushin Il-62M | 1951525 | |
| ☐ UK 86579 | Ilyushin Il-62M | 2951636 | |
| ☐ UK 76351 | Ilyushin Il-76TD | 1013408240 | Lst ESL |
| ☐ UK 76353 | Ilyushin Il-76TD | 1023414454 | Lst ESL |

| | | | |
|---|---|---|---|
| ☐ UK 76358 | Ilyushin Il-76TD | 1023410339 | |
| ☐ UK 76359 | Ilyushin Il-76TD | 1033414483 | |
| ☐ UK 76426 | Ilyushin Il-76TD | 1043419644 | |
| ☐ UK 76428 | Ilyushin Il-76TD | 1043419648 | |
| ☐ UK 76448 | Ilyushin Il-76TD | 1023413443 | Lst ESL |
| ☐ UK 76449 | Ilyushin Il-76TD | 1023413443 | Lst ESL |
| ☐ UK 76782 | Ilyushin Il-76TD | 0093498971 | std |
| ☐ UK 76793 | Ilyushin Il-76TD | 0093498951 | |
| ☐ UK 76794 | Ilyushin Il-76TD | 0093498954 | std |
| ☐ UK 76805 | Ilyushin Il-76TD | 1003403109 | |
| ☐ UK 76811 | Ilyushin Il-76TD | 1013407223 | std |
| ☐ UK 76813 | Ilyushin Il-76TD | 1013408246 | |
| ☐ UK-76824 | Ilyushin Il-76TD | 1023410327 | std |
| ☐ UK 86016 | Ilyushin Il-86 | 51483202014 | std |
| ☐ UK 86052 | Ilyushin Il-86 | 51483202019 | std |
| ☐ UK 86053 | Ilyushin Il-86 | 51483203020 | std |
| ☐ UK 86056 | Ilyushin Il-86 | 51483203023 | |
| ☐ UK 86057 | Ilyushin Il-86 | 51483203024 | std |
| ☐ UK 86064 | Ilyushin Il-86 | 51483203031 | std |
| ☐ UK 86072 | Ilyushin Il-86 | 51483204039 | std |
| ☐ UK 86083 | Ilyushin Il-86 | 51483206054 | std |
| ☐ UK 86090 | Ilyushin Il-86 | 51483207061 | std |
| ☐ UK 85286 | Tupolev Tu-154B | 78A-286 | std |
| ☐ UK 85344 | Tupolev Tu-154B-2 | 79A-344 | |
| ☐ UK 85370 | Tupolev Tu-154B-2 | 79A-370 | std |
| ☐ UK 85397 | Tupolev Tu-154B-2 | 80A-397 | std |
| ☐ UK 85398 | Tupolev Tu-154B-2 | 80A-398 | |
| ☐ UK 85401 | Tupolev Tu-154B-2 | 80A-401 | std |
| ☐ UK 85416 | Tupolev Tu-154B-2 | 80A-416 | std |
| ☐ UK 85423 | Tupolev Tu-154B-2 | 80A-423 | std |
| ☐ UK 85438 | Tupolev Tu-154B-2 | 80A-438 | std |
| ☐ UK 85449 | Tupolev Tu-154B-2 | 80A-449 | |
| ☐ UK 85575 | Tupolev Tu-154B-2 | 83A-575 | |
| ☐ UK 85578 | Tupolev Tu-154B-2 | 83A-578 | |
| ☐ UK 85600 | Tupolev Tu-154B-2 | 84A-600 | Govt |
| ☐ UK 85711 | Tupolev Tu-154M | 91A-887 | |
| ☐ UK 85764 | Tupolev Tu-154M | 93A-947 | |
| ☐ UK 85776 | Tupolev Tu-154M | 93A-958 | dam |
| ☐ UK 11369 | Antonov An-12P | 00346909 | |
| ☐ UK 11372 | Antonov An-12 | 5343204 | |
| ☐ UK 31001 | Airbus A310-324 | 574 | |
| ☐ UK 31002 | Airbus A310-324 | 576 | |
| ☐ UK 31003 | Airbus A310-324 | 706 | |
| ☐ UK 75700 | Boeing 757-23P | 731/28338 | Govt |
| ☐ UK 80001 | Avro RJ85 | E2312 | |
| ☐ UK 80002 | Avro RJ85 | E2309 | |
| ☐ UK 80003 | Avro RJ85 | E2319 | |
| ☐ UK 91000 | Ilyushin Il-114 | 101348328025 | std |
| ☐ UK-76701 | Boeing 767-33PER | 635/28370 | |
| ☐ VP-BUB | Boeing 757-23P | 875/30060 | |
| ☐ VP-BUD | Boeing 757-23P | 886/30061 | |
| ☐ VP-BUZ | Boeing 767-33PER | 650/28392 | |
| ☐ | Boeing 767-33PER | | o/o |
| ☐ | Boeing 767-33PER | | o/o |

## UN - KAZAKHSTAN

### AEROTRANS — ATG

| | | | |
|---|---|---|---|
| ☐ UN-85422 | Tupolev Tu-154B-2 | 422 | |

### AIR ASTANA — SXA

| | | | |
|---|---|---|---|
| ☐ P4-BAS | Boeing 737-8Q8 | 752/30627 | |
| ☐ P4-CAS | Boeing 737-7Q8 | 1011/30629 | |
| ☐ P4-DAS | Boeing 737-7Q8 | 1097/30642 | |

### AIR KAZAKSTAN — KZK

| | | | |
|---|---|---|---|
| ☐ UN-86068 | Ilyushin Il-86 | 51483204035 | Jow ESL |
| ☐ UN-86071 | Ilyushin Il-86 | 51483204038 | std |
| ☐ UN-86077 | Ilyushin Il-86 | 51483205047 | |
| ☐ UN-86086 | Ilyushin Il-86 | 51483206057 | std |

| | | | |
|---|---|---|---|
| ☐ UN-86101 | Ilyushin Il-86 | 51483207069 | std |
| ☐ UN-86116 | Ilyushin Il-86 | 51483209084 | std |

| | | | |
|---|---|---|---|
| ☐ UN-85478 | Tupolev Tu-154B-2 | 81A-478 | Lst UGN |
| ☐ UN-85173 | Tupolev Tu-154B-1 | 76A-173 | |
| ☐ UN-85221 | Tupolev Tu-154B | 77A-221 | |
| ☐ UN-85337 | Tupolev Tu-154B-2 | 79A-337 | |
| ☐ UN-85396 | Tupolev Tu-154B-2 | 80A-396 | |
| ☐ UN-85431 | Tupolev Tu-154B-2 | 80A-431 | |
| ☐ UN-85521 | Tupolev Tu-154B-2 | 82A-521 | |
| ☐ UN-85775 | Tupolev Tu-154M | 93A-957 | |
| ☐ UN-85780 | Tupolev Tu-154M | 93A-964 | |
| ☐ UN-85781 | Tupolev Tu-154M | 93A-965 | |
| ☐ UN-85782 | Tupolev Tu-154M | 93A-966 | |

| | | | |
|---|---|---|---|
| ☐ UN-A3101 | Airbus A310-322 | 399 | |
| ☐ UN-A3102 | Airbus A310-322 | 412 | |
| ☐ UN-B3703 | Boeing 737-2T4 | 1154/23444 | |
| ☐ UN-B3705 | Boeing 737-2Q8 | 748/22453 | |
| ☐ UN-B3706 | Boeing 737-2M8 | 664/22090 | |
| ☐ UN-B6701 | Boeing 767-2DXER | 861/32954 | Govt |
| ☐ UN-65147 | Tupolev Tu-134A-3 | 61012 | std |
| ☐ UN-76371 | Ilyushin Il-76TD | 1033414485 | Jow TIS |
| ☐ UN-76374 | Ilyushin Il-76TD | 1033416520 | |
| ☐ UN-76810 | Ilyushin Il-76TD | 1013409282 | |

## ATYRAU AIR WAYS — JOL

| | | | |
|---|---|---|---|
| ☐ UN-65069 | Tupolev Tu-134A-3 | 49908 | |
| ☐ UN-65070 | Tupolev Tu-134A-3 | 49912 | |
| ☐ UN-65610 | Tupolev Tu-134A | 40150 | |
| ☐ UN-65619 | Tupolev Tu-134A | 31218 | |
| ☐ UN-85742 | Tupolev Tu-154B-2 | 78A-320 | Lsf JAK |

## BERKHUT AIR — BEK

| | | | |
|---|---|---|---|
| ☐ UN-B5701 | Boeing 757-2M6 | 102/23454 | Govt |
| ☐ UN-B1111 | BAC One-Eleven 401AK | 078 | Govt |
| ☐ UN-11373 | Antonov An-12BP | 02348304 | |

## SAYAKHAT — SAH

| | | | |
|---|---|---|---|
| ☐ UN-76384 | Ilyushin Il-76TD | 1003401015 | Jow TIS |
| ☐ UN-76385 | Ilyushin Il-76TD | 1033416515 | Jow TIS |
| ☐ UN-76434 | Ilyushin Il-76 | 1023412395 | Jow TIS |
| ☐ UN-76442 | Ilyushin Il-76TD | 1023414450 | Jow TIS |
| ☐ UN-85835 | Tupolev Tu-154M | 85A-716 | |
| ☐ UN-85837 | Tupolev Tu-154M | 86A-724 | |
| ☐ UN- | Tupolev Tu-154M | 86A-725 | Lst Qeshm |
| ☐ UN-85852 | Tupolev Tu-154M | 86A-726 | |
| ☐ UN-85853 | Tupolev Tu-154M | 86A-728 | |
| ☐ UN-85854 | Tupolev Tu-154M | 86A-729 | |
| ☐ UN-85855 | Tupolev Tu-154M | 89A-823 | |
| ☐ UN- | Tupolev Tu-154M | 86A-734 | o/o |
| ☐ UN- | Tupolev Tu-154M | 89A-815 | o/o |
| ☐ UN- | Tupolev Tu-154M | 90A-855 | o/o |

# UR - UKRAINE

## AEROSVIT AIRLINES — AEW

| | | |
|---|---|---|
| ☐ UR-BVY | Boeing 737-2Q8 | 852/22760 |
| ☐ UR-VVA | Boeing 737-3Q8 | 1808/24492 |
| ☐ UR-VVB | Boeing 737-529 | 2296/26537 |
| ☐ UR-VVC | Boeing 737-529 | 2298/26538 |
| ☐ UR-VVD | Boeing 737-529 | 2165/25419 |
| ☐ UR-VVE | Boeing 737-448 | 1778/24521 |
| ☐ UR-VVF | Boeing 767-383ER | 274/24476 |

## AIR KHARKOV — KHV

| | | |
|---|---|---|
| ☐ UR-65037 | Tupolev Tu-134A-3 | 48850 |
| ☐ UR-65073 | Tupolev Tu-134A | 49980 |
| ☐ UR-65114 | Tupolev Tu-134A-3 | 60395 |
| ☐ UR-65746 | Tupolev Tu-134A-3 | 2351608 |

| | | | |
|---|---|---|---|
| ☐ UR-65752 | Tupolev Tu-134A-3 | 61079 | |
| ☐ UR-65761 | Tupolev Tu-134A-3 | 62244 | |
| ☐ UR-65764 | Tupolev Tu-134A-3 | 62305 | |
| ☐ UR-65773 | Tupolev Tu-134A-3 | 62495 | Lst OTL |
| ☐ UR-65877 | Tupolev Tu-134A-3 | 31250 | |

## AIR UKRAINE — UKR

| | | | |
|---|---|---|---|
| ☐ UR-65077 | Tupolev Tu-134A-3 | 60028 | |
| ☐ UR-65107 | Tupolev Tu-134A | 60328 | |
| ☐ UR-65135 | Tupolev Tu-134A-3 | 60648 | |
| ☐ UR-65757 | Tupolev Tu-134A-3 | 62215 | |
| ☐ UR-65765 | Tupolev Tu-134A | 62315 | |
| ☐ UR-85379 | Tupolev Tu-154B-2 | 79A-379 | |
| ☐ UR-85460 | Tupolev Tu-154B-2 | 81A-460 | |
| ☐ UR-85482 | Tupolev Tu-154B-2 | 81A-482 | |
| ☐ UR-85490 | Tupolev Tu-154B-2 | 81A-490 | |
| ☐ UR-85513 | Tupolev Tu-154B-2 | 81A-513 | |
| ☐ UR-85526 | Tupolev Tu-154B-2 | 82A-526 | |
| ☐ UR-85535 | Tupolev Tu-154B-2 | 82A-535 | |
| ☐ UR-85701 | Tupolev Tu-154M | 91A-876 | Lst UDD |
| ☐ UR-85707 | Tupolev Tu-154M | 91A-882 | |
| ☐ UR-76705 | Ilyushin Il-76MD | 0063472158 | Lsf UKW |
| ☐ UR-86133 | Ilyushin Il-62M | 1138234 | |
| ☐ UR-86135 | Ilyushin Il-62M | 1748445 | |
| ☐ UR-86580 | Ilyushin Il-62M | 2343554 | |

## ANTONOV AIRLINES — ADB

| | | | |
|---|---|---|---|
| ☐ UR-82007 | An-124-100 | 19530501005 | |
| ☐ UR-82008 | An-124-100 | 19530501006 | |
| ☐ UR-82009 | An-124-100 | 19530501007 | |
| ☐ UR-82027 | An-124-100 | 19530502288 | |
| ☐ UR-82029 | An-124-100 | 19530502630 | |
| ☐ UR-82070 | An-124-100 | 9773051359127 | std |
| ☐ UR-82072 | An-124-100 | 9773053359136 | |
| ☐ UR-82073 | An-124-100 | 9773054359139 | |
| ☐ UR-11315 | Antonov An-12BP | 4342307 | |
| ☐ UR-11765 | Antonov An-12BP | 401705 | |
| ☐ UR-13395 | Antonov An-26 | 2605 | |
| ☐ UR-21510 | Antonov An-12BP | 0901404 | |
| ☐ UR-74010 | Antonov An-74T | 36547030450 | |
| ☐ UR-NTP | Antonov An-140 | | std |
| ☐ UR-82060 | Antonov An-225 | 01-01 | |

## ATI INTERNATIONAL — TII

| | | | |
|---|---|---|---|
| ☐ UR-76629 | Ilyushin Il-76MD | 0053458745 | |
| ☐ UR-76700 | Ilyushin Il-76MD | 0063471134 | |
| ☐ UR-76716 | Ilyushin Il-76MD | 0073474211 | |
| ☐ UR-76767 | Ilyushin Il-76MD | 0083487598 | |
| ☐ UR-76777 | Ilyushin Il-76MD | 0083482490 | |
| ☐ UR-78129 | Ilyushin Il-76MD | 0083489683 | Lst AHC |
| ☐ UR-78130 | Ilyushin Il-76MD | 0043454611 | Lst AHC |
| ☐ UR-78752 | Ilyushin Il-76MD | 0083483519 | |
| ☐ UR-78758 | Ilyushin Il-76MD | 0083484551 | |
| ☐ UR-78772 | Ilyushin Il-76MD | 0083487627 | |

## CABI — CBI

| | | | |
|---|---|---|---|
| ☐ UR-CAE | An-74TK-100 | 36547095905 | Lst MTL |
| ☐ UR-74057 | An-74-200 | 36547098960 | |

## KHORS AIR — KHO

| | | | |
|---|---|---|---|
| ☐ T9-CAD | Antonov An-12BP | 4342202 | Lsf BIO |
| ☐ UR-BYL | Douglas DC-9-51 | 787/47657 | |
| ☐ UR-CAN | McDD MD-83 | 1539/49822 | Lst DAL |
| ☐ UR-TSI | Antonov An-12BP | 6344701 | Opf UN |
| ☐ UR-UCJ | Ilyushin Il-76MD | 0083484531 | Lsf UKS |
| ☐ UR-11326 | Antonov An-12BP | 2400802 | |

## UKRAINE INTERNATIONAL AIRLINES — AUI

| | | |
|---|---|---|
| ☐ UR-GAC | Boeing 737-247 | 1071/23188 |
| ☐ UR-GAG | Boeing 737-35B | 1626/24238 |
| ☐ UR-GAH | Boeing 737-32Q | 3105/29130 |
| ☐ UR-GAJ | Boeing 737-5Y0 | 2262/25192 |
| ☐ UR-GAK | Boeing 737-5Y0 | 2374/26075 |
| ☐ UR-GAL | Boeing 737-341 | 1637/24275 |
| ☐ UR-GAP | Boeing 737-529 | 2165/25419 |

## UKRAINIAN CARGO AIRWAYS — UKS

| | | | |
|---|---|---|---|
| ☐ UR-UCA | Ilyushin Il-76MD | 0073479394 | |
| ☐ UR-UCB | Ilyushin Il-76MD | 0063467003 | |
| ☐ UR-UCC | Ilyushin Il-76MD | 0083489647 | |
| ☐ UR-UCD | Ilyushin Il-76MD | 0083488643 | |
| ☐ UR-UCE | Ilyushin Il-76MD | 0083484522 | |
| ☐ UR-UCF | Ilyushin Il-76MD | 0083488638 | |
| ☐ UR-UCG | Ilyushin Il-76MD | 0083482478 | |
| ☐ UR-UCH | Ilyushin Il-76MD | 0083484536 | |
| ☐ UR-UCJ | Ilyushin Il-76MD | 0083484531 | Lst KHO |
| ☐ UR-UCL | Ilyushin Il-76MD | 0043456692 | |
| ☐ UR-UCO | Ilyushin Il-76MD | 0053458749 | |
| ☐ UR-UCQ | Ilyushin Il-76MD | 0063465963 | |
| ☐ UR-UCR | Ilyushin Il-76MD | 0073475270 | |
| ☐ UR-UCS | Ilyushin Il-76TD | 0063470113 | |
| ☐ UR-UCT | Ilyushin Il-76MD | 0063470089 | Lst AZV |
| ☐ UR-UCU | Ilyushin Il-76MD | 0073476275 | |
| ☐ UR-UCV | Ilyushin Il-76TD | 0043451517 | |
| ☐ UR-UCW | Ilyushin Il-76MD | 0054358733 | |
| ☐ UR-UCX | Ilyushin Il-76MD | 0063470112 | |
| ☐ UR-UCY | Ilyushin Il-76MD | 0083485566 | |
| ☐ UR-UDB | Ilyushin Il-76MD | 0043455686 | |
| ☐ UR-UDC | Ilyushin Il-76MD | 0063467011 | Lst GLS |
| | | | |
| ☐ UR-UCK | Antonov An-12BP | 0346905 | ex |
| ☐ UR-UCN | Antonov An-12BK | 01347604 | Lst VPB |
| ☐ UR-UCZ | Tupolev Tu-154B-2 | 82A-561 | |

## VETERAN AIRLINES — VPB

| | | | |
|---|---|---|---|
| ☐ UR-PAS | Antonov An-12AP | 2401105 | |
| ☐ UR-PLV | Antonov An-12 | 4342308 | |
| ☐ UR-UCN | Antonov An-12BK | 00347604 | Lsf UKS |
| ☐ UR-YMR | Antonov An-12BP | 9346302 | |

## VOLARE AVIATION ENTERPRISE — VRE

| | | | |
|---|---|---|---|
| ☐ UR-BWM | Antonov An-12BP | 00347004 | Lst ESL |
| ☐ UR-LAI | Antonov An-12V | 8345505 | |
| ☐ UR-LMI | Antonov An-12BK | 6344605 | |
| ☐ UR-LTG | Antonov An-12V | 00347201 | |
| ☐ UR-SMA | Antonov An-12BK | 7345208 | |
| ☐ UR-SVG | Antonov An-12BK | 04342409 | Jow ESL |
| | | | |
| ☐ UR-76628 | Ilyushin Il-76MD | 0053458741 | |
| ☐ UR-76636 | Ilyushin Il-76MD | 0053459781 | |
| ☐ UR-76687 | Ilyushin Il-76MD | 0063469051 | |
| ☐ UR-76704 | Ilyushin Il-76MD | 0063471150 | |
| ☐ UR-76727 | Ilyushin Il-76MD | 0073475268 | |

# VH - AUSTRALIA

## ALLIANCE AIRLINES — FWQ

| | | | |
|---|---|---|---|
| ☐ VH-FNY | Fokker 100 | 11484 | |
| ☐ VH-FWH | Fokker 100 | 11316 | |
| ☐ VH-FWI | Fokker 100 | 11318 | |
| ☐ VH- | Fokker 100 | | o/o |
| ☐ VH- | Fokker 100 | | o/o |

## ASIAN EXPRESS AIRLINES — AXF

| | | | |
|---|---|---|---|
| ☐ VH-DHE | Boeing 727-2J4F | 1598/22080 | Lsf BCS |

## AUSTRALIAN AIR EXPRESS — XME

| | | | |
|---|---|---|---|
| ☐ VH-AUP | Boeing 727-277F | 1481/21695 | |
| ☐ VH-TBS | Boeing 727-77C | 768/20278 | |
| ☐ VH-VLD | Boeing 727-281F | 1316/21455 | |
| ☐ VH-VLE | Boeing 727-277F | 989/20549 | |
| ☐ VH-VLG | Boeing 727-277F | 1054/20551 | |
| ☐ VH-VLH | Boeing 727-277F | 1759/22642 | |
| ☐ VH-VLI | Boeing 727-277F | 1753/22641 | |
| | | | |
| ☐ VH-NJF | BAe 146 Srs.300QT | E3198 | Opb NJS |
| ☐ VH-NJM | BAe 146 Srs.300QT | E3194 | Opb NJS |
| ☐ VH-NJV | BAe 146 Srs.100QT | E1002 | Opb NJS |

## AUSTRALIAN AIRLINES — AUZ

| | | | |
|---|---|---|---|
| ☐ VH-OGI | Boeing 767-338ER | 387/25246 | Lsf QFA |
| ☐ VH-OGJ | Boeing 767-338ER | 396/25274 | Lsf QFA |
| ☐ VH-OGK | Boeing 767-338ER | 397/25316 | Lsf QFA |
| ☐ VH-OGL | Boeing 767-338ER | 402/25363 | Lsf QFA |

## NATIONAL JET SYSTEMS — NJS

| | | | |
|---|---|---|---|
| ☐ VH-NJA | BAe 146 Srs.100 | E1004 | |
| ☐ VH-NJC | BAe 146 Srs.100 | E1013 | Lst QFA |
| ☐ VH-NJD | BAe 146 Srs.100 | E1160 | Lst QFA |
| ☐ VH-NJE | BAe 146 Srs.100 | E1104 | Lst QFA |
| ☐ VH-NJF | BAe 146 Srs.300QT | E3198 | |
| ☐ VH-NJG | BAe 146 Srs.200 | E2170 | Lst QFA |
| ☐ VH-NJH | BAe 146 Srs.200 | E2178 | Lst QFA |
| ☐ VH-NJJ | BAe 146 Srs.200 | E2184 | Lst QFA |
| ☐ VH-NJL | BAe 146 Srs.300 | E3213 | Lst QFA |
| ☐ VH-NJM | BAe 146 Srs.300QT | E3194 | |
| ☐ VH-NJN | BAe 146 Srs.300 | E3217 | Lst QFA |
| ☐ VH-NJQ | BAe 146 Srs.200 | E2072 | Lst QFA |
| ☐ VH-NJR | BAe 146 Srs.100 | E1152 | |
| ☐ VH-NJT | Avro RJ70A | E1228 | |
| ☐ VH-NJU | BAe 146 Srs.200 | E2073 | Lst QFA |
| ☐ VH-NJV | BAe 146 Srs.100QT | E1002 | |
| ☐ VH-NJW | BAe 146 Srs.200 | E2034 | |
| ☐ VH-NJX | BAe 146 Srs.100 | E1003 | Lst QFA |
| ☐ VH-NJY | BAe 146 Srs.100 | E1005 | Lst QFA |
| ☐ VH-NJZ | BAe 146 Srs.100 | E1009 | Lst QFA |
| | | | |
| ☐ VH-JSH | DHC-8-202 | 411 | |
| ☐ VH-JSI | DHC-8-103 | 229 | |
| ☐ VH-JSJ | DHC-8-103 | 170 | |
| ☐ VH-JSQ | DHC-8-311A | 399 | |
| ☐ VH-ZZA | DHC-8-202 | 419 | |
| ☐ VH-ZZB | DHC-8-202 | 424 | |
| ☐ VH-ZZC | DHC-8-202 | 433 | |
| ☐ VH-ZZI | DHC-8-202 | 550 | |
| ☐ VH-ZZJ | DHC-8-202 | 551 | |

## QANTAS AIRWAYS — QFA

| | | | |
|---|---|---|---|
| ☐ VH-EBA | Airbus A330-201 | 508 | |
| ☐ VH-EBB | Airbus A330-201 | 522 | |
| ☐ VH-EBC | Airbus A330-201 | 506 | o/o |
| ☐ VH-EBD | Airbus A330-201 | 513 | o/o |
| ☐ VH-EBE | Airbus A330-201 | 569 | o/o |
| ☐ VH-EBF | Airbus A330-201 | 562 | o/o |
| ☐ VH-EBG | Airbus A330-201 | 571 | o/o |
| ☐ VH-EBH | Airbus A330-301 | 553 | o/o |
| ☐ VH-EBI | Airbus A330-301 | | o/o |
| ☐ VH-EBJ | Airbus A330-301 | | o/o |
| ☐ VH-EBK | Airbus A330-301 | | o/o |
| | | | |
| ☐ VH-TAB | Boeing 737-3Q8 | 2355/26282 | |
| ☐ VH-TAF | Boeing 737-376 | 1225/23477 | |
| ☐ VH-TAG | Boeing 737-376 | 1251/23478 | |
| ☐ VH-TAH | Boeing 737-376 | 1259/23479 | |
| ☐ VH-TAI | Boeing 737-376 | 1264/23483 | |
| ☐ VH-TAJ | Boeing 737-376 | 1270/23484 | |
| ☐ VH-TAK | Boeing 737-376 | 1277/23485 | |
| ☐ VH-TAU^ | Boeing 737-376 | 1286/23486 | |

| | | | |
|---|---|---|---|
| ☐ VH-TAV | Boeing 737-376 | 1306/23487 | |
| ☐ VH-TAW | Boeing 737-376 | 1352/23488 | |
| ☐ VH-TAX | Boeing 737-376 | 1356/23489 | |
| ☐ VH-TAY | Boeing 737-376 | 1390/23490 | |
| ☐ VH-TAZ | Boeing 737-376 | 1391/23491 | |
| ☐ VH-TJA | Boeing 737-376 | 1649/24295 | |
| ☐ VH-TJB | Boeing 737-376 | 1653/24296 | |
| ☐ VH-TJC | Boeing 737-376 | 1740/24297 | |
| ☐ VH-TJD | Boeing 737-376 | 1761/24298 | |
| ☐ VH-TJE | Boeing 737-476 | 1820/24430 | |
| ☐ VH-TJF | Boeing 737-476 | 1863/24431 | |
| ☐ VH-TJG | Boeing 737-476 | 1879/24432 | |
| ☐ VH-TJH | Boeing 737-476 | 1881/24433 | |
| ☐ VH-TJI | Boeing 737-476 | 1912/24434 | |
| ☐ VH-TJJ | Boeing 737-476 | 1959/24435 | |
| ☐ VH-TJK | Boeing 737-476 | 1998/24436 | |
| ☐ VH-TJL | Boeing 737-476 | 2162/24437 | |
| ☐ VH-TJM | Boeing 737-476 | 2171/24438 | |
| ☐ VH-TJN | Boeing 737-476 | 2265/24439 | |
| ☐ VH-TJO | Boeing 737-476 | 2324/24440 | |
| ☐ VH-TJP | Boeing 737-476 | 2363/24441 | |
| ☐ VH-TJQ | Boeing 737-476 | 2371/24442 | |
| ☐ VH-TJR | Boeing 737-476 | 2398/24443 | |
| ☐ VH-TJS | Boeing 737-476 | 2454/24444 | |
| ☐ VH-TJT | Boeing 737-476 | 2539/24445 | |
| ☐ VH-TJU | Boeing 737-476 | 2569/24446 | |
| ☐ VH-TJV | Boeing 737-4Q8 | 2264/25163 | |
| ☐ VH-TJW | Boeing 737-4L7 | 2517/26961 | Lsf RON |
| ☐ VH-TJX | Boeing 737-476 | 2773/28150 | |
| ☐ VH-TJY | Boeing 737-476 | 2785/28151 | |
| ☐ VH-TJZ | Boeing 737-476 | 2829/28152 | |
| ☐ DQ-FJF | Boeing 737-7X2 | 96/28878 | Lsf FJI |
| ☐ VH-VXA | Boeing 737-838 | 1042/29551 | |
| ☐ VH-VXB | Boeing 737-838 | 1045/30101 | |
| ☐ VH-VXC | Boeing 737-838 | 1049/30897 | |
| ☐ VH-VXD | Boeing 737-838 | 1063/29552 | |
| ☐ VH-VXE | Boeing 737-838 | 1071/30899 | |
| ☐ VH-VXF | Boeing 737-838 | 1096/29553 | |
| ☐ VH-VXG | Boeing 737-838 | 1102/30901 | |
| ☐ VH-VXH | Boeing 737-838 | 1137/33478 | |
| ☐ VH-VXI | Boeing 737-838 | 1141/33479 | |
| ☐ VH-VXJ | Boeing 737-838 | 1157/33480 | |
| ☐ VH-VXK | Boeing 737-838 | 1160/33481 | |
| ☐ VH-VXL | Boeing 737-838 | 1172/33482 | |
| ☐ VH-VXM | Boeing 737-838 | 1177/33483 | |
| ☐ VH-VXN | Boeing 737-838 | 1180/33484 | |
| ☐ VH-VXO | Boeing 737-838 | 1183/33485 | |
| ☐ VH-VXP | Boeing 737-838 | 33722 | o/o |
| ☐ VH-VXQ | Boeing 737-838 | 33723 | o/o |
| ☐ VH-VXR | Boeing 737-838 | 33724 | o/o |
| ☐ VH-VXS | Boeing 737-838 | 33725 | o/o |
| ☐ VH-EBR | Boeing 747-238B | 464/22614 | Lst FJI |
| ☐ VH-EBT | Boeing 747-338 | 602/23222 | |
| ☐ VH-EBU | Boeing 747-338 | 606/23223 | |
| ☐ VH-EBV | Boeing 747-338 | 610/23224 | |
| ☐ VH-EBW | Boeing 747-338 | 638/23408 | |
| ☐ VH-EBX | Boeing 747-338 | 662/23688 | |
| ☐ VH-EBY | Boeing 747-338 | 678/23823 | |
| ☐ VH-NLH | Boeing 747-436 | 779/24050 | Lsf BAW |
| ☐ VH-OEB | Boeing 747-48E | 983/25778 | |
| ☐ VH-OEC | Boeing 747-4H6 | 808/24836 | |
| ☐ VH-OED | Boeing 747-4H6 | 858/25126 | |
| ☐ VH-OEE | Boeing 747-438ER | 1308/32909 | |
| ☐ VH-OEF | Boeing 747-438ER | 1313/32910 | |
| ☐ VH-OEG | Boeing 747-438ER | 1320/32911 | |
| ☐ VH-OEH | Boeing 747-438ER | 1321/32912 | |
| ☐ VH-OEI | Boeing 747-438ER | 32913 | |
| ☐ VH-OEJ | Boeing 747-438ER | 32914 | |
| ☐ VH-OJA | Boeing 747-438 | 731/24354 | |
| ☐ VH-OJB | Boeing 747-438 | 746/24373 | |
| ☐ VH-OJC | Boeing 747-438 | 751/24406 | |
| ☐ VH-OJD | Boeing 747-438 | 764/24481 | |
| ☐ VH-OJE | Boeing 747-438 | 765/24482 | |
| ☐ VH-OJF | Boeing 747-438 | 781/24483 | |
| ☐ VH-OJG | Boeing 747-438 | 801/24779 | |
| ☐ VH-OJH | Boeing 747-438 | 807/24806 | |
| ☐ VH-OJI | Boeing 747-438 | 826/24887 | |
| ☐ VH-OJJ | Boeing 747-438 | 835/24974 | |
| ☐ VH-OJK | Boeing 747-438 | 857/25067 | |
| ☐ VH-OJL | Boeing 747-438 | 865/25151 | |
| ☐ VH-OJM | Boeing 747-438 | 875/25245 | |
| ☐ VH-OJN | Boeing 747-438 | 883/25315 | |
| ☐ VH-OJO | Boeing 747-438 | 894/25544 | |
| ☐ VH-OJP | Boeing 747-438 | 916/25545 | |
| ☐ VH-OJQ | Boeing 747-438 | 924/25546 | |
| ☐ VH-OJR | Boeing 747-438 | 936/25547 | |
| ☐ VH-OJS | Boeing 747-438 | 1230/25564 | |
| ☐ VH-OJT | Boeing 747-438 | 1233/25565 | |
| ☐ VH-OJU | Boeing 747-438 | 1239/25566 | |
| ☐ VH-EAJ | Boeing 767-238ER | 119/23304 | |
| ☐ VH-EAK | Boeing 767-238ER | 120/23305 | |
| ☐ VH-EAL | Boeing 767-238ER | 125/23306 | |
| ☐ VH-EAM | Boeing 767-238ER | 129/23309 | |
| ☐ VH-EAN | Boeing 767-238ER | 133/23402 | |
| ☐ VH-EAO | Boeing 767-238ER | 137/23403 | |
| ☐ VH-EAQ | Boeing 767-238ER | 183/23896 | |
| ☐ VH-OGA | Boeing 767-338ER | 231/24146 | |
| ☐ VH-OGB | Boeing 767-338ER | 242/24316 | |
| ☐ VH-OGC | Boeing 767-338ER | 246/24317 | |
| ☐ VH-OGD | Boeing 767-338ER | 247/24407 | |
| ☐ VH-OGE | Boeing 767-338ER | 278/24531 | |
| ☐ VH-OGF | Boeing 767-338ER | 319/24853 | |
| ☐ VH-OGG | Boeing 767-338ER | 343/24929 | |
| ☐ VH-OGH | Boeing 767-338ER | 344/24930 | |
| ☐ VH-OGI | Boeing 767-338ER | 387/25246 | Lst AUZ |
| ☐ VH-OGJ | Boeing 767-338ER | 396/25274 | Lst AUZ |
| ☐ VH-OGK | Boeing 767-338ER | 397/25316 | Lst AUZ |
| ☐ VH-OGL | Boeing 767-338ER | 402/25363 | Lst AUZ |
| ☐ VH-OGM | Boeing 767-338ER | 451/25575 | |
| ☐ VH-OGN | Boeing 767-338ER | 549/25576 | |
| ☐ VH-OGO | Boeing 767-338ER | 550/25577 | |
| ☐ VH-OGP | Boeing 767-338ER | 615/28153 | |
| ☐ VH-OGQ | Boeing 767-338ER | 623/28154 | |
| ☐ VH-OGR | Boeing 767-338ER | 662/28724 | |
| ☐ VH-OGS | Boeing 767-338ER | 665/28725 | |
| ☐ VH-OGT | Boeing 767-338ER | 710/29117 | |
| ☐ VH-OGU | Boeing 767-338ER | 713/29118 | |
| ☐ VH-OGV | Boeing 767-338ER | 796/30186 | |
| ☐ VH-ZXA | Boeing 767-336ER | 288/24334 | |
| ☐ VH-ZXB | Boeing 767-336ER | 293/24338 | |
| ☐ VH-ZXC | Boeing 767-336ER | 298/24339 | |
| ☐ VH-ZXD | Boeing 767-336ER | 363/24342 | |
| ☐ VH-ZXE | Boeing 767-336ER | 364/24343 | |
| ☐ VH-ZXF | Boeing 767-336ER | 365/25203 | |
| ☐ VH-ZXG | Boeing 767-336ER | 419/25443 | |

## QANTASLINK     QFA

| | | | |
|---|---|---|---|
| ☐ VH-IMD | Boeing 717-2K9 | 5014/55055 | |
| ☐ VH-IMP | Boeing 717-2K9 | 5013/55054 | |
| ☐ VH-LAX | Boeing 717-2K9 | 5020/55057 | |
| ☐ VH-VQA | Boeing 717-2CM | 5002/55001 | |
| ☐ VH-VQB | Boeing 717-2CM | 5003/55002 | |
| ☐ VH-VQC | Boeing 717-2CM | 5041/55151 | |
| ☐ VH-VQD | Boeing 717-23S | 5031/55062 | |
| ☐ VH-VQE | Boeing 717-23S | 5034/55063 | |
| ☐ VH-VQF | Boeing 717-231 | 5077/55092 | |
| ☐ VH-VQG | Boeing 717-231 | 5083/55093 | |
| ☐ VH-VQH | Boeing 717-231 | 5084/55094 | |
| ☐ VH-VQI | Boeing 717-231 | 5087/55095 | |
| ☐ VH-VQJ | Boeing 717-231 | 5093/55096 | |
| ☐ VH-VQK | Boeing 717-231 | 5095/55097 | |
| ☐ VH-NJC | BAe 146 Srs.100 | E1013 | Lsf NJS |
| ☐ VH-NJD | BAe 146 Srs.100 | E1160 | Lsf NJS |
| ☐ VH-NJE | BAe 146 Srs.100 | E1104 | Lsf NJS |
| ☐ VH-NJG | BAe 146 Srs.200 | E2170 | Lsf NJS |
| ☐ VH-NJH | BAe 146 Srs.200 | E2178 | Lsf NJS |
| ☐ VH-NJJ | BAe 146 Srs.200 | E2184 | Lsf NJS |
| ☐ VH-NJL | BAe 146 Srs.300 | E3213 | Lsf NJS |
| ☐ VH-NJN | BAe 146 Srs.300 | E3217 | Lsf NJS |
| ☐ VH-NJQ | BAe 146 Srs.200 | E2072 | Lsf NJS |

| | | | |
|---|---|---|---|
| ☐ VH-NJU | BAe 146 Srs.200 | E2073 | Lsf NJS |
| ☐ VH-NJW | BAe 146 Srs.200 | E2034 | |
| ☐ VH-NJX | BAe 146 Srs.100 | E1003 | Lsf NJS |
| ☐ VH-NJY | BAe 146 Srs.100 | E1005 | Lsf NJS |
| ☐ VH-NJZ | BAe 146 Srs.100 | E1009 | Lsf NJS |
| ☐ VH-YAD | BAe 146 Srs.200 | E2097 | |
| ☐ VH-YAE | BAe 146 Srs.200 | E2107 | |
| ☐ VH-YAF | BAe 146 Srs.200 | E2040 | |
| | | | |
| ☐ VH-SBB | DHC-8Q-311 | 539 | |
| ☐ VH-SBG | DHC-8Q-315 | 575 | |
| ☐ VH-SBJ | DHC-8Q-315 | 578 | |
| ☐ VH-SBT | DHC-8Q-315 | 580 | |
| ☐ VH-SDA | DHC-8Q-202 | 482 | |
| ☐ VH-SDE | DHC-8Q-202 | 453 | |
| ☐ VH-TND | DHC-8-102 | 036 | |
| ☐ VH-TNG | DHC-8-102 | 041 | |
| ☐ VH-TNU | DHC-8-103 | 203 | |
| ☐ VH-TNW | DHC-8-103A | 243 | |
| ☐ VH-TNX | DHC-8-102 | 033 | |
| ☐ VH-TQA | DHC-8-314A | 365 | |
| ☐ VH-TQB | DHC-8-314 | 400 | |
| ☐ VH-TQC | DHC-8-314 | 423 | |
| ☐ VH-TQF | DHC-8-102 | 067 | |
| ☐ VH-TQG | DHC-8-201 | 430 | |
| ☐ VH-TQN | DHC-8-102 | 062 | |
| ☐ VH-TQO | DHC-8-102 | 004 | |
| ☐ VH-TQP | DHC-8-102 | 135 | |
| ☐ VH-TQQ | DHC-8-102 | 204 | |
| ☐ VH-TQR | DHC-8-102 | 208 | |
| ☐ VH-TQS | DHC-8-202 | 418 | |
| ☐ VH-TQT | DHC-8-102A | 349 | |
| ☐ VH-TQU | DHC-8-102A | 346 | |
| ☐ VH-TQV | DHC-8-102A | 362 | |
| ☐ VH-TQW | DHC-8-103A | 306 | |
| ☐ VH-TQX | DHC-8-202 | 439 | |
| ☐ VH-TQY | DHC-8-315 | 552 | |
| ☐ VH-TQZ | DHC-8-315 | 555 | |
| ☐ VH-WZI | DHC-8-102 | 014 | |
| ☐ VH-WZJ | DHC-8-102 | 027 | |
| ☐ VH-WZS | DHC-8-102 | 005 | |
| ☐ VH- | DHC-8Q-314 | | |
| ☐ VH- | DHC-8Q-314 | | |
| ☐ VH- | DHC-8Q-314 | | |

## REX – REGIONAL EXPRESS

| | | | |
|---|---|---|---|
| ☐ VH-EKD | SAAB SF.340A | 155 | |
| ☐ VH-EKG | SAAB SF.340B | 367 | |
| ☐ VH-EKH | SAAB SF.340B | 369 | |
| ☐ VH-EKN | SAAB SF.340B | 372 | |
| ☐ VH-EKT | SAAB SF.340A | 085 | |
| ☐ VH-EKX | SAAB SF.340B | 257 | |
| ☐ VH-KDB | SAAB SF.340A | 008 | |
| ☐ VH-KDI | SAAB SF.340A | 131 | |
| ☐ VH-KDK | SAAB SF.340A | 016 | |
| ☐ VH-KDP | SAAB SF.340A | 052 | |
| ☐ VH-KDQ | SAAB SF.340B | 325 | |
| ☐ VH-KDV | SAAB SF.340B | 322 | |
| ☐ VH-KEQ | SAAB SF.340A | 011 | |
| ☐ VH-LIH | SAAB SF.340B | 316 | |
| ☐ VH-OLL | SAAB SF.340B | 175 | |
| ☐ VH-OLM | SAAB SF.340B | 205 | |
| ☐ VH-OLN | SAAB SF.340B | 207 | |
| ☐ VH-SBA | SAAB SF.340B | 311 | |
| ☐ VH-TCH | SAAB SF.340B | 362 | |
| ☐ VH- | SAAB SF.340B | 209 | o/o |
| ☐ VH- | SAAB SF.340B | 275 | o/o |
| ☐ VH- | SAAB SF.340B | 279 | o/o |
| ☐ VH- | SAAB SF.340B | 285 | o/o |
| ☐ VH- | SAAB SF.340B | 290 | o/o |
| ☐ VH- | SAAB SF.340B | 291 | o/o |
| ☐ VH- | SAAB SF.340B | 293 | o/o |
| ☐ VH- | SAAB SF.340B | 303 | o/o |
| ☐ VH- | SAAB SF.340B | | o/o |
| ☐ VH- | SAAB SF.340B | | o/o |

## TRANSAUSTRALIAN AIR EXPRESS    XME

| | | | |
|---|---|---|---|
| ☐ VH-AUP | Boeing 727-277F | 1481/21695 | |
| ☐ VH-TBS | Boeing 727-77C | 768/20278 | |
| ☐ VH-VLD | Boeing 727-281F | 1316/21455 | |
| ☐ VH-VLE | Boeing 727-277F | 989/20549 | |
| ☐ VH-VLG | Boeing 727-277F | 1054/20551 | |
| ☐ VH-VLH | Boeing 727-277F | 1759/22642 | Lsf BCS |
| ☐ VH-VLI | Boeing 727-277F | 1753/22641 | Lsf BCS |

## VIRGIN BLUE AIRLINES    VOZ

| | | | |
|---|---|---|---|
| ☐ VH-VBA | Boeing 737-7Q8 | 817/28238 | |
| ☐ VH-VBB | Boeing 737-7Q8 | 832/28240 | |
| ☐ VH-VBC | Boeing 737-7Q8 | 858/30638 | |
| ☐ VH-VBD | Boeing 737-7Q8 | 975/30707 | |
| ☐ VH-VBF | Boeing 737-7Q8 | 1032/30630 | |
| ☐ VH-VBH | Boeing 737-7Q8 | 1080/30631 | |
| ☐ VH-VBI | Boeing 737-7Q8 | 1107/30644 | |
| ☐ VH-VBJ | Boeing 737-7Q8 | 1159/30647 | |
| ☐ VH-VBK | Boeing 737-7Q8 | 1171/30648 | |
| ☐ VH-VBL | Boeing 737-7Q8 | 1220/30633 | |
| ☐ VH-VBM | Boeing 737-76N | 1090/32734 | |
| ☐ VH-VBN | Boeing 737-76N | 1134/33005 | |
| ☐ VH-VBO | Boeing 737-76N | 1226/33418 | |
| ☐ VH-VBP | Boeing 737-7BX | 922/30743 | |
| ☐ VH-VBQ | Boeing 737-7BX | 989/30744 | |
| ☐ VH-VBR | Boeing 737-7BX | 1027/30745 | |
| ☐ VH-VBS | Boeing 737-7BX | 1085/30746 | |
| ☐ VH-VBT | Boeing 737-7BX | 776//30740 | |
| ☐ VH-VOA | Boeing 737-8BK | 991/30620 | |
| ☐ VH-VOB | Boeing 737-8BK | 1108/30622 | |
| ☐ VH-VOC | Boeing 737-8BK | 1136/30623 | |
| ☐ VH-VOD | Boeing 737-8BK | 1193/30624 | |
| ☐ VH-VOE | Boeing 737-86Q | 824/30272 | |
| ☐ VH-VOF | Boeing 737-86Q | 845/30274 | |
| ☐ VH-VOG | Boeing 737-86N | 839/28644 | |
| ☐ VH-VOH | Boeing 737-86N | 1094/29884 | |
| ☐ VH-VOI | Boeing 737-81Q | 1138/30786 | |
| ☐ VH-VOJ | Boeing 737-81Q | 1234/30787 | |
| ☐ VH- | Boeing 737-8 | | o/o |
| ☐ VH- | Boeing 737-8 | | o/o |
| ☐ VH- | Boeing 737-8 | | o/o |
| ☐ VH- | Boeing 737-8 | | o/o |

## VN - VIETNAM

### PACIFIC AIRLINES    PIC

| | | | |
|---|---|---|---|
| ☐ S7-RGJ | Airbus A321-131 | 0604 | Lsf RGA |
| ☐ S7-RGK | Airbus A320-131 | 0614 | Lsf RGA |
| ☐ S7-RGL | Airbus A320-232 | 0542 | Lsf RGA |
| ☐ S7-RGO | Airbus A300B4-605R | 584 | Lsf RGA |
| ☐ S7-RGP | Airbus A310-324 | 549 | Lsf RGA |

### VIETNAM AIRLINES    HVN

| | | | |
|---|---|---|---|
| ☐ VN-B202 | ATR 72-201 | 215 | |
| ☐ VN-B204 | ATR 72-201 | 341 | |
| ☐ VN-B206 | ATR 72-212 | 419 | |
| ☐ VN-B208 | ATR 72-212 | 416 | |
| ☐ VN-B210 | ATR 72-212A | 678 | |
| ☐ VN-B212 | ATR 72-212A | 685 | |
| ☐ VN-B214 | ATR 72-212A | 688 | o/o |
| ☐ VN-B246 | ATR 72-202 | 523 | Lsf UKA |
| | | | |
| ☐ S7-ASA | Airbus A320-214 | 0590 | Lsf RGA |
| ☐ S7-ASB | Airbus A320-214 | 0594 | Lsf RGA |
| ☐ S7-ASC | Airbus A320-214 | 0601 | Lsf RGA |
| ☐ S7-ASD | Airbus A320-214 | 0605 | Lsf RGA |
| ☐ S7-ASE | Airbus A320-214 | 0607 | Lsf RGA |
| ☐ S7-ASF | Airbus A320-214 | 0611 | Lsf RGA |
| ☐ S7-ASG | Airbus A320-214 | 0617 | Lsf RGA |
| ☐ S7-ASH | Airbus A320-214 | 0619 | Lsf RGA |
| ☐ S7-ASI | Airbus A320-214 | 0648 | Lsf RGA |
| ☐ S7-ASJ | Airbus A320-214 | 0650 | Lsf RGA |
| ☐ VN-A342 | Airbus A321-131 | 0591 | Lsf RGA |
| ☐ VN-A346 | Airbus A321-131 | 0597 | Lsf RGA |

| | | | |
|---|---|---|---|
| ☐ VN-A761 | Boeing 767-33AER | 780/27477 | |
| ☐ VN-A762 | Boeing 767-324ER | 568/27392 | |
| ☐ VN-A763 | Boeing 767-352ER | 575/26261 | |
| ☐ VN-A764 | Boeing 767-324ER | 571/27393 | |
| ☐ VN-A765 | Boeing 767-324ER | 593/27568 | |
| ☐ VN-A766 | Boeing 767-33AER | 591/27909 | |
| ☐ VN-A768 | Boeing 767-33AER | 545/27310 | |
| ☐ VN-A769 | Boeing 767-352ER | 583/26262 | |
| | | | |
| ☐ VN-A502 | Fokker 70 | 11580 | VIP |
| ☐ VN-A504 | Fokker 70 | 11585 | VIP |
| ☐ VN-A141 | Boeing 777-2Q8ER | 28688 | o/o |
| ☐ VN-A142 | Boeing 777-2Q8ER | 32701 | o/o |
| ☐ VN- | Boeing 777-200ER | | o/o |
| ☐ VN- | Boeing 777-200ER | | o/o |

## VP-C - CAYMAN ISLANDS

### CAYMAN AIRWAYS                                      CAY

| | | |
|---|---|---|
| ☐ VP-CAL | Boeing 737-205 | 616/22022 |
| ☐ VP-CKX | Boeing 737-236 | 1056/23162 |
| ☐ VP-CYB | Boeing 737-2S2C | 608/21929 |

## VT - INDIA

### AIR INDIA                                            AIC

| | | |
|---|---|---|
| ☐ VT-EJG | Airbus A310-304 | 406 |
| ☐ VT-EJH | Airbus A310-304 | 407 |
| ☐ VT-EJI | Airbus A310-304 | 413 |
| ☐ VT-EJJ | Airbus A310-304 | 428 |
| ☐ VT-EJK | Airbus A310-304 | 429 |
| ☐ VT-EJL | Airbus A310-304 | 392 |
| ☐ VT-EQS | Airbus A310-304 | 538 |
| ☐ VT-EQT | Airbus A310-304 | 544 |
| ☐ VT-EVE | Airbus A310-324 | 501 |
| ☐ VT-EVF | Airbus A310-324 | 548 |
| ☐ VT-EVG | Airbus A310-304 | 447 |
| ☐ VT-EVH | Airbus A310-304 | 481 |
| ☐ VT-EVU | Airbus A310-304 | 519 |
| ☐ VT-EVV | Airbus A310-324 | 634 |
| ☐ VT-EVY | Airbus A310-324 | 589 |
| ☐ VT- | Airbus A310-324 | 598 |
| ☐ VT- | Airbus A310-324 | 695 |
| | | |
| ☐ VT-EFU | Boeing 747-237B | 390/21829 |
| ☐ VT-EGA | Boeing 747-237B | 414/21993 |
| ☐ VT-EGB | Boeing 747-237B | 431/21994 |
| ☐ VT-EGC | Boeing 747-237B | 434/21995 |
| ☐ VT-EPW | Boeing 747-337M | 711/24159 |
| ☐ VT-EPX | Boeing 747-337M | 719/24160 |
| ☐ VT-ESM | Boeing 747-437 | 987/27078 |
| ☐ VT-ESN | Boeing 747-437 | 1003/27164 |
| ☐ VT-ESO | Boeing 747-437 | 1009/27165 |
| ☐ VT-ESP | Boeing 747-437 | 1034/27214 |
| ☐ VT-EVA | Boeing 747-437 | 1089/28094 |
| ☐ VT-EVB | Boeing 747-437 | 1093/28095 |
| ☐ VT-EVJ | Boeing 747-4B5 | 739/24199 | Lsf KAL |

### AIR SAHARA

| | | |
|---|---|---|
| ☐ VT-SID | Boeing 737-4Q8 | 1971/24705 |
| ☐ VT-SIF | Boeing 737-2K9 | 709/22416 |
| ☐ VT-SIG | Boeing 737-73A | 216/28497 |
| ☐ VT-SIJ | Boeing 737-81Q | 424/29049 |
| ☐ VT-SIK | Boeing 737-81Q | 444/29050 |
| ☐ VT-SIQ | Boeing 737-4Q8 | 1627/24234 |
| ☐ VT-SIR | Boeing 737-76Q | 1010/30279 |
| ☐ VT-SIS | Boeing 737-76Q | 1025/30280 |
| ☐ VT-SIU | Boeing 737-7K9 | 205/28090 |
| ☐ VT-SIV | Boeing 737-7K9 | 223/28091 |
| ☐ VT-SIW | Boeing 737-31S | 2925/29056 |
| ☐ VT-SIX | Boeing 737-31S | 2923/29055 |

### ALLIANCE AIR                                          LLR

| | | |
|---|---|---|
| ☐ VT-EGE | Boeing 737-2A8 | 679/22281 |
| ☐ VT-EGF | Boeing 737-2A8 | 681/22282 |
| ☐ VT-EGG | Boeing 737-2A8 | 689/22283 |
| ☐ VT-EGH | Boeing 737-2A8 | 739/22284 |
| ☐ VT-EGI | Boeing 737-2A8 | 798/22285 |
| ☐ VT-EGJ | Boeing 737-2A8 | 799/22286 |
| ☐ VT-EGM | Boeing 737-2A8C | 747/22473 |
| ☐ VT-EHE | Boeing 737-2A8 | 899/22860 |
| ☐ VT-EHF | Boeing 737-2A8 | 902/22861 |
| ☐ VT-EHG | Boeing 737-2A8 | 903/22862 |
| ☐ VT-EHH | Boeing 737-2A8 | 907/22863 |

### BLUE DART AVIATION

| | | |
|---|---|---|
| ☐ VT-BDE | Boeing 737-2A8F | 434/21163 |
| ☐ VT-BDF | Boeing 737-2A8F | 435/21164 |
| ☐ VT-BDG | Boeing 737-2K9F | 702/22415 |

### INDIAN AIRLINES                                       IAC

| | | |
|---|---|---|
| ☐ VT-EDW | Airbus A300B2-1C | 036 |
| ☐ VT-EDY | Airbus A300B2-1C | 059 |
| ☐ VT-EDZ | Airbus A300B2-1C | 060 |
| ☐ VT-EFV | Airbus A300B2-1C | 088 |
| ☐ VT-EFX | Airbus A300B2-1C | 113 |
| ☐ VT-EHC | Airbus A300B4-203 | 181 |
| ☐ VT-EHD | Airbus A300B4-203 | 182 |
| ☐ VT-ELW | Airbus A300B2-1C | 026 |
| ☐ VT-EVC | Airbus A300B4-203 | 262 |
| ☐ VT-EVD | Airbus A300B4-203 | 240 |
| | | |
| ☐ VT-EPB | Airbus A320-231 | 0045 |
| ☐ VT-EPC | Airbus A320-231 | 0046 |
| ☐ VT-EPD | Airbus A320-231 | 0047 |
| ☐ VT-EPE | Airbus A320-231 | 0048 |
| ☐ VT-EPF | Airbus A320-231 | 0049 |
| ☐ VT-EPG | Airbus A320-231 | 0050 |
| ☐ VT-EPH | Airbus A320-231 | 0051 |
| ☐ VT-EPI | Airbus A320-231 | 0056 |
| ☐ VT-EPJ | Airbus A320-231 | 0057 |
| ☐ VT-EPK | Airbus A320-231 | 0058 |
| ☐ VT-EPL | Airbus A320-231 | 0074 |
| ☐ VT-EPM | Airbus A320-231 | 0075 |
| ☐ VT-EPO | Airbus A320-231 | 0080 |
| ☐ VT-EPP | Airbus A320-231 | 0089 |
| ☐ VT-EPQ | Airbus A320-231 | 0090 |
| ☐ VT-EPR | Airbus A320-231 | 0095 |
| ☐ VT-EPS | Airbus A320-231 | 0096 |
| ☐ VT-EPT | Airbus A320-231 | 0097 |
| ☐ VT-ESA | Airbus A320-231 | 0396 |
| ☐ VT-ESB | Airbus A320-231 | 0398 |
| ☐ VT-ESC | Airbus A320-231 | 0416 |
| ☐ VT-ESD | Airbus A320-231 | 0423 |
| ☐ VT-ESE | Airbus A320-231 | 0431 |
| ☐ VT-ESF | Airbus A320-231 | 0432 |
| ☐ VT-ESG | Airbus A320-231 | 0451 |
| ☐ VT-ESH | Airbus A320-231 | 0469 |
| ☐ VT-ESI | Airbus A320-231 | 0486 |
| ☐ VT-ESJ | Airbus A320-231 | 0490 |
| ☐ VT-ESK | Airbus A320-231 | 0492 |
| ☐ VT-ESL | Airbus A320-231 | 0499 |
| ☐ VT-EVO | Airbus A320-231 | 0247 |
| ☐ VT-EVP | Airbus A320-231 | 0257 |
| ☐ VT-EVQ | Airbus A320-231 | 0327 |
| ☐ VT-EVR | Airbus A320-231 | 0336 |
| ☐ VT-EVS | Airbus A320-231 | 0308 |
| ☐ VT-EVT | Airbus A320-231 | 0314 |

### JET AIRWAYS                                            JAI

| | | |
|---|---|---|
| ☐ VT-JCA | ATR 72-212A | 572 |
| ☐ VT-JCB | ATR 72-212A | 575 |
| ☐ VT-JCC | ATR 72-212A | 593 |
| ☐ VT-JCD | ATR 72-212A | 636 |
| ☐ VT-JCE | ATR 72-212A | 640 |
| ☐ VT-JCF | ATR 72-212A | 674 |
| ☐ VT-JCG | ATR 72-212A | 679 |
| ☐ VT-JCH | ATR 72-212A | 681 |

| | | | |
|---|---|---|---|
| ☐ VT-JAE | Boeing 737-4H6 | 2426/27086 | |
| ☐ VT-JAF | Boeing 737-4H6 | 2435/27168 | |
| ☐ VT-JAM | Boeing 737-48E | 2905/25773 | |
| ☐ VT-JAN | Boeing 737-48E | 2925/25775 | |
| ☐ VT-JAR | Boeing 737-45R | 2943/29032 | |
| ☐ VT-JAS | Boeing 737-45R | 2963/29033 | |
| ☐ VT-JAT | Boeing 737-45R | 3015/29034 | |
| ☐ VT-JAU | Boeing 737-45R | 3046/29035 | |
| ☐ VT-JGA | Boeing 737-85R | 1228/30410 | |
| ☐ VT-JGB | Boeing 737-85R | 30411 | |
| ☐ VT-JGC | Boeing 737-85R | 30410 | |
| ☐ VT-JGD | Boeing 737-95R | 33740 | |
| ☐ VT-JNA | Boeing 737-86N | 89/28578 | |
| ☐ VT-JNB | Boeing 737-86N | 91/28575 | |
| ☐ VT-JNC | Boeing 737-85R | 164/29036 | |
| ☐ VT-JND | Boeing 737-85R | 177/29037 | |
| ☐ VT-JNE | Boeing 737-71Q | 138/29043 | |
| ☐ VT-JNF | Boeing 737-71Q | 152/29044 | |
| ☐ VT-JNG | Boeing 737-71Q | 169/29045 | |
| ☐ VT-JNH | Boeing 737-71Q | 181/29046 | |
| ☐ VT-JNJ | Boeing 737-85R | 297/29038 | |
| ☐ VT-JNL | Boeing 737-85R | 326/29039 | |
| ☐ VT-JNM | Boeing 737-85R | 465/29040 | |
| ☐ VT-JNN | Boeing 737-85R | 489/29041 | |
| ☐ VT-JNP | Boeing 737-76N | 664/28630 | |
| ☐ VT-JNQ | Boeing 737-76N | 734/28635 | |
| ☐ VT-JNR | Boeing 737-85R | 749/30403 | |
| ☐ VT-JNS | Boeing 737-73A | 775/28498 | |
| ☐ VT-JNT | Boeing 737-76N | 417/28609 | |
| ☐ VT-JNU | Boeing 737-75R | 835/30404 | |
| ☐ VT-JNV | Boeing 737-75R | 927/30405 | |
| ☐ VT-JNW | Boeing 737-75R | 1016/30406 | |
| ☐ VT-JNX | Boeing 737-85R | 1073/30407 | |
| ☐ VT-JNY | Boeing 737-85R | 1146/30408 | |
| ☐ VT-JNZ | Boeing 737-85R | 1185/30409 | |

### VISAA AIRWAYS

| | | | |
|---|---|---|---|
| ☐ VT-VA | DHC-8Q-202 | 463 | o/o |
| ☐ VT-VA | DHC-8Q-202 | 536 | o/o |

## V2 - ANTIGUA

### CARIBBEAN STAR AIRWAYS — GFI

| | | |
|---|---|---|
| ☐ V2-LFF | DHC-8-314 | 410 |
| ☐ V2-LFG | DHC-8-106 | 268 |
| ☐ V2-LFH | DHC-8-106 | 253 |
| ☐ V2-LFI | DHC-8-106 | 317 |
| ☐ V2-LFJ | DHC-8-102 | 007 |
| ☐ V2-LFM | DHC-8-311A | 267 |
| ☐ V2-LFN | DHC-8-106 | 351 |
| ☐ V2-LFO | DHC-8-102 | 106 |
| ☐ V2-LFR | DHC-8-102A | 251 |
| ☐ V2-LFU | DHC-8-311 | 250 |
| ☐ V2- | DHC-8-102 | 141 |

### CBJ CARGO

| | | |
|---|---|---|
| ☐ V2-LFQ | L-1011-200F Tristar | 1212 |

### LIAT – THE CARIBBEAN AIRLINE — LIA

| | | |
|---|---|---|
| ☐ V2-LCY | DHC-8-110 | 035 |
| ☐ V2-LDP | DHC-8-102 | 140 |
| ☐ V2-LDQ | DHC-8-102 | 113 |
| ☐ V2-LDU | DHC-8-102A | 270 |
| ☐ V2-LEF | DHC-8-103 | 144 |
| ☐ V2-LES | DHC-8-311B | 412 |
| ☐ V2-LET | DHC-8-311B | 416 |
| ☐ V2-LEU | DHC-8-311 | 408 |
| ☐ V2-LFT | DHC-8-102 | 261 |
| ☐ V2-LFV | DHC-8-311A | 283 |
| ☐ V2-LFW | DHC-8-311A | 305 |
| ☐ V2-LFX | DHC-8-311A | 315 |

## V5 - NAMIBIA

### AIR NAMIBIA — NMB

| | | | |
|---|---|---|---|
| ☐ V5-ANA | Boeing 737-25A | 1422/23790 | Lsf SFR |
| ☐ V5-CAN | CASA CN.235-10 | 12-C007 | |
| ☐ V5-NMA | Boeing 747-48EM | 1131/28551 | std |
| ☐ ZS-JAV | F-28 Fellowship 4000 | 11183 | Lsf AQU |
| ☐ ZS-OGE | CASA CN.235-10 | C010 | Lsf SFR |

## V8 - BRUNEI DARUSSALAM

### ROYAL BRUNEI AIRLINES — RBA

| | | | |
|---|---|---|---|
| ☐ V8-RBF | Boeing 767-33AER | 414/25530 | |
| ☐ V8-RBG | Boeing 767-33AER | 442/25532 | |
| ☐ V8-RBH | Boeing 767-33AER | 477/25534 | |
| ☐ V8-RBJ | Boeing 767-33AER | 454/25533 | |
| ☐ V8-RBK | Boeing 767-33AER | 504/25536 | |
| ☐ V8-RBL | Boeing 767-33AER | 521/27189 | |
| ☐ V8-RBM | Boeing 767-328ER | 586/27428 | |
| ☐ V8-RBN | Boeing 767-328ER | 579/27427 | |
| | | | |
| ☐ V8-RBA | Boeing 757-2M6 | 94/23452 | |
| ☐ V8-RBB | Boeing 757-2M6 | 100/23453 | Lst HRH |
| | | | |
| ☐ V8- | Airbus A319-132 | 2023 | o/o |
| ☐ V8- | Airbus A319-132 | | o/o |

## XA - MEXICO

### AEROCALIFORNIA — SER

| | | |
|---|---|---|
| ☐ XA-ACZ | Douglas DC-9-32 | 619/47514 |
| ☐ XA-ADA | Douglas DC-9-32 | 926/48112 |
| ☐ XA-ADK | Douglas DC-9-31 | 214/47131 |
| ☐ XA-AGS | Douglas DC-9-15 | 90/45786 |
| ☐ XA-BCS | Douglas DC-9-14 | 88/47043 |
| ☐ XA-CSL | Douglas DC-9-14 | 29/45743 |
| ☐ XA-GDL | Douglas DC-9-15 | 139/47085 |
| ☐ XA-LAC | Douglas DC-9-15 | 405/47126 |
| ☐ XA-LMM | Douglas DC-9-14 | 45/45736 |
| ☐ XA-RKT | Douglas DC-9-15 | 224/47122 |
| ☐ XA-RNQ | Douglas DC-9-15 | 125/47059 |
| ☐ XA-RRY | Douglas DC-9-15 | 64/45785 |
| ☐ XA-RXG | Douglas DC-9-14 | 7/45714 |
| ☐ XA-SWG | Douglas DC-9-32 | 395/47230 |
| ☐ XA-SWH | Douglas DC-9-32 | 450/47236 |
| ☐ XA-SYD | Douglas DC-9-32 | 397/47283 |
| ☐ XA-SYQ | Douglas DC-9-14 | 15/45702 |
| ☐ XA-TAF | Douglas DC-9-32 | 154/47039 |
| ☐ XA-TBQ | Douglas DC-9-32 | 642/47553 |
| ☐ XA-THB | Douglas DC-9-32 | 761/47648 |
| ☐ XA-THC | Douglas DC-9-32 | 772/47666 |
| ☐ XA-TNT | Douglas DC-9-32 | 930/48113 |

### AEROCARIBE — CBE

| | | |
|---|---|---|
| ☐ XA-ABQ | Douglas DC-9-31 | 943/48119 |
| ☐ XA-ABR | Douglas DC-9-31 | 949/48120 |
| ☐ XA-ABS | Douglas DC-9-31 | 942/48118 |
| ☐ XA-ABT | Douglas DC-9-31 | 1030/48141 |
| ☐ XA-AEB | Douglas DC-9-31 | 1048/48147 |
| ☐ XA-AEC | Douglas DC-9-31 | 1050/48155 |
| ☐ XA-SSW | Douglas DC-9-14 | 25/45735 |
| ☐ XA-SVZ | Douglas DC-9-15 | 388/47125 |
| ☐ XA-TVB | Douglas DC-9-31 | 1042/48145 |
| ☐ XA-TVC | Douglas DC-9-31 | 1044/48146 |

### AEROLINEAS INTERNACIONALES — LNT

| | | |
|---|---|---|
| ☐ XA-AAD | Boeing 727-223 | 1185/20991 |
| ☐ XA-AFB | Boeing 727-232 | 1164/21149 |
| ☐ XA-AFC | Boeing 727-225F | 831/20383 | std |
| ☐ XA-SKC | Boeing 727-23 | 265/19181 |

| | | | |
|---|---|---|---|
| ☐ XA-SNW | Boeing 727-23 | 140/18450 | |
| ☐ XA-SPU | Boeing 727-223 | 699/20181 | |
| ☐ XA-TPV | Boeing 727-223 | 657/19493 | |
| ☐ XA-TQT | Boeing 727-223 | 730/20188 | |

## AEROLITORAL · SLI

| | | | |
|---|---|---|---|
| ☐ XA-AAO | SAAB SF.340B | 164 | Lsf CRX |
| ☐ XA-ACB | SAAB SF.340B | 179 | |
| ☐ XA-ACK | SAAB SF.340B | 183 | |
| ☐ XA-ACR | SAAB SF.340B | 186 | |
| ☐ XA-ADH | SAAB SF.340B | 178 | |
| ☐ XA-ADY | SAAB SF.340B | 363 | |
| ☐ XA-AEM | SAAB SF.340B | 161 | Lsf CRX |
| ☐ XA-AFR | SAAB SF.340B | 176 | Lsf CRX |
| ☐ XA-ASM | SAAB SF.340B | 197 | |
| ☐ XA-CGO | SAAB SF.340B | 270 | |
| ☐ XA-TJI | SAAB SF.340B | 188 | |
| ☐ XA-TJR | SAAB SF.340B | 226 | |
| ☐ XA-TKA | SAAB SF.340B | 288 | |
| ☐ XA-TKL | SAAB SF.340B | 217 | |
| ☐ XA-TKT | SAAB SF.340B | 189 | |
| ☐ XA-TQO | SAAB SF.340B | 251 | |
| ☐ XA-TQX | SAAB SF.340B | 321 | |
| ☐ XA-TTW | SAAB SF.340B | 255 | |
| ☐ XA-TUB | SAAB SF.340B | 248 | |
| ☐ XA-TUC | SAAB SF.340B | 196 | |
| ☐ XA-TUM | SAAB SF.340B | 246 | |
| ☐ XA-TUN | SAAB SF.340B | 187 | |
| ☐ XA-TUQ | SAAB SF.340B | 190 | |
| ☐ XA- | SAAB SF.340B | 196 | |

## AEROMAR AIRLINES · TAO

| | | | |
|---|---|---|---|
| ☐ F-GPYM | ATR 42-500 | 520 | Lsf LIT |
| ☐ XA-RNP | ATR 42-320 | 213 | |
| ☐ XA-RXC | ATR 42-320 | 257 | |
| ☐ XA-SJJ | ATR 42-320 | 039 | |
| ☐ XA-SYH | ATR 42-320 | 062 | |
| ☐ XA-TAH | ATR 42-500 | 471 | |
| ☐ XA-TAI | ATR 42-500 | 474 | |
| ☐ XA-TIC | ATR 42-320 | 058 | |
| ☐ XA-TKJ | ATR 42-500 | 561 | |
| ☐ XA-TLN | ATR 42-500 | 564 | |
| ☐ XA-TPR | ATR 42-500 | 586 | |
| ☐ XA-TPS | ATR 42-500 | 594 | |
| ☐ XA-TRI | ATR 42-500 | 607 | |
| ☐ XA-TRJ | ATR 42-500 | 608 | |

## AEROMEXICO · AMX

| | | | |
|---|---|---|---|
| ☐ | Boeing 737-700 | o/o | |
| ☐ | Boeing 737-700 | o/o | |
| ☐ | Boeing 737-700 | o/o | |
| ☐ | Boeing 737-700 | o/o F | |
| | | | |
| ☐ N301AM | Boeing 757-2Q8 | 957/30045 | |
| ☐ N801AM | Boeing 757-2Q8 | 541/25624 | |
| ☐ N802AM | Boeing 757-2Q8 | 558/26270 | |
| ☐ N803AM | Boeing 757-2Q8 | 590/26268 | |
| ☐ N804AM | Boeing 757-2Q8 | 592/26271 | |
| ☐ N805AM | Boeing 757-2Q8 | 594/26272 | |
| ☐ N806AM | Boeing 757-2Q8 | 597/26273 | |
| ☐ XA-TQU | Boeing 757-29J | 588/27203 | |
| | | | |
| ☐ XA-APB | Boeing 767-3Q8ER | 727/27618 | |
| ☐ XA-JBC | Boeing 767-284ER | 307/24762 | |
| ☐ XA-RVZ | Boeing 767-284ER | 297/24716 | |
| ☐ XA-TNS | Boeing 767-283ER | 305/24728 | |
| ☐ XA-TOJ | Boeing 767-283ER | 301/24727 | |
| | | | |
| ☐ N1003P | Douglas DC-9-32 | 1014/48150 | |
| ☐ XA-AMA | Douglas DC-9-32 | 947/48125 | |
| ☐ XA-AMB | Douglas DC-9-32 | 951/48126 | |
| ☐ XA-AMC | Douglas DC-9-32 | 961/48127 | |
| ☐ XA-AMD | Douglas DC-9-32 | 964/48128 | |
| ☐ XA-AME | Douglas DC-9-32 | 968/48129 | |

| | | | |
|---|---|---|---|
| ☐ XA-DEI | Douglas DC-9-32 | 771/47650 | |
| ☐ XA-DEK | Douglas DC-9-32 | 718/47602 | |
| ☐ XA-DEL | Douglas DC-9-32 | 721/47607 | |
| ☐ XA-DEM | Douglas DC-9-32 | 723/47609 | |
| ☐ XA-JEB | Douglas DC-9-32 | 458/47394 | |
| ☐ XA-JEC | Douglas DC-9-32 | 235/47106 | |
| ☐ XA-SDF | Douglas DC-9-32 | 99/47006 | |
| ☐ XA-TFO | Douglas DC-9-32 | 1017/48151 | |
| | | | |
| ☐ EI-BTX | McDD MD-82 | 1445/49660 | |
| ☐ EI-BTY | McDD MD-82 | 1466/49667 | |
| ☐ N158PL | McDD MD-88 | 1623/49761 | |
| ☐ N160PL | McDD MD-88 | 1626/49763 | |
| ☐ N161PL | McDD MD-88 | 1632/49764 | |
| ☐ N162PL | McDD MD-88 | 1645/49765 | |
| ☐ N168PL | McDD MD-88 | 1854/53174 | |
| ☐ N169PL | McDD MD-88 | 1868/53175 | |
| ☐ N204AM | McDD MD-87 | 1430/49404 | |
| ☐ N205AM | McDD MD-87 | 1525/49405 | |
| ☐ N214AM | McDD MD-87 | 1457/49585 | |
| ☐ N216AM | McDD MD-87 | 1472/49586 | |
| ☐ N491SH | McDD MD-82 | 1087/49150 | |
| ☐ N501AM | McDD MD-82 | 1172/49188 | |
| ☐ N505MD | McDD MD-82 | 1086/49149 | |
| ☐ N583MD | McDD MD-83 | 1438/49659 | |
| ☐ N753RA | McDD MD-87 | 1541/49587 | |
| ☐ N755RA | McDD MD-87 | 1621/49727 | |
| ☐ N803ML | McDD MD-87 | 1610/49726 | |
| ☐ N831LF | McDD MD-83 | 1704/53050 | |
| ☐ N838AM | McDD MD-83 | 1331/49397 | |
| ☐ N861LF | McDD MD-83 | 1578/49826 | |
| ☐ N881LF | McDD MD-83 | 1718/53051 | |
| ☐ N944AM | McDD MD-82 | 1304/49440 | |
| ☐ N945AS | McDD MD-83 | 1423/49643 | |
| ☐ N946AS | McDD MD-83 | 1461/49658 | |
| ☐ N957AS | McDD MD-82 | 1080/49126 | |
| ☐ N1003X | McDD MD-82 | 1028/48067 | |
| ☐ N1003Y | McDD MD-82 | 1031/48068 | |
| ☐ N1075T | McDD MD-87 | 1549/49724 | |
| ☐ XA-AMQ | McDD MD-82 | 1180/49190 | |
| ☐ XA-AMS | McDD MD-88 | 1715/49926 | |
| ☐ XA-AMT | McDD MD-88 | 1716/49927 | |
| ☐ XA-AMU | McDD MD-88 | 1732/49928 | |
| ☐ XA-AMV | McDD MD-88 | 1741/49929 | |
| ☐ XA-MRM | McDD MD-82 | 1938/53066 | |
| ☐ XA-SFO | McDD MD-87 | 1508/49673 | |
| ☐ XA-SHJ | McDD MD-87 | 1670/49779 | |
| ☐ XA-SWW | McDD MD-87 | 1592/49848 | |
| ☐ XA-SXJ | McDD MD-83 | 1573/49845 | |
| ☐ XA-TLH | McDD MD-83 | 1956/53119 | |
| ☐ XA-TPM | McDD MD-87 | 1463/49671 | |
| ☐ XA-TRD | McDD MD-82 | 1016/48079 | |
| ☐ XA-TWA | McDD MD-87 | 1674/49780 | |
| ☐ XA- | McDD MD-82 | 1088/49151 | |
| ☐ XA- | McDD MD-83 | 1630/49741 | |
| ☐ XA- | McDD MD-83 | 1680/49904 | |

## AEROMEXPRESS CARGO · MPX

| | | | |
|---|---|---|---|
| ☐ XA-SXL | Boeing 727-2K5F | 1553/21852 | |

## AEROUNION · TNO

| | | | |
|---|---|---|---|
| ☐ XA-TUE | Airbus A300B4-203F | 078 | |
| ☐ XA-TVU | Airbus A300B4-203F | 074 | |

## ALLEGRO AIR · GRO

| | | | |
|---|---|---|---|
| ☐ XA-AAQ | Boeing 727-231 | 1454/21628 | std |
| ☐ XA-ABL | Boeing 727-232 | 935/20640 | std |
| ☐ XA-ABM | Boeing 727-260 | 1520/21978 | std |
| ☐ XA-GRO | Boeing 727-231 | 1466/21634 | |
| ☐ XA-SXO | Boeing 727-247 | 764/20268 | std |
| ☐ XA-TLZ | Boeing 727-2B7 | 1735/22163 | |
| ☐ XA-TMA | Boeing 727-2B7 | 1743/22164 | |
| ☐ XA-TRR | Boeing 727-231 | 1456/21629 | |
| ☐ N102RK | Boeing 727-2A1 | 1320/21343 | |

| | | | |
|---|---|---|---|
| ☐ N118DF | Boeing 727-2A1 | 1322/21344 | |
| ☐ N369FA | Boeing 727-2K5 | 1551/21851 | |
| | | | |
| ☐ XA-TSW | McDD MD-83 | 1630/49741 | |
| ☐ XA-TTC | McDD MD-83 | 1680/49904 | |
| ☐ XA-TUP | McDD MD-82 | 1594/49877 | |
| ☐ XA-TWL | McDD MD-83 | 1380/49568 | |
| ☐ XA- | McDD MD-82 | 1071/49120 | |

## AVIACSA        CHP

| | | | |
|---|---|---|---|
| ☐ XA-SDR | Boeing 727-276 | 1056/20555 | |
| ☐ XA-SIE | Boeing 727-276 | 1661/22069 | |
| ☐ XA-SIJ | Boeing 727-276 | 1564/22017 | |
| ☐ XA-SJE | Boeing 727-276 | 1357/21479 | |
| ☐ XA-SJU | Boeing 727-276 | 906/20552 | std |
| ☐ XA-SLG | Boeing 727-276 | 1232/21171 | |
| ☐ XA-SLM | Boeing 727-276 | 1483/21696 | |
| ☐ XA-SMB | Boeing 727-276 | 1434/21646 | |
| ☐ XA-SXC | Boeing 727-225 | 902/20619 | std |
| ☐ XA-SXE | Boeing 727-225 | 898/20615 | |
| | | | |
| ☐ XA-ABC | Boeing 737-205 | 1245/23467 | |
| ☐ XA-NAF | Boeing 737-219 | 1186/23470 | |
| ☐ XA-NAK | Boeing 737-219 | 1199/23474 | |
| ☐ XA-NAV | Boeing 737-219 | 1194/23472 | |
| ☐ XA- | Boeing 737-219 | 1189/23471 | |
| ☐ XA- | Boeing 737-219 | 1197/23473 | o/o; std |
| ☐ XA- | Boeing 737-219 | 1203/23475 | |
| ☐ XA-SIW | Boeing 737-2T4 | 716/22370 | |
| ☐ XA-SIX | Boeing 737-2T4 | 717/22371 | |
| ☐ XA-TTM | Boeing 737-201 | 865/22753 | |
| ☐ XA-TTP | Boeing 737-201 | 963/22868 | |
| ☐ XA-TUK | Boeing 737-201 | 961/22867 | |
| ☐ XA-TVD | Boeing 737-201 | 889/22758 | |
| ☐ XA-TVL | Boeing 737-201 | 964/22869 | |
| ☐ XA-TVN | Boeing 737-201 | 845/22752 | |
| ☐ XA- | Boeing 737-2Q9 | 625/21976 | o/o |
| ☐ XA- | Boeing 737-201 | 606/21818 | o/o |
| ☐ XA- | Boeing 737-201 | 837/22445 | o/o |
| ☐ XA- | Boeing 737-201 | 940/22866 | o/o |
| | | | |
| ☐ XA-TBX | Douglas DC-9-14 | 13/45716 | std |
| ☐ XA-TGJ | Douglas DC-9-15 | 128/45783 | std |
| ☐ XA-TIM | Douglas DC-9-15 | 82/45778 | |
| ☐ XA-TIZ | Douglas DC-9-15 | 114/45782 | |
| ☐ XA-TJS | Douglas DC-9-15 | 140/45784 | |

## AZTEC AIRLINES        TED

| | | | |
|---|---|---|---|
| ☐ XA-AAU | Boeing 737-3K9 | 1623/24211 | |
| ☐ XA-AAV | Boeing 737-3K9 | 1796/24214 | |
| ☐ XA-AEP | Boeing 737-7EA | 859/32406 | |
| ☐ XA-AEQ | Boeing 737-7EA | 904/32407 | |
| ☐ XA- | Boeing 737-3K2 | 1198/23412 | |
| ☐ XA-TWF | Boeing 737-76N | 124/28577 | |

## ESTAFETA CARGA AEREA        ESF

| | | | |
|---|---|---|---|
| ☐ XA-ABX | Boeing 737-210C | 344/20917 | |
| ☐ XA-ACP | Boeing 737-2T4C | 989/23065 | |
| ☐ XA-TRW | Boeing 737-275C | 139/19743 | |

## MAGNICHARTERS        GMT

| | | | |
|---|---|---|---|
| ☐ XA-MAB | Boeing 737-2C3 | 406/21016 | |
| ☐ XA-MAC | Boeing 737-2C3 | 397/21014 | |
| ☐ XA-MAE | Boeing 737-277 | 789/22648 | |
| ☐ XA-MAF | Boeing 737-2K9 | 815/22505 | |
| ☐ XA-MAG | Boeing 737-205 | 440/21184 | |

## MAS AIR CARGO        MAA

| | | | |
|---|---|---|---|
| ☐ N314LA | Boeing 767-316ERF | 848/32573 | Lsf LCO |
| ☐ N871MY | Douglas DC-8-71F | 343/45970 | Lsf LCO |
| ☐ XA-MAY | Douglas DC-8-71F | 252/45810 | Lsf LCO |

## MEXICANA        MXA

| | | | |
|---|---|---|---|
| ☐ N62TY | Airbus A319-112 | 1625 | |
| ☐ N429MX | Airbus A319-112 | 1429 | |
| ☐ N588MX | Airbus A319-112 | 0588 | |
| ☐ N612MX | Airbus A319-112 | 1612 | |
| ☐ N618MX | Airbus A319-112 | 1618 | |
| ☐ N634MX | Airbus A319-112 | 1634 | |
| ☐ N706MX | Airbus A319-112 | 1706 | |
| ☐ N750MX | Airbus A319-112 | 1750 | |
| ☐ N866MX | Airbus A319-112 | 1866 | |
| ☐ N872MX | Airbus A319-112 | 1872 | |
| ☐ N882MX | Airbus A319-112 | 1882 | |
| ☐ N925MX | Airbus A319-112 | 1925 | |
| | | | |
| ☐ F-OHME | Airbus A320-231 | 0252 | |
| ☐ F-OHMF | Airbus A320-231 | 0259 | |
| ☐ F-OHMG | Airbus A320-231 | 0260 | |
| ☐ F-OHMH | Airbus A320-231 | 0261 | |
| ☐ F-OHMI | Airbus A320-231 | 0275 | |
| ☐ F-OHMJ | Airbus A320-231 | 0276 | |
| ☐ F-OHMK | Airbus A320-231 | 0296 | |
| ☐ F-OHML | Airbus A320-231 | 0320 | |
| ☐ F-OHMM | Airbus A320-231 | 0321 | |
| ☐ F-OHMN | Airbus A320-231 | 0353 | |
| ☐ N225RX | Airbus A320-231 | 0225 | |
| ☐ N280RX | Airbus A320-231 | 0280 | |
| ☐ N291MX | Airbus A320-231 | 0291 | |
| ☐ N292MX | Airbus A320-231 | 0292 | |
| ☐ N304ML | Airbus A320-231 | 0373 | |
| ☐ N332MX | Airbus A320-231 | 0332 | |
| ☐ N347TM | Airbus A320-231 | 0347 | |
| ☐ N361DA | Airbus A320-231 | 0361 | |
| ☐ N368MX | Airbus A320-231 | 0368 | |
| ☐ N369MX | Airbus A320-231 | 0369 | |
| ☐ N405MX | Airbus A320-231 | 0405 | |
| ☐ N415MX | Airbus A320-231 | 0415 | |
| ☐ N467RX | Airbus A320-231 | 0467 | |
| | | | |
| ☐ XA-HOH | Boeing 727-264 | 1379/21577 | |
| ☐ XA-HON | Boeing 727-264 | 1416/21617 | |
| ☐ XA-HOV | Boeing 727-264 | 1429/21637 | std |
| ☐ XA-HOX | Boeing 727-264 | 1457/21638 | |
| ☐ XA-IEU | Boeing 727-264 | 1497/21836 | |
| ☐ XA-MEB | Boeing 727-264 | 1545/21837 | |
| ☐ XA-MEC | Boeing 727-264 | 1547/21838 | |
| ☐ XA-MED | Boeing 727-264 | 1607/22156 | |
| ☐ XA-MEE | Boeing 727-264 | 1619/22157 | |
| ☐ XA-MEF | Boeing 727-264 | 1642/22158 | |
| ☐ XA-MEH | Boeing 727-264 | 1676/22409 | |
| ☐ XA-MEI | Boeing 727-264 | 1678/22410 | |
| ☐ XA-MEK | Boeing 727-264 | 1720/22412 | |
| ☐ XA-MEL | Boeing 727-264 | 1728/22413 | |
| | | | |
| ☐ N101LF | Boeing 757-2Q8 | 688/26332 | |
| ☐ N380RM | Boeing 757-2Q8 | 836/29380 | |
| ☐ N755MX | Boeing 757-2Q8 | 424/24964 | |
| ☐ N758MX | Boeing 757-2Q8 | 438/24965 | |
| ☐ N762MX | Boeing 757-2Q8 | 819/29442 | |
| ☐ N763MX | Boeing 757-2Q8 | 821/29443 | |
| ☐ N764MX | Boeing 757-2Q8 | 639/27351 | |
| ☐ N765MX | Boeing 757-2Q8 | 954/30044 | |
| ☐ XA-TRA | Boeing 757-230 | 267/24737 | |
| | | | |
| ☐ PH-JXW | Fokker 100 | 11390 | |
| ☐ PH-KXJ | Fokker 100 | 11400 | |
| ☐ PH-KXR | Fokker 100 | 11410 | |
| ☐ PH-LXG | Fokker 100 | 11420 | |
| ☐ XA-SGE | Fokker 100 | 11382 | |
| ☐ XA-SGF | Fokker 100 | 11384 | |
| ☐ XA-SHI | Fokker 100 | 11309 | |
| ☐ XA-SHJ | Fokker 100 | 11319 | |
| ☐ XA-TCG | Fokker 100 | 11374 | |
| ☐ XA-TCH | Fokker 100 | 11375 | |
| ☐ XA-TKP | Fokker 100 | 11266 | |
| ☐ XA-TKR | Fokker 100 | 11339 | |

## XT - BURKINA FASO

### AIR BURKINA

| | | | |
|---|---|---|---|
| ☐ XT-FZP | F-28 Fellowship 4000 | 11185 | |
| ☐ XT-TIB | F-28 Fellowship 2000 | 11108 | Lsf LIB |

### FASO AIRWAYS — FSW

| | | | |
|---|---|---|---|
| ☐ XT-FCB | Ilyushin Il-76TD | 1023408265 | std |

## XU - CAMBODIA

### IMTREC AVIATION CAMBODIA — IMT

| | | |
|---|---|---|
| ☐ XU-315 | Antonov An-12BP | |
| ☐ XU-365 | Yunshuji Y-8 | |

### KAMPUCHEA AIRWAYS — KMP

| | | |
|---|---|---|
| ☐ XU-100 | L-1011-1 Tristar 1 | 1156 |
| ☐ XU-122 | L-1011-1 Tristar 100 | 1221 |
| ☐ XU-200 | L-1011-1 Tristar 1 | 1200 |
| ☐ XU-300 | L-1011-1 Tristar 50 | 1129 |

### MEKONG AIR INTERNATIONAL — MKN

| | | |
|---|---|---|
| ☐ XU-735 | Boeing 737-524 | 2748/26319 |

### PRESIDENT AIRLINES — PSD

| | | | |
|---|---|---|---|
| ☐ B-16802 | Boeing 737-8Q8 | 739/28236 | Lsf MDA |
| ☐ XU-881 | F-27 Friendship 100 | 10168 | |
| ☐ XU-888 | F-28 Fellowship 1000 | 11012 | std |

### SIEM REAP AIR INTERNATIONAL — SRH

A wholly owned subsidiary of **Bangkok Air** and leases aircraft from parent as required – some wear joint titles

## XY - MYANMAR

### MYANMA AIRWAYS — UBA

| | | | |
|---|---|---|---|
| ☐ XY-ADT | F-27 Friendship 600 | 10523 | |
| ☐ XY-AEQ | F-27 Friendship 400 | 10294 | |
| ☐ XY-AEU | F-27 Friendship 600 | 10343 | |
| ☐ XY-AEV | F-27 Friendship 600 | 10347 | |
| ☐ XY-AEW | F-27 Friendship 600 | 10352 | |
| ☐ XY- | F-27 Friendship 600RF | 10569 | std |
| ☐ XY-ADU | F-28 Fellowship 1000 | 11019 | |
| ☐ XY-ADW | F-28 Fellowship 4000 | 11114 | |
| ☐ XY-AGA | F-28 Fellowship 4000 | 11232 | |
| ☐ XY-AGB | F-28 Fellowship 4000 | 11184 | |

### MYANMAR AIRWAYS INTERNATIONAL

| | | | |
|---|---|---|---|
| ☐ S7-RGM | Boeing 737-3Q8 | 1598/24299 | Lsf RGA |

## YA - AFGHANISTAN

### ARIANA AFGHAN AIRLINES — AFG

| | | | |
|---|---|---|---|
| ☐ YA-BAB | Airbus A300B4-203 | 180 | |
| ☐ YA-BAC | Airbus A300B4-203 | 190 | |
| ☐ YA-FAL | Boeing 727-200 | | |
| ☐ YA-FAM | Boeing 727-223 | 1255/21088 | |
| ☐ YA-FAS | Boeing 727-223 | 1345/21388 | |
| ☐ YA-FAY | Boeing 727-228 | 1719/22289 | |
| ☐ YA- | Airbus A300B4-203 | 177 | o/o |
| ☐ YA- | Boeing 747-238B | 310/21352 | |

## YI - IRAQ

### IRAQI AIRWAYS — IAW

| | | | |
|---|---|---|---|
| ☐ YI-AGK | Boeing 727-270 | 1186/21197 | std |
| ☐ YI-AGL | Boeing 727-270 | 1191/21198 | std |
| ☐ YI-AGM | Boeing 727-270 | 1203/21199 | std |
| ☐ YI-AGQ | Boeing 727-270 | 1647/22261 | std |
| ☐ YI-AGR | Boeing 727-270 | 1686/22262 | std |
| ☐ YI-AGS | Boeing 727-270 | 1809/22263 | std |
| ☐ YI-AOY | Boeing 727-200 | | |
| ☐ YI-AGE | Boeing 707-370C | 889/20889 | std |
| ☐ YI-AGG | Boeing 707-370C | 892/20891 | std |
| ☐ YI-AGN | Boeing 747-270C | 287/21180 | std |
| ☐ YI-AGO | Boeing 747-270C | 289/21181 | std T |
| ☐ YI-AGP | Boeing 747-270C | 565/22366 | std |
| ☐ YI-ALM | Boeing 747SP-70 | 567/22858 | std |
| ☐ YI-ALV | Ilyushin Il-76MD | 0033448409 | |
| ☐ YI- | Boeing 747SP-09 | 445/22298 | |

## YJ - VANUATU

### AIR VANUATU

| | | |
|---|---|---|
| ☐ YJ-AV18 | Boeing 737-3Q8 | 3016/28054 |

## YK - SYRIA

### SYRIANAIR — SYR

| | | |
|---|---|---|
| ☐ YK-AKA | Airbus A320-232 | 0886 |
| ☐ YK-AKB | Airbus A320-232 | 0918 |
| ☐ YK-AKC | Airbus A320-232 | 1032 |
| ☐ YK-AKD | Airbus A320-232 | 1076 |
| ☐ YK-AKE | Airbus A320-232 | 1085 |
| ☐ YK-AKF | Airbus A320-232 | 1117 |
| ☐ YK-AGA | Boeing 727-294 | 1188/21203 |
| ☐ YK-AGB | Boeing 727-294 | 1194/21204 |
| ☐ YK-AGC | Boeing 727-294 | 1198/21205 |
| ☐ YK-AGD | Boeing 727-269 | 1670/22360 |
| ☐ YK-AGE | Boeing 727-269 | 1716/22361 |
| ☐ YK-AGF | Boeing 727-269 | 1788/22763 |
| ☐ YK-AQA | Yakovlev Yak-40 | 9341932 |
| ☐ YK-AQB | Yakovlev Yak-40 | 9530443 |
| ☐ YK-AQD | Yakovlev Yak-40 | 9830158 |
| ☐ YK-AQE | Yakovlev Yak-40 | 9830258 |
| ☐ YK-AQF | Yakovlev Yak-40 | 9931859 |
| ☐ YK-AQG | Yakovlev Yak-40K | 9941959 |
| ☐ YK-AHA | Boeing 747SP-94 | 284/21174 |
| ☐ YK-AHB | Boeing 747SP-94 | 290/21175 |
| ☐ YK-ANA | Antonov An-24B | 87304203 |
| ☐ YK-ATA | Ilyushin Il-76M | 093421613 |
| ☐ YK-ATB | Ilyushin Il-76T | 093421619 |
| ☐ YK-ATC | Ilyushin Il-76M | 0013431911 |
| ☐ YK-ATD | Ilyushin Il-76M | 0013431915 |
| ☐ YK-AYE | Tupolev Tu-134B-3 | 66187 |

## YL - LATVIA

### AIR BALTIC — BTI

| | | | |
|---|---|---|---|
| ☐ YL-BAK | Avro RJ70 | E1223 | Lst DRK |
| ☑ YL-BAL | Avro RJ70 | E1224 | |
| ☐ YL-BAN | Avro RJ70 | E1225 | |
| ☐ YL-BAR | Fokker 50 | 20149 | |
| ☐ YL-BAS | Fokker 50 | 20162 | Lsf SAS |
| ☐ YL-BAT | Fokker 50 | 20163 | Lsf SAS |
| ☐ YL-BAU | Fokker 50 | 20126 | |

### CONCORS LATVIAN AIR SERVICE — COS

| | | |
|---|---|---|
| ☐ YL-KAE | LET L-410UVP-E | 790209 |
| ☐ YL-LAO | Ilyushin Il-18D | 2964017102 |

| | | | |
|---|---|---|---|
| ☐ YL-LBV | Yak-42D | 4520424116664 | |
| ☐ YL-LBZ | Yak-42D | 4540424116669 | |
| ☐ YL-LBY | Yak-42D | 4540424116677 | o/o |

### INVERSIJA — INV

| | | |
|---|---|---|
| ☐ YL-LAK | Ilyushin Il-76T | 0003424707 |
| ☐ YL-LAL | Ilyushin Il-76T | 0013433984 |

### LAT CHARTER — LTC

| | | |
|---|---|---|
| ☐ YL-LBE | Tupolev Tu-134B-3 | 63285 |
| ☐ YL-LBG | Tupolev Tu-134B-3 | 63333 |
| ☐ YL-LBT | Yak-42D | 4520424404018 |
| ☐ YL-LBU | Yak-42D | 4520423403018 |

### LATPASS AIRLINES — LTP

| | | |
|---|---|---|
| ☐ YL-LAB | Tupolev Tu-154B-2 | 81A-515 |

### RAF-AVIA — MTL

| | | | |
|---|---|---|---|
| ☐ YL-RAA | Antonov An-26B | 97311206 | DHL c/s |
| ☐ YL-RAB | Antonov An-26 | 07310508 | DHL c/s |
| ☐ YL-RAC | Antonov An-26 | 07309903 | DHL c/s |
| ☐ YL-RAD | Antonov An-26B | 47313909 | DHL c/s |
| ☐ YL-RAF | An-74TK | 36547095905 | Lsf CBI |

# YR - ROMANIA

### CARPATAIR — KRP

| | | | |
|---|---|---|---|
| ☐ YR-VGA | Yakovlev Yak-40 | 9810757 | |
| ☐ YR-VGM | SAAB SF.340B | 208 | Lsf CRX |
| ☐ YR-VGN | SAAB SF.340B | 200 | Lsf CRX |
| ☐ YR-VGO | SAAB SF.340B | 215 | Lsf CRX |
| ☐ YR-VGP | SAAB SF.340B | 228 | Lsf CRX |

### ION TIRIAC AIR — TIH

| | | | |
|---|---|---|---|
| ☐ YR-ITA | Antonov An-26 | 6407 | DHL c/s |

### ROMAVIA — RMV

| | | | |
|---|---|---|---|
| ☐ YR-ABB | Boeing 707-3K1C | 883/20804 | |
| ☐ YR-BRC | BAC One-Eleven 561RC | 403 | |
| ☐ YR-BRE | BAC One-Eleven 561RC | 405 | Govt |
| ☐ YR-BRH | BAC One-Eleven 561RC | 408 | Lst PFO |
| ☐ YR-BRI | BAC One-Eleven 561RC | 409 | Lst PFO |
| ☐ YR-IMM | Ilyushin Il-18D | 187009904 | |
| ☐ YR-IMZ | Ilyushin Il-18GrM | 187009802 | Lst EXV |

### TAROM — ROT

| | | | |
|---|---|---|---|
| ☐ YR-ATA | ATR 42-500 | 566 | |
| ☐ YR-ATB | ATR 42-500 | 569 | |
| ☐ YR-ATC | ATR 42-500 | 589 | |
| ☐ YR-ATD | ATR 42-500 | 591 | |
| ☐ YR-ATE | ATR 42-500 | 596 | |
| ☐ YR-ATF | ATR 42-500 | 599 | |
| ☐ YR-ATG | ATR 42-500 | 605 | |
| ☐ YR-BGA | Boeing 737-38J | 2524/27179 | |
| ☐ YR-BGB | Boeing 737-38J | 2529/27180 | |
| ☐ YR-BGC | Boeing 737-38J | 2662/27181 | |
| ☐ YR-BGD | Boeing 737-38J | 2663/27182 | |
| ☐ YR-BGE | Boeing 737-38J | 2671/27395 | |
| ☐ YR-BGF | Boeing 737-78J | 795/28440 | |
| ☐ YR-BGG | Boeing 737-78J | 827/28442 | |
| ☐ YR- | Boeing 737-78J | | |
| ☐ YR- | Boeing 737-78J | | |
| ☐ YR-BGY | Boeing 737-36M | 2809/28332 | |
| ☐ YR-ABA | Boeing 707-3K1C | 878/20803 | |
| ☐ YR-LCA | Airbus A310-325 | 636 | |
| ☐ YR-LCB | Airbus A310-325 | 644 | |

# YS - EL SALVADOR

### TACA INTERNATIONAL AIRLINES — TAI

| | | | |
|---|---|---|---|
| ☐ N59106 | Airbus A300B4-203F | 106 | std |
| ☐ N59107 | Airbus A300B4-203F | 107 | |
| ☐ N59139 | Airbus A300B4-203F | 139 | std |
| ☐ N59140 | Airbus A300B4-203F | 140 | |
| ☐ N68142 | Airbus A300B4-203F | 142 | |
| ☐ N471TA | Airbus A319-132 | 1066 | Lst PTU |
| ☐ N472TA | Airbus A319-132 | 1113 | Lst PTU |
| ☐ N473TA | Airbus A319-132 | 1140 | Lst PTU |
| ☐ N474TA | Airbus A319-132 | 1159 | Lst PTU |
| ☐ N475TA | Airbus A319-132 | 1575 | |
| ☐ N | Airbus A319-132 | | o/o |
| ☐ EI-TAA | Airbus A320-233 | 0912 | Lsto CUB |
| ☐ EI-TAB | Airbus A320-233 | 1624 | |
| ☐ EI-TAC | Airbus A320-233 | 1676 | |
| ☐ EI-TAI | Airbus A320-233 | 0916 | |
| ☐ N340LA | Airbus A320-232 | 0425 | Lst LRC |
| ☐ N451TA | Airbus A320-233 | 0733 | |
| ☐ N452TA | Airbus A320-233 | 0741 | |
| ☐ N453TA | Airbus A320-233 | 0747 | |
| ☐ N454TA | Airbus A320-233 | 0789 | |
| ☐ N455TA | Airbus A320-233 | 0874 | |
| ☐ N457TA | Airbus A320-233 | 0902 | |
| ☐ N460TA | Airbus A320-233 | 1007 | |
| ☐ N461TA | Airbus A320-233 | 1300 | |
| ☐ N462TA | Airbus A320-233 | 1334 | |
| ☐ N463TA | Airbus A320-233 | 1339 | |
| ☐ N464TA | Airbus A320-233 | 1353 | Lst CUB |
| ☐ N465TA | Airbus A320-233 | 1374 | Lst CUB |
| ☐ N470TA | Airbus A320-233 | 1400 | |
| ☐ 481TA | Airbus A320-233 | 1500 | Lst LRC |
| ☐ N482TA | Airbus A320-233 | 1482 | Lst LRC |
| ☐ N483TA | Airbus A320-214 | 1509 | |
| ☐ N484TA | Airbus A320-233 | 1523 | |
| ☐ N486TA | Airbus A320-233 | 1730 | |
| ☐ N941LF | Airbus A320-233 | 0461 | Lst LRC |
| ☐ N981LR | Airbus A320-233 | 0558 | Lst TAI |
| ☐ N991LR | Airbus A320-233 | 0561 | Lst TAI |
| ☐ N | Airbus A320-233 | 1799 | o/o |
| ☐ N | Airbus A320-233 | 1804 | o/o |
| ☐ N | Airbus A320-233 | 1827 | o/o |
| ☐ N | Airbus A320-233 | 1814 | o/o |
| ☐ N231TA | Boeing 737-2K5 | 763/22596 | |
| ☐ N232TA | Boeing 737-296 | 675/22277 | |
| ☐ N233TA | Boeing 737-2K5 | 833/22601 | Lst OCA |
| ☐ N235TA | Boeing 737-205 | 595/21765 | Lst LRC |
| ☐ N238TA | Boeing 737-242 | 630/22075 | Lst LRC |
| ☐ N240TA | Boeing 737-205 | 572/21729 | Lst OCA |
| ☐ N251LF | Boeing 737-2L9 | 705/22408 | Lst LRC |
| ☐ N261LR | Boeing 737-230 | 744/22402 | Lst LRC |
| ☐ N281LF | Boeing 737-2L9 | 620/22071 | Lst LRC |
| ☐ N371TA | Boeing 737-3S1 | 1896/24834 | Lst VRG |

# YU - SERBIA & MONTENEGRO

### AVIOGENEX — AGX

| | | |
|---|---|---|
| ☐ YU-AKD | Boeing 727-2L8 | 1142/21040 |
| ☐ YU-AKH | Boeing 727-2L8 | 1146/21080 |
| ☐ YU-AKM | Boeing 727-243 | 1814/22702 |
| ☐ YU-ANP | Boeing 737-2K3 | 1401/23912 |

### JAT – YUGOSLAV AIRLINES — JAT

| | | | |
|---|---|---|---|
| ☐ YU-AKB | Boeing 727-2H9 | 1045/20931 | std |
| ☐ YU-AKE | Boeing 727-2H9 | 1094/21037 | std |
| ☐ YU-AKF | Boeing 727-2H9 | 1118/21038 | std |
| ☐ YU-AKG | Boeing 727-2H9 | 1119/21039 | std |
| ☐ YU-AKI | Boeing 727-2H9 | 1681/22393 | |
| ☐ YU-AKJ | Boeing 727-2H9 | 1691/22394 | std |

| ☐ YU-AKK | Boeing 727-2H9 | 1786/22665 | Lst UKM |
| ☐ YU-AKL | Boeing 727-2H9 | 1790/22666 | |

| ☐ YU-AND | Boeing 737-3H9 | 1134/23329 | |
| ☐ YU-ANF | Boeing 737-3H9 | 1136/23330 | |
| ☐ YU-ANH | Boeing 737-3H9 | 1171/23415 | |
| ☐ YU-ANI | Boeing 737-3H9 | 1175/23416 | Lst MAK |
| ☐ YU-ANJ | Boeing 737-3H9 | 1305/23714 | |
| ☐ YU-ANK | Boeing 737-3H9 | 1310/23715 | |
| ☐ YU-ANL | Boeing 737-3H9 | 1321/23716 | Lst MAK |
| ☐ YU-ANV | Boeing 737-3H9 | 1524/24140 | |
| ☐ YU-ANW | Boeing 737-3H9 | 1526/24141 | Lst MAK |
| ☐ YU-AON | Boeing 737-3Q4 | 1490/24208 | |
| ☐ EI-CXH | Boeing 737-4Q8 | 1665/24070 | Lsf ADH |
| ☐ | Boeing 737-400 | | Lsf ADH |

| ☐ YU-AHN | Douglas DC-9-32 | 591/47470 | std |
| ☐ YU-AHU | Douglas DC-9-32 | 626/47532 | std |
| ☐ YU-AHV | Douglas DC-9-32 | 627/47460 | std |
| ☐ YU-AJH | Douglas DC-9-32 | 685/47562 | std |
| ☐ YU-AJI | Douglas DC-9-32 | 687/47563 | Lst OSL |
| ☐ YU-AJJ | Douglas DC-9-32 | 688/47567 | |
| ☐ YU-AJK | Douglas DC-9-32 | 689/47568 | Lst BLV |
| ☐ YU-AJL | Douglas DC-9-32 | 695/47571 | |
| ☐ YU-AJM | Douglas DC-9-32 | 701/47582 | Lst BLV |

| ☐ YU-ALN | ATR 72-201 | 180 | |
| ☐ YU-ALO | ATR 72-201 | 186 | |
| ☐ YU-ALP | ATR 72-201 | 189 | Lst SBK |
| ☐ YU-AMB | Douglas DC-10-30 | 278/46988 | elgrade |

### MONTENEGRO AIRLINES — MGX

| ☐ YU-AOJ | F-28 Fellowship 2000 | 11184 |
| ☐ YU-AOK | Fokker 100 | 11272 |
| ☐ YU-AOL | Fokker 100 | 11268 |
| ☐ YU-AOM | Fokker 100 | 11321 |

### PELIKAN BLUE LINE — PBL

| ☐ YU-BXX | LET L-410UVP-E | 902422 | Lst MGX |
| ☐ YU-BYY | LET L-410UVP-E | 892316 | |

## YV - VENEZUELA

### AEROPOSTAL — LAV

| ☐ YV-10C | Douglas DC-9-51 | 820/47713 | |
| ☐ YV-11C | Douglas DC-9-21 | 462/47306 | |
| ☐ YV-12C | Douglas DC-9-21 | 475/47360 | |
| ☐ YV-13C | Douglas DC-9-21 | 382/47301 | |
| ☐ YV-14C | Douglas DC-9-51 | 830/47738 | Lsf FIN |
| ☐ YV-15C | Douglas DC-9-51 | 883/47771 | Lsf FIN |
| ☐ YV-20C | Douglas DC-9-51 | 842/47705 | |
| ☐ YV-21C | Douglas DC-9-51 | 845/47719 | |
| ☐ YV-22C | Douglas DC-9-51 | 841/47703 | |
| ☐ YV-24C | Douglas DC-9-32 | 848/47727 | |
| ☐ YV-25C | Douglas DC-9-32 | 847/47721 | |
| ☐ YV-32C | Douglas DC-9-51 | 892/47770 | |
| ☐ YV-33C | Douglas DC-9-51 | 893/47782 | |
| ☐ YV-35C | Douglas DC-9-51 | 815/47712 | |
| ☐ YV-37C | Douglas DC-9-34CF | 872/47752 | |
| ☐ YV-42C | Douglas DC-9-51 | 783/47656 | |
| ☐ YV-43C | Douglas DC-9-51 | 805/47694 | |
| ☐ YV-44C | Douglas DC-9-51 | 806/47695 | |
| ☐ YV-46C | Douglas DC-9-32 | 610/47535 | |
| ☐ YV-47C | Douglas DC-9-32 | 560/47490 | |
| ☐ YV-48C | Douglas DC-9-32 | 394/45847 | |
| ☐ YV-49C | Douglas DC-9-32 | 637/47539 | |

| ☐ YV-18C | Boeing 727-231 | 1574/21984 | |
| ☐ YV-40C | Boeing 727-231 | 1462/21632 | |
| ☐ YV-41C | Boeing 727-231 | 1565/21968 | |
| ☐ N64346 | Boeing 727-231 | 1464/21633 | Lsf FAO |
| ☐ N79749 | Boeing 727-224 | 1767/22451 | Lsf FAO |
| ☐ N79750 | Boeing 727-224 | 1772/22452 | Lsf FAO |

### ASERCA AIRLINES — OCA

| ☐ YV-703C | Douglas DC-9-15 | 59/45798 |
| ☐ YV-705C | Douglas DC-9-31 | 283/45867 |
| ☐ YV-706C | Douglas DC-9-31 | 365/45875 |
| ☐ YV-707C | Douglas DC-9-31 | 390/47272 |
| ☐ YV-708C | Douglas DC-9-31 | 130/45864 |
| ☐ YV-709C | Douglas DC-9-31 | 151/47005 |
| ☐ YV-710C | Douglas DC-9-31 | 389/47271 |
| ☐ YV-714C | Douglas DC-9-31 | 87/47007 |
| ☐ YV-718C | Douglas DC-9-31 | 282/47187 |
| ☐ YV-719C | Douglas DC-9-31 | 322/47157 |
| ☐ YV-720C | Douglas DC-9-31 | 103/45837 |

| ☐ N233TA | Boeing 737-2K5 | 833/22601 |
| ☐ N235TA | Boeing 737-205 | 595/21765 |
| ☐ N240TA | Boeing 737-205 | 572/21729 |

### AVENSA — AVE

| ☐ YV-89C | Boeing 727-22 | 181/18851 |
| ☐ YV-94C | Boeing 727-281 | 1029/20877 |
| ☐ YV-97C | Boeing 727-2D3 | 1055/20885 |
| ☐ YV-765C | Boeing 727-22 | 195/18855 |
| ☐ YV-823C | Boeing 727-2D3 | 1701/22269 |
| ☐ YV-838C | Boeing 727-35 | 292/19165 |
| ☐ YV-69C | Douglas DC-10-30 | 133/46944 |

### LASER — LER

| ☐ YV-881C | Douglas DC-9-32 | 217/45789 |
| ☐ YV-977C | Douglas DC-9-14 | 32/45745 |
| ☐ YV-1121C | Douglas DC-9-32 | 437/47281 |
| ☐ YV-1122C | Douglas DC-9-32 | 325/47219 |

### RUTACA – RUTAS AEREAS — RUC

| ☐ YV-215C | Boeing 737-2M6 | 462/21231 |

### SANTA BARBARA AIRLINES — BBR

| ☐ YV-1014C | ATR 42-320 | 368 |
| ☐ YV-1015C | ATR 42-320 | 360 |
| ☐ YV-1016C | ATR 42-320 | 358 |
| ☐ YV-1017C | ATR 42-320 | 300 |
| ☐ YV-1018C | ATR 42-320 | 340 |
| ☐ YV-1019C | ATR 42-320 | 363 |
| ☐ YV-1023C | ATR 42-320 | 351 |
| ☐ YV-1036C | ATR 42-320 | 366 |

### SERVIVENSA — SVV

| ☐ YV-79C | Boeing 737-229 | 352/20908 |
| ☐ YV-92C | Boeing 727-281 | 954/20724 |
| ☐ YV-608C | Boeing 727-227 | 816/20394 |
| ☐ YV-844C | Boeing 727-2D3 | 1709/22270 |
| ☐ YV-845C | Boeing 727-27 | 454/19534 |

### VENESCAR INTERNACIONAL — VEC

| ☐ YV-846C | Boeing 727-35F | 325/19167 | Lsf BCS |
| ☐ YV-848C | Boeing 727-31F | 712/20114 | Lsf BCS |

## Z - ZIMBABWE

### AIR ZIMBABWE — AZW

| ☐ Z-WPA | Boeing 737-2N0 | 1313/23677 | Lst LAM |
| ☐ Z-WPB | Boeing 737-2N0 | 1405/23678 | |
| ☐ Z-WPC | Boeing 737-2N0 | 1415/23679 | |
| ☐ Z-WPE | Boeing 767-2N0ER | 287/24713 | |
| ☐ Z-WPF | Boeing 767-2N0ER | 333/24867 | |

## ZA - ALBANIA

### ADA AIR
ADE

| | | | |
|---|---|---|---|
| ☐ LZ-DOF | Yakovlev Yak-40 | 9521541 | Lsf HMS |
| ☐ LZ-DOM | Yakovlev Yak-40 | 9620447 | Lsf HMS |
| ☐ ZA-ADA | Embraer EMB.110P2 | 110303 | |

### ALBANIAN AIRLINES
LBC

| | | | |
|---|---|---|---|
| ☐ LZ-DOB | Yakovlev Yak-40 | 9340432 | Lsf HMS |
| ☐ LZ-HMS | Tupolev Tu-154M | 87A-751 | Lsf HMS |
| ☐ LZ-TUH | Tupolev Tu-134A | 60142 | Lsf HMS |
| ☐ ZA-MAL | BAe 146 Srs.200 | E2054 | OpbHMS |

## ZK - NEW ZEALAND

### AIR NEW ZEALAND
ANZ

| | | | |
|---|---|---|---|
| ☐ ZK-FRE | Boeing 737-3U3 | 2992/28742 | |
| ☐ ZK-NAW | Boeing 737-219 | 1197/23473 | std |
| ☐ ZK-NGA | Boeing 737-33R | 2975/28873 | |
| ☐ ZK-NGB | Boeing 737-36Q | 3013/29140 | |
| ☐ ZK-NGC | Boeing 737-36Q | 3057/29189 | |
| ☐ ZK-NGD | Boeing 737-3U3 | 2966/28732 | |
| ☐ ZK-NGE | Boeing 737-3U3 | 2969/28733 | |
| ☐ ZK-NGF | Boeing 737-3U3 | 2974/28734 | |
| ☐ ZK-NGG | Boeing 737-319 | 3123/25606 | |
| ☐ ZK-NGH | Boeing 737-319 | 3126/25607 | |
| ☐ ZK-NGI | Boeing 737-319 | 3128/25608 | |
| ☐ ZK-NGJ | Boeing 737-319 | 3130/25609 | |
| ☐ ZK-NGK | Boeing 737-3K2 | 2731/26318 | |
| ☐ ZK-NGM | Boeing 737-3K2 | 2722/28085 | |
| ☐ ZK-NGN | Boeing 737-33S | 3012/29072 | |
| ☐ ZK-NGO | Boeing 737-37Q | 2961/28548 | |
| ☐ ZK-NBS | Boeing 747-419 | 756/24386 | |
| ☐ ZK-NBT | Boeing 747-419 | 815/24855 | |
| ☐ ZK-NBU | Boeing 747-419 | 933/25605 | |
| ☐ ZK-NBV | Boeing 747-419 | 1180/26910 | |
| ☐ ZK-NBW | Boeing 747-419 | 1228/29375 | |
| ☐ ZK-SUI | Boeing 747-441 | 971/24957 | |
| ☐ ZK-SUJ | Boeing 747-4F6 | 1161/27602 | |
| ☐ ZK-NBA | Boeing 767-219ER | 124/23326 | |
| ☐ ZK-NBB | Boeing 767-219ER | 134/23327 | |
| ☐ ZK-NBC | Boeing 767-219ER | 149/23328 | |
| ☐ ZK-NCE | Boeing 767-319ER | 371/24875 | |
| ☐ ZK-NCF | Boeing 767-319ER | 413/24876 | |
| ☐ ZK-NCG | Boeing 767-319ER | 509/26912 | |
| ☐ ZK-NCH | Boeing 767-319ER | 555/26264 | |
| ☐ ZK-NCI | Boeing 767-319ER | 558/26913 | |
| ☐ ZK-NCJ | Boeing 767-319ER | 574/26915 | |
| ☐ ZK-NCK | Boeing 767-319ER | 663/26971 | |
| ☐ ZK-NCL | Boeing 767-319ER | 677/28745 | |
| ☐ ZK-NCN | Boeing 767-319ER | 785/29388 | |
| ☐ ZK-NCO | Boeing 767-319ER | 808/30586 | |

### AIR NEW ZEALAND LINK
NZA

| | | | |
|---|---|---|---|
| ☐ ZK-MCA | ATR 72-212A | 597 | |
| ☐ ZK-MCB | ATR 72-212A | 598 | |
| ☐ ZK-MCF | ATR 72-212A | 600 | |
| ☐ ZK-MCJ | ATR 72-212A | 624 | |
| ☐ ZK-MCO | ATR 72-212A | 628 | |
| ☐ ZK-MCP | ATR 72-212A | 630 | |
| ☐ ZK-MCU | ATR 72-212A | 632 | |
| ☐ ZK-MCW | ATR 72-212A | 646 | |
| ☐ ZK-MCX | ATR 72-212A | 687 | |
| ☐ ZK-M | ATR 72-212A | 703 | o/o |
| ☐ ZK-EAA | Beech 1900D | UE-424 | |
| ☐ ZK-EAB | Beech 1900D | UE-425 | |
| ☐ ZK-EAC | Beech 1900D | UE-426 | |

| | | |
|---|---|---|
| ☐ ZK-EAD | Beech 1900D | UE-427 |
| ☐ ZK-EAE | Beech 1900D | UE-428 |
| ☐ ZK-EAF | Beech 1900D | UE-429 |
| ☐ ZK-EAG | Beech 1900D | UE-430 |
| ☐ ZK-EAH | Beech 1900D | UE-431 |
| ☐ ZK-EAI | Beech 1900D | UE-432 |
| ☐ ZK-EAJ | Beech 1900D | UE-433 |
| ☐ ZK-EAK | Beech 1900D | UE-434 |
| ☐ ZK-EAL | Beech 1900D | UE-435 |
| ☐ ZK-EAM | Beech 1900D | UE-436 |
| ☐ ZK-EAN | Beech 1900D | UE-437 |
| ☐ ZK-EAO | Beech 1900D | UE-438 |
| ☐ ZK-EAP | Beech 1900D | UE-439 |
| ☐ ZK-JND | Beech 1900D | UE-302 |
| ☐ ZK-FXA | SAAB SF.340A | 120 |
| ☐ ZK-FXB | SAAB SF.340A | 122 |
| ☐ ZK-FXD | SAAB SF.340A | 088 |
| ☐ ZK-NLC | SAAB SF.340A | 132 |
| ☐ ZK-NLE | SAAB SF.340A | 067 |
| ☐ ZK-NLG | SAAB SF.340A | 151 |
| ☐ ZK-NLH | SAAB SF.340A | 137 |
| ☐ ZK-NLM | SAAB SF.340A | 038 |
| ☐ ZK-NLN | SAAB SF.340A | 136 |
| ☐ ZK-NLO | SAAB SF.340A | 153 |
| ☐ ZK-NLP | SAAB SF.340A | 042 |
| ☐ ZK-NLQ | SAAB SF.340A | 124 |
| ☐ ZK-NLR | SAAB SF.340A | 097 |
| ☐ ZK-NLS | SAAB SF.340A | 134 |
| ☐ ZK-NLT | SAAB SF.340A | 116 |
| ☐ ZK-NSK | SAAB SF.340A | 084 |

### AIR POST
PST

| | | |
|---|---|---|
| ☐ ZK-NAN | F-27 Friendship 500 | 10365 |
| ☐ ZK-NAO | F-27 Friendship 500 | 10364 |
| ☐ ZK-NQC | Boeing 737-219C | 928/22994 |
| ☐ ZK-POH | F-27 Friendship 500 | 10680 |

### FREEDOM AIR INTERNATIONAL
FOM

| | | |
|---|---|---|
| ☐ ZK-FDM | Boeing 737-3M8 | 2004/25016 |
| ☐ ZK-SJB | Boeing 737-33R | 2881/28868 |
| ☐ ZK-SJC | Boeing 737-3U3 | 2988/28738 |
| ☐ ZK-SJE | Boeing 737-3K2 | 2721/27635 |

### JETCONNECT

| | | | |
|---|---|---|---|
| ☐ VH-CZG | Boeing 737-377 | 1292/23659 | Lsf QFA |
| ☐ ZK-CZR | Boeing 737-33A | 1831/24460 | Lsf QFA |
| ☐ ZK-CZS | Boeing 737-33A | 1654/24030 | Lsf QFA |
| ☐ ZK-CZU | Boeing 737-33A | 2600/27267 | Lsf QFA |
| ☐ ZK-JNE | Boeing 737-33A | 2069/25119 | Lsf QFA |
| ☐ ZK-JNF | Boeing 737-376 | 1286/23486 | Lsf QFA |

### ORIGIN PACIFIC AIRWAYS
OGN

| | | |
|---|---|---|
| ☐ ZK-JSE | BAe Jetstream 41 | 41046 |
| ☐ ZK-JSK | BAe Jetstream 41 | 41049 |
| ☐ ZK-JSM | BAe Jetstream 41 | 41052 |
| ☐ ZK-JSN | BAe Jetstream 41 | 41053 |
| ☐ ZK-NSO | BAe Jetstream 41 | 41056 |
| ☐ ZK-JSY | ATR 72-212 | 379 |
| ☐ ZK-JSZ | ATR 72-212 | 385 |
| ☐ ZK-NES | DHC-8-102 | 125 |
| ☐ ZK-NET | DHC-8-102 | 197 |

## ZS - SOUTH AFRICA

### AIRQUARIUS AVIATION
AQU

| | | | |
|---|---|---|---|
| ☐ ZS-JAS | F-28 Fellowship 4000 | 11225 | Lsf RSS |
| ☐ ZS-JAV | F-28 Fellowship 4000 | 11183 | Lst NMB |
| ☐ ZS-JES | F-28 Fellowship 4000 | 11236 | Lsf RSS |

| ] ZS-XGW | F-28 Fellowship 4000 | 11130 | |
|---|---|---|---|
| ] ZS- | F-28 Fellowship 3000 | 11151 | |
| ] ZS- | F-28 Fellowship 3000 | 11143 | |
| ] ZS-NPX | Boeing 727-23F | 218/19131 | |

## AIRWORLD — SPZ

| ] ZS-NWA | Boeing 727-230F | 1002/20757 | Lsf SFR |
|---|---|---|---|
| ] ZS-OBN | Boeing 727-232F | 920/20637 | Lsf SFR |

## CIVAIR — CIW

| ] ZS- | Douglas DC-9-32 | 750/47643 | o/o |
|---|---|---|---|

## COMAIR — CAW

| ] ZS-NNG | Boeing 737-236 | 635/21793 | |
|---|---|---|---|
| ] ZS-NNH | Boeing 737-236 | 653/21797 | |
| ] ZS-OKD | Boeing 737-236 | 677/21803 | |
| ] ZS-OKE | Boeing 737-236 | 710/21807 | |
| ] ZS-OKF | Boeing 737-2L9 | 550/21686 | Lsf SFR |
| ] ZS-OLA | Boeing 737-236 | 1058/23163 | |
| ] ZS-OLB | Boeing 737-236 | 1074/23167 | |
| ] ZS-OLC | Boeing 737-230 | 714/22119 | Lsf SFR |
| ] ZS-SBN | Boeing 737-244 | 214/20229 | |
| ] ZS-SBO | Boeing 737-244 | 250/20329 | |
| ] ZS-SBR | Boeing 737-244 | 260/20331 | |
| ] ZS-NOU | Boeing 727-230 | 1176/21113 | std |
| ] ZS-NVR | Boeing 727-230 | 922/20673 | std |

## HYDRO AIR — HYC

| ] ZS-OOS | Boeing 747-258C | 272/21190 | Opf DHL |
|---|---|---|---|

## INTER-AIR AIRLINES — ILN

| ] ZS-IJH | Boeing 727-116C | 594/19813 | |
|---|---|---|---|
| ] ZS-IJI | Boeing 707-323C | 614/19517 | |
| ] ZS-IJJ | Boeing 737-2H7C | 309/20591 | |
| ] 3D-ZZM | Boeing 737-2H7C | 304/20590 | Lst LAM |

## KULULA.COM

| ] ZS-OTF | Boeing 737-436 | 2147/25305 | Lsf SFR |
|---|---|---|---|
| ] ZS-OTG | Boeing 737-436 | 2197/25840 | Lsf SFR |
| ] ZS-OTH | Boeing 737-436 | 2222/25841 | Lsf SFR |

## MILLIONAIR CHARTER

| ] ZS-IJF | Boeing 727-23 | 114/18444 | std |
|---|---|---|---|
| ] ZS-NNN | Douglas DC-9-32 | 630/47516 | |
| ] ZS-NRA | Douglas DC-9-32 | 609/47430 | |
| ] ZS-NRB | Douglas DC-9-32 | 611/47468 | |
| ] ZS-OLN | Douglas DC-9-32 | 312/47218 | |

## NATIONWIDE AIR CHARTER — NTW

| ] ZS-NMS | BAC One-Eleven 509EW | 186 | std |
|---|---|---|---|
| ] ZS-NMT | BAC One-Eleven 518FG | 201 | std |
| ] ZS-NNM | BAC One-Eleven 409AY | 108 | |
| ] ZS-NUG | BAC One-Eleven 531FS | 237 | std |
| ] ZS-NUH | BAC One-Eleven 537GF | 257 | std |
| ] ZS-NUI | BAC One-Eleven 537GF | 258 | |
| ] ZS-NUJ | BAC One-Eleven 537GF | 261 | |
| ] ZS-NYZ | BAC One-Eleven 416EK | 132 | std |
| ] ZS-OAF | BAC One-Eleven 408EF | 114 | |
| ] ZS-OAG | BAC One-Eleven 401AK | 066 | std |
| ] ZS-OAH | BAC One-Eleven 408EF | 115 | |
| ] ZS-OEZ | Boeing 737-230 | 704/22118 | |
| ] ZS-OIV | Boeing 737-230 | 840/22634 | |
| ] ZS-OMG | Boeing 737-230 | 793/22140 | |
| ] ZS-OOC | Boeing 737-258 | 910/22856 | |

| □ ZS-OOD | Boeing 737-258 | 919/22857 | |
|---|---|---|---|
| □ ZS-OVE | Boeing 737-228 | 944/23006 | |
| □ ZS-OVF | Boeing 737-228 | 952/23008 | |
| □ ZS-OVG | Boeing 737-236 | 661/21800 | |
| □ ZS-OWM | Boeing 737-2R8C | 573/21711 | |
| □ ZS-NYX | Boeing 727-116F | 520/19811 | std |
| □ ZS-NYY | Boeing 727-95 | 315/19251 | |
| □ ZS-ODO | Boeing 727-231 | 1063/20843 | |

## ROSSAIR — RSS

| □ ZS-DHL | ATR 42-300F | 050 | Opf DHL |
|---|---|---|---|
| □ ZS-JAS | F-28 Fellowship 4000 | 11225 | Lst AQU |
| □ ZS-JES | F-28 Fellowship 4000 | 11236 | Lst AQU |
| □ ZS-OSN | ATR 42-300 | 139 | Lst TRQ |
| □ ZS-OVO | Boeing 737-2A9C | 242/20205 | |

## SAFAIR — SFR

| □ ZS-JAG | L-382G Hercules | 5027 | |
|---|---|---|---|
| □ ZS-JIV | L-382G Hercules | 4673 | Opf ABR |
| □ ZS-JIX | L-382G Hercules | 4684 | |
| □ ZS-JIY | L-382G Hercules | 4691 | |
| □ ZS-JIZ | L-382G Hercules | 4695 | UN/WFP |
| □ ZS-JVL | L-382G Hercules | 4676 | Opf ABR |
| □ ZS-RSC | L-382G Hercules | 4475 | |
| □ ZS-RSI | L-328G Hercules | 4600 | |
| □ ZS- | Boeing 737-700 | | o/o |
| □ ZS- | Boeing 737-700 | | o/o |

## SOUTH AFRICAN AIRLINK — LNK

| □ ZS-NRE | BAe Jetstream 41 | 41048 | |
|---|---|---|---|
| □ ZS-NRF | BAe Jetstream 41 | 41050 | |
| □ ZS-NRG | BAe Jetstream 41 | 41051 | |
| □ ZS-NRH | BAe Jetstream 41 | 41054 | |
| □ ZS-NRI | BAe Jetstream 41 | 41061 | |
| □ ZS-NRJ | BAe Jetstream 41 | 41062 | |
| □ ZS-NRK | BAe Jetstream 41 | 41065 | Lst SZL |
| □ ZS-NRL | BAe Jetstream 41 | 41068 | |
| □ ZS-NRM | BAe Jetstream 41 | 41069 | |
| □ ZS-NUO | BAe Jetstream 41 | 41044 | |
| □ ZS-NYK | BAe Jetstream 41 | 41095 | |
| □ ZS-OEX | BAe Jetstream 41 | 41103 | |
| □ ZS-OMF | BAe Jetstream 41 | 41034 | |
| □ ZS-OMS | BAe Jetstream 41 | 41035 | |
| □ ZS-OMY | BAe Jetstream 41 | 41036 | |
| □ ZS-OMZ | BAe Jetstream 41 | 41037 | |
| □ ZS-OTM | Embraer ERJ-135 | 145485 | |
| □ ZS-OTN | Embraer ERJ-135 | 145491 | |
| □ ZS-OUV | Embraer ERJ-135 | 145493 | |
| □ ZS-OUW | Embraer ERJ-135 | | o/o |
| □ ZS-SJW | Embraer ERJ-135 | 145423 | |
| □ ZS-SJX | Embraer ERJ-135 | 145428 | |
| □ ZS- | Embraer ERJ-135 | | o/o |
| □ ZS- | Embraer ERJ-135 | | o/o |
| □ ZS- | Embraer ERJ-135 | | o/o |
| □ ZS- | Embraer ERJ-135 | | o/o |

## SOUTH AFRICAN AIRWAYS — SAA

| □ ZS-SNA | Airbus A340-642 | 410 | o/o |
|---|---|---|---|
| □ ZS-SNB | Airbus A340-642 | 417 | o/o |
| □ ZS-SNC | Airbus A340-642 | 426 | o/o |
| □ ZS- | Airbus A340-642 | 531 | o/o |
| □ ZS- | Airbus A340-642 | 547 | o/o |
| □ ZS- | Airbus A340-642 | 557 | o/o |
| □ ZS- | Airbus A340-642 | 534 | o/o |
| □ ZS-SXA | Airbus A340-313X | 544 | o/o |
| □ ZS-SIA | Boeing 737-244 | 787/22580 | Lsf SFR |
| □ ZS-SIB | Boeing 737-244 | 796/22581 | Lsf SFR |
| □ ZS-SIC | Boeing 737-244 | 805/22582 | Lsf SFR |

| | | | | |
|---|---|---|---|---|
| ☐ ZS-SID | Boeing 737-244F | 809/22583 | Lsf SFR | |
| ☐ ZS-SIE | Boeing 737-244 | 821/22584 | Lsf SFR | |
| ☐ ZS-SIF | Boeing 737-244F | 828/22585 | Lsf SFR | |
| ☐ ZS-SIG | Boeing 737-244 | 829/22586 | Lsf SFR | |
| ☐ ZS-SIH | Boeing 737-244 | 835/22587 | Lsf SFR | |
| ☐ ZS-SII | Boeing 737-244 | 836/22588 | Lsf SFR | |
| ☐ ZS-SIJ | Boeing 737-244 | 843/22589 | Lsf SFR | |
| ☐ ZS-SIL | Boeing 737-244 | 859/22591 | Lsf SFR | |
| ☐ ZS-SIM | Boeing 737-244 | 881/22828 | Lsf SFR | |
| ☐ ZS-SIN | Boeing 737-236 | 670/21802 | Lsf SFR | |
| ☐ ZS-SIO | Boeing 737-236 | 628/21792 | Lsf SFR | |
| ☐ ZS-SIP | Boeing 737-230 | 701/22116 | Lsf SFR | |
| ☐ ZS-SIR | Boeing 737-236 | 697/21805 | Lsf SFR | |
| ☐ ZS-SIS | Boeing 737-236 | 669/21801 | Lsf SFR | |
| ☐ ZS-SIT | Boeing 737-236 | 599/21790 | Lsf SFR | |
| ☐ ZS-SIU | Boeing 737-236 | 644/22026 | Lsf SFR | |
| ☐ ZS-SIV | Boeing 737-236 | 662/22029 | | |
| ☐ ZS-SIW | Boeing 737-236 | 722/22031 | | |
| ☐ ZS-SJA | Boeing 737-8S3 | 561/29248 | | |
| ☐ ZS-SJB | Boeing 737-8S3 | 653/29249 | | |
| ☐ ZS-SJC | Boeing 737-85F | 565/28828 | | |
| ☐ ZS-SJD | Boeing 737-85F | 582/28829 | | |
| ☐ ZS-SJE | Boeing 737-85F | 669/28830 | | |
| ☐ ZS-SJF | Boeing 737-85F | 688/30006 | | |
| ☐ ZS-SJG | Boeing 737-8S3 | 711/32353 | | |
| ☐ ZS-SJH | Boeing 737-8S3 | 725/32354 | | |
| ☐ ZS-SJI | Boeing 737-85F | 746/30007 | | |
| ☐ ZS-SJJ | Boeing 737-85F | 761/30567 | | |
| ☐ ZS-SJK | Boeing 737-8BG | 807/32355 | | |
| ☐ ZS-SJL | Boeing 737-8BG | 819/32356 | | |
| ☐ ZS-SJM | Boeing 737-85F | 789/30476 | | |
| ☐ ZS-SJN | Boeing 737-85F | 850/30569 | | |
| ☐ ZS-SJO | Boeing 737-8BG | 918/32357 | | |
| ☐ ZS-SJP | Boeing 737-8BG | 955/32358 | | |
| ☐ ZS-SJR | Boeing 737-844 | 1176/32631 | | |
| ☐ ZS-SJS | Boeing 737-844 | 1205/32632 | Lsf SFR | |
| ☐ ZS-SJT | Boeing 737-844 | 1225/32633 | Lsf SFR | |
| ☐ ZS-SJU | Boeing 737-844 | 32634 | o/o | |
| ☐ ZS-SJV | Boeing 737-844 | 32635 | o/o | |

| | | | |
|---|---|---|---|
| ☐ ZS-SAC | Boeing 747-312 | 598/23031 | |
| ☐ ZS-SAJ | Boeing 747-312 | 583/23027 | |
| ☐ ZS-SAK | Boeing 747-444 | 1162/28468 | |
| ☐ ZS-SAL | Boeing 747-244B | 154/20237 | |
| ☐ ZS-SAM | Boeing 747-244B | 158/20238 | |
| ☐ ZS-SAN | Boeing 747-244B | 160/20239 | |
| ☐ ZS-SAP | Boeing 747-244B | 198/20557 | |
| ☐ ZS-SAT | Boeing 747-344 | 577/22970 | |
| ☐ ZS-SAU | Boeing 747-344 | 578/22971 | |
| ☐ ZS-SAV | Boeing 747-444 | 827/24976 | |
| ☐ ZS-SAW | Boeing 747-444 | 861/25152 | |
| ☐ ZS-SAX | Boeing 747-444 | 943/26637 | |
| ☐ ZS-SAY | Boeing 747-444 | 995/26638 | |
| ☐ ZS-SAZ | Boeing 747-444 | 1187/29119 | |
| ☐ ZS-SBK | Boeing 747-4F6 | 1158/28959 | |
| ☐ ZS-SBS | Boeing 747-4F6 | 1167/28960 | |
| ☐ ZS-SKA | Boeing 747-357 | 586/22996 | |
| ☐ ZS-SKB | Boeing 747-357 | 585/22995 | |
| ☐ ZS-SPC | Boeing 747SP-44 | 288/21134 | |
| ☐ ZS-SPE | Boeing 747SP-44 | 298/21254 | |

| | | | |
|---|---|---|---|
| ☐ G-WWBB | Airbus A330-243 | 404 | Lsf BMA |
| ☐ G-WWBD | Airbus A330-243 | 401 | Lsf BMA |
| ☐ ZS-SRB | Boeing 767-266ER | 98/23179 | |
| ☐ ZS-SRC | Boeing 767-266ER | 99/23180 | |

### SOUTH AFRICAN EXPRESS AIRLINES          EXY

| | | |
|---|---|---|
| ☐ ZS-NMI | Canadair RJ-200 | 7153 |
| ☐ ZS-NMJ | Canadair RJ-200 | 7161 |
| ☐ ZS-NMK | Canadair RJ-200 | 7198 |
| ☐ ZS-NML | Canadair RJ-200 | 7201 |
| ☐ ZS-NMM | Canadair RJ-200 | 7234 |
| ☐ ZS-NMN | Canadair RJ-200 | 7237 |

| | | | |
|---|---|---|---|
| ☐ ZS-NLW | DHC-8-315 | 338 | 30 |
| ☐ ZS-NLX | DHC-8-315 | 348 | 30: |
| ☐ ZS-NLY | DHC-8-315 | 352 | 30: |
| ☐ ZS-NLZ | DHC-8-315 | 354 | 30- |
| ☐ ZS-NMA | DHC-8-315 | 358 | 30: |
| ☐ ZS-NMB | DHC-8-315 | 368 | 30( |
| ☐ ZS-NMP | DHC-8-315B | 420 | 30: |

### SUNAIR

| | | |
|---|---|---|
| ☐ ZS-NNN | Douglas DC-9-32 | 630/47516 |
| ☐ ZS-NRA | Douglas DC-9-32 | 609/47430 |
| ☐ ZS-NRB | Douglas DC-9-32 | 611/47468 |

# Z3 - MACEDONIA

### MACEDONIAN AIR TRANSPORT          MAK

| | | | |
|---|---|---|---|
| ☐ YU-ANW | Boeing 737-3H9 | 1526/24141 | Lsf JA |
| ☐ Z3-AAA | Boeing 737-3H9 | 1175/23416 | Lsf JA |
| ☐ Z3-ARF | Boeing 737-3H9 | 1321/23716 | Lsf JA |

# 3B - MAURITIUS

### AIR MAURITIUS          MAU

| | | | |
|---|---|---|---|
| ☐ 3B-NAU | Airbus A340-312 | 076 | |
| ☐ 3B-NAV | Airbus A340-312 | 094 | |
| ☐ 3B-NAY | Airbus A340-313X | 152 | |
| ☐ 3B-NBD | Airbus A340-313X | 194 | |
| ☐ 3B-NBE | Airbus A340-313X | 268 | |
| ☐ 3B-NAK | Boeing 767-23BER | 206/23973 | |
| ☐ 3B-NAL | Boeing 767-23BER | 214/23974 | |
| ☐ 3B-NBF | Airbus A319-112 | 1592 | |
| ☐ 3B- | Airbus A319-112 | 1936 | o/( |

# 3C - EQUATORIAL GUINEA

### AIR BAS          RBS

| | | |
|---|---|---|
| ☐ 3C-KKJ | Ilyushin Il-18V | 184006903 |
| ☐ 3C-KKK | Ilyushin Il-18D | 186009202 |
| ☐ 3C-KKL | Ilyushin Il-18D | 187010204 |
| ☐ 3C-KKR | Ilyushin Il-18E | 185008603I |
| ☐ 3C-OOZ | Antonov An-12V | 9346509 |

### AIR CARGO PLUS          CGP

| | | | |
|---|---|---|---|
| ☐ 3D-ALJ | Boeing 707-323C | 354/18689 | st( |
| ☐ 3D-FNK | Douglas DC-8F-55 | 208/45683 | |
| ☐ 3D-NGK | Boeing 707-399C | 601/19415 | |

### ECUATO GUINEANA DE AVIACION          ECV

| | | |
|---|---|---|
| ☐ 3C-QQH | Embraer ERJ-145 | 145076 |

### GATS AIR          GTS

| | | |
|---|---|---|
| ☐ 3C-KKE | Ilyushin Il-76TD | 1023411368 |
| ☐ 3C-KKF | Ilyushin Il-76TD | 1023411384 |
| ☐ 3C-KKG | Ilyushin Il-76TD | 1023410360 |

### JETLINE INC          JLE

| | | |
|---|---|---|
| ☐ P4-DCE | Douglas DC-8-62H | 469/46071 |
| ☐ 3C-QRF | BAC One Elevan 401AK | 061 |
| ☐ 5A-DKS | Ilyushin Il-76TD | 1033418584 |
| ☐ 5A-DKT | Ilyushin Il-62M | |

# 3D - SWAZILAND

## AFRICAN INTERNATIONAL AIRWAYS — AIN

| | | |
|---|---|---|
| ] ZS-OSI | Douglas DC-8F-62F | 516/46098 |
| ] 3D-ADV | Douglas DC-8F-54 | 410/46012 |
| ] 3D-AFR | Douglas DC-8F-54 | 247/45802 |

## NORTHEAST AIRLINES — NEY

| | | |
|---|---|---|
| ] 3D-NEC | L-1011-50 Tristar | 1096 |
| ] 3D- | L-1011-50 Tristar | 1060 |
| ] 3D- | L-1011-50 Tristar | 1066 |

## ROM ATLANTIC INTERNATIONAL

| | | |
|---|---|---|
| ] 3D-ROK | Boeing 707-323C | 19587 |

## SKY AVIATION

| | | |
|---|---|---|
| ] 3D-BOB | Boeing 727-2H3 | 1210/21235 |
| ] 3D-JAA | Boeing 707-321B | 774/20022 |
| ] 3D-JAB | Boeing 727-2H3 | 1252/21318 |
| ] 3D-PAF | Boeing 747SP-09 | 304/21300 |
| ] 3D-PAH | Boeing 747-246B | 166/20333 |
| ] 3D-PAJ | Boeing 747-246B | 181/20504 |
| ] 3D-SGH | Boeing 727-224 | 1151/20666 |
| ] 9Q-CBP | Boeing 727-2H3 | 1271/21320 |

# 3X - GUINEA

## AIR GUINÉE — GIB

| | | |
|---|---|---|
| ] 3X-GCB | Boeing 737-2R6C | 779/22627 |

# 4K - AZERBAIJAN

## AZAL AZERBAIJAN AIRLINES — AHY

| | | |
|---|---|---|
| ] 4K-65496 | Tupolev Tu-134B-3 | 63468 |
| ] 4K-65704 | Tupolev Tu-134B-3 | 63410 |
| ] 4K-65705 | Tupolev Tu-134B-3 | 63415 |
| ] 4K-65708 | Tupolev Tu-134B-3 | 63447 |
| ] 4K-65709 | Tupolev Tu-134B-3 | 63484 |
| ] 4K-65711 | Tupolev Tu-134B-3 | 63498 |
| ] 4K-65712 | Tupolev Tu-134B-3 | 63515 |
| ] 4K-65713 | Tupolev Tu-134B-3 | 63520 |
| ] 4K-65714 | Tupolev Tu-134B-3 | 63527 |
| ] 4K-AZ10 | Tupolev Tu-154M | 98A-1013 |
| ] 4K-85548 | Tupolev Tu-154B-2 | 82A-548 |
| ] 4K-85698 | Tupolev Tu-154M | 91A-871 |
| ] 4K-85729 | Tupolev Tu-154M | 92A-911 |
| ] 4K-85738 | Tupolev Tu-154M | 92A-921 |
| ] 4K-AZ1 | Boeing 727-235 | 531/19460 |
| ] 4K-AZ8 | Boeing 727-230 | 870/20525 |
| ] VP-BBR | Boeing 757-22L | 894/29305 |
| ] VP-BBS | Boeing 757-22L | 947/30834 |

## AZAL CARGO — AHC

| | | | |
|---|---|---|---|
| ] ER-IBB | Ilyushin Il-76 | | |
| ] ER-IBS | Ilyushin Il-76 | | |
| ] 4K-AZ14 | Ilyushin Il-76TD | 1023412389 | Lsf TWN |
| ] 4K-AZ15 | Ilyushin Il-76TD | 1033417569 | |
| ] 4K-AZ16 | Ilyushin Il-76TD | 1023412411 | Lsf TWN |
| ] 4K-AZ19 | Ilyushin Il-76MD | 0053460820 | |
| ] 4K-AZ27 | Ilyushin Il-76MD | 0053460827 | Opb AZQ |
| ] 4K-78129 | Ilyushin Il-76MD | 0083489683 | Lsf TII |
| ] 4K-78130 | Ilyushin Il-76MD | 0043454611 | Lsf TII |
| ] 4K-AZ18 | Antonov An-12 | 9346308 | |

## SILK WAY AIRLINES — AZQ

| | | | |
|---|---|---|---|
| □ 4K-AZ23 | Antonov An-12 | | |
| □ 4K-AZ25 | Douglas DC-8-62F | 319/45920 | |
| □ 4K-AZ27 | Ilyushin Il-76MD | 0053460827 | Opf AHC |

## TURANAIR — URN

| | | | |
|---|---|---|---|
| □ 4K-325 | Tupolev Tu-154B-2 | 78A-325 | |
| □ 4K-473 | Tupolev Tu-154B-2 | 81A-473 | |
| □ 4K-474 | Tupolev Tu-154B-2 | 81A-474 | |
| □ 4K-727 | Tupolev Tu-154M | 86A-727 | Lst BUC |
| □ 4K-733 | Tupolev Tu-154M | 86A-733 | Lst BUC |
| □ 4K-85524 | Tupolev Tu-154B-2 | 82A-524 | |

# 4L - GEORGIA

## ABAVIA — BVZ

| | | |
|---|---|---|
| □ 4L-65061 | Tupolev Tu-134A-3 | 49874 |

## AIRZENA — TGZ

| | | | |
|---|---|---|---|
| □ D-AHLF | Boeing 737-5K5 | 1968/24927 | Lsf HLF |

# 4R - SRI LANKA

## SRILANKAN — ALK

| | | |
|---|---|---|
| □ 4R-ABB | Airbus A320-231 | 0406 |
| □ 4R-ADA | Airbus A340-311 | 032 |
| □ 4R-ADB | Airbus A340-311 | 033 |
| □ 4R-ADC | Airbus A340-311 | 034 |
| □ 4R-ALA | Airbus A330-243 | 303 |
| □ 4R-ALB | Airbus A330-243 | 306 |
| □ 4R-ALC | Airbus A330-243 | 311 |
| □ 4R-ALD | Airbus A330-243 | 313 |
| □ 4R- | Airbus A320-230 | 0304 |

# 4X - ISRAEL

## ARKIA ISRAELI AIRLINES — AIZ

| | | |
|---|---|---|
| □ 4X-AVU | ATR 72-212A | 587 |
| □ 4X-AVW | ATR 72-212A | 583 |
| □ 4X-AVX | ATR 72-212A | 656 |
| □ 4X-AVZ | ATR 72-212A | 577 |
| □ 4X-BAU | Boeing 757-3E7 | 906/30178 |
| □ 4X-BAW | Boeing 757-3E7 | 912/30179 |
| □ 4X-BAZ | Boeing 757-236 | 183/24121 |

## CARGO AIR LINES — ICL

| | | | |
|---|---|---|---|
| □ 4X-ICL | Boeing 747-271C | 416/21964 | Lsf GTI |
| □ 4X-ICM | Boeing 747-271C | 438/21965 | Lsf GTI |

## EL AL ISRAEL AIRLINES — ELY

| | | | |
|---|---|---|---|
| □ 4X-EKA | Boeing 737-858 | 204/29957 | |
| □ 4X-EKB | Boeing 737-858 | 249/29958 | |
| □ 4X-EKC | Boeing 737-858 | 314/29959 | |
| □ 4X-EKD | Boeing 737-758 | 327/29960 | |
| □ 4X-EKE | Boeing 737-758 | 442/29961 | |
| □ 4X-EKI | Boeing 737-86N | 192/28587 | |
| □ 4X-EKJ | Boeing 737-86N | | o/o |
| □ 4X-AXF | Boeing 747-258C | 327/21594 | |
| □ 4X-AXH | Boeing 747-258B (SCD) | 418/22254 | |
| □ 4X-AXK | Boeing 747-245F | 478/22151 | |
| □ 4X-AXL | Boeing 747-245F | 476/22150 | |
| □ 4X-AXQ | Boeing 747-238B | 233/20841 | |
| □ 4X-ELA | Boeing 747-458 | 1027/26055 | |
| □ 4X-ELB | Boeing 747-458 | 1032/26056 | |

| | | | | |
|---|---|---|---|---|
| ☐ 4X-ELC | Boeing 747-458 | 1062/27915 | |
| ☐ 4X-ELD | Boeing 747-458 | 1215/29328 | |
| | | | |
| ☐ 4X-EBI | Boeing 757-258 | 745/27622 | |
| ☐ 4X-EBM | Boeing 757-258 | 156/23918 | Opf ISR |
| ☐ 4X-EBS | Boeing 757-258ER | 325/24884 | |
| ☐ 4X-EBT | Boeing 757-258ER | 356/25036 | Lst ERO |
| ☐ 4X-EBU | Boeing 757-258 | 529/26053 | |
| ☐ 4X-EBV | Boeing 757-258 | 547/26054 | |
| | | | |
| ☐ 4X-EAA | Boeing 767-258 | 62/22972 | |
| ☐ 4X-EAB | Boeing 767-258 | 68/22973 | |
| ☐ 4X-EAC | Boeing 767-258ER | 86/22974 | |
| ☐ 4X-EAD | Boeing 767-258ER | 89/22975 | |
| ☐ 4X-EAE | Boeing 767-27EER | 316/24832 | |
| ☐ 4X-EAF | Boeing 767-27EER | 326/24854 | |
| | | | |
| ☐ 4X-ECA | Boeing 777-258ER | 319/30831 | |
| ☐ 4X-ECB | Boeing 777-258ER | 325/30832 | |
| ☐ 4X-ECC | Boeing 777-258ER | 335/30833 | |
| ☐ 4X-ECD | Boeing 777-258ER | 405/33169 | |

### ISRAIR — ISR

| | | | |
|---|---|---|---|
| ☐ 4X-ATL | ATR 42-320 | 089 | |
| ☐ 4X-ATM | ATR 42-320 | 069 | |
| ☐ 4X-ATN | ATR 42-320 | 053 | |
| ☐ 4X-ATO | ATR 42-320 | 064 | |
| ☐ 4X-EBM | Boeing 757-258 | 156/23918 | Opb ELY |

### SUN D'OR INTERNATIONAL AIRLINES — ERO

| | | | |
|---|---|---|---|
| ☐ 4X-EBT | Boeing 757-258ER | 356/25036 | |
| ☐ 4X-EKI | Boeing 737-86N | 192/28587 | |

## 5A - LIBYA

### AFRIQIYAH AIRWAYS — AAW

| | | | |
|---|---|---|---|
| ☐ D-AHLU | Boeing 737-4K5 | 2677/27831 | Lsf BPA |
| ☐ I-BPAC | Boeing 737-4Z9 | 2043/25147 | Lsf BPA |

### AIR ONE NINE

| | | | |
|---|---|---|---|
| ☐ YU-AOJ | F-28 Fellowship 2000 | 11184 | Lsf MGX |

### BURAQ AIR TRANSPORT — BRQ

| | | | |
|---|---|---|---|
| ☐ UN-76005 | Ilyushin Il-76 | | |
| ☐ 5A-DMN | Boeing 727-228 | 1710/22287 | |
| ☐ 5A-DMO | Boeing 727-2F2 | 1088/20983 | |
| ☐ 5A-DMP | Boeing 727-2F2 | 1086/20981 | |

### LIBYAN ARAB AIR CARGO — LCR

| | | | |
|---|---|---|---|
| ☐ 5A-DKL | Antonov An-124 | 19530502761 | |
| ☐ 5A-DKN | Antonov An-124 | | |

### LIBYAN ARAB AIRLINES — LAA

| | | | |
|---|---|---|---|
| ☐ 5A-DIB | Boeing 727-2L5 | 1109/21051 | |
| ☐ 5A-DIC | Boeing 727-2L5 | 1110/21052 | std |
| ☐ 5A-DID | Boeing 727-2L5 | 1213/21229 | std |
| ☐ 5A-DIE | Boeing 727-2L5 | 1215/21230 | std |
| ☐ 5A-DIF | Boeing 727-2L5 | 1257/21332 | |
| ☐ 5A-DIH | Boeing 727-2L5 | 1371/21539 | |
| ☐ 5A-DII | Boeing 727-2L5 | 1386/21540 | |
| | | | |
| ☐ JY-AGV | Airbus A310-203 | 306 | Lsf RJA |
| ☐ TS-IAZ | Airbus A300B4-622R | 616 | |
| ☐ OD-AGO | Boeing 707-321C | 570/19269 | Lsf TMA |
| ☐ TS-IAX | Airbus A300B4-622R | 601 | Lsf TAR |
| ☐ TS-IGU | Airbus A310- | | |
| ☐ 5A-AGU | Airbus A310-203 | 295 | Lsf RJA |

## 5B - CYPRUS

### AEROTRANS — PFO

| | | | |
|---|---|---|---|
| ☐ YR-BRH | BAC One-Eleven 561RC | 408 | Lsf RMV |
| ☐ YR-BRI | BAC One-Eleven 561RC | 409 | Lsf RMV |

### CYPRUS AIRWAYS — CYP

| | | | |
|---|---|---|---|
| ☐ 5B-DAT | Airbus A320-231 | 0028 | |
| ☐ 5B-DAU | Airbus A320-231 | 0035 | |
| ☐ 5B-DAV | Airbus A320-231 | 0037 | |
| ☐ 5B-DAW | Airbus A320-231 | 0038 | |
| ☐ 5B-DBA | Airbus A320-231 | 0180 | |
| ☐ 5B-DBB | Airbus A320-231 | 0256 | Lst ECA |
| ☐ 5B-DBC | Airbus A320-231 | 0295 | Lst ECA |
| ☐ 5B-DBD | Airbus A320-231 | 0316 | |
| ☐ 5B-DBJ | Airbus A320-231 | 0414 | Lst ECA |
| ☐ 5B-DBK | Airbus A320-231 | 0430 | Lst ECA |
| | | | |
| ☐ 5B-DAQ | Airbus A310-203 | 300 | |
| ☐ 5B-DAR | Airbus A310-203 | 309 | |
| ☐ 5B-DAS | Airbus A310-203 | 352 | |
| ☐ 5B-DAX | Airbus A310-204 | 486 | |
| ☐ 5B-DBO | Airbus A319-112 | 1729 | |
| ☐ 5B-DBP | Airbus A319-112 | 1768 | |
| ☐ 5B-DBS | Airbus A330-243 | 505 | |
| ☐ 5B-DBT | Airbus A330-243 | 526 | |

### EUROCYPRIA AIRLINES — ECA

| | | | |
|---|---|---|---|
| ☐ 5B-DBB | Airbus A320-231 | 0256 | Lsf CYP |
| ☐ 5B-DBC | Airbus A320-231 | 0295 | Lsf CYP |
| ☐ 5B-DBJ | Airbus A320-231 | 0414 | Lsf CYP |
| ☐ 5B-DBK | Airbus A320-231 | 0430 | Lsf CYP |
| | | | |
| ☐ 5B-DBU | Boeing 737-8Q8 | 1272/32796 | |
| ☐ 5B-DBV | Boeing 737-8Q8 | | o/o |
| ☐ 5B-DBW | Boeing 737-8Q8 | | o/o |
| ☐ 5B-DBX | Boeing 737-8Q8 | | o/o |

### HELIOS AIRWAYS — HCY

| | | | |
|---|---|---|---|
| ☐ 5B-DBH | Boeing 737-86N | 790/30806 | |
| ☐ 5B-DBI | Boeing 737-86N | 829/30807 | |

## 5H - TANZANIA

### AIR TANZANIA — ATC

| | | | |
|---|---|---|---|
| ☐ 5H-ATC | Boeing 737-2R8C | 546/21710 | |
| ☐ 5H-TCA | Boeing 737-33A | 1955/24790 | |

## 5N - NIGERIA

### ADC AIRLINES — ADK

| | | | |
|---|---|---|---|
| ☐ 5N-BED | Boeing 737-204 | 858/22638 | |
| ☐ 5N-BEE | Boeing 737-204 | 700/22365 | |

### ALBARKA AIR SERVICE — NBK

| | | | |
|---|---|---|---|
| ☐ 5N-BBP | BAC One-Eleven 518FG | 202 | |
| ☐ 5N-BBQ | BAC One-Eleven 520FN | 230 | |
| ☐ 5N-BBU | BAC One-Eleven 561RC | 252 | |
| ☐ 5N-IMM | Boeing 727-256 | 915/20603 | |
| ☐ | Boeing 727-256 | 912/20600 | |

### AMOKO AIR — OBK

| | | | |
|---|---|---|---|
| ☐ 5N-KHA | Boeing 707-347C | 745/19967 | |
| ☐ 5N-KMA | Boeing 707-3K1C | 884/20805 | |

## BELLVIEW AIRLINES — BLV

| | | | |
|---|---|---|---|
| ☐ F-GHXK | Boeing 737-2A1 | 514/21599 | ex |
| ☐ F-GHXL | Boeing 737-2S3 | 570/21775 | |
| ☐ YU-AJK | Douglas DC-9-32 | 689/47568 | Lsf JAT |
| ☐ YU-AJM | Douglas DC-9-32 | 701/47582 | Lsf JAT |

## CHANCHANGI AIRLINES — NCH

| | | | |
|---|---|---|---|
| ☐ 5N-BCF | Boeing 727-2M7 | 1452/21655 | |
| ☐ 5N-BDE | Boeing 727-2M7 | 1675/21346 | |
| ☐ 5N-BDF | Boeing 727-2M7 | 1302/21457 | |
| ☐ 5N-BDG | Boeing 727-225 | 1798/22558 | |
| ☐ 5N-BEU | Boeing 727-225 | 1800/22559 | |
| ☐ 5N-BCG | BAC One-Eleven 510ED | 141 | |
| ☐ 5N-BCH | BAC One-Eleven 510ED | 140 | |

## CHROME AIR SERVICES — CHO

| | | | |
|---|---|---|---|
| ☐ 5N-SEO | BAC One-Eleven 487GK | 267 | |
| ☐ 5N-UJC | BAC One-Eleven 525FT | 255 | |

## DASAB AIR — DSQ

| | | | |
|---|---|---|---|
| ☐ 5N-BEG | Boeing 727-256 | 914/20602 | |

## EARTH AIRLINES SERVICES

| | | | |
|---|---|---|---|
| ☐ 5N-BEI | Boeing 737-244 | 87/19708 | |

## EAS AIR LINES — EXW

| | | | |
|---|---|---|---|
| ☐ 5N-BEY | Boeing 737-2K9 | 804/22504 | |
| ☐ 5N-ESA | BAC One-Eleven 501EX | 174 | |
| ☐ 5N-ESB | BAC One-Eleven 501EX | 175 | |
| ☐ 5N-ESD | BAC One-Eleven 561RC | 402 | |
| ☐ 5N-ESE | BAC One-Eleven 525FT | 254 | |
| ☐ F-GYAL | Boeing 737-222 | 95/19074 | Lsf BIE |

## FREEDOM AIR SERVICES — FFF

| | | | |
|---|---|---|---|
| ☐ 5N-BCY | Boeing 727-235 | 538/19461 | |
| ☐ 5N-BEJ | Boeing 727-227 | 1132/21044 | |

## IRS AIRLINES — LVB

| | | | |
|---|---|---|---|
| ☐ 5N-AKR | Boeing 727-223A | 1121/20984 | |
| ☐ 5N-RIR | Boeing 727-223A | 1250/21087 | |

## KABO AIR — QNK

| | | | |
|---|---|---|---|
| ☐ 5N-CCC | BAC One-Eleven 401AK | 069 | VIP |
| ☐ 5N-GGG | BAC One-Eleven 414EG | 154 | std |
| ☐ 5N-HHH | BAC One-Eleven 401AK | 064 | std |
| ☐ 5N-KBW | BAC One-Eleven 407AW | 106 | ex std |
| ☐ 5N-KKK | BAC One-Eleven 423ET | 160 | |
| ☐ 5N-VVV | BAC One-Eleven 401AK | 080 | |
| ☐ 5N-EEE | Boeing 747-243B | 134/19732 | |
| ☐ 5N-JJJ | Boeing 747-136 | 111/19766 | |
| ☐ 5N-NNN | Boeing 747-287B | 274/21189 | |
| ☐ 5N-OOO | Boeing 747-136 | 246/20952 | |
| ☐ 5N-PDP | Boeing 747-238B | 238/20842 | |
| ☐ 5N-PPP | Boeing 747-238B | 241/20921 | |
| ☐ 5N-RRR | Boeing 747-136 | 109/19765 | |
| ☐ 5N-MMM | Boeing 727-224 | 938/20656 | std |

## NIGERIA AIRWAYS — NGA

| | | | |
|---|---|---|---|
| ☐ 5N-ANN | Douglas DC-10-30 | 231/46957 | |
| ☐ 5N-ANY | Boeing 737-2F9 | 893/22773 | |
| ☐ 5N-AUB | Boeing 737-2F9 | 925/22986 | |
| ☐ 5N-AUF | Airbus A310-222 | 285 | std |

## OKADA AIR — OKJ

| | | | |
|---|---|---|---|
| ☐ 5N-USE | BAC One-Eleven 524FF | 235 | |

## ORIENTAL AIRLINES — OAC

| | | | |
|---|---|---|---|
| ☐ 5N-ENO | BAC One-Eleven 515FD | 208 | |
| ☐ 5N-EYI | BAC One-Eleven 523FJ | 211 | std |

## SAVANNAH AIRLINES — SNI

| | | | |
|---|---|---|---|
| ☐ 5N-BDU | BAC One-Eleven 523FJ | 193 | |
| ☐ 5N-BDV | BAC One-Eleven 530FX | 233 | |

## SOSOLISO AIRLINES — OSL

| | | | |
|---|---|---|---|
| ☐ YU-AJI | Douglas DC-9-32 | 687/47563 | Lsf JAT |

## TRANSAHARAN AIRLINES

| | | | |
|---|---|---|---|
| ☐ 5N-DEC | Boeing 727-256 | 1080/20975 | |

# 5R - MADAGASCAR

## AIR MADAGASCAR — MDG

| | | | |
|---|---|---|---|
| ☐ 5R-MFA | Boeing 737-2B2 | 204/20231 | |
| ☐ 5R-MFB | Boeing 737-2B2 | 314/20680 | |
| ☐ 5R-MFH | Boeing 737-3Q8 | 2651/26305 | |
| ☐ 5R-MJC | ATR 42-300 | 132 | |
| ☐ 5R-MJD | ATR 42-310 | 155 | |
| ☐ 5R-MVT | ATR 42-300 | 044 | |

# 5T - MAURITANIA

## AIR MAURITANIE — MRT

| | | | |
|---|---|---|---|
| ☐ 5T-CLG | F-28 Fellowship 4000 | 11093 | |
| ☐ 5T-CLH | F-28 Fellowship 4000 | 11138 | |
| ☐ 5T-CLK | Boeing 737-7Q8 | 22/28210 | |

# 5V - TOGO

## AIR TOGO

| | | | |
|---|---|---|---|
| ☐ 5V-TAI | F-28 Fellowship 1000 | 11079 | Lsf Govt |

## TRANS AFRICAN

| | | | |
|---|---|---|---|
| ☐ 5V-TTK | Douglas DC-9-32 | 302/47198 | |

# 5W - SAMOA

## POLYNESIAN – AIRLINES OF SAMOA — PAO

| | | | |
|---|---|---|---|
| ☐ 5W-SAM | Boeing 737-8Q8 | 701/30039 | |
| ☐ 5W-SAO | Boeing 737-8Q8 | 935/30639 | |

# 5X - UGANDA

## AFRICA ONE — AFI

| | | | |
|---|---|---|---|
| ☐ 5X-ONE | Douglas DC-10-30 | 185/46952 | |
| ☐ 5X-TRE | Douglas DC-9-51 | 864/47746 | |
| ☐ 5X-TWO | Douglas DC-9-51 | 861/47732 | |
| ☐ 5X- | Douglas DC-9-51 | 860/47731 | |

### DAS AIR CARGO — DSR

| | | |
|---|---|---|
| ☐ N400JR | Douglas DC-10-30F | 254/46976 |
| ☐ N401JR | Douglas DC-10-30F | 266/46590 |
| ☐ N402JR | Douglas DC-10-30F | 327/47831 |
| ☐ 3C-QRO | Boeing 707-351C | 540/19411 |
| ☐ 5X-JOE | Douglas DC-10-30CF | 115/47906 |
| ☐ 5X-ROY | Douglas DC-10-30F | 305/47818 |

### GREAT LAKE AIRWAYS — GLU

| | | |
|---|---|---|
| ☐ 5X-GLA | Boeing 707-379C | 718/19821 |

## 5Y - KENYA

### AFRICAN AIRLINES INTERNATIONAL — AIK

| | | |
|---|---|---|
| ☐ 5Y-AXI | Boeing 707-330B | 454/18927 |

### AFRICAN EXPRESS AIRWAYS — AXK

| | | | |
|---|---|---|---|
| ☐ 5Y-AXB | Boeing 727-231 | 603/19565 | |
| ☐ 5Y-AXD | Douglas DC-9-32 | 180/47088 | Lsf RLL |
| ☐ 9L-LDG | Douglas DC-9-32 | 237/47093 | Lsf RLL |

### AIRKENYA

| | | |
|---|---|---|
| ☐ 5Y-BMJ | DHC-7-102 | 83 |
| ☐ 5Y-BMP | DHC-7-102 | 80 |
| ☐ 5Y-BPD | DHC-7-102 | 32 |
| ☐ 5Y-BPZ | Boeing 737-2P6 | 564/21733 |

### ASA – AFRICAN SAFARI AIRWAYS — QSC

| | | | |
|---|---|---|---|
| ☐ 5Y-VIP | Airbus A310-308 | 620 | Lsf HLF |

### KENYA AIRWAYS — KQA

| | | | |
|---|---|---|---|
| ☐ 5Y-KQA | Boeing 737-3U8 | 2863/28746 | |
| ☐ 5Y-KQB | Boeing 737-3U8 | 2884/28747 | |
| ☐ 5Y-KQC | Boeing 737-3U8 | 3034/29088 | |
| ☐ 5Y-KQD | Boeing 737-3Q8 | 3095/29750 | |
| ☐ 5Y-KQJ | Boeing 737-248 | 565/21714 | |
| ☐ 5Y-KQK | Boeing 737-248 | 579/21715 | |
| ☐ 5Y-KQV | Boeing 767-3Y0ER | 487/26206 | |
| ☐ 5Y-KQW | Boeing 767-3Y0ER | 503/26207 | |
| ☐ 5Y-KQX | Boeing 767-36NER | 844/30854 | |
| ☐ 5Y-KQY | Boeing 767-36NER | 841/30841 | |
| ☐ 5Y-KQZ | Boeing 767-36NER | 837/30853 | |
| ☐ 5Y-KQE | Boeing 737-76N | 877/30133 | |
| ☐ 5Y-KQF | Boeing 737-76N | 1145/30136 | |
| ☐ 5Y-KQG | Boeing 737-7U8 | 1242/32371 | |
| ☐ 5Y-KQH | Boeing 737-7U8 | 32372 | o/o |

## 6V - SENEGAL

### AIR SENEGAL INTERNATIONAL — SNG

| | | | |
|---|---|---|---|
| ☐ 6V-AHK | Boeing 737-2B6 | 456/21216 | ex Lsf |

### RAM

| | | |
|---|---|---|
| ☐ 6V-AHM | Boeing 737-5K5 | 2044/25062 |
| ☐ 6V-AHN | Boeing 737-7BX | 716/30738 |
| ☐ 6V-AHO | Boeing 737-7BX | 758/30739 |

## 6Y - JAMAICA

### AIR JAMAICA — AJM

| | | |
|---|---|---|
| ☐ 6Y-JAF | Airbus A320-214 | 0624 |
| ☐ 6Y-JAG | Airbus A320-214 | 0626 |

| | | | |
|---|---|---|---|
| ☐ 6Y-JAI | Airbus A320-214 | 0628 | |
| ☐ 6Y-JAJ | Airbus A320-214 | 0630 | |
| ☐ 6Y-JMA | Airbus A320-212 | 0528 | |
| ☐ 6Y-JMB | Airbus A320-212 | 0422 | |
| ☐ 6Y-JMD | Airbus A321-211 | 0666 | |
| ☐ 6Y-JME | Airbus A321-211 | 0775 | |
| ☐ 6Y-JMF | Airbus A320-214 | 1213 | |
| ☐ 6Y-JMG | Airbus A320-214 | 1390 | |
| ☐ 6Y-JMH | Airbus A321-211 | 1503 | |
| ☐ 6Y-JMI | Airbus A320-214 | 1747 | |
| ☐ 6Y-JMJ | Airbus A320-214 | 1751 | |
| ☐ 6Y- | Airbus A320-214 | | o/o |
| ☐ 6Y- | Airbus A321-211 | 1905 | |
| ☐ 6Y- | Airbus A321-211 | 1966 | |
| ☐ 6Y- | Airbus A321-211 | 1988 | |
| ☐ 6Y-JAB | Airbus A310-324ER | 676 | |
| ☐ 6Y-JAC | Airbus A310-324ER | 678 | |
| ☐ 6Y-JAD | Airbus A310-324ER | 682 | |
| ☐ 6Y-JAE | Airbus A310-324ER | 686 | |
| ☐ 6Y-JMC | Airbus A340-312 | 048 | |
| ☐ 6Y-JMM | Airbus A340-313X | 216 | |
| ☐ 6Y-JMP | Airbus A340-313X | 257 | |

## 7O - YEMEN

### YEMENIA — IYE

| | | | |
|---|---|---|---|
| ☐ F-OGYO | Airbus A310-324ET | 568 | |
| ☐ F-OHPR | Airbus A310-325 | 702 | |
| ☐ F-OHPS | Airbus A310-325 | 704 | |
| ☐ 7O-ACQ | Boeing 737-2R4C | 1034/23129 | |
| ☐ 7O-ACR | Boeing 737-2R4C | 1040/23130 | |
| ☐ 7O-ACU | Boeing 737-2N8 | 478/21296 | |
| ☐ 7O-ACV | Boeing 727-2N8 | 1518/21844 | |
| ☐ 7O-ACX | Boeing 727-2N8 | 1549/21846 | |
| ☐ 7O-ACY | Boeing 727-2N8 | 1557/21847 | |
| ☐ 7O-ADA | Boeing 727-2N8 | 1512/21842 | Govt |
| ☐ 7O-ADF | Ilyushin Il-76TD | 1033418578 | |
| ☐ 7O-ADG | Ilyushin Il-76TD | 1023412402 | |
| ☐ 7O-ADJ | Airbus A310-324 | 535 | |
| ☐ 7O-ADL | Boeing 737-8Q8 | 1129/30645 | |
| ☐ 7O-ADM | Boeing 737-8Q8 | 1195/28252 | |
| ☐ 7O-ADN | Boeing 737-8Q8 | 1186/30661 | |

## 7T - ALGERIA

### AIR ALGERIE — DAH

| | | |
|---|---|---|
| ☐ 7T-VEA | Boeing 727-2D6 | 850/20472 |
| ☐ 7T-VEB | Boeing 727-2D6 | 855/20473 |
| ☐ 7T-VEI | Boeing 727-2D6 | 1111/21053 |
| ☐ 7T-VEM | Boeing 727-2D6 | 1204/21210 |
| ☐ 7T-VEP | Boeing 727-2D6 | 1233/21284 |
| ☐ 7T-VET | Boeing 727-2D6 | 1662/22372 |
| ☐ 7T-VEU | Boeing 727-2D6 | 1664/22373 |
| ☐ 7T-VEV | Boeing 727-2D6 | 1711/22374 |
| ☐ 7T-VEW | Boeing 727-2D6 | 1723/22375 |
| ☐ 7T-VEX | Boeing 727-2D6 | 1801/22765 |
| ☐ 7T-VEF | Boeing 737-2D6 | 332/20759 |
| ☐ 7T-VEG | Boeing 737-2D6 | 361/20884 |
| ☐ 7T-VEJ | Boeing 737-2D6 | 407/21063 |
| ☐ 7T-VEK | Boeing 737-2D6 | 409/21064 |
| ☐ 7T-VEL | Boeing 737-2D6 | 416/21065 |
| ☐ 7T-VEN | Boeing 737-2D6 | 454/21211 |
| ☐ 7T-VEO | Boeing 737-2D6 | 459/21212 |
| ☐ 7T-VEQ | Boeing 737-2D6 | 473/21285 |
| ☐ 7T-VER | Boeing 737-2D6 | 482/21286 |
| ☐ 7T-VES | Boeing 737-2D6C | 486/21287 |
| ☐ 7T-VEY | Boeing 737-2D6 | 853/22766 |
| ☐ 7T-VEZ | Boeing 737-2T4 | 885/22700 |
| ☐ 7T-VJA | Boeing 737-2T4 | 897/22800 |
| ☐ 7T-VJB | Boeing 737-2T4 | 900/22801 |
| ☐ 7T-VJJ | Boeing 737-8D6 | 610/30202 |

| | | | |
|---|---|---|---|
| ☐ 7T-VJK | Boeing 737-8D6 | 640/30203 | |
| ☐ 7T-VJL | Boeing 737-8D6 | 652/30204 | |
| ☐ 7T-VJM | Boeing 737-8D6 | 691/30205 | |
| ☐ 7T-VJN | Boeing 737-8D6 | 751/30206 | |
| ☐ 7T-VJO | Boeing 737-8D6 | 868/30207 | |
| ☐ 7T-VJP | Boeing 737-8D6 | 896/30208 | |
| ☐ 7T-VJQ | Boeing 737-6D6 | 1115/30209 | |
| ☐ 7T-VJR | Boeing 737-6D6 | 1131/30545 | |
| ☐ 7T-VJS | Boeing 737-6D6 | 1150/30210 | |
| ☐ 7T-VJT | Boeing 737-6D6 | 1152/30546 | |
| ☐ 7T-VJU | Boeing 737-6D6 | 1164/30211 | |
| | | | |
| ☐ 7T-VJC | Airbus A310-203 | 291 | |
| ☐ 7T-VJD | Airbus A310-203 | 293 | |
| ☐ 7T-VJG | Boeing 767-3D6ER | 310/24766 | |
| ☐ 7T-VJH | Boeing 767-3D6ER | 323/24767 | |
| ☐ 7T-VJI | Boeing 767-3D6ER | 332/24768 | |
| ☐ 7T-VKL | Airbus A340-313X | 117 | Lsf KZW |

### ANTINEA AIRLINES — DJA

| | | | |
|---|---|---|---|
| ☐ 7T-VVA | Boeing 737-210C | 256/20440 | |

### KHALIFA AIRWAYS — KZW

| | | | |
|---|---|---|---|
| ☐ F-OHGM | ATR 72-212A | 644 | |
| ☐ F-OHGN | ATR 72-212A | 648 | |
| ☐ F-OHGO | ATR 72-212A | 652 | |
| ☐ F-OHGP | ATR 72-212A | 672 | |
| ☐ F-OHGQ | ATR 72-212A | 677 | |
| ☐ F-OHGR | ATR 72-212A | 684 | o/o |
| ☐ F-OHGT | ATR 72-212A | 698 | o/o |
| ☐ F-OHRN | ATR 42-320 | 268 | |
| ☐ F-OHRO | ATR 42-320 | 304 | |
| ☐ F-OHRP | ATR 42-320 | 178 | |
| ☐ F-OHRQ | ATR 42-320 | 203 | |
| ☐ 7T-VVQ | ATR 72-212A | 676 | gt |
| ☐ 7T-VVR | ATR 72-212A | 683 | gt |
| ☐ 7T-VVS | ATR 72-212A | 694 | |
| ☐ 7T-VVT | ATR 72-212A | 699 | o/o |
| ☐ | ATR 72-212A | | o/o |
| ☐ | ATR 72-212A | | o/o |
| | | | |
| ☐ F-OGYM | Airbus A310-324 | 457 | std |
| ☐ F-OGYN | Airbus A310-324 | 458 | std |
| ☐ F-OGYS | Airbus A310-324 | 467 | std |
| ☐ F-OHPU | Airbus A310-324 | 439 | |
| ☐ F-OHPV | Airbus A310-324 | 449 | |
| ☐ F-OHPY | Airbus A310-324 | 452 | std |
| ☐ F-OIHS | Airbus A310-304 | 674 | |
| | | | |
| ☐ D-AILH | Airbus A319-114 | 0641 | Lsf DLH |
| ☐ D-AILI | Airbus A319-114 | 0651 | Lsf DLH |
| ☐ D-AILK | Airbus A319-114 | 0679 | Lsf DLH |
| ☐ F-OHJV | Airbus A319-112 | 1048 | |
| ☐ F-OHJX | Airbus A320-214 | 1086 | |
| ☐ F-OHJY | Airbus A319-112 | 1124 | |
| ☐ F-OHJZ | Airbus A319-112 | 1054 | |
| ☐ 7T-VKO | Airbus A320-211 | 0094 | Lsf DLH |
| ☐ C-FRAE | Airbus A330-322 | 143 | Lsf SSV |
| ☐ C-FRAV | Airbus A330-322 | 171 | Lsf SSV |
| ☐ TC-AFJ | Boeing 737-4Y0 | 1661/23979 | Lsf PGT |
| ☐ TC-APD | Boeing 737-42R | 2997/29107 | Lsf PGT |
| ☐ TC-APM | Boeing 737-809 | 117/28403 | Lsf PGT |
| ☐ TC-APY | Boeing 737-86N | 233/28591 | Lsf PGT |
| ☐ 7T-VKL | Airbus A340-313X | 117 | Lst DAH |
| ☐ 7T-VKM | Airbus A340-313X | 139 | |
| ☐ 7T-VKN | Airbus A340-313X | 149 | |
| ☐ 7T-VKP | Boeing 777-236 | 17/27108 | o/o |
| ☐ | Boeing 777-236 | 19/27109 | o/o |
| ☐ | Boeing 747-409 | 904/25879 | o/o |

### SAHARA AIRLINES — SHD

| | | | |
|---|---|---|---|
| ☐ 7T-VVJ | Fairchild FH-227B | 544 | ex |
| ☐ 7T-VVK | Fairchild FH-227B | 562 | |

### TASSILI AIRLINES — DTH

| | | | |
|---|---|---|---|
| ☐ F-GVZA | ATR 42-300 | 503 | Lsf ARF |
| ☐ HB-IVX | DHC-7-102 | | 91Lsf Benavia |
| ☐ HB-IVY | DHC-7-102 | | 74Lsf Benavia |

## 8R - GUYANA

### UNIVERSAL AIRLINES — UVG

| | | | |
|---|---|---|---|
| ☐ SP-LPB | Boeing 767-35DER | 577/27902 | Lsf LOT |

## 9A - CROATIA

### AIR ADRIATIC — AHR

| | | | |
|---|---|---|---|
| ☐ 9A-CBC | McDD MD-82 | 1095/49143 | |
| ☐ 9A-CBD | McDD MD-82 | 1049/48093 | |

### CROATIA AIRLINES — CTN

| | | | |
|---|---|---|---|
| ☐ 9A-CTF | Airbus A320-212 | 0258 | |
| ☐ 9A-CTG | Airbus A319-112 | 0767 | |
| ☐ 9A-CTH | Airbus A319-112 | 0833 | |
| ☐ 9A-CTI | Airbus A319-112 | 1029 | |
| ☐ 9A-CTJ | Airbus A320-214 | 1009 | |
| ☐ 9A-CTK | Airbus A320-214 | 1237 | |
| ☐ 9A-CTL | Airbus A319-112 | 1252 | |
| ☐ 9A | Airbus A319-112 | | o/o |
| ☐ 9A- | Airbus A319-112 | | o/o |
| ☐ G-OZRH | BAe 146 Srs.200 | E2047 | Lsf FLT |
| ☐ 9A-CTS | ATR 42-300QC | 312 | |
| ☐ 9A-CTT | ATR 42-300QC | 317 | |
| ☐ 9A-CTU | ATR 42-320 | 394 | |

## 9G - GHANA

### GHANA AIRWAYS — GHA

| | | | |
|---|---|---|---|
| ☐ SU-LBD | Airbus A320-214 | 1372 | Lsf TAS |
| ☐ 9G-ADT | Douglas DC-9-51 | 796/47665 | |
| ☐ 9G-ADU | Douglas DC-9-51 | 803/47692 | |
| ☐ 9G-ANA | Douglas DC-10-30 | 369/48286 | |
| ☐ 9G-ANB | Douglas DC-10-30 | 234/46959 | |
| ☐ 9G-ANC | Douglas DC-10-30 | 159/46933 | |

### JOHNSONS AIR — JON

| | | | |
|---|---|---|---|
| ☐ 5Y-BOR | Boeing 707-399C | 601/19415 | Lst ETC |
| ☐ 9G-FIA | Boeing 707-331C | 815/20069 | std |
| ☐ 9G-JET | Boeing 707-323C | 655/19372 | |
| ☐ 9G-LAD | Boeing 707-323C | 439/18940 | std |
| ☐ 9G-OLD | Boeing 707-324C | 537/19350 | |
| ☐ 9G-LCA | Canadair CL-44-0 Guppy | 16 | |

### MK AIRLINES — MKA

| | | | |
|---|---|---|---|
| ☐ 9G-MKA | Douglas DC-8F-55 | 254/45804 | std |
| ☐ 9G-MKC | Douglas DC-8F-55 | 207/45692 | std |
| ☐ 9G-MKE | Douglas DC-8-55F | 223/45753 | |
| ☐ 9G-MKF | Douglas DC-8F-55 | 246/45820 | |
| ☐ 9G-MKG | Douglas DC-8-62F | 437/46027 | |
| ☐ 9G-MKH | Douglas DC-8-62AF | 551/46153 | |
| ☐ 9G-MKK | Douglas DC-8-62F | 417/46022 | |
| ☐ 9G-MKN | Douglas DC-8-63CF | 540/46151 | |
| ☐ 9G-MKO | Douglas DC-8-63AF | 549/46147 | |
| ☐ 9G- | Douglas DC-8-62F | 461/46028 | std |
| ☐ 9G- | Douglas DC-8F-55 | 251/45674 | |
| | | | |
| ☐ 9G-MKJ | Boeing 747-244SF | 486/22170 | |
| ☐ 9G-MKL | Boeing 747-2R7F | 354/21650 | |
| ☐ 9G-MKM | Boeing 747-2B5B (SF) | 484/22482 | |
| ☐ 9G-MKP | Boeing 747-245F | 396/21841 | |

## 9H - MALTA

### AIR MALTA     AMC

| | | |
|---|---|---|
| ☐ 9H-ABE | Boeing 737-2Y5 | 1414/23847 |
| ☐ 9H-ABF | Boeing 737-2Y5 | 1418/23848 |
| ☐ 9H-ABR | Boeing 737-3Y5 | 2446/25613 |
| ☐ 9H-ABS | Boeing 737-3Y5 | 2467/25614 |
| ☐ 9H-ABT | Boeing 737-3Y5 | 2478/25615 |
| ☐ 9H-ADH | Boeing 737-33A | 3007/27459 |
| ☐ 9H-ADI | Boeing 737-33A | 3021/27460 |
| ☐ 9H-ADM | Boeing 737-382 | 1695/24365 |
| ☐ 9H-ADN | Boeing 737-382 | 2226/25161 |
| | | |
| ☐ 9H-ABP | Airbus A320-211 | 0112 |
| ☐ 9H-ABQ | Airbus A320-211 | 0293 |
| ☐ 9H-ADY | Airbus A320-214 | 1769 |
| ☐ 9H-ADZ | Airbus A320-211 | 0331 |

## 9K - KUWAIT

### KUWAIT AIRWAYS     KAC

| | | | |
|---|---|---|---|
| ☐ 9K-AHI | Airbus A300C4-620 | 344 | |
| ☐ 9K-AMA | Airbus A300B4-605R | 673 | |
| ☐ 9K-AMB | Airbus A300B4-605R | 694 | |
| ☐ 9K-AMC | Airbus A300B4-605R | 699 | |
| ☐ 9K-AMD | Airbus A300B4-605R | 719 | |
| ☐ 9K-AME | Airbus A300B4-605R | 721 | |
| | | | |
| ☐ 9K-ALA | Airbus A310-308 | 647 | |
| ☐ 9K-ALB | Airbus A310-308 | 649 | |
| ☐ 9K-ALC | Airbus A310-308 | 663 | |
| ☐ 9K-ALD | Airbus A310-308 | 648 | |
| ☐ 9K-ADB | Boeing 747-269M | 335/21542 | |
| ☐ 9K-ADD | Boeing 747-269M | 553/22740 | |
| ☐ 9K-ADE | Boeing 747-469M | 1046/27338 | |
| ☐ 9K-AKA | Airbus A320-212 | 0181 | |
| ☐ 9K-AKB | Airbus A320-212 | 0182 | |
| ☐ 9K-AKC | Airbus A320-212 | 0195 | |
| ☐ 9K-AKD | Airbus A320-212 | | o/o |
| ☐ 9K-ANA | Airbus A340-313 | 089 | |
| ☐ 9K-ANB | Airbus A340-313 | 090 | |
| ☐ 9K-ANC | Airbus A340-313 | 101 | |
| ☐ 9K-AND | Airbus A340-313 | 104 | |
| ☐ 9K-AOA | Boeing 777-269ER | 125/28743 | |
| ☐ 9K-AOB | Boeing 777-269ER | 145/28744 | |

## 9L - SIERRA LEONE

### AIR LEONE     RLL

| | | | |
|---|---|---|---|
| ☐ 9L-LCW | Ilyushin Il-76TD | 0033448404 | |
| ☐ 9L-LCX | Ilyushin Il-76TD | 0043453575 | |
| ☐ 9L-LDF | Douglas DC-9-32 | 180/47088 | Lst AXK |
| ☐ 9L-LDG | Douglas DC-9-32 | 237/47093 | Lst AXK |
| ☐ 9L-LDI | Yakovlev Yak-40 | 9542043 | |
| ☐ 9L-LDJ | BAC One-Eleven Srs 531FS | 242 | std |
| ☐ 9L-LDK | BAC One-Eleven Srs 518FG | 203 | o/o |
| ☐ 9L-LDL | BAC One-Eleven Srs 518FG | 232 | std |

### AIR UNIVERSAL     UVS

| | | |
|---|---|---|
| ☐ 9L-LDC | L-1011-100 Tristar | 1231 |
| ☐ 9L-LDE | L-1011-250 Tristar | 1244 |

### HA AIRLINES     BEY

| | | |
|---|---|---|
| ☐ 9L-LCU | Boeing 727-256 | 1010/20818 |
| ☐ 9L-LCY | Boeing 727-256 | 912/20600 |

### QUIKMAY AIRLINES     AMM

| | | |
|---|---|---|
| ☐ 9L-LCK | Boeing 727-256 | 1006/20814 |
| ☐ 9L-LCS | Boeing 727-256 | 910/20598 |

## 9M - MALAYSIA

### AIR ASIA     AXM

| | | |
|---|---|---|
| ☐ 9M-AAA | Boeing 737-3Y0 | 2013/24907 |
| ☐ 9M-AAB | Boeing 737-36N | 2846/28555 |
| ☐ 9M-AAC | Boeing 737-3Q8 | 2854/28200 |
| ☐ 9M-AAD | Boeing 737-3Y0 | 2001/24905 |
| ☐ 9M-AAE | Boeing 737-3L9 | 1800/24570 |
| ☐ 9M-AAF | Boeing 737-33A | 1739/24096 |
| ☐ 9M-AAG | Boeing 737-3 | 2347/27061 |

### BERJAYA AIR CHARTER     BVT

| | | |
|---|---|---|
| ☐ 9M-TAH | DHC-7-110 | 109 |
| ☐ 9M-TAK | DHC-7-110 | 110 |
| ☐ 9M-TAL | DHC-7-110 | 112 |
| ☐ 9M-TAO | DHC-7-110 | 62 |

### MALAYSIA AIRLINES     MAS

| | | | |
|---|---|---|---|
| ☐ 9M-MKA | Airbus A330-322 | 067 | |
| ☐ 9M-MKC | Airbus A330-322 | 069 | |
| ☐ 9M-MKD | Airbus A330-322 | 073 | |
| ☐ 9M-MKE | Airbus A330-322 | 077 | |
| ☐ 9M-MKF | Airbus A330-322 | 100 | |
| ☐ 9M-MKG | Airbus A330-322 | 107 | |
| ☐ 9M-MKH | Airbus A330-322 | 110 | |
| ☐ 9M-MKI | Airbus A330-322 | 116 | |
| ☐ 9M-MKJ | Airbus A330-322 | 119 | |
| ☐ 9M- | Airbus A330-223 | 290 | o/o |
| ☐ 9M- | Airbus A330-223 | 296 | o/o |
| ☐ 9M- | Airbus A330-223 | 300 | o/o |
| | | | |
| ☐ 9M-MMA | Boeing 737-4H6 | 2272/26443 | |
| ☐ 9M-MMB | Boeing 737-4H6 | 2308/26444 | |
| ☐ 9M-MMC | Boeing 737-4H6 | 2332/26453 | |
| ☐ 9M-MMD | Boeing 737-4H6 | 2340/26464 | |
| ☐ 9M-MME | Boeing 737-4H6 | 2362/26465 | |
| ☐ 9M-MMF | Boeing 737-4H6 | 2372/26466 | |
| ☐ 9M-MMG | Boeing 737-4H6 | 2378/26467 | |
| ☐ 9M-MMH | Boeing 737-4H6 | 2391/27084 | |
| ☐ 9M-MMI | Boeing 737-4H6 | 2395/27096 | |
| ☐ 9M-MMJ | Boeing 737-4H6 | 2399/27097 | |
| ☐ 9M-MMK | Boeing 737-4H6 | 2403/27083 | |
| ☐ 9M-MML | Boeing 737-4H6 | 2407/27085 | |
| ☐ 9M-MMM | Boeing 737-4H6 | 2410/27166 | |
| ☐ 9M-MMN | Boeing 737-4H6 | 2419/27167 | |
| ☐ 9M-MMQ | Boeing 737-4H6 | 2441/27087 | |
| ☐ 9M-MMR | Boeing 737-4H6 | 2445/26468 | |
| ☐ 9M-MMS | Boeing 737-4H6 | 2450/27169 | |
| ☐ 9M-MMT | Boeing 737-4H6 | 2462/27170 | |
| ☐ 9M-MMU | Boeing 737-4H6 | 2479/26447 | |
| ☐ 9M-MMV | Boeing 737-4H6 | 2491/26449 | |
| ☐ 9M-MMW | Boeing 737-4H6 | 2496/26451 | |
| ☐ 9M-MMX | Boeing 737-4H6 | 2501/26452 | |
| ☐ 9M-MMY | Boeing 737-4H6 | 2507/26455 | |
| ☐ 9M-MMZ | Boeing 737-4H6 | 2521/26457 | |
| ☐ 9M-MQA | Boeing 737-4H6 | 2525/26458 | |
| ☐ 9M-MQB | Boeing 737-4H6 | 2530/26459 | |
| ☐ 9M-MQC | Boeing 737-4H6 | 2533/26460 | |
| ☐ 9M-MQD | Boeing 737-4H6 | 2536/26461 | |
| ☐ 9M-MQE | Boeing 737-4H6 | 2542/26462 | |
| ☐ 9M-MQF | Boeing 737-4H6 | 2560/26463 | |
| ☐ 9M-MQG | Boeing 737-4H6 | 2568/27190 | |
| ☐ 9M-MQH | Boeing 737-4H6 | 2624/27352 | |
| ☐ 9M-MQI | Boeing 737-4H6 | 2632/27353 | |
| ☐ 9M-MQJ | Boeing 737-4H6 | 2657/27383 | |
| ☐ 9M-MQK | Boeing 737-4H6 | 2673/27384 | |
| ☐ 9M-MQL | Boeing 737-4H6 | 2676/27191 | |
| ☐ 9M-MQM | Boeing 737-4H6 | 2685/27306 | |
| ☐ 9M-MQN | Boeing 737-4H6 | 2852/27673 | |
| ☐ 9M-MQO | Boeing 737-4H6 | 2877/27674 | |

| | | | |
|---|---|---|---|
| ☐ TF-ATX | Boeing 747-236B (SF) | 672/23711 | Opb ABD |
| ☐ TF-ATZ | Boeing 747-236B (SF) | 697/24088 | Opb ABD |
| ☐ 9M-MHI | Boeing 747-236 (SCD) | 502/22304 | |
| ☐ 9M-MHJ | Boeing 747-236 (SCD) | 526/22442 | |
| ☐ 9M-MHM | Boeing 747-4H6M | 745/24405 | |
| ☐ 9M-MPA | Boeing 747-4H6 | 932/27042 | |
| ☐ 9M-MPB | Boeing 747-4H6 | 965/25699 | |
| ☐ 9M-MPC | Boeing 747-4H6 | 974/25700 | |
| ☐ 9M-MPD | Boeing 747-4H6 | 997/25701 | |
| ☐ 9M-MPE | Boeing 747-4H6 | 999/25702 | |
| ☐ 9M-MPF | Boeing 747-4H6 | 1017/27043 | |
| ☐ 9M-MPG | Boeing 747-4H6 | 1025/25703 | |
| ☐ 9M-MPH | Boeing 747-4H6 | 1041/27044 | |
| ☐ 9M-MPI | Boeing 747-4H6 | 1091/27672 | |
| ☐ 9M-MPJ | Boeing 747-4H6 | 1130/28426 | |
| ☐ 9M-MPK | Boeing 747-4H6 | 1147/28427 | |
| ☐ 9M-MPL | Boeing 747-4H6 | 1150/28428 | |
| ☐ 9M-MPM | Boeing 747-4H6 | 1152/28435 | |
| ☐ 9M-MPN | Boeing 747-4H6 | 1247/28432 | |
| ☐ 9M-MPO | Boeing 747-4H6 | 1290/28433 | |
| ☐ 9M-MPP | Boeing 747-4H6 | 1296/29900 | |
| ☐ 9M-MPQ | Boeing 747-4H6 | 1301/29901 | |
| ☐ 9M- | Boeing 747-4H6 | | o/o |
| ☐ 9M- | Boeing 747-4H6 | | o/o |
| | | | |
| ☐ 9M-MRA | Boeing 777-2H6ER | 64/28408 | |
| ☐ 9M-MRB | Boeing 777-2H6ER | 74/28409 | |
| ☐ 9M-MRC | Boeing 777-2H6ER | 78/28410 | |
| ☐ 9M-MRD | Boeing 777-2H6ER | 84/28411 | |
| ☐ 9M-MRE | Boeing 777-2H6ER | 115/28412 | |
| ☐ 9M-MRF | Boeing 777-2H6ER | 128/28413 | |
| ☐ 9M-MRG | Boeing 777-2H6ER | 140/28414 | |
| ☐ 9M-MRH | Boeing 777-2H6ER | 151/28415 | |
| ☐ 9M-MRI | Boeing 777-2H6ER | 155/28416 | |
| ☐ 9M-MRJ | Boeing 777-2H6ER | 222/28417 | |
| ☐ 9M-MRK | Boeing 777-2H6ER | 231/28418 | |
| ☐ 9M-MRL | Boeing 777-2H6ER | 329/29065 | |
| ☐ 9M-MRM | Boeing 777-2H6ER | 336/29066 | |
| ☐ 9M-MRN | Boeing 777-2H6ER | 394/28419 | |
| ☐ 9M-MRO | Boeing 777-2H6ER | 404/28420 | |
| ☐ 9M- | Boeing 777-3H6 | o/o | |
| ☐ 9M- | Boeing 777-3H6 | o/o | |
| ☐ 9M- | Boeing 777-3H6 | o/o | |
| ☐ 9M- | Boeing 777-3H6 | o/o | |
| | | | |
| ☐ 9M-MGA | Fokker 50 | 20150 | |
| ☐ 9M-MGB | Fokker 50 | 20156 | |
| ☐ 9M-MGC | Fokker 50 | 20161 | |
| ☐ 9M-MGD | Fokker 50 | 20164 | |
| ☐ 9M-MGE | Fokker 50 | 20166 | |
| ☐ 9M-MGF | Fokker 50 | 20167 | |
| ☐ 9M-MGG | Fokker 50 | 20170 | |
| ☐ 9M-MGI | Fokker 50 | 20175 | |
| ☐ 9M-MGJ | Fokker 50 | 20204 | |
| ☐ 9M-MGK | Fokker 50 | 20248 | |
| ☐ 9M-BBJ | Boeing 737-7H6 | 397/29274 | |

### TRANSMILE AIR SERVICES — TSE

| | | | |
|---|---|---|---|
| ☐ 9M-TGA | Boeing 727-2F2F | 1808/22993 | Lst AMU |
| ☐ M-TGB | Boeing 727-2F2F | 1810/22998 | Lst AMU |
| ☐ 9M-TGE | Boeing 727-247F | 1471/21697 | |
| ☐ 9M-TGF | Boeing 727-247F | 1474/21698 | |
| ☐ 9M-TGG | Boeing 727-247F | 1485/21699 | |
| ☐ 9M-TGG | Boeing 727-247F | 1493/21701 | |
| ☐ 9M-TGH | Boeing 727-223F | 661/19494 | |
| ☐ 9M- | Boeing 727-223F | 545/19480 | |
| ☐ 9M- | Boeing 727-223F | 710/20185 | |
| | | | |
| ☐ 9M-PML | Boeing 737-275C | 427/21116 | |
| ☐ 9M-PMM | Boeing 737-205C | 278/20458 | |
| ☐ 9M-PMP | Boeing 737-248C | 215/20220 | Lst TSD |
| ☐ 9M-PMW | Boeing 737-209 | 1581/24197 | |
| ☐ 9M-PMZ | Boeing 737-209 | 1420/23796 | |

## 9N - NEPAL

### ROYAL NEPAL AIRLINES — RNA

| | | | |
|---|---|---|---|
| ☐ 9N-ACA | Boeing 757-2F8 | 142/23850 | |
| ☐ 9N-ACB | Boeing 757-2F8C | 182/23863 | |
| ☐ B-2856 | Boeing 757-2Z0 | 833/29793 | Lsf CXN |

## 9Q - CONGO KINSHASA

### ROYAL NEPAL AIRLINES — RNA

| | | | |
|---|---|---|---|
| ☐ 9Q-CAD | Douglas DC-8-63F | 386/46000 | |

### HEWA BORA AIRWAYS — ALX

| | | | |
|---|---|---|---|
| ☐ 9Q-CHA | L-1011-250 Tristar | 1227 | w/o 02? |
| ☐ 9Q-CHB | L-1011-500 Tristar | 1209 | |
| ☐ 9Q-CHC | L-1011-500 Tristar | 1237 | |
| ☐ 9Q-CKB | Boeing 707-366C | 744/19844 | |
| ☐ 9Q-CKK | Boeing 707-366C | 867/20761 | |
| ☐ 9Q-CKZ | Boeing 737-293 | 47/19309 | |
| ☐ 9Q-CRG | Boeing 727-30 | 28/18361 | |
| ☐ 9Q-CRS | Boeing 727-214 | 573/19687 | |
| ☐ 9Q-CWA | Boeing 727-227 | 998/20775 | std |

### WETRAFA AIRLIFT

| | | | |
|---|---|---|---|
| ☐ 9Q-CWF | Douglas DC-9-32 | 638/47531 | |
| ☐ 9Q-CWT | Boeing 727-25 | 204/18291 | |

## 9V - SINGAPORE

### SILKAIR — SLK

| | | | |
|---|---|---|---|
| ☐ 9V-SBA | Airbus A319-132 | 1074 | |
| ☐ 9V-SBB | Airbus A319-132 | 1098 | |
| ☐ 9V-SBC | Airbus A319-132 | 1228 | |
| ☐ 9V-SBD | Airbus A319-132 | 1698 | |
| ☐ 9V-SLA | Airbus A320-232 | 0872 | |
| ☐ 9V-SLB | Airbus A320-232 | 0899 | |
| ☐ 9V-SLC | Airbus A320-232 | 0969 | |
| ☐ 9V-SLD | Airbus A320-232 | 1422 | |
| ☐ 9V-SLE | Airbus A320-232 | 1561 | |
| ☐ 9V-SLF | Airbus A320-232 | | o/o |

### SINGAPORE AIRLINES — SIA

| | | | |
|---|---|---|---|
| ☐ 9V-STA | Airbus A310-324 | 665 | |
| ☐ 9V-STB | Airbus A310-324 | 669 | |
| ☐ 9V-STC | Airbus A310-324 | 680 | |
| ☐ 9V-STD | Airbus A310-324 | 684 | |
| ☐ 9V-STE | Airbus A310-324 | 693 | |
| ☐ 9V-STF | Airbus A310-324 | 697 | |
| ☐ 9V-STQ | Airbus A310-324 | 493 | |
| ☐ 9V-STU | Airbus A310-324 | 548 | |
| ☐ 9V-STV | Airbus A310-324 | 570 | |
| ☐ 9V-STW | Airbus A310-324 | 589 | |
| ☐ 9V-STY | Airbus A310-324 | 634 | |
| ☐ 9V-STZ | Airbus A310-324 | 654 | |
| | | | |
| ☐ 9V- | Airbus A340-541 | 478 | o/o |
| ☐ 9V- | Airbus A340-541 | 492 | o/o |
| ☐ 9V- | Airbus A340-541 | 495 | o/o |
| ☐ 9V- | Airbus A340-541 | 499 | o/o |
| ☐ 9V- | Airbus A340-541 | 560 | o/o |
| ☐ 9V- | Airbus A340-541 | 563 | o/o |
| ☐ 9V-SJK | Airbus A340-313X | 202 | |
| ☐ 9V-SJL | Airbus A340-313X | 212 | |
| ☐ 9V-SJM | Airbus A340-313X | 215 | |
| ☐ 9V-SJN | Airbus A340-313X | 236 | |
| ☐ 9V-SJO | Airbus A340-313X | 282 | |
| ☐ 9V- | Airbus A340-313X | 528 | o/o |
| ☐ 9V- | Airbus A340-313X | 554 | o/o |

| | | | |
|---|---|---|---|
| ☐ 9V-SMA | Boeing 747-412 | 717/24061 | std |
| ☐ 9V-SMB | Boeing 747-412 | 722/24062 | std |
| ☐ 9V-SMC | Boeing 747-412 | 736/24063 | |
| ☐ 9V-SMD | Boeing 747-412 | 755/24064 | std |
| ☐ 9V-SME | Boeing 747-412 | 761/24065 | |
| ☐ 9V-SMF | Boeing 747-412 | 791/24066 | |
| ☐ 9V-SMG | Boeing 747-412 | 809/24226 | |
| ☐ 9V-SMH | Boeing 747-412 | 831/24227 | |
| ☐ 9V-SMI | Boeing 747-412 | 838/24975 | |
| ☐ 9V-SMJ | Boeing 747-412 | 852/25068 | |
| ☐ 9V-SMK | Boeing 747-412 | 859/25127 | |
| ☐ 9V-SML | Boeing 747-412 | 860/25128 | |
| ☐ 9V-SMM | Boeing 747-412 | 921/26547 | |
| ☐ 9V-SMN | Boeing 747-412 | 923/26548 | |
| ☐ 9V-SMO | Boeing 747-412 | 940/27066 | |
| ☐ 9V-SMP | Boeing 747-412 | 953/27067 | |
| ☐ 9V-SMQ | Boeing 747-412 | 955/27132 | |
| ☐ 9V-SMR | Boeing 747-412 | 962/27133 | |
| ☐ 9V-SMS | Boeing 747-412 | 981/27134 | |
| ☐ 9V-SMT | Boeing 747-412 | 990/27137 | |
| ☐ 9V-SMU | Boeing 747-412 | 1000/27068 | |
| ☐ 9V-SMV | Boeing 747-412 | 1010/27069 | |
| ☐ 9V-SMW | Boeing 747-412 | 1015/27178 | |
| ☐ 9V-SMY | Boeing 747-412 | 1023/27217 | |
| ☐ 9V-SMZ | Boeing 747-412 | 1030/26549 | |
| ☐ 9V-SPA | Boeing 747-412 | 1040/26550 | |
| ☐ 9V-SPB | Boeing 747-412 | 1045/26551 | |
| ☐ 9V-SPC | Boeing 747-412 | 1049/27070 | |
| ☐ 9V-SPD | Boeing 747-412 | 1056/26552 | |
| ☐ 9V-SPE | Boeing 747-412 | 1070/26554 | |
| ☐ 9V-SPF | Boeing 747-412 | 1072/27071 | |
| ☐ 9V-SPG | Boeing 747-412 | 1074/26562 | |
| ☐ 9V-SPH | Boeing 747-412 | 1075/26555 | |
| ☐ 9V-SPI | Boeing 747-412 | 1082/28022 | |
| ☐ 9V-SPJ | Boeing 747-412 | 1084/26556 | |
| ☐ 9V-SPL | Boeing 747-412 | 1101/26557 | |
| ☐ 9V-SPM | Boeing 747-412 | 1241/29950 | |
| ☐ 9V-SPN | Boeing 747-412 | 1266/28031 | |
| ☐ 9V-SPO | Boeing 747-412 | 1270/28028 | |
| ☐ 9V-SPP | Boeing 747-412 | 1276/28029 | |
| ☐ 9V-SPQ | Boeing 747-412 | 1289/28025 | |
| ☐ 9V- | Boeing 747-412 | | o/o |
| ☐ 9V- | Boeing 747-412 | | o/o |
| | | | |
| ☐ 9V-SQA | Boeing 777-212ER | 67/28507 | |
| ☐ 9V-SQB | Boeing 777-212ER | 83/28508 | |
| ☐ 9V-SQC | Boeing 777-212ER | 86/28509 | |
| ☐ 9V-SQD | Boeing 777-212ER | 90/28510 | |
| ☐ 9V-SQE | Boeing 777-212ER | 122/28511 | |
| ☐ 9V-SQF | Boeing 777-212ER | 126/28512 | |
| ☐ 9V-SQG | Boeing 777-212ER | 226/28518 | |
| ☐ 9V-SQH | Boeing 777-212ER | 237/28519 | |
| ☐ 9V-SQI | Boeing 777-212ER | 390/28530 | |
| ☐ 9V-SQJ | Boeing 777-212ER | 406/30875 | |
| ☐ 9V-SQK | Boeing 777-212ER | 428/33368 | |
| ☐ 9V-SRA | Boeing 777-212ER | 144/28513 | |
| ☐ 9V-SRB | Boeing 777-212ER | 149/28998 | |
| ☐ 9V-SRC | Boeing 777-212ER | 150/28999 | |
| ☐ 9V-SRD | Boeing 777-212ER | 153/28514 | |
| ☐ 9V-SRE | Boeing 777-212ER | 239/28523 | |
| ☐ 9V-SRF | Boeing 777-212ER | 330/28521 | |
| ☐ 9V-SRG | Boeing 777-212ER | 337/28522 | |
| ☐ 9V-SRH | Boeing 777-212ER | 343/30866 | |
| ☐ 9V-SRI | Boeing 777-212ER | 348/30867 | |
| ☐ 9V-SRJ | Boeing 777-212ER | 372/28527 | |
| ☐ 9V-SRK | Boeing 777-212ER | 389/28529 | |
| ☐ 9V-SRL | Boeing 777-212ER | 409/32334 | |
| ☐ 9V-SRO | Boeing 777-212ER | 32321 | o/o |
| ☐ 9V-SRP | Boeing 777-212ER | 33369 | o/o |
| ☐ 9V-SRQ | Boeing 777-212ER | 33371 | o/o |
| ☐ 9V-SVA | Boeing 777-212ER | 350/28524 | |
| ☐ 9V-SVB | Boeing 777-212ER | 353/28525 | |
| ☐ 9V-SVC | Boeing 777-212ER | 355/28526 | |
| ☐ 9V-SVD | Boeing 777-212ER | 366/30869 | |
| ☐ 9V-SVE | Boeing 777-212ER | 374/30870 | |

| | | | |
|---|---|---|---|
| ☐ 9V-SVF | Boeing 777-212ER | 378/30871 | |
| ☐ 9V-SVG | Boeing 777-212ER | 398/30872 | |
| ☐ 9V-SVH | Boeing 777-212ER | 407/28532 | |
| ☐ 9V-SVI | Boeing 777-212ER | 412/32316 | |
| ☐ 9V-SVJ | Boeing 777-212ER | 415/32335 | |
| ☐ 9V-SVK | Boeing 777-212ER | 419/28520 | |
| ☐ 9V-SVL | Boeing 777-212ER | 422/32336 | |
| ☐ 9V-SVM | Boeing 777-212ER | 30874 | o/o |
| ☐ 9V-SVN | Boeing 777-212ER | 30873 | o/o |
| ☐ 9V-SYB | Boeing 777-312 | 184/28516 | |
| ☐ 9V-SYC | Boeing 777-312 | 188/28517 | |
| ☐ 9V-SYD | Boeing 777-312 | 192/28534 | |
| ☐ 9V-SYE | Boeing 777-312 | 244/28531 | |
| ☐ 9V-SYF | Boeing 777-312 | 360/30868 | |
| ☐ 9V-SYG | Boeing 777-312 | 364/28528 | |
| ☐ 9V-SYH | Boeing 777-312 | 420/32317 | |

## SINGAPORE AIRLINES CARGO — SQC

| | | |
|---|---|---|
| ☐ 9V-SFA | Boeing 747-412F | 1036/26563 |
| ☐ 9V-SFB | Boeing 747-412F | 1042/26561 |
| ☐ 9V-SFC | Boeing 747-412F | 1052/26560 |
| ☐ 9V-SFD | Boeing 747-412F | 1069/26553 |
| ☐ 9V-SFE | Boeing 747-412F | 1094/28263 |
| ☐ 9V-SFF | Boeing 747-412F | 1105/28026 |
| ☐ 9V-SFG | Boeing 747-412F | 1173/26558 |
| ☐ 9V-SFH | Boeing 747-412F | 1224/28032 |
| ☐ 9V-SFI | Boeing 747-412F | 1256/28027 |
| ☐ 9V-SFJ | Boeing 747-412F | 1285/26559 |
| ☐ 9V-SFK | Boeing 747-412F | 1298/28030 |
| ☐ 9V-SFL | Boeing 747-412F | 1322/32897 |

# 9Y - TRINIDAD & TOBAGO

## BWEE EXPRESS

| | | |
|---|---|---|
| ☐ 9Y-WIL | DHC-8Q-311 | 489 |
| ☐ 9Y-WIN | DHC-8Q-311 | 499 |
| ☐ 9Y-WIP | DHC-8Q-311 | 538 |

## BWIA WEST INDIES AIRWAYS — BWA

| | | | |
|---|---|---|---|
| ☐ 9Y-ANU | Boeing 737-8Q8 | 697/28235 | |
| ☐ 9Y-BGI | Boeing 737-8Q8 | 547/28232 | |
| ☐ 9Y-GEO | Boeing 737-8Q8 | 433/28225 | |
| ☐ 9Y-GND | Boeing 737-86N | 1251/33419 | |
| ☐ 9Y-KIN | Boeing 737-8Q8 | 680/28234 | |
| ☐ 9Y-POS | Boeing 737-8Q8 | 506/28230 | |
| ☐ 9Y-TAB | Boeing 737-8Q8 | 598/28233 | |
| ☐ N3140D | L-1011-500 Tristar | 1233 | std |
| ☐ 9Y-TGJ | L-1011-500 Tristar | 1179 | |
| ☐ 9Y-TGN | L-1011-500 Tristar | 1191 | std |
| ☐ 9Y-THA | L-1011-500 Tristar | 1222 | Lsf GAT |
| ☐ 9Y-THQ | McDD MD-83 | 1313/49448 | |
| ☐ 9Y-THX | McDD MD-83 | 1642/49789 | |
| ☐ 9Y-TJN | Airbus A340-313 | 093 | |

## TOBAGO EXPRESS — TBX

| | | |
|---|---|---|
| ☐ 9Y-WIT | DHC-8Q-314B | 487 |
| ☐ 9Y-WIZ | DHC-8Q-311 | 557 |

# TRY OUR COMPANIONS TO AFQR 2003 . . .

## BUSINESS JETS – BJQR 2003

Contains 72 A5-pages listing all currently active civil or military business jets and corporate airliners by country in registration/serial order. Correct to January 7th 2003 and also includes US reserved registrations.                    *Price £4-95  (or £4-50 to Air-Britain members)*

## UK/IRELAND CIVIL/MILITARY REGISTERS – UKQR 2003

Around 144 A5-size pages giving the regns and types of all current UK, Irish and foreign-registered aircraft based in the UK, serials and types of all current UK military aircraft, and lists of which aircraft are based at all of the major and many of the minor UK civil airfields and microlight strips.                    *Price £6-95 (or £6 to Air-Britain members)*

# . . . AND THEIR BIG BROTHERS

## AIRLINE FLEETS 2003

800+ pages of around 3000 fleet lists with many extra features, including jet and turboprop airliners in non-airline use.  Now in its 32nd edition, this is the indispensable companion for the serious airline enthusiast.                    *Price £22-50 (or £18 to Air-Britain members)*

## UK/IRELAND CIVIL REGISTERS 2003

The 39th annual edition of our longest-running title lists all current G- and EI- allocations, plus overseas-registered aircraft based in the UK, alphabetical index by type, military-civil marks de-code, full BGA and microlight details. New museum aircraft section this year, this is the UK civil aircraft register bible.                    *Price £22 (or £17-50 to Air-Britain members)*

## BUSINESS JETS INTERNATIONAL 2003

The only publication that gives full production lists for all biz-jets in c/n order with details of all regns/serials carried, model numbers and fates, plus a 48,000+ index of biz-jet regns, now in its 18th edition at around 400 pages.

## EUROPEAN REGISTERS HANDBOOK 2003

With some 600 A4 pages, the 18th edition contains the current civil aircraft registers of 43 European countries – expanded this year to the borders of Russia. The only such publication with full previous identities, ERH includes balloons, gliders and microlights.

For full details and prices of these and scores of other Air-Britain books, visit our web-site on **www.air-britain.co.uk**

# AIR-BRITAIN MEMBERSHIP
## Join on-line at www.air-britain.co.uk

Air-Britain was founded in 1948 and today has over 4,200 current members including over 700 from outside the United Kingdom.

Air-Britain News (monthly – average 160 pages) continuously updates this annual publication and all our other annual publications. For January-December 2003 the cost is £36 (UK), £45 (Europe), £51 (Rest of the World). This includes all the benefits listed below. If you join during the year you may pay a pro-rata subscription covering the balance of the year (if back magazines to January are not required).

Membership of 'Air-Britain' includes the following benefits:

➤ A quarterly house magazine, AIR-BRITAIN AVIATION WORLD, illustrated in colour and black & white, containing 48 pages of news and photographs.

➤ Three additional magazines (NEWS, AEROMILITARIA, ARCHIVE) available on subscription in any combination. All rates include the basic membership cost and benefits, and also offer a substantial saving on the cover prices of the magazines.

➤ Discounts on 'Air-Britain' Books. We publish 10-20 books per annum.

➤ Access to ab-ix, the 'Air-Britain' e-mail Information Exchange Service.

➤ Access to an on-line database of UK airfield residents.

➤ Access to Local Branches and the Specialist Information Service.

➤ Access to Air-Britain Trips

➤ Access to black & white and colour photograph libraries

➤ An annual Fly-In

➤ An annual Aircraft Recognition Contest

You can join Air-Britain direct from this advert on-line at **www.air-britain.co.uk**, where full details of the magazines and membership subscription rates are given.

Membership normally runs January-December, but a number of alternative options are available to get new members started with a subscription.

**Alternatively, you can contact us for a membership pack containing samples of our magazines, subscription rates, and a book list. Please write to: Air-Britain Membership Enquiries, 1 Rose Cottages, 179 Penn Road, Hazlemere, High Wycombe, Bucks, HP15 7NE, UK. Tel/fax: +44 (0)1394 450767. E-mail: Barry.Collman@air-britain.co.uk.**